"America is usually viewed as the poor cousin of European intellectual life when it comes to producing canonical social theory. As well-known authority Charles Lemert shows in this sweeping reinterpretation, Americans of all kinds have been intrepid contributors to attempts to conceive of how social order is imagined and made, and under what conditions the agents that society produces can transform it in turn."

Samuel Moyn, *Chancellor Kent Professor of Law and History, Yale University, USA*

"The story of American social theory is often overshadowed by US appropriations of European texts. But it is a vigorous tradition in its own right, helping to shape the country as well as advance social science. Charles Lemert tells this story beautifully, with warmth and engagement as well as insight and breadth of perspective. An important contribution and a pleasure to read."

Craig Calhoun, *University Professor of Social Sciences, Arizona State University, USA*

"This is no typical social theory book. Charles Lemert, one of the most original theorists of the last half century, creates a compelling new narrative of 'America' that weaves together history, politics, philosophy, sociology, and anthropology. Spanning the ideas and contexts of everyone from Franklin to Jefferson, Lincoln to Thoreau, Tubman to Du Bois, to more contemporary scholars of globalization, environment, culture, and urban life, Lemert illuminates and explains the connections, fractures, and changes over more than two centuries of Americans thinking America."

Andrew Deener, *Professor of Sociology, University of California, Santa Barbara, USA*

"This book is beyond words in its brilliance. This curated theoretical magnum opus delves into the rich tapestry of American social theory, offering a detailed homage to the American theoretical tradition and its intellectuals. It highlights the evolution of a nation by analyzing historical and cultural milestones through the insights of thinkers such as Emerson, Thoreau, Du Bois, and Dewey. This book addresses pragmatism, identity, social movements, and marginality, crafting a vivid narrative of the American experiment. It traces the journey from premodern to modern to postmodern frameworks, providing a rich, sophisticated overview of the history and theories that shape the United States. Moreover, it underscores America's unique contributions to global intellectual discourse in a landscape dominated by European philosophical traditions. *Americans Thinking America* is beyond measure, like its author, who, given his life's contributions to the discipline, can easily be revered as the Godfather of social theory."

Waverly Duck, *North Hall Chair Endowed Professor of Sociology, University of California, Santa Barbara, USA*

"Charles Lemert's *Americans Thinking America* is the master work of one of the greatest American social theorists of the twenty-first century. The book offers a comprehensive guide to theory in what would become the United States from the early 1700s through to the present. This is essential reading for all who seek to better understand the trajectory of American social thought and all its contradictions."

Kristin Plys, *J. Clawson Mills Scholar, Metropolitan Museum of Art, New York City, USA, and Associate Professor of Sociology and History, University of Toronto, Canada*

"In this brilliant masterpiece of social theory, Lemert weaves a rich, diverse, and inclusive tapestry of ideas that shine a spotlight on the complex debates shaping our social world and the very essence of America itself. By skilfully placing often overlooked scholars in dialogue with the traditionally revered voices in knowledge production, Lemert offers a fresh and nuanced perspective on how we collectively understand and engage with our surroundings. Through captivating storytelling and profound philosophical inquiry, this book is an essential guide for understanding the intricate ways in which the collective of American thinkers, including scholars denied, make sense of a shared social landscape. A must-read for anyone seeking to understand social theory, past, present, and future."

Victor Rios, *Professor of Sociology, University of California, Santa Barbara, USA*

Americans Thinking America

In this dynamic book, Charles Lemert elaborates a vigorous, distinctive, and creative American tradition in social thought.

American social theory has tended to be overshadowed by European social thought. Yet, looking deeper, Americans have always made important contributions to social theory. Drawing upon the work of a dazzling array of both seminal and unjustly overlooked philosophers, sociologists, litterateurs, and political activists, Lemert constructs a coherent yet variegated intellectual framework for understanding American social theory and culture from the colonial era to the present. In doing so, Lemert analyzes American intellectual attitudes on race, gender, popular culture, political thought, capitalism, and social movements, while also exploring schools of thought from transcendentalism and pragmatism to interactionism and intersectionality.

In his inimitable style, Charles Lemert, a master of "finding theory where you'd least expect it," offers a masterful rendering of the American tradition in social theory. In doing so, Lemert shines new light on social theory and American history. Both authoritative and accessible, this indispensable work will be essential reading for students, scholars, and general readers with interests in social theory and American social history.

Charles Lemert is University Professor and John C. Andrus Professor of Social Theory Emeritus at Wesleyan University, USA. He has written extensively on social theory, globalization, and culture. He is author of *Globalization: An Introduction to the End of the Known World* (Routledge, 2015), *Why Niebuhr Matters* (Yale University Press, 2011), *Structural Lie: Small Clues to Global Things* (Routledge, 2008), *Thinking the Unthinkable: The Riddles of Classical Social Theories* (Routledge, 2007), *Postmodernism is Not What You Think: Why Globalization Threatens Modernity* (Routledge, 2005), and *Muhammad Ali: Trickster in the Culture of Irony* (Polity Press, 2003). He is also co-author of *Introduction to Contemporary Social Theory* (Second Edition, Routledge, 2022) and *Capitalism and Its Uncertain Future* (Routledge, 2021), editor of *Social Theory: The Multicultural, Global, and Classic Readings* (Seventh Edition, Routledge, 2021) and co-editor of *Globalization: A Reader* (Routledge, 2010).

A New Order of Social Things

Edited by Waverly Duck, *University of California, Santa Barbara*, Kristin Plys, *University of Toronto*, Charles Lemert, *Wesleyan University*, and Katharine Wallerstein, *University of California, Davis*

The social and human sciences may well be going through a sea change similar to what they experienced after the revolutionary moment of 1968. Today, it is fair to say, there are several obvious spheres of thought and research where this new order is beginning to show itself:

- The Global South
- Cultural and Critical Theories
- Multicultural Urban Ethnographies
- The Instability of Social Democracies
- Theorizing the Virtual World

To address these important questions we look to theorists of multiple geographies, genders, races, castes, and perspectives—established theorists who will levy this forum to take their existing work in new directions, along with early-career theorists whose ideas will chart new avenues for a renewal of critical theory. This breadth embraces both the plurality and ambiguity of theory today while also exploring bold solutions to the current impasse.

Titles in this series:

Americans Thinking America
Elements of American Social Thought
Charles Lemert

Americans Thinking America
Elements of American Social Thought

Charles Lemert

Routledge
Taylor & Francis Group
NEW YORK AND LONDON

Designed cover image: Frederic Edwin Church, West Rock, New Haven, Oil on canvas, 1849, New Britain Museum of American Art

First published 2025
by Routledge
605 Third Avenue, New York, NY 10158

and by Routledge
4 Park Square, Milton Park, Abingdon, Oxon, OX14 4RN

Routledge is an imprint of the Taylor & Francis Group, an informa business

© 2025 Charles Lemert

The right of Charles Lemert to be identified as author of this work has been asserted in accordance with sections 77 and 78 of the Copyright, Designs and Patents Act 1988.

All rights reserved. No part of this book may be reprinted or reproduced or utilised in any form or by any electronic, mechanical, or other means, now known or hereafter invented, including photocopying and recording, or in any information storage or retrieval system, without permission in writing from the publishers.

Trademark notice: Product or corporate names may be trademarks or registered trademarks, and are used only for identification and explanation without intent to infringe.

ISBN: 978-1-138-62974-5 (hbk)
ISBN: 978-1-138-62977-6 (pbk)
ISBN: 978-1-315-21023-0 (ebk)

DOI: 10.4324/9781315210230

Typeset in Sabon
by Newgen Publishing UK

For Geri Thoma Lemert and Anna Julia Lemert, who with their love, kept me alive through the years of grief in which we three lived on after the deaths of Matthew and Noah—sons and brothers

Contents

List of Figures xii
Preface and Acknowledgments xiii
Books by Charles Lemert xvi

PART I
Americans Thinking America 1

1 What is Theory? How Can There Be a Theory of America? 3

2 Elements of American Social Theory 23

PART II
American Social and Natural Spaces, 1727–1861 39

3 The First Fires of America's Revolutionary Culture: Benjamin Franklin, Jonathan Edwards, Thomas Paine 41

4 America's Revolutionary Culture Burns Bright: George Washington and Thomas Jefferson 55

5 Nation-State in the Making: James Madison and Alexander Hamilton 74

6 America Faces Its Fate: Ralph Waldo Emerson, Henry David Thoreau, Margaret Fuller 92

PART III
Civil War and American Pragmatism, 1861–1917 and After 119

7 A Suffering Republic and its Culture: John Brown and Harriet Tubman 121

8 Balm for the Nation's Wounds: Frederick Douglass and Walt Whitman 145

9 Abraham Lincoln's Implicit Practical Social Theory and A New America 172

10 Suffering as the Seed of Pragmatism: Abraham Lincoln and
   Oliver Wendell Holmes, Jr. 185

11 Pragmatism, the Hard Realities of Change: William James,
   Charles Sanders Peirce, John Dewey, Jane Addams, George Herbert Mead,
   Richard Rorty, Cornel West 200

PART IV
American Culture Tries to Explain its Disorder, 1919–1968 219

12 The Function of American Culture: Henry Adams, Talcott Parsons,
   Robert K. Merton 221

13 Interpreting Cultures: Robert Bellah, Clifford Geertz, Alvin Gouldner,
   George Marcus, Michael Fischer, Jeffrey Alexander 237

14 On Excluded Cultures: W.E.B. Du Bois, Zora Neale Hurston, Paula Gunn
   Allen, James Baldwin, Medgar Evers, Martin Luther King, Jr., Malcolm X ... 258

15 The Fungible Interaction Order: David Riesman, Erik Erikson,
   Edwin Lemert, Erving Goffman, Harold Garfinkel 284

16 Ethnographies and American Social Theory: Robert E. Park, W.E.B. Du Bois,
   W.I. Thomas, Florian Znaniecki, Elliot Liebow, Carol Stack,
   William Julius Wilson 307

17 The New Ethnographers of Urban Disorder: AbdouMaliq Simone, Elijah
   Anderson, Waverly Duck, Victor Rios, Matthew Desmond, Nikki Jones,
   Alice Goffman 330

18 Power, Domination, and the World Revolution of 1968: Herbert Marcuse,
   Kwame Ture, Bob Moses, Fannie Lou Hammer, Ella Baker, C. Wright Mills,
   Angela Davis 359

PART V
Reprise 387

   Social Theories in America and the Six Elements 389

PART VI
Identities and Differences in an Unsettled America, 1968 and Beyond 405

19 The Feminist Standpoint as Critical Theory: Charlotte Perkins Gilman,
   Dorothy Smith, Nancy Hartsock, Sandra Harding, bell hooks 407

20 Fractured Identities and Queer Analytics: Anna Julia Cooper,
    Patricia Hill Collins, Donna Haraway, Kimberlé Crenshaw Williams,
    Gloria Anzaldúa, Judith Butler   430

21 States, Social Movements, and Revolutions: The Roosevelts,
    Reinhold Niebuhr, Charles Tilly, Theda Skocpol, James Scott   477

22 Rethinking the World in the Unsettled 1960s: W.W. Rostow, Daniel Bell,
    C. Wright Mills, Students for a Democratic Society   524

23 Global Structures and Exclusions: Immanuel Wallerstein, Saskia Sassen,
    David Harvey, Nancy Fraser   556

PART VII
American Futures, 1542 and 1619 to When?   589

24 The TimeSpace of Traveling Theory: Edward Said, Sam Han, Trịnh Thị Minh
    Hà, Cabeza de Vaca, Black Elk, Phillis Wheatley, Gyatri Chakravorty Spivak,
    Howard Zinn, E.O. Wilson   591

    Index   611

Figures

6.1 Frederic Edwin Church, *West Rock, New Haven*, Oil on canvas, 1849, New Britain Museum of American Art 108
R.1 Diagram of the atomic structure of acetic acid 398

Preface and Acknowledgments

Chemistry Lessons: Why Elements?

In my college days at Miami University in Ohio, I was a premed major which in the day was a major that required chemistry and biology. I was fine with biology which, as it was taught then, involved mostly counting and identifying parts of living (or once living) things—birds, skeletal bones, floral species, embryos, spiders, and such like. Chemistry was another matter. One cannot count chemical events. H_2O is an event in which two hydrogen atoms combine with one oxygen atom to make water. H_2O does many good things for all creatures. But, if you have it nearby, the only thing some would count are the bacteria it may carry from a polluted stream to your gullet. Or, it is possible to measure how acidic the water is—more if there is an extra hydrogen ion, less if less. All-in-all water is a compound without which life would not be.

I did well enough with less complex compounds, but organic chemistry is more about those unimaginably complex compounds out of which human and other organic bodies are made and by which they live. As a premed student, I was told that organic chemistry was one of the courses medical schools viewed as indicative of a student's right to admission. So when it came to this subject I was determined to prepare well for the final exam. In those days late in the 1950s students often took drugs, less to get high, than to stay awake while preparing for exams. The drug I took later came to be known as speed, about which I knew nothing. I wanted only to get A+ in a subject that, truth be told, made little sense to me. I took the pill. In the exam I did very well for the first three-quarters. Then I crashed. My grade on that exam was exactly 77—perfect when I had my mind; zero when it was gone. Then and here my interest in medical school ended. I went on to study theology, become a minister, and a civil rights activist, then to return to Harvard to finish a PhD which led eventually to my becoming a sociologist. Along the way, my interest in drugs of the kind I took for that exam never grew. It wasn't worth it.

But the aspect of organic chemistry that stayed with me over the many years since that exam was the mystery of how elements combine to make a compound that serves, for a while, to be a structure that works for a good while anywhere that life exists. This is a theorem I defend as being as true for *social* compounds as for natural ones. Hence, the full title of this book: *Americans Thinking America: <u>Elements</u> of American Social Thought*.

More than a few dear friends have wondered: *Why Elements?* Inelegant they said. Perhaps, but this failed organic chemist believes elements work for this book because—now some nearly 70 years after losing his mind in a chemistry exam—he has come to understand that the elements of a culture come together for a while to become a working compound that serves a people often well, sometimes not so well. They serve well enough until some new social agent forces them to change.

This too is why I have chosen to introduce each chapter with a local story drawn from my experience in my current hometown, New Haven. The point here is to keep before the reader my literary and theoretical belief that all big social things begin as little ones. America cannot be thought of without some narrative reference to a local time and place where events come together to be what American culture and its theories are, for a time, definite. How they got from something that happened to me while on a walk along the local Mill River is a mystery that will always frustrate those who want to know every link along a causal chain. Yet, it must be true that a grand culture like the American one has somehow grown from local events each chemically bound by the social ions that hold the elements of ordinary life in place, for a time. Some readers may not warm to the chemistry figure of speech. Yet, the basic fact of social life is that it helps not at all to introduce the analytic cleaver that cuts off local practices from powerful, if invisible, general structures without which social being cannot exist. Mysteries abound!

If there is one further prefatory word, it is one so obviously true that it is seldom mentioned. Nothing in this universe, nor in any of its countless human social relations, is *ever* fixed in time. Life does not work that way. Death is always a lingering presence—whether it is the death of a loved one or the decline and collapse of what was once a structural necessity that some thought could never die. Yet, Rome died. America, as we think of it, will too. If not, then it will pass on into some lesser version of what it once was.

Thanking and Remembering Others Without Whom What We Have Done Would Not Be

I begin by thanking those without whom I would not have lived to write this book in the way it has been written, for better or worse. I suffer from no disease that others my age have not suffered. I am old, just the same. But I thrive in the life I have because of my wife Geri Thoma Lemert and my daughter Anna Julia Lemert (my Cooper). We three have been a family together for twenty-six years. We have lived through the final decades of Geri's professional career as a literary agent working mostly for many of the historians whose books figure in this book. She already knew much of what I had to learn. Anna Julia has grown into a beautiful and brilliant woman who gives us joy that makes the trouble life hands down seem like nothing. Though Anna knew Matthew hardly at all, we three together mourn his death by suicide at 29 years in 2000 when Annie had but two years. Noah had more time to give but died in 2020, at 46 years of cancer. Though the boys are gone the family remains what keeps us still seeking better things for ourselves but also for others we know who have so little.

As for the book, I thank our dear friend Christa Dove who proofed it all with a keen eye for errors and typos. She is amazing for this, in part, because English is her third language, yet, she reads and diagnoses as if she had used this language all her nearly 89 years. I also thank Craig Calhoun and Andrew Deener who read an earlier version of the manuscript rife with errors. Their reviews suggested how I could fix errors of content and organization. Both are busy people, but they took the time to help me, as they have helped others.

Another pleasure of recent years is that I have made deepening friendship with others. Waverly Duck, for years now, has been a virtual member of our family. He visits us often and tolerates our imperfections. Kathy Wallerstein became a close friend in the years when her father, Immanuel, and her mother, Beatrice, were aging, then dying. Kathy lived in California in those days, so it fell to me to be on call when there was an emergency at their home in Branford. Those moments made us the close friends we are after her parents are gone. I miss Immanuel and Beatrice almost as much as she does.

I first met Kristin Plys when she was a graduate student in sociology at Yale. Then I became a member of her dissertation committee. After Yale she took a position at the University of Toronto during when our interests converged on a book, *Capitalism and Its Uncertain Future*, which has been well enough received for us to start another, *The Certain Future of Marxism*. Kristin is on the way to being the super star of her generation, which Waverly is —though he keeps trying to do and be more. Waverly, Kathy, Kristin, and I have joined as co-editors of a new book series, *The New Order of Social Things*, in which we seek to publish books by social theorists willing to break the mold of our disciplines and to write on subjects outside the stream those older have set down.

I could not thank friends like these without mentioning Dean Birkenkamp. Dean and I have worked together as author and editor for thirty years plus—all the while developing a friendship that goes beyond books. Dean believed in this book since a visit here in New Haven several years ago when he took the time to read a few of the first chapters. He has never failed to stand with me on this or any of the many book projects we've worked on.

Finally, I must give thanks and remembrances to those about whom I have written. Even those in the long ago like Thomas Paine and Alexander Hamilton who touched me for the ways they moved about in life and thought, often irritating others or lapsing into the stupid arguments that, in Hamilton's case, got him killed. It is hard not to admire Abraham Lincoln for his genius, but also for how he came from nowhere in a rural backcountry to become the leader America then so much needed—and this while losing a beloved son, whose death sent his wife into a life-long depression.

Then too there were those I came to know personally. Talcott Parsons was my teacher and was helpful to all ways that allowed me to figure out what he was driving at. I was sitting with Pierre Bourdieu in Paris when we learned of Parsons' death. Bourdieu told me of a time when Parsons drove him recklessly somewhere in New Jersey. Speaking of Parsons, there was Alvin Gouldner who, in the day, was Parsons' most articulate critic in *Coming Crisis in Western Sociology* in 1970. Al Gouldner invited me up to Washington University in St. Louis when I was doing hard time in Southern Illinois, and his marriage with Janet Gouldner was coming undone. Al was a difficult person to some but kind to me in the sense that he apologized when he knew he had been harsh for no good reason. There are more relationships, some in passing, some enduring. Of these the most unusual was my relationship with Immanuel Wallerstein who for many years allowed me nothing more than a passing relation. But, in time (and before he fell ill) somehow he warmed to me. He and Beatrice often had Geri and me (and Anna once) over for an evening meal with others who included among many Jim Scott—who by the way had me once to his farm in Durham where I learned of how he lived rural in keeping with those in villages of Southeast Asia with whom he lived to study their ways. Sadly, Jim died just recently. Also, I got to know Dorothy Smith, who died recently. We came to know each other at a distance. I once chaired a public seminar in which Dorothy was the only woman who took a strong voice. She used that voice to attack and demoralize most of the proud men who, in the day, thought of themselves the cat's meow. This she could and would do, while, more often, being kind and supportive to younger feminists at a time late in the 1970s when a third wave was beginning to crash the shores of the then-mainstream. There were many others over the years.

I could go on, but won't. The challenge for me in this book has been to write honestly about many including those few whom I knew, in a book that, while it contains criticisms, is meant to paint all the theorists on a larger canvas. If I have been wrong in my interpretations or perhaps too little critical of some, I beg their forgiveness.

—*Charles Lemert*,
New Haven,
August 16, 2024

Books by Charles Lemert

Silence and Society: Below the Bottom Turtle (2025)
Americans Thinking America: Elements of American Social Thought (2025)
Social Theory: The Multicultural and Classical Readings (8e, 2025)
Introduction to Contemporary Social Theory, with Anthony Elliott (3e, 2024)
Capitalism and Its Uncertain Future, with Kristin Plys (2022)
Globalization: An Introduction to the End of the Known World (2015)
Uncertain Worlds: World-Systems Analysis in Changing Times, with Immanuel Wallerstein and Carlos Aguirre Rojas (2012)
Social Things: An Introduction to the Sociological Life (5e, 2012)
Why Niebuhr Matters (2011)
The Structural Lie: Small Clues to Global Things (2011)
Globalization: A Reader with Anthony Elliott, Daniel Chaffee, Eric Hsu (2010)
The Race of Time: A Charles Lemert Reader, edited by Daniel Chaffee and Sam Han (2010)
The New Individualism, with Anthony Elliott (2010)
Thinking the Unthinkable: The Riddles of Classical Social Theories (2007)
Durkheim's Ghosts: Cultural Logics and Social Things (2006)
Deadly Worlds: The Emotional Costs of Globalization, with Anthony Elliott (2006)
The Souls of WEB Du Bois, with Alford A. Young, Jr., Jerry G. Watts, Manning Marable & Elizabeth Higginbotham (2006)
Postmodernism Is Not What You Think (2005)
Sociology After the Crisis (2e, 2004)
Muhammad Ali: Trickster and the Culture of Irony (2003)
Dark Thoughts: Race and the Eclipse of Society (2002)
The Goffman Reader, edited with introductions, with Ann Branaman (1997)
Crime and Deviance: Essays and Innovations by Edwin Lemert, edited with Michael Winter (2000)
The Voice of Anna Julia Cooper, edited, with Esme Bhan (1998)
Intellectuals and Politics: Social Theory Beyond the Academy (1990)
Michel Foucault: Social Theory and Transgression, with Garth Gillan (1983)
French Sociology: Rupture and Renewal since 1968 (1981)
Sociology and the Twilight of Man: Homocentrism and Discourse in Sociological Theory (1979)

Part I
Americans Thinking America

1 What is Theory?
How Can There Be a Theory of America?

$$E=mc^2$$
—*Albert Einstein, Theory of Special Relativity, 1905*

$$\Delta x\, \Delta p \geq \frac{\hbar}{2}$$
—*Werner Heisenberg, The Uncertainty Principle, 1927*

There is no theory of the universe.
Events cannot be predicted beyond a certain point
but occur in a random and arbitrary manner.
—*Stephen Hawking, A Brief History of Time, 1988*

Gilgamesh the tall, magnificent and terrible, …
who restored the cult-centers destroyed by the Deluge,
and set in place for the peoples the rites of the cosmos.
—*The Coming of Enkidu in The Epic of Gilgamesh, 1300–1000 BCE*

In the beginning God created the heaven and earth.
—*Genesis 1, Not Moses; Probably a Priestly Source, 6th Century BCE*

Cogito, Ergo Sum
—*René Descartes, Discourse on the Method, 1637*

All our knowledge begins with the senses, proceeds then to the understanding,
and ends with reason. There is nothing higher than reason.
—*Immanuel Kant, Critique of Pure Reason, 1781*

Spirit alone is Reality. It is the inner being of the world,
that which essentially is, and is per se; it assumes objective, determinative form,
and enters into relations with itself …
—*Georg Hegel, The Phenomenology of Mind, 1807*

The history of all hitherto existing society is the history of class struggles.
—*Karl Marx and Friedrich Engels, The Manifesto of the Communist Party, 1848*

DOI: 10.4324/9781315210230-2

> *Amongst the novel objects that attracted my attention during my stay in the United States, nothing struck me more forcibly than the general equality of conditions. ... Consequentially each man undertakes to be sufficient to himself and glories in the fact that his beliefs about everything are peculiar to himself.*
> —Alexis de Tocqueville, Democracy in America, 1835

What is Theory?

All of the verbal and numeric lines just above are theories. Theories here are of many kinds, to be sure, but they are theories, nonetheless. The English word *theory* comes from the Greek *theōria* which meant *contemplation*, or, by extension, *speculation*. Some of the above, like the creation myths in *Genesis* and *The Epic of Gilgamesh*, are more on the speculative side, while Einstein's famous **E=mc²** and others of a scientific nature are closer to contemplation. In the second case, it is fair to interpret *contemplation* as *looking deeply*, as Werner Heisenberg did upon discovering his uncertainty principle[1]:

$$\Delta x \, \Delta p \geq \frac{\hbar}{2}$$

Neither the authors of the *Genesis* line nor whoever wrote *The Epic of Gilgamesh*—nor the authors of other theories of the kind—looked deeply at the world about them. They do, however, look broad and high for a way to explain the social things they live on and with. More recently Stephen Hawking's bold statement in 1988 calls theories of this kind into question: "There is no theory of the universe. Events cannot be predicted beyond a certain point but occur in a random and arbitrary manner..."[2] Just the same, and again, in one sense or another, all those listed here, even the most scientific, wrote theories.

Then too there are theories that fit neither of these two categories—at least not exactly. René Descartes' *Cogito, Ergo Sum* is a theory that came to be without speculating or looking deeply at anything in particular even though he published it in a book called *Discourse on the Method*. Descartes did, however, think deeply. Theories of this kind are certainly not mere speculation. They may be, in a loose sense, contemplative in that they arise from systematic, even logical, thinking about some or another aspect of the world as it must be, or ought to be—where *must* and *ought* are not moral and religious modifiers. The *ought* of theories like this is logical in the sense of having been thought-through against all that the author knows from having read and pondered others who wrote about the same problem. In Descartes' day early in the 1600s, theoreticians of this kind would likely have been called *metaphysicians* or, in still more modern times, they came to be called *philosophers* which is to say lovers of wisdom—from the ancient Greek φίλος (*philos*: "love") and σοφία (*sophia*: "wisdom"). Over the centuries, philosophy took on a more precise meaning,

---

1 There are many sophisticated explanations of Heisenberg's 1927 *The Uncertainty Principle* of which the one at *Stanford Encyclopedia of Philosophy* (July 12, 2016 @ https://plato.stanford.edu/entries/qt-uncertainty/) is the best so far as I can judge. The arithmetic formula in Heisenberg's original article is at Heisenberg, W. (1927) [1927-03-01]. "Über den anschaulichen Inhalt der quantentheoretischen Kinematik und Mechanik". *Zeitschrift für Physik (in German).* **43** (3): 172–198. Bibcode:1927ZPhy...43..172H. doi:10.1007/BF01397280. ISSN 0044-3328. S2CID 122763326. Heisenberg, W (1983) [1927]. "*The actual content of quantum theoretical kinematics and mechanics*". No. NAS 1.15: 77379. 1983. *43* (3–4): 172. Bibcode:1983ZhPhy..43..172H. Archived from the original on 2023-09-02. Retrieved 2023-08-28. English translation of *Über den anschaulichen Inhalt der quantentheoretischen Kinematik und Mechanik.*
2 Stephen Hawking, *A Brief History of Time* (Bantam Books, 2017), 183.

roughly, love of knowledge, where knowledge is neither scientific nor religious. Just the same, there are, today, philosophies of both science and religion or (for those who would prefer another term) myth. In time, philosophies in various fields of knowledge became sciences of the field. By late in the twentieth century, thinkers like Robert K. Merton, Robert Bellah, and Mircea Eliade were primarily sociologists of science (Merton) or religion (Bellah) or historians of mythology (Eliade).[3] Had they written late in the eighteenth century they would have been considered philosophers. But then, we need to realize, late in the eighteenth century there was nothing like sociology and history of the kind Eliade wrote was just beginning to become what now it is. Changes like these suggest that still another brand of theory was in the offing.

The drift in the tides of theory can be identified, all-too-simply perhaps, by reference to Immanuel Kant's distinction in his *Critique of Pure Reason* in 1781 between pure knowledge and practical knowledge. Kant's philosophy of knowledge was very much at the heart of the Enlightenment, during when most, if not all, things came under scrutiny by other philosophers of the day. Kant's philosophy soon became a turning point. His philosophy came to be known as *idealism* but it was quite at odds with the idealism of Georg Wilhelm Friedrich Hegel who wrote *The Phenomenology of Mind* in 1807. Hegel was a generation younger than Kant so, as younger ones do, he took it upon himself to criticize Kant's idealism which, he thought, went too far into practical knowledge. Details aside, it can be said that the Kant-Hegel differences became an important early version of the debate over dichotomies in theoretical and philosophical thinking—a difference that was central to the legend that Karl Marx, after 1845 when *Camera Obscura* appeared in *German Ideology*,[4] meant to turn Hegel on his head by composing a grand social philosophy in which all history is the story of the struggle of the worker to escape the alienation that capitalist economies, and their precursors, impose on the lower working classes—a classic example of the materialism/idealism distinction. For Marx, material reality was basic, ideals were no more than a passive reflection of economic forces.

So, it is now plain to see, the drift away from pure philosophy toward something different was in fact a drift that turned social philosophies, such as they were, into *social sciences*, such as they would soon become. But long before theory would make that big leap into social sciences, there emerged a new type of theory. Marx was an early progenitor of this type of theory but there were others, who without claiming to be theorists of any kind actually did one or another kind of empirical research in order to formulate what would not for a long while be considered theories.

The 1835 book by Alexis de Tocqueville, *Democracy in America*, actually formulated for the first time since the revolutionary era, a theory about America that revolutionaries like Thomas Jefferson and James Madison could only hope would come to be. By 1835, those hopes had become an observable reality, as Tocqueville began his famous book:

---

3 For Robert Bellah, see *Religion in Human Evolution: From the Paleolithic to the Axial Age* (2011). For Robert K. Merton, see *Science, Technology and Society in Seventeenth Century England* (1938), and for Mircea Eliade *The Myth of the Eternal Return: Cosmos and History* (1971).

4 Karl Marx, "German Ideology," in *The German Ideology, Part I* Robert C. Tucker, editor, *The Marx-Engels Reader* (W.W. Norton, 1978 [second edition]), 154. It should be explained that the phrase *Camera Obscura* occurs (so far as I know) only once. As a metaphor it refers to the fact that, for one example, in early cameras the real image appears in the photographic image upside down; hence *camera obscura*. Yet, it has come to be an expression so vivid as to stand on its own as a key word reflecting his stand on materialism—thus, it occurs in a section Tucker and others have entitled "Feuerbach: Opposition of the Materialistic and Idealistic Outlook," a short section just before Marx begins his argument with Hegel.

> Amongst the novel objects that attracted my attention during my stay in the United States, nothing struck me more forcibly than the general equality of condition… Consequentially each man undertakes to be sufficient to himself and glories in the fact that his beliefs about everything are peculiar to himself.[5]

In short, Americans value equality which allows them to be confident individuals. This was 1835 but it is today still true that Americans think of themselves as free individuals because they believe they live in a society where all are free to think and do as they choose because all are equal, in principle if not in the reality of any given moment. More on this to come, a lot more, but for now let Tocqueville stand for an early instance of disciplined empirical study of social things like America, by which he identified an element of America's enduring values.

In Tocqueville's day few were they who acknowledged that there could be such a thing as social science. Yet, before long, Tocqueville's early nineteenth-century French contemporaries Henri de Saint-Simon and Auguste Comte introduced *sociology* as a science. Comte began to write of sociology as a positive science, while Saint-Simon wrote, without using the term, an early version of the sociology of the new industrial world. By the end of the nineteenth century, and well into the twentieth, social sciences of several kinds had become institutionally recognized academic disciplines. Disciplinary social sciences then began to present themselves to the world as "real" sciences able to represent empirical findings in relation to what came to be called variously: sociological, political, economic, anthropological, historical theories.

Then in the second half of the twentieth century, things changed again. Racial, feminist, and queer theories emerged out of the ignorance that silenced those who became their theorists. Even daring members of self-satisfied academic fields like sociology and anthropology, economics and political science, began to refer to their theories as *social theory*. This even when trying to keep their more scientific theoretical work similitudinously scientific. By the early decades of the twenty-first century, social theories were ubiquitous. All these changes, for which Tocqueville and Émile Durkheim in France, Marx in exile in London, and Max Weber in Germany, and others aplenty were pioneers of theories as different from Descartes and Hegel, not to mention the authors of *Genesis* and *Gilgamesh*, who just the same served as deep background to theory as it has become.

What is Theory?

After this all-too-cursory review of the kinds of theories, one might be tempted to say that theory is as theory does. Too clever perhaps, and too vague, yet there is something to this paraphrase of the Forest Gump line. The difference is that, in the movie, Tom Hanks used the line "Stupid is as stupid does." Whatever else theory is, or does, it is not stupid. In fact, in any of its versions, theory aims to make good sense of some or another, little or big thing. Even when, at the extreme, theory tries to make sense of things like gods or beginnings that in themselves are real if unknowable. Worlds begin somewhere. But, as Stephen Hawking put it, there can be no theory of the universe. Even as scientists currently agree that the universe began some 13.8 billion years ago, they don't agree on how, much less why.

---

5 Alexis de Tocqueville, *Democracy in America* (Project Gutenberg Ebook, 1835), Book I, Introductory Chapter. @ https://www.gutenberg.org/files/815/815-h/815-h.htm#link2H_4_000

Scientists and theorists do not, and cannot, agree among themselves with what even the most brilliant of other theorists think. In 1927, for remarkable example, at the 5th Solvay Conference in Austria, 29 of the world's most brilliant physicists (17 of whom won a Nobel Prize) spent a full week debating each other's theories. Niels Bohr and Albert Einstein continued their disputes over quantum mechanics. Einstein famously challenged Heisenberg's Uncertainty Principle. Even when they agreed on some things, Stephen Hawking was correct that there is a limit to what we can know about aspects of the universe—and one need not be a well-trained and respected scientist or theorist of any kind to recognize these limits.

On this, anyone of but modest intelligence or insufficient formal education, need only look at the night sky. Can anyone without a professional trick to play truly believe that we earthlings are the only sentient beings amid all those planets and stars which are countless? There may be, but no one knows or can know. If that doesn't do it for you, try the claim that no two snowflakes are the same—a supposition created by Wilson Bentley of Vermont who, between 1891 and 1935, photographed 5,000 snowflakes. But how would anyone know this for sure without studying a larger sample of every single flake that has fallen? Interesting idea, it may be said to be a theory, but not one based on confirmable facts. Even with an N of 5,000, Bentley had just begun a study of the countless number of fallen flakes.

Theories of all kinds are always subject to challenges. This is their nature. They are thrown into a sea of skeptics who will question them. This, of course, is partly due to the fact that theories are not, and cannot be, realities. They tell the story of realities—and often tell their stories very well. Even $E=mc^2$, like Heisenberg's more inscrutable uncertainty formula, are stories that, like stories of all kinds, inspire other stories like those told at the 1927 Solvay Conference in Austria where geniuses met after hours for drink and food to tell each other what they thought of the scientific stories told during the day. Everything tradition has taught people to believe is defied by the insistence, made here, that all theories—of whichever kind—are stories told to an audience in order to make a claim about the world in which the tellers and listeners live. Einstein's $E=mc^2$ is as much a story as the Gilgamesh legend. How? Because both are the final or tentatively final story issuing from a long line of arithmetic, oral, or written stories that, for whatever reason, lead to a conclusion like $E=mc^2$. Some will say that this is playing games with well-honored ways of thinking. This righteous skepticism brings us to the third question of the chapter.

How Can There Be a Theory of America?

First, it must be said that, here and throughout, we are referring to *America*, not *the United States of America*, or the *USA*, except when they are linked as part of the book's ongoing narrative. There can be, and are, theories of the *USA*—the nation with discrete territorial borders and social, political, economic and other institutions established over time in that territory. Nations are different from each other. Many of those who believe strongly in *America* also may believe that the *USA* is, for example, different, and in crucial ways, better than all other nations. But, strictly speaking, as a factual claim this is not so. Nations have each been formed over time since the Peace of Westphalia in 1648. The Thirty Years War from 1618 to 1648 had created chaos among the different territories in Europe and their leaders—from the Hapsburg Emperor to the France of Cardinal Richelieu, *stadtholders* who would govern the early Dutch Republic and others among the remnants of the Holy Roman Empire. They agreed to respect borders such as they were. It hardly need be said that the respect wavered and all too often collapsed into war and other encroachments.

All the same, this is where the idea of discrete nations began. Nations were, simply put, native institutions that prevailed within their borders. A nation or, as it came to be called, a nation-state was first and foremost a political entity or, to use the technical term, a *polity* which is to say: an organized people with enough sense of a common identity that they are able to develop institutions governing their relations with each another. The United States of America is a nation-state and has been, in principle, since 1789 when the former colonies ratified the terms of the Constitutional Convention held in Philadelphia from May to September 1787.

USA is shorthand for a nation. *America* refers to the values that nation's people have come to share, imperfectly. In other words, *America* is a cultural thing. Cultures cannot be givens—neither by the gods nor the laws of nature. Cultures are made by the people of a given reasonably well-bordered region or nation. Some cultures go beyond the places where they arose. The values of the Enlightenment arose in the proto-nations of early modern Europe but then spread across the Atlantic when Thomas Jefferson freely borrowed from John Locke and others to fashion the ideal of America as a land of the free able to pursue, at will, "life, liberty, and the pursuit of happiness"—a declaration, its limits notwithstanding, that came to be a foundational slogan for Americans and their America. Needless to say, this slogan is a theory—one held and abused by people who pledge allegiance to the theory and its flag as if those pledging (some very young school children) knew what it meant. Theories like this one are themselves social things that rise to a transcending level by virtue of being shared among members—shared, that is by talking, writing, singing, drawing, painting, signing, and all other ways of imagining what they think they are or might become. They arise, that is, from storytelling, which is never as simple as some think. Stories are often, perhaps always, told during and about differences, sometimes bitter, sometimes bloody.

> That suffering is a way of life
> that suffering is a virtue
> that suffering is the price
> we pay for seeing the future.
>
> Some of us are still hung up
> substituting words for relationships
> substituting writing for living.[6]

Stories are never just words or pictures or songs, they come to be because those who tell them, and those who read or hear them, have, with rare exception, lived through suffering. Often, if not always, they find in the stories relief from their agonies. We tell stories to our infant children when they're sick or sad, or can't get to sleep, or wish they could be downstairs with the older kids, or are just plain unhappy. At the same time, we tell, as our ancestors told, vivid stories before, during, and after wars of revolution or merely in the defense of their nation. Some of these stories were songs—*The Star Spangled Banner* was written by Francis Scott Key during the War of 1812 as he watched the British attack on Fort McHenry in Baltimore's inner harbor. Some stories of this kind became flags. They are sung and told and woven during very many agonal moments from the smallish to the enormous—some petty, some grand.

---

6 Gloria Anzaldúa, "The New Speakers," in *The Gloria Anzaldúa Reader*, AnaLouise Keating, editor (Duke University Press, 2009), 24–25.

So then, how can stories about America rise to this grand level of cultural meaning? The crude but necessary first answer. They do it just like other nations. The French still sing *La Marseillaise* that tells French citizens who sing that they came from the 1789 Revolution. Germans today still sing *Das Deutschlandlied* after lyricists recovered from their quite checkered past under Hitler in WWII.[7] Wars seem always to find a way into national anthems, surely because they were all, one way or another, created out of wars defending or enlarging national borders.

If it be granted that America is a cultural thing, then it is because of stories told—in bars or pubs or, more publicly, in constitutional conventions or meetings of the *États Généraux de 1789* in France or, for that matter, in meetings of a *Politburo*, according to the whims of Mao or Stalin and their successors. Stories of all kinds are told here and there in homes and neighborhoods. Some stories rise high to join others that may come to be part of such historic documents like the *Constitution of the United States*. This document was handed down for ratification in 1787, written by James Madison and Alexander Hamilton, among others, and was of course formalized as the nation's first law of being. One might say that the *Constitution* is a cultural thing that made a nation. Just the same, even as the framers of the *Constitution* came to a written conclusion, members of the Constitutional Convention (especially Alexander Hamilton and Benjamin Franklin) told the stories which, at that point, they had come to hear and tell in their daily lives before the Convention. But the *Constitution* itself was not simply a story. In a figurative sense, it was a flag that waved Americans into a new national world.

Words and other means of public storytelling matter. When, by narrative or song, or any other of the ways stories are told, they call to mind heroic and, sometimes banal, moments of the past of a people. They are, if not a flag as such, a symbolic message. *Symbol* comes down from the Greek σύμβολον and the French *symbolon*, "from a verb meaning *throw together*, put together, *compare*, – which alludes to the Classical practice of breaking a piece of ceramic in two and giving one half to the person who would receive a future message, and the other half to the person who had sent it. If and when the two fit together, the receiver could be sure that the messenger bearing it did indeed also carry a genuine message from the intended person."[8] This awkward definition of *symbol* helps, nonetheless, to explain the symbolic nature of stories which are nothing if not an attempt to fit two separate, if not broken, pieces of life together so that, when told, those who hear or read the story know that it is authentic. *Authenticity*, it should be said, does not denote *true*. It only means that the story was told by one who knew in her own way from where and by what the parts the story came—and that it thereby seemed worth retelling.

Stories themselves may obscure their inner meanings. And a story itself may not be true, as the Gilgamesh myth is not true. Our stories are myths. *Myth*, it happens, is from the Greek *mythos* which has several etymological meanings in English: *speech, thought, word, discourse,* and *story*! *Discourse* is from Late Middle English. It denotes *reasoning* but, oddly, from the Old French, *discursus* conveyed the sense of *running to and fro* before, in our time, it came to mean *argument*. In a sense, if we think of a myth as separated parts

---

7 The melody of *Das Deutschlandlied* was composed in 1797 by Joseph Haydn as a personal anthem to Francis II, then Emperor of the Holy Roman Empire. The text comes from a patriotic poem written in 1841. In 1922, during the Weimar Republic, it was adopted as Germany's national anthem. Its first stanza with the notorious line "*Deutschland uber alles*" was retained by Hitler as the prelude to the Nazi anthem *Das Horst Wessel Lied*. When WWII was over and Hitler dead, the *Deutschlandlied* was dropped for seven years before being reinstated as the national anthem with its uncontroversial last stanza only.
8 Alain Rey et al., eds., *Dictionnaire historique de la langue française*, new edition, vol. 2 (Paris: Dictionnaires Le Robert, 1995), 2082. English translation of these lines is from the Wikipedia entry for *symbol* [July 31, 2023].

matched, this is not far from the nature of a story whose teller must somehow, probably unconsciously, argue with herself which of the two parts fit together and how.[9] Stories, in this sense, can be, and often are, a a kind of mending of differences. When the authors of *Genesis* said: "In the beginning God created the heaven and earth"—they were putting together their heaven and earth. In the same way that, when Einstein "said" $E=mc^2$ he was putting together energy and mass. And so on.

Erving Goffman would remind us that we tell our stories to others seeking their cooperation in accepting us as we want to be seen in their eyes. If they accept our story, then our self is presented and real enough for the time being. In other words, for Goffman, being a self is a drama in which our performance must be persuasive. At the same time, in the process, we often must lie when telling our story. The lies often cover dark secrets that, if others knew the truth, our presentations would be damaged and, in that moment, we would not exist as the self we want others to accept. If found out, we must repair the damage. "The performer who is dramaturgically prudent will have to adapt his performance to the conditions under which it must be staged."[10]

The same is true of mythological stories we tell about some aspect of our world. We don't know all the background of the story we tell. In some cases, the mythic story tells of a past so ancient that we can only tell what others have told us—as when, in a case like *Gilgamesh*, the stories told are necessarily fraught with errors. But this is also true when we are condemning capitalism as Karl Marx analyzed it. Marx's writings are so many that hardly anyone reads the entire corpus. Marx's three volume master work *Capital: A Critical Analysis of Capitalist Production* is well more than 2,200 pages.[11] Few if any have *carefully* read it all line by line. Most study the better organized and theoretically meaty first volume.

Theories like *Marx's* of Capitalism can be considered myths since, Louis Althusser notwithstanding, no one can possibly cover all of Capitalism's important facts in its emergence to compose anything like a scientific Marxism.[12] If this, then, even more so, stories we tell of ourselves can only hint at the relatively few remembered incidents of a past we cannot fully recall. Some of it we don't want to remember. Some of it sneaks into consciousness through dreams. Some in pre-technomedia days kept diaries that help—but even these are but a part of the truth. When we tell stories of others we know, we can only offer a narrative sketch not a full-blown biography. Still the story can mean something to others if told in terms they might understand. But even well told it could be said that our stories, and by implication, our *selves* are myths we tell to get by with others who might or might not trust what we say.

Here, and in all the chapters in *Americans Thinking America*, I will tell stories of places and people local to the town where I live—this to make the point that even we in local

---

9 For one example of a well-known and respected literary story teller, see Mary Gaitskill, *The Art of Fiction, No. 257* in *The Paris Review 243* (Spring, 2023), 34–68. At the start of this interview Gaitskill says, referring to one of her early stories: "That's why I would call it fiction. "Something Nice" also definitely describes an experience I had, when I worked briefly as a prostitute, and that one was told entirely from the man's point of view—an invented character with an invented life. That dynamic wasn't as antagonistic, but it still took something to imagine myself into another person who was very different from me. I was pretty young when I wrote that story, and he's an old guy in an unsatisfying marriage."
10 Erving Goffman, "Informative Control and Personal Identity," in Goffman, *Stigma: Notes on the Management of a Spoiled Identity* (Anchor Books/Doubleday, 1959), 222.
11 Karl Marx, *Capital Unabridged/Three Volumes*, edited by Frederick Engels (International Publishers, 1967).
12 Louis Althusser, "The Merits of Classical Economics," in Althusser and Etienne Balibar, *Reading Capital* (New Left Books, 1970 [1968]), chapter 3. Also Althusser's classical essay "Ideology and Ideological State Apparatus (Notes towards an Investigation)" in Althusser, *Lenin and Philosophy and Other Essays* (New Left Books, 1971 [1970]), 127–198. See also Althusser, "On the Materialist Dialectic," in his *For Marx* (Verso, 1969 [1965]), chapter 6.

American towns tell and hear stories that, one way or another, fit America's stories of itself. Still, when I wrote them for this book, my retelling is meant to put together broken, if local, parts of America's story. They do not in so many words rise to discernible elements of American culture, but neither are they alien to the culture in which they were bred.

Paul Crowe: A Rugged Individual Living Pragmatically Against a Looming, if Local, Nature

Somewhere in the East Rock Park on the outskirts of New Haven, Connecticut, a sturdy soul lives in a makeshift lean-to home with tarp above and below where he sleeps on many blankets gathered here and there from the leavings of the well-off in the town. His name is Paul Crowe. I've known him for at least the 15 years he has lived among the rocks and sheltering trees and brush of a heavily wooded and elevated town park. Though I walk regularly in the surrounding hills, I have never seen Paul's camp site and never asked to see it. I know him to be a nice but very private person. Somehow, he is always clean, well-shaven, and dressed in neat but minimalist clothing.

One November day I saw Paul walking toward downtown, in jeans and a tank top. I offered him a ride. He took it because we like each other. When he got into my modest, shabby but high-end Lexus, I asked if he wasn't cold. He said no. Though that day was preternaturally warm for late autumn, I was chilled by the light rain that soaked through my two layers to cool the sweat below expelled during a longish walk I just finished. It had been a while since I'd seen Paul. This because in recent years the times he spent in town changed because he had found a late-night job cleaning a restaurant. The pay, I believe, is not near minimum wage. Paul mentioned in passing that he was down to the last few dollars from the week's wages. Paul is resourceful. He gets a bit of food from the restaurant and a bit more in shops along the way from his home in the woods to town. He is thin but not emaciated. In the past, when Geri and I owned a house along his route, he would stay with us on bad winter nights. He never overstayed his welcome. In good weather before work, he usually hangs out on the downtown church steps. I often stop before going to a meeting or whatever. We talk then as when he stayed over.

So, the reader may wonder, why tell a story so local and otherwise off the charts after a reasonably nuanced and high-minded discussion of theory and stories? Surely, it might be said, there is a better story to begin such an ambitious book composed around America's historical stories and personages. The answer here is simple. Big stories begin with little ones. Story-telling is always in some sense a collective enterprise. Not all little stories like this one grow big as part of a collective enterprise. Before this book appears in print no one will know this story as I tell it.

I tell the story of Paul Crowe because, in all the important ways, he lives the life of the earliest American settlers. He is the very archetype of the rugged individualist living against and with the wild and looming Nature. Paul makes his life in and against nature's rocks and woods, and he does so in little and big ways by virtue of his well-formed pragmatic skills. He has a cell phone (what the homeless here once called Obama-phones that they were given by a public agency). Before he found the job, he charged his phone at an outdoor socket used by Park & Recreation workers to power snow and leaf blowers, grass mowers, and the like. Paul makes his way up and down city streets, avoiding the angry and unfriendly who are always on or about the Town Green. Yet, also, he makes friendly contacts with those he knows will welcome him. And he does this and more without begging for money. He just doesn't ask, even if he needs the help. He never attends church services, but members of the downtown church on his way who have come to recognize him give him a little from time to time. Unlike other homeless people, people who know Paul, however slightly, know that he is not a drug user nor what some call a panhandler. He presents as decent and responsible. Those who may doubt what I say about Paul Crowe should know that I have worked with homeless people for many years. I know the good and the not-so-good. Though I've formed relations with many of them, none stands out as Paul does. By "stands out" I don't mean "better" than all others, or the like—but better than what many well-housed people think of the unhoused.

Even such a story, once told and heard, can inspire bigger and related stories—ultimately theories. For example, if a nation can think of itself as "exceptional," then certainly one can identify an individual like Paul as exceptional. Observations of the kind of similar persons are the planted seeds from which a theory may bloom. What is exceptional about Paul Crowe is that he does not think of himself as special in any way. To be sure here, already, is a difference from stories Americans tell of their exceptional nation. Some might think Paul is somehow afflicted by a personal or mental failure of some kind. Perhaps. But I know him well enough to know, at least, that he is no more free of personal issues than I and most of my friends are. Mental problems are human and, in this world, normal. As a matter of fact, in this world thinking of oneself as exceptional may be a disorder of some kind. The latest Diagnostic and Statistical Manual (*DSM-5*) of the American Psychiatric Association lists only one new disorder that might cover such a state of mind. This new disorder is "Intellectual Disability" which includes among its symptoms an inability to cope in the social domain, which refers to "empathy, social judgment, interpersonal communication skills, the ability to make and retain friendships, and similar capacities." Even this vaguely defined symptom does not come close to the American belief that its nation is exceptional. But here the attempt to make sense of the Paul Crowe story arrives abruptly at its limits in a discussion of the lesser stories as the beginning of much larger ones. Paul may be exceptional for the way he gets by against the odds, but he is not a personal instance of the kind of exceptionalism that is, one could say, a pathological aspect of a national culture that has in fact bred the idea that America is endowed with what Walter Russell Mead calls its *Special Providence*.[13]

What is One to Make of a Story Like This?

First, it is obvious that Paul's story is, like all stories, tendentious to some degree. There is no such thing as a story free of its teller's peculiar ideas, even prejudices. Or, I should add that, in this instance, I am the author of the story—and I am surely factually wrong in several ways at once. Authors of all kinds write what they know, *or think they know*, and what they want to say. *Non-fiction* is a mistakenly named genre of literature. There is no such thing as writing free of fiction. When a story is told all that is required is that the parts fit together well enough to confirm the teller's identity. Even when the two parts are ceramic—as in the classical definition, they were—they are unlikely to fit perfectly or come free of imperfections in the parts of a once hand molded piece of clay or the like. Ceramics are compounds of various natural and (today) a few unnatural elements. This is more true of stories told from memory or some other imperfect source. Leaving aside the classic notion of broken ceramic parts, the underlying fact of stories is that they are made up out of various separate parts that are drawn together by the storyteller. For awkward example, consider Einstein's **E** for Energy and **M** for Mass that, only after he mathematically derived

---

[13] Walter Russell Mead, *Special Providence: American Foreign Policy and How It Changed the World* (Routledge, 2002). Walter Mead does *not* think of America's Special Providence as pathological.

the C² for the Constant [speed of light squared], came together to make sense of a natural story about how different universal parts somehow fit together—until, that is, some yet to be born Heisenberg-type confirms the uncertainty of the fit. This is much the same as the line from *Genesis 1:* "In the beginning God created heaven and earth." Here the constant G² puts Earth together with its Beyond; Or: B=EG². Silly perhaps. But I happen to be what is commonly called a *believer* and stories like this make imperfect sense to me whether it is a story told by a sixth-century BC priest in Israel or a different story told by Martin Heidegger in *Sein und Zeit* in Marburg in 1927. Earth *und* its Beyond or Being and Time are parts of fundamental mysteries of human life and belief.

But the point here is not any individual's state of mind, but how, in the case of Paul Crowe, he *seems* to live according to at least three elements attributable to American culture—individualism, pragmatism, life against and among Nature. This comparative glimpse of a man who has what some would consider trouble in his life might, just might, suggest a kind of relation between a mental state and the collective mind, or culture. If an individual can get by in life without exaggerating his special qualities, what are we to say about a good enough nation that, in spite of its several virtues, still thinks of itself as utterly exceptional? Is it possible that such a state of collective mind is, if not insane, at least pathological in a global world where national realities and culture are in constant flux? That cultures can be insane we know from the Nazi era in Germany. Still, in that era when there were many, if not all, who were utterly sane and competent individuals—Dietrich Bonhoeffer for example.[14]

Is a small, very local story like that of Paul Crowe inherently indicative of elements of American culture? If by *inherent* one means that Paul himself, as he lives his life, is thinking about America, the answer is not likely. Paul is smart but not by any means a theorist of culture. But then he is not the story teller here. I am, and this book is a story about American culture. So, for now the question is: Can any story be told without becoming a theory of something?

Charlotte Bronte's *Jane Eyre*, for example, is one of the modern world's most famous stories. Jane begins as a disinherited young woman who works as a governess who comes to work in Rochester's household. Soon she is loved by her wealthy master who, in time, invites her into marriage. But at their wedding ceremony an intruder enters to give a reason the marriage cannot go forward—Rochester is already married. Charlotte immediately leaves Thornfield Hall to work as a teacher in a small rural school. Yet, one day she imagines hearing Rochester calling her. Jane returns to discover Thornfield Hall all-but destroyed by fire. Rochester is blind, but Charlotte finds him and loves him still. They embrace. The book ends.

Charlotte Bronte's story turns on a mystery. To whom was Rochester married? The novel answers that his wife, Bertha Mason, is insane and lives in the attic from which, in early days, strange noises were heard. But the story says little more about her than that Bertha set the suicidal fire that also destroyed Rochester's life—until, that is, Jane returns. The love affair is redeemed. The reader is left with an improbable happy ending. Many read the novel with satisfaction if not pleasure at some of the twists and turns. But then there is the otherwise untold story of Bertha.

---

14 Eberhard Bethge, *Dietrich Bonhoeffer: Theologian, Christian, Man for His Times: A Biography* (Fortress Press, 2000; revised edition, edited by Victoria J. Barnett). Bethge was a student, minister, and close friend of Bonhoeffer. He served alongside Bonhoeffer in his anti-Nazi confessing church. Bonhoeffer was hanged by the Nazis on April 19, 1945, at 39 years, in the Flossenbürg concentration camp but days before the defeat of Germany in WWII. Bethge, however, survived to die at 91 years in 2000.

The Madwoman in the Attic: The Woman Writer and the Nineteenth-Century Literary Imagination (1979), by Susan Gubar and Sandra Gilbert, uses Bertha Mason's imprisonment in Rochester's attic as a figure characterizing the exclusion and isolation of women writers, as if they were in the same boat as an insane woman of color from colonized nineteenth-century Jamaica. Gubar and Gilbert compose an important theory of women in the literary imagination of the period, but theirs does not focus as much on the racial and imperialist aspects of the exclusion as does Edward Said in *Culture and Imperialism* (1993). Said mentions *Jane Eyre* only a few times in his study of how imperialism sneaks into a culture that devalues women and racially different others. Still, of *Jane Eyre* he says plainly: "Bertha Mason, Rochester's deranged wife in *Jane Eyre* is a West Indian, and also a threatening presence, confined to an attic room."[15] Though Said's book discusses Jane Austen's stories in greater detail,[16] his *Culture and Imperialism* reveals how books like *Jane Eyre* tacitly reveal the role of stories in the making and sustaining of an imperialistic culture.

This is to say, in effect, that fiction is real, even empirical in its way. This has been recognized as long ago as 1759 when Laurence Sterne—author of what some take as a classical literary work, *The Life and Opinions of Tristram Shandy, Gentleman*—is reported to have said that fiction is as much data-based as any other truth telling story. Sterne, in 1759, wrote: "Fiction is never just a plot: it is a microcosmos consisting of all manner of things, including events, characters, places, local and national memories, myths, maps, title pages, blank pages, blacked-out pages, gallons of ink, reams of paper, and, above all, writing—writing of seemingly any kind. Such a cosmos accommodates travelers moving in many directions, or none at all."[17] Though written several centuries ago, today such a line might be considered, by some, postmodern and, by others, just plain radical progressive thinking before its day. Just the same, few are they of whichever age who could plausibly dismiss it out of hand.

Returning now to Paul Crowe, though he does not specifically think of himself as an instance of elements of American culture, it could be said that I am pretending to be an Edward Said to his story. Such is the way with cultures. They are made up out of countless stories told and retold, every time with some or another inflection, until some find a way to come together with other separated parts that fit together to become a living or working myth of America and of what she is and wants to be. When I refer to the stories as "made

---

15 Edward Said, *Culture and Imperialism* (Knopf, 1993), 62.
16 Just before the Charlotte Bronte line, Said discusses Jane Austen's *Mansfield Park* (1814) for the way "… Thomas Bertam's slave plantation in Antigua is mysteriously necessary to the poise and the beauty of Mansfield Park, a place described in moral and aesthetic terms well before the scramble for Africa, or before the age of empire officially began." See Said, *ibid*, 59. On the same page he, first, quotes John Stuart Mill's *Principles of Political Economy* (1848) on the West Indian colonies as places "where England finds it convenient to carry on the production of sugar, cotton, and few other tropical commodities." Then, as an illustration of Said's remarkable intellectual range, he refers (again on the same page) to Walter Rodney's classically well entitled book *How Europe Underdeveloped Africa* (1972) while also identifying Aimé Césaire, Frantz Fanon, and Albert Memmi as having been on the same track. [For several views, including mine, on this issue see Charles Lemert, "Said & 'Edward': Dispossession and Overcoming Nostalgia," in *Sociological Practice* (2005 / Special issue on the legacy of Edward Said). The journal is no longer in print but this article and others in the special issue can be found at https://www.okcir.com/product/proceedings-journal-article-said-edward-dispossession-and-overcoming-nostalgia-by-charles-lemert/]. Better yet, Lemert, "Said & 'Edward': Dispossession and Overcoming Nostalgia," in Lemert, *The Structural Lie: Small Clues to Global Things* (Paradigm/Routledge, 2011), 152–167.
17 Richard Hughes Gibson, "On Fiction's Lawlessness in Which the Digressive and Progressive Are Reconciled," in *The Hedgehog Review Web Features* (March 23, 2023) @ https://hedgehogreview.com/web-features/thr/posts/on-fictions-lawlessness

up," I do not mean they are false. I mean they are made into something that means. This is what storytelling can do and often does.

This Being Said, Where Does One Begin to Tell the Story of American Culture?

The first answer is straightforward enough: Not with a formal academic theory. I have no objections to academic theories. I have made a living writing about and composing them. But when it comes to thinking through the stories of American culture one must, as I have, patch together elements from many different sources gathered over time from different corners of American spaces. Time and space, important to say, are integral to the context for all stories. Paul Crowe's time and space, one could say, are in the here and now. Charlotte Bronte's story was in a very English place in its long gone past—but it contains elements that allow it to have meaning in the here and now of its readers. But even more, there are stories about American personages who have played a role in patching together elements of American culture. One is Thomas Jefferson who, in a letter to John Holmes on April 22, 1820, wrote that maintaining slavery is like "holding a wolf by the ear and we can neither hold him nor safely let him go. Justice is in one scale and self-preservation in the other."[18] As was Jefferson's way, here he is saying much in a few words about what now is known to have been the deep unsolved contradiction in the great man's life. He welded many important parts of the American story while, against his better angel, he kept slaves to the end, while failing to make good on his wish to emancipate them.[19] Then too, he seems to have loved a slave, with whom he bore children, and who was in effect his virtual common law wife.[20] Jefferson was a brilliant writer and leader, but also a human being who lived outside the norms of the day.

Then too others among the so-called founding fathers spoke poignantly in one or another personal situation so as to offer a line able to grow into a larger story. Benjamin Franklin loved chess but not to the exception of his political wit. Walter Isaacson reports two moments of his chess playing sometime during his first diplomatic mission to Paris (1776–1778) when the Revolution against George III was well under way:

> During one of Franklin's late-night chess matches, a messenger arrived with an important set of dispatches from America. He waved him off until the game was finished. Another time, he was playing with his equal, the Duchess of Bourbon, who made a move that inadvertently exposed her king. Ignoring the rules of the game, he promptly captured it. "Ah," said the duchess, "we do not take kings so." Replied Franklin in a famous quip: "We do in America."[21]

A simple story like this can serve as counter-instance to the one of the ever-serious Thomas Jefferson. Franklin's wit was just one among other aspects of his genius. He was a world-recognized scientist for his studies of electricity—surely a Nobel Prize winner had there been such a prize then. Perhaps also, Franklin was America's greatest diplomat for having successfully negotiated with both London and Paris, and winning financial support for

---

18 *The Jefferson Monticello* @ https://www.monticello.org/research-education/thomas-jefferson-encyclopedia//wolf-ear-quotation/
19 Ken Burns, *Thomas Jefferson* (Florentine Films, 1997; PBS at Prime Video).
20 For the full story, including doubts about the deeper nature of their relationship, see Annette Gordon-Reed, *Thomas Jefferson and Sally Hemings: An American Controversy* (University of Virginia Press, 1997).
21 Walter Isaacson, *Benjamin Franklin: An American Life* (Simon & Schuster, 2003), 372.

the Revolution from France. Some even think he was—Jefferson notwithstanding—the very best writer of the day. Franklin was real, as was Jefferson. But they were also the sources of stories among the stories that in time were both hidden and remembered in the American story.

Then too, there are so many stories about Abraham Lincoln such that it is hard to say which is the most worth retelling. One good prospect is the account of his struggle with Jefferson's dilemma—and how where Jefferson failed, Lincoln succeeded. Lincoln is known to have said in 1864: "I am naturally anti-slavery. If slavery is not wrong, nothing is wrong. I cannot remember when I did not so think, and feel."[22] This more than a year *after* he decreed the *Emancipation Proclamation*. Among much else, the very fact that so long after his most important decision, he was still debating the slave issue with, in this case, a lawyer practicing in Frankfort, Kentucky, shows how his own position was caught in the tangle of national attitudes as to the freeing of slaves. Before Lincoln arrived at the moment on January 1, 1863 when he would declare their emancipation, he had wavered on the practical question of what to do with and for freed people. For a long while Lincoln held to the idea of colonization by which freed slaves would be returned to Africa. That so intelligent a man could entertain such an impossible solution is a sign of the depth to which he shared with the nation at large a struggle in the bloody confusion of war. Yet, in due course, moved in part by the chastisement of Frederick Douglass who let him know how silly colonization was, Lincoln made the ever-since crucial decision to declare the slaves emancipated. Even here he did so against the advice of many of his closest advisors, and by relying on the legal provision that allowed a President to act freely in the national interest during war. It was a war time decision made on military grounds. Its effect, however, was military in that he saw, all the more clearly, the importance of freed men as uniformed members of the Union Army. Black soldiers played an increasingly vital role in the war effort, especially in Grant's and Sherman's invasion of the South. Thus it is that a few lines in a letter a year later is part of the story of Lincoln's presidency during war—a story that still today supports the widely held conviction that he was the greatest of all American presidents.

Stories about Jefferson, Franklin, and Lincoln make a pertinent and enchantingly serious contribution to the American story during its first settled years after 1776 until 1865. But they were just a beginning. Yet these three worked their good deeds at a distance in space and time from each other. Better, however, would be an historical situation where story telling was central to a community's existence in such a way that its theories were a culmination of those before—thus a clearing of the field for new growth in America's story. This would be Concord, Massachusetts from roughly 1836 when Ralph Waldo Emerson published *Nature* and 1837 delivered his *American Scholar Address* at Harvard to 1888 when Louisa May Alcott died.

The Concord Moment, 1836–1888

However one dates the Concord Moment, it was the most important locally connected group of theorists and story tellers for a good 50 years in the middle of America's most momentous century. Among much else, the Concord Moment began before the Civil War when the United States came close to coming undone and, after, when American culture had to redefine its values. America's classical values formulated in the Revolutionary era

---

22 Letter to Albert G. Hodges, April 4, 1864, *Abraham Lincoln Online/Speeches & Writings* @ http://www.abrahamlincolnonline.org/lincoln/speeches/hodges.htm

remained in place even as they were eclipsed by those of a new urban society that had to deal with acute social differences. By the 1880s, differences between North and South would remain, made all the more troublesome by rapid urbanization in the North, where still more differences came to the fore. These were, as still now, differences normal to all serious urban societies that embrace people who left the countryside for the city where, then already, as now, they found a mélangerie of immigrants—from rural to urban, from south to north, from Europe to the East coast, from Asia to the West, with their many differences of all kinds. All urban people must live and get by with each other in spite of differences in languages, races, habits, and especially cultures—which is to say, theories of how things ought to be.

Though Concord, in its moment, was a suburb of Boston, New England's hub, it never, not even today, became anything like a city as did Worcester and Springfield to the West, Providence to the East, and Manchester to the North, or Hartford and New Haven to the South. That it remained small in the day meant that those who lived there in the mid-nineteenth century day knew one another, whether closely or in passing. So when intellectual and literary notables gathered in mid-nineteenth century Concord, the town's intellectual genius exceeded that of Harvard's, whose day would not come for another generation.[23] It may also have rivaled even Boston for its literary brilliance[24]—a brilliance encouraged by the shared belief that America, while benefitting from its European past, was by then free to pursue its own distinctive intellectual and literary intuitions. Robert D. Richardson, the late great intellectual biographer, said of Concord in the day:

> Concord in the 1830s and 1840s—Emerson's Concord—was to America what Goethe's Weimar had been to Germany. In each case, a small if not humble society came to have enormous moral and intellectual importance for a country, coming eventually to symbolize the best of the national culture.[25]

Concord also came to be called, by Susan Cheever, the American Bloomsbury in her short but trenchant book, *American Bloomsbury: Louisa May Alcott, Ralph Waldo Emerson, Margaret Fuller, Nathaniel Hawthorne, and Henry David Thoreau*.[26] All of those mentioned lived in Concord during its Weimar or Bloomsbury moment. Others of comparable note were part of the mix—Bronson Alcott lived there for a while, John Brown lectured before his end, and Herman Melville visited Hawthorne often. All were major literary or public figures of the day and all told stories.

For the time being, however, let Emerson and Thoreau serve as the exemplars of Concord's story-based theorists. Emerson literally made his living lecturing around the country. These were the days before any kind of media, except newspapers in towns across the land. The big news in towns and small cities was when a famous lecturer like Emerson came to lecture. Emerson never spoke down to his audiences in packed meeting halls. His stories, however, were not really stories. His stories, such as they were, were tales of ideas that pertained to the lives of those attending—tales of those who to him represented America itself. He

---

23 On the pathetic state of Harvard in Thoreau's day, see Laura Dassow Walls, *Henry David Thoreau: A Life* (University of Chicago Press, 2017), 70–73.
24 On Oliver Wendell Holmes, Sr. and Boston as the Hub "of the planet," see Louis Menand, *The Metaphysical Club* (Farrar, Strauss and Giroux, 2001), 5–7. More generally on Boston, see Mark Peterson, *The City-State of Boston: The Rise and Fall of an Atlantic Power, 1630–1865* (Princeton University Press, 2019).
25 Robert D. Richardson, *Henry Thoreau: A Life of the Mind* (University of California Press, 1986), 54.
26 Susan Cheever, *American Bloomsbury: Louisa May Alcott, Ralph Waldo Emerson, Margaret Fuller, Nathaniel Hawthorne, and Henry David Thoreau—Their Lives, Their Loves, Their Work* (Simon & Schuster, 2006).

often began with a snippet that sets the tone and place of his topic. One of Emerson's most important lectures, *The Transcendentalist* in 1842, was delivered in the Masonic Temple in Boston. He began: "The first thing we have to say respecting the *new views* here in New England, at the present time, is, that they are not new, but the very oldest thoughts cast into the mold of these new times."[27] Most often the lectures were cast around plenteous references to older thinkers. A few pages on, in *The Transcendentalist*, an essay on his unique view of idealism, Emerson introduces his view of materialism, beginning with reference to a classical materialist, Étienne Bonnot de Condillac. Then Emerson creates an imaginary story of a capitalist who relies on the work of granite cutters whom his auditors might have assumed to be the epitome of hard-nosed materialists:

> The sturdy capitalist, no matter how deep and square on blocks of Quincy granite he lays the foundations of his banking-house or Exchange, must set it, at last, not on a cube corresponding to the angles of his structure, but on a mass of unknown materials and solidity, red-hot or white-hot, perhaps to the core, which rounds off to an almost perfect sphericity, and lies floating in soft air, and goes spinning away, dragging bank and banker with it at a rate of thousands of miles the hour, he knows not whither,—a bit of a bullet, now glimmering, now darkling through a small cubic space on the edge of an unimaginable pit of emptiness.[28]

Well, one might wonder, is this a story of the kind that could become part of a theory? The puzzle is soon solved in Emerson's next paragraph.

> In the order of thought, the materialist takes his departure from his consciousness, and reckons the world an appearance. The materialist respects sensible masses, Society, Government, social art, and luxury, every mass, whether majority of numbers, or extent of space, amount of objects, every social action. The idealist has another measure, which is metaphysical, namely the *rank* which things themselves take in his consciousness; not at all size or appearance. Mind is the only reality, of which men and all other natures are better or worse reflectors. *Nature, literature, history, are only subjective phenomena.*[29]

Even if the last, italicized statement might stump a modern critical theorist, the paragraph as a whole is jam-packed with lucid explanations of a mystery of the day. This was 1842. Hegel had passed nine years earlier, leaving behind the most ambitious and analytically strict idealism in the emerging modern world. It would be another three years after Emerson's lecture before Marx would publish his 1845 *Camera Obscura*, in which he turned idealism on its head by announcing that ideas and ideals are "interwoven with the material activity and material intercourse of men." But Emerson, who read everything and everyone, here collapses the differences into a daringly original concept of idealism. Did his audience in Boston Masonic Hall that day understand every word? Probably not. But remember—they paid a price to attend the lecture by one of America's rising intellectual stars. They had no cellphones to distract. They surely listened intently to the story of the granite cutter. One can only suppose that most there got the story's theoretical point about idealism's relation to the dawning capitalist world. In the day, the material things of America's fast growing

---

27 Emerson, *The Transcendentalist*, in *Ralph Waldo Emerson: Essays and Lectures* (Penguin Books/Library of America, 1983), 193. [Punctuation is correct here. It is in the published text.]
28 *Ibid*, 194.
29 *Ibid*, 195; emphasis added.

capitalism were on the minds of those in the nation's small towns—some of whom worried that the mental and the spiritual would drown under the wave of economic materialism.

Henry Thoreau was close to Waldo Emerson and his family. The two of them often met and walked in the woods. Thoreau's cabin on Walden Pond was on Emerson's land. He lived for a long stretch in Emerson's house. In fact, on September 6, 1847, Thoreau closed his cabin on Walden Pond and moved into the Emerson house, encouraged by Lidian, Waldo's wife, who needed his help with the house and kids while Emerson was away on a yearlong lecture tour of Europe where his *Transcendentalism* was quite the rage. "Never again would Henry live alone."[30] After, he lived with others in Concord, including Louisa May Alcott and her family. But the most cherished and well-used of the homes he shared with others was the Yellow House on Main Steet, bought in 1849 by his brother John where his mother Cynthia made a list of needed repairs that Henry made sure were taken care of. "The Yellow House attic became his bedroom, parlor, workshop, nature museum, and window on the world."[31] From this house by the river he set off by boat for some of his exploratory trips and many of his jobs as a surveyor. There too he died May 6, 1862 at only 44 years of life.

Robert Frost said of Thoreau and his *Walden* that "he surpasses everything we have in America."[32] Frost would know because he told the story of America in much the same way, nearly a century after Thoreau. Many have told that story, but a case can be made that the tale told in *Walden* in 1854—three years after Herman Melville's *Moby Dick* and Nathaniel Hawthorne's *House of the Seven Gables* (both in 1851)—is more deeply Americana, planted in the local soil of Salem. By contrast *Moby Dick* was set at sea where Ahab was obsessed with a great whale and *House of the Seven Gables* was a story of a tragically fallen family trapped in a haunted house. The whale and the house were also, one way or another, metaphors of America differently carried away by the waters of time. *Walden* is pure America. Thoreau's life at the Pond brought together the full membership of the still young nation—immigrant farmers, native peoples, modern railroad men, freed slaves, the tax collector, the bean field farmer seeking to modernize, and more. In this sense it was more fully an American story—so much so that not even Mark Twain's *Huckleberry Finn* in 1888 reaches so broadly into the American story, except perhaps in the final note where Jim is left freed but alone and Huck sets off to the West. Not even William Faulkner who won the 1949 Nobel Prize for Literature for, as the Prize Committee put it, "his powerful and unique contribution to the modern American novel." Faulkner's *As I Lay Dying* in 1930 was as local as local gets and indubitably a great American novel, but Thoreau was not writing fiction, not even a little. He told true stories that fiction writers would then (less so now) find hard to tell. Thoreau's stories were of real people in Concord or fictionalized people who could have lived in Concord.

Walden is composed in such a way that Thoreau quilts his big story out of patches, each colorful in its own way and each telling more than a story but a story that offers explicit ideas. And the ideas were so universal that they became part of the thinking of American writers and public figures—including Louise Erdrich, Wendell Berry, John F. Kennedy, John Muir, many others —who planted Thoreau ever deeper in the American culture.[33]

---

30 Laura Dassow Walls, *Henry David Thoreau: A Life* (University of Chicago Press, 2017), 231.
31 *Ibid*, 285.
32 Robert Frost, Letter to Wade Van Dore, June 24, 1922, in Richard Ruland, editor, *Twentieth Century Interpretations of Walden* (Prentice Hall, 1968), 285.
33 Douglas Brinkley, "Thoreau's Wilderness Legacy, Beyond the Shores of Walden Pond," *New York Times Sunday Book Review* (July 9, 2017), 12. See also, on Thoreau's influence on the sciences, Olivia Box, "Using Thoreau's Notebooks to Understand Climate Change," *JSTOR Daily* (March 16, 2022) @ https://daily.jstor.org/using-thoreaus-notebooks-to-understand-climate-change

More on this last point to come. But for now, let's start at the beginning where Thoreau responds to questions about why he would do such a thing as leave town to live alone by a pond. Some thought he must be lonely or afraid. Some asked how much the cabin cost (for which his answer was $28.12 1/2.). And so on. Then, a bit further on, he begins to tell stories, first mysteriously, of Brahmins "sitting exposed to four fires and looking in the face of the sun"; then:

> The twelve labors of Hercules were trifling in comparison to those which my neighbors have undertaken; for they were only twelve, and had an end; but I could never see that these men slew or captured any monster or finish any labor. They have no friend Iolaus to burn with a hot iron the root of the hydra's head, but as soon as one head is crushed, two spring up. ... I see young men, my townsmen, whose misfortune it is to have inherited farms, houses, barns, cattle, and farming tools; for these are more easily acquired than got rid of. Better they had been born in open pasture and suckled by a wolf, that they might have seen with clearer eyes what field they were called to labor in. ... But men labor under a mistake. The better part of the man is soon plowed into the soil for compost.[34]

So here, at the beginning of *Walden*, Thoreau tells several kinds of stories—those of the classical Iolaus who does the bidding of Hercules; then of his laboring neighbors who were worse off even than those Hercules had burned with a hot iron.

Then, a few paragraphs on, Thoreau offers the most memorable line in the book: "The mass of men lead lives of quiet desperation."[35] This is his answer, not just to the mass of desperate men, but, ultimately, to the question of what America had been and was becoming. No one would insist that *Walden* is a critical theory of America even after it had come to be viewed that way. The 1854 book was composed as a whole in the seven years after its author left the Pond. Thoreau's story telling method must be taken for what it is. It was, first, different from that of his mentor and friend, Emerson—who always came out with the point of the theory he was declaiming. Emerson's passions were muted but fully discernible. Thoreau was more the story teller—stories told with strong clues as to the theory they are composing—but stories nonetheless. This being said, *Walden* was in fact a criticism, subtly made, of the new industrializing economy that in the 1850s was already imposing itself into the daily affairs of Concord's townspeople and farmers alike. Nowhere in the book is this more clear than in "The Bean-Field" which is an early lesson on the evils of the Anthropocene Age, just then dawning. (More on "The Bean-Field" to come later.)

For now, here, at the beginning of *Americans Thinking America*, the point is to state the underlying theory at work in this book, which is: *America and its culture are what, over the centuries, Americans thought both about their America and, as citizens, looked to those who were prominent and talented enough to lead its armies, to write its laws, to compose its poetry, to tell its stories, to rethink its worn out ideas, and to invent new ones needed for changing times.* No $E=mc^2$ here. Our subject, thereby, is far more complicated, in its way, than the subject matter of astrophysics. Complicated, that is, because the study of a culture like this one cannot be reduced to mathematics or any other analytic shorthand. Einstein's mass and energy, like the stars, are part of an unfathomably remote and enormous universe so beyond human observation that one only has numeric data to represent its activities. To

---

34 Henry David Thoreau, *Walden; or, Life in the Woods* in Brooks Atkinson, editor, *Walden, and Other Writings of Henry David Thoreau* (Random House/Modern Library Edition, 1992), 4–5.
35 *Ibid*, 8.

conclude what Einstein did was to translate *"Energy must equal Mass times a Constant Squared [where the constant is the Speed of Light]"* is to translate his theory into a neat and efficient statement for others to debate. **E=mc²** is the language of those debates. Crudely put, science of this kind is at best a supremely intelligent guess based on what can be thought based on the debates of the day. This is true even if a pesky Werner Heisenberg says:

$$\Delta x \, \Delta p \geq \frac{\hbar}{2}$$

The natural sciences rely on a language and method of their own in order to simplify their countless possible data for others to see what they are driving at.

A science of culture trying to get at the nature of a thing like *America* must try to explain something that can *never* be reduced to a formula. The study of cultures must contend with at least three major problems.

(1) Cultures are always changing but, when changed, they retain threads of what came before. *Cultures are, thereby, always several things at once.*
(2) Cultures change because those subject to them want and demand something different and better. *Cultures are, thereby, always and necessarily rent with different features their various subject groups want.*
(3) Cultures, thereby, are primarily what practical people subject to them need or want or desire. Aspects of a given culture are sometimes agreed upon by those professionally trained in making theories of cultural things. *Cultures therefore comprise both practical and professional theories—both derived from stories told.*

Simply put: *(1) Cultures change. (2) Cultures always deal with differences. (3) Culture's stories are both practical and professional.* Put more inclusively, theories of culture are always also social theories because, even though a culture is an analytic thing unto itself, cultures always arise from stories and thoughts told by the people who make up the society to which they refer. To make all this ever more complicated—social theories, always and necessarily, are influenced, if not determined, by the cultures in which they originate. All this makes one wish vainly for an **E=mc²** of culture.

So What Is Theory When it Comes to Culture?

I verge on the outrageous when, now, I pull together the separate pieces of this chapter with the now familiar assertion that culture itself is a working theory made out of stories told here and there over centuries. When a culture is planted in a well-enough bordered nation like the United States of America, then its America comes into being—from the first stories told on land at Plymouth or St Augustine or some still unknown place near Roanoke to today's nation-wide celebrations based on legends from New England, Florida, Virginia. There were, we must assume, in these early times and places, memorable lines that turned into stories. They may well have been some version of "What have we done coming here?" Whether it was the weather (different in all three places), or the looming wilderness, or the first recognition of strange others living thereabouts, or any of any number of worries they could have had—what those first settlers thought and said to their stranded companions came to be first stories of America. One of these is the legend of a first harvest time meal with the Massasoit near Plymouth Rock in November 1621 or the less well-known celebration allegedly held just after 38 English landed on December 4, 1619, somewhere on the

James River in Virginia. There were stories told when and where by whomever that led over time, two and a half centuries later, to Abraham Lincoln's declaration of the last Thursday in November as a national day of Thanksgiving.

The Thanksgiving legend, true or not, has been melded into a number of other stories, many certifiably true, others not, to become part and parcel of American culture. Or, stated from the more elevated, often academic, side of these things, any formally stated analytic theory of American culture need not mention this or any other story, but such a theory would be worthless were it not able somehow to embrace these first thanksgivings. In fact, it could even be said that when certain formal theories of America refer to its exceptional qualities relative to other national cultures it is drawing on the many Thanksgivings from 1619 and 1621 to 1863 when Lincoln proclaimed a national holiday for many other lesser stories in villages, towns, and cities across the land.

Americans Thinking America is a theory book, of course. It is a book about the major figures who, down through the years, told in their actions, speeches, and writings of the larger story of America. This is a book of cultural theory, yes, but only in the sense that Americans have thought, as they still do, and tell stories of what America means. Also, before turning to a second chapter, don't be surprised when each of the chapters to come begins with a local story—this to remind you that all big cultural stories begin in some very local place which, for me, is New Haven, Connecticut.

2 Elements of American Social Theory

What went yee out in the wilderness to see?
—Samuel Danforth, A Brief Recognition of New England's Errand into the Wilderness, 1670

Our day of dependence, our long apprenticeship
to the learning of other lands, draws to a close. ...
Who can doubt, that poetry will revive and lead to a new age,
as the star in the constellation Harp, which now flames in our zenith,
shall one day be a polestar for a thousand years.
   —Ralph Waldo Emerson, American Scholar, 1837

Easily the most dramatic episode in American history
was the sudden move to free four million black slaves in an effort to stop a great civil war,
to end forty years of bitter controversy, and to appease the moral sense of civilization.
   —W.E.B. Du Bois, Black Reconstruction in America, 1860–1880, 1935

The American Negro problem is a problem in the heart of the American.
   — Gunnar Myrdal, The American Dilemma:
   The Negro Problem and Modern Democracy, 1944

This world is white no longer, and it will never be white again.
   —James Baldwin, Notes of a Native Son, 1955

Once I thought to write a history of the immigrants in America.
Then I discovered that the immigrants were America.
   —Oscar Handlin, 1951
   The Uprooted: The Epic Story of the Great Migrations that Made the American People

Before the city, there was the land.
Go back just over a century and a half to the place that became Chicago,
and our familiar distinction between city and country vanishes.
   —William Cronon, Nature's Metropolis: Chicago and the Great West, 1991

We choose to go to the Moon in this decade and do the other things,
not because they are easy, but because they are hard.
   —John F. Kennedy, Speech at Rice University, Houston, 1962

TimeSpace reflects the view that for every kind of SOCIAL TIME,
there exists a particular kind of SOCIAL SPACE.

DOI: 10.4324/9781315210230-3

*Thus, time and space in social sciences should not be thought of as separate,
measured separately, but as irrevocably linked into a number of combinations.*
—**Immanuel Wallerstein, World-Systems Analysis, 2004**

*I would say that as our struggles mature,
they produce new ideas, new issues, and new terrains on which we engage in the quest for freedom.
Like Nelson Mandela, we must be willing to embrace the long walk toward freedom.*
—**Angela Davis, Freedom Is a Constant Struggle, 2016**

Americans Thinking Their Culture

Samuel Danforth (1626–1674) was an early Puritan minister in today's Roxbury, Massachusetts.

He began one of his sermons with a question that would ask what future Americans were doing in their new, wild land: "What went yee out in the wilderness to see?" The question soon was revised as a formal doctrine of America's manifest destiny which, in turn, became the basis for its theory of American exceptionalism.

Two centuries later, in 1836, Ralph Waldo Emerson would publish one of his most famous books, *Nature*. The following year, he would deliver his *American Scholar* lecture at Harvard, which declared: "Our day of dependence, our long apprenticeship to the learning of other lands, draws to a close. …Who can doubt, that poetry will revive and lead to a new age, as the star in the constellation Harp, which now flames in our zenith, shall one day be a polestar for a thousand years." It was so controversial in already stuffy Harvard that he was no longer permitted to speak on campus. Nevertheless, this declaration came to be understood as America's declaration of *cultural* independence. When understood in relation to his book, *Nature*, it completed the three elements of American culture suggested in the courageous if ill-liberal thinking of the early Puritans. These three were: the *individualism* and *pragmatism* directed at living against, and with, *nature* and the wilderness that in time it would overcome to form a continental nation.

Yet these three themes would not stand alone. Not long after Emerson's important writings in the 1830s, Americans would lapse into a Civil War that would become the first of a series of national troubles that challenged this then still new nation. In 1935, W.E.B. Du Bois published *Black Reconstruction in America, 1860–1880* which began with these words: "Easily the most dramatic episode in American history was the sudden move to free four million black slaves in an effort to stop a great civil war to end forty years of bitter controversy, and to appease the moral sense of civilization."[1] Du Bois, one of America's most dazzling thinkers and writers, meant these words ironically. *Black Reconstruction* is the story of how the freeing of Black slaves was at best weak-kneed. After the Civil War the short period of relative progress for freed men and women under the nation's program of Reconstruction of the South and this most terrible of its institutions would fall away. The southern planters still had their fields producing the cotton that brought them wealth. Without slavery, they construed a plan whereby poor whites would join them in keeping poor Blacks as field and domestic labor. Slavery continued without the name under a Jim Crow system that would endure at least until the Civil Rights Act of 1964, and long after in the continuing structural racism of the United States. *Black Reconstruction* ends "One reads the truer deeper facts of Reconstruction with great despair."[2]

---

1 W.E.B. Du Bois, *Black Reconstruction in America, 1860–1880* (Oxford University Press, 2017 [1935]), 3.
2 *Ibid*, 728.

Just more than a century later, Gunnar Myrdal the Swedish economist and Nobel Prize winner declared: "The American Negro problem is a problem in the heart of the American."[3] Myrdal's *The American Dilemma: The Negro Problem and Modern Democracy* published in 1944 is still read with interest today. In due course, the very idea of a "Negro problem" was challenged by Black writers, notably James Baldwin in the essay "Stranger in the Village," in *Notes of a Native Son* in 1955: "The world is white no more, and it will never be white again."[4]

So, the troubles that erupted after the Civil War grew more serious in the twentieth century when another, to some, troubling presence of immigrants from abroad. Immigrants gave as much as they got. Eventually many realized that they too were immigrants, as Oscar Handlin put it at the beginning of *The Uprooted: The Epic Story of the Great Migrations that Made the American People* in 1951: "Once I thought to write a history of immigrants in America. Then I discovered that the immigrants were America."[5] To be sure, there were troubles associated with changes in urban neighborhoods but nothing like the divisive ones associated with slavery and race. In fact there were ways in which new cities like Chicago, rebuilt after the fire of 1871, became *both* home to new immigrations *and* vital centers open to the vast Western lands. "Before the city, there was land. Go back just over a century and a half to the place that became Chicago, and our familiar distinction between city and country vanishes."[6] This was William Cronon in 1991 in his book *Nature's Metropolis: Chicago and the Great West*.

The original three elements continued to be central to American culture. Individualism remained, and remains, a basic American value as did pragmatism which became all the more prominent as the uniquely American school of pragmatism of philosophy came into being early in the twentieth century. Then, after mid-century, nature became important in a new way. The plains had been settled, Alaska would be the new frontier, but then the moon became the first stellar object to serve as a new natural frontier. On September 12, 1962, then President John F. Kennedy spoke at Rice University in Houston, Texas to call attention to America's then new program of lunar exploration: "We choose to go to the Moon in this decade and do the other things, not because they are easy, but because they are hard."[7] The words gave flight to the basic American value of hard-work against unthinkably distant natural odds.

Then ironically just a decade-plus after Kennedy's speech on space exploration, Immanuel Wallerstein introduced the early versions of what became his theory of world history. TimeSpace was an historian's reversal of the term used in astrophysics, SpaceTime. The first tacit elements of Wallerstein's theory could be found in the first volume of his four-volume work on modern historical time in global spaces, *The Modern-World System, Vol I* in 1974. Eventually, he made the concept central to his theory of the modern world as a global system: "TimeSpace reflects the view that for every kind of SOCIAL TIME, there exists a particular kind of SOCIAL SPACE. Thus, time and space in social sciences should not be thought of as separate, measured separately, but as irrevocably linked into a number

---

3 Gunnar Myrdal, *The American Dilemma: The Negro Problem and Modern Democracy* (Harper and Brothers, 1944), xlvii.
4 James Baldwin, "Stranger in the Village," *Notes of a Native Son* (Beacon Press, 1944), 175.
5 Oscar Handlin, *The Uprooted: The Epic Story of the Great Migrations that Made the American People* (Little Brown and Company, 1951), 3.
6 William Cronon, *Nature's Metropolis: Chicago and the Great West* (W.W. Norton, 1991), 23.
7 John F. Kennedy, *Address at Rice University in Houston, Texas on the Nation's Space Effort, 12 September 1962*. (John F. Kennedy Presidential Library and Museum @ https://www.jfklibrary.org/asset-viewer/archives/jfkwha-127-002.)

of combinations."[8] Wallerstein's *world-system* was one that allowed him to examine the world's history as extended over the time of the modern world from 1500 until 1991, when that system fell apart. The system during that long half-millennium was one in which world space was settled and dominated by a series of core states—from the Spanish settlers of the new world through Dutch, French, English and American world powers. These core states dominated and exploited the mineral and labor wealth in what he called the peripheral regions of the world in what came to be called the Global South. But his analytic theory was anything but an abstract theory. In point of fact, the modern world was a world in which emergent capitalist states stole the personal and natural resources of the world's poorest. It was (and in a way still is) a colonizing system. Wallerstein himself was a scholar (when he was not being political) but in his scholarship he refrained from using words like greed, exploitation, and evil.

Since the 1960s many became more and more outspoken about the evils in their world. None more so than Angela Davis, a political radical who refused to give up in her efforts to improve the political and economic realities that oppressed so many people: "I would say that as our struggles mature, they produce new ideas, new issues, and new terrains on which we engage in the quest for freedom. Like Nelson Mandela, we must be willing to embrace the long walk toward freedom."[9]

Through the years (perhaps until recent times) the basic elements of American culture and its social theories have endured with more than a few adjustments to the times Americans had to deal with and understand. Now for a good decade from 2015 to 2025, America, like much of world at large, has faced troubles that, while short of those that led to Civil War, are shaking the foundations of its culture. Since we got over that war in the 1860s, it is reasonable, if not certain, that we and our values will somehow overcome the neo-fascism that in our time puts the American experiment at risk.

Story Tellers Come and Go

J.P. Dempsey's closed the other night. In its day it was a joint of a certain kind—dark but for the bar signs advertising beers, muted lights here and there, and flat screens tuned to one or another sports channel. Weekends the place grew loud. Some in the crowd shuffled about as if to dance to the juke music. The larger crowd had to shout to be heard. But weeknights were muted. A lonely fugue filled the air. Regulars sipped their drinks, flirted with Jo when she was at the bar, muttered vague protests on the state of the world.

Just the same, in spite of it all, a gentle humanity stood its ground. Dennis sat alone by the door sipping something dark. He lived alone. He complained with good reason about his job. Henry, who at 40 years still played ice hockey, sat at the far end of the bar near the kitchen. He downed whiskeys with beer chasers after long days at the beck and call of his bosses. Depending on the night, one might have met Bob from a town some fifteen-miles distant. He came so far because his wife did not approve of drinking. He was never drunk. Joe was a craftsman so gifted that he traveled often and far to ply his skill. His drink was DeWars. He read conservative magazines except when James came with him. John was a small-particle physicist at Yale. He came after meetings with graduate students for a beer and something to eat. I once tried to describe what I thought I knew of the Higgs boson. He listened patiently, then responded with a smile and something like, "Can I buy you a

---

8 Immanuel Wallerstein, *World-Systems Analysis: An Introduction* (Duke University Press, 2004), 98.
9 Angela Davis, *Freedom Is a Constant Struggle* (Haymarket Books, 2016), 11.

drink?" More often than one might suppose, Dempsey's quietly desperate scene allowed for talk about very human things. Why didn't Jo marry her boyfriend and move on in life? What will Dennis do when he retires? Why didn't Henry get a better job? What kind of a job requires flying to Geneva every three weeks? And so on.

In spite of the silences and disagreements, people who gather at places like Dempsey's are talking about their lives, yes; but also, about life itself—about its wounds, and what comforts can be had. Not just in bars in New Haven, but also in coffee houses in Delhi, or among grieving groups beside the Ganges; in tea houses in Cardiff or pubs in Bristol; while sipping coffee in cafés off Boulevard St. Germain or Pernod in the bar near the *gendarmerie* in Montargis; in truck stops at Effingham where I-70 west and I-57 south cross; in the once-Starbucks now a Party-approved coffee house in the Forbidden City or in the Party-monitored community room in the disappearing *Hutong* off Tiananmen; in the late spring poppy fields south of Bishkek on the way to the national park in the *Kyrgyz Ala-Too* mountains; beside the food trucks in Porto Alegre by the *Lagoa dos Patos*; on the park benches near the South Terrace in Adelaide or at the D'Arenberg Cellar Door in McClaren Vale; during potlatches in Tanana, Alaska, or in the hunting cabin east on the Yukon River; in the Buddhist monastery in the mountains northeast of Daegu; on sidewalks after morning prayers at mosques in Bridgeport, Connecticut or during ham suppers in the church in East Alstead, New Hampshire; in near empty strip joints in the winter in Essen, or in rowdy Saturday night camp grounds in Split; even in the late night, nude-normal hot tub in the upscale massage place next to the Cafe Beaujolais in Mendocino; or strolling on the *Çukurcuma Caddesi* in Istanbul before visiting the Museum of Innocence; or on dark and rainy nights in the only pub in Ballingskelligs where three lonely men drink to keep warm in the emptiness of it all—or anywhere in the world where people meet each other, strangers or friends, seeking some small measure of ordinary wisdom.

Even as very local gatherings for drink and pleasure or grief and pain or any other of the all-but countless reasons people gather in small groups away from their homes, these gatherings don't last all that long. Participants come for a time, then go elsewhere. Those who gathered at Dempsey's on State Street in New Haven just went away when it closed. Several may have died. Some went to AA. Another switched to Archie Moore's on Willow Street. Rumor has it that Jo the barkeep finally got married and moved away. Remarkably, one man switched for a while to a bar well out on rural Route 80 the last I heard of him. The lovely couple who came from time to time may have come back to Ward 9, the bar that took over Dempsey's place. I just don't know. Bar life no longer appealed to me, much to Geri's satisfaction. I still drink martinis in the evening. She doesn't drink so even that bothers her. Yet, we love each other which means we tolerate what we don't like.

Gatherers come for a time, then go some other place—home, a graveyard or ashes borne on a river or ocean, northern-most Minnesota of all places, some another bar, wherever. Stories told one time in a gathering place may still be retold by those who leave. Such it is with stories. They are told until they are not. Many of the dead are remembered as loved ones tell stories of their beloved long after they are gone.

Yet, the remarkable thing is that stories told everywhere in this world's TimeSpace may linger for a good while until they are, shall we say, swallowed up in the mysterious clouds of a culture where no one remembers from where or whom they came.

The TimeSpace of Culture in America

If cultures are territorial, as they are, then they are embedded in Nature. So too, thereby, must be social theories. Yet, one common failure of many social theories is that they have lost a connection with Nature—with, that is, the winds, waters and stars, rocks, and soil that surround and support all living things. Even materialistic theories, like those that issue from Marx miss this point when they treat the material world as if it were not much more than machines, markets, and commodities.[10] There are exceptions to the habit of those who think of social things as utterly outside of Nature. Of these the theories of Bruno Latour are notable by virtue of his ferocious attack on the artificial line drawn between the social and the natural.[11] Still, when all is said and done, the problem exists—not only in specifically social theories but in the modern West's generic ideas about cultures. The earth in all its material and immaterial aspects is, literally and figuratively, the ground on which all forms of natural life—most especially human social life—move and have their being.

Already in the earliest days of settlement, America's colonizers could not escape the looming trees and lands of North America's natural geography. The first Pilgrims crossed the dangerous North Atlantic seas to what, for them, was a vast unexplored wilderness. In 1670, Samuel Danforth's sermon, *A Brief Recognition of New England's Errand into the Wilderness*. It's New Testament text was from *Matthew 11*: "*What went yee out in the wilderness to see?*" Danforth went on to remind his congregation that they were on a religious mission[12]—and then added that the new world's natural environment was the surface on which his new Americans were meant to live out their sense of moral purpose. Those millions who came after these first settlers followed the rebellious Pilgrims in Massachusetts and the loyal Cavaliers in Virginia by heading West through Kentucky to the vast plains beyond which now are no longer frontiers but satisfactorily settled. Yet, well into the twenty-first century's still newer world of globalization in which, among much else, America's popular culture obsesses before countless plays on the theme of Alaska as the last frontier.[13] If Alaska is thought to be a current last American frontier on land, it is almost a given that somewhere and somehow in the inner workings of American culture, there will be another, as there was in 1962 when President John F. Kennedy rallied the nation to support space exploration.

After the Moon landing in 1969, the 1977 Voyager space missions sailed to Mars and Saturn and then beyond our solar system into the unthinkably vast universe. On a day to come, long after today's space missions, men and women will almost certainly report back to a latter-day version of NASA's Webb Space Telescope. Alaska, the Moon, Mars, and beyond. The wilderness of American culture is a culture of open, unknown, wild, or barren spaces, of hard work against the odds, of a present oriented toward an unknown future, and, above all, of winning against the odds.

Not all of American culture, and surely not all of its social theories, are based on frontier cultures. Still, and more to the point, it is true enough that what common culture Americans share is shaped by the natural territories and barriers upon which its different people attempt to inscribe definite and shared meanings that were part of the local culture of its English settlers, then many others, down through time to today when globalization has ballooned nature into the hard and watery surfaces of planet earth.

---

10 As, by the way, Marx himself did not ignore nature. He began with it. See the beginning of his 1844 essay "Estranged Labor," where he writes: "The worker can create nothing without nature, without the *sensuous external world*." In Robert C. Tucker, editor, "The Economic and Philosophical Manuscripts of 1844," in *The Marx-Engels Reader* (W.W. Norton, 1978 [second edition], 72.
11 For two instances among many: Bruno Latour, *Politics of Nature: How to Bring the Sciences into Democracy* (Harvard University Press, 2004); *Facing Gaia: Eight Lectures on the New Climatic Regime* (Polity Press, 2017).
12 Perry Miller, *Errand into the Wilderness* (Harvard University Press, 1956).
13 *Alaska: The Last Frontier* is but one of no fewer than, on recent count (June 2017), 22 television series or films featuring Alaska. At last count well into the 2020s there were still more.

American culture from its earliest days has passed through a series of pivotal moments that themselves turned on the country's distinctive geographic nature. They are:

- its settlement early in the seventeenth century of coastal outposts on the edge of an indeterminate, forested wilderness;
- its eighteenth century wars of independence against the then most powerful North Atlantic colonizer and the naval power that controlled the seas;
- then too, in the eighteenth and early nineteenth centuries when America's great religious awakenings led to the burning-over of upper New York State which opened yet another trail toward the Western frontier;[14]
- then America's terrible nineteenth century Civil War that divided a feudal, agrarian South[15] from its industrializing North, a war begun in large part in a political struggle over whether the then new Western frontier states would be free or enslaved;
- then too, early in the twentieth century when a progressive era did what it could to come to terms with multi-racial and multi-ethnic migrant populations in new frontier urban centers like Chicago, *Nature's Metropolis*;
- and in mid-twentieth century when the United States had to adjust to the new geopolitical reality that, after the ravages of World War II, America had become the only true world power—a power that, ever since, required America to cast its presence on all parts of the earth;
- then, late in the twentieth century and early in the twenty-first when the hard realities of global geographical distances and real economic and political differences made it all the more clear that globalization meant America had to adjust to a multipolar world in which neither its economic brilliance nor its military prowess could win the day in remote places on nature's globe.

These historical junctures were never aligned along a linear trajectory from lesser to more developed. From the earliest of its days, this then new world was itself multipolar, contested by no fewer than four global powers, not to mention its many indigenous nations.[16] Well before the seventeenth century, when British colonizers were first encountering Indian nations interior to their coastal settlements, the Spanish were already a presence in Florida, along the Gulf of Mexico and Rio Grande, in the Southwestern deserts and up the Pacific Coast. At much the same time, the French had designs on New England but had to settle for a northerly presence from which they gained control of the Saint Lawrence River, the Great Lakes, and the upper Mississippi Valley, where, along the way down, they encountered the Spanish coming upriver. When the French were colonizing the lower Mississippi River and eventually New Orleans in 1682, the Dutch were colonizing the lower Hudson River before New Amsterdam gave way to New York in 1664. In the 1740s, Russians crossed the Bering Sea to attempt a permanent settlement in North America, but the native Aleutians held them off then and again. By 1800, the Russians gave up after a promising colony in Kodiak was

---

14 Whitney R. Cross, *The Burned-over District: The Social and Intellectual History of Enthusiastic Religion in Western New York, 1800–1850* (Cornell University Press, 1950).
15 Though a feudal slave economy, the South's cotton production made it a force in ante-bellum American foreign policy; see Matthew Karp, *The Vast Southern Empire: Slaveholders at the Helm of American Foreign Policy* (Harvard University Press, 2016). The now classic work on the feudal workings of the South's slave system is Eugene Genovese, *Roll, Jordan, Roll* (Random House, 1972).
16 Alan Taylor, *American Colonies: The Settling of North America* (Penguin Books, 2001). And for the same point in a later period, see Steven Hahn, *A Nation Without Borders: The United States and Its World in an Age of Civil Wars, 1830–1910* (Penguin/Random House, 2016).

overwhelmed in 1794, only to leave behind in our time, Nikolaevsk, a Russian Orthodox village of just more than 300 people on the Kenai Peninsula.

Then too there would not have been an American Frontier, had not France, having over-reached financially before and during its 1789 Revolution,[17] been forced for financial reasons to sell off its Louisiana Territory west of the Mississippi—thereby making the United States territory larger than England's and France's combined. Immediately after the Louisiana Purchase in 1803, the Lewis and Clark expedition (1804–1806) explored and mapped the continent's far Northwest up the Missouri River from St. Louis at the Mississippi to the Columbia to the Pacific. After settlement by European nations, down to the present, the North American land mass from the Atlantic to the Pacific Oceans, from the Arctic ice fields to the Gulf of Mexico and the *Río Bravo del Norte* and as far south as *Chiapas* has been, one way or another, prominent in the TimeSpace of the modern world-economy.

The very use of a concept like Immanuel Wallerstein's *TimeSpace*[18] may seem to be not much more than academic theoretical jargon. Still, just as practical social theories can do certain things that professional ones cannot, so the reverse is true. In this instance, there may be no better concept than *TimeSpace* to account for the unusual way American culture is grounded in natural spaces on which its historical time has traveled. Few other nations are planted on the edge of so grand an open space. The notable others include Australia settled around its Outback; Brazil settled mostly close to its long Atlantic coast well-distant of its Amazon rainforests; the Democratic Republic of Congo centered in Kinshasa on the Congo River near the Atlantic well apart from its mineral rich interior where, under Mobutu Sese Seko's vicious rule, enslaved Congolese people mined wealth for him and Belgian colonizers.[19] Most Canadians live along a thin southern tier below its forested and Arctic northern territories, much as most Russians live in Russia's European West below the Arctic north and far from Siberia to the East. Most Mongolians live in its capital city Ulaanbaatar because the rest of the country is barren desert and grassy steppes. In all of these cases, with rare exceptions, the open spaces are given over to the mining of carbon fuels and other mineral wealth or timber harvesting or grazing land or as reserves for indigenous or traditional people.

Unlike North America, these other global open spaces are not settled in a network of culturally salient population centers. Only the United States has settled its vast interior plains from the Mississippi River valley to the Rocky Mountains—some 500,000 square miles of mostly open prairie that serves for more than the production of grains and meat producing animals. Iowa City, Omaha in Nebraska, Columbia in Missouri, Lawrence in Kansas, Rochester in Minnesota are examples of small but culturally cosmopolitan centers with universities and institutions known the world over for contributions to science and technology, medicine and health care, literature and the arts, social sciences and philanthropy. No other major nation has so fully lived out so much of its historical time on such an empty but prominent aspect of its physical geography.

TimeSpace, awkward though it may sound, is a social theoretical concept that erases the categorical differences between time and space, thereby moving social theory closer

---

17 Theda Skocpol, *States and Social Revolutions: A Comparative Analysis of France, Russia, & China* (Cambridge University Press, 1979), 174–185.
18 Among other of Immanuel Wallerstein's works, see in also: "The Inventions of TimeSpace Realities: Toward an Understanding of our Historical Systems," in Wallerstein, *Unthinking Social Science: The Limits of Nineteenth-Century Paradigms* (Polity Press, 1991).
19 Adam Hochschild, *King Leopold's Ghost: A Story of Greed, Terror, and Heroism in Colonial Africa* (Houghton-Mifflin, 1998).

to modern theoretical physics since 1905 when Einstein's theory of special relativity first proposed a theory of spacetime[20]—which itself is a concept that describes both cosmic and particulate nature. At the least, it can be said with reliable conviction that American culture is a very good instance of the extent to which collective social life with all its cultures and theories takes place in nature, on what solid ground there may be amid the rocks and deserts, rivers and lakes, oceans, and atmospheres.[21]

Because of America's unusual historical play on its natural environment and open spaces, one can understand why from the beginning its culture has been preoccupied with moral errands on a series of wild places that, one after another, became its several frontiers. Hence a corollary to these basic principles is that American culture, as it has come down over four centuries, has long encouraged retreat as a way to respond to over-bearing social circumstances. Americans all have come from somewhere else, as Oscar Handlin said in *The Uprooted*—almost always from places torn by violence or poverty or political tyranny. Most who today call America home are no more than distant descendants of immigrants who came generations before. Some owe their right of place to the English who came to Jamestown or Plymouth or to the Spanish and the French who came to St. Augustine or to the Irish in Boston or New York City, or Poles in Chicago, or Germans in Cincinnati or St. Louis or many others who crossed the Atlantic. Still others owe their lives here to bone weary kin who made their furtive way by land to *El Norte* or those who came in shackles across the Middle Passage from West Africa, and others over the years from all parts of the world—from East Africa and the Caribbean, from South and East Asia, from nearly every place, no matter how remote, where people vulnerable to enslavement or others who were free to leave for a dream. Then, of course, there are those who left the American East to cross the prairies to escape cities and towns they felt were suffocating their sense of economic and social purposes. More than any other national culture, America is a culture of strangers, thus of differences.

The General and the Particular: Trouble for Social Theories

All social theories suffer a necessary contradiction. On the one hand, there can be no such thing as an abstract theory of any living social group. On the other, it is in the nature of a theory to suggest, if not stipulate, the general nature of any particular, practical social arrangement. For social theories to break with the practical is for them to break with the social realities they represent. In this case, granting the particular and practical importance of America's natural environment and its immigrant peoples, it could well be asked whether it is too general a claim that its social theory has been deeply formed by the American TimeSpace.

The crucial moment in the codification of America's theory of itself was in the period of relative calm between the end of the Revolutionary War until the ratification of the *Constitution* in 1788 and the *Bill of Rights* in 1791 and a near half-century later when Lincoln decreed the *Emancipation Proclamation* in 1863 and the end of the Civil War in 1865. In the between of the nation's two transformative wars, a uniquely American concept of individualism was mostly in the background of its culture. It was, of course,

---

20 So far as I can tell, among physicists *spacetime* is the preferred expression, perhaps because their definitive mystery is cosmic space. It might thus be that among social analysts like Immanuel Wallerstein *TimeSpace* is used because historical time is the pivotal puzzle.

21 The first now classical historical demonstration of the importance of natural and physical spaces to human settlement is: Fernand Braudel, *The Mediterranean and the Mediterranean World in the Age of Philip II* (Harper Torchbooks, 1972–73 [1949]).

there in Jefferson's rhetoric in the *Declaration of Independence,* as it had been earlier in Benjamin Franklin's awakening of the spirit of community associations to serve the public need. Then too there was the first great religious awakening in the 1740s that was given both inspiration and theory by Jonathan Edwards' revision of Calvinist doctrine in favor of the relative free will of the Christian to save himself from damnation. And to be sure, James Madison's deep scholarship that led to his own revision of the enlightenment ideas of Adam Smith and Dave Hume, among others. As a result, Madison's contributions of the *Federalist Papers* even as he focused on the question of the crisis of factions that he believed would have destroyed the young Republic, drew upon his first political principle of the free individual. Also, Madison's *Federalist 10* turned on an Americanized notion of the rights of the individual in a republican democracy—a notion that was planted in solid constitutional earth in the *Bill of Rights* which he authored. Still, it remained for the likes of Thoreau and Emerson and the Concord Bloomsbury movement to replant and nourish an explicit theory of the American individual—a theory Thoreau composed by giving witness to a robust individual parting of ways from the then-prevailing desperation of the mass of men. Thoreau's down-to-earth idea of desperation as normal to America in the day was a conviction that could have been written in tandem with Emerson's high theory of an American intellectual culture cut away from Europe's old traditions. Emerson's idea of "Man Thinking" turned toward the sublime power of transcending Nature itself. Just the same it was a philosophical cousin to Thoreau's escape to life along by the Pond. In both cases, and others of the day in Concord, Nature both permitted and shaped the American individual as one able to face the challenges of life in a still new world where *man thinking* is meant to live on his own terms against a still imposing wilderness.

If, however, this individualism arises against an environment so formidable that a people cannot know what lies beyond the seas and the forests, they are forced to be seriously practical. They must find ways, if they can, to endure the sea sickness, the loneliness of a bare-bones settlement, the fear of dark forests, and more. First and foremost, they must survive. Many did not. The English colony in Popham, Maine in 1607 quickly failed, while Jamestown in the Colony of Virginia (also in 1607) suffered terribly the first years but survived. Much earlier, the lost Roanoke colony in Virginia, settled in 1585, disappeared entirely, never to be found. The Massachusetts Bay colonists endured after 1628 but the Dorchester colony on Cape Ann failed in 1623. Hardy and unrelentingly practical souls they had to be. Their all-too-simple cultural beliefs served to lend embracing purpose to their miseries.

The idea that the early settlers were somehow on an errand to establish a new Israel in the new world must have seemed to some implausible. According to Perry Miller, the Massachusetts Bay Company "was not a battered remnant of suffering Separatists thrown up on a rocky shore; it was an organized task force of Christians, executing a flank attack on the corruptions of Christendom."[22] This vainglorious conceit served them well enough, if at the cost of a "haunting fear that someone, somewhere, may be happy."[23] It introduced a moral purpose that over the centuries came to assume, shorn of the religious wool, a central place in the way Americans thought about themselves. Over time God's errand became the manifest destiny of America's special providence. As all exaggerated expressions of national purpose must, this one is a fundamental, if crude, practical social theory of collective origins, responsibilities, and destinies.

---

22 Perry Miller, *Errand into the Wilderness* (Harvard University Press, 1956), 11.
23 H. L. Mencken, "Arcana Coelestia," *A Mencken Chrestomathy* (Alfred A. Knopf, Inc, 1949), 624.

The Three Primal Elements of American Social Theory

First, important to say, the word *elements* is appropriate here because, as I said in the first chapter, both cultures and theories are like the ceramic parts of old that must fit each other well enough that their recipient can know that the message is real, if not utterly true. Ceramic pieces are compounds. The definition that comes up on *Wikipedia* is useful enough: "A ceramic is any of the various hard, brittle, heat-resistant, and corrosion-resistant materials made by shaping and then firing an inorganic, nonmetallic material, such as clay, at a high temperature." I risk quoting a source once sneered at by the intellectual elite because there could hardly be a better definition for a cultural ceramic which is hard and brittle elements but must be shaped and fired to fuse its component parts. Then too, among the several ingredients is clay, itself a compound of soil and hydrous aluminum phyllosilicates such as kaolinite $Al_2Si_2O_5(OH)_4$. One only need know that the compound includes what chemists in my day called elements, of which H_2O may be the element known by most. This is to say that here the *elements* of American social theory should not be read as though its parts are different and separate. They are as fused as is any chemical compound. Water is not water without Oxygen, H_2O.

Hence, coming to American culture itself, the primary, but not exclusive, elements of American social theory are: 1) an inclination toward *individualism*, 2) a sense that *nature* is both a challenge and a resource, and 3) a hardy *pragmatism* needed to face the challenges and fashion the resources of the new worlds ahead.

None of these three was ever a singular element standing on its own. Each was developed in relation to the others. Each also emerged as a familiar and evident theme in early American culture, most obviously in the seventeenth century settlement of the coastal colonies on through the eighteenth century's war of independence; but also, of course, in the settlement of the western frontier during the long nineteenth century from 1776 to 1917.[24] Yet it remained for the Concord era, in its broadest sense, to fix the three themes in terms by which they could be understood over the years since.

These three are considered *primary* in the double-meaning of *first—foundational*, but also *partial*. The Civil War brought Concord's idyllic moment to an end, forcing a painful reconsideration of American culture and, thereby, of American social theory. Nothing in Europe's nineteenth century, not even 1848, came close to the enduring structural discord that bled for all to see in the American Civil War. Ever after the War's end in 1865, the American Republic has suffered a relentless disorder over racial differences—a disorder sometimes ignored, or buried from view, but one that in the long run always came out to force both practical and professional social theories to face up to a difficult reality that, even as late as the 2020s, hides behind a low-lying tyranny.[25]

In 1944, Gunnar Myrdal described this persisting wound on America's moral and political body, and please note his use of the expression "American Creed":

> The American Negro problem is a problem in the heart of the American. It is there that the interracial tension has its focus. ... [The "American Dilemma"] is the ever engaging conflict between, on the one hand, the valuations preserved on the general plane which

---

24 The idea of a long nineteenth century owes to Eric Hobsbawm's trilogy, *The Age of Revolution: Europe 1789–1848*, *The Age of Capital: 1848–1875*, and *The Age of Empire: 1875–1915* (Random House: 1962, 1975, 1987 respectively).

25 Here I refer to an authoritarian one-time President who has often been called "the former guy," who at the same time bears the name Donald J. Trump.

we shall call the "American Creed," where the American thinks, talks, and acts under the influence of high national and Christian precepts, and, on the other hand, the valuations preserved on specific planes of individual and group living, where personal and local interests; economic, social, and sexual jealousies; considerations of community prestige and conformity; group prejudice against particular persons or types of people; and all sorts of miscellaneous wants, impulses, and habits dominate his outlook.[26]

Plus which, there could hardly be a better description of the mundane sources of practical social theories—and especially so of American ones that must contend with the contradictions of a culture in which disordering elements confuse and frustrate high-minded ordering values. Because Americans think so highly of their moral purposes, their more vulgar prejudices grind hard and fine.

When the equilibrium between order and disorder remains broken for a long time, the culture of the disordered nation emerges as all important for its presumed ability to heal the differences. But when it comes to deep structural conflicts, a culture is markedly less able to resolve the normal practical questions of differences of identities among its members. Plus which, differences arising from identity politics, so-called, are all the more severe when the national society is meant to embrace so many people who have emigrated from so many different origins. National cultures present themselves as able to calm troubles by ordering the disorders natural to any and all modern complex societies. Yet, unlike other national cultures, the American one is, in effect, crosscut by its unique historical tensions. The trunk of the American tree of liberty has grown not so much from a deep tap root as from a subterranean rhizome of stray and wandering roots—its immigrating peoples.

Hence, an additional emergent feature of American social theories derives from the tension between the ordering functions of the nation's public culture and the disordering assaults of its local cultural prejudices. No culture of so grand an assemblage as the United States can possibly impose order when it must contend with a society cut several ways at once—when, that is, its disordering movements are part and parcel of the deep structure of the society.

After the Civil War: America Faces Conflicting Values Arising from New Troubles

When, therefore, a nation's culture is meant to do what cannot be done well enough, then the powers-that-be must enter the fray among the disordering differences.[27] Here, a good part of the trouble lies with popular notions of the nature of culture itself. Cultures are commonly thought of as high-minded, immaterial, or above the fog rising from the darker side of social life. Thus it is often thought that power is hard, and darker still, relative to culture, which is considered soft, perhaps gentle, even palliative—thus passive before power's ability to get its way. This is not an entirely silly assumption. It is obvious, for example, that regimes intent upon dominating their populations deploy power to distort aspects of the shared culture, beginning with signs and words, the media, and even the inability of people to communicate honestly.[28] The Nazis, for obvious example re-appropriated the ancient

---

26 Gunnar Myrdal, *The American Dilemma: The Negro Problem and Modern Democracy* (Harper and Row, 1944), xlvi.
27 Juergen Habermas, *Legitimation Crisis* (Beacon Press, 1975).
28 For example, Herbert Marcuse, *One-Dimensional Man: Studies in the Ideology of Advanced Industrial Society* (Beacon Press, 1964).

Asian swastika as a symbol for their pseudo-religious political propaganda, which in turn silenced the German people before Hitler's murderous outrages.

Power and culture cannot, therefore, be taken as separate social spheres. Power relies on culture to do its dirty deeds. Culture rises to public prominence only when its messages are broadcast by a power elite. Since knowledges, including social theories, are at the heart of any given culture, even the most mundane of practical ideas fly on the wings of power. No one has made this point more persuasively than Michel Foucault:

> The *relations of power* are not in a position of exteriority to other types of relations (economic processes, *knowledge relationships*, sexual relations), but are immanent in the latter; they are the immediate effects of the divisions, inequalities, and disequilibriums which occur in the latter, and conversely, they are the internal conditions of these differentiations ...[29]

Hence, the neologism that Foucault invented: *powerknowledge*. However one chooses to put it, Foucault's description of the entangled relations between power and knowledge, among other social relations, is apt to Myrdal's dilemma of race in America. Cultural knowledge's intimate relation with power explains a good deal about American history and culture—acutely so because of the contradiction between its all-too-lofty idea of its special providence and the base reality of its local, tribal differences and prejudices. American culture has been, at least, hot enough to melt-down, if not fuse, the nation's inherent conflicts among ethnic, religious, racial, and other identities.

American culture's soft attitude toward its values renders the American people weak before raw power at the highest levels of State power. The evident discord in the Revolutionary generation between, in particular, Thomas Jefferson's idyllic republicanism and Alexander Hamilton's strong federalism injected into the nation's life blood a dispute that even now, centuries later, is as poisonous as ever. The Civil War is said to have been the "birth of modern America,"[30] but that America was born amid the still vulgar dispute over states' rights and national unity. At the end of that War in 1865, Abraham Lincoln's commitment to preserving the Union seemed to have settled matters until his assassination doomed Reconstruction. Upon the North's decision in 1877 to withdraw troops from the former Confederacy, Reconstruction collapsed, and the Jim Crow South soon revealed itself to be de facto slavery.[31] If, closer to our time, the hard-bitten racism that irrationally incited hatred of Barack Obama and his presidency means anything, it means that states' rights have little to do with republican values. More generally, recourse to states' rights ultimately has more to do with a long-bred resistance to federal authority—in particular with respect to racial and other of America's several unreconcilable multicultural differences.

That the American state must attempt to govern an assemblage of different, often conflicted, groups is also tied up with the fact that, over the centuries, American federal authority has been subject to social movements of just as many kinds as there are differences. Neither right nor left can begin to define the contesting movements, many of which owe their histories to the several sides of the Civil War. Even now, the remnants of the Ku Klux Klan and the Southern Poverty Law Center can trace their purposes to that War and its entailments.

---

29 Michel Foucault, *The History of Sexuality: Volume 1* (Random House, 1978 [1976]), 94. Emphases added.
30 Lous Menand, *Metaphysical Club: A Story of Ideas in America* (Farrar, Straus and Giroux, 2001), ix.
31 W.E.B. Du Bois, *Black Reconstruction in America, 1860–1880* (Oxford University Press, 2017 [1935]).

The extent of this distinctive feature of American politics is measurable. For one among other metrics: The United States does not come close to having the largest number of Non-Governmental Organizations (NGOs). India does.[32] Still, the US ranks high among postmodern societies in the number and kind of political advocacy social movements since the 1960s.[33] NGOs are commonly devoted to the social well-being of their host society. But in the United States, NGOs of discernible political purposes are commonly allied with social movements seeking to support, or reform, *challenge or undermine* the nation's federal agencies. Public controversies over the legality of formally charitable organizations like those supporting a woman's right to an abortion and its right-wing opponents are examples of politically minded movements.

Movements of this kind are at the heart of the nation's long tradition of voluntary associations going back at least to Benjamin Franklin's community organizing of public interest organizations in the mid-eighteenth century. Post offices, hospitals, insurance companies, schools, even militia, and more were organized by Franklin in Philadelphia beginning with small groups often meeting informally, often in taverns after the workday. These modest voluntary associations were, in effect, social movements acting in civil society for the common good. Ever since these pre-Revolutionary beginnings, voluntary associations have functioned as social movements that energize—for better or worse—America's public life. The story of these movements is neither strikingly linear nor void of ill-purposes. Even so, two centuries later, especially after the world revolution of 1968, social movements became, if anything, more notably oppositional than ever. For the most part they serve common needs. Yet, some, to be sure, strike out against health service organizations like Planned Parenthood, local school boards that permit the use of textbooks thought to be politically woke, gun clubs resistant to the most oblivious of legal restrictions, charitable groups that care for "undesirable" populations like the poor and homeless, and so on. It's a mixed history. Then too, well more than two centuries after the *Constitution of the United States* in 1789, and the *Bill of Rights* in 1791, guaranteed the right of free association in the public sphere, leading constitutional scholars are still called upon to debate or defend social movements and controversial associations.[34] It could well be said that when American people organize to change or challenge, there will be factions *and* fractures in the body politic. The same may be true of other modern democratic states, but in America it is the more striking because of its belief that this nation and its culture are exceptional. Cultures like this one can and do stumble on the contradictions they breed.

These traditions and the turmoil and benefit they make are among the reasons that social movement theory has become a distinctive feature of American social, political, and legal thought not to mention political ideologies and actions including the legitimacy of State authority.[35] For a somewhat Jacobin center-right State, America's federal government over

---

32 India leads the world with 3.1 million NGOs (*Indian Express*, August 1, 2015). The United States has 1.5 million NGOs (*US Bureau of Democracy, Human Rights, and Labor*, January 20, 2017), which means that, per capita, it has 40% more than India. Also, the U.S. ranks in the top 15% of nations in the more reliable (than the Cato index) freedom rankings, while India is barely in the top 40% ("Freedom in the World," Freedom House, July 2017).

33 Kenneth T. Andrews and Bob Edwards, "Advocacy Organizations in the U.S. Political Process," *Annual Review of Sociology* 30 (2004): 479–506.

34 For examples: Jack M. Blakin and Riva B. Siegel, "Principles, Practices, and Social Movements," *University of Pennsylvania Law Review* 154 (2006): 927–950; Jack M. Blakin and Riva B. Siegel, eds., *The Constitution in 2020* (Oxford University Press, 2009); Owen Fiss, "Criminalizing Political Advocacy," *A War Like No Other* (The New Press, 2015), 200–224 and *inter alia*.

35 Charles Tilly, "Future Social Science," in *Roads from Past to Future* (Rowman & Littlefield, 1997), 17–33.

the years has twisted and turned around an impossible-to-define political center that remains stable and markedly free without beheadings of those thought to be troublemakers. All these years since 1789, there has been no Reign of Terror, even if, at times, the federal state did despicable evil to many. The Founders ignored slavery because many of them owned slaves. Andrew Jackson sent native peoples on a Trail of Tears to arid lands. Well after the Indian Wars were over, federal militia slaughtered Lakota Sioux in 1890 at Wounded Knee. And so it goes.

If there is a reason to give the United States a small benefit of doubt as to its worst democratic failures, that reason would be that it is the one national society that has made democracy work relatively well over a good stretch of its history while, at the same time, being willing to be home to so many different people. America was never a melting pot, nor could it have been. But, somehow, so far, it has worked even in the worst of times.[36] And when it works, it does because its ever-multiplying voluntary associations and social movements have lit the fires for changes of one or another kind. Not always to the good, but without the fires the pot doesn't cook.

The Six Distinctive Elements of American Social Theory

This being said, it is possible to propose the several *secondary* elements of American social theory, which are secondary only in the sense that the nation had to grow into itself before Emerson's American *man thinking* could come into its own. If American social theory's *primary* elements are cultural themes native to the nation's early formation, then the *secondary* ones came to the fore in the conjuncture marked by the Civil War and the nation's subsequent industrialization. It was then, late in the nineteenth century, that America's fate as a body politic of many and different members was the most salient domestic product of the nation's already apparent emergence as a global power.

Hence, the distinctive qualities of American social theory as they came to be:

1) an inclination toward the *individual*,
2) who is seen as understanding *nature* as both a challenge and a resource,
3) in respect to which the individual must possess a strong sense of *pragmatism*.

Yet, in their social relations, Americans thinking must also come to terms with

4) *disordering* obstacles to the ability of its culture to maintain a vital *interaction order*,
5) in which what common cultural knowledge that could be had must be had against the powerful effects of historically formed *identity differences*,
6) which, in turn, came to be as waves of immigrants and their social movements struggled among themselves to unsettle the nation state which itself struggles with *exclusions* inevitable to the fact that no one nation, especially not a Global one, can be everything to everyone.

None of the six distinctive elements of American social theory sprang full blown from the nation's beginnings. Some arose late in the nation's history. Some faded over time. Some faded then rose again. Some changed in content and orientation as history changed. None was ever purely and simply American. Some were borrowed. All were conditioned by American culture's geographical imagination, at the heart of which is a historically unique

---

36 Richard Hofstadter, *The American Political Tradition: And the Men Who Made It* (Alfred Knopf, 1948).

TimeSpace—itself a formal concept that explains many of the culture's practical social theories.

In thinking about these elements of American culture, it seems normal to ask, as most Americans would—is there one of them more important that the others? Since they are *elements*, the answer must be no because they are parts of the culture's parcel. In time—a time we in this moment cannot imagine, perhaps another element might spring up from the mix. This cannot be known now because it might never happen. We are speaking here of some interstellar-like eruption in the American TimeSpace in which, like a distant star exploding, it then gathers itself back into a different gaseous whole. Those who study the universe know that things like this happen—or, better put, they happened so far away and so lost in millions and more of light years ago that, measured by our TimeSpace here on this earth, the light they sent to our night horizons is, at best, televisual—no longer really there wherever it once was.

Still, returning to America's cultural elements, it is possible to suggest a glue, if you will, for the broken and refitted ceramic of our culture. What might that be? In a book like this one it must surely be a surprise that shocks by its undeniable authenticity. No better way to put it than by the words of one who has spent her life shocking the world with the aggressive truth of her thinking. That would be, again, Angela Davis who sees her people—who by implication are *all* people—in a never-ending struggle for freedom: "I would say that, as our struggles mature, they produce new ideas, new issues, and new terrains on which we engage in the quest for freedom."

Part II
American Social and Natural Spaces, 1727–1861

3 The First Fires of America's Revolutionary Culture
Benjamin Franklin, Jonathan Edwards, Thomas Paine

The world of misery, that Lake of burning brimstone is extended abroad under you ...
You are probably not sensible of this; you find you are kept out of hell,
but do not see the hand of God in it, but you look at other things.
  —*Jonathan Edwards, Sinners at the Hand of an Angry God, 1741*

A great Empire, like a great Cake, is most easily diminished at the Edges. Turn your Attention therefore first to your remotest Provinces; that as you get rid of them, the next may follow in Order.
That the Possibility of this Separation may always exist, take special Care the Provinces are never incorporated with the Mother Country, that they do not enjoy the same common Rights, the same Privileges in Commerce, and that they are governed by severer Laws, ... without allowing them any Share in the Choice of the Legislators.
By carefully making and preserving such Distinctions, you will (to keep to my Simile of the Cake) act like a wise Gingerbread Baker, who, to facilitate a division, cuts his Dough half through in those Places, where,
when bak'd, he would have it broken to Pieces.
  —*Benjamin Franklin, Rules by Which a Great Empire May Be Reduced To a Small One, 1773*

These are times that try men's souls,
The summer soldier and the sunshine patriot will in this crisis shrink from the service of their country;
but he that stands it now, deserves the love and thanks of man and woman.
Tyranny, like hell is not easily conquered; yet we have this consolation with us,
that the harder the conflict, the more glorious the triumph.
  —*Thomas Paine, American Crisis, 1776*

Fireworks and West Rock / Imagining When it All Began

On a clear day, once the leaves have fallen, I was able to see East Rock from my work desk in the house we have since left. East Rock is part of the Metacomet Ridge that runs north from the Long Island Sound at New Haven along the Connecticut River Valley through Massachusetts and Vermont to the Canadian border. East Rock was formed some 200 million years ago probably early in the Jurassic period. Today it is popular for hiking and picnicking in good weather. From its summit one can see the whole of urban New Haven, including our house in the day. On the 4th of July the city celebrates the nation's Independence Day to fireworks set off from the top of the Rock.

Some few miles off, East Rock faces West Rock which also is part of the Jurassic Metacomet Ridge. Today, West Rock is less amenable to summer fun, though part of the year it is possible to drive to the summit to enjoy the scenery and to consider the mysteries of the Three Judges Cave. The judges memorialized were not, however, eminent New Haven judges; rather, they were three of the 59 English judges (then called Commissioners) who signed the death warrant that led to the execution of King Charles I in 1649. They were regicides—king-killers. Thereafter, the Long Parliament ruled in a republican sort of way until the Royalist Restoration in 1660 when the regicides still living were themselves bound over and executed. New Haven's three judges—Edward Whalley, John Dixwell, and William Goffe—escaped retribution by fleeing England for New England. Legend has it that when warrants for their arrest were presented in the then small colonial village of New Haven, Whalley and Goffe hid in the cave atop West Rock. Dixwell hid elsewhere in the village. Today, only the deeply nerdy know the facts of the three judges, after whom three of New Haven's four axial streets are named. Whalley and Dixwell Avenues, and Goffe Street, thus, are modern day constructions along or across which the people of New Haven pass, often many times a day, without knowing much, if anything, about the three English king-killers of 1649.

In contrast to the East Rock, few are the hikers and picnickers who visit the West Rock. Still, apart from the judges, West Rock is more famous for another reason—Frederic Edwin Church's 1849 landscape painting, *West Rock, New Haven* (see Figure 6.1, p.108). Like many landscapes of the day, Church's *West Rock* is cast southerly toward the West against an afternoon sky. Church's West Rock is illuminated from the right of the canvas by a late in the day sun shining through cumulus clouds in the distance framed by dark but not quite foreboding clouds at the top of the tableau. The clouds, bright and darkening, occupy the uppermost half of the image. Just up from the bottom of West Rock, Church introduces a meandering stream as it flows down from the Rock. Today that stream rushes briskly aside a playing field eventually to become the West River—now as then, a geographic fence that cuts easterly toward Long Island Sound while the Metacomet Ridge veers north and west, defining the space of what in Church's day was a sparsely settled village.

Church was within his artistic rights to have painted the stream as a fulsome, but necessary, complement to the lush field that itself is a visual marker for the clouds above and the open face of the Rock just below midline. In the field, at the bottom of the tableau, and visually near the widening stream, men are at work pitching new-mown hay in wagons with a single cow in the shade of the wagon close to the river at the bottom of the painting. This pastoral scene is set off from West Rock by a dark green line of woods that frames the bottom third of the canvas, drawing the eye to the open Rock and the clouds above that fill the remaining two-thirds of the painting. A solitary, white steeple peeks its head through the trees as if to point beyond the Rock to the far West that, for the men in the field, it may have inspired a dream of the world they are too old to explore.

These geographic and historic wonders are there to be imagined as I worked, day after day at my desk. Were I to focus my mind's eye, I could also see the geologic lines—North to the Canadian arctic, West to the West Rock and beyond to the American West. All this, both the possible and the improbable can come together in an individual's imagination. When my attention wandered from work to the window to the geological Rock that is linked along the Metacomet Ridge to the West Rock, I often thought of the fireworks shot from the peak of the East Rock in the town-wide party each American Independence Day. It is a conceit of some American sociologists when they speak blithely of the *sociological* imagination as somehow unique to their way of thinking. In fact, the personal life runs on imaginations of many kinds—the social, yes; but also: the geological, the geographical, the historical, and others. None of these invokes a hard factual given. Whatever we ought to be doing in those moments it would likely go better if we dreamt with discipline of all the many structural things that are there to enrich, when they are not frustrating, the daily grind. And of this no other imaginable thing is more to the point of our mundane lives than culture.

Cultures and American Social Spaces

Cultures are necessarily territorial. Once established in a given territory, a culture may invade the whole of the space it names and claims. It is the work of border police and customs agents to certify, when they can, that those who enter either belong or, if not, that they pose no known threat to those who do. Yet, as debates in most late modern nations illustrate, borders are always porous—equally so to those with evil intentions as to migrants seeking a better world. But it is impossible to see, first-hand, the territorial boundaries of any given nation, nor even those of the smallest, most local neighborhoods and villages.

Borders are, in a sense, comparable to the frames of a painting like Frederick Edwin Church's *West Rock, New Haven*. Borders literally frame a space that only exists in the cultural imagination. Political figures responsible for border security can do no more than build (or promise to build) walls of some kind along their borders. Some walls—like the Berlin Wall—hold for an historical while until those closed out or those locked in tear it down. Some walls—like America's at check points on roadways at its border with Canada—provide no more than a hint of control, thereby reflecting an unwitting accord that those who can walk in snow-covered fields in either direction are unlikely to be many in number or dangerous in purpose. Then, of course, there are more porous walls—like the one a recent American president insisted he could build at the border with Mexico or others thought to be able to serve as China's Great Wall once did to keep out foreign foes. China's Wall served its purpose more or less well until 1600 CE when the Manchus invaded China proper, crushed the Ming Dynasty, and established a Manchurian Qing Dynasty in China—whereupon the Wall itself became, in due course, little more than a tourist mecca.

If walls cannot forever protect a people's borders, then what can? There is an answer that will not satisfy those who work in border police units. The answer is indeed soft and easily abused: Cultures alone are able to certify and protect those who belong. Only when a person reasonably grasps what other members of the culture understand to be the rules of the cultural game will that person be trusted as one on the in. Not even the inability to use one of a nation's languages is nearly so disqualifying as a serious mistake in grasping the rules of ordinary life. In Rwanda, I am told, it is illegal to ask a stranger whether she is Hutu or Tutsi. The rule is one of Rwanda's attempts to overcome the lingering effects of the 1994 genocidal war in which militant Hutus slaughtered some 800,000 Tutsis. Whether or not such a rule exists, it is at best foolish to inquire into another's tribal background. In North America much weaker versions of this rule may apply. Be careful when asking someone who they voted for. If a man, do not ask a woman when her baby is due unless you already know she is pregnant, not overweight. In some places in Europe, make sure you know when to greet with how many cheek kisses appropriate to which level of familiarity. In Korea, wait for the host to pour your beverage and don't forget to bring a gift. In Australia, upon ordering coffee, don't say "no worries" if you don't know what a flat white is. Cultures pervade the micro-encounters of strangers. They determine how one is to view the other. Some mistakes are forgivable. Some are not.[1] Either way, they reveal whether, and to what degree, the other belongs.

---

1 In Brad Pitt's 2009 film *Inglorious Bastards* with Quentin Tarantino and Christoph Waltz, the cover of American soldiers in a Nazi occupied cafe was blown when the one American who was fluent in German mistakenly used the wrong hand signal for two. Violence began.

Very often cultures change in mysterious ways and especially so when, of a sudden, revolutionaries rise up to change the rules of the game. Revolutions are mysterious because, more times than not, the final result of contrary cultural forces is delayed in time and transformed in aspect from what either side anticipated. The revolutionary culture that changed American political and social realities in the 1770s actually was energized by imperceptible changes in the 1740s—and they were inspired by very different thinkers coming to terms with different underground flaws in late colonial cultures of resistance.

Benjamin Franklin and Jonathan Edwards—the Awakenings of the 1740s

Surely some will balk before the idea that two men so completely unlike each other as Benjamin Franklin and Jonathan Edwards might have been of common purpose. Yet, a leading expert of the subject has said:

> Edwards and Franklin, though opposite in temperament, were both sons of pious New England Calvinist families at a time when their heritage faced a severe crisis. Each was precocious and, growing up in an era when print was the medium by which news and views spread,[2] each read everything he could get his hands on. Each as an extraordinarily curious boy delved into the mysteries and rigors of the theological volumes in his father's library. … Each soon realized that the Calvinist theology that dominated New England's intellectual life was sadly out of date according to fashionable British standards. Edwards and Franklin each spent a lifetime dealing with the clash of these two worlds. Each worked vigorously to use what he saw as essential in his New England heritage to meet the challenges of a rapidly changing modern age.[3]

They were different in more ways than temperament. Though they were both born early in the eighteenth century (Edwards, 1703; Franklin, 1706) and both were prominent in mid-eighteenth-century American culture, there is no evidence that they ever met. Edwards was the century's most important American intellectual of Christian thought, while Franklin was colonial America's unrivaled polymath—scientist, community organizer, early pragmatic wise-man, diplomat, and more.

Differences aside, each in his way awakened an aspect of American colonial culture that in time made a revolutionary culture possible. As still young men, each had established himself as a leading figure in his sphere of influence. In 1727 Franklin, age 21, ventured the profits earned in his printing business to buy the *Pennsylvania Gazette* which soon became the most widely read paper in all the Colonies. He not only printed the paper but wrote for it. Here began his career as a sage of the common man, notably in his *Poor Richard's Almanack* which he published from 1732 to 1758—a commercial and popular success and an early instance of mass popular culture.

About nearly the same time, Edwards in 1729, age 26, became the pastor of the Church in Northampton he would serve until 1750. Edwards was already known as an intellectual prodigy with two degrees from Yale. In 1734 he would deliver the first of his more famous sermons, *A Divine and Supernatural Light*. Then, in 1734–35, in Northampton and the Connecticut Valley the seeds of a great spiritual awakening began to grow by the

---

2 Though telegraphy service had begun in France in 1791, it wasn't until well into the nineteenth century that the United States were wired and the telegraph widely used—most famously in the Civil War.
3 George M. Marsden, *A Short Life of Jonathan Edwards* (William B. Eerdmans Publishing, 2008), 3. Also: Marsden, *Jonathan Edwards: A Life* (Yale University Press, 2003), 202–203.

inspiration of Jonathan Edwards' preaching.[4] The awakening then spread when he reported news of the early awakenings to clergy throughout New England. Accordingly, Edwards' fame spread. Then in 1740, George Whitefield, the brilliant English evangelical preacher, visited Northampton on a tour of New England in 1740 and sparked the more widespread revival that solidified Jonathan Edwards' identity as the American preacher most responsible for the First Great Awakening. His 1741 sermon, *Sinners in the Hands of an Angry God*, was in the day stirring rhetoric but also a work of literary and intellectual brilliance.

Still, one might ask: great awakenings, *plural*?—Edwards *and* Franklin? Admittedly the inclusion of Franklin with Edwards is disarming. Yet, when the question concerns the forbears of American revolutionary culture, the claim makes sense. Among Franklin's many and varied contributions to an independent America, the one least well appreciated may be the one of most enduring consequence. Benjamin Franklin almost single-handedly spawned the voluntary associations that, then as now, are essential to a vibrant civil society. First among the many civic clubs and associations he organized when he had but 21 years was a Junto, the Leather Apron Club. This association's name alludes to its intended membership—ordinary working men gathered to discuss ways they could improve themselves and their community:

> Franklin was the consummate networker. He liked to mix his civic life with his social one, and he merrily leveraged both to further his business life. ... Franklin's small club was composed of enterprising tradesmen and artisans, rather than the social elite who had their own fancier gentlemen's clubs. At first, the members went to a local tavern for the Friday evening meetings, but soon they were able to rent a house of their own. There they discussed the issues of the day, debated philosophical topics, devised schemes for self-improvement, and formed a network for the furtherance of their careers.[5]

Among the founding figures of the nation no one, with the possible exception of Abigail Adams,[6] was nearly so good at forging enduring social relations. Sociability was in Franklin's blood.[7] "He likes to be with people, sipping tea with young women, raising a glass with other men, playing chess, telling jokes, singing songs."[8] His voluntary clubs became social movements that led to many of Philadelphia's social and public institutions—all initiated without calling attention to himself. Who knew that Philadelphia's (and the nation's) post offices, libraries, clinics, insurance programs, and more grew from the seed of a young man's strangely named club?[9] Even, and remarkably, in 1747 Franklin organized Pennsylvania's first colonial militia by a subscription program that recruited men to service and bought armaments to defend the city.[10] In time, beginning with his years as a diplomat in London, Franklin's all-too-clever denunciations of British arrogance stung abroad as they inspired at home. For example, his address to the British Parliament in 1773 which began: "A great

---

4 Edwards, "A Faithful Narrative of the Surprising Work of God" (Northampton, 1737); cited in George Marsden, *Jonathan Edwards: A Life* (Yale University Press, 2003), 25. For a primary source of this and other of Edwards' writings, see John E. Smith, Harry S. Stout, and Kenneth P. Minkema, eds., *A Jonathan Edwards Reader* (Yale University Press, 2003).
5 Walter Isaacson, *Benjamin Franklin: An American Life* (Simon & Schuster, 2003), 55.
6 Joseph J. Ellis, *First Family: John and Abigail Adams* (Vintage Books, 2010), especially chapters 6 and 7.
7 Of particular interest on this and other aspects of Franklin's social and intellectual life is Stacy Schiff, *A Great Improvisation: Franklin, France, and the Birth of America* (Henry Holt and Company, 2005), 39–45 (on his sociability).
8 Edmund S. Morgan, *Benjamin Franklin* (Yale University Press, 2002), 1.
9 *Ibid*, 47–49. Also, Isaacson, *Benjamin Franklin*, 55–66.
10 Morgan, *Benjamin Franklin*, 67–70.

Empire, like a great Cake, is most easily diminished at the Edges. Turn your Attention therefore first to your remotest Provinces; that as you get rid of them, the next may follow in Order."[11]

There could be no better witness to the essential role of voluntary associations in a vibrant, even revolutionary, civil society than Franklin's social enterprises. In late colonial America, the willingness of men and women of all social statuses to break ranks with the formal structures of British colonial rule made possible the Boston Tea Party, the militia in Concord, the Continental Army, the universities of Pennsylvania and Virginia, and more. The colonizing forces aligned with Britain were many and powerful in the colonies. Without the generation of the 1740s, George Washington and Thomas Jefferson decolonizing movement in the 1770s would not have been. The Virginia tidewater patriarchs deserve credit for the courage by which their personal moral habits broke the stranglehold of George III and his armies. They and the others, including John Adams, were leaders, in action and rhetoric, demonstrating and defining the necessity of a new civil sphere over which the British colonizers had no final authority. But there would have been no civil sphere without the likes of Franklin and his clubs. If such a Franklin had not existed, we would have had to invent one.

True religious believers will, I realize, continue to balk at the idea that Franklin deserves to be counted as the one who ignited a secular great awakening comparable to Jonathan Edwards' religious awakening. Still, what Edwards inspired in the Connecticut Valley and across New England and what Franklin encouraged among tradesmen and common people in Philadelphia and beyond was, in the long run, crucial to the leveling of British colonial rule.

Then too, there is an odd historical fact that lends weight to the claim that Franklin, a man of vague (at best) religious beliefs, was an awakener of another kind. He was a fond friend and outspoken admirer of George Whitefield. If anything, on personal terms, Whitefield may have been closer to Franklin than to Edwards. Their personalities were quite the same—warm, outgoing, well-read and able to form lasting personal relations. So drawn to Whitefield was Franklin that when Anglicans and other denominations in Philadelphia closed their doors to one of Whitefield's revival meetings, Franklin sparked a community-wide movement to build a hall big enough for Whitefield's revivals. Franklin became, as ever, a behind the scenes trustee of that building which thereafter served many subsequent large group meetings. In time that meeting hall became the Academy of Philadelphia, which in due course became the University of Pennsylvania.

At the same time, it is also right to ask just how Edwards, who was so intellectual by nature, could have inspired anything like a Great Awakening. He was not the spine-tingling public speaker that Whitefield was. Yet, his mind was so naturally gifted and well trained—and his writing so eloquent—that Edwards in Northampton's pulpit was a force to be reckoned with. Another reliable source describes him this way: "His expositions compellingly combined unrelenting reason and poetic mysticism, and his writing was often matched by stirring revival oratory that reflected his vivid imagination and mastery of Congregational preaching."[12] Edwards had his faults, chief among them was being so tone-deaf to the wishes of his parish as to introduce an unwanted, overly strict requirement for church membership that led to his dismissal from the Northampton church in

---

11 Franklin, "Rules by Which a Great Empire Can be Diminished to a Small One," *The Public Advertiser* (September 11, 1773) @ https://founders.archives.gov/documents/Franklin/01-20-02-0213
12 Bruce Kuklick, *Churchmen and Philosophers: From Jonathan Edwards to John Dewey* (Yale University Press, 1985), 15.

1750, whereupon he moved to Stockbridge for missionary work among frontier settlers and Indians.

Faults notwithstanding, Edwards was the greatest philosophical thinker in America prior to (and including) the Revolutionary generation and, very likely, the most brilliant until Charles Sanders Peirce late in the nineteenth century. But few today will find it easy to appreciate his qualities of mind for all the unforgiving theological formulations and biblical allusions in his sermons. Consider, if you will, his most famous sermon in 1741 at the height of the Great Awakening—*Sinners in the Hands of an Angry God*, for which the biblical text was *Deuteronomy* 32:35, "Their foot shall slide in due time." What?—one might ask. Even the first lines of the sermon will not help the skeptic to appreciate the biblical text. Edwards continues: "…the wicked unbelieving Israelites, that were God's visible people…and notwithstanding God's wonderful works that he had wrought toward his people, yet…brought forth bitter and poisonous fruit."[13]

It may, however, help to put the sermon in its setting. Northampton in the 1740s was a settled river town of some 1,000 people. The Connecticut River was its geographic vector toward a more settled world to the South—to the Hartford and New Haven colonies and Yale. Boston, to be sure, was then, as since, the true Hub of New England, but it was more than two days off by horseback over roughhewn roads. Just a dozen miles to the north of Northampton lay the frontier village Deerfield. Edwards was born the year before the Deerfield Massacre in 1704. Two of his cousins and an aunt were killed by Abenaki, Iroquois, Wyandot, and Pocumtuc Indians marshaled by French colonial troops fighting a rear-guard action against the English during Queen Anne's War. In the 1740s stories were known and told in Northampton where, even then, the frontier was close by. No one can know if Edwards had this particular aspect of local lore in mind in *Sinners in the Hands of an Angry God*. Yet, it is certain that he was aware of the homiletic value of a comparison between Israel's ancient journey across sea and wilderness to its promised land and (in the phrase Perry Miller made famous in our time) the errand into the wilderness of the settlers of New England.

As good preachers, then and now, do, Edwards makes the text the organizing principle of his discourse: *Deuteronomy* 32:35, "Their foot shall slide in due time." Those, here, whose feet shall slide are the wicked Israelites, in respect to whom, Edwards makes four exegetical insistences:

1. "That they were *always* exposed to destruction… .
2. …They were always exposed to *sudden* unexpected destruction… .
3. …They are liable to fall *of themselves* … .
4. …that the reason why they are not fallen already, and don't fall now, is only that *God's appointed time is not come*."[14]

Students of classical social theories who are familiar with Max Weber's *Protestant Ethic and the Spirit of Capitalism* (1904–05) might discern the important departure Edwards takes from the strict Calvinism of which Weber wrote. Sixteenth century Calvinism in Protestant Europe and later among the Puritan pilgrims in the Massachusetts Bay Colony was ever more unforgiving than eighteenth century Edwardsian revivalism in Western Massachusetts.

---

13 Jonathan Edwards, "Sinners in the Hands of an Angry God," in *A Jonathan Edwards Reader*, edited by John E. Smith, Harry S. Stout, and Kenneth P. Minkema (Yale University Press, 1995), 89–90. All subsequent references to Edwards are from sermons or essays in this collection.
14 *Ibid*, 89–90.

For Calvin, there was nothing the Christian could do to undo the possibility that God had elected her for damnation from the beginning of time.

True, those not familiar with the finer points of Protestant doctrine are unlikely to appreciate the difference Edwards draws—much less how any of this could have contributed to American revolutionary culture. Here's how: The four exegetical points about the fate of the wicked Israelites served as a framework for the words addressed to Edward's Northampton congregation in 1741, the year in which the earlier awakening in the Connecticut Valley began to surge into the *Great Awakening* of New England. As hair-raisingly obscure as *Sinners in the Hands of an Angry God* may seem, the sermon at least allows believers to do something about their fate: "They are liable to fall of *themselves*..." and have not fallen yet only because "God's appointed time is not come." For Calvin, God's time is in the past at the beginning of time. For Edwards, God's time is more open to some unknowable future. This does not mean that God in his time will not destroy those within hearing of these words. It does mean that in human time, there is time to change. Then, in a social theoretically interesting way, Edwards speaks directly to those before him:

> The world of misery, that Lake of burning brimstone is extended abroad under you ... You are probably not sensible of this; you find you are kept out of hell, but don't see the hand of God in it, but look at other things, as the good state of your bodily constitution, your care of your own life, and the means you use for your own preservation. But these things are nothing; if God should withdraw his hand. ...[15]

First, important to note, is the eloquence of the language and figures of speech such as "the Lake of burning brimstone" / [into which you shall fall] "if God should withdraw his hand." At this point in a sermon in 1741 one supposes that few congregants are dozing off—or forgetting the opening biblical figure "the feet of the wicked Israelites shall slide." Second, as to the doctrinal theory, notice the crucial point underlying the frightening imagery: *There is time to change.* There is, in religious principle, time to prevent God from dropping you into that Lake of hell. Edwards here is appealing to what he calls religious affections[16] (where Calvin appealed to the mind and the moral will). For Edwards, to put it loosely, your life and all you have is in your hands.

Though it would require a good bit more reading and interpreting fully to present Edwards the social theorist, this is enough to see the broader intellectual program at work. Edwards, by focusing on religious feelings, was calling attention to the *individual*—by calling attention to the ability of the individual to do something about her fate; and by putting the individual in the hands of *even* an angry God. In this, odd though it may seem, Edwards introduces a theory of time—God's time to be sure, but still a time that opens to the promise of salvation. The skeptic might still dismiss this as mere homily instead of a serious philosophy of free will. Against which the evidence is that he eventually formulated a moral theory of free will. Late in life, after he had left Northampton for Stockbridge (and before he would become President of Princeton, and promptly die in 1758 of a bad inoculation), Edwards wrote a systematic theory of moral freedom, *Freedom of the Will* (1754) and *Concerning the End for Which God Created the World,* and *The Nature of True Virtue* (both 1755). Here, long separated from the enthusiasms of the Northampton awakenings, Edwards the philosopher appears.

---

15 *Ibid*, 95.
16 "A Treatise Concerning Religious Affections," in *A Jonathan Edwards Reader*, 137–171.

> The faculty of the will is that faculty or power or principle of mind by which it is capable of choosing: an act of will is the same as an act of choosing or choice. ... I think that 'tis enough to say it's that by which the soul chooses; for in every act of will whatsoever, the mind chooses one thing rather than another. ...So that whatsoever names we call the act of the will by—choosing, refusing, approving, disapproving, liking, disliking, embracing, rejecting, determining, directing, commanding, forbidding, inclining or being averse, a being pleased or displeased with—all may be reduced to this of choosing. For the soul to act voluntarily, is evermore to act electively.[17]

Both the tone and the content of this statement in 1754 are notably different from those in *Sinners in the Hands of an Angry God* in 1741. The seventeen years between were, in some ways, worlds apart.

In 1741 Edwards was preaching in the quake between the awakenings that began in 1734 and the Great Awakening of the 1740s that swept across New England and beyond. The ground of religious being shook, leaving in its path the conditions that broke into the open again in the nineteenth century in the Second Great Awakening from 1790 to 1840. Even after, there were other revivalist movements to come—another awakening from 1850 to 1900, then still another evangelical revival from 1960 to 1980. And, as religious habits changed, so too did other elements of American political and social culture. The Second Great Awakening was particularly important to the future of post-revolutionary America. It is known for the burning over of western New York State fired by the revivalist Charles Finney.[18] This awakening was not limited to New York State. It brought the burn to the western frontier in Ohio and Kentucky, even the Tidewater. It was a national phenomenon that, in its way, could be said to have burned off the religious and social structures of the colonial era and opened the way to an ever-advancing settlement of the far west, eventually to Oregon and California and the Pacific.

Edwards did not cause all this. He was a lesser force in a wide and diverse social movement that had spread from England to New England in the 1740s then across the new nation. Whatever one thinks about its religious language and values, the Great Awakening was an indigenous social movement that arose from American values fixed on the free individual as the engine of voluntary social action. Edwards surely did not offer anything like a *social* theory of the coming new society. Then too neither did Franklin, even if he wrote and acted in ways that today are more consistent with how we think and speak of political and social things.

Benjamin Franklin and Jonathan Edwards—two very different men possessed of different intellectual languages; yet, they were oddly aware of each other and drawn toward a common purpose. For a revolution and a revolutionary culture to grow late in the eighteenth century it was necessary somehow that the shrubs of colonial culture be burned away once and for all. Franklin did this as witnessed by the voluntary associations he spawned and inspired. Edwards did it by the rhetoric of a God who in his own time allowed the wicked of this world to choose whether to live or not. Neither was sufficient unto the revolutionary fire in the 1770s, but empirically both were necessary.

---

17 "Freedom of the Will," *A Jonathan Edwards Reader*, 193–194. See also Marsden, *Jonathan Edwards*, chapter 27 ("Original Sin 'in This Happy Age of Light and Liberty'").
18 On the Second Great Awakening in the nineteenth century, see Whitney R. Cross, *The Burnt-Over District: The Social and Intellectual History of Enthusiastic Religion in Western New York: 1800–1850* (Cornell University Press, 1950).

As seemingly remote in time as the awakenings of Franklin and Edwards in the 1740s were to American revolutionary culture in the 1770s, they focused historical attention on an easily overlooked aspect in the prehistory of dramatic cultural transformations. Though no historical conjuncture like the revolutionary events of the 1770s ever takes place all of a sudden, their apparent suddenness usually bursts forth from some or another underground shaking of the foundations of a long-enduring order of things. The two awakenings of the 1740s were foremost (if not exclusively) the first of the open explosions in the 1770s. When revolutionary moments break into the open, bursts of change come down so suddenly that it takes a while before those affected realize that they must learn to think about (and think in) the new order of things. Even historical figures most commonly identified as principals in the new order are subject to social forces beyond (or below) their accustomed spheres of influence. Though Franklin knew the common people he organized, Edwards was surely surprised by the resistance of the ordinary townspeople who in 1750 rejected him because of his strict membership policy. Something similar was just as true of the first formal expression of America's revolutionary culture in 1776.

Everyone knows that Thomas Jefferson drafted the *Declaration of Independence* signed by delegates at the Second Continental Congress on July 4, 1776. The signers were all men of rank, the elite of the colonies. Yet, their declaration was not news that early summer day. Other forces inspired by the awakenings of the 1740s had well before begun to move common people toward their own ideas of independence. Even before July 4, 1776, local military clashes had been under way for more than a year since April 1775 when patriots repulsed a British attempt to confiscate an armory of weapons belonging to Concord's militia. Jefferson's lyrically defiant opening words would not for some time become common wisdom in the far-flung colonies. High rhetoric seeps slowly into a culture's pores. A more basic, even raw, language floods the common sense all at once.

Thomas Paine—A Theorist of Revolutions

Thomas Paine was born in 1737 to a modest if marginally respectable family in Thetford, Norfolk, England. In his youth, he worked as an apprentice to his father, a corset-stay maker. He left home at a young age to become a merchant marine, an independent staymaker, a shop keeper, a tax collector, a labor organizer, and a teacher. In 1757 (at 20 years), he tried his hand at various enterprises in London, then again in provincial towns. But in all this, including marriage, Paine failed—except for managing to educate himself by independent reading of literature, history, languages, the sciences. Ultimately, in 1774, with a letter of introduction from Benjamin Franklin, he migrated to Philadelphia where he found a living sufficient to support his calling as a revolutionary pamphleteer and political theorist. His gifts as a self-taught but brilliantly informed and uncommonly powerful writer led Paine to a new life in America where he became first among equals as an intellectual force in the new nation's independence movement.

From the earliest stirrings of revolution, certainly after the Boston Tea Party in 1773, independence minded colonists were considered—as much by themselves as by their colonizers—to be rebels engaged in a civil war against the British throne. Months before Jefferson's *Declaration of Independence* in the summer of 1776, Thomas Paine had stirred a revolutionary spirit among the colonists. Paine's *Common Sense* was published January 10, 1776. The essay immediately came to the attention of common people and future leaders of the revolution. George Washington is reported to have said of it in a note to a friend in Massachusetts: "…by private letters which I have lately received from Virginia I find that

Common Sense is working a powerful change there in the minds of many men."[19] The power of Paine's famous essay issued from its expansive political and social vision that was, one could say, even more global and insistent than Jefferson's call to revolution. Paine's *Common Sense* began:[20]

> The cause of America is in a great measure the cause of all mankind. Many circumstances hath, and will arise, which are not local, but universal, and through which the principles of all Lovers of Mankind are affected, and in the Event of which, their Affections are interested. The laying a Country desolate with Fire and Sword, declaring War against the natural rights of all Mankind, and extirpating the Defenders thereof from the Face of the Earth, is the concern of every Man to whom Nature hath given the Power of feeling…

Paine's pamphlet became an immediate bestseller. As many as 100,000 copies sold fresh off the press.

By the end of 1776, the war was going badly for the revolutionary army. Late December that year George Washington's ill-equipped and poorly trained army was stalled in the bitter cold in New Jersey. Paine's *The American Crisis* was read aloud to the dispirited Continental Army on December 23, 1776, who went on the next day to cross the Delaware, then on December 25–26, they marched through the bitter cold to defeat British mercenaries in the Battle of Trenton. Though addressed in large measure to Washington's troops, the memorable words soon were read in all the colonies, as today they are remembered across the land:[21]

> These are times that try men's souls. The summer soldier and the sunshine patriot will in this crisis, shrink from the service of their country; but he that stands it *now*, deserves the love and thanks of man and woman. Tyranny, like hell, is not easily conquered; yet we have this consolation with us, that the harder the conflict, the more glorious the triumph. What we obtain too cheap, we esteem too lightly: it is dearness only that gives everything its value.[22]

While Jefferson's *Declaration of Independence* is properly considered the formal call to revolution, Paine's raw political fervor produced the words that impassioned the political will to fight against the odds of winter and defeat. By contrast, Jefferson's famous words are elegantly composed in the passive voice as if from on high. "When in the Course of human events it becomes necessary for one people to dissolve the political bands which have connected them with another…" Paine's famous words are active, direct, even insistent. "These are times that try men's souls." If legend has it right, Paine's words inspired Washington's army frozen in its winter encampment enough to move them across the Delaware River to surprise the enemy at Trenton.

Yet, though Paine was first and foremost a polemicist of radical political intent, he was far more than that. His *Rights of Man* in 1791–92 (also a bestseller in the day) is a rigorously

---

19 Among other sources, John E. Remsburg includes these lines in *Thomas Paine: Apostle of Liberty* @ https://www.gutenberg.org/files/40210/40210-h/40210-h.htm
20 *Common Sense*, in *The Thomas Paine Reader*, edited by Isaac Kramnick and Michael Foot (Penguin, 1987), 65–66.
21 On the enduring importance of *Common Sense*, see Craig Nelson, *Thomas Paine: Enlightenment, Revolution, and the Birth of Modern Nations* (Penguin, 2007), 108–114 and elsewhere.
22 Isaac Kramnick and Michael Foot, eds., *The Thomas Paine Reader*, 116.

argued political and social theory, the bulk of which is devoted to a systematic critique of Edmund Burke's *Reflections on the Revolution in France* (1790), a text that is often (if not entirely fairly) referred to as a classic of conservative political theory.[23] Burke was appalled that France's 1789 Revolution had so severely overthrown the *ancien régime* as to destroy its national structures without any intelligent consideration of what they were doing. "Already there appears," wrote Burke,

> ...a poverty of conception, a coarseness, and a vulgarity in all the proceedings of the Assembly and of all their instructors. Their liberty is not liberal. Their science is presumptuous ignorance. Their humanity is savage and brutal.[24]

As literature, Burke's essay was eloquent; as political criticism, it was ferocious; but as political theory Burke was more concerned with the ways France's revolution threatened all of Europe and, especially, England.

Paine's judgment on Burke is just as ferocious and just as evident as to his radical liberalism. If anything, Paine was the more intent on writing a well-informed political theory:

> I give to Mr Burke all his theatrical exaggerations for facts, and then I ask him if they do not establish the certainty of what here I lay down? Admitting them to be true, they show the necessity of the French Revolution, as much as any one thing he could have asserted. These outrages were not the effect of the principles of the revolution, but of the degraded mind that existed before the revolution, and which the revolution is calculated to reform.[25]

The substance of Paine's theory of revolutionary liberalism is straightforward and it is robustly social as well as political.

Paine turns Burke on his head. For Paine, the failure was not in the "presumptuous ignorance" of the revolutionaries, so much as the *ancien* political culture ("the degraded mind") 1789 meant to reform.

> I am not contending for nor against any form of government, nor any party here or there. That which a whole nation chooses to do, it has a right to do. Mr Burke says, No. Where then *does* the right exist? I am contending for the rights of the *living* and against their being willed away, and controlled and contracted for, by the manuscript assumed authority of the dead over the rights and freedoms of the living.[26]

The locution *the rights of the living* is code for what later would be called *the will of the people*. Both are rhetorically loose expressions; both (especially the latter) subject to nonsensical application. But both, properly used, refer to the political authority of those embedded in ordinary, often gruesome, mundane life. However it is expressed, this idea was the core idea of both the American and French revolutions—an idea that suffered terrible distortions and false expression in actual political histories. Burke was within his rights to

---

23 For an exceptionally concise summary of Burke's complicated politics see Alan Ryan, "An Anglo-Irish Cicero," *The New York Review of Books* (January 18, 2018), 45–47—a review essay on Richard Bourke, *Empire and Revolution: The Political Life of Edmund Burke*.
24 Edmund Burke, *Reflections on the Revolution in France* (Jonathan Bennett, 2017 [1790]) @ https.www.earlymoderntexts.com, 44.
25 Paine, *The Rights of Man (1791–92)* in *The Thomas Paine Reader*, 214.
26 *Ibid*, 204.

wish for an old order, but wrong to claim that any and all new orders are, by their novelty, dangerous.

As the prologue to Paine's argument continues, he becomes more explicit in his political theory:

> It requires but a very small glance of thought to perceive that although laws made in one generation often continue in force through succeeding generations, yet they continue to derive their force from the consent of the living. A law not repealed continues in force, not because it *cannot* be repealed, but because it *is not* repealed; and the non-repealing passes for consent. ... The circumstances of the world are continually changing, and the opinions of men change also; and as government is for the living, and not for the dead, it is the living only that have any right in it. That which may be thought right and found convenient in one age may be thought wrong and found inconvenient in another. In such cases, Who is to decide, the living or the dead?[27]

The rights of man are, first, those of the living gathered in a recognized state—in effect, in a nation. And nations are themselves living states of affairs embedded in history and, therefore, changing or, at least, subject to changes.

In Paine's day the issue at hand was politics pure and simple, but even revolutionary politics are based on and express practical theories that, of necessity, are the beginning of an explicit social theory. *The Living* are never individuals. They are people living together under one or another of the several kinds of political regimes. What choices people living on the ground can (and sometimes do) make are always, to varying degrees, revolutionary—efforts to adjust to, or alter, or to overthrow the structures of political authority with or under which they must live. Paine's basic principle is therefore historical or what today we would call an historical social theory. For him, the importance of Burke's horror at the French Revolution is that it served as foil for his own sharper historical argument.

In more than a few important ways, Thomas Paine was a harbinger of elements of American social theory that would not undergo disciplined expression until well into the twentieth century. It may not be quite right to call him a social movement theorist. But he was at the least a social theorist of the State and its capacity for domination. Plus which, well before Marx, Paine put forth a theory of revolution from below and of the inherent revolutionary potential of the excluded. His theories of the State, thus, bore a surprising attitude toward differences between Jefferson's republicanism and Hamilton's federalism. Paine's politics of *the living* were consistent with the republican commitment to the primacy of local, even agrarian, values—with, that is, Jefferson's idealization of the agrarian ideal of public things (of, that is: *res publica* or republican values) that was behind his hostility to and distrust of federalism. Yet, Paine's embrace of the spirit of republican politics also allowed him to be sympathetic to the elements of Hamilton's federalism—in particular his support of both a strong federal judiciary and of a national banking system able to set limits on the State.[28] As time went by, however, Paine's strong kind of republican political theory set him apart from the federalist politics that became necessary if the post-revolution colonies were to form themselves into a nation. Then the torch passed to George Washington, John Jay, James Madison, and Alexander Hamilton who fashioned both the theory and practice of a new nation of *united* states.[29]

---

27 *Ibid*, 206–207.
28 See Nelson, *Thomas Paine*, chapter 6.
29 Joseph Ellis, *The Quartet: Orchestrating the Second American Revolution, 1783–1789* (Penguin Books, 2015), especially "*Pluribus* to *Unum*," xi–xx.

Just the same, Paine's social theory, in particular, had its own staying power. Like Emerson and Thoreau, Paine was deeply influenced by the broad spectrum of Enlightenment philosophies (including Kant's ideas on nature and the sublime). As a result, his thinking anticipated the same transcendent Nature that Emerson in 1837 would ordain as the identifying principle of American cultural independence. For example, Paine in *Agrarian Justice* (1795): "To understand what the state of society ought to be, it is necessary to have some idea of the natural and primitive state of man ..." And Emerson on American man thinking in *American Scholar* (1837): "The first in time and the first in importance of the influences upon the mind is that of nature."[30]

As fertile as his thinking was, Paine's central theoretical themes are, first, his appeal to "the living," and, second, his robust theory of social revolution as a natural right of the living, then also, his idea of the State as a necessary evil. Taken together, they are, at the least, an elemental political sociology: "Society in every state," he said at the beginning of *Common Sense*, "is a blessing, but government even in its best state is a necessary evil; in its worst state an intolerable one. ..."[31] The radical liberal, like today's nostalgic conservative, adheres to a conservatism that, now as then, is troubled by the necessities attended to a vital, democratic nation-state.

---

30 This is the first line of Emerson's *American Scholar* in 1837.
31 Paine, *Common Sense in The Thomas Paine Reader*, 66.

4 America's Revolutionary Culture Burns Bright
George Washington and Thomas Jefferson

> *When in the course of human events it becomes necessary*
> *for one people to dissolve the political bonds which have connected them with another,*
> *and to assume among the powers of the earth separate & equal station to which*
> *the laws of nature and of nature's God entitle them, a decent respect to the opinions of mankind*
> *requires that they should declare the causes which impel them to the separation.*
> *We hold these truths to be self-evident that all men are created equal. ...*
> —Thomas Jefferson, Declaration of Independence, 1776

> *I am now embarked on a tempestuous Ocean*
> *from whence perhaps no friendly harbor is found. ...*
> *It is an honor I wished to avoid. ... I can answer but for three things—a firm belief*
> *in the justice of our Cause—close attention to the prosecution of it—and the strictest of integrity.*
> —George Washington on his appointment as head
> of the Continental Army, June 6, 1775

> *Having had occasion to mention the particular situation of Monticello for other purposes,*
> *I will just take notice that its elevation affords an opportunity of seeing a phenomenon which*
> *is rare on land, though frequent at sea. The seamen call it looming. Philosophy is as yet in the*
> *rear of the seamen, for so far from having accounted for it she has not given it a name.*
> *Its principal effect is to make distant objects appear larger,*
> *in opposition to the general law of vision, by which they are diminished.*
> —Thomas Jefferson, Notes on the State of Virginia, 1781

> *Observe good faith and justice towards all nations; cultivate peace and harmony with all;*
> *religion and morality enjoin this conduct,*
> *and can it be that good policy does not equally enjoin it?*
> *It will be worthy of a free, enlightened, and, at no distant period, a great nation,*
> *to give to mankind the magnanimous and too novel example of a people always guided by*
> *an exalted justice and benevolence.*
> *Who can doubt that in the course of time and things*
> *the fruits of such a plan would richly repay any temporary advantages*
> *which might be lost by a steady adherence to it?*
> —George Washington, Farewell Address, September 17, 1796

In 1779, New Haven was approaching its second century since settlement and would soon join the other colonies in quitting its subjugation to Britain. Still, as it was with many smaller towns throughout the colonies, New Haven played a negligible role in the American Revolution. In the day New Haven was a bustling harbor on the Southern New England coast. This fact may well be why the British chose to attack the surrounding towns on the Connecticut coast. The invasion on October 16, 1779 began at Savin Rock in today's West Haven and spread up the coast to New Haven and East Haven and down to Bridgeport in the Southwest.[1]

The British assault force was 2,600 men—preposterously large for an attack that the British command ought to have realized would serve no military purpose.[2] Apparently, the strategic purpose of this costly attack was to draw George Washington's troops away from New York—thus, to leave the much more important port and town vulnerable to a stronger British attack. The idea was to make way for a Southern strategy that, no doubt, was seen by the British as, at the least, risky because of Lord Cornwallis's embarrassment at having been driven north two years before when he was defeated by the Continental Army on January 2, 1777, just days after Washington's near-miraculous crossing of the Delaware River December 25–26.[3] The British had only to regret their later blunder based on a theory with no evidence that New Haven and its surrounds would draw Washington away from his own Southern strategy.

These historical sketches invite further consideration of the question at hand. What, in fact, constitutes a successful revolution? The now near classic definition of a social revolution is Theda Skocpol's in her *States and Social Revolutions* (1979): "Social revolutions are rapid, basic transformations of a society's state and class structures, and they are accompanied and in part carried through by class-based revolts from below."[4] Skocpol takes France, China, Russia—the three historically orthodox revolutions—as empirical case studies for the testing of her definition. As her *States and Social Revolutions* in 1979 goes through the history of these revolutions, Skocpol characterizes each as falling short of modern democratic orders, namely: a "Modern State Edifice" (France), a "Dictatorial Party State" (Russia), and a "Mass-Mobilizing Party State" (China). None of these types is close to being democratic—with the qualified exception of the French democratic edifice in which then, as now, a dominant social class tends to rule. Of course Skocpol was not at the time focused on democratic social and political orders—even though social revolutions are distinctly modern therefore democratic in intent, if not in fact.

Yet, in our time, verging on a half-century after Skocpol's book, we still must wonder what a social revolution might be. At the very end of *States and Social Revolutions*, Skocpol offers a prescient statement that is pertinent to the question of democracy:

> Yet for true democratization to become possible within any given advanced industrial country, it would surely be necessary for democratizing movements to proceed roughly

---

1 The following is based on: http://www.ctamericanrevolution.com/images/maps/5_New_Haven_July_2 013_PDF.pdf, which in turn draws on Charles Harvey Townshend, *The British Invasion of New Haven, Connecticut: Together with some account of their landing and burning the towns of Fairfield and Norwalk, July 1779* (Tuttle, Morehouse & Taylor Publishers, 1879).
  See also Neil Olsen's quite thorough and engaging book on early New Haven, of which his *The First Yankee: Isaac Doolittle of Connecticut* (Nonagram Publications, 2022) provides a historically rich background to the 1789 New Haven invasion.
2 Neil Olsen offers the only sensible reason for the invasion. Doolittle was a manufacturer of what was then the best gunpowder around. See Olsen, *The First Yankee*, chapter 3.
3 For the full account of the campaigns in New York, see, "The Fall of New York," in David Hackett Fischer *Washington's Crossing* (Oxford University Press, 2004), 81–114 especially.
4 Theda Skocpol, *States and Social Revolutions* (Cambridge University Press, 1979), 4.

simultaneously in advanced countries, with each movement making a key objective to achieve steady progress toward disarmament and international peace.[5]

This was a lofty ideal, but one that in our day has yet to be achieved. Revolutions are, for the most part, dreams of a well-meaning kind. Since Skocpol's book in 1979, the very nature of social revolutions has undergone definite change due to changes in the global structures. In the period since the world revolution of 1968, the global decolonizing revolutions that began in 1947 sprouted into a variety of state and class structures, many edging toward something like social democratic states—Ukraine, South Africa, India of course, Chile after the election of Diego Paulsen in 2020, Mexico, Cuba after the Castros perhaps. Then too there are modernizing states of mixed recent histories—The Democratic Republic of Congo after Mobuto Sese Seko, even socialist Vietnam after Ho, Kenya to a degree after the 2010 Constitution. Still others in the Global South have fallen back into their earlier unstable times—Venezuela after Chavez, Brazil under Bolsanaro, Haiti after the earthquakes and prolonged civil violence. This is quite a mixed recent history.

Yet there is one clear case of a successful revolution that came into its own when its populace supported a revolutionary War and a new democratic State with hardly more than the normal political tension between factions. The War itself was well led as was the postwar process of state formation. This was, of course, the American revolution after 1775. It was not long after that, in 1789, that the very new United States of America had fashioned a mature, if not perfect, Constitution with a Bill of Rights and inaugurated its first democratic president, George Washington. Plus which, the American is the classic example of a successful decolonizing revolution. Jack Goldstone, in his *Revolution and Rebellion in the Early Modern World* (1991), updates Skocpol's definition so that it can include better rebellions that today would be labeled decolonizing revolutions from the American one after 1775 and those in the Global South after India in 1947. Goldstone allows for this nuance in the theory of revolutions by indicating the structural aspects that must simultaneously be present: "… (1) a state financial crisis …; (2) severe elite divisions …; (3) a high potential for mass mobilization …."[6] Goldstone's book is limited, as the title says, to early modern rebellions up to France in 1789 and does not get into decolonizing rebellions in the twentieth century, and does not systematically examine the American revolution of 1775—even though it actually fits his definitional terms quite well. Britain's financial crisis is represented by its foolish taxation policies for its American colonies that brought on the Boston Tea Party in 1773 and other complaints by the Americans. The severe elite divisions were, most obviously, those between colonial leaders and the colonizer's appointed governors. The potential for mass mobilization is represented by the growing number and kind of complaints by the colonized. The historical realities of these factors opened the breach into which George Washington, Thomas Jefferson, and other decolonizing leaders entered, ultimately to make a new nation.

George Washington, a brilliant Commander of the Revolutionary Army, was also a practical genius as a political leader. There were others, as Edmund S. Morgan put it in *The Genius of George Washington*: "What was extraordinary about the Revolution was the talent it generated, the number of men of genius who stepped out of farmyards and plantations, out

---

5 *Ibid*, 293.
6 Jack A. Goldstone, *Revolution and Rebellion in the Early Modern World* (Routledge, 2016 [University of California Press, 1991]), xxiii.

of countinghouses and courtrooms, to play a leading role in winning the war."[7] Thomas Jefferson was arguably first among equals of these others—not only because he fashioned the *Declaration of Independence*, the first lines of which are known to many of the nation's citizens, but also because he served so many political roles in Virginia as Governor, in the Continental Congress, as diplomat to France, as member of Washington's cabinet, as third President of the United States—not to mention interventions in the Continental Congress that lent credence to republican values.

Washington and Jefferson were not alone as supreme founders, but they stand tall among others who joined in making a revolution that made a nation.

Washington—An Interactional Genius[8]

Edmund S. Morgan has said of Washington that "...[his] genius lay in his understanding of power, both military power and political power, an understanding unmatched by that of any of his contemporaries."[9] The claim is particularly sharp to his point in that, just before this, Morgan remarked persuasively that at no other time in the nation's history after the revolutionary generation were there as many leaders who have been considered great with good reason. Among many others, Benjamin Franklin, James Madison, Alexander Hamilton, John Adams who were indisputably great to various degrees,[10] there are those not usually put in this category. Among these (following Joseph Ellis[11]), there was John Jay, who with Adams and Franklin steadily negotiated the Treaty of Paris in 1783 that gave the United States all of Britain's land West to the Mississippi River. Then too, Robert Morris,[12] a financial genius who single-handedly lent his wealth to cover the debts of the bankrupt revolutionary colonies. Yet, Washington, in spite of his lack of higher education, stood out at a time when the new nation was blessed with exceptional political and intellectual talent.

Washington's genius was exceptional in that he invented himself as one who embodied the understanding that power can only be gained and well deployed when one disciplines himself in his interactions with others—including the public on behalf of which power is exercised. Many of the others, with the notable exceptions of Benjamin Franklin and John Jay, suffered one or another failure of personal discipline. Jefferson was too often missing in action while belligerently clinging to the republican values of America as a rural, agrarian nation. Hamilton, the most intuitively brilliant of them all, was so flawed of character that, when he left the tutelage of Washington, he destroyed himself ultimately by a needless death in the 1804 duel with Aaron Burr. Madison was the most disciplined of scholars and no less patient in working the vote count in back rooms, but he was shy in public and bound himself too tightly to Washington. And John Adams, brilliant in his own way, simply could not keep himself from politically silly and embarrassing behavior, as in his signing the *Alien and Sedition Act* of 1789 and his truculence in leaving the White House at 4 AM the morning of Jefferson's inauguration on March 4, 1801.

---

7 Edmund S. Morgan, *The Genius of George Washington* (W.W. Norton, 1977), 4.
8 A good bit of this section owes to Ron Chernow, *Washington: A Life* (Penguin, 2010); and Edmund S. Morgan, *The Genius of George Washington* (a short but pungent essay). Chernow's relevant chapters are 49 (where Washington is introduced for his "rays of genius") and 47 where the title is "Acting the Presidency" (a title Erving Goffman would have appreciated).
9 Morgan, *The Genius of George Washington*, 6.
10 Adams for example was a terrible president.
11 Ellis, *The Quartet: Orchestrating the Second American Revolution, 1783–1789* (Penguin Random House, 2015), 67–93, and elsewhere.
12 *Ibid*, 32–46.

George Washington was not, by any means, a perfect man. But he did perfect the art of self-presentation. His personal power was conveyed on first encounter by his judicious, even aloof, demeanor in personal and public relations. Those about him, and those subject to his authority, knew to keep him at respectful bay. This was not an easy trick. Several others had a similar effect by different means—Jay by his always calm and welcoming manner; and Franklin by his world-famous scientific achievements. But others lacked the ability to manage themselves with others. Hamilton, for particular example, was a miraculous writer and speaker whose genius kept those present at his public displays of wisdom at once entranced and weary—on at least one occasion during a six-hour filibuster. All (except Madison and of course Washington) shrank before Hamilton's mastery but not all held him in lasting respect. Washington—who in fact had little of Hamilton's intellectual brilliance—did not need to present grand displays of anything more than his dignity. He was, to be sure, aloof, but in a way that was seldom off-putting. Washington was the epitome of gravitas. As a result, he could work effectively with both Hamilton, the brash financial wizard from New York, and Madison, the Virginia planter who was the judicious scholar.

But Washington's genius for power in politics and much else was not ethereal—not merely a quality of an interior determination or personal ambition. He knew who he was and what he was doing. Washington was completely aware of the social effects of his presentation of self—what Erving Goffman called face-work.[13] Goffman's idea was that in all social interactions there must be basic interaction rituals that are equally well understood by those who enact them and those before whom they are enacted. In this respect, social interaction is theatrical, even when not dramatic. Anyone who presents a particular personal performance of self requires an audience that understands the competent interaction ritual without which the performance fails.

As for Washington's approach to this dynamic, one instance among many illustrates his mastery of this basic rule of personal power in public. When he was elected President of the Second Continental Congress in 1775, Washington presented himself to the gathered congress dressed in full military regalia, thereby to remind those who needed no reminding of his competence as Commander in Chief of the Revolutionary Army. Then he gave a short acceptance speech much like others of the kind he used. As James Madison reported on the event, Washington "reminded them of the novelty of the scene of business in which he was to act, lamented his want of [better qualifications], and claimed the indulgence of the house towards the involuntary errors which his experience might occasion."[14] The genius of Washington's performance lay in his presenting by his dress an unmistakable sign of his prowess, while calling attention to the duties that lay before him, then begging their indulgence of his inabilities. What can be more powerful than a play on a well understood *interaction ritual* in a truly democratic society—that those with the power to lead know what they are meant to do in spite of their pretense of inadequacy unto the power they assume.

All this may seem far removed from Jacques Derrida's ever more abstract theory of *inscriptions*[15] that came before today's well-articulated understanding of the nature of *interaction rituals*. Social rituals of all kinds—and especially those at play in the social understanding of the rules of social behavior—are also inscribed, nonverbally, in the order of social things. There is no guidebook to interaction rituals. They just are what they are. Much like the miracle of language learning that arises, in most cases, all of a sudden fully

---

13 Goffman, "On Face-work: An Analysis of Ritual Elements in Social Interaction," *Psychiatry* 18 [1955] (3): 213–231; also, *Interaction Ritual: Essays on Face-to-Face Behavior* (Doubleday, 1967).
14 Quoted from Washington's diaries by Ron Chernow, *Washington: A Life*, 530. Bracketed phrase is Chernow's.
15 Jacques Derrida, *Writing and Difference* (University of Chicago Press, 1978), especially chapter 10, "Structure, Sign, and Play in the Discourse of the Human Sciences."

blown sometime around eighteen months, social competency seems to appear more slowly and later but normally it comes all at once as if it was inborn from the beginning. To be sure, the first infantile displays of language competence require fine tuning, as does competence in knowing and doing the rituals of social interaction. Neither is perfectly well understood, but both are known to be present by the social fact that however strangely the other may speak or act they are accepted as normal enough when their performances work within a range of acceptability. Even eloquent public speakers make grammatical errors—misusing pronouns, confusing singular and plural accord, more. Likewise, from time to time everyone slips by saying the wrong thing at the wrong time or greeting another too warmly or too coolly.

It is possible to say that a competent display of self-presentation in interactions with others is a monument to definitive rules of social accord—rules that are in fact never completely definite—and, when they are presumably being obeyed, they are never perfectly what they are understood to be by the abstract grammars of manners and normal behavior. Washington's interactional genius was in the fact that, in almost everything he did in public, he came so close to performing late eighteenth century social rituals for a man of power who in the day was also everyone's father figure. He was the father of the American nation not because he was warm and cuddly but precisely because he was cool and distant—thus powerful to the needs of the day.

And the precise needs of his day were—first, the desire to escape British rule; second, having won independence, the need to establish and maintain a more perfect national union. At the risk of overplaying the notion of inscriptions as a communication based on an absence,[16] it is at least fair to say that George Washington inscribed a new nation based on the absence of colonial rule that required a war that, once won, could no longer serve merely as a monument to the reality of independence. Much gritty work by him and others was needed.

For telling example: The Treaty of Paris might have meant little in the long run had not John Jay won the agreement that the new nation would extend at least to the Mississippi River. At the time this accomplishment was more than Jefferson's dreams of the far Pacific. It was, in the day, a political necessity. Had there not been an international accord that the new nation had rights to territory some five hundred miles beyond its well settled Eastern Coast, that territory would have been fair game for the imperial designs of, in particular, Spain and France, not to mention Great Britain again. All of them would surely have coveted the western lands to the Mississippi River after American independence. Washington himself understood the importance of the western lands because his wealth was largely gained from the vast acreage of the Blue Ridge in Virginia eventually purchased in 1848, after his expedition there as a surveyor.[17] Because he owned the lands before the War, he knew their value would soar after the War.

Foreign colonizers, even when they lose a colony or two or more will attempt to colonize again. At the same time, for the new United States to hold its territorial claim, it had to become a nation able to assert a coherent and powerful foreign policy. The Spanish, especially, sought to block American access to the lower Mississippi, but John Jay saw that the Spanish empire was in decline. As things turned out, of course, Spain was unable to enforce

---

16 See Derrida, *Writing and Difference*, 280, where he says, wordily: "...in the absence of a center or origin, everything became discourse—provided we can agree on this word—that is to say, a system in which the central signified, the original of the transcendental signified is never absolutely present outside a system of difference. The absence of the transcendental signified extends the domain and the play of signification infinitely." Derrida is not everyone's cup of tea, I know. But if one considers these lines with Washington as the transcendental signifier of the founding of America it is possible to see a hint of how Derrida's inscription may fit.

17 Ron Chernow, "Fortune's Favorite," in his *Washington: A Life*, chapter two.

its waning imperial claims. His sense of American space was a key part of Washington's repertoire that inspired him to think and act with calm ferocity.

More generally, in *Washington's Farewell Letter to the States on Disbanding the Army* (June 8, 1783), he put before the newly independent states the four principles to which they had to adhere if they were to become a liberal nation among the world's still ancient regimes:

> There are four things, which I humbly conceive, are essential to the well-being, I may even venture to say, to the existence of the United States as an independent power: First, an indissoluble union of the states under one federal head. Secondly, a sacred regard to justice. Thirdly, the adoption of a proper peace establishment. Fourthly, the prevalence of that pacific and friendly disposition, among the people of the United States, which will induce them to forget their local prejudices and policies… These are the pillars on which the glorious fabric of our independency and national character must be supported.[18]

This was Washington at the end of the war, saying farewell to the Army, reflecting on the necessities before the newly independent states, but before the work of fashioning a national constitution had begun. Whatever he lacked as a theorist, he more than made up for in the intelligence of his practical understanding of what a nation must do to endure. This was Washington before the modern democratic nation-state began to come into being anywhere else in the world, before even the Constitutional Congress had begun to come to terms with these four points and others essential to the survival of the nation.

All this was context and content for the agenda of the Constitutional Convention of 1787 in which George Washington deployed his authority to broker the accord that allowed the nation's Constitution to displace the loose Confederation that would never have held the independent states together. Again, Washington was the healing balm behind the negotiations. The Constitution in the name of "the People" as opposed to "the States" was the result of drafts and debates in which Madison, the Republican, and Hamilton, the Federalist, played primary roles, even though they were, in the end, party to the opposing grand factions. Once the nation was settled on a legal foundation, it remained for Washington, to accept the Presidency he would have preferred not to have been imposed on him. The figurative father did his duty. Neither he nor the People could have willed otherwise.

Washington served eight years as President during when he literally invented the nation's executive administration. Article 2. Section 2. of the Constitution gives to the President the right to create executive departments but the only responsibility explicitly assigned to the first President was that of Commander in Chief of the Army and Navy. The Confederate Congress had allowed for four departments—foreign affairs, treasury, war, and post office. Washington had to develop these four then to invent all the rest. He was fortunate to have had Jefferson for Secretary of State and Hamilton for the Treasury. He soon appointed Edmund Randolph as Attorney General and Henry Knox as secretary of War. Had he not built an executive cabinet there would have been no enduring coherence to the national state. He did it at some considerable damage to his health not the least of which was his dental health. He had lost all but one of his teeth by the end. Over time his presentation as aloof was aggravated by the practical fact that he had to keep his false teeth clenched to avoid embarrassment and relieve the near constant pain.

All of Washington's accomplishments notwithstanding, it may be said that his most enduring contribution was refusing a third term which he would have won with ease. As

---

18 See *Founders Online*: https://founders.archives.gov/documents/Washington/99-01-02-11404

difficult as his health problems were, he did not quit for that reason. He said farewell to the nation in 1797 for, once again, the higher purpose of duty to the nation. It was in his nature, not only to be reluctant to assume the office, but also to stand adamant against setting a precedent of long presidential reigns. More than a decade after the ratification of the Constitution the fear that a President of the United States might (just might) revert to the British tradition of something like a hereditary royal throne still haunted the post-Revolutionary generation.

Apart from his countless letters and occasional circular letters like his 1783 Farewell to the Army, Washington left behind one document as remarkable as it was poignant—his *Farewell Address* of September 17, 1796. Washington's farewell to the nation was true to form. As with other of his public addresses, this last one began with the obligatory confession of "the inferiority of [his] qualifications," after which he said:

> In looking forward to the moment which is intended to terminate the career of my public life, my feelings do not permit me to suspend the deep acknowledgment of that debt of gratitude which I owe to my beloved country for the many honors it has conferred upon me...[19]

After this, he went into uncharacteristic detail on the challenges the country would face after he was gone—the threat of sectionalism, especially North versus South; and the necessity for a clear and firm foreign policy. These two—as if to say that failure in either respect would aggravate the very threat he and the Constitutional Congress had been determined to avoid: the sharpening of crippling factions. Having spent much of his life from 1783 to 1796 determined to mediate the differences between republicanism and federalism, he was no fan of political parties. Yet, Washington succeeded in getting Jefferson and Hamilton to work together early in his presidency, in part by heeding his close Virginia friend James Madison's initial warnings that a confederation cannot succeed because it has no way to calm the strife caused by factions. In his behind-the-scenes manner, Washington encouraged Madison to work with Hamilton to put aside the differences in their politics in order to compose and ratify the Constitution. The monument to their cooperation is of course *The Federalist Papers*, which is judged by many to be the most important and nuanced theory of democratic governments, ever.

Then, concluding his farewell, Washington turned homiletical with an affecting sermon on the centrality of what today we call American civil religion:

> Observe good faith and justice towards all nations; cultivate peace and harmony with all; religion and morality enjoin this conduct, and can it be that good policy does not equally enjoin it? It will be worthy of a free, enlightened, and, at no distant period, a great nation, to give to mankind the magnanimous and too novel example of a people always guided by an exalted justice and benevolence. Who can doubt that in the course of time and things the fruits of such a plan would richly repay any temporary advantages which might be lost by a steady adherence to it?

Washington died December 14, 1799, two years after saying farewell to a nation that would endure after he was gone—mostly for the better, occasionally for the worse. He is today

---

19 Washington, *Farewell Address*, 1796 @ https://avalon.law.yale.edu/18th_century/washing.asp (Lillian Goldman Law Library, Yale Law School).

remembered by a monumental obelisk pointing skyward above the capital city named after him. As visually stunning as this monument is most ordinary Americans still referred to him more personally as the father of their country.

Thomas Jefferson: Virginia and the Differences among the Colonies

Above all else, Thomas Jefferson longed for a life he was never quite able to enjoy except perhaps for his love of books and his famously irregular domestic relations with Sally Hemings. That he did not have what he dreamed of is ironic because, otherwise, he had everything a Virginia gentleman of the time could want. He was formally educated at William and Mary College. He inherited land and wealth and slaves which allowed him to have and hold his lovely plantation home, Monticello. When he was not serving his state and country, Jefferson retreated to Monticello. Even late in life, after he had retired from politics, he devoted himself to building the University of Virginia, down mountain from Monticello. Jefferson's dream of the good life was in keeping with the rights and privileges of an elite Virginia gentleman. So consumed was he by the desire to be such a gentleman, that even in retirement, Monticello was a virtual hotel. Notables and commoners presented themselves at his door assuming they would be welcome to stay. Jefferson would pour the finest of wines at the evening table. His commitment to an extreme version of the patriarch's code of honor was among the factors—alongside his indifference to managing Monticello's farming enterprises until retirement. It was this deferral of a planter's job that put him in debt so great that, in the end, all this was lost. Upon Jefferson's death in 1826, his plantation, his personal possessions, and his slaves who were not emancipated, were liquidated to compensate his creditors. Only then did Sally Hemings—his enslaved companion and mother of his unwhite children—win the freedom she could have had under French Law had she remained in Paris when Jefferson returned to America in 1789.[20]

Then too, the travel required by Jefferson's many spectacular successes as a patriarch compounded the pain of his personal failure to achieve his dream of an enveloping domestic life at Monticello. His young wife, Martha Wayles Skelton Jefferson, died in 1782 at twenty-four years after bearing six children, only two of whom survived to adult life. Jefferson was, just the same, the *paterfamilias* of the children he fathered by Martha and those by his slave Sally Hemings, who was Martha's half-sister by her slave-holding bio-father.[21]

When Mary, the younger of his adult daughters, died in 1804, her death prompted Abigail Adams to write a tender letter of condolence that, in spite of Jefferson's clumsy reply, eventually opened the way for Jefferson's late in life reconciliation with John Adams after 1812 until their deaths in 1826. Adams and Jefferson began their relations in 1777. Thereafter, during the revolutionary years, they necessarily worked together amicably—notably when in 1884 they, along with Benjamin Franklin, were appointed ministers to negotiate trade and diplomatic agreements in Europe on behalf of their new nation. But political and personal differences arose after Washington's presidency (1789–1797) when they were rivals in the 1796 campaign to succeed Washington. Adams, the federalist, won. Their relationship fell apart completely after the acidic presidential campaign of 1800 when Adams lost his bid for a second term to Jefferson.[22] Adams belligerently left Washington, D.C. for his Quincy home just when Jefferson was being sworn in on March 4, 1801.

---

20 Annette Gordon-Reed, *The Hemingses of Monticello* (W.W. Norton, 2008), chapters 28–30.
21 *Ibid*, chapters 14–18 on his early personal and kin relations with Sally Hemings.
22 David McCullough, *John Adams* (Simon & Schuster, 2001), 535–536.

Beyond their political and personal differences, the two patriarchs could be thought of as the elegant tokens of the internal struggles of the new American nation. It is more than ironic that they died, each thinking of the other, on July 4, 1826, the fiftieth anniversary of the *Declaration of Independence*. Jefferson was the elegant patriarch of good manners who could not overcome the imperfections of his domestic life. Adams, by contrast, and garrulous though he was, enjoyed fifty-four years of marriage and a happy family life. Jefferson was the all-but pure-perfect Virginia gentleman. Adams was, in a secular way, the hard-edged Massachusetts puritan. Their underlying, if interrupted, friendship represented the differences and affections that, to this day, are at work in the American cultural psyche.

Yet, as much as he shared with Adams, Jefferson was drawn more to his fellow Virginia gentlemen—James Monroe, his neighbor on the mountain outside Charlottesville; and James Madison, not far off in Montpelier, who was a close friend for a good half-century.[23] The Virginia patriarchs were not of one mind on politics and policy. Conspicuously, during Washington's presidency, there were times when relations were openly hostile owing to the acute differences between Jefferson's republican politics and the President's alliance with Hamilton, the federalist. Yet, these and similar oppositional dynamics were not personal but structural. Still, differences aside, in bearing and outlook Washington and Jefferson represented the common status of wealthy Virginia gentlemen.

The importance of Virginia—alongside the two other prominent colonies, Massachusetts and Pennsylvania—can be (and often is) underestimated. The prominence of these three colonies owes as much to their place in the nation's cultural imagination as to their actual historical importance, not to mention that they were the three largest colonies.[24] When it comes to the collective cultural imagination, Massachusetts is, far and away, the source of the more enduring legends and historical narratives—Plymouth Rock in 1620, the Salem Witch Trials in 1691–92, the Boston Massacre in 1771, and the Tea Party in 1773, the battles of Bunker Hill, then Lexington and Concord in 1775, and especially the Thanksgiving ritual of the colony's earliest days in the Plymouth Colony. Even from a scholarly point of view, it is the settlement of Massachusetts Bay by the Puritans that has been widely taken as defining the early and subsequent cultural tradition of the nation, 1619 notwithstanding.

By comparison, Pennsylvania offers less to the American popular culture. Independence Hall in Philadelphia is its best-known historical site. There the *Declaration of Independence* was signed in 1776, but as a tourist destination it barely surpasses Faneuil Hall in Boston which is important historically, if at all, for a few revolutionary speeches. Today both are just as well known for their proximity to shopping. Pennsylvania's hold on the popular imagination owes mainly to Benjamin Franklin, the founding generation's unrivaled polymath. As diplomat and founder, Franklin was as much an international as a national figure. In more ways than even Adams and Jefferson, Franklin was the icon of America—in Europe, honored for his scientific work, as in America where his accomplishments survive as a seldom recognized model for America's pragmatic culture. Still, Franklin so transcended Philadelphia, the city he loved, that he cannot be purely identified with either Philadelphia or Pennsylvania as John Adams is with Massachusetts and Jefferson with Virginia.

---

23 Andrew Burstein and Nancy Isenberg, *Madison and Jefferson* (Random House, 2010).
24 For more facts that one can bear on the social differences among these colonies according to their British origins, see David Hackett Fischer, *Albion's Seed: Four British Folkways in America* (Oxford University Press, 1989). The four folkways were: East Anglia to Massachusetts, the South of England to Virginia, North Midlands to Delaware Valley, North Britain to the West.

By contrast to Massachusetts, Pennsylvania and Jefferson's Virginia Colony are less prominent in the public imagination. Virginia is generally thought of for its famous patriarchs, just as Pennsylvania is imaged as Franklin's cultural territory. Otherwise, the Jamestown Settlement in Virginia is not nearly as mythic as Plymouth, Massachusetts. And the Colonial Williamsburg restoration is what it is—a generic reconstruction of a colonial town more historically salient than Sturbridge Village in Massachusetts with which it shares the aura of a righteous Disney production.

Yet, there is a deeper aspect to the neglect of Virginia. Even the most serious of scholars of the colonial era is implicated. Perry Miller's *Errand into the Wilderness* remains the gold standard for understanding the cultures of the earliest seventeenth-century colonizers as having been on God's errand to the American wilderness to build a New Jerusalem. Miller's errand keepers were, principally, the Massachusetts Puritans. Yet, Miller was aware that the Virginia settlers troubled his theory. "Obviously," wrote Miller in his attempt to include the Virginians in the Puritan errand, "the desire of achieving a holy city was less explicit in the dreams of the Virginia Company …; still the colonizing impulse was fulfilled within the same frame of universal relevance as the Puritans assumed."[25] That the Virginia Colony can be "assumed" to have been on the same errand as the Massachusetts Puritans is not obvious at all. Miller's theory required him to dismiss the fact that the Virginia Company was more mercantile than the Massachusetts Puritans. Still, while arguing that the Virginians were not only Christian, but Protestant, Miller made a mistake in church history. The earliest British mission to Virginia was commissioned under the aegis, first of the Crown, then in effect by the Church of England which was decidedly not even close to the Calvinist culture of the Puritans. The distinction is important. A good two centuries after the lost Roanoke Colony in 1585, Virginia gentlemen were at best cultural Anglicans and, more often in the case of the Virginia patriarchs, Enlightenment Deists. The differences between the stern irascibility of John Adams[26] and the delicately well-mannered Thomas Jefferson[27] illustrates reasonably well the differences between latter day secularized Puritans and cultural Anglicans. Certainly the settlers of Virginia were not mere mercantilists, any more than the Massachusetts Bay settlers were merely religious. If they shared a common interest, it was the wish to leave urbanizing Europe. Still, the differences are salient. Just the same, Jefferson made Virginia important in a way seldom recognized.

Thomas Jefferson—Republican Patriarch as Ethnographer of Virginia

Beyond the comparisons, the important question is just how Thomas Jefferson, in particular, contributes to anything even remotely close to a social theory.

Strange though it may be to suggest, a good case can be made for Jefferson's *Notes on the State of Virginia* in 1781 as the first American original empirical social study of theoretical value. Even more, in the day only Montesquieu's *De l'esprit des loix* in 1740 was a stronger theoretical work based on empirical evidence. Jefferson's *Notes* was his only book but arguably his generation's most carefully researched book. That Jefferson worked on it over many

---

25 Perry Miller, *Errand into the Wilderness* (Harvard University Press, 1956), 99; for the following see 106–115.
26 On John Adams's temperament, see Joseph Ellis, *First Family*, chapter 7.
27 On Jefferson's preternaturally well-mannered ways, see his letter of July 7, 1791 to John Adams in *Thomas Jefferson Writings* (Library of America, 1984), 981 where he signs with the following: "Be so good as to present my respectful compliments to Mrs. Adams and to accept assurances of the sentiments of sincere esteem and respect with which I am Dear Sir, Your friend and servant."—very seventeenth century to be sure but still over the top.

On the back-and-forth between Jefferson and Adams see, again, Joseph Ellis, *First Family*, chapter 7.

years—from 1781 to 1787 when the definitive English language edition was published—demonstrates how committed he was to the project. Plus which, *Notes* was his only book of public interest. It may well be, as some have suggested, the most important American book before 1800. One prominent historian said of *Notes*: "Everything else Jefferson wrote about America is epiphenomenal to this work, which had no precedent at the time and is widely revealing of Jefferson's attitudes on a wide range of subjects."[28]

Otherwise, in respect to method, *Notes* calls to mind other comparably exhaustive treatments of a clearly boundaried and coherent social setting—in particular, W.E.B. Du Bois's *Philadelphia Negro* (1899) and Fernand Braudel's *The Mediterranean and the Mediterranean World in the Age of Phillip II* (1949). Though these two works were very different in purpose, both presented facts drawn from field notes, observations, and archives to make a point. *Philadelphia Negro* (1899) demonstrated that Philadelphia's all-Black Seventh Ward was a complex and vital community and not at all the disorderly slum whites assumed. *The Mediterranean*, a book of many theoretical purposes, is best-known for the way it demonstrated just how traditional event-history could never begin to capture the historical nature of a region without examining the geological and climatic histories and the structural conjunctures that shaped social life.

Jefferson's *Notes* was neither as nuanced as Du Bois's *Philadelphia Negro* nor as theoretically grand as Braudel's *The Mediterranean*. Still it stands up well for its range of explanations. Plus which, much like Du Bois's fieldwork in Philadelphia, Jefferson's study of Virginia was researched by him alone in a time when there were few available archives or no established idea of sociological fieldwork. Where Jefferson made broader theoretical points, he drew largely on his personal experience. Where he erred (notably on the mental abilities of African people), he also began to correct then current beliefs on questions of slavery and emancipation. It would be silly to suggest that *Notes* stood the test of empirical time on these issues. But what it lacks in enduring methodological quality, it retains in the distinctiveness of research at a given historical moment in American social history. Jefferson did social research in a way that still today many social theorists would find hard to consider legitimate. Still, Annette Gordon-Reed and Peter Onuf, two of the most authoritative commentators on Jefferson, wrote that *Notes* exceptionally combined the personal with the theoretical:

> *Notes on Virginia* was an extraordinarily personal text, much more revealing than the autobiography Jefferson started and quickly abandoned in old age to explain his public life away from home to his family at Monticello. He began locating Virginia—and himself—in space, describing the new state's boundaries, rivers, mountains, and other physical features.[29]

Anyone reading *Notes* for the first time is likely to be puzzled by this observation. A personal book that begins with geography—really? Indeed the opening chapters on boundaries, rivers, mountains, and other physical features read as sheer description (much as Braudel's *Mediterranean* might appear to the novice).

Yes, Jefferson is writing descriptively about Virginia, so in what way is he also writing about himself? The personal elements of Jefferson's book are not always on the surface of the text. Rather they are embedded in the book's narrative structure. *Notes* began in 1781

---

28 John B. Boles, *Jefferson: Architect of American Liberty* (Basic Books, 2017), 170.
29 Annette Gordon-Reed and Peter S. Onuf, *Most Blessed of the Patriarchs: Thomas Jefferson and the Empire of the Imagination* (Liveright, 2016), 86.

as a reply to questions posed by the Marquis de Barbé-Marbois, a member of the French legation in Philadelphia. In the years following, Jefferson grew impatient with what he considered scandalous misrepresentations of facts about North American wildlife and a particularly poor entry on "America" in the French *Encyclopédie méthodique*. More questions were asked by Barbé-Marbois. Jefferson tweaked the queries to suit his purposes. By 1787, the English version had more obviously become Jefferson's personal statement of the facts of the State of Virginia. One must read the geographic, even the demographic, sections of *Notes* before getting to what is personal. But also, one must realize that Jefferson's personal dispositions were shaped by the fact that his life was lived in a welter of social and natural forces. For Jefferson, being who he was in a revolutionary conjuncture, those forces could not help but have been emotionally and personally troubling to the point of turning his heart and mind to the home he missed.

Still, for those determined enough to read through the first ten of the queries (almost half of the total length of *Notes*) it is hard not to wonder what's going on, in general, and, in particular, what could possibly be personal—about boundaries, rivers (of which many from the Roanoke to the Mississippi and the Missouri), sea ports (of which none), mountains, cascades, minerals, animals, vegetables, climate, population (stated in sheer demographic terms by numbers of settlers and inhabitants generally from 1607 to 1782; then free males and females, slaves, horses, cattle, and more)? Only in *Query XI, Indians*, do the raw numbers take on anything like a social form. But before getting into the more sociological entries, it is important to try to say something about what might have been personal about even the raw descriptive data entries.

Jefferson started writing *Notes* in 1781, just after his second term as Governor of Virginia, leaving him free to ponder his immediate future. Sadly, the following year his young wife, Martha, died. Yet, in spite of terrible grief, Jefferson took up public duties in 1783, serving as Virginia's delegate to Congress, then in 1784 accepting diplomatic assignments in Europe, eventually succeeding Franklin in Paris in 1785. He published the first French edition of *Notes* in 1785. The first English edition appeared in 1787 when he was still in France. This, while Paris was already moving toward its Revolution. Jefferson was at Versailles in May 1789, when the *Estates General* presented their demands for change. Soon after, Jefferson witnessed the storming of the Bastille on July 14, 1789. He left France for home that autumn when the French Revolution was full blown.

Notes was more or less continuously on Jefferson's mind during the nearly five years he was in Paris. Perhaps acutely so in those last months when he was ending his time in Paris where he was culturally so well suited—though not enough, one supposes, to cover the late stages of grief over Martha's death and his Monticello dream. It is even likely that Jefferson's romantic (if not sexual) relation in Paris with Maria Cosway, a beautiful younger woman (twenty-seven years old to Jefferson's forty-three) was an emotional acting out of his grief. Like Martha, Maria was beautiful—as was, not incidentally, Sally Hemings who was in Paris with him. Both younger women were also intelligent in their different ways. By the time Sally Hemings made the decision to leave Paris with Jefferson she was, at sixteen years, mature enough to understand the risks of returning to Monticello. The year they returned, Sally bore her first child who died in infancy.

What might all this have to do with Jefferson's apparent preoccupation with a seemingly formal book like *Notes on the State of Virginia*? From what can be discerned about the deeper undercurrents of his character, Jefferson was little likely to have talked publicly about the emotional contradictions behind his public presentations of self. Unlike John Adams and Alexander Hamilton, but like George Washington (most of the time)—Jefferson in public usually kept his personal feelings to himself. It is, therefore, fair to assume that the conflicting feelings of his new relations in Paris covered both what he had lost in losing Martha and, at another level, what he lost while in Paris of the romance of domestic life in Virginia. Jefferson would not have been the first or last to pour himself into book writing as a way of acting out feelings that otherwise would have no place to go for their expression. One of the clearest observations about Jefferson's feelings for Virginia is found in an 1872 article by a nineteenth century historian, James Parton: "From his youth up, Jefferson had gazed westward from Monticello, wondering what there might be between his mountain-top and the Pacific Ocean."[30]

Late in 1789 Jefferson quit revolutionary France for post-revolutionary America. But his hopes of spending his days at his Virginia mountain-top home were dashed, again, by a call to public service as President Washington's Secretary of State. It would be three presidential terms after 1789 (Washington's two and John Adams's one), before Jefferson in his first term (1801–1805) would be in a position to learn what lay west of his Virginia mountain top. The long-term economic costs of France's revolution caused Napoleon to sell the Louisiana territory to the United States in 1803 to help cover France's economic crisis. Soon after, Jefferson commissioned Meriwether Lewis and William Clark to explore the vast territory from the Mississippi River to the Pacific Ocean of which the then new president had dreamed. Lewis and Clark departed from St. Louis in May 1804. They returned from their expedition in September 1806—a quarter century after Jefferson wrote the first draft of *Notes on the State of Virginia* in 1781. Strange as it may seem in respect to Jefferson's implicit social theory, the opening of the Atlantic colonies to the Pacific offers a strong explanation for why he composed *Notes* as he did.[31]

Notes begins (in *Query I, An exact description of the limits and boundaries of the State of Virginia*) with a short, but technical description of the boundaries of Virginia, measured according to degrees longitude between the Atlantic and the Mississippi River and by latitude from the Ohio River to the Roanoke—an area he is quick to state is "one third greater than the islands of Great Britain and Ireland." In *Query II, A notice of its rivers, rivlets, and how far they are navigable?* Again, as often in the twenty-three queries, the contents are particular, exact, and at first seemingly unremarkable. He begins, of course, with the Roanoke and James rivers where the first colonists settled. As it happens, the Roanoke was at best a stream and not navigable, but the James River was both navigable and prominent in the founding of the Virginia Colony and in Jefferson's life. He studied at William and Mary College on the James. Williamsburg was the early capital of Virginia where he served in the House of Burgesses and as Governor. Monticello was not far off. This was the heartland of Jefferson's Virginia. But in reading on in *Query II* there are surprises. After notes on the familiar Appomattox and Rappahannock rivers (both notable in the Civil War) the reader suddenly finds herself in strange waters when Jefferson pays close attention to the Mississippi, Illinois, Ohio ("the most beautiful river on earth"), and the Missouri rivers. The Missouri River is America's largest, the river that more than any other feeds the Mississippi of which he wrote: "...*the Missouri* ...is remarkably cold, muddy, and rapid." These were all rivers to the far west of Virginia, rivers he would never see in person. One can well imagine the kind of research and reading that allowed Jefferson to speak clearly and authoritatively of these western lands and waters.

---

30 James Parton, "Jefferson's Return from France in 1789," *The Atlantic* (November 1872).
31 All lines and passages quoted from *Notes on the State of Virginia* are easily found in any one of several online sources, like the one at *The Library of Congress* which presents the 1832 version published in Boston by Lilly and Wait. See https://tile.loc.gov/storage-services/service/gdc/lhcbcb/04902/04902.pdf . Readers can check passages by simply entering the query number in Roman numerals; for example: *Query XIV. The administration of justice and description of laws?*

Thereafter, from *Query III. Sea Ports?* (of which, none) through *Query VII. Climate?* in which the material presented seems straightforward, except for clues here and there as to one of his reasons for writing *Notes* to correct errors of the French commentaries. In the longish *Query VI, Minerals, plants, animals?* Jefferson routinely cites the views of Voltaire, Linnaeus, Buffon (none of whom could have had direct knowledge of the subject). This is Jefferson the scholar and public intellectual. Yet, after the citations, he, almost incidentally, corrects their views. *Query VII. Climate* calls to mind Braudel's grand theory in its header: *Climate. A notice of all what can increase the progress of human knowledge?* Here one comes upon a striking instance of Jefferson's personal attitude toward Virginia:

> Having had occasion to mention the particular situation of Monticello for other purposes, I will just take notice that its elevation affords an opportunity of seeing a phenomenon which is rare on land, though frequent at sea. The seamen call it *looming*. Philosophy is as yet in the rear of the seamen, for so far from having accounted for it she has not given it a name. Its principal effect is to make distant objects appear larger, in opposition to the general law of vision, by which they are diminished.[32]

Though the reference is to *his* mountain, Jefferson deploys *looming* as a critical tool that may have been lacking in the philosophy of his day but was present in his philosophical vision. In *Notes* he makes Virginia seem larger than it was or, in time, would be. His vision is not of Virginia alone but of the America beyond Virginia's mountains, and beyond the Mississippi, Ohio, and Missouri rivers—the America that in 1803 he sent Lewis and Clark to open it up. The geographical imagination always gazes beyond the diminished terrain of local living to explore the possibilities that loom beyond the horizon.

After *Query VII*, *Notes* becomes more sociological. In *Query VIII. Number of inhabitants?* Jefferson begins to describe the demographics of Virginia, of which specific elements in his data portend the facts and troubles of his own life, in particular such descriptive statistics for 1781 as:

296,852 free inhabitants of all ages…
270,762 slaves of all ages…

567,614 inhabitants of every age, sex, and condition

One wonders what fellow Virginians of the day must have thought of the fact that there were nearly as many slaves as free (predominantly white) people. We know that across the Southern slave-holding states white people knew and feared the great number of enslaved people who could reasonably become a mass uprising able to overthrow their economic and social system. Their fears were ultimately confirmed by the revolution in Haiti from 1791 to 1804 in which French colonizers were overthrown by slaves. Then too, the 1781 raw data must have worked on Jefferson's confused, if not entirely ambivalent, feelings for Sally Hemings.

Query XI. Aborigines? reveals Jefferson the amateur ethnologist of the variety of Indians in the State based in part on his own rather crude archaeology of bones that he, apparently, dug up himself. But also here Jefferson, drawing on what was a natural assumption in the day, asks "from whence came those aboriginal inhabitants of America?" Here he proves

---

32 Jefferson, "*Query VII, Climate: A notice of all what can increase the progress of human knowledge.*" Notes on the State of Virginia, *Jefferson/the Library of America* (Viking Press, 1984), 207. Emphasis on *looming* added.

himself at least a good critical theorist. After addressing the notion that Indians came as did primitive whites (from Europe by way of Norway, Greenland, Iceland, and Labrador), he then seems to commit to the correct version of human migrations. If "the two continents of Asia and America be separated at all, it is only by a narrow streight [sic]," then this would explain "the resemblance between the Indians of America and the Eastern inhabitants of Asia." The subtlety of his theory is noteworthy. This observation was consistent with his Westward dream of the new America, a dream dreamt well before Lewis and Clark would return in 1806. Again geographical imagination seems to have enlarged his limited ethnological assumptions as to the conviction that the aborigines of Virginia in 1787 were likely to have come from across the Pacific.

After *Query XII* (a stub that says little about the State's towns and villages), Jefferson settles into serious social history in *Query XIII. The constitution of the state, and its several charters?* Here, he outlines the history of Virginia from settlement on, through the elaboration of British colonial law as thoroughly rational if prejudicial, then to the *doléances* of the colonists on the threshold of state formation. After which, Jefferson comes to the chapter where he is at once astute politically and disgraceful morally.

Query XIV. The administration of justice and description of laws? gets into the social theoretical meat of the book. As before, the chapter starts off as the kind of bland description that its title implies. Then, almost in passing, Jefferson turns to a description of how the poor, foreigners, sick, and vagabonds are dealt with (not uncharitably). Then *Query XIV* comes to the subject we today have been waiting for: laws and practices concerning slaves, their purchase and selling. Outrageously, slaves are here considered as among other commodities: gaming debts, flour and beef, useful animals, and the acquiring of lands from the Indians. Soon enough, amid all this, the following: "To make slaves distributable among the next of kin, as other moveables" (where the kin in question are heirs of the owners of these "moveables"). This was Jefferson probably in 1783 or 1784 when Sally Hemings was at most 11 years old. It is hard to know when exactly in the six-year history of the drafts to *Notes*, Jefferson would take Sally Hemings and *her* kin not as mere distributables but as *de facto* domestic companions of a certain kind—as slaves but more than merely slaves. To be generous, one might attribute this unnerving passage to the second draft just after Martha Wayles, his wife, died and before his relations with the Hemings family were as close as they would be after the Paris years when Sally would bear her first child by Jefferson.

Whenever the line about slaves being "distributable ... moveables" was written, suddenly, within a few lines in the text as we have it, the discussion changes abruptly in tone and style—but not necessarily for the better. Here (a third of the way through *Query XIV*) Jefferson launches into another of his amateur ethnological disquisitions, now about slaves and other Blacks of African descent. The offensive remark about slaves as moveables is part of a section that means to consider how various legal matters in the Virginia Colony can be revised to deal with issues unique to the State of Virginia in the day. Hence, he turns to the question of the emancipation of slaves and a bill on the subject that either was not taken up or not passed. Then he turns to why the bill failed and here we see the morally better Jefferson who, of a sudden, turns the racial tables to write of "the deeply rooted prejudices entertained by whites ... ." But, and not surprisingly, given the times and his own relations to slaves, Jefferson turns the table back away from the source of white prejudice to the differences of black people, beginning with their "color": "Whether the black of the negro resides in the reticular membrane between the skin and scarfskin, or in the scarfskin itself"... and so on. This is Jefferson the bio-ethnologist and not the Jefferson of 1776 of "all men are created equal". There were at least two different Jeffersons as there are any number of dispositions in each of us. But, I think, the contrast is well worth noting.

Everything that follows in this section of *Query XIV* turns on the contradictions of Jefferson, the man. For us all, beliefs and practices and the justifications of the latter we make are seldom perfectly in line. It may not be fair, but it is normal to criticize Jefferson for failing to do well at what we all fail. Jefferson goes on to dig himself into a deeper hole. "Is this difference [in skin color] of no importance?" To which he answers, astonishingly: "Are not the fine mixtures of red and white, the expressions of every passion by or lesser suffusions of color in the one preferable to that eternal monotony, which reigns in the countenance, that immoveable veil of black which covers all the emotions of the other race?"

If these words were indeed written in 1784, then Sally Hemings would have been eleven. The year following, she would be part of his household in Paris. When they left for their Virginia home in 1789, Sally was a young woman. If the baby she bore in 1790 was his (as it very likely was), we can respect early remarks on the conviction that, as a decent person, he had come to realize that her skin tone was hardly a veil of black. Not white like the skin of her half-sister Martha, his then dead wife, but surely capable of the expression of color arising from emotions. One would expect that in time he knew better as to skin and blushing.

There's more: black people have good enough memory but "in reason they are inferior" to whites, and the like. He makes particularly ridiculous judgments, such as elsewhere in *Notes* (*Query XIV. The administration of justice, and the description of the laws?*):

> Many millions of them have been brought to and born in America. Most of them have indeed been confined to tillage, to their own homes, and their own society: yet many have been so situated, that they might have availed themselves of the conversation of their masters.... Some have been liberally educated, and all have lived in countries [*sic*] where the arts and sciences are cultivated; and have had before their eyes samples of the best works from abroad.

In 1784, he may well have been romanticizing the slaves of Monticello who, upon the death of John Wayles (Martha's father), became part of Jefferson's mountaintop extended family in which Robert and Sally Hemings (Martha's half-siblings) would become especially close to Jefferson.

The commentary on slaves in this section is, at best, ambivalent. Black people had many qualities (memory, music, religion, and poetry) but none very well developed, he thought, in spite of their exposure to the culture of their masters. The ambivalence is to Jefferson's credit, if one is willing to credit him with a degree of unconscious confusion over the contradictions in his personal life. If *Query XIV* was written more or less at once, then one might dare to suggest that, even early in his own personal relations with Sally and Robert Hemings, among other of his extended Black kin, Jefferson seems to have realized he was in moral hot water. This surely is the most acutely personal section of *Notes*.

In *Query XIV. The administration of justice and description of laws?* Jefferson suddenly heads toward a conclusion in which he reverts to a list of crimes associated with the administration of justice, the alleged topic of the query. The remaining ten queries in *Notes* wander matter of factly over subjects like colleges, religions, customs, commerce and manufacturing, weights and measures, incomes, before coming to a recitation of public sources for his and other histories of the State of Virginia. Almost in passing, in *Query XVIII*, he makes what for the time was a theoretically coherent complaint against slavery that the careful reader will come to realize was also very personal:

> And with what execration should the statesman be loaded, who permitting one half the citizens thus to trample on the rights of the other, transforms those into despots, and

these into enemies, destroys the morals of the one part, and *amor patriae* of the other. For if a slave can have a country in this world, it must be any other in preference to that in which he is born to live and labour for another; in which he must lock up the faculties of his nature, contribute as far as depends on his individual endeavors to the envanishment of the human race; or entail his own miserable condition on the endless generations proceeding from him. With the morals of the people, their industry also is destroyed.

Then at the very end of this short but pungent query at the very end of *Query XVIII*:

The Almighty has no attribute which can take side [*sic*] with us …—But it is impossible to be temperate and to pursue this subject through the various considerations of policy, of morals, of history natural and evil. We must be contented to hope they will force their way into every one's mind. I think a change already perceptible, since the origin of the present revolution. The spirit of the master is abating, that of the slave rising from the dust, his condition mollifying, the way I hope preparing, under the auspices of heaven, for a total emancipation, and that this is disposed, in the order of events, to be with the consent of the masters, rather than by their extirpation.

Here, at long last, is Thomas Jefferson, author of the *Declaration of Independence*, a very personal, if appropriately vexed man, who longed for a domestic life he could only find in relation to the enslaved half-sibling of his dead wife.

Empire of the Eye

It would be another half-century after the end of the revolutionary generation with the deaths of Thomas Jefferson and John Adams on July 4, 1826, that Frederic Edwin Church would emerge as the successor to Thomas Cole as the foremost artist of American landscape art. In *Empire of the Eye*, Angela Miller says of Church that "he came of age in the 1850s and identified with the mission of his generation: to give to nationalism an organic basis, to root it in the geography of the continent."[33] The men haying the field in Church's *West Rock, New Haven*, worked below the Metacomet Ridge that occluded their eyes from the far West beyond which the already setting sun was heading. Whatever they may have dreamt of that beyond, in 1849 they knew that theirs was a continental nation stretching to an unthinkable Pacific. They were digging and harvesting their local field, but they surely had a geographical imagination that allowed them to suppose that their children or their children's children might well see those distant seas.

There would have been no *Empire of the Eye* had it not been for leaders of several different stripes in the eighteenth century—Franklin and Edwards, Paine and Jefferson were chief among those who forged the culture that made the nation's collective geographical imagination possible. They were not alone. Nor were they perfect. Edwards got himself fired from the pulpit of his fame. Paine was imprisoned in France during its revolution. Jefferson was confused as to his personal relation to his slave holding. Only Franklin was relatively immune to moral blemish any more severe than his dalliances with beautiful women in Paris. They each contributed to the ways Americans would think America for years to come.

Franklin gave us the nation's first example of American pragmatism and a foundational demonstration of the importance of voluntary associations. Edwards, in his theologically

---

33 Angela Miller, *The Empire of the Eye: Landscape Representations and American Cultural Politics, 1825–1875* (Cornell University Press, 1993), 167.

abstract way, broke the Calvinist spell and opened a muted but evident idea of the individual's ability to save himself in God's time, which in turn introduced a philosophically serious notion of historical time. Paine was America's first social theorist of what now we call revolutions from below and this he did in his critique of Edmund Burke which spawned a theory of the State as a living thus plastic structure. It is always tempting to grant Jefferson privilege of place among the founders—and there is some good reason for this in his concept of *looming* as a figure for more than the geographical imagination but, if thought through, looming was a conceptual tool (if to him an unconscious one) for seeing beyond the moral evil of slavery. Then too his odd little book *Notes on the State of Virginia* must have been the empirical dream on which in 1803 he bought the American West from Bonaparte thus to make the nation continental.

5 Nation-State in the Making
James Madison and Alexander Hamilton

Among the numerous advantages promised by a well constructed union,
None deserves to be more accurately developed
than its tendency to break and control the violence of faction ...
There are ... two methods of removing the causes of faction:
The one, by destroying the liberty which is essential to its existence;
The other by giving to every citizen the same opinions, the same passions, and the same interests.
It could never be more truly said of the first remedy that it is worse than the disease.
Liberty is to faction, what air is to fire, an aliment without which it instantly expires. ...
The inference to which we are brought is, that the causes of faction cannot be removed,
and that relief is only to be sought in the means of controlling its effects.
— *James Madison, The Federalist No. 10, 1787*

A firm Union will be of the utmost moment to the peace and liberty of the States,
as a barrier against domestic faction and insurrection. ...
If momentary rays of glory break forth from the gloom, while they dazzle us with a transient
and fleeting brilliancy, they at the same time admonish us to lament that the vices of government
should pervert the direction
and tarnish the luster of those bright talents and exalted endowments
for which the favored soils that produced them have been so justly celebrated.
— *Alexander Hamilton, The Federalist No. 9, 1787*

New Haven Colony was founded in 1637 by a Puritan minister, John Davenport, and Theophilus Eaton, a wealthy merchant, also a Puritan. Eaton's wealth was sufficient to buy the rights to settle a colony at a *new harbor* on the north shore of Long Island Sound. The year following, 1638, this new haven was settled when some 250 Puritans came down from Massachusetts with the intention of establishing a different, presumably better, colony.

Departures from John Cotton's Massachusetts Colony were several in the day. Thomas Hooker settled the Connecticut River Colony (today's Hartford) in 1636, the same year Roger Williams settled the Providence Colony in today's Rhode Island. Hooker and Williams objected (for different reasons) to Cotton's strict (even ruthless) Puritanism, while Davenport objected to what he considered too liberal a Puritan doctrine as to membership. Whatever their religious motives the essential fact is that Theophilus Eaton was wealthy enough to venture £3000 (a minor fortune in 1638) to buy land for a port town. We can fairly conclude that the New Haven pilgrims were true to the underlying motivation of all colonizers. Colonizing ventures, however high minded their professed purposes, are always also, and with rare exception, economic enterprises.

DOI: 10.4324/9781315210230-7

Like most early New England colonies, New Haven was built up around a green space left open for parades, cattle grazing, public orations, and other common purposes. New Haven's Town Green was (and still is) a 16-acre public space designed to be an open central square around which settlers built homes according to a primitive town plan of nine squares. New Haven, then as now, faces the Long Island Sound and is geographically embraced on either side by the West and Quinnipiac Rivers. To the North the Metacomet Ridge sheltered the town, as still today, from severe Nor'easters. By 1641 all of the town squares were assigned to families. Davenport and Eaton enjoyed much larger plots of land outside and to the East of the nine square grid which is said to have made New Haven the first planned town.

In 1639 a Puritan church was organized. Soon it began to use a central space just off the Green as its burial grounds. A first Meeting House was built in 1640. A century later, in the 1740s during the First Great Awakening, the congregation of that first church split over doctrinal matters. Today their successor congregations—Center Church on the Green and United Church on the Green—stand side by side serving dwindling and aged congregations. Town greens were often the common ground where differences were settled, or not, for better or worse. Just the same, their place in New England legend is that these common grounds were a symbol, if not an instance, of an early democratic impulse in the American colonies. As it turns out, over the several centuries since its establishment, New Haven's Town Green is not, in the usual sense, even a little bit democratic. It is, in fact, owned privately by five proprietors not subject to popular contradiction even though they depend on public funds to maintain their plot of land. The owners of the space are, oddly, proprietors for life. When one dies, the remaining four choose the successor. In legal principle, they have the theoretical right of ownership to do what they want with the Green.

Still now, centuries later, the Green remains a town square for many of the same activities for which it was set aside in 1638. Yale students and townspeople amble across it in good weather—as do more than a few homeless people, of which there must have been some in 1638 as other pilgrims or drifters sought shelter from Indians or Baptists. Today's homeless people are, in fact, the first citizens of the Green. With no place to go they nap or sleep there until local police run them off without good or legal reason (unless the proprietors in their autonomous wisdom tell them to). True, some of those without shelter beg for money. Righteous townspeople assume that the begging is not for food but for drugs and drink. True in some cases, but not all. Otherwise, on any given day you might find some hard-to-identify military people engaged in exercise routines where once local militia did something of the kind. In summer, concerts; in winter, a holiday tree, and a menorah; in autumn, a 12K road race that ends in front of the churches; in spring, parades of various purposes like St. Patrick's Day and another that involves beds racing to commemorate something or another. To the east off the lower Green is the town's City Hall where small crowds will protest various issues to the profit of the nearby hotdog vendor. On the west side of the upper Green, opposite the seat of local government, is the local college. As for the other two boundaries of the Green, one finds the public library and a court house on the north and to the south a series of small, constantly changing providers of munchable foods, coffee shops that come and go, a few ice cream places offering an ever changing number of flavors, and any number of shops offering a bizarre variety of cell phones (including the one the poor call Obama phones—which is to say subsidized), and recently smoke shops selling pot.

With the obvious exceptions of the vendors and drug dealers, or the number of poor and unhoused, this Town Green does today what it was meant to do in 1638. It remains a kind of neutral district—open to the public within vague, even arbitrary limits, owned by proprietors of little real power to enforce much more than errant car parking. Whoever owned the space in 1638, if it was not Davenport or Eaton. At the least one assumes that townspeople tried to keep horses, if not goats, off their grass which was meant for cattle.

Is it a coincidence that after 1783, by when the independent colonies were free to transform themselves into a nation, they too established something of a national green? By 1789, after years of debate and compromise, Revolutionary era patriarchs gave the phrase "United States of America" enduring meaning by ratifying a national Constitution that began in earnest: "We the People of the United States... ." The year following, 1790, Congress approved the new nation's capital district as something like the open greens of towns like New Haven. The District of Columbia on the Potomac came to be where it is by means of a political deal struck between Alexander Hamilton of New York and James Madison of Virginia. The Residence Act was adopted in 1790, in a compromise with Hamilton that resolved one of the issues structured into the creation of this new nation. There were several competing sites for the national capital—New York and Philadelphia notably. But Hamilton brokered the votes of the New York delegation to join with Madison's Virginia delegates who, for obvious reasons, wanted the capital on the Potomac in the near South. Hamilton, the financial genius, got the federal government to assume the war debts of the thirteen states. Madison, always the well-informed theorist of solutions to the nation's challenges, argued for the federal district plan in *Federalist 43*. It was agreed that George Washington would pick the exact site. Unsurprisingly he chose a site close by his Virginia estate, Mount Vernon. Hence, the federal district was planted in land taken equally from Maryland, a border state committed to the union, and Virginia, an outright slave state that would secede in 1861.

In another, more general but apparent sense, Washington, D.C. would not have become what it is today were it not desirable (perhaps necessary) for the new nation to have as its capital a neutral green space, open to all; but also somewhere on the always tense border between North and South. And such a space would not have come to be had not the thirteen colonies, independent of Great Britain, found a way to unite into a federal, united nation. The District of Columbia was named Washington, D.C., after George Washington, who, in the popular imagination, was the only true spiritual father of the country.

The District, like New Haven's Green, is not owned or governed by those who live in the district. Though the District has its own elected officials, including a single Representative to the United States Congress (without the right to vote), residents of D.C. also have little say over the management of their city. Washington, D.C., now a city of some 700,000 residents, is governed, when all that matters is said and done, by the Congress of the United States.

Except for its National Mall, the District of Columbia is no longer a truly open green space. Still there is something of a cultural affinity between common spaces in early American towns and the National Mall. As town greens like New Haven's are bounded by religious, administrative, legal, educational, and commercial buildings, so in a similar fashion is the national Mall that extends along an axis from the Lincoln and Washington monuments to the White House with prominent museums and monuments arrayed on either side. It could be said that the National Mall serves a sacred purpose symbolized by the fact that the Capitol looks down the Mall to the Lincoln Monument and its reflecting pool to the Washington Monument, thereby offering an elaborate shrine to symbolic figures of America's civil religion. Hence also this national space, in its way, is a homologue of the greens of America's earliest settlements and towns—green spaces framed by secular political buildings and monuments to religious life. Construction of the United States Capitol Building began in 1793 and was not completed until 1800 just after the end of George Washington's second term as President. John and Abigail Adams moved into the White

House in 1800 before it was completed and when the Capital district was but a silhouette of what it would become.

There were political compromises behind the decision to settle the District of Columbia adjacent to Maryland and Virginia, the site on the Potomac also pulled together, however uncertainly, a national geographic imagination linking North and South. The Potomac River flows 400 miles to the Chesapeake Bay from headwaters at the confluence of the Potomac and Shenandoah rivers at the near North just above Harper's Ferry in West Virginia. As the Potomac runs from the North to the South, so the District of Columbia was established as a somewhat neutral space between two very different political economies—an already modernizing, industrial North and the feudal, agrarian South. It would be another twenty years until 1820 and the Missouri Compromise would hold together, for a while, a fragile union against the coming war between North and South. The agreement that Missouri would be admitted to the Union as a slave state balanced by the admission of Maine as a free state held uncertainly until the Kansas-Nebraska Act in 1854 tore the unstable compromise apart, opening the way for Civil War in 1861. The 1820 Missouri Compromise was no more than a papering over of the foundational factions of the nation. That both sides were able to join to fight free of the British is a tribute to a deeper current below the surface waves of post-colonial American original culture.

That nation's capital district straddled North and South. The National Mall has become a built environmental tribute to the eventual, if still uncertain, accord between the nation's original factions. The Capitol Building is set on the Mall such that Abraham Lincoln gazes across the Reflecting Pool to the Washington Monument to suggest the national Father who saved the Union looks back to the founding Father who made the new nation possible. General George Washington of the Revolutionary War had to become, against his own wishes, the President who presided over the Second American Revolution from 1783 to 1789.[1] After the War, there was a Confederation of States already straining the compromise by which Washington, D.C. was built. But before a national capital could be built, a new generation of revolutionary leaders were needed to transform the *Articles of Confederation* into a Constitution that, in our time, is, for better or worse, the longest enduring republican Constitution on the planet.

A Second American Revolution: After the Violence, a New Nation

To speak of a *second* American revolution might be interpreted as a play on words. In one sense it is since the reference here is to the events after the American War of Independence ended in 1783. Then the now liberated former colonists quickly came to the realization that the by-then independent, once-colonization states could not make good on the War they together won. The war was fought by a Confederation of colonies that came together to liberate themselves from British colonizers. After, many came quickly to realize that they were still vulnerable to foreign forces. They needed to invent a nation, of which, strictly speaking, there were none in the world. A nation could not hold together if it remained a loose confederation of independent states. Among other concerns was that foreign nations, including the British they defeated, would be interested in the lands west of the Mississippi. Interests of the kind always, then as now, can lead to wars, as in fact they already had all over North America. War-like violence was, therefore, always in the offing.

---

1 Joseph Ellis, *The Quartet: Orchestrating the Second American Revolution, 1783–1789* (Random House/ Vintage, 2016).

More than a threat, actual violence has always been part of the American story—from the earliest Indian Wars on. Richard Slotkin has written of this in his classic book, *Regeneration Through Violence: The Mythology of the American Fronter, 1600–1860*. In his long and brilliantly nuanced book, Slotkin reports on the contributions of many American story tellers whose writings were composed around tales of violence—deer slaying, Indian killings, whale hunting, buffalo slaughters, and more. Among many other tales of endemic violence are stories told by James Fenimore Cooper, Henry Thoreau, Walt Whitman, Herman Melville, Nathaniel Hawthorne, Daniel Boone, Buffalo Bill, and others who contributed to the American mythology of the frontier. Slotkin concluded:

> Under the aspect of mythology and historical distance, the acts and motives of the woodchopper, the whale and bear hunter, the Indian fighter and the deerslayer have an air of simplicity and purity that makes them seem finely heroic expressions of an admirable quality of the human spirit. … But their apparent independence of time and consequences is an illusion: a closely woven chain of time and consequence binds their world to ours. Set the statuesque figures and their piled trophies in motion through space and time and a more familiar landscape emerges---the whale, buffalo, and bear hunted to the verge of extinction for pleasure in killing and "scalped" for fame and the profit in hides by Buffalo Bill; the meat left to rot…the Indian debased and killed in return for his gifts; its land and its people, its "dark" peoples especially, economically exploited and wasted; the warfare between man and nature, between race and race, exalted as a kind of heroic ideal. … [2]

My interpretation of Slotkin's theory is that violence is at the heart of each successive regeneration of the American story as fact and myth. Skirmishes like Concord in 1775 or wars like America's Revolution a year later—or John Brown's vicious slaughter of five men and boys he believed to be pro-slavery at Pottawatomie Creek in 1856 or his failed assault at Harper's Ferry in 1859 which was, for many, an important motivation for the ever more deadly Civil War in 1861—and countless other local and national, lesser and grand, conflicts that became part of the American story of itself. America the beautiful—yes of course; but also Harper's Ferry and Gettysburg in 1863—and on and on.

America is made of troubles and triumphs, including the threat and reality of deadly violence. Here, the Second American Revolution is the revolution in nation building after its war of decolonization. The *Articles of Confederation* composed in war time in 1777 would not do in peace time. America as a democratic nation could come to be only after the *Constitution of the United States* became settled law after 1791.

The *Articles of Confederation and Perpetual Union* were such that the confederation they instituted could hardly be a perpetual union. The problem was already apparent in Article 2 where the basic principle of the 1777 *Articles* stated: "Each state retains its sovereignty, freedom, and independence, and every power, jurisdiction, and right, which is not expressly delegated to the United States, in Congress assembled."[3] Then, immediately following, in Article 3, the union is described as "a league of friendship" to serve for a series

---

2 Richard Slotkin, *Regeneration Through Violence: The Mythology of the American Fronter, 1600–1860* (Wesleyan University Press, 1973), 564–565.
3 *Articles of Confederation and Perpetual Union Between The States Of New-Hampshire, Massachusetts-Bay, Rhode-Island And Providence Plantations, Connecticut, New-York, New-Jersey, Pennsylvania, Delaware, Mary-Land, Virginia, North-Carolina, South-Carolina And Georgia* (1777), Library of Congress: Article 2. This and all other quotations are from this source @ https://tile.loc.gov/storage-services/service/rbc/bdsdcc/n001001/n001001.pdf

of generalities of which one ("common defence") was specific and urgent given the war in progress. But the others listed were both obvious and without nuance. The confederated states were expected, in "friendship," to provide for the general welfare of all, the liberties of each, and a common readiness to assist the others against attacks and offenses. Later, obvious restrictions were laid upon the separate states—notably, not to enter into independent treaties or wars with a foreign power (Article 6)—which rights to war and peace were reserved exclusively to the common Congress (Article 9).

When the Revolutionary War was settled in 1783 by the Treaty of Paris, the former colonies, now states, had no unifying purpose beyond their league of friendship. No less a personage than George Washington worried that the Western territories could become subject to European influence and that new independent states would form outside the union, which would make the idea of a United States an illusion. At one point, he wrote to Benjamin Harrison on the vulnerability of American territories to foreign interests: "I need not remark to you Sir, that the flanks & rear of the United States are possessed by other powers—& formidable ones, too; nor, how necessary it is to apply the cement of interest, to bind all parts of the Union together by indissoluble bonds—especially that part of it, which lies immediately west of us with the middle states."[4] Joseph Ellis reminds us that in the day there were two attitudes on the issue of whether the West offered the American people an evidently optimistic future or, on the contrary, a darker, more pessimistic one. On the optimistic side, Ellis wrote. "This kind of political redemption of the east by the west could occur, of course, only if the two sections remained politically connected." But then Ellis adds the full truth of the matter. "Both optimists and pessimists were just guessing, but the increasing dysfunctional character of the Confederation Congress seemed to tilt the argument toward the pessimists, since the emergence of a gigantic American nation required the existence of a national government that did not exist."[5] Hence, a national government had to be invented by means of constituted laws and rights agreeable to all.

The *Constitution of the United States* was composed out of proposed articles that were debated and clarified over the better part of five years, then ratified in 1791. Its important difference from the *Articles of Confederation* is that the *Constitution* began with the familiar words: "We the People of the United States, in Order to form a more perfect Union ..." This in sharp contrast to the opening of the *Articles of Confederation*: "To all to whom these Presents [sic] shall come, we the undersigned Delegates of the States affixed to our Names send greetings... ." The *Constitution* constitutes a nation of people for whom its several states are secondary to the ideal of a perfect union. Those who framed the document realized almost immediately that they had neglected to assure the rights of *the People* in whose name their constituting document was composed. Hence, the *Bill of Rights* was agreed upon in 1789 and ratified in 1791 as Amendments I–X to the *Constitution*.

But even this strong platform for a singular federal state, though necessary, would have been insufficient had not George Washington set aside his personal desire to retire to Mt. Vernon in order to become the union's first President. If ever there was an imperative that one person alone could be President of the new republic, this was it. The Commander of the Colonial Armies was also a man of abiding pragmatism in his dealings with others—whether individuals or parties or nations. Washington led while others worked out the abiding contents of the 1791 Constitution.

---

4 From George Washington to Benjamin Harrison, 10 October 1784, *Founders Online/the National Archive* @ https://founders.archives.gov/documents/Washington/04-02-02-0082
5 Ellis, *The Quartet*, 83. Line on the optimist position just before this is from the same page.

James Madison: Political Theorist of Factions and the Nation State

If Thomas Paine was America's first serious practical political and social theorist and Jonathan Edwards its first great philosopher, then James Madison was—as much, perhaps more than Hamilton—America's first disciplined scholar of democratic political theory. Madison tackled and explained what remains the fundamental, almost surely, unresolvable dilemma of a modern democratic state. Madison's word, still a good one, for this dilemma was *factions*—a term common in the day. Though *factions* may not today be in common use, it enjoys more analytic depth than other words have. *Differences* is too vapid at best, too abstract at worse. *Multiplicities?*—well, the less said, the better if what is wanted is a concrete term that expresses the social dynamics of a political system that appreciates the freedom of parties and people to pursue their own interests. *Conflict-ridden* comes closer to the problem except for the fact that not all conflicts between factions break into the open.

The foremost threat to a political system is that conflict could break the system apart. Such a break happens only when opposing factions in the political dynamics struggle ferociously enough over time that they come to a point of no return. This of course is what happened after 1774 with the Boston Tea Party and 1775 when local militia in Lexington and Concord repelled British forces. The British were at the time the global superpower. They had assumed that all they needed do was to send over their trained and well-equipped armies to put the colonies in their place. The war that began in 1775, however, would last more than eight years. Lexington and Concord were the breaking point after which there was no turning back.

Then, in the end, once the Revolution was won, the conflict with Britain left the scars that wars always cut on the flesh of winners and losers. For the Americans surely one such scar was an acute sensitivity to domestic conflict—a sensitivity that was anything but trivial. The independent slave-holding and free colonies were well aware that they might go their separate ways. This deep structural lesion aggravated the less acute but real worries about factions or dug-in parties like the federalists and republicans. These two major parties were themselves subdivided into factions of their own as those between James Madison and Patrick Henry among the republicans. Then too there were, as always there are, the factions that arise in civil societies structurally torn by conflicting interests—in the day, the salient ones were the many factions in the manufacturing and trade centers in the North and, in the South, the grinding differences between rebels in the slave-holding states in the deep South and middle of the road moderates in border states. The prospect of unresolvable differences among factions became a threat to the new nation as still today they are in the purportedly more mature nation. Then, however, the task for members of the Constitutional Convention in 1787 who sought to do something about factions that were deeply held while trying to build some kind of political union out of the thirteen former colonies that, having agreed only that the British must go, had not much else in common after the Revolution.

Whatever factions may be called, James Madison was the first American to study the problem historically, then to formulate a theory of the perils facing those who left them unattended. Madison published this theory in what many consider the most important document of early American history, *The Federalist Papers* in 1788. Then too, he worked the back rooms of the Constitutional Convention to fashion the political accords that ratified the *Constitution of the United States* and its ten initial amendments, its *Bill of Rights*—without which a United States of America would not have come to be. Many beside Madison engaged in the political work, but none—not even Alexander Hamilton, his only intellectual peer in the day—engaged in the scholarly research necessary to the enduring theory that is little appreciated today because its truth is embedded in the nation's Constitution.

If, as I suggest, Thomas Jefferson's *Notes on the State of Virginia* in 1785 is an early instance of ethnography, then Madison's *Notes on Ancient and Modern Confederacies* in 1786 is an early, unqualifiedly scholarly study of the political history of confederacies— with an eye to their various types that were, he concluded, failures. As Jefferson, in writing *Notes,* had no archives or data sources of the kind we enjoy today, so Madison had no historical sources readily at hand near his home in Montpelier, Virginia or in Philadelphia or Mount Vernon where he travelled to consult with George Washington as they and others were preparing for the Constitutional Congress. What Madison did have was his friend Thomas Jefferson in Paris from whom he requested all the books available there on the history of confederacies. He received from Jefferson in relatively short order two trunks of the books and documents he needed. These were sufficient for the disciplined Madison to prepare his *Notes on Ancient and Modern Confederacies* which was, literally, notes in a way that Jefferson's *Notes of the State of Virginia* were not. Madison's text (probably compiled between April and June 1786) was a meticulous summary (much of it in the original Latin) of the Lycian and Amphychtyonic confederacies in Greece that lasted for a good millennium after 1522 BCE until the Persian invasion led by Darius I in 522 BCE. On the point that would be crucial to his subsequent political theory, he wrote: "It happened but too often that the Deputies of the strongest Cities awed and corrupted those of the weaker, and that Judgment went in favor of the most powerful party."[6]

Madison's report on the history of confederacies was his way of preparing for the Constitutional Congress in 1787 where the foremost issue of concern was how a federal republic would assure the rights of States in respect to representation in a national Congress. Virginia was far and away the largest state and among the most powerful. Pennsylvania and Massachusetts were comparably powerful, and New York's power was on the rise. Yet, even New York was, as the debate played out, skeptical of the ability of the more powerful states to respect the rights of the smaller former colonies. If New York, then surely Delaware and Rhode Island; then also the lesser slave-holding states of the southern colonies. Slavery aside for the moment, the issue was how to apportion votes in the Constitutional Congress, much less in a given national election. Hence, the electoral college problem (as unsettled today as then) was a chronic symptom of the founders' inability to settle the apportionment issue—a function of the concern over proportional representation and the balance of power between the larger states with the great number of representatives allotted according to population in the Congress and Senators of equal number regardless of a state's population.

Madison's *Notes* went on to summarize and comment on the most important confederacies in occidental history (as world history was then understood)—the Achaean League of Alexander the Great that fell in 184 CE when the Macedonians were defeated by the Romans, the Helvetic confederacy in fourteenth century CE in Central Europe, the Belgic in seventeenth century Utrecht, the Germanic after the Diet of Worms in 1663. That Madison's research was fair to variations in the historical cases is evident in the fact that he drew different conclusions as the data required. In respect to the Achaean League, for example: "After the death of Alexander, this Union was dissolved by various dissensions raised chiefly thro' the arts of the Kings of Macedon."[7] The Helvetic "had no common treasury [and in the end] … in disputes force was used against the party refusing to submit." As for the Germanic: "the laws were despised … Jealousy of the Imperial

---

6 Madison, *Notes on Ancient and Modern Confederacies,* @ //founders.archives.gov/documents/Madison/ 01-09-02-001.

7 The Achaean, Helvetic, and Germanic are the confederacies, each of which are discussed in distinct sections of Madison's *Notes on Ancient and Modern Confederacies*, where the passages quoted can be found.

authority seems to have been a great cement of the confederacy." And so on. Today's scholars on the subject have likely corrected and filled in what Madison missed. But, apart from the limitations of his sources, Madison deserves credit for attending to what variance there was in the record he had at hand.

No one would say, as it was said of Jefferson's *Notes*, that Madison's *Notes* were a very personal text. But anyone of fair mind would have to say that Madison's *Notes* were perspicaciously scholarly. In addition to which Madison was also, in the moniker used in our time, a public intellectual. He, as much as anyone in the day, and (with the possible exception of Alexander Hamilton), was the behind-the-scenes intellectual force in the framing and defending of the Constitution of the United States and the Bill of Rights. Though the number of his contributions to the *Federalist Papers* was less than those of Hamilton, Madison's were certainly less tendentious than Hamilton's and, in their way, more enduring for the concerns of our day. Of these, no subject to which Madison attended continues to haunt democratic societies in the twenty-first century more than factions.

Madison's intellectual contributions to the foundations of America as a constitutionally framed nation were significant to be sure, but they might not have found their way into constitutional law without others. Washington, for one example, kept himself aloof, thus he lent gravitas to the debates, thereby opening the discursive space for "Hamilton's charisma, and Madison's cerebral power".[8] Washington figured in the framing of the groundwork documents of the Republic mostly by being the transcendent figure looming (Jefferson's word again) in the background. He was the mostly silent one whose approval was required for passage. By contrast to Washington, Hamilton, whose intellect was powerful in itself, was the charismatic figure who forced the issues and actually inspired and sustained *The Federalist Papers* which he began in *Federalist 1* by dramatizing the human importance of the ratification of the Constitution:

> After an unequivocal experience of the inefficiency of the subsisting federal government, you are called upon to deliberate on a new Constitution for the United States of America. The subject speaks its own importance; comprehending in its consequences nothing less than the existence of the *union*, the safety and welfare of the parts of which it is composed, the fate of an empire in many respects the most interesting in the world. It has been frequently remarked that it seems to have been reserved to the people of this country, by their conduct and example, to decide the important question, whether societies of men are really capable or not of establishing good government from reflection and choice, or whether they are forever destined to depend for their political constitutions on accident and force. If there be any truth in the remark, the crisis at which we are arrived may with propriety be regarded as the era in which that decision is to be made; and a wrong election of the part we shall act may, in this view, deserve to be considered as the general misfortune of mankind.[9]

Thereafter, Hamilton wrote 51 of the 85 *Federalist* essays, Madison 29 (and John Jay, who had fallen ill, but 5).

Yet, as before, it was Madison who lent the scholarly and intellectual depth to *The Federalist Papers*. Nowhere is this more evident than in his cooperative effort with Hamilton in *Federalist 9 and 10* on factions. Hamilton wrote *Federalist 9, The Utility of the Union*

---

8 Joseph Ellis, *The Quartet*, 71.
9 *Federalist 1* and the papers as a whole can be found at *Federalist Papers: Primary Documents in American History* (Library of Congress) @ https://guides.loc.gov/federalist-papers/full-text

as a Safeguard Against Domestic Faction and Insurrection. Madison wrote *10, The Same Subject Continued.* It might seem by the two titles that Madison's *10* is but a footnote of no special quality to Hamilton's *9* with its expansive even alarming title. But just the opposite is the case. To be sure Hamilton's paper introduces and addresses the issue of factions and their potential for insurrection that were feared after the colonies had defeated Great Britain and were presumed by many to no longer have a shared interest in their friendly Confederation.

As if he had read Madison's *Notes on Ancient and Modern Confederacies* (as probably he had), Hamilton begins and ends his essay on factions with reference to the failures of the Lycian League's interference in the proper business of confederated cities that generated "a state of perpetual vibration between the extremes of tyranny and anarchy."[10] This was the fear of what might occur in the post-war American colonies without a stable but respectful national administration. So far so good. But then Hamilton abandons his charismatic opening lines and lurches into a generic defense of the new Constitution in what at first appears to be strangely abstract language: "I mean the *enlargement* of the *orbit* within which such systems are to revolve, either in respect to the dimensions of a single State, or the consolidation of several small States into one great Confederacy." The idea of a single State as the sun around which the states would orbit was a figure first used by Edmund Randolph, Madison's friend and fellow Virginia delegate. Randolph meant to characterize the promise of the enlargement of governmental authority that a nation-state would allow—an enlargement that was loathed by those, like Patrick Henry (another Virginian), who was rabidly opposed to any kind of federal arrangement that would diminish the autonomy of the several states.[11] Hamilton is addressing the question that was central to the Constitution—that of "the dimensions of a single State, or the consolidation of several small States into one great Confederacy." His essay then rather haphazardly discusses sources like Montesquieu and the Lycian Confederacy on the matter and comes to a wan conclusion that history's lessons often rest on "erroneous theory." On the whole, Hamilton's *Federalist 9* does not do justice to its own title, *The Utility of the Union as a Safeguard Against Domestic Faction and Insurrection*. It reads almost as though he is turning the substance at hand, factions, over to Madison's *Federalist 10*.

Federalist 10 was published in November 1787, months after another of Madison's scholarly reports, *Vices of the Political System of the United States* (April 1787). *Vices* was much like *Notes on Ancient and Modern Confederacies* in 1786 and both are background to Madison's *Federalist 10* which deals forthrightly and systematically with factions—with the effects of discord among states and against the Confederacies to which they are affiliated. He begins more succinctly than Hamilton: "Among the numerous advantages promised by a well-constructed union, none deserves to be more accurately developed than its tendency to break and control the violence of faction ..."[12] Among Madison's several intellectual qualities, he thought and wrote more as a lawyer preparing a brief. In fact, during the extremely bad winter weather of 1783–84 when he was confined to his home at Montpelier until Spring, Madison devoted the months to the study of the classic works on common law, *Coke Upon Littleton*.[13]

---

10 Hamilton, *Federalist 9* (November 21, 1787), in *Alexander Hamilton: Writings* (Library of America, 2001), 196; compare ending at 201 which is a note on the Lycian confederacy. Then too, *Federalist 9* is of course in the *Federalist Papers: Primary Documents in American History* (Library of Congress).
11 Noah Feldman, *The Three Lives of James Madison* (Random House, 2017), chapter 3, especially 97–101.
12 Quotations from *Federalist 10*, here and below, are from *Madison: Writings* (Library of America, 1999), 160–167.
13 Feldman, *The Three Lives of James Madison*, 54–55.

"A Madisonian argument lacked all the emotional affections but struck with the force of pure thought."[14]

Madison's brief on factions goes straight to a definition astonishing for a parsimony that condenses all the structural issues in a single sentence:

> By a faction I understand a number of citizens, whether amounting to a majority or a minority of the whole, who are united and actuated by some common impulse of passion, or of interest, adverse to the rights of other citizens, or to the permanent and aggregate interests of the community.

Think of the theoretical gift by which Madison coherently dealt with majority/minority status, impassioned interests adverse to the rights of others, as to the interests of the community. I know of no social theoretical line that says so much in so few words—and especially none of recent times. Then Madison continues to describe "the two methods of curing the mischiefs of faction." Remove the cause; control its effects—neither of which in the abstract would seem either possible or desirable. But Madison, in the next lines of *Federalist 10*, has the solution—less abstract perhaps but now robustly logical and practically coherent. The former destroys liberty; the other aggravates passions and interests. "Liberty is to faction, what air is to fire, an aliment without which it instantly expires." Then, as regards controlling the effects of factions, a still more nuanced argument:

> The second expedient is as impracticable, as the first is unwise. As long as the reason of man continues fallible, and he is at liberty to exercise it, different opinions will be formed. As long as the connection subsists between his reason and his self-love, his opinions and passions will have a reciprocal effect on each other; ... The diversity in the faculties of men from which the rights of property originate, is not less an insuperable obstacle to an uniformity of interests. The protection of these faculties is the first object of government. ... And from the influence of these on the sentiments and views of the respective proprietors, ensures a division of the society in different interests and parties.[15]

As for the social theory, Madison is here writing twenty years before Hegel's *Phenomenology of the Mind*, forty years before Harriet Martineau's *Woman,* and just shy of fifty years before Marx's *Economic and Philosophical Manuscripts of 1844*—to mention but a few of the earliest classics of disciplined social theory in modern times. Madison matters in particular because he sustains a theoretical tension between what came to be called the agency of the subject and the force of general social structures—between the subjective mind and human passions, on the one side, and, in this instance, the purpose of government. But also, he juxtaposes human nature and mankind's social constructs without lapsing into the theoretically depilating notion of opposing dichotomies.

Federalist 10 comes to a conclusion with, again, a coherent definition of the solution to the problems posed by factions, namely: "A republic, by which I mean a government in which the scheme of representation takes place, opens a different prospect, and promises a cure for which we are seeking." This may sound dreamy, but at the very end, Madison makes it clear that there are no easy solutions to factions:

---

14 Ellis, *The Quartet*, 117. Also, Joseph Ellis, *Founding Brothers: The Revolutionary Generation* (Knopf, 2000), 53–54.
15 Still *Federalist 10, op cit.*

In the extent and proper structure of the union, therefore, we behold a republican remedy for the diseases most incident to republican government. And according to the degree of pleasure and pride, we feel in being republicans, ought to be our zeal in cherishing the spirit and supporting the character of the federalists.

Madison concludes by making it clear that factions are not ideal types.

The Federalist Papers would not have come to be without the two principal authors setting aside their very political differences that, if not held in check, would have doomed the Constitution and the nation to failure. Madison, the Republican, and Hamilton, the Federalist, were aligned with several of the union's most threatening factions—South against North, Republican versus Federalist, rural planters as opposed to urban bankers and manufacturers; and they were as different in temperament as two could be—a methodical man of logical brilliance; a charismatic figure of rhetorical genius. Yet they held their differences in check and, with Washington looking on, made the United States of America possible for better or worse.

After *The Federalist Papers* were completed (August 16, 1788), Madison and Hamilton drifted apart.[16] By late 1791, Madison changed his mind about what he took to be Hamilton's position in favor of a stronger centralized government. Then too in December 1791 Hamilton would publish his then controversial *Report on Manufactures*, which was not well received by the Virginian planters whose republican ideals inclined toward an agrarian America. Madison then drew closer still to Jefferson and in due course to James Monroe as well. Washington remained customarily neutral as to the differences between Madison and Hamilton; and this in spite of the fact that his financial interests were based on agriculture and his Western land holdings. By the end of Washington's first term in 1793 Madison was a leader of a newly formed Republican Party that stood in opposition to Hamilton's Federalist Party. Still they both must be honored for comprising differences that would become factions in order to write *The Federalist Papers* and to see the Constitution ratified.

Since the point of the Constitution was to form a federal government and a unified nation, Hamilton was more in his federalist element in their joint labors. Madison's compromise was the greater which is clear in his *Federalist 51* where he all but argues for a centralized government in an awkwardly recast definition of pure republican values: "It is of great importance in a republic not only to guard one part of the society against the oppression of its rulers; but to guard against the injustice of the other part."[17] Here factions are more specific as they are more abstractly put—one *part* against another prefigures one *party* against another. At the end of *Federalist 51* Madison again blesses a party romance with Hamilton: "Happily for the *republican cause*, the practicable sphere may be carried to a very great extent, by a judicious modification and mixture of the *federal principle*."[18]

As in all unnatural romances where the partners must strain against their separate ways, the romance ended in divorce. Madison in effect reverted to an earlier, more primitive Republican commitment. He broke with Hamilton to the point that in the years remaining to Hamilton they became enemies.

---

16 The following relies on Feldman, *The Three Lives of James Madison*, 337–371.
17 *Federalist 51* in *Madison's Writings* (Library of America, 1999), 297.
18 *Ibid*, 298.

Alexander Hamilton: Banks and Manufactures

If, among the patriarchs, there was a genius comparable to Benjamin Franklin, it may have been Alexander Hamilton, who was the youngest of them all. He had but 50 years when he died July 12, 1804 in a duel with Aaron Burr. Into a short adult life of 30 years he packed more than others did in twice the time.

Hamilton left St. Croix, Virgin Islands for New York at 16. He entered King's College (today's Columbia University) at 19. In his first year of college, he also began a serious writing career by publishing a pamphlet, *A Full Vindication of the Measures of Congress*, that initiated an on-going exchange with Samuel Seabury who was a loyalist opposed to the very idea of a Continental Congress. In 1776, Hamilton left college and began a military career after the Colonial Army suffered the Kip's Bay defeat. He fought in the battle of Princeton in 1777 at 22 years when he also became aide-de-camp of George Washington. He was Washington's advisor on matters military, political, presidential until the President's last months in office. In the end he wrote the final draft of Washington's Farewell Address in 1796 after leaving Washington's cabinet the year before. And on it went—successful New York lawyer, member of Congress, an author of most of the *Federalist Papers* among other enduring writings, founding leader of the Federalist Party, first Secretary of the Treasury, founder of the Bank of the United States, and more. In the end, however, after leaving George Washington's paternal-like discipline, Hamilton unraveled—got into fights of all kinds. In the last he got himself killed by Aaron Burr. "You've invented a new kind of stupid, a damage you can never undo. Kind of stupid."[19] The most brilliant of men, turned stupid.

Stupid though Hamilton's end was, only Franklin of his era was more brilliantly accomplished in so many different fields. The best way to convey Hamilton's accomplishments is to say that, amid all else—including founder and coauthor of the *Federalist Papers*, one of the key figures in the design and elaboration of the Constitutional union—his most important achievements were in respect to making the case for the nation's banking system and for becoming a manufacturing economy. This in three long and nuanced papers published between December 1790 and December 1791—*Report on a National Bank, Opinion on the Constitutionality of a National Bank, Report on Manufactures*—, of which the third on manufacturing can reasonably be considered his most brilliant paper. All the more astonishing is that 1791 was the year when the two contrary dispositions of his political and personal life exposed him at once to public honor and disgrace. In the year from late 1790 to late 1791, he organized, raised the funds for, and won a charter for the *Society for Useful Manufacturing* as the institutional structure for a manufacturing mill town on the Passaic River at today's Paterson, New Jersey. His *Report on Manufactures* was anything but pure theory.

At the same time, in July 1791, Hamilton began his adulterous affair with 23-year-old Maria Reynolds who, as things turned out, seduced Hamilton in a scheme contrived with her husband James to blackmail Hamilton financially and for other considerations. Hamilton paid up, at least $1000 (a considerable sum in 1791). Early in 1792, the affair had ended. Maria had divorced her husband. But Hamilton was haunted politically for years to come. When the affair surfaced in public, Hamilton's political enemies made hay not just of his morals but also of his corruption in paying the Reynolds' bribe. As late as 1797, Hamilton published what became known as *The Reynolds Pamphlet* in which, remarkably for the day, he admitted to the affair but defended himself against charges of corruption.

---

19 Lin Manuel Miranda, "Congratulations Lyrics [Eliza]," *Hamilton the Musical* (2015).

As in other of his writings the pamphlet was articulate and convincing in defending himself against the charge of using his public office to enrich himself. The sexual matter faded into the backstage of Hamilton's dazzling rhetorical genius in defending himself against financial corruption. Most striking is the subtle use of a kind of double entendre in respect to his reputation:

> I dare appeal to my immediate fellow citizens of whatever political party for the truth of the assertion, that *no man ever carried into public life a more unblemished pecuniary reputation*, than that with which I undertook the office of Secretary of the Treasury; a character marked by an indifference to the acquisition of property rather than an avidity for it.[20]

Having admitted the blemish on his sexual reputation, Hamilton emphatically asserted the purity of his pecuniary reputation. Somehow the ploy worked well enough—perhaps in part because he had left the office of Secretary of the Treasury at the end of 1795, well before the affairs came to public attention in 1796. Still, the affair with Maria Reynolds, with its delayed public trouble for Hamilton, serves to frame his three important essays of 1790 and 1791 when the affair was hot and heavy. Even while all that was going on, Hamilton was able to think decisively about two issues of deep consequence for the nation—banks and its financial system; manufacturing and its economic future.

Hamilton's *Report on a National Bank* was published December 13, 1790 by the still new first Secretary of the Treasury. The Constitution had been ratified on June 21, 1788. George Washington assumed office April 30, 1790. The new national government was still filling in its administrative structures when *Report on a National Bank* was published. Hamilton had previously offered a *Report on Public Credit* early in 1790. A national bank was required for a coherent policy about liquid credit. The assumption of the war debts of the states remained unsettled. It is safe to say that no one in the day knew as much as Hamilton about credit and banking. Plus which, he had the authority needed to set forth the policy. He faced opposition in Congress, notably from the Virginians who, while accepting the reality of a constitutionally defined nation state, still resisted the financial terms entailed in paying the bills.

Report on a National Bank begins plain and simple.[21] Banks are common in all commercial nations. "Theorists and men of business unite in the acknowledgement of ...their utility."[22] It is not incidental that Hamilton starts off by referencing banking practices in all the modern economies: Italy, Germany, Holland, England, and France.[23] The very idea of a national bank was foreign to a new nation, especially this one where so many remained deeply suspicious of anything centralized. Hamilton then turns to the three main advantages of a national bank. Put simply, they are: The *first* is that when gold and silver have no other purpose than coinage for transactions, their greater financial value to the community is lost. If fungible wealth in cash is deposited in a bank its value grows for the benefit of all because the bank's holdings can produce surplus value by lending to borrowers who, in turn, pay back the interest charges. Simpler yet: a national bank supports a system of public credit

---

20 *The Reynolds Pamphlet* or: *Observations on Certain Documents ... In Which the Charge of Speculation Against Alexander Hamilton, Late Secretary of the Treasury, is Fully Refuted. Written by Himself. Alexander Hamilton Writings* (Library of America, 2001 [1797]), 884. Emphasis added.
21 Quotations and general allusions in the following, when not specifically noted, are from *Report on a National Bank* in *Alexander Hamilton Writings* (Library of America, 2001), 575–612.
22 *Ibid*, 575.
23 At the time, all listed were early modern nations except Germany which remained a confederation.

for the common good. The *second* advantage of a national bank is that the cash reserves are available for sudden financial emergencies. A *third* advantage is that of "facilitating ... the payment of taxes."[24]

Thus, in the first few pages of the *Report*, Hamilton makes his strongest general point: "It is one of the properties of Banks to increase the active capital of a country."[25] Simple, but smart. But he is just beginning. Always aware of the lingering opposition, Hamilton devotes the remaining 85% of the report to countering the criticisms of a National Bank— as increasing usury, preventing other kinds of lending, tempting the practice of over trading, allowing fraudulent traders to get around the system, banishing gold and silver. The complaints had merit as we know today when there are limits as to who can borrow, when gold and silver are indeed all but banished except as commodities, when fraudulent trading is rampant. Yet, for his day, Hamilton was ingenious in responding to these concerns. One example, and not the strongest, is that banks are unlikely to be deceived by fraudulent traders because the nation's banks will be run by directors who are thoroughly familiar with how these matters work. Here Hamilton has in mind himself and others in the New York banking community. His stronger case is against the fear that gold and silver will be banished:

> It is immaterial what serves the purpose of money, whether paper, or gold and silver ... [if] the effect on industry is the same; and [if] the intrinsic wealth of a nation is to be measured, not by the abundance of precious metals, contained in it, but by the quantity of the *productions of its labor and industry*.[26]

Years later, Karl Marx in 1867 would have been pleased at least that a banker like Hamilton got the point he would make in *Capital I* about labor as foundational to a capitalist economy. Hamilton put the forces of production—labor and industry—forward as the key not only to monetary value but also to surplus value. *Report on a National Bank* goes on and on in ever spiraling detail and exceptionally refined arguments—for some 16,000 words. How many in the day read it is hard to say. Clearly it was persuasive enough to convince members of the Congress.

A bill chartering the Bank of the United States passed the Senate on January 20, 1791, just more than a month after Hamilton's report was published. On February 8 it passed the House and was sent to President Washington for his signature. Madison was dead set against the bill. Secretary of State Thomas Jefferson, and Attorney General Edmund Randolph recommended against the signing, whereupon the President asked the opinion of his Secretary of the Treasury, Hamilton, who set about replying explicitly to Jefferson, Randolph, and Madison. Weeks later, February 23, 1791, he answered their objections in *Opinion on the Constitutionality of a National Bank*. The principle motivating their objections was that the Constitution makes no mention of a National Bank or more generally to government's right to charter corporations of any kind. Hamilton's reply (another 14,000 words) is a complex but coherent theory meant to put down an early instance of strict constitutional constructionism:

> Now it appears to the Secretary of the Treasury, that this *general principle* is *inherent* in the very *definition* of *Government* and *essential* to every step of the progress to be

---

24 *Ibid*, 579.
25 *Ibid*, 578.
26 *Ibid*, 586. Emphasis added.

made by that of the United States; namely—that every power vested in a Government is in its nature *sovereign*, and includes by *force* of the *term*, a right to employ all the *means* requisite, and fairly *applicable* to the attainment of the *ends* of such power; and which are not precluded by restrictions & exceptions specified in the constitution; or not immoral, or not contrary to the ends of political society.[27]

As can be seen from words I've italicized throughout the statement, Hamilton meant from the first to drive home his points—much in the manner of a legal brief meant to be read by both judge and opposing counsel. His point was well taken by Washington who signed the bill chartering the National Bank two days later, February 25, 1791. The *Opinion* may have been legal theory, but it was also social and political theory. Traces of *Federalist 9* on factions as a threat to the union are evident between the lines. If a government cannot act with sovereign authority, with morality and concern for political society, and without violating explicit Constitutional prohibitions there is no government.

Hamilton was a cool hand—even amid the most embarrassing of circumstances. The Maria Reynolds affair would blossom that summer in July of 1791. Still, late that year Hamilton turned to his December 5, 1791 *Report on Manufactures*. Since April, he had been preparing the way for the *Society for the Establishment of Useful Manufacturing* with its site at the Great Falls on the Passaic River. By the end of the year $600,000 had been raised as stock for the enterprise. By the end of 1791 the Board of the *Society* approved textile and bleach contracts and the personnel needed for a factory that Hamilton alone had developed.[28] Few if any among the founders of the nation—not even Washington and certainly not Jefferson and Madison or Adams—were able to work on several fronts at once with such intensity and productive results. Here too Hamilton, like Franklin, and his mentor, the President, was a strong proponent of early American practical pragmatism. If such a judgment is fair, then it was a kind of pragmatism that flowed from one of the most powerful intellects of the day.

Report on Manufactures at the end of 1791 was the concluding intellectual masterpiece of Hamilton's miraculous, if troubled, year. This report takes the republican interests in small town, agricultural politics head on by a method similar to the one deployed in *Report on a National Bank* of the previous December. He begins with a general theory of how manufacturing does not undercut an agrarian economy, then answers the objections by elaborating seven salient ways that manufacturing is beneficial, even necessary, for the nation's economic and social viability. He begins, quoting unnamed opponents of manufacturing:

In every country ... Agriculture is the most beneficial and *productive* object of human industry. This position, generally, if not universally true, applies with peculiar emphasis to the United States, on account of their immense tracts of fertile territory, uninhabited and unimproved. ...Nothing equally with this, can contribute to the population, strength and real riches of the country.[29]

Here Hamilton gives Virginia opponents their due: "This mode of reasoning is founded on facts and principles, which have certainly respectable pretension."[30] He graciously concedes that agricultural labor "has *intrinsically a strong claim to pre-eminence over every other*

---

27 *Constitutionality of a National Bank, Alexander Hamilton Writings*, 613. Emphases added.
28 Ron Chernow, *Hamilton* (Penguin Books, 2004), 370–374.
29 *Report on Manufactures, Alexander Hamilton Writings*, 647–648. Emphasis is Hamilton's.
30 *Ibid*, 649. Quote just following same page. Emphasis is Hamilton's.

kind of labor." Then, immediately after, Hamilton argues that, this being so, one ought to exercise "great caution" before concluding that this is exclusively so of agrarian production.

At this point Hamilton offers a kind of soft history of the movement already in motion in Europe. Once agricultural production at a certain point in its development yields a profit beyond the expenses entailed in production, then that surplus can serve other purposes. Though the costs of production and labor are different this is also true of manufacturing—in effect Hamilton is making the already by then familiar observation that the means of production in farming are fixed by land rent but in manufacturing they can be costly but also fungible. Then the comparative point is hammered home:

> The annual produce of the land and labour of a country can only be en-creased in two ways—by some improvement in the *productive powers* of the useful labour, which actually exists within it, or by some increase in the quantity of such labour. ... *Artificers* being capable of greater subdivision and simplicity of operation, than that of *Cultivators*, it is susceptible, in proportionately greater degree, of improvement in the *productive powers*...[31]

Hamilton does not quite take back his generous argument as to the special role of Cultivators in a country. But he does tip his hand in favor of the greater productive potential of Artificers, which is to say Manufacturers.

Hamilton then launches into a longish discussion comparing profits earned by Cultivators and Artificers before concluding that "the *nett* [sic] produce of Capital engaged in manufacturing enterprises is greater than that of Capital engaged in Agriculture."[32] But just after this he qualifies that the point is not to suggest that manufacturing is more productive than farming. The back and forth is in the rhetorical logic. However superior tillage might be for the good of the country, Agriculture's productivity ought *not* be a basis for opposing Manufacturing. In fact, he adds that manufacturing benefits the farming by allowing the Cultivator to use his profits to supply "himself with the manufactured articles of which he stands in need."[33]

This being said, Hamilton rests his case as to manufacturing not being a threat to agriculture and turns to the productive and revenue benefits of manufacturing, of which there are seven major facts of the matter:

1. Division of Labour.
2. An extension of the use of Machinery.
3. Additional employment to the class of the community not ordinarily engaged in the business.
4. The promoting of emigration from foreign countries.
5. The furnishing greater scope for the diversity of talents and dispositions which discriminate men from each other.
6. The affording of a more ample and various field for enterprise.
7. The creating in some instance a new, and securing in all, a more certain and steady demand for the surplus produce of the soil.[34]

---

31 *Ibid*, 651. Emphases added, and "en-creased" (from Old English) is Hamilton's spelling but "increased" later is his also—the difference may be due to an error in transcription or transmission.
32 *Ibid*, 655.
33 *Ibid*, 658.
34 *Ibid*, 658–659.

Without going into the details, the list is stated as an enunciation of self-evident prospects, which indeed they have been proven to be. He adds many pages of elaboration of each point and in the process touches on background structural issues behind the debate, notably: "Ideas of a contrariety of interests between the Northern and southern regions, are in the Main as unfounded as they are mischievous."[35]

The *Report* ends with a still longer discussion of products that manufacturing can provide the economy: iron, copper, lead, wood, skins, grains, flax and hemp, cotton, wool, silk, glass, gun powder, paper, printed books, refined sugars, and chocolate.[36] This section reads a bit like the majority of entries in Jefferson's *Notes on the State of Virginia*—more detail than the reader needs or wants. Still, Hamilton's list, read straightforwardly as a list, stands on its own as entirely convincing. In 1791 it would have been hard to suppose that a farmer would not have immediately seen the advantages of manufacturing in the production of particular grains, flax, wool, sugars, and cotton. Eli Whitney, for example, had already invented the cotton gin in 1794—a machine that, one supposes, planters in the South would have wished for in 1791 and were glad after the gin was available. Cotton production was the region's most profitable crop. It is possible to suppose that planters were so committed to slavery as a means of cotton production that they would have refused to use the cotton gin. They did not. Whitney's cotton gin came to be employed along with slave labor to increase their production.

Alexander Hamilton was, to be sure, a man of flawed character but, then too, in other respects so were others. Washington, Madison, and Jefferson kept themselves in a false position by professing a loathing of slavery while being unable to free their slaves. Still, whatever Jefferson's feelings for Sally Hemings, he kept her close-by until his death, probably for a degree of companionship but certainly for sexual satisfaction. Even Benjamin Franklin was a bold womanizer in the Paris years. And so on. At the least none of these (except perhaps for Jefferson) got themselves into public trouble and certainly none got himself killed as Hamilton did. Then too there is John Adams who had little ability to keep quiet when his temper got the best of him. None was perfect.

One might want to conclude that Hamilton was the least perfect of them all. Perhaps he was, but he was also the one (with the exception of Washington) who did more in so many ways to win the War of Independence, to assure the passage of the Constitution, to settle the new nation's financial institutions, and to propose the logic of manufacturing that was proven to be right for the United States to become an industrial power that is also the keeper of the world's breadbasket on its Great Plains.

---

35 *Ibid*, 694 and following.
36 The *Report on Manufactures* adds up to 36,000 words, compared to the 16,000 of the *Report on a National Bank* and 14,000 on the Constitutionality *of a National Bank*—66,000 words in a year, all while managing the Department of the Treasury and the pending crisis of his affair with Maria Reynolds, not to mention duties associated with being a founder of a new nation. Not even Stephen King could do that.

6 America Faces Its Fate
Ralph Waldo Emerson, Henry David Thoreau, Margaret Fuller

To go into solitude, a man needs to retire as much from his chamber, as from society.
I am not solitary whilst I read and write, though nobody is with me.
But if a man would be alone, let him look at the stars.
—Ralph Waldo Emerson, *Nature*, 1836

This is a delicious evening, when the whole body is one sense,
And imbibes delight through every pore.
I go and come with a strange liberty in Nature, a part of herself.
—Henry David Thoreau, *Walden*, 1854

Male and female represent the two sides of the great radical divide.
But in fact they are perpetually passing into one another.
Fluid hardens to solid, solid rushes to fluid.
There is no wholly masculine man, no purely feminine woman.
—Margaret Fuller, *Woman in the Nineteenth Century*, 1845

The Mill River False Pond: Waldens Everywhere

At the base of East Rock on the Metacomet Ridge north of New Haven is a reservoir created by the damning of Lake Whitney, creating the waterfalls that provided energy for Eli Whitney's early industrial enterprise. Below the falls the waters flow on to become the Mill River. Just after the dam on one side is the Eli Whitney Museum and Workshop. Today children enjoy workshops on water and the falls.

Walkers can cross the Mill River just below the falls over a covered bridge originally built early in the 1800s after the design of Ithiel Town, a prominent architect in the day who also designed Center Church and Trinity Church on New Haven's Town Green. Over the bridge, near by the falls, are the remains of the corner stone of the factory where in 1789 Eli Whitney manufactured guns, five years after he invented the cotton gin. A site of early industrial manufacturing is today the crossroad for recreational hikers. From one walk path a bit off from the Mill River, one can look up to see the rocky side East Rock. For those looking for a serious hike, they must choose a branch of this trail that ascends to the peak of East Rock. Otherwise, those on a stroll through the woods take the riverside trail that meanders, when not flooded, beside the Mill River toward a pond-like expansion of the waterway.

Here the Mill River becomes a false pond before it flows on to join the Quinnipiac River that marks the eastern edge of New Haven. Just where they join, both rivers dump

DOI: 10.4324/9781315210230-8

their waters into the city's original new harbor, a protected city-side basin in which fresh waters mix with Atlantic salt. Back upriver, both sides of the false pond are lined with reeds. Ducks and geese live, feed, and reproduce among them. Rumor has it that, since the climate has turned warmer in winter, ducks and geese who no longer migrate south have a kind of natural world agreement. In cold months the ducks get the lower water and the geese the higher reservoir. They are said to trade environments when the water warms. I walk there year-round. At best I have a vague sense this might be true if only because I'm not always sure which is a duck and which a goose. I've been told that the geese are actually swans. Whichever birds do whatever, that the rumor is passed around—no doubt on the authority of bird watchers who know their birds—is a tribute to the endurance of not-necessarily-authoritative gossip as a source of local wisdom. People today still amble about in nature, passing on to strangers what they had heard on the trail.

In Henry Thoreau's day as now, Walden Pond outside Concord, Massachusetts, was similar to the Mill River's false pond outside New Haven. Neither is far from its town center. Both were, and still are, protected areas where townspeople can retreat for an hour or two of repose. In Thoreau's day the industrial world was not far off. Across Walden Pond from his cabin ran the Fitchburg-Boston Railroad. Behind East Rock the Hartford-New Haven rail line passes today as it did in Thoreau's day. Like Whitney's pond-side gun factory in New Haven, in Concord not far from Walden Pond John Thoreau and Company made the best pencils in America in a factory of sorts behind the family home. Henry not only worked there with his brother and father, but here too he engineered the technique and the machinery by which high quality graphite could be inserted into wood such that the pencils were sharpened into cylindrical as opposed to square points.

America, even in Eli Whitney's and Henry Thoreau's days, was shaped by a geographical imagination that loomed from sea to sea over the Alleghenies, the Great Plains and the Rockies and the Sierras. Two great rivers—the Mississippi and the Missouri—divided West from East and watered the South with northern waters. Water is in American blood in a way that it is not among peoples of the world's deserts, ice lands, and deep forests. The geographical imagination of the American people is, it could be said, liquid—always flowing from a source to deltas at one or another of the three North American coasts.[1] Walden Pond in Concord is one of the local ponds that feeds the Sudbury River that flows North to join the Assabet where both flow into the Concord River that flows North to Lowell and Lawrence, where it joins the Merrimack that in turn eventually empties into the sea at Portsmouth, New Hampshire.

It is all too easy to suppose that America's ponds are lesser waters. They are in respect to volume but not at all in the wider range of geographical imagination. They are resting places where thoughtful people walk and ponder, sit and think. Thoreau's *Walden* is surely the world's best known and most cherished story of the spiritual value of pond pondering.[2] It is common to assume that the view from beside an ocean is the one most likely to promote human inspiration. This may well be, but such an inspiration is one fixed on the daunting and endless vision against which the individual is in some inner spiritual sense diminished,

---

1 It is better perhaps to say four shores by taking into account the southern shores of the St. Lawrence Seaway and the Great Lakes that to the north are just as coastal in their way as are the Atlantic, Gulf, and Pacific coasts to the east, south, and west.

2 The Pond remains today an environmental and historical monument long after Thoreau's shack was taken down. See W. Barksdale Maynard, *Walden Pond: A History* (Oxford University Press, 2004).

reminded of her finitude. Not even the stars above have the same effect, if only because on a clear night one can dream that there are other beings out there on some faraway where. Not so with ocean views where one thinks of his solitary self, alone. But pond-side can inspire a different order of imagination. One may wonder about the train passing opposite or the cabins elsewhere on the water or of the dogs running free, even of the surrounding forests. Along the trail by the Mill Pond there remains today a make-shift shelter made of fallen limbs by a father and his son one summer some five or more years ago. Before it collapsed in a winter storm, a few of its limbs served as supports for a make-believe tepee or yurt, perhaps.

By a pond, one peers into passing waters that lead to the sea. Emerson said it well in his eulogy for Thoreau in May 1862. "To him there was no such thing as size. The pond was a small ocean; the Atlantic, a large Walden Pond."

Concord, 1836–1868, Sees and Tells of America's Fate

In the Concord Moment in mid-nineteenth century America, the town's sages saw things others could not see and wrote of them at such a high philosophical level that for some what they saw was a revelation. Still, as the century turned toward its Gilded Age after the Civil War and a long period of urbanization in the North where immigrants were welcomed to work hard for a new home, what the Concord thinkers understood was that America's fate was not what previously had been promised.

From Waldo Emerson's *Nature* in 1836 to Louisa May Alcott's *Little Women* in 1868, Concord was home to thinkers who rewrote the American story as it had come down to them. Emerson's *Nature* in 1836 and his *American Scholar* in 1836 were both declarations of American cultural independence—the former declared a new transcending idea of human nature, while the latter declared the independence of America's culture from Europe's. Oversimplifying, Alcott's *Little Women* in 1868 when considered in relation to Margaret Fuller's *Woman in the Nineteenth Century* in 1845, though very different kinds of literature, brought women young and mature into the picture of a coming more modern world. And, in the between, Henry Thoreau's *Walden* in 1854 and his *Plea for Captain John Brown* in 1859 addressed their desperation of these times. These, among many others party to the Concord Moment, serve for now to demonstrate the extent to which those who lived or gathered in that small Massachusetts town in those days rethought American culture at a moment during when America and its nation were at mortal risk of Civil War.

Yet, paradoxically as much as the Concord Moment was when America's best thinkers of the day were rethinking American thinking itself, writers like Emerson and Thoreau drew on their fathomless knowledge of European thought to declare that America's way of thinking was heading off on its own way. Hence the oft-repeated line of Robert D. Richardson that "Concord in the 1830s and 1840s—Emerson's Concord—was to America what Goethe's Weimar had been to Germany." America's Weimar was at once local and global in its redirecting the German *Bildung* in a distinctively American notion of *Self-culture* in which the thinking subject is at once individual and natural, in the sense of nature's many aspects including *human* nature.[3] Then too, Henry Thoreau, like the others, could see that social things were changing to such an extent that it was time to tell the world to make way for the new. In this sense they all offered a prophetic word on how the American world after the Civil War would be different and demanding in more ways than the Revolutionary Age

---

3 Robert D. Richardson, *Henry Thoreau: A Life of the Mind* (University of California Press, 1986), 54–57.

from 1776 to 1861 had been. Civil War put everyone on notice that a new world was in the offing so long as the ship of State survived this War.

Those who told of this new world, however mutedly, were not prophets in the Old Testament sense. They did not shout loudly at those in power as Amos did in the eighth century BCE. The Concord prophets were, by comparison, quiet and calm, all-too-philosophical some might say—but they knew what needed to be said about America's fate.

Concord and its Prophets

Emerson began the Concord Moment in American history with his first book, *Nature*, in 1836, and his sensational paper at Harvard, "American Scholar" in 1837. That literary moment ended, many say, with Alcott's *Little Women* in 1868. Thoreau's *Walden* in 1854 is the most avidly read. Alcott's *Little Women* is to me, but not others, unreadable.[4] Yet, all three endure, perhaps because they together, along with other of the books of Concord authors—must notably Margaret Fuller's *Woman in the Nineteenth Century* in 1845— reoriented American literature so sharply that a distinctly American way of thinking came into its own.

In 1837 Concord was a satellite town of Boston. It was small and still relatively remote. Just the same, its local geography set it amid much larger social forces. By land, Concord was bound historically to Lexington and the start of the Revolutionary War. In Thoreau's day, though smallish, Concord was a bustling town of 2,200—not rural, but still twenty miles remote from Boston. Yet, the Fitchburg-Boston rail line was rapidly making Concord an exurb, if not yet a suburb, of the Boston Hub.[5] And by water, the Concord River provided Thoreau access to the Merrimack River and the industrial cotton mills at Lowell to the north.[6] Like all populated settlements, whatever their size, Concord was part of a surround that, in principle, was a local place on the map of the world. At the least, Emerson, Thoreau, Fuller, Hawthorne and the others brought the far world home in their writings as they drew deeply from the literary resources of Europe and Asia.

From Thoreau's home in town on the Sudbury River just below its confluence with the Concord River, he could not, of course, see more than the river waters he devoted himself to charting and studying.[7] But in his mind's eye the waters led him to the burgeoning factory center—the American Ruhr Valley and the nation's coming industrial power. Cultural geography is the art of geographical imagination. Thoreau and Emerson in particular, in their similar but distinct ways, put Concord on the practical map of American culture. Concord itself was neither an economic nor a political force in the young nation. But it was a force in creating the more expansive aspects of America's cultural imagination. Robert D. Richardson, who did not incline toward exaggeration, put it this way, as I previously mentioned:

> Concord in the 1830s and 1840s—Emerson's Concord—was to America what Goethe's Weimar had been to Germany. In each case, a small if not humble society came to have

---

4 Clearly, I am wrong about this: Sarah Lyall, "'Little Women' Marches On: Fans Celebrate the Novel's 150th Anniversary," *The New York Times*, September 14, 2018, C17.
5 Mark Peterson, *The City-State of Boston: The Rise and Fall of an Atlantic Power, 1630–1865* (Princeton University Press, 2019).
6 Thoreau, *A Week on the Concord and Merrimack Rivers* (1849).
7 Robert M. Thorson, *The Boatman: Henry David Thoreau's River Years* (Harvard University Press, 2017). For "American Ruhr," just below, see chapter 3.

enormous moral and intellectual importance for a country, coming eventually to symbolize the best of the national culture.[8]

If Concord was an American Weimar, it was because of the towering intellect of Emerson who, like Goethe, read and wrote across a good number of literary and intellectual genres. In another, more inclusive sense, Susan Cheever had it better in describing Concord in the day as an American Bloomsbury in which Louisa May Alcott, Margaret Fuller, and Nathaniel Hawthorne joined Emerson, Thoreau, and Bronson Alcott, and a good many others, to form a cultural band of brothers and sisters who were midwives to the birth of important new ways of thinking.[9]

Emerson, Thoreau, and Fuller were at the intellectual and spiritual core of the Concord Moment. They and their wider cohort of writers and transcendentalists took up the task of defining a distinctly American theory of America. This they achieved by inventing an implicit social theory that set America in and against Nature where that nature was understood as the vital source of a globally fresh idea of what a new nation set in a new continent must come to terms with. No one, so far, has put it better than Larzer Ziff:

> Nature also seemed opposed to the acculturation of the citizenry despite its promise of abundant prosperity. The brooding weight of the vast, primitive continent stretching beyond the western horizon made the seaboard effort at civilization trivial. The task of taming, it seemed, would have to go on for a century at least before a culture, in the traditional sense, would emerge.[10]

Nature, in other words, was both the challenge and the promise of what America could be. It still is.

The tension between the nation and its Nature has been, from the beginning, an underlying element in the constituent tension of American culture. America still today thinks of itself as the land of the free and home of the brave but it is also a nation of factions never ending—of slavery and its consequences, of the enduring scars of Indian removal, of economic inequalities ever more acute, of contesting social movements, and of social differences owing in large part to America being a nation of immigrants. To be sure, these tensions are present, in differing ways, in a good many, perhaps most, modern nations built on the edges of vast natural spaces. But in none—not Australia, not Brazil, not Canada, not Russia—has a "vast primitive continent" posing irremediable challenges while also being the "horizon" toward which its civilization would be drawn and in respect to which it would define its sense of itself. America's settlement of its vast continent was, of course, a conquest of Nature—where nature was the wilderness beyond but also the living bodies of the enslaved, removed, and economically deprived among its many different people.

In the Concord Moment, these tensions came to the fore in ways that earlier generations could not have imagined. These were the days when the network of railroads brought East and West together, when civil strife eventuated in a terrible Civil War splitting North from South. The great rivers of the West, the Great Lakes to the North, sparked the first of the nation's natural imaginary even while the deep fissures between a still-feudal South and industrial North tore the nation's connective tissues. In Concord itself the strong

---

8 Richardson, *Henry Thoreau: A Life of the Mind*, ibid, 54.
9 Susan Cheever, *American Bloomsbury: Louisa May Alcott, Ralph Waldo Emerson, Margaret Fuller, Nathaniel Hawthorne, and Henry David Thoreau—Their Lives, Their Loves, and Their Work* (Simon & Schuster, 2006).
10 Larzer Ziff, "Introduction," to *Ralph Waldo Emerson: Selected Essays* (Penguin, 1982), 8.

early reception of *Nature* emboldened Emerson to bring together a remarkable group of New England intellectuals who met some thirty times mostly in the wider Boston area. Though referred to by several different names, the group came to be thought of as the Transcendentalist Club. Among the notables participating were Thoreau and Fuller, but also Henry Hedge, George Ripley, Bronson Alcott, Orestes Brownson. As to accomplishment and brilliance, the Transcendentalist Club rather easily surpassed Harvard's senior faculty at the time.[11] By the same measure, this group at least equaled those founders who wrote the Constitution between 1783 and 1789. Only the metaphysical club of William James, Charles Sanders Peirce, and Oliver Wendell Holmes, Jr. late in the nineteenth century and early in the twentieth were a gathering of comparable intellectual genius.[12] Once one gets well into the twentieth century it is hard to find other coherent groups of scientific or intellectual genius—among the few were, perhaps, the early days of social science at the University of Chicago in the 1920s[13] or J. Robert Oppenheimer, Enrico Fermi, and others in the Manhattan Project that created the atomic bomb in the 1940s.

Yet, none of the nation's enduring important intellectual and scientific groups set about, as did the Transcendentalist Club, to formulate a basis for national consciousness. Not even the founding generation and the framers of the Constitution in 1783–89 were nearly so well aware that nationhood required more than a constitutionally legal structure. Nationhood requires a lived collective history that, over time, allows a nation's adherents a shared consciousness—one that gets under the political and legal skin always there ready to warm the blood of shared collective life or to interrupt movements that would cripple the sinews of social muscle.

Benedict Anderson in *Imagined Communities* (1983) persuasively argued that it was the invention of print media that made possible a sense of national consciousness; in particular one fed by "the convergence of capitalism and print technology on the fatal diversity of human language [that] created the possibility of a new form of imagined community, which in its basic morphology set the stage for the modern nation."[14] The United States was no exception. From Thomas Paine, Benjamin Franklin, and the authors of the *Federalist Papers* on down through the years, print media of all kinds nurtured and spread a national consciousness among the American people who, as a matter of demographic fact, could have had little more than local and personal contacts with other Americans and fewer still once the westward migrations became the salient reality of national life. A nation, being a generalized structural notion, exists in its collective imagination by its imaginary[15]—that is, an aspect of collective culture necessary to, but utterly beyond, the day-to-day events of national life. We can suppose that local markets are a concrete feature of *the economy*, that elections are visible features of a *political system*, that professed values and beliefs are aspects of a *shared culture* plain and simple. But a *nation* is a pure, abstract feature of a shared and territorially bordered sociological imagination. One can point to a nation on a map but there is no such visible social thing available to the naked eye.

Though neither Emerson nor Thoreau nor Fuller thought in these terms—not even in terms of a national consciousness, they (and especially Emerson) were social theorists in another sense. For them, the operative sphere of an individual's capacity to belong to a

---

11 Robert D. Richardson, *Emerson: The Mind on Fire* (University of California, 1995), 246.
12 Louis Menand, *The Metaphysical Club* (Farrar, Straus and Giroux, 2001).
13 Andrew Abbott, *Department and Discipline: Chicago Sociology at 100* (University of Chicago Press, 1999).
14 Benedict Anderson, *Imagined Communities: Reflections on the Origins and Spread of Nationalism* (Verso, 1985), 45.
15 Cornelius Castoriadis, *L'Institution imaginaire de la société* (Seuil, 1975); *The Imaginary Institution of Society* (Blackwell/MIT Press, 1987).

wider world was, obviously, Nature. Social things were always and unavoidably natural things. Concord transcendentalism would not endure even into the twentieth century in anything like what it was in the Concord Moment. Still Emerson, Thoreau, Fuller and the others who represented that moment were, as some have said, the leaders of still another revolution—this time, a cultural one—that would infuse the already modernizing nation with, in effect, a social theory of itself: *Americans thinking America*.

A Theoretical Excursus: The Gaia Hypothesis, Nature, and the Anthropocene

When reading Emerson and Thoreau on Nature, one wants to capitalize the N in Nature, as I have done. This temptation arises from the extent to which the Concord transcendentalists often refer to Nature in intimate, even reverential terms. Thoreau, for example: "In midsummer we are of the earth—confounded with it—and covered with its dust. Now we begin to erect ourselves somewhat and walk upon its surface."[16] Emerson, always the more philosophical, writes of Nature as a God in and of which he is a part:

> Standing on the bare ground, —my head bathed by the blithe air, and uplifted into infinite space, —all mean egotism vanishes. I become a transparent eyeball; I am nothing, I see all; the currents of Universal Being circulate through me; I am part and particle of God.[17]

The intimacy of passages like these is homologous to a current general theory of man's relation to the natural world—the Gaia Hypothesis.

The modern version of the hypothesis owes to James Lovelock who in the 1960s, just more than a century after the zenith of Concord transcendentalism, drew on the Ancient Greek legend of the birth of Gaia, which is to say, roughly: Mother Earth. Lovelock put forth the hypothesis as a theory of all the living and material aspects of the Earth as part of an integrated system in which living things, including humans, are coequals with the seas and sands—the Earth itself. "Gaia theory is about the evolution of a tightly coupled system whose constituents are the biota and their material environment, which comprises the atmosphere, the oceans, and the surface rocks."[18] Lovelock is[19] a scientist not embarrassed to base a serious theory of geophysics on one of the ancient world's creation myths.

The Gaia myth derives from the Greek a creation narrative, Hesiod's *Theogony*, which begins: "Verily at the first Chaos came to be, but next wide-bosomed Earth, the every-sure foundations of all the deathless ones who hold the peaks of snowy Olympus…" Gaia is the wide-bosomed Earth who promises life by calming the primordial chaos. Hesiod's story has many of the same elements of the Yahwist story in the Jewish Pentateuch of about the same time. "In the beginning when God created the universe, the earth was formless and desolate" (Genesis 1:1–2)—after which the full array of natural elements was created: light, the seas, the land, plants, the sun and the moon, day and night, the creatures of the water and the birds of the air, all kinds of animal life; then, and only then, man and woman were set in this garden of Nature. Hesiod's narrative differs in the order of created things. In *Theogony* the natural wonders are created, first out of chaos, out of a "black Night that gave birth to the day, then the starry skies over which Mother Earth exposed her nurturing breasts."

---

16 Thoreau, *Journal* (August 7, 1854).
17 Emerson, *Nature* (1836), chapter 1, paragraph 4.
18 James Lovelock, "Geophysiology, the Science of Gaia," *Reviews of Geophysics* 17 (1989), 216.
19 As I write, in late 2022, Lovelock had just died in March. He was 102 years old and still writing to the end; for example *Novacene: The Coming Age of Hyperintelligence* (Allen Lane, 2019).

Thus Hesiod also differs from the Yahwist storyteller in that the Earth was created out of love, even lust. The creator is not a distant God but the voluptuous Earth mother. Themes of this sort and variations of the same appear in most of the notable creation myths.[20]

While Lovelock did not delve into a full range of creation myths, his use of the Gaia story with its emphasis on Mother Earth made his scientific geophysiological point. The Earth entire—including *all* of its material *and* immaterial members—is a living whole brought into being by an emblematic nurturing mother who (by implication) should be loved and nurtured in return. I exaggerate Lovelock's figure of speech to draw the connection between the Concord transcendentalists and more current theoretical attempts to refigure the relation between social man and his natural world. The emergent name for the issue is an expression borrowed from geological history, the Anthropocene—the period that came just after the Precambrian. The Anthropocene period is when human life dominated geological time for better or worse, as it so apparently does in our time.

Foremost among recent social theorists of a Gaia theory of our globalized Earth was Bruno Latour, who, until his death late in 2022, was the most prominent and inventive thinker among French social theorists. In *We Have Never Been Modern* (1991) and *An Inquiry into Modes of Existence: Anthropology of the Moderns* (2013), Latour agued, in effect, that the central premise of modern culture is quite wrong. Modernity got its own history wrong by conceiving of generic Man as the central figure in the modern period of Earth history. Modernity's strong concept of human society has had a deadly effect on social thought not to mention on social life itself. By conceiving of human society as the be-all and end-all of geologic history, modernity put Nature outside and beyond man's endeavors—as a pure, abstract idealization of Nature's resources being unlimitedly abundant.

This means, as a corollary, that social thought has had little to say about the future of humans on planet earth—which could not possibly be forever unlimited in its abundance as liberal modern culture foolishly supposed. In respect to Gaia theory, Mother Earth will die if she is not cared for. "[We] …have to take into account even more entanglements that will conflate the order of Nature with the order of Society; tomorrow and even more than yesterday we're going to feel ourselves bound by ever more numerous and diverse living beings."[21]

To be sure, Emerson and the Concord transcendentalists, writing more than a century before Latour, were not thinking in these terms. Still, it could be said that they were Gaia theorists before the fact, even though these were the times in America when some (notably Thoreau) had an inkling that generic man was becoming a danger to his natural home. The nation then was still engaged in settling its great plains, rocky mountains, and pacific coast. Nature was therefore a state of promise. At the same time, even though the Concord thinkers had no strong idea of society, their idea of Nature could have softened America's modernizing culture. Had transcendentalism outlived the American Civil War, the culture of the Concord Moment might have prevailed well-enough to allow America to embrace its environing Nature in a less instrumental and commodified way than what came to pass in the Gilded Age, from the 1870s on. When the modernizing North defeated the agrarian South, the Union was set on being modern in a way that used natural resources without regard for the future of Nature. Ever since, as heavy industry came to dominate the American economy, its culture encouraged the belief that America can exploit its vast

---

20 For primary passages of the important creation myths see Charles Lemert et al, *Globalization: A Reader* (Routledge, 2010), 10–23.
21 Bruno Latour, *An Inquiry into Modes of Existence: An Anthropology of Moderns* (Harvard University Press, 2018), 10. Emphasis added.

natural world as a limitless resource offering itself in service to the accumulation of economic and cultural capital.

Emerson's Transcendentalism: Nature and the Conduct of Life

Philosophically, Emerson's transcendentalism was derived from Goethe, of course, but also, perhaps mainly, from Immanuel Kant whom he cites at the crucial place in his general essay on the subject.[22] Kant's theory of pure practical reason is rightly considered one of (perhaps *the*) foundational documents of Enlightenment thought. Late eighteenth-century philosophy spawned many different enlightenments—German, Scottish, English, French, even American if you count thinkers like Thomas Jefferson. But it was Kant who provided the parsimonious statement of the prevailing belief that—in the decline of theology and pure rational metaphysics—enlightened human knowledge is meant to understand not the external world of objects but the method by which objects in the natural world are known. "I entitle transcendental," said Kant in 1780, "all knowledge which is occupied not so much with objects as with the mode of our knowledge of objects in so far as this mode of knowledge is possible a priori."[23] Crudely put, Kant's transcendentalism, far from dismissing man's ability to know the natural world, begins with the belief that Nature itself implants the possibility of knowing *a priori*—before the fact of knowing.

The formal name for Kant's basic theory of knowledge is idealism which, in the day, cleared the intellectual table in Europe. After Kant came Georg Wilhelm Frederic Hegel as the most systematic interpreter of social history by means of a dialectic of opposing social ideas—of *theses* and *antitheses* encountering each other to resolve the differences in a fresh *synthesis* upon which history turns to another dialectic of opposing ideas engaging each other in order to develop still another synthesis. Idealism, thus, asserts the primacy of ideas and ideals—of, we are likely to say, culture—over material factors. It hardly needs be said, that Karl Marx's theories of modern capitalism became, in the generation following Hegel, the pure perfect materialism. Emerson, to be sure, well understood this classic dichotomy between idealism and materialism. Emerson's 1842 Boston lecture, *The Transcendentalist*, began:

> As thinkers, mankind has ever divided into two sects, Materialists and Idealists; the first class founding on experience, the second on consciousness ... The materialist insists on facts, on history, on the force of circumstances, and the animal wants of man; the idealist on the power of Thought and Will, on inspiration, on miracle, on individual culture. These two modes of thinking are both natural, but the idealist contends that his way of thinking is in higher nature.[24]

Emerson's view of the two general philosophical positions is extraordinarily well balanced. Just after this passage from *The Transcendentalist*, Emerson says: "Every materialist will be an idealist; but an idealist can never go backward to be a materialist." Thus Emerson's Kantian theory of the relation between Soul and Nature is, obviously, an idealism that, among social theorists today, is odd because it is far easier to think of Nature as materialist if one is to account for the geographic, geologic, and geophysiological aspects of the natural world.

---

22 *The Transcendentalist*, in *Emerson: Essays and Lectures* (The Library of America, 1983), 198–199.
23 Kant, *Critique of Pure Reason*, VII (1780).
24 Emerson, *The Transcendentalist*, in *Emerson: Essays and Lectures* (The Library of America, 1983), 193.

Emerson's *Nature* is a short book but one systematically organized. After a brief introduction there are eight chapters arranged in an ascending series from the most foundational elements of Nature to the most high-minded; thus: 1. *Nature*, 2. *Commodity*, 3. *Beauty*, 4. *Language*, 5. *Discipline*, 6. *Idealism*, 7. *Spirit*, 8. *Prospects*. The chapter on Idealism, thus, is put at the crucial midpoint in the series after the four more evidently social aspects of Nature—commodity, beauty, language, discipline. Idealism thus functions as a theoretical transition to spirit and prospects, where *Spirit* is a presentation of Emerson's distinctive post-Unitarian idea of religion and *Prospects* refers to the laws of the world. In other words, *Nature*, the book, is a philosophical travel guide from socio-economic values to the moral necessities of life with others to the higher spheres of human yearning. In the book's *Introduction*, Emerson sets the theme as he wants it:

> Philosophically considered, the universe is composed of Nature and Soul. Strictly speaking, therefore, all that is separate from us, all which Philosophy distinguishes as the NOT ME, that is, both nature and art, all other men and my own body, must be ranked under this name NATURE.[25]

So, obviously, he is *not* thinking of Nature as simply trees and animals and the like—but of a much wider range of aspects of the world outside our souls or senses of self.

Emerson then forges the link to Chapter 1. *Nature*, where he completes the general idea in more poetic but Kantian terms:

> To go into solitude, a man needs to retire as much from his chamber as from society. ... If a man would be alone let him look at the stars. ... Standing on bare ground, —my head bathed by the blithe air, and uplifted into infinite space, —all mean egotism vanishes. I become a transparent eyeball; I am nothing; I see all; the currents of Universal Being circulate through me; I am part or particle of God.[26]

There is here not a touch of modern-day couplets, least of all the *self/other* couplet. Emerson's soul is thoroughly part of Universal Being. Ultimately, one sees by means of the sublime, transparent eyeball of God.

With this grand notion as the book's frame, Emerson then begins the journey along the path of Nature's particular elements, beginning with chapter 2. *Commodity*. "Nature, in its ministry to man, is not only the material, but is also the process and the result."[27] Wind, sun, ice, rain, plants are among Nature's elements that minister to man by such gifts as sowing seeds, making rain, feeding animals; and, more generally, the nourishing gifts of Nature itself. Emerson adds that these "useful arts are reproductions or new combinations by the wit of man, of the same natural benefactors."[28] By extension we might say, in today's normal social scientific language, that human subjects and the natural world of objects are not distinguished by barriers or levels of separating differences. Again: no micro/macro differences. They are each and all part of the dynamic system of life and being. In addition to being very Kantian, Emerson's theory of Nature and its commodities is in effect true to the Gaia hypothesis.

---

25 Emerson, *Nature* in Emerson, *Essays and Lectures* (Library of America, 1983), 9.
26 *Ibid*, 9.
27 *Ibid*, 12.
28 *Ibid*.

Thereafter come two chapters that account for a still higher social level of natural wonders: 3. *Beauty* and 4. *Language*. In respect to Beauty, Emerson begins with the striking point that the natural world offers the eye and senses aesthetic forms. "The tradesman, the attorney comes out of the din of the street, and sees the sky, and woods, and is man again."[29] Then he adds the aspect of the sublime in Nature. Its grandeur and well composed lines and shadows inspire a sense of the spiritual. Then, and this point is particularly interesting in respect to the mundane mind: Nature can be "an object of the intellect" that generates creative thought and action. Finally, Emerson points beyond Beauty. "Beauty in nature is not ultimate. …It must stand as a part, and not as yet the last or highest expression of the final cause of Nature."[30]

Language, chapter 4, begins with the strong theory that "*Nature* is the vehicle of thought," in three ways: First, "words are signs of natural facts." Second, "some natural facts are symbols and spiritual facts." Third, "nature is the symbol of spirit."[31] More modern linguists—like Ferdinand de Saussure or Noam Chomsky—would not find this a good enough linguistics. Just the same, it is in its way a powerful and notably Idealist theory of the range of language facts: words, symbols, and transcendent symbols.

Discipline, chapter 5, is where Emerson comes as close as ever he does to a somewhat formal social theory.

> Nature is a discipline of the understanding in intellectual truths. Our dealing with sensible objects is a constant exercise in the necessary lessons of difference, of likeness, of order, of being and seeming, of progressive arrangement, of ascent from particular to general; of combination to one end of manifold forces.[32]

Taken alone, this passage can be seen as a skeletal social theory of categories, or better yet, a sketch of Kant's tableau of philosophical categories. But the passage does not stand alone. The chapter begins with a litany of social forces: "Space, time, society, labor, climate, food, locomotion, the animals, the mechanical forces, give us sincerest lessons, day by day, whose meaning is unlimited."[33] Here is a stronger blink of a social theory in which Emerson identifies the centrality of social action. "The central Unity is still more conspicuous in actions. Words are finite organs of the infinite mind. They cannot cover the dimensions of what is in truth. They break, chop, and impoverish it. An action is the perfection of what is in truth."[34] This is not, of course, pragmatism as it came to be at the end of the nineteenth century with Charles Sanders Peirce, but it is, again, a shadowy sketch of the nature of social action—of the social actions that constitute the whole of collective life.

Then comes chapter 6 *Idealism* which, unlike the 1842 lecture, *The Transcendentalist*, is not a programmatic statement but a linking chapter between Nature's more basic, almost social, elements and the higher nature of spirit itself. This becomes evident in Emerson's notably linear and ascending aspects of Idealism.[35] The *first* is: "Nature is made to conspire with spirit to emancipate us." He brings this point home with a qualified, but detectably Kantian, notion of the sublime: "Hence arises a pleasure mixed with awe; I may say, a low

---

29 *Ibid*, 14.
30 *Ibid*, 19.
31 *Ibid*, 20.
32 *Ibid*, 26.
33 *Ibid*.
34 *Ibid*, 30.
35 All quotations concerning Emerson's *Idealism* chapter are at *ibid*, 33–39.

degree of the sublime is felt from the fact, probably, that man is hereby apprized, that, whilst the world is a spectacle, something in himself is stable." The qualifications point to a special aspect of man, which becomes clear a *second* feature of Idealism: "In a higher manner, the poet communicates the same pleasure. By a few strokes, he delineates, as on air, the sun, the mountain, the camp, the city, the hero, the maiden, not different from what we know them, but only lifted from the ground and afloat before the eye." "The gift of poetry," it would seem, is that more "stable" aspect of human being. Hence, *three*: "The poet animates nature with his own thoughts, he differs from the philosopher only herein, that the one proposes Beauty as his main end; the other Truth." Hereafter poetry becomes the dominant theme of the chapter. Then, Emerson discusses intellectual science; after which: religion and ethics "which may be fitly called the practice of ideas, or the introduction of ideas into life".

The chapter on *Idealism* is a high-minded rehearsal of Emerson's version of the philosophical position that leads to the natural field toward which the soul aspires; namely: 7. *Spirit*, which surprises if one is holding to a strict Kantian attitude: "We are as much strangers in nature, as we are aliens from God."[36] Really? This seems to contradict Emerson's starting point. But the poet comes to the rescue.

> Is not the landscape, every glimpse of which hath a grandeur, a face of him? Yet this may show us what discord is between man and nature, for you cannot freely admire a noble landscape, if laborers are digging in the field hard by. The poet finds something ridiculous in his delight, until he is out of sight of men.[37]

In the last two chapters, *Spirit* and *Prospects*, there are places where a modern reader might suppose that Emerson's idealization of the poet comes close to what today, in social theory, we would call a cultural theory of that state of social being in the human self (or soul) which is drawn toward her higher nature. Yet, Emerson's idea of culture was not close enough to what social theory today has in mind. His was still within the range of the German *Bildung*, or formation in the sense of personal development, also characterized as self-culture.[38]

The human soul, it seems, is not just drawn toward Nature itself, but to the highest, if imperfectly attained, communion with Nature. Soul and Nature together comprise the true meaning of the world Gaia herself made and suckles. When Emerson turns, in chapter 7, to *Prospects*, he writes in his own poetic manner, to just this point: "The problem of restoring to the world original and eternal beauty, is solved by the redemption of the soul. The ruin or the blank, that we see when we look at nature, is in our own eye."[39] Thereupon *Nature* ends where it began. Nature and Soul are the constituent aspects of the Universe:

> So shall we come to look at the world with new eyes. It shall answer the endless inquiry of the intellect, —What is the truth? and of the affections, —What is good? By yielding itself passive to the educated Will. Then shall come to pass what my poet said; 'Nature is not fixed but fluid. Spirit alters, moulds, makes it. The immobility or bruteness of nature, is the absence of spirit; to pure spirit, it is fluid, it is volatile, it is obedient.

---

36 *Ibid*, 42.
37 *Ibid*, 42.
38 Richardson, *Emerson: The Mind on Fire*, 271–274. On *self-culture*: Laura Dassow Walls, *Henry David Thoreau: A Life* (University of Chicago Press, 2017); 86–90; and Richardson, *Thoreau: A Life of the Mind*, 53–57.
39 Emerson, *Nature*, 47.

Every spirit builds itself a house; and beyond a house a world; and beyond its world a heaven ...'[40]

Nature, the book, is a masterpiece of parsimoniously well-styled theory. Not perhaps a recognizable social theory in today's sense but an American theory done in the manner of Emerson's "American Scholar" in 1837 in which *man thinking* is the enduring slogan of America's cultural independence. If this, then *Nature* in 1836 is the text that instructs and illustrates the groundwork principles of Americans thinking America—the individual's soul as the driving force in Nature which from the beginning was, as still it is, the primal environmental fact of the new nation.

Emerson with Thoreau and Fuller, were foremost among the Concord Transcendentalists because all set Nature and Soul in relation to strong political and social commitments. All three were abolitionists, all outspokenly against slavery, and all were feminists in the sense that, from the beginning, the Transcendentalist Club intentionally included and respected women. Fuller was decidedly the foremost feminist of the day. Thoreau's 1859 lecture, *A Plea for Captain John Brown*, was a prominent event in a series of Concord meetings to support and defend Brown, who had visited Emerson and Thoreau in Concord in 1857. Emerson, above all, was in the mix in all the political concerns of the day. He was particularly appalled by the Cherokee Trail of Tears and the Indian Removal policies of Andrew Jackson.[41]

Emerson, while a leader and activist, tended to express his social and political views in texts like *Man the Reformer* in 1841 and between the lines in his 1850 book, *Representative Men*, and *The Conduct of Life* in 1860. The last mentioned is notable for the prominence Emerson gives to power and wealth in an otherwise moral and behavioral discussion of, as the title suggests, ideas leading to rules for living. *The Conduct of Life* includes chapters on culture, behavior, worship, and beauty. But the first three chapters are worthy of note: 1. Fate, 2. Power, 3. Wealth. In the first is where he applies the idea that the laws of Nature limit social life: "...in race, in retardations of strata, and in thought and character as well."[42] Then in the chapter on power he writes:

All power is of one kind, a sharing of the nature the world. The mind that is parallel with the laws of nature will be in the current of events and strong with their strength. One man is made of the same stuff of which events are made; is in sympathy with the course of things; can predict it.[43]

This is what we today understand as a zero-sum theory of power. For Emerson it can only be that way because the world is bound up between Soul and Nature into a system in which all things are equal. "Society is a troop of thinkers, and best heads among them take the best places."[44] In respect to wealth, Emerson comes to what is surely his most critical theory of the then modern political economy. "Men of sense esteem wealth to be the assimilation of nature to themselves, the converting of the sap and juices of the planet to the incarnation and nutriment of their design. Power is what they want, not candy—power to execute their design... ."[45]

---

40 *Ibid*, 48.
41 Emerson, Letter to Martin Van Buren President of the United States, 1836.
42 *The Conduct of Life* in *Emerson/Essays and Lectures* (Library of America, 1983), 941–1011.
43 *Ibid*, 973.
44 *Ibid*, 974.
45 *Ibid*, 993.

These few traces of a theory of power and wealth do not, of course, constitute an out-in-the-open social theory of political economy. But they are the beginnings of a systematic theory of Nature that allows for, even as it does not explicitly affirm, a theory of social actions within the limitations of the Soul/Nature universe.

Thoreau's Time/Space: Walden

Thoreau, by contrast to his friend and mentor Emerson, was not inclined toward strictly non-fiction philosophical essay writing. Thoreau's most important writings were stories, often with fictional elements, about his adventures in Nature—climbing mountains, boating, exploring forests and woods near Concord and around New England. *Walden; or Life in the Woods* is the story of his life on the pond for two years, two months, and two days between July 4, 1845 and early September 6, 1847.

Walden is revered because it captures the imagination in a number of ways. Its radical individualism is conveyed by a complicated series of stories and observations. Readers who value *Walden* for its moral and social philosophy miss the point if they fail to realize that Thoreau, the storyteller, is playing a literary game by mixing and matching fiction and non-fiction, by interrupting *Walden*'s story line with asides and digressions, by pretending that the timeline is simple when it is not. Thoreau's writings are different from Emerson's expository style.

Just the same, Thoreau's writing, like Emerson's, is replete with delicately placed references to classic sources from the Greeks down through history to Goethe and Kant. Though Emerson read all of Goethe and wrote extensively about him, Thoreau, in effect, lived Goethe's ideal of *self-culture*[46] which Goethe summarizes in his view of biography:

> For the principal task of biography, I believe, is to present a man in the conditions of his time, and to show to what extent those conditions, taken as a whole, thwart him or favor him, *how he forms from it all a view of the world and of man, and how, if he is an artist, a poet, or a writer, he then takes that view and projects it back into the world.*[47]

The world thwarts or favors the individual who must live with Nature's limitations. Still the individual, against the world's limitations, must form a view of that world and of himself as one among others who, even if not a poet or a writer, must think the world into existence. This is Goethe, to be sure, but already one can see a glimmer of Kant's idea that we know the world *a priori,* but *synthetically.*

In the months after graduating from Harvard in 1837, Thoreau was devoted to reading classic poets from Virgil to the English and German poets—especially Goethe. At the same time, he was translating Goethe's *Italian Journey*.[48] On Thoreau's interest in Goethe, consider the following two passages:

> The morning was misty, calm, and beautiful, and this seemed a good omen. The upper clouds were like streaked wool, the lower heavy. After a wretched summer, I look forward to a fine autumn. The sun was hot, and it occurred to me that this place lay on the same latitude as my own native town.

---

46 Richardson, *Thoreau*, 57.
47 Goethe, *The Autobiography of Johann Wolfgang von Goethe,* Preface to Vol I (University of Chicago Press, 1974), 2c [*sic*]. Emphasis added.
48 Richardson, *Thoreau*, 7–8.

And:

> The air was so elastic and crystalline that it had the same effect on the landscape that a glass has on a picture, to give it an ideal remoteness and perfection. The landscape was clothed in a mild and quiet light, in which the woods and fences checkered and partitioned it with a new regularity, and rough and uneven fields stretched away with lawn-like smoothness to the horizon, and the clouds, finely distinct and picturesque, seemed a fit drapery to hang over a fairyland.

In tone and visual acuity they are so similar that, in a blind test, it would be hard to say which is Goethe and which Thoreau. The first appears among the opening lines of *Italian Journey* just when Goethe began his wandering on September 7, 1786. The second appears as the hypothetical Sunday entry in Thoreau's first book, *A Week on the Concord and Merrimack Rivers*—a journey with his brother John that began August 31, 1839. Both Goethe and Thoreau were famous for the wonder of their visual portraits of what they saw along their ways. It is widely believed that Goethe's self-culture lay behind his abiding influence on German culture.[49] So too in respect to Thoreau's contributions to American culture.

As much as Goethe's Weimar may be compared to Emerson's and Thoreau's Concord for having been small towns of enduring national importance, there is a difference between the two national cultures. Norbert Elias, in *The Germans*, makes the telling point that in German culture dominating political figures like Frederick the Great and Otto von Bismarck operated outside the sphere of German culture. German heroes like Goethe and Beethoven were "culture heroes outside politics, but not 'makers' of 'history,' not counter heroes on a national scale".[50] If Elias is to be trusted, then other modern cultures, including the American one, have a different division of cultural labor between their culture heroes and their political leaders. Indeed by the end of the Concord Moment in 1868, the United States had already given birth to a long list of culture heroes who were also political forces to be reckoned with—Thomas Paine, Ben Franklin, Thomas Jefferson, James Madison, Alexander Hamilton, John Adams, Abraham Lincoln, and Frederick Douglass, to mention but the most notable.

Thus, to consider American social theory such as it was from the colonial settlement in the 1600s to 1868, allows a better understanding of the importance of Emerson, Thoreau, and Fuller as culture heroes. They were, in effect, at once the Weimar and Bloomsbury elites who, if not on the order of Goethe and Beethoven, were America's first stellar cultural figures who, though political in their ways, were not political authorities. The politics of the wider Transcendentalist Club were real and influential—but they were not power brokers. They were, to use Elias's idea, cultural "counter-heroes on a national scale."

Thoreau, as much as Emerson, became, like Fuller, a counter-hero whose literary art and personal self-culture decisively shaped what may be the most enduring theme in America's sense of its national culture.[51] Today that theme has evolved into the more technical social theoretical concept *Time-Space*—the idea that captures the sense in which a world of real people gathered in social groups of all kinds are fated to live at a definite time in well-bordered spaces. The time of human living is necessarily limited by the hard-spatial reality

---

49 Adam Kirsch, "Life Lessons from Goethe: What's so great about Goethe?" *The New Yorker* (February 1, 2016).
50 Norbert Elias, *The Germans: Power Struggles and the Development of Habitus in the Nineteenth and Twentieth Centuries* (Columbia University Press, 1996), 328.
51 On the question of the differences among the United States and other nations see Jill Lepore, "The New Americanism: Why a Nation Needs a National Story," *Foreign Affairs* (February 5, 2019).

of Nature. Interstellar times and spaces may be infinite, they may warp or be caught up in dead zones and dark holes, they may be infinite for all we know. But human times are lived in finite spaces. We may migrate from one or another geographical and political territory to escape misery or to find a better time in which to live. But, when we do, we land as immigrants in some or another new world. There we can only do and be what that space allows or makes possible. The time of such spaces as these is the TimeSpace of ordinary life—always lived from moment to moment *as if* it were unlimited in spite of the fact that it is and must be. In this sense, TimeSpace, when viewed from the perspective of the day-to-day living, must reside in the Unconsciousness of collective life on the ground.

Thoreau had no expressed idea of an Unconscious dimension of life. Yet, in his wanderings on land and waters, Thoreau saw, as Goethe did, that a particular self-culture is required in order to see that otherwise it is invisible. In particular, the geographical and environmental imagination sees only what presents itself to a certain kind of well-formed eye, as in: "The air was so elastic and crystalline..."; or "... the landscape was clothed in a mild and quiet light. ..." In these words, metaphor is the literary eye by which we see what is right there before us, unnoticed. Of course, air is not crystalline, and landscapes are not clothed, but we see them with a fresh, otherwise blind, eye.[52] In seeing afresh, we see a moment in a place that would not have come to mind without a metaphoric probe into what is not available to the conscious mind. Seeing, thus, is to see what the naked normal eye does not—to see beyond the moment and the locale through and over which one passes without seeing. Thinking is seeing. Theory is seeing what is not visible.

Emerson of course understood the general concept of self-culture and was not without the poetic capacity to see what others did not, but Thoreau was the original American genius who saw, and did, what others could not. In this sense, his radical individualism was, first and foremost, an aesthetic expression of social and natural things and the Gaia-like system they comprise. In many ways, *Walden; or Life in the Woods* has not been fully appreciated. Apart from its inspiring, sometimes irritating qualities, the book's genius is that it is in its way like a tone poem or a landscape painting. Thoreau was able to write discursively so as to make available to the careful reader his vision of the metaphoric quality of the natural and social surroundings of his cabin. His narrative books are, each in their way, an extended probe below the surface of the social norms then prevalent in his time and place.

Thoreau is known to have described his literary method as the weaving of "a kind of basket of a delicate texture."[53] He weaves into an apparently straightforward narrative all manner of observations of the wider world and insights from his own experience. For example, in the chapter *Spring* in *Walden*:

> When the ground was partially bare of snow, and a few warm days had dried its surface somewhat, it was pleasant to compare the first tender signs of the infant year just peeping forth with the stately beauty of the withered vegetation which had withstood the winters,—life-everlasting, goldenrods, pinweeds, and graceful wild grasses...[54]

The passage seems to be descriptive of what one winter day might have been before Thoreau's eyes. But, on closer look, the passage and, for that matter, the chapter as a whole,

---

52 To venture into these thickets in respect to Thoreau is to be, once again, indebted to Robert Richardson, *Henry Thoreau: A Life of the Mind*, 50–54, "The Eye of Henry Thoreau."
53 Walls, *Henry David Thoreau: A Life*, ibid, 254–255.
54 Thoreau, *Walden* in *Walden, and Other Writings* edited by Brooks Atkinson (The Modern Library/Random House, 1992), 290.

Figure 6.1 Frederic Edwin Church, *West Rock, New Haven*, Oil on canvas, 1849, New Britain Museum of American Art

is composed outside any particular time or field. True, Thoreau had observed grasses of the kind as have any of us who have walked in late winter fields. It is the way of literary nonfiction to tell a story as if the telling is more immediate to the teller's eye than it could be. But Thoreau, in the lines immediately following, goes beyond even the necessary beyond of his story:

> I am particularly attracted by the arching and sheaf-like top of the wool-grass; it brings back the summer of our winter memories and is among the forms which art loves to copy, and which, in the vegetable kingdom, have the same relation to types already in the mind of man that astronomy has. It is an antique style, older than the Greek or Egyptian.[55]

The narrative leaps from grass, winter's summer memories, to art, to the vegetable kingdom, to Greek astronomy. By the end of these lines, the astute reader realizes that she is not in any particular place relative to the cabin on Walden Pond, in some indeterminate time in the winters of 1846 or 1847. There is of course little in this that is unique to Thoreau—*except* for the way he plays with his time and with the spatial surround of Walden Pond. *Walden*, the book, is a tapestry—better still, think of it as a landscape painting.

To think of *Walden* as a landscape painting is possible if the reader envisions Thoreau's home on Walden Pond as the figurative frame for a more complicated canvas than it might

---

55 *Ibid*, 291.

first appear. Consider Frederic Edwin Church's *West Rock, New Haven* painted in 1849 just two years after Thoreau left Walden Pond and five years before he finished the book. West Rock itself is such a frame in that the field and stream at the bottom of the canvas exist in no particular space and time except as a figment of rural American imagination. The skies and clouds above point to a time to come when the sons of farmers might leave for that West beyond the Rock.

Church's *West Rock, New Haven* appears to be purely pastoral—except for the darkening clouds in the upper canvas; then too, there are the men in the foreground who are hard at work with all but no chance of following the sun beyond the Rock to the West. That dream will remain, if at all, for their sons. Behind even the most idyllic of landscapes hides the not-always-visible prospect of life being uprooted and uncertain, even apocalyptic as Lawrence Buell has put it.[56]

How much Thoreau studied landscape artists like Church, not to mention other world renowned landscape artists, including Thomas Cole, exhibited at the Boston Atheneum in his day, is not entirely clear. But it has been suggested as likely.[57] What is clear is that he shared the American landscape *zeitgeist* that also influenced his literary method in *Walden*. What is not hard to imagine is the way *Walden*, in particular, far from being purely representational, probes behind the scenes of Thoreau's life on the pond.

> Thoreau's most interesting visual writing comes not when he is being most pictorial, most representational, most "photographic," but when he can use the visual scene to convey his awareness of the energy behind nature, creating and animating the scene we see, or when he describes a scene in such a way as to draw out or articulate the feelings of the observer.[58]

Call the literary effect of *Walden* what you will, it is all but indisputable that it stirs feelings *and* challenges readers to consider what they feel about what Thoreau puts before them to see (if they will). This is an effect he creates by collapsing the time of the narrative in order to enrich the reader's experience of the places; —again, TimeSpace.

Walden is a popular book because it is rooted in the pond's natural spatial surround in a way that draws the reader ever out and beyond the pond. As a result, the time of the story creates a matrix of vectors that serve to intensify not just the energy of Nature but the energy of Thoreau's relation to Nature. While theoretically consistent with Emerson's philosophical transcendentalism, Thoreau's literary and visual joining of the Soul and Nature is decidedly not straightforward. Emerson's writing follows what could be called a pedagogical line. Thoreau's captivates the reading eye by forcing it to enter the literary time the author creates; for example, in the book's focal chapter, *Where I Lived, and What I Lived For*:

> Time is but the stream I go a-fishing in. I drink it; but while I drink, I see the sandy bottom and detect how shallow it is. Its thin current slides away but eternity remains. I would drink deeper; fish in the sky, whose bottom is pebbly with stars. I cannot count one. I know not the first letter of the alphabet. I have always been regretting that I was not as wise as the day I was born.[59]

---

56 Lawrence Buell, "Environmental Apocalypticism," *The Environmental Imagination: Thoreau, Nature Writing, and the Formation of American Culture* (Harvard University Press, 1995), chapter 5.
57 Richardson, *Henry Thoreau*, 51; and especially Buell, *The Environmental Imagination*, 258–268 and throughout this masterful book.
58 Richardson, *Henry Thoreau*, 53.
59 Thoreau, *Walden*, in *Thoreau/Walden, and Other Writings*, 93.

Just count the time vectors that cut across his pond—*time* is a stream of food and drink ..., the current points him and the reader to *eternity*..., as it does anyone who looks skyward at *night*—... that wisdom is never greater than the innocence of *the day we were born*. The passage would be jumbled confusion were it not for the way metaphors allow the divergent times to float on the fishing stream.

Thoreau's literary and artistic method brings an implicit theory home in ways that were original in his day. By situating social things in the interstices between Nature in all its array and the individual Soul, Thoreau's transcendentalism avoids the clumsiness of level-thinking by floating the variety of times and spaces, grand or small, in a single stream in which the elements are not linked systematically. When they are set as if they were floating in a local scene that moves the imagination, they point to the natural and social whole of things. So long as theorists divide their empirical attention between the study of local (hence, micro) social things as distinct from structural (hence, macro) things there will never be—as so far there has not been—a realistic but plausibly complete portrait of the systematic relations between the actions of subjects and the enabling and disabling effects of their objective surround; which is to say: a Gaia-like theory of social action.

Walden presents Thoreau himself as the subject of a story that begins: "When I wrote the following pages, or rather the bulk of them, I lived alone in the woods, a mile from any neighbor, in a house which I built myself, on the shore of Walden Pond, in Concord, Massachusetts, and earned my living by the labor of my hands only."[60] These might seem to be the opening lines of a personal story—which they are; but the story is personal only in Thoreau's complicated and non-linear sense of the time of his adventures. For one thing, the time of *Walden*, the book, is different from the time of Thoreau's life on Walden, the pond. Important to add that the book as we have it is Thoreau's sixth draft undertaken in the winter of 1853, a good decade after his 1843 "A Winter Walk" in *The Dial*. This preliminary sketch nearly two years before the fact of his time on the Pond is considered a foundational source for the lyric passages in *Walden* and, it would seem, for the book's seasonal structure.[61] The book thus is composed as if he lived by the Pond for one year, through the four seasons. Though from time to time he refers to a previous summer and the like, the timeline of the story is that of a single year.[62] Yet, and here is the genius of Thoreau's literary subterfuge, the year such as it appears to be is but a connivance for a matrix of temporal vectors that cut across the year—thereby creating the complicated TimeSpace of the story for which the house on the Pond is the allegorical space for the corresponding matrix of spaces. The story compounds the times and spaces of Thoreau's year on Walden in a way that avoids the confusion of his many vectors.

But where is summer? As it happens, in this story of many twists and turns, summer is covered by the book's most controversial chapter, *The Bean-Field*. In many ways, this chapter is the hook on which hangs the fictional frame of *Walden* as an annual cycle of events in Thoreau's story of his time on the Pond. *The Bean-Field* is also a metaphorical portrait of Thoreau's particular brand of transcendental philosophy. It begins: "Meanwhile my beans, the length of whose rows, added together, was seven miles already planted... ."[63] These two and a half acres of beans were planted in the spring before he moved into his

---

60 *Ibid*, 3.
61 Richardson, *Henry Thoreau: A Life of the Mind*, 140–141; 305–310. "The Winter Tale" has also been described as symphonic in structure; see Jessica Stout, "Swinging Sound of Cymbals": Symphonic Form in "A Winter Walk," *The Thoreau Society* (2015) @ https://www.thoreausociety.org/news-article/. Stout also lists the considerable literature on the musical tone of Thoreau's writing in general.
62 Just as, for example, *A Week on the Concord and Merrimack Rivers* condenses two weeks into one.
63 Thoreau, *The Bean-Field, Walden* in *Thoreau / Walden, and Other Writings*, 146.

cabin on July 4, 1846. Yet, his bean-field by the side of the road exposed him to rebuke for the time of the planting: "Beans too late! Peas so late!"[64]—comments he means to suggest are more than passing observations.

The field-side complaints are at the center of the controversy of the bean-field chapter. Thoreau wrote *The Bean-Field* as a response to Henry Colman, a one-time Unitarian minister turned to the surveying of crop lands in Massachusetts, whereupon he became an authority on agriculture in the East. These were the days when some of the farmers depicted in Frederic Edwin Church's *West Rock, New Haven* were starting to venture to the West for land and better farming conditions. Colman sought to justify farming in Massachusetts by a method Thoreau strenuously opposed. Colman argued that farmers even in the East could be productive if they would learn and apply scientific methods of cultivation. Thoreau would have nothing of it. His bean-field was, he wrote, "one field not in Mr. Colman's report." Robert A. Gross goes so far as to say of Thoreau's purpose here: "*The Bean-Field* chapter, as one scholar has observed, represents 'a microcosm of the entire *Walden*,' an epitome of the techniques and the themes he uses throughout the book."[65] Robert Richardson adds that Thoreau "made his Walden Pond bean field a major metaphor for his particular idea of self-cultivation."[66] Similarly Richard Schneider has offered the phrase "seeds of virtue" for Thoreau's bean field.[67] Then too, Thoreau comments with sarcasm on the scientific farmers:

> In the winter of '46–7 there came a hundred men of Hyperborean extraction swoop down on to our pond one morning, with many carloads of ungainly-looking farming tools – sleds, plows, drill-barrows, turf-knives, spades, saws, rakes, and each man was armed with a double-pointed pike-staff, such as is not described in the *New-England Farmer* or *the Cultivator*. I did not know whether they had come to sow a crop of winter rye, or some other kind of grain recently introduced from Iceland.[68]

The Bean-Field chapter is only apparently a simple story of faming in the summer of 1846 when in fact it is a political manifesto of the extent to which then modernizing science is ruining local well-being. Thoreau was planting the seeds of a transcendentalist declaration of his own self-culture—a declaration asserted by the planting of his bean field.

Thus it is that *The Bean-Field* and the model farm movement were part and parcel of the Anthropocene era:

> Thoreau could see that the ground was shifting, and in the sheer audacity of his genius, he decided it was up to him to witness the changes and alert the world. From his watchtower by the railroad, deep in Walden Woods, he would sound the alarm and point to a better way.[69]

Concord transcendentalism was anything but apolitical. *The Bean-Field* turns out to be a running critical dialogue with Henry Colman's model farm and the coming of scientific

---

64 *Ibid*, 148.
65 Robert A Gross, "The Great Bean Field Hoax: Thoreau and the Agricultural Reformers," *Virginia Quarterly Review Online* (61: 3, Summer, 1985). He doesn't say who the other scholar is.
66 Richardson, *Thoreau: A Life of the Mind*, 54.
67 Richard J. Schneider, "Walden," in Joel Myerson, *Cambridge Companion to Henry David Thoreau* (Cambridge University Press, 1995), 94.
68 *The Bean-Field*, 276.
69 Walls, *Henry David Thoreau: A Life*, 8–9. See also Walls, "Henry David Thoreau and the Necessity of Conviction," *Chicago Humanities Festival* (November 29, 2017) at https://chicagohumanities.org/shows/.

agribusiness. The chapter ends: "The true husbandman will cease from anxiety, as the squirrels manifest no concern whether the woods will bear chestnuts this year or not and finish his labor with every day and sacrificing in his mind not only his first but his last fruits."[70] No one would blame those who read this as hopelessly naive. But then again this could be radical anti-Anthropocene politics.

Margaret Fuller's Revolutionary Transcendentalism

No one, not even Emerson, was a more important personal and intellectual influence on Thoreau than Margaret Fuller. At the same time, she was close to Emerson in a different more complicated way. From her first visit with Lidian and Waldo Emerson in 1836, she and Waldo grew close and remained so over the years. If anything, theirs was an intellectual, even spiritual, romance. Nathaniel Hawthorne—who at best had mixed feelings about Fuller—noted in his journals that Emerson said of her: "He apotheosized her as the greatest woman, I believe, of ancient or modern times and the one figure in the world worth considering."[71]

Fuller was educated from early childhood by her father. Timothy Fuller was a demanding teacher who pressed his four-year-old daughter to begin to read history, literature, and languages, both ancient and modern. Through the years he was unrelenting. If she disappointed him, he rebuked her harshly—a practice that recurred even into her young adult life. In Fuller's *Autobiographical Sketch* in 1840, in an early section aptly entitled "Overwork," she wrote of her father's effect on her childhood: "I was put under discipline of considerable severity, and, at the same time, had a more than ordinary high standard presented me."

The father's demanding, if harsh, standards explain Margaret's exceptional intellectual and literary achievements. Her childhood was, as Vivian Gornick puts it, a double inheritance—the first cause of her adult life as a public intellectual, also, "[she] paid for this gift with lifelong migraines, permanent insomnia and impaired eyesight, as well as a debilitating inability to believe that her intellectual output was sufficient."[72] Still, as much as she suffered, Fuller gave much more in many areas. Fuller was a popular lecturer, as well as a successful editor of *The Dial* from 1840 to 1842. Then too, she was also a scholar who translated Goethe and wrote a biography of the German poet. She was a poet in her own right, as well as author of many non-fiction essays and, among other book length works, two books popular in her day and important still in ours. Plus which Fuller contributed literary and social commentary to Horace Greeley's *New-York Tribune*—and more. All this in the mere fifteen years between her father's death in 1835 and her death in 1850.

The relations among Emerson, Thoreau, and Fuller served each in their way. They were earnestly mutual in spite of their obvious differences. Still, Fuller stood out among the three, not simply because she did so much in so few years; nor because she was at least their intellectual equal; but because she broke the mold of Concord's transcendentalist attitudes—this by introducing what we now clearly recognize to be a feminist theory that became the central feature of her life's work. However much her father formed her intellectually and

---

70 *The Bean-Field*, 157.
71 Cited in Susan Cheever, *American Bloomsbury*, 82.
72 Vivian Gornick, "A Double Inheritance: On Margaret Fuller," *The Nation* (April 3, 2012); compare Judith Thurman, "An Unfinished Woman," *The New Yorker* (April 1, 2013). Even more so, see John Matteson, *The Lives of Margaret Fuller* (W.W. Norton, 2012), especially the poignantly titled chapter 2, "Misfit"; and Megan Marshall, *Margaret Fuller: A New American Life* (Houghton Mifflin, 2013), especially chapter 7, "My Heart Has No Proper Home."

injured her emotionally, when she was free of him upon his death, she grew more and more focused on girls and women. Upon his death, she had to help support the family financially. Fuller turned naturally enough to teaching—first at Bronson Alcott's Temple Street School in Boston, then at the Greene Street School in Providence where she took special interest in the girls. When she returned to Massachusetts in 1839, she finished her biography of Goethe, *Conversations with Goethe in the Last Years of His Life*—from which she developed the practice of offering public conversations about Goethe, then on an increasing number of subjects. Her audiences were, primarily, educated women in the Boston area. Fuller and other of the transcendentalists engaged in the debates with William Lloyd Garrison on methods for ending slavery which for her entailed the liberation of women. Between 1841 and 1843 her conversations grew increasingly political in respect to gender roles, women's suffrage and rights, as well as abolition. The political conversations were context for, if not cause of, her feminism.

In 1842 Fuller turned over the editing of *The Dial* to Emerson, and began work on her first feminist essay, *The Great Lawsuit: Man versus Men, Woman versus Women*. In the summer of 1843 Fuller set off with friends, Sarah and James Clark, for Illinois. Fuller left them in Illinois to begin her wilderness journey across the Great Lakes to Mackinaw on Michigan's Upper Peninsula. Upon her return home, Fuller began to compose *Summer on the Lakes* which was published June 1844. Soon after, she began to revise *The Great Lawsuit* into her most famous book, *Woman in the Nineteenth Century*, published in 1845. After which, she moved to New York City upon accepting Horace Greeley's offer to write regularly for the *New-York Tribune*. Fuller's contributions to the *Tribune* were remarkable because she wrote broadly on political and social issues; notably: *Our City Charities: Visit to Bellevue Alms House, to the Farm School, the Asylum for the Insane, and Penitentiary on Blackwell's Island* (March 1845). The plight of women was a common thread in her newspaper columns. In 1847 she traveled to Italy, where she began to write on Italian politics. There she fell in love with Giovanni Angelo Ossoli. Their son Nino was born before they decided to sail to the United States. In 1850, all three drowned in a shipwreck off Fire Island. She had had but forty years, fewer than fifteen of them for productive intellectual work. Who knows what she might have done had she survived?

Still, Fuller did quite a lot, not just in formulating the first American feminist theory, but in adding that important element to transcendental thought which, without her, would have remained confined to Emerson's generic Soul/Nature dichotomy. This she did by taking what she learned from Goethe and Emerson as background to an original rethinking of Nature as having the definitive social aspect that was lacking in Emerson and tacit in Thoreau. Fuller introduced the gendered soul as an active force that viewed gender relations as inherently social by understanding the degree to which male and female are fluid categories. Hence the famous passage in *Woman in the Nineteenth Century:*

Male and female represent the two sides of the great radical divide.
But in fact they are perpetually passing into one another.
Fluid hardens to solid, solid rushes to fluid.
There is no wholly masculine man, no purely feminine woman.[73]

Here is the radical move. Emerson's Soul/Nature formula now is decidedly social and plural. Individual differences enter the discussion.

---

73 Fuller, *Woman in the Nineteenth Century* in Mary Kelley, ed., *The Portable Margaret Fuller* (Penguin, 1994), 293.

Some today might consider Fuller's move here part of a deconstruction of the cultural norm of "the *ideal* man," as Fuller puts it at the beginning of the book. If so, it is also an historical claim that she is writing and living "a new hour in the day of man."

Margaret Fuller's Feminist Social Theory

All too often theory is considered a practice in and of itself and one practiced without an explicit method. Yet, as Thoreau's method in *Walden* suggests, there is a sense in which even literary non-fiction can be used to formulate and communicate a general theory. Thoreau's bean-field story of a summer's planting and hoeing deploys the transcendentalist theory of self-culture as a weapon critical of the scientific cultivation of the day. *Walden*, thus, can be read as plowing a field of beans Thoreau did not need. It was instead a latent theory of his opposition to what came to be called agribusiness. But the important thing here is that Thoreau used, and expanded upon, a method he learned from Fuller in 1843, two years before he moved to the pond.

Fuller's method was already fixed in *Summer on the Lakes* in 1844, when she began revisions of her 1843 essay, *The Great Lawsuit: Man versus Men, Woman versus Women,*—which in turn would become *Woman in the Nineteenth Century* in 1845. In just more than two years, Fuller thought through and composed a coherent theory based on a self-conscious literary method—one that would issue in an original feminist theory that corrected Concord transcendentalism's inability to put forth an explicit social theory of modern society. Mary Kelley has gone so far as to pronounce Fuller's role in the scheme of nineteenth century social thought as the "model of *woman thinking*"[74]—as, that is, a gender play on Emerson's *man thinking* in "American Scholar."

Fuller's method was evident in *Summer on the Lakes*, which at first presents as a disorderly travel narrative in which Fuller's journal notes are randomly deployed as sources for a literary collage. Yet it would seem, as James Matteson observes, that Fuller knew what she was doing, that she "*pointedly* shunned the appearance of connectedness and linearity."[75] The intended jumble includes, among much else:—poems of her own making;—an extended friendly conversation beside Niagara Falls with James Freeman Clarke and his sister Sarah (her travel companions on the early weeks of their wandering);—a good many observations on native people she visited especially the Ottawa and Chippewa on Mackinaw Island who demonstrated that, far from being savages, "their decorum and delicacy are striking,"[76];—a long and hard to follow review of the writings of the German poet Justinus Kerner;—then also, passages evocative of Goethe's lyric style such as one inspired by the Rock River in Illinois:

> The river flows sometimes through these parks and lawns, then betwixt high bluffs, whose grassy ridges are covered with fine trees, or broken with crumbling stones ... Along the face of such crumbling rocks, swallows' nests are clustered, think as cities, and eagles and deer do disdain their summits. One morning out in the boat, along the base of these rocks, it was amusing and affecting too, to see these swallows put their heads out to look at us. There was something very hospitable about it, as if man had never shown himself a tyrant near them. What a morning that was![77]

---

74 Mary Kelley, "Introduction," *The Portable Margaret Fuller*, xviii.
75 John Matteson, *The Lives of Margaret Fuller* (W.W. Norton, 2012), 235. Emphasis added.
76 Matteson, 230.
77 *Summer on the Lakes, Portable Margaret Fuller*, 94–95.

Amid all the seemingly disconnected elements in the book, what is to be made of passages of such lyric beauty as this one that punctuate the book?

It could well be that Fuller wrote *Summer* in rather a hurry, late into the fall after she returned. Possible of course, but there is also the possibility that there was a method to her madness. Again Matteson: "*Summer on the Lakes* is, indeed, a subterranean text—the upward emanation of a consciousness that could remain beneath the surface for only so long."[78] "Method" might not be the word for a subterranean consciousness that leaks into conscious life, but the ability to allow for the leaks can be a literary method in the sense that, for notable example, poetry functions in such a way. Poetry is neither fact nor fiction. It is nothing if not metaphoric. Poems point to what is possible even if the reader cannot say what they mean. Poetry, in effect, creates probabilities that invite the reader or listener to enter. *Summer on the Lakes* is not, however, a prose poem. However the reader chooses to view *Summer on the Lakes,* a close reading comes upon its subterranean elements—the personal feelings below the surface that flow naturally from her reflections on her own childhood, her early teaching of young girls, her conversations with cultured women in Boston. All this, and more, leaked into *The Great Lawsuit*. Then, after *Summer on the Lakes,* the underground steam gushed into the open in *Woman in the Nineteenth Century.*

In *Summer on the Lakes* there is, among many instances, a personage who surfaces out of the blue—Mariana. Fuller's Mariana, interpreters agree,[79] is at least a fictional throwback to Margaret's childhood, especially the days at Miss Prescott's School in Groton, when her father was serving his last year as a Congressman in Washington. Margaret was but fifteen. Her year at Miss Prescott's was at once an insistence that she needed to have the formal instruction of a proper school, not to mention a degree of freedom from her father's imprecations. Mariana is a stand-in for Margaret's rebellion against the school's all too proper schooling. She appears in *Summer on the Lakes* when Margaret had returned to Chicago after exploring the downstate prairies of Illinois. In a Chicago hotel, she claims to have met a Mrs. Z who is portrayed as an aunt of Mariana's, her fictional self presented as a school mate. The news was that Mariana "so full of life, was dead." Then two pages on:

> Among Mariana's irregularities was a great aversion to the mealtime ceremonial. … Often as possible she excused herself on the ever-convenient plea of headache. … Today I found her on the balcony lost in gazing on the beautiful prospect. I have heard her say afterwards, she had rarely in her life been so happy, —and she was one with whom happiness was still a rapture. It was one of the most blessed summer days. … Pure blue were the heavens, and the same hue of contentment was in the heart of Mariana.[80]

Soon the tale reverts to Mariana's disagreeable relations with the other girls in the school who found her as strange as she found them. In the end, Margaret expresses through Mariana her prodigality:

> Never was forgotten the vow of the returning prodigal. Mariana could not resent, could not play false witness. The terrible crisis, which she so early passed through, probably prevented the world from hearing much of her. A wildfire was tamed in that hour of

---

78 Matteson, 237.
79 For discussions, see Matteson's chapter 2, "Misfit," especially 58–60; Marshall's chapter 4, "Mariana"; and Kelley's introduction to *Portable Margaret Fuller*, xii–xvi.
80 *Summer on the Lakes,* in *Portable Margaret Fuller*, 120–121; passage below, 126–127.

penitence at the boarding school, such as has sometimes wrapped court and camp in itself destructive glow.

Then immediately following: "Mariana was a very intellectual being, and she needed companionship."

Why this fictional self-presentation in *Summer on the Lakes* in 1843? And why is it a story of death—of Mariana representing Margaret's spiritual death to her childhood under the harsh hand of her father's expectations. The Mariana tale, so finely composed amid an otherwise unevenly organized book, is clearly a stream of thought that would break into the open two years later.

Woman in the Nineteenth Century in 1845 is, however, roughly organized into three parts. *First*, an extended discussion on liberty and law drawn from the principles of the American *Declaration of Independence*; *second*, a shorter but trenchant central section serving as context for Fuller's feminist theorem; *third*, a much longer final section that serves to document the long history of exceptional women who serve as models for the liberated women of her new age.

The first section begins with the *ideal man* cultural trope which she sharply criticizes in the manner of the Old Testament prophets:

> Yet, no doubt, a new manifestation is at hand, a new hour in the day of man. We cannot expect to see any one sample of completed being, when the mass of men lie engaged in sod, or use the freedom of their limbs only with wolfish energy. The tree cannot come to flower till its root be free from the cankering worm, and its whole growth open to air and light. While any one is base, none can be entirely free and noble. *Yet something new shall presently be shown of the life of man, for heart's crave, if minds do not know how to ask it.*[81]

Fuller here makes no bones. The ideal man is stuck as sod in the mud, wolfish, and infected with canker sores, but there is new order of life that will clean, clear, and heal "his" afflictions.

Then Fuller turns to her implicit declaration of woman's independence: "It should be remarked that, as the principle of liberty is better understood, a broader protest is made on behalf of Woman."[82] In the pages following Fuller anticipates Simone de Beauvoir by almost a century, when, in *The Second Sex* in 1949, Beauvoir equated the woman's position with those of the Slave and the Jew. Then, some pages on, Fuller comes to Miranda through whom she takes her stand with other literary and intellectual feminists of the day—Mary Wollstonecraft, George Sand, Harriet Martineau, and Angelina Grimké. The first section is long and not nearly as neat as a short summary may make it seem. But there is no mistaking her main point.

Then, of a sudden, the book comes to its main theoretical point in the book's short but paramount second section that starts by proclaiming the nature of woman in an unmistakable allusion to the transcendentalist soul:

> The especial genius of woman I believe to be electrical in movement, intuitive in function, spiritual in tendency. ... More native is it to her to be the living model of the artist than to set apart from herself any one form of objective reality. ... In so far as *soul* is in her

---

81 *Ibid*, 233. Emphasis added.
82 *Ibid*, 235.

completely developed, all soul is the same; but as far as it is modified in her as woman, it flows, it breathes, it sings, rather than deposits soil, or finishes work...[83]

Woman is not like man the dirt of sod, or the wolf, or the canker. Nor is she objectively One; —rather, in her electrical movement, she is Many.

Yet, this poetic rendering of woman's spiritual nature is not meant to make her superior to man. Her nature makes her part of man's nature. Then the theorem (again):

Male and female represent the two sides of the great radical divide.
But in fact they are perpetually passing into one another.
Fluid hardens to solid, solid rushes to fluid.
There is no wholly masculine man, no purely feminine woman.

These few strong lines of Fuller's theoretical feminism occur almost precisely half-way through the book. The third section following is very long. Here she reverts to her mix and match method to generate a rough history from the classical era down to her time of notable women—actual and literary—who serve as empirical evidence for her feminism.

When all is read and done, with the digressions set aside, Fuller's feminist theory is true to her transcendentalist convictions, while at the same time deconstructing and revealing the deeper possible meanings of Emerson's Soul/Nature dichotomy. She in effect comverts the singular Soul into many by turning from the generic ideal man to the nature of woman who is fluid enough to pass into the nature of man. Neither man nor woman is wholly masculine or feminine. By consequence, Nature itself must be several even many.[84] Without in the least criticizing Emerson, Fuller revolutionizes his and Thoreau's implicit Gaia theory of nature as mother. Her feminism has this radical effect even as it is not stated or even as it could not in her time have been thought. Amazingly, by transforming transcendentalist terms, she brings the philosophy around full circle by her feminist theorem.

Her book ends not at the end, but in a striking passage near the end of its second section: "Every relation, every gradation of nature is incalculably precious, but only to the soul, which is poised upon itself, and to whom no loss, no change, can bring dull discord, for it is in harmony with the central soul."[85]

Pragmatism or Transcendentalism?

Which of the two is the first indisputably, well-formed American school of social philosophy? It is commonly held that pragmatism is. If the question concerns the first overtly social theory based on principles distinctively American, pragmatism is a fair answer. But, even then, it is hard to ignore the role of the Concord transcendentalism of Emerson,

---

83 *Ibid*, 293; quote just below same place.
84 It is hard not to use "deconstructing" here because this precisely is what Fuller is doing. But, contrary to popular abuse of the term, *to deconstruct* does NOT mean to *take apart*; rather Derrida meant it to refer, not to a method, but to the need of serious readers of any philosophical concept to dig into its deeper not always obvious meaning. Christopher Norris has put it plainly: "...deconstruction is the vigilant seeking out of ... blind spots or moments of self-contradiction where a text betrays the tension between rhetoric and logic, between what it manifestly *means to say* and what it nonetheless *constrained to mean*." See Norris, *Derrida* (Harvard University Press, 1987), 19. For Derrida himself, see "Writing Before the Letter," in Derrida, *Of Grammatology* (Johns Hopkins University Press, 1974 [1967]), Part I; and Gayatri Chakravorty Spivak's brilliant "Translator's Preface," xv–xx. Or look again at how, above, I explain Fuller's way of dealing with Emerson's Soul/Nature dichotomy. [On deconstruction, see also Gayatri Chakravorty Spivak, chapter 24.]
85 *Ibid*, 295.

Thoreau, and Fuller for having developed not just an indigenous school of crypto-social philosophy but for having so coherently initiated what we can see as the richest, first instance of Americans thinking America—a school of thought that not only drew upon social ideas already by then well formed in early American traditions but one that, by its engagement with the political and social turmoil of its time, was actually focused on America as such. Pragmatism, as it came to be, was about democratic action in the world. Concord transcendentalism was about the world as such—a world of rivers, ponds, and lakes that flowed through time and space.

Part III
Civil War and American Pragmatism, 1861–1917 and After

7 A Suffering Republic and its Culture
John Brown and Harriet Tubman

We still live in the world of death the Civil War created…
We still seek to use our deaths to create meaning where we are not sure any exist.
The Civil War generation glimpsed the fear that still defines us---
The sense that death is the only end.
—Drew Gilpin Faust, *This Republic of Suffering*, 2008

I am quite cheerful in view of my approaching end,
—being fully persuaded that I am worth inconceivably more to hang than any other purpose.
—John Brown to a New England Anti-Slavery Convention, May 1859

All over the North men were singing the John Brown song.
His body was in the dust, but his soul was marching on. …
His death was giving new life and power to the principles of justice and liberty.
—*Life and Times of Frederick Douglass*, 1882

I was the conductor of the Underground Railroad,
and I can say what most conductors can't say—I never ran my train off the track
and I never lost a passenger.
—Harriet Tubman, probably 1896

Most that I have done and suffered in the service of our cause has been in public, and I have received much encouragement at every step of the way. You, on the other hand, have labored in a private way.
I have wrought in the day – you in the night.
I have had the applause of the crowd and the satisfaction that comes of being approved by the multitude,
while the most that you have done has been witnessed
by a few trembling, scarred, and foot-sore bondmen and women,
whom you have led out of the house of bondage.
—Frederick Douglass to Harriet Tubman, August 29, 1868

The Suffering Republic

Before Drew Gilpin Faust became Harvard University's 28th President (and the first since 1672 without a degree from Harvard), she was a distinguished American historian. So much so that her 2008 book *This Republic of Suffering* won many prestigious prizes including the Bancroft Prize and the American History Book Prize, while also being short-listed for the National Book Award and the Pulitzer Prize. Among the many good reasons for the book's recognition is how it captured the many deaths of the Civil War and our nation's struggle to understand death itself—both then and now. The full title says it all: *This Republic of Suffering: Death and the American Civil War*. Notice that she means *this* republic—*ours*. Hence, its closing lines:

> We still live in the world of death the Civil War created...We still seek to use our deaths to create meaning where we are not sure any exist. The Civil War generation glimpsed the fear that still defines us—The sense that death is the only end.[1]

And she meant that the deaths and suffering by America's Civil War would be ground deep into the nation's collective Unconsciousness—from which it would continually pester the consciousness of all Americans.

Just before the mid-nineteenth century when Concord's Bloomsbury culture was formulating a fresh version of Americans thinking America, that same America was staggering toward the Civil War in 1861—a war that could well have torn it apart. That war, as much as any other America has fought, is particularly well remembered on both sides of the national divide—remembered for the dead lost and the lingering omnipresence of death in the nether regions of the country's culture. No war killed so many. None, not even our World Wars, so touched the nation's emotional heart.

The Civil War Troubles America's Future

It is hard to go anywhere in America without coming upon a memorial to the dead of its wars—of which the Civil War was, and still is, the deadliest. On East Rock, the highest prominence overlooking the town, stands New Haven's Soldiers and Sailors Monument. There are more than a few such monuments in towns and cities nationwide. Since 1887, the New Haven monument stands some 112 feet above the East Rock which itself is 366 feet above sea level. From that vantage, on a clear day, one can enjoy a panoramic vista of the far reaches of the town from its harbor on Long Island Sound to the Mill River as it flows down from its headwaters in the North beyond the Metacomet Ridge.

The Monument honors those who fought and died in the nation's major wars prior to 1887—the Revolutionary War, that of 1812, the Mexican American War, and of course the Civil War. The quadrant memorializing the Civil War faces New Haven to the southwest. It is thereby open to the expansive nation beyond the setting sun. Monuments, as a category, are a mixed bag of remembrances—from small and forgotten ones to the grand and unforgettable. Memorials to the Civil War remember at once, and strangely so, both the unforgettable and the forgotten.

The Civil War, as we now know, was a war the ravages of which would shred the nation long after its end in 1865. Some thought that the Voting Rights Act, a century later in 1965, would heal the breach, but that too was an illusion. Now, in and after, the 2020s, the better part of a half-century after that, the shredding may be less bloody in some ways but just as threatening to the national culture. By 2065, two centuries after the Civil War was fought over race and slavery, the nation will be neither white nor ethnically European as it was in that day. By then, should the whole still be knit together, even if loosely, the civil wars raging through the two centuries will have been won by the descendants of former slaves and immigrants from the other Americas, from the Caribbean and Africa, and from the Middle East and all parts of Asia.

---

1 Drew Gilpin Faust, *This Republic of Suffering: Death and the American Civil War* (Knopf, 2008), 271.

The minority white nation of the days to come will have to rethink that new America, for which they will be able to draw from the cultural genius of the nation's revolutionary and post-revolutionary generations. Even if, by then, Concord transcendentalism will have been buried somewhere in the nether tissues of a nation cut and healed, then cut again in the present situation when tyrants are tunneling into the body politic hoping to bolster a renewal of white dominance. If a semblance of those times remains in 2065 it will remain somewhere in the still deeper tissues of American culture. Cultures and the theories they breed seldom die forever and, by 2065, the American culture will have endured less than half-a-millennium if we take 1619 as the first instance of what America would come to be. Who knows what it will be in times to come and how, in the most practical of terms, people will think it and speak of it? No one knows of course. Futures are, at best, part of several imaginations by which a people try to aim ahead—even when, like Frederic Edwin Church's farmers below West Rock in 1849, they will never live to see that land looming beyond the setting sun.

Still, if it is true, as so far it has been, that cultures endure for countless setting suns, then whatever America will be in 2065 it will surely be something more than a pragmatic culture of individuals living in and against a vast natural surround. If these three themes—*pragmatism, individualism, transcending Nature*—were the founding elements of American social theory, then the Civil War was at once the end of the founding era of the nation's theory of itself and the conjuncture that demanded a new series of social and cultural themes out of those three. That new series would become, in time, theoretical themes that paid fresh attention to the disorders in the nation's culture that were typified by a brutal Civil War. These were themes that arose in and after the War in the nation's need to formulate, first, a stable *interaction order* in an increasingly complex society. The Civil War was, in many ways, the null point through which America passed on its way to becoming stoutly modern. "The modern" was initially imagined as the triumph of a technologically sophisticated economy. But in the century after the 1820s, the waves of immigrant laborers and farmers and the northward migration of freed people added a different, if ill-considered, modernity—one in which a growing, seemingly endless, number of *identities* that in their differences aggravated the number and kind of *social exclusions*. Yet, before these emergent themes—*interaction order, identities, exclusions*—would settle into what they have become today, the nation had to work through the threats of a Civil War that, once settled, made it necessary for Americans to think America in fresh, if troubling, terms.

The Civil War and the Divided Republic of Suffering

Faust, in *This Republic of Suffering*, writing on the historical impact of the great number of deaths in the Civil War, asserted that "death transformed the American nation as well as hundreds of thousands of individuals directly affected by loss."[2]

This Republic of Suffering is a book about the many ways deaths in the Civil War preoccupied the nation, during and long after. From the start, these deaths of young men occasioned widespread evidence of the cultural influence of the ideal of the good death—of, that is, dying fully prepared to give up life in the confidence that a better world awaits.[3] The good death ideal had been prevalent for centuries but by the nineteenth century in America

---

2 Drew Gilpin Faust, *This Republic of Suffering: Death and the American Civil War* (Knopf, 2008), xiii; and the book as a whole for the following paragraphs.
3 On the good death and the work of mourning, see Faust, *This Republic of Suffering*, chapter 5, "Realizing, Civilians and the Work of Mourning."

it had become an acute element in the general culture in part because a more evangelical Christianity had largely replaced the Calvinism of the colonial era (John Brown's Calvinism notwithstanding). The decisive evidence of a good death were the last words of the dying taken as evidence of their readiness to pass on to life with God. On the battlefields and in surgery tents, chaplains, nurses, and companions were recruited to convey to family and friends news of just how their soldier had died a good death.

The good death cultural norm spread through the population such that no more than a few of the nation's thirty-two million-plus people were unaware of it. Fewer still were unaffected by the omnipresence of death itself. After deadly battles on the fields, the suffering was acute. Survivors and family members searched the battlefields to identify their dead for proper burial. Then, after the War was over, they continued to search for remains of dead loved ones. A movement grew to disinter bodies and rebury them closer to home or, as more time went by, in national cemeteries for the Civil War dead. Then too there was a near universal process by which civilians affected by a death engaged in "the work of mourning." Virtually everyone struggled to discern what to believe about the meaning of the War and the deaths. Through it all, there was the question of how many had actually died. The numbers themselves aggravated the pain of suffering and questions of how the living were meant to survive it all. These are foremost among the reasons why death transformed America.

It goes without saying that the suffering that coursed through the nation was due to the lesion that broke the nation's skin in Civil War. Before the dying began in earnest the nation was already divided, as it remained after the War; then too down into our time, and on into a future yet to come. The primal division was that between the slavery-based agrarian economy in the South and the emergent industrial capitalism in the North that grew out of the originating differences associated with the 1619 movement—*slavery* and *settlement* of the wilderness were two sides of the same American coin. This foundational division was hidden under the blanket of a culture meant to heal the bruises caused by the insistent political factions and the harsh moral struggles of the nation's leaders—of whom none more tormented than Abraham Lincoln. As prodigious as Lincoln came to be in America's historical imagination, he struggled over the meaning of the nation's divisions and how they might be resolved.

For the first two years of Abraham Lincoln's presidency, his Civil War policy was focused not on slavery but on preserving the Union. He, of course, was perfectly clear that slavery was a cause of the War but, for Lincoln, preservation of the Union was the overriding issue. This conviction he kept well in mind in the years before he became president, perhaps most famously in the memorable lines of his June 16, 1858 "House Divided" speech where, after quoting the New Testament line, Lincoln stipulated that the national crisis over slavery was, in effect, an either/or choice for *both* North and South:

> "A house divided against itself cannot stand." I believe this government cannot endure, permanently half slave and half free. I do not expect the Union to be dissolved—I do not expect the house to fall—but I do expect it will cease to be divided. *It will become all one thing, or all the other.* Either the opponents of slavery will arrest the further spread of it and place it where the public mind shall rest in the belief that it is in course of ultimate extinction; or its advocates will push it forward till it shall become alike lawful in all the States, old as well as new—North as well as South.[4]

---

4 Lincoln, "House Divided," in *Abraham Lincoln/Speeches and Writings 1832–1858* (Library of America, 1989), 426. "A house divided against itself cannot stand" is in the Bible at Mark 3:25.

This was just shy of four years before, with all the authority of his presidency, Lincoln would draft the *Emancipation Proclamation*. Late summer of 1862 he still held to a version of the House Divided ambivalence. In a famous August 22 letter responding to Horace Greeley's complaint in the *New York Tribune* the President made it clear that he was not prepared to win the War in order to end slavery. Lincoln said: "My paramount object in this struggle *is* to save the Union and is *not* either to save or destroy slavery. What I do about slavery, and the colored race, I do because I believe it helps to save the Union; and what I forbear, I forbear because I do *not* believe it would help to save the Union."[5]

Lincoln's ambivalence toward dealing with slavery softened when, on January 1, 1863, he authoritatively issued the *Proclamation* without even a hint of the either/or uncertainty of the 1858 speech and the Horace Greeley letter of late summer 1862:

> I do order and declare that all persons held as slaves within said designated States and parts of States are and henceforward shall be free: and that the executive government of the United States, including the military and naval authorities thereof, will recognize and maintain the freedom of said persons.[6]

Yet, even then, Lincoln came under fire from members of his own cabinet, notably Salmon P. Chase, who served as Secretary of the Treasury and never quite gave up on his belief that he, not Lincoln, should have been President. Chase (who became Chief Justice of the Supreme Court in 1864) was predictably troubled about the legal justification for the *Proclamation*. To which the President responded on September 2, 1863 with legal, political, and moral subtlety:

> The original proclamation has no constitutional or legal justification except as a military measure. ... If I take the step, must I not do so, without any argument, except the one that I think the measure is politically expedient, or morally right? Would I not thus give up all footing upon constitution and law? Would I not thus be in the boundless field of absolutism?[7]

In spite of political turmoil over the *Proclamation*, 1863 was a turning point in the War and thus a moment of progress that, in time, allowed subsequent history to view his *Emancipation Proclamation* as both militarily necessary and morally right. Still, even after the *Proclamation* was decreed, Lincoln tried to stir the waters for a colonization policy whereby freedpeople could be resettled in Africa or the Caribbean. Frederick Douglass, who had established a relationship with Lincoln, was appalled by this scheme and told the President so.

Early summer of 1863 the Union armies won the Battle of Gettysburg on July 3rd and forced the surrender of the Confederate encampment at Vicksburg on July 4th. In those two days the Union ended the South's hopes of invading the North and of blockading the Mississippi River from invasion of the deep South. The North had the Confederacy effectively surrounded and exposed to the penetration of the Union armies deep into

---

5 Lincoln to Horace Greeley, August 22, 1865 in *The Portable Lincoln* edited by Andrew Delbanco (Penguin, 1992), 240.
6 *Final Emancipation Proclamation*, January 1, 1863, in *Abraham Lincoln: Speeches and Writings, 1859–1865* (Library of America, 1989), 425. [As for the adjective *"Final,"* see Lincoln's *Preliminary Emancipation Proclamation*, September 22–24, 1862 in *Abraham Lincoln: Speeches and Writings, 1859–1865, ibid*, 368–370.]
7 Lincoln to Salmon Chase, September 2, 1863, in *Abraham Lincoln: Speeches and Writings, 1859–1865, ibid*, 501.

the South. The Union penetration of the South culminated on December 24, 1864 with William Tecumseh Sherman's March through Atlanta to the Sea at Savannah. After that, it remained only for Ulysses S. Grant, who had won Vicksburg the year before, to lead the conquest of Petersburg and the Confederate capital at Richmond on April 2, 1865. Robert E. Lee surrendered a week later on April 9 at Appomattox. The War was over. Lincoln was assassinated five days later on Good Friday, April 14, 1865 and died the next morning. He had gone to Ford's Theatre that evening to relax after administering a long and trying war. Few then, and fewer still today, would have wished him dead the morning of April 15. Still, one could entertain the thought that, had he survived, Lincoln would not have had a magical solution to Reconstruction. He lived the divisions in the nation.

Needless to say, the tragic end of the President's life dimmed the glow of victory. In a way, the five days between Appomattox and the assassination at Ford's Theatre revealed two sides of American culture—one bright, the other dark. On the bright side, the Reconstruction program Lincoln had already begun under Union control in Louisiana and elsewhere in the South was a bright, if short-lived, light. Even under the seriously racist, President Andrew Johnson, Reconstruction programs developed to good enough effect. Freedpeople made important advances in social and economic progress. Institutions of secondary and higher education took shape supported by the Freedmen's Bureau and Northern philanthropists. Literacy rates soon were dramatically improved. The Freedman's Saving Bank with offices in 17 states and supported by the Government rapidly grew to nearly $60 million in assets, then a significant degree of collective wealth (roughly $1 billion today). The Bank, however, was crippled by the Long Depression that began in 1873. It collapsed in the decade following. Still, these and other instances of progress were the bright side of the post-Civil War era.

American culture, as it evolved over the centuries, has generally favored history's bright side—which is to say: the inevitability of progress. In a definite, if limited, sense there assuredly has been progress that endures today. It could be said that the first and surest post War embodiment of that progress was Frederick Douglass—born a slave, Frederick Augustus Washington Bailey, in 1818 in Maryland. Twenty years later he escaped to the North, eventually to become a public figure known across the nation. Even in bondage Douglass had learned, by hook and crook, to read and write, which made possible not only his reading knowledge of history and the classics but, more importantly, his world-wide fame as a public speaker who fought for the abolition of slavery. By the time of his death in 1895, Douglass had written three best-selling memoirs. In the last of those, *The Life and Times of Frederick Douglass* (1892), he could say, with good conscience and a clear eye:

> Servitude, persecution, false friends, desertion and depreciation have not robbed my life of happiness or made it a burden. I have been, and still am, especially fortunate, and may well indulge sentiments of warmest gratitude for the allotments of life that have fallen to me."[8]

This is progress. Then too Douglass' story is one among others of the day. By the end of the century the stories of Martin R. Delaney, Booker T. Washington, and W.E.B. Du Bois, Ida B. Wells Barnett, Anna Julia Cooper, among many others, formed a collective narrative of progress. The Great Migration to the North of some six million freedpeople after 1910— and, in the same year, the founding of the National Association for the Advancement of the Colored People turned the page for Blacks in American history. Then, in the 1920s, the

---

8 Frederick Douglass, *Life and Times of Frederick Douglass* (The Library of America, 1994 [1892]), 1045.

brilliance of the Harlem Renaissance shone upon the narrative of the progress of American Black people such that it revealed the deep structural racism of a changing American culture.

But this mostly bright side shone against a darker side that extended the era of *ersatz* slavery. Whatever the progress, Reconstruction failed.

> It must be remembered and never forgotten that the civil war in the South which overthrew Reconstruction was a determined effort to reduce black labor as nearly as possible to a condition of unlimited exploitation and build a new class of capitalists on this foundation.[9]

This is W.E.B. Du Bois, writing in 1935. The "civil war" he refers to was not the Civil War from 1861–1865, but the war by which the South's capitalist agricultural interests reversed most of the gains of Reconstruction after 1873. The White Planter regained his prior position of domination over the Black Worker while using White Workers to function—with no extra remuneration other than the privilege of being white (the racial wage[10])—as the go-between enforcer of a new class of exploited Black Workers who had, by then, become virtual slaves, free in name only. Such is the way of actual progress as distinct from its rhetorical idealization. There is no ever-onward and -upward line of history.

Whenever an ideology of necessary progress infects a culture, the infection eats away at the fiber of social life, seeping up from the lives of those who suffer most. The straightforward fact of such an ideology is that, if ever there were a just world, it would be, at the least, a world in which, whatever differences there may be, none would be excluded to the point of virtual or actual death. Clearly, over the years in America many have died both kinds of death. Nevertheless, many think that the importance of progress to modern cultures is prototypically an American idea. Even now, still early in the twenty-first century, there are those who want to come to America in spite of its pathetically distracted, uncertain, and sometimes evil public politics. One might assume that I am referring narrowly to America's terrible moment after 2016. But, in truth, there are numerous historical moments of the kind—the cruelty of Puritan religious attitudes; the Salem Witch Trials in the earliest years; the long history of enslavements of various kinds after 1619; Andrew Jackson's Indian removal policy in the 1830s; James K. Polk's Mexican-American War that in 1848 legitimated America's quasi legal theft of Mexican lands; the Fugitive Slave Law in 1850; Chief Justice Roger B. Taney's dreadful Dred Scott Decision in 1857; Andrew Johnson's disastrous presidency after 1865 that undermined Reconstruction; the slaughter of Lakota women and children at Wounded Knee in 1890; Woodrow Wilson's segregationist policies during the War of 1914; in 1942 Franklin Roosevelt's internment of 120,000 Japanese-American citizens; then closer to the present situation, the New Jim Crow that calls attention to a culture that imprisons black men in outrageously disproportionate numbers.[11] In these cases, the names are little more than authoritative markers of a deep underlying racism by which America morbidly brutalized people and seized lands on its perverse presumption of continental rights and privileges. Then too, there is a long history since the 1870s of union busting and violence against workers and their families, including the systematic economic

---

9 W.E.B. Du Bois, *Black Reconstruction in America: 1860–1880* (Atheneum, 1992 [1935]), 670.
10 David Roediger, *The Wages of Whiteness: Race and the Making of the American Working Class* (Verso Books, 1999).
11 Michelle Alexander, *The New Jim Crow: Mass Incarceration in the Age of Colorblindness* (The New Press, 2010). Also, by the same author: "Injustice on Repeat," *The New York Times Sunday Review* (January 19, 2020).

marginalization of working women in domestic industrial, business positions, and other sectors of an all too rich economy.

It is true of course that structured social evils have afflicted other modern societies in obvious instances like Nazi Germany, Soviet Russia, Maoist China. These exclusions were systematically justified by extreme nationalist ideologies that, so far, have proven ever more destructive than those operating in American history. Still, America's demonic cultural Unconscious energizes impulses that can be, in their way, nearly as awful. This because, over the years, so many in the wider world have exaggerated the inevitability of the American idea of itself as a society where progress is a given because its people are good and its natural resources abundant. America's pride of its exceptional place in the world order, until well into the twenty-first century, had been taken for granted. At the same time, the pride has fostered a homegrown contradiction that has caused American culture to lumber on in the tension between its conscious sense of America the Beautiful—whose "alabaster cities gleam, undimmed by human tears!"—and its innocence as to its unconscious cultural mind that darkens those gleaming cities. Again, Gunnar Myrdal put it just so in his definition of "The American Creed" at the beginning of his *An American Dilemma* in 1944:

> [T]he American thinks, talks, and acts under the influence of high national and Christian precepts, and, on the other hand, the valuations of specific planes of individual and group living, where personal and local interests; economic, social, and sexual jealousies; considerations of community prestige and conformity; group prejudice against particular or types of people; and all sorts of miscellaneous wants, impulses, and habits dominate outlook.[12]

This passage bears repeated reading. Myrdal's theory of *The American Dilemma* addressed, of course, America's inability to apply its high-minded values to the practical conditions of life with others where jealousies bewilder, desires rule, and prejudices flourish. But it applies just as well to the whole of American culture.

Like any other culture, whatever the extent of its domain, American culture serves, in part, to cover the sins of its past. To be sure, cultures tell truths and express high values. Yet to the very extent that cultures—especially national ones—are meant to glorify and inspire, they must either repress or camouflage the not-so-glamorous sides of their national natures.

Progress and the Origin of Human Cultures

Still, there remains a basic question: Where do cultures come from? If they are organic, as it seems they are, then they grow from a rich but dirty ground. When they blossom, they appear brighter than any flower or weed could be. Wendell Berry, farmer poet, has written:

> Memory,
> native to this valley, will spread over it
> like a grove, and memory will grow
> into legend, legend into song, song
> into sacrament.[13]

---

12 Gunnar Myrdal, *An American Dilemma: The Negro Problem and Modern Democracy* (Harper & Row, 1964 [1944]), xlvii.
13 Quoted by Amanda Petrusich in "Going Home with Wendell Berry," *The New Yorker* (July 14, 2019).

Cultures are nothing if they do not grow out of the memory of a past in a native valley or a grove where stories are told and songs sung, some of which are treasured enough to turn, ultimately, into something akin to a sacrament. Yet, as is well known, memory is selective. A sacramental memory comes from the dirt that nourishes even as it covers the dead. The ground of memories is cross plowed by desires and deprivations between which passions and differences are energized. The ground plowed is the prejudice infused dirt of daily life. The irony is that from such a soil, sacramental cultures often grow and blossom.

This may sound weirdly religious. In a sense it must be. Religion is that aspect of human cultures which attempts to justify human realities by appealing to one or another of the notions that serve as higher powers to ordinary life. They may be as abstract as Being itself or as concrete as a local sphere of storytelling gods. The Concord transcendentalists got this notion quite right. As Anne Rose has put it: "What the Transcendentalists advocated was no longer Christianity per se but simply religion."[14] In this historical sense, religion as such is at least homologous, if not analogous, to culture.

Even, and especially, in modern times, cultures are forced to account as best they can for the memory of historical evils perpetuated under the illusion of doing or pursuing a good. The result is what Mircea Eliade, the great historian of religion, calls "the normality of suffering." Eliade concludes his best-known book, *Cosmos and History: The Myth of the Eternal Return*, with a dire but true statement: "[T]o the extent to which modern man is irremediably identified with history and progress, and to which history and progress are a fall, both implying the final abandonment of the paradise of archetypes and repetition."[15] Eliade is referring here to the specific influence of the Judeo-Christian myth of the fall of man, but more generally he is pointing to the general human experience of the memory of failures that cultures of historical progress must somehow erase from the collective memory of humankind's fallen nature—or, better said: of humanity's inability to prevent people from doing evil, of which the most common form is violence against those with whom we share what ground there is.

Once Americans began to invent formal social theories of their emergent culture, they were inclined to believe that culture was something like a collective common mind that regulated the many organic functions of the social body. Formal social theory in America did not begin in earnest until late in the nineteenth century.[16] These theories did not flourish, however, until after World War II, when, for a while, America was the world's economic and military super power which encouraged the not very well thought-through cultural idea that culture itself was the head of the nation's body—as, that is, the central nervous system that directs the functioning of, in particular, the legal, political, economic systems for the good of all.[17] In effect, in his theory of culture took a bit too seriously the idea that the political realm is one in which practical solutions to competitive differences can be found. This idea, when it took on formal expression, was that individuals seek to survive and thrive by trying to get ahead in the race for well-being, if not wealth. In this scheme, surviving and thriving were understood as direct (or indirect) mastery of the resources of the natural world. This way of thinking was true to the predominant ideology of American culture after World War II when the nation was flourishing on the upward slope of progress. At the same time, the core ideas of the day, when a modern America had won a global war, were a kind of

---

14 Anne C. Rose, *Transcendentalism as a Social Movement, 1830–1850* (Yale University Press, 1981), 38.
15 Mircea Eliade, *Cosmos and History: The Myth of the Eternal Return* (Harper Torchbooks, 1959), 162.
16 Louis Menand, "Pragmatisms," in his *The Metaphysical Club: Story of Ideas in America* (Farrar, Straus, and Giroux, 2001), chapter 13. Also, "Pragmatism, The Hard Realities of Change," chapter 11 below.
17 The major theorist in this way of thinking was Talcott Parsons in such books as *The Social System* (The Free Press, 1951). For a closer analysis of his and related theories, see "The Function of American Culture," chapter 12 below.

short-term regression to the foundational themes of American social thought in its classical post-Revolutionary era—*individuals acting pragmatically in and against Nature.*

But the Civil War was the beginning of a more complicated shared theoretical culture of America's enduring dilemma. After the Civil War, the doctrine of necessary historical progress implicit in these foundational themes prevailed, but against persistent contrary forces of national *disorder*, new and sometimes *conflicting social identities* as the nation modernized, and the lingering *threat of exclusions* different from slavery but, in many ways, much the same. The assumption that American culture is good in and of itself endured for nearly a century as true to the modern progressive ideal and good enough to deny the inherent troubles of disorder, conflict, and exclusions.

America's triumph in World War II seemed for a time to seal the protective cultural crust that covered the stew of troubles that never went away after the Civil War. But the crust would soon crumble—first around the edges, slowly opening enough to reveal the spoiled meat within. By 1950, the Cold War was in full frost which led to a war in Korea for which even now, well into a new century, there is no peace treaty. The unsettled war in Korea was followed a decade later by a war lost in Vietnam; then not long after the Cold War ended in 1989–1991; a decade later a new century opened after 9/11, with failed and unbearably long wars in Iraq and Afghanistan; then another decade plus on, there was a war in Ukraine that may turn out to be endless. It would seem that, these days, no one wins what wars there are—and still not in involving a series of high-tech guerrilla strikes and special force responses covered by littoral or air counterstrikes.

Still, whatever may have changed in global warfare, there have been times in American history when various theories of the nation's divine errand into the wilderness—including its sense of manifest destiny or special providence, and other generic if lesser versions of its exceptionalism—have occluded honest memory of the realities. Even well into the twenty-first century a movement of Americans shouting "Make America Great Again"—a slogan that concedes slippage in the nation's exceptional nature, while supposing the age-old grand ideas of America's place in the world could be restored.

Historically, these grand ideas came strongly to the fore in the years prior to the Civil War. As early as 1835, Alexis de Tocqueville, in his *Democracy in America*, attributed a special historical purpose to America—this during Andrew Jackson's assault on America's indigenous people in the 1830s. Then in the 1840s the Manifest Destiny doctrine inspired a false sense of the nation's exceptional trajectory just when slavery was gnawing at the nation's heart strings such that the Civil War was, by then, all but inevitable. Then too, in 1941 when the world was lapsing into a second global war, Henry Luce announced the American century. If these historical moments are to be trusted, it would seem that thoughts of the nation's greatness are exaggerated during times of collective awareness that crisis and failure are in the offing. In the striking case of the *Star-Spangled Banner* which was composed during the War of 1812 when American forces in Fort Henry were being hammered by British artillery. All along, cultural tropes of the nation's special virtues were pronounced when its ordinary failures were beginning to break the crust of popular consciousness. These irruptions of national grandeur were not so much defensive as symptomatic of the repressed awareness that the nation was not all *that* special.

It could be said, therefore, that, since America's collective culture serves to guide and enrich its people, it is also much like a collectively conscious mind—which, in turn, invites comparison to an individual's mind. If the comparison is apt, then too it is fair to suggest that the collective mind, like the individual mind, also functions to forget and otherwise repress whatever is too unbearable to face. America's national culture thinks well of all that it surveys but, as any probative historian would agree, such a culture is not very good at taking stock of the reality of the nation's social evils—of which none is more persistently deep rooted than the racism essential to slavery proper, then the virtual slavery under Jim Crow, and other degradations that endured well after 1865. The good/evil duplicity of American culture was at work from the first in 1619 and continues now, as it will for time to come. Social evils, when engrained in the institutional structures of a nation, are not forces that can be willed or washed away—as they often are for individuals. Social evils are so ingrained in the character of the nation that at best they can be recognized and tolerated only cursorily, if at all. Intolerable evils, or merely embarrassing ones, surface only in collective repetition compulsions[18] that over time make trouble for the nation similar to the trouble they make for the individual. For America, the collective repetition compulsion is that, unlike most other nations, it believes it can win unwinnable wars, or be greater than any other nation has been. This, perhaps because, in its unconscious collective mind, the nation needs to prove it is better than, deep down, it knows it is not.

If we take the Massachusetts Puritans and their idea of a mission into the wilderness in 1620 as the foundational culture of the American idea of inevitable progress, then it is just as fair to take the Virginia settlement in 1619 as the foundation of the colony's evil side—slavery. Everything that came after the earliest colonies—the Revolution and the *United States Constitution* in 1789 and the states that came to be—were torn between the progress made in its revolution and the early state formation, and the underlying racism that produced the cotton wealth that divided the nation in War in the 1860s. Not one of America's foundational institutions avoided the shredding —even the most liberal of modern constitutions, drawn up as it was by slave holders, was agonally silent on the rights of slaves.

America's culture is good enough and has done much good. But the awkward fact of cultures is that, when social theorists attempt to think them, they must think in the terms their culture provides. As a result, when all is said and done, social theorists are baffled by an Unthinkable[19]—by, that is, contrary forces that lurk below the surface of any national culture. The problem is all the more acute in American culture which so exaggerates its higher moral values as to blind the national eye to failures that embarrass its good intentions. This is quite a different matter from being inherently evil. Evil is done from time to time but once done the culture tends to erase the memory of it. In American history, there are surprisingly important cases of those who used evil to do good—among them John Brown and Harriet Tubman.

Violence Against Social Evil: John Brown and Harriet Tubman

Just as George Washington was a nearly pure practical social theorist, so too were John Brown and Harriet Tubman. Washington was first among equals in thinking through the basic structure of the national ethos, and then justifying these thoughts by his disciplined presentation of himself as the nation's paternal self. In somewhat the same ways, but to different ends, the earnest values of Brown and Tubman were expressed less by what they said than by what they did.

John Brown, the radical warrior against slavery, and Harriet Tubman, the militant leader on the Underground Railroad, demonstrated for all to see, if only they would look hard,

---

18 Sigmund Freud, "Remembering, Repeating, and Working-through," *Standard Edition of the Complete Psychological Works of Sigmund Freud* (Hogarth Press, 1919 [1914]), 12: 147–156.
19 For a general discussion of this term, consider: Charles Lemert, *Thinking the Unthinkable: Riddles of Classical Social Theory* (Routledge, 2016 [2007]).

that the Civil War and the end of slavery were necessary if the nation Washington brought into its own was to survive. Brown and Tubman, however, chose methods different from Washington's. They were willing to use violence to attack the social evil of slavery. For John Brown, a strict Calvinist as to moral determination, violence came to be a strategic method by which he meant to raise a slave rebellion and destroy the slave system.[20] Harriet Tubman, in her way, was more the organizer and leader of the means by which slaves could escape the American South. Yet, like Brown, she did not shrink from arming herself when necessary to protect the hundreds of slaves she guided along the Underground Railroad.

Though Brown was white, he understood and genuinely appreciated Negro slaves and freedpeople, some of whom, from time to time, lived with him and his family. Tubman of course knew the situation of the slaves she led out from bondage because she herself was a fugitive. Her many trips down South and back with escaped slaves led to her becoming known as the Moses of her people.[21] This moniker invites comment on the culture of those who embodied the dark thoughts of the dominant mid-nineteenth-century American culture. Slaves not only understood the Biblical stories, but they passed on stories that demonstrated a long cultural tradition that has been traced back to Africa.[22] Among these are the trickster tales, of which the best known is the story of Tar-Baby and Br'er Rabbit, in which he aims to catch Br'er Rabbit by setting a Tar-Baby in his path whereupon he himself is tricked by being stuck in the tar. All seems lost for Br'er Rabbit but then the trick is turned when he says "please, Br'er Fox, don't fling me in dat brier-patch." Br'er Fox does just that without realizing that a brier-patch is home to the rabbit, who scratches his way free.

Trickster tales are more than children's stories. In the day, they were sophisticated narratives widely shared in slave communities—stories that contributed to the enslaved Negro's arsenal of tricks they could turn on white masters for what gain could be had. Frederick Douglass for one learned to read in a master's household in Baltimore by just such a trick.[23] Not incidentally, Toni Morrison used the fact that whites called black people tar-babies—a notion that is at play in her 1981 novel, *Tar Baby*. Morrison was, thus, enriching a long tradition of tactical narratives that became prominent in American literary culture. In the 1920s, Harlem Renaissance writers like Nella Larsen wrote literary fiction featuring black female tricksters.[24] In the 1930s, Zora Neale Hurston, the folklorist and cultural anthropologist, collected Negro trickster and other folk tales, and wrote trickster fiction in the vein of folk tales of Negro life in the deep south.[25] It might be a stretch to think of

---

20 Much of the following discussion of John Brown is indebted to David S. Reynolds, *John Brown, Abolitionist: The Man Who Killed Slavery, Sparked the Civil War, and Seeded Civil Rights* (Vintage Books/Random House, 2005)—a book that is widely praised in large part because it so boldly defends the strong claims, enunciated in its subtitle, as to Brown's historic importance.
21 Catherine Clinton, *Harriet Tubman: The Road to Freedom* (Little Brown, 2004), chapter 6.
22 Henry Louis Gates, Jr., *The Signifying Monkey: A Theory of African American Literary Criticism* (Oxford University Press, 1988). Also, Lawrence W. Levine, "Patterns of African American Culture," in *The Unpredictable Past: Explorations in American Cultural History* (Oxford University Press, 1993), 35–136; but especially, 59–77 ["The Meaning of the Slave Trickster"].
23 David W. Blight, *Frederick Douglass: Prophet of Freedom* (Simon & Schuster, 2018), 37–42. Though his mistress in Baltimore voluntarily taught him reading, she had to keep the fact from the household's master who, when he found out, forced her to stop. In a sense they had to trick the master to pursue early literacy lessons. Douglass also learned language in his play with literate children in the household. See Frederick Douglass, *Life and Times of Frederick Douglass*, chapter 10.
24 Nella Larsen, *Quicksand* and *Passing* (Rutgers University Press, 1986). Larsen's two novels were originally published in 1928 and 1929, respectively.
25 Zora Neale Hurston, *Their Eyes Were Watching God* (J.B. Lippincott, 1937). Also, Hurston's memoir, *Dust Tracks on a Road* (J.B. Lippincott, 1942) is of particular interest.

the very serious and strategic John Brown as a trickster. But it is not hard to imagine how Harriet Tubman relied on trickster tactics to lead enslaved people through the thickets, where slavecatchers lurked, on the Underground Railroad to the North where they found freedom. At the least, both went about trying to destroy the slave system by using, or being willing to use, violence against the system's inherently violent ways.

John Brown: Righteous Terrorism

Even if John Brown was not self-consciously a trickster, he did turn the tables on whites by repaying their violence in kind. He was a righteous rebel against an evil but powerful dominating order. Brown, the radical Abolitionist, was both a proponent of violence against the Slave Caste System and an engaged practitioner of systematic terrorist politics. Yet, as W.E.B. Du Bois said of him, Brown was also a man of serious moral and personal values:

> John Brown was a stalwart, rough-hewn man, mightily yet tenderly carven. To his making went the stern justice of the Cromwellian "Ironside," the freedom-loving fire of a Welsh Celt, and the thrift of a Dutch housewife. And these very things it was—thrift, freedom, and justice—that early crossed the unknown seas to find Asylum in America. Yet, they came late, for before them came greed, and greed brought black slaves from Africa.[26]

Here is a picture of Brown, a man of well-settled American and Calvinist values, but also a picture framed by the social evil against which Brown fought and died. In respect to his role in the murderous attack on five proslavery men he orchestrated in May 1856 at Pottawatomie Creek, Kansas, Brown said: "I have only a short time to live, only one death to die, I will die fighting for this cause. There will be no peace in this land until slavery is done for."[27] But Brown did not think of his death as merely symbolic. It was also a political response to the slavery system. Brown said, at court on November 2, 1859, after he was sentenced to hang for the Harper's Ferry raid: "Now, if it is deemed necessary that I should forfeit my life for the furtherance of the ends of justice, and mingle my blood further with the blood of my children and with the blood of millions in this slave country whose rights are disregarded by wicked, cruel, and unjust enactments, I submit; so let it be done!"[28]

At first, Brown's violent attacks on proslavery people and institutions appear to have been a straightforward turning of the table on a violent system. But, deeper still, they were energized by a fierce strategy that called for violence to the point of murder when the time was right. As all strict Calvinists must, Brown had his own over-determined idea of history. The Pottawatomie killings were meant to teach a lesson by terrorist means. Proslavery men had killed antislavery people in Lawrence, Kansas. Pottawatomie was their just dessert.

But the question remains: Why was John Brown in Kansas in the first place? His home was in North Elba, New York. The answer turns on the conjuncture of two seemingly

---

26 W.E.B. Du Bois, *John Brown* (George W. Jacobs & Company of Philadelphia, 1909), 15. Compare Henry David Thoreau's similar portrait of Brown in "A Plea for Captain John Brown" (1859) in *Walden and Other Writings of Henry David Thoreau* (The Modern Library, 1992), 717–744.

27 Quote is from a talk given by Brown after the Pottawatomie massacre he led in the Kansas territory on May 24–25, 1856. Brown's words were probably spoken on August 30, 1856 after another battle in Bleeding Kansas; see *Battle of Osawatomie*, Kansas State Historical Society at www.kshs.org/kansapedia/battle-of-osawatomie/19722

28 John Brown's *Final Speech* upon his conviction at his trial on November 2, 1859, www.gilderlehrman.org/sites/default/files/inline-pdfs/05508.051_FPS.pdf

different but inexorably joined structural circumstances that simultaneously inspired and tormented the young American nation in its first full century of independence. These two—one so promising, the other so troubling—were made possible by two structural realities of American history: *first*, the purchase and settling of America's vast western territories; and *second*, the nation's oldest political crisis between Free and Slave holding factions. Across the early decades of the nineteenth century, the deep structural conflict between the promise of the prairies and the dirty soil of the cotton South was always teasing the dream of a good and orderly continental nation. Until the Civil War, open conflict was, for the most part, held at bay. When the Western territories came ready to be states in the Union, it had to be determined whether they would be Free or Slave. Then the hell broke into the open.

The crisis came to a head in 1820 when Missouri was readying for admission to the Union. Missouri, on the near edge of the Great Plains, was a territory bordering to the North a free state, Illinois (admitted in 1818), and, to the South, slave states, Kentucky and Tennessee (both admitted in the 1790s). Which would Missouri become? The Missouri Compromise in 1820 settled the matter with a degree of equity by setting the line between Freed and Slave States at parallel 36°30′ or, roughly, a line cutting across Tennessee and Kentucky to the West at the Mississippi River and beyond. The Compromise was that Maine was admitted as Free and Missouri as a Slave State. The 1820 Compromise held uncertainly for some three decades. Yet, as with all flawed political compromises, the terms were vulnerable to the very social forces they were meant to settle.

As the Western plains were filling with settlers, land was made available by the taking of land from people native to the plains. The most notorious of these land thefts was, of course, Andrew Jackson's Indian Removal Act of 1830. From then on until December 29, 1890 when some 300 Lakota Sioux men, women, and children were slaughtered at Wounded Knee, the history of the American West was fraught with official pillage, government sponsored displacement, and military assassination of the West's native populations. Hence, still another layer of America's unconscious collective mind played out in the nation's deep structural racism.

The lands west of the Mississippi River were, thereby, settled amid the tension between the nation's contradictory structural aspects—on the one hand, the extraordinary promise of a virtually limitless, looming future in the West and, on the other, America's economic investment in racial differences. Black slaves were the indispensable source of ultra-cheap field labor on the South's land. They produced the commodity that, more than tobacco and sugar, was the nation's first mass produced commodity that generated the early modern capital surplus of a nation that would become, by century's end, the rising core of global capitalism. In the beginning, everything was land. The vast plains of the West and the cotton fields in the South were recto and verso of the nation's geographical imagination that energized, for better or worse, its cultural and economic histories. Though slavery was the foremost public issue in respect to admission to the Union of territories on the Plains, then much the same, the lands taken from native peoples were always in the background as the ghosts of dead and wounded people from whom it was taken.

In the decade before the Civil War, the right of new Western states to choose freedom for all or slavery came to the fore with the Kansas-Nebraska Act of 1854—an ill-intended act of Congress that repealed the fragile accords of the Missouri Compromise. The Kansas-Nebraska Act created two territories (not yet states) that were allowed to determine whether they would permit slavery or not. The fate of these territories was left to the will of their settlers. There were two consequences. For one, settlers demanded access to lands granted by treaty to the native nations. For another, the Kansas territory, in particular, was exposed to settlement and intrusion by pro-slavery agitators from Missouri. The result was that the

Kansas Territory became a battleground between "Free Staters" and "Border Ruffians." From the year of the Kansas-Nebraska Act in 1854 until the start of the Civil War in 1861, Kansas came to be known by tropes of violence, among them: "bleeding Kansas."

Already by 1850 John Brown's commitment to destroying slavery by any means necessary was a well-settled disposition. This was when Brown became definitively the American Cromwell—a Calvinist so fixated on a systemic evil that violence, even murder, was called for. Yet Brown's ways and means were different from Cromwell's. Brown was the one with the morally superior position. Oliver Cromwell writing of his leadership of the slaughter of some 3,500 Irish in 1649, said:

> I am persuaded that this is a righteous judgment of God upon these barbarous wretches, who have imbrued their hands in so much innocent blood and that it will tend to prevent the effusion of blood for the future, which are satisfactory grounds for such actions, which otherwise cannot but work remorse and regret.[29]

By contrast, Brown's violence was not for revenge but for a far more enlightened purpose, as he wrote to his wife on December 2, 1859 just before his hanging: "I have been whipped, as the saying is, but I am sure I can recover all the lost capital occasioned by that disaster by only hanging a few moments by the neck; I feel quite determined to make the utmost out of this defeat."[30] The sentence of death for Brown was for his role in the Harper's Ferry raid in which seventeen people died. Just the same, he claimed in his Final Speech on the occasion of his sentencing on November 2, 1859: "I never did intend murder, or treason, or the destruction of property, or to excite or incite slaves to rebellion, or to make insurrection."[31] In one sense, this was a gratuitous statement because he and those who joined him in Pottawatomie in 1856 murdered five Missouri proslavery men. Brown, thus, was motivated by at least some degree of Cromwell's violence as religiously justified revenge.

But, granting Cromwell's influence on Brown, and given the difference in their principles and methods, what else may have been central to Brown's moral vision? The answer is suggested by David S. Reynolds' bold subtitle to *John Brown, Abolitionist: The Man Who Killed Slavery, Sparked the Civil War, and Seeded the Civil Rights Movement*. Such an expansive claim for Brown seems at first preposterous in its claim that John Brown was so central to American racial politics down to the twentieth century (and by implication, after). Yet, as Reynolds' book pursues its strong narrative line, the author makes a plucky case for what he calls his cultural historical method (which could just as well be considered a cultural sociology) of Brown's place in history. Reynolds leads with his argument for Oliver Cromwell as Brown's philosophical anchor.[32] Then, he makes the case for Brown's centrality to the most persistent, unyielding cultural confusion in American history with a nuanced discussion of the use Brown made of the prehistory of what could be called

---

29 Cromwell to Speaker Lenthall, 17 September 1649, *The Cromwell Association* at www.olivercromwell.org/wordpress/cromwell-to-speaker-lenthall-17-september-1649
30 For context to these words and other words in his last days, see David S. Reynolds *John Brown, Abolitionist: The Man Who Killed Slavery, Sparked the Civil War, and Seeded the Civil Rights Movement* (Vintage, 2005), especially his remarkable chapter 15, "The Passion."
31 As before: www.gilderlehrman.org/sites/default/files/inline-pdfs/05508.051_FPS.pdf—among other sources.
32 David S. Reynolds, *John Brown, Abolitionist*, 18–19; also 164–65.

righteous terrorism.³³ Whatever may have been the contributions of Cromwell's historical example, Jonathan Edwards' sermon "Sinners in the Hands of an Angry God" was for Brown the more important resource for his Calvinist activism.

Still, just as important as these influences on Brown were, more significant historical figures lent nuance to Brown's strategic thinking. Toussaint Louverture's 1791 leadership of the Black rebellion against French colonizers in Haiti that led to independence in 1804—and, of course, Nat Turner's slave rebellion in Virginia in 1831—inspired Brown's tactical principle that Blacks in oppressed conditions with little or no power are able, through violent rebellion, to unsettle dominant populations of colonizers and slaveholders. It is well known that, after Haiti's revolution and Nat Turner's rebellion, whites in the ante-bellum American South lived with the fear that they too could be overthrown by their slaves. Though Reynolds concedes that Brown's reading was "broad not deep," he also makes a compelling case for Brown's careful understanding of the example of the *maroons*—black slaves brought by Spanish colonizers to South Carolina in 1526 who fled into the wilderness even before the Spanish colony failed.³⁴ Hence the English term "maroon" comes from the Spanish *cimarrones* for "wild". The maroons were, thus, an early legendary source for the ante-bellum South where fugitive slaves fled into the wild woods and swamps.³⁵ Clearly Brown learned from their example. In this sense Harriet Tubman and all those she led North were maroons disappearing into the wilderness, seeking the Underground Railroad to Canada.

To put it simply, Brown's primal sources of Calvinism, Oliver Cromwell and Jonathan Edwards, took on strategic force in his knowledge from the witness of the maroons, Toussaint Louverture, and Nat Turner.³⁶ From these models Brown formulated his tactics for the Harper's Ferry Raid—to mobilize slaves, to flee with them to the mountains of today's West Virginia, and to inspire other slaves (and the nation as a whole) by attacking the Federal armory that served as the focus of the raid while also arming mobilized slaves.³⁷ Brown failed of course. Slaves did not rebel in significant numbers. Federal troops took back the Armory. Brown and his cadre were captured. Some seventeen people had been killed. He was hanged. Yet, failure aside, Brown had thoughtfully, if not wisely, settled upon a serious theory of righteous terrorism.

In our day, still early in the twenty-first century, many terrorist movements are anything but righteous, especially not among the likes of the Islamic State of Iraq and the Levant (ISIS) and other fundamentalist Islamic terrorists that claim high righteous purpose based on distorted interpretations of the Qur'an. Much the same can be said of Hindu nationalists in India and fringe, extreme right Christian nationalists in the US. But in Brown's day what he meant to do could well have been, as Reynolds argues, a morally grounded combustible for the Civil War; then too, a century later, for the Civil Rights Movement, notably when nonviolence gave way to the Black Power Movement after 1966. Oddly, Brown's righteous terrorism does seem to have contradicted the principle behind his claim at sentencing for the Harper's Ferry Raid that he intended no violence or harm, nor that he meant to incite slaves

---

33 *Ibid*, 98–99; and all of chapter 6 on Brown's plan is an historically helpful presentation of John Brown's strategic theory. "Righteous terrorism" is my expression, used to represent my view that Edward's Calvinism was likely more central than Cromwell's to Brown. Reynolds prefers to describe Brown's theory as a guerrilla action.

34 *Ibid*, 106, and 106–109 on the *maroons* and, more generally, Haiti and Toussaint L'Ouverture.

35 Reynolds's succinct discussion of these early sources for Brown's strategic theory is at *ibid*, 106–110.

36 And on Brown's regard for Nat Turner see *Reynolds*, 54–55, 167–68 and, especially, 408 for Charles Langston's observation that "He admired Nat Turner as well as George Washington."

37 *Ibid*, 296 and the whole of chapter 12. Also, Du Bois, *John Brown*, 204–253.

to rebellion. Many in the day argued that he was mentally ill. But none who did studied this contradiction. In a sense, his ultimate righteous purpose was to free slaves and end slavery, not to kill or be killed. This leads to one of the most important qualities of Brown's thinking and being.

Brown thought and lived as if he were Black. Again, Reynolds on Brown's crucial difference from other serious abolitionists like William Lloyd Garrison and Wendell Phillips: "Brown was the only one to model both his own lifestyle and plans for abolishing slavery on black culture. ... He immersed himself in black culture, learning much from it and giving much back to it."[38] This fact of Brown's life is important both to American culture's tendency to dismiss or ignore him and his ultimate importance to the nation's cultural history. It is not hard to imagine that, in Brown's day and since, there was a pervasive cultural resistance to supposing that a white man who did not shrink from violence was necessary to the destruction of slavery—and that such a man must be somehow pathological.

Yet, Brown's legacy did live on in the higher culture of the nation—most strikingly is the fact that Julia Ward Howe's 1861 *Battle Hymn of the Republic* became a Union anthem in the Civil War as a version of the just as famous anthem to Brown's martyrdom: "John Brown's body lies a-mouldering in the grave, His soul is marching on"—a line that Frederick Douglass quoted late in life in 1892 to accentuate John Brown's enduring value to the nation. That the lines could serve as a kind of countercultural national anthem long after the Civil War suggests the degree to which the dominant white culture could not ignore John Brown. Still, it is also not a stretch to suggest that Brown was the white nation's worst nightmare—a dream arising from the collective unconscious of its common culture. Brown wrote his way into the future of America's collective mind by well thought-through actions against an evil system.

Harriet Tubman: A Practical Genius Ready to Fight

Harriet Tubman secured her place in American culture by the sheer courage of returning through the thickets of racial evil to rescue those left behind. She returned "time and again."[39] She saved some hundreds of enslaved people from the thorns of the South's demonic ways with black workers exploited for the South's place in the global cotton empire. Even if the number saved was only one hundred, the number is small when considered against the millions enslaved. Yet, it is a prodigious number when measured by the efforts of a single woman, herself ever at risk, who faced the danger of countless trips back and down to lead others forward and upward.

Together Brown and Tubman stand out over time as figures who, both, engaged the culture's cavernous racism in ways that went well beyond lectures, sermons, or moral platitudes. They were action figures who acted in ways that even the most liberal of cultural patriots could not fathom. Yet, in important ways they were different. Their differences were due, in no small part, to the fact that Harriet had been a slave who until the end of the Civil War remained technically a fugitive. She was continuously on the run. She had little time for formal or informal education. She was, thereby, illiterate. John Brown, however, though not a scholar, was highly literate in the sense that he set aside enough time in his crowded

---

38 *Ibid*, 118.
39 There are various differing estimates of the number of rescue trips she made to the South and back again, but the best practice by a reliable scholar like Catherine Clinton is to keep that number open by saying that Tubman returned "time and again." The number of slaves freed is equally hard to determine, though Clinton says that it may have been as many as 750. Again, see "The Moses of Her People," chapter 6 in Clinton, *Harriet Tubman: The Road to Freedom*.

daily life to read in order to study so he could think seriously about what he meant to do. This is not to say that Tubman utterly lacked her own thoughtful method for destroying the slave system. One might say, without underestimating her intellectual determination, that her method was clear enough as to strategy but ever more resourceful as to tactics. Brown's well formulated strategy for the raid on Harper's Ferry was well-enough grounded in both religious and historical literatures but it was a tactical disaster. Strategically, it allowed him to fulfill the terms of a morbidly Calvinist purpose of getting hanged in order to end the slave-system. If David S. Reynolds is right, the failure at Harper's Ferry galvanized opposition to slavery, incited the Civil War, and in the long run led to a more aggressive civil rights movement a century later.

By contrast to Brown, Harriet Tubman was a genius at making her way through the wild woods to the upper South and north to St. Catherines, Ontario, where she had established a home that served as the terminal of the Underground Railroad (UGRR, as it came to be known). Depending on where in Maryland she met slaves for the journey on foot, or by boat and train, to Canada, the one-way to freedom took many days if entirely by walking, mostly at night through swamps and undergrowth, over hills and around centers of population.[40] When she did not stay over in St. Catherines, Harriet[41] all but immediately turned around, often for another rescue. John Brown had a firm strategic plan, well enough informed by reading to qualify in our time as a social theory of radical politics. This, in spite of the prior fact of his life, that Brown was rightly known for his disciplined practical identification with Black people from whom he derived hints and context for his tactical actions against slavery from Pottawatomie to Harper's Ferry. His actual assaults were relatively few in contrast to Harriet Tubman's multiple rescue missions back and forth between the upper South and Canada. Each of her missions had its own risks and challenges. It was as if she was instructed by a divine voice on how to escape traps set for her and those she was leading to freedom. One story, reported at length with emendations on the basis of a conversation with Harriet herself, tells of the peril she faced:

> … And so, hunted and hiding and wandering, they found themselves at last at the entrance of the long bridge that crosses the river at Wilmington, Delaware. No time had been lost in posting up advertisements and offering rewards for the capture of these fugitives; for Joe in particular the reward offered was very high. First a thousand dollars, then fifteen hundred, and then two thousand, "an' all expenses clar an' clean for his body in Easton Jail." This high reward stimulated the efforts of the officers who were usually on the lookout for escaping fugitives, and the added rewards for others of the party, and the high price set on Harriet's head, filled the woods and highways with eager hunters after human prey. When Harriet and her companions approached the long Wilmington Bridge, a warning was given them by some secret friend, that the advertisements were up, and the bridge was guarded by police officers. Quick as lightning the plans were formed

---

40 Google maps estimates the distance from Eastern Shore Maryland is just less than 500 miles; if on foot on today's roads, the walk would take 158 hours or about 4 days walking *without relief*, 8 days walking at night only. Thus, even when the journeys were by water or by actual railroads (often they were), there were delays waiting for connections.

41 Here and elsewhere academic norms would have me refer to "Tubman" not "Harriet," yet it seems wrong even disrespectful to do so. When even now one spends so much time with her story, it seems wrong to use the academic formality for her, especially since those on the UGRR who knew of her called her Moses or General, later on. It is not that she was intimate with all who knew and worked with her but that she was such a force that 'Harriet' seemed more respectful as often happens with unusually great leaders like, for examples, Alexander or Abe or Ike.

in her ready brain, and the terrified party were separated and hidden in the houses of different friends, till her arrangements for their further journey were completed.

There was at that time residing in Wilmington an old Quaker, whom I may call my "friend," for though I never saw his face, I have had correspondence with him in reference to Harriet and her followers. This man, whose name was Thomas Garrett, and who was well known in those days to the friends of the slave, was a man of a wonderfully large and generous heart, through whose hands during those days of distress and horror, no less than three thousand self-emancipated men, women and children passed on their way to freedom. He gave heart, hand, and means to aid these poor fugitives, and to our brave Harriet he often rendered most efficient help in her journeys back and forth.

He was the proprietor of a very large shoe establishment; and not one of these poor travelers ever left his house without a present of a new pair of shoes and other needed help. No sooner had this good man received intelligence of the condition of these poor creatures, than he devised a plan to elude the vigilance of the officers in pursuit and bring Harriet and her party across the bridge. Two wagons filled with bricklayers were engaged and sent over; this was a common sight there and caused no remark. They went across the bridge singing and shouting, and it was not an unexpected thing that they should return as they went. After nightfall (and, fortunately, the night was very dark) the same wagons recrossed the bridge, but with an unlooked-for addition to their party. The fugitives were lying close together on the bottom of the wagons; the bricklayers were on the seats, still singing and shouting; and so they passed the guards, who were all unsuspicious of the nature of the load contained in the wagons, or of the amount of property thus escaping their hands.[42]

This is but one of many reliable accounts of Harriet's tactical genius deployed in dangerous situations where friends and fellow agents on the UGRR warned of announcements of rewards for the capture of fugitives and of the police at the bridge—among them the Quaker Underground Railroad agent, Thomas Garrett, and the bricklayers he organized to help the slaves and their Moses.

Genius is the right word for Harriet Tubman, if it is granted that genius includes a powerful intuitive wisdom, both intellectual and spiritual. Tubman was religious, as was Brown. But she was not, even remotely, a Calvinist. Her faith was nurtured by the evangelical awakenings that were current in slave communities of the day.[43] She was illiterate, so what she knew of the Bible was heard in local gatherings both on plantations and along the ways she traveled. She was widely respected by those who knew her and had heard of her. One of the most commonly quoted observations was by abolitionist Thomas Garrett that "he had never met a person of any color, who had more confidence

---

42 For this close to first-hand account, see Sarah H. Bradford, *Harriet: The Moses of Her People* (Geo. R. Lockwood & Son, 1886), 43–45; also https://docsouth.unc.edu/neh/harriet/harriet.html. Bradford's book is based on the notes and recollections of conversations with Harriet Tubman which were, naturally, edited to an unknown extent. In particular it is hard to know the status of the one line put in quotes and meant to be read as Negro dialectic. It was common in the day for white writers like Bradford to "translate" sayings into what they considered Negro dialect. This being said it is fair to assume that she and Harriet (who was famously a generous conversationalist) were friendly. This was the second of two books Bradford wrote on Tubman. The first was *Scenes from the Life of Harriet Tubman* (W.J. Moses, 1869), which quotes Harriet but to a lesser extent than the 1889 version and is shorter, less well written. Also, see Clinton, *Harriet Tubman*, 90.
43 For an excellent discussion of Harriet's religious formation, see Kate Clifford Larson, *Bound for the Promised Land: Harriet Tubman, Portrait of an American Hero* (One World/Random House, 2005 [2003]), 44–54.

in the voice of God as spoken direct to her soul ... and her faith in a Supreme Power truly was great."[44]

Hers was the rarest of gifts—a spiritual genius that informed Harriet's intuitive practical genius for finding a way out of lurking dangers:

> Who would suspect a fugitive with such a price set upon her head, of rushing at railway speed into the jaws of destruction? With a daring almost heedless, she went even to the very village where she would be most likely to meet one of the masters to whom she had been hired; and having stopped at the Market and bought a pair of live fowls, she went along the street with her sunbonnet well over her face, and with the bent and decrepit air of an aged woman. Suddenly on turning a corner, she spied her old master coming towards her. She pulled the string which tied the legs of the chickens; they began to flutter and scream, and as her master passed, she was stooping and busily engaged in attending to the fluttering fowls. And he went on his way, little thinking that he was brushing the very garments of the woman who had dared to steal herself, and others of his belongings.[45]

To Harriet's spiritual and practical geniuses was added a supernatural courage that allowed her without fear to come face to face with the beast who would most want to devour her. Others would have quaked, but she calmly passed close by and set the chickens loose on him. It was the kind of thing hard to imagine in our day. In recent hard times, the courage of some Jews and their gentile protectors before the Nazis comes close. The difference even here is that Harriet Tubman did what she did alone except for the station masters and scattered agents of the Underground Railroad. A good many people, white and black, were crucial helpers. She galvanized them all.

Harriet was also brilliant at organizing and participating in what today we would call an actor-network.[46] She was the Moses who led the way and brought countless agents into her network from 1851 until 1859. 1859 was the year that William H. Seward (who would become Lincoln's Secretary of State) gave her favorable terms that allowed her to buy a home on his property outside Auburn, New York. Seward was part of Harriet's network. 1859 was also the year after she had met with Frederick Douglass in Rochester. Then too, in 1858, Douglass had a long strategic meeting with John Brown before he declined the following year to participate in Brown's raid. The same year that John Brown met with her in St Catherines, Ontario before his failure in 1859 at Harper's Ferry.[47]

Douglass, Brown, and Tubman confided in one another.[48] Given their prominence in the anti-slavery movements, it is hard not to think of them as the legendary figures whose methods triangulated opposition to the slave system. Frederick Douglass hints at this in this letter to Harriet in August 1868:

---

44 Quoted by Larson, *Bound for the Promised Land: Harriet Tubman*, 46. Larson also provides an excellent discussion of Harriet Tubman's particular brand of evangelical Christianity in the pages surrounding this quote. Also see Clinton and Bradford biographies, among other sources.
45 Bradford, *Harriet: The Moses of Her People*, 34–35.
46 Bruno Latour, *Reassembling the Social: An Introduction to Actor-Network Theory* (Oxford University Press, 2005).
47 The best timeline for these and other dates for Harriet Tubman's life is in Larson, *Bound for the Promised Land*, 300–304. For Douglass, see *Douglass: Autobiographies* (Library of America, 1994), 1049–1077.
48 A good source for Harriet Tubman's relations with John Brown, is Larson, 156–160, even better is Bradford, 96–98; and for Douglass' esteem for her see his 1868 letter to Harriet in Bradford (1889), 135 and Bradford (1869), 7. The quote just below are lines from that letter.

The midnight sky and the silent stars have been the witnesses of your devotion to freedom and of your heroism. Excepting John Brown – of sacred memory – I know of no one who has willingly encountered more perils and hardships to serve our enslaved people than you have. Much that you have done would seem improbable to those who do not know you as I know you.[49]

Douglass was, to be sure, *the* public voice of the movement. Brown necessarily kept mostly out of the public eye because, as his method of righteous terrorism took shape, he had to live and plan underground in order to sneak up on those he meant to wound or kill for just purposes. Harriet was *a* prominent voice on the lecture circuit where she gave compelling accounts of her exploits on the Underground Railroad. She was, as we know, not a strategic theorist as were Brown and Douglass.

Harriet Tubman worked intuitively by very practical actions on the ground—actions that did not exclude the threat of violence. Bradford quotes her as saying: "Dead niggers tell no tales; you go on or die!"[50] One of the most striking stories to which this line applied tells of a time when Harriet was guiding twenty-one escaped slaves north by a path that required spending all day and evening in a swamp. They were cold, wet, and famished. One among them announced he was turning back to take his chances with his master. Harriet knew that those chances were slim to none and that his return would put all in the group in danger. She pulled out the revolver she often carried and said: "Move or die!" He moved and escaped to Canada with the others.[51]

By 1860, it was not by chance, especially with war in the offing, that Harriet's efforts on behalf of those enslaved began to change. In 1850 the despicable Fugitive Slave Act was passed by the United States Congress. One of the episodes Harriet told of in her speaking events was of her part in the rescue of a fugitive slave, Charles Nalle, on April 27, 1860 in Troy, New York. She was in town that day to visit a cousin when she heard a commotion. Harriet quickly investigated and learned that local police were attending to the letter of the Fugitive Slave Act by attempting to lead Nalle away. A crowd of townspeople blocked the police, whereupon he was led to the courthouse. A judge ruled in favor of the police. Thereupon Harriet became the leader of the protesting crowd. Soon there was fighting. Harriet and others were injured. Yet she fought on:

> Tubman gave the signal to the crowd below, then rushed down the stairs and made an attempt to wrestle Nalle from the grasp of the sheriff and his deputies as they were exiting the building. Hanging on the neck of one officer, Tubman began choking him, but she was beaten back. Again, she struck, fighting to keep hold of Nalle as the sheriff and other officers dragged him into the angry crowd. ... A fight ensued. Nalle and Tubman were dragged and beaten as the crowd tried to pry him from the grip of the officers. ... Pistols were drawn, and one officer threatened to kill a rescuer he had grabbed from the crowd, instantly a knife was drawn under the throat of the policeman, and the pistol was dropped.[52]

Eventually, Nalle escaped to freedom. The local newspaper in Troy reported favorably on Tubman's defiant example that encouraged many colored women to join the struggle. Word

---

49 Letter from Frederick Douglass to Harriett Tubman (Rochester, August 29, 1868) at www.blackpast.org/african-american-history/1868-letter-from-frederick-douglass-to-harriet-tubman/
50 Bradford, *Harriet: The Moses of Her People*, 33.
51 The account is reported by Clinton, *Harriet Tubman: The Road to Freedom*, 90–91.
52 Larson, *Bound for the Promised Land*, 181.

spread. Harriet became a national figure. The fate of fugitive slaves in the North became a national *cause célèbre*.

Then, almost exactly a year later, the Civil War began on April 12, 1861. Harriet was thereby forced to quit the Underground Railroad. She turned to service for the Union armies—caring for the needs of the soldiers. More in line with her experience in the 1850s, she applied her geographical knowledge as a conductor of the Underground Railroad to work as a spy and a scout for Union forces in the South. Most famously, she engineered the assault by boat on plantations up the Combahee River in South Carolina. Major plantations in the area were burned and 700 slaves were liberated with no harm to them or their rescuers. The mission was perfectly executed.

Late in life, Harriet was able to pay off the mortgage on her Auburn home, after her benefactor, William H. Seward, had died. In 1896, she determined that her home in Auburn should become a home for older and ill people of color. In 1903, she gave the property over to the AME Zion Church in Auburn with the expectation that it would remain in service for the needy. She died on March 10, 1913.

Americans Forced to Think Differently of America

The Civil War was a cut that had to be made for there to have been some hope of healing the effects of the nation's original sin. Whatever skeptics might think, slavery was there from the beginning of the first possibility of an America. What the nation came to be some two centuries after 1619 was a body politic riven under the skin. In the last years of the Revolutionary Generation (roughly 1775–1826) the pain of that cut was suppressed as the new nation knit itself together. Yet, even then, half of the states were beholden to a slave labor economy. After the Missouri Compromise in 1820 and the opening of the Western territories to inclusion in the already torn Union, the 1619 wound began to ooze subcutaneous pus. In 1854, the Kansas-Nebraska Act tore through the thin skin. Once it became necessary to assign freedom of choice as to slavery or freedom to the potential states among the Western territories there was no way to dam the bleeding—in Kansas at first, later the nation. The Dred Scott decision of 1857, then the Lincoln-Douglas debates in 1858, and the election of Abraham Lincoln late in 1860 made war inevitable, not in the sense that Civil War was either a logical conclusion or a determination ordained by some higher power—but inevitable in the sense that the global time of America's first settlements foreshadowed the structural fracture of its TimeSpace. America in the beginning did not spring up *sui generis* on the eastern edge of a vast wilderness. The wilderness was not wild. The first settlements in America, as we now know, were settled by European whites as part of the global thrust of European states across the North Atlantic in search of profitable mineral and agricultural resources. America, therefore, was settled according to proto capitalist purposes that in the South soon enough flourished. It was not long before cotton, sugar, and tobacco production grew great enough to become the nation's first global products that made possible the capital surplus which, late in 1800s, made the nation a leading global power. The Civil War was a conjuncture of all the historical times that created the defining lexicon of the nation's destiny.

The Civil War, thus, was much more than a war between North and South. It was also a war between a rising industrial region and a stubbornly agrarian South. Hence, if South against North, then slave-farmed cotton land in the South versus the vast settler-invaded wilderness to the West; then, by consequence, an unstable relation between the past as possibility and the future as promise. Then too, agricultural origins built by a social evil rose toward an asymptote where they could never quite join with industrial growth based on ingenuity—so too, in the interstices of the nation, the dilemma that a people of high moral self-regard were, and still are, at unbreachable odds with an economic system based on capital greed and indifference to those it excludes.

In other words, to say that the nation has always been divided is also to say that it has been multiply torn along a number of vectors that have converted a relatively straightforward either/or dichotomy into an unfathomable matrix of cross-cutting trajectories of social times and competing dispositions. The vectors comprise the historical leavings of different times (1619, 1775, 1789, 1803, 1820, 1830, 1854, 1861, 1865, 1873, and so on) that have punctuated the nation's many spatial relations (Atlantic Massachusetts, Atlantic Virginia, Colonial Britain, Great Plains, New Territories in the Pacific West, South-North, North-South, and so on). These and other vectors reinvent themselves endlessly, or so it would seem. Together, they are among the elements of America's TimeSpace—an unthinkably complicated matrix of moving parts. Individuals, thereby, live on several vectors at the same time. In the Civil War, families mourned equally for their dead sons, cousins, or nephews who fought each other—one for the Union, the other for the Confederacy. As almost everyone living in a societal mix like this must know (more or less consciously), such a system leaks through its pores. Identities, friendships, clubs and schools, neighborhoods and towns—and all the countless institutions small and large, not to mention the individuals trying to find their way—are never able to maintain perfectly well-defined borders as members, citizens, self-identities, and all of the like. These skins must breathe. They are therefore open to all manner of intrusions from adjacent porous skins.

This may well seem a highfalutin way to characterize the revelatory effect of the Civil War. Yet, when so much blood was shed and so many died over four long years, the aftereffects are not simply held as remembered horrors. They are necessarily inscribed in the deep tissue of the body torn. They remain as scars exposed when the political body attempts to wash away the scabs of its filthy past—or, alternatively, to memorialize the dead and the cause for which they died. Scrubbing and fantasizing are the two extreme ways of overcoming a cut so grave that it cannot be sutured.

The Civil War altered but did not eliminate the nation's original sin. Slavery was destroyed only to be replaced by a new form of slavery when Reconstruction was killed after 1873. Even when Jim Crow faded away, the nation remained torn by racial differences that in effect perpetuated the slave-master mentality[53] that is behind the anti-immigrant policies and prejudices have grown uglier than ever in the second decade of the twenty-first century. The suffering continues without an obvious ointment.

For severe chronic wounds of mind or body, it is necessary to expose the infected cut to fresh air. This is what John Brown and Harriet Tubman did with surgical precision. Brown's martyrdom was celebrated in the spoken words and song that turned Harper's Ferry into a monument reminding all of the evil of slavery. Harriet Tubman and those she organized and inspired were no less clear in cutting open how far and hard was the road to freedom.

---

53 The most vivid description of the slave-master mentality is in *Life and Times of Frederick Douglass: From 1817–1882*, part I, chapter 21. Here in a chapter entitled "Escape from Slavery," Douglass begins: "My condition during the year of my escape (1838) was comparatively a free and easy one, so far, at least, as the wants of the physical man were concerned; But the reader must bear in mind that my troubles from the beginning had been less physical than mental, and he will thus be prepared to find that slave life was adding nothing to its charms for me as I grew older, and became more and more acquainted with it." *Life and Times of Frederick Douglass: From 1817–1882*, in Henry Louis Gates, Jr., ed., *Frederick Douglass: Autobiographies* (Library of America/Random House, 1994), 635. The book can also be found @ https://oll.libertyfund.org/title/lobb-the-life-and-times-of-frederick-douglass-from-1817-1882

Brown and Tubman, and the others who joined them did more than open the wound for diagnosis. They were first among equals who emboldened others courageous enough to think differently about America's history and its future. To be sure, cultural thinking of this kind is necessarily fortuitous and uneven, not even close to a latter-day declaration of independence. John Brown and Harriet Tubman were fore-runners who made a difference—a difference that burrowed its way into post-Civil War American culture.

Once the evil of slavery and the suffering of the war were exposed the nation had to come to terms that its national order could not to be taken for granted. The Civil War—and those like John Brown and Harriet Tubman who exposed its deeper wound for what it was—contributed to the end of the ideology of a pure perfect national order. Wise and good people like these two do not choose to die or risk death for an abstract idea that flies in the face of realities on the ground—and none were as well grounded as John Brown and Harriet Tubman.

The Civil War was the conjuncture that established a new principle of social order in America. Thereafter, the innocent belief in social order as a possible permanent feature of American life became, at best, a cultural dream, not an attainable social fact. Then and there, naïve innocence had to face wide-awake guilt. A good century after the end of the Civil War, writers like Erving Goffman in his 1963 book, *Stigma: Notes on the Management of a Spoiled Identity*, formalized the concepts made necessary the century before by the Civil War. The subtitle hints at the generic social theory. Identities, whether of individuals or societies, are always spoiled; or better: social order is always defenseless before the disorders that intrude. As a consequence, when it comes to social things, order and disorder are always coupled in an interaction order. What order there may be is a vulnerable condition that arises from continuous interactions that always put it at risk. A social interaction order is not a dialectical synthesis so much as a never resolvable condition of life with others.

Such was the reality Americans had to live with and think about after the Civil War that, for all its tragic suffering, required a new sense of social reality—one in which interaction orders were also disorders wrought of the ever growing number of social identities in conflict with each other from which came too many exclusions upon which the nation's alabaster cities could not gleam. But before these new realities could be faced, the nation required a palliative that would heal the wounds by telling the truths a better America might think and sing. This was the contribution made by Walt Whitman and Frederick Douglass.

8 Balm for the Nation's Wounds
Frederick Douglass and Walt Whitman

What, to the American slave, is your Fourth of July?
I answer: a day that reveals to him, more than all other days in the year,
the gross injustice and cruelty to which he is a constant victim.
To him, your celebration is a sham; your boasted liberty, an unholy license;
your national greatness, your swelling vanity;
your sounds of rejoicing are empty and heartless;
your denunciations of tyrants, brass fronted impudence;
your shouts of liberty and equality, hollow mockery; your prayers and hymns,
your sermons and thanksgivings, with all your religious parade, and solemnity,
are to him, mere bombast, fraud, deception, and hypocrisy—a thin veil
to cover up crimes that would disgrace a nation of savages.
There is not a nation on earth guilty of practices, more shocking and bloody,
than are the people of these United States, at this very hour.
— *Frederick Douglass, What to the Slave Is the Fourth of July? 1852*

I celebrate myself, and sing myself,
And what I assume you shall assume,
For every atom belonging to me as good belongs to you. ...
The runaway slave came to my house and stopt outside,
I heard his motions crackling the twigs of the woodpile,
Through the swung half-door of the kitchen I saw him limpsy and weak,
And went where he sat on a log and led him in and assured him,
And brought water and fill'd a tub for his sweated body and bruis'd feet,
And gave him a room that enter'd from my own, and gave him some coarse clean clothes,
And remember perfectly well his revolving eyes and his awkwardness,
And remember putting plasters on the galls of his neck and ankles;
He staid with me a week before he was recuperated and pass'd north,
I had him sit next me at table, my fire-lock lean'd in the corner.
— *Walt Whitman, Song of Myself, 1855*

Ministers of Healing and Justice

Frederick Douglass *and* Walt Whitman? One might very well wonder what these two have to do with each other. Douglass, an escaped slave turned public figure; Whitman, a Brooklyn white boy grown into a poet—what indeed? The answer is that these two, in their different ways, were among the most prominent of those in the Civil War era to help Americans think

DOI: 10.4324/9781315210230-11

differently about America. It could even be said that they ministered to America by their faith in its transcending culture.

The years on either side of the War itself, from 1854 to 1873, overlapped with the nation's first great literary and philosophical movement—the Concord transcendentalists who, more than any other group, solidified America's foundational cultural principles. Those principles survive today, but after such a brutal war they could not, and have not, been able to stand alone. The Civil War changed everything that had come before. It was long in coming and, when it came, no one thought it would last four bloody years, much less a century and more after Appomattox. Those years of violent conflict essentially overwhelmed popular assumptions about what America had been and still could be. Not least among changes that could not be gotten around was the omnipresence of death—not just the dead in the War but the cultural death of aspects of America's foundational thought. No longer could Americans think of themselves simply as a nation of independent pragmatic individuals able to live in, and with, the demands of a vast natural world that transcended all that could be thought and done. But what were they to think and do in order to face a new seemingly morbid national reality?

Drew Gilpin Faust again: "We still work to live with the riddle that they—the Civil War dead and their survivors alike—had to solve so long ago."[1] The riddle of death remained unsolved well after the War. David Blight suggests that the memory of those deaths continued in the cultural contradictions the War aggravated and left for subsequent history to deal with:

> Americans faced an overwhelming task after the Civil War and emancipation: how to understand the tangled relationship between two profound ideas—*healing* and *justice*. On some level both had to occur but, given the potency of white supremacy in nineteenth century America, these two aims never developed in historical balance. One might conclude that the imbalance was simply America's inevitable historical condition, and thus celebrate the remarkable swiftness of the reunion. But sometimes reconciliations come with terrible costs, both intentional and unseen. The sectional reunion after so horrible a civil war was a political triumph by the late nineteenth century, but it could not have been achieved without the resubjugation of many of those people the war had freed from centuries of bondage. That is the tragedy lingering on the margins and infesting the heart of American history from Appomattox to World War I.[2]

Blight was being both prophetic and a bit too optimistic. The tragedy of the resubjugation of former slaves and their descendants continued well after World War I. Even now—however much the more acute aspects of this national tragedy may have softened—the pain remains poignant even in the face of those who would pretend it isn't.

Then too, there is little reason to believe that the deeper underlying forms of racism are amenable to healing much less to a more robust kind of justice. Those willing to learn have long ago learned that racism is not a simple matter of psychological or social prejudice—not even when racial prejudice breeds specific kinds of social and economic injustices like housing or employment discrimination. Racisms of all kinds have histories and histories leave behind the debris of their dirty business. As a result, the institutions they build on

---

1 Drew Gilpin Faust, *The Republic of Suffering: Death and the American Civil War* (Knopf, 2008), 271.
2 David W. Blight, "The Civil War in History and Memory," *The Chronicle of Higher Education* (Section 2, July 12, 2002), B8. [An extract from Blight's *Beyond the Battlefield: Race, Memory, and the American Civil War* (University of Massachusetts Press, 2002).]

ground thus soiled can never be more than superficially fair. They never come close to justice. They cannot.

American racism against people of African descent is part and parcel of the modern world-system—in particular, of its triumphant economic system. Capitalism, it hardly need be said, is viciously greedy. It seeks to accumulate evermore capital. It judges enterprises and their workers by a bottom line that is never good enough. If that, then no one who works in, or otherwise depends on, capitalist corporations or shops or firms is ever good enough. Eventually, if lucky, employees may get a farewell party at a Chinese restaurant and, perhaps, a watch or some other absurd gift to remind them of what once was. Soon enough those retired die to become spiritual brothers and sisters to field hands and workers—from slaves to early factory workers—who died serving ruthless masters who believed they owned their labor by right.

Whatever may be good about the modern world (and much is), little of it is good enough to heal the daily wounds the capitalist world-system inflicts on those who must live in it. And, while those subject to capitalism suffer—both the several rich and the many poor—none have suffered as have those who paid for the system in the first place. From the beginning, capitalism has exploited those who live on the periphery of the global core from which it runs the world. But, in America, even now, those who have come down from African slaves after 1619 bear the marks on their backs as if they too, like their ancestors, had been whipped by slave masters. The marks may be invisible to most naked white eyes. As when a father is walking with his very young daughter in a stroller and she must hear him say to white women who don't get it: "Don't touch the hair." Or, when, years later, the same child, whose name is Anna, is asked by a substitute teacher: "Is your name pronounced a certain way?" Or, when she is in high school, a therapist *begins* treatment with "So what do you feel about having white parents?" Or, years later, she applies for jobs for which she is over-qualified and is not hired, in one case because "You aren't fast enough at the cash register." (Needless to say, the person who got the job was white. How fast must one be to register?) Small things, some might say. Small perhaps, but they are etched on a person's spiritual skin and must be scratched. There's no balm for such an itch. So how could there be for a national itch?

Can there be a balm for the imperfect entanglement of healing and justice? If so, what might it be? Whatever it might be, it would have to be something that, even today, we have not yet seen—except perhaps for a glimmer here and there in the remote corners of America's times and spaces. Yet, since America has always aspired to be better than it could be, even in the worst of times, it is in the nature of how Americans think about America that they must imagine their nation healing, if not entirely justly. Many have, from time to time, but none quite like Frederick Douglass and Walt Whitman.

Douglass and Whitman, different though they were, stood out during and after the Civil War era as public figures qualified by experience and personal gifts to present truth to the times. Douglass, the fugitive slave, knew slavery first-hand by reading and hard work mastering the language to such an extent that he became America's unrivaled spokesman on the single most deadly continuous aspect of its culture—slavery and the racism that irritates its heartstrings. Whitman, the intellectual and personal wanderer to the corners of American life, who from his early years in Brooklyn did what few (except perhaps Ben Franklin) did to engage directly and respectfully with the many people of America—from freedpeople in the South to immigrant workers in the North—who were changing the demographic nature of the American people. Whitman was the poet who told stories in *Leaves of Grass* of that new America—stories told in ways that allowed Americans "to think anew their nature." Douglass, no less, was a poet of the spoken word who, like Emerson, was a star of the athenaeum circuit, but one who told not of an abstract Nature but of the broken bodies of slaves whose nature was not considered human.

In short, Douglass made the death of an old order real, as Whitman made an image of a possible new America real. Plus which, they are bound by the not incidental fact that both were poets. Whitman wrote prose poems; Douglass prose poetry.

Frederick Douglass, the Biography of Slavery and Exclusion

Frederick Douglass wrote three autobiographies—*The Narrative of Frederick Douglass* (1845), *My Bondage and My Freedom* (1855), and *Life and Times of Frederick Douglass* (1881). Each was a bestseller. Each was different from the others, reflecting both his changing perspective on his life's experiences and changing thinking about slavery and race in America. Each telling of his life's stories repeats, embellishes, and supplements details of his remembered life.[3]

Taken together, and read alongside his many speeches and published essays, and set against the history of the American nineteenth century, they represent Douglass' historical biography of slavery and racial exclusions in America. Though it is common these days to entitle a book as a biography of a subject not exactly personal,[4] it remains strange to encounter the phrase "a biography of slavery and racial exclusions." Yet, if ever there could be a biography of any social thing or of any being or material thing other than a human individual, it would be Frederick Douglass' personal history of slavery and racism as he lived them before and after the Civil War until his death in 1895. In his days, no one, not even Harriet Tubman, better understood and more thoroughly reflected on the emotional and practical conditions of the American slave system and racism after slavery—none, that is, until 1899 when W.E.B. Du Bois published *The Philadelphia Negro*. That Douglass did what he did in spreading the ugly story of American racism with no education other than what he taught himself, is a story of its own—a story, important to say, of just what it takes for the solitary individual to be joined (as all individuals are) with the grand story of the nations and worlds that provide them with the resources, supports, conflicts, ideas, and all else normal and necessary to life on the ground. Not only did Douglass tell versions of his own story three times over, but the thread of his story is emblematic (perhaps even paradigmatic) of the nature and effects of the American system of racial domination and exclusion.

Douglass did much more than write three biographies. His countless speeches, in all parts of the country (even in the South after the War), were written for publication. Many were published in national newspapers. He founded and edited periodicals and newspapers—*North Star* in Rochester, New York (from 1847); *Frederick Douglass' Paper* (after 1851); *Douglass' Monthly* (then, 1859); and served as an editor of *The New Era* (1870) and rolled it over to found *The New National Era* in Washington, D.C. (1871). He contributed widely to prestigious intellectual magazines, notably *North American Review, Harper's Weekly,* and *The Atlantic Monthly*. He was friendly with Abraham Lincoln, served as delegate to Haiti for Ulysses S. Grant's administration, was appointed Marshall of Washington, D.C. by Rutherford B. Hayes, headed the Freedman's Bank after it was ruined by unscrupulous silent partners, was appointed by Benjamin Harrison general consul and minister to

---

3 For a presentation of how Douglass altered his personal story in each of the three narratives, see John Stauffer, "On Genealogical Self-Fashioning," in John Stauffer and Henry Louis Gates, *The Portable Frederick Douglass* (Penguin Classics, 2016), 539–554.

4 For examples, Jack Miles, *God: A Biography* (Knopf, 1995); Fay Bound Alberti, *A Biography of Loneliness* (Oxford University Press, 2019).

Haiti. He was a spokesperson and political operative for the Republican Party until 1884 when the Democrat Grover Cleveland and his party swept the national elections and broke the already weakened hold Republicans had as the liberal party in national politics. He served as a member and leader in all the obvious Anti-Slavery organizations, and countless other black organizations including as a Trustee of Howard University, as well as a not so obvious leadership role in the National Council of Women. He was a committed feminist and suffragist. In addition to his relationships with John Brown and Harriet Tubman, he was friendly with Susan B. Anthony and Elizabeth Cady Stanton. Over the years, he became famous in Europe where he toured as speaker and traveler several times. Many of his projects were supported financially and personally by prominent Europeans who were attracted to his intellectual and rhetorical genius. Both Julia Griffiths Crofts, an English Abolitionist, and Ottilie Assing, a German radical feminist, lived from time to time with the Douglass family while helping with his publications and raising funds from abroad. All this and more. In short, no other Black person in the day achieved such international prominence; few have since.

What characterized Douglass' trajectory over a long life was his ability to change his life as the world changed—after his escape from slavery; after his fugitive status was resolved; after he perfected his rhetorical skills; after he rose to national prominence as America's most eminent lecturer on slavery; after the Civil War when slavery had been taken down and replaced by Jim Crow; after he became friends with Ida B. Wells and encouraged her campaign against lynching; after many of his many children died; after his faithful wife of many years Anna Murray Douglass died; after his second marriage late in life to Helen Pitts; after he suffered criticism for marrying a white woman; after joining Susan B. Anthony on the platform at a meeting of the National Council of Women on February 20, 1895, then dying at his Cedar Hill home that evening. Douglass suffered failures of course and many times was beaten and bruised by racist protestors who interrupted his speaking engagements, but he was relentless in meeting every challenge, personal and public, many of which led as much to pain and criticism as to pleasure and success. Only heart disease could stop him.

Douglass' Greatest Speech: What to the Slave Is the Fourth of July?

If one had to choose a single word to describe Douglass' underlying method in all he did, it would be "prophet." Where John Brown was a Calvinist and Harriet Tubman an evangelical, Frederick Douglass was an Old Testament Prophet. Though he could be comforting and intellectually rigorous as well as poetically elegant, Douglass was most Douglass when declaiming a jeremiad over the fate of black people in America. His most famous public lecture was just this—a lament cloaked in anger and disgust: *What to the Slave Is the Fourth of July?* David W. Blight begins his quite brilliant interpretation of this speech with a verse from the Prophet Jeremiah (1:10): "I have this day set thee over the nations and the kingdoms, to root out, and to pull down . . . to build, and to plant."[5] This precisely is the kind of prophet Frederick Douglass was in his Fourth of July homilies—stern in his condemnation of the white world, encouraging of the revolutionary possibilities of the Black world, and looking to the promise of a day when a better America could build and plant anew. *What to the Slave Is the Fourth of July?* was, in effect, a sermonic word for slaves and their heirs—a sermon meant to inspire a fresh declaration of independence.

---

5 David Blight, *Frederick Douglass: Prophet of Freedom* (Simon & Schuster, 2018), chapter 13, "By the Rivers of Babylon," 228.

Douglass delivered a version of *What to the Slave Is the Fourth of July?* many times, usually on July 5th, a black tradition in New York and beyond. His first was on July 5, 1852 presented to some 600 (mostly white) people in Corinthian Hall, Rochester, New York. The tradition was meant to signal that so long as Blacks were enslaved or otherwise excluded from white America, its Independence Day was to be respected but not unqualifiedly embraced. In 1852 the nation was still divided between the slave-holding South and a benighted North that, with notable exceptions, kept hands off the South's slave system. Just a year and months before July 5, 1852, the Fugitive Slave Act was passed by Congress on September 18, 1850. The Fugitive Slave Act not only allowed slave catchers to pursue their prey in the North, it also encouraged (required, some thought) northern police and constabularies to participate in the return of captured slaves. 1852 was a year in the eye of a national storm over slavery. Two years later, the Kansas-Nebraska Act of 1854, with all its gratuitous dusting of arithmetic logic dividing the West into two hypothetical parts, revealed the mockery of the 1820 Missouri Compromise. When the coin of the realm is true freedom, a nation cannot be fairly organized when the measuring rod is the extent to which slavery—the most abominable form of unfreedom—is to be apportioned. From 1820 on it was only a matter of time before a civil war would render America shredded by a storm of apparent doom.

Frederick Douglass rode the very winds he helped stir. Yet, unlike John Brown's sloppily planned and forlorn storm at Harper's Ferry, Douglass' was as well tended as a rhetorical storm could be. *What to the Slave Is the Fourth of July?* was composed in a way that the prophetic winds blew from diverse directions and forces. A long and potent middle declamation was set between an affirmative introduction and hopeful conclusion that graced his prophetic condemnations of the slave system and its racist entailments.

Douglass began by feigning his unworthiness to address the crowd at Corinthian Hall, a gesture that he immediately turned back on his audience: "The fact is, ladies and gentlemen, the distance between this platform and the slave plantation, from which I escaped, is considerable—and the difficulties to be overcome in getting from the latter to the former, are by no means slight."[6] Then Douglass turned to the Fourth of July and its meaning for America—an America that, he said, was "under a dark cloud," after which he deployed an extended metaphor of exceptional eloquence:

> There is consolation in the thought that America is young. —Great streams are not easily turned from channels, worn deep in the course of ages. They may sometimes rise in quiet and stately majesty, and inundate the land, refreshing and fertilizing the earth with their mysterious properties. They may also rise in wrath and fury, and bear away, on their angry waves, the accumulated wealth of years of toil and hardship. They, however, gradually flow back into the same old channel, and flow on serenely as ever. But while the river may not be turned aside, it may dry up, and leave nothing behind but the withered branch, and the unsightly rock, to howl in the abyss-sweeping wind, the sad tale of departed glory. As with rivers so with nations.[7]

This is Douglass at his disarmingly poetic best. The extended metaphor of the river plays with his audience. Rivers refresh and fertilize, rise in wrath and fury, flow back in the same old channel, [but also:] dry up and leave nothing behind. *As with rivers so with nations.*

---

6 All quotations from Douglass' *What to the Slave Is the Fourth of July?* are to be found in John Stauffer and Henry Louis Gates, editors, *The Portable Frederick Douglass* (Penguin Classics, 2016), 196.
7 *Ibid*, 197.

The prophet warns of the nation's possible sad fate of departed glory—a warning handed down on a day it is meant to celebrate its noble stately origins. Think of 600 white people in Corinthian Hall on that warm early summer afternoon. They came to hear Rochester's leading citizen who was famous the nation over. What they heard crept up on them, one supposes. They went to be entertained. They got a warning cloaked in poetic imagery and honest praise for the nation's founding fathers. "I cannot contemplate their great deeds with less than admiration."[8]

The section ends however with an unambiguous twist: "I leave, therefore, the great deeds of *your* fathers to other gentlemen whose claim to have been regularly descended will be less likely to be disputed than *mine*."[9] The simple *yours/mine* dichotomy firmly corrects the speech's opening lines of false embarrassment. His white audience is put in its historic place. Then and there the tone changes, even with the disarmingly apt lines of poetry from Henry Wadsworth Longfellow's "A Psalm of Life":

My business, if I have any here to-day, is with the present. The accepted time with God and his cause is the ever-living now.

"Trust no future, however pleasant,
  Let the dead past bury its dead;
Act, act in the living present,
  Heart within and God overhead."

We have to do with the past only as we can make it useful to the present and to the future.[10]

These lines transform Douglass' rhetorical *yours/mine* dichotomy into a sharp merciless point; and they open the section labeled "The Present" which, in turn, introduces the long main argument that denounces the white world in no uncertain terms.

Here is the mature Douglass in 1852 saying what, he thought, needed to be said about white America's celebration of its past; and saying with an intellectually acute understanding how memory works in the writing of personal *and* collective memorials. Depending on the past a group may have had, memories of surrounding national celebrations are likely to be false to any included group. Neither slaves nor their heirs can fully embrace a national past that excludes them. The white world's Fourth of July may be good enough in its own right, but it cannot (especially not in 1852) begin to get at the past of slavery, the past of blacks who then, and since, must look for the future in the present. Douglass' *yours/mine* dichotomy is a clever cut between the white and black worlds—a rhetorical gesture that sharpens the point of his most famous speech:

The Fourth of July is *yours*, not *mine*. *You* may rejoice, *I* must mourn. To drag a man in fetters into the grand illuminated temple of liberty and call upon him to join you in joyous anthems, were inhuman mockery and sacrilegious irony. Do you mean, citizens, to mock me by asking me to speak today? If so then there is a parallel to your conduct. And let me warn you that it is dangerous to copy the example of a nation whose crimes, towering up to heaven, were thrown down by breath of the Almighty, burying that

---

8 *Ibid*, 200.
9 *Ibid*, 202.
10 *Ibid*, 202.

nation in irrecoverable ruin! I can to-day take up the plaintive lament of a peeled and woe-smitten people![11]

Then Douglass' discourse on the American present turns to his answer to the paper's titular question—an answer that is the speech's most powerful, memorable, and poetic moment:

> *What, to the American slave, is your Fourth of July?*
> *I answer:* a day that reveals to him, more than all other days in the year,
> the gross injustice and cruelty to which he is a constant victim.
> To him, your celebration is a sham; your boasted liberty, an unholy license;
> your national greatness, your swelling vanity;
> your sounds of rejoicing are empty and heartless;
> your denunciations of tyrants, brass fronted impudence,
> your shouts of liberty and equality, hollow mockery; your prayers and hymns,
> your sermons and thanksgivings, with all your religious parade, and solemnity,
> are to him, mere bombast, fraud, deception, and hypocrisy—a thin veil
> to cover up crimes that would disgrace a nation of savages.
> *There is not a nation on earth guilty of practices more shocking and bloody than are*
> *the people of these United States, at this very hour.*[12]

Here is Frederick Douglass, the escaped slave who knows of what he speaks; and he speaks unhesitantly to the white audience in Corinthian Hall and, through them, to the white nation in which, whatever their moral values, local whites are privileged by race. *No nation on earth*, he roars, *is so much a nation of savages—so guilty of practices more shockingly bloody than are the American people at this very hour.* Celebrate Independence Day? —Really?

After the prophetic poem at the heart of *What to the Slave Is the Fourth of July?* Douglass assumes a stern, even scholarly, and intermittently sarcastic tone on the topics that complete the paper's no longer oblique denunciations of white America. Douglass turns first to the internal slave trade and artificial Mason-Dixon line that by 1850 and the Fugitive Slave Law had nationalized slavery (his words)—a law that he calls a gross infringement of Christian Liberty. He adds: "…if the churches and ministers of our country were not stupidly blind, or most wickedly indifferent, they, too, would so regard it." But, as often he does, Douglass inserts personal experiences, affectingly described:

> In the deep still darkness of midnight, I have often been aroused by the dead heavy footsteps, and the piteous cries of the chained gangs as they passed our door. The anguish of my boyish heart was intense; and I was often consoled when speaking to my mistress in the morning to hear her say that the custom was very wicked; that she hated to hear the rattle of chains, and the heart-rending cries.[13]

This is Douglass, writing in 1852 (when he was probably thirty-four) recalling his experience in Baltimore of hearing slaves being led to the auction block (when he was a boy of eight or nine years).

---

11 *Ibid*, 204.
12 *Ibid*, 207–208. This passage is lined out to suggest the extent to which, especially here, Douglass' prose is also poetry. Emphases are added.
13 *Ibid*, 210.

What to the Slave Is the Fourth of July? then expands on the wickedness of the churches with a series of criticisms of American religious institutions. Why does not "...the church of our country (with fractional exceptions) ... esteem the Fugitive Slave Law as a declaration of war against religious liberty?"[14] Then, as if to answer this question: "The church of this country is not only indifferent to the wrongs of the slave, [it] takes sides with the oppressors."[15] He makes it clear that he is not attacking Christianity itself or all churches, but: "the great mass of churches of our land. ... There are exceptions, and I thank God that there are."[16] He then cites Henry Ward Beecher and Douglass' friend Samuel J. May as among the small band of righteous religious leaders. After which, Douglass launches a longish discussion of the ways churches in England are, by and large, morally superior in respect to slaves and their colonial subjects.

Why, one might ask, these severe condemnations of organized American religion? One answer is simply factual. Slave holders were themselves religious in their distorted way. As a result, their churches were at least silent with respect to the evils of the slave system. But the better answer is that Hebrew Prophets from the eighth through the sixth centuries BCE were central to his religious views. They were the rock upon which he built both his political criticism of slavery and race in America and the hope he held for the future. As in most things, David Blight helps bring this aspect of Douglass' thinking to the fore:

> Isaiah, Jeremiah, and Ezekiel were his constant companions, a confounding but inspiring source of intellectual and emotional control. Their great and terrible stories provided Douglass the deepest well of metaphor and meaning for his increasingly ferocious critique of his own country. Their Jerusalem, their temple, their Israelites transported into Babylonian Captivity, their oracles to the nation of woe to be inflicted upon them by a vengeful God for their crimes, were his American "republic" ... . Their awesome narratives of destruction and apocalyptical renewal, exile and return, provided scriptural basis for his mission to convince Americans they must undergo the same. ... As Isaiah "came and said" and Jeremiah followed God's call to "go and cry in the ears of Jerusalem," so Douglass proclaimed anti-slavery oracles to vast public audiences in proslavery America. ... *He was an American Jeremiah chastising the flock as he also called them back to their covenants and creeds.*[17]

Blight has this right.

One might add only that, like the prophet Jeremiah, Douglass called those to whom he spoke to a new and different sense of common life. Norman Gottwald in his classic work on the Old Testament prophets adds the important point that their messages were not spoken to individuals, nor were they nihilistic; rather the Hebrew prophets of the eighth through sixth centuries presented images of a strong communal revival. Gottwald:

> That the prophets were able to think of a communal view of life outlasting the two ancient states of Israel and Judah was itself remarkable. Also, that they were able to

---

14 *Ibid*, 213.
15 Also, 213, but at the beginning of a new section, "The Church Responsible." Hence the irony in my header at the beginning of this chapter—*Ministers of Healing and Justice*. Douglass was a Hebrew Prophet if anything; and certainly not a Christian minister.
16 *Ibid*, 215.
17 *Ibid*, 207–208. This passage is lined out to suggest the degree to which Douglass' rhetoric was also poetry. Emphasis added.

envision the acceptance of that life by other states on equal terms was quite unusual for ancient times.[18]

In modern times much the same view can be found in Reinhold Niebuhr's views on the importance of the prophet Amos to Christian social ethics.[19] Douglass, the prophet, therefore viewed his America as in exile from its foundational values, as being, by virtue of its slave system, in a Babylonian Captivity of its own: "By the rivers of Babylon, there we sat down. Yea! We wept when we remembered Zion. ... How can we sing the Lord's song in a strange land? If I forget thee, O Jerusalem, let my right hand forget her cunning."[20]

Then, after a long discourse on aspects of America's history, Douglass comes to his conclusion. The conclusion to *What to the Slave Is the Fourth of July?* ends abruptly with a clear turn that is neither like the obsequious opening nor the denunciatory main argument. Douglass, the prophet, concludes that the nation and his people must look to a communal future:

> Allow me to say, in conclusion, notwithstanding the dark picture I have his day presented, of the state of the nation, I do not despair of this country. There are forces in operation, which must inevitably, work the downfall of slavery. *"The arm of the Lord is not shortened,"* and the doom of slavery is certain. I, therefore, leave off where I began, with hope.[21]

The quoted line is an allusion to the first verse of Isaiah 59, which reads in full: "Behold, the Lord's hand is not shortened, that it cannot save; neither his ear heavy, that it cannot hear." Thereafter, the next 16 verses are a litany denouncing the ways the faithful have separated themselves from their God. Then at verse 19, Isaiah 59 turns hopeful:

> ... When the enemy shall come in like a flood, the Spirit of the Lord shall lift up a standard against him.
> And the Redeemer shall come to Zion, and unto them that turn from transgression in Jacob, saith the Lord.
> As for me, this *is* my covenant with them, saith the Lord; My spirit that *is* upon thee, and my words which I have put in thy mouth, shall not depart out of thy mouth, nor out of the mouth of thy seed, nor out of the mouth of thy seed's seed, saith the Lord, from henceforth and forever.

These verses from the end of Isaiah 59 are the Biblical context for the fragment that Douglass mentions in passing—*"The arm of the Lord is not shortened."* Why such a fragment? Douglass was almost always clear because he was always well prepared. This was a talk he spent three weeks preparing. That he abbreviated so crucial a reference to Isaiah must mean

---

18 Norman K. Gottwald, *All the Kingdoms of the Earth: Israelite Prophecy and International Relations in the Ancient Near East* (Harper & Row, 1964), 392. It is also worth adding that Gottwald was famous, among biblical theologians, for having been a Marxist Old Testament Scholar.
19 Reinhold Niebuhr, *Nature and Destiny of Man, Volume II* (Scribner's, 1949), 10–11. Also, Charles Lemert, *Why Niebuhr Matters* (Yale University Press, 2011), chapter 5.
20 Douglass, *What to the Slave Is the Fourth of July?* in John Stauffer and Henry Louis Gates, *The Portable Frederick Douglass*, 204. Douglass quotes these lines from Psalm 137 in the transitional section of *What to the Slave Is the Fourth of July?* just before he offers his poetic answer after which he launches into his criticism of American religion and its role in supporting the slave system.
21 *Ibid*, 220.

that he assumed his listeners and readers knew the passage; or, if they did not know the words exactly, they would get their drift. His audience, after all, were neighbors in his city. They came to his July 5th talk prepared for a prophecy. Even if the sharp denunciations of white America were more than they bargained for, his readers also knew Douglass' ways and means.

They also trusted him because of all that he said and prophesied about how America's abiding racism rooted in slavery spoiled whatever was noble in its founding principles. All that he said was certified by his occasional offer to show his audiences the scars on his back, cut by the vicious methods of the slave system. This offer was itself rhetorical. No one needed to look at his naked and scarred back to know the truth of what he said. One way or another, they were familiar with his personal experiences as a slave on Eastern Shore Maryland and, in particular, with the brutality he suffered at the hands of a notorious negro breaker.

Covey, the Negro Breaker

Douglass tells of Edward Covey, the Negro Breaker, in all three of his memoirs. He revised the three memoirs as from one to the next he changed his attitudes toward various events and people. But his account of Covey is much the same for the years from 1845 to 1855, and only slightly modified in 1892 [1881].[22] Covey was the narrative anchor of his biography of slavery in America and to his sense of his life's meaning.

> There was, in the Bay Side, very near the campground where my master got his religious impressions, a man named Edward Covey, who enjoyed the execrated reputation, of being a first-rate hand at breaking young negroes. This Covey was a poor man, a farm renter; and his reputation (hateful as it was to the slaves and to all good men) was, at the same time, of immense advantage to him. It enabled him to get his farm tilled with very little expense. ... Some slaveholders thought it an advantage to let Mr. Covey have the government of their slaves for a year or two, almost free of charge, for the sake of the excellent training such slaves got under this happy management![23]

This passage is remarkable for the way it outlines the terms of the racial wage that would come to govern the post-Civil War slave system—a system by which the poor white remains poor but, relative to poor blacks, is compensated by the benefits of being white.[24]

At the same time, and nearly as important, there is the easily missed early line about Covey's place being "near the place where my master got his religious impressions"—to

---

22 The 1892 edition of Douglass' *Life and Times* is an enlarged version of the 1881 edition that did not sell well. Douglass was near the end of his days—a time when one would want to write honestly of a central experience in life. Oddly the 1892 edition was dated 1893 in the Library of America collection *Douglass Biographies* in 1994, which seems to suggest that the title page printed in this collection was based on an early publisher's title page. In several places including here I use 1892 [1881] for the original version of the third narrative even while quoting from Library of America's 1892 expanded version. The alert reader will notice in the next note that I try to get out of this mess by using the 1855 version, *My Bondage and My Freedom*. [PS: This is the kind of thing academics worry about even when they no longer are one. CL]
23 Frederick Douglass, *My Bondage and My Freedom* in Henry Louis Gates, editor, *Frederick Douglass: Autobiographies* (Library of America, 1994), 256 (quote following, 257). This, the 1855 version of Douglass' three autobiographies devotes three chapters to his experiences with Covey. *Life and Times of Frederick Douglass* devotes four chapters more or less entirely to the negro breaker.
24 W.E.B. Du Bois first sketched the racial wage concept in his *Black Reconstruction in America: 1860–1880* (Atheneum, 1992 [1935]), 670. For a systematic discussion of Du Bois's idea, see David Roediger, *The Wages of Whiteness: Race and the Making of the American Working Class* (Verso Books, 1999).

which Douglass adds: "Covey was said to 'enjoy religion,' and was as strict in his cultivation of piety, as he was in the cultivation of his farm." As much as Douglass' long passage at the heart of *What to the Slave Is the Fourth of July?* was prophetic in a biblical sense, Douglass also notably frames his disgust with the slave holders as a stern rebuke of their religious habits: "your prayers and hymns, ... your sermons and thanksgivings, with all your religious parade, and solemnity, are to him, mere bombast, fraud, deception, and hypocrisy."[25] This turn in *What to the Slave Is the Fourth of July?* is sharper even than the denunciatory lines that opened its strong middle section. Neither the calming politesse of the opening lines, nor even the denunciatory passages that answer. Douglass' titular question is as cutting as the underlying theme in his speech—a theme for which his experience with Covey, the negro breaker, serves as the personal and figurative mooring.

After the very young Frederick's stay from 1826 to 1833 in Baltimore with Hugh and Sophia Auld (where she taught him to read), Douglass was sent back to St Michaels, Maryland and Thomas Auld, who in turn sent him on for one year to Edward Covey for breaking. Douglass' introduction of Covey, the negro breaker, written well after the experience, is stark for its pathos:

> If, at any one time of my life, more than another, I was made to drink the bitterest dregs of slavery, that time was during the first six months of my stay with Mr. Covey. We were worked all weathers. It was never too hot or too cold; it could never rain, blow, snow, or hail too hard for us to work in the field. Work, work, work, was scarcely more the order of the day than of the night. The longest days were too short for him, and the shortest nights were too long for him. I was somewhat unmanageable when I first went there; but a few months of this discipline tamed me. Mr Covey succeeded in breaking me. I was broken in body, soul and spirit. My natural elasticity was crushed; my intellect languished; the disposition to read departed; the cheerful spark that lingered about my eye died; the dark night of slavery closed in on me; and behold a man transformed into a brute![26]

This was the beginning, but not the whole story.[27]

Eventually Douglass had enough. On an extremely hot summer day he fell ill from heatstroke, too weak even to stand. Covey ignored the symptoms and demanded that Douglass get back to work. He couldn't get up. He crawled as best he could toward some shade. He was beaten. Covey persisted before giving up and returning to his own work. Douglass decided to run away to his master in St. Michaels. Covey saw Douglass leaving across the field and pursued him on horseback. Douglass knew he could not outrun Covey on the road, so he entered the woods and walked through the brush all the night to Thomas Auld's home. Auld showed some sympathy for his condition but sent him back to Covey after a night's rest. Douglass made his way back, stopping for a night with Sandy, "a man as famous among slaves of the neighborhood for his good nature, as for his good sense... ." After feeding Douglass and giving him another night's rest, Sandy advised Douglass to go

---

25 Douglass, *What to the Slave Is the Fourth of July?* in *Portable Frederick Douglass*, 207–208.
26 *My Bondage and My Freedom*, "Covey, the Negro Breaker," chapter 15, 267–268. Important to say that this passage in the 1855 edition is an internal quotation by Douglass of this first telling of the Covey story in the 1845 edition. All the more evidence of how central the Covey story was to him.
27 The report following is mostly my paraphrase of passages from Douglass' account in chapter 16, "Another Pressure of the Tyrant's Vice" and chapter 17, "The Last Flogging."

back to Covey's "with all speed, and to walk up bravely to the house, as though nothing had happened."²⁸

He arrived on a Sunday morning. Covey's religious disposition, such as it was, kept his evil nature at bay. But Monday morning Covey set about to break Douglass anew. But Douglass resolved to fight and fight he did. Just when Covey thought he had the upper hand, Douglass sprang to his feet, fought back, grabbed Covey by the throat. "Covey soon cried out lustily for help; not that I was obtaining any marked advantage over him, or was injuring him, but because he was gaining none over me, ..." Others from the household, a handyman and a household slave, heard Covey's cries and came to the scene in the barn. But neither would help Covey. The negro breaker was broken by a boy of sixteen years. It was the last flogging and the decisive event in Douglass' life as a slave, as he made clear:

> Well, dear reader, this battle with Mr. Covey,—undignified as it was, and as I fear my narration of it is—was the turning point in my "*life as a slave.*" It rekindled in my breast the smouldering embers of liberty; it brought up my Baltimore dreams, and revived a sense of my own manhood. I was a changed being after that fight. I was *nothing* before; I was A MAN NOW. It recalled to my life my crushed sense of self-respect and my self-confidence and inspired me with a renewed determination to be a FREEMAN.²⁹

These lines appear in "The Last Flogging" chapter in all three of Douglass' narratives. They were of course written well after the fact, but they are written in a way that tells of their importance to Douglass' adult sense of himself. David Blight writes of the Covey memories: "Douglass likely never forgot the sense of his hands gripping Covey's throat, his fingernails drawing blood as he strangled the slave master. Whether it happened or not as Douglass later described it, the feeling became real in memory."³⁰ To be sure, memoirs like memories are necessarily only partly true. Therefore, what is remembered in the kind of detail that Douglass offers cannot help but be the facts of the matter wrapped in a fiction that, in itself, is determined by the importance of the facts to the one who remembers.

Douglass, the Prophet

We become (and, in time, are) what we remember from our pasts well enough to put into service in our presents in the hope of making a future. This precisely is what Douglass meant in the section he labeled "The Present" that began the strong middle section of *What to the Slave Is the Fourth of July?* "We have to do with the past only as we can make it useful to the present and to the future." This line is another of the theoretically subtle remarks Douglass made as if he were just trying to finish a poem, and perhaps he was, since the line seems meant to complement the verse from Longfellow's "A Psalm of Life":

> "Trust no future, however pleasant,
>   Let the dead past bury its dead;
> Act, act in the living present,
>   Heart within and God overhead."

---

28 For the two quotes above in context see Douglass' account of episode with Sandy, see "The Last Flogging," in *My Bondage and My Freedom*, 279–282.
29 *Ibid*, 286.
30 Blight, *Frederick Douglass*, 67.

Douglass was a prophet who realized that to prophesy a future requires acceptance of the past, for what it was, in order to deal with the present, such as it is, with all its reminders of the dead past. Without this, one cannot possibly imagine a future into which life might flow.

Futures are never guaranteed. When we find ourselves living in a future like (or sometimes unlike) one we may have dreamt of, we are often surprised to find there the traces of a past that linger in a present. The arc of the temporal universe is long, but it bends toward whatever comes in its own time to the local spaces where people must live. Prophecy is the telescope of memory. When Douglass reminded us of Longfellow's line that we must *let the dead bury the dead*, he meant to complete a prophetic insistence that *we can trust no future* because life is *action in the living present*. Douglass' poetic fragment comes to a conclusion that sounds strangely off key: *Act, act in the living present, Heart within and God overhead.* It is as though Douglass had in mind Immanuel Kant's categorical imperative in *Critique of Practical Reason*: "two things fill my mind with ever-increasing wonder and awe: the starry heavens above me and the moral law within me."[31] If not Kant, then Isaiah 59: "My spirit that is upon thee, and my words which I have put in thy mouth, shall not depart out of thy mouth, nor out of the mouth of thy seed, nor out of the mouth of thy seed's seed, saith the Lord, from henceforth and forever."

Douglass was a prophet of no particular philosophical or religious tendency. His poetry was framed by his sense of the arch of his temporal universe, put simply: He could not live with his past as a Covey-broken slave. He lived fully in a series of presents, each requiring a change, but each change was set against a new future—for himself, and his race. Near the end of his life, he wrote tenderly in 1892 [1881] in *Life and Times of Frederick Douglass*:

> What may remain of life to me, through what experiences I may pass, what heights I may attain, into what depths I may fall, what good or ill may come to me in this breathing world where all is change and uncertainty and largely at the mercy of powers over which the individual man has no absolute control; *all of this, if thought worthy and useful, will be told by others when I have passed from the busy stage of life*. I am not looking for any great changes in my fortunes or achievements in the future. The most of the space of life is behind me and the sun on my day is nearing the horizon.[32]

Douglass wrote these words perhaps as late as 1892 when he had fewer than two years to live. He was busy up to the end. He died upon returning to Cedar Hill from a meeting of the National Council of Women elsewhere in the District of Columbia. Given how he lived, his could not have been a better death—in the midst of active life, suddenly, with, it would seem, very little pain; and knowing his day would come soon. At the very end of *Life and Times*, he adds:

> Forty years of my life have been given to the cause of my people, and if I had forty years more, they should all be given to the same great cause. If I have done something for that cause, I am, after all, more a debtor to it than it is debtor to me.[33]

---

31 Longfellow surely knew Kant: " 'Who is the greater?' says the German moralist; 'the wise man who lifts himself above the storms of time, and from aloof looks down upon them, and yet takes no part therein, – or he who from the height of quiet and repose throws himself boldly into the battle-tumult of the world?' " Longfellow, *Outre-Mer, A Pilgrimage Beyond the Sea* (William D. Ticknor, 1846), 196.

32 Douglass, *Life and Times of Frederick Douglass*, in Henry Louis Gates, editor, *Frederick Douglass: Autobiographies* (Library of America, 1994), 912. Emphasis added.

33 *Ibid*, 914.

For a lesser personage, this benediction might seem pretentious. But Douglass did what he did because he was who he became after suffering the pains of his people. He had earned the right to speak of his life this way.

Frederick Douglass could prophesy a future for his people and the nation because, more than anyone in his day, he was a paradigmatic figure who experienced and therefore embodied what slaves and racially excluded men and women had lived through, as he had—the terrors of ante-bellum beatings, the promises of a Civil War and emancipation, the disappointments at the failure of Reconstruction. Douglass did not so much rise above his days with Covey or his several disappointments that the hope of emancipation was empty. What he did was let the past be past in order to think and speak out as he lived his experiences of America in the day.

Who, one might ask, writes three autobiographies of the same life? Only one whose stories are in demand by those who need to read and hear them. It was not that he was an author of best-selling books but there was in the day a very human demand for the telling of his story as the story of millions of others. It was a story that could be told only by one who had lived it. And by living it as he did, Douglass was an in-the-flesh prophet of what could be—and could be even when as now it has not come to be. A *could-be* is still a promise and a possibility.

Frederick Douglass' story was thereby a balm for a nation bleeding from the cut of centuries of slavery and racial exclusion. The scars are several. Whether on the back or in the soul the one who is cut cannot pretend the scars aren't there. Showers, whether of water on the body or blessings on the soul, do not wash them away. What washings of this sort do, however, is (as the saying goes) *they keep hope alive*. When so many have been cut such that the nation itself bleeds on, then there is balm in the story of one who suffered it all yet could still look to a future. Douglass was not a saint or a hero—one who inspires others to rise to his or her standard. Frederick Douglass was an open prophetic book into which those who need his story can enter. He was one who, in the end, could say with all human honesty: *If I have done something for that cause, I am, after all, more a debtor to it than it is debtor to me.*

Walt Whitman, the Poet of Many Americas

Whitman was the first American who tried both to engage the experiences of all the several Americas of his day and, in his poetry, to bring them into being—or, if not that, into America's imagination of what it was and could still be. He was, first, a poet of America's then major cities—Brooklyn and Manhattan. Yet, he also lived and taught school on then-rural Long Island. More still, he sung of Americans in all their many kinds of labor in *I Hear America Singing* in the first 1855 edition of *Leaves of Grass*:

> I hear America singing, the varied carols I hear,
>   Those of mechanics, each one singing his as it should be blithe and strong,
>   The carpenter singing his as he measures his plank or beam,
>   The mason singing his as he makes ready for work, or leaves off work,
>   The boatman singing what belongs to him in his boat, the deckhand
>   singing on the steamboat deck,
>   The shoemaker singing as he sits on his bench, the hatter singing as
>   he stands,
>   The wood-cutter's song, the ploughboy's on his way in the morning,
>   or at noon intermission or at sundown,

> The delicious singing of the mother, or of the young wife at work,
>   or of the girl sewing or washing,
> Each singing what belongs to him or her and to none else,
> The day what belongs to the day—at night the party of young
>   fellows, robust, friendly,
> Singing with open mouths their strong melodious songs.[34]

Whitman was America's first true multicultural poet. David S. Reynolds explains this quality by referring to Whitman's uncommon idea of race: "*Race* for Whitman was an inclusive word that took into account all that is associated today with race, class, and gender. He scoured working class and African American cultures in search of idioms and slang expressions ordinarily banished from polite literature."[35]

To the end of composing poetry that conveyed a sense of these American subcultures and identity groups, Whitman was a kind of amateur ethnographer. He learned urban working-class slang, for example, by listening to and studying Bowery youth—and African American slang by studying the language of slaves in the American South. For an interesting example, Whitman wrote in his *Notebooks*:

> The nigger dialect furnishes hundreds of outre words, many of them adopted into the common speech of the mass of people. ... The nigger dialectic has the hints of a future theory of the modifications of all words in the English language, for musical purposes, for a native grand opera in America.[36]

If these lines seem strange to us today, remember they were written in mid-nineteenth century, light years before the identity politics of the twenty-first century when the word "nigger" has become unspeakable to the point that a new word had to be invented, the "n-word." In some ways this fact of our culture today is an illustration of what Whitman meant when, in his New York urban days in 1848 and after, he sought out direct contact with African Americans in order to learn of the ways and means of cultures different from the then dominant literary culture. In many ways Whitman's note on "nigger dialectic" is entirely consistent with his poetic method.

Song of Myself is nothing if not a play on the words he professed to have heard in his America—a play that, in lyrical effect, strings together a host of social realities to create a "native grand opera"[37] of America. Here again, as throughout *Leaves of Grass*, is an explicit expression of the book's metaphoric title. *Leaves of Grass* is a figure in which the individual blade or leaf is nothing without the field of grass that itself is many leaves in one—a notion that plays out in the book's first poem, *One's-Self I Sing*:

> One's-Self I sing, a simple separate person,
> Yet utter the word Democratic, the word En-Masse.

---

34 Selections from Whitman's *Leaves of Grass* are from the Project Gutenberg e-book edition (last updated February 12, 2020) @ https://www.gutenberg.org/files/1322/1322-h/1322-h.htm. I use the organizational format of this edition which may *not* be the same in other editions, for example: *Walt Whitman The Complete Poems* (Penguin Classics, 1975).

35 David S. Reynolds, *Walt Whitman's America: A Cultural Biography* (Knopf, 1995), 319–321; quote below on Whitman's curious interpretation of the word "nigger," 320.

36 Whitman's theory of "nigger dialect" here is quoted by Reynolds, *ibid*, 320.

37 Whitman, *An American Primer* (Boston: Small, Maynard & Company, 1904), 24.

> Of physiology from top to toe I sing,
>   Not physiognomy alone nor brain alone is worthy for the Muse, I say
>   the Form complete is worthier far,
>   The Female equally with the Male I sing.
>   Of Life immense in passion, pulse, and power,
>   Cheerful, for freest action form'd under the laws divine,
>   The Modern Man I sing.[38]

One's-Self I Sing opens *Leaves* and is followed by *I Hear America* near the end of Book I. The two seem to frame the basic poetic principles of *Leaves*. Later (in Book III) is *Song of Myself*—the poem Jay Parini has called America's most important poem.[39]

Here too is Whitman's most original, if latent, social theoretical principle, stated as poetry. *Song of Myself* begins:

> I celebrate myself, and sing myself,
>   And what I assume you shall assume,
>   For every atom belonging to me as good belongs to you.
>
> I loafe and invite my soul,
>   I lean and loafe at my ease observing a spear of summer grass.[40]

It may sound strange to suggest that even a brilliant poem is also in some sense social theory. But clearly, whatever one wants to call it, something like theory is going on here. The opening line of *Song of Myself* makes an intellectually interesting point about social life: "For every atom belonging to me as good belongs to you." Later in *Song of Myself* Whitman offers a related point that could be said to complete an axiom of sorts: "(I am large, I contain multitudes.)"[41] The poem is a dialogue of the poet speaking to and about himself understood as a multilogue with all others. Poetry can say and think what discursive prose cannot. Prose explains. Poetry hints. In reference to Whitman's poetry, David S. Reynolds makes the astute observation: "Poetry just might help restore the togetherness that politics and society had destroyed."[42] At the least it is fair to say that Whitman's *Song of Myself* clearly suggests a solution to a problem social theorists have stumbled on, in that this poem is a journey of the self who is particular, personal, and multiple:

> I tramp a perpetual journey, (come listen all!)
>   My signs are a rain-proof coat, good shoes, and a staff cut from the woods,
>   No friend of mine takes his ease in my chair,
>   I have no chair, no church, no philosophy,
>   I lead no man to a dinner-table, library, exchange,
>   But each man and each woman of you I lead upon a knoll,
>   My left hand hooking you round the waist,
>   My right hand pointing to landscapes of continents and the public road.[43]

---

38 *Leaves of Grass*, I, 1. [In the Gutenberg version of *Leaves* Roman numerals indicate the Book, Arabic refers to the stanza.]
39 Jay Parini, "The Ten Best American Poems," *The Manchester Guardian* (March 11, 2011).
40 *Leaves of Grass*, "Song of Myself," III, 1.
41 *Ibid*, III, 51.
42 Reynolds, *Walt Whitman's America*, 309.
43 *Ibid*, III, 46.

After journeying hither and yon in a vast poetic space that can only be his America, even though the name of the space does not appear. That poetic space is, obviously, a social space—that of America.

To be clear I am not saying that Whitman was somehow a crypto sociologist or social theorist. Yet, here in *Song of Myself* his poetic method of immersing himself in America's many and various cultures becomes a narrative thread that links a charming rural countryside to the ravages of slavery. Compare the two following stanzas from *Song of Myself*. First, from stanza 9:

> The big doors of the country barn stand open and ready,
>   The dried grass of the harvest-time loads the slow-drawn wagon,
>   The clear light plays on the brown gray and green intertinged,
>   The armfuls are pack'd to the sagging mow.[44]

And second, from stanza 10:

> The runaway slave came to my house and stopt outside,
> I heard his motions crackling the twigs of the woodpile,
> Through the swung half-door of the kitchen I saw him limpsy and weak,
> And went where he sat on a log and led him in and assured him,
> And brought water and fill'd a tub for his sweated body and bruis'd feet,
> And gave him a room that enter'd from my own, and gave him some coarse clean clothes,
> And remember perfectly well his revolving eyes and his awkwardness,
> And remember putting plasters on the galls of his neck and ankles;
> He staid with me a week before he was recuperated and pass'd north,
> I had him sit next to me at table, my fire-lock lean'd in the corner.[45]

The first selection from *Songs* with the grass of an enormous field is, obviously, meant to call forth an image of American farms. But, at the same time, the mode of reference is clearly a welcoming of others to join him because they are many *and* one looking for the looming West: Again: "But each man and each woman of you I lead upon a knoll, / My left hand hooking you round the waist, / My right hand pointing to landscapes of continents and the public road."[46] Then, the second selection from *Songs* about the runaway slave tells of his being embraced as they *both* gazed to the landscapes beyond. The slave sat next to him at table (the locked gun set in the corner). One can well imagine their arms locked as the slave leaves not for the West with its landscapes, but for the looming North where freedom awaits. But who is embracing whom?

Song of Myself ends with the mystery of not knowing who the poet is, even though he has composed verse upon verse of personal thoughts and feelings that could:

> I bequeath myself to the dirt to grow from the grass I love,
>   If you want me again, look for me under your boot-soles.
>
>   You will hardly know who I am or what I mean,
>   But I shall be good health to you nevertheless,
>   And filter and fibre your blood.

---

44 *Ibid*, III, 9.
45 *Ibid*, III, 10.
46 *Ibid*, III, 45.

> Failing to fetch me at first keep encouraged,
> Missing me one place search another,
> I stop somewhere waiting for you.[47]

Whitman's Poetry of the Social Many as One

Again, the opening stanza to *Song of Myself*:

> I celebrate myself, and sing myself,
>   And what I assume you shall assume,
>   For every atom belonging to me as good belongs to you.

In a sense, these lines and the poem itself could be read as a radical theory of the relations between individuals and their wider society. A dyed-in-the-wool, all-too-serious social theorist might even read this as the (to him, usually a him) familiar *micro/macro* or *subject/object* dichotomies in which the lesser member is somehow of a different order of things from the greater one—as if there could be a human subject cut off from the whole of her object world.

Needless to say, these latter-day technical concepts would never have occurred to Whitman, even though the seeds of the dichotomies were already well introduced by eighteenth century philosophers like Adam Smith and Immanuel Kant. Whitman was well read. He knew the then-modern philosophers. But the basic philosophical idea in *Song of Myself* was not true to classically modern categories—which, to reach for an approximate way of describing them, were, in Whitman's own poetic way, figuratively networked so as to include, in his word, multitudes. Modern philosophy after Thomas Aquinas, the Renaissance, and Martin Luther[48] developed an analytic method that cut the cosmos into its constituent parts. Yet, there is irony in the fact that microphysics and astrophysics, different though they are, hold to essentially the same analytic laws—that the particulars of their spheres are the dynamic elements of a nation's subatomic and cosmic being. This strange fact allows for the possibility that Whitman was on to something, without realizing it.

Whitman could hardly be considered an analytic or categorical philosopher in the modern sense. Nevertheless, his poetry was earnestly philosophical, composed in his own lyrical terms. *Song of Myself*, especially, and *Leaves of Grass* as a whole, turned on his theoretical fusion of the self and its atomic being: "For every atom belonging to me as good belongs to you." To the hyper-analytic reader this makes little sense. We should not, however, cast stones. All but a few of us were brought up on the very Enlightenment philosophies that consolidated the method of putting everything into an analytic taxonomy of different states of being each divided off from the others. All little/big, micro/macro dichotomies—and their derivatives—are among the more pretentious taxonomic cuts.

"For every atom belonging to me as good belongs to you." What sense to be made of Whitman's line is made as a song. He is composing "the narrative grand opera" of America.[49] Later in the poem, Whitman adds a disarming lyrical texture to his unusual

---

47 *Ibid*, III, 52.
48 Perhaps the single most succinct instance of cutting the human subject off from its object world is Martin Luther's *Treatise on Christian Liberty* (November 1520) which includes the somewhat famous lines: "A Christian is a perfectly free lord of all, subject to none. A Christian is a perfectly dutiful servant of all, subject to all."
49 Mark Swed, "Walt Whitman's Operatic America," *Los Angeles Times* (May 27, 2018).

atomic theory by linking speech and vision as twins of a sort—not a dichotomy but a joining, perhaps, and an equating:

> My voice goes after what my eyes cannot reach,
> With the twirl of my tongue I encompass worlds and volumes of worlds.
> Speech is the twin of my vision, it is unequal to measure itself,
> It provokes me forever, it says sarcastically,
> Walt you contain enough, why don't you let it out then?

Still more disarming is that here, he appears to be talking to himself—advising himself that he ought to let go of the provocative interior. But is the Walt spoken to, the poet himself? If indeed the self and the collective others of society are one, then any given self, by whichever name, must necessarily be indistinguishable from any other, including the self himself who speaks.

Hence the still more perplexing aspect of the line: "Speech is the twin of my vision; it is unequal to measure itself…"[50] Is this a misprint? Does he mean "unequal" or "unable" to measure itself? The first stanza explains: "My voice goes after what my eyes cannot reach…" *Leaves of Grass* can be a bit prosaic in places, but the power of the book and of poems like *Song of Myself* arises from the lyrical vision that hints at what cannot be seen. This must be the sense of the telling lines in the first stanza: "My voice goes after what my eyes cannot reach, / With the twirl of my tongue I encompass worlds and volumes of worlds." This stanza goes a long way toward making sense of Justin Kaplan's interesting but ill-explained interpretation of Whitman's poetic method. Not only, according to Kaplan, is "speech the twin of my vision" but he adds:

> *Leaves of Grass* was to celebrate the conquest of loneliness through the language of common modern speech. It invokes the profoundest pun in the English language, "eye" and "I," and links the seer with the sayer. … This "Walt" speaks for the collective, timeless "I."[51]

Justin Kaplan's pithy few lines plant the interpretive seed of Whitman's mature, if early, method.

Whitman's poetic method was, in and of itself, many things at once. Not only is "speech the twin of [his] vision" but the radical collapsing of the visual eye into the ample tongue of song and speech allows the poetic "I" to grasp the vastness of worlds such that his "eye" could see their plentiful volume. Whitman knew what he was doing and saying because the homophonic doubling here deploys a word that itself has a double meaning. Volume is at once a measure of space and of sound. For all but the utterly deaf, proximate sound can be fully heard, but the full volume of space can never be measured by the individual "I" and especially not in respect to the space of Whitman's capacious America.

Whitman's poetic method attempts to turn everything available to the senses over and over, seemingly without limit. The self is doubled upon itself *because* the I of the individual self is at once the self of all others which, by extension, leads to the strange notion in the first two lines of *Song of Myself*: "One's-Self I sing, a simple separate person / Yet utter the word Democratic, the word En-Masse."[52] In language, subject and object are one in the sense

---

50 *Leaves of Grass*, "Song of Myself," III, 25. Lines quoted just below [My voice goes after…], same place.
51 Justin Kaplan, *Walt Whitman: A Life* (Simon and Schuster, 2008), 189. The stanza of poetry is from *Song of Myself*.
52 *Leaves of Grass*, Inscriptions, "One's-Self I sing," I, 1.

of being indistinguishable. The individual and the whole are a voluminous but continuous mass. There is no Being; only beings.

> Do I contradict myself?
> Very well then, I contradict myself,
> (I am large, I contain multitudes.)[53]

To tell the truth of so unthinkable a thing as America, contradiction is necessary, even beautiful. *I contain multitudes*. Poetry works when it plays on mysteries like this. The words create a vision of what is real but unseen *and* unseeable. America is just that. Though Whitman looked for and listened to many of those about whom he sang, he imagined many more he could not have seen or heard. Poetry, thus, plays on the social imaginary.

War, Lincoln's Death, and the Healing of a Nation

The first edition of *Leaves of Grass* in 1855 in which "I contain multitudes"[54] focused his latent theory of the self/other dilemma was a decade before the end of the Civil War. The book was already a settled statement. Yet, in a later edition, there is a strange insertion in *Song of Myself* of another pungent line: "...my book and the war are one."[55] The line was written during the War, when Whitman had moved to Washington. David Reynolds says of the line that it could not have meant that the War inspired his best poetry: "In his eyes, the Civil War accomplished for America what he had hoped his poetry would accomplish."[56] Still one might ask, how can it be that the Civil War with all the lingering suffering could be the balm for the suffering that *Leaves* was meant to heal? Not of course a snake-oil balm but a medicinal ointment that stings upon application but may ease the pain enough to allow healing—if not perfect healing—in the long run of an individual or national life.

In Washington, during the Civil War, Whitman lived *with* the War which was always close by the District of Columbia. Many of the early battles were in Northern Virginia. Whitman gave himself over to minister to the wounded and dying soldiers in hospitals in Washington. In a sense these lent him occasion to love, even if not sexually, these brave and lovely young men. Elsewhere in *Native Moments* Whitman was quite out:

> Native moments—when you come upon me—ah you are here now,
> Give me now libidinous joys only,
> Give me the drench of my passions, give me life course and ranks,
> I am for those who believe in loose delights,
> I share the midnight orgies of young men,
> I dance with dancers and drink with drinkers...[57]

Whitman was bisexual. He enjoyed multiple partners of both genders, which is to say that he was polyamorous.

---

53 *Leaves of Grass*, III, 51. For context and discussion see Reynolds, *Walt Whitman*, Chapter 10, 'I Contain Multitudes: The First Edition of *Leaves of Grass*." Reynolds makes the interesting point that these lines were written first for the 1855 Edition which made it more of a utopian document because "the boundaries of section, class and race had become glaringly visible" (Reynolds, 309).
54 *Leaves of Grass*, III, 51.
55 *Leaves of Grass*, I, "To Thee Old Cause."
56 Reynolds, *Walt Whitman's America*, Chapter 6 "My Book and the World Are One," 413.
57 Whitman, *Native Moments in Leaves*, Book IV, *Children of Adam*.

> A woman waits for me, she contains all, nothing is lacking,
> Yet all were lacking if sex were lacking,
> or if the moisture of the right man were lacking.[58]

In his day, tender loving, even sexual relations with partners of the same sex, men and women both, was common if not widely condoned. Still, Whitman's sexual desires were, it seems, uncommonly diverse and robust. Here then is another sense in which Whitman's "I" was many things at once. "I contain multitudes." His kindnesses to the dying and his desire for them, even as they were at death's door, was still another way in which he was as multiple as the America of which he sang.

The ointment Whitman spread over the nation's wounds—wounds that bled grotesquely in the Civil War—was a balm long needed. Well before the open wounds of that War, boils and cankers infected America's fetal body. Even in 1619 the newborn nation-to-be was crying to cut the cord that had fed them even as they labored out of Britain's womb. Soon after 1619, the arterial system of the American colonies began to burn with hot blood stirred by its original faction—North against South, Freedom or Slavery. The Revolution of 1776 and the settled Constitution of 1789 promised what they could not deliver. The Constitution that began with "We the People..." was a gloss on the underlying pushing and pulling over slavery. Here, obviously, Whitman and Douglass were in perfect accord. Abraham Lincoln tried to hold the Republican line that saving the Union was, first and foremost, not abolishing slavery. The Civil War, however, was the purgative that cleansed the ill-disposed Union. "My book and the war are one."

It is not that Whitman held a strong line against slavery. He was not perceptibly ideological or, even, ethical. What he *felt* (probably the best word) about the War was that it regurgitated all the fever inducing intestinal lesions the etiology of which was a collective attempt to swallow hard the obvious strains the body political had to ignore in order to believe it was in fact a Union. Truth be told, Whitman's poetic method was based on his own deep emotional disposition to sing out of one's self—a multitudinous welter of personal selves. "I contain multitudes." And: "My book and the war are one." Again, for Whitman there is no purely individual "I"; nor is there a global whole of the masses. One might even say, poetically, that everything is multiple because, over the years, America traveled through prosperity and anguish:

> To the drum-taps prompt,
> The young men falling in and arming,
> The mechanics arming, (the trowel, the jack-plane, the blacksmith's
>   hammer, tost aside with precipitation)
> The lawyer leaving his office and arming, the judge leaving the court,
> The driver deserting his wagon in the street, jumping down, throwing
>   the reins abruptly down on the horses' backs,
> The salesman leaving the store, the boss, book-keeper, porter, all leaving;
> Squads gather everywhere by common consent and arm,
> The new recruits, even boys, the old men show them how to wear
>   their accoutrements, they buckle the straps carefully,
> Outdoors arming, indoors arming, the flash of the musket-barrels,
> The white tents cluster in camps, the arm'd sentries around, the
>   sunrise cannon and again at sunset,

---

58 Whitman, *A Woman Waits for Me* in *Leaves* IV, *Children of Adam*.

> Arm'd regiments arrive every day, pass through the city, and embark
>   from the wharves,
> (How good they look as they tap down to the river, sweaty, with
>   their guns on their shoulders!
> How I love them! How I could hug them, with their brown faces and
>   their clothes and knapsacks cover'd with dust!)[59]

This from *Drum Taps*, one of the Civil War poems in *Leaves*, in which Whitman is more openly emotional. Here his multitudes are joined with those of the nation—the nation's children embody America's emotions. The multitudes of both are emotional multitudes in which, so to speak, the visual element is feelings—feelings that could not be ignored in a republic suffering from a necessary but terrible war. Also, and not incidentally, the feelings are expressed in a litany of what some would call, empirical—or fictional facts—observations of people living and leaving their lives as war is in the offing. Suffering was already staring them in the face as they descended to the streets for the marches to come.

For Whitman that suffering was never so desperate as when, at War's end, Abraham Lincoln was murdered. Hence, the best known and much-admired poem in *Leaves of Grass*:

> When lilacs last in the dooryard bloom'd,
>   And the great star early droop'd in the western sky in the night,
>   I mourn'd, and yet shall mourn with ever-returning spring.
>
> Ever-returning spring, trinity sure to me you bring,
>   Lilac blooming perennial and drooping star in the west,
>   And thought of him I love.[60]

This of course is the lead stanza of *When Lilacs Last in the Dooryard Bloom'd*, in which its lyrical form carries the reader from Lincoln's death and the nation's mourning. The first eight stanzas, then return in a fashion to the discursive manner of the early parts of *Leaves* by refocusing from Lincoln's death to visions of America—in stanza fourteen:

> Then with the knowledge of death as walking one side of me,
>   And the thought of death close-walking the other side of me,
>   And I in the middle as with companions, and as holding the hands of
>   companions,
>   I fled forth to the hiding receiving night that talks not,
>   Down to the shores of the water, the path by the swamp in the dimness,
>   To the solemn shadowy cedars and ghostly pines so still.[61]

Then in the concluding stanza sixteen, Whitman moves beyond grieving to singing with full throat of the many wonders of America:

> I cease from my song for thee,
>   From my gaze on thee in the west, fronting the west, communing with thee,
>   O comrade lustrous with silver face in the night.
>
> Yet each to keep and all, retrievements out of the night,

---

59 *Leaves of Grass*, XXI, *Drum-Taps*, "First O Songs for a Prelude."
60 *Leaves of Grass*, XXII, "Memories of President Lincoln," *When lilacs last in the dooryard bloom'd*, 1.
61 *Ibid*, XXII, 14.

> The song, the wondrous chant of the gray-brown bird,
> And the tallying chant, the echo arous'd in my soul,
> With the lustrous and drooping star with the countenance full of woe,
> With the holders holding my hand nearing the call of the bird,
> Comrades mine and I in the midst, and their memory ever to keep, for the dead I loved so well,
> For the sweetest, wisest soul of all my days and lands—and this for his dear sake,
> Lilac and star and bird twined with the chant of my soul,
> There in the fragrant pines and the cedars dusk and dim.[62]

The song now moves beyond the dead President to the fronting vision of the West—of America's still unsettled future where fragrant pines and cedars replace the sad blooming lilacs. The chant of his soul—of America's soul—revives. Even in *O Captain! my Captain!*—the most dramatic of Whitman's grievings for President Lincoln, there is a strong note of promise that "the prize we sought is won."

> O Captain! my Captain! our fearful trip is done,
> The ship has weather'd every rack, the prize we sought is won,
> The port is near, the bells I hear, the people all exulting,
> While follow eyes the steady keel, the vessel grim and daring…[63]

The grief poems—*O Captain!* and *Lilacs*—were written late in 1865 and were placed, along with *Drum Taps* (another important Civil War poem later in the final edition of *Leaves*). These three have all of the verve of *Song of Myself*. Yet, another literary riddle: oddly, Whitman edited Book I of *Leaves* to insert *Eidolons*, a poem composed in 1876. In Greek literature an *eidolon* appeared as a ghost or, perhaps, a spiritual projection by which a thing or a person, living or dead, is portrayed as a transcending embodiment of all that is feared or admired by a presumptive group. In American literature, a prime example is Moby Dick, the incarnation of an evil power. In American culture, Abraham Lincoln served (and still does) as a spiritual projection of all that is good (or presumptively good) in America. The spiritualizing eidolon of Lincoln and the transcendent "I" with which *Leaves* began are now eclipsed, peeking out from time to time in the bulky remainder of *Leaves*, which began: "One's-Self I sing, a simple separate person, / Yet utter the word Democratic, the word En-Masse." *Eidolons*, by contrast, floats in a wholly, even spiritualized, ether. It ends:

> And thee my soul,
> Joys, ceaseless exercises, exaltations,
> Thy yearning amply fed at last, prepared to meet,
>   Thy mates, eidolons.
> Thy body permanent,
> The body lurking there within thy body,
> The only purport of the form thou art, the real I myself,
>   An image, an eidolon.
> Thy very songs not in thy songs,
>   No special strains to sing, none for itself,

---

62 *Ibid*, XXII, 14.
63 *Ibid*, "Oh Captain! My Captain!"

> But from the whole resulting, rising at last and floating,
>   A round full-orb'd eidolon.⁶⁴

What lies hidden beneath the poetic imagery is the formulaic self/other/whole—a whole without categorical distinctions? The grief poems late in *Leaves* are suggested by the insertion of the 1876 *Eidolons* in Book I, the earliest and most expansive of the book's collection of early poems. Hence, a kind of magical realism haunts the book.

Leaves begins in lyrical songs of America, the land of the many people who in their multitude embrace the selfhood of the poet and of the selves of the many. The magic here is that Lincoln's death transfigured the nation's culture by transforming America—by, in effect, resurrecting it from the dead bodies of Civil War. This was the beginning of what came to be called America's *Civil Religion*⁶⁵—Father Abraham's death and resurrection (so to speak) completed Washington's paternal leadership of the nation out from bondage to its land flowing with milk and honey. Lincoln was Christ to Washington's Moses. To be sure, Whitman did not think or write in these terms. Still, the final two lines of *Eidolons* could be read as a kind of resurrection theme: "But from the whole resulting, rising at last and floating, /A round full-orb'd eidolon."⁶⁶ The lines owe a debt to Whitman's latent transcendentalism. Whichever way they are read, they represent the extent to which Whitman contributed to American culture the general terms of a transcendentalist civil religion.

Hence, Whitman's lyrical balm for America's divisions, losses, and possibilities. He sang of America in all of its classes, sexes, races, and other differences. No one before had done anything like this for America. Then too, with a special kind of genius, he tied the individual and individuals to one another by uncategorically joining them together—not by fusion but by an open and loose chain of spiritual natures. He lived the songs he sang—not perfectly well, but better by far than most. He lived in the big cities and the rural islands; he visited white working-class and African-American neighborhoods; he cared for, even as he loved, injured young men in Civil War hospitals; he read widely, but wrote in his own (until then) utterly unique voice; he mourned the fallen President until his grief had subsided; he lived a long life until 1892; he knew the early antebellum, rural America but also the modern America becoming a global industrial and technological force; he received gilded age capitalists like Andrew Carnegie and poets like Oscar Wilde; he longed for fame based on *Leaves of Grass* mid-century, and found it belatedly, near his century's end.

If Whitman lent balm to America suffering, the ointment he gave—or meant to give—through his songs did not completely heal the cuts and bruises, as a balm of his kind never could. Whitman was multitudes, never thereby fully one, always open, always in a way scratching the scars we all suffer as we seek to live as one among the many. At the least he stood for all, in his day and ours, who must face the American multitude before which we are personally a multitude. Perhaps more than any other culture, America encourages its more sentient citizens to be as many as we choose to be, while doing our best to live humbly as one among many. We all have scars in need of healing, the scars we cut by scratching ourselves.

---

64 *Leaves of Grass*, I, "Eidolons."
65 Robert Bellah, "Civil Religion in America," *Daedalus, Journal of the American Academy of Arts and Sciences* (Winter 1967, Vol. 96, No. 1), 1–21. Compare: Philip Gorski, *American Covenant: A History of Civil Religion: From the Puritans to the Present* (Princeton University Press, 2017). My presentation of civil religion is a paraphrase in my terms of Bellah's essay, published when I was his graduate student.
66 *Leaves of Grass*, I, "Eidolons."

Frederick Douglass and Walt Whitman: America's Cultural Future

They were not the same, to be sure. They were not friends. It seemed, however, that they would have understood each other. They were both poets of a sort, each a master of the language in his own way. As for their personal origins and the trajectories of their lives, they could not have been more different. But they should not be considered an historical odd couple; nor should they be thought of being some kind of analytic recto/verso of culture at a given time in America. Yet, differences granted, they each made life-giving contributions to America's sense of herself at a time when the very idea of America was in ruin.

It may seem too much to say that together Douglass and Whitman were balm for the nation's wounds. Yet, to extend the metaphor, for a balm to begin to heal a wound, the lesion must be cleaned before the ointment can be applied. Cleaning a cut is painful. All cuts, whether superficial or deep, expose the nether tissues of the body. Even a torn hang nail exposes the nailbed to the air that stings. When the injury is deep in the national body its historical tissues cannot escape infection. But it does no good to pretend the infection is not real. This was Frederick Douglass' contribution to treating America's wound—a wound that was first cut in 1619—and had to be exposed before it could heal. Opening the flesh stings. *What to the Slave Is the Fourth of July?* may not have stung the 600 people in Corinthian Hall in 1852. They knew what they were in for. But Douglass' life as lived, and told of, rubbed hard at the open sore. He was not, of course, the only one to participate in exposing the subcutaneous infection of America. It may well be that John Brown's righteous terrorism was, as many believe, the cut that broke the skin of denial. Harriet Tubman, too, did her part by leading slaves up from the slave states to the North and, important to add, out of the country to Canada, a safer and healthier place. Others too of course—from President Lincoln to Ida B. Wells and more still, whether famous or unknown—exposed the truth of the disease of slavery on the nation as a whole. It could even be said that Abraham Lincoln himself was paradigmatic of just how hard it was to look deep under the skin to slavery. That a very good man like Lincoln had so much trouble coming to terms with slavery—then, after emancipation, being unable to see just how freedpeople could live in the United States—explains how hard it was to face the pain of America's failure. Lincoln tried again and again to get the differential diagnosis right. He hoped against hope that saving the Union was sufficient reason for the War. It was not. The threat to the Union was slavery itself because, as Douglass said, it was slavery that made a mockery of the Declaration of Independence. But, in the end, before and during the Civil War, and in the bitter years after, it was Douglass who lived the life that told the story of how terrible slavery was. It would not be too far wrong to say that Douglass' story of Covey, the Negro Breaker, was a harsh tincture in the cut John Brown tore open.

Without Douglass, in particular, and many others who exposed the nation's wound, there would have been no balm for Whitman to spread over the open flesh. As Douglass put the lie to the classic notion that American culture inspired pragmatic individuals to pursue progress against a limitless wilderness, so Whitman gently sang of the bond that all individuals in the land had to the several selves of many others. He dreamt of an America reborn to a lyrical future. It is not that Douglass was morbid. He was a prophet of a possible future—a future that could only be if Americans came to terms with their differences. *The Fourth of July is yours, not mine.* Whitman, however, sang of the America that was already many. *I contain multitudes.* Both moves were necessary and complementary. The multitudes cannot be celebrated until the deep differences are embraced.

It is not that the classical themes by which Americans thought America were no longer in play. Even now, centuries on, Americans think of themselves as pragmatic individuals who require space in order to make progress. But Douglass and Whitman set us on the hard road to understanding America's racial cleavage. What progress we've made, limited though it is, sets us on the path toward accepting the global realities that people everywhere are different. And those differences, once seen for what they are, invite the possibility (even the necessity) of multitudes as being who we are—collectively and individually.

9 Abraham Lincoln's Implicit Practical Social Theory and A New America

The mystic chords of memory,
stretching from every battlefield, and patriot grave, to every living heart and hearthstone,
all over this broad land, will yet swell the chorus of the Union,
when again touched, as surely it will be, by the better angels of our nature.
    —*Abraham Lincoln, The Gettysburg Address, November 19, 1863*

The Address

In Putney, Vermont—a small town in a remote region—there is a remarkable school that, in a sense, lives by the words of Abraham Lincoln. The school cares for and teaches 50 teenage boys, grades 6 through 12. This is the Greenwood School. Its curriculum, and the community of which it is a part, are designed to serve boys who suffer complex learning problems. In their previous schools, most of them were emotionally brutalized by being stigmatized as "learning disabled." This all-too-clinical designation, when freely used in "regular" (private as well as public) schools, has the effect of stigmatizing students thus classified as stupid. Greenwood seeks to help students thus abused. Most of their diagnoses are for severe learning problems—Dyslexia, Executive Function Disorder, and Dysgraphia. But the one that may be the most debilitating is Attention Deficit Hyperactivity Disorder (ADHD): "A syndrome, usually diagnosed in childhood, characterized by a persistent pattern of impulsiveness, a short attention span, and hyperactivity, interfering with academic, occupational and social performance."[1] Whatever a person's social background, no one thus diagnosed is exempt from the damage done by being publicly classified as learning disabled. Greenwood, however, is a surprisingly therapeutic place for one reason.

At the heart of the Greenwood School's curriculum is the requirement that all students learn to recite the Gettysburg Address in public. Why this? For young people with severe speech disorders arising from their learning issues, the Address is a challenge. It challenges because it is so poetic—thus, at once emotionally moving but, also, for boys who suffered in other schools, it is strangely relative to the standard American English used elsewhere. Yet, in their efforts to learn Lincoln's most famous speech they must also confront the limits of

---

1 Ken Burns, *The Address* (Walpole, NH: Florentine Films, 2014). The description of executive function disorder is comparably severe: "The cognitive process that regulates an individual's ability to organize thoughts and activities, prioritize tasks, manage time efficiently and make decisions." *The Address* tells the story of the Greenwood School and of the Gettysburg Address.

their ability to read and recite—to learn. Even those with the more severe learning problems eventually succeed—all with evident pride.

Abraham Lincoln's Practical Nature

The lesson here in respect to Lincoln's practical social ethic is that the spoken word is both basic to practical life and, when well spoken, can lift that life out of the mundane. Words can heal when put to those special events where ordinary suffering meets the need to go on living with others. They heal by breathing fresh air into the deflated lungs of a people otherwise pressed in by the dull, often dangerous, routines of daily life. Literally, this is what *in-spiring* means and can be. People, especially the commonly oppressed, gasp for this good air where the practical rises to higher human possibilities. Lincoln was a genius of this sort of well-purposed intervention.

In this and other ways, Abraham Lincoln was pragmatic without being a philosophical pragmatist. To be pragmatic and to hold fast to a practical attitude about daily life is *not* necessarily pragmatism. The former is a cultural attitude that orders ordinary life; the latter is a philosophical movement that came to be late in the nineteenth and early in the twentieth century. They are related, to be sure. But, first and foremost, pragmatism—whether merely practical or loftily philosophical—is (and long has been) a primordial aspect of American culture. Lincoln did not invent it, but he did drink of its deep lake in this nation's history at a time when that nation was at risk of being drowned by division and war.

Everything Lincoln gained, and everything he came to think, began in the hard soil of his earliest days on the frontier. He passed his childhood under the most impoverished of frontier conditions. Hardscrabble barely begins to describe the circumstances of his early childhood homes. Yet, his father Thomas, who could barely read, was strong in character and body—a true frontiersman who occasionally guided others in the wilderness. He farmed the several homesteads they lived on in Kentucky and Indiana. Abraham's biomother was Nancy Hanks. She died in 1818 when Abraham was but 9. The year following, Thomas married Sarah Johnston, a widow with three children. Two years later still, the family moved to Illinois. These years seem to have been happy ones for Abraham, who in adolescence hired himself out to labor for others. In 1828, he navigated, on a flatboat he had built, down the Mississippi to New Orleans where he sold produce grown in Illinois.

Lincoln had scant formal education.[2] His schooling, such as it was, amounted to little more than a few scattered months from age 7 to 17. Yet he became an avid reader—of teaching guides and schoolbooks, of the Bible, of Aesop's fables and the like—from which he memorized passages that, in later life as President, lent him the gift of seemingly always being able to tell a story or quote a pithy line to distract petitioners and political adversaries. In respect to Lincoln's pragmatic nature, it is significant that he had closely read biographies of Benjamin Franklin and George Washington—two of the nation's most eminent practical doers and thinkers.

In 1831, Lincoln left the family home to live independently for six years in New Salem, a small town in rural, if not frontier, Illinois. These were the years when he characterized himself as "a piece of floating driftwood."[3] Then and there he participated in a remarkable number of activities, all supported by his ability to move from task to practical task, mostly with success. He made a second trip downriver to New Orleans, was partner in a grocery

---

2 On Lincoln's childhood and young adult formation, David S. Reynolds is particularly good. See Reynolds, *Abe: Abraham Lincoln in His Times* (Penguin Press, 2020), chapters 2–6.
3 David Herbert Donald, *Lincoln* (Simon & Schuster, 1995), chapter 2.

store and meeting place in town, became local postmaster, joined the local militia ready for action in the Black Hawk Indian War, and more. He was admired and friendly with the men about town for his hard work and good humor. Lincoln, to be sure, as he grew older, came to terms with the frontier but, as Eric Foner says, he "never romanticized his backwoods youth."[4] What he did was to learn from it (and in spite of it) in order to move beyond his frontier days. The years in New Salem were the first step beyond the backwoods. Here he made his first ventures into politics as a candidate for State Legislature (to which he was elected after an initial defeat). Then too he began the study of law, a career choice that was anything but inspired by the backwoods. Soon enough, Lincoln's political stock rose. He became politically prominent state-wide for his role in effecting the move of the Illinois state capital from Vandalia to Springfield. By 1837 he had settled in Springfield where he began the practice of law.

On January 27, 1838, Lincoln delivered his first notable public address to the Young Men's Lyceum of Springfield, "The Perpetuation of Our Political Institutions."[5] Just more than a year before, he had been in New Salem, working and hanging out with men of the town. Yet this speech in 1838 was eloquent, inspiring, deeply practical, as well as directly on target to the consuming issue his nation would face during his lifetime, and after. Still, the Lyceum Address, while raw by comparison to the Gettysburg Memorial, had enough literary beef on its bones to suggest what was to come. He began, for example, with warm respect for the nation's first and subsequent leaders: "Their's was the task (and nobly they performed it) to possess themselves, and through themselves us, of this goodly land: and to uprear upon its hills and its valleys, a political edifice and equal rights." Though far from the most eloquent of Lincoln's best-known speeches, this earliest of his public talks is eloquent in another way. It reaches expansively for a vision of America's unique place in the world—a "goodly land" inviting liberty and equality. In this, he captures the spirit of his times, while expressing his own vision of the nation's place in history.

The year after the Lyceum speech, Lincoln's legal practice was sufficiently well established that he could join the band of lawyers and judges on their twice-yearly rural circuits to small towns in Central Illinois.[6] They usually traveled on horseback over rough dirt roads, often overrun by flooding streams. The small towns where they held court offered little for rest. When the make-shift court hearings were over for the day they stayed in crude, filthy, inns or farmhouses where the food was bad. They often slept two to a bug-ridden bed. But Lincoln took it all in stride. He led the way across flooded roads and actually enjoyed the evenings when the legal teams would gather to swap stories. Lincoln was the star of these evening get-togethers for the hilarity of his stories. Yet, still more important to Lincoln's life experience on these circuit rides were his relations with those he represented. He was famous for remembering their names and the nuances of their various life conditions that shaped their positions as plaintiffs or defendants. Even more, he was able to listen to them and speak to the court itself in terms all could understand.

Lincoln's circuit court experience began in 1839—the year he first met Mary Todd, his wife to be, and when he had his first public encounter with Stephen A. Douglas. After 1854 and the Kansas-Nebraska Act, he then traveled the state in 1858 for the debates with

---

4 Eric Foner, *The Fiery Trial: Abraham Lincoln and American Slavery* (W.W. Norton, 2010), 37.
5 *Address to the Young Men's Lyceum of Springfield, Illinois, January 27, 1838* in *Abraham Lincoln/Speeches and Writings 1832–1858* (Library of America, 1989), 28–36. Or in *The Portable Abraham Lincoln*, edited by Andrew Delbanco (Viking Penguin, 1992), 17–28.
6 The details following are told with particular relish by David S. Reynolds in *Abe: Abraham Lincoln and His Times*, in chapter 7, "Law and Culture: Lessons of the Law Circuit."

Stephen Douglas, by then his rival for the U.S. Senate. The circuit days were behind him. He had become a state-wide political figure and was beginning to build a national reputation. Still, it is hard to avoid the conclusion that those early days on the circuit had compounded the experience of his frontier childhood and young adult life in New Salem. Lincoln had his nose to the ground of ordinary life. Nothing affected his legal and political careers more. In 1850 (or thereabouts) he wrote "Notes on the Practice of Law" where he wrote, with wisdom: "The leading rule for the lawyer, *as for the man, of every calling*, is diligence. Leave nothing for tomorrow, which can be done today. ... *Discourage litigation. Persuade your neighbors to compromise* whenever you can. Point out to them how the nominal winner is often a real loser—in fees, and expenses, and waste of time."[7] Lincoln was diligent in the preparation of cases but not to the singular end of playing a dramatic role in court. He worked for compromise. And above all he encouraged honesty. "Resolve to be honest at all events; and if, in your own judgment, you cannot be an honest lawyer, resolve to be honest without being a lawyer."

Lincoln's code of radical honesty was anything but an abstract ethical rule. It was (and remains) a way of living based on presenting oneself as truly as possible and by taking others seriously for what they present themselves to be—neither necessarily good nor bad. Some would say that the underside of this quality of character is that those thus formed are likely to be slow to make up their minds, as Lincoln was on the question of slavery. Still, Lincoln's radical honesty as a pragmatic manner of living with others grew from his life and work dealing with people on the frontier and the circuit—an energizing element in his pragmatic disposition that was, in turn, a precursor of the philosophy to come long after he was gone.

Slavery and Lincoln's Practical Politics

The Civil War changed, even transformed, the nation—from agrarian to industrial, from regional to continental, from cultivated by Nature to riveted on the Mechanical. These changes, and many more, were in play before the War. Yet the War—its causes and consequences—turned on the issue of slavery and its abolition. In the end it was Lincoln who would bear ultimate responsibility for doing whatever could be done about slavery. He had no choice but to deal with it in practical terms—terms that were restricted by the still more pressing principle that the preservation of the Union was the more urgent purpose of the War.

Well before he became President, Lincoln in the 1850s was drawn into public debates over what to do about slavery. Yet, he held fast to his disposition of methodical honesty—which led, in practical terms, to his ability to see both sides. There is no better example of this than his 1858 *House Divided Speech* in Springfield, Illinois which began, famously:

> "A house divided against itself cannot stand."
> I believe this government cannot endure, permanently, half-*slave* and half-*free*.
> I do not expect the Union to be *dissolved*—I do not expect the house to *fall*—but I do expect it will cease to be divided.
> It will become *all* one thing, or *all* the other.
> Either the *opponents* of slavery will arrest the further spread of it,

---

[7] "Notes on the Practice of Law," in *The Portable Abraham Lincoln*, edited by Andrew Delbanco (Viking Penguin, 1992), pp. 33–35. Emphases added. Exact publication date unknown. Quote just below same place.

or that its *advocates* will push it forward, till it shall become alike lawful in *all* of the States, *old* as well as *new*—North as well as South.[8]

At first blush, this passage alone could be read to conclude that Lincoln was unable to decide the slavery issue that, soon after, he would have to face head on. It is well known that in due course late in 1862 he did thus decide. But here, in 1858, the *House Divided* speech also expresses a keen sense of the practical historical context in respect to which a decision, if any, must be made.

The *House Divided* speech was not simply a general policy statement, even if it was presented to the Illinois State convention where he was named the Republican candidate to oppose Stephen A. Douglas for the U.S. Senate. Just after the speech's familiar words of principle, Lincoln launched right into an analysis of the 1854 Kansas-Nebraska Act, the effects of which sharpened the knife of the slavery question. This it did by beginning the political crisis that devolved from the uncertainty as to how new states made from territories might become slave or free—and how those determinations would affect the nation as a whole. Lincoln summarizes the main points of the Kansas-Nebraska Act: 1) that no Negro slave can ever become a citizen, 2) that neither Congress nor territorial legislatures can exclude slavery, 3) only a slave state can determine whether a freed slave may be forced back into slavery. Then, Lincoln came to the issue of the uncertainty of the concrete aspects of Kansas-Nebraska and the slavery problem: "We shall lie down pleasantly dreaming that the people of Missouri are on the verge of making their State free; and shall awake to the reality, instead, that the Supreme Court has made Illinois a slave State."[9] Lincoln closed: "Wise councils may accelerate, or mistakes delay, it, but sooner or later the victory is sure to come."[10]

One might look at "House Divided" as a typical political speech in the manner of most in our day and as Stephen A. Douglas's always were. Lincoln, by contrast, was one who, with rare exception, spoke in respect to possibilities, not promises—and possible ways to act, not definitive actions. All of his major addresses as President had this quality; notably, from—the first inaugural: "…the mystic chords of memory… all over this broad land, will yet swell the chorus of the Union, when again touched, as surely they will be, by the better angels of our nature"[11];—to Gettysburg: "…that this nation, under God, shall have a new birth of freedom, and that government of the people, by the people, for the people, shall not perish from the earth"[12];—to the second inaugural: "…with malice toward none; with charity for all; firmness in the right, let us strive on to finish the work we are in; to bind up the nation's wounds…".[13]

The genius of Lincoln's speech-making was that he knew how to win over people, even those whose attitudes were at first at odds with his. This quality was well in evidence in the Cooper Union Speech in New York City—the speech that some say made Lincoln

---

8 *"House Divided" Speech at Springfield, Illinois, June 16, 1858*, in *Lincoln Speeches and Writings 1832–1858*, 426. Or *The Portable Lincoln*, 89. The biblical line at the first is at Matthew 12:25.
9 *Ibid*, 452. [Or, *Portable*, 95.]
10 *Ibid*, 434. [Or, *Portable*, 97.]
11 *"First Inaugural Address, March 4, 1861"* in *Lincoln Speeches and Writings, 1859–1865* (Library of America, 1989), 224. Or, in *The Portable Abraham Lincoln*, *ibid*, 204.
12 *"Address at Gettysburg, Pennsylvania, November 19, 1863,"* in *Lincoln Speeches and Writings, 1859–1865*, *ibid*, 536; Or, in *The Portable Abraham Lincoln*, *ibid*, 295.
13 *"Second Inaugural Address, March 4, 1865,"* in *Lincoln Speeches and Writings, 1859–1865*, 687; Or, in *The Portable Abraham Lincoln*, *ibid*, 321.

president.[14] Before the event on February 27, 1860, Lincoln's national reputation was already prominent. Two years before he had lost the Senate race to Stephen Douglas, but the news of their debates had spread beyond Illinois—such that Lincoln was increasingly mentioned as a possible presidential candidate of the Republican Party.

In the end, many commentators could hardly believe that Lincoln was nominated over the favorite, Seward, much less elected over Douglas.[15] But he was successful because of what Doris Kearns Goodwin calls his political genius or what, here, I call his pragmatic approach to politics—his, that is, ability to be as perfectly honest as humanly possible with himself, with those about him, and with the general public. There could be no better illustration of this skill than the February 27, 1860 Cooper Union Address in New York City before a packed house of Easterners eager to learn more about Lincoln. Lincoln began by calling up Senator Douglas's pivotal statement that his own view on slavery was justified by the founders. Douglas said: "Our fathers, when they framed the Government under which we live, understood this question just as well, even better, than we do now."[16] Douglas was not, of course, in the audience except insofar as Lincoln brought him in as he proceeded to decompose Douglas's theorem step by step with a clever arithmetic device. Lincoln began with evidence from the 39 who signed the original Constitution 1787, then moved to 1789, in the first Congress to formally consider the prohibition of slavery when there were but 16 of the original 39, he repeats what turns out to be his refrain that there was "no line dividing local from federal authority on the question of slavery, nor anything in the Constitution, forbade the Federal Government, to control as to slavery in federal territory."[17] The arithmetic device is effective because it goes to the heart of Douglas's idea by demonstrating that, as time went by, and the number of framers absent from decisions on slavery increased, the principle of the original framers on slavery remained intact. "This is all Republicans ask—all Republicans desire—in relation to slavery. As those fathers marked it, so let it be again marked, as an evil not to be extended, but to be tolerated…"[18]

Then just after this, Lincoln addressed the Southern people: "…you are not inferior to other people." This was before the 1860 election, thus before he was President and the Southern states had left the Union. By addressing the South as it was before the Civil War, he brings his Cooper Institute audience into a rhetorical feeling for whether or not the slave holding South was a threat to the nation as a whole. In a word, he was addressing, one might say, the unconscious suspicions of his Northern, mostly liberal, audience—their

---

14 Harold Holzer, *Lincoln at Cooper Union: The Speech That Made Abraham Lincoln President* (Simon & Schuster, 2004).
15 Other likely candidates for the nomination—Salmon P. Chase of Ohio, William H. Seward of New York, and Edward Bates of Missouri—were, in their ways, better known because of longer careers in state and federal government and for the saliency of their positions in respect to slavery. All three were major figures who had good reason to suppose they ought to be president. Chase and Seward were both more radical as to slavery than Lincoln, and Bates was a Border State conservative until he too came out opposed to slavery—then in 1864 Bates left the Republican Party because Lincoln appointed Chase instead of him Chief Justice of the Supreme Court. Each of the three rivals came from a state whose votes were crucial to the election. Each was politically conspicuous in his own right, each more politically explicit than Lincoln who had played his ideological cards close to the chest. And, as is well-known, each possessed political sophistication and administrative skills that upon election, Lincoln would appoint each to his cabinet—Chase to Treasury, Seward to State, and Bates as Attorney General. See Doris Kearns Goodwin, *Team of Rivals* (Simon & Schuster, 2005).
16 "Address at Cooper Institute, New York City, February 27, 1860" in *Lincoln Speeches and Writings, 1859–1865*, 111. [Or, in *The Portable Abraham Lincoln, ibid*, 176.]
17 *Ibid*, 115–116. [Or, *Portable*, 172.]
18 *Ibid*, 120. [Or, *Portable*, 176.]

deeper war worries. Then, a bit later in the speech, he said (referring to the nation's original confederation of colonies): "It is exceedingly desirable that all parts of the Confederacy shall be at peace, and in harmony, one with another. Let us Republicans do our part to have it so."[19] Lincoln calms by recalling America's original harmony.

The genius of the Cooper Institute Address is the double-play Lincoln makes by deploying ideas, historical facts, and words in ways that allow him to speak at once to the Republican before him in New York City, to the generic South, to the coming crisis of slavery's structural threat to the Union and, thereby, to the American nation itself. Thus, he concludes: "Wrong as we think slavery is, we can yet afford to let it alone where it is, because that much is due to its actual presence in the nation."[20]

Then he returns to Douglas and the Kansas-Nebraska Act as the issue at hand early in 1860: "…[B]ut can we, while our votes will prevent it, allow it to spread in the National Territories, and to overrun us here in the Free States?"[21] This concluding question is, again, a trademark of Lincoln's rhetorical and political genius. He did not declare what must be done. He opens the issue to those before him that evening in the Cooper Union. The Address was printed in full in newspapers nationwide. People realized he was fully qualified to become President—thus, to hold the Union together, if such could be.

Even though Lincoln remained faithful to the pragmatic politics, his Presidency was quite another matter. He was no longer as free to joke and play in public. He tried some of this early in the trip from Springfield to the White House but was subjected to searing criticism mostly from Southern newspapers. Well before he was inaugurated, South Carolina had quit the Union in December 1860. In January 1861 other States followed. The Confederacy had become a reality on February 8, 1861 when all the States of the Deep South withdrew. Not long after Lincoln's inauguration a month later on March 4, 1861 he would have to face the crisis of whether to resupply Fort Sumter. He so decided but before the relief arrived off Charleston, Confederate forces began firing on the Fort, on April 12, 1861 forcing Union troops to abandon it. The War was on.

Lincoln's first inaugural address took place amid this turmoil, leaving him all but alone with few serious moments of relief from the War and its ever more acute crises. Already in the Inaugural Address, with its memorably poetic final lines, he began much as he had at Cooper Union just more than a year before. But this time, appropriately enough, he uses the facts of the nation's founding to place himself in the lineage of its presidents:

> It is seventy-two years since the first inauguration of a President under our national Constitution. During that period fifteen different and greatly distinguished citizens, have, in succession, administered the executive branch of the government. They have conducted it through many perils; and, generally, with great success. I now enter upon the same task for the brief constitutional term of four years, under great and peculiar difficulty. A disruption of the Federal Union heretofore only menaced, is now formidably attempted.[22]

Of course, there is nothing remarkable for anyone so fresh to a high political office declaiming the challenges that lay ahead. But, for Lincoln, measured against his past, to state the plain facts of the Nation's perils was to indicate that he fully realized the risks at hand as he assumed the office, of which many believed he was not worthy.

---

19 *Ibid*, 128. [Or, *Portable*, 184.]
20 *Ibid*, 129–130. [Or, *Portable*, 186.]
21 *Ibid*, 130. [Or, *Portable*, 186.]
22 "*First Inaugural Address, Abraham Lincoln Speeches and Writings, 1859–1865*, 217. [Or, *Portable*, 197.]

The very idea of a unified American nation, Lincoln continued, was from the first, even before its Constitution, a cultural ideal before it become a political reality. Though the 1774 Articles of Confederation were, strictly speaking, not a formal Union, the Revolution itself served to bind the Colonies together such that, by the time of the Constitution itself in 1778, the ideal of forming "a more perfect union"[23] was fixed in the collective mind. The freshly minted President made it clear that he believed that the Union cannot be taken down by the actions of one or several of its constituent States (a belief held against the realities). Then, he changed tone by speaking firmly of those "who seek to destroy the Union … I need address no word to them." Then he turns to those "who really love the Union."[24]

But speaking thus is fraught with issues beyond the reality that some believed in slavery, others not. He added that, among the attendant issues, was the "…foreign slave trade, now imperfectly suppressed would be ultimately revived without restriction, in one section; while fugitive slaves, now only partially surrendered, would not be surrendered at all, by the other."[25] This is the conundrum that had long been at the practical center of the differences between the nation's two sections. More than a decade after the 1850 Fugitive Slave Act planted the venomous thorn in the side of what hope of Union there might have been, the War began. Civil War would not be, as Lincoln had hoped, about preserving the Union. Slavery and its social entailments had long before torn the flesh of the national ideal. Then too, 1861 was but four years after the infamous 1857 Dred-Scott Decision of the Supreme Court that no Negro could ever be a citizen. Both the Fugitive Slave Act and the Dred-Scott Decision stirred feeling and thinking in the North. Harriet Tubman had already been the Moses who led many slaves out of the South. John Brown had failed in his Harper's Ferry raid in 1859, but his name lived on as *John Brown's Body*—the popular marching song of the Union troops.

Frederick Douglass was chief among abolitionists who stirred the pot that brewed the idea that fugitive slaves who wished to be (and in time became) members of the Union armies would be part of the victorious force that ended the Confederacy. Douglass's *Narrative of the Life of Frederick Douglass, An American Slave* had been a bestseller since it was published in 1845. The splintered sections, North and South, were seriously anxious over the crises provoked by slavery. Lincoln may not have known what would come to pass more than two years later when his *Emancipation Proclamation* of January 1, 1863 would stir the motivation of slaves to escape bondage and join the Union military to overcome its reluctance to organize, train, and assign Negroes to Civil War battles. But this fact sealed the deal of his *Proclamation*.

Lincoln pointedly ended his First Inaugural by addressing those who had already broken from the Union: "In your hands, my dissatisfied fellow countrymen, and not in mine, is the momentous issue of civil war. … You can have no conflict, without being yourselves the aggressors."[26] Then he concludes with the famously musical lines:

I am loth to close. *We are not enemies, but friends.* Though passion may have strained, it must not break our bonds of affection. *The mystic chords of memory, stretching from every battlefield, and patriot grave,* to every living heart and hearthstone, all over this broad land, will yet swell the chorus of the Union, when again touched, as surely it will be, by *the better angels of our nature.*[27]

---

23 *Ibid*, 218. [Or, *Portable*, 198.]
24 *Ibid*.
25 *Ibid*, 221. [Or, *Portable*, 201.]
26 *Ibid*, 223–224. [Or, *Portable*, 204.]
27 *Ibid*, 224. [Or, *Portable*, 204.] Emphases added.

The "better angels of our nature" is a phrase as well-known as any in the Gettysburg Address. "We must not be enemies," he said. They thought otherwise, but Lincoln, to his credit, never thought they were enemies, except in a military sense. He refused to recognize their claim to be an independent national entity. When he spoke of the "mystic chords of memory, stretching from every battlefield, and patriot grave," the President was referring to those who died in the Revolution. Yet, as we read the words from a distance in time, it is hard not to read them as an uncanny extension of Lincoln's unconscious obsession with his own death, with death itself, with the deaths that would come in the Civil War.

Emancipation, Death, and Suffering at Gettysburg

In the Gettysburg Address on November 19, 1863, two and a half years after Lincoln became President, death on a battlefield of that War and its many dead had become the theme of Lincoln's most famous speech. It is commonly ranked among the greatest speeches of all time and certainly the greatest in American history. It came late in the year that began with the *Emancipation Proclamation*—the life promising decree that was framed by so many deaths.

Lincoln had made public a draft of the *Proclamation* to his Cabinet and others on September 22, 1862. The definitive *Proclamation* was promulgated on January 1, 1863. The delay provided time for him to learn what others thought, negatively as well as positively. The thought of freeing the slaves had haunted him for a good long while. He knew not what to do with all those freed men and women. Lincoln clumsily preferred colonization, a perfectly unworkable notion for some four million freed slaves. The War itself caused him to give up this notion, especially after he consulted Negro leaders in August 1862. Frederick Douglass, in particular, sternly rebuked him: "The President of the United States seems to possess an ever-increasing passion for making himself appear silly and ridiculous."[28] The muscle in the rebuke is interesting because the two men had good, if not perfectly good, relations. There were other reasons that the President needed the time to ponder. In particular, Lincoln needed time to assess the often-outrageous criticisms of his plan to free the slaves, some much more severe than Douglass's rebuke. Then too, as the late 1850s and early 1860s rolled on, an increasing number of slaves escaped to the North and became quite a bit more than a mere presence, even when the War was going badly for the Union. The North had vastly superior industrial resources and much greater population, but Union armies were regularly outfoxed by Robert E. Lee.

Very probably the most important lesson Lincoln learned was that he came to see the practical importance of freeing the slaves. He shrewdly came to realize that Emancipation could be decreed as part of his presidential responsibility for the Union's military operations. All he needed was at least one decisive defeat of Lee. It came in a bloody battle at Antietam on September 1862—a rare victory in the day and one of the War's most deadly.

When all was said and done, the *Emancipation Proclamation* was unambiguous and unwavering:

> Now, therefore I, Abraham Lincoln, President of the United States, by virtue of the power vested in me as Commander-in-Chief, of the Army and Navy of the United States in time of actual armed rebellion against authority and government of the United States in the 1838 Address, and as a fit and necessary war measure for suppressing said rebellion, do,

---

28 "The President and His Speeches" (1862), in *Douglass Monthly* (September 1862); in *The Portable Frederick Douglass*, edited by John Stauffer and Henry Louis Gates (Penguin Classics, 2016), 479.

on this first day of January, in the year of our Lord, one thousand eight hundred and sixty three.[29]

Then, after listing the slave States affected by the freeing of slaves, Lincoln handed down the game changing new decree: "And by virtue of the power, for the purpose aforesaid, I do order and declare that all persons held as slaves within said designated States and parts of States, are, and henceforward shall be free ..." In the long run, it was the Proclamation itself that changed things, North and South. While it did not immediately give the Union the upper hand, it did lead to an important bolstering of its Army with hard fighting former slaves. By May 1863, Negro troops were inducted in the Army. They soon began to demonstrate their courage and commitment to the Union, most legendarily in the attack on Fort Wagner, South Carolina on July 18, 1863 by the all-Negro Massachusetts 54th, led by a white commander, Robert Gould Shaw. Most of their number, including Shaw, were ferociously slaughtered.[30] Still, it is fair to suppose that, had the Negro regiment faltered in the attack, the experiment might have failed and the already long war prolonged.

Still, as momentous as the July 18, 1863 attack on Fort Wagner was, just more than two weeks before, two battles in distant places were more important to the eventual outcome of the War. On July 3, 1863, in Mississippi, Ulysses S. Grant finally won a months-long assault on Vicksburg by the brilliant but arduous tactic of ferrying his troops across the Mississippi River from the South and West then marching them North to create an impenetrable front on Vicksburg's East. There, after failing to break through the Confederate artillery defenses, Grant's army simply blockaded the city long enough to starve its people and troops into surrender. The battle gave the Union control of the entire length of the Mississippi as well as access from the West to the interior of the Confederate States.

On the same day as Grant's victory at Vicksburg, the Union battle at Gettysburg, Pennsylvania came to its climax. There, for three days, Robert E. Lee led his first, and only serious, attack in the North. For two days, the forces, North and South, fought to a stand-off even though both sides together suffered some 50,000 casualties in the bloodiest battle of the war. Then, on July 3, Lee ordered what came to be known as Pickett's Charge—after the Confederate General George E. Pickett, whose infantry bore the brunt of a murderous assault on the Union line on Cemetery Ridge. Lee believed so much in himself that he was sure he had softened the Union troops up the previous day, making the Ridge vulnerable. It was not. Lee's troops were defeated. In shame for his rare failure of judgment, Lee rode out to apologize to his retreating troops. His army fled the battleground to return to the South, never seriously to cross into the North again. Gettysburg could have ended the war had the Union's Commanding General George G. Mead pursued and crushed Lee's army but, like so many previous Union generals in the futile tradition of General George McClellan, Mead held back. Lincoln was furious. The war continued for the better part of another two years. Still, Gettysburg was the battle that broke the spiritual back of Lee and the Confederacy.

Some four months later, on November 19, 1863, thousands gathered at the Gettysburg battlefield where so many had died. Lincoln here delivered a two-minute address commemorating the meaning wrought by those many who died there. He thought his short address had failed. Most present could not hear what he said. Many were prepared to settle in for a much longer speech. The speaker before him, the distinguished Edward Everett—the

---

29 *Final Emancipation Proclamation, January 1, 1963* in *Lincoln Speeches and Writings, 1859–1865*, 424. [Or, in *Portable Abraham Lincoln*, 271.]
30 The story of the 1863 attack on Fort Wagner is told in the 1989 film *Glory*, starring Matthew Broderick, Denzel Washington, and Morgan Freeman.

nationally renowned public speaker and politician, president of Harvard University, and much else—had held forth for more than two hours. Lincoln's two minutes were not enough time for photographers to ready their lenses. Still Everett strikingly wrote to Lincoln: "I should be glad if I could flatter myself that I came as near to the central idea of the occasion in two hours as you did in two minutes." It was in fact two minutes or less:

> Four score and seven years ago our fathers brought forth, on this continent, a new nation, conceived in Liberty, and dedicated to the proposition that all men are created equal.
>
> Now we are engaged in a great civil war, testing whether that nation, or any nation so conceived, and so dedicated, can long endure. We are met on a great battlefield of that war. We have come to dedicate a portion of that field, as a final resting-place for those who here gave their lives, that that nation might live. It is altogether fitting and proper that we should do this.
>
> But, in a larger sense, we cannot dedicate, we cannot consecrate, we cannot hallow this ground. The brave men, living and dead, who struggled here, have consecrated it far above our poor power to add or detract. The world will little note, nor long remember what we say here, but it can never forget what they did here. It is for us the living, rather, to be dedicated here to the unfinished work which they who fought here have thus far so nobly advanced. It is rather for us to be here dedicated to the great task remaining before us that from these honored dead we take increased devotion to that cause for which they here gave the last full measure of devotion – that we here highly resolve that these dead shall not have died in vain that this nation, under God, shall have a new birth of freedom, and that government of the people, by the people, for the people, shall not perish from the earth.[31]

Seldom has so much been said in so few words. The words are pure Lincoln in their poetic effect. They are also mysterious in their way. Poetically speaking, what is plain to see and hear is, as Adam Gopnik puts it: "Lincoln had mastered the sound of the King James Bible so completely that he could recast abstract issues of constitutional law in Biblical terms, making the proposition that Texas and New Hampshire should be forever bound by a single post office sound like something right out of Genesis."[32] Lincoln's poetic voice was classically Elizabethan.

Here again, and perfectly so, is Lincoln's uncommon practical method of addressing not-so-much an audience as an historical moment where the moment is a conjuncture in which the long-term history of the nation intrudes upon the local events at hand so as to put them in a new and surprising light.[33] The Gettysburg Address came nearly a quarter century after his first public speech to The Young Men's Lyceum of Springfield, Illinois in 1838. He was then young and callow, yet the fugue theme is much the same. In 1863, he had perfected his rhetorical art—an art that was tested by a war so much more terrible than either side thought possible. The killing and misery of war would continue after Gettysburg for a year

---

31 There are at least five different versions of the Address. This is the fifth version written, well after the event, by Lincoln for his stepson Alexander Bliss. It is not known whether there are other versions by Lincoln's hand.
32 Adam Gopnik, "Angels and Ages: Lincoln's Language and Its Legacy," *The New Yorker* (May 28, 2007).
33 Fernand Braudel is the theoretical founder of the tripartite theory of historical times: long-enduring, conjunctural, and event history. See Fernand Braudel, *The Mediterranean and the Mediterranean World in the Age of Philip II* (Harper & Row, 1972 [1949]). On conjunctural time, see Braudel, *The Perspective of the World* (Harper & Row, 1984 [*Le Temps du Monde*, 1979]), 21–88. But compare Immanuel Wallerstein, "Time and Duration," in *Uncertainties of Knowledge* (Philadelphia: Temple University Press, 2004), 71–82.

and a half. Yet, the Address ranged high and wide to cover the suffering with an inspiring blanket of purpose—so much so that its third stanza bears repeating and remembering the words that reveal the tacit pragmatism ever-present in what he said and did across the all-too-few years of his adult life:

> The world will little note, nor long remember what we say here, but it can never forget what they did here. It is for us the living, rather, to be dedicated here to the unfinished work which they who fought here have thus far so nobly advanced. It is rather for us to be here dedicated to the great task remaining before us that from these honored dead we take increased devotion to that cause for which they here gave the last full measure of devotion – that we here highly resolve that these dead shall not have died in vain that this nation, under God, shall have a new birth of freedom, and that government of the people, by the people, for the people, shall not perish from the earth.[34]

There is not a line too long nor a word too many. Yet one is inspired to reread and ponder the series of Elizabethan couplets:

The world will little note what we say here /
  but it can never forget what they did here.
It is for us the living, rather, to be dedicated here to the unfinished work /
  they who fought here have thus far so nobly advanced.
It is rather for us to be here dedicated to the great task remaining before us /
  from these honored dead we take increased devotion to that cause for which they here gave the last full measure of devotion –
that we here highly resolve that these dead shall not have died in vain /
  that this nation, under God, shall have a new birth of freedom,
that government of the people, by the people, for the people,
  shall not perish from the earth.

Lincoln's verse is lyrical, but free.

Foremost among the tasks before Lincoln—and before the large gathering before which he spoke so parsimoniously in a corner of the field at Gettysburg—was to embrace the suffering of those who gave their lives, of those they left behind to mourn, of the nation's collective suffering. The war was still on. No sure end in sight. The cemetery was only partially built. Remains of the dead were visible to those willing to look.

Lincoln, the War, and a New Necessary America

Abraham Lincoln was, at the very least, the pivotal public figure in the nation—at the most, he was the single most important public figure in American political culture. He merits consideration as the most conspicuously public and practical social theorist at the beginning of America's modern age.

This for three reasons. The *first* of course is that he embodied that pragmatic culture that was necessary to America's beginnings and would emerge in the modern era as America's most distinctive formal social philosophy—one that, if anything, played an even more salient role as the nation's new urban structural social conflicts. The *second* reason for

---

34 *Address at Gettysburg, Pennsylvania on November 19, 1863* in *Lincoln Speeches and Writings, 1859–1865*, 530. [Or, *Portable*, 295.]

Lincoln's enduring prominence is the one first defined by Robert Bellah—his status as the savior in American Civil Religion.[35] The memory of his death and suffering has sunk deep into the nation's collective consciousness[36]—a cultural fact that served as an antidote to the lingering negative dimension of American history.

The *third* reason for Lincoln's importance to America's story is how his personal story allowed him access to the evil buried in the breast of the Nation's political body. No other president was as familiar with America's endemic malevolence. The underside of Lincoln's frontier days and those in New Salem was not, as Eric Foner says, something to be romanticized. Hardscrabble is hard. But the hard living included all the many obstacles in the way toward a more perfect union—poverty yes, but also bad, even violent behavior, more and worse. Then too Lincoln's days on the circuit court meant direct contact with people who faced the court because of their misdeeds. For the most part Lincoln's story is sanitized to protect his image as a transcendent hero. Still, quite apart from the unspeakable horrors of the Civil War, he lived through any number of social evils—attacks on indigenous people, the brutality caused by the Fugitive Slave Law, the grinding poverty he grew up with, traditional practices toward women of which his wife was a victim (though not necessarily by the actions of her husband). All this and more was overshadowed by the extreme evil of the war itself—one more deadly and destructive than any other in the nation's history. Lincoln well understood the negative side of America's history, even though he did not, as presidents seldom do, speak openly of it.

No one has told this larger story more completely than Howard Zinn in *A People's History of the United States*.[37] Zinn and others tell of how from the first great numbers of the American people suffered long and hard under the nation's oppressive force—an aspect too seldom recognized as common among so-called modern democratic nations. Zinn says at the beginning of *A People's History*: "The pretense is that there really is such a thing as 'the United States' subject to occasional conflicts and quarrels, but fundamentally a community of people with common interests." True believers will find this attitude wrongheaded in every which way. Whatever one thinks, the reality lends plausibility to Zinn's idea. Lincoln himself did not believe this about the United States. He could not have of course; and did not. But he would have understood its insight.

---

35 Robert Bellah, "Civil Religion in America," *Journal of the American Academy of Arts and Sciences* (Winter 1967) 96: 1–21.
36 This aspect of Lincoln's significance is developed in Chapter 10.
37 Howard Zinn, *A People's History of the United States, 1492–Present* (HarperCollins, 2001 [1988]).

10 Suffering as the Seed of Pragmatism
Abraham Lincoln and Oliver Wendell Holmes, Jr.

With malice toward none; with charity for all; with firmness in the right,
as God gives us to see the right, let us strive to finish the work we are in;
to bind up the nation's wounds;
to care for him who shall have borne the battle, and for his widow, and his orphan
—to do all which may achieve and cherish a just, and lasting peace,
among ourselves and with all nations.
—Abraham Lincoln, Second Inaugural Address, March 4, 1865

The life of the law has not been logic; it has been experience.
The felt necessities of the time, the prevalent moral and political theories,
intuitions of public policy, avowed or unconscious,
even the prejudices judges share with their fellow men,
have had a good deal more to do than syllogism
in determining the rules by which men should be governed.
—Oliver Wendell Holmes, Jr. Common Law, 1881

Freddie Fix-it Day on Dixwell

Over the Hill, as well-off white folk here say, is one of the town's mixed race and poorer neighborhoods. Each Spring, Dixwell Avenue, the neighborhood's main street, hosts its Freddie Fix-it Parade. The Parade first began in 1962, when racial troubles and conflict were worse and more public than, even now, they are—when mostly black neighborhoods were for the most part ignored. The Parade is thought to be the oldest of such events in the Northeast. New Haven's Freddie Fix-it Parade started for the very practical purpose of cleaning up the streets especially in neighborhoods where the elderly were beset by trash of all kinds, including drug paraphernalia, littering the sidewalks.

The irony of the Parade's founding in 1962 is that this was the year after Yale political scientist Robert Dahl published *Who Governs? Democracy and Power in an American City*[1] (1961)—a book once taken as the best explanation of democratic pluralism in American politics. Hence, a second irony, Robert Dahl's book used the City of New Haven as the exemplar of his political theory, as the subtitle suggests. It was written, to some good extent, to contradict top-down theories of political power, for which C. Wright Mills' 1956 book *Power Elite* was, in the day, the primary instance. Dahl admitted that the American democratic system was not perfect. Still, he argued that it was open, dynamically competitive, and inclusively democratic. In 1962 this would have been news to the founders of the Freddie Fix-it Parade. For most in the neighborhood, Yale itself was so far over the hill that

---

1 Robert Dahl, *Who Governs? Democracy and Power in an American City* (Yale University Press, 1961).

Who Governs? would have made little sense, had they time to read it. Some of the Parade's founders were well educated, several were administrators and teachers in the local schools. But, one supposes, their attentions were directed toward the needs of their neighborhood and homes.

In 1962 one of the prominent buildings off Dixwell Avenue was the Elm Haven public housing project—everything public housing used to be: uncared for, crudely built, without amenities save for those residents made and kept up. Today Elm Haven is gone, torn down in the 1980s. Those who grew up there still call themselves "brick babies." They put on an occasional picnic to remember the old days. Not long ago, they celebrated the passing of one of theirs, Ray Roberson, a homeless but much beloved brick baby who was mercilessly hacked to death by the railroad tracks. Some three hundred members of the community, many of them brick babies, packed every pew at the Varick Memorial Church to share fond memories of him, after which doves were released to fly over the site of the Elm Haven project which today is occupied by modern, clean, more than livable, rental homes with yards and safe parking. In the sixty years since the first Freddie-Fix-it day in 1962, much has changed on this side of the hill. The neighborhood is coming back. Did the Freddie Fix-it Parade start all this? Hard to say. But it certainly didn't hurt. Today the Dixwell community is far from perfect, but it is on the way to better. The Freddie-Fix-it Parade celebrates what can be. The Parade, it seems, inspired pragmatic work to clean up and rebuild a community. People generally want to change things for the better. They just needed to start in. Not always easy.

The Longer Story of America's Fix-it Culture

From the first, Americans in particular had to be pragmatic to deal with the new land and its looming wilderness. To be sure, it is far from obvious how this works; but work it did. For one thing, even in the first days of settlement after 1619, Americans had no choice but to make something work. They were the first Europeans to attempt to settle the vast North American spaces. The aboriginal first peoples, who had been there for thousands of years, had little to teach them—that first Thanksgiving at Plymouth notwithstanding. Corn and turkeys were fine but, to survive as a people, the settlers had to learn how the high European values that to some degree encouraged them to leave for a better place could be refashioned to help them make livable worlds in such strangely empty places.

Then too, as time went by, there was the necessity of embracing the disposition to live according to a future-oriented economic ethic—what Max Weber called the Spirit of Capitalism. To be sure this ethic was also found in Europe in the eighteenth and nineteenth centuries. But it was particularly apt in North America where it became more robust and independent, more encompassing of life itself. American capitalism in those days was different and no more so than in the 1820s when the new textile mills in Lawrence and Lowell, Massachusetts perfected and expanded Alexander Hamilton's 1792 industrial mills in Paterson, New Jersey. The massive Lawrence and Lowell milling complex introduced new technologies that fostered nearly a hundred lesser mills in Massachusetts alone. Plus which, by drawing cotton from the slave plantations in the South, they contributed to the Cotton Empire[2] that was at the heart of global capitalism in the day.

Still the question arises, if the claim is made that America's pragmatic values arose from the earliest settler's decision to leave Europe for a new, presumably better, place—how then did this ethical attitude persist down through many years to become an ongoing feature of

---

2 Sven Beckert, *Empire of Cotton: A Global History* (Penguin/Vintage Books, 2015).

the culture—a habitus somehow stronger than similar pragmatic notions in other cultures? The first answer is that it must be practiced by national and community leaders for all to see and be influenced by. Of these there are obvious examples: Governor Bradford of the Plymouth Colony, Benjamin Franklin, George Washington—but also, perhaps unexpectedly, Alexander Hamilton who, though a brilliant intellectual, was driven to solve practical problems of government, banking, and industry; and among others even less obvious, Jonathan Edwards whose all-too-abstract preaching led nonetheless to the awakening of hundreds of Calvinist souls in the Upper Connecticut River Valley. Yet, of all these and others, there was one national figure whose pragmatic ways were still more important to the nation, ways that cut deep into its social body. This was Abraham Lincoln.

Lincoln's Death and the Republic of Suffering

Abraham Lincoln was a deeply practical person, a personal quality he learned in his youth on the frontier. Yet, in a larger sense, it may have been his capacity for suffering that served the nation more after he was gone. At the least, it is hard to erase the memory of this man who rose so high to face unbearable responsibilities only to be killed at the very instant when he might have enjoyed relief from the misery. His dreadful death is so unfathomable that its memory haunts on, conceivably to good enough practical effect.

Can the indelible memory of a leader serve practical—as opposed to simply inspirational—purposes? George Washington comes first to mind as possibly similar to Lincoln. But Washington's presentational genius entailed, at first glance, his having been aloof, above the fray. This quality contributed to his military and presidential genius and had a vital, enduring effect on the nation's formation. But it was not primarily practical in the sense of having entered deeply into the collective passions of the people. Lincoln's practical genius did just that. During his presidency and the War, what people saw (mostly through the photographs by Matthew Brady) was a tired, lonely, and world-weary man. His countenance was that of one who suffered the troubles of the War and its miseries. The Civil War itself was a long trial of suffering. All were touched by it—where "all" embraces nearly everyone, South as well as North. Lincoln's terrible death came to embody the suffering and death that everyone experienced, directly or indirectly. If not their sons, the sons of neighbors, relatives, acquaintances.

Those who think of Lincoln as the fallen and risen Christ of an American Civil Religion may well be thinking of the fact that his death, but days after the War ended, was also the death of the first, foundational America. Historians rightly bemoan how Lincoln's death doomed Reconstruction and true liberty for freed men and women, not to mention the liberation of the United States from its soiled reputation as a nation that held on to, or refused to end, slavery. Still it is worth asking: What might have been had Lincoln lived after the War? The nation was already changed by the War and by the economic transformations well under way. Industrialization was a fact of life in the North. Cotton production had long been caught in a global economic network of demand. Yet, the nation remained soiled by its history of white supremacy. Lincoln too was historically tainted by the nation's slave-holding South and the North's moral confusion as to what to do about the slaves when freed.

It is downright impossible to expunge, much less ameliorate, the moral and human stain that had colored the American dream since 1619. Healing and cleansing of that order require something like a deadly War and a prolonged suffering in its aftermath. In clinical language, it requires a long grievous working-through of the deep damaging injury—a working-through so raw that, well into the twenty-first century, it is still oozing with pus.

Could Reconstruction have been begun otherwise and better? Perhaps, but how exactly? By whom? This is not to make light of the decades still of suffering by the emancipated slaves and their descendants. The heavy fact that they carried the burden for so long, and to heroic effect, must be respected.

The memory of the characterologically suffering Lincoln served the nation at least to the extent of providing a cultural sign of the virtue of necessary suffering. To heal a wound cut at birth in 1619 requires more than time. It requires a remedy all-but-impossible to concoct. Emancipation in 1863 prevented further infection, but as things turned out it was a Band-Aid. Just the same, the death of the suffering President gave subsequent generations of ordinary folk a shared memory. Abraham Lincoln became the nation's good ghost of the then real but not yet obvious changes the Civil War had worked into the nation's story of itself—a story that, so long after, has still to realize itself in the moral means by which Americans think their collective identity. Structurally pervasive economic and technological changes do not require the same kind of story. They are, very often, myth-making miracles coming from nowhere. But moral changes are encountered slowly in the mysteries of ordinary life when people start talking differently. There is some good reason, therefore, to consider the basic premise underlying this attempt to reconstruct the what-was and might-have-been of Lincoln's death. Necessarily, moral change can only be pragmatic.

In *The Republic of Suffering*, Drew Gilpin Faust calls meticulous attention to the poets and writers of Lincoln's day who wrote of his suffering and death, and, especially, of the unknown dead who died in the War.[3] Among them, Walt Whitman enjoys a place of privilege as the poet who, still today, is known mostly for his poems of Lincoln's death and the pain Whitman himself and others felt:

When lilacs last in the dooryard bloom'd,
  And the great star early droop'd in the western sky in the night,
  I mourn'd, and yet shall mourn with ever-returning spring.

Ever-returning spring, trinity sure to me you bring,
Lilac blooming perennial and drooping star in the west,
And thought of him I love.[4]

Thus began the best-known of Whitman's poems written in the wake of Lincoln's murder. That continued with lines directed at the multitudes as the slain President was taken to burial in Illinois:

Coffin that passes through lanes and streets,
  Through day and night with the great cloud darkening the land,
  With the pomp of the inloop'd flags with the cities draped in black,
  With the show of the States themselves as of crape-veil'd women standing,
  With processions long and winding and the flambeaus of the night,
  With the countless torches lit, with the silent sea of faces and the
    unbared heads,
  With the waiting depot, the arriving coffin, and the sombre faces,
  With dirges through the night, with the thousand voices rising strong

---

3 Drew Gilpin Faust, *The Republic of Suffering: Death and the American Civil War* (Knopf, 2008), chapters 4 and 8.
4 "When Lilacs Last in the Dooryard Bloom'd," *Memories of President Lincoln/Leaves of Grass* (Penguin Classics, 1986), 351.

> *and solemn,*
> *With all the mournful voices of the dirges pour'd around the coffin,*
> *The dim-lit churches and the shuddering organs—where amid these*
> *you journey,*
> *With the tolling bells' perpetual clang,*
> *Here, coffin that slowly passes,*
> *I give you my sprig of lilac.*[5]

It was Lincoln's death that lent meaning to Whitman's earlier puzzling line in 1855: *I am large, I contain multitudes.*[6] As poet, he saw himself at one with the American multitudes. Much later, well after Lincoln's death, Whitman composed a prose essay, *Specimen Days*, that was more to the point of what the actual multitudes felt about death and suffering arising from their feelings for the unknown dead:

> And everywhere among these countless graves—everywhere in the many soldier Cemeteries of the Nation, (there are now, I believe, over seventy of them)—as at the time in the vast trenches, the depositories of slain, Northern and Southern, after the great battles—not only where the scathing trail passed those years, but radiating since in all the peaceful quarters of the land—we see, and ages yet may see, on monuments and gravestones, singly or in masses, to thousands or tens of thousands, the significant word UNKNOWN.[7]

This was Whitman, in 1882, writing prose as a kind of social history of collective grief. Even in prose his irrepressible poetic voice rings true nearly two decades after Lincoln was killed. So long after the terrible events of 1865, Whitman continues to write with pathos of the graves of the dead killed in that war—those for whom the dead president was the metonymic ghost.

Walt Whitman was chief among other writers of the day[8] who kept alive the experience of morbid suffering the War had inflicted on American culture. With Emily Dickinson, Ralph Waldo Emerson, Herman Melville, others still, he shared the sense that poetic literature need also be, in effect, social history. The Civil War—and Lincoln's death—comprised a conjunctural event in American history. They brought the mundane realities of suffering into the nation's long-enduring history. Like most cultures, the American found it hard to deal with the worst in its history.

In effect, Whitman was America's first out of the closet, if anonymous, pragmatist. He wrote as he traveled about to visit any and all among the still new America's people, always to feel with them and to take them in. He meant to *be* the American people—more importantly, to write poetry that made the people the pragmatic substrate of high thinking, of philosophy. No less a sympathizer of pragmatism than Richard Rorty puts Whitman in the company of John Dewey, arguably the true founder of American philosophical pragmatism:

---

5 *Ibid*, 352–353.
6 The line from *Song of Myself* first appeared in 1855 and was revised slightly over the years. This version is from the 1892 edition of *Leaves of Grass*—verse 51.
7 "The Million Dead, Too, Summ'd Up," *Specimen Days* (1882) in *Gutenberg EBook Complete Prose Works by Walt Whitman*.
8 Drew Gilpin Faust emphasizes the role of death in Emily Dickinson and Herman Melville, alongside Whitman and other writers prior to and contemporary with the War and Lincoln, see, *The Republic of Suffering*, especially chapter 8, "Believing and Doubting."

Both Dewey and Whitman viewed the United States as an opportunity to see ultimate significance in a finite, human, historical project, rather than in something eternal and nonhuman. ... They want to put hope for a casteless and classless America in the place traditionally occupied by knowledge of the will of God. They want that utopian America to replace God as the unconditional object of desire. They wanted the struggle for social justice to be the nation's animating principle, the nation's soul.[9]

In 1891, his last year of life, Whitman composed, "The Pallid Wreath," which exhibits just this quality of thought and, not incidentally, returns to the War and his poetic imagination of Lincoln's death:

> Somehow, I cannot let it go yet, funeral though it is,
>   Let it remain back there on its nail suspended,
>   With pink, blue, yellow, all blanch'd, and the white now gray and ashy,
>   One wither'd rose put years ago for thee, dear friend;
>   But I do not forget thee. Hast thou then faded?[10]

Philosophical pragmatism this is not, but it does meet the standard set down by Rorty and others as to what pragmatism means to do—to turn thought and, thereby, culture away from abstractions toward the ground of daily life and those who populate it. No wonder then that Whitman was so drawn to Lincoln in whom he saw those standards at work.

What Whitman knew and wrote in his poetry was, in effect if not in fact, an early sketch of Drew Gilpin Faust's *The Republic of Suffering and the American Civil War*. The phrase "republic of sufferings" owes to Frederick Law Olmstead's experience of young men wounded and dead in the War.[11] It is not too far wrong to suppose that Olmstead's lifetime career beautifying American cities as a landscape architect was somehow inspired that a desire to cover the dark grief of that War, as it may have similarly inspired others like Oliver Wendell Holmes, Jr. to do what they did. "Death transformed the American nation as well as the hundreds of thousands of individuals directly affected by loss."[12] Faust, writing in 2008, said what remains true in our time:

> We still live in the world of death the Civil War created. ... We still struggle to understand how to preserve our humanity and our selves with such a world. ... The Civil War generation glimpsed the fear that still defines us—the sense that death is the only end. We still work to live with the riddle that they—the Civil War dead and their survivors alike—had to solve so long ago.[13]

A Disclaimer on Lincoln as America's Holy Man

For many still today, Lincoln is a hero. To some, he is a saint. In this respect he is not unlike more than a few ordinary dead who, while alive, had done good among those who knew

---

9 Richard Rorty, *Achieving Our Country: Leftist Thought in Twentieth-Century America* (Harvard University Press, 1998), 17–18.
10 "The Pallid Wreath" (1891), *The Walt Whitman Archive*.
11 Faust, *The Republic of Suffering and the American Civil War* (Knopf, 2008), xiii.
12 *Ibid*, xiii.
13 *Ibid*, 272.

them. When we memorialize our beloved dead, we usually exaggerate their better nature and seldom mention their faults and failures. Memorials of the common kind, like those of the better known, are offered close after the death when memories of the ones lost are still fresh and painful. Walt Whitman, among the many who mourned Lincoln's death, was no exception. He felt that terrible loss for decades until the end of his life. It was Whitman's poetic mourning that contributed to the elevation of the dead President to the status of a national Holy Man—a transcendent symbol very much more than a simple belief or a theoretical idea.

Sociologically, holy things are, by their nature, quite beyond social things. Abraham Lincoln, the man, was decidedly a social creature who did both great things and some not so great. He was human. Perhaps the best, most balanced, account of this duplicitous fact of Lincoln's life is the PBS Documentary, *Looking for Lincoln*, by Henry Louis Gates.[14] The film includes a full range of attitudes toward Lincoln's special nature. Presidents like George W. Bush and Bill Clinton (himself a bit of a Lincoln scholar) represented those with more or less unqualifiedly positive views of Lincoln. On the other extreme, Lerone Bennett Jr., whose book, *Forced Into Glory: Abraham Lincoln's White Dream* (2000), declaims the negative, as in: "Everything you think you know about Lincoln and race is wrong." Scholars like David Blight and Harold Holzer deliver the nuanced between of the humanity of Lincoln. Lincoln has been, in fact, not the pure perfect human being that many—most notably former slaves and their descendants—believed he was. He was, fair to say, an outstanding President during the worst possible War. Even so, his temper often blinded him, just as his caution made him slow to fire incompetent generals. Even worse, he deserves history's blame for favoring the colonization of freed slaves—a position so absurdly impossible as to be, at the least, "silly" as Frederick Douglass said.

Drew Gilpin Faust, years later, was correct in focusing first on the suffering and death that the Civil War caused all in the day and the nation thereafter to struggle to learn of the good death. Young soldiers dying with a heaven on their lips was one thing. But a still young nation, looking for an uncertain future after the passing, if not death, of the founding generation was still another. It may seem strange to suggest, as Faust does, that we are still dealing "with the world of death the Civil War created." But it is not all that strange. Deep believers in America's most disturbing War may prefer, as surely most do, to cast their believing eyes back before the Civil War to the heroic Revolution. "All men are created equal," indeed. It was easier in those days to swallow Jefferson's line without choking. Such a line on the eve of a good War was a more palatable canon of national faith. It would be more than a generation after 1776 when it began to dawn that, truth be told, social things are what they must be—complicated, sometimes evil, always less than what decent people hope for.

As things turned from bad to worse after the Missouri Compromise in 1820 and the Kansas-Nebraska Act in 1858, war was upon the nation. This is where Lincoln the sacralized figure became possible, perhaps even necessary. Lincoln's murder by the hand of one who hated him on behalf of others who shared John Wilkes Booth's dastardly thinking turned Lincoln into more than he was or could have been even at his human-most best. So many then, and since, have been transported to the Beyond of the Lincoln myth because of the way he died, as in life he did so much that was truly great and wise. A good death ending a good life made it hard—even in a way pointless—to pay close attention to his human failures.

---

14 Henry Louis Gates, and others, *Looking for Lincoln* (PBS: THIRTEEN @ Educational Broadcasting Corporation, 2022 [2011]).

This book's attempt to ferret out Lincoln's role in the way Americans think America may seem at times to give in to the myth of the man—except for one thing. If he was in any way simply practical, much less a proto pragmatist, he was necessarily soiled with the ordinariness of life itself. Practical life cannot be lived in some Beyond of this world. It must be lived with others on the ground in the dirt of human behavior. Lincoln, the man, was no exception. Lincoln, the sacral political figure, was one who made the dirt tolerable.

Lincoln: The Buried Seed of American Pragmatism

Lincoln, to repeat, was pragmatic without being a pragmatist. The Civil War demanded pragmatic methods and strategies. It was a war said to have been the first modern war but one in which, as of old, men faced each other across fields, walls, and woods. They were directed by military orders meant to disentangle immediate life-and-death enigmas.

Deep down, Lincoln, when faced with the realities of a terrible war, was more than simply practically minded. He was the hidden kernel of what, after the War and his death, would slowly sprout into a philosophical pragmatism. As President he had no choice but to focus on the events at hand. This he did in a manner born in his frontier beginnings that, unavoidably, became the hard root of a persistent philosophy. Presidents faced with a War like the one Lincoln had to deal with must do what they do before a public eye that is slow to praise and quick to condemn. Only the most poisoned of persons enjoys war. Even when they profit from it—as industrialists in the North did—joy is not what they experience in their money making. Lincoln did not financially profit from the Civil War and he certainly experienced little if any joy from it—but he did benefit from the way it hardened his practical disposition into a thorough going practical philosophy for managing the events at hand. Of which there is no better illustration of his mature sense of practical thinking than how he grew into this role as a reluctant military strategist and sometime tactician when dealing with a series of inept or overly cautious generals. None more so than the pathetic General George B. McLellan who again and again refused to deploy his mighty, well equipped Army of the Potomac against Confederate forces. Lincoln's temper rose to the point of all-but-ordering the General to attack, which did little good. On November 5, 1862, he dismissed McClellan as General of the Army of the Potomac.

The lesson learned was that Lincoln, as President, needed to direct his military or find a general who could and would. This he did until he found Ulysses S. Grant who himself had come forth as a decisive and intently practical field commander. After Grant's victory at Vicksburg Lincoln eventually promoted him to Commander of the Army with the rank of Lieutenant General of the Army (previously held only by George Washington). Lincoln was so determined to win the War and save the Union that he entered the military realm more than any president until well into the twentieth century, when, among other instances, Lyndon B. Johnson in the 1960s became similarly involved in the War in Vietnam (with very different results).[15] Reunifying the nation was an unequivocally practical goal. Slavery, though viciously hateful, was an institution derived from an abstract theory of the nature of human differences.

Then too, the Civil War and its aftermath led to changes that were deep and dark— changes that were very different from the more apparent, progressive macro-changes usually ascribed to the second half of the nineteenth century—those from rural to urban life,

---

15 Franklin Delano Roosevelt was active with Churchill (remotely with Stalin) in World War II but not obsessed with America's role. Woodrow Wilson was all but indifferent to World War I which he did not want to enter. Theodore Roosevelt was driven by a desire to engage in a war to assert his masculinity, but all he had was the contrived assault on San Juan Hill by his Rough Riders.

from agriculture to industry, and those from preoccupation with Nature to the challenges of dealing with modern urban cultures. It is true that all of these macro-changes (especially the third) became, in time, the source of chronic domestic conflicts. Before the Civil War, the avaricious needs of industrial capitalism dramatically encouraged the many European immigrants who, over decades, populated the industrial North and as well as the modernizing agricultural regions of the Upper Midwest. Chinese people came to work in mining, agriculture, and building the railroad system. In time, after 1916, the Great Migration of freedpeople from the South to the industrial North changed the newly urbanized nation forever. What had begun early in the nineteenth century had made America, in the twentieth, a nation of wildly different ethnic groups, many not speaking English, most wanting to maintain elements of their original cultures that were strange in their host nation. None of these latent, sometimes patent, conflicts were as terrible as the dark consequences of the Civil War, but they were hard felt.

Needless to say, Lincoln himself knew nothing of what would come after him. In the years before, he was functionally naïve in thinking that the Civil War could renew the unifying energy of the nation's Revolutionary founding—a Union meant to be characterized by, as he said, "a just and lasting peace among ourselves and with all nations." Here Lincoln was dreaming the primeval American dream of a gloriously original democratic nation made by and for its mythic people. The problem is that *the people* were (as now they still are) a wish not a fact, a belief not a reality.

It must be said, with more than a little shame, that from its earliest days the so-called *United* States of America has always thought of itself as a culturally pure-bred nation. Nikole Hannah-Jones's 1619 Project rightly identifies the founding moment of this putative white dominating nation with the landing of the first African slaves in Virginia who were destined for exclusion. The important qualification of her attribution is that in 1565, well before the Virginia Colony was settled, Pedro Mendez de Aviles landed 20 miles north of today's St. Augustine, Florida to establish what became a thoroughly multicultural settlement of white Europeans from Spain, freed and escaped blacks, and indigenous Americans. When Spain was forced to cede its holdings in Florida in the First Treaty of Paris in 1763 what remained of this multicultural moment waned.[16] That there is this one exception to the founding history of white-America, makes all the more remarkable the fact that the nation was founded to be—in effect, if not in intent—a white nation.

This may be a reason why, when four million slaves were emancipated, Lincoln at first could only think of the utterly unrealistic solution of their colonization outside the United States. Like many in his day, as in ours, it has been (and still is) difficult to speak of the United States as historically a white nationalist State—as, that is, a nation governed of, by, and for *white* people.[17] Then too there is an often-ignored link to America's tacit white supremacy in its long tradition of unjustified abuse of its indigenous, native people. White cultural thinking necessarily sees all other racial people as other-therefore-different, hence: lesser.

---

16 Eugene Lyon, *The Enterprise of Florida: Pedro Menendez de Aviles and the Spanish Conquest Of, 1565–1568* (University of Florida Press, 1983). Lyon spent six years in the archives in Aviles, Spain, unearthing the story of the St. Augustine Colony. One of the few nationally prominent historians to mention the Florida settlements is Alan Taylor who says little directly about the unique nature of the early Spanish colony. Just the same see Alan Taylor's *American Colonies* (Viking, 2001), chapters 2–4. Then, too, the story of multicultural Spanish settlers and explorers goes beyond *La Florida*. Also, there is the story of Cabeza de Vaca (see Annette Gordon-Reed's, "Estebanico's America" in *The Atlantic* (June 2021)) where she mentions Andrés Meséndez, *A Land So Strange: The Epic Journey of Cabeza de Vaca* (Basic Books, 2007).

17 This is a disturbing thought, to be sure. But it is harder to deny it if in fact the reference is to a deeply tacit aspect of the American people—thus in much the same way that racism is tacit. See Anne Warfield Rawls and Waverly Duck, *Tacit Racism* (University of Chicago Press, 2020).

The Civil War in and of itself did little to change ante-bellum thinking about enslaved Negro people, except of course to grant them a slight degree of freedom. As short-lived as that freedom was when the post-war Reconstruction of the South was cut short in 1877, it was more potent than even liberals in the North could have imagined. Though freed men and women were kept in economic bondage for the better part of a century after 1865, what they began in the all-too-brief moment of Reconstruction from 1865 to 1877 endured in Black churches and juke joints—not to mention in the institutions supported by the Freedman's Bureau that kept the still underground culture sufficiently alive until it could move into the open after the *Brown v. Board of Education* decision in 1954. It was the whites in the South who imposed Jim Crow laws; and in the North it was the allegedly liberal whites who turned deaf ears and blind eyes from what was going on in border towns and major cities where the whites-only bathrooms were replaced by just as effectively segregated urban ghettos.

Abraham Lincoln did not, and could not have, thought in terms like these. But he did understand the nature of the conflict caused by social differences. Had he not, he would have never played a significant role in strategically commanding the Union armies in the War. He was, very probably, the greatest of American presidents because none other (not even Franklin Delano Roosevelt) faced a war that was as likely as the Civil War to destroy the nation—a threat that was never out of the collective mind over four long years. In the long run, Lincoln faced the threat and changed his mind—about slavery, about Negro troops, about colonization, about the purpose of the War itself. This was his proto-pragmatism—high thoughts planted in the soil of daily life. This was the sturdy disposition that moved him from his earliest days, and the one that dwelt openly in the last of his great writings, the *Second Inaugural Address*.

On March 4, 1865 Lincoln was inaugurated into his second term as president. The War was still on, to continue erratically for a few weeks more. Yet, in his *Second Inaugural Address,* he spoke of the War and slavery as if no end was in sight. "Fondly do we hope—fervently do we pray—that this mighty scourge may speedily pass away." When Lincoln comes to the last word in this short homily, he quotes Psalm 19:9 of the King James Version, "the judgements of the Lord are true and righteous altogether." Lincoln's last major Address ends with an unequivocal blessing for both sides:

> With malice toward none, with charity for all, with firmness in the right as God gives us to see the right, let us strive on to finish the work we are in, to bind up the nation's wounds, to care for him who shall have borne the battle and for his widow and his orphan, to do all which may achieve and cherish a just and lasting peace among ourselves and with all nations.

Just more than a month later, Lee surrendered to Grant at Appomattox on April 9, 1865. Lincoln was murdered five days later. He left behind more than words. President Lincoln left the American people with a good but difficult challenge—one that would require them to live with the death and suffering the War burned into the flesh of America's body politic. "To strive on to finish the work we are in, to bind up the nation's wounds ..."

Oliver Wendell Holmes, Jr. and the Beginnings of Philosophical Pragmatism

The Civil War saved the Union. "But, in almost every other respect, the United States became a different country. The war alone did not make America modern, but the War marks the birth of modern America."[18] With this statement, Louis Menand begins *The Metaphysical Club*, his history of the social and scientific theorists who, more than others, introduced the intellectual movements that—from the Civil War through the first decades of the twentieth century—restructured America's collective social thought in ways that were distinctly and irreversibly modern.

Among the thinkers who led the way beyond the nation's ante-bellum culture were Oliver Wendell Holmes, Jr., Charles Sanders Peirce, William James, and John Dewey. All of whom were, in one way or another, important contributors to the foundations of philosophical pragmatism.[19] Though others, who were less explicitly pragmatist, also contributed in starkly different ways that academic philosophers began to think in distinctively American terms. Among them are Jane Addams and Theodore Roosevelt who were among those commonly overlooked as leaders who provided cover for pragmatism during its early formative period from the 1890s through the 1910s.

Yet, of them all, Holmes was the only one who not only lived through, and fought in, the Civil War, then remained active into the period, more than a half-century later, when the pragmatism movement was well-settled in American philosophical culture. Holmes was born March 8, 1841 and died March 6, 1935, days short of his 94th birthday and just three years after retiring as Associate Justice of the US Supreme Court. When Holmes fought in the Civil War, he was neither close to Lincoln who was much his elder; nor, as the years went by, was his philosophy commonly considered central to the pragmatist tradition, though Richard Posner has shown it should have been.[20] Of all the historical figures usually overlooked in the study of the early American social theories, Holmes is chief among those who should have been given a place in the social theoretical canon.

Holmes fought in the War. After it ended in 1865, he set out to become what might be called a social philosopher of the Law. Holmes was seriously injured three times in the Civil War. Each time he returned to duty. Through the years we held dear those with whom he fought and suffered. On December 11, 1897, speaking to a reunion of surviving members of the 20th Regimental Association, Holmes said:

We are getting old fellows ... things have not stood still. The list of ghosts grows long. The roster of men grows short. My memory of those stirring days has faded to a blurred dream. Only one thing has not changed. As I look into your eyes I feel as always I do that a great trial in our youth has made you different—made all of us different from what we could have been without it. It has made us a brotherhood of man. And best of all it has made us believe in something else besides ourselves and getting all the loaves and fishes we could.[21]

Earlier, Memorial Day 1884, he said more succinctly: "Through our great good fortune, in our youth our hearts were touched by fire."[22] The War was always on his mind. Yet,

---

18 Louis Menand, *The Metaphysical Club* (Farrar, Strauss, and Giroux, 2001), ix.
19 Holmes, James, and Peirce were members of the Metaphysical Club that met in Cambridge early in the 1870s. Only Peirce mentioned the Club. What is certain is that a circle of younger intellectuals, including these three, gathered for intellectual discussion. Most had some relation to Harvard. See Menand, *The Metaphysical Club*, 201–205 (and the whole of chapter 9).
20 See Richard A. Posner's *The Essential Holmes*, edited and introduced by Richard A. Posner (University of Chicago Press, 1992), especially his essay at xi–xxii.
21 Posner, *The Essential Holmes*, 73.
22 Stephen Budiansky, *Oliver Wendell Holmes: A Life in War, Law, and Ideas* (W.W. Norton, 2019), 127.

his gallantry—so singular among gentlemen of his social status among Boston's elite—was not nearly so remarkable as his method of discovering what kind of philosophy he would devote his life's work to advancing. When his Civil War duty was over, he went to Concord to talk to a family friend, Ralph Waldo Emerson, about his future.[23] He came away with the decision to study law, which he thought provided him a better way to write philosophy. Holmes meant to do something different.

One recent pragmatist, Cornel West, identified Emerson as among "the grand spiritual godfathers of American pragmatism," along with Jefferson and Lincoln. This in part because, West continues, all three shared a sense of the ultimately tragic deep structural nature of democracy—of its acute sense of "individuality within participatory communities, heroic action of common folk in a world of radical contingency, and a deep sense of evil that fuels struggles for justice."[24] This is a sense of pragmatism that served Lincoln tacitly and Holmes explicitly. Yet, Holmes would do philosophy but not as Emerson did. His pragmatism such as it was sunk down in the bottomless chain of practical actions and precedents upon which the law does its work.

In the years to come, when Holmes became a judicial associate of both the Massachusetts and the United States Supreme Courts, he deployed his profound knowledge of the law—a knowledge he composed as the rhetorical harmony over the primary melody of his unique brand of pragmatism. Nowhere is this more evident than in his masterful book, *The Common Law* in 1881; for example:

> The object of this book is to present a general view of the Common Law. To accomplish the task, other tools are needed besides logic. It is something to show that the consistency of a system requires a particular result, but it is not all. *The life of the law has not been logic: it has been experience.*

Then Holmes added a very specific statement that conforms judiciously to pragmatism as it would come to be. "The law embodies the story of a nation's development through many centuries and it cannot be dealt with as if it contained only the axioms and corollaries of a book of mathematics."[25]

In time, Holmes came to be known for his critique of legal formalism—the belief that legal decisions can be reached entirely by resort to agreed-upon principles applied to the case at hand. Holmes trusted the ability of judges to decide cases on the basis of their own experience with the facts of the world as they apply to the case before them.

Holmes's pragmatic legal reasoning is particularly evident in his famous dissent in *Lochner v. New York* (198 U.S.). Holmes is said to have dissented only a few times among the many hundreds of cases he heard. But of the few, one in particular is said to be studied in most law schools today—a dissent that Posner described as a "rhetorical masterpiece ... merely the greatest judicial opinion of the last hundred years."[26] Holmes's 1904 dissent in *Lochner v. New York* is brief but jam-packed:

---

23 *Ibid*, 58–61, 152–153.
24 Cornel West, "Pragmatism and the Sense of the Tragic," in *Keeping Faith* (Routledge, 1993), 107–108.
25 Both quotes here are from Holmes, "Early Forms of Liability," Lecture 1, *The Common Law*. See Posner, *The Essential* Holmes, 237. Emphasis added.
26 Posner, *Law and Literature* (Harvard University Press, 1988), 346–347; cited by Budiansky, *Oliver Wendell Holmes*, 294.

> I regret sincerely that I am unable to agree with the judgment in this case, and that I think it my duty to express my dissent. This case is decided upon an economic theory which a large part of the country does not entertain ... .The liberty of the citizen to do as he likes so long as he does not interfere with the liberty of others to do the same, which has been a shibboleth for some well-known writers, is interfered with by school laws, by the Post Office, by every state or municipal institution which takes his money for purposes thought desirable, whether he likes it or not. The 14th Amendment does not enact Mr. Herbert Spencer's Social Statics. ... *I think that the word liberty in the Fourteenth Amendment is perverted when it is held to prevent the natural outcome of a dominant opinion, unless it can be said that a rational and fair man necessarily would admit that the statute proposed would infringe fundamental principles as they have been understood by the traditions of our people and our law.*[27]

The average reader might not find this a rhetorical masterpiece. Yet today, as in 1904, given that it is addressed to lawyerly readers, it is. It avoids the customary legalese. But more importantly, whatever may be obscure to some, is the straightforwardness with which Holmes stands against the majority's position in *Lochner v. New York*.

At issue was the right of plaintiff, Lochner, who ran a bakery in Utica, New York, to defy a state law that limited the employer from contracting with workers to work more than 10 hours a day, 60 a week. The principle at issue was whether the rights of a business owner are protected by the Fourteenth Amendment. The majority ruled in favor of Lochner by judging that "the right to purchase or to sell labor is part of the liberty protected by this amendment unless there are circumstances which exclude the right."[28] Encouraged by the due process provision of the Fourteenth Amendment, the majority concluded that no individual employer of laborers can be deprived of his right "to life, liberty, and property." They believed that the property in question was the worker's time which the Court decided was a right to liberty as such for the employer. The decision's not very subtle political attitude was consistent with the economic theories of the Gilded Age in which the dominant class was, in effect, the only actor with true and unbridled rights.

Holmes's dissent is excruciatingly lethal to the majority's idea of liberty. For one, he points to instances where the State infringes regularly on these rights. It imposes school and Sunday laws, plants a Post Office in local communities, while also demanding and collecting taxes. The pragmatic summit of his dissent is that the very idea of liberty is "perverted" when the principle is deployed in a way that is foreign to the long-held traditions of the people *and* their laws. The people here served are the ground for a legal decision—one that required no abstract law or exaggerated judicial theory. Of course, Holmes, as always, is formally respectful of his "brethren" (as the saying went) on the Court.[29] But no reasonable reader could miss the bull's eye of his dissent.

---

27 Holmes's dissent is readily available online as part of *Lochner v. New York* (198 U.S. 45). The version here omits certain of the less sections less relation to his pragmatism. The omissions are short and indicated. Also, Posner, *The Essential Holmes*, 305–306. Emphasis added.
28 Here and below, for the majority's opinions on *Lochner v. New York*, see p. 58 at: https://tile.loc.gov/storageservices/service/ll/usrep/usrep198/usrep198045/usrep198045.pdf
29 Holmes's sideswipe at Herbert Spencer is the sole instance of a righteous dig at the Court's majority. In the day Spencer's *Social Statics* (1851) was still a widely read classic of social science. In the book's conclusion (para. 7),

American Pragmatism Comes to Be

If it be granted that Lincoln and Holmes, in their different ways, were proto-pragmatists, then, in them and others of the day, there is confirmation for a general fact of Americans thinking America. There has always been a pragmatic feature in the settled nation's culture. This was, to be sure, a matter of necessity. The first settlers had to deal with a sparsely populated and otherwise raw natural wilderness. Some might wonder: Is it too strong to suggest that seeds from the earliest days gave rise to the pragmatic attitude of the nation? Yet, the common sense of it is that, as America sprouted into the broad-branched state of our day, many of the seeds planted by the settlers and founders came to decorate its branches with individual, pragmatic leaves, each a tribute to its having made itself against a looming wilderness. Culturally, what matters is that seeds sown on bad soil came from somewhere and took root. When, in the earliest days, the cultural soil is wild and barren, what grows matters. The moment when buds peeked out were the Civil War and its aftermath. In a sense, it is fair to say that Abraham Lincoln was the last of the great practical proto-pragmatists—in respect to whom, Oliver Wendell Holmes, Jr. was the first out-in-the-open, if small flowered, philosophical pragmatist.

It would not be until the writings of Charles Sanders Peirce on signs and semiotics in—for example, "What is a Sign?" in 1894—that an analytic move toward philosophical pragmatism began to make way for what was to come in William James's *Pragmatism: A New Name for Old Ways of Thinking* in 1907. Roughly, 1890 to 1920 was the highwater mark for the formation of classic American pragmatism. Yet, in the between, two figures, one obvious and well-known, were identifiably associated with what was to come, Theodore Roosevelt and Jane Addams.

Theodore Roosevelt—though author of many well-regarded books[30] and a respected intellectual—took a pragmatic approach to his presidency. This was the Gilded Age. Roosevelt was from a well-off family. But he was dead serious in his efforts to limit the control of the capitalists who controlled most of the nation's wealth. While not even a practical pragmatist as was Lincoln, there can be little doubt either that he came along at the right time for pragmatism, or that the emergent culture made Roosevelt possible. Either way, there were strains of the philosophy in what he did and said—for example, his uncompromising attitude toward those of extreme wealth, his own class of origin:

> It is unhappily true that we inherit the evil as well as the good done by those who have gone before us, and in the one case as in the other the influence extends far beyond the mere material effects. ... So it is with the equally dangerous criminals of the wealthy classes. The conscienceless stock speculator who acquires wealth by swindling his fellows, by debauching judges, and by corrupting legislatures and who ends his days with the reputation of being among the richest men in America, exerts on the minds of the rising generation an influence worse than that of the average murderer or bandit...[31]

If these lines seem to be little more than cantankerous, consider them in light of his somewhat more explicitly pragmatic ideas on philanthropy:

Spencer writes lucidly of the highfalutin generalization that Holmes despised: "The candid reader can now see his way out of the dilemma in which he feels placed, between a conviction, on the one hand, that the perfect law is the only safe guide, and a consciousness, on the other, that the perfect law cannot be fulfilled by imperfect men." Neither conviction nor consciousness figured in OWH's thinking about the law.

30 An example: *The Naval War of 1812* (1882) was long considered a classic in military history. It is thought to have provided the argument for Roosevelt's appointment as Assistant Secretary of the Navy where he began the work that continued into his presidency to strengthen America's naval forces.

31 Theodore Roosevelt, *American Ideals* (G.P. Putnam's Sons, 1897), 21.

The soup-kitchen style of philanthropy is worse than useless, for in philanthropy as everywhere else in life almost as much harm is done by soft-headedness as by hard-heartedness. The highest type of philanthropy is that which springs from the feeling of brotherhood, and which, therefore, rests on the self-respecting, healthy basis of mutual obligation and common effort.[32]

Roosevelt did not let the case rest with impassioned pronouncements. His work ethic was not far from Lincoln's practical politics. Most famously, he said—with respect to J.P. Morgan's attempt to "fix" his differences with the President in mind: "All I ask is a square deal for every man. Give him a fair chance. Do not let him wrong anyone, and do not let him be wronged." *Square Deal* was the motto of his presidency, especially of his unrelenting political opposition to the captains of industry like J.P. Morgan he repeatedly cut down to size by breaking up their monopolies.[33]

Theodore Roosevelt was not a pragmatist, but his practical politics were assuredly apt to the coming of this new philosophical disposition. Others in the day were out-and-out pragmatists. None more so than Jane Addams who founded Hull House in Chicago to care for recent immigrants and was a leader in the Settlement House Movement. Like Roosevelt, she won the Nobel Peace prize (Addams for her work for world peace). Unsurprisingly, she was a supporter of Theodore Roosevelt and his progressive politics. She was, among many other activities, a founding member of the National Conference of Charities and Corrections, a leader in the National American Suffrage Movement, the National Association of Colored People, the International League for Peace and Freedom, among other leadership roles.

Then too, based on her years of experience serving newly urbanized immigrants, she was instrumental in the University of Chicago establishing a School of Social Work. She had founded Hull House in 1889, three years before the University itself was founded. More importantly, three years earlier John Dewey established his no less famous Laboratory School that provided him the experience that advanced his pragmatist philosophy. Once Dewey heard Addams lecture on her work, he sought her out and soon enough they became close friends as well as intellectual collaborators. Addams was not a philosopher by any means. She was too preoccupied with the practical needs of the poor and otherwise needy. Just the same it is easy to see that her relations with Dewey were influences on her thinking, as hers was on his. For one example, *Democracy and Social Ethics* (1902): "As the acceptance of democracy brings a certain life-giving power, so it has its own sanctions and comforts. Perhaps the most obvious one is the curious sense which comes to us from time to time, that we belong to the whole, that a certain basic wellbeing can never be taken away from us whatever the turn of fortune." Compare this to Dewey in his most famous book, *Democracy and Education* (1916): "[Democracy entails] not only more numerous and more varied points of shared common interest, but greater reliance upon the recognition of mutual interests as a factor in social control." Two different writers, each treating the same subject some fifteen years apart, each writing in their own style, coming to nearly the same conclusion. When people come together democratically, they create more encompassing communities that serve their members' well-being. Not for certain the kind of thing that Lincoln or Holmes might have said, but at the least such a thought is typical of pragmatism came to be.

---

32 *Ibid*, 345–346.
33 On Roosevelt's dramatic rebuke of J.P. Morgan's arrogant attempt to "fix" his relations with the President, see Edmund Morris, *Theodore Rex* (Random House, 2001), 90–92.

11 Pragmatism, the Hard Realities of Change
William James, Charles Sanders Peirce, John Dewey, Jane Addams, George Herbert Mead, Richard Rorty, Cornel West

The Pragmatist clings to facts and concreteness,
observes truth at its work in particular cases, and generalizes.
Truth, for him, becomes a class-name for all sorts of working-values in experience.
—William James, Pragmatism: A New Name for Some Old Ways of Thinking, 1907

The <u>final</u> upshot of thinking is the exercise of volition,
And, of this thought no longer forms a part;
but belief is only a stadium of mental action, an effect upon our nature due to thought,
which will influence future thinking.
—Charles Sanders Peirce, How to Make Our Ideas Clear, 1878

Society not only continues to exist by transmission, by communication,
but it may fairly be said to exist in transmission, in communication.
There is more than a verbal tie between the words common, community, and communication.
—John Dewey, Democracy and Education, 1916

As the acceptance of democracy brings a certain life-giving power,
so it has its own sanctions and comforts.
—Jane Addams, Democracy and Social Ethics, 1902

The 'I,' then, in this relation of the 'I' and the 'Me'
is something that is, so to speak, responding to a social situation
which is within the experience of the individual.
—George Herbert Mead, Mind, Self and Society, 1934

National pride is to countries what self-respect is to individuals:
a necessary condition for self-improvement.
Too much national pride can produce bellicosity and imperialism,
just as excessive self-respect can produce arrogance.
—Richard Rorty, Achieving Our Country, 1997

The pragmatist conception of human beings is one of an organism
Whose faculties are integrated, who is interested and integrated with an environment.
So that when you are talking about the consensus forged by human beings
who agree upon certain common aims and ends.
—Cornel West, Pragmatism and the Tragic in Prophetic Thought in Postmodern Times, 1993

The American Philosophy: Where It Started and Where It Has Gone

Some may consider pragmatism America's only indigenous philosophy. Of course it is not, one only has to consider the Concord Moment in the 1860s when Waldo Emerson, Henry Thoreau, and Margaret Fuller wrote as then only American intellectuals could about all manner of issues. Then there is the Revolutionary Era when John Madison, Thomas Jefferson, and Alexander Hamilton put theoretical meat on the democratic bones George Washington laid down. And more, if less notable, since then.

But Pragmatism, the philosophy, was truly indigenous in the sense that it played on practical pragmatism that the first settlers after 1619 *and* their slaves lived by to survive the cruel new wilderness of their new worlds. The founders of the philosophy some three centuries later live good enough lives in a far more than settled world in Cambridge, Massachusetts where the bright lights and shadows of Harvard were sun and cloud to their creative thinking. In the day, the elites in and around Harvard were in some or another degree of relationship. The founders themselves, William James and Charles Sanders Peirce were friends to such an extent that when Peirce was ill and destitute near the end of his life, James organized friends to donate money that would give Peirce some comfort. Yet, beyond friendship it was James who introduced Pragmatism to the world, with lines like these: "The Pragmatist clings to facts and concreteness, observes truth at its work in particular cases, and generalizes. Truth, for him, becomes a class-name for all sorts of working-values in experience."[1] Here, is James at his best writing for those willing to read plain yet important language. Yet, it comes at the beginning of the chapter in which he introduces Pragmatism with reference to Charles Peirce's own initial statement on the subject in 1878, in "How to Make Our Ideas Clear." Peirce's ideas, however, were seldom clear. But in the 1878 essay James refers to, Peirce is clearer than usual:

> The *final* upshot of thinking is the exercise of volition. And, of this thought no longer forms a part; but belief is only a stadium of mental action, an effect upon our nature due to thought, which will influence future thinking.[2]

Clarity is always in the eye of the beholder. Here the words seem to make sense because they occur in a section on thought and belief. Where they begin to confuse even a well-intended reader is if this is a defining statement of Pragmatism as it would come to be, why not just say so, straight on? The answer is that Peirce always kept two or more ideas in mind in any given discussion. This is not to say that James was simple-minded. Rather it is to say that Pragmatism itself is much more than working ideas in action.

As a consequence Pragmatism is a philosophical attitude that can only make common sense when it is used in relation to practical subjects. Two who could be said to have deployed applied Pragmatism were John Dewey, who studied and directed schools, and Jane Addams, who was a leader in the Settlement House Movement, who were both deeply interested in how democracy works for good. Dewey, for example: "Society not only continues to exist by transmission, by communication, but it may fairly be said to exist in transmission, in communication. There is more than a verbal tie between the words common,

---

[1] William James, *Pragmatism: A New Name for Some Old Ways of Thinking* (Longmans, Green and Co., 1949 [1907]), 69.

[2] Charles Sanders Peirce, "How to Make Our Ideas Clear [1878]," in *Charles Sanders Peirce: The Essential Writings*, edited by Edward C. Moore (Prometheus Books, 1972), 143–144.

community, and communication."³ Then Jane Addams: "As the acceptance of democracy brings a certain life-giving power, so it has its own sanctions and comforts."⁴

Much later, George Herbert Mead wrote in the Pragmatist tradition, in his *Mind Self and Society*, a line that many students of social theory have memorized: "The 'I,' then, in this relation of the 'I' and the 'Me' is something that is, so to speak, responding to a social situation, which is within the experience of the individual."⁵ He wrote in other outlets of Pragmatism but, as he put it, he was more interested "in the American scene"⁶—an interesting remark because the book in itself was not in any way focused on American culture, except possibly in the sense that Mead thought of himself as writing in the American tradition of pragmatism. I can't be sure, but if this was why he composed the remarkable ideas, the possibility gives justification to mentioning Norman Denzin who was a prolific leader in the Iowa School of Symbolic Interactionism.⁷ I should also mention the role of Herbert Blumer who was an important theorist at the University of Chicago for much of his active academic career. In 1996 while at UC-Berkeley he published a definitional work on Symbolic Interaction plainly influenced by Mead and through him the American tradition of Pragmatism.⁸

As this chapter's title suggests, Pragmatism entails facing the hard realities of social change. This, in part, is why those presented here lived and wrote at different times and with respect to changes that demand a practical method for thinking them. Richard Rorty was a deeply serious philosopher who was known for writing a book *Achieving Our Country: Leftist Thought in Twentieth-Century America*. The book was first of the 1997 William E. Massey Sr. Lectures in the History of American Civilization. In 1997 America had lived through a good decade of post-Cold War change and trouble. The lectures were welcome at normally stodgy Harvard because they spoke to the times with what he said to begin his first lecture.

National pride is to countries what self-respect is to individuals: a necessary condition for self-improvement. Too much national pride can produce bellicosity and imperialism, just as excessive self-respect can produce arrogance.⁹

Cornel West was Rorty's graduate student at Princeton where he learned, not just Pragmatism, but deep and widely cast philosophical thought. He is, in addition to being an author and admired teacher, an ordained minister and the much admired, if controversial, public figure.

---

3 John Dewey, *Democracy and Education* (Gutenberg eBook, 2008 [1916]), chapter 7, Part 1.
4 Jane Addams, *Democracy and Social Ethics* (Macmillan & Co, 1902), 62.
5 George Herbert Mead, *Mind, Self and Society* (University of Chicago Press, 1934), 174.
6 *Ibid*, 289n.
7 Norman Denzin, *The Qualitative Inquiry Reader*, edited with Yvonna S. Lincoln (Sage, 2002). As time went by, Norman, interestingly, left the Sociology Department at the University of Illinois for the College of Communications where he founded the International Institute for Qualitative Inquiry. He and those who shared his broad interest in social issues and the developing qualitative research, acknowledge George Herbert Mead and Pragmatism as chief among the influences of their international movement. (See for example the article by two Turkish sociologists: Sebnem Caglar and Füsun Alver, "The impact of symbolic interactionism on research studies about communication science". *International Journal of Arts and Sciences* 8 (2015), 479–484.) Norman published well more than 50 books on many subjects. He was also a courageous and generously kind human being who faced up to a problem with alcoholism so that he could continue his ever robust writing and thinking and his many relations with others (including those like me who worked and thought differently) . -CL
8 For an, at the time, off-beat interpretation of Blumer, see Charles Lemert, *Sociology and the Twilight of Man: Homocentrism and Discourse in Sociological Theory* (Southern Illinois University Press, 1979), Chapter 5. [This is not an advertisement!]
9 Richard Rorty, *Achieving Our Country: Leftist Thought in Twentieth-Century America* (Harvard University Press, 1998), 1.

All this explains his prophetic view of Pragmatism's sense of the tragic: "The pragmatist conception of human beings is one of an organism whose faculties are integrated, who is interested and integrated with an environment."[10]

A Local Pragmatist

James Thomas is well-known about town but especially in the Hill, New Haven's second major poor and mostly Black neighborhood. James grew up there. In high school he was an outstanding basketball player—so good that he won a scholarship to play at a major university whose team challenged for, and once won, the NCAA championship. James did not star in college and did not finish his degree program. After, he returned home to care for his many siblings and their children and his mother who was confined to her home due to age-related weakness.

For reasons not entirely clear to the many who love him as a friend, he became homeless. For eight years he walked the streets, eating what he could find in dumpsters or thrown aside by those who couldn't be bothered to dispose properly of their garbage. For him this was good fortune. The food wasn't clean, but it kept him going. Nights, whatever the weather, he slept under the bleachers at one of the City's two larger high schools. He covered himself as best he could, often with clothes and an occasional torn blanket found here and there. For eight years he kept this life going as best as anyone could.

Then, one spring day, James was walking in an upscale downtown neighborhood. Joe, a resident, saw him coming. He hated giving money to homeless people wandering by. James approached. Joe grew irritable. He was ready to say a firm No when James asked for a bar of soap. Joe was taken aback but liked the idea. He offered James a shower, then lunch. They are friends to this day, years later. They are truly an odd couple. Joe is white, of medium height and weight, well employed and housed. James is not white, of considerable height and robust weight, at the time homeless with no means whatsoever. When they are together, among those who don't know them, heads turn. Yet, soon enough, after first meeting, Joe took him to his church. Knowing Joe, heads did not turn but some wondered who this new person was. In time, James was hired by the church as a part-time sexton. This, it would seem, lent James a degree of respectability such that he found a public housing apartment. It was offered rent free, paid for by his teaching night basketball to the City's drifting youth. Park and Recreation workers remembered James as a basketball player and a good family man from the Hill where he grew up.

It was not long before the Church recognized his special qualities. The rector offered James the use of the Church's undercroft for weekly meetings. James wanted to organize a weekly meeting for homeless men and women. At first there were no more than four or five attending. It did not take long for the number to grow to an average of fifty or more each week including former prisoners, recovering drug addicts, and despairing homeless people. The meetings were simple, consisting of Bible lessons and religious talks offered, at first by James, but in time by a group of men and women comprising a spiritual team. Eventually, members of the community made simple lunches for those attending. Then too community agencies that serve the homeless sent staff to the meetings. They helped a good many of the group find housing funded by the State. In time James's reputation grew such that he was invited to speak in other parts of the state. A church in Middletown called James to start a similar group there. He is now officially the outreach minister of his church in New Haven and has been offered a similar position in Middletown.

---

10 Cornel West, "Pragmatism and the Tragic" in *Prophetic Thought in Postmodern Times* (Monroe Maine, Common Courage Press, 1993), 50.

All this, but James, though well enough housed, remains poor, if not impoverished. He does not gain more than modest pay for his work as sexton, and little for the meetings. Needless to say, James Thomas is an unusual and good man—now famous across the City, and beyond, for reasons more than his now faded athletic prowess. But that is not all. His story is a near perfect illustration of pragmatism as lived. James is not a philosopher, but he is among those Americans who have imbibed pure practical pragmatism. He came to terms with eight years homeless on the streets. He did not let those years destroy the core beliefs that would flourish after—and had been there under the surface all along. Otherwise, once settled in a new life, he would not have won over Joe and members of his church nor, just as significantly, would not have gathered the men and women in his weekly spiritual group, many of whom knew him when he was young. An athletic star he was no longer. But he is a thoroughly real person. In the simplest of terms his pragmatism lies in realizing that the individual and the social come together for the good of all. As Cornel West put it: "We have to recognize that there cannot be relationships unless there is commitment, unless there is loyalty, unless there is love, patience, persistence."[11]

William James Codifies Pragmatism

William James was born in 1842 a year after Oliver Wendell Holmes, Jr. The two became the best known and arguably the most innovative intellectuals in modernizing America late in the nineteenth century. James's friend and colleague in the intellectual culture of Cambridge, Massachusetts Charles Sanders Peirce was, at the least, philosophically more innovative but not well known because his writings were all but impossible for the general reader to understand.

Holmes and James advanced two new approaches to traditional, even ancient, practices. For Holmes it was the Law; for James it was Psychology. Strictly speaking, neither was an out-and-out pragmatist. Holmes was an early practitioner of pragmatism before the fact. James contributed to pragmatism by popularizing what Charles Sanders Peirce rather inscrutably invented. Yet, in this respect, James was the one whose writings on psychology and other subjects, while not explicitly pragmatist, bore some relation to the philosophy. He, more than anyone (other than John Dewey), made pragmatism known to the wider world.

More to the point of William James, he was slow to settle on an intellectual focus after years of wandering about Europe, then Harvard and Cambridge. Though James returned to Europe many times, he did not take to Europe as did his brother Henry, the author of great works of fiction, who did not take to the United States. Henry James became an expatriate, living and working in England. William James was, if not an expatriate, uprooted in his own way. William's early adult years were where in a sense he drifted about in Harvard's neighborhoods where many brilliant men, many Harvard College alumni lived and worked without finding a permanent place in the College. Hence, they were inclined toward regular gatherings like the one Peirce remembered as The Metaphysical Club—an ironic name for thinkers who wanted nothing to do with metaphysics.

But, more precisely, James's wandering was intellectual. He had learned French and German in Europe and studied art and science in Geneva. Back home, while still young, he studied art in Newport, Rhode Island. After which, he entered the Lawrence Scientific School of Harvard. There he tried, variously, physiology, anatomy, and a bit of chemistry,

---

11 Cornel West in "Interview by bell hooks," in bell hooks and Cornel West, *Breaking Bread: Insurgent Black Intellectual Life* (South End Press, 1991), 55.

before going to Harvard Medical School in 1864. After a year, he signed on to Louis Agassiz's research venture to the Amazon River where Agassiz hoped to find evidence for glaciers in the Southern Hemisphere—this to prove his theory that all species arise in their own locale and not because they evolve from earlier life forms. Agassiz was wildly popular as a public lecturer until his reputation started to fade as Charles Darwin's *On the Origin of the Species* in 1859 changed everything by demonstrating the greater scientific merits of evolutionary theory.[12] James, it turned out, found the Amazon research venture uninteresting. He returned home early and renewed his studies at the Medical School. He graduated in 1869 but never practiced medicine. That year he suffered one of several extended periods of depression, from which he recovered in 1873 when he was appointed instructor in Anatomy and Physiology at Harvard. In 1875 James began teaching Psychology. In 1880 he added Philosophy to his resume. In 1885 he became Professor of Philosophy. Two years later James was also Professor of Psychology.

In 1890, after his academic meandering, James published his masterpiece, *Principles of Psychology*, well over 1300 pages in two volumes. Today a good bit of what James covered in this book is passé. Yet, *Principles* remains a model for anyone daring enough to write a comprehensive textbook introducing—actually inventing—a new field of scientific endeavor. In James's day, only Oliver Wendell Holmes' *Common Law* in 1881 (like *Principles*, still in print) was of the same ilk. *Principles* is twenty-eight nuanced chapters ranging from *The Scope of Psychology* and *The Functions of the Brain* to *Habit*, *The Relations of Minds to Other Things*, and *Stream of Thought*, then to *Attention*, *Conception*, *Perception of Time*, and *Memory*. These and other subjects are Book One. Book Two includes: *Sensation*, *Imagination*, *The Perception of Reality*, *Instinct*, *The Emotions*, and *Hypnosis*—topics that today may or may not be taken up in psychological research and teaching. Just the same while Book One tends to consider issues that, as James put it, treat psychology as a natural science; Book Two, by contrast, reaches beyond to subjects that now, as then, would not be thought of as available to scientific study—especially imagination, instinct, emotions, and hypnosis.[13] Still, Book One is closer to scientific psychology, then and now; and Book Two in 1890 was a venture toward a comprehensive and original catalogue of psychology's range of research possibilities. *Principles* was after all a serious, and in the day, systematic textbook that set the field of psychology on new ground.

What is also clear from *Principles* is just how much an incipient pragmatist philosophy was already sprouting roots in 1890, many years before James would write *Pragmatism*. The ambition and scope of the book is made clear in Chapter 1 of Book One under the topic header: "Psychology is the Science of Mental Life, both of its phenomena and of their conditions." He continues:

The phenomena are such things as we call feelings, desires, cognitions, reasonings, decisions, and the like; and, superficially considered, their variety and complexity is such as to leave a chaotic impression on the observer. The most natural and consequently the earliest way of unifying the material was, first, to classify it as well as might be, and, secondly, to affiliate the diverse mental modes thus found, upon a simple entity, the

---

12 An important recent book on Darwin's influence in America is Randall Fuller, *The Book That Changed America: How Darwin's Theory of Evolution Ignited a Nation* (Viking, 2017).
13 Today neuroscience somewhat tangentially studies sensations and perception of reality, while some brands of psychoanalysis attend to instincts. As for emotions, the term amygdala (coined in 1996) or its equivalent does not appear in *Principles*. *Hypnosis* today is kin to such new experimental medical procedures for eating disorder, anxiety, depression, PTSD.

personal Soul, of which they are taken to be so many facultative manifestations. Now, for instance, the Soul manifests its faculty of Memory, now of Reasoning, now of Volition, or again its Imagination or its Appetite.[14]

As it happens, James's idea of the Personal Soul figures in the one chapter that today still matters to social theorists—Book One, Chapter 10, "The Consciousness of Self." One of James's more important, but seldom recognized, contributions to social theory is how he, single-handedly, erased the Soul as the center of individual human beings and replaced it with a theory of the social Self.[15] In his words, "the constituent of the Self may be divided into two classes: ... the feelings and emotions they arouse,--*Self-feelings* and the actions to which they prompt,--*Self-seeking and Self-preservation.*"[16] Those in the first are a) the material Self; b) the social Self; c) the spiritual Self; and d) the pure Ego. The second class is curious but telling as to James's careful thinking through. It contains but one aspect associated with the material Self by which he greatly expands even on his notion of the social Self:

> The body is the innermost part of *the material Self* in each of us; and certain parts of the body seem more intimately ours than the rest. The clothes come next. The old saying that the human person is composed of three parts—soul, body and clothes—is more than a joke. We so appropriate our clothes and identify ourselves with them that there are few of us who, if asked to choose between having a beautiful body clad in raiment perpetually shabby and unclean, and having an ugly and blemished form always spotlessly attired, would not hesitate a moment before making a decisive reply. Next, our immediate family is a part of ourselves. Our father and mother, our wife and babes, are bone of our bone and flesh of our flesh. When they die, a part of our very selves is gone. … Our home comes next. Its scenes are part of our life; its aspects awaken the tenderest feelings of affection. … All these different things are the objects of instinctive preferences coupled with the most important practical interests of life. We all have a blind impulse to watch over our body, to deck it with clothing of an ornamental sort, to cherish parents, wife and babes, and to find for ourselves a home of our own which we may live in and improve.[17]

Considered straight-on the passage may seem a wordy expansion on his idea of the Self. But considered more closely one sees early-on that, for James, personal life is always drawn toward the social Self—a relation that became theoretically explicit in the two more dynamic constituents of the Self—the Social Self and the Pure Ego. He provided memorable definitions of each.

In *Principles of Psychology*, he wrote of the Social Self: "*A man has as many social selves as there are individuals who recognize him* and carry an image of him in their mind. To wound any one of these images is to wound him."[18] This doctrine was repeatedly deployed by later pragmatists, notably George Herbert Mead's *Mind, Self, and Society*—and it was evident in W.E.B. Du Bois's idea of the double consciousness of the American Negro in *Souls*

---

14 James, *The Principles of Psychology I* (Harvard University Press, 1981 [1890]), 15.
15 Charles Lemert, "A History of Identity: The Riddle at the Heart of the Mystery of Life," *Routledge Handbook of Identity Studies*, edited by Anthony Elliott (Routledge, 2011), chapter 1.
16 *James, Principles I*, 280. The five aspects of the Self are found in *Ibid*, 292–93. Italics are in the original.
17 *Ibid*, 280.
18 *Ibid*, 281–282. Emphasis original.

of *Black Folk* (1903) and Charles Horton Cooley's the looking glass self (1902).[19] James's discussion of the Pure Ego is, if anything, even more influential because it offers a classic statement of personal identity theory:

> The sense of personal identity is ... the sense of sameness perceived *by* thought and predicated of things *thought about*. These things are a present self and a self of yesterday. The thought not only thinks them, but thinks they are identical. The psychologist looking-on, and playing the critic, might prove the thought wrong. In either case the personal identity would not exist as a *fact,* but it would exist as a *feeling* all the same; and the consciousness of it would still be there ...[20]

Then he concludes the passage with the unforgettable definition of personal identity as a conviction always hovering, usually unspoken in the back of the individual's mind: "*I am the same self that I was yesterday.*"[21]

Hence the theoretical pair, when joined, are not a dichotomy but a dialectical account of the individual's necessary relation to society: *A man has as many social selves as there are individuals who recognize him/ I am the same self that I was yesterday.* This same dialectic stands behind pragmatism's central principle that truth is neither an abstraction nor an empirical fact but the practical idea that individuals come to be in their ongoing relations with society.

Later in 1907, in *Pragmatism: A New Name for Old Ways of Thinking,* James begins Chapter 1, *The Present Dilemma in Philosophy*, with much the same idea: "Philosophy is at once the most sublime and the most trivial of human pursuits. It works in the minutest crannies, and it opens out the widest vistas."[22] Pragmatism, he continues, is not about scientific method or abstraction. It is about experiential facts about the world. The most interesting chapter is 5, *Pragmatism and Common Sense* that, near its beginning, puts the idea in down-to-earth terms:

> Our fundamental ways of thinking about things are discoveries of exceedingly remote ancestors, which have been able to preserve themselves throughout the experience of all subsequent time. They form one great stage of common sense. Other stages have grafted themselves upon this stage but have never succeeded in displacing it. Let us consider this common-sense stage first as if it may be final. In practical talk, a man's common sense means his good Judgement, his freedom from eccentricity, his GUMPTION, to use the vernacular word.

Hence the book's subtitle insisting that pragmatism is a "new name for old ways of thinking."

The eight chapters of *Pragmatism* cover a good many of those older ways of thinking: the one and the many, the concept of truth, and pragmatism's relation to humanism and religion. In Chapter 6, "Pragmatism's Conception of Truth," James makes his definitive statement of the basic nature of pragmatist theory:

---

19 Importantly, Du Bois was James's student at Harvard and Cooley knew Mead and worked with Dewey at the University of Michigan.
20 James, *Principles*, 315–316.
21 *Ibid*, 316. Emphasis original.
22 Concerning quotations from James's *Pragmatism*, I give chapter numbers or other identifications of their location in the text because there are so many editions with different paginations that not even the online Gutenberg text gives page numbers. See https://www.gutenberg.org/files/5116/5116-h/5116-h.htm—this is the

> What, in short, is truth's cash-value in experiential terms? The moment pragmatism asks this question, it sees the answer: *True Ideas Are Those That We Can Assimilate, Validate, Corroborate And Verify. False Ideas Are Those We Cannot.* ... The truth of an idea is not a stagnant property inherent in it. Truth HAPPENS to an idea. It BECOMES true, is MADE true by events. Its verity is in fact an event, a process: the process namely of its verifying itself ...[23]

One cannot help but understand at least the drift of James's clear enough definition of pragmatism. For better or worse pragmatism's acknowledged founder, Charles Sanders Peirce was seldom able to make himself clear to the general reader as James did. Just the same, Peirce must be understood as best one can.

Charles Sanders Peirce Overcomes the Limits of Binary Theory

Pragmatism, as it developed after the deaths of James in 1910 and Peirce in 1914, grew beyond philosophy in two major ways such that, early in the twenty-first century, it has become important to many brands of social theory. James in his way stood behind the brand that came to have an effect in sociology, social ethics, religion, and related topics including democratic theory and education. Peirce was more important to the second way that pragmatism developed in respect to language and the theory of signs (or semiotics). Though both James and Peirce touched on both subjects, the common, if occasionally implicit, theme in both aspects of pragmatism was, in James's words, the Social Self and the Pure Ego—or, as things developed, Society and the Individual.

Peirce was a kind of philosophical wizard. James, who had been Peirce's friend to the end, once told of attending a talk by Peirce of which he said that he could not understand a word, but he was enchanted listening as the words passed over him. James was not the only one affected this way by Peirce. So prescient was Peirce that he anticipated the more familiar but classic theory of semiotics of the Swiss linguistic Ferdinand de Saussure, whose *Course in General Linguistics* was not published until 1916 some two decades after Peirce first laid down the foundations for a more prudent theory of language and signs. Simply put, Saussure's scheme rested on the distinction between language (*langue*) and speech (*parole*) from which he derived the notion that the sign (itself comprising a signifier and a signified) is arbitrary, which is to say, all-too-simply, that words bear no relation to things. This means that the word "cow" when spoken is taken from language, not from an actual bovine animal in a field. Peirce by contrast, and well before Saussure, did not believe that any such dichotomous scheme for languages works—that only a tripartite one will do. He wrote almost as if he were responding to Saussure (which he could not have been): "The action of a sign calls for a little closer attention. Let me remind you of the distinction between dynamic or dyadic action; and intelligent, or triadic action."[24] Peirce continues:

> An event, A, may, by brute force, produce an event, B; and then the event, B, may in its turn, produce a third event, C. The fact that the event, C, is about to be produced by B,

---

best source for searches of James's *Pragmatism*. By contrast to these many different versions, there is only one standard edition of *Principles of Psychology*.
23 *Ibid*, emphases in original.
24 Charles Sanders Peirce, "Survey of /The Valency of Concepts," *The Collected Papers of Charles Sanders Peirce*, Vol V (Harvard University Press, 1960 [1932]), 323.

has no influence at all upon the production of B by A. It is impossible that it should, since the action of B in producing C is a contingent future event at the time B is produced.[25]

As algebraic as the statement seems, it conveys Peirce's sense of triadic action as ongoing over time.

Hence, Peirce developed his theory of the sign as comprising three elements—or, in his terms, three *actions*—sign, object, interpretant. The three have the effect of signifying "by means of another mental sign" which, he adds ironically, is not purely and simply "mental" in the sense of being ideal as opposed to real. Later he provides an illustration:

> Suppose, for example, an officer of a squad or a company of infantry gives the word of Command "Ground arms!" The order is, of course, a *sign*. The thing that causes a sign is called the *object* (according to the usage of speech, the "real" but more accurately, the *existent object*) represented by the sign: the sign is determined to some species of correspondence to that object. In the present case the object the command represents is the will of the officer that the butts of the muskets be brought down to the ground. Nevertheless the action of the will upon the sign is not simply dyadic; for if he thought the soldiers were deaf mutes, or did not know a word of English, or were raw recruits utterly undrilled, or were indisposed to obedience, his will would not produce the word of the command. However, although this condition is most usually fulfilled, it is not essential to the action of the sign. … In [this case], however, a mental representation of the index is called the *immediate object* of the sign; and this object does triadically produce the intended, or proper, significant outcome of a sign, I propose the name, the *interpretant* of the sign. The example of the imperative command shows that it need not necessarily be of a mental mode of being.[26]

Though the example is relatively clear it also illustrates the extent to which Peirce was always turning his own language and thoughts over in his head.

In respect to Peirce's pragmaticism, his claim that thinking is a semiosis of signs breaks open the confining binary idea that the thinking subject thinks about external objects. Or, better put, Peirce means to say that the thinking subject acts against *and* in relation to structured objective realities. Instead, the practical actions themselves—whether thinking, communicating, or plain old acting—are described by Peirce as being simultaneously inside and outside the individual concept, sign, or action. Then too, according to Peirce, there can be no outcome (no conclusive result of a sign signifying) unless there is (in his word) an *interpretant* in the pragmatic relations. The interpretant creates the significant action—an action that signifies by becoming the object of the sign.

Like James and others in the day, but even more so, Peirce took Darwin's scientific method of chance variation as the key to modern science.[27] In one of Peirce's earliest essays on pragmatism, "How to Make Our Ideas Clear" in 1878, he dismissed the "distinctness of logicians" in a most congenial manner: "We have there found that the action of thought is

---

25 *Ibid*, 323.
26 Peirce, *Collected Papers Vol V*, 324–325.
27 See Louis Menand, "The Law of Errors," *The Metaphysical Club* (Farrar, Straus and Giroux, 2001), chapter 8. On Darwin's chance variation, see *Ibid*, 121–123. Again, on Darwin's influence on American social thought see Randall Fuller, *The Book That Changed America: How Darwin's Theory of Evolution Ignited a Nation*, and for the particular influence of Darwin's theory of chance variation, 224–230. Also of interest to those who use libraries is Philip P. Wiener, *Values in a Universe of Chance: Selected Writings of Charles S. Peirce, 1839–1914* (Doubleday Anchor, 1958).

excited by the irritation of doubt, and ceases when belief is attained, so that the production of belief is the sole function of thought."[28] It would be hard to find a more perfect early statement of pragmatism as it became early in the twentieth century. In "Man's Glassy Essence" in 1892 Peirce reframes the classical concept of logic in respect to the meaning making (his locution) of consciousness in which consciousness depends on the prior sense of a person being an ego: "The consciousness of a general idea has a certain 'unity of ego' in it, which is identical when it passes from one mind to another. It is, therefore, quite analogous to a person; and, indeed, a person is only a particular kind of idea."[29] Again, Peirce here may have been influenced by William James's concept of the Pure Ego in *Principles of Psychology* in 1890. In turn, he influenced James's *Pragmatism* in 1907.

John Dewey and Jane Addams, Pragmatism and Democracy

John Dewey was quite a different intellectual from Peirce and James, though he was familiar with the writings of both.[30] Then too, he was different in the sense that he was from Burlington, Vermont, where he began his studies of philosophy and did graduate work not at Harvard but at Johns Hopkins University. These differences may well be a reason that Dewey was very much his own thinker. Peirce was radically original but, in his way, focused on rethinking his several fields as they came down academically. Dewey, by contrast, knew no limits. He was a social and political activist—commitments encouraged by his work in schools (notably the University of Chicago Laboratory School) and intellectual concern for democracy. He wrote in clear language on a range of subjects—notably, among his books: *Democracy and Education: An Introduction to the Philosophy of Education* (1916), *German Philosophy and Politics* (1915), *The Influence of Darwin on Philosophy* (1910), *How We Think* (1910), *Letters from China and Japan* (1920), *Psychology and Social Practice* (1901), *Critical Theory of Ethics* (1891), *Leibniz's New Essays Concerning Human Understanding* (1902), more. In each he reads closely, while opening up to the importance of their subjects to issues at hand early in the twentieth century.

The best example perhaps of Dewey's personal seriousness about politics was his relationship with Jane Addams, who if anything was more wide ranging than Dewey. Addams founded Hull House in Chicago in 1899 to care for recent immigrants and was a leader in the Settlement House Movement. Like Theodore Roosevelt, she won the Nobel Peace prize. Unsurprisingly, she was a supporter of Roosevelt and his progressive politics. She was, among many other activities, a founding member of the National Conference of Charities and Corrections, a leader in the National American Suffrage Movement, the National Association of Colored People, the International League for Peace and Freedom. Then too, she was instrumental in establishing the University of Chicago School of Social Work. She had founded Hull House the year before the University itself was founded in 1890 and six years before John Dewey established the University's Laboratory School in 1896. Once Dewey heard Addams lecture on her work, he sought her out and soon enough they became

---

28 Charles Sanders Peirce, "How to Make Our Ideas Clear [1878]," in *Charles Sanders Peirce: The Essential Writings*, edited by Edward C. Moore (Prometheus Books, 1972), 141.
29 Charles Sanders Peirce, "Man's Glassy Essence, [1892]" in *Charles Sanders Peirce: The Essential Writings*, 235–236.
30 See, among other of Dewey's writings, his supplemental essay on Peirce's *Chance, Love, and Logic* (where he presents a supplemental essay on Peirce's pragmatism and makes it clear that he has thoroughly understood both Peirce and James; for example "In the literal sense of the word pragmatist, therefore, Peirce is more of a pragmatist than James." Dewey, *The Pragmatism of Peirce*, in Peirce, *Chance, Love, and Logic* (Forgotten Books, 2016 [1923]), 307.

close friends as well as intellectual collaborators. Addams was not, by any means, a philosopher. She was too preoccupied with the practical needs of the poor and otherwise needy. Just the same it is easy to see that her relations with Dewey were influences on her thinking, as hers were on him. For one example, Addams in *Democracy and Social Ethics* (1902):

> As the acceptance of democracy brings a certain life-giving power, so it has its own sanctions and comforts. Perhaps the most obvious one is the curious sense which comes to us from time to time, that we belong to the whole, that a certain basic wellbeing can never be taken away from us whatever the turn of fortune.[31]

Compare this to Dewey in *Democracy and Education* (1916):

> [Democracy entails] not only more numerous and more varied points of shared common interest, but greater reliance upon the recognition of mutual interests as a factor in social control.[32]

Two different writers, each treating the same subject some fifteen years apart, coming to nearly the same conclusion. When people come together democratically, they create more encompassing communities that serve the collective well-being. No one thinks of Addams as a philosophical pragmatist, but she was at least a practitioner of the art; as Dewey, not primarily an activist, practiced what he did in a manner for which, Addams was in the day the global exemplar.

In the historical background of Jane Addams's social activism and John Dewey's pragmatism was the Progressive Era from, roughly, 1890 to 1920, of which Theodore Roosevelt's politics were the most conspicuous instance. The Social Gospel and Settlement House movements were among a good many down-to-earth progressive movements. Progressive politics in the day were largely if not exclusively a response to the outrages of the Gilded Age that were, for example, revealed for what they were by Mark Twain's 1873 book *The Gilded Age* and Upton Sinclair's 1906 *The Jungle*. The extremely wealthy comprised less than 1% of the population while controlling the banking and corporate spheres such that 99% in the day were all-but-excluded from access to any form of wealth, even home ownership.

As for Dewey, he begins his most popular book, *Democracy and Education* with strikingly sound sociological judgment that is also obviously pragmatist:

> Society not only continues to exist by transmission, by communication, but it may fairly be said to exist in transmission, in communication. There is more than a verbal tie between the words common, community, and communication. Men live in a community by virtue of the things which they have in common. … What they must have in common in order to form a community or society are aims, beliefs, aspirations, knowledge—a common understanding—like-mindedness as the sociologists say.[33]

Then, in chapter 5, Dewey dismisses the widely held notion that education is meant to contribute to the student's development. Rather, he says: that education works when it is "the unfolding of latent powers toward a definite goal."[34] Which to us today may seem an

---

31 Jane Addams, *Democracy and Social Ethics* (Macmillan & Co, 1902), 62.
32 John Dewey, *Democracy and Education* (Gutenberg eBook, 2008 [1916]), Chapter 7, Part 2.
33 *Ibid*, Chapter 1, Part 2.
34 *Ibid*, Chapter 5, Part 2.

unremarkable statement. But in his day, *unfolding* affirmed that even the young possess "latent powers" that can, and ought to be, nurtured. The powers that he had earlier described (chapter 4) as "plasticity, the power to learn from experience means the formation of habits." Right off, the individual is at the center of social things and the individual is far from being a cipher subject to social forces or a mere vessel for cultural norms and values. Democracy is the key to his pragmatist theory of education, as he puts it:

> Society is one word, but many things. Men associate together in all kinds of ways and for all kinds of purposes. One man is concerned in a multitude of diverse groups, in which his associates may be quite different. It often seems as if they had nothing in common except that they are modes of associated life. Within every larger social organization there are numerous minor groups: not only political subdivisions, but industrial, scientific, religious, associations. ... From this standpoint, many a minor political unit, one of our larger cities, for example, is a congeries of loosely associated societies, rather than an inclusive and permeating community of action and thought.[35]

Then in the same chapter he characterizes the democratic ideal as, *first*, more than a mere variety of aspects but a coherent arrangement in which there is a "greater reliance upon the recognition of mutual interests as a factor in social control" and, *second*, a change in habits such that individuals readjust "through meeting the new situations produced by varied intercourse." These two aspects, he continues, are at the foundation of a democratic society from which is derived "the devotion of democracy to education."[36]

The details of his theory are worth close reading because they reveal just how Dewey's range of competencies and his ability to probe ideas deeply and plainly led him to propose a social philosophy available at once to ordinary folk and professional social theorists. In particular, Dewey generates a fresh understanding of the individual as at once engaged in, and by, society to the effect of joining in the democratic associations all about by virtue of a natural plasticity that is nurtured in schools that, in being democratic themselves, make societal democracy possible.

George Herbert Mead Revises Pragmatism as a Social Psychology

George Herbert Mead became friends with John Dewey when both were at the University of Michigan, then during their years at the University of Chicago. Dewey was an important influence on Mead until Dewey left in 1904 to become Professor of Philosophy at Columbia University, where Dewey's intellectual interests and public life continued to multiply while Mead's turned back to a relatively narrow social psychology of the self.

One notable, and early, similarity in their thinking was Dewey's 1896 hyper-scientific paper, "The Reflex Arc Concept in Psychology,"[37] which seems to have inspired Mead's 1903 paper "The Definition of the Psychical." Dewey's earlier paper discussed the relation between a neural stimulus and a cognitive reflex. He argued that the reflex is indistinguishable from the stimulus—that therefore there is no arc in time between the two. This, as we have seen, was a crucial idea for his brand of pragmatism because it amounted to the deeper conclusion that action is not first and foremost mental or cognitive—that thoughts arise not

---

35 *Ibid*, Chapter 7, Part 1.
36 *Ibid*, Chapter 7, Part 2.
37 John Dewey, "The Reflex Arc Concept in Psychology," *Psychological Review 3* (1896), 357–370.

in the mind but in the experience of action. Mead, in his own way, examined what was then called "the psychical" (or, more generally, mental process or, even mind):

> The value and content of the conditions is continually changing as the meaning as the problem develops and the meaning grows as it recognizes and accepts the conditions that face it. It is evident ... that in this state of reflection it is impossible to present the elements out of which the new world is to be built up in advance.[38]

This may appear to be a small difference, but it does illustrate how, early in their careers, both shared an idea that Peirce had already announced as James would in a few years—that thinking begins not in the mind but in experience.

Soon enough, their differences materialized as Mead gravitated toward language and signification as a source of meaning that was first introduced by Peirce. Mead's famous book *Mind, Self, and Society* was composed by Charles W. Morris in 1934 from student notes, three years after Mead's death. Oddly it was Morris who exaggerated Mead's social behaviorism.[39] Mead himself abandoned his earlier idea that it is experience that unifies thought and action. What he adds in *Mind, Self, and Society* is the role of symbols and language that became the center of his thinking:

> Only in terms of gestures as significant symbols is the existence of mind or intelligence possible; for only in terms of gestures which are significant symbols can thinking—which is simply an internalized or implicit conversation of the individual with himself by means of such gestures—take place. The internalization in our experience of the external conversations of gestures which we carry on with other individuals in the social process is the essence of thinking; and the gestures thus internalized are significant symbols because they have the same meanings for all individual members of the given society or social group. ... Otherwise the individual could not internalize them or be conscious of them and their meanings. As we shall see, the same procedure which is responsible for the genesis and existence of mind or consciousness—namely, the taking of the attitude of the other toward oneself, or toward one's own behavior—also necessarily involves the genesis and existence at the same time of significant symbols, or significant gestures.[40]

Though Mead was foremost a philosopher, he was also a social psychologist. What, thereby, made Mead's use of meaningful gestures and significant symbols so valuable to sociologists and social theorists was how he understood them as the integrating and dynamic elements of the two sides of the consciousness of experience—the attitude toward oneself and the attitudes others take toward oneself. And here we encounter, once again, William James's dilemma of self-consciousness, namely: How does one maintain a sense of personal identity while also contending with the realities of social selves? Where James kept the identity/pluralist dichotomy separate, Mead's theory kept them together. Thus, Mead famously reconfigured James's original description of the 'I' and the 'Me' on self-consciousness:

---

38 George Herbert Mead, "The Definition of the Psychical," *The Decennial Publications of the University of Chicago Vol. 3* (University of Chicago Press, 1903), 112.
39 One sign of the exaggeration by Morris is the book's subtitle: *Mind, Self, and Society: From the Standpoint of Social Behavior* which the University of Chicago wisely chose to print in a point so small and nearly of the same color as the jacket cover that one must search to find it. Morris can be forgiven by the fact that in the day behaviorism, as we know it today, was just then distinguishing itself from what then was a more general noun in academic psychology.
40 Mead, *Mind, Self, and Society* (University of Chicago Press, 1934), 47–48.

> The "I," then, in this relation of the "I" and the "me," is something that is, so to speak, responding to a social situation which is within the experience of the individual. It is the answer which the individual makes to the attitude which others take toward him when he assumes an attitude toward them. ... The "I" gives the sense of freedom, of initiative. The situation is there for us to act in a self-conscious fashion. ... We are aware of ourselves, and of what the situation is, but exactly how we will act never gets into experience until after the action takes place. ... Such is the basis for the fact that the "I" does not appear in the same sense in experience as does the "me." ... So there is always that distinction, if you like, between the "I" and the "me." The "I" both calls out the "me" and responds to it. Taken together they constitute a personality as it appears in social experience.[41]

He is a bit prolix but the point he makes is discernible enough, especially when one recalls the most quoted line in Mead's book: "The 'I' of this moment is present in the 'me' of the next moment."[42] The key is the subtle interjection of the word 'present' as if to suggest that the 'I' and the 'me' are always ever present one to another. Still, how does this work? Here is where Mead's implicit semiotics comes in. The I/Me relation is a symbolic dialogue in which the 'Me' presents the social situation to the 'I' which, in that instant, to use Peirce's term, interprets the experience. Though Mead had little to say about Peirce, it is hard to miss the suggestion that symbolic meanings, even gestures, are the interpretants that, in effect, hold together the straining parts of self-consciousness while also carrying forward the self itself. He could very well have said, after Peirce's triadic scheme, that the interpretant of this moment is presented in the meaning of the next.

Then, to turn to a distinctive aspect of Mead's sociology (and one for which that Dewey's Laboratory School must have provided some evidence), the key to his Self-theory is in his distinction between the play and game stages of early childhood development. A young child's play is no more than taking the role of the other, often an imaginary other—a doll becomes the "child" as the actual child becomes the "mother." The play stage is necessary for emotional development, but it is insufficient for full social participation. Try to teach four-year-olds to play American football and you will get a strange set of runnings-about. Even hide-and-seek is a game that the very young can play by means of pretending to be where they are not. Social activity becomes possible when the child fully enters the game-stage, which demands that everyone playing the game know all its rules to know what to do. Therefore, for Mead, day-to-day social activity depends on the fact that even strangers can be expected to know and obey the normal rules of the game of life with others. For example, queues for tickets or services don't work unless everyone in the line knows what the rules are. Those who try to cut the line will be told where to go. (Except at the airport in Hong Kong where, queue rules are, it seems, nonexistent.) Visualizing what others are doing, or meant to do, involves visualizing what one is meant to do in the same situation. Knowing the rules and symbolically appreciating the meaning of the actions of all others is the foundation of the self's social ability to be conscious of herself through dialogue with the attitudes others take toward her. This Mead called the competence of possessing a sense of the Generalized Other.

---

41 *Ibid*, 177–178. On my comment just after this quoted line that "he," Mead, was a bit prolix, I should qualify this by reminding that *Mind, Self, and Society* came into being three years after Mead's death on the basis of notes made by students who had been in his classes. Transcription by those without recording devices is at best a hard practice to do perfectly well. Then too class notes are themselves unable to be literal, as are even stenographic ones as one section of the book was. See, Charles Morris' Preface to *Mind, Self, and Society, ibid*, v–vii.
42 *Ibid*, 174.

Cornel West and Richard Rorty: Tragic America and Radical Pragmatism

Cornel West, since birth in Tulsa, Oklahoma, in 1953, has always been on a fast-track—one accomplishment after another. After graduating high school in 1970 in Sacramento, California, he went to Harvard College and graduated in 1973—three years with high honors. He then went to Princeton for graduate studies which seems to have been the one sojourn where he took time before graduating with the PhD in 1980.

The single most important guidebook to West's philosophical writing is *The Cornel West Reader* published in 1999. He was, that year, but 46—middle aged to be sure, but still young by today's standards among authors and scholars. He had by then explored and developed a position with respect to American pragmatism and begun the serious study of culture as a social structure alongside politics and the economy. He was ahead of specialists in cultural sociology who had tended to treat culture as a discrete sphere unto itself. For West, culture is a social structure of comparable importance to political and economic structures because culture is the energizing force of the ineluctable social differences and conflicts in late modern societies. In particular it was cultural movements that led the way in defining racial differences as more than a "Negro Problem." West was among those who came to realize that racial differences were, and are, a basic structural aspect of American society and that, as a result of their being embedded in historically pliable configurations, cultural ideas about race, they are contingent not fixed.

West's radicalism is original (and just shy of weird), as has been his way of describing his intellectual position. His introduction to *The Cornel West Reader* starts: "I am a Chekhovian Christian with the deep democratic commitments. By this I mean I am obsessed with confronting the pervasive evil of unjustified suffering and unnecessary social misery in the world."[43] He then clarifies: Why Chekov? "Chekhov leads us through our contemporary inferno with love and sorrow, but no cheap pity or promise of ultimate happiness." The Chekhovian theme is meant to account for the fact that American pragmatism (Dewey's included) has no room for the tragic. Why Coltrane?—because Coltrane's music is a leaven for Chekhov's tragic sour dough. "With Coltrane and Chekhov, the tragic and the comic are in fascinating tension and hence they actually need one another."[44]

Princeton was essential to West's intellectual formation because there in graduate studies he got to know Richard Rorty. These were during the crucial days when Rorty was working on *Philosophy and the Mirror of Nature* (1979), his great pragmatist critique of early modern notions of philosophy. Rorty, more focused in an academic way than West, introduced the book with an uncommonly clear summary of very complicated modern philosophies—those, he thought, that sought to see the world as if it were "a glassy essence," a mirror. He addresses this philosophical dilemma by subdividing the field into two groups. The first group is Descartes, Locke, and Kant—the early modern philosophers who advanced the classical notion of "the mind as a great mirror"[45] harboring representations of the world through which philosophers could study reality by "pure, nonempirical methods." Against them, Rorty sets Wittgenstein, Heidegger, and (importantly) Dewey. After conceding that Wittgenstein offers greater "dialectical acuity" and Heidegger better "historical learning,"

---

43 Cornel West, *The Cornel West Reader* edited by Cornel West (New York: Basic Books, 1999), xv; quote on Coltrane following is on page xvi.
44 Cornel West, "Chekhov, Coltrane, and Democracy," *The Cornel West Reader*, 557.
45 Richard Rorty, *Philosophy and the Mirror of Nature* (Princeton University Press, 1979), 45–69. This is a section mostly on Descartes in a chapter named "The Invention of the Mind," in which the section header is "Ability To Exist Apart from the Body," followed by another under "Dualism and Mind-Stuff." The book is meticulously argued, as is the section where Rorty refutes the classic notion of the mind as a great mirror.

he points to Dewey, who "wrote his polemics against traditional mirror imagery out of a vision of a new kind of society."[46]

Rorty does not engage in a lot of arm-waving about American pragmatism, but it is clear he is thinking here of America late in the twentieth century—a fact that Rorty more openly discusses in *Achieving Our Country: Leftist Thought in Twentieth-Century America*, where he associates John Dewey with Walt Whitman (arguably the nation's first out-and-out pragmatist):

> Both Dewey and Whitman viewed the United States as an opportunity to see ultimate significance in a finite, human, historical project, rather than in something eternal and nonhuman. ... They want to put hope for a casteless and classless America in the place traditionally occupied by knowledge of the will of God. They want that utopian America to replace God as the unconditional object of desire. They wanted the struggle for social justice to be the nation's animating principle, the nation's soul.[47]

These days one doesn't think of Cornel West as having been influenced by anyone. He's just too *sui generis*. But clearly Rorty was an enduring influence, one whose high-minded but down-to-earth pragmatism prepared for the way he learned from others and from the world.

West's pragmatism was always planted in the soil of down-to-earth real and dirty issues. As things turned out over the two decades after graduate school, race and American democracy were foremost among these issues. And truly the relations were then, and still are, dirty. In a 1993 essay, "Pragmatism and the Sense of the Tragic," he begins: "The recent revival of pragmatism provides a timely intellectual background for the most urgent problematic of our postmodern moment: the complex cluster of questions and queries regarding the meaning and value of democracy."[48] This was 1993, still West frames pragmatism by calling upon "the grand spiritual godfathers of American pragmatism"—Thomas Jefferson, Ralph Waldo Emerson who each in turn settled America's pragmatic foundations. "These foundations consisted roughly of the irreducibility of individuality within participatory communities, heroic action of ordinary folk in a world of radical continuity, and a deep sense of evil that fuels struggles for justice."[49] Some historians would quibble with West's characterizations of Jefferson, Emerson, Lincoln, but it would be hard to deny that each stood for, at the least, the basic principles well-woven into early American culture and practice.

West may not be an historian, but he is a very good historical philosopher—one who here and elsewhere is inclined to use the witness of major public figures. There is, at least, no doubt that the Black prophetic tradition had been on his mind since his first breakout book, *Race-Matters* in 1993. Well before his disappointment with Barack Obama, he mentions many of the same prophets that figure in *Black Prophetic Fire*. But in the earlier book he is already sharply criticizing Black leaders whom he castigates for reflecting the cautious values of the then new Black middle class. But by 2014 in *Black Prophetic Fire* he is ever-so-much more specific at the outset about what is needed:

---

46 *Ibid*, 13.
47 Richard Rorty, *Achieving Our Country: Leftist Thought in Twentieth Century America* (Harvard University Press, 1998), 17–18.
48 Cornel West, "Pragmatism and the Sense of the Tragic," in *Keeping the Faith: Philosophy and Race in America* (Routledge, 1993), 107; quote just below, same place.
49 *Ibid*, 107.

I want to reinvigorate the Black prophetic tradition and to keep alive the memory of Black prophetic figures and movements. I consider the Black prophetic tradition one of the greatest treasures in the modern world. It has been the leaven in the American democratic load. Without the Black prophetic tradition, much of the best of America would be lost and some of the best of the modern world would be forgotten.[50]

We today live in a time when the global-those who believe in facts are more than likely to agree with West in respect to the historical idea that our world is being reconstituted because of its decolonization by the African Diaspora—from whom we all, skin color and culture aside—are genetically descended.

Cornel West remains today a pragmatist of his own sort—provided we can grant that among all the ever-growing crop of social theories pragmatism, as he understands it, holds a unique place, a place hard to define amid all the extraordinary abundance of themes and subjects he touches upon. But, if there is one that takes the theoretical cake it would be the lead essay in a book he co-edited in 1991, with "The New Cultural Politics of Difference," in *Marginalization and Contemporary Cultures* that presents selections from theorists and writers as different as Gilles Deleuze and Toni Morrison, as Homi Bhabha and Gloria Anzaldúa, as Trinh T. Minh-ha and Edward Said. The authors in the book are different only in their theoretical dispositions—all were agreed on the importance of the marginalized to how social theorists must view the world as it is. West begins this way:

Distinctive features of the new politics of difference are to trash the monolithic and homogeneous in the name of diversity, multiplicity and heterogeneity; to reject the abstract, general and universal in light of the concrete, specific and particular; and to historicize, contextualize, and pluralize by highlighting the contingent, variable, tentative, shifting and changing. Needless to say these gestures are not new in the history of criticism or art, yet what makes them novel—along with the cultural politics they produce—is how and what constitutes difference, the weight and gravity it is given in representation and the way in which highlighting issues like extremism, empire, class, race, gender, sexual orientation, age, nation, nurture and religion at this historical moment acknowledge some discontinuity and disruption from previous forms of cultural critique.[51]

So many words, but none wasted. This could well be a declaration of independence for a new pragmatic social theory of life as it is lived, daily.

---

50 Cornel West with Christa Buschendorf, *Black Prophetic Fire* (Beacon Press, 2014), 2.
51 "The New Cultural Politics of Difference," in *Out There: Marginalization and Contemporary Cultures*, edited by Russell Ferguson, Martha Gever, Trinh T. Minh-ha, and Cornel West (The New Museum of Contemporary Art / The MIT Press, 1990), 19.

Part IV
American Culture Tries to Explain its Disorder, 1919–1968

12 The Function of American Culture
Henry Adams, Talcott Parsons, Robert K. Merton

Between the dynamo in the gallery of machines and the engine-house outside,
the break of continuity amounted to an abysmal fracture for an historian's objects.
No more relation could he discover between the Cross and the cathedral.
The forces were interchangeable if not reversible, but he could see only an absolute fiat in electricity as in faith.
—Henry Adams, **The Dynamo and the Virgin**, 1907

An "act" involves: (1) an agent, an "actor"... (2) and an "end" toward which the process of action is oriented. (3) It must be initiated in a "situation" ... (4) a certain mode of relationship between those elements.
—Talcott Parsons, **The Structure of Social Action**, Vol 1, 1937

No society lacks norms governing conduct.
But societies do differ in the degree to which folkways, mores and institutional controls
are effectively integrated with the goals
which stand high in the hierarchy of cultural values.
—Robert K. Merton, "Social Structure and Anomie," 1949

How Do Cultures Work?

Today this would be a strange question. We now do not think of social things as somehow working—an all too mechanical way of thinking about living things. But in early days it was common to think of culture as a mechanism whereby societies come together to act for some or another good—hence, functionalism.

The first to think this was the late nineteenth and early twentieth century polymath Henry Adams who seemed to know something about everything he turned his acute attention to. His most famous, though seldom read, short essay was a chapter in *The Education of Henry Adams: A Study of Twentieth Century Multiplicity* in 1906. That chapter, "The Dynamo and the Virgin," where he made the remarkable argument that, in effect, Western culture as we think of it now began in the design of early medieval cathedrals and became what we today think of the modern world.

> Between the dynamo in the gallery of machines and the engine-house outside, the break of continuity amounted to an abysmal fracture for an historian's objects. No more relation

could he discover between the Cross and the cathedral. The forces were interchangeable if not reversible, but he could see only an absolute fiat in electricity as in faith.[1]

Between the Virgin and the modern Dynamo, there was an important transformation between the cultural objects that held the world together so that it, in our word, functioned.

Functionalism as a theory of social thought that came to be in 1937, some thirty years after Adams' essay in 1906. This was Talcott Parsons' first volume of *The Structure of Social Action*, in which he began by laying out the structural elements in respect to which a social act functions with its several analytic elements to work within a coherent mode of relationship:

> An "act" involves: (1) an agent, an "actor"... (2) and an "end" toward which the process of action is oriented. (3) It was be initiated in a "situation" ... (4) a certain mode of relationship between those elements.[2]

In time, *The Structure of Social Action* came to be regarded as the foundational text of the American tradition of functionalism. This in spite of the fact that many who do not like hard reading considered it impossible to understand.

Not long after, in 1949, Robert K. Merton published the first of several revised editions of his classic book *Social Theory and Social Structure*, which included his widely-read essay "Social Structure and Anomie." Here he wrote similar to, but different from, Parsons on what also came to be thought of as a brand of functionalism:

> No society lacks norms governing conduct. But societies do differ in the degree to which folkways, mores and institutional controls are effectively integrated with the goals which stand high in the hierarchy of cultural values.[3]

Both Parsons at Harvard and Merton at Columbia inspired a good many followers who until the 1960s all but governed (so to speak) American sociology, in which culture was widely considered the structural source that integrated a society's several action systems. Even the already famous social thinkers at the University of Chicago, including George Herbert Mead and others, were for a while eclipsed by the functionalist traditions. But even Chicago was strongly affirmative of culture's role in making sense of social things.

Celebrating a Culture

Like many towns, New Haven has an annual Fourth of July Fireworks celebration. The fireworks are fired from the top of East Rock, the promontory that overlooks the town and its seaport. When the sun begins to set, crowds slowly gather below the Rock after finishing their holiday picnics. When the fireworks light the sky, most are in some kind of awe.

> And the rockets' red glare
>   The bombs bursting in air
>   Gave proof through the night
>   That our flag was still there

---

[1] Henry Adams, *The Education of Henry Adams: A Study of Twentieth Century Multiplicity* (Houghton Mifflin, 1918 [1907], chapter 25.
[2] Talcott Parsons, *The Structure of Social Action, Vol 1* (Free Press, 1937), 44.
[3] Robert K. Merton, "Social Structure and Anomie," in *Social Theory and Social Structure* (Free Press, 1949), 134.

Every American has sung America's national anthem—some in broken English. Love of one's country is, at best, a sometime thing. It floats mysteriously over public fireworks, school and military ceremonies. The patriotic feeling dwells within, lodged somewhere in the back of the emotional minds of those thus devoted.

This is one of the things cultures do. They can inspire and engage members. "Cultures are dramatic conversations about things that matter to their participants, and American culture is no exception."[4] Cultures may, and do, carry forth the salient contents of songs, pledges, memories of leaders and founders, of loved ones killed in war, and more. More generally, cultures most notably provide the down-to-earth norms that tell members what to do: "No society lacks norms governing conduct. But societies do differ in the degree to which folkways, mores, institutional controls are effectively integrated with the goals which stand high in the hierarchy of cultural values."[5] Theories of cultures, on the other hand, can, and do, change over time; hence Talcott Parsons' first line of *The Structure of Social Action* where he asks: "Who now reads Spencer?" In this Parsons in 1937 was distinguishing his theory of cultures and social action from Herbert Spencer's evolutionary theory that had long been dominant late in the nineteenth century and early in the twentieth.

Henry Adams: The First American Theorist of the Function of Culture

Henry Adams was not a direct influence on any of the recent American theorists of culture. Their neglect of Adams is, in some part, due to the far-reaching changes in American social theory between 1900 and 1945 when academic formalism had cleared the decks of any traces of the aesthetic and literary attitudes so apparent in *The Education of Henry Adams*.

Adams, in his day, was many things to many people—a disciplined (if mostly non-academic) historian; a Harvard College professor (he resigned in 1877 at 39 years); a world traveler who wrote astutely about the places he visited; an acquaintance or friend of many of the nation's political leaders; a friend to many of England's and Europe's leading literary, intellectual, and social figures; and much more. Then too, Henry Adams was also the great grandson of President John Adams, grandson of President John Quincy Adams, son of Charles Francis Adams a prominent diplomat and political personage, and thereby a member of the Adams and (by marriage) Brooks families—two of Massachusetts' oldest and most prominent clans. He inherited money sufficient to support an independent life pursued in order (in the titular phrase of his memoir) to educate Henry Adams, in which he refers, oddly, to himself in the third person. Yet, Henry Adams has not been afforded the attention he deserves—this perhaps because, as David S. Brown suggests in *The Last American Aristocrat*, Adams was all-too-much above the fray even while being so well connected to the nation's intelligentsia and political elite.[6]

Still Adams put forth a serious theory of culture in *The Education of Henry Adams: A Study of Twentieth Century Multiplicity* (1906) which is an elegant and original study of the cultural ties and differences from Roman Christianity's thirteenth century to the industrial and machine age at the end of the nineteenth. *The Education of Henry Adams* draws on research that appeared in his *Mont-Saint-Michel and Chartres: A Study of Thirteenth*

---

4 Robert N. Bellah with Richard Madsen, William M. Sullivan, Ann Swidler, and Steven M. Tipton, *Habits of the Heart: Individualism and Commitment in American Life* (University of California Press, 1985), 27.
5 Robert K. Merton, "Social Structure and Anomie," in *Social Theory and Social Structure* (The Free Press, 1957 [1949]), 134.
6 David S. Brown, *The Last American Aristocrat: The Brilliant Life and Improbable Education of Henry Adams* (Scribner, 2020), 5–6, 25–27, 104–105, *et passim*.

Century Unity where he provides architectural and historical details of the iconic medieval cathedrals he used to paint a portrait of thirteenth-century Christian culture.[7] The two books are different in kind but intimately related to Adams's theory of culture.

The yoke between the two is "The Dynamo and the Virgin," chapter 25 in *The Education of Henry Adams*, where Adams presents what in retrospect might be called a literary social theory of culture. Beautifully written for those with a taste for somewhat over-the-top elegance. More to the point, this single chapter is as original and wide-ranging as any cultural theory stated in fewer than 5,000 words could be. Its originality turns on the rather nineteenth century method of thinking historically—a method that was, one might say (at some risk), linear. Modern social science and its theories tend to have become comparative—or lateral in the sense of comparing across a period in time. Adams's method was more severely linear, as he says in a chapter (29) called "The Abyss of Ignorance (1902)":

> Any schoolboy could see that man as a force must be measured by motion, from a fixed point. Psychology helped here by suggesting a unit—the point of history when man held the highest idea of himself as a unit in a unified universe. *Eight or ten years of study had led Adams to think he might use the century 1150–1250, expressed in Amiens Cathedral and the Works of Thomas Aquinas, as the unit from which he might measure motion down to his own time, without assuming anything as true or untrue, except relation.* The movement might be studied at once in philosophy and mechanics. Setting himself to the task, he began a volume which he mentally knew as "Mont-Saint-Michel and Chartres: A Study of Thirteenth Century Unity." From that point he proposed to fix a position for himself, which he could label: "The Education of Henry Adams: A Study of Twentieth-Century Multiplicity." With the help of these two points of relation, he hoped to project his lines forward and backward indefinitely, subject to correction from anyone who should know better.[8]

The historical occasion for Adams's modern fixed point was the 1900 World Exposition in Paris that featured the new electricity generated by dynamos. He had previously visited the lesser but comparably interesting 1893 exposition in Chicago, of which he said: "Chicago was the first expression of American thought as a unity; one must start there."[9]

The Dynamo and the Virgin—A Linear History of Culture

Though dated serially, all but a few chapters in *The Education of Henry Adams*[10] range far and wide—none more so than "The Dynamo and the Virgin." The method, however, is not

---

7 *The Education of Henry Adams: A Study of Twentieth Century Multiplicity* (Houghton Mifflin, 1918 [1907]) and *Mont Saint Michel and Chartres: A Study of Thirteenth Century Unity* (Project Gutenberg eBook [1904]). Both books were initially printed privately only to be published later. There are many current editions of *Mont-Saint-Michel and Chartres*. I have chosen the Gutenberg version due to its accessibility.
8 *Education*, 435. Emphasis added. Note: Throughout Henry Adams writes of himself in the third person; thus, in the emphasized sentence "Adams" and "he" is the author referring to himself.
9 *Ibid*, 343—in Chapter 22, "Chicago," just before he begins the next chapter, 23, "Silence (1894–1898)" with: "The convulsion of 1893 left its victims in dead-water and closed much education." The line seems to refer as much to the epochal machine age as to the financial crisis of that year. Also, on Adams and Chicago, see Brown, *ibid, Last American Aristocrat*, 283–287.
10 Adams, *The Education of Henry Adams* (Houghton Mifflin, 1918 [1906]). For reasons hard to understand the book first was published in 1906, but the Pulitzer was not awarded until 1918 after Adams had died, also the year of the book's second edition.

comparative but a kind of theoretical spiral around the two points that anchor the story historically—the medieval Virgin and the modern Dynamo.

"The Dynamo and the Virgin" is an original, if long ignored, contribution to a theory of cultures. Adams began with what at first seems to be an utterly abstract concept—as he put it, the *unity* of American thought. But *unity* is not an independent concept. Unity is a point in his spiral of time—one from which a linear trajectory can be drawn back and forth between the Dynamo and the Virgin. In a later chapter (33), "A Dynamic Theory of History," Adams presents a theory of history, that begins: "A dynamic theory, like most theories, begins by begging the question: it defines progress as the development and economy of forces."[11] Thus, the unity of a culture is determined by a *force* that produces the effect of that unity—a force, he argues, that was missing in America until the end of the nineteenth century, when the Chicago Exposition in 1893 dramatized the Industrial (hence Mechanical) Age that had been coming into its own since the Civil War. Chicago 1893 represented what Paris 1900 made all the more visible to the eye of the modern world. The differences between the medieval and modern worlds were, thereby, clear to him. "All the steam in the world could not, like the Virgin, produce Chartres." Then, immediately after in "The Dynamo and the Virgin", he continues:

Yet in mechanics, whatever the mechanicians [sic] might think, both energies acted as interchangeable forces on man, and by action on man all known force may be measured. Indeed, few men of science measured force in any other way. ... Symbol or energy, *the Virgin had acted as the greatest force the Western world ever felt and had drawn man's activities to herself more strongly than any other power, natural or supernatural, had ever done; the historian's business was to follow the track of the energy*; to find where it came from and where it went to; its complex source and shifting channels; its values, equivalents, conversions. It could scarcely be more complex than radium; it could hardly be deflected, diverted, polarized, absorbed more perplexingly than other radiant matter. Adams knew nothing about any of them, but as a mathematical problem of influence on human progress, though all were occult, all reacted on his mind, and he rather inclined to think the Virgin easiest to handle.[12]

This is the crux of Adams's cultural theory. The Virgin and the Dynamo are not the same cultural forces. Yet, in their very different historical ages, they were cultural forces that lent unity to their times—of the Virgin in the great cathedrals and the theology of Aquinas, 1150–1250; and of the Dynamo dramatized in the Chicago and Paris expositions, 1893–1900. In *Mont-Saint Michel and Chartres*, Adams draws upon the relationship between Aquinas's intellectual representation of the cathedrals and the modern machine:

The Church Intellectual, like the Church Architectural, implied not one architect, but myriads, and not one fixed, intelligent architect at the end of the series, but a vanishing vista without a beginning at any definite moment; and if Thomas pressed his argument, the twentieth-century mechanic who should attend his conferences at the Sorbonne would be apt to say so. "What is the use of trying to argue me into it? Your inference may be sound logic but is not proof. Actually, we know less about it than you did. All we know is the thing we handle, and we cannot handle your fixed, intelligent prime motor. To your old ideas of form, we have added what we call force, and we are rather further

---

11 *Ibid*, 474.
12 *Ibid*, 388–389. Emphasis added. Quote above same place.

than ever from reducing the complex to unity. In fact, if you are aiming to convince me, I will tell you flatly that I know only the multiple and have no use for unity at all."[13]

Here Adams states his principle of cultural change along the line from the Virgin to the Dynamo—from Unity to Multiplicity the key words in the subtitles to the two books: *Mont Saint-Michel and Chartres: A Study of Thirteenth Century Unity* and *The Education of Henry Adams: A Study of Twentieth Century Multiplicity*. Between the two historical moments Adams allowed for this difference but, it seems, he misstated the difference as it came to be. His remark, just above, that the modern is moved only by multiplicity such that the age of dynamo has "no use for unity at all" contradicts the lesson of the Dynamo taught in the Paris exposition. This was his conclusion just after seeing and studying Chartres and the Virgin that, unquestionably, lent unity to the Christian Middle Ages after 1250–1340.

Then later, after pondering the Dynamo in 1903, he takes quite a different position in one of his characteristically subtle statements of his experience of the dynamo:

> To him, the dynamo itself was but an ingenious channel for conveying somewhere the heat latent in a few tons of poor coal hidden in a dirty engine-house carefully kept out of sight; but to Adams the dynamo became a symbol of infinity. *As he grew accustomed to the great gallery of machines, he began to feel the forty-foot dynamos as a moral force, much as the early Christians felt the Cross.* The planet itself seemed less impressive, in its old-fashioned, deliberate, annual or daily revolution, than this huge wheel, revolving within arm's length at some vertiginous speed, and barely murmuring—scarcely humming an audible warning to stand a hair's-breadth further for respect of power—while it would not wake the baby lying close against its frame. Before the end, one began to pray to it; inherited instinct taught the natural expression of man before silent and infinite force. Among the thousand symbols of ultimate energy the dynamo was not so human as some, but it was the most expressive.[14]

If his dynamic theory of history entails periods when a force like the Virgin produces a unity, then why does not the force of the dynamo do the same as, here, he says it does? "The stupendous acceleration after 1800 ended in 1900 with the appearance of the new class of super sensual forces, before which the man of science stood at first as bewildered and helpless as, in the fourth century, a priest of Isis before the Cross of Christ."[15] The multiplicities of the modern are fast coming and going but they too bow before super sensual forces somewhere out there.

Adams offers the elements of a theory of culture—one well done at a time when there were no explicit theories of culture. No surprise then that he did not draw all elements of his theory together. What he did, however, was provide an early example of how theories of culture today might still be done. Thus, he modeled a loose theory of culture that might have avoided many of the errors of omission and neglect that the American functionalists succumbed to. He, at least, had a theory of modern multiplicities that later day functionalists could not fathom.

---

13 *Mont Saint-Michel and Chartres* (Project Gutenberg eText), 353 [in this case Project Gutenberg provides page numbers because it is an eText copy of the 1913 original in the Cornell University Library].
14 *Education*, 380.
15 *Ibid*, 486–487.

Talcott Parsons: Functional Theory Comes into Its Own

Talcott Parsons was born in 1902. His father Edward was a Congregational minister who had been aligned with the Social Gospel Movement of the day as well as a student of Jonathan Edwards' much earlier writings. Though years later, after the younger Parsons became famous, radicals scorned the abstract nature of his sociology. Yet, as a teacher at Harvard, Talcott Parsons taught with the well-documented but plain spoken manner of a Protestant minister devoted to his gospel.[16] His early life experiences with religion may well have predisposed him to the importance of culture as a force that aims to make good sense of twists and turns of social life.

Talcott Parsons became a social scientist of a unique kind. After college at Amherst, he studied with the intellectual stars then at the London School of Economics—L.T. Hobhouse, R.H. Tawney, Harold Lasky, but was most influenced by the social anthropologist, Bronislaw Malinowski. He then won a fellowship to Heidelberg where he was able to earn the PhD in three semesters. He chose to major in economics while also reading sociology.[17] Parsons began at Harvard in 1927 where he was a lesser figure until 1937, when his first still great book, *The Structure of Social Action*, soon enough made him not only Harvard's principal sociologist but America's as well. Though today overlooked, in the day *The Structure of Social Action* was an astonishing masterpiece. It was the first major and thorough-going theoretical book designed to reframe sociological theory. And, for its time, it was the first important book to import European ideas into American sociology in a way that ironically, if cryptically, put forth American values as the organizing resource of sociology. Social action is a general concept that renders actors and their actions central to the order of social structures.

By "social action" Parsons did not mean political activism. Yet he managed to include politics, in a general sense, as one of his scheme's four important structural aspects of a functioning action system: *economic* adaptation, *political* competition in respect to goals, *legal* integration of the resulting conflicts, and *culture* as the latent system that maintains a society's collective rules and norms. These four elements in *The Structure of Social Action* in 1937 served as a foundation for the theoretical work that followed in two important ways. The first is the principle that agents, ends, situations, means, and conditions of action are always in a systemic relation. The second—and somewhat surprisingly—is that action systems are at once analytic *and* empirical—general principles necessary to each other. Parsons's tacit theorem meant to attribute a system-like property to action of all kinds in order to describe how things work in the real world. *But* the analytic concepts he used to describe real action systems are not in themselves *in* or *from* the real world even though they (the analytic concepts) are themselves real (in an analytic way), therefore empirically effective. This sounds odd. What does it mean?

First off, important to note, it is not exactly absurd to suggest that we, like all living creatures, live in systems that include conditions that we, as actors, cannot control even though we must deal with them. Then too, structural conditions beyond our control are not *completely* beyond our control. We at least use some of them as means—school systems, for example. The social conditions involved in an educational system do not readily bend

---

16 One year, sometime around 1960, I took Parsons's course on American society. Though I have had many wonderful teachers, but none was better organized and more inspiring than Parsons. Somewhere, I still have my notes from that class. I may have found him easy to follow in part because I had switched over from the study of the then supremely abstract systematic theology in the Divinity School to sociology. CL

17 On Parsons's education see Talcott Parsons, "On Building Social System Theory: A Personal History," *Daedalus* 99:4 (1970), 826–827.

to the wishes of students; nor even to those of local or state officials who might want them changed. As a result, many children on their first days of school are overwhelmed by the school environment—just as are immigrants or tourists in foreign places, or workers new to factories or offices, not to mention prisoners facing their first lock-down. Yet eventually school children come to deal with the system. When they leave school, they then must face the wider social system for which their schools may or may not have prepared them. Then too tourists, unlike immigrants, go home. Immigrants may too, but more often than not, if they got in legally, they stay and, like graduating students, figure out the wider system as best they can. Even prisoners who stand no chance of parole deal with their carceral institutions, sometimes well enough.

Everyone who lives anywhere that is organized to any degree must deal with the structured conditions that limit their agency while, in some cases, enhancing it. Life with others is a sometime thing. Most of us do our best to get somewhere. When we come to the end of our lives, we enjoy memories of what pleased us and regret those that don't. Death, many suppose, is a silence. If we are alert in those waning days, we accept that the social systems we leave behind will remain for others. Otherwise put, in a manner closer to what Parsons meant in his grand theory: What we know about the facts of life are not facts pure and simple. Facts are taken out of the reality they represent. Facts are, thereby, of the same analytic order as the theories we compose to explain the realities out there, somewhere. In this sense, school-going kids, like high-minded social scientists, must live in a world outside the realities that condition all of us as we struggle with what means we have to achieve ends that are never what we had in mind in the first place. "Theory," Parsons said, as only he could say, "is an independent variable in the development of science, but the body of theory in a given time constitutes to a greater or lesser degree an integrated 'system.' Another way of putting this is to say that any system of theory has a determinate logical structure."[18]

What he meant by this counterintuitive statement is that theories themselves are action systems. From which Parsons derived his method, *analytic realism*. Much later in the *Structure of Social Action*, he pulls his general theory of social actions together with an unusually clear summary statement. This was what came to be called analytic realism. When all is said and done, analytic realism is neither real nor analytic, but a method that yields representations of reality, one of which may function well enough to yield an adequate representation of the alleged reality.

Keep in mind that this was 1937. America was still suffering its long Depression. Hitler was pushing Europe and the world to the verge of war. The global realities were troubling to anyone who was willing to look. Yet, Parsons at Harvard writes a book that seems to ignore all this. Even so, examining *The Structure of Social Action* more closely, one can be less harsh as to his abstract theorizing. Parsons did an astonishing thing in his honest and original idea of functional theory as, at best, "adequate" for any scientific system willing to get by in the wilderness between facts and ideas. *The Structure of Social Action* laid the groundwork of a colossally nuanced and ample functionalist theory of social action that, though not announced as such, served as a program for the rethinking of scientific social theory.

But that is not all. Parsons's book cleared the field for a fresh approach to social theory and especially culture. *The Structure of Social Action* is more important for having watered then pruned the theories that came before the bouleversements of economic depression and world war in the 1930s and 1940s. His criticisms of those who came before were unexceptionally careful if controversial. He began with the classical social philosophers

---

18 Parsons, *The Structure of Social Action Vol I* (McGraw Hill, 1937), 7.

whom he typified, somewhat surprisingly, as individualistic positivists—Hobbes, Locke, Malthus, Marx, the Social Darwinists. With Marx on the list some will find this characterization strange. It is actually more than strange to identify collective bargaining as somehow more important to Marx than, say, the accumulation of capital.[19] Yet the major sections of Parsons's big book served to introduce European social theorists like Alfred Marshall and Vilfredo Pareto who were in 1937 all-but-unknown in America. In relatively short essays in Part I of *The Structure of Social Action*, they served to define the background to action theories as they moved away from positivism. After which, Parsons famously presented more nuanced expositions of Émile Durkheim and Max Weber who, in addition to being sources of what he called "Voluntaristic Theories of Action," were well known for their studies of the role of religion in society. Parsons was but 25 years old when he came to Harvard in 1927. In the ten years following he mastered these giants of social thought on the way to composing what remains a seldom read systematic masterpiece.[20]

Few who write one major book, write another, much less two others. Parsons did with *The Social System* in 1951 and, in the same year, *Toward a General Theory of Action*. The former was Parsons' masterly, if sometimes obscure, theoretical statement of action theory. The latter was a joint project edited with Edward Shils that included a number of other contributors especially in the key Part I, "Some Fundamental Categories of the Theory of Action: A General Statement."[21] There is a story behind the two books. In 1944 Parsons had a bid from another university. Harvard responded by promoting him to the Chair of its Sociology Department but also by gratifying his wish to form a separate Department of Social Relations meant to integrate the major social sciences—initially sociology, psychology, and anthropology. As time went by the associated faculty greatly expanded the range of new social sciences to include cognitive psychology, cybernetics, others. *Toward a General Theory of Action* in 1951 was an early product of the new Department's cooperative ventures.

Also in 1951, *The Social System* was the result of the maturation in Parsons's thinking into newly acquired interests—culture and personality: "The focus of this work, then, is … concerned both with personality and culture, but not for their own sakes, rather in their bearing on the structure and functioning of social systems."[22] Personality as a topic stands out because this is the first major work in which Parsons began to discuss personality in itself as an action system and the means by which individuals are socialized into social systems; hence Chapter 6, "The Learning of Social Role-Expectations and the Mechanisms of Socialization of Motivation." More important are the two chapters following which, in 100 pages (close to 25% of the book), examine belief systems and expressive symbols—which is to say: culture. *The Social System*—in contrast to *The Structure of Social Action* in 1937—offered a much more dynamic theory of the interactions of action systems and of how they change. But it was far from the final word in the theory he was inventing. In some ways *Toward a General Theory of Action* was closer still to that theory. In spite of (or perhaps, because of) its having been a joint enterprise, this book is, at least, more clearly ordered around a general

---

19 *Structure Vol I*, 108–109.
20 Curiously, Parsons claimed to have had a weak knowledge of Weber and a low opinion of Durkheim when he first came to Harvard. See Parsons, "On Building Social System Theory: A Personal History," *Daedalus*, 866. Also here (page 868), he says that in his studies he had had teachers and mentors who introduced him to all the rest but Durkheim who, as things turned out, became a major influence on his functionalist theory of culture.
21 Talcott Parsons and Edward A. Shils, *Toward a General Theory of Action* with contributions by Edward C. Tolman, Gordon W. Allport, Clyde Kluckhohn, Henry A. Murray, Robert R. Sears, Richard D. Sheldon, Samuel A. Stouffer (Harvard University Press, 1951).
22 Parsons, *The Social System Vol I* (Free Press, 1951), 18–19.

theory of action systems with independent chapters on personality, social and value systems. What stands out, however, is the statement that "cultural systems have their own forms and problems of integration which are not reducible to those of personality and social systems or both together. ... and are on a different plane." This important statement of culture's unique nature relative to the other action systems continues:

> The cultural tradition in its significance both as an *object* of orientation and as an *element* in the orientation of action must be articulated both conceptually and empirically with personalities and social systems. Apart from embodiment in the orientation systems of concrete actors, culture, though existing as a body of artifacts and as systems of symbols, is not itself organized as a system of action. Therefore, culture as a system is on a different plane from personalities and social systems.[23]

How? In brief, culture, strictly speaking, is not an action system but, to repeat Parsons's words, "an element in the orientation of action [that] must be articulated both conceptually and empirically with personalities and social systems." Not a statement easily unpacked. But, in general terms, Parsons is saying that culture may have the features of an action system, but it stands out from other systems by being uniquely important in contrast to personality and social systems. When this mysterious remark, made in 1951, is considered in respect to what he wrote a decade later one can see that he came to explain that culture plays the crucial role of, one might say, supervising, while directing, the functional integrity of the social system as a whole.

Thus, Parsons's clearest statement of the role of culture in the social system, is in another, still later, jointly authored and edited book and major book, *Theories of Society: Foundations of Modern Sociological Theory* in 1961—an ever more massive, two volume compendium composed with Edward Shils, Kaspar D. Naegele, and Jesse R. Pitts. *Theories of Society* is organized in such a way that it makes obvious the scheme presented in the two 1951 books. This is because the staple of the book's selections that fill the table with a feast of texts from the history of modern social thought from Hobbes and Machiavelli down through the years until 1961 when, one could say, that Parsons with colleagues represented the then latest in what then was known as *sociological* theory. In respect to Parsons's thinking, his general introduction is the remarkably clear and readable introductory essay, "An Outline of the Social System." It is here that Parsons outlined his legendary *AGIL* paradigm that codifies the four functional structures of action systems: *Adaptation, Goal Attainment, Integration, Latent Pattern Maintenance.*

In principle, the paradigm applies to any functioning action system, but here, at the end of a long theoretical journey, the system is (as the book's title states) *society*. Parsons's social systems theory identifies four functions with respect to the *AGIL* paradigm beginning with *Adaptation,* as the function by which a social system adapts to its natural environment. The economy, thereby, is the system by which societies extract natural resources (including human bodily labor power) by hunting, gathering, cultivating, or manufacturing to produce

---

23 Parsons, "Some Fundamental Categories of the Theory of Action: A General Statement," in Parsons and Shils, eds., *Toward a General Theory of Action*, 7. Quote following, same place. *Note on Attribution*: I am assuming that this particular section was written by Parsons himself because it sounds like him (and I've read and listened to him over several years). Then again as noted above in footnote 21, there were seven contributors to the book as a whole, in addition to his co-editor Shils. That each played some role, if only advisory, in this introductory statement is clear from a footnote to this passage, stated with remarkable care and formality: "Mr. [Richard] Sheldon dissents from this view. His grounds are stated in Chapter II."

products useful—hence, valuable—for human life. *Goal Attainment* is the function whereby individuals and groups are motivated to pursue wants and goals. This then is the motivational aspect of a social system that moves individuals to engage in the many institutional groups that provide members with access to the goods harvested from nature. *Integration*, thereby, is the function whereby strains associated with the competition entailed when members struggle to acquire the goods that no known social system has ever provided to *all* members equally. Here enters the plain fact that inequality is a given in modern societies (a fact that Parsons did not emphasize). The poor get by on what they can get. The wealthy go beyond needs to gratify their desires to win more than anyone actually needs. In the vast between are those motivated by more than surviving. They seek pleasures, for which they need resources to eat well, maintain friendships, have and enjoy children. As decent as these goals are, there are rivals for the means to attain them. Weekends they may have neighborhood picnics. Mondays they return to work to fight for what they want. Yet no one in the middle of all this gets all they desire and some fall back into poverties of one or another kind for lack of the most basic goods.

To this point, the reality of inequality means that in modern social systems there is always a greater or lesser degree of turmoil that may or may not lead to changes in the system itself. Hence, Parsons's fourth function suffers the ignominy of a terrible name: *Latent Pattern Maintenance*. "Latent" points to the fact that this element operates behind the scenes of ordinary life actions and institutions. When we work for what we want, or try to settle arguments, seldom, if ever, do we wonder why we are acting in these ways. In his 1961 "Outline of the Social System," Parsons explains: "Pattern-maintenance ... plays a part in the theory of social systems, as of other systems, comparable to that of the concept of inertia in mechanics."[24] This is why earlier he resisted referring to culture as a full-fledged functional system among the other three. At the same time, it is disturbing but obvious, that, if one is to buy into anything like an *AGIL* paradigm, the functioning of a society necessarily drifts toward turmoil. Something *must*, theoretically speaking, maintain the pattern. Better put, this is the key to Parsons's theory of culture. But then, whatever his apparent earlier reservations about culture as a system, he came around to the primacy of culture in any functioning society. "The structure of cultural meanings constitutes the ground of any system of action."[25] With Parsons, nothing was ever simple. In 1961 he was surprisingly quick to say that cultural systems are, in fact, systems in their own right without ever being identical with a social system. Patterns must be maintained but always by a latent force.

Parsons was not a cultural theorist as so many are today. Yet, he was the one who put culture on the theoretical map, notably in America. Today he is read, if at all, more in Europe than America. Many of the rising revolutionaries of the 1960s who had of a sudden discovered Marx made their careers by attacking Parsons's scheme. Today you will have very few confessing structural functionalists anywhere, yet the ghosts of Parsons's brilliance lurk about nowhere more than behind American ideas of cultural theory.

Robert K. Merton: The Analytic Nuances of Culture and Social Structures

Robert K. Merton (1910–2003) was young enough to have taken courses with Talcott Parsons at Harvard in the 1930s. In Merton's major book, *Social Theory and Social Structure*, he acknowledges his debt to Parsons as his "teacher and friend ... who so early

---

24 Parsons, "An Outline of the Social System," in Parsons and others, *Theories of Society* (The Free Press, 1961), 39.
25 Parsons, "Introduction to Culture and the Social System," in *ibid*, 963.

in his career conveyed his enthusiasm to so many."[26] There is a widely held myth that he and Parsons formed a kind of partnership to advance functionalist theory. In fact, though Merton did write about functionalism, his doctoral thesis at Harvard became the book *Science, Technology and Science in Seventeenth Century England* (1938)—a product of his graduate research with George Sarton, founder of the history of science. Sarton's influence endured in Merton himself who became the founder of the sociology of science, but also in the elegant seriousness with which he contributed to the science of sociology.[27]

As important as Sarton and Parsons were to him, when Merton left Harvard he set off on his own. Merton differed from Parsons in that, however analytic his subject, with rare exception, did he ever fail to consider original empirical evidence. His life-long interest in science studies inspired his insistence that sociology must be equally rigorous theoretically *and* empirically—both at once. At Columbia, Merton formed a lasting friendship with Paul Lazarsfeld, the Viennese mathematician, and founder of Columbia's Bureau of Applied Social Research, which set the trend for post-World War II American empirical sociology. Together, with Parsons at Harvard, the Merton-Lazarsfeld partnership taught or otherwise influenced the majority of American sociologists other-than those under the sway of the Chicago tradition.

Merton's distinctive approach to sociology was *middle-range* theory which in a sense was a rebuke of analytic theory as much as it was an insistence, against crude empiricism, that theory must inform and guide research.

> I attempt to focus attention on what might be called *theories of the middle range*: theories intermediate to the minor working hypotheses in abundance during the day-to-day routines of research, and all-inclusive speculations comprising a master conceptual scheme from which it is hoped to derive a very large number of empirically observed uniformities of social behavior.[28]

Though Merton published many books and articles, his major work is one of the most unusual books in American social theory. *Social Theory and Social Structures* (1949, twice revised and enlarged in 1957 and 1968) is a collection of Merton's important shorter writings, some of them first published in editions of this book, most reworked from edition to edition. The book as a whole represents the range of Merton's intellectual interests, for examples: "Bureaucratic Structure and Personality," "Role of the Intellectual in Public Bureaucracy," "Theory of Reference Groups," "Patterns of Influence: Locals and Cosmopolitans," "The Self-Fulfilling Prophecy," "Science and Economy in 17th

---

26   Robert K. Merton, *Social Theory and Social Structure* (The Free Press, 1957 [1949]), x.
27   George Sarton was exceptional among historians of science in the day because of this interest in language and literature. He said, in the Preface to *Ancient Science through the Golden Age of Greece* (Harvard University Press, 1952), on pages vii–viii: "My main regret as a teacher of ancient science is that my large audiences hardly ever included students of classical philosophy, and yet my course might have been a revelation to them; the probable reason for their absence is that their advisors were not concerned about science, nor even about the history of science. Too Bad!" In this he paved the way for Harvard's most literary of biologists, Edward O. Wilson, who among much else wrote *The Future of Life* (Random House, 2002) which begins with an enchanting and mind-changing letter to [which is to say: about] Henry Thoreau. George Sarton was also the father of May Sarton, who, according to *The Poetry Foundation*, wrote 53 books, including 19 novels, 17 books of poetry, 15 nonfiction works, 2 children's books, a play, and additional screenplays. [Confession: I once read a good dozen of her books while estranged from a girlfriend who had a house in Maine not far from York where May Sarton spent her last years. Today I don't remember any of them save for the fact that they provided some solace for a grown up baby.]
28   Merton, "Introduction," *Social Theory and Social Structures*, 5–6.

Century England," and a famous article with Paul Lazarsfeld, "Studies in Radio and Film Propaganda."

Merton's is a textbook not necessarily intended for students, but in the sense of scientific texts meant to renew or define a working paradigm. The role of paradigms in science, according to Thomas S. Kuhn's classic 1962 work *The Structure of Scientific Revolutions*, is to organize a normal condition for scientific research on a particular topic. In time, Kuhn argued, paradigms break down as new knowledge demands a new normal. Darwin and Einstein are examples. For Merton, functionalism was a revolutionary paradigm in sociology. The lead essay in *Social Theory and Social Structure*, "Manifest and Latent Functions," is the definition and defense of a paradigm in the making: "Functional analysis is at once the most promising and possibly the least codified of contemporary orientations to the problems of sociological interpretation."[29]

Then he adds: "the first and foremost purpose [of the functionalist paradigm] is to supply a provisional codified guide for adequate and fruitful functional analysis."[30] Merton's purpose here is to present definition, history, postulates, and working concepts necessary for functionalist research in sixty-five pages each dense with an astonishing number of references, many to sources quite outside sociology. The paradigm itself is:

> [The] distinction between manifest and latent functions [refers,] first to those [manifestly] objective consequences for a specified unit (person, subgroup, social or cultural system) which contribute to its adjustment or adaptation and were so intended; the second [refers] to unintended or unrecognized [latent] consequences of the same order.[31]

This is to say that the manifest function of school, for example, is to educate the young; their latent function is to create good citizens, just as the manifest function of war is to defend a nation, while its latent function can be to stimulate a nation's war-time economy. Merton, to be sure, intended to define a paradigm for functional analysis, but just as much he created a paradigm for structural analysis. Structures, he made clear in "Manifest and Latent Functions," may be objective but they are not simply created by the intentions of actors, who more often than not stumble upon unintentional consequences structures seem to demand.

Merton's important contribution to a theory of cultures was made in an article that first appeared in 1938 in the *American Sociological Review* before republication in *Social Theory and Social Structure*. "Social Structure and Anomie" could be said to have made two paradigmatic contributions. Even before Parsons worked through the role of culture in his AGIL model, Merton demonstrated in this article both the structural importance of culture *and* how culture's relations to social structures can vary under different social circumstances. Merton, thereby, initiated an American structuralist movement at the same time that Claude Lévi-Strauss was inventing a different kind of structuralism in France.

"Social Structure and Anomie" turns on Merton's reinterpretation of Émile Durkheim's definition of anomie as the social condition in which society fails to provide moral guidance to individuals. This was Durkheim's basic idea in 1897 in *Suicide* where he gathered evidence to demonstrate that suicide was not an individual choice but a social consequence when society fails to provide a sufficient social bond in times of structural crisis—among

---

29 *Ibid*, 19.
30 *Ibid*, 55.
31 *Ibid*, 63.

bourgeois capitalist men who committed disproportionately high rates of suicide during economic crises, for example. Where Merton differed from Durkheim was by emphasizing that, from culture to culture, and among different groups in society, the power of culture depends on the "institutional means" that may be unequally available. *Anomie*—a sense of aimlessness or of not knowing how to behave—becomes acute when cultural goals encounter a deficiency of institutional means. When anomie (thus defined) occurs, the individual must adapt as best one can. Adaptation for Merton (unlike Parsons) is less the goal of dealing with an environment than a practical effort to deal with a conflict in structures that puts the individual in crisis for want of the means to achieve a cultural goal. Durkheim understood the problem and Parsons' theory allowed for it, but Merton worked out the structural relations.

Merton's "Social Structure and Anomie" may be the clearest instance in post-classical sociology of an attempt to cultivate an analytic paradigm. Merton's working concepts are *cultural goals* and *institutionalized means* as embedded alongside *anomie* and *modes of adaptation*. "Social Structure and Anomie" takes American cultural and social structures as his empirical references. In his typically careful manner, he identifies America's foremost cultural goal as monetary success. The culture may not demand wealth of its adherents, but it does require *sufficient* monetary success to certify an actor's social worth. Put this way, the interpretation gets at an arguable fact of the American way of life in the long transition from the first inklings of a middle-class late in the nineteenth century through the emergence of a consumption-oriented culture in the 1950s. The article first appeared in 1938 when the long depression still drastically limited the institutionalized means for monetary success. That so many were out of work was, for Merton, more than an economic problem. It was just as much a cultural one in that the most impoverished people were unable to present themselves as worthy members of society—unable, that is, to be true Americans. Again, Merton effectively made analytic sense of the morally insane fact that the poor are virtually nothing—a fact of American life that has been true since 1619.

From this general scheme, Merton postulated five modes of adaptation. The first and ideally most normal is *conformity*, where the cultural goal is displayed for all to see as monetary success attained through a job, sometimes called "honest labor." This is the ideal state shaken by the widespread anomie caused dramatically in the 1929 economic collapse that devastated the exaggerated grandeur of the Roaring 20s, causing the nation to fall into deep depression. While Durkheim insisted that severe economic crises led many to suicide, Merton argued that there are other less morbid modes of adaptation. Hence, his second mode was *innovation* in which the cultural goal of sufficient (or extreme) income is gained by deviant means that turn out to be more normal than pure cultural morality might allow. Among these are begging, sex work, drug dealing, numbers running in the day, even outright theft as when a mother steals to provide for her hungry children. Over-the-top instances of innovation are drug dealing that turns to gang banging, embezzling for no other reason than greed, pimping of working girls by enslaving them to drug addiction. On the other hand, in the case of sex work, stripping can be a short cut to income when the alternative is street prostitution can be a desperate and dangerous attempt to survive.

Merton's other three modes of adaptation were: *ritualism*—where individuals no longer believe in the cultural goal of success but keep digging away at some or another life because that is what is done in their neighborhood; *retreatism*—where some just plain give up on being normal worthy members of society by becoming drop-outs, vagrants, addicts, and more or less unabashed ne'er-do-wells; *rebellion*—where people leave the normal order altogether to join a utopian community meant to build society back better. It is evident that for Merton (and most thinking people) the only viable modes are *conformity* and *innovation*. While the other three can be seen everywhere by those willing to look, they are at best limited life possibilities: *ritualism* stifles generational change, *retreatism* is a dead-end, *rebellion* almost never leads to deep structural changes in society.

Merton's five modes of adaptation in "Social Structure and Anomie" made a deep and enduring impression on American sociology's theory of deviance. Not all deviance is deviant. Even more, it has served as a model for social theoretical structuralism in America where hitherto its most native theoretical tradition was pragmatism. Plus which, Merton's paradigm demonstrates very appealingly how social theories rooted in empirical evidence can broaden the range of social thought to include what today are known as outlying or deviant social practices. But, when all is said and done, Merton's scheme gave the generations following him a sense of just how the tensions between culture and economic reality are necessarily part-and-parcel of a mature social science. Strictly speaking, Merton was not a cultural theorist in today's sense, but his guidance toward an understanding of the social and economic entanglements with culture made possible early versions of a sociological cultural theory.

Cultural Theory as a Global Enterprise that Changes as the World Changes

Since the days of Parsons and Merton, not to mention Adams, cultural theory has spawned many progenies such that their number and variety requires the plural—cultural *theories*. But there was good historical reason in their days for a general theory of culture as such. In these earlier theoretical times global crises had inspired a rethinking of how, if at all, the world can be held together. At the end of the nineteenth century, Émile Durkheim was the first then to understand this fact of global life and to remake sociology with respect to the then new crisis of urban societies within a definite culture able to order the many disorders associated with the newly splaying cities. In this sense he was not expressly a functionalist. Still he was Parsons's guide to what became known as functionalism. In America, Henry Adams was Durkheim's contemporary, and, in his strangely elitist way, he could be said to have been doing much the same as Durkheim for whom the decline of religion created the normative void modern societies needed to fill somehow. For Adams it was the Dynamo that did just this as the Virgin had done well before the Age of the Machine. The dynamo was to Adams, what urban disorder was to Durkheim. It would be ridiculous to call Henry Adams a functionalist. His theory of culture was, one could say, so linear that he could not (or would not) think the modern in and of itself. He was not a theorist. Still Adams's basic question was: What serves the unity of society in the modern era as the Virgin had in the medieval long before? No one then would have thought of the Machine as a unifier. Today the Machine is as remote from public thought as it was in a remote corner of the 1893 Chicago exposition.

Yet, the issue returned all the more urgently after World War II when all the world was in ruins and America was riding high in its century (as Henry Luce put it). What then might represent the underlying unity of the modern world when the dynamo is no longer a curiosity? There are many reasons why neither Parsons nor Merton, both extraordinarily widely read, did not happen upon Henry Adams, who was not of their intellectual kind. At the same time, it is perfectly obvious why the functionalist question would stand behind their theories. Crudely put, America even more during the War, stood out—first, for having begun to solve the global economic crisis in a way different from what Germany under Hitler; then second, after the War, for having stood alone among the shambles it had righteously helped create. Put more crudely still, the social scientific question of the day was: Can modern societies be made whole again? It is important to add that structuralism quickly dominated post-war French social thought, overwhelming existentialism's emphasis on personal engagement. It is not by accident that Claude Lévi-Strauss's inaugural lesson at the *Collège de France*, *The Scope of Anthropology*, began as an extended homage to Durkheim. To be sure, Durkheim played a different role in the thinking of Parsons and Merton—one closer to Durkheim than to Lévi-Strauss. Yet, Parsons' analytic method and his emphasis on culture were interestingly close in purpose to Lévi-Strauss's emphasis on myth. While there may be a good bit of wishful social thinking in the comparisons, it is fair enough to say that in the day when they arose, French structuralism and American structural functionalism served a common purpose—as much for their appeal to readers as to the intentions of their authors.

The ideas of Merton and Parsons influenced at least two, if not more, generations of American sociologists. If their ideas have today faded into the shadows of passé classics—neither quite Weberian or Durkheim nor comparable to Judith Butler and Cornel West today—they hover about in the works of those who, to varying degrees, took their leave of the functionalists. Robert Bellah, Clifford Geertz, Jeffrey Alexander—for instructive examples—all enjoyed a relation with Parsons; as Alvin Gouldner, his generation's most prominent radical, remained loyal to his teacher Merton until his dying day in Madrid. These four were leaders among those who lead the way in teaching their students that the point of cultural studies is to interpret cultures, not analyze them—an important distinction that makes today's cultural theories what they are.

13 Interpreting Cultures
Robert Bellah, Clifford Geertz, Alvin Gouldner, George Marcus, Michael Fischer, Jeffrey Alexander

So long as it is vital, the cultural tradition of a people—its symbols,
ideals, and ways of feeling—is always an argument about
the meaning of the destiny its members share.
Cultures are dramatic conversations about things that matter to their participants,
and American culture is no exception.
— Robert N. Bellah, Habits of the Heart, 1985

The concept of culture ... is essentially a semiotic one.
Believing, with Max Weber, that man is an animal suspended in webs of significance
he himself has spun,
I take culture to be those webs, and the analysis of it
to be therefore not an experimental science in search of a law
but an interpretative one in search of meaning.
— Clifford Geertz: Thick Description: Toward an Interpretative Theory of Culture, 1973

The culture of critical discourse (CCD) is an historically evolved set of rules,
a grammar of discourse which (1) is concerned to justify its assertions,
but (2) whose mode of justification does not proceed by invoking authorities,
and (3) prefers to elicit the voluntary consent of those addressed solely on the basis of arguments adduced.
— Alvin W. Gouldner, The Future of Intellectuals and the Rise of the New Class, 1979

Social and cultural anthropology has promised its still largely Western readership enlightenment on two fronts. The one has been the salvaging of distinct cultural forms of life from a process of apparent global Westernization. ... the other promise... has been to serve as a form of cultural critique for ourselves. In using portraits of other cultural patterns to reflect self-critically on our own ways, anthropology disrupts common sense and makes us reexamine our taken-for-granted assumptions.
— George Marcus and Michael Fischer, Anthropology as Cultural Critique, 1986

Every action, no matter how instrumental and reflexive vis-à-vis its external environments, is embedded in a horizon of meaning. ... Every institution no matter how technical, coercive, or seemingly impersonal can only be effective if related to a patterned set of symbols. ...
For this reason, every subfield of sociology must have a cultural dimension.
— Jeffrey Alexander, ASA Culture Section Newsletter, 1996

What, After All, Is Culture?

Almost everyone uses the word "culture." Almost no one can say what it is. It is one of those things, if it is a thing, that demands interpretation. While the early students of social functions who were influenced by Parsons and Merton, tended to treat culture as an analytic category. These were the days in the 1940s and 1950s when America reigned supreme among the democratic nations. It was natural, thereby, to assume that its culture was what culture was.

Then, late in the 1960s all this changed when social moments demanded, in effect, that there were *cultures*—plural and lower case; not *a* Culture. Consequently, by the 1970s and 1980s and well into the 2000s, those interested in cultures had to set-out to say what they were—to interpret them.

Two of those prominent in defining cultures were Robert Bellah and Clifford Geertz. From Bellah, came:

> So long as it is vital, the cultural tradition of a people—its symbols, ideals, and ways of feeling—is always an argument about the meaning of the destiny its members share. Cultures are dramatic conversations about things that matter to their participants, and American culture is no exception.[1]

Cultures are dramatic conversations! They are not remote analytic categories. This is quite a different interpretation from Bellah's one-time teacher and colleague, Talcott Parsons.

Clifford Geetz and Robert Bellah were friends who saw culture somewhat the same way. Geertz:

> The concept of culture ... is essentially a semiotic one. Believing, with Max Weber, that man is an animal suspended in webs of significance he himself has spun, I take culture to be those webs, and the analysis of it to be therefore not an experimental science in search of a law but an interpretative one in search of meaning.[2]

Bellah, a sociologist, and Geertz, an anthropologist, differed in their methods and topics, but they together established that cultures were interpretive as well as necessarily interpreted.

Alvin Gouldner, by contrast, was a very different, openly left social thinker who came to culture late in his days when he developed a still important, if sadly ignored, theory of a new class of actors who worked not on the shop floor but in technomedia. His main organizing concept was *Culture of Critical Discourse*:

> The culture of critical discourse (CCD) is an historically evolved set of rules, a grammar of discourse which (1) is concerned to <u>justify</u> its assertions, but (2) whose mode of justification does not proceed by invoking authorities, and (3) prefers to elicit the <u>voluntary</u> consent of those addressed solely on the basis of arguments adduced.[3]

---

1 Robert Bellah, *Habits of the Heart: Individualism and Commitment in American Life* with Richard Madsen, William M. Sullivan, Ann Swidler, and Steven M. Tipton (University of California, 1985), 27.
2 Geertz, "Thick Description: Toward an Interpretive Theory of Culture," *Interpretation of Cultures* (Basic Books, 1973), 5.
3 Alvin Gouldner, *The Future of Intellectuals and the Rise of the New Class* (Oxford University Press, 1982 [1979]), 28.

While Gouldner obviously was intent upon creating a new more critical way of thinking culture, George Marcus and Michael Fischer in *Anthropology as Culture Critique* in 1986 attempted to bring forth the critical element of their work as anthropologists—work that converts their field into a method of culture critique:

> Social and cultural anthropology has promised its still largely Western readership enlightenment on two fronts. The one has been the salvaging of distinct cultural forms of life from a process of apparent global Westernization. ... the other promise... has been to serve as a form of cultural critique for ourselves. In using portraits of other cultural patterns to reflect self-critically on our own ways, anthropology disrupts common sense and makes us reexamine our taken-for-granted assumptions.[4]

Marcus and Fischer meant to revise cultural anthropology so that its native critical aspect would become an up-front *critique* of culture.[5]

Jeffrey Alexander means to identify cultural sociology as an independent aspect of social theory alongside studies of the social, political, and economic aspects of a society:

> Every action, no matter how instrumental and reflexive vis-à-vis its external environments, is embedded in a horizon of meaning. ... Every institution no matter how technical, coercive, or seemingly impersonal can only be effective if related to a patterned set of symbols. ... For this reason, every subfield of sociology must have a cultural dimension.[6]

Generally, after the 1970s culture became a subject of interpretation under a principle adhered to by the theorists mentioned here—that cultures cannot be taken at face value. They require interpretation to make common sense.

Cultures Meeting/Trying To Make Sense of Themselves

Once-homeless James Thomas is a member of the church in New Haven that is on its Green at the very center of the town. This Town Green is unlike most in New England where all is calm and clean, quiet places where residents and visitors can rest after lunch close to one of those very white churches from olden times. New Haven's Green overflows with activities, many of which fit the picturesque image of those small remote towns. Arts and musical events take place there, as do Memorial Day remembrances. At the end of the year there is a Menorah and a Christmas tree, both lighted. In warmer weather, National Guard troops exercise on the Lower Green.

There's more, but among the more are activities that trouble the all-too-comfortable who think of the Green as down and dirty. New Haven's Green is the daytime home of homeless people. Nights, the police chase them away. But days the homeless gather with others in their unsheltered state. Some ask for money for food or coffee. Others, but not as many as some think, join better-off users in buying and using drugs. The Green is a focal market for the region's drug dealers. Not long ago there was a fentanyl crisis on the Green with hundreds ill, more than a few hospitalized, a few dead.

---

[4] George Marcus and Michael Fischer, *Anthropology as Cultural Critique* (University of Chicago Press, 1986), 1.
[5] Marcus and Fischer distinguish *critical* theory from their sense of *Critique*, see their "Repatriation of Anthropology as Cultural Critique," chapter 5 in *Anthropology as a Cultural Critique*.
[6] Jeffrey Alexander, *ASA Culture Section Newsletter* 10:3–4 (1996), 1–3.

Normally, James leads his Tuesday mid-day Spiritual Fellowship for current and former homeless people in his church's undercroft—which is to say its basement, refurbished for meetings like this one. Some members of the Spiritual Fellowship started attending the Sunday service upstairs. This was fine until homeless people also came to the Church's after service coffee hour in the undercroft. They were hungry, so they took generous portions from the snacks. This was not fine with some members, one of whom reportedly said: "They eat so much that there won't be any for the choir boys." Others were appalled at this attitude. The choir boys are very well fed day after day. About the same time, a nasty little book called *Toxic Charity* circulated among members, several of whom organized a well-attended study group on the book. Its theme was, roughly: Don't give money to the poor and homeless because this will keep them from getting a job and getting their lives together. At the time, in New Haven the cost of renting an affordable single room—of which there were very few—was about twice the average monthly pay for beginning hourly labor. For a time, controversy in the Church, as in the town, raged. People were upset. It seemed to them that the homeless were everywhere, begging and bothering. Many who had not read *Toxic Charity* thought it was the homeless who were toxic.

Still the question remains. *Aren't Christians meant to serve the poor?* "*Inasmuch as you have done it unto the least of these you have done it unto me.*"[7] To which the answer is: *Of course, Yes*! But meaning to do something and being able to do it are two different things. The principles of a religion are one thing. Putting those principles to work is another. Then one day, as if out of nowhere, attitudes and behaviors toward homeless people changed. People in the Church seemed to have learned to bring principles down to practices. I was part of the discussions but couldn't say how this happened. It just did. In time, honest thinking and talking prevailed. Simply put, people learned to reinterpret the culture that loomed over their Church—a culture whose values they repeated in hymns and prayers week after week. Cultures often work for good without those they affect realizing.

Robert Bellah: Habits of the Heart

There came a moment in the 1960s when American social theorists started to break away from the functionalist theories of Talcott Parsons and, to a lesser extent from Robert K. Merton's. In most cases, the breaks were respectful of both; some, less so. Robert Bellah was first among equals among those who left the functionalist camp without tearing it down. He sought less to use culture analytically, more to interpret it.

Bellah was born in 1927 in Oklahoma, grew up in Los Angeles, went to Harvard College from where his honors thesis, *Apache Kinship* (1952), was published by Harvard University Press. He graduated in 1950 *summa cum laude*. Thereafter, few of his endeavors were anything short of *summa*. He completed doctoral studies in Sociology and Far Eastern Languages at Harvard in 1955, after which he was a postdoctoral scholar at McGill University's Institute for Islamic Studies.[8] In 1957 he published his doctoral thesis, *Tokugawa Religion: The Values of Preindustrial Japan*.[9] Also in 1957, Bellah returned to Harvard's Sociology Department and its Center for Middle Eastern Studies. All this goes to say that

---

7   Matthew 25:40.
8   An important instance of Bellah's integrity has to do with the reason he went to McGill. "He was a graduate student completing his doctorate in 1954 when McGeorge Bundy, then Harvard's dean of faculty, pressured him to confess his activities and name his former Communist associates. Bellah refused and headed to McGill when his Harvard fellowship was canceled." [Elaine Woo, "Robert N. Bellah Dies at 86; UC Berkeley Sociologist," *LA Times* (August 2, 2013) @ https://www.latimes.com/local/obituaries/la-me-robert-bellah-20130804-story.html]
9   Bellah, *Tokugawa Religion: The Values of Preindustrial Japan* (Beacon Press, 1957).

Bellah's varied and remarkable education went hand-in-glove with his in-depth study of three important religious cultures, Islamic, Japanese, Apache.

As a result, at a time when religion was out of fashion sociologically, Bellah was unafraid to devote his long career to the sociology of *religions*, plural. Bellah's first venture was his 1964 article in the *American Sociological Review*, "Religious Evolution," in which he put forth a generic definition of religion with respect to six historical ages: the *primitive/tribal*, the *archaic, historic/early modern*, and the *axial* ages from which Bellah extracts for the purposes of this article *archaic, historic, early modern*, and *modern* religions for his analysis of religious evolution.[10] Bellah deployed a definition of religion that owes equally to one of his teachers, Talcott Parsons, and to Paul Tillich—filtered, one supposes, through Clifford Geertz. "So, for limited purposes only, let me define religion as a set of symbolic forms and acts which relate man to the ultimate conditions of his existence."[11]

Historically, Bellah's *primitive* referred, for the most part, to aboriginal cultures where religious actions are "identification, 'participation,' acting-out" and *not* worship or sacrifice.[12] His *archaic* period is conceptually but not empirically distinct from the primitive:

> The characteristic feature of archaic religions is the emergence of true cult [*sic*] with the complex of gods, priests, worship, sacrifice, and in some cases divine or priestly kingship. The myth and ritual complex characteristic of primitive religion continues within the structure of archaic religion, but it is systematized and elaborated in new ways.[13]

Here is where Bellah's sociology of religions also entails a theory of cultures:

> *Primitive* man can only accept the world in its manifold givenness. *Archaic* man can through sacrifice fulfill his religious obligations and make peace with the gods. But the *historic* religions promise man for the first time that he can understand the fundamental structure of reality and through salvation participate actively in it.[14]

As the primitive may be viewed as proto-archaic so the religions of the historic era can be viewed as having paved the way for the early modern period. In the historic period a religious elite emerges as social conflict enters in respect to the interpretation of the otherworldly. Here religious organization is quite different:

> The differentiation of a religious elite brought a new level of tension and the possibility of conflict and change onto the social scene. Whether the confrontation was between the Israelite prophet and king, Islamic ulama and sultan, the Christian pope and emperor or even better between the Confucian scholar-official and his ruler, it implied that political acts could be judged in terms of standards that the political authorities could not finally control.[15]

---

10 Bellah, "Religious Evolution," *American Sociological Review* 29:3 (1964), 364–373—or the bulk of the paper. Important to add that this historical analysis became, in the day, a rage among scholars of religious studies, theologians, and sociologists of religion who had their traditional assumptions challenged but also illuminated.
11 *Ibid*, 359.
12 Bellah, "Religious Evolution," 364.
13 *Ibid*, 364.
14 *Ibid*, 367. Emphases added. Some might wonder what here became of the Axial Age he refers to. He dealt with that in a later book but for now he is referring to religions as such and not their historical ages; and in 1964 the issue at hand was modern thus historic religion. The later book is *Religion in Human Evolution: From the Paleolithic to the Axial Age* (Harvard University Press, 2011).
15 *Ibid*, 368.

Clearly Bellah's historic period anticipates the early modern for which the paradigmatic case is the Protestant sects born of the sixteenth-century Reformation—especially Calvinism. Since Bellah means to lay down the authoritative historical scheme for the study of religions and their cultures, the Protestantized early modern period is historically exemplary, even pivotal. Protestant Christianity did two things at once. It gave the individual believer unmediated access to the transcendent power *and* (somewhat ironically) "conceived *religious action* as identical with the whole of life."[16] This obviously is Weber's idea of the Calvinist strain in the Protestant Ethic that, in time, led to a secular capitalist work ethic. Yet, for Bellah the this-worldly aspect of the early modern period may effectively fade into the modern which changes the analytic terms of religions:

> To concentrate on the church in a discussion of the modern religious situation is already misleading, for it is precisely the characteristic of the new situation that the great problem of religion, as I have defined it, the symbolization of man's relation to the ultimate conditions of his existence, is no longer the monopoly of any groups explicitly labeled religious.[17]

In a way, Bellah ended up only where he could have given his definition of religion. While the Parsonsian evolutionary element is frustrated by the modern realities, the Tillichian aspect of his definition of religion, like Geertz's, may have foreordained the conclusion. The very idea of defining religion generically was famously attacked by Talal Asad.[18] Though controversial, the critique makes sense inasmuch as, in Bellah's case, it seems that religion, once defined in respect to symbolic forms and acts, is destined to lead to a religious type where the enduring primitive/archaic fusion of this-worldly cultures must be broken by an other-worldly sphere. Otherwise there could be no differences among types of religions—and no evolution to speak of.

Not many scholars who might write an essay like "Religious Evolution" early in their career come back to the subject again and again in order, at the end of their lives, to publish a massively comprehensive book on the same subject. *Religion in Human Evolution: From the Paleolithic to the Axial Age* in 2011, nearly a half century later, did just that[19]—and did so by refining his 1964 theory both conceptually and empirically, while, unsurprisingly, making no effort to consider the early modern and modern religions. It is as if he conceded the limits, if not the error, of "Religious Evolution." If those limits are to be taken seriously, they may be excused by all that he did between 1964 and 2011. As important as the 2011 book is in its own right—and it is the most important contemporary sociological study of premodern religions—for present purposes of examining Bellah's social theory of culture two books written between 1964 and 2011 are more important.

Though Bellah clearly began with a robust analytic theory of religious cultures, he soon enough turned from religion to culture as his subject—in particular American culture. The

---

16 "Religious Evolution," 369.
17 *Ibid*, 372.
18 See Talal Asad, "The Construction of Religion as an Anthropological Category," in *Genealogies of Religion: Discipline and Reasons of Power in Christianity and Islam* (Johns Hopkins University Press, 1993 [1982]), 27–54. Bellah later defended Geertz and himself without actually stating why Asad was wrong especially in his attack on Geertz; see Robert Bellah, *Religion in Human Evolution: From the Paleolithic to the Axial Age* (Harvard University Press, 2011), n. 19, 610–11. Though today social theorists of culture and religion hardly mention Talal Asad, his *Genealogies of Religion* ought to be read in comparison to Bellah's *Religion in Human Evolution*.
19 For a brilliant review of this book, see Jack Miles, "Review Essay on *Religion and Human Evolution*," *Journal of the American Academy of Religion*, 83:3 (September 2013), 852–864.

first step in this direction was in 1967 in "Civil Religion in America," the one article that may have been read more than "Religious Evolution." "Civil Religion in America"[20] turns out to have been more a theory of the unique strains in American culture than a study of religion as he portrayed it in the earlier 1964 article. Bellah presents civil religion in America according to three times of trial: first, *the revolutionary era*—when George Washington represented the new nation's transcendent ideas; second, *the civil war*—when Abraham Lincoln bore the burden of suffering that resurrected the nation; and third, *the crisis of 1960s* that came to a head in 1968, a time where the crisis was "responsible action in a revolutionary world"—for which there was no single transcendent figure.

Bellah's distinctive contribution to the interpretation of cultures is in two books that sought to come to terms with the third time of trial: *Habits of the Heart: Individualism and Commitment in American Life* with Richard Madsen, William M. Sullivan, Ann Swidler, and Steven M. Tipton in 1985; and *The Good Society* with the same four co-authors in 1991. *Habits of the Heart*—a book with a most intriguing title—begins with a clear statement of the structural issue affecting American culture in the nation's struggle to come to terms with a global revolution that by 1980 was: "...the division of life into a number of separate functional sectors: home and workplace, work and leisure, white collar and blue collar, public and private [... divisions] suited to the needs of the bureaucratic, industrial corporations ..."[21] The late twentieth century time of trial is represented by figurative case studies of Brian, Joe, Margaret, and Wayne whose lives are presented to suggest the conversations they *might* have had, which is to say conversations the collective American "we" might have had in the 1980s. The solution in *Habits of the Heart* in 1985 is the proposal of a rather opaque social movement toward a new social ecology that reconstitutes a web of commitments.[22]

It is apparent why *Habits of the Heart* is about culture—about, that is, the way culture determines individuals and their social commitments. This in spite of the fact that the book makes ample reference to changes in the political economy. In *Habits*, Bellah uses a definition of *culture* that differs from the ones he used earlier in his articles on religion—here culture becomes: "Those patterns of meaning that any group or society uses to interpret and evaluate itself and its situation."[23] More concretely, the book appealingly says: "Cultures are dramatic *conversations* about the things that matter to their participants. ..."[24] While Bellah's theory of culture owes its origin to Parsons, here he is less analytic and more empirically attuned to the function of culture in American society—a function meant to keep the social order workably together.

The Good Society in 1991—Bellah's second book with Richard Madsen, William M. Sullivan, Ann Swidler, and Steven M. Tipton—was published but six years after *Habits of the Heart*, but it refers to a different world and does not dwell on the individual. If 1968 was the year of a world revolution, then 1989, when the Soviet Union collapsed, was the year that revolution turned truly global—and not just for this geopolitical fact of

---

20 "Civil Religion in American," *Daedalus* 96:1 (1967), 1–21.
21 Bellah, *Habits of the Heart: Individualism and Commitment in American Life* with Richard Madsen, William M. Sullivan, Ann Swidler, and Steven M. Tipton (University of California, 1985), 43. [Note: For both of Bellah's books *with* his four associates, I often use Bellah's name as if he were the sole author for shorthand purposes. This seems easy but to me it is also fair. I studied with Bellah in the 1960s well before these two books in the 1980s and, time difference notwithstanding, the language and themes are his—or so I believe. Madsen, Sullivan, Swidler, and Tipton all went on to distinguished careers of their own.]
22 *Ibid*, 283–291.
23 *Ibid*, 333.
24 *Ibid*, 27. Emphasis added.

this-worldly life, but because the world was coming into local view in new ways. This was a revolution that grew out of the decolonization movements in the Global South a generation earlier and the impressions they made in the 1960s within the nations of the North where students, workers, women, gays and lesbians, Blacks and other people of color resisted the white, characterologically straight male domination of their worlds and of the world itself. By 1991 all this was viral to the faint of heart. As a result, in one chapter, "America in the World," *The Good Society* covers these issues.[25] *The Good Society*, as distinct from *Habits of the Heart*, takes a radically different empirical world as its subject.

Theoretically, however, the key innovation in *The Good Society* is the importance of institutions. For one thing, early in the book a point is made that sociologists in the day needed to appreciate, what even now they are still beginning to consider.[26] "The idea that institutions are objective mechanisms that are essentially separate from the lives of the individuals who inhabit them is an ideology that exacts a high moral and political price."[27] Bellah adds, two paragraphs on, that "responsibility is something we exercise as individuals but within and on behalf of institutions."[28] It would be hard to imagine a better thematic statement for the book as a whole. Where *Habits of the Heart* turned on the stories of individuals, *The Good Society* turns on sketches of major institutional sectors of American society each presented after a bracing chapter, "The Rise and Fall of the American Century," that is spot on still today:

> One way of summing up the difficulty Americans have in understanding the fundamental roots of their problems is to say that they still have a Lockean political culture, emphasizing individual freedom and the pursuit of individual affluence (the American Dream) in a society with a most un-Lockean economy and government.[29]

Thereafter, the substance of the book wrestles with this dilemma in chapters on the political economy, government and politics, technical and moral education, and the public church. Each, predictably, is an astute diagnosis of the cultural effects of these institutional sectors.

Of the two books, *Habits of the Heart* was an academic bestseller—all but required reading for many. *The Good Society* never quite rose to the same level of popularity, but it is the better book. It corrects the impression of the earlier book's singular emphasis on the individual in American culture. Not incidentally, in its Appendix, "Institutions in Sociology and Public Philosophy," *The Good Society* offers a quite compelling statement of Bellah's thinking as a social theorist addressing issues at the end of the twentieth century.[30] Though there is much else in both books, together they are an important contribution to the theory of culture, done as the authors say, in a Tocquevillian manner, "combining an analytic with a narrative method."[31]

More generally, *The Good Society* reframes the classic American idea of individualism from its Lockean origins as a struggle against natural and social odds into a social theory

---

25 Bellah, "America in the World," in *The Good Society* with Richard Madsen, William M. Sullivan, Ann Swidler, and Steven M. Tipton (Knopf, 1991), chapter 7.
26 *Ibid*, 9–12 [a section, with the header "Why Americans Have Trouble Understanding Institutions"].
27 *Ibid*, 12.
28 *Ibid*, 13. Here they are following the lead of Mary Douglas, *How Institutions Think* (Syracuse University Press, 1986), 124.
29 *Ibid*, 79. [the first line of a section headed by "The Present Impasse" in chapter 2, "The Rise and Fall of the American Century."]
30 *Ibid*, 287–306.
31 *Ibid*, 289.

whereby individuals achieve what goals they have by joining with others in institutions meant to make their worlds better.[32] Yet Bellah stops short. *The Good Society* discusses the social conflicts associated with the institutional sectors, of which the most poignant is "The Tyranny of the Market."[33] But the book doesn't fully engage the implications of its important idea that individuals and their institutions must contend with the emergent global realities—realities that brought down conflict upon conflict on local and national societies the world over. Just the same, their step in the right direction opened the way for a rethinking of culture. Where there are differences and thereby conflict, culture can no longer simply be defined and analytically deployed. Culture itself must be interpreted against facts that very often lead to the recognition that there is no such thing as *culture* (singular). There are *cultures* that can cause trouble for other cultures. Cultures have as much to do with disorder as with order. Bellah did not go that far. But he opened the door, a door that Clifford Geertz walked through.

Clifford Geertz: A New Paradigm for the Interpretation of Cultures

If there is a single text that could be called the lodestar for the once-new interpretative cultural theories, it is Clifford Geertz's "Thick Description: Toward an Interpretive Theory of Culture"—the lead essay in his 1973 collection of essays, *The Interpretation of Cultures*, itself a classic.

Geertz was born in San Francisco in 1926, served in the Navy (1943–45), before going to Antioch College, then to Harvard University for graduate work with Talcott Parsons and Clyde Kluckhohn, graduating in 1956. After the doctorate, he did extensive ethnographic field work in Modjokuto, a small town in Java, from which he gained the empirical and theoretical basis for his first important book, *The Religion of Java* in 1960. The same year, Geertz began his teaching career at the University of Chicago. His formative experiences were remarkably similar to Bellah's except that Geertz became a cultural anthropologist which, at the least, made cultural differences all the more central to his cultural theory. In 1970 Geertz moved to the Institute for Advanced Studies in Princeton.[34]

Geertz also published *Peddlers and Princes: Social Development and Economic Change in Two Indonesian Towns* in 1963, *Agricultural Innovation: The Process of Ecological Change in Indonesia* in 1964, *Islam Observed: Religious Development in Morocco and Indonesia* in 1968, *Negara: The Theatre State of Nineteenth Century Bali* in 1980, *Local Knowledge: Further Essays in Interpretive Anthropology* (1983), among other books and many articles. After his fieldwork days were over, Geertz eventually began to write a number of shorter books that were more or less memoiristic reflections on his experiences in anthropology. Among these are *After the Fact: Two Countries, Four Decades, One Anthropologist* (1996) and *Available Light: Anthropological Reflections on Philosophical Topics* (2000). The titles alone indicate an important constant in Geertz's intellectual journey—always thinking of field work, always thinking theoretically. *Works and Lives: Anthropologist as Author* (1988), in particular, is a valuable indicator of a theoretical lineage Geertz advanced because it offers a brilliant *explication de texte* of Claude Lévi-Strauss's *Tristes Tropiques* in

---

32 *Ibid*, 66–70; and the whole of "The Rise and Fall of the American Century."
33 *Ibid*, 90–95.
34 Geertz remained friendly with Bellah over the years, clearly holding Bellah's work in high regard—sufficiently so that he joined in the nomination of Bellah for a permanent position at the Institute for Advanced Studies. The appointment was voted down by some of its natural science members. His supporters moved for reconsideration of the vote. A bitter fight ensued, but Bellah withdrew because of grief over the death of his daughter.

a chapter entitled "The World in a Text: How to Read *Tristes Tropiques*." As Lévi-Strauss honored Émile Durkheim and used Ferdinand de Saussure's theory of signs, so here Geertz deploys Lévi-Strauss's famously controversial book and the tradition he took for himself to signal the importance of signs in his theory of cultures.

In a passage of such literary elegance as to rival the best writing in *Tristes Tropiques* in 1955, Geertz in 1973 provided what remains one of the most explicitly succinct definitions of culture as a semiotic of signs:

> Culture, this acted document, ... is like a burlesqued wink or a mock sheep raid. Though ideational, it does not exist in someone's head; though unphysical, it is not an occult entity. ... The thing to ask about a burlesqued wink or a mock sheep raid is not what their ontological status is—they are things of this world. The thing to ask is what their import is: what it is, ridicule or challenge, irony or anger, snobbery or pride, that, in their occurrence and through their agency, is getting said.[35]

Burlesqued winks and mock sheep raids? To what is Geertz referring? Nothing less than his most famous concept—*thick description* as the method of cultural studies.[36]

Geertz borrowed *thick description* from the Oxford philosopher Gilbert Ryle who also introduced the example of the burlesqued wink. From the outside, said Ryle, a wink does not reveal its meaning. It could be a meaningless twitch or a meaning-filled gesture—a burlesque upon the events passing before those gathered about. And, Geertz adds: Is the wink, if meaningful, a gesture according to a local code opaque to the outsider? Does it convey a particular message about the situation? Or might it be a convention of some sort not particularly tied to the context but only to ones like it? And so on. These are the kind of questions asked by anyone who would study the cultures of people different from theirs. The sheep raid figure is, thus, an extension upon Ryle's wink—that of a Jewish trader who was taken by the colonial French army to be a Berber who lost his sheep, but they spared his life because a joke was taken for serious by those unable or uninterested in doing a thick description of the events unfolding on a North African plain.

Thick description entails, in effect, a decoding of the meanings of human conduct occurring in public where actions of all kinds are susceptible to being mistaken and where meaning can make all the difference in the world at hand. In culture-filled public situations meanings are decided *not* by a hermeneutic of the actor's intention—or, even, by a probe to the inner meaning of the structured systems—, but by a reading of the cultural code at play in the situation. Though "reading" has been surcharged with jargon in some theoretical quarters, there is a difference between a reading and a hermeneutic. Strictly speaking, *hermeneutics* dig for secreted intentions behind a scene; while *readings* take the surfaces of social things for what they are—thus, to decode their differential relations with the multiple but finite possibilities a culture allows (hence Lévi-Strauss's idea that the study of cultures is a transformational semiology). When faced with a wink, the question is not *What do these people mean when they do that?* Rather, it is *When they do that, which of the possible meanings are they signifying?* The difference between may seem small, but it is a salient difference.

---

35 Geertz, "Thick Description: Toward an Interpretive Theory of Culture," *Interpretation of Cultures* (Basic Books, 1973), 10.
36 The following long section on Geertz and semiology is taken from Charles Lemert, *Durkheim's Ghosts: Cultural Logics and Social Things* (Cambridge University Press, 2006), 56–58 (in the chapter "What is Culture?").

The thickness of the description must refer thereby not to operational concepts, strong protocols directing the science, or the N of valid data and reliable interpretations of them. The thickness lies in getting down to the small differences the wink could mean among the others it could not—down to, that is, the fine line that reveals the cultural code as it pertains to concrete events. In other words, thick description is less about the mass of data than the fineness of the clue.

The wink is neither a weed masking a true intention nor a seed of pure cultural understanding. It is a flower in the garden of meanings—a flower for which the seed was sown sufficiently long before it could have grown up amid weeds without losing its bloom. Not even the ethnographer can know that there was in fact an original sower of the seeds, nor for that matter that there was a Manichean rival who sowed the evil weeds. All that matters is that the events occur in public, which is to say: that they are meaningful in the sense that they signify something to those about. This is culture—and the challenge for the interpreter is reading the code by which the meanings are signified, an interpretative act that is thick, not by virtue of the mass of its detail, but by the specific gravity of its meanings.

Call it what you will, culture by any name is that social thing which cultivates the conditions for participation in some local social whole, no matter what its size or prominence in the flux and reversals of historical time. Culture cultivates the microscopic details of the social. How can it be otherwise?[37] Social things are lived in the micro spaces of the social whole the naked eye cannot see. Meanings are not general, but concrete. Signs are not neon displays over the squares of time in all the big cities, but the slightest gesture that signifies the small difference in the possible meanings that may be many but limited enough to mean something.

All in all, Geertz, even more than Bellah, opened the flood gates to more than a few departures in the study of culture. His "Thick Description: Toward an Interpretive Theory of Culture" is close to having been a paradigm shifter in Thomas Kuhn's sense. After Geertz's *The Interpretation of Culture* in 1973, many of his ideas functioned to invite a new and thicker seriousness in the study of cultures. Three of those departures barely mentioned Geertz. Yet they deserve discussion here because they were early ventures toward new cultural studies that embraced the notion that cultures had to contend with the disordering aspects of societies after the 1980s when the disordering of the 1960s had settled into the warp and woof of late modern societies.

Exemplars of these innovations are Alvin Gouldner's *The Future of Intellectuals and the Rise of the New Class* in 1979, George Marcus and Michael Fischer's *Anthropology as Cultural Critique* in 1986, and Jeffrey Alexander's steps toward a strong program in cultural sociology that culminated in his magnum opus, *The Civil Sphere* in 2006.

Alvin W. Gouldner: The Culture of Critical Discourse

Alvin W. Gouldner was born in the Bronx in 1920. He was educated in New York City schools. After Baruch College in the City University of New York, he studied for the PhD at Columbia University, after which he rose rapidly to the ranks of the globally famous (in his case, some would say, notorious) sociologists.

---

37 Geertz has called the method "microscopic" which is to say: "Small facts speak to large issues, winks to epistemology, or sheep raids to revolutions, because they are made to." *The Interpretation of Cultures*, 23; for "microscopic," 21.

Through the years Gouldner advertised himself as "a street tough kid from the Bronx."[38] He was truly tough and often given to anger and outrage over events that stirred his soul, for good or ill. Street tough though he could be, at Columbia and ever after he enjoyed a friendship with his advisor, Robert K. Merton.[39] It is at least possible that one of the reasons their relationship grew from teacher/student to friends is that Merton also had grown up on tough streets in Philadelphia. Through the years, Merton's influence was apparent, especially in Gouldner's first two books: *Patterns of Industrial Bureaucracy* (1954) and its companion volume, *Wildcat Strike* (1954).[40] The former came to be recognized as a modern classic in industrial sociology. Gouldner's growing up in the Bronx in the 1930s is reflected in his decision to study the social conditions of workers in a bureaucratized factory system. In the years following, Merton's influence was occasionally hidden behind Gouldner's turn to a critical post-Marxist theory. Yet, it is there between the lines by which he came to straddle the then major differences in America between the cultures of Sociology and Marxism.[41]

Gouldner's most famous book in the day was *The Coming Crisis of Western Sociology* in 1970 which appeared just when academic sociology was facing up to the turmoil of the 1960s. It was widely read by left-leaning sociologists (many of them veterans of the Civil Rights and Anti-Vietnam War movements). *Coming Crisis* attacked Talcott Parsons, then waning as the most prominent American sociological theorist. Parsons's structural functionalism, Gouldner argued, furtively advanced the idea that the American social system was the prototype for all modern societies. Gouldner sarcastically referred to "The World of Talcott Parsons"—a world that ignored Marxism and Socialism. This critique could be said to have been Gouldner's way of breaking with the old order of cultural theory.[42] Even before *Coming Crises,* Gouldner's writings touched on aspects of culture, but the most important of these was *Enter Plato* in 1965 where he interpreted culture in respect to the objectivism/subjectivism dilemma. In the book's remarkable closing chapter of *Enter Plato,* "Death and the Tragic Outlook," Gouldner decisively located knowledge as the most fundamental of personal realities—as, that is, reflexivity as the dynamic aspect of culture.

At the time of Gouldner's death in Madrid of a heart attack at 60 years in 1980, he had just finished a remarkably inventive trilogy, *The Dark Side of the Dialectic*. The three books were a leap into his brand of cultural theory. The three books were: *The Dialectic of Ideology and Technology: The Origins, Grammar, and Future of Ideology* (1976); *The Future of Intellectuals and the Rise of the New Class: A Frame of Reference, Theses,*

---

38 The line about his being a tough kid from the Bronx was in a CV I found in his home office in St. Louis after his death in 1980. To near the end, he remained the street tough character. On one occasion Al and I were having dinner at a nice restaurant in the city. The waitress [sic!] came by for a third time to ask if we needed anything else. Al said: "We need for you to stop bothering us." She stopped. I shrank in amazement.
39 Robert K. Merton, "The Genesis and Growth of a Friendship," *Theory and Society* 11/6 (1982), 915–938.
40 Alvin W. Gouldner, *Patterns of Industrial Behavior* (Free Press, 1954) and *Wildcat Strike* (Harper & Row, 1954). See also "Metaphysic Pathos and the Theory of Bureaucracy," *American Political Science Review* 62/3 (1955), 496–507.
41 The discussion of Gouldner following depends on an essay written with the late Paul Piccone that appeared first in *Theory and Society* (November 1983) before being republished with a tribute to Piccone under the title "Cruelty and Murder in the Academy" that functions as a preface of sorts to the article we wrote on Gouldner: "Alvin Gouldner and Post-Marxist Critical Theory," in Charles Lemert, *The Structural Lie: Small Clues to Global Things* (Routledge/ Paradigm, 2011), 49–75.
42 Though Geertz did not figure in Gouldner's emergent theory of cultures, he did use Geertz's "Ideology as a Cultural System" to support his critique of Parsons as essentially Comtean positivism. See Gouldner, *Dialectic of Ideology and Technology* (Continuum Books/Seabury Press, 1976), 10.

Conjectures, Arguments, and an Historical Perspective on the Role of Intellectuals and Intelligentsia in the International Class Contest of the Modern Era (1979); *The Two Marxisms: Contradictions and Anomalies* (1980). Of these, it was the second, and shortest of the three, that is the odd book out for more reasons than its ridiculously long subtitle. It is, actually more a long pamphlet than a fully developed discursive book.[43] Just the same, *The Future of Intellectuals and the Rise of the New Class* is a densely packed, substantive outline of Gouldner's view of the interpretation of cultures. The book begins with a schematically stated history of the rise of the New Class:

(1) the rise of secularization, (2) the rise of diverse vernacular languages, (3) a breakdown of the feudal and old regime system of *personalized patronage*, (4) a corresponding growth of an anonymous market for the products and services of the New Class, (5) [the rise] of the multinational structure of European politics, (6) the nuclear family [and] the autonomy of children, (7) public [schooling], (8) socialization of the young by ... a *semi-autonomous group of teachers*, (9) public education system becomes a major cosmopolitanizing influence on students, (10) making all *authority-referencing* claims potentially problematic, (11) the new culture of discourse often diverges from assumptions fundamental to everyday life, (12) the social position of humanistic intellectuals, *particularly in a technocratic and industrial society*, becomes more marginal and alienated than that of the technical intelligentsia. ... (13) Revolution itself becomes a technology to be pursued with "instrumental rationality."[44]

This was more than twenty years before September 11, 2001 when Osama bin Laden's attack on America was organized and initiated by a handheld technological device. Since, mobile phones, weaponized drones, social networks, ever more sophisticated computer systems, and more are at the center of postmodern societies, revolutionizing how people communicate, attack others, get what "news" they get, and study the world. Gouldner was years ahead of his times.

In respect to his cultural theory, Gouldner was particularly persuasive with his distinctive idea of cultural capital that was much more carefully worked out than the one Pierre Bourdieu was developing at the same time in France. If Gouldner may have been overly optimistic about the power of a New Class, he was far from wrong in describing it as a new cultural bourgeoisie able to challenge the older money class in a kind of *"civil war within the upper classes."*[45] About this there is little reason to doubt. Again, in our day, especially in America, there has risen a largely ill-educated class of those excluded from the benefits (such as they are) of the capitalist system had joined in a political attack on the remnants of a New Class because they—especially the technomedia—are, in their way, attacking the dug-in political figures beholden to the Old Class of money brokers.

---

43 All three books were published by Seabury Press which in the day published academic books. Why Gouldner resorted to this publisher is itself a question for which no answer can be found. Seabury seems to have disappeared leaving behind a remnant of religious books. It would be helpful to know if Gouldner's *Two Marxisms* published in 1980 had been in production before *The Future of Intellectuals* and, for whatever reason, he needed to foreshorten it. He was undergoing trouble at home that put his marriage in doubt which, may or may not, have been the reason he died of a cardiac arrest late in 1980. His widow, Janet, told me that during lunch on the day he died, Gouldner said: "You never know when you'll have your last plate of beans." After lunch, they left, and he died on the sidewalk in Madrid.
44 Gouldner, *The Future of Intellectuals and the Rise of the New Class* (Oxford University Press, 1982 [1979]). [Edited.]
45 *Ibid*, 18; and the whole of Thesis Five: There was a Cultured Bourgeoisie, 18–27.

Gouldner's New Class Theory was also original in respect to American culture in following the semiotic line already well developed in Europe and by Geertz. His version was the New Class as a Speech Community. Here the operative idea is of a culture of critical discourse (CCD) in which "there is nothing that speakers will on principle permanently refuse to discuss or make problematic."[46] The tensions among the triangulated sectors in American society (and others) are largely due to aggravated speech that respects no limits—a bizarre inversion of the Constitution's first amendment protecting free speech. It is not just the New Class elite but all factors in the cultural and political system that are willing and able to say anything, no matter how silly or, more importantly, provocative.

Gouldner's interpretation of culture was not, strictly speaking, a full-blown theory of cultures. Just the same, so long now after he died, his leftish interpretation of culture merits more attention. Gouldner's contribution to cultural theory is that he was a pioneer in interpreting cultures and societies structurally—with disciplined attention to political realities (especially those arising in the 1960s)—realities that were as much disordering as ordering.

George Marcus and Michael Fischer: Anthropology as Cultural Critique

In retrospect, *Anthropology as Cultural Critique: An Experimental Moment in the Human Sciences* by George Marcus and Michael Fischer is a strange kind of book. It appeared in 1986 just when the study of cultures was booming. For many, the book made this experimental moment (as they called it) a necessary engagement. The book itself is less the statement of a position in respect to the interpretation of culture than a compendium of the state of the art. If, as we have seen, the 1960s where the decade when, as Immanuel Wallerstein put it, the modern world system began to unravel, then in the 1980s was when the human sciences began to take that world seriously, even as it was changing dramatically.

George Marcus, today, is Chancellor's Professor at the University of California Irvine after serving as a distinguished professor of Anthropology at Rice University, where he chaired the Department of Anthropology for a good quarter-century. In both places he has spawned programs for the study of ethnography and more than a few journals and other academic enterprises focusing on culture studies and ethnography. Michael Fischer is Andrew W. Mellow Professor in the Humanities and Professor of Anthropology and Science and Technology Studies at M.I.T. while also holding a position at Harvard Medical School. Fischer had formerly been Director of the Center for Cultural Studies at Rice University. He too is active in encouraging a new look in cultural anthropology—for example, his 2018 book, *Anthropology in the Meantime: Experimental Theory, Method, for the Twenty-first Century*. Both are prominent cultural anthropologists. Each has pursued his own intellectual trajectory. But their *Anthropology as Cultural Critique* in 1986 stands on its own for having defined and described the paradigm breakdown occurring in the 1980s—a shift that radically crashed the barriers between and among fields opening the way for experiments in and around the study of culture. Early on, their book starts by referring to Clifford Geertz's paper, "Blurred Genres" (1980) as an attempt "... to characterize the current trend by noting the fluid borrowing of ideas and methods from one discipline to another."[47] Marcus

---

46 *Ibid*, 28.
47 *Anthropology as Cultural Critique: An Experimental Moment in the Human Sciences* (University of Chicago Press, 1986), 7. They also, as few did in the day, included Pierre Bourdieu, 84. Their qualified acknowledgment of Geertz's importance to the field begins chapter 1 of their book (page 7) partly repeated to identify the qualification: "Clifford Geertz's paper, 'Blurred Genres' (1980), attempted to characterize the current trend

and Fischer come close to naming Geertz, Pierre Bourdieu, and Marshall Sahlins as co-originators of this shift, but they stop short.[48] They are more interested in the coming apart of the old and the rise of the new.

Hence, the title of their first chapter, "A Crisis of Representation in the Human Sciences," and the following striking statement:

> Present conditions of knowledge are defined not so much by what they are as by what they come after. In general discussion with the humanities and social sciences, the present indeed is often described as "postparadigm"—postmodernism, poststructuralism, post-Marxism, for example.[49]

The chapter then ranges over sources so different that, in the day, they were seldom juxtaposed—Talcott Parsons and the neofunctionalists (notably Jeffrey Alexander), Walter Benjamin, Robert Musil, Ludwig Wittgenstein, Louis Althusser and the Two Marxisms, Hayden White's *Metahistory* (1973), but also Durkheim and Weber, and Nietzsche, Anthony Giddens and Alvin Gouldner, and more. Their general point is well-enough made that it serves to lend background to the second chapter, "Ethnography and Interpretative Anthropology." Though earlier they had stopped short of naming Geertz as a paradigm originator, the key chapter, "Ethnography and Interpretative Anthropology," returns again and again to Geertz, for one: "The metaphor of cultures as texts, popularized by Clifford Geertz in 1973, served to mark vividly the difference between the behavioral scientist and the cultural interpreter."[50]

By presenting a nuanced account of the history of interpretative anthropology and its "after," Marcus and Fischer come to one of their most important conclusions about the study of cultures:

> Ethnography thus must be able to capture more accurately the historical context of its subjects, and to register the constitutive workings of impersonal international political and economic systems on the local level where fieldwork usually takes place. These workings can no longer be accounted for as merely external impacts on local, self-contained cultures. Rather, external systems have their thoroughly local definition and penetration, and are formative of the symbols and shared meanings within the most intimate life-worlds of ethnographic subjects.[51]

This is a nugget in a field of theories then still worrying about what has been called the macro-micro link. Theories of culture, Marcus and Fischer argued, will get nowhere unless they break open the dichotomy between subjects and objects. What they proposed in 1986

---

by noting the fluid borrowing of ideas and methods from one discipline to another. Geertz did not, however, attempt to analyze the dilemmas of the various disciplines." In my several, separate meetings with George and Michael I found them each to be very generous people. Perhaps the issue is that, like most authors of books meant to define a new paradigmatic departure, they felt obliged to criticize, however politely, those who may have made the departure before them. Then too, in their Introduction they seem to have conceded the importance of Geertz by beginning the book itself (page 1) by castigating Edward Said for his failure to take Geertz seriously.

48 *Ibid*, 84; also 141–146.
49 *Ibid*, 8.
50 *Ibid*, 26. [The Geertz reference is to his "Deep Play: Notes on the Balinese Cockfight," in *The Interpretation of Cultures* (1973).]
51 *Ibid*, 39.

was so much more ingenious and useful than, in the same period, Pierre Bourdieu's *habitus* and Anthony Giddens's *structuration theory*—both of which narrow the dichotomous divide without suggesting, as Marcus and Fischer do, just how the inner workings of universal and local do what they do—in reality and in cultural theory.[52]

The result of their ingenuity is demonstrated in the two most indispensable chapters in *Anthropology as Cultural Critique*. Their titles suggest just how they develop the book's main idea: "Conveying Other Cultural Experiences: The Person, Self, and Emotions" (chapter 3) and "Taking Account of World Historical Political Economy: Knowable Communities in Larger Systems" (chapter 4). Chapter 3 is just what its title suggests, for example: "Regional analysis should ... involve not only geographic-economic mapping of what happens where, but also the relative power-linked articulation and conflict over ideologies, world views, moral codes, and the locally bounded conditions of knowledge and competence."[53] The idea here is best, if loosely, characterized by the section header following this line, "Historicizing the Ethnographic Present." In chapter 3 on "Conveying Other Cultural Experiences," the reader encounters not general theorizing but concrete (one might say, middle-range) characterizations of the relation between working ethnographers' concepts and the "personhood" of those studied, a term used to represent three groups of "culturally variable experiences of reality": psychodynamic, realist, and modernist.[54] As before, each of the three is discussed with respect to texts appropriate to the topic, among them Robert Levy's *Tahitians: Mind and Experience in the Society Islands* (1973), with the unsurprising allusion to Geertz.[55] "Psychodynamic" is not a term commonly used in reference to cultural ethnography, but Marcus and Fischer use it to enrich their discussion of personhood.

> [The] mark of contemporary experiments in psychodynamic texts is the display of discourse—self-reflective commentaries on experience, emotion, and self; on dreams, remembrances, associations, metaphors, distortions, displacements, and on transference and compulsive behavior patterns—all of which reveal a behaviorally significant level of reality reflecting, contrasting with, or obscured by, public cultural forms.[56]

Passages like this one stir heart and mind because, in other of the social sciences, one seldom encounters such an honest deployment of psychoanalytic concepts—presented not as a programmatic tendency but as part of a larger literature of different but related ideas. This

---

52 Bourdieu's *habitus* was first clearly stated in his *Outline of a Theory of Practice* (1977 [1972]); and Giddens's *structuration theory* was most fully developed in *The Constitution of Society* (1984) after being introduced in *New Rules of Sociological Method* (1976). For a comparison and critique of both see Charles Lemert, *Sociology after the Crisis* (Routledge/Paradigm, 2004), chapter 7 ("Three Ways to Think Structures and Ignore Differences"). Bourdieu, whom I never once considered addressing as Pierre, fought hard to win his Chair at the Collège de France. Once won, he was generous to visiting, often younger, Americans (of which I was one). He arranged several long stays at the *Maison des sciences de l'homme* and made time for me—once at the *Gare de Lyon* when he was rushing off for the Cannes Film Festival. He died at 71, too young for one who had more to give, including the likelihood that he would have used the years to respond to the criticisms of his ideas that had come to be by 2002.
53 *Anthropology as Cultural Critique*, 94.
54 Ibid, 48.
55 Ibid, 50. In spite of the initial qualified characterization of Geertz he is, far and away, the most frequently cited author. In the book's Index—20 mentions to 10 for Sahlins and 3 for Bourdieu. Only "Marxism" and "Science" equal "Geertz"—an interesting fact in itself.
56 Ibid, 54.

chapter alone shines bright on Marcus and Fischer who, here, and elsewhere in the book are taking stock not just of cultural ethnography but of culture as such.

Anthropology as Cultural Critique is not, to be sure, an attempt to redefine culture or, even, culture studies. If one realizes that its purpose is modest—to summarize the present and past of cultural ethnographies. Yet, in another sense, it does just this with an élan and brilliance not often encountered in academic texts, among which it stands on its own.

Jeffrey Alexander: Cultural Sociology

Jeffrey Alexander does something similar to what Marcus and Fischer have done. But he does it over time and for a quite different purpose. Over many years, Alexander has devoted his intellectual energies to the founding and developing of cultural sociology by which he means something quite well defined.

Alexander took his BA at Harvard in 1969 and his PhD at the University of California at Berkeley in 1978. At Berkeley he studied with Neil Smelser and Robert Bellah, both associates of Talcott Parsons. Alexander's first major book grew out of his doctoral thesis. Upon publication many thought it had all the appearance of being a remake of Parsons's major first work, *The Structure of Social Action*. Alexander's big book is *Theoretical Logic in Sociology*. One review was titled "Parsons Junior"[57]—harsh, to say the least. Yet even the book's title makes it clear that, granting the influence of Parsons, Alexander was addressing a different subject. His books were about theoretical logic, a subject related of course to Parsons's analytic realism. Yet Alexander, at the beginning of his career, takes Parsons's analytic realism as a template for reopening the door of theoretical logic nearly a half-century after *The Structure of Social Action* in 1937. In 1983 Parsons had declined as the major figure of American social thought as the field grew massively (if not always deeply) through the consumption by American sociologists of new European sources— sources as far afield as Alfred Schutz's phenomenological logic that set the frame for Peter Berger's and Thomas Luckman's *Social Construction of Reality* (1969) to Juergen Habermas's early exploration of communicative competence in *Legitimation Crisis* (1973). At the same time, Michel Foucault, Claude Lévi-Strauss, and proto-third wave feminisms were breaking down still other doors. For Alexander to have written as he did so much in the Parsonsian line was daring and, in its way, breathtakingly brilliant. Then too, looking back in time at Alexander's theoretical career he was far from trapped in the cage of his first important book.

As early as 1987 he called for a strong program of cultural theory in which he parted ways definitively from Parsons—and to a degree from both Bellah and Geertz.[58] By 1989 his strong program was announced, in French, as "Cultural Sociology or Sociology of Culture: Towards a Strong Program for Sociology's Second Wind," then later in English in 1996, most prominently in the American Sociological Association's *Culture Section Newsletter* as "Cultural Sociology or Sociology of Culture: Toward a Strong Program." Here especially he made clear that the strong program means all sociological research must take account of the cultural dimension of all sectors of society:

---

57 The review was written by Alan Sica. Alexander was, understandably, annoyed by it. Alan and Jeff are friends of mine. In time I came to see the moniker as clever but not to the point of Jeff's book.

58 Alexander, *Twenty Lectures: Sociological Theory Since World War II* (Columbia University Press, 1987); on Parsons see lectures 2 through 6 and 7 ("The Revolt Against the Parsonian [sic] Synthesis") and on Bellah and Geertz, 17 ("Cultural Sociology (2): Clifford Geertz's Rebellion Against Determinism"), especially 306–310.

Every action, no matter how instrumental and reflexive vis-à-vis its external environments, is embedded in a horizon of meaning. ... Every institution no matter how technical, coercive, or seemingly impersonal can only be effective if related to a patterned set of symbols. ... For this reason, every subfield of sociology must have a cultural dimension.[59]

Important to add that this relatively short proclamation of the strong program idea appeared later, several times. First, and professionally significant, in *The Handbook of Sociological Theory* in 2001; then again in *The Meanings of Social Life: A Cultural Sociology* (2004), in chapter 1 as "The Strong Program in Cultural Sociology."[60] The latter is noteworthy because in some obvious ways it was a collection of previously published essays representing Alexander's step toward his major 2006 book, *The Civil Sphere*. In addition to another version on "The Strong Program in Cultural Sociology," *The Meanings of Social Life* includes "The Discourse of American Civil Society: A New Proposal for Cultural Studies" (both with Philip Smith).

The Civil Sphere is important because it represents another American turn in the interpretation of culture—one that takes America itself as the focus. *The Civil Sphere* appeared a good quarter century after Gouldner's Culture of Critical Discourse proposal, yet, it sought, differently, to establish an explicit link between American political society and its culture. Where Gouldner meant to reframe cultures in terms that were a post-Marxist critical theory of discourse with traces of sociology, and Marcus and Fischer ranged far and wide beyond their discipline to expose an emerging anthropological critique of culture, Alexander sought to reframe sociological thinking as a cultural sociology of American political society. Though Alexander is an acknowledged international figure in the field, in *The Civil Sphere* he returned to the tune if not the refrain that American society as such could be a model for a general theory of culture. To be sure, he parted ways with both Parsons and Bellah. Just the same, Alexander's strong program is set in the liminal noise of their views of culture.

The Civil Sphere begins with a litany of the sources that influenced Alexander's thinking since 1979, notably: "Gramsci's cultural Marxism, Durkheim's civic morals, Weber's fraternization, and Parsons's societal community."[61] Yet, in the same place, he suggests just how long the civil sphere has been on his mind—going back at least to 1991 when he published an early draft of what turns out to be chapter 3 in *The Civil Sphere* as "Bringing Democracy Back In: Reality, Morality, Solidarity."[62] Democracy is the fugue line in *The Civil Sphere*—a contrapuntal topic set against the harmonic line, culture. Thus, he writes,

> We need a new concept of civil society as a civil *sphere*, a world of values and institutions that generates the capacity for social criticism and democratic integration at the same time. Such a sphere relies on solidarity, on feelings for others we do not know but whom we respect out of principle, not experience, because of our putative commitment to a common secular faith.[63]

---

59 *ASA Culture Section Newsletter* 10:3–4 (1996), 1 and 3.
60 Jeffrey Alexander with Philip Smith, "The Strong Program in Cultural Sociology: Elements of a Structural Hermeneutics" in Alexander, *The Meanings of Social Life: A Cultural Sociology* (Oxford University Press, 2003), chapter 1. Important to say: Each of these versions is not the exact same paper; but they are all clear statements of Alexander's strong program of cultural sociology—which, in many ways, was his main contribution to the study of culture.
61 Alexander, *The Civil Sphere* (Oxford University Press, 2006), ix–xii.
62 Alexander, "Bringing Democracy Back In: Universalistic Solidarity and the Civil Sphere," in Charles Lemert, ed., *Intellectuals and Politics: Social Theory in a Changing World* (Sage Publications, 1991), chapter 9.
63 *The Civil Sphere*, 4.

Here Alexander lends texture to his strong program for cultural sociology by taking with utter seriousness the complex nature of the civil sphere as fluid to the point of being "contradictory and fragmented." Then:

> The ideas of civil society are never completely negated. They hold before us alternative possibilities, and from these general principles there emerge counterproposals for reform. It is the idea of civil society that allows divisions to be reconstructed. That solidarity can be broadened is the project of civil repair.[64]

But where is culture in this? The answer is found in his basic idea of cultural sociology (quoted earlier) "[that] every institution no matter how technical, coercive, or seemingly impersonal can only be effective if related to a patterned set of symbols." In this sense, cultures are ubiquitous. The embracing idea is that the cultural element in the civil sphere is both embedded in the divisions in a society and able to repair them.

One of the better features of *The Civil Sphere* is that it does not replay Alexander's long journey toward defining and institutionalizing his strong program in cultural sociology. Just the same, the book itself is a deployment of aspects of his program in cultural sociology in his theory of the civil sphere and democracy. "Any discussion of the civil sphere is inextricably intertwined with an analysis of democracy as a political form."[65] Thus begins the book's key chapter 3, "Bringing Democracy Back In: Realism, Morality, Solidarity." Here Alexander advances one of his more ingenious theoretical moves. He sharpens traditional dichotomies in order to make analysis true to the state of social life, then dulls their effect so that his theoretical conclusions are honestly realistic. This chapter, thereby, identifies the inherent "fallacies of twentieth century evolutions" (as he puts it[66]) in order to dismiss utopianism as a failed ideal for civil politics. Then, he turns to realism where he calls to mind Plato's reference to Thrasymachus (as a foil to Socrates' idealism)—this to contend with the modern error of stipulating an evil-other in order to emphasize the good, but utopian, standard for politics—for which he mentions Marx's attack on democracy as a sham in a stern materialist political economy.[67] All too briefly put, this is a taste of Alexander's realism, after which (as the chapter's title suggests), he turns to morality and solidarity which are carefully discussed as shared provisions of a healthy civil society. Here he deploys Tocqueville's (and Bellah's) "habits of the heart" to insist that such a society requires a culture "that pays attention to shared feelings and symbolic communications, to what and how people speak, think, and feel about politics and, more generally, about democratic politics."[68] Hence, his realist notion of the deep structural link of morality and solidarity. But, just after, he qualifies: "I wish to understand civil society as the arena not of solidarity defined in a communitarian and particularistic way but in universalistic terms." He continues, "…the we-ness of a national, regional, or international community, the feeling of connectedness to 'every-member' of that community." Then later on: "If we wish to develop an approach to democratic social life that acknowledges the role of solidarity and moral ideals, we must start from a more realistic conception of the difficulties and challenges faced by complex societies."[69]

---

64 *Ibid*, 7.
65 *Ibid*, 37.
66 *Ibid*, 38.
67 *Ibid*, 41; but see footnotes 28 and 29 to chapter 3; *ibid*, 562.
68 *Ibid*, 43.
69 *Ibid*, 46.

Then, and importantly for his cultural sociology, Alexander ends this densely packed chapter with a short concluding section on "Cultural Codes and Democratic Communications" which, in turn, ends with a lucid statement as to what is to follow in the remaining seven hundred-plus pages of *The Civil Sphere*: "The paradox in the very construction of the language of civil society is intensified by the contradictions that inevitably accompany organizational efforts to institutionalize it. There remains the possibility of justice, but it is devilishly difficult to obtain."[70]

Since the topic at hand is theories of cultures, it would be a stretch to try to engage the details in the rest of a very long book. Just the same Alexander's cultural sociology may be well-enough introduced by a précis of the remainder. After its first introductory part, *The Civil Sphere* comprises three parts. Their titles might suggest each is pure theory, thereby a contradiction of Alexander's premise about civil society. As it happens, only Part II. *Structures and Dynamics of the Civil Sphere* would seem to justify this expectation. Yet, each of the five chapters in the very long Part II, is meant to dig down into structural specifics and dynamics of the civil sphere. Chapter 4, for example, "Discourses: Liberty and Repression," starts with an abstract analytic presentation of the binary structures of motives, relationships, institutions, but then continues with a more concrete discussion of the tensions between good and evil civil narratives that are illustrated, rather sparsely, with historical examples alluded to in the text, but made concrete by notes (of which, some 25% of the book). In the case at hand the incongruity between the high and good civil values of the American revolutionary era are set against the nation's normal national capacity for evil illustrated charmingly by "Uncle Remus and the Malevolent Rabbit" and Richard Slotkin's *Regeneration through Violence* (1973).[71]

After this chapter on discourses, Alexander turns to the more grounded chapters of Part II where the dynamics of the empirical structures are nicely and plainly discussed: chapters (5), "Communicative Institutions: Public Opinion, Mass Media, Polls, Associations"; and (6) "Regulative Institutions 1: Voting, Parties, Office" and (7) "Regulatory Institutions 2: The Civil Force of Law." Each with nuggets like the difference between fictional media and allegedly factual media (like news). Part II ends with Chapter 8, "Uncivilizing Pressures and Civil Repair," that includes two sections. "Space: The Geography of Civil Society" that sets forth the differences of territorial spaces as a source of evil (so to speak), which is parsimoniously brilliant. Then just after: "Time: Civil Society as Historical Sedimentation," which is an instance where the dialectic method all-too-optimistically requires that time and history allow for civil repair.

Then, as Alexander drills down to the concrete, Part III turns to social movements—with generous attention to the two most important. Chapter 10, "Gender and Civil Repair: The Long and Winding Road through M/otherhood"; and chapters 11–14 on "Race and Civil Repair" – where "Black Civil Society" (11), the "Civil Rights Movement and Communicative Solidary" (12), "Civil Trauma" (13), and "Regulatory Reform and Ritualization" (14) are discussed at great length. At first glance a reader might say something is wrong here. Why one chapter on Gender, and four on Race? The not entirely satisfying answer must be that

---

70 *Ibid*, 50. It may be worth adding that *The Civil Sphere* is one of the few books (of nearly 800 pages) that is worth reading through. I don't agree with all Jeff does in the book, but none of it is without interest. When it came out, I was on a panel at a New Haven book store with several of Yale's prestigious scholars none of whom tackled the book's main theme. I thought I might have (one member of the audience, himself a major figure, seemed to say I had); but, if I did, it was more or less by chance because in the day in 2006 it was easy enough to have an opinion but hard to master the whole thing. I hope that here I've done the book credit (if not full credit, due to my several criticisms) in this discussion, the better part of twenty years later.

71 *Ibid*, 63; also note 23 on 577.

Part III is about social movements. Some will find this overdone. But in fairness when Alexander was writing this book (from, in effect, 1991 to 2006) the American Civil Rights Movement was still the model for the leading school of social movement theory—resource mobilization theory. By comparison, Part IV is about *Modes of Incorporation into the Civil Sphere* and includes two long chapters (18 and 19) about the Jewish Question, which in places is very, very interesting; for examples "Making the Good Jew 'Bad': Philip Roth's Confidence" and "The Universality of Jewish Difference: Woody Allen as Cultural Icon." The former is an intriguing short essay that, for the most part attends to the early and middle fictions to suggest that Roth's fiction serves to out the "Bad Jew"—a challenging proposition but one wonders what Alexander might have said about *The Human Stain* (2006) where Coleman Silk buries himself in the closet such that when he is outed he loses everything and everyone. Alexander lists all of Roth's novels prior to this one which seem to be right down his cultural alley. Here, as in other of the many latter chapters, time has moved beyond gender studies, social movements, race and ethical theories as they were in 2006. Of course, civil repair remains now, as then, a vital question for Americans after when it has become hard to know just how the fractures haunting American culture and politics in the 2020s can be repaired. Still, when an author slips into troubled empirical waters, the fair reader can always reach up for the long and sturdy bridge of the book as a whole. Then too, no one can be blamed for not knowing what would come to pass so relatively soon after the early years of a new century.

No one—not even Homer (if he was one)—writes a great book without going too far from home. Theories of cultures are, in themselves, many, by definition. In their manifold incarnations they come upon against insurmountable differences—troubled waters for which there is no bridge. From Bellah and Geertz to Gouldner, Marcus and Fischer, and Alexander their incompatible ideas of the theory of cultures, becomes another bridge that leads from cultures as order to cultures as disorder.

14 On Excluded Cultures

W.E.B. Du Bois, Zora Neale Hurston, Paula Gunn Allen, James Baldwin, Medgar Evers, Martin Luther King, Jr., Malcolm X

One ever feels his twoness,
—an American, a Negro; two souls, two thoughts, two unreconciled strivings;
two warring ideals in one dark body,
whose dogged strength alone keeps it from being torn asunder.
—W.E.B. Du Bois, *Souls of Black Folk*, 1903

"They musta come from Zar, and dat's on de other side of far." "Uh, hunh!" Gold gloated. "Ah knowed you didn't know whut you was talkin' about. Now Ah'm goin' ter tell you how come we so black:
Long before they got thru makin' de Atlantic Ocean and haulin' de rocks for de mountains, God was makin' up de people. But He didn't finish 'em all at one time. Ah'm compelled to say dat some folks is walkin' 'round dis town right now ain't finished yet and never will be. Well, He give out eyes one day. All de nations come up and got they eyes. Then He give out teeth and so on. Then He set a day to give out color. So seven o'clock dat mornin' everybody was due to git they color except de niggers. So God give everybody they color and they went on off. Then He set there for three hours and one-half and no niggers. It was gettin' hot and God wanted to git His work done and go set in de cool. ...
So God hollered "Get back! Get back!"
And they misunderstood Him and thought he said, "Git black,"
and they been black ever since.
—Zora Neale Hurston, "Why Negroes Are Black,"
Mules and Men, 1935

In the beginning was thought, and her name was Woman. The Mother, the Grandmother, recognized from earliest times into the present among those peoples of the Americas who kept to the eldest traditions, is celebrated in social structures, architecture, law, custom, and the oral tradition. To her we owe our lives, and from her comes our ability to endure, regardless of the concerted assaults on our, on Her, being, for the past five hundred years of colonization. She is the Old Woman who tends the first of life.
She is the Old Woman Spider, who weaves us together in a fabric of interconnection.
She is the Eldest God, the one who Remembers and Re-members;
and through the history of the past five hundred years has
taught us bitterness and helpless rage, we endure into the present, alive, certain of our significance, certain of her centrality, her identity as the Sacred Hoop of Be-ing.
—Paula Gunn Allen, *The Sacred Hoop: Recovering the Feminine in American Indian Traditions*, 1986

Medgar Evers annoyed confetti and assorted / brands of businessmen's eyes.
The shows came down: to maxims and surprise. / And palsy.
Roaring no rapt arise-ye to the dead, he
leaned against tomorrow. People said that
he was holding clean globes in his hands.
—Gwendolyn Brooks, Medgar Evers, 1968

All of our people have the same goals, the same objective.
That objective is freedom. justice, equality. All of us want recognition
and respect as human beings.
We don't want to be integrationists. Nor do we want to be separationists. We want to be human beings.
—Malcolm X, The Black Revolution, 1964

Black Power is a cry of disappointment.
The Black Power slogan did not spring from the head of some philosophical Zeus.
It is born from the wounds of despair and disappointment.
It is a cry of daily hurt of persistent pain.
—Martin Luther King, Jr. Where Do We Go from Here?
Chaos or Community? 1967

Three men—Medgar, Malcolm, and Martin—were very different men.
I want these three to bang against each other and reveal each other, as in truth they did ...
and use their dreadful journey as a means of instructing those the people they loved so much,
who betrayed them and for whom they gave their lives.
—James Baldwin, Remember This House, 1979 [in I'm Not Your Negro, 2017]

Thinking Exclusions

With the exception of Frederick Douglass, no Black American was more justly famous for his thinking than W.E.B. Du Bois whose *Souls of Black Folk* is now known by the sensible as a call to marching if not to arms.

> One ever feels his twoness,—an American, a Negro; two souls, two thoughts, two unreconciled strivings; two warring ideals in one dark body, whose dogged strength alone keeps it from being torn asunder.[1]

One of Du Bois's many accomplishments, cultural and political, was that he played a major leadership role in the Harlem Renaissance in the 1920s.

Zora Neale Hurston was one of many Black creative writers who was part of the Renaissance. What made her unusual in their company is that she studied anthropology with Franz Boas. These studies equipped her to return to the South to collect Negro folk tales which were eventually published in her books—notably *Mules and Men*, in which the selection from the tale of "Why Negroes Are Black" appears:

> "They musta come from Zar, and dat's on de other side of far."

---

1 W.E.B. Du Bois, "Of Our Spiritual Strivings," in *Souls of Black Folk*, introduced by Henry Louis Gates (Bantam, 1989 [1902]), 3.

"Uh, hunh!" Gold gloated. "Ah knowed you didn't know whut you was talkin' about. How come we so black:

Long before they got thru makin' de Atlantic Ocean and haulin' de rocks for de mountains, God was makin' up de people. But He didn't finish 'em all at one time. Ah'm compelled to say dat some folks is walkin' 'round dis town right now ain't finished yet and never will be. Well, He give out eyes one day. All de nations come up and got they eyes. Then He give out teeth and so on. Then He set a day to give out color. So seven o'clock dat mornin' everybody was due to git they color except de niggers. So God give everybody they color and they went on off. Then He set there for three hours and one-half and no niggers.

It was gettin' hot and God wanted to git His work done and go set in de cool. ...
So God hollered "Get back! Get back!"
And they misunderstood Him and thought he said,
"Git black," and they been black ever since.[2]

Paula Gunn Allen, a Native American woman who identified with her mother's tribal people, the Laguna Pueblo, did much the same with people of her first nation culture that Hurston did with the tales of her people. For example:

In the beginning was thought, and her name was Woman. The Mother, the Grandmother, recognized from earliest times into the present among those peoples of the Americas who kept to the eldest traditions, is celebrated in social structures, architecture, law, custom, and the oral tradition. To her we owe our lives, and from her comes our ability to endure, regardless of the concerted assaults on our, on Her, being, for the past five hundred years of colonization.

She is the Old Woman who tends the first of life.
She is the Old Woman Spider, who weaves us together in a fabric of interconnection.
She is the Eldest God, the one who Remembers and Re-members;
 and through the history of the past five hundred years has taught us bitterness and helpless rage, we endure into the present, alive, certain of our significance, certain of her centrality, her identity as the Sacred Hoop of Be-ing.[3]

It need not be said that many others beside those of whom Hurston and Allen told their stories. But among those others excluded who found their voices, in America there was no moment more potent with a blast of insistences than those of the many who discerned their public calling in the mid-1960s—feminists, queer people, and of course Blacks. It is hard to pick one group to represent the others, but James Baldwin makes a case for the three everyone knows:

Three men—Medgar, Malcolm, and Martin—were very different men.

---

2 Zora Neale Hurston, "Why Negroes Are Black," *Mules and Men* in *Hurston: Folklore, Memories, & Other Writings* (Library of America, 1993 [1935]), 38–39.
3 Paula Gunn Allen, *The Sacred Hoop: Recovering the Feminine in American Indian Traditions* (Beacon Press, 1992 [1996]), 11.

I want these three to bang against each other and reveal each other, as in truth they did … and use their dreadful journey as a means of instructing those the people they loved so much, who betrayed them and for whom they gave their lives.[4]

Medgar Evers worked on the ground as a civil rights activist, for which he was assassinated. Gwendolyn Brooks, the poet, sung his praises in 1968:

Medgar Evers annoyed confetti and assorted / brands of businessmen's eyes.
   The shows came down: to maxims and surprise. / And palsy.
       Roaring no rapt arise-ye to the dead, he
       leaned against tomorrow. People said that
       he was holding clean globes in his hands.[5]

In a "The Black Revolution," a speech in New York City on April 8, 1964 Malcom X pronounced the words that on that day shook liberals and others. He said:

All of our people have the same goals, the same objective. That objective is freedom. justice, equality. All of us want recognition and respect as human beings. We don't want to be integrationists. Nor do we want to be separationists. We want to be human beings.[6]

Martin Luther King, Jr., ever the soul of Black life in America as many thought of him, wrote in a different tone but not one hostile to Malcolm's purposes:

Black Power is a cry of disappointment. The Black Power slogan did not spring from the head of some philosophical Zeus. It is born from the wounds of despair and disappointment. It is a cry of daily hurt of persistent pain.[7]

The world as it has been was built on the backs and deprivations of excluded peoples the world over from time immemorial. America, remarkably, was not late to the realization of that tragedy. Those discussed here are important examples of what so many have done to try to change this fact of global life—a fact that persists down into our time.

Color All the Way Back

In 1638, when English Puritans led by the Reverend John Davenport and Theophilus Eaton settled the New Haven Colony, the land all about had long been home to the Quinnipiack people, a nation in the Algonquin family of North American aboriginal people. The English soon entered into a treaty with the Quinnipiack on the promise to protect them from rival indigenous people (including the Pequot) in exchange for possession of their tribal lands. The protection quickly turned into reservations to the East of the Harbor. By the 1760s, the Quinnipiack had migrated north to Massachusetts. Shortly after, the last known of their people had passed on, leaving only archaeological traces going back some 8,000 years. It

---

4 James Baldwin, "Remember This House," in James Baldwin and Raoul *Peck, I'm Not Your Negro* (Vintage Books 2017 [1979]), 6.
5 "Medgar Evers," by Gwendolyn Brooks, *Poetry Explorer / Your Free Poetry Website* @ https://www.poetryexplorer.net/poem.php?id=10023771
6 *Malcolm X Speaks* (Merit Publishers and Betty Shabazz, 1965 [1964]), 51.
7 Martin Luther King, Jr., "Black Power," in *Where Do We Go From Here / Chaos or Community* (Beacon Press, 1968 [1967]), 33.

is fair to say that the first New Haveners were these long-gone indigenous people. They are remembered today by a river, a college, a medical practice, and businesses named after them.

In 1844, when America was heading toward Civil War, Black[8] members of Trinity Episcopal Church left to establish their own church, St. Luke's Episcopal Church. Today that church makes it clear that their founding ancestors left Trinity because, as they say on their website, "these 'colored members' believed themselves to be victims of racial discrimination." St Luke's today is a thriving, if smallish, congregation of people mostly of Afro-Caribbean descent. Among its members in the nineteenth century was Alexander Du Bois, grandfather to W.E.B. Du Bois. St. Luke's is one of the oldest Black Episcopal churches in the nation. One of its early rectors was the Reverend James Theodore Holly (1829–1911), the first African American Bishop in the American Episcopal Church who became a missionary who led over a hundred Black Christians to a new life in Haiti. Today, St. Luke's and Trinity are engaged in a number of joint ventures and shared services. Trinity itself now has a good many Black members. St. Luke's is on Whalley Avenue not far from the town's oldest African American Church, Varick African Methodist Episcopal Church, on Dixwell Avenue which was established in 1818. Not far off is the Bethel Methodist Episcopal Church on Goffe Street. William Goffe, John Dixwell, Edward Whalley were the three judges who, in the 1660s, had fled the British seeking them for the crime of regicide.

The three predominantly Black churches are located near the apex of the three avenues named after the judges. Goffe, Dixwell, and Whalley avenues converge close to the town center at the Broadway business district to the northwest of Yale University. Today most in the New Haven's larger Black churches are to be found clustered in that apex or not far outside it. This is the neighborhood known for the Freddie Fix-It Parade. It is mostly Black and mostly lower income, with more drug dealing and violent crime than the vast majority of residents in the area want. The City Jail is located in this troubled area. Most of the town's Black population lives here or in The Hill which is, if anything, more severely cut off from the predominantly white neighborhoods located in the shadows of East and West Rocks. Today, nonwhite people are major players in New Haven's government and its prominent social service agencies. The town's public schools and businesses are somewhat integrated, even if two of its major High Schools located close by the Goffe/Dixwell/Whalley triangle mostly serve students of color. New Haven is demographically segregated. The vast majority of its people of color are, at the least, unable to afford the cost of homes in the well-off white neighborhoods. *The more things change, the more they remain the same.*

From 2010 to 2020, the greatest demographic change in this town was the surge in the Latinx population to 31%. Latinx[9] people edged out the number of Blacks living in New Haven, in part because they brought and cared for significantly more children into the world, 43%–34%.[10] In a striking case of statistical exclusion, sources that

---

8 I capitalize Black when it is used to designate the racial group out of respect for W.E.B. Du Bois's long and successful battle with New York media to get Negro capitalized. He considered negro with lower case n a gratuitous insult. Curiously, *The New York Times* recently reminded readers that its use of Black with B goes back to Du Bois's insistence on Negro many years before. See Nancy Coleman, "Why We're Capitalizing Black," *The New York Times* (July 5. 2020) @ https://www.nytimes.com/2020/07/05/insider/capitalized-black.html

9 To many, *Latinx* may seem odd, at least, or all-too-woke, at worst. In truth there is an issue here in that *Latino* is a masculine plural that, in a once robustly masculinist ethnic group like others, it would be right to replace *Latino* with a more generic plural, like *Latinx*. I hope and believe that a better plural will one day be found. For now, in a world where *LGBTQ+* is commonly used, *Latinx* is reasonable.

10 Kelley Davila and Mark Abraham, "New Haven Neighborhood Changes 2010 to 2020," *Data Haven/2020 Demographic Changes in Connecticut Town and City Neighborhoods* (on line @ https://www.ctdatahaven.org/reports/2020-census-data-demographic-change-connecticut-town-and-city-neighborhoods/new-haven-neighborhood-changes-2010-2020)

meant to advertise New Haven as a good place to buy homes underestimated the Latinx population and exaggerated the white percentage by lumping white Latinx people with generic whites. Skin color wins! In spite of this, anyone who walks the streets of New Haven realizes that the town is populated, and visited, by people of color. In 2020 only 28% of the town's citizens were white. Latinx people—who are largely Puerto Rican and others from island nations—tend to settle where people of their original culture live. They live in a burgeoning neighborhood to the East, Fair Haven and its adjacent neighborhoods. Fair Haven is a bustling business community, with many restaurants and other businesses catering to Latinx wants and needs. The Latinx population is also growing in Newhallville—a developing neighborhood just off the Goffe/Dixwell/Whalley apex that once was all but entirely Black.

The institutional heart of the town is Yale University. Though Yale does its best to admit students of color and to colorize its staff and faculty it ranks with Harvard and Princeton as one of the most prestigious *white* universities in the land. Students of whichever color admitted are superior scholars and destined for big things. Then too, as a prevailing symbol of the town, Yale bears the burden of its own history and of New Haven's for having created itself amid a long history of exclusions—of the Quinnipiack, of its African American and Afro-Caribbean people, of its Puerto Rican and other Latinx immigrants, of its homeless, of its poor who cannot afford the rent of the many rising apartments in the downtown area much less the housing in the mostly white East Rock and Westville neighborhoods.[11] Yale has tried to scrub from its buildings the names of slave holders. Still, Yale suffers the burdens of being "great" which in America is still, this late in the day, taken by the elite of the elite to be rhetorically the same as "white."[12]

New Haven may be more famous than many towns of its size, but, in respect to its structural exclusions, it is like most, if not all, cities and towns in America. If the exclusion of commonly targeted people is to be more than a general, even abstract, moral principle, those who care must realize that exclusions always take place on the ground where people come together over the centuries. In this sense, America is like all settlements the world over. If we are to have an honest theory of cultures, we must pay disciplined attention to cultures wrought of exclusions—cultures that ever and always rub against all other cultures with whom they share a common space.

---

11 It must be said that Yale is responsible for some but not all of these exclusions. Still, try as it might, it is institutionally possible for Yale to bend more toward the poor and people of color who beg outside Phelps Gate, or clean its halls and classrooms.

12 This statement requires some justification. I grew up in the 1940s in Cincinnati, Ohio, where the only Black people most upper middle-class whites knew worked in their homes—as did Florence Lyons who, over the years, I came to realize was, in effect, my adoptive mother. On his death bed my very white father said to Florence, among his last words: "Thank you for taking care of our boys. We just couldn't do it." Otherwise few of those we knew as kids in the day, saw little of Blacks—not on early television, not even on the field where the Cincinnati Reds played. Jackie Robinson didn't break into the major leagues until 1947 in Brooklyn, which to Reds fans in the day was the other side of the moon. We who are from places and times like there and then, are regularly astonished at the racial world in which we have grown old. Still, most of us subliminally handed down the whiteness of our youth, many of us struggled to overcome it. I for one am hurt but not surprised when our still young Black daughter, Anna Julia, is injured by racist gestures by people who think white.

W.E.B. Du Bois: Those Excluded in Spite of the Power of Their Double-Consciousness

W.E.B. Du Bois (1868–1963) was born in Great Barrington, Massachusetts—then, and still, a town with few black households.[13] So white was Great Barrington in Du Bois's day that, it seems, few whites were troubled by their Negro neighbors. In early childhood Du Bois had little sense that his skin color was at issue until, well along in primary school, a snotty white girl startled him by rejecting his party card. This likely was his first conscious experience of the color line. Du Bois was an excellent student at Great Barrington High School, after which he meant to attend Harvard College. For whatever reason, Harvard, being what it is, rejected the young Du Bois. His racial difference was a factor.[14] Du Bois redeemed the College's initial rejection when, years later, Harvard admitted him in 1888 after he studied at Fisk University. He graduated from Harvard College *cum laude* in 1890 with a major in philosophy, after which he began doctoral studies both at the University of Berlin and Harvard. Du Bois completed the PhD at Harvard in 1896 with a thesis on *The Suppression of the African Slave Trade to the United States of America, 1638–1870*.

His time at historically Black Fisk University allowed Du Bois to live, for the first time, in a robustly all-Negro community. Even more significant to this experience were the two summers of 1886 and 1887 when he left Fisk and Nashville to serve as a schoolteacher in Alexandria—a poor, rural community of Black folk in the hills of Eastern Tennessee. There he truly lived among the poorest of marginalized Negroes, an experience that shaped one of the most original, if seldom read, chapters in *The Souls of Black Folk* (1903), "On the Meaning of Progress." The more famous chapter in *Souls* is the first, "Of Our Spiritual Strivings," which contains Du Bois's memorable and oft-quoted lines on the double-consciousness of the American Negro: "One ever feels his twoness,—an American, a Negro; two souls, two thoughts, two unreconciled strivings; two warring ideals in one black body, whose dogged strength alone keeps it from being torn asunder."[15] As poetically and theoretically elegant as Du Bois's twoness maxim is, "On the Meaning of Progress" speaks more directly to the intersectionality between race and class, even gender and perhaps sexuality. It was, in a sense, the meat on the bones of his theory of double consciousness—a consciousness that Du Bois called attention to later by, among much else, pressuring the white publishing world to capitalize the N in Negro. In his consciousness, the American Negro was a joining of two *culturally equal* social forces.

During his two summers in the hills of Tennessee, Du Bois grew especially close to the family of a young woman, Josie, who serves as his literary icon for the oppression of economically impoverished, rural Negroes in the South one generation after the end of the Civil War. "On the Meaning of Progress" is, without question, a defiant criticism of the white world's ideology of progress—hence, by implication, of Capitalism's commitment to endless economic growth. It is not, however, an abstract critique. "On the Meaning of Progress" includes the tale of Du Bois's later visit to Josie's village, ten years after he had left Fisk. What he found was anything but progress. Josie had left the hills to work in Nashville, there to earn what she had hoped would contribute to the economic prospects of her family. But Alexandria was unchanged. In the end, Josie was dead. He left sad, perhaps depressed, not just for Josie but for all those cut off by the color line:

---

13 Much of the following on Du Bois is drawn from my contributions to Kristin Plys and Charles Lemert, *Capitalism and Its Uncertain Future* (Routledge, 2021), 134–144. And from chapters 6 and 8 on Du Bois in Charles Lemert, *Dark Thoughts: Race and the Eclipse of Society* (Routledge, 2002).
14 David Levering Lewis, *W.E.B. Du Bois, 1868–1919: Biography of a Race* (Henry Holt, 1994), 54.
15 W.E.B. Du Bois, *The Souls of Black Folk* (Bantam Books, 1903), 3.

My journey was done, and behind me lay hill and dale, and Life and Death. How shall man measure Progress there where the dark-faced Josie lies? How many heartfuls of sorrow shall balance a bushel of wheat? How hard a thing is life to the lowly, and yet how human and real! And all this life and love and stress and failure, —is it the twilight of nightfall or the flush of some faint-dawning day? Thus, sadly musing, I rode to Nashville in the Jim Crow car. [16]

Du Bois rode that car to a brilliant academic career but also to a long life marked as much by political action and cultural leadership as by scholarship.

After the Harvard PhD, Du Bois taught briefly at Wilberforce College in Ohio before spending a year engaged in fieldwork in Philadelphia studying the Negro community in the City's Seventh Ward. The research was supported half-heartedly by the University of Pennsylvania which declined to grant him so much as a title commensurate with his Harvard pedigree. The result of his insulting tenure at Penn was his first important book, *The Philadelphia Negro* (1899), which demonstrated that the urban Negro community was anything but a slum of socially undisciplined people. The University of Pennsylvania belatedly appointed Du Bois Professor of History Emeritus in 2012, a half-century after he died. In this, Penn was a day late and a dollar short.

When, in July 1900, Du Bois participated prominently in the first Pan-African Congress in London, he threw himself into a global sea of political action and literary work that consumed most of the remaining 63 years of his life. He died on African soil in 1963—after visits to Africa over many years, after having become a leader in the Pan-African movement, after giving meaning to the African roots of the American Negro, after having migrated to Accra, Ghana at the encouragement of Kwame Nkrumah. But in those 63 intervening years Du Bois did more than all but a few ever have—and he always defied expectations. For one, many then, and since, have been surprised by Du Bois's frankly socialist values and Pan-African politics that seemed at odds with his better known literary and political service to the American Negro.

Early in his public life, Du Bois had earned his status as a race-man (to use the expression then in vogue) on the wings of his sophisticated intellectual work. He was not quite an elitist, but he knew that his education allowed him to engage in racial politics in a unique way; hence, he emphasized the power of the educated as leaders of racial uplift. His program—*the talented tenth*—was shaped specifically by his differences with Booker T. Washington—since 1881, the President of Tuskegee Normal and Industrial Institute (later, of course, Tuskegee Institute). Washington's racial politics were based on the idea that hard manual labor in fields and factories were the only certain route to what racial uplift could be had. In still another chapter in *Souls*, "Of Booker T. Washington and Others," Du Bois presented an opening salvo against the Tuskegee ideal. Washington betrayed himself in his infamous 1895 Atlanta Compromise Speech, of which the irritating line was quite explicitly a compromise with the white South. "In all things that are purely social we can be as separate as fingers yet one as the hand in all things essential to mutual progress."[17] Du Bois's outspoken differences with Washington were surely determined by his first-hand knowledge of the hard-working Josies of the world who were powerless in the face of the harsh racialized economic inequalities.

---

16 *Ibid*, 52.
17 Booker T. Washington's Atlanta Exposition Speech, September 18, 1895 @ (among many other online places) https://history.iowa.gov/sites/default/files/history-education-pss-areconstruction-atlanta-transcription.pdf

Already, by the time of *Souls* in 1903, *The Philadelphia Negro* in 1899 had certified Du Bois's reputation as a social scientist of Negro life in America. But in 1910, his work changed when he was among the founders of the National Association for the Advancement of Colored People (NAACP). He immediately joined the organization's staff in New York City as Director of Publicity and Research, a role he used to establish *The Crisis*—the monthly magazine he edited for 25 years. The underlying crisis that stood behind *The Crisis* was of course the inherent dilemma of the American Negro—the crisis in the souls of Black folk who ever feel their twoness: "…two souls, two thoughts, two unreconciled strivings; two warring ideals in one black body… ." From 1911 to 1934, *The Crisis*, under Du Bois, served as the voice of the African Diaspora in America. At the height of its influence, the magazine had 100,000 subscribers and many more readers as copies of the magazine were passed around in local communities. Then, in 1934, Du Bois quit his position at the NAACP in a dispute with its leadership that for years had sought to remove him for fear that his aggressive racial politics would cost the organization financial support. Du Bois returned to Atlanta University to write what may well be his most important book.

Du Bois's *Black Reconstruction in America, 1860–1880* in 1935 is the first major work of structural social history in the United States, and arguably the first in North Atlantic historiography. It is also Du Bois at his Marxist best. It was not a literal application of Marx's ideas so much as an application of his structural ideas. For Du Bois, the fate of Reconstruction was determined by the structural actors he introduces in the book's first three chapters—the *planter class* (1) set against the differences between the *Black worker* (2) and the *white worker* (3). Then in the fourth chapter Du Bois makes the compelling point that the Civil War was a General Strike by the black worker—as he put it in his epigraph to the fourth chapter: "How the Civil War meant emancipation and how the Black worker won the war by a general strike which transferred his labor from the Confederate planter to the Northern invader, in whose army lines workers began to be organized into a new labor force."[18] This is Du Bois the poet summarizing a more than 700-page book of empirical historical sociology.

Black Reconstruction makes the general if ironic point that the promise of labor would remain even after 1877 when Reconstruction was dismantled, returning the Black worker to the conditions from which she had been emancipated. Jim Crow was slavery in all but name. Du Bois remarks: "We must remember the Black worker was the ultimate exploited; that he formed the mass of labor which had neither wish nor power to escape from the labor status, in order to directly exploit other laborers, or indirectly, by alliance to share in their exploitation."[19] He then goes on to say that, when Black workers tried to "join white capital," they were "driven back into the mass of racial prejudice before they had time to establish a foothold." Still, Du Bois holds to the idea of the promise of Black workers.

Here Du Bois strikes back at the then prevailing liberal theory that Reconstruction's failure was somehow due to the inability of the Black workers as freed men and women to pull their lives and communities together. Nothing could have been farther from the truth. If one takes Lincoln's *Emancipation Proclamation* on January 1, 1863 as the beginning of the idea of Reconstruction[20]—and the beginning of the Long Depression from 1873–1896

---

18 W.E.B. Du Bois, *Black Reconstruction in America: 1860–1880* (Harcourt Brace [Free Press] 1935[1992]), 55.
19 *Ibid*, 15. [Even here, I capitalize Black where Du Bois did not. This out of respect for his insistence on capitalizing Negro.]
20 Some argue, with good reason, that when the Union captured New Orleans in 1862, Reconstruction began then. This as opposed to 1867 when the official postwar policy began. It is fair enough, I think, to take the *Proclamation* in 1863 as the legal basis for what came in full after the Civil War.

as the beginning of its end, then the irony of Du Bois's theory of Black labor is evident. In the relatively short time of Reconstruction, freed men and women made enormous strides in education in schools supported by white, Northern philanthropists;—in savings and financial development with the help of the federally supported Freedmen's Saving and Trust Company;—in the development of mutual aid and religious societies;—in the beginning of political participation, and more. Yet all this was taken away, first and foremost, by the economic crisis that endured more than two decades that, secondarily, opened the way for white racists to close down federal support for Reconstruction in 1877. And yet, Jim Crow notwithstanding, Du Bois concludes the opening chapter on the Black worker remarkably with a hopeful and global statement:

> It was thus the Black worker, *as founding stone of a new economic system in the nineteenth century and for the modern world*, who brought civil war in America. He was itself the underlying cause, in spite of every effort to base strife upon union and national power. That dark and vast sea of human labor in China and India, the South Seas and all Africa; in the West Indies and Central America and in the United States—that great majority of mankind, on whose bent and broken backs rest today the founding stones of modern industry—shares a common destiny; it is despised and rejected by race and color; paid a wage below the level of decent living; driven, beaten, prisoned and enslaved in all but name; spawning the world's raw material and luxury—cotton, wool, coffee, tea, cocoa, palm oil, fibers, spices, rubber, silks, lumber, copper, gold, diamonds, leather. How shall we end the list and where?[21]

Then he concludes: "The emancipation of man is the emancipation of labor, and the emancipation of labor is the freeing of the basic majority of workers who are yellow, brown and black."[22] Without intellectual arm waving, here Du Bois is locating the American Negro not just among the African Diaspora but as part of a global movement of people of color whose time would not come for at least another century after 1877—if not then, or yet. In *Black Reconstruction* in 1935, Du Bois was clearly influenced by the economic crisis after 1929. He declared that Black workers were central to the evolution of modern industrial labor. To explain this seemingly preposterous idea, Du Bois argued that it was necessary to look backward from the economic crisis of the 1930s to that of the 1870s.[23]

This he knew of course in 1961 when he returned to his African roots—a move he had long considered:

> Africans awake, put on the beautiful robes of Pan African socialism.
> You have nothing to lose but your chains!
> You have a continent to regain!
> You have human freedom and human dignity to regain![24]

Du Bois is not always thought of as a leader of the global decolonizing movement against capitalism. Yet, relative to others, great as they were, he lived longer, wrote more, did more on more fronts, while devising a remarkable number of theoretical interventions. With all

---

21 *Ibid*, 15; emphasis added.
22 *Ibid*, 16.
23 Charles Lemert, "The Race of Time: Deconstruction, Du Bois, and Reconstruction, 1935–1873," in *The Race of Time: The Charles Lemert Reader* (Routledge/Paradigm, 2009), 130.
24 W.E.B. Du Bois, *The Autobiography of W.E.B. DuBois: A Soliloquy on Viewing My Life from the Last Decade of Its First Century* (International Publishers, 1968), 404.

this, there is so much that one tends not to see—that, of all the decolonizing leaders, none was honored more the world over. The Soviet Union gave him the Lenin Peace Prize. A talk in China before what he thought was a local audience was actually broadcast nationally. Africa welcomed and adopted him as a son.

Many know his double-consciousness lines by heart. Few remember that it was introduced by a forceful global assertion—one that puts the exclusion of the American Negro in dynamic tension with her identity:

> After the Egyptian and Indian, the Greek and Roman, the Teuton and Mongolian, the Negro is a sort of seventh son, born with a veil, and gifted with second sight in this American world, —a world which yields him no true self-consciousness,
>
> but only lets him see himself through the revelation of the other world. It is a peculiar sensation, this double consciousness, this sense of always looking at one's self through the eyes of others, of measuring one's soul by the tape of a world that looks on in amused contempt and pity. One ever feels his twoness, —an American, a Negro; two souls, two thoughts, two unreconciled strivings; two warring ideals in one dark body, whose dogged strength alone keeps it from being torn asunder.[25]

It would be difficult to imagine a more poetic account of the extent to which the American Negro's exclusion is simultaneously the source of the ability to see what the excluders cannot see—that this global Negro can "see himself through the revelation of the other world." This fact alone gives the American Negro a power that enslaving and segregating whites do not have. The power lies in the fact that Du Bois himself lived fully with the "dogged strength" that the American Negro's double consciousness requires *and* allows. Again: "One ever feels his twoness, —an American, a Negro; two souls, two thoughts, two unreconciled strivings; two warring ideals in one dark body, whose dogged strength alone keeps it from being torn asunder." Too often readers of this passage overlook the power of being a *global* seventh son. Those veiled are hidden from the Other, who in turn do not realize that those on whom they have imposed the veil look back without their noticing. Those on the occluded side of the color line are indeed "gifted with a second sight in this American world." This second sight is the power to know their oppressors better than the oppressors know themselves. The veiled are excluded, yes. But their exclusion segregates them for use and abuse that ironically lends to the oppressed the strange power that only the excluded possess to see what their oppressors cannot. "The color line trope, delicately applied to protect to sensibilities of the reader, saves the situation from the ruin of *mere* subjective experience. This is the method of the standpoint—not personal but social in its embrace, not local but global in its reach."[26] Or, better put by James Baldwin: "You never had to look at me, / I had to look at you. / I know more about you than you know about me. / Not everything that is faced can be changed; / but nothing can be changed until it is faced."[27]

---

25 W.E.B. Du Bois, "Of Our Spiritual Strivings," in *The Souls of Black Folk* (Vintage Books/The Library of America, 1990), 8–9.
26 Charles Lemert, "Cultural Politics in the Negro Soul," in Alford A. Young, Jr., Manning Marable, Elizabeth Higginbotham, Charles Lemert, and Jerry G. Watts, *The Souls of W.E.B. Du Bois* (Routledge/Paradigm, 2006), 90.
27 James Baldwin, *I Am Not Your Negro*, edited by Raoul Peck (Vintage Books/Random House, 2017), 103.

Zora Neale Hurston, *Their Eyes Were Watching God*

Zora Neale Hurston was born January 7, 1891 in Notasulga, Alabama. In 1894 her family moved to Eatonville, Florida, then one of a very few towns governed by Negroes. In contrast to Du Bois, and some others who wrote out of their exclusion, Hurston never quite left home.

Of course, in a strict biographical sense, she did leave Eatonville;—for Jacksonville after her mother died in 1904;—then to Memphis to live with her brother in 1914, shortly after to Baltimore where she served as a maid to the lead singer in a Gilbert & Sullivan production and worked as a waitress;—then, after 1919, to Howard University for college where in 1921 she met Alain Locke and other Harlem Renaissance figures including Du Bois;—then to New York after 1925 where she published short stories and scholarly articles and began studies at Barnard College;—then in 1926 when she began field work in Harlem encouraged by the anthropologist Franz Boas;—and in 1927 back in the South when Boas secured a fellowship for her to collect and study folklore;—then after 1928 when she continued folklore research while staying with her brother John in Jacksonville;—in 1930 when she continued her research in the Bahamas;—and back in New York City in 1934 where in 1935 she published *Mules and Men* and began doctoral studies at Columbia;—then in 1936 when a Guggenheim Fellowship supported research in Jamaica and Haiti;—then, in 1937, she was back in New York City where her fame and literary productivity flourished;—in 1939 when she returned to the South to teach at North Carolina College for Negroes then to lecture on Black theatre in Durham;—then in 1941 when she moved to Los Angeles to live with a friend and begin her memoir *Dust Tracks on a Road*;—and in 1942 she was back in the South for lectures and more work on folklore. She moved here and there until she suffered a stroke in 1959 in St Lucie, Florida where she died in 1960 in poverty to be buried in an unmarked grave not that far from Eatonville.[28]

Zora Neale Hurston traveled far and wide. But spiritually she never left Florida. She was in a sense, the most spiritual of thinkers—one, that is, who never ceased probing the inner depths of the culture and people who brought her into their world. "Like the dead-seeming, cold rocks. I have memories within that came out of the material that went to make me. Time and place have had their say."[29] It was in the rural Negro small towns, mostly in Florida, where time and again she heard the folk stories of her people—where "her people" is much more than a convenient commonplace. She began her first collection of folk tales with a spark of her spirituality. "I was glad when somebody told me, 'You may go and collect Negro folklore'." That somebody was Franz Boas. Just the same, she did need such an authority to tell her where to go for what. She continues:

> In a way it was not a new experience for me. When I pitched headforemost into the world, I landed in the crib of negroism. From the earliest rocking of my cradle, I had known about the capers Brer Rabbit is apt to cut and what the Squinch Owl says from the treetop. But it was fitting me like a tight chemise. I couldn't see it for wearing it. It was only when I was off to college, away from native surroundings, that I could see myself like somebody else and stand off and look at my garment. Then I had to have the spy glass of Anthropology to look through at that.[30]

---

28 In 1973 Alice Walker found her grave and marked it.
29 Zora Neale Hurston, "My Birthplace," *Dust Tracks on the Road* (Harper Perennial Classics 2006 [1942]), 1.
30 Zora Neale Hurston, "Introduction," *Mules and Men* (Penguin Books/Library of America, 1995 [1935]), 9.

From beginning to end, *Mules and Men* is a blend of folktales and memoir that more times than one might suppose rendered sweet theory, cut with bitters. First memoir, then folktale:

> When I was rounding Lily Lake, I was remembering how God had made the world and the elements and the people. He made souls for people, but he didn't give them out because he said:
> "Folks ain't ready for souls yet. De clay ain't dry. It's de strongest thing Ah ever made. Don't aim to waste none through loose cracks. And then men got to grow strong enough to stand it. De way things is now, if Ah give it out it would tear them shackly bodies to pieces. Bimeby, Ah gave it out."
> So folks went 'round thousands of years without no souls. All de time de so soul-piece it was setting 'round covered up wid God's loose raiment. Every now and then de wind would blow and hist up de cover and then the elements would be full of lighting and de winds would talk. So people told one 'nother that God was talking in de mountains. ... [31]

This tale is not theology. Folktales may draw on religious ideas, but they are practical theories about people's worlds.

Maya Angelou, in her foreword to *Dust Tracks on a Road* (Hurston's full-fledged memoir), says of these folktales: "There is an eerie, sometimes pathetic, oft-times beautiful urge that prevails in Black American lore, lyrics and literature. The impulse, simply put, is to tell the story . . . to tell one's own story . . . as one has known it, and lived it, and even died it."[32] There could hardly be a better way to portray pure practical social theory than by allusion to Black American lore. All the more so because Negro folklore comprises, with scant exception, trickster stories. Mostly famously, the Brer Rabbit tales. But here, in Hurston's tale of her return to Eatonville, she tells the story of "folks [going] 'round for with no souls for thousands of years" which has the effect of making God the trickster of whom "people told one 'nother that God was talking in de mountains." In *Trickster Makes This World*, Lewis Hyde writes:

> Trickster is a boundary crosser. Every group has its edge, its sense of in and out, and the trickster is always there, at the gates of the city and the gates of life, making sure there is no commerce. He also attends to the internal boundaries by which groups articulate their social life. We constantly distinguish—right and wrong, sacred and profane, clean and dirty, male and female, young and old, living and dead—and in every case trickster will cross the line and confuse the distinction. Trickster is the creative idiot, therefore, the wise fool, the gray-haired baby, the cross dresser, the speaker of sacred profanities. ... Trickster is the mythic embodiment of ambiguity and ambivalence, doubleness and duplicity, contradiction and paradox.[33]

Thus, when Hurston is headed back home to Eatonville, thinking of the joy of being told to collect Negro folklore, she was thinking of the doubleness and duplicity that marginalized, small town Southern Negroes must live with.

This, important to note, is the very state of mind that W.E.B. Du Bois wrote of in his line on the twoness of the American Negro—a concept born of his personal experience with Josie's excluded family in the impoverished mountain village in Tennessee. Yet, Du Bois

---

31 *Ibid*, 11.
32 Zora Neale Hurston, *Dust Tracks on a Road* (Harper Perennial Classics, 2006 [1942]), vii.
33 Lewis Hyde, *The Trickster Makes This World* (Farrar, Strauss, and Giroux, 1998), 7.

wrote at a remove from Josie's world. He was straddling the fate of Josie's morbid poverty against the nation's high-minded notion of progress—a twoness that Hurston understood ever more practically, even while stopping short of formulating a general theory of it. In a society as riven by race as the American one, anyone pressed to the margins—the Negro above all—can be a trickster or, at least, appreciate the trickster stories. Closer to our day, Muhammad Ali was, for a good while, the most famous personage on earth because he made himself the trickster figure that brought to the surface the deep irony of an allegedly liberal white world that in itself was duplicitous and double-minded.[34]

Perhaps the most astute discussion of the trickster in pan-African culture is Henry Louis Gates's brilliant *The Signifying Monkey: A Theory of African American Literary Theory* (1988). The trickster central to this book is the West African Yoruba figure Esu-Elegbara and its homologues in Negro America, of which one of the best known is the Tar Baby. Gates writes:

> Of the many colorful figures that appear in black vernacular tales, only the Tar Baby is as enigmatic and compelling as is that oxymoron, the Signifying Monkey. The ironic reversal of a racist image of the black as simianlike, the Signifying Monkey, he who dwells at the margins of discourse, ever pruning, ever troping, ever embodying the ambiguities of language, is our trope for repetition and revision, indeed our trope of chiasmus, repeating and reversing simultaneously as he does in one deft discursive act.[35]

More simply, and closer to Hurston's trickster, Toni Morrison, author of the novel *Tar Baby* (1981), has said: "Tar baby is a name ... that white people call black children, as I recall. For me, the tar baby came to mean the black woman who can hold things together."[36] This is a common theme in Morrison's fiction, as it was of Hurston's—as, also, it was true of Hurston herself as a kind of trickster in the very culture that formed her.

Gates, in Chapter 5 of *Signifying Monkey*—"Zora Neale Hurston and the Speakerly Text"—presents Hurston as a key figure in the history of Black literature from Paul Lawrence Dunbar's rhetorical strategy *Lyrics of Lowly Life* in 1895 down to the 1930s.[37] "Zora Neale Hurston is the first writer that our generation of black and feminist critiques has brought into the canon, or perhaps I should say the cannons."[38] Gates contends that Hurston, first among Black equals on the issue, was most influential in inventing a double-edged account of how the American Negro must be represented in Black literary theory. He offers the following interpretation:

> Their mode of narration of *Their Eyes* consists, at either extreme of narrative commentary (rendered in third-person omniscient and third-person restricted voices) and of characters' discourse (which manifests itself as a direct speech rendered in what Hurston calls dialect). Hurston's innovation is to be found in the middle spaces between these two extremes of narration and discourse, ... It was Hurston who introduced free indirect discourse into Afro-American narration. It is this innovation ... which enables her to represent various traditional modes of Afro-American rhetorical play while

---

34 Charles Lemert, *Muhammad Ali: Trickster in the Culture of Irony* (Polity Press, 2003).
35 Gates, *The Signifying Monkey: A Theory of African-American Literary Theory* (Oxford University Press, 1988), 52.
36 Morrison apparently said this in a 1995 interview with Karin L. Badt, cited in the Wikipedia entry on Morrison's *Tar Baby*.
37 *The Signifying Monkey*, 173–180. See also Henry Louis Gates, "Afterword," 244–254.
38 *Ibid*, 180.

simultaneously representing her protagonist's growth in self-consciousness through her indirect discourse.[39]

Theory *and* method—one and the same—is only possible when they are at work in a fiction of real practical living where people talk with, and of, each other.

There is no better illustration of Hurston's breathtakingly original method than what she writes near the end of *Their Eyes Were Watching God* where Hurston tells of the sad end of Janie's relationship with Tea Cake. Janie and Tea Cake had long settled into a deep love for each other and a series of homes in Florida. Then one day a merciless hurricane strikes. While they are fleeing for high ground, Tea Cake is bitten by a rabid dog. He falls into madness when the infection deranges his mind. Tea Cake suffers the delusion that Janie is cheating on him. He tries to kill her. She saves herself by killing him. An all-white jury later declares her not guilty. Hurston continues:

> So, she was free and the judge and everybody up there smiled with her and shook her hand. And the white women cried and stood around her like a protecting wall and the Negroes, with heads hung down, shuffled out and away. The sun was almost down, and Janie had seen the sun rise on her troubled love and then she had shot Tea Cake and had been in jail and had been tried for her life and now she was free. Nothing to do with the little that was left of the day but to visit the kind white friends who had realized her feelings and thank them. So, the sun went down.
>
> She took a room at the boarding house for the night and heard the men talking around the front.
>
> "Aw you know dem white mens wuzn't gointuh do nothin' tuh no woman dat look lak her."
>
> "She didn't kill no white man, did she? Well, long as she don't shoot no white man she kin kill jus' as many niggers as she please."
>
> "Yeah, de nigger women kin kill up all de mens dey wants tuh, but you bet' not kill one uh dem. De white folks will sho hang yuh if yuh do."
>
> "Well, you know whut dey say 'uh white man and uh nigger woman is de freest thing on earth.' Dey do as dey please."[40]

Janie buried Tea Cake in Palm Beach. She knew he loved the 'Glades but it was too low for him to lie with water maybe washing over him with every heavy rain. Anyway, the 'Glades and its waters had killed him. She wanted him out of the way of storms, so she had a strong vault built in the cemetery at West Palm Beach. Janie had wired to Orlando for money to put him away. Tea Cake was the son of Evening Sun, and nothing was too good. The Undertaker did a handsome job and Tea Cake slept royally on his white silken couch among the roses she had bought. He looked almost ready to grin. Janie bought him a brand-new guitar and put it in his hands. He would be thinking up new songs to play to her when she got there.

The day of the gun, and the bloody body, and the courthouse came and commenced to sing a sobbing sigh out of every corner in the room; out of each and every chair and

---

39 *Ibid*, 191.
40 Zora Neale Hurston, *Their Eyes Were Watching God* (HarperCollins eBook), 237–238. @ https://uniteyouthdublin.files.wordpress.com/2015/01/88253919-their-eyes-were-watching-god-by-zora-neale-hurston.pdf

thing. Commenced to sing, commenced to sob and sigh, singing and sobbing. Then Tea Cake came prancing around her where she was, and the song of the sigh flew out of the window and lit in the top of the pine trees. Tea Cake, with the sun for a shawl. Of course, he wasn't dead. He could never be dead until she herself had finished feeling and thinking. The kiss of his memory made pictures of love and light against the wall. Here was peace. She pulled in her horizon like a great fishnet. Pulled it from around the waist of the world and draped it over her shoulder. So much of life in its meshes! She called in her soul to come and see.[41]

How can a fiction like this be said to be a theory? And what here is the free indirect discourse Gates attributes to Hurston?

Read it again and again—perhaps as one might read a poem—and you begin to feel yourself caught up in the doubled-over and duplicitous trick of narration in a dialect that turns what is being said back on itself while ever turning around and onward. The death of Tea Cake in repose with a grin is the resolution of the American Negro's duplicitous state of being. A white jury exonerates Janie. She overhears Black men gossiping in their dialect. Again the telling line: "Yeah, de nigger women kin kill up all de mens dey wants tuh, but you bet' not kill one uh dem. De white folks will sho hang yuh if yuh do." Here is the doubled over indirect discourse in which the American Negro tells the discursive truth of her Negritude against the deadly fact of the exclusions of white culture.

Without taking anything away from Du Bois, it must be said that thirty-four years after *Souls of Black Folk*, Hurston redoubled the gift of second sight, several times over until the full weight of twoness can bear down on the Black American. "…An American, a Negro, two souls, two thoughts, two unreconciled strivings; two warring ideals in one dark body, whose dogged strength alone keeps him from being torn asunder." This is Du Bois at his poetic best, but there is no room for Josie who was in fact torn asunder. By contrast, at the end of *Their Eyes Were Watching God*, Hurston's Tea Cake must be torn asunder to put life and death in their necessary duplicitous relation. "Of course, he wasn't dead. He could never be dead until she herself had finished feeling and thinking. The kiss of his memory made pictures of love and light against the wall." Tea Cake died of Janie's love—a love that would never quit. He lives on in memory, which, when all is said and done, is what culture is and does—and especially so for the excluded who live in its long dark shadow.

Paula Gunn Allen: Ritual Gynocracy in Native America

Paula Gunn Allen was born in 1939 in Albuquerque, New Mexico and grew up in Cubero, New Mexico, a small village adjacent to the Laguna Pueblo reservation. Her mother was native Laguna Pueblo and a poet of her culture. Paula's father was Lebanese American and the proprietor of a store in Cubero before becoming prominent in New Mexican politics. Allen's childhood experiences in a good family and close to her mother's Indian culture nurtured her in several ways at once. After attending mission schools in Albuquerque and time taken to raise two children, Allen's education advanced steadily from college and MA degrees at the University of Oregon to a PhD at the University of New Mexico. Then too, her background in Cubero was context for the direct influence of her mother's poetry that drew her into the literary life as a poet and novelist then, ultimately, as author or editor of books on American Indian traditions.

---

41 *Ibid*, 242.

It is not far wrong to suggest that Paula Gunn Allen was to American Indian cultures what Zora Neale Hurston was to American Negro folk culture. Yet, Allen faced challenges in a different era that Hurston did not. American Indian cultures were, and are, many and different. They are spread across a vast space from the Southwest to the Pacific Coast, Northwest to Canada and Alaska, then back across the Rocky Mountains in the Midwest to upper New York State and parts of New England. No one could possibly engage in the nuanced folkloric field studies that Hurston compiled in the American South and the Caribbean. The homology to Zora Neale Hurston's study of the American Negro cultures is that, well into the end of the twentieth century, Paula Gunn Allen collected representative literatures of American Indian cultural texts in books like *Voice of the Turtle: American Indian Literature, 1900–1970* (1994) and *Song of the Turtle: American Indian Literature, 1974–1994* (1996).

Then, in addition, Allen published discursive works of her own that served to recover the feminine in Indian cultures—of these *The Sacred Hoop: Recovering the Feminine in American Indian Traditions* (1992) is best known for breaking open the patriarchal and white biases of the colonizer's culture. Here too, as the title suggests, Allen returns to the folk traditions of American Indians. Their stories may not have been as available as those of the American Negro. Still, the ones Allen introduces are, in their way, central to American Indian culture. *The Sacred Hoop* begins with "The Ways of Our Grandmothers" presented as ubiquitous, if not universal, in American Indian traditions:

> In the beginning was thought, and her name was Woman. The Mother, the Grandmother, recognized from earliest times into the present among those peoples of the Americas who kept to the eldest traditions, is celebrated in social structures, architecture, law, custom, and the oral tradition. To her we owe our lives, and from her comes our ability to endure, regardless of the concerted assaults on our, on Her, being, for the past five hundred years of colonization. She is the Old Woman who tends the first of life. She is the Old Woman Spider, who weaves us together in a fabric of interconnection. She is the Eldest God, the one who Remembers and Re-members; and through the history of the past five hundred years has taught us bitterness and helpless rage, we endure into the present, alive, certain of our significance, certain of her centrality, her identity as the Sacred Hoop of Be-ing.[42]

These lines are discursive, obviously, but they are at least built upon the folkways of Paula Gunn Allen's people.

The Sacred Hoop, then, begins with an essay written in 1984, "The Grandmother of the Sun: Ritual Gynocracy in Native America"—which is to say, the Grandmother of all women. Though Allen composed in the discursive mode, this essay identifies those folk traditions of American Indians for whom the Woman dominates the culture. Of which, there are many forms, including: the Old Spider Woman, the Corn Woman, the Earth Woman—and, in Gunn's words: "what they together have made is called Creation, Earth, creatures, plants, and light."[43] Quite understandably, Allen begins with reference to her own tribal culture, the Keres Indians of the Laguna Pueblo: "Central to the Keres theology is the basic idea of the Creatrix as She Who Thinks rather than She Who Bears, of woman as a creation thinker

---

[42] Paula Gunn Allen, *The Sacred Hoop: Recovering the Feminine in American Indian Traditions* (Beacon Press, 1992 [1996]), 11. The book is a collection of Allen's writings dating back to 1984.
[43] *Ibid*, 13.

and female thought as origin of material and nonmaterial reality. ... She is 'both Mother and Father to all people and to all creatures.' "[44]

In one sense, Allen deploys something like Zora Neale Hurston's theory-method by going home for the source that allowed her to tell the tale of American Indian gynocracy. At a crucial point in her elaboration of the pipe of the Sacred Woman, she tells a story her great-grandmother told her—the tale of "Iyatiku, or Corn Woman, the mother goddess of the Keres, who is called the mother of the people, [and] is in a ceremonial sense another aspect of Thought Woman."[45] The tale is of a time in the long ago when Iyatiku lived in the White Village during hard times caused by drought. Iyatiku gave them a gambling game to occupy themselves during these troubled times. But, in due course, the men abused the game by squandering the people's meager resources while failing to engage in the required ritual—for which the women rebuked them even though they were included in the male ritual places. Iyatiku was angered and abandoned the village which soon enough perished. The people built a new village that thrived because Iyatiku left her power with them. The lesson was learned. The people came to detest violence. "They are," the tale continues, "very careful to contain their emotions and to put a smooth face on things, for rain is essential to the very life of their villages. Without it the crops can't grow, the livestock will starve, there will be no water for drinking or bathing—in short, all life, physical and ceremonial, will come to a halt."[46] "Grandmother of the Sun" then surveys a number of other tales of this kind and comes to a muscular conclusion: "A strong attitude integrally connects the power of Original Thinking or Creation Thinking to the power of mothering."[47]

The Sacred Hoop was followed in 1991 by an elegantly composed collection, *The Grandmothers of the Light: A Medicine Woman's Source Book*. The book's first chapter, "The Living Reality of the Medicine World," begins with Allen's declaration that the stories in her collection have drawn upon the numerous oral traditions of the American Indian cultures.[48] Most are not collected first-hand as Hurston collected her tales of the American Negro. Some are, of course, but most are found in reliable prior collections of ethnographers and historians of native America. Yet Allen's stories are retold to represent, as she puts it, "... the four directions and seven directions, they span North America from the Yucatán to Washington State, from Arizona to New York State. Among them, stories about the Great Goddess in a variety of guises—Xmucané, Sky Woman, Six Killer (Sutalidihi), Thinking Woman, Changing Woman, White Shell Woman, Tonan, Scomalt, Iyatiku, Ic'sts'ity, and Nau'ts'ity—tell how the cosmos was formed and the ways of magic."[49] That in these first lines of the preface to *Grandmothers of the Light*, Allen does not try to "explain" the given names of the Great Goddesses but suggests that she means to address native people who can be assumed either to know some of them or to have a native interest in learning about them. Then, soon after, *Grandmothers of the Light* turns discursive to call attention to the strange double meanings of *"myth"* as "synonymous with *fable*, from the Greek where it had the connotation of a moral story."[50] Myths are not, thereby, irrational much less false on the surface. Myths, Allen goes on to say, can be traced from the Greek down to the Germanic root syllable *Mu*, that in turn leads to a relation to the German *die Mutter*,

---

44 *Ibid*, 15. Allen in turn cites a leading authority on the Keres, Anthony Purley, "Keres Pueblo Concepts of Divinity," *American Indian Culture and Research Journal* 1:1 (Fall 1974).
45 *The Sacred Hoop*, 17. Story of Iyatiku following is paraphrased from the same place.
46 *Ibid*, 18.
47 *Ibid*, 29.
48 *Ibid*, 3.
49 Paula Gunn Allen, *Grandmothers of the Light: A Medicine Woman's Source Book* (Beacon Press, 1991), xiii.
50 *Ibid*, 7.

"mother." Hence: "myth and mother—both discredited in the modern world—are nevertheless essential to the modern world's existence."[51] But then Allen expands her semantic journey by reference to the "muttering"—and comments that muttering is a common practice in magical rituals of which, I would add, that the mothering of troubled infants very often takes the form of muttering songs and sayings that make little obvious sense save for their calming effect on the child.

Then in the book's first chapter, "The Living Reality of the Medicine World," after introducing ritual magic, Allen turns to a section on "The Seven Ways of the Medicine Woman"—the Way of the Daughter, The Way of the Household, the Way of the Mother, the Ways of the Gatherer and of the Ritualist, the Way of the Teacher and the Way of the Wise Woman. Each is drawn from its roots in American Indian traditions in order to present a general history of woman that culminates in a theory of contemporary women, concluding with the most powerful of statements:

> It should surprise no one that the modern age from its beginnings in the Renaissance to the present, has become more and more thoroughly separated from womanity, from ritual magic, from tribal social systems, and from harmony with the earth. The four have ever danced together: woman, magic, tribes, and earth, and the dance goes on, even yet.[52]

Grandmothers of the Light concludes with a long chapter on "Myth, Magic, and Medicine in the Modern World," which returns to the traditional American Indian fables in order to pull together her view of medicine as ritual magic. The idea, of course, is that the Indian way is healing because it binds people harmoniously with nature. But the modern world is killing all that. "Native people are convinced that disharmonious actions toward plant and animal communities turn them against human health and life. They become poisonous, where, before being mistreated, they were nutritious and safe for human use and consumption. Another consequence is that they quietly disappear."[53]

Her earlier essay "Who Is Your Mother? Red Roots of White Feminism" in *The Sacred Hoop* is a still stronger statement of just how American Indian women can contribute to the healing of modern society. It begins, again, with the classic question of her own Laguna Pueblo people, "Who Is Your Mother?"—a sacramental query founded on the matrilineal structure of Laguna society in which "your mother's identity is the key to your own identity." She continues:

> Of course, your mother is not only that woman whose womb formed and released you—the term refers in every individual case to an entire generation of women whose psychic, and consequentially physical, "shape" made the psychic existence of the following generation possible. But naming your own mother (or her equivalent) enables people to place you precisely within the universal web of your life, in each of its dimensions: cultural, spiritual, personal, and historical.[54]

It goes without saying that this is a strong structural theory of mothers, of women. This, alone, makes an important potential contribution to White Feminism. It was written in the 1980s when Second Wave White feminism dominated the scene with a program that fell

---

51 *Ibid*, 7.
52 *Ibid*, 24.
53 *Ibid*, 170.
54 Paula Gunn Allen, "Who Is Your Mother? Red Roots of White Feminism," in *The Sacred Hoop*, 209.

short of naming the many types of women called to a feminist identity. But Allen's "Red Roots of White Feminism" goes well beyond identity politics. It means to say that life itself, in all its adumbrations, is mothered. Men may be good hunters, but women mother the tribe—the social home of all people. "The feminist idea of power as it ideally accrues to women stems from tribal sources."[55]

In this Paula Gunn Allen closes the circle that Zora Neale Hurston's more literary method left implied, even open. The tales of the excluded American Negroes and of the excluded American Indians are stories of power—the power of survival against all odds, of being real in real relations that are considered at least strange, at worst evil, by their excluders. Theirs is a power not of revolutionary potential by a lesser class of people in but not of the system. They are out of the system entirely. Yet, they have the power to remember, to re-member, and to tell the stories of their ancient pasts—near pasts of the Negroes, distant pasts of the Indians. Yet these otherwise different pasts, and different peoples, hold to stories of where they came from—whether Negro Spirituals in Du Bois's case, or of loves and deaths in Hurston's, or of tribal mothering rituals in Allen's. In *On Juneteenth*, a highly personal book, Annette Gordon-Reed writes tellingly of just this tangle of historical forces associated with America's excluded people:

> In the twenty-first century, the United States has come to a point of reckoning about its past, including the story of the dispossession of Native peoples, who are still very much present. At the same time where appropriate, Native peoples are now being asked to come to grips with their relationship to African Americans, the descendants of people whom they enslaved, and with whom, in some cases, they share a blood line.[56]

Even now, Allen's benedictory message can be heard and attended to: "The four have ever danced together: woman, magic, tribes, and earth, and the dance goes on even yet."[57]

I'M NOT YOUR NEGRO:
James Baldwin/Medgar Evers/Malcolm X/Martin Luther King, Jr.

The book *I'M NOT YOUR NEGRO* is by, *and about*, James Baldwin. It appeared in 2017 thirty years after Baldwin died in 1987. It is a parsimonious but delicately selected compilation of what Baldwin wrote and said during a special moment in his life when Jimmy[58] decided to return to America in 1957, ten years after he had left home for Paris. *I'M NOT YOUR NEGRO* is so emphatic in its titular subject that it demands all caps. That inspiration is most vividly on display in the fast-moving film of the same name directed by Raoul Peck.[59]

---

55 *Ibid*, 220.
56 Annette Gordon-Reed, *On Juneteenth* (Liveright, 2021), 95–96.
57 *Grandmothers of Light*, 24.
58 I may seem pretentious for me to use *Jimmy*, but I do it following others who have written on Baldwin, some of whom knew him well. But also because I think *Jimmy* is all-but-required when referring to a man who was so brilliantly down with his people *and* his nation that it would be strange to use, for example, *James*. *Jimmy* was not a *James*. He was, and still is, a world famous author who, at the same time, engaged the people in his life with vitality and honesty. To be sure, in writing about the man it is necessary to use *Baldwin*, according to authorial norms, just to be clear to readers about the subject. *Jimmy* softens the hardness of necessary norms. But to be *perfectly* clear, I did not have a personal relation with him.
59 James Baldwin *I'M NOT YOUR NEGRO*, compiled, edited, and introduced by Raoul Peck (Vintage International/Random House, 2017), based on the film *I'M NOT YOUR NEGRO* (*Vélvet Film, Inc.* and *Vélvet SAS*, 2016).

I'M NOT YOUR NEGRO, the film and the book, are set in a crucial period in Baldwin's life and the nation's life, roughly from 1955 to 1968—or: *from* the first important modern Civil Rights movement in the Montgomery Bus Boycott in 1955–1956 led by a very young Martin Luther King, Jr. *to* 1968 near the end of a decade when three great Black leaders had been murdered—Medgar Evers on June 12, 1963 in Jackson, Mississippi; Malcolm X on February 21, 1965 in New York City; and King himself on April, 8, 1968 in Memphis, Tennessee. These were *times* that Eddie S. Glaude, Jr. has called, using Walt Whitman's expression, *after times*—the times of Whitman's and the nation's mourning after Lincoln's assassination—a time Glaude applied to the *after times* of early Black rebellion and the assassinations of that multi-pronged movement's leaders.[60]

Though Baldwin did not, so far as I am aware, use this or any other expression like *after times,* but he did, quite clearly, mourn the deaths of the three figures of the racial movements of the 1960s that can have no single covering name. Eerie though it may be to suggest it, it is possible, on some level, Jimmy may have known that Medgar, Malcolm, and Martin would die tragic deaths. Death was always on his mind. He came to know his own mind, after years of tortuous personal struggles and lost lovers and all else that forces any sentient being to look deep inside while looking honestly outside to the truths of the history with which one must live. Baldwin did just that through all the necessary pain one must suffer in order to see clearly, and write with human passion:

> One writes out of one thing only—one's own experience. Everything depends on how relentlessly one forces from this experience the last drop, sweet or bitter, it can possibly give. This is the only real concern of the artist, to recreate out of the disorder of life that order which *is* art. The difficulty then, for me, of being a Negro writer was the fact that I was, in effect, prohibited from examining my own experience too closely by the tremendous demands and very real dangers of my situation.[61]

This was Jimmy Baldwin in *Notes of a Native Son* published in 1955 when he had turned just 31 years old. By then, young though he was, he had already published a novel, *Go Tell It On The Mountain*, in 1953 and the play *Amen Corner* in 1954—plus a good many articles in prestigious magazines ("Many Thousands Gone," in *Partisan Review* in 1951 and "Stranger in the Village" in *Harper's Magazine* in 1953, for examples). At the end of *Notes of a Native Son* in "A Question of Identity," which appeared in *Partisan Review* in 1954, he made an astute social theoretical observation that for him expressed a fact of his mental life about American culture's confusion about the relation of the person and the social forces with which one must live:

> [This confusion] which has so grandiose and general a ring, is, in fact, most personal—the American confusion seeming to be based on *the nearly unconscious assumption that it is possible to consider the person apart from all the forces that have produced him*. This assumption, however, is itself based on nothing less than our history, which is the history of the total and willing, alienation of entire peoples from their forbears. What is overwhelmingly clear, it seems, to everyone but ourselves is that this history has created

---

60 Eddie S. Glaude, Jr., *Begin Again: James Baldwin's America and Its Urgent Lessons for Our Own* (Crown/Random House, 2020), 16. For Walt Whitman's *after times*, Whitman, *Democratic Vistas* (The Cato Institute [Liberatarianism.Org], 2017), 44.
61 James Baldwin, *Notes of a Native Son* (Beacon Press, 1985 [1955]), 7. [Or, in *James Baldwin: Collected Essays*, edited by Toni Morrison (The Library of America/Penguin, 1998.]

an entirely unprecedented people, with a unique and individual past. It is, indeed, this past which has thrust upon us our present so troubling role. It is the past lived on the American continent, as against the past, irrecoverable now on the shores of Europe, which must sustain us in the present. The truth about that past is not that it is too brief, or too superficial, but only that we, having turned our faces so resolutely away from it, have never demanded from it what it has to give. It is this demand which the American student in Paris is forced, at length, to make, for he has otherwise no identity, no reason for being here. From the vantage point of Europe, he discovers his own country.[62]

This from a young native son whose highest academic degree was from DeWitt Clinton High School in the Bronx. It is not just the passage's intellectual maturity but, even more, the emotional depth of Baldwin's thinking. He never dismissed his native nation, and always and regularly returned to it both in his soul and on many return visits. He died in 1987 in his home at Saint Paul-de-Vence, France, but surely his soul left his remains to fly back to America. Well before that figurative ideal is the fact of his many returns in life to New York City,—in 1952 on money borrowed from Marlon Brando after four years in Paris and Europe,—again soon after, in 1954 on a Guggenheim,—then again in 1957 when he made an extended trip to the South where he met Martin Luther King and his wife Coretta Scott King.[63] In NYC in the 1950s he was greeted as what he had become—an emerging international literary figure to be reckoned with.

But the third of these early returns was a very different story. His purpose in 1957 was to experience the American South as it was and would be for just a few years more. He knew he had to engage the people and places where the persistent racial war was still injuring and killing Blacks, yes, but also whites. In a sense, one could say that this trip to the American South was the sequel to what he said of his initial trip to Paris in 1948:

> I left America because I doubted my ability to survive the fury of the color problem here. (Sometimes I still do.) I wanted to prevent myself from becoming *merely* a Negro; or, even, merely a Negro writer. I wanted to find out in what way the *specialness* of my experience could be made to connect me to other people instead of dividing me from them.[64]

The sequel then is found in what Baldwin wrote years later in 1972 about a photograph he saw while in a cafe with Richard Wright in 1956 in a newspaper kiosk on the Boulevard Saint-Germain in Paris:

> Facing us on every newspaper kiosk on that wide, tree-shaded boulevard, were photographs of fifteen-year-old Dorothy Counts being reviled and spat upon by the mob as she was making her way to school in Charlotte, North Carolina. There was unutterable pride, tension, and anguish in that girl's face as she approached the halls of learning, with history, jeering, at her back. ... It made me furious, it filled me with both hatred

---

62 Ibid, 136–137. [Or, *Baldwin, Collected Essays, ibid*, 100.] Important to add that *Notes of a Native Son* is itself a compilation of previously published articles written between 1948 (when he was but 24) and early 1955.
63 These and other dates on Baldwin's life are from the superb chronology in *Baldwin: Collected Essays, ibid*, 845–855. It worth adding that all of the *Library of America* collections of American writers have chronologies which are invaluable.
64 Baldwin, "The Discovery of What It Means to be an American," in Baldwin's *The Price of the Ticket: Collected Nonfiction: 1948–1985* (Beacon Press, 1985 [1959]), 179. [Originally published in *The New York Times Book Review* (January 25, 1959).]

and pity, and it made me ashamed. Some one of us should have been there with her! I dawdled in Europe for nearly another year, ... but it was on that bright afternoon that I knew I was leaving France. I could, simply, no longer sit around in Paris discussing the Algerian and black American problem. Everybody else was paying their dues, and it was time I went home and paid mine.[65]

Interestingly, there is some minor difference as to when, or if, Baldwin first saw the photographs in Paris. David Leeming takes the passage at face value, while Eddie Glaude seems to doubt it because Baldwin made no mention of the photograph in *Nobody Knows My Name* in 1961.[66] This may seem a minor point, except for the fact that Baldwin himself much later reflects on his first sight in Paris of the Dorothy Counts photographs in 1956 with an observation he made while on his homeward journey to the South in 1957 with another remark on another photograph of Counts:

I must add for the benefit of my so innocent and criminal countrymen, that, today, fifteen years later, the photograph of Angela Davis has replaced the photograph of Dorothy Counts. *These two photographs would appear to sum up the will of Americas—heirs of all the ages—in relation to blacks.*[67]

These lines appeared in 1972 in *No Name in the Street*, when for Baldwin and all Americans troubled by the tragedies in the 1960s, still suffered deep inside the pain of the losses of Medgar Evers, Malcolm X, and Martin Luther King, Jr.

On this point in *No Name*, Eddie Glaude sets his biographic record straight in respect, at least, as to the symbolic value of Dorothy's pain that day at Harding High School in Charlotte in 1956:

Looking back, after the deaths of Medgar Evers, Malcolm X, and Martin Luther King, Jr., the photo with all its pathos, anguish, and pride represented for Baldwin in 1972 the demand to bear witness to what was happening in 1957 and to what had transpired since.... Dot's eyes captured the trauma of that journey. Baldwin sought to narrate what happened on the eve of a social movement that sought to transform the country, and to testify to that odd combination of trauma and grit, which he now knew so well, seen in a fifteen-year-old black girl's courage that spurred *him*, so he believed, to leap into the fire.[68]

Baldwin was a man who moved, and was pulled, in many directions at once. Not just back and forth between Europe and America, but also between a refusal to make white America solely responsible for the racial tensions at home and a commitment to the deeper truth of those tensions. As much as he came to respect Malcolm X, and grieved his passing, Baldwin at first rejected Malcolm's early attacks on white America—an attitude he struggled with just as much as he did with Stokely Carmichael's Black Power and the violent threats of the Black Panthers. But neither did he unqualifiedly embrace Martin's notion of love as the power of resistance. David Leeming puts Baldwin's mixed mind as to Martin Luther King's ability to move toward Malcolm X:

---

65 Baldwin, *No Name in the Street* (1972) in *Baldwin, Collected Essays* [1998], 383.
66 David Leeming, *James Baldwin a Biography* (Arcade Publishing/Knopf, 1994), 139; and Glaude, *Begin Again* (2020), *ibid*, 33.
67 Baldwin, *No Name in the Street* (1972) in *Baldwin, Collected Essays* [1998], 384. Emphasis added.
68 Glaude, *Begin Again* (2020), *ibid*, 43.

Everywhere he went people asked about the Muslims. Yet angry as he was, and fascinated as he had become by Malcolm X, and as skeptical as he sometimes felt about the methods of Martin Luther King Jr., Baldwin could never give up on King's nonviolent program nor his at this point turn to the more muscular approach of the followers of the Honorable Elijah.[69]

But most surprising of the three Baldwin cast as the principals of this *Remember This House* in 1979 proposal that in turn became the players in Raoul Peck's 2017 *I'M NOT YOUR NEGRO* might well be Medgar Evers—this because his primary association was with the NAACP in Mississippi. Since at least 1934 when W.E.B. Du Bois, a cofounder of the NAACP, resigned the organization because of its failure to take a radical position on the economic exclusion of Blacks, there had been a line of thought that the NAACP was the Uncle Tom of civil rights organizations. Through the years it had been all-too-inclined to huddle under white culture and philanthropy. Yet, in the deep South in the early 1960s before Fannie Lou Hammer and the Mississippi Freedom Summer in 1964, the NAACP was the most prominent and, in its liberal way, most radical movement of racial politics. Medgar Evers became the organization's field secretary in November 1954, just after the *Brown V. Education* decision of the U.S. Supreme Court declared school segregation unconstitutional. Evers thereafter became all the more aggressive protest leader, not just in school desegregation, but to stop segregation on Mississippi's Gulf Coast beaches and to integrate buses and public parks. As his leadership grew more effective, members of the KKK and White Citizen's Council like Bryon De La Beckwith were determined to put an end to him. Beckwith assassinated Medgar late in the day on June 12, 1963 at his home in Jackson, Mississippi. He was mortally wounded but lived on the margin of death long enough to break another race line. Medgar or, better put, his body was the first Black ever to be admitted to an all-white hospital in Mississippi. Over the years since, Medgar Evers did the day-to-day, on the ground work that is necessary for anything like a Civil Rights Movement to come to be. "Medgar Evers did a lot to bring the NAACP to Mississippi. But one of his main contributions was to take news of the struggle in Mississippi to the people of the U.S. and the world through news releases, interviews, and speeches."[70]

Still, one might ask why these three? *I'M NOT YOUR NEGRO* begins with a poignant reference to Baldwin's unwritten *Remember This House* in which he meant to tell his story of America through the lives of his murdered friends, Medgar, Martin, and Malcolm. In Baldwin's letter to his agent Jay Action on June 30, 1979, he wrote of a very personal insistence on *Remember This House* as a "… journey, to tell the truth, which I always knew I'd have to make, but had hoped, perhaps (certainly, I had hoped), not to make it so soon."[71] Then on the very next page, in Jimmy's words, composed as a poem:

The three men, Medgar, Malcolm, and Martin—
were very different men.
Consider that Martin was only twenty-six in 1955.
He took on his shoulders the weight of the crimes,
and the lies and the hopes of the nation.

---

69 Leeming, *James Baldwin: A Biography, ibid*, 219.
70 Ronald W. Bailey, *Remembering Medgar Evers … for a New Generation* (Distributed by Heritage Publications in cooperation with the Mississippi Network for Black History and Heritage, 1988). The quoted passage as it appears here cites this book in "The Struggle of Medgar Evers" on the Medgar Evers College website @ https://www.mec.cuny.edu/history/life-of-medgar-evers/. Some of the details of Evers' life here are also taken from https://en.wikipedia.org/wiki/Medgar_Evers --an unusually well-documented entry.
71 Baldwin [with Peck], *I'M NOT YOUR NEGRO, ibid*, 5.

> I want these three lives to bang against
> and reveal each other,
> as, in truth, they did …
> and use their dreadful journey
> as a means of instructing the people
> whom they loved so much,
> who betrayed them,
> and for whom they gave their lives.

Here you can hear, if you will, Jimmy Baldwin the very young preacher he was in Harlem in 1938, and in some quiet way that he remained to his own end.[72] The second verse, where he leads with "these three lives" ends with a tacit resurrection belief: *these three men revealed themselves/life is a dreadful journey/ they loved so much/those who betrayed them/and for whom they gave their lives.* Yet, there was nothing naively optimistic about Baldwin's view of life and death in America. One of his most embracing quotations from a 1961 radio interview was: "To be a Negro in this country and to be relatively conscious is to be in a rage almost all the time." Or, in *Open Letter to the Born Again* in 1979:

> *Inasmuch as ye have done unto the least of these my brethren, yet have done it unto me.* That is a hard saying. It is hard to live with that. It is a merciless description of our responsibility for one another. It is a hard light under which one makes the moral choice. That the Western world has forgotten that such a thing as moral choice exists, my history, my flesh, my soul bear witness.[73]

This was written September 29, 1979, just two months after his proposal to write about Medgar, Malcolm, and Martin—when he remained the crypto-preacher of Christian doctrine. Baldwin, on this score, was torn every which way, seeking always to pull it all together.

But that is not all. There were internal tensions concerning his sexuality and many failed affairs, and also his failed relations with his stepfather, but his good relationship with his brother David who was among those at his deathbed. Then, more broadly, there were the dynamics in his intellectual life, some surprising—he was influenced by and wrote about Henry James and William Faulkner and read Henry Adams with respect while rejecting his linear history of the modern world in "The Dynamo and the Virgin" that portrayed American culture as arriving at its modern industrial zenith along a trajectory could be traced back to the unifying power of early medieval cathedral at Chartres—a lineage that did not allow for the racial world that for half that millennium, shaped and thwarted the lives of his forbears. At the same time, Jimmy Baldwin was a close friend of Marlon Brando

---

72 For an interesting comment on Baldwin's early religious thinking, see Campbell, *Talking at the Gates, ibid*, 23: "[His early meetings with Richard Wright] … had their effect on Baldwin the preacher. The sacred, it turned out, was not the domain to scrutinize in search of 'everlasting life'; looked at another way, perhaps the Holy Ghost might be identified here on earth, among human beings, in works of art. (Baldwin had not yet reached the point where salvation would be pursued vis the profane.)"

For a description of Baldwin's early years as a preacher beginning in 1938 before he finished junior high school, see Leeming, *ibid*, 24–31. Leeming, who knew Jimmy well in his later life, suggests that at 14 years-of-age being a successful preacher meant so much to him because it gave him a second family, and a degree of separation from his abusive stepfather. Also (Leeming, 25): "Jimmy's second birth and later his success in the pulpit led to greater self-assurance at home. He began consciously to stand up to his stepfather and to side openly against him."

73 *Open Letter to the Born Again*, in Baldwin, *The Price of the Ticket: Collected Nonfiction: 1948–1985* (Beacon Press, 1985), 663.

and Toni Morrison, among many others. But he also handed down surprising criticisms of those with whom he had once been close—most notably Richard Wright who helped Jimmy in his early years in Paris just after Wright's *Native Son* had been published in 1940. But by late 1951 Baldwin came out with "Many Thousands Gone," in which he lumps *Native Son* with *Uncle Tom's Cabin* by arguing initially that Bigger Thomas in *Native Son* was Uncle Tom's spiritual descendant by being compliant with the white society that "denies him life."[74] Then, two years later, in a longer criticism of Wright, Baldwin wrote: "*Native Son* finds itself at length so trapped by the American image of Negro life and by the necessity to find the ray of hope that it cannot pursue its own implications."[75] In all these ways Baldwin was, at the least, a complex person. This as a result of his personality, to be sure; but even more to the way that personality drove his intellectual pursuit of a bewildering number of sources and issues. An early biographer of Baldwin, James Campbell put it just right: "No one, Baldwin used to say, can be described. In my view, it is more true of him than anyone."[76]

Perhaps he could not finish *Remember This House* because he understood deeply well that no one, himself included, can be described. Somehow W.E.B. Du Bois is always in the background of meditations like this.

> *It is a peculiar sensation, this double-consciousness, this sense of always looking at one's self through the eyes of others, of measuring one's soul by the tape of a world that looks on in amused contempt and pity. One ever feels his twoness,—an American, a Negro; two souls, two thoughts, two unreconciled strivings; two warring ideals in one dark body, whose dogged strength alone keeps it from being torn asunder.*

Could there be a better way to illuminate the inner dynamics of *I'M NOT YOUR NEGRO*—or more to the point, to define the cultural exclusion that lay behind the deaths of Medgar, Malcolm, and Martin whose journeys through American life caused its culture to tremble in fear at what lay ahead after their deaths of the 1960s—deaths Jimmy wanted to account for as part of the exclusion of the American Negro. This was his journey through a life that ended, ironically, in Saint-Paul-de-Vence, outside the country he, to the surprise of many, loved even as it excluded him.

---

74 Baldwin, "Everybody's Protest Novel," in 1949 in *The Price of the Ticket*, ibid, 44. For a spot on view of Baldwin's criticism of Wright, see Ayana Mathis and Pankaj Mishra, "James Baldwin Denounced Richard Wright's 'Native Son' As a 'Protest Novel.' Was He Right?", *The New York Times Bookend* (February 24, 2015) where Mishra writes:

"Baldwin's essay "Everybody's Protest Novel," published when he was only 24, initiates a lifelong battle to overcome his own vulnerability as well as his society's fantasies and prejudices. His main objection to "Native Son" was that it confirmed the damning judgment on African-Americans delivered by their longstanding tormentors."

75 Baldwin, "Many Thousands Gone," *Notes of a Native Son*, ibid, 40. [Or, *Baldwin, Collected Essays* [1998], 31.]
76 James Campbell, *Talking at the Gates: A Life of James Baldwin* (University of California Press, 2002 [1991]), xii.

15 The Fungible Interaction Order
David Riesman, Erik Erikson, Edwin Lemert, Erving Goffman, Harold Garfinkel

*The society of incipient population decline develops its typical members
as a social character whose conformity is insured by their tendency to be sensitized
to the expectations and preferences of others. These I shall call other-directed people
and the society in which they live dependent on other direction.*
—David Riesman, The Lonely Crowd, 1950

*We must try to formulate the way in which self-contradictions in American history
may expose her youth to an emotional and political short circuit and thus endanger her dynamic
potential.*
—Erik Erikson, Childhood and Society, 1950

*When a person begins to employ his deviant behavior,
or a role based on it as a means of defense, attack, or adjustment to the overt and covert
problems created by the consequent societal reaction to him, his deviation becomes
secondary.*
—Edwin Lemert, Social Pathology, 1951

*In their capacity as performers, individuals will be concerned with maintaining the impression
that they are living up to the many standards by which they and their products are judged.*
—Erving Goffman, The Presentation of Self in Everyday Life, 1959

*I use the term "ethnomethodology"
to refer to the investigation of the rational properties of indexical expressions
and other practical actions as contingent on ongoing accomplishments
of organized artful practices of everyday life.*
—Harold Garfinkel, Studies in Ethnomethodology, 1967

Fungibility, An Unexplored Fact in Modern Societies

Fungibility—what could that be? In the simplest of terms it is the exchange of items of presumably equal value. We do it every time we pay cash for something we want. Yet we know very well—whether it is cash for apples or apples for oranges—that it is unlikely that the trade is fair and equal.

The same lack of logic appears in our interactions with others. We may think we have a good exchange on a first date, it may turn out to seem that way after a first night, but soon enough we realize that relational trades of time and feelings, always fade away. For a relationship to endure those party to it must engage in a series of supposedly fungible gives and gets. Any give and get is unlikely to be a fair trade. What matters, if the relationship endures, is that partners tolerate those all-too-common moments when what they give is not equal to what they get. Yet, in many instances, the relationship continues. Geri and I have been together for many years. We each remember the times we got the short end of the stick. Sometimes we laugh about them. Life goes on.

A similar dynamic occurs on a larger scale when in a society—or, diplomatically speaking, between societies—the traditional patterns of exchange somehow fall apart to be replaced by another. In personal relations when things fall apart, divorce is the answer. But in societal relations divorce is impossible. Members and nations must remake their relations until some eschatological moment when the ice melts and we all drown in the waters we could have held off.

One of those moments occurred when in America things changed once—not morbidly but decisively. The old was replaced by something new—not necessarily something better, but different and perhaps workable. As we shall see, the years on either side of 1950 were for Americans such a moment. David Riesman, for one, saw that the older inner-directed ideals that American's thought they obeyed, for the most part, were falling away to be replaced by something very different:

> The society of incipient population decline develops its typical members as a social character whose conformity is insured by their tendency to be sensitized to the expectations and preferences of others. These I shall call other-directed people and the society in which they live dependent on other direction.[1]

Other-directed attitudes lead to conformity to what others expect—which is not the kind of rugged individualism earlier Americans believed in.

Riesman was not alone in his concern. Two other thinkers of the same day, Erik Erikson and Edwin Lemert, had much the same idea expressed very differently. Erikson, the most famous psychoanalyst of his day, wrote in *Childhood and Society* of the way the then emerging society was undercutting the dynamic independence of young people:

> We must try to formulate the way in which self-contradictions in American history may expose her youth to an emotional and political short circuit and thus endanger her dynamic potential.[2]

More generally Edwin Lemert, a leading sociologist of crime and deviance, put forth societal reaction as an explanation for why some individuals come to see themselves as deviant:

> When a person begins to employ his deviant behavior, or a role based on it as a means of defense, attack, or adjustment to the overt and covert problems created by the consequent societal reaction to him, his deviation becomes secondary.[3]

Lemert's theory all-but put an end to biological or characterological theories of deviances.

Then, later, two other notables who thought of themselves as sociologists, came up with theories of social behavior that were in tune with these earlier theorists. To the weak-hearted their ideas were strange, but to others they were a revelation. Erving Goffman, for one, came up with the idea that far from being an interior sensibility, the self is social in nature:

---

1 David Riesman, *The Lonely Crowd* (Yale University Press, 1969 [1950]), 8.
2 Erik Erikson, *Childhood and Society* (W.W. Norton, 1950), 287.
3 Edwin M. Lemert, *Social Pathology: A Systematic Approach to the Theory of Sociopathic Behavior* (McGraw Hill, 1951), 75.

In their capacity as performers, individuals will be concerned with maintaining the impression that they are living up to the many standards by which they and their products are judged.[4]

For Goffman, the self is a social performance that others make real by judging their authenticity for better or worse.

Once the reader stays with Goffman, what he argues may be unsettling, but it is understandable. Harold Garfinkel's ethnomethodology tends to be more inscrutable:

I use the term "ethnomethodology" to refer to the investigation of the rational properties of indexical expressions and other practical actions as contingent on ongoing accomplishments of organized artful practices of everyday life.[5]

Yes, that's a mouthful but, as we shall see, he means to say that all social interactions are indexical, which is to say that they point to other interactions that the actor needs to understand. This is close to saying when we interreact with others we must become sociologists of our interactions.

So when all is said and begun, what follows is a discussion of how at a given time, American attitudes toward themselves and toward others changed, for better or worse.

Newhallville: An Improbably Rising Neighborhood

Newhallville, like much of the town itself, was once a farming area outside New Haven proper. In the 1820s the only notable man-made structure was a canal meant to link the town to prosperous towns as far north as Northampton, Massachusetts. Naturally, it was hoped that the canal would bring prosperity to Newhallville. It did not. Yet, that would come after 1870 when the Winchester Repeating Arms Company established its base of operations there. Over the years the Company brought the area long sought economic benefits by employing an increasing number of workers to a high of 19,000 during World War II.[6] Along the way, two- and three-unit apartment housing for workers were constructed close-by the factory where most in the neighborhood worked. Then, when deindustrialization set in, Winchester Repeating Arms moved elsewhere before it was sold in 1965 under a different name.[7] The last of its employees lost their jobs in 2006.

As these things happen in America, by 2006 Newhallville had already started its decline. When Winchester Arms disappeared so of course did its jobs, leaving the once thriving workforce abandoned. The tenements went the way of mixed-use urban housing—unpainted, ill-repaired, variously empty. It is far from clear where the unemployed workers went—as seldom it is. Some migrated to nearby towns, but their number could not possibly have been even close to 19,000 decades before. Crime rose such that early in 2000s murder rates were the talk of the wider town. Well-off whites over the hill whispered to one another that the crime was Black. It was not, of course—at least not exclusively. Some of it was caused by whites among others passing through Newhallville in search of drugs to fuel their nasty

---

4 Erving Goffman, *The Presentation of Self in Everyday Life* (Anchor Books, 1959), 251.
5 Harold Garfinkel, *Studies in Ethnomethodology* (Prentice-Hall, 1967), 11.
6 "'The Gun That Won the West' becoming just part of history," *USA Today*, 1/18/2006. Otherwise most of this history of Newhallville is, admittedly, from the Wikipedia *Newhallville* entry which seems, as best as one can tell, to be well documented (as here) and otherwise deserving of a reader's confidence.
7 National Register of Historic Places Inventory-Nomination: Winchester Repeating Arms Company Historic District.

ways. Even the nastiest of New Haven's real estate investments firms—one named Mandy another named Pike—stayed away with rare exception. Even slum lords realized that there was little gain to be had from the neighborhood's skid to nowhere.

Then things in Newhallville began to change, slowly. Though Yale kept its hands off the real estate market it did invest in a Science Park on its near side of the neighborhood. The hope was that this would become what the Farmington Canal did not, and the Winchester Arms did for a while—a source of hope if not prosperity. The hope was warranted to a degree. Soon enough part of the old Winchester building was redeveloped into what appeared to have been upscale apartments. Then too across from the Science Park buildings and the new apartments a well-meant but oversized building appeared meant to be a food court presumably for Yale people in the Science Park and residents of Winchester apartments. So far, no more than three of its many service units have been occupied—a Chinese take-out (now closed), a barbeque-ribs place, and a coffee shop some say offers the best coffee in a town overflowing with coffee offerings. The empty store fronts advertised how the Park has fallen short of expectations.

On the other hand, there are stirrings in the residential neighborhood. Yale, rather diffidently, started rehabbing a few buildings mostly to give its architecture students experience. There is a kind of village center to Newhallville occupied by an elementary grade school and a few shops. The school has been troubled in the sense that it has suffered an uncommon rate of administration turnover. The shops, however, seem to hold on, though none is a full-fledged grocery. Hair salons are the most numerous around the neighborhood, followed by a few bars and liquor stores here and there, and somewhat more than a few delis.

Across from the school there is a lovely church—granite style exterior, a number of classrooms, a large meeting room, and a nice enough sanctuary. But sometime in the 2010s, the Episcopal Diocese of Connecticut closed the church as a place of worship—too few paying parishioners to keep it open and heated. Somehow it never occurred to the weirdly adorned bishops with their robes and miters that they could have used the building as a social service center. An independent and charismatic pastor from the neighborhood occupied it for a while as just that—and successfully so. He and others committed to the people of Newhallville used it for community meetings with, for one example, police officers and town administrators to discuss a resurgence of violent crime. Even in its declined state, Newhallville has managed to hold on to a sense of community participation and loyalty.

Then, somewhere in the recent history of the neighborhood, a rather remarkable man came on the scene. The first instance of this man's unusual character is the fact that, at the beginning of his career, Jim pursued and gained a PhD in Sociology from Cornell University. Legend has it that he never intended to be an academic sociologist. What he fully intended to do was urban work for the poor. The degree, it seems, was his ticket to legitimacy when he knocked on the doors one needs to open to help the poor. In 1980, the year Jim Paley finished his degree at Cornell, he became Executive Director of Neighborhood Housing Services of New Haven, a national organization with chapters in many similar cities. Neighborhood Housing Services (or NHS) offers home ownership and redevelopment services to neighborhoods like Newhallville where residents often lack the independent financial means and know-how to own or repair their own homes.

Forty plus years later, Jim was still NHS's leader and has led it to important progress in housing in Newhallville and throughout the town. From the first, his goal at NHS in New Haven was to increase homeownership. For which (as its website says): "We began community organizing to help residents take charge of their neighborhoods. [And] during the 1990s, when housing values were declining sharply, we increased homebuyer education and counselor programs."⁸ By the 2020s, NHS had a strong staff that today provides leadership for a nonprofit Real Estate Agency, a Real Estate Development program that oversees the rehabilitation of houses in Newhallville, a community organizer who, among much else, has led residents to build a quite wonderful community garden and other smaller gardens here and there. These are but a few of the staff departments by which NHS serves New Haven and Newhallville. In 2021, NHS assisted more than 400 new homeowners, helped 42 customers with mortgage problems, provided 36 virtual workshops for nearly 800 new customers. It may surprise some (as it did me) that NHS in 2020 offered 2 homebuyer education seminars for 49 Yale University employees eligible for the University's employer-assistance programs. (You'd think it would occur to Yale to offer such a program.) And, one striking example of the way NHS thinks of everything is that they have a tool lending library for residents.

The effect of all this is apparent to anyone who knew the neighborhood a decade or more before NHS came into its own. Lilac Street, that runs down toward the local school, was in shambles. But now, with more than a few houses redeveloped and occupied by homeowners, it is as different as different can be—not perfect but so much better than it was. People visiting Newhallville today know something important is going on. Now there are other agencies in the town involved, most inspired by NHS which has reached deep into New Haven's town leadership and its community culture. Yale seems now to have gotten more interested. Members of the NHS Board include city and agency leaders. People talk about the neighborhood. There is still crime. Much else needs to be done.

But Newhallville is changing—and it is changing even when its interaction order boils over. The community meeting with town police and leaders of the community was held after a particularly vicious murder on the far northern border of the neighborhood. Before, it had been a while when Newhallville experienced few violent crimes and no murders. It did not help for the residents to learn that both the victim and perpetrators were not from Newhallville. This only aroused concern local drug dealing was on the increase. The meeting with the police did not completely calm the community's concern. The meeting was contentious. In the end, however, the coming together of residents and the police, and other town officials had the entirely good effect of letting people know that others cared and were doing what could be done to reduce the dealing and crime. Not long after, the town made the local police station more open to visits by citizens. On the other hand, in respect to the neighborhood's relations with the town itself, early in January 2022, residents learned of a plan to move a methadone clinic from a non-residential area to an abandoned school near Newhallville. Local community leaders organized a zoom protest in which some 160 residents protested the move and the fact that they had not been informed.⁹

In many ways Newhallville today has the prospect of becoming better than ever. Its nineteenth century farming days were overrun and lost. The prosperity of the Winchester Arms days were what capitalist anchored factories always are—a sometime thing. Yes, tenements were built to house workers meant to serve the interests of the corporation not the future of the community. When Winchester Arms left, it left behind ruins. Today the larger part of its crumbling factory is still undeveloped as the developed apartments are themselves far short of the promise of bringing a better off population to the area. All this being granted, Newhallville, even with its remaining troubles, promises more for its future than ever before. It is, in effect, a fungible community to which the town can look with some hope because the people who live in Newhallville can see a better day.

---

8 For this passage and the data following, see: https://nhsofnewhaven.org/about/annual-report/. [Full disclosure: for quite a few years I served on the organization's Board of Trustees. CL]

9 Allan Appel, "Newhallville Blasts Methadone Clinic Plan," *The New Haven Independent* (January 13, 2022): https://www.newhavenindependent.org/article/apt_move_to_newhallville_in_community_crosshairs.

Fungible? What could that mean here? Technically, "fungible" refers to any item (including cash money) that could be exchanged for a product of equal value. In fact, fungibility is at best an approximation of actual exchange values. It is well known that the value of cash money rises and falls wildly depending on market fluctuations. Actual material products are seldom what their advertisers promise them to be. Houses, cars, tools, even foods are too often made to appear better than they are. The skill and commitment of workers never yields the income needed to pay for the goods they need and desire in order to live well. Weather, illness, competition, and more cut into the promises of the quality of time and effort employed. Fungible is as fungible does.

Newhallville today is fungible in the sense that it can become more than it has been, if not fungibly equivalent to other communities in the town except in its own unique way. The white and well-off community over the hill in East Rock is better in a real estate sense. It thinks of itself as "safe" but in fact it too is beset by theft, murders, and other troubles different and lesser than Newhallville's but no less affecting. Newhallville is considerably more real in the sense that life lived there is life as it is in a middling town dominated by a prestigious over-the-top university which in its own famous way is not real. Newhallville is what it is, for better and worse, because it now enjoys a viable, if troubled, interaction order. Interaction orders are what you might expect of people who create and maintain social orders in which members interact with one another in a local well-bordered place. Not always but often they are able to create what to them is a good enough degree of order—an order in which the interactions allow social relations to work for some at least, for many in time, if never all the time. Newhallville is an interaction order in this sense. At any given time on any given street things work when the people affected accept or otherwise deal with the troubles they face—as best they can.

Truth be told, all communities, to varying degrees, are fungible interaction orders in the sense that members create what order there can be. When a social interaction order is created against the odds—as most must—they may work no more than well enough. In that sense they are fungible—able to present themselves as possessing the qualities that can be had. In the case of Newhallville today its fungibility rests in its promise—of better homes, stronger knit community relations, even the possibility of redeeming Yale's stalled encroachment on the neighborhood. The Science Park will never be what Winchester Arms was. Nor should it be. The Park is not meant to employ residents of Newhallville. Nor will it turn the neighborhood into an East Rock, much less a Greenwich or a Westport or any other of the superrich towns down the shoreline. These are the communities that are not fungible. They are neither equivalent nor exchangeable for any social order than each other and the few others like them scattered in unreal places around the world. In the world as it is, Newhallville is what a struggling neighborhood can be when capital greed sucks up the best of possible human interactions.

Newhallville, therefore, is unlikely to become America's dream of an ideal community—an ideal that, in and of itself, is little more than a dream. Dream communities—of which in America, Levittown suburbs were its postwar first fantasy—suffered a short life before they became no more than what they were bound to be—mostly forlorn mass-produced homes meant for those who can afford no better. Plus which it was soon discovered that in the Cold War era for the housewives abandoned during the day with no work and no place to go they were a nightmare.[10] Even the better ones held to the unspeakable belief that these were

---

10 Betty Friedan, *Feminine Mystique* (Basic Books, 1963) is the *locus classicus* of feminist complaints about women in American Suburbs. Elaine Tyler May, *Homeward Bound: American Families in the Cold War Era* (Perseus/ Basic Books, 1988) is (in my opinion) the best study of the issue of Cold War suburban families. There

places where *their* kind of people live—places where the streets are named Cranberry Lane, Willow Court, Strawberry Fields, and after other flora and fauna of their once wild land. These places want to remain the same as other similarly dream-like neighborhoods here and there where people have risen just so far with little hope of going higher. By contrast the Newhallvilles of the world are places where some real hope can be had. They are places of which a fungibly similar place can be found.

A fungible on-the-ground interaction order is necessarily always changing if also becoming much the same again and again. This, it turns out, is a theoretical way of describing one of the six major elements of American culture. In the long century after the Civil War America rose to global prominence on the wings of an astonishing economic growth. By mid-twentieth century, the American economy had overcome the Depression of the 1930s and was fueled for the nation's unheard-of rate of production of military armaments. After 1945 it had leapt to a hitherto unthinkable place as the sole Global Power still standing after World War II—a worldly stature that made Rome seem, if not puny, rather local by comparison. America's sheer economic grip on the world as it was then led in time to its own slump into a degree of confusion about itself. So many were the enticements of postwar affluence that in America the world about seemed not only new but ever changing—household gadgets meant to make homelife and homework easy, shopping malls, the first black-and-white television sets that seemed to bring the world into the living room, and more of such like.

Lonely Crowds, Acted Selves, Suburbs, and a Shocking World Revolution

Post WWII America became sooner than anyone would have guessed a nation largely of consumption consumed people. Which in turn led to a number of high-level social theoretical musings around 1950, of which David Riesman's *The Lonely Crowd* was the runaway bestseller. It was so popular because it seemed to announce a deep structural change in American culture—one in which the new person of the era had abandoned the classic values of pragmatic individuals devoted to progress in favor of a culture in which Americans were more intent upon conforming to social expectations. It was, he thought, a new but ugly culture of conformism. Others in Riesman's day said something similar though without the mild hysteria of *The Lonely Crowd*. Not long after *The Lonely Crowd*, Erving Goffman, in *Presentation of Self in Everyday Life* (1959), wrote of the self as essentially a dramatic performance for and with others. In effect, he eliminated the free personal self as a factor in the individual's dealings with others. Then in 1967, Harold Garfinkel pulled together and advanced emergent ideas in previous writings to put forth a startlingly different, if confusing, program in *Studies in Ethnomethodology* (1967). If to the average reader of social thought, Goffman's ideas were inimitable, Garfinkel's were that and more as he introduced indexicality as crucial to social research—this at a time when such a concept was all but alien in America. It all seemed to many a decline toward nowhere.

Still, Riesman's plainspoken lament was a first sign of a growing transformation in how high and practical social theories viewed America and its culture. In the two plus decades after 1950 that could be said to have culminated in the world revolution of 1968, a new line of thinking reconsidered the classic principle of human being as driven by a soul or self on its head.[11] Early in the 1970s, for example, there appeared a different but fresh line

---

are countless articles and essays on the general subject, as there are for studies of the American suburb, notably Robert C. Wood, *Suburbia: Its People and Politics* (Houghton Mifflin, 1958).

11 Charles Lemert, "A History of Identity: The Riddle at the Heart of the Mystery of Life," in Anthony Elliott, ed, *Routledge Handbook of Identity Studies* (Routledge UK, 2011), 3–29.

of thinking about what by then had become "the Subject." Dorothy Smith's 1974 essay "Knowing a Society from Within: A Woman's Standpoint" is, for many, the *locus classicus* of feminist standpoint theory—a theory that, generally speaking, argued that a woman's subjecthood is shaped by different social factors from those of men. Then began a long line of feminist then queer theoretical studies of identity that culminated in 1990 with Judith Butler's *Gender Trouble: Feminism and the Subversion of Identity*.

Though it might seem that this short history of interaction theories and their entailments diverges awkwardly from a central theme in American social thought, this is the way things happened. World War II so fundamentally changed the modern world-system that had prevailed since roughly 1500 such that the coming new global order after 1950 was, from the first, headed toward dissolution. The Cold War began as early as 1946 with Winston Churchill's declaration of an Iron Curtain descending between East and West. America had become thereafter the last of the modern core states to rule so totally the global system. Russia then China ruled where the United States did not. This, in effect, spelt the coming end of the modern system. In the five centuries from Gutenberg's invention of the moveable type press in the 1440s to the world revolution in the 1960s the modern world arose as a system, at the center of which there were a series of core states that, in effect, controlled the global interaction order.[12] Looked at one way, it is tempting, and not wrong, to suggest that it was the spreading literacy made possible by Gutenberg who began it all—a world that had in common to a kind of endpoint of information saturation, after the 1960s when techno-data all but drowned the world as the popularization of techno-media reached deep into the most marginal of regions and communities. This is not an entirely strange proposition. It was, in fact, the case that global literacy was among the forces that brought the modern world into the consciousness of the global poor which in turn led to a revolutionary consciousness that broke out in, say 1947, when India left Britain's global colonial system. That consciousness spread both horizontally across the globe and vertically into the oppressed sectors of the core states including those of the United States after 1945 and its semi-peripheral allies in Europe and, later, the other Americas. According to Immanuel Wallerstein all this boiled over in 1968 and drowned the system itself with the collapse of the Cold War in 1989–91. Since, and down to present times, it has been far from clear what kind of a world we are living in and where, if anywhere, it is headed.

In a sense, the world as it has become is both disorderly and little else but interactions. Everything has been drifting, even and especially in the once peripheral regions in the Global South. In a word, the capitalist world itself had grown deadly.[13] In such a chaotic global interaction order, where does one turn to find some promise of social order, however fungible? One answer—and by no means the only one—is to geographically local communities like Newhallville where what individual worth one can attain depends on her interactions with others, where interactions are not conforming so much as cooperative, where what order there is is a sometime thing that comes and goes from street to street—to a strangely vital locale where no particular analytic category supports even the possibility of a fixed identity much less a coherent and singular self. One of the several movements in social theory that has helped those with a will to face this world is a band of new ethnographers that came upon the empirical social science scene in the 2010s—a full half century after

---

12 Immanuel Wallerstein, *World-Systems Analysis: An Introduction* (Duke University Press, 2004), among numerous other of his writings.
13 "Exploitative Capitalism in the Global South" and "Capitalism's Zones of Exclusion and Necropolitics" in Kristin Plys and Charles Lemert, *Capitalism and Its Uncertain Future* (Routledge, 2022), 323–353.

Riesman and others posed the question of how the future oriented individual can keep what remains of her individual nature.

The new ethnographers provide a fresh answer to the old theoretical question that in the generations before them had become: *How does the subject survive as subject against the objective forces of the wider society?* Though none of those presented here put it just this way, their answer is: *One survives by becoming part of an interaction order that is always and ever real when it takes place on the ground of daily life with others.* These new ethnographers are part of a wide movement that transformed urban ethnography from its roots in a rather placid, even monotonic community studies. Each in his or her different way takes the local urban neighborhood as the subject of field work—field work that issues less in a general descriptive community study than in the empirical study of interactions that, for better and sometimes worse, allow heroic if flawed people to contend with their experiences as punished boys, people evicted from their homes, and those who lived precariously against insults of poverty and drug dealing, fugitives, and similar life crises. The titles of the books representing the new ethnographers tell the story of how each digs into the structural actions of American cities: *No Way Out: Precarious Living in the Shadow of Poverty and Drug Dealing* (by Waverly Duck), *Punished: Policing the Lives of Black and Latino Boys* (by Victor Rios), *Evicted: Poverty and Profit in the American City* (by Matthew Desmond), *On the Run: Fugitive Life in an American City* (by Alice Goffman).

David Riesman's Lonely Other-Directed People

David Riesman (1909–2002) was born in Philadelphia. He was educated at Harvard College and Harvard Law School. He had a short but prominent career in the law as a Supreme Court Clerk for Justice Louis Brandeis, as an assistant district attorney in New York for Thomas Dewey, and as a law school professor at the University of Chicago. It would seem that this University looked down on his popularizing teaching to courses packed with undergraduate students. Still it was there that he wrote and published *The Lonely Crowd* in 1950 before moving, in 1956, to Harvard's Department of Social Relations as Ford Professor of Social Sciences. There he taught another popular course, "American Character and Social Structure" obviously thereby organized around the central theoretical themes of *The Lonely Crowd*.

The Lonely Crowd in 1950 was not a deeply theoretical book, much less one that could be said to have anticipated in so many words the concept of an interaction order. In truth, an underlying theoretical resource of the book was Max Weber's classic distinction between traditional and modern rational cultures of legitimate authority. For Riesman, Weber's types were the basis for his three types of social character: traditional, inner-directed, other-directed. Still, these types are easily seen as deep background to Riesman's own general notion of social character as "that part of 'character' which is shared among significant social groups and which, as most contemporary social scientists define it, is the product of the experience of these group."[14] *The Lonely Crowd* is often considered an interpretative

---

14 Riesman, *The Lonely Crowd* (Yale University Press, 1969 [1950]), 4. In many ways Riesman's use of *social character* is a concept borrowed in part from psychoanalysts interested in social problems. As a result, Riesman begins *The Lonely Crowd* with a section "Character and Society" that follows his mention of Erich Fromm and Karen Horney, among others (including anthropologists with a working knowledge of psychoanalysis like Margaret Mead). This before beginning the section "Character and Society" in which Erik Erikson provides an empirical definition of social character among Yurok Indians as "unconscious attempts at creating out of human raw material that configuration of attitudes which is (or once was) the optimum under the tribe's particular natural conditions, and economic-historic necessities." See Riesman, *ibid*, 5.

but popular account of American social character in the postwar era. It is that, but much more. Riesman's comparative categories, while in one sense Weberian, also anticipated W.W. Rostow's *The Stages of Economic Growth* (1960) in which the transition from tradition to early stages of growth was followed by "the drive of economic maturity" and "the stage of mass-consumption." Rostow doesn't mentioned Riesman who seems to have driven on the same track, for example:

> The society of high growth potential develops in its typical members a social character whose conformity is insured by their tendency to follow tradition: these I shall term tradition-directed people and the society in which they live a society dependent on tradition-direction. The society of transitional population growth develops in its typical members a social character whose conformity is insured by their tendency to acquire early in life an internalized set of goals. These I shall term inner-directed people and the society in which they live a society dependent on inner-direction. Finally, the society of incipient population decline develops in its typical members a social character whose conformity is insured by their tendency to be sensitized to the expectations and preferences of others. These I shall term other-directed people. ...[15]

None of these suppositions turned-out to be earth shaking. Yet, they suggest how Riesman toyed with the concept of social character in a fashion that for the most part avoided all the false dichotomizing of couplets like subject/object and micro-macro, and the like. *The Lonely Crowd* was the best-selling sociology book in the twentieth century. Just the same, its notion of social character has not been recognized for its distinctive manner of using the psychoanalytic notion of character as a divisible aspect of human consciousness able to expose its social side to the influence of the group and society in general.

Nevertheless, if not intentionally, Riesman's scheme foretold the concept of fungible interaction orders. While not a theorist as such, there are theoretically rich sections of *The Lonely Crowd*. For one example, in Chapter 12 ("Adjustment or Autonomy?") he inserts Durkheim's anomie into his own tripartite formula to make the vital qualification that the types he deploys are not fixed and impermeable:

> These three universal types (the adjusted, the anomic, the autonomous), like our three historical types (tradition-directed, inner-directed, and other-directed) are, in Max Weber's sense, "ideal types," that is, constructions necessary for analytical work. Every human being will be one of these types to some degree; but no one could be completely characterized by any one of these terms.[16]

The book thereby is wound around and around the dynamics of these analytic types. This is what gives the book its literary texture and made it of such broad and enduring value to readers of all kinds (even a lesser number of hard-core academics found it intriguing and teachable).

The spine of *The Lonely Crowd* is the American social character that holds together the tissues of Riesman's analytic body of topics—from parenting to teaching of children, from storytelling to mass media, from craft skill to manipulative and from free trade to fair trade (these being the elements of what he calls the difference between the inner-directed round

---

15 *Ibid*, 8.
16 *Ibid*, 243; for Durkheim, 240ff.

of life and the other-directed), from the wheat bowl to the salad bowl (figures for the two types of food and of consumption—including sex), and much more. Just these few elements suggest the degree to which *The Lonely Crowd* is an argument built out of popular cultural references and allusions. These are why it was such a popular read in its day, down until the present when all of this seems to have been covered by the shadow of meta-technologies that make the very idea of an inner-directed personage all but a wisp of a faint past.

Yet in the day, when the distinction was a matter of some urgency, Riesman's method (if that is the word) was that it served to compare the contrasting interaction orders between inner- and other-directed social characters. For example, the interaction order of inner-direction parenting:

> We may say, then, that parents who are themselves inner-directed install a *psychological gyroscope* in their child and set it going; it is built to their own and other authoritative specifications; if the child has good luck, the governor will spin neither too fast, with the danger of hysteric outcomes, nor too slow, with the danger of social failure.[17]

Against the psychological gyroscope, other-directed parenting installs a psychological radar set—which is "a device not tuned to control movement in any particular direction while guiding and steadying the person from within but rather tuned to detect the action, and especially the symbolic action, of others."[18] As a result, according to Riesman, other-directed parents send out enduring signals that may be attuned to signals in the social environment. This, of course, means that the other-directed parent has far less control over the child as she moves eventually out of the family home. This and other of the interaction orders that run through *The Lonely Crowd* work by juxtaposing the order such as it is in the two different types of social character.

Shortly after Riesman died May 10, 2002, his close Harvard colleagues said that he "was an interpretive sociologist who drew upon more specialized work and on other disciples ... in his effort to distinguish forest from trees. His craft was distinguished by his remarkable curiosity about all aspects of American life, his meticulous interviewing and recording, and his skillful use of insights gained from pointed discussions and a vast correspondence with persons from all walks of life."[19] Riesman was nothing if not deeply attentive to American life in the years before 1950. It is unlikely to be an accident that George Orwell's *1984* was published in 1949. The ghost of new social order was disquietingly in the air.

Erik Erikson: Personal Identity at Risk in a Conflict-Ridden Society

Such a ghost haunted others about the same time. One was Erik Erikson (1902–1994) who was born in Frankfurt. His mother, a Jewish-Dane, moved from Copenhagen to Germany while pregnant, leaving her estranged husband. Erik, who grew up in Germany, may well have suffered his own identity confusion due to the estrangement of his parents. He broke off his education in Germany to wander about, then to work with young children of parents who were in analysis with Anna Freud. Upon noticing his care in dealing with children, Freud encouraged him to consider becoming a psychoanalyst. He took up the trade, training

---

17 *Ibid*, 45. Emphasis added.
18 *Ibid*, 55.
19 Daniel Bell, Nathan Glazer, Christopher Jencks, Ezra Vogel, Orlando Patterson, *Memorial Minute Read to Harvard Faculty*, October 13, 2003.

at the Vienna Psychoanalytic Institute. Erikson moved to the United States in 1930 and rose quickly in the ranks of American analysts.

In 1950, Erikson published *Childhood and Society* in which he applied his psychoanalytic theory of the eight stages of psychological development. For Erikson, the psychoanalyst, the stage (or "age" as he put it) most aggravated in postwar America was youth, during when an individual struggles with the tension between identity and role confusion—or, otherwise put, when the new youth in the day faced a conflict-ridden social experience of different social expectations. Here, in particular, Erikson makes historical sense of the book's title, *Childhood and Society*:

> All countries and especially large ones complicate their own progress with the very premises of their beginnings. We must try to formulate the way in which self-contradictions in American history may expose her youth to an emotional and political short circuit and thus endanger her dynamic potential.[20]

In a more academically precise, if not entirely different, manner, Erikson, like Riesman, presents his arguments through case studies and comments on aspects of then-prevailing American cultural attitudes toward childhood. Two Indian communities (the Sioux and the Yurok) are the subject of Part Two. Legends of Hitler's childhood and Maxim Gorky's youth are the subjects of chapters 9 and 10 which comprise the penultimate section of the book. Then too there are shorter vignettes—the case of Jean, an early ego failure; toys and reasons (chapters 5 and 6 meant to illustrate Part Three, The Growth of the Ego); and more throughout. Some of these are the customary psychoanalytic method of case presentations; but others reach to what Riesman called social character.

None of these is more poignant than the key chapter 8 in Part Four, Youth and American Identity, on parental relations with children and youth. The subject is important enough that some years later in what Erikson labels an Afterthought in the 1985 edition of *Childhood and Society*, he reviews what over the years he still considered the key issue, beginning with a remarkable statement: "So let me now, again, reflect on one of the truly original 'nuclear conflicts' in human life, namely the role of *motherhood* and *fatherhood*, and relate it to what to us has now become the all-encompassing danger of nuclear armament."[21] To which one might reasonably say: What? Parenting as a nuclear conflict that, he seems to say, is at the heart of the postwar threat of nuclear war, and more. For example:

> Our psychoanalytic references to the conflict of two parental types dominant in modern nations with the dilemma of an all-influential *American "Mom"* and an, at times, historically destructive parental type of the *German father*. "Momism" was said to represent a composite image of traits none of which could be present all at once in a single woman" (page 289) but, to quote here one generalization "Mother" became 'Mom' only when Father became 'Pop' under the impact of identical historical discontinuities. For, if you come down to it, Momism is only misplaced paternalism.[22]

Though the book itself naturally gives a great deal more detail, it is plain to see that Erikson's general idea is the interaction order between parents and their post-puberty (when youth

---

20 Erik Erikson, *Childhood and Society* (W.W. Norton, 1950), 287.
21 Erik Erikson, "Afterthoughts 1985," *Childhood and Society* (W.W. Norton, 1985 [1950]), 9.
22 *Ibid*, 9. Passage, including the interior quote, refers to page 289 in the 1950 edition where he first introduces the cultural role of "Mom" or momism in American culture.

begins)[23] children is the crucial turning point in an individual's personal development. The developmental tension between identity and role confusion is the definitive adolescent stage when a youth's relationship to parents and the world determines whether or not he [sic][24] matures into an adult who knows who he is or who is confused about himself and the world about. Implicit to *Childhood and Society* is that the ability of a child to learn how to function well in society is that he (and in principle she) manages the conflictual dynamic to move from parental authority to an autonomous person.

Erikson's book is rooted in the same historical moment Riesman meant to explain. In its way *Childhood and Society* is the better book, except for the fact that *The Lonely Crowd* provides the better, if more general, description of the new social character that entails a fungible interaction order in which what happens on the ground in families and communities can transform itself into a different interaction order that may or may not have been for the better. Just the same, they are driving at a similar if not the same point and each contributes to a set of facts that historically, and analytically, contribute to the later theory of interaction orders and how they are vulnerable to change.

Edwin Lemert: Social Pathology and Secondary Deviance

Edwin M. Lemert (1912–1996) was born in Cincinnati, Ohio, to a family that aspired to the upper classes. His father, a successful insurance agent, managed to do just this by moving to Cincinnati's prestigious Eastern Hills. Edwin studied at Miami University in Ohio where he studied with Reed Bain and Fred Cottrell, the leading lights of sociology at the school. Instead of studying for the law as his parents expected, Lemert set out for travel to the West and Mexico and tried a turn at amateur boxing. He was, thereby, the black sheep in his family. In 1939, he took his PhD in Sociology at Ohio State University. After, he made his way to the University of California Los Angeles before becoming founding chair of sociology at UC Davis.

In 1951, Lemert published *Social Pathology: A Systematic Approach to the Theory of Sociopathic Behavior* in which he invented what came to be called labelling theory. Lemert's important idea was the distinction between primary and secondary deviation. Here the interaction order is plain to see. Any individual might engage in any number of socially deviant acts—excessive drinking, petty stealing, an occasional tough-guy punch. This is primary deviation (where Lemert defines deviation as "other than normal in a statistical sense"). These behaviors remain primary so long as:

> ...the deviant individuals ... react symbolically to their own behavior aberrations and fix them in their sociopsychological patterns. The deviations remain primary deviations or symptomatic as long as they are rationalized or otherwise dealt with as functions of a socially acceptable role.[25]

The bully for example can mend his ways or the sexually loose girl can change her ways. But the deviation becomes secondary when a person identifies himself to himself as a tough guy or loose girl thinks of herself as just that way. When the one becomes a gangster and

---

23 *Ibid*, 261.
24 [sic] ... because in his day and perhaps still, the issue, according to psychoanalytic theory, seems to be true of boys more than girls.
25 Edwin M. Lemert, *Social Pathology: A Systematic Approach to the Theory of Sociopathic Behavior* (McGraw Hill, 1951), 75. The definition of primary deviation as "other than normal in a statistical sense" is on page 447.

the other a working girl their deviations are secondary. "When a person begins to employ his deviant behavior or a role based on it as a means of defense, attack, or adjustment to the overt and covert problems created by the consequent societal reaction to him, his deviation becomes secondary."[26] This then is the societal reaction theory of deviance. The thorough-going out of the closet secondary deviant is one who accepts society's definition of his or her identity—an identity that began primarily as a sort of accidental slip toward a deviant behavior out from which she or he could climb. Secondary deviance is when the individual cannot take back his fall into a selfhood by which the same individual has come to be known by social others in his or her circle.

One of Lemert's more famous illustrations of his societal reaction theory is his empirical account of check forgers or "check-men" as they identified themselves. They had deployed their own method of passing bad checks. Because of the secrecy required they had to keep their identity hidden which meant moving on from bank to bank. As a result, if those who may have started by passing bad checks from time to time while maintaining an otherwise normal life routine, once they became check-men their lives were necessarily and utterly organized around this activity—which is to say they were always on the move. The important and surprising result of Lemert's interviews with check-men in prison was that they differed from other criminals in that they were cooperative upon arrest and during adjudication and were model prisoners upon conviction. Lemert explained this by the unusual societal circumstances of their profession:

> Systematic check-forgers do not seem to have had criminal associations. For this as well as for technical reasons, they are not likely to seek out or to be comfortable in informal associations with other criminals who have been products of early and lengthy socialization and learning in a criminal subculture. It also follows that their morality and values remain essentially "middle" or "upper" class and that they seldom integrate these with the morality of the professional criminal. ... In addition to these factors, the class characteristics and backgrounds of systematic forgers inclines them to avoid intimate association with other criminals.[27]

In a word, the systematic check-forger was a loner, never able to exhibit to others his exceptional criminal skill. Today check-forgers are no longer what once they were. Forgery as such has become not a matter of passing paper but of internet-based criminal theft.

Interestingly, Erving Goffman turns to Lemert in the key chapter in *Stigma*, "The Self and Its Other" to say, at first, that he rejects Lemert's seemingly limited view of the secondary deviant as having been forced into a seemingly permanent and isolating identity.[28] Then, just after this remark, Goffman turns Lemert on his head by citing an essay in which Lemert had said that the number of deviants could be as high as one wanted to make it.[29] This to

---

26 *Ibid*, 76.
27 Edwin Lemert, "The Behavior of the Systematic Check Forger," *Social Problems* 6:2 (Fall 1958), 147. For easier reference to this paper in the context of Lemert's work as a whole, see Charles C. Lemert and Michael F. Winter, eds., *Crime and Deviance: Essays and Innovations of Edwin M. Lemert* (Rowman and Littlefield, 2000), 93–103 (chapter 9, "Fast-Living, Big Spending, a Life on the Edge: The Check Forger").
28 Goffman's comment is on the extreme individuation in Lemert's discussion of the secondary deviant in *Social Pathology* (75–76). Goffman's quibble with Lemert on this point is in Erving Goffman, *Stigma: Notes on the Management of Spoiled Identity* (Simon & Schuster, 1963), 127 (footnote to *Social Pathology*).
29 Goffman's second Lemert reference is to "Some Aspects of a General Theory of Sociopathic Behavior," *Proceedings of the Pacific Sociological Society*, Research Studies, State College of Washington, 16:1 (1948), 23–29.

Lemert, Goffman follows with his entertainingly wild line to the effect that almost no one is normal: "In an important sense there is only one completely unblushing male in America: a young, married, white, urban, northern, heterosexual Protestant father of college education, fully employed, of good complexion, weight and height, and a recent record in sports."[30]

Erving Goffman: The Performed Self in an Interaction Order

Erving Goffman (1922–1982) was born in Manville, Alberta and passed the better part of his youth and early adulthood in Canada, studying in Manitoba while also being engaged for several years with the National Film Board of Canada in Ottawa. By 1945 he had earned a BA in sociology and anthropology at the University of Toronto, after which he pursued graduate studies at the University of Chicago where he did fieldwork in a small town in the Shetlands, which became his 1953 doctoral thesis ("Communication Conduct in an Island Community"). It would not be wrong to suggest that whatever else may have created his unusual sociological eye, Goffman's time in small towns in Canada and Scotland lent him the gift of being outside the busy world while looking in.

The Shetlands fieldwork and thesis became *The Presentation of Self in Everyday Life*—very possibly the *locus classicus* of interaction order theory. *Presentation* first appeared in 1956 as a research paper at the University of Edinburgh's Social Science Research Centre, before being published in 1959 by Doubleday/Anchor. It was, however, preceded by two classical essays—"Cooling the Mark Out: Some Aspect of Adaptation to Failure" and "On Face-work: An Analysis of Ritual Elements in Social Interaction."[31] Then too, in respect to Goffman's important early writings on the self's interaction with others, there is *Stigma: Notes on the Management of Spoiled Identity* in 1963. Few others have produced such an original and out-of-the-mainstream corpus of original theoretical texts.

The first, "Cooling the Mark Out," was published before even *Presentation of Self* was a finished draft of the doctoral thesis. It is important to say that this essay, in particular, is a case that ought to embarrass today's sociology with all its fandangled scholarly apparatus—lit review, hypothesis, method, findings, conclusions, etc. Goffman, the graduate student, here writes what would become a scholarly classic without any of this. Plus which, there are no data, to speak of. He simply writes in elaborate detail about a phenomenon he assumes a reader will understand—and here is the key to Goffman's literary and theoretical genius. He assumes that a normal adult reader knows what he has in mind and can be made to rethink it in his terms.

"Cooling the Mark Out" begins with a sketch of the phenomenon at hand. The mark is one who is victim to a confidence game that costs him money or some other tangible valuable. Goffman begins with the slim sort of empirical reference he often makes: "The con is said to be a good racket in the United States only because most Americans are willing, nay eager, to make easy money and will engage in any action that is less that legal."[32] The con-game is described as beginning with a "potential sucker" whose confidence is won by being given a chance to make easy money if he reinvests his gains. After several rounds of investment, suddenly the mark finds he has lost it all. The confidence team then disappears.

---

30 Goffman, *Stigma*, 128.
31 Erving Goffman, "Cooling the Mark Out: Some Aspect of Adaptation to Failure," *Psychiatry* 15:4 (1952), 451–463; and: "On Face-work: An Analysis of Ritual Elements in Social Interaction," *Psychiatry* 18:3 (1955), 213–231. "On Face-work" was later republished in Goffman's *Interaction Ritual* (Anchor Books, 1967), 5–45.
32 "Cooling the Mark Out," in Charles Lemert and Ann Branaman, eds., *The Goffman Reader* (Blackwell Publishers, 1997), 3.

Then follows more than twenty journal pages of *explication* of the mark as an individual, beginning with the following:

> For the purposes of analysis, one may think of the individual in reference to the values or attributes of a socially recognized character which he possesses. Psychologists speak of a value as a personal involvement. Sociologists speak of a value as status, role, or relationship. In either case, the character of the value that is possessed is taken in a certain way as the character of the person who possesses it.[33]

Clearly Goffman's idea of social character is different from those of Riesman, Erikson, and Lemert in that his locates the individual's social character as neither in the individual nor given to him by society but an attribution assigned to the individual by his or her interaction in a social setting. This, of course, is the underlying notion of *Presentation of Self*. But staying with "Cooling the Mark Out" suggests just how Goffman develops the desiderata of how a mark is cooled out and what happens when he won't budge from the scene. Perhaps the most interesting is the first of the ways a person can deal with the end of an involvement:

> He may withdraw from one of his involvements or roles in order to acquire a sequentially related one that is considered better. This is the case when a youth becomes a man, when a student becomes a practitioner, or when a man from the ranks is given a commission.[34]

Goffman here has passed from the mark and the confidence man to a more general issue—one that turns out to be the first full-blown instance (if not by name) of the fungible interaction order. The man, the practitioner, and the commissioner all have, by implication, at least advanced to different but still fungibly comparable characters arising from an interaction order. One example of the authority, so to speak, of the mark in the relationship is he may "go into business for himself" by organizing his own con-game—a practice meant to establish a status similar to the one he has lost, as when the mark is rejected in a marriage "makes a better remarriage." That this is the anticipation of an interaction order is found in Goffman's surprising statement of fungibility that "... a mark can refuse to be cooled out [which can] have consequences for other persons."[35] Whether he does or not, the game has consequences for both parties. Goffman's article ends with a number of instances of the dilemma entailed, for example: "In the United States, the jobs of waitress, cab driver, and night watchman, and the profession of prostitution, tend to be ending places where persons of certain kinds, starting from different places, can come to rest."[36]

Three years after "Cooling the Mark Out," in 1955, Goffman published "Face-work" which is an outgrowth of the scheme that bloomed in *Presentation of Self*. Here, Goffman keeps with his method of writing about a now universally recognizable phenomenon without the bother of "data" so-called, not even anecdotes that sometimes sneak into other books. Just the same in "Face-work" Goffman provides one of his most memorable ironies: "Universal human nature is not a very human thing. By acquiring it the person becomes a kind of construct built up not from inner psychic propensities but from moral rules that are impressed upon him from without."[37] That this irony was later published in

---

33 *Ibid*, 5.
34 *Ibid*, 6.
35 *Ibid*, 14.
36 *Ibid*, 19.
37 Goffman, "On Face-work," in *Interaction Order* (Anchor Books, 1967), 45.

Goffman's *Interaction Ritual: Essays on Face-to-Face Behavior* (1967) is important because it also serves as an early form of his concept of interaction rituals that, in turn, served in later writings to transcend the impression that face-to-face interactions can be reduced to social psychology.

"On Face-work," otherwise, could also be viewed as a development of the scheme in "On Cooling Out the Mark." Goffman was not, like other social theorists, inclined to compose a literary trajectory that led to a strong position or a school of thought. He was nothing if not indifferent to anything of this sort. Still, it would not be wrong to view "On Face-work" as an early step toward clarifying a theory of face-to-face behavior for which, as he put it, this hitherto unclear subject can be sketched but not well defined: "It is that class of events which occurs during co-presence and by virtue of co-presence."[38] This line is little more than what some might see as mere repetition. But it is one thing to stipulate "co-presence" as the subject matter, and something more to add that "co-presence" is the *cause* of the phenomenon.

Co-presence, however, turns out to be the occasion whereby the individual can develop a "line" which is where a "face" can be claimed. Or, it is "the positive social value a person effectively claims for himself by the line others assume he has taken in a particular contact."[39] Goffman adds later on: "Members of every social circle may be expected to have some knowledge of face-work and some experience of its use."[40] Here he reverts to a very practical sense of knowledge, "sometimes called tact, *savoir-faire*, diplomacy, or social skill" whereby a person loses face by making a "*faux pas, gaffe*, a boner, or brick" (again Goffman's reliance on ordinary language to describe his phenomena). One who has lost face then has two choices—either to be defensive in order to save his own face or protective by saving the other's face, or both. When a basketball player, for example, wildly misses a long shot she can either look at the ground as if she had slipped or pat the butt of a mate as if the other is forgiven for not taking the shot in the first place. The essay goes on at length to reveal the details of face-saving work.

The details of these early writings reappear full blown in *Presentation of Self* in 1959, which is also the first major book in which he reverts to a more scholarly presentation (likely because it came to be as a doctoral thesis at the University of Chicago). Yet, alongside footnotes to academic texts there are also ample references to popular writings, anecdotes, and high literature—as when he offers a passage from Evelyn Waugh in which he describes the performance rituals of the elite class or from Kafka's *The Trial* when he describes K's sense of being out of place when the inspector does not encourage to sit for the interview.[41] Yet, his nods to formal academic practices serve to support what can fairly be called his analytic presentation which is clearly outlined in the chapter headers: Performances (1), Teams (2), Regions and Region Behavior (3), Discrepant Roles (4), Communication Out of Character (5), The Arts of Impression Management (6).

"Regions and Region Behavior" is central to a dramaturgical model whereby the self presents a performance of the impression she wants the audience at hand to see. This region is, in effect, the stage. The backstage is where the individual keeps secret those aspects of the self not to be known by a given audience. For example upon a first meeting with a potential date one does not want the other to know that he is still in a sexual relationship with a third. If the date leads to a relationship, he may have a good reason to share the truth about his

---

38 *Ibid*, 1.
39 *Ibid*, 5.
40 *Ibid*, 13.
41 Goffman, *Presentation of Self in Everyday Life* (Anchor Books, 1959), 100 (Waugh) and 96 (Kafka). "K" is the lead character in Kafka's novel.

sexual background, if for example the other confesses that she is having an affair. Some secrets, however, are truly dark as when a member of a new relationship had been either a pimp or a street girl to pay for college (for example). The backstage secrets are important in that whether or not, or how, the secrets are revealed, they have everything to do with how an impression is managed. With rare exception, selves are performed before others, either in the moment or over time as word gets around. Hence, she who presents her-self requires a team that shares for a time at least certain defensive attributes and practices, of which are dramaturgical loyalty, discipline, and circumspection.[42] Circumspection is the practical attitude of anticipating changes that require a change in the joint performance, as when—in an example Goffman gives—a fellow teacher refuses to enter the active classroom of a colleague for fear of disrupting his performance. Goffman concludes his discussion of impression management with a wonderfully apt statement of the dramaturgical: "Shared staging problems; concern for the way things appear; warranted and unwarranted feelings of shame; ambivalence about oneself and one's audience: these are some of the dramaturgic elements of the human situation."[43] Goffman was not known personally to be an emotional sympathetic man, but here is about the best possible comment on the emotional element in an interaction order.[44]

Stigma, four years later, completes the early formulation of his view of what is now called the fungible interaction order. As he says in concluding the book:

> In conclusion, may I repeat that stigma involves not so much a set of concrete individuals who can be separated into two piles, the stigmatized and the normal, as a pervasive two-role social process in which every individual participates in both roles, at least in some connections and phases of life.[45]

Yet, this was far from his last word, though sadly his last word was in his American Sociological Association presidential address (that was read by Robert K. Merton because Erving Goffman's stomach cancer had disabled him), "The Interaction Order." Unsurprisingly, he complicates the very idea:

> In speaking of the interaction order I have so far presupposed the term "order," and an account is called for. I mean to refer in the first instance to a domain of activity—a particular kind of activity, as in the phrase, "the economic order." No implications are intended concerning how "orderly" such activity ordinarily is, or the role of norms and rules in supporting such orderliness as does obtain. Yet, it appears to me that *as an order of activity*, the interaction one, more than any other perhaps, is in fact orderly, and that this orderliness is predicated on a large base of shared cognitive presuppositions, if not normative ones, and self-sustained restraints.[46]

There could hardly be a better, more fungible benedictory conclusion to an idea and to the man himself. To the very end Goffman always looked for fresh angles on the issue at hand, the truth of which was never settled.

---

42 *Ibid*, 212–228.
43 *Ibid*, 237.
44 For a particularly clear and pungent summary of Goffman's concept of the interaction order that rejects the primacy of autonomous structural effect, see Anne Rawls, "The Interaction Order Sui Generis: Goffman's Contribution to Social Theory," *Sociological Theory* 5:2 (1987): 136–149.
45 Goffman, *Stigma*, 137–138.
46 Goffman, "The Interaction Order," *American Sociological Review* 89:1 (1983): 1–17. The passage is in a selection from the same article, reprinted in Lemert and Branaman, *The Goffman Reader*, 240.

Harold Garfinkel: Indexical Expressions and the Artful Practices of Everyday Life

Harold Garfinkel (1917–2011) was born in Newark, New Jersey, to a Jewish family of modest means. His early education through college at the University of Newark (later Rutgers) was in and around Newark. In the day, courses at the University of Newark were often taught by Columbia graduate students who introduced Garfinkel to high-level theoretical cultures not normally offered in a then very local college. In due course, he learned of the University of North Carolina's graduate program in sociology where he took a master's degree after interrupting studies in 1942 to serve in the Air Force during the Second World War.

From there, having become familiar with Talcott Parsons's theoretical program, he went on to doctoral studies at Harvard in 1947. During the Harvard years, Garfinkel taught for two years at Princeton, where he helped organize a Ford Foundation conference that brought major innovative theorists to campus, notable among them was Alfred Schutz whose phenomenological theory—who combined with Parsons to lend him a most unusual combination of early influences! Garfinkel's varied sources suggest the extent to which he became the most idiosyncratically original of social theorists. Curiously, in 1941 Garfinkel published a short story, "Color Trouble,"[47] which is curious to his development because its plot concerned a seldom recognized theme of his work, race—and because as fiction it represents the basic themes of his social theory.

Looking back over the years, readers may well be intrigued by the fact that Garfinkel's first major book length manuscript of social theory, *Seeing Sociologically: The Routine Grounds of Social Action* (2006 [1948]), was written while he was a graduate student at Harvard. In this text (recently published by Anne Rawls) Garfinkel began (predictably) with reference to his teacher Talcott Parsons's key idea *action*, then turns to a longer phenomenological reference to Alfred Schutz's 1945 essay "On Multiple Realities."[48] Just before this, Garfinkel introduces *Seeing Sociologically* with what he calls the "home plate" of his early theory:

> First, the leading aim of this project is to translate the concept of the social relationship into the terms of communicative effort between actors. Second, our is to study this communicative endeavor with regard to contents, organizations of meanings, the processes and logics of communicative expressions, and the tactics of communication and understanding using the fact that the experience of incongruity can be experimentally induced as the means for teasing these various facets out of the closely woven fabric of social intercourse.[49]

While neither pure Parsons nor simple Schutz, the passage works between the two by introducing communication as basic to what Goffman two decades later would call the interaction order, with a notable mention of *incongruity* which anticipates Garfinkel's use of reflexivity in his ethnomethodological program. Later in the same book he elaborates on the communicative kernel of interaction studies.[50] Here he makes the sociologically incongruous statement that all-but-eliminates the formal concept of a personal communicating subject:

---

47 Garfinkel, "Color Trouble," in Edward J. O'Brien, ed., *The Best Short Stories 1941* (Houghton Mifflin, 1941), 97–119.
48 Anne Rawls, "Respecifying the Study of Social Order," in Garfinkel, *Seeing Sociologically: The Routine Grounds of Social Action* (Routledge/Paradigm, 2006 [1948]), 101–107.
49 Garfinkel, *Seeing Sociologically*, 99–100.
50 *Ibid*, 179–188.

From the actor's point of view social communication takes place between an identified self and an identified other. From an observer's point of view communication takes place between actors where "actors" means the animal symbolicum employing a cognitive style. The concept of communication has nothing whatsoever to do with the concept of concrete person, except that *one cannot say* the communication occurs between "concrete persons." For the scientist "concrete person" is a reification of the possibilities he entertains as "fulfillable" that an object occupies exactly the same logical status as *io* [= identified other].[51]

Early in graduate studies, Garfinkel defied the basic idea of his mentor's (Parsons) concept of systemic actor.

Studies in Ethnomethodology (1967) begins with an arguably better definition of his program: "I use the term "ethnomethodology" to refer to the investigation of the rational properties of indexical expressions and other practical actions as contingent ongoing accomplishments of organized artful practices of everyday life."[52] In the same place, he explains the importance of constantly changing indexical elements in the communications that take place in what others came to call the interaction order. Here the difference from Goffman's idea is the introduction of *indexicality* by which Garfinkel means to make available for better understanding the (scientific) observer's reified "concrete person"—as, in effect, one who is not there in the real interaction order but created by the scientific observer. Here is where Garfinkel turns what he calls "Durkheim's aphorism" on its ear. The aphorism is Durkheim's idea that sociology begins with social facts[53] that are, according to Garfinkel, perversely related to ethnomethodology:

[You] can use Ethnomethodology to recover in ordered phenomenal details the accountable work that makes up, in and as its work sites the design, administration, and carrying off of investigations with the use of formal analytic practices. These are recovered as the phenomenal field properties of the investigation's procedural ordered appearances. You can't do it the other way around. That is to say, you can't use the methods of formal analysis to recover the work and the findings that Ethnomethodology is coming up with. So EM's [Ethnomethodology's Method] takes on *Durkheim's aphorism indeed they are not only alternate they are asymmetrically alternate. And that they are asymmetrically related is itself a social fact.*[54]

Or, as Anne Rawls puts this: "Ethnomethodology understands Durkheim's aphorism differently. Ethnomethodology has been respecifying Durkheim's aphorism so that it reads differently. 'The objective reality of social facts' is sociology's fundamental *phenomenon*."[55] Either way, Garfinkel's is an amazingly coherent statement when you think about it.

---

51 *Ibid*, 180. Emphasis added. Note: *io* is an algebraic symbol for "identified other" that Garfinkel deploys in series of analytic formulae early in the book; *Ibid*, 166.
52 *Studies in Ethnomethodology* (Prentice-Hall, 1967), 11.
53 Durkheim first stated this aphorism in *Rules for Sociological Method* (1895) and applied in his empirical study of *Suicide* (1897). Also, for an interesting discussion of Durkheim by an important scholar of Garfinkel's work, see Anne W. Rawls / Émile Durkheim, *De la Division du Travail Social: Vers une théorie sociologique de la justice* (Paris: LE BORD DE L'EAU: la bibliothèque de Mauss, 2019).
54 Harold Garfinkel, *Ethnomethodology's Program / Working Out Durkheim's Aphorism* (Rowman & Littlefield, 2002), 117. Emphasis added.
55 *Ibid*, 66. The allusion to Durkheim's "objective reality of facts" is to his *Rules of Sociological Method* (Free Press, 1982 [1895]), 45.

It turns out that the easiest way to think about Garfinkel's program is in respect to his case reports or phenomenal accounts of empirical fieldwork, several of which appear throughout *Studies in Ethnomethodology*. Most are on institutional settings where formal reports compress a record of what transpired in, for example, clinical settings. Early in the book under "The 'Uninteresting' Essential Reflexivity of Accounts" he analyzes records in the *Los Angeles Suicide Prevention Center* for the way they "to produce, accomplish, recognize, or demonstrate rational-adequacy-for-all-practical-purposes of their procedures and findings."[56] In the process, reports omit certain otherwise important facts like how the person discussing her suicide thinks she might do it. In order to make a proper clinical report a good deal of editing in the reporting and the actual intervention takes place. Otherwise put, the practical reasoning of volunteers is in itself an attempt to repair the indexicality of the clinical conversation. This point is all-the-better made by the oft referred to Chapter 6, "Good organizational reasons for 'bad' clinic records"[57] where the key statement is on clinical records in the Out-Patient Psychiatric Unit of the UCLA Medical Center:

In our view the contents of clinic folders are assembled with regard for the possibility that the relationship may have to be portrayed as having been in accord with expectations of sanctionable performances by clinicians and patients. ... By calling a medical record a "contract" we are not claiming that the record contains only statements of what should have happened as opposed to what did happen. ... Clinic records are consulted upon many different occasions and for many different interests. But for all the different uses to which records may be put and for all the different uses that they serve, considerations of medico-legal responsibility exercise an overriding priority of relevance as prevailing structural interests whenever procedures for the maintenance of records and their eligible contents must be decided.[58]

The point is that the very reporting of clinical data entails a good degree of trouble in respect to the facts of the matter because there are so many others who have a stake in the contract implied by the report itself—patients, persons referred to in the report, those who contributed to the report, and so on.[59] These are the organizational factors that make the reports "bad" clinical records.

Here it is important to say that whatever else it may be, *Studies in Ethnomethodology* is also about the relation between Garfinkel's method and sociological methods. The first words of the book are: "In doing sociology, lay and professional, every reference to the 'real world,' even where the reference is to physical or biological events, is a reference to the organized activities of everyday life."[60] Thus at the end the book returns to this question in Chapter 8, "Rational Properties of Scientific and Commonsense Activities" where Alfred Schutz's phenomenology served to draw a direct line between scientific and commonplace reasoning based on the sensibilities that link while distinguishing them. The book's concluding idea: "Instead of the properties of rationality being treated as a methodological principle for interpreting activity, they are to be treated only as empirically problematical

---

56 Garfinkel, *Studies in Ethnomethodology*, 8.
57 Anne Rawls, in her brief bio of Garfinkel, has uncovered the fact that at the University of Newark he studied some insurance and business courses that, she observes, were the first source of this famous chapter. See Rawls, "Harold Garfinkel," George Ritzer, ed., *The Blackwell Companion to Major Social Theorists* (Blackwell Publishing 2000), 555–556.
58 *Studies in Ethnomethodology*, 199–200.
59 *Ibid*, 206.
60 *Ibid*, vii.

material. They would have the status only of data and would have to be accounted for in the same way that the more familiar properties of conduct are accounted for."[61] Before which he offers a relatively clear statement of the fungibility of interaction orders:

> The person assumes a particular "form of sociality." Among other things the form of sociality consists of the person's assumption that some characteristic disparity exists between the "image" of himself that he attributes to the other person as that person's knowledge of him, and the knowledge that he has of himself in the "eyes" of the other person. He assumes too that alterations of this characteristic disparity remain within his autonomous control.[62]

It is not far wrong to say that, for Garfinkel, practical sociological reasoning is the basic social fact of ethnomethodology's attempt to repair the indexicality of the communications of "real" (so to speak) actors. Not unashamedly a coherent program, but it serves a purpose for those willing to meditate on it.

Order and Disorder and the Fungibility of All Social Things

It almost goes without saying that it would be impossible for human beings to live together unless there is some stable order that they agree to respect. At the same time, social orders, whether small or grand, come unglued more often than one would hope. At the worst they come apart when members fail to respect the rules or, alternatively when they are attacked by other groups pursuing their different interests. Rome was an example of the former. After centuries of decline, aggravated by its overextended empire, by AD 410 Rome simply fell to the Goths. On the other hand, there are those grand social contrivances that invite, even require, others to destroy them even when they are thriving. Adolf Hitler's short-lived Germania fell in 1945 because the Nazi dream of a thousand-year Reich soon enough became a nightmare. The very idea was madness in the hands of a mad man who foolishly began wars on his Western and Eastern Front—wars that so provoked the Soviets to the East and the Anglo-American Allies to the West to destroy him and his all-but insane dreams. Yet, between these two extremes there is the historical fact that all social orders—from friendships and marriages to Empires and nations—are fungible.

Fungibility is itself, as we have seen, a state of social *disorder* that sooner or later (usually sooner) frays at the seams of its cloak of permanence. As much as their founders and leaders, not to mention their members and citizens, rely on their organizing social cloaks, they are necessarily loosely knit. Not even social theorists of the boldest ambition are able to design a pattern of a pure perfect social fabric. The reason for this is plain to see even when few among us dare to look hard at the unravelling seams of any given society. Some have tried to take such a hard look but, with rare exception, none so far dared to look deeply at the worst possible fate that could be. This is because they want to live on with a social blanket that keeps them warm during dark days when all about is cold and bone-chilling. We should not blame them.

Social sciences mean to be sciences when in fact the ultimate fact of all social orders is apocalyptic—which is to say that any attempt to understand social orders is, ultimately, theological. Why would any god make a world doomed to die? This is the theological question of theodicy. Why is there ultimate evil? Even if any given god is thought to be

---

61 *Ibid*, 282.
62 *Ibid*, 275.

good, her goodness cannot extend to freezing her creatures in ice—in, that is, a state of affairs in which those thus created have no freedom to move about and have whatever they may desire or need.

One social theorist who tried to imagine a social order in which all things worked together for good was Talcott Parsons, son of a Congregational minister. Parsons himself, underneath his brilliance, was a good man. He meant to design a theoretical pattern for the world as *he* saw it. The problem was that the world he saw in 1937 when he published his first great book, *The Structure of Social Action*, was wrought with economic misery and a coming world war that would soon renew the terrors of the deadly war of 1914. *Kristallnacht* would crash the vulnerable windows of global peace in 1938—the year after *The Structure of Social Action* would so delicately conceive of a world in which social orders offer guiding cultures that provide the rules that would collectively manage political differences generated by the social actions individuals and groups pursuing needs and wants in a zero-sum desert. In real social orders there simply is not enough for everyone. In principle it would be possible for worlds to provide enough food, shelter, water, and other of the needs of human animals as well as plants and lesser animals. The problem is wants. Humans are desiring creatures. We want more—and, if there is a god of social worlds, she or he gives us freedom to want more—a more that may be little more than the ability to move about to make new homes or to make new friends and lovers and such like.

In the abstract this may sound very gloomy. On the ground, however, it is possible to study and explain ordinary local social communities. This is the work of ethnographies that, in spite of what some think, are able magically to explain the larger social worlds in which they must exist. The irony is that any given descriptive ethnography may seem to be merely empirical. But here the key word, ethno*graphy*—writing about people,—changes everything. The *writing* about, or telling the story of, an actually existing commonplace community always creates a theory. All stories, whether nonfiction or fiction, have narrative plots without which they would make no sense. Even James Joyce's *Ulysses*, mind-numbing though it may seem, is a story with a plot—a story of Leopold Bloom's ventures. I've been in Dublin on a June 16th, Bloomsday, when the city and all Joyce readers reenact, or otherwise ponder, Leopold's reenactment of Homer's Ulysses. Theory is a story—often a grand story. Parsons's theory was a grand story of a social order that, in the day, did not exist on the ground—as never it has.

In the modern world, the story to be told is one of a fungibility in which an earlier social order changes enough to call into question whether what came before will survive. In a certain definite sense, this story is most acutely the story of late modern cities. The New Ethnographers are those who take seriously those changes among urban America's most vulnerable. These are stories that cannot be told without some prominent plot as to the deep structural effects of power and domination.

16 Ethnographies and American Social Theory
Robert E. Park, W.E.B. Du Bois, W.I. Thomas, Florian Znaniecki, Elliot Liebow, Carol Stack, William Julius Wilson

The city is a state of mind, a body of customs and traditions, and
organized attitudes that adhere in these customs and are transmitted with these traditions.
The city is not merely a physical mechanism and an artificial construction.
—Robert E. Park, The City, 1925

No city played a more important role in shaping the landscape and economy
of the mid-continent during the second half of the nineteenth century than Chicago.
—William Cronon, Nature's Metropolis: Chicago and the Great West, 1991

This study of the central district of Negro settlement furnished a key to the situation in the city;
in other words a general survey was taken to ascertain the general distribution of these people. ...
This general inquiry, while it lacked precise methods of measurement in most cases,
Served nevertheless to correct the errors and illustrate the meaning of the
statistical material obtained in the house-to-house survey.
—W.E.B. Du Bois, The Philadelphia Negro, 1899

The Polish peasant community has developed during many centuries complicated systems of
beliefs and rules of behavior sufficient to control social life under ordinary circumstances,
and the cohesion of the group and the persistence of its membership are strong enough to withstand passively the influence of eventual extraordinary occurrences...
—W.I. Thomas and Florian Znaniecki,
The Polish Peasant In Europe and America, 1918–1920

The streetcorner man wants to be a person in his own right, to be noticed, to be taken account of,
but in this respect, as well as in meeting his money needs, his job fails him.
The job fails the man and the man fails the job.
—Elliot Liebow, Tally's Corner:
A Study of Negro Streetcorner Men, 1967

Kin expect to help one another out. That one can repeatedly join households of kin is
a great source of security among those living in poverty,
and they come to depend on it.
—Carol Stack, All Our Kin, 1974

By "new urban poverty," I mean poor, segregated neighborhoods in which a substantial majority
of individual adults are either unemployed or dropped out of the labor force altogether.
—William Julius Wilson, When Work Disappears:
The World of the New Urban Poor, 1996

Writing People's Communities Across the Century

It is sometimes assumed that all things ethnographic began in and around the University of Chicago, which was founded in 1890, late for a great university when measured against Harvard, Yale, and the College of New Jersey. Some took this to suggest that the Chicago university would be ahead of the times. In one sense it was in that the University came to be when Chicago itself was rapidly rebuilding due to its location on the frontier between the rural West and the urban East.

> No city played a more important role in shaping the landscape and economy of the mid-continent during the second half of the nineteenth century than Chicago.[1]

True to be sure; but when it comes to ethnographies, not so much. As it happened the first enduringly great American ethnography was *The Philadelphia Negro* by W.E.B. Du Bois in 1899.

> This study of the central district of Negro settlement furnished a key to the situation in the city; in other words a general survey was taken to ascertain the general distribution of these people. ...This general inquiry, while it lacked precise methods of measurement in most cases, served nevertheless to correct the errors and illustrate the meaning of the statistical material obtained in the house-to-house survey.[2]

Du Bois did many things well. Here he demonstrates his mastery of a then somewhat new sociological method, ethnography.

This being said, as we will see later in this chapter, Chicago did become mostly in the 1920s a center of urban ethnography for which the early programmatic statement was by Robert E. Park:

> The city is a state of mind, a body of customs and traditions, and organized attitudes that adhere in these customs and are transmitted with these traditions. The city is not merely a physical mechanism and an artificial construction.[3]

Before Park wrote his statement, in 1918 two Chicago ethnographers published a remarkable study, *The Polish Peasant in Europe and America* in which they set the Polish community in Chicago against its long prior roots in Poland:

> The Polish peasant community has developed during many centuries complicated systems of beliefs and rules of behavior sufficient to control social life under ordinary circumstances, and the cohesion of the group and the persistence of its membership are strong enough to withstand passively the influence of eventual extraordinary occurrences...[4]

---

1 William Cronon, *Nature's Metropolis: Chicago and the Great West* (W.W. Norton, 1991), xv.
2 W.E.B. Du Bois, *The Philadelphia Negro: A Social Study* (The University of Pennsylvania Press, 1899), 3.
3 Robert E. Park, "The City: Some Suggestions For the Investigation of Human Behavior in the Urban Environment," in Robert E. Park, Ernest W. Burgess, Roderick D. McKenzie, *The City* (University of Chicago Press, 1925), 1.
4 William Isaac Thomas and Florian Znaniecki, *The Polish Peasant In Europe and America: Monograph of an Immigrant Group* (Boston, Richard G. Badger, The Gorham Press [Originally published by the University of Chicago Press, 1918]), 2.

Though early in the ethnographic game, Park's programmatic statement and the expansive approach of Thomas and Znaniecki inspired a deeper and more insistent approach by subsequent ethnographers.

In the later 1960s and the early 1970s, two late modern classic ethnographies were written, about men and women on the margins of urban life. *Tally's Corner* by Elliot Liebow studied streetcorner men who had, for reasons Liebow explained, given up on their lives:

> The streetcorner man wants to be a person in his own right, to be noticed, to be taken account of but in this respect, as well as in meeting his money needs, his job fails him. The job fails the man and the man fails the job.[5]

By sharp contrast, Carol Stack, in *All Our Kin* in 1974, has shown that women in a similar economic plight manage to get by because they form a network of relations with each other:

> Kin expect to help one another out. That one can repeatedly join households of kin is a great source of security among those living in poverty, and they come to depend on it.[6]

It is not by accident that Stack, writing in 1974, was writing just when feminist standpoint theory was coming to wider attention.

Finally, William Julius Wilson's *When Work Disappears: The World of the New Urban Poor* in 1996 must be mentioned. Wilson is not an ethnographer but his research focuses attention on poor neighborhoods of *the world of the new urban poor*. His definition cuts sharp to his purposes:

> By "new urban poverty," I mean poor, segregated neighborhoods in which a substantial majority of individual adults are either unemployed or dropped out of the labor force altogether.[7]

Wilson's clarity of concept and focus is one of the reasons that, as we shall also see later in this chapter, he was at the center of debates over how to understand urban ghettos. *When Work Disappears* was published in 1996, but some decades later it remains at the center of attention for those who care about the poor trapped, in most instances, in urban ghettos.

The Hill, An Enclosed Urban Neighborhood

The Hill, so-called, in New Haven is not much of a hill—certainly not when compared to East and West Rocks that soar over the City. Over the years, the Hill has been referred to as Mount Pleasant, Oyster Point, Sodom Hill, Trowbridge Square, Spireworth Village—names so unfamiliar that an article on "the Hill" put the moniker in quotation marks.[8] These names go back, one assumes, to its early history. Mid-nineteenth century the neighborhood welcomed Irish and German immigrants, while simultaneously being open to Blacks from the South for whom it was a station of the Underground Railroad. Today the Hill is populated mostly by Latinx people and African Americans.

---

5 Elliot Liebow, *Tally's Corner: A Study of Negro Streetcorner Men* (Rowman & Littlefield, 2003 [1967]), 39.
6 Carol Stack, *All Our Kin: Strategies in a Black Community* (Harper & Row, 1974), 123.
7 William Julius Wilson, *When Work Disappears: The World of the New Urban Poor* (Knopf, 1996), 19.
8 Jim Shelton, "Old As 'the Hill'," *New Haven Register*, April 3, 2011. Other facts of its early history, same source.

Truth be told, the neighborhood is largely cut off from the rest of the City. To the north it is bordered by the Oak Street connector, a multiple lane highway that was originally meant to connect the interstate highways in the East of New Haven to towns in the North West with their own multi-lane roadways. The connector was never finished. Though efforts have been made to eliminate this barrier between the Hill and downtown, progress has been slow. Instead the Yale Medical School and Yale New Haven Hospital function as an institutional barrier on the Hill side of the connector. The Hospital's many and ever-growing number of medical buildings have taken up the land that formerly might have otherwise provided affordable residential housing. Then too the southern border of the Hill is hemmed in by frontage roads and Interstate 95 that runs along the near side of the Long Island Sound. To the West, another busy street serves as a blockade between New Haven and West Haven. The town's largest cemetery keeps the Hill from expanding to the West. To the East the Union Terminal and its rail tracks form still a fourth wall around the Hill. For a long while, a well populated housing project stood opposite the railroad station. But it was torn down for reasons hard to remember, leaving an enormous empty lot of many acres separating the Hill from the convenience of train travel.

In the interior of this urban moat, the Hill carries on as best a generally poor neighborhood can. Oddly a recent survey of the neighborhood's livability measures rates the Hill as D- with respect to housing and C- with respect to jobs, schools, and off-the-scale with respect to crime and safety—but A+ for nightlife![9] One never knows where rankings like this one—*Niche/Best Places*—come from. This one frankly admits that they come from experts, who have studied some or another data. Since *Niche/Best Places* is a national project, it is likely that the experts have never even visited the Hill. Instead, like most surveys of this kind, they probably did little more than take the numbers available from the City and compare them nationwide by some algorithmic process only the experts can understand. But such a measure can say where the people go for nightlife. If is beyond unlikely that they go to Toad's downtown which is packed with area college students jumping about to music by bands unknown to most others. Then too there are shadier rankings like *Area-vibes*[10] that ranks the Hill as A+ for commute (d'uh!) and A for amenities—a still more vague category, which might refer to the neighborhood's easy access to health care—not just Yale's hospitals, but, Cornell Scott Hill, the major general hospital for the poor and underinsured is located in the center of the neighborhood.

Reporting sites like *Niche/Best Places* and *Area-vibes* might use scientifically produced data such as the census data compiled by the Census Bureau in the U.S. Department of Commerce, but they use them for their own entrepreneurial purposes. The problem with data gathered by the U.S. Department of Commerce is that places like the Hill in New Haven, which they presume to characterize are, when all is said and seen, much more complicated in ways that no grading scale can represent.

In addition to the Hill's several hospitals there is, on the Eastern border of the Hill, New Haven's adult education school located near Columbus House, the agency that cares for homeless people. The schools may not be the best in the town, but Hill Regional Career High School is a long-established institution (once named Lee High School after Richard C. Lee a former mayor who in the 1960s revitalized downtown New Haven). Graduates of the school, including James Thomas, remain active in and about the town. Speaking of whom, a good many of the men and women belonging to Thomas's Spiritual Fellowship have been helped to find housing. This informal group works in concert with Columbus

---

9 See *Niche/Best Places* @ https://www.niche.com/about/where-niche-grades-come-from/
10 *Area-vibes* @ https://www.areavibes.com/new+haven-ct/hill/?ll=41.29776+-72.93646

House and other agencies in the Hill to care not only for the homeless, but the ill, the once incarcerated, and other excluded people.

Also there are some active enterprises in the neighborhood. The Hill Museum is home to the quite remarkable pencil drawings by Krikko Obbott of huge cityscapes of New York City, Tokyo, Boston, and many other global cities. Some of them are as large as 20 × 15 feet. They are displayed in Obbott's museum on West Street. Reproductions are sold the world over. Yet hardly anyone in the town, much less the Hill, knows about them. Another adjacent amenity is City Point, on the extreme South West tip of the Hill. City Point is a somewhat upscale neighborhood on the Long Island Sound which is home to one of the best restaurants in the state. Shell and Bones Oyster Bar and Grill may well have been named in honor of the oyster fishermen who, in the past, built homes in the Point. Farther to the West on the Sound are a number of sea-side condominiums. Some of their residents have taken responsibility to clean and plant flowers and other greens around the traffic circle near-by.[11] Though the average Hill resident cannot afford to live or dine there, City Point adds a degree of stability and prestige to the area.

Down from City Point into the Hill, near Riverside High School, is a neighborhood of nice if not glamorous homes for those of modest income. Well into one of the Hill's more marginal sections lives a socially concerned couple who have turned their home and back-yard into an informal home and campground for a good many of the unhoused poor in the City. There those in acute need find housing and meals paid for by various church and public agencies. None of these institutions in the Hill is particularly prominent in the larger City yet they are instances of good work and will for and by those who live there.

And so it goes in this one otherwise unremarkable neighborhood. What does it mean to rate if D- or F+ in some respect and A for amenities. Short answer: very little. It does nothing more than to say it is not as good as Westport or even near-by Woodbridge—and that is why surveys like *Niche/Best Places* exist: to steer the well-off to places they'd like to live. To be sure more scientific social surveys are not, neither by intent nor method, so crass. But even the best of these cannot tell the whole story of any particular place.

Ethnographies of Disorder in Neighborhoods

The Hill is the kind of neighborhood that could well be the subject of research for ethnographers interested in urban disorder. As those who came to invent the concept of fungible interaction orders have taught, disorder is a distinctly (if not exclusively) social theoretical idea—and especially in the sense that urban disorder never exists without some important degree of order. Ever since the Civil War so memorably disordered the nation, the fungibility of its national interaction order has served to dramatize America's peculiar contradictions—that, from its first settlements, it was, as it remains, a high-minded culture seeking perfect democratic order while also being disordered by the scourge of slavery upon which its appalling white nationalism was founded. Then too, in time, the original blight of white nationalism afflicted the nation's values by its ever expanding violence against, and disregard of, Native peoples; as well as the abuse of Asian people who helped build its West; then also of others from Ireland and remote Europe who built its industry while being painted as "might-as-well-be-Negros"; and down to present times when Latinx migrants coming from the South to work are treated as enemies by too many. The subjects change,

---

11 Ed Stannard, "The Rotary in New Haven's City Point Does More Than Slow Traffic. It's Bringing Folks Together," *New Haven Register* (May 19, 2022). The author of this article is a prominent member of the downtown church where James Brown's Spiritual Fellowship is based.

but not the story. America's peculiar theory and practice of white supremacy endures down into today's postmodern era. The proponents of this perverse value of white supremacy are today very often people who live on the vast American nether regions—the rural South and open West, the still confederate villages of the Deep South, the superior suburban ghettos and exurbs of the Northern cities. Yet, those who cling to an unspoken doctrine of white supremacy have become an army at war with what they now call militant replacement theory. The supremacists fight under the false flag that America was founded by white Europeans who are its proper members. This bizarre, if to some persuasive, lie is born these days on a fear that whites will soon lose the place of privilege they never had. The truth they are unable to embrace is that it was their ancestors who killed and exiled the indigenous people of the New World, then did the same to Africans imported to build their new world's economic order—and more, and worse.

One might wonder: *Why now, this? These last few paragraphs may belong in this book, but here? Why this digression in a chapter on ethnography?* The short answer is that ethnographies achieve little unless they recognize and tell of the disorder that makes the communities they study what they are. *And* local disorders are never simply local. Disorder always comes down from the wider world where a larger body of people are forced to deal with disputes and real conflicts among groups of members. Where there is racial conflict in America that discord always sinks into and alters its local communities, one way or another. Some communities—like Ferguson, Missouri in 2014 or Harrison, Arkansas[12] which has been called, in 2023, the most racist town in America—experience the conflict directly; while others—like Westport, Connecticut or Palm Beach, Florida or Newport, Rhode Island in the Gilded Age with the hyper-wealthy built their 40 room plus "cottages" for summer vacations—who, in the rare moments when they are overheard by their housekeepers complain, experience the condemnations of those disgusted by their racial exclusions.

Which brings to mind the underlying condition of stories told: For those who tell stories, their stories only matter if those to whom they are told are actually listening or seeing deeply. As David Brooks has put it: "There is one skill that lies at the heart of any healthy person, family, school, community organization, or society: the ability to see someone else deeply and make them feel seen—to accurately know another person, to let them feel valued, heard, and understood."[13] Seeing and hearing are essential to storytelling. When the other neither sees nor hears the story's point, the story is not told. This too is why ethnographies *can be* so much better at telling an empirical story than numeric or formulaic theorists. Try as most might, the story told by $E=mc^2$ is all but impossible to see or hear. But stories about places like the Hill almost always get the attention of those willing to listen or read them thoughtfully—and usually because they already have an interest in the community—or ones like it. Then too, generally speaking, nothing attracts deep attention more than tales of trouble and conflict.

This leads me back to the question that's been brewing for some pages now: Why are ethnographies of such special importance to research intent upon *making* theory, as distinct

---

12 https://www.cbc.ca/radio/thecurrent/the-current-for-oct-26-2020-1.5775035/residents-of-the-most-racist-town-in-america-say-they-re-working-hard-to-shake-that-reputation-1.5775050

13 David Brooks, *How to Know a Person: The Art of Seeing Others Deeply and Being Deeply Seen* (Random House, 2023). Also, David Brooks, "The Gift of Your Attention," *The New York Times Opinion Section* (October 22, 2023), 6.

from confirming or changing settled theories? The answer has two parts. *First*, a fair and full study of neighborhoods like the Hill can only be done by an ethnography—the study of the way a people live (*ethnos* = people, folk). *Second*, an ethnography is exceptionally suited for the study of people whose lives are determined by deep structural disorder in their wider world—a world itself dominated by people so above the ground of daily life that they see no problem in acting toward those cut off—like many in the Hill—as if they were, at the least, undeserving of the benefits of their world. This because ethnography is a story-telling method, which means it is at one and the same time, and by definition, a *theory-making* activity. Each of the two parts demands explanation.

As for the *first*, when it comes to saying something accurate and meaningful about a "people," it is necessary to know that something on the basis of first-hand acquaintance. It may sometimes be helpful to refer to indirect measures like, for primary examples: demographic reports on their ethnic and racial composition; the current rate of child birth whether up or down; the source of personal income whether a job or a street deal; and more of the like. But then, the information like this can introduce sometimes awkward nuances. As, for example, how many of people living in the Hill are well-enough employed at, for example, Yale's nearby hospitals perhaps cleaning floors or pushing wheelchairs for patients on the way to a Cat-scan. If employed by illegal street dealing, then it makes a difference how many are selling pot on the street by the Deli on Howard Avenue as compared to those who were among those recently arrested by the FBI Safe Streets/Gang Task Force for trafficking fentanyl. And so on. No numeric demographic category can be fine-grained enough to capture differences like these—and certainly not the *where* and *when* of dealing *which* drugs. Quantitative measures can help but only incompletely as in: What does it mean to conclude, as the report above on the Hill's ranking does, that a generally poor and imperfect neighborhood is A for amenities while in other measures it is F+/D-? If this is so, it is necessary to talk to and observe people as they live their lives to find out if, and to what extent, they agree.

Here *Area-vibes* at least indicates the sources of its information. One source is called *OpenStreetMap* from which they identify the 45,000 cities and neighborhoods they rank in the US. Interestingly *Area-vibes* is a Canadian company that makes these rankings for a profit. Still, in referring to their method *Area-vibes* says, blandly, "Our Livability Score is created from science, data and statistics." That's comforting, to be sure, if only we were told which ones. But, leaving aside the business aspect of this enterprise, it is clear that a (if not *the*) principal resource for American communities is The United States Department of Commerce which just so happens to be the governmental home of the U.S. Census Bureau. So again it is clear that politicians at least assume that the most important consumers of census data are commercial enterprises and businesses. To be sure, there is no Cabinet position for a Secretary of Social Sciences, though there is a lower level National Science Foundation which is located in Alexandria, Virginia that has a program of funding for the Social, Behavioral, and Economic Sciences.

OK. Enough of this already. The point should be clear. A good many other interests apart from scientific demographers care about demographic data. What these others have in common is that their interests are not particularly well served by carefully collected local information about the populations of people they advertise and sell. Only something like ethnography can give honest information about communities, whether large cities or very local neighborhoods like the Hill.

Now the *second* reason ethnography is necessary to the study of places like the Hill is because ethnography is by its very nature a theory-making activity. Put crudely:

- Ethnographies are stories about a people.
- Stories are necessarily theories.
- Theories, like stories as normally understood, are interesting (if sometimes tragically so) only because they try to put together broken or otherwise separated parts of a situation.
- Urban ethnographies are about communities broken by the fact that some who live in them are deprived of the goods others in the larger population readily have.

Some surely will find this litany a bit strange. But think of a story like Maurice Sendak's *In the Night Kitchen* which is as strange as strange gets. Mickey, a quite young boy, while asleep, is disturbed by noises from outside his room. He is disturbed in the dream-like sense of seeing himself out of bed, drifting nakedly into the Night Kitchen where bakers are preparing the morning's breakfast cakes. Mickey is suddenly in the mixing bowl with butter and batter. He complains to the bakers that he is not dough, at which point he flies in a sort of magic airplane up from the batter to a milk bottle meant to pour milk into the dough before it is put in the oven. At that point, however, Mickey so enjoys the milk that he jumps into the bottle. Just before the bakers are ready to put the batter into the oven, Mickey rises to the top of the bottle, his coating of batter slides off, he is once again naked. He then helps the bakers finish the batter and put the dough in the oven. Mickey slides off the bottle naked into his bed. He awakes, however, clothed and unharmed. He falls asleep again until he is awakened ready to enjoy the morning cake. This is one of the stories I loved reading to my children when they were as young as Mickey. They loved it. Why? And how can a story like this be a theory?

For one thing it is a story that has all the characteristics of a dream and dreams tell us what we are feeling. Of course, there are those who believe that dreams mean nothing—that they are nothing more than perturbations in the physiology of the brain. A number of neuro-scientists believe this. If that is true then how is it possible that we remember our dreams? Why do we remember them sufficiently well to talk about them to others, including our analysts? After a number of years in psychoanalysis I reported a repetitive dream—of traveling West from Cincinnati along the Indiana side of the Ohio River. When this dream occurred again, the details were different but the direction of my escape to the West remained the same. Years later after a good many iterations of my mental story, I decided that I was looking for my father from whom I wanted to run. My psychoanalyst did not disagree. She had already heard enough about that relationship.

Now a well-prepared skeptic would say, *So what?* For which, the well-enough treated dreamer thought to himself: "Well, it's something like what I feel and think about my longing for my father to be more of a father to me than he was able." Still, *So what?* remains a fair question for anyone not willing to listen to stuff like that. As it happens a few years after I hit upon this rebus of my longing for something I couldn't have, I became a teacher in the Culture Program of the accredited doctoral program at the Boston Graduate School of Psychoanalysis. The teaching entailed listening to students tell their stories as a way of connecting to the academic materials assigned for the class. And this, in turn, led to my attending the School's regular clinical presentations by candidates in training of their patients' stories and dreams and treatment history. Their case reports seemed to make sense to me. One might again wonder: *So What?* Isn't this little more than the hermeneutics of a group of believers in the same basic truths of mental life and the Unconscious mind? For which the reply must be, *Could be*. Obviously, hard core cause-and-effect methodologists would reject this supposition out of hand. Yet, for the time being, we are talking about ethnography which is not a cause-and-effect science. It is, in fact, a *hermeneutic* of stories—that is, an interpretation of stories told and the retelling of them for others to read or hear.

Stories, as I've said many times before, are theories. If so then what to make of the stories told for different purposes, including different analytic purposes. If, for one, an utterly abstract telling of a story told and retold in Vienna over drinks in the 1920s between Einstein and Heisenberg, who disagreed then. Also, what is to be made when psychoanalysts tell stories of their patients in Brookline in the 1990s, or when a dad reads *In the Night Kitchen* to Anna in Killingworth in the 2000s. All these possibilities, different as they are, raise the question of what they might have in common that could make them all a theory of whatever kind? Well, to start, they are all based on observations—of, in the case of $E=mc^2$, what other physicists have said about the relation between Energy and Mass in the universe of all things; or, in the case of psychoanalysts listening to case reports had previously heard of what another patient said about his feelings about his father; or, in the case of Mickey's dream-like experience in a night kitchen, I know first-hand that very young Anna at bedtime was less worried about being naked than about whether she'd get a cake in the morning. In all three cases the stories, however they are told, are based on direct observations of human experiences and actions. And all are told as theories, always and ever susceptible to challenge. Heisenberg did not agree with Einstein's $E=mc^2$, a dear friend found my story about my father ridiculous, and my three-year-old daughter liked *In the Night Kitchen,* but she would have ignored any attempt I would have made to explain it. Some theories are meant to be argued over or studied by experts; others are meant to be told then set free to have what effect they might have.

Yes, theories are everywhere. This is why it is necessary when studying a neighborhood like the Hill to use a method that recognizes that the people who live there are themselves story tellers—hence, theorists—of what goes on there. Even today well into the 2020s, James Thomas tells the story of his home having been burned down when he was young, and of his father disappearing and his mother being disabled, requiring him in his teens to care for his younger siblings, then when a homeless adult walking the city hungry sleeping under bleachers nightly. When James Thomas tells this story repeatedly to members of his Spiritual Fellowship, his theory of having overcome impossible obstacles became their theory of how they can do the same. Theories can be confirmed in the telling—and passed forward, or rejected for some other theory; so too when one tells a story to a group and one or more of the group are inspired to tell their stories that may or may not be similar. Theories are stories told to others who pass them around for confirmation or rejection.

This precisely is what all stories do. The higher they are, like $E=mc^2$, the fewer are they who can confirm or reject them. When the stories are told among psychoanalysts in an institute or among believers in that institute or believers in a schul or church or mosque many are they who will take them in, while others, if doubting, keep silent. The more inscrutable they are, like the one of Mickey *In the Night Kitchen*, the more are they who can pass them on and in that way confirm them. It makes no sense to reject a good enough story, even when unaware adults are puzzled by them, while somehow enjoying them. But whatever kind of story is told it sparks thoughts about what is going in the world is all about.

Ethnographers Are Story Tellers Who Specialize in Collective Disorders

Ethnography began as the disciplined practice of studying the world's peripheral and, usually, excluded people. Yet, for the most part, ethnography, as we know it today, arose in the modern era. Sociologists borrowed the artful practice of fieldwork studying people in their grounded lives from anthropologists who, with rare exception, studied remote cultures of people as they were being discovered by white explorers and capitalists. Ethnography in this sense has always been more or less the local study of people displaced by the New World Order. Trobriand Islanders, Blacks and other urban people of color in America, indigenous cultures in Australia's outback, workers in Industrial England, others.

In due course, urban ethnography has slowly but surely come into its own as the one modern empirical science that is, by nature, deeply theoretical. This understanding has grown out of theoretical attempts to understand the deep structural nature of the modern world-system. However remote early ethnography reports on faraway places there was always, somewhere lurking behind accounts of sometimes alien places a comparison to the worlds of those who read the ethnographies. However we presume to understand lives and loves of these peoples might seem strange to writers and their readers in the Global North, it remains hard if not impossible *not* to see in them a theory of who they are. For example, Yale political theorist and ethnographer, Jim Scott, in his remarkable book, *The Art of Not Being Governed*, describes *Zomia*, The Great Mountain Kingdom in Southeast Asia. *Zomia* extends from Cambodia and Thailand to China, Vietnam, and Laos to the Northeast and Burma, India, and Bangladesh to the Northwest. This Great Mountain Kingdom is home to as many as 100 million people, all living at least two hundred, some three hundred, meters above sea level in an area of 2.5 million square kilometers.[14] Their shared culture is anarchism. They have fled the state and colonial ruled lowland nationalities governed by one or another state government. They refuse state control which is why they moved to *Zomia*. The idea should be shocking to highly educated people of the Global North. Thus shocked, they are forced to refresh their theory of the State as the *sine qua non* of modern democratic societies.

Those already familiar with what ethnographers do might well say two things: "No one can do an ethnography of so many different people spread across such a vast territory." True, but it must be said that ethnographers can theorize about the general even when they have studied local places. Local stories would make no sense unless they point to the general. And, in Scott's case he has done more than a few ethnographies of communities in Southeast Asia (about which more later). He knows the people and their ways—including the fact that in some instances even, when resisting a dominant class, villagers can and do join together to safeguard their way of life. No one can do an on-the-ground ethnography of a place like Zomia—so Jim Scott came as close to something like it as anyone can imagine. Perhaps because his books, while based on fieldwork, are so enticingly theoretical. For example, among those who know Scott's work his ethnographic books have had a significant influence on American ethnographers for such books as *Seeing Like a State* (1989) and *Two Cheers for Anarchism* (2012). He at least made the study of disorder in villages a salient subject of research.

In one sense, since early in the 1900s when sociological ethnography took up the study of urban communities, notably Chicago, in a day when tensions among immigrant

---

14 James Scott, *The Art of Not Being Governed* (Yale University Press, 2009), 13–18. Also see the section on Scott, Chapter 21.

communities and between them and long-settled white migrants to the city disorder and conflict became an important theme in emerging American social ethnography. In America, ethnography took on a distinctive nature once it divorced itself from earlier practices that were, in a word, married more to community studies—of, if not communities in America, then of premodern cultures the world over. Then their communities were no longer innocent by-standers to the developing ravages of global capitalism. As it happens, ethnography as a practice has changed time and again. In due course, an important group of American ethnographers have made a discovery that has begun to have an important effect on social theory generally.

A Theoretical Excursus: Subjects/Objects, Locals/Social Structures—and the Micro/Macro Dichotomies They Created

Across the field of social theories an ugly weed has spread to corrupt, if not kill, the theoretical wheat that could otherwise have flourished. Attempts have been made to mow these weeds—thus to allow the better plants to thrive. Some have done this by simply changing the root structure in which the soil of modern societies has nourished more tares than wheat. Foremost among these gardeners was Donna Haraway whose 1985 essay, "The Cyborg Manifesto and Fractured Identities," inspired a group of feminists who had turned from chaste gender studies toward, if not natural science, to the study of nature. Not long after, Judith Butler's 1990 book *Gender Trouble: Feminism and the Subversion of Identity* cut down altogether the troubled past of identity studies in which the feminine was trapped in male-dominate analytic categories.[15] More on this to come!

Otherwise, modern social theory since Martin Luther's *Treatise on Christian Liberty* in 1520 and, more familiarly, René Descartes' *Discourse on Method* in 1637 set down the categories that in time became a prison house for social thought. Luther was the first clearly to affirm that the individual can think for himself, even about God. Descartes, instead, wrote about the thinking self. For example: "I think that a stone is a substance, that is to say, a thing that is suitable for existing in itself; and likewise I think that I too am a substance." And: "For I am indeed of such a nature that, while I perceive something very clearly and distinctly, I cannot help believing it to be true."[16] In this, Descartes' famous theorem – *I think therefore I am*—joins his method of *clear and distinct ideas* to lay down the classical formula for the ontological distinction between *self* and *other*—or, *of* the *self* as *a thinkable element in the objective world*. To be sure this is no more than a prime instance of early modern philosophy's classical commitment to a notion of Being as such in which all beings therein enjoy a distinct position in the universe of such things.

Other philosophers of the early modern era developed their own versions of this all-too generic theory of things—Montesquieu's *Spirit of Laws*, Rousseau's *Social Contract*, Spinoza's *Improvement of Understanding*, Leibnitz's *Explication of Binary Arithmetic Codes*, Kant's *Critique of Pure Reason*, many more. One might suppose that Hegel's dialectic might have sprouted a line that would lead to an eventual end to the philosophy of

---

15 For Donna Haraway, see her *Simians, Cyborgs, and Women: The Reinvention of Nature* (Routledge, 1991 [1985]) and Butler, *Gender Trouble: Feminism and the Subversion of Identity* (Routledge, 1990).
16 René Descartes, *Discourse on Method* (Hackett Publishing Co, 1998 [1637]), 76; quoted line following, 91. Or online: https://grattoncourses.files.wordpress.com/2017/12/rene-descartes-discourse-on-method-and-meditations-on-first-philosophy-4th-ed-hackett-pub-co-1998.pdf

the binaries, but no. *The Phenomenology of Mind,* for example, includes strong statements like: "The spirit of the world is spiritual essence permeated by a self-consciousness which knows itself to be directly present as a self-existent particular and knows that as an objective actuality over against itself."[17] Even here it is easy enough to see traces of the wrong-headed idea that there are ontological differences between large and distant macro social structures and small and local micro subjects and their communities.

It is hard to underestimate the ways this utterly mistaken and unproveable dichotomy has created problems for empirical and theoretical social theory. At the least, social theory's use of binaries like macro/micro and structure/subjects might have done better had its proponents gone back to a careful rereading of those who established the classical philosophical dichotomies—Descartes, Rousseau, Kant, Spinoza, Leibnitz, and others. Kant in 1789 began to understand the issues, as did Marx in 1844. But both gave in to an overly strong thinking subject or an overly unthinking social structure—Kant's *synthetic a priori* and Marx's *estranged labor.* Late in the nineteenth century Nietzsche *could* be said to have been the first to attack classical thinking. But *could* is the most that can be said of Nietzsche, who was more or less against every prevailing philosophical concept in European culture of the day. Even he, in his brilliant intellectual meandering, seems to have come close to the corrosive dichotomizing, as in 1874: "Let me give a picture of spiritual events in the soul of modern man. Historical knowledge streams on him from sources that are inexhaustible, strange incoherences come together, memory opens all its gates and yet is never wide open enough."[18] Still it happened that, after the nineteenth century, social theories borrowed unthinkingly one of classical philosophy's central schemes. Some social theorists are well enough read in philosophy, a few have read some, many not much at all. Hence the irony: A not-particularly philosophical discipline has borrowed for the longest time one of early modern philosophy's classic attitudes about human individuals and their wider world.

The problem with social theoretical attempts to play the classical game is that philosophy, even late in its day, was still, at least latently, metaphysical in the sense that it held fast to the idea that the universe of beings demands an ontology of things as such. Ontology, literally, is the logic of being. The problem for social thought is that *social ontologies* must deal with the nature of social being in which the things of human imagination and practice are, in fact, ill-defined, constantly in motion, ever remaking the worlds they live in.

It took a while until the 1970s after the world revolution of 1968 for prominent social theorists to *attempt* to break out of the classical straight jacket.[19] Pierre Bourdieu in *Outline of a Theory of Practice* (1972) introduced his fungible concept of structures and practices, namely: the *habitus:*

> The structures constitutive of a particular type of environment (e.g. the material conditions of existence characteristic of a class condition) produce *habitus,* systems of durable, transposable, *dispositions*, structured structures predisposed to function as structuring structures, that is as principles of the generation and structuring of practices and representations which can be objectively "regulated" and "regular" without in any

---

17 G.W.F. Hegel, *The Phenomenology of Mind* (Dover Publications, 2005 [1807]), 287.
18 Friedrich Nietzsche, *The Use and Abuse of History* (Bobbs-Merrill 1949 [1874]), 23.
19 On the philosophical background of the dichotomies and the attempts of Pierre Bourdieu and Anthony Giddens to overcome them, see also, if you wish: "Three Ways to Think Structures and Ignore Differences," in Charles Lemert, *Sociology After the Crisis* (Routledge/Paradigm, 2004 [1995]), 131–167.

way being the product of obedience to rules, objectively adapted to their goals without presupposing a conscious aiming at ends or an expressed mastery of the operations necessary to attain them and, being all this, collectively without being the product of the orchestrating action of a conductor.[20]

High intellectual literature goes on like this—sentences without end, dependent clauses, qualifications and more. Just the same the point of *habitus* is here well-enough stated in the phrase: "…systems of durable, transposable, *dispositions*, structured structures predisposed to function as structuring structures." He did what he did in phrases like this one which in Paris in the day was language of the *École normale supériere*—the grande école of which none greater. In his way, Bourdieu was trying to put together what the dichotomies tore apart.

Similarly, Anthony Giddens, writing in the clear, if ornate, literary manner of Oxbridge intellectuals, made his first stab at something similar to Bourdieu's *habitus* in his *New Rules of Sociological Method* in 1976. The book begins with a straightforward announcement of the need to challenge the micro/macro analytic scheme. Then, at the book's end, Giddens, in a few jam-packed words, puts forth his plain but original way of thinking that suggests terms for overlooking the old: "[The] primary tasks of sociological analysis are the following: (a) The hermeneutic explication and mediation of divergent forms of life within descriptive metalanguages of science; (b) Explication of the production and reproduction of society as the accomplished outcome of human agency."[21]

Later, in *The Constitution of Society* (1984), Giddens's major comprehensive book on social theory, he develops his idea of structure as a *virtual* social thing:

> Structure thus refers, in social analysis, to the structuring properties allowing the 'binding' of time-space in social systems, the properties which make it possible for discernibly similar social practices to exist across varying spans of time and space and which lend them 'systemic' form. To say that structure is a 'virtual order' of transformative relations means that social systems, as reproduced social practices, do not have 'structures' but rather exhibit 'structural properties' and that structure exists, as time-space presence, only in its instantiations in such practices and as memory traces orienting the conduct of knowledgeable human agents.[22]

The high theoretical tone of the passage reveals at the least Giddens' similarity to and difference from Bourdieu's project. Bourdieu wants to invent a new category, *habitus*, that absorbs into itself both structures and subjects. Giddens, in his way, is aiming for something similar but turns structures into virtual, if transformative, relations that, while not real as such, sneak into the memory of agents.

Meanwhile, in spite of the efforts of Bourdieu and Giddens, social theorists concerned with structures and subjects persisted in taking the micro-macro link as a coherent way to think about complex social things. Notable among them are the contributors to the collection, *The Micro-Macro Link* (1987) edited by Jeffrey C. Alexander, Bernhard Giesen, Richard Munch, Neil J. Smelser. Then too Randall Collins published *Macro History: Essays in Sociology of the Long Run* in 1999 and twenty years later *Charisma: Micro-Sociology of Power and Influence* in 2020. Don't get me wrong, these are among the world's most

---

20 Pierre Bourdieu, *Outline of a Theory of Practice* (Cambridge University Press, 1977 [1972]), 72.
21 Anthony Giddens, *New Rules of Sociological Method* (Stanford University Press, 1993 [1976]), 170.
22 Anthony Giddens, *The Constitution of Society* (University of California Press, 1984), 17.

prominent social theorists, yet neither Giddens nor Bourdieu figure in their arguments.[23] It is too simple to put this off to a rather natural tendency among scholars to keep to their own kind. As a general dilemma in social studies the macro-micro tandem is a hard nut to crack. Jeffrey Alexander, for example, begins his introduction to *The Micro-Macro Link* with the confession that the link is a problem that resists easy solution, then he retreats to a solution that—even though it bears up well to Giddens' insistence that structures must be treated as virtual things—still reverts to an escape that leads to the same old trouble. "Only if it is viewed analytically, moreover, can the linkage between micro and macro be achieved."[24] But analytic solutions belong entirely to theoretical method and cannot lead to a description of a purported reality. One may object to Bourdieu's *habitus* and Giddens' *virtual structures* but close readings of each show that they are concepts meant to be descriptive of realistic situations. Some may consider this a distinction without a difference. Yet, in fact, when dealing primarily with facts, this is a real difference. On the ground of interactions, if they are to be described, theory of all kinds requires terms that fit on-the-ground facts of the matter. This is where trouble lingers. *Subjects/ structures or micro/macro* are pure, abstract dichotomies, and—in a word, merely analytic categories. Ethnographies cannot afford to propose theories that are simply analytic.

Early Ethnographies in America

For a long while early in the twentieth century, American ethnographies were part of community studies, which is to say studies that took a given community as a whole as the frame of reference for research. The University of Chicago was founded in 1892 and its sociology in the day offered what was one of its better-known programs, ethnography. Unsurprisingly, since then sociology in America was ill-formed—immature, if not academically deformed. In the 1890s Chicago was, in many ways, a laboratory for the emerging American city. In many wars, it was, as William Cronon (an historian, not an ethnographer) has written, the American city that most represented the role of Nature in America because it was the place where, late in the nineteenth century, the wilderness gave way to urban life. He wrote: "No city played a more important role in shaping the landscape and economy of the mid-continent during the second half of the nineteenth century than Chicago."[25] Then too, the famous 1871 fire burned through most of the then smallish city, making way for new construction that, in time, led to a modern urban space with today's high rising buildings. Already by then Chicago had become a rail and canal hub that linked West to East and far North to South. The resulting industry attracted workers from rural America and immigrants from Europe and freedpeople from the South. By late in the nineteenth century Chicago was transformed into one of middle America's most complex multi-ethnic and bi-racial cities.[26]

---

23 In the *Micro-Micro Link*, the eighteen contributing authors from around the North Atlantic world (notably France and Germany as well as the US), cited Giddens four times and Bourdieu once. One of them, Raymond Boudon, who cited neither, had an office at the *Maison des science de l'homme* in Paris but two floors from Bourdieu's while both were alive.

24 Jeffrey Alexander and Bernhard Giesen, "From Reduction to Linkage: The Long View of the Micro-Macro Debate," in Alexander et al, *The Micro-Macro Link* (University of California Press, 1987), 1.

25 William Cronon, *Nature's Metropolis: Chicago and the Great West* (W.W. Norton, 1991), xv.

26 As an aside: the fact that James Scott, a political theorist, and William Cronon, an historian, can properly be mentioned in a discussion of social ethnographies says a lot about how open and embracing ethnographers are. Academically, ethnographers today are usually found in both sociology and anthropology departments—which all-too-often tempts administrators to merge them—this against the outrages of both departments.

When the University of Chicago's sociology program was established in 1892, Chicago itself was the obvious, even necessary, subject of its research and education. John Dewey and Jane Addams were examples of the University's commitment to urban communities. Chicago's study of urban neighborhoods was, for a while, called ecological sociology—an attribution set down by Robert E. Park a leader in the early years of Chicago sociology and inventor of the idea and practice of human ecology.[27] Yet Park's ecological method for urban research was very well derived from his more general social theory of the city: "The city is a state of mind, a body of customs and traditions, and organized attitudes that adhere in these customs and are transmitted with these traditions. The city is not merely a physical mechanism and an artificial construction."[28]

In some ways Chicago as it had developed early in the twentieth century was a city that, in the day, required a totalizing ecological perspective. By consequence, in the early years American urban ethnography tended to study specific cities or their neighborhoods environmentally—as, that is, situated in surrounding social, cultural, and natural environments—and not, by the way, from the point of view of a particular set of social dynamics. Prominent among many examples from the Chicago School was W. I. Thomas and Florian Znaniecki, *The Polish Peasant in Europe and America: Monograph of an Immigrant Group* (1918–1920, five volumes).[29] As the title suggests the book means to trace the historical background of Polish people of peasant background to their settlement in America, for which the Chicago community was their primary place of settlement. Much of the five volumes of *The Polish Peasant* comprise all-but-literal reports on activities in the Chicago Polish community, including line-for-line conversations, court documents, and the like.

That the major content of Thomas and Znaniecki's book is so particular as to have caused readers to ignore the quite sophisticated methodological note at the book's beginning which aims to reframe, if not invent, a methodology appropriate to the work of urban ethnographers.

> Thus—to take an example—the Polish peasant community has developed during many centuries complicated systems of beliefs and rules of behavior sufficient to control social life under ordinary circumstances, and the cohesion of the group and the persistence of its membership are strong enough to withstand passively the influence of eventual extraordinary occurrences, although there is no adequate method of meeting them. ... But when, owing to the breakdown of the isolation of the group and its contact with a more complex and fluid world, the social evolution becomes more rapid and the crises more frequent and varied, there is no time for the same gradual, empirical, unmethodical elaboration of approximately adequate means of control, and no crisis can be passively borne, but every one must be met in a more or less adequate way, for they are too various

---

Wesleyan and Yale, for examples, have separate departments, but at different times tried to collapse one into the other.

27 Robert Ezra Park, "Human Ecology," *American Journal of Sociology*, vol. 42, no. 1 (University of Chicago Press, 1936), 1–15. Among Park's many books, see also *The City: Suggestions for the Study of Human Nature in the Urban Environment*, with R. D. McKenzie & Ernest Burgess (Chicago: University of Chicago Press, 1925).

28 Robert E. Park, "The City: Some Suggestions for the Investigation of Human Behavior in the Urban Environment," in Robert E. Park, Ernest W. Burgess, Roderick D. McKenzie, *The City* (University of Chicago Press, 1925), 1.

29 William Isaac Thomas and Florian Znaniecki, *The Polish Peasant in Europe and America: Monograph of an Immigrant Group* (Boston, Richard G. Badger, The Gorham Press [Originally published by the University of Chicago Press, 1918–20]).

and frequent not to imperil social life unless controlled in time. The substitution of a conscious technique for a half-conscious routine has become, therefore, a social necessity, though it is evident that the development of this technique could be only gradual, and that even now we find in it many implicit or explicit ideas and methods corresponding to stages of human thought passed hundreds or even thousands of years ago.[30]

Though it may not be entirely apparent from a first reading, looking closer one can see what is going on here, at least three significant notions. *First*, ecological sociology appears in the mention of the history of Polish migrations from the old world to the new—where, *second*, they encounter evolution "more rapid and the crises more frequent and varied," which is to say: modern urban life; which requires a methodology that, *third*, permits a gradual, slower technique in which research encounters "stages of human thought passed hundreds or even thousands of years ago."

This methodological note (said to have been written mostly by Znaniecki) goes on to discuss at such considerable nuance and range of ethnic life that it might be thought of as a manifesto—for, in effect, ethnographic research itself. Of particular interest in Znaniecki's note is its insistence that, whatever the particular object of research might be, the study must attend to the "whole life of a given society."[31] Manifesto or not, Znaniecki's "Methodological Note" ends with a statement that well represents, not just the Chicago School, but urban ethnography in general: "The Polish peasant finds himself now in a period of transition from the old forms of social organization that had been in force, with only insignificant changes, for many centuries, to a modern form of life."[32] In fact, urban ethnographies—as opposed to those engaged in numeric nomothetic studies—cannot help but examine the way a community changes. Though Robert E. Park was the early intellectual leader of the Chicago school of sociology, a methodological note like Znaniecki's with Thomas nicely illustrates the underlying methodology and theoretical sophisticated behind these early ethnographies.

Other Chicago ethnographies fit much the same pattern of *The Polish Peasant*, in particular Louis Wirth's study of the Jewish Ghetto in *The Ghetto* (1928). Then too, there is Frederick Thrasher's *The Gang: A Study of 1313 Gangs in Chicago* (1927) and, somewhat later, William Foote White's *Street Corner Society* (1943). Later still, W. Lloyd Warner's multiple volume *Yankee City Series* (1941–1952) on Newburyport, Massachusetts, was, for a long while, considered the most important (and certainly most ambitious) ethnography in its day. The fifth book in the series, *The Living and the Dead: A Study of the Symbolic Life of Americans* is still considered the greatest book in the series and perhaps among all of early American ethnographies.[33]

Du Bois's The Philadelphia Negro in 1899 to the Moynihan Scandal in 1965

Though the Chicago sociologists led the way in exemplifying an American ethnographical style, they were not alone. Before, for example, came the first enduringly important American ethnography, *The Philadelphia Negro* (1899). This was W.E.B. Du Bois's ethnography of

---

30 *Ibid*, 2.
31 *Ibid*, 18.
32 *Ibid*, 74.
33 W. Lloyd Warner, *The Living and the Dead: A Study of the Symbolic Life of Americans* (Yale University Press, 1952). For an abridged volume of all five Yankee City Books, see W. Lloyd Warner, *Yankee City* (Yale University Press, 1963).

Philadelphia's all-Black Seventh Ward. Du Bois studied the neighborhood exhaustively in order to demonstrate that those who lived there lived good lives not all that different from the lives of whites—thus to dispel the racist idea that urban Blacks were different socially. Again, like the Chicago ethnographers, Du Bois, working alone, presents his own methodological note: "This study of the central district of Negro settlement furnished a key to the situation in the city; in other words a general survey was taken to ascertain the general distribution of these people. This general inquiry, while it lacked precise methods of measurement in most cases, served nevertheless to correct the errors and illustrate the meaning of the statistical material obtained in the house-to-house survey."[34]

Then, well-after Du Bois and the Chicago studies, Herbert Gans in *The Urban Villagers: Group and Class in the Life of Italian Americans* (1963) studied a neighborhood of Italians to describe how their in-grown culture prevented them from resisting Boston's redevelopment program that in the end destroyed the integrity of the community. Though Du Bois had no relation to the University of Chicago, Gans had studied there. Yet, though he was influenced by David Riesman and Everett Hughes, Gans was, in a way, the first to break with Chicago's wholistic approach by inserting a strong idea into his interpretation of—as the subtitle suggests: the group was broken by class differences.

Then in 1965 the classic tradition of community studies was fractured by Daniel Patrick Moynihan's infamous report, *The Negro Family: The Case for National Action*. The Moynihan Report was not an ethnography but a well-intended liberal proposal for action that all-but destroyed its own purpose by describing the Negro family as "pathological." The year, 1965, was not the year to say such a thing even if it was generously meant to support Negro communities.

Elliot Liebow's Men and Carol Stack's Women

Shortly after Moynihan's controversial report, two notable ethnographies appeared, and both avoided the problem of racializing the negative. One was the still highly respected *Tally's Corner: A Study of Negro Streetcorner Men* (1967 [2003]) by Elliot Liebow who managed to write an engaging book on a group of Black men who were all but lost to modern urban life. In a sense he continued the traditional American ethnographic method by focusing entirely on Tally and his companions. Yet, Liebow added to his description of their troubles a compelling analytic point for the reasons they were where they were. Simply put, he makes the point descriptively in a long and pungent chapter, "Men and Jobs." The men are kept on the hook of craven unfair job driver who arrives each morning to hire a few who work for a minimum at dirty labor with no assurance of gaining the job the next day. "The Streetcorner man is under continuous assault by his job experience and job fears."[35] Liebow worked at the Center for the Study of Work and Mental Health at the National Institute of Mental Health, so it is not surprising that he interprets the fate of the men with an emphasis on their states of mind. In brief, they fail every role in their lives—marriage, family, fatherhood, friendship—because of the debilitating effect of the job experience and failure to provide for themselves and others economically.

Then seven years later, another ethnographer took another step toward what came to be called the ethnography of interaction orders: Carol Stack's *All Our Kin: Strategies in a Black Community* (1974). Stack's idea can be summarized by her response to Moynihan

---

34 W.E.B. Du Bois, *The Philadelphia Negro: A Social Study* (The University of Pennsylvania Press, 1899), 3.
35 Elliot Liebow, *Tally's Corner: A Study of Negro Streetcorner Men* (Rowman & Littlefield, 2003 [1967]), 44.

and others who had recently studied black families and communities: "Many descriptions of Black American domestic life by both Blacks and Whites (Frazier 1939; Drake and Clayton 1945; Abrahams 1963; Moynihan 1965; Rainwater 1966) have overlooked the interdependence and cooperation of kinsmen in Black communities."[36] What she does not say here is that all these studies were about men. Stack's *All Our Kin*, by contrast, is about women who are part of kin groups that help them to deal with poverty and other troubles in their neighborhood, the Flats. Kin and actual relatives and others who function as kin—occasional fathers or other men. But it is the women who build the kin groups by which they survive in better conditions than one might suppose by means of what Stack called the elasticity of their relations with others who remain kin as they come and go.

> A consequence of the elasticity of residence patterns is that even when persons move to separate households, their social, economic and domestic lives are so entwined with other kin that they consider themselves simultaneously a part of the residential groups of their kin. Kin expect to help one another out. That one can repeatedly join households of kin is a great source of security among those living in poverty, and they come to depend on it.[37]

Here is a strong theory of a local interaction order—and one that anticipates by thirty-seven years Waverly Duck's important idea of collective efficacy (about which more to come).[38] *All Our Kin* has long been a respected book. So much so that there is a national organization All Our Kin, Inc with a chapter in New Haven. The organization "trains, supports, and sustains family child-care providers."[39] Yet, as widely as the book is read, Carol Stack's acute theoretical interpretations are seldom quoted as such.

William Julius Wilson Expands the Theoretical Scope of Urban Studies

In the period after Liebow and Stack, the major figure in the study of race relations in the inner city was William Julius Wilson, who is not himself an ethnographer. Beginning with *Power, Racism and Privilege: Race Relations in Theoretical and Sociohistorical Perspectives* in 1973 and *The Declining Significance of Race: Blacks and Changing American Institutions* in 1978, and continuing through to what may rightly be called a masterpiece, *When Work Disappears: The World of the New Urban Poor* (1996), Wilson led teams of field researchers at the University of Chicago in studies of empirical sophistication. And not just that but his books led over time to what may be the most important body of work on the changing circumstances of the urban poor. Wilson always situated his empirical data with reference to national issues of the economic and cultural factors at work in respect to race. *The Declining Significance of Race* is the first of these interventions in the history of the study of the racial poor. You can imagine how controversial the book was, but it was written with such authority that Wilson was subjected to none of the public outrage that fell upon Moynihan. After Wilson moved to Harvard, he published *When Work Disappears: The World of the New Urban Poor* (1996) which identified the extent to which rapid changes in the global economy left the long-term poor in the lurch. Young people in the West and

---

36 Carol Stack, *All Our Kin: Strategies in a Black Community* (Harper & Row, 1974), 44.
37 Ibid, 123.
38 Waverly Duck, *No Way Out: Precarious Living in the Shadow of Poverty and Drug Dealing* (University of Chicago Press, 2015), 2–19.
39 "About All Our Kin, Inc," https://allourkin.org/mission.

South Sides of Chicago when he studied these areas were born to families so poor that they seldom knew of anyone who got and held a job. The jobs were not there. One example:

> A 30-year-old welfare mother of two children from an impoverished South Side neighborhood of Chicago put it this way: 'A lot of them is having babies 'cause they ain't got nothing better to do. Now I have one 13 and one 8 years old. I had mine when I was 16 years old. I had mine 'cause I was curious. I wanted to see what it was like.'[40]

For a good quarter century and more Wilson, though not an ethnographer, has pretty much set the tone for the study of local communities of poor Black people. At the highest level that tone is set by Wilson's theoretical and policy argument about the new urban poor at the end of the twentieth century:

> As we examine the adaptations and responses of ghetto residents to persistent joblessness in this chapter, it should be emphasized that the disappearance of work in many inner-city neighborhoods is the function of a number of factors beyond their control. Too often, as reflected in the current public policy debates on welfare reform, the discussion of behavior and social responsibility fails to mention the structural underpinnings of poverty and welfare. The focus is mainly on the shortcomings of individuals and families and not on the structural and social changes in the society at large that have made life so miserable for many inner-city ghetto residents or that have produced certain unique responses and behavior patterns over time.[41]

This was published quite a while ago when, as a new century was about to be born, the *Myth of the Welfare Queen* was still very much in vogue, as today it still is in some quarters.[42] *When Work Disappears* is jam packed with numeric data as well as ample quotations from field studies, but always it leads to a strong, even insistent, theoretical claim that challenges the public to think and think again.

An Overwrought Criticism of Some Ethnographies

There was, however, an unusual moment early in the twenty-first century when Loïc Wacquant published in the *American Journal of Sociology* a very, very long, occasionally nasty, rebuke of trends in American ethnography. The article, "Scrutinizing the Street: Poverty, Morality, and the Pitfalls of Urban Ethnography," in 2002, presented itself as a review of three then recent ethnographies, all published in 1999. They were *Sidewalk* by Mitchell Duneier, *Code of the Street: Decency, Violence, and the Moral Life of the Inner City* by Elijah Anderson, and *No Shame in My Game: The Working Poor in the Inner City* by Katherine Newman. Wacquant's complaint against these three ethnographers is that "all three authors put forth truncated and distorted accounts of their object due their abiding wish to articulate and even celebrate the fundamental goodness—honesty, decency, frugality—of America's urban poor."[43] Though he won his PhD at Chicago under William Julius Wilson, Wacquant is French. He came to know Pierre Bourdieu very well while in Paris (where he also took

---

40 William Julius Wilson, *When Work Disappears: The World of the New Urban Poor* (Alfred A. Knopf, 1996), 107–108.
41 *Ibid*, 253.
42 For example, in 2019 see: Bruce Covert, "The Myth of the Welfare Queen," *The New Republic* (July 2, 2019).
43 Loïc Wacquant, "Scrutinizing the Street: Poverty, Morality, and the Pitfalls of Urban Ethnography," *American Journal of Sociology* 107: 6 (May 2002), 1479.

quite a number of degrees). Wacquant obviously knew quite a lot about American ethnography and did so with the analytic precision and condescension common to many French intellectuals.[44] Yet, whatever one thinks of Wacquant's attitudes, behind them all he made good enough sense of possible and often actual problems represented by Duneier, Anderson, and Newman.

> I will suggest that the proximate causes of the common limitations and liabilities of these three tomes—their uncontrolled skid from morality to moralism, their naïve acceptance of ordinary categories of perception as categories of analysis, their utter subservience to policy prescriptions and propaganda—can be found in the parochialism of the U.S. tradition of poverty research, the unwarranted empiricist disjunction of ethnography from theory, and the changing economics of social science publishing. ... And it spotlights a watershed moment in the politics of urban sociology in the United States: just as the romantic ethnographies of the cool, the marginal, and the lowly produced during the progressive sixties in the style of the second Chicago school were organically tied to the liberal politics of America's semi-welfare state and its then-expanding "social-problems complex," the neo-romantic tales spun by Duneier, Anderson, and Newman at the close of the regressive nineties suggest that U.S. sociology is now tied and party to the ongoing construction of the neoliberal state and its "carceral-assistential complex" for the punitive management of the poor, on and off the street.[45]

Harsh perhaps—but there is a sense in which Wacquant inadvertently clears the ground for an ethnographic approach that is, as he put it, as much theoretical as empirical—and in both aspects able to focus on local interaction orders with a more robust consideration of the wider structural pressures on the poor. At his best, Wacquant did this exceedingly well. For example, in one of his studies of prisons, he writes (in the vein of Michel Foucault) that the ghetto is a manner of "social prison" while the prison functions as a "judicial ghetto." Both are entrusted with enclosing a stigmatized population so as to neutralize the material and/or symbolic threat that they pose for the broader society.[46]

Then too in Wacquant's ethnography, *Body and Soul: Notebooks of an Apprentice Boxer*, he makes a sharp point of what he considers the shortcomings of American ethnographies: "I recused the false idea, deeply rooted in the American sociology of the relations between racial division and urban marginality since the earliest works of the Chicago School, that the ghetto is a "disorganized" universe, characterized by lack, want, and absence."[47] This at the start of an ethnography of a boxing gym of Black men in South Chicago where he remarks on the absence of racial differences among those, poor and Black though they were, who became part of a body culture. "The equalitarian ethos and pronounced color blindness of pugilistic culture are such that everyone is accepted into it so long as he submits to the common discipline and 'pays his dues' in the ring."[48]

Yet, Carol Stack for one is all but universally appreciated, while Loïc Wacquant is not. Just the same, these two, so different in many other ways, each pointed to a faint vision of a fungible interaction order in the communities they studied. It would remain for others

---

44 Admittedly the remark on condescension is a bit too strong. Bourdieu himself was, in my experience, capable of quite generous relations with others. But then while Bourdieu, the good cop, was still alive, Wacquant was his bad cop.
45 *Ibid*, 1470–71.
46 Wacquant, *Punishing the Poor: The Neoliberal Government* (Duke University Press, 2009), 198.
47 Wacquant, *Body and Soul: Notebooks of an Apprentice Boxer* (Oxford University Press, 2004), xi.
48 *Ibid*, 10.

to advance the idea, starting with one of the three ethnographers Wacquant dismissed, *mistakenly*—Elijah Anderson who in many ways has been the spiritual leader of the New Ethnographers.

Ethnographers May Not Be Perfect, But Ethnographies Are Necessary

Loïc Wacquant's criticism was widely read and discussed—in part because it consumed an unheard-of 64 pages of the ultra-prestigious *American Journal of Sociology* (that just so happens to be published by the University of Chicago Press). Clearly some approved of his general attitude not just to the three ethnographers he criticized but to ethnography itself, which is indicated by his tone in the first lines of the article:

> After a long decade during which researchers, following journalists and policy pundits, focused on the alleged rise, (mis)conduct, and threat of an "underclass" characterized by its presumed social isolation and antisocial behaviors, students of race and poverty in the U.S. metropolis have recently turned to issues of work, family, morality, and individual responsibility, in keeping with the newfound political concern for and media interest in those topics fostered by the "welfare reform" and the bipartisan rightward turn of social policy.[49]

Whenever you read a passage with words like "underclass," without a footnote, it is probably an instance of literary sarcasm. Then too when one writes about sociologies of any kind and refers to their borrowing from "journalists and policy pundits" it is an open insult. Nothing disturbs sociologists more than to be called mere journalists.

But why would Wacquant be so nasty in attacking three ethnographers when he too is an ethnographer? He is perfectly capable of being quite charming, for example, at an on-line event at NYU Institute for Public Knowledge in 2022, where in fact he presents on his book *The Invention of the "Underclass": A Study in the Politics of Knowledge* (2022)—written some 20 years after his 2002 *American Journal of Sociology* article.[50] It is evident that he had been meditating on the "underclass" for quite some time. Another reason may be that he is French and had been Pierre Bourdieu's literary representative in America[51] in the years before Bourdieu's death in 2002. Parisians, in particular, in the day very much wanted to be clear and distinct in expressing their views. So that too. But the basic thing is that he is brilliant. This no one can deny. His basic criticism of the ethnographies of Duneier, Anderson, and Newman illustrates this perfectly well.

> Their blindness to issues of class power and their stubborn disregard for the deep and multisided involvement (or, to use their own language, "responsibility") of the state in producing the social dereliction and human wretchedness they sensibly portray

---

49 Loïc Wacquant, "Scrutinizing the Street," 1468.
50 https://www.youtube.com/watch?v=KRjgyCm0pzQ . Also at https://loicwacquant.org/.
51 I know a little about this because well before Wacquant came on the scene Pierre Bourdieu seemed to be trying me out for this role at a time when he was not at all widely known in the US. He sent me warmly signed copies of his books and, though he never said so in so many words, he wanted me to find a publisher for them. I was able to find a publisher for two of them, and he was pleased. But then I decided against going farther with the project and politely bowed out. He remained friendly but books stopped coming. I liked Bourdieu very much, but I wanted my independence. I don't know for certain what Pierre Bourdieu had in mind, but it is clear that Loïc Wacquant was willing and able to serve while advancing his own writing career. In this sense Wacquant is more brilliant than I, probably by a significant degree.

condemn Duneier, Anderson, and Newman to elaborating variants of the classical fallacy of *argumentum ad populum*, in which a thesis is asserted, even acclaimed, because it resonates with the moral schemata and expectations of its audience, but at the cost of a dangerous suspension of analytic and political judgment.[52]

He makes a good enough point especially about Duneier's *Sidewalk*, but not at all about Eli Anderson's *Code of the Street* where the basic theme of the book is implicitly about how class power structures the street/decency dichotomy that produces what Wacquant calls "social dereliction and human wretchedness." *Code of the Street* is, in fact, seriously analytical without a great deal of analytic arm waving. No surprise then that shortly after Wacquant's *AJS* appeared, Anderson published his retort to Wacquant in the *American Journal of Sociology*. Anderson's "The Ideologically Driven Critique" begins angrily:

> It is clear from the outset that Wacquant has a particular "theoretical" ax to grind—one with an ideological blade—and that in doing so he seriously misreads *Code of the Street*, distorting its findings to fit his polemical purposes. At best, he seriously misunderstands my work; at worst, he willfully misrepresents it in his review. Regardless, Wacquant fails to engage the main thrust of the book: As a result of the breakdown or weaknesses of civil law in the most distressed inner-city communities, a survival strategy with implications for local public order has emerged—a "code of the street" that relies on "street justice," whose transactions involve a currency of reputation, respect, retribution, and retaliation.[53]

It is no surprise that authors dispute one another's way of thinking. But here the tone and content of the dispute makes a difference for, at least, understanding how and why ethnography can be so open to complaint.

Still, why this concluding tangent? It is not that other sociologists do not disagree but when they do, if the work is quantitative, they speak in numeric terms, much as Einstein and Heisenberg did in 1927 in Vienna over $E=mc^2$. These two surely talked in words over beers when the day was over, but, during the daily round of theoretical debates, arithmetic formulae were the language. Between qualitative research like ethnographies and quantitative research *in the social sciences, especially* there is an enormous gulf. Quantoids, as qualitoids sometimes call them, want precision of expressive *and* maximum scope of empirical reference. This is a fair-enough wish but like all desires it comes at a risk. The quantoids put at risk the descriptive nuance and story-like readability qualitoids, like ethnographers, value. Anyone can read Anderson's *Code of the Street* and not get at least the drift of the story if not the author's precise point? Hardly anyone can read $E=mc^2$ (even in translation) and know very much about what it means because the c^2 in $E=mc^2$ is a *constant*, as formulae writers put it, and such a thing complicates the discourse about the relation of E to M—of, that is, the relation of **Energy** to **Mass** in the universe of all thinkable things. So, as I said at the first, where there is theory there are differences. No theory can be beyond controversy.

---

52 Wacquant, "Scrutinizing the Street," 1470.
53 Elijah Anderson, "The Ideologically Driven Critique," *American Journal of Sociology* 107:6 (May, 2002): 1533. If anything, Katherine Newman's criticism of Wacquant in the same issue of the *AJS* is all the more ferocious (for an academic; for instance, her "No Shame: The View from the Left Bank," is a sneer at his Parisian attitude: "In the end, there is almost no link between these three books and what Wacquant makes of them. Long before its publication in *AJS*, Wacquant has been busy distributing his attack around the globe and across the profession."

So here is the unique role of ethnographies in the human sciences. Ethnographies are stories that come to be heard and read as theories when those hearing or reading are willing to see the theory in the story. This is not always easy. I've read and discussed more than a few times Eli Anderson's *Code of the Street*—some of those times he was present.[54] I haven't always gotten the drift right. This at first was due to the fact that I had an early interest in semiotics—so I was more interested in how he used the word code—which, by the way, I have long thought he could have done more with. In a word, Eli is a good ethnographer but not a good semiologist, and that was my problem. I could have carried on about this, as several times I did, but I never became aggressive as Wacquant did with *his* theoretical preferences at the time in 2002. I didn't because it made no sense to me to behave that way. Still, I could be difficult and imagine that Wacquant made no sense because he was, in 2002, suffering a bit of a Parisian intellectual hang up—even such thoughts on my part are themselves aggressive in their way. But then Loïc now praises William Julius Wilson who became one of his mentors and he is neither Parisian nor anything but kind in temperament. In fact once when Wilson was visiting Wesleyan for a lecture series I organized, he told me how shocked he was that his Harvard colleagues refused to invite Loïc to a seminar there because they thought he behaved *nastily* or some such word.

Okay, enough of this rigmarole. It may seem that I am just carrying on about various ones I know to varying degrees. But, ideally, that is the way ethnographies can have an effect on others—and were it as easily done, it is how all theories including numeric ones should be received and passed on. Quantitative theorists like the Yale physicist I often met at J.P. Dempsey's before it closed would try to tell what he did every three weeks with the CERN Large Hadron Accelerator in Geneva. Even though I couldn't make out how the Higgs boson wave accounts for small particles in the universe, he inspired me to try—and he refused to laugh when I failed. He smiled at my cluelessness and bought me drink instead. But even this is a story that matters. This is the second time I've told this story of drinks in a now closed bar in this book, and I returned to it again now because it is too much to, once again, tell the Einstein-Heisenberg discussion over drinks in Vienna in 1927. In other words, and finally to be short all theories inspire stories among the elect or the average. As a kind of theory none is more available than those that arise from ethnographies. That they are available, unlike the Higgs boson wave, makes them all the more controversial, which controversies lead to more stories.

---

54 For a few years I was a senior fellow in Elijah Anderson's Yale Urban Ethnography Workshop.

17 The New Ethnographers of Urban Disorder

AbdouMaliq Simone, Elijah Anderson, Waverly Duck, Victor Rios, Matthew Desmond, Nikki Jones, Alice Goffman

In a fundamental way, this cityness has become and always has been largely peripheral to city life. That is, the very dimension that characterizes the city—its capacities to continuously reshape the ways in which people, places, materials, ideas, and affect are intersected—is often the very thing left out of the larger analytic picture.
—AbdouMaliq Simone,
City Life From Jakarta to Dakar, 2010

Almost everyone residing in poor inner-city neighborhoods is struggling financially and therefore feels a certain distance from the rest of America, but there are degrees of alienation, captured by the terms "decent" and "street" or "ghetto," suggesting social types.
—Elijah Anderson, *Code of the Street: Decency, Violence, and the Moral Life of the Inner City,* 1999

Trust, mutual understanding, and reciprocity form
the bedrock of social organization in this community.
In order to survive, everyone must become competent in the normally expected practices
that constitute the situations they walk into and out of during the course of daily life …
—Waverly Duck, *No Way Out: Precarious Living in the Shadow of Poverty and Drug Dealing,* 2015

The youth control complex is the combined effect of the web of institutions, schools, families, businesses, residents, media, community centers, and the criminal justice system that collectively punish, stigmatize, monitor, and criminalize young people in an attempt to control them.
—Victor Rios, *Punished: Policing the Lives of Black and Latino Boys,* 2011

Affordable housing should be a basic right in this country.
The reason is simple: without stable shelter, everything falls apart.
—Matthew Desmond, *Evicted: Poverty and Profit in the American City,* 2016

People do not make good on their own: people make good with others.
—Nikki Jones, *The Chosen Ones: Black Men and the Politics of Redemption,* 2018

The threat of prison and the heavy presence of police, the courts, and the prisons come to permeate the social fabric of the community in more than subtle ways,

DOI: 10.4324/9781315210230-21

shifting the currency of love and commitment and creating
a new moral framework through which residents carve out their identities and relationships.
—Alice Goffman, On the Run: Fugitive Life in an American City, 2014

Recasting Ethnographies for a New Day

Ethnographies in America are not all that old that most would say that they are in need of recasting. But in a sense they are because earlier ethnographers like Elliot Liebow, Carol Stack, and even Loïc Wacquant, along with wise thinkers like William Julius Wilson, and many others, have opened the door to new considerations made all the more acute by changes evident in the early history of the twenty-first century.

To begin, consider one whose work has been so deeply done in the Global South far from even the southern-most borders of America. AbdouMaliq Simone who has roots in America before he became a global person living for the time being in the UK, visiting universities in the US and Europe, as well as Africa and Southeast Asia. In his book *City Life from Jakarta to Dakar* Simone proposes a new concept:

> In a fundamental way, this cityness has become and always has been largely peripheral to city life. That is, the very dimension that characterizes the city—its capacities to continuously reshape the ways in which people, places, materials, ideas, and affect are intersected—is often the very thing left out of the larger analytic picture.[1]

Does such a one belong in a book about American social theories? Yes because, as will become apparent, Simone is a global figure whose ethnographies give Americans clues how that work can and must be done in a globalized world—certainly the kind of novelty the practice needs.

Among Americans, if there is an inspiration for, if not a practitioner of, the New Ethnography, it would be Yale's Elijah Anderson who has taught or otherwise worked with many of the younger new ethnographers. An example of the novelty of Anderson's ethnography is his 1999 book: *Code of the Street: Decency, Violence, and the Moral Life of the Inner City*, where he writes:

> Almost everyone residing in poor inner-city neighborhoods is struggling financially and therefore feels a certain distance from the rest of America, but there are degrees of alienation, captured by the terms "decent" and "street" or "ghetto," suggesting social types.[2]

For one important thing, Anderson always looks for the complications in urban life even as his elegant writing presents them clearly.

Waverly Duck at the University of California at Santa Barbara (UCSB) provides an original theory of local interaction orders based on his research for *No Way Out: Precarious Living in the Shadow of Poverty*:

> Trust, mutual understanding, and reciprocity form the bedrock of social organization in this community. In order to survive, everyone must become competent in the normally expected practices that constitute the situations they walk into and out of during the course of daily life...[3]

---

1 *City Life from Jakarta to Dakar: Movements at the Crossroads* (Routledge, 2010), 5.
2 Anderson, *Code of the Street: Decency, Violence, and the Moral Life of the Inner City* (W.W. Norton, 1999), 25.
3 Waverly Duck, *No Way Out: Precarious Living in the Shadow of Poverty and Drug Dealing* (University of Chicago Press, 2015), 6.

You can see from this passage that Duck views interaction orders as fungible.

Victor Rios, also at UCSB, which is fast becoming a center for new ethnographers, writes of the dire straits of young Black and Latino boys on the streets of Oakland:

> The youth control complex is the combined effect of the web of institutions, schools, families, businesses, residents, media, community centers, and the criminal justice system that collectively punish, stigmatize, monitor, and criminalize young people in an attempt to control them.[4]

Yet Rios studied them closely enough that he could say that they devised schemes whereby they used personal resources to get out from under such a brutal complex.

Matthew Desmond's new ethnography is one in which his long and careful field work including living among those he studied resulted in a book that included a manifesto: Sociology must engage, he said, in what then was a new subfield of work: *eviction*. Housing is, he argues, that without which people fall into a hopeless pit:

> Affordable housing should be a basic right in this country. The reason is simple: without stable shelter, everything falls apart.[5]

Desmond backed up his manifesto by investing the money he won from a MacArthur Genius Grant in projects that would put eviction studies on the sociological map.

Nikki Jones is Professor and Chair of African American Studies *and* African Diaspora Studies at the University of California at Berkeley. The title alone tells something of why she is part of the New Ethnographers movement—as does her powerful turn of phrase in her 2018 book, *The Chosen Ones: Black Men and the Politics of Redemption*: "People do not make good on their own: people make good with others."[6] Many of the men she studied on the streets of the Filmore District of San Francisco found their way out of urban misery by working together to join their individual redemptive powers. The book concludes with a stunning statement: *Free people, free people.*

Alice Goffman's *On the Run: Fugitive Life in an American City* in 2014—a thoroughly brilliant book in which she says, new ethnographically:

> The threat of prison and the heavy presence of police, the courts, and the prisons come to permeate the social fabric of the community in more than subtle ways, shifting the currency of love and commitment and creating a new moral framework through which residents carve out their identities and relationships.[7]

Alice Goffman has been attacked by cowards in unsigned statements claiming that she was too close to her subjects. More than Desmond? More than any new ethnographer?

New Ethnography, by going beyond the more formalist methods of some of the earlier ethnographers, requires careful work in many of its aspects.

---

4 Victor Rios *Punished: Policing the Lives of Black and Latino Boys* (New York University Press, 2011), 40.
5 Matthew Desmond, *Evicted: Poverty and Profit in the American City* (Penguin Random House, 2016), 300.
6 Nikki Jones, *The Chosen Ones: Black Men and the Politics of Redemption* (University of California Press, 2018), 5.
7 Alice Goffman, *On The Run: Fugitive Life in an American City* (University of Chicago Press, 2014), 198.

Fair Haven: Decent Enough To Pass Its Street Code

Fair Haven is New Haven's fastest growing and far and away most interesting neighborhood. Yet, few of those who live elsewhere know anything about it and seldom visit this community. The same is not so for Fair Haven's residents who have relatively easy access to downtown New Haven, some two miles away. Hence, an irony. Those who live in the Hill neighborhood are closer to the New Haven Green, by far. But the urban moat that surrounds them makes the trip hard and longer. Not so of Fair Haven.

Looking at a map, one would think that Fair Haven seems to be similarly cut off. It is, after all, bordered on East and West by the Quinnipiac and Mill Rivers, and to the North by the Quinnipiac Marsh. Interstate 91 runs across its Northern border before descending along its West border beyond the Mill River. Yet, the highway and a goodly number of bridges to the main city connect Fair Haven readily to New Haven. Oddly, Fair Haven's once local medical center has partly moved to Sargent Drive in New Haven into a center that serves its patients but also those of Yale New Haven Hospital and of Cornell Scott Hill Health Center. Just the same the long-standing Fair Haven Community Health Care still operates two of its three clinics on Grand Ave—Fair Haven's axial street where, also, many of its commercial and social service facilities are located.

Similar to the Hill, Fair Haven is ranked A+ for amenities. But here it is easier to see what that might be. There are a number of accessible pharmacies, groceries, restaurants, and other commercial offerings along Grand Avenue, but also there are a good many schools around Fair Haven, as well as churches and other religious and social enterprises. But also the neighborhood enjoys easy access not just to New Haven proper but its vast and inviting East Rock Park where many who live in Fair Haven can be seen enjoying picnics and the playgrounds in the warmer months. Fair Haven is ranked C overall—higher than the Hill's D-/F (–this difference is an illustration of how these rankings function to establish hierarchies among different local neighborhoods[8]).

The most distinctive social feature of Fair Haven is its large Puerto Rican and African American populations. This alone is surely one of the reasons residents of New Haven's adjacent upscale East Rock neighborhood seldom shop or otherwise visit Fair Haven—except for an occasional visit to the artist studios and shows at Erector Square or to the District (a work-offices, gym, and restaurant facility), both of which are the border with Fair Haven. Still, there is crime throughout New Haven. East Rock is plagued by property theft and a few murders. The crime rate is higher in Fair Haven, especially property theft. Most striking of all is that at the very center of the neighborhood at Grand and Ferry Streets the city has joined with local leaders of Fair Haven's "harm reduction coalition" to establish an "engagement center" to serve and support sex workers, day laborers, drug users, and other struggling populations.[9] There could hardly be a better instance of a fungible interaction order. Generally speaking, Fair Haven would be an interesting place for ethnographic research, of which none worthy of public notice has been done.

By contrast to Fair Haven, which is relatively orderly, the Hill, with its more tacit, but vibrating, disordering aspects, is the kind of neighborhood that could well be of particular interest to the New Ethnographers. There can be little doubt that Fair Haven offers a good many amenities, especially for its Latinx population which is growing rapidly with migrants of Caribbean origin. Also housing is ample. Along Front Street by the

---

8 The flimsy value of these comparative rankings on neighborhoods and communities are discussed in chapter 16 on the unique scientific purpose of ethnographies.
9 "Engagement Center Eyed for Problem Block," *New Haven Independent* (August 16, 2022).

Quinnipiac River there is a clean and quite lovely low-income housing project perched on a hill slightly above a row of smaller mostly nicely kept and decorated and well gardened houses presumably owned by the modestly well off. On Front Street there happens to be an excellent Oyster House that rarely has an open table. Up from Front Street there are many blocks of grand houses from an older time, many of them attractive if not well kept—and then too there are more modest homes up and across Grand Ave nearer to New Haven town center. Still *Niche/Neighborhood* ranks *housing* in Fair Haven D-, while ranking the neighborhood *good for families* at C+ and much better for the ever-ambiguous *amenities*. But the real curve ball on the whole is *crime* where Fair Haven is literally off the chart—no grade, just a blunt *minus*. The data show that Fair Haven has a crime rate some 30% higher than New Haven and 100% higher than the national average[10]—of which theft and burglary are far and away the most common, while violent crimes are lower.[11]

All in all the most striking fact about Fair Haven is that it is today populated by people many of whom have migrated to New Haven from the islands and elsewhere in the world. And this brings us to the ethnographer whose presence in this chapter may well be a surprise to many, some of whom might even say who is AbdouMaliq Simone?

AbdouMaliq Simone: Cityness and the Global New for Ethnographies

The moniker *New Ethnographers* is coined to account for structural changes in the first decades of the twenty-first century. To be sure urban disorder is itself a structural feature of late or post-modern cities, globally South as well as North. These dramatically changed cities experience waves of migrations from drought and war riddled rural areas to urban areas increasingly flooded with waves of migrants seeking safety and better lives. AbdouMaliq Simone, since 1977, has lived in and studied this migratory pattern from sub-Saharan Africa where new cities have arisen on the periphery of African cities like Johannesburg, Freetown, Kinshasa, Dakar, and Lagos and Southeast Asian cities like Jakarta.[12]

Simone has invented the concept of *cityness* to account for ways these migrations have changed many cities the world over and altered how urban studies must be done. Simply put, he writes: "Cityness refers to the city as a thing in the making."[13] He means by this at first odd notion of cityness to take account of the way cities across the world are ever more in flux than they had been through the twentieth century. We must, he argues, think of a city as a place where people are part of the infrastructure, living as part of a geographic, economic, cultural, and social entity that is ever changing. Not all cities of course, but many. Hence, the surprising but oft-ignored fact of cities:

> In a fundamental way, this cityness has become and always has been largely peripheral to city life. That is, the very dimension that characterizes the city—its capacities to continuously

---

10 https://www.areavibes.com/new+haven-ct/fair+haven/crime/ . Here the important fact is that Fair Haven's is so much higher than New Haven's.

11 https://www.niche.com/places-to-live/n/fair-haven-new-haven-ct/#crime-safety. I will not provide the numbers given because they are based on comparison to national averages. Here again are all the flaws of this kind of commercial ranking systems. But at least these provide a sketch of the neighborhood.

12 AbdouMaliq Simone, *Under Siege: Four African Cities-Freetown, Johannesburg, Kinshasa, Lagos* (Hatje Cantz Verlag, 2003); *For the City Yet to Come: Changing African Life in Four Cities* (Duke University Press, 2004); *City Life from Jakarta to Dakar: Movements at the Crossroads* (Routledge, 2010).

13 AbdouMaliq Simone, *City Life from Jakarta to Dakar*, ibid, 3.

reshape the ways in which people, places, materials, ideas, and affect are intersected—is often the very thing left out of the larger analytic picture.[14]

Then in a long chapter on *Intersections*, Simone plants a section on the capital city of the People's Republic of Congo, Kinshasa—which may have suffered the worst instance of European colonization by King Leopold early in the twentieth century and Mobutu Sese Seko later. The viciousness of that ruling order has been replaced by cityness—a condition of intersections in which people are part of Kinshasa's infrastructure.[15] In today's Kinshasa, the people who live there, the Kinois, live between continuously oscillating poles of deep respect for simple truths and a regular practice of exaggerations—as Simone puts it in the header of one section: "When Confidence and Fear, Precision and Exaggeration Prove Too Difficult to Reconcile".[16] One example is of the omnipresence of police, thereby of surveillance which encourages a high degree of public dissemblance that cuts against the grain of their deeply religious commitments and faith in basic honesty. Geographically Kinshasa is a city of 9 million people spread out over an area of 100 square kilometers—so far that many live in quasi rural areas between city and the countryside—again a tug in two directions at once. And most also live on $1 a day—many of whom hide or exaggerate what wealth they have or wish they had. They are in a word people always on the move from place to place, from truth to exaggeration and deception. They can be called part of Kinshasa's infrastructure because this constant movement is itself multidimensional in a way that makes of the city's geographic boundaries a figure of practical speech. Many came by way of migration. Once there they continue to migrate several ways at once within Kinshasa; hence its cityness. Similarly, Simone sees the same in a very different city in a section under still another intriguing header: "Once Upon Many Different Times in Inner City Johannesburg."[17]

Johannesburg, of course, unlike Kinshasa, has come out from a very different kind of colonization, apartheid, which has caused it to change itself radically again in both the geographical and social senses, among others. Its cityness has caused it to rearrange all of the normal institutional and sector divisions to accommodate the new presence of the former forbidden into political, economic, and social life.

Predictably, the book ends with "Reclaiming Black Urbanism: Inventive Methods for Engaging Urban Fields from Dakar to Jakarta" (chapter 6). From the start, Simone is *not* trying to narrow the focus on Black people. Rather, by Black Urbanism he means to rethink global cities altogether. He does this in a way that is more convincing and vastly more original than others who are better known for their writings on the subject. The global city, for Simone, is something more than the larger cities of greater importance for their place in global interactions. They are again new cities that require a new theory:

> Black urbanism is a way of addressing a situation where the theorization of global urban change has paid insufficient attention to practices and technologies that bring an increasing heterogeneity of calculations, livelihoods, and organizational logics into a relationship with each other.[18]

---

14 *Ibid*, 5.
15 Adam Hochschild, *King Leopold's Ghost: A Story of Greed, Terror, and Heroism in Colonial Africa* (Random House, 1998).
16 *Ibid*, 134–141.
17 *Ibid*, 237–262. See also Simone, "People as Infrastructure: Intersecting Fragments in Johannesburg," *Public Culture* 16(3), 2004: 407–429.
18 *Ibid*, 280.

This may sound all too theoretical in a pure analytic sense. But Simone means it in the most empirical sense. He immediately follows with:

> Increasingly, urban economies are focusing on how intersections are actually practiced and performed. ... There are scores of small stories: The stock exchange in Lagos opens up an office in Shanghai. Rich Congolese businessmen buy auto parts distributors in Dubai. Businessmen from Nairobi buy into a Bangkok-based shipping company.[19]

Thus a high powered conceptual statement is illustrated by a series of empirical stories of connections the world-over. They are stories meant to ground a theory of Black urbanism by references to events so dispersed and so particular that only one who has lived and studied in all these places might know or realize that they must be googled.

Who, then, is AbdouMaliq Simone? Well first off, though he makes no fuss about it, Simone was born in Wisconsin, studied at Hampshire College in Massachusetts and took a graduate degree at the Wright Institute in Berkeley. At least this qualifies him for a place in a book on American social theory—not that he needs to be thus qualified. He is the very archetype of a global person working and living across the Global South while holding academic positions across the Global North from Sheffield (his home base for now) and Cambridge University in the UK to the Max Planck Institute to Berkeley and NYU in New York, and too many other places to name. "He lives between London, Turin, Jakarta, and Bangkok."[20]

Simone is a migrant himself who has studied and lived among people the world over who, one might say, live in a constant state of migration. When he writes about these far flung places he tells sharp and telling stories of who the people are and how their lives are the result cityness. His on the ground direct studies tell of how people got there and how they get on since arriving to become part of an urban flux that could well be the story of our urban world for time to come. Simone is, in short, an ethnographer and much else. He belongs in this discussion because he studies people who live without exception in the kind of disordering that accompany migrations from, to, and within rural and urban places which are themselves in a state of dramatic change.

It has long been held that the rural migrations to cities was over and done with early in the twentieth century. But that of course is not true early in the twenty-first century when, even in America, the daily domestic news other than mass shootings is of the migrants who come from the South in search of heaven only to find hell, as the title of a new and important book suggests, *We Thought It Would Be Heaven: Refugees In An Unequal America* by Blair Sackett and Annette Lareau.[21] This book actually studies migrants from the Democratic Republic of Congo, but their suffering and shocking loss of a promised land is also the story of those who come to America's southern borders seeking the relief from violence and poverty that *El Norte* once promised.

To be sure, the new ethnographies that are featured in this chapter only indirectly deal with people who have come to various cities seeking what was seldom to be found.

---

19 *Ibid*, 280–281.
20 Biographical details are from: https://www.sharjahart.org/sharjah-art-foundation/people/abdoumaliq-simone.
21 Blair Sackett and Annette Lareau, *We Thought It Would Be Heaven: Refugees In An Unequal America* (University of California Press, 2023).

New Ethnographies of North America As It Has Come To Be

The distinguishing fact of American history is not of its revolutionary origins, but of its utter transformation from a once rural country into one so radically and dramatically urban at a central moment in its history. And, with this transformation came unrelenting conflicts and the disordering that accompanies urban life.

Ever since the Civil War so memorably disordered the Nation, the fungibility of its national interaction order has served to dramatize the Nation's peculiar contradictions— *first*, from its first settlement it was, as it remains, a high-minded culture seeking perfect democratic order while always being disordered by the scourge of slavery upon which its unspeakable white nationalism was founded; and *second*, America's racial corruption caused the Civil War that reordered the Nation such that the corruption of what began in slavery migrated in more modern times to its cities. America's peculiar theory and practice of white supremacy down into today's postmodern era has been a perversion of its otherwise good cultural values. The proponents of this perverse value of white supremacy are today very often people who live on in the vast American nether regions—the rural South and West, the still confederate villages of the Deep South, the inferior exurbs of the Northern cities. Yet, they are the army of what has come to be called militant replacement theory—the false notion that America was founded by white Europeans who are its only proper members. This bizarre if to some persuasive lie is born these days of a fear that whites will soon lose the place of privilege in the continental culture they never had. For it was their ancestors who killed and exiled the indigenous people of the New World, and did the same in effect to Africans imported to build their new world's economic order.

This may seem a far-fetch from ethnographies of urban disorder, except for the fact that sociologists, and others of their kind, borrowed the practice of ethnography as the written study of people in their grounded lives from anthropologists who in turn, with rare exception, studied remote cultures of people who were being discovered by white explorers and capitalists. Ethnography in this sense has always been more or less the local study of people displaced by the New World Order. Trobriand Islanders, Blacks and other people of color in America, the Indigenous settlers of land, workers in Industrial England, among others.

In this sense, then, New Ethnographers are not all that new—except for one important thing. Urban ethnography has slowly but surely divorced itself from earlier practices that were, in a word, married more to community studies—of, if not communities in America, the study of premodern cultures the world over as though their communities were innocent by-standers to the developing ravages of global capitalism. As it happens, as time has passed ethnography as a practice has changed time and again. In due course, an important group of American Ethnographers have made a discovery that had an important effect on social theory generally.

The New Ethnographers departed from the earlier traditions by studying order and disorder in troubled communities from within, but more importantly, they did so with keen descriptive attention to the interactions of particular groups of people whose lives depended on getting by as best they could and escaping patterns of living that all-but ruined them in the eyes of the wider world. Without exception, the disorderly inner cities came to be as a result of migrations from within the nation of those whose ancestors had come from abroad bringing values and life styles their descendants today barely understand.

Limits on Upward Migration: Elijah Anderson's Code of the Street

If there is a *locus classicus* for a robust New Ethnography, it would be *Code of the Street: Decency, Violence, and the Moral Life of the Inner City* (1999) by Elijah Anderson.

The book was written near the end of his long tenure at the University of Pennsylvania (he moved to Yale in 2007). Anderson's *Code of the Street* was informed by his thorough familiarity with Philadelphia and its neighborhoods which allowed him to write an unqualifiedly nuanced ethnographic study of the urban neighborhood down toward town on Germantown Avenue.

His book is introduced by this geographic fact of the neighborhood studied for *Code of the Street*—a literary tactic that suggests the degree to which Anderson's ethnographic site is situated at the juncture of temporal and spatial vectors. Not only does Germantown Avenue date back to colonial times, but spatially it reaches out far from downtown Philadelphia and its neighborhoods into the well-off outlying areas. "The story of Germantown Avenue can therefore serve in many respects as a metaphor for the whole city."[22] This may seem a small feature to characterize Anderson's book as the beginning of new ethnographies but it takes on greater salience when the book's orthogonal narrative line is introduced—that between *street* and *decent families*.[23] Every element of Anderson's ethnographic book turns on this difference within the Germantown neighborhood—a difference that generates a dynamic tension in the life of the neighborhood. A particularly striking passage in *Code of the Street* is the long (ten page) field note on the struggles of Yvette, a twenty-year-old woman from a decent family, who was forced to deal with street challenges.[24] The long report on Yvette's situation, as she saw it, looks back on her teen years. Her father was out on his own. Her mother ran the home. She made sure that Yvette attended church regularly and, when it became obvious that public schools were "too street" (so to speak), she got Yvette into a private school where she did well enough. Yet even though her home life was largely closed to the outside world, Yvette could not avoid contact with the street people who disliked her. She describes one incident with the mother of children she had looked out for:

> I was tutoring her children in math and science, just trying to help them out because they're kind of failing. One's at Simon Gratz High and one's at James Middle School. And I wanted them out. And she caught me one day when my mother wasn't there. She's like, "You know Yvette, you make people hate you." And I'm like, "What are you talking about? What is the problem?" She was like, "You come around here. You think you're better than everyone else. Da-da-da." It's just a whole spiel that she goes on. But that just tells me—I didn't do anything. I tried to help her kids and she saw me trying to help her kids as me thinking I'm better than her. Which is twisted. That's just wrong.[25]

That's just wrong! Indeed. Faced with the twisted attitude of the mother whose kids she was helping, Yvette understood what was going on. She was who she was—a young woman trying to lead a decent life. Those who thought she thought she was better than they, were right in the sense that they had sunk under the stultifying cloud of street culture.

This is but one story among many, but it goes to the heart of *Code of the Street* which is about the struggle street people have in a neighborhood where decent others do better than they do. At the same time Anderson concludes the book with a sad note about the decent

---

22 Anderson, *Code of the Street: Decency, Violence, and the Moral Life of the Inner City* (W.W. Norton, 1999), 15.
23 On the decent/street dichotomy see, especially Chapter 1 in *Code of the Str ibid*, 35–65.
24 *Ibid*, 53–63. BTW, Anderson is an excellent writer who often reads his elegantly composed field notes in seminars. It is one of the important ways he influences others. Though he might well object to my saying so, I think it is also the way he turns these small groups into a kind of interaction order. A class is nothing but a class unless the teacher interjects direct information from the field. More than once I've seen his classes turned into something else, a more fungible order.
25 *Ibid*, 56.

people: "Surrounded by violence and what many view as municipal indifference to innocent victims of drug dealers and users, as well as common street criminals, the decent people are finding it increasingly difficult to maintain a sense of community."[26] Here is the elementary interaction order in so many urban neighborhoods. Though Anderson does not use the term, here and elsewhere he saw the communities he studied as caught up and organized in an interaction order.

In a much later book—*The Cosmopolitan Canopy: Race and Civility in Everyday Life* (2011)—Anderson writes of Philadelphia's Center City where Blacks commonly share public spaces and work environments with whites. The picture drawn is of settings where Blacks and whites get along well, if not perfectly well. But, in the book's most stunning chapter—"The Nigger Moment"—Anderson tells of those all but ubiquitous moments in an idealized interracial culture where the ideal is shattered by the all-too-familiar insensitivity of white people. He tells of Jesse, a college graduate who became a paralegal in a white shoe law firm where he enjoyed friendly social relations with partners and fellow workers. Then just before Jesse was to leave for a vacation in Lima, Peru, one senior partner gave Jesse advice in front of other white partners: "When you get to Peru, don't hang out too much with banana eating monkeys! And don't hang out too much with drug dealers." There was an uncomfortable silence and nervous chuckles from the group. But Jesse wasn't laughing—he was stunned. He was not only deeply offended by the behavior of this highfalutin partner but also shaken by the accommodating reactions of others who heard the remark.[27] In this Nigger Moment the self-satisfied decent professionals felt they could engage in street talk with a Black colleague. Similar perhaps but it was a reversal of the struggles of decent folk in *Code of the Street*.

It is not at all clear that Elijah Anderson is an out-and-out interaction order theorist. In truth he is not a theorist in the usual sense at all. Just the same, his writings do describe a fungible order by whatever name—and his teaching and mentoring of others does seem to have had one or another kind of influence on a younger group of urban ethnographers—who, wittingly or unwittingly, put to work the ideas and methods in the older tradition of interaction order studies.[28]

A Defining Theory of the New Ethnography: Waverly Duck on the Interaction Order as Collective Efficacy

Waverly Duck (1976–) is North Hall Professor of Sociology at the University of California at Santa Barbara. He had taught at the University of Pittsburg for a number of years, after having been Senior Fellow in Urban Ethnography at Yale where he was a close associate of Elijah Anderson.

Professor Duck is one of the new ethnographers who, more than any other, explicitly wrote of an interaction order among the people in and around the community he calls Bristol Hill. His first book, *No Way Out: Precarious Living in the Shadow of Poverty and Drug Dealing* (2015), begins by acknowledging Elijah Anderson's contribution to the problem of studying people who live in precarious communities:

---

26 Ibid, 325.
27 Anderson, *The Cosmopolitan Canopy: Race and Civility in Everyday Life* (W.W. Norton, 2011), 260.
28 Of the younger New Ethnographers here discussed Alice Goffman and Nikki Jones were Anderson's students at Penn and Waverly Duck was his postdoctoral associate at Yale. Also, for a number of years he held annual conferences at Penn and Yale to which he invited most of the leading ethnographers at one time or another. Matthew Desmond may have been an exception, but I know for a fact that he knows Anderson and that, at the least, they met a time or two at Yale.

> The code of the street, as initially defined by Anderson, refers to the set of informal but commonly understood rules that govern interpersonal behavior in public when law enforcement and other formal means of settling conflicts are absent. In neighborhoods that are isolated from mainstream institutions and plagued by concentrated poverty and endemic unemployment, this code functions alongside the norms and values residents call "decent" which most of them share with white, middleclass Americans.[29]

Here Duck is faithful to Anderson's idea but, interestingly, he tweaks Anderson's tendency to make street/decent an oppositional dichotomy. Duck, here and throughout *No Way Out*, sneaks in a small but important modification by stating clearly that even those who live and act by the street code share the decency code normal to white, middle-class Americans.[30] Just after this, Duck makes it clear that his study of Bristol Hill follows a program that goes beyond Anderson's in crucial ways: "I expand the concept of the code [of the street] to encompass the entire set of interactions among residents and between themselves and outsiders on Lyford Street."[31] Duck, quite explicitly turns to a more robust sense of a fungible interaction order:

> Trust, mutual understanding, and reciprocity form the bedrock of social organization in this community. The social obligations that exist between residents are essential to understanding how people navigate the neighborhood. In order to survive, everyone must become competent in the normally expected practices that constitute the situations they walked into and out of during the course of daily life, accurately interpreting what is going on there and responding in ways others deem appropriate.[32]

What Duck is doing here is using both Goffman and Garfinkel to buttress his original interpretation of interaction order in a way that puts earlier, less well-formulated theoretical movements of the kind in a fresh and more available form.

To be sure, David Riesman, Erik Erikson, and Edwin Lemert were, while original in their own domains, background to the later movement of fungible interaction orders. It is Goffman and Garfinkel, in their different ways, who not only lend important dimensions to the general idea of an interaction order but bring "fungibility" into the open. Though Duck did not use the adjective fungible (and perhaps this was wise for a then younger scholar coming into his own), but he astutely realizes that Goffman and Garfinkel—though strictly speaking not empirical sociologists—offered the building blocks for a fresh perspective in the study of local communities. For example, here is Duck referring to the ordering shared by people in Bristol:

> The local order practices they share create a constitutive framework for social action, without which interactions and identities in this context would make no sense. In Erving Goffman's terms [in *The Presentation of Self* in 1959] they constitute performance criteria for establishing identity, competence, and loyalty in this place. As Harold Garfinkel in 1967 [in *Studies in Ethnomethodology*], they both require and demonstrate mutual

---

29 Waverly Duck, *No Way Out: Precarious Living in the Shadow of Poverty and Drug Dealing* (University of Chicago Press, 2015), 7.
30 For example, see Anderson's straightforward definition of the street code as "... not the goal or product of any individual's actions but is the fabric of everyday life, a vivid and pressing milieu within which all local residents must shape their personal routines..." Anderson, *Code of the Street*, 326; compare 9.
31 *Ibid*, 5.
32 *Ibid*, 6.

commitment and a high degree of reciprocity. Treating the practices of such places as an interaction order that requires a high degree of commitment and attention from residents challenges the prevailing understanding of poor Black neighborhoods. The interaction order constitutes an important but overlooked form of *collective efficacy*, even though forged as it is in a context of poverty and isolation, it often works against the visible expression of middleclass values.[33]

It is all too easy to read through the generative ideas and textured descriptive sections of this book and fail to see just how important this passage is in respect to the general idea of a fungible interaction-order. In part, the concept of *collective efficacy* offers a solution to a problem that has been puzzling social theorists since, at least, Riesman and Erikson, down through more general subsequent attempts to figure out how subjects live each day with, and against, prevailing social structures *and* the interaction orders that make and inhabit them. Just after this stunning passage, Duck adds: "Because of the constitutive character of local interaction-order practices, it is a mistake to use standards that come from elsewhere to judge individuals who grow up there as if they were free to follow whatever rules they choose or to measure the solidarity and efficacy that characterizes the neighborhoods."[34]

This is what others were looking to see in and say about their research. It is what Carol Stack saw without saying it in the Flats. And what Loïc Wacquant apparently meant to say and couldn't because he gave in to his own oppositional impulses that cluttered his thinking in the attack on American ethnographers. In effect what Waverly Duck is explaining is that the poor and Black urban neighborhoods are (1) not disordered, (2) not set in stone, (3) not necessarily outside the wider cultural norm. In short, they are in constant motion, while making and remaking the social order in which they live *together*. Yet, Duck makes his own important qualification. The interaction order he observed in Bristol Hill is defined by the combined structural intrusions of poverty and drugs. Hence the book's subtitle: *No Way Out: Precarious Living in the Shadow of Poverty and Drug Dealing*—in respect to which he offers the important sociological note that not all communities suffering in the shadow of poverty are the same: "Communities where drug dealing structures the economy have different local order practices than where sex work or working off the books are the main illegal enterprises."[35] This remark may seem off-the-cuff. But those who have had experience with these, and similar, communities know just what is meant.

Back in the long ago, in Paris, France, there were several different kinds of sites where sex workers did their work. One, more active in the summer months, was a field in the *Bois de Boulogne*. Here the sex workers turned tricks where they could—often behind trees, occasionally in the john's car. Another site where sex workers plied their trade was a now gentrified street that ran East from a *Super-Marché* of sorts, now torn down. Then the street was, if not run-down, lined with marginal apartment buildings. Sex workers offered themselves by standing outside entrances to various of the buildings. Their place of business was evidently more up-scale than that of those who worked in the woods. Today in the US and elsewhere sex work is often associated with massage parlors run by absent landlords. Obviously, whether in a field, or on a street, or in parlors, sex workers deal with very different interaction orders. Some are self-employed. Others are beholden to bosses of a kind. Even on the street they must deal with many interactions, notably johns who cheat and beat them. In the US, the police are more the problem—especially when

---

33 Duck, *No Way Out*, 19. Emphasis added.
34 *Ibid*, 19.
35 *Ibid*, 47.

righteous local authorities seek to close the parlors down. Along a famous red-light canal in Amsterdam, sex workers have their own shops where they are not subject to official harassment. Anyhow it is evident—even to those who have not sought their services, sex-workers have their own interaction orders—much different in most ways than those housed in poor neighborhood streets like Bristol's Lyford Street—that function at night as a service center where white customers can buy their drugs from local dealers and leave the area quickly. What this rather amateurish portrayal of the interaction orders of sex workers suggests is the importance of Waverly Duck's observation that interaction orders have their own interactive natures—and especially those among the poor and otherwise excluded.

By further implication, the idea is that interactions are not set in stone. They are in constant motion. Their relations with the wider world are different from setting to setting and, in principle, the settings are also in constant motion. Duck has not worked all this out theoretically but empirically *No Way Out* begins to outline the oft-ignored fact that structures themselves fluctuate as time and conditions change. This notion could lead to a revolution in the way structures are conceived in relation to subjects—*could* lead, to be sure. Yet in *No Way Out* there are more than a few case studies where the promise of such a possibility is evident.

What *No Way Out* does is to describe vividly the several interaction orders at play in Bristol Hill. Quite reasonably, the first is that of the drug dealer—a subject to which the first three chapters are devoted, beginning with "Jonathan's World." Duck served as an expert witness for a drug trial which led him to meet Jonathan in prison, but also his family—and thereby to learn the background that led Jonathan to drug dealing. His defense attorney intended to make the case that Jonathan's crime, such as it was, was due to the social conditions of his upbringing in Bristol Hill about which Duck had already done extensive ethnographic research. "Jonathan's first association with drug dealing came by earning small sums for doing errands at the store for a dealer."[36] This was a first step along a familiar downward path toward drug dealing and all the trouble that brings.

Chapter 2 then expands the horizon from Jonathan to "Drug-Dealing Careers" (plural!). Much like sex workers, dealers must work in a variety of circumstances—dealing on the street, contending with drug-dealing areas, being known as "corner-boys," working the day shift when younger, and working the night shift as old heads, dealing in vacant lots and abandoned playgrounds. All of these factors require an on-the-ground ingenuity which entails at least a tacit understanding of the interaction order, notably on the main venue, Lyford Street. Then follows a particularly instructive observation on the way interaction orders shape the choices individuals make:

> While participants in orderly social settings can exercise some choice over the actions they perform, the social situation and the expectations it generates frame their choices. ... The local order on Lyford Street both constructs and enables the choices and resources available to people. The specific location in which people find themselves can profoundly shape their personal feelings and attitudes. ... The social order of such neighborhoods rests on the nature of the underground or illegal enterprise and the orderly practices necessary to succeed in it, not in what people believe, value, or want for themselves or others.[37]

---

36 Waverly Duck, *No Way Out: Precarious Living in the Shadow of Poverty and Drug Dealing* (University of Chicago Press, 2015), 30.
37 *Ibid*, 45–47.

What is suggested here is a reframing of the subject/object dichotomy, and more. Subjects and their worlds, as previously noted, are in constant motion such that it makes little empirical sense to say that the world in which these men live embraces analytically distinct layers—and, for that matter, this has become just as true of the worlds in which all of us live.

No Way Out, by its careful description of the interaction orders of drug dealing, introduces a temporal element in a local ethnography. It begins with Jonathan's world then moves on to the interaction orders associated with drug-dealing in Bristol, then turns to the sad but predictable fact that "drug-careers rarely end well." This leads logically to chapter 3, "The Rise and Fall of Lyford Street," where Duck quotes an old head, Mr. John, who was one of the first Black men to move to the Lyford Street neighborhood in the 1960s:

> The neighborhood started turning. I'll tell you exactly when it started turning. It started turning when they started closing down the projects. Until they started turning down the projects, you'd have one [black] family here, one [black] family there, which was cool by me. But when they started closing down the projects, instead of that one family moving in you had five or six families moving in. And white people started getting up and fleeing. I'm not going to say moving, they were fleeing. And I used to say 'Well you known I'm black. They didn't flee when I moved in.'[38]

Of course this sounds as if the decline of Lyford Street is a race issue. But no, Duck goes on to say: "The accounts that blame the drug trade on the people who moved from the projects fail to recognize that both the drug trade and the neighborhood's decline began well before their arrival."[39] Duck's interpretation arises from his probing below the surface event to a "history that few people knew." Then he continues:

> The interaction-order practices that flourish here have incorporated those who came from the projects and those who were here beforehand. While the historical account reconstructed [here] is distinct from that offered by residents, it differs mostly in pointing to political developments that lay behind the visible process of neighborhood change. Policies and practices implemented by outsiders did not improve but rather damaged a densely populated, thriving, and integrated neighborhood triggering a cascade of negative consequences that continues to this day.[40]

The fault of drug dealing and decline a neighborhood owes, not to race, but to outsiders—notably those who ordered the closing of the projects, thereby intruding on Bristol Hill in the name of doing good. This kind of good was bad indeed, and famously so. Redevelopment, which was intended to "clean up" urban neighborhoods, actually destroyed a good many of them.[41]

The middle three chapters of *No Way Out* present the important dynamics of Bristol Hill's interaction orders—"Snitching, Gossip, and the Power of Information," "The Politics of Murder and Revenge," and "Collective Punishment: Black Men's Reflections on

---

38 Ibid, 57.
39 Ibid, 59.
40 Ibid, 65.
41 For an apt and classical study on this very subject, see Herbert Gans, *Urban Villages: Group and Class in the Life of Italian Americans* (1962) about the way that a thriving ethnic community in Boston was destroyed by the City's Planning Department in the name of reclaiming their neighborhood for upper-middle class condominiums.

Everyday Life in Bristol Hill." Each of these are narratives told by introducing individuals who represent the topic at hand. The third of these (chapter 6) tells of the lives of six men who had all been subject to penalties made all the more acute by poverty. Here Duck takes Elliot Liebow's "theory of manly flaws," in *Tally's Corner*, along with other concepts in the literature, as an orienting notion. Like Liebow's men, Duck's men are caught in a web of troubles that compound their already troubled lives. Yet in the end, he concludes that these men face "constraints [that are] multiple, overlapping, and to some extent mutually exacerbating: the absence of higher-wage jobs, inadequate education, radical contraction of social safety nets, a judicial-police system whose attentions make things worse.... Yet many of the men found workable solutions to the problems they face that could easily be incorporated by policy makers."[42]

For the most part, to this point in *No Way Out*, the people presented thoroughly are, for the most part, men. But in the last chapter, "Benita's Story," a woman enters, and for good reason. Benita in Bristol Hill is, in many ways, the counter-figure to Ruby Banks and other of the women in the Flats in Carol Stack's *All Our Kin*. Benita is poor, Black, with three children, living in poorly kept up and temporary housing; she has trouble finding and keeping jobs, and more. The difference, Duck explains, is that previously the women on the Flats got by on Aid-to-Families with Dependent Children—a welfare program that was closed down and no longer existed in Benita's day. Benita had to make-do. She did find a job as a nurse's aide—poorly paid, but income. The father of her children was addicted and unreliable. Benita's kin came and went, but she found networks of a sort through local churches and their social service agencies. But she had no regular access to childcare or financial help. She was once arrested for failure to pay debts. She was regularly evicted for lack of rent money. She did have a car but had an accident without a license. More trouble, but:

> When the police arrived, she recognized both officers from previous traffic stops. She quickly explained that she did not have a license and that she was in the process of paying off the previous fines but stressed that she had to drive to work every day in order to support her family. Still in nursing scrubs and obviously upset, she was then comforted and hugged by one of the officers who explained that most people in her circumstances would have left the scene of the accident.[43]

Trouble averted. Overall Benita lived on a "housing merry-go-round." In two years, says Duck,[44] "she moved five times and [had] four different jobs."

Here Carol Stack appears again as a standard for getting by with help from kin and neighbors—*even* though Benita had nothing like the strong sustaining group comparable to kin-network on the Flats. Yet she had a lesser version of it:

> Consistent with Stack's findings, Benita consistently maintained a positive relationship with all of her neighbors. They initially looked after her children when Benita spent a few days in jail because she was unable to pay off her accumulated traffic fines. Her next-door neighbor even transported all her children to a relative's house while Benita strategized to raise funds for her release. ... Benita believed she would have been stranded without these vital relationships with family and friends. After her arrest she received money from her children's father, her sister and a neighbor she had known for a short time. She even

---

42 *No Way Out*, 113.
43 *Ibid*, 122.
44 *Ibid*, 128.

accepted help from a former lover, a drug dealer whom she had broken up with because she did not want him around her children.[45]

Benita got-by with various kinds of help from the cop who hugged her to the absent father of her children to a new neighbor to, even, the drug dealer she had rejected.

Hence, Waverly Duck's strong case for the importance of a vibrant interaction order in a neighborhood that suffered more than a few of the worst troubles of urban life today. "An interaction-order approach not only offers a different way of understanding these communities but also aids in resolving contested questions about culture, social disorganization, and collective efficacy."[46] In his second book, *Tacit Racism* (with Anne Rawls), Duck reaches for, but does not quite find, the new and much needed structural theory. But the idea of racism as tacit—which is to say unconscious to normal actors—is a very important suggestion. The problem with social theories in the modern day is that so many of them try somehow to conceive of structures as things in themselves—as opposed to virtual social things (as Anthony Giddens put it) that cannot in fact be seen and observed except by numeric and grand social historical methods, neither of which touches the ground of ordinary life. The workings of interaction-orders as Duck thinks of them are themselves tacit. In Bristol Hill people like Benita and others get by through their fragile but real interactions with others whom they find and keep in, precisely, a working interaction-order—a good order. "The local interaction order is not an impoverished culture. It is a powerful and creative response to the poverty and divisions of Race and class that seek to isolate and oppress residents of the neighborhood—a response that restores the social supports that residents need in order to flourish as autonomous human beings."[47]

In *No Way Out* Duck has pulled together an important strain of ethnographic method and thought that makes it possible, now, to speak of New Ethnographers. That strain draws, first and foremost, on Erving Goffman and Harold Garfinkel before allowing Elliot Liebow and Carol Stack to alter more traditional methods in which poverty, race, and class were seen as nothing more than the oppressing forces among poor Blacks. Elijah Anderson's code of street was a mediating concept that encouraged Duck's interpretation of interaction-orders and the strong use of collective efficacy—interpretations that make it possible for ethnographers to take a new perspective, one that appreciates what came before—going back to the Chicago School early in the twentieth century. Still, they set off on their own. The New Ethnographers may not have drawn directly on the lineage that inspired *No Way Out*—still, one can say, somewhat feebly, that there is something in the ethnographic air that has changed one of American social thought's most distinctive traditions.

Victor Rios: The Youth Control Complex

Victor Rios's *Punished: Policing the Lives of Black and Latino Boys* appeared in 2011 well before Waverly Duck's *No Way Out* in 2015. Yet, though Rios does not use the expression *interaction-action order*, he could have. *Punished* is clearly a book every bit as much of a similar, if not the same, methodological orientation—as well as, coming so early in the game, as much a classic in among New Ethnographies as any other. Though Duck was

---

45 *Ibid*, 128.
46 *Ibid*, 138.
47 Waverly Duck, "The Interaction Order of a Poor Black American Space: Creating Respect, Recognition, and Value in Response to Collective Punishment," in Anne Warfield Rawls and Waverly Duck, *Tacit Racism* (University of Chicago Press, 2020), 225.

born into extreme poverty in Detroit, he avoided being caught up in gang-life and any other of the miseries that can affect the early lives of poor Black boys. Rios, remarkably, given his distinguished academic achievements, was caught in all that and worse. As a result, *Punished: Policing the Lives of Black and Latino Boys* is a kind of ghost story of Rios's early life—and, if he were to accept this characterization, it is in some large part a deeply moving and troubling memoir especially in its Preface. Here Rios writes vividly and honestly of his early days of gang life, crime, punishment, time in juvenile hall, probation. One personal story is especially agonal—the shooting of his best friend:

> Hearing gunshots I leaped between two cars for protection. I turned back: our enemies had faded away as they scattered behind apartment buildings. I checked my body to see if I'd been shot. I was fine. ...We looked for Smiley. He was nowhere in sight. I turned the corner on the car I hid behind. There he was face flat on the ground. I ran over to him, kneeling over his body and grabbing him and trying to get him to stand up. Smiley had been shot. The bullet hit him in the head. ... Fresh human blood painted a picture of death on my brand-new pair of white Nike Cortez tennis shoes. I stood on that dark street knowing that my friend was dying. I thought, as the movies taught me, he should have been dead the instant the bullet hit his skull, but he continued to twitch and shake as we drove him to the hospital.[48]

After, the police threatened to arrest him for no other reason than being on the scene. He asked if they were going to "catch the murderer." To which the cop answered: "What for? ... We want you to kill each other off." Such was the kind of treatment he and other young men on Oakland's streets encountered unrelentingly. Rios came to call it criminalization.

Not long after, as he tells the story, Rios was befriended by a teacher who urged him back to school, found university students to mentor him, talked to his probation officer for him, and helped him get into the California State University, East Bay. An Officer Wilson who caught him drinking and fighting on the street then, after hearing his story, chose not to arrest him but laid down the law. He gave him a second chance. The chance was that if he ever found Rios in similar trouble, he would arrest him on multiple charges. This was just what he needed. He finished high school and college while working full time, living in a shack in the "lower Bottom of West Oakland," and caring for his family. After college he was accepted in the doctoral program in sociology at the University of California, Berkeley. He became a sociologist, eventually a professor and dean at UC Santa Barbara, and a distinguished scholar and author of *Punished*, and more.

As I said, Rios does not use the language of interaction orders. But he could have. And probably did not because of his training at Berkeley at a time when Erving Goffman was long gone and dead when Rios began graduate studies. Just the same, the concepts he used—youth control complex and criminalization—are well within the long tradition of fungible interaction-order studies, as is evident in how he defines his leading concepts:

> The *youth control complex* is a ubiquitous system of *criminalization* molded by the synchronized system punishment meted out by socializing and social control institutions. This complex is the unique whole derived from the sum of the punitive parts that young people encounter. While being called a "thug" by a random adult, told by a teacher that he or she will never amount to anything, and frisked by a police officer, all in the same

---

48 Victor Rios *Punished: Policing the Lives of Black and Latino Boys* (New York University Press, 2011), x–xi. Story retold below continues at *ibid*, xi–xii.

day, this combination becomes greater than the sum of its parts. It becomes a unique formation—the youth control complex—taking a toll on the mind and future outcomes of the young person. This complex is the combined effect of the web of institutions, schools, families, businesses, residents, media, community centers, and the criminal justice system that collectively punish, stigmatize, monitor, and criminalize young people in an attempt to control them.[49]

It is important upon reading this, to recall the subtitle of the book, *Policing the Lives of Black and Latino Boys*. The subject is boys, but as Rios's careful definition of the youth control complex makes clear, the community and its institutions are all engaged in the control of the boys (and other young people). Rios also makes it clear that he studied, not the actual crimes (if any) of the boys, but how they were criminalized—treated as criminals even when they are guilty of nothing as Rios himself was after the death of his friend Smiley. The criminalization system is woven deep into Oakland's structure—a city that has a large Black population and has long been considered a troubled community in the Bay Area. Not only this, but Rios is clear that "poor and racialized populations have been criminalized and violently punished in the United States since its inception."[50]

Victor Rios, without using the term, has introduced the idea of fungible interaction-order in what later could be described as a new perspective. While focusing on a part of the Flatlands of Oakland (the Black and Latino boys), he invented a concept (youth control complex) that required consideration of the entire community. Though their criminalization "entrapped" these boys in a destructive system, "… [that] developed within them an oppositional consciousness…[that] led to direct opposition to punitive control. … This resistance carried the seeds of redemption, self-determination, resilience, and desistance."[51] In other words, in Rios's "Youth Support Complex," he means to suggest, as a general possibility beyond Oakland, the kind of social order where young people, by resisting the system, can gain dignity and freedom. Hence another basic attitude of the New Ethnographers—that there can be order in the disorder, an order arising among members of communities facing seemingly impossible odds. Again, fungibility in the ordering of disorder.

Matthew Desmond: Home and Hope

Matthew Desmond's *Evicted: Poverty and Profit in the American City* in 2016 is, as the title suggests, about eviction, a problem that before his book has been largely ignored in American cities where owners profit from the poverty of those who rent, for a while, their properties. He writes, powerfully:

> We need a robust sociology of housing that reaches beyond a narrow focus of policy and public housing. We need a new sociology of displacement that documents the prevalence, causes, and consequences of eviction. And perhaps most important, we need a committed sociology of inequality that includes a serious study of exploitation and extractive markets.[52]

---

49 *Ibid*, 40. Emphases added.
50 *Ibid*, 160.
51 *Ibid*, 102–103.
52 Matthew Desmond, *Evicted: Poverty and Profit in the American City* (Penguin Random House, 2016), 333.

Desmond's manifesto is one of the reasons he is among the most respected younger sociologists to date of the twenty-first century. The other reason is the book itself which is so thoroughly well researched and empirically sound as to represent the new sociologies he calls for. Still another is that, after Desmond had won many awards and prizes for *Evicted*, he did not stop there. He donated money he gained by winning a MacArthur Genius Fellowship to initiate and support on-going in-depth studies of eviction in Milwaukee, which studies have become a stimulus for the new sociology of displacement he calls for.

Evicted begins by describing the dire straits of those who are evicted and why his manifesto is so on point:

> Eviction's fall-out is severe. Losing a home sends families to shelters, abandoned homes, and the street. It invites depression and illness, compels families to move to degrading housing in dangerous neighborhoods, uproots communities, and harms children. Eviction reveals people's vulnerabilities as well as their ingenuity and guts.[53]

Until the reader gets to the last line here one might think this is the very opposite of anything like an interaction order. But Desmond is clear that eviction reveals the ingenuity and guts of its victims. And it is possible to add, that Desmond writes with such detail that the reader also learns how eviction reveals the limited compassion of property owners—like Sherrena; for example:

> Petite with chestnut kin, Sherrena wore a lightweight red-and-blue jacket that matched her pants, which matched her off-kilter NBA cap. She liked to laugh, a full, open-mouthed hoot, sometimes catching your shoulder as if to keep from falling. But as she turned off North Avenue on her way to pay a visit to tenants who lived near the intersection of Eighteenth and Wright Streets, she slowed down and let out a heavy sigh. Evictions were a regular part of the business, but Lamar didn't have any legs. Sherrena was not looking forward to evicting a man without legs.[54]

In the book's Prologue, "Cold City," Desmond introduces right-off the property owner, Sherrena, and Arleen, the renter with two small children who is to be evicted.

The story of Sherrena and Arleen sets up the narrative line of the book as a whole, told with particular poignancy in "Christmas in Room 400" (chapter 8). Arleen had fallen behind in her rent due to the costs of a funeral and other debts. She owed $870 in a place and at a time when that was a considerable sum for anyone living on the economic margins. Sherrena filed for a hearing at the Milwaukee County Courthouse, Room 400. Curiously, she called to remind Arleen of the date, two days before Christmas. Had Arleen not shown up it is likely that Sherrena would have won the case. Here is another even more poignant example of Desmond's ethnographic elegance in describing the scene that day:

> A black woman whose hearing had just concluded stepped back into the room, holding her child's hand. Her head was wrapped, and she kept on her blue winter coat. She continued down the middle aisle of Room 400, walking by an anemic white man with homemade tatoos, a white woman in a wheelchair wearing pajama pants and Crocs, a blind black man with a limp hat on his lap, a Hispanic man wearing work boots and a shirt that read PRAY FOR US—all waiting for their eviction cases. Tenants in eviction

---

53 *Ibid*, 5.
54 *Ibid*, 10.

court were generally poor, and almost all of them (92%) had missed rent payments. The majority spend at least half of their household income on rent. One-third devoted at least 80 percent on it. Of the tenants who did come to court and were evicted, only 1 in 6 had another place lined up: shelters or the apartments of friends or family. A few resigned themselves to the streets. Most simply did not know where they would go.[55]

In one jam-packed but very readable paragraph the people in Room 400 are described in their different but quite human natures, while at the same time we are told the statistical reality of their fates.

Sherrena's experience in the court room then takes a turn as Arleen appears. Upon seeing her Sherrena says "Girl,' Sherrena said, "I got to get you outta this house or get my money. Genuine ... I mean, 'cause I got bills." She then pulls a bill out of her file and shows it to Arleen and asks: "Do you see what I have to *go through* ..."[56] Time passes. Arleen leaves the room. The lawyers are done for the day. The case is in the hands of Commissioner Laura Gramling Perez, who, like the judicial system often is, procedures in case like this one tend to be strict but forgiving of the problems both must deal with. When their case is called Sherrena calls Arleen in. "We up." Before Perez they go back and forth. Arleen offers to get out by New Year's Day. Sherrena argues that will mean she can't get a new tenant in and that the extra days mean another month's rent is due. Commissioner Perez tries to work out a plan. Sherrena resists. Arleen introduces the unrepaired damages she had to endure in the apartment. On it goes until Perez works out a deal such that she knows Sherrena can keep the security deposit to cover her lost rent, leaving a balance of $320. Finally the case concludes with the Commissioner concluding: "Here's the deal. Ma'am you're getting to move out voluntarily by January first. ... If you don't do that, then your landlord is entitled to come back here for without further notice and she can get a writ of eviction. And the sheriff will come"[57] Neither gets what they want, though in the end Sherrena holds the better card. Arleen is permitted to stay the extra days and, more importantly, she does not have an eviction on her record.

Arleen and Sherrena walk out together. Sherrena offers to drive Arleen home. They chat in the car. As they pass rental properties, Sherrena remarks "Some of these tenants ... they nasty as hell. They bring roaches with them. ... So Arleen, if you ever thinking about becoming a landlord don't. It's a bad deal. Get the short end of the stick ever time."[58] Needless to say it's always the renter who is always shorted. Yet, Sherrena is talking with Arleen in the moment as if they were and could be in the same boat. Then they arrived at Arleen's building. As she steps out of the car, she turns back to Sherrena to say: "Merry Christmas."

Here is the nub of Desmond's story. The evicted and their landlords are by no means equals. Hence, from his manifesto: "... we need a committed sociology of inequality that includes a serious study of exploitation and extractive markets." True. But Desmond, rather remarkably, makes his point by telling the true stories of the exploited and extractors with due respect for their humanity *and* the actual relations in which they and theirs live together in the sense of dealing with each other.

Arleen's Christmas greeting to Sherrena ends Part One of *Evicted*, "Rent." Then follows Part Two, "Out," and Part Three, "After." The scenes change in each. The descriptive and

---

55 *Ibid*, 97.
56 *Ibid*, 100 [both quotes].
57 *Ibid*, 106.
58 *Ibid*, 107.

literary virtues continue. Since the general theme is now plain to see, there is no need to replay more of the book. Desmond does that better than anyone other could. He comes to his conclusion in the book's *Epilogue: Home and Hope* where he makes the telling point that won Desmond so much praise: "Affordable housing should be a basic right in this country. The reason is simple: without stable shelter, everything falls apart."[59]

Whether interaction order is the word for Desmond's ethnographic approach might be arguable. Yet, in an important sense, the term works. As the case of Sherrena and Arleen makes clear he is looking not so much for generic aspects of communities of the evicted as for the very local and, in effect, very personal issues the evicted suffer. Just as much, and more than most, Desmond intends to put himself in the picture in the scenes he observed. He is not just *looking at* the people he lived with in Milwaukee's South End and elsewhere, he was *being with them*. Hence, most tellingly, he describes what he was doing in the field and after as "ethnography as a way of being in the world."[60]

Desmond followed *Evicted* in 1986 with a different but just as engaging book in 2023, *Poverty, By America*. Those unfamiliar with his first book may find the title to this one a little too clever with its comma after *Poverty,*—but not so. Much as he argued in *Evicted*, poverty is not something that just happens to people any more than it is the fault of the poor who are thought to lack the moral and personal qualities to earn money. Poverty, he says, is created by America, and it can be repaired by America. As before, not even here is *America* an abstraction. For Desmond, America is about *Americans* and what they can and ought to do:

> There are a good many challenges facing this big, wide country, but near the top of the list must be concerns about basic needs. We must ask ourselves—and then ask our community organizations, our employers, our places of worship, our schools, our political parties, our courts, our towns, our families: What are we doing to divest from poverty? *Every person, every company, every institution has a role in perpetuating poverty but also a role in ameliorating it.*[61]

If you skipped or skimmed over these lines, read them again. This is a manifesto to be sure, but not one serving to cast blame on someone like the poor herself or the politician himself. These are lines in which the key words are *we, our, every*. No one is excluded. We all made poverty and we can ameliorate it.

Could he have written this book this way without having first dug deep into the lives of evicted poor? In principle, yes. But would it then have had its urgent sense of universal responsibility? Is he dreaming? The cynic might ask. But how else can the world be free of senseless poverty? And who else but all of us can do it? Desmond is not given to theoretical language, but it is hard to believe that he would object to the idea that interaction-orders are everywhere and, because they are, they allow for the fungibility of a social order. When some are poor we all are poor. We all together can fix it. Social things are fungible. No exceptions!

Nikki Jones: Free People, Free People

In general ways, each of the ethnographers presented in this chapter has made his or her own distinctive contribution that permits their consideration as New Ethnographers. Elijah

---

59 *Ibid*, 300.
60 *Ibid*, 404.
61 Matthew Desmond, *Poverty, By America* (Crown, 2023), 189.

Anderson writes with literary elegance that allows him to change with flare and wisdom the course of ethnographic research in books like *Code of the Street*. Waverly Duck, in *No Way Out*, recovers and invents working concepts like *interaction order* and *collective efficacy* to provide a fresh way of appreciating the ability of people in otherwise miserable communities to get by and get along by dealing creatively with the meager hand that has been dealt them. Similarly, Victor Rios in *Punished* has deployed his concept of Youth Control Complex in order to discern just how much the Black and Latino boys in Oakland got by and beyond such that their story suggests the promise of a youth *support* complex. Matthew Desmond's *Evicted* demonstrates the need for his manifesto calling out a new sociology of eviction and the trouble it makes. Desmond helps the reader both to see his proposed new sociologies in action and to see them as elements of his inspiring motto for ethnography as "a new way of being in the world."

Turning now to Nikki Jones, her two urban ethnographies, when read together, juxtapose differences and similarities between men in the Filmore District of San Francisco and young women in West Philadelphia in order to identify a politics of redemption, as she puts it in *The Chosen Ones: Black Men and the Politics of Redemption* (2018). To this end, Jones' descriptive findings are presented with enlightening reference to the long and serious tradition of studies of (mostly) Blacks in violent and otherwise troubled communities. Jones' earlier ethnography tells a story well suggested by the book's title, *Between Good and Ghetto: African American Girls and Inner-City Violence* (2010). One should not miss that the titles of both books, published eight years apart, reveal an underlying sense of hope for and about young people living in all-but insufferable circumstances.

Looking first at *The Chosen Ones* it is important to see that this title is, if not ironic, at least touched with irony given the situation of the boys and men Jones studied while living in their neighborhood. The book begins with a note to "Nicky [sic]" Jones from Eric Johnson written July 5, 2013. Its subject line is "Corey was murdered last night."[62] In a certain odd way *The Chosen Ones* is composed around the different fates of Corey, dead *from* the first—and Eric, headed for death *at* first, then in time very much alive. Eric, in the end, is redeemed after a long struggle over his years with the back and forth "turf wars" between groups of young drug-dealing men "that mimic, in some ways, the block-by-block battles... [that] reinforce the social organization and objectives of the crime-fighting community and, in turn, shape the life trajectories of men like Eric..."[63] This composite quote from the introduction of *The Chosen Ones* very well conveys the nuances of the emergent life of Eric and others who, in the long run, came to be considered redeemed.

After a long first chapter on "Eric's Awakening," Jones presents, in the second chapter, "The Crime Fighting Community"—in other words, the two sides of a coin of the realm shaped by wider social forces in the Filmore District. Jones, as always, never fails to introduce historical context where it is important and, too, she is respectful of the nuances in those contexts. She points out that crime-fighting in San Francisco arose when an earlier peacekeeping movement, in the 1960s, was gradually overwhelmed when heroin came on the scene eroding the effectiveness of peacekeeping. At its best it employed neighborhood young men to engage community groups to reduce the tension. Then in the 1970s law-and-order became the political watchword across the nation.

Throughout all this, caretaking was evident in the poor neighborhoods where Blacks had long been accustomed to caretaking among themselves. More generally there were, and are,

---

62 Nikki Jones, *The Chosen Ones: Black Men and the Politics of Redemption* (University of California Press, 2018), 1.
63 *Ibid*, 4.

internal caretakers—members of the community, and external caretakers—like social welfare agencies. In other words, in the 1960s and 1970s there were local and cosmopolitan agents at work in these communities. Plus which, race was integral. What Jones calls "the politics of representation" was, in effect, a complex matrix of agents:

> Insiders included Black politicians and professionals who were often selected by powerful Whites to represent the Black community. The outsiders included African Americans who came to Midwestville looking for a better life. Insiders often found themselves in a bind when called upon to advance the interests of the Black community, since their authenticity and legitimacy within the Black community was commonly questioned by others, especially the militant young.[64]

It is easy to see how the insider/outsider dynamics comprise a matrix of many vectors in which Black community members are actors *and* subjects.

Then in the 1980s and 1990s came *crime-fighting* for which the exemplar was the so-called Boston Miracle in the second half of the 1990s where homicides dropped dramatically. Crime-fighting in Filmore was no less complex, notably in the oft uneasy relations between police and representative spokespersons in the Black community. The crucial local group, however, was Brothers Changing the Hood (BCH) of which Eric was a member. Jones presents an especially compelling account of a BCH meeting—compelling because it is so much like ordinary meetings anywhere. The men spoke and listened to one another's troubles. A visiting Lawyer's Committee on Civil Rights wished he had known of the group earlier. Jones herself commented: "This meeting, particularly efforts like the gang injunction and the 'call in,' illustrates the new contours of crime fighting."[65] The results were not generally what the BCH members might have wanted but the meetings lent a degree of "civic-legitimacy" to the group and the efforts (occasionally intrusions) of law-enforcement and the wider crime-fighting community.

After the chapter on the crime-fighting community, *The Chosen Ones* deals with the targeting of the Filmore community *because* it was predominantly Black—of which the most appalling instances were the strip searches of Black male bodies. Then, in chapter 4, "Buffers and Bridges," the story turns back to Eric, by then a man in his thirties with a family. This was a good decade after he had been dealing drugs. He was by then the leader of Brothers Changing the Hood, which had become "a caring community of accountability for Black men not only to redeem themselves for past wrongs but also to redeem themselves as men and fathers."[66] Hence the expression "Buffers and Bridges" out of their former ways into a new life.

The narrative line of *The Chosen Ones* had, thus, been announced in the book's introduction: "People do not make good on their own: people make good *with* others."[67] And this is where the fugue element in the story comes in, *Black Men and the Politics of Redemption*. The men who came to be in Brothers Changing the Hood worked with each other, to be sure, but their work was always amid the larger political structures that all too often were punitive. Their politics of redemption came to be against and with this larger, not always kind, political system. The motto Jones provides at the very end is *Free people, free people*.

This is not a story with a surprise ending. It is not a televisual crime story of a hero. As written *The Chosen Ones* begins with a spoiler. Chapter 1, "Eric's Awakening" tells the

---

64 *Ibid*, 63–64.
65 *Ibid*, 77. Longer discussion of this meeting, 74–80.
66 *Ibid*, 120.
67 *Ibid*, 5.

story from his drug-dealing to his redemption. Jones obviously wanted readers to make no mistake about her story. Again: *Free people, free people.*

The Chosen Ones was published in 2018 when Nikki Jones was at the University of California Berkeley, where she had become Professor and Chair of African American Studies. *Between Good and Ghetto: African American Girls and Inner-City Violence* began as her doctoral thesis field research under Elijah Anderson at the University of Pennsylvania. It was published in 2010 when she was assistant professor of sociology at the University of California, Santa Barbara. *Between Good and Ghetto* offers many of the qualities of *The Chosen Ones* though, quite understandably, less fully developed. Still, Jones in the first ethnography provides a rich location of her observations with respect to the literature which in *The Chosen Ones* is one of the best there is for an empirical study. Then too *Between Good and Ghetto* shows the importance of Elijah Anderson, her teacher, to good effect—especially in one of the book's definitive conclusions about girls and the streets of West Philadelphia:

Inner-city girls are cognizant of the code of the street as a system of accountability in the same way they understand gender expectations. African American, inner-city girls must reconcile the dilemmas and contradictions they encounter while navigating potentially dangerous settings. ... [T]hey are committed to behaving in ways that others evaluate as good, yet they also come to believe that they must present a tough demeanor and be ready to fight. At the same time, these girls will rely heavily on strategies of situational avoidance or relational isolation to minimize their involvement in potential interpersonal battles. Girls with reputations as fighters work the code of the street in ways that directly and often deliberately challenge both traditional and local expectations regarding femininity.[68]

Then follows what may be the most theoretically poignant observation about the girls. "In developing survival strategies that work for them, these girls embrace, challenge, reinforce, reflect, and contradict elements of mainstream and local masculinity *and* femininity." Jones introduces a concept that seldom figures in social theories of identities: "...*fluidity* between and within competing and controlling expectations of good and ghetto."[69]

For an early book, the field work and scholarship are quite mature. Mature enough that Jones does two things that few ethnographers do. First, she captures and applies the sensibility of *the stranger* that the classical social theorist, Georg Simmel, first sketched in 1908. She felt herself to be a stranger among these girls whose situations she understood without fully accepting the why and wherefore of their dilemmas. Second, Jones finishes this book with a strong feeling about those circumstances:

I also feel an anger that I know is familiar to these girls, and to other Black women across the country, regardless of their class position or the shade of their skin. Despite all the advances made over the last century, survival remains a struggle for many Black women in America, but especially for the poor.[70]

Jones' anger puts an edge on the slogan of her books. *Free people/Free people*. Still it applies. The girls of West Philadelphia depended as much on each other, as did the boys and men of Filmore.

---

68 Nikki Jones, *Between Good and Ghetto: African American Girls and Inner-City Violence* (Rutgers University Press, 2010), 154.
69 *Ibid*, 155 [both quotes here].
70 *Ibid*, 162; and 166 [for the Simmel reference].

Alice Goffman's Trials and Tribulations

Alice Goffman's *On The Run: Fugitive Life in An American City* (2014) has been more severely criticized than any other I know of in recent years. The criticisms of the book have been, with rare exceptions, vulgar, to say the least. One of the fairest is by Victor Rios in the *American Journal of Sociology* who complains mostly that the book is actually two books—one, on "punitive policing and fugitive status"; the other an illumination of "pathological criminality."[71] Rios's complaint is that Goffman fails, in his opinion to analytically link the two books—and, secondarily, that the number of individuals studied is too small.[72]

There are differences of opinion always in academic culture. Nothing too new or terrible here. At the same time there is viciousness in the academy—all of which is inexcusable. Alice Goffman has been subjected to more than a little of that. After she received her PhD from Princeton, she took a position in Sociology at the University of Wisconsin Madison—a program that from time to time has been considered the best in the field. During her tenure there her book won many accolades. She was in demand as a speaker across the nation and even gave a TED talk, which has become proof positive that the speaker had done something worthy of public interest. Yet, Alice Goffman was denied tenure. When asked by a public source why, the University hid behind the ever-more absurd excuse that they couldn't discuss the case because, in effect, it was a "personnel matter." Colleges use this excuse all the time, but at some point, these institutions need to stand up for their own values, above all those surrounding the principle of freedom of information.

After leaving Wisconsin, Goffman accepted a position as McConnel Visiting Professor of Sociology at Pomona College. The appointment gave rise to a grievance over the hiring and demanded that she be dismissed for alleged methodological errors and violations. The principal source for this complaint was an anonymous 60-page accusation of her intellectual dishonesty posted without identification of any kind on https://pastebin.com/BzN4t0VU. The statement itself makes points that merit an explanation—again a normal expectation in the academy. But the sources of these 60 pages are not given, except for the fact that the authors claim to have checked city records for evidence of what she wrote about one of her subjects, Alex—and other similar concerns. Such like were made by a nameless critic. If you can't name yourself then you lose your right to complain against an author whose name was, by then, very well known. Then too the 128 people who complained about Goffman's appointment to Pomona themselves refused to publicize their names—presumably because they were students, but that, again, does not justify their attacks on a case about which they had little primary knowledge. And again where were the faculty, the provost, and the President of Pomona in all this? In either case the authors of the demands, even if students, end their attack with: "Should we not receive a response to our demands by Tuesday, April

---

71 Victor Rios, Review of *On The Run: Fugitive Life in An American City*, *American Journal of Sociology* 121–1 (July 2015), 307. The one exception to this review's better nature is a gratuitous remark about Goffman's book being a *Jungle Book* story which means to suggest that Alice Goffman is doing little more than going native among people she could not comprehend. NOTE: as should already be evident, I respect Victor Rios as an ethnographer and a person. That he was drawn into the then predominant nastiness about *On the Run* goes to show that, even the best among us, can step over the line.

72 The two-books-in-one observation has been made by Owen Fiss, a distinguished professor of Constitutional Law at Yale. His observation was not a complaint. It was in one of our Yale Senior Research Seminars held sometime in 2019, as I remember. Goffman's "two books" were, he said, retributive justice and fugitive status. The discussion of the book by seminar members was without rancor and with keen interest.

25, 2017 at 5PM, we will take direct action."[73] What actions? I've been around students for decades, and have been attacked by some, but they were always clear as to what they would do and who they were.

Depending on one's point of view, there are at least two sides to this sad story. Those who don't find it sad, must in their lonely nights wonder what happened to their sense of decency. Whatever they may think, she was at the time of her research young by professional academic standards—and now she is unemployed!

There is one uncommonly balanced article on "The Trials of Alice Goffman," by Gideon Lewis-Kraus in *The New York Times Magazine*.[74] Lewis-Kraus fully presents both the criticisms and defenses of Goffman and her book and puts each in context. He mentions those who praised Goffman's book. Malcolm Gladwell called the work "extraordinary" and in *The New York Review of Books*, Christopher Jencks called it an "ethnographic classic." Randall Collins is quoted as saying of Goffman: "She got in deep enough so that not only does she understand things from their point of view, she doesn't give priority to laws, official morals, all the things that conventional people take for granted."

Like Collins, Lewis-Kraus puts her honors and awards in context. He writes: "The American Sociological Association gave "On the Run" its Dissertation Award, and many of Goffman's peers came to feel as though she had been specially anointed by the discipline's power elite—that she had been allowed, as the future public face of sociology, to operate by her own set of rules." Then he adds:

> The discipline as a whole does not seem to know quite how to react to Goffman's case. Sociologists are proud that the work that comes out of their departments is so heterodox and wide-ranging—and, especially when it comes to issues like mass incarceration, so influential in policy debates—but it is a fractured field, and many sociologists worry that over the last few decades they have ceded their great midcentury prestige and explanatory power to economists on one side and social psychologists on the other. There has been a lot of hand-wringing about Goffman, and even her sympathizers mostly declined to speak to me on the record for fear of contamination.

When Lewis-Kraus turns the focus on the discipline of sociology itself, he is spot on. Many, perhaps most, of the more vulgar criticisms like the anonymous *Pastebin* 60-pager rant page upon page to the effect of "How can this be?"—sociology ought not allow this kind of thing? Sociology is indeed a fractured field as it ought to be.

In fact, Lewis-Kraus is particularly apt to this point when he alludes to the curious fact that Alice Goffman's thinking may well be at least in tune with Erving Goffman's:

> Erving's work was varied and deliberately unsystematic, he is best known for his elaboration of the self as a series of performances. His daughter has taken over his idea that static character is less interesting or relevant than the dynamics of exchange. "I don't think," she once told me—after calling herself "chameleonlike"—"that I have real preferences, just desires that emerge in social interactions."

---

73 https://medium.com/@5csociologystudents/april-21st-letter-to-the-pomona-college-sociology-department-2d6aa210b19b
74 Gideon Lewis-Kraus, "The Trials of Alice Goffman," *The New York Times Magazine* (January 12, 2016) at https://www.google.com/search?q=New+York+Times+Alice+Goffman. [In the online source there are no page numbers.]

Here the journalist may be stretching a good point. It is hard to know to what extent her bio-father's thinking may have influenced Alice Goffman. If it did, it certainly was not directly and personal. He had died when she was but an infant. Surely, she read his writings, as have thousands of others. In some ways, Erving Goffman was, in a way, an important figure in fracturing the field. Whatever one thinks of *On the Run* it is at least good sociology with all the fractures and disputes appertaining thereto.

Why all this time and space on Alice Goffman and her book? There are two good enough reasons: The *first* is that she is clearly a New Ethnographer, who started on her way when Elijah Anderson was her teacher. It shows. But *second*: In books on social theory over the centuries there have been many disputes and a few outrages over the truth of a theoretical matter—from Jonathan Edwards being fired, to Alexander Hamilton getting himself shot, and John Brown getting himself hanged—not to mention Malcolm X and Martin King being assassinated, and on and on without mentioning the myriad of firings and abuses that take place down academic hallways every day everywhere.

Of all the dangerous games social theorists can play, ethnography—new or old—is perhaps the most dangerous because it requires its practitioners to get down in local dirt, then to survive long enough to tell the story of those she or he spent day upon day with over years.

Alice Goffman's *On the Run: Fugitive Life in an American City*

"This book is an on-the-ground account of the US prison boom: a close-up look of young men and women living in one poor and segregated Black community transformed by unprecedented levels of imprisonment and by the more hidden systems of policing and supervision that have accompanied them."[75] This is how *On the Run* begins. The research began when Goffman was a sophomore at the University of Pennsylvania in her early 20s. The field work had its beginning not in the classroom but when she met Aisha, a high school sophomore, Black and poor, whom she was tutoring. One thing led to another. Alice Goffman met Aisha's family then her friends in the neighborhood. Among them were the boys she came to call the 6th Street Boys in Philadelphia; hence the title of the book's first chapter, "The 6th Street Boys and Their Legal Entanglements." Reggie, Chuck, Mike, and Harry, Alex and Anthony are significant figures throughout the book. She came to know them because in due course she moved into the neighborhood to work on her PhD thesis for Princeton. Their legal troubles, she reports, were many and complex. All began with drug possession and dealing. "On 6th Street, the fear of capture and confinement weighs on the young with warrants out for their arrest but also those going through a court case or trying to complete probation or parole sentences."[76]

Chapter 2, "On the Art of Running," tells of the beginning of trouble that leads to their fugitive status. "Running wasn't always the smartest thing to do when the cops came but the urge to run was so engrained that sometimes it was hard to stand still."[77] One of the basic consequences of fugitive status is that the fugitive cannot call the police even when he has been harmed. Among the required skills is "cultivating an unpredictable routine" and being prepared to pay the price, which is often the simple, if risky, act of presenting oneself to the cops as someone they are not. At the extreme they must snitch on another whom the police might want more.[78] Chapter 3, "When the Police Knock Your Door In," develops

---

75 Alice Goffman, *On the Run: Fugitive Life in an American City* (University of Chicago Press, 2014), ii.
76 *Ibid*, 20.
77 *Ibid*, 27.
78 *Ibid*, 37–53.

The New Ethnographers of Urban Disorder 357

these themes in the previous chapter with an emphasis on the violent methods the police often use—one of whom she interviewed to the following effect: "Warrant Unit officers explained to me that this violence represents official (if unpublicized) policy, rather than a few cops taking things too far."[79] Just before this reference Goffman reports on an incident she and Aisha observed of four cops chasing down and strangling Aisha older sister's boyfriend.

The pivotal chapter in *On the Run*, is the fourth, "Turning Legal Troubles into Personal Resources." The headers alone in the early sections of Chapter 4, refer to what would surprise and impress those not in the know. They are: "Jail as a Safe Haven," "the Bail Office as a Bank," "Being Wanted as a Means of Accounting for Failure." One might well imagine how, for these young men, jail would be a safe-haven from the dangers of life on the streets. Most of them would be puzzled about the Bail Office as a bank. When they are released, they are due some 80% of the bail refundable with a year. Some leave it as a way of saving until a need arises. Overall being wanted can have other practical benefits. They can, for example, always check themselves into jail, so to speak, to get out of harm's way. Generally, Goffman writes:

> [Men] and women in the neighborhood turn the presence of the police, the courts, and the prisons into a resource they make use of in ways the authorities neither sanction nor anticipated. Taken together, these strategies present an alternative to the view that 6th Street residents are simply the pawns of the authorities, caught in legal entanglements that constrain and oppress them.[80]

This last line of the quote ends the chapter on personal resources. It might, to some, seem a little understated. The chapters that follow make the point of the book's story.

Again, titles say a lot. Chapter 5, "The Social Life of Criminalized Young People" emphasizes the one basic fact of their lives—that they have lives that, in spite of it all, provide them support and encouragement. Their mothers are beset by troubles caused by their young people's criminal lives—court dates, the bail payments, jail visits, phone calls to public defenders. These troubles and more complicate their already burdened lives. But, at the same time, they give them a sense of being good mothers—not a small thing in those circumstances. Then too, penal events provide occasions for celebration among friends and family. Even more, and tellingly: "Just as the criminal justice system now furnishes the social events around which young people work out their relationship with one another, it has provided the social material with which young people construct a sense of themselves as brave and honorable."[81] A fugitive community offers the occasion for maintaining relations, which, as we know, often requires giving up something of personal value in order to purchase a sense of personal worth.

On the Run carries forth the story with a sixth chapter, "The Market in Protections and Privileges." Here it should not be hard, even for critics, to see the point. Privileged folk outside this kind of poor and excluded community call this kind of thing networking. But even among these young men there can be material gains like income and jobs, and more. As throughout Goffman tells this part of the story with thoughtful and very human tales of the 6th Street boys and girls and their friends. Chapter 7, "Clean People," strays a little too much off target in order to deploy a figure of speech. That said, a good enough point

---

79 *Ibid*, 72.
80 *Ibid*, 106.
81 *Ibid*, 120.

is made. What counts here is the way the terms and accounts of people in and around 6th Street live with what the outside world, including the police, think of them and their community as dirty. The vast majority of those living on and around 6th Street lead clean lives. Goffman ends the chapter with an important and engaging statement. "The people featured here are all, in a variety of way, *leading clean lives in a dirty world*."[82]

Dirty world indeed. If there is a generic answer to those who wanted to read more about the legal system and how it creates fugitive communities, it may be that those likely to read such a book are likely to have a good enough sense of the dirtiness of this world. This is not an entirely good defense if one finds fault with the ethnographic narrative that drives the story. Whatever some may say, *On the Run* is a book rich with details of how young people fall into lives of crime—then, having suffered the consequences, *including* those imposed by local police action, some work themselves into better, even good, lives. At the very end Alice Goffman makes the main point of *On the Run*:

> [These] cases involve as many differences as similarities. In many instances those seized by the authorities didn't circulate back into the general population; once they were gone, they didn't return. The fear of torture and death isn't the same as the fear of prison or deportation. But these cases share enough so that a deep knowledge of one may teach us about the experience of people living in others.[83]

---

82 *Ibid*, 194.
83 *Ibid*, 204.

18 Power, Domination, and the World Revolution of 1968

Herbert Marcuse, Kwame Ture, Bob Moses, Fannie Lou Hammer, Ella Baker, C. Wright Mills, Angela Davis

The idea of the power elite rests upon and enables us to make sense of the decisive institutional trends that characterize the structure of our epoch, in particular, the military ascendancy in a privately incorporated economy, and more broadly, the several coincidences of objective interests between economic, military, and political institutions.
—*C. Wright Mills, The Power Elite, 1956*

The political needs of society become those individual needs and aspirations, their satisfaction promotes business and the commonwealth and the whole appears to be the embodiment of Reason. ...
And yet this society is irrational as a whole.
—*Herbert Marcuse, One-Dimensional Man, 1964*

The question is, will white people overcome their racism and allow for that to happen in this country? If that does not happen, brothers and sisters, we have no choice but to say very clearly, "Move over, or we goin' to move on over you."
—*Stokely Carmichael, Black Power Speech at Berkeley, 1966*

The questions that we think face the country are questions which in one sense are much deeper than civil rights. They're questions which go very much to the bottom of mankind and people. They're questions which have repercussions in terms of a whole international affairs and relations. They're questions which go to the very root of our society.
What kind of society will we be?
—*Bob Moses, Stanford University, 1964*

I'm sick and tired of being sick and tired...
—*Fannie Lou Hammer, Somewhere in Mississippi, 1964*

Strong people do not need strong leaders.
—*Ella Baker, Sometime after she left SCLC and joined SNCC in 1964*

We cannot go on as usual. We cannot pivot the center. We cannot be moderate.
We will have to be willing to stand up
and say no with our combined spirits, our collective intellects, and our many bodies.
—*Angela Davis, Freedom is a Constant Struggle, 2016*

I'm Sick and Tired of Being Sick and Tired[1]

This now famous statement by Fannie Lou Hammer was made after Mississippi Freedom Summer, 1964, which led to the Mississippi Freedom Democratic Party's challenge to the all-white party delegation. Fannie Lou Hammer was the Mississippian who played a central role in Freedom Summer's effort to register Black voters. Young people, Black and white, came from all over the nation to help in this effort—which turned out to be the beginning of the people's civil rights movement as distinct from the more prominent movement led by the Southern Christian Leadership Conference (SCLC) in which ministers like Martin Luther King, Jr. led a more top-down movement.

Ella Baker was also active in the Mississippi Freedom Party. By 1964, after a good while with the SCLC, she began an important shift to supporting young men and women in the movement. This led to the formation of Student Non-Violent Coordinating Committee (SNCC). Her most famous quote is "Strong people do not need strong leaders,"[2] reflects her disillusionment with the minister-led SCLC and her commitment to younger people.

Chief among the younger people involved in Freedom Summer was Bob Moses. In 1961, Moses was teaching high school in New York after graduating from Harvard. That summer, however, he moved to Mississippi where he was the organizer with Fannie Lou Hammer of the voter registration drive that became the Freedom Summer of 1964. That April he spoke at Stanford University, saying:

> The questions that we think face the country are questions which in one sense are much deeper than civil rights. They're questions which go very much to the bottom of mankind and people. They're questions which have repercussions in terms of a whole international affairs and relations. They're questions which go to the very root of our society. What kind of society will we be?[3]

Moses went on, we shall see, to develop an important educational program based on what he learned working in Mississippi.

One among the many outcomes of the 1964 programs was the beginning of SNCC of which Ella Baker was part. More famous internationally was Stokely Carmichael who is generally recognized as the one who coined the term Black Power, of which he said in a speech at Berkeley:

> The question is, will white people overcome their racism and allow for that to happen in this country? If that does not happen, brothers and sisters, we have no choice but to say very clearly, "Move over, or we goin' to move on over you."[4]

---

1 Fannie Lou Hammer said this on December 20, 1964 at the Williams Institutional CME Church, Harlem, New York, organized to support the Mississippi Freedom Democratic Party's Congressional Challenge. Downloaded source is *The Archives of Women's Political Communication* at Iowa State University @ https://awpc.cattcenter.iastate.edu/2019/08/09/im-sick-and-tired-of-being-sick-and-tired-dec-20-1964/

2 Almost every source I could find lists this line as Baker's most widely quoted. I have not been able to track down its origin. But it helps to know that the Ella Baker Center for Human Rights in Oakland, California (@ https://ellabakercenter.org/) is an on-going institution that serves to carry on Baker's life work. The line endures down through the years. As recently as April 17, 2024, Maya Gay, a *New York Times* editorial writer, used it on the *Morning Joe* show on MSNBC.

3 Robert P. Moses, Speech at Stanford University on Freedom Summer, April 24, 1964 (@ https://americanradioworks.publicradio.org/features/blackspeech/bmoses.html.

4 Stokely Carmichael, Speech at UC Berkeley, October 29, 1966 (@ https://americanradioworks.publicradio.org/features/blackspeech/scarmichael.html).

But it was a moment that included many who were not young or Black. Chief among them was Herbert Marcuse.

Marcuse's 1964 book, *One-Dimensional Man*, described the deeper cultural issues that required protest and change:

> The political needs of society become those individual needs and aspirations, their satisfaction promotes business and the commonwealth and the whole appears to be the embodiment of Reason. ... And yet this society is irrational as a whole.[5]

Then too there was Angela Davis who in 1970 became involved in her own legal defense for a case arising from her political activism. Many years later she would write with the passion and wisdom that characterized her life and work:

> We cannot go on as usual. We cannot pivot the center. We cannot be moderate.
> We will have to be willing to stand up and say no with our combined spirits, our collective intellects, and our many bodies. [6]

The Over-Others Who Think So Well of Themselves

The poorer and more troubled neighborhoods in my small New England city form a kind of geographic border for the city proper. Interior to this border the East Rock neighborhood serves as home for many Yale people. Then too in New Haven's increasingly affluent downtown upscale apartment buildings are rising day-by-day. The historical center of this growing zone is Wooster Square. David Wooster, after whom it is named, was a revolutionary war hero. Long after his day, it became known as Little Italy because of its world-famous pizza restaurants. Early in the nineteenth century, ship captains and grocery magnates began to build large Greek-revival homes around the district's central square. Today that square is home to those who can afford to live in this lovely park surrounded by houses only the well-to-do can own. Then too, Wooster Square today is itself being developed to its West with new condominiums and rentals that are expensive, with but a minority of so-called affordable units. This in a city where early in the 2020s "affordable rents" can be $1500 and up for not much more than a studio. Gradually this newly developed city housing extends west from Ninth Square (one of New Haven's original blocks laid out after 1638) into the downtown South of its Green, then on toward the West.

Somewhat more remote is Westville, also with mostly higher income residents with shopping and restaurants close by Westville proper. Westville, as the name implies, is the upscale neighborhood to the West. It is, in many ways, the ideal of an American suburb—no urban fuss, many parks and playgrounds, a few churches, and more than a few synagogues. Westville is the site of Yale's golf course and a kind of shallow lake district as well as the prestigious Hopkins preparatory school on its highest hill. Geographically, Westville is hemmed in by the West Rock, the sister promontory to East Rock, to its northeast and the West River to its East, the relatively calm Wilbur Cross highway to the West, and the very exclusive, mostly rural town of Woodbridge to the northwest.

---

5 Herbert Marcuse, *One-Dimensional Man: Studies in the Ideology of Advance Industrial Society* (Beacon Press, 1964), ix.
6 Angela Y. Davis, *Freedom Is a Constant Struggle: Ferguson, Palestine, and the Foundations of a Movement* (Haymarket Books, 2011), 145.

Westville's Mc Kinley Street is usually regarded as the neighborhood's most prestigious address with fine homes near parks and greenspaces. Yet, from all appearances it is not nearly so wealthy as the three super rich streets in East Rock—St. Ronan, Everit, and "Rich" Livingston streets. The last mentioned so-named colloquially for its block of elegant, million-dollar-plus homes facing East Rock Park. East Rock Park itself is a 427-acre park that offers many miles of hiking trails, some gentle, some steep.

Homes on Everit and St. Ronan streets house families of considerable wealth and prestige. St. Roman Street is up the hill from the main axis through the district, Whitney Ave. After a few blocks it becomes Edgehill Road, only slightly less upscale, that passes by Edgerton Park—lovely gardens, magnificent trees and shrubs, and leisurely walking paths enclosed all around by a wall originally built to enclose the remains of the twenty-acre estate that Frederic F. Brewster, a Standard Oil magnate, built in 1906 for his wife. Brewster willed the grounds to the City upon his widow's death on the condition that his mansion be destroyed. It was, in 1964. What remains are a carriage house, an elegant outbuilding (now used for public events including regular classes on growing bonsai trees, a large greenhouse open to the public with well-nurtured plants, a public outdoor garden, a fountain, public walking paths, and a large open lawn for children, families, and the young to picnic and play. The bonsai tree classes say enough about what kind of a neighborhood East Rock is! To its east, is a modest area known as Goatville, where there is relatively affordable housing for, among others, Yale graduate students who of course run into Yale faculty and administrators in the upscale delis up and down Orange Street. Of course, many others of means live here as well.

East Rock and, to a lesser extent, Westville are, therefore, where the elite and powerful of New Haven live. The story of one resident and her many children who also live there well illustrates not just how the status-conscious powerful live and have their pretentious being. Marjorie is, one could say (as many do), the town's foremost saint. After an early career in nursing and an MA in Public Health from Yale, she somehow got together enough money to purchase from Albertus Magnus College a large house the College no longer had use for when it developed nearby properties closer to campus. Marjorie is white but extraordinarily committed to gender, diversity issues, and the needs of disabled people—and is especially comfortable with Blacks. Most of her many children are Black. Her home is where she has cared for some 30 or more children, some today with their own children. Years ago she founded *There's No Place Like Home* where she cares for children and adults. Her home is *not* a foster care facility. She has *adopted all* her children who now range from a developmentally disabled young man to grown adults, two with children of their own—Vanessa, Emily, KC, and Eric. Among the others are functioning young people who go to school and are trying as best they can to find their way in life.

There's No Place Like Home is just up from Edgehill Road—near the thick of all too wealthy East Rock. The neighborhood was in an uproar when Marjorie set up her massive brick house. Of course they did not confess to racism so much as to the fact that she had bought the house for the social agency she still operates—which is the way others disguise their racism. Others of her grown children have been killed, died of cancer, or, in one recent case, Steve, who died apparently of an overdose. All but a few of her adopted children are Black. Many of the bio-mothers of her adopted kids are addicts or otherwise out of life's mainstream.

This much being said, you can well imagine why so many all-too comfortable East Rock neighbors objected from the first to *There's No Place Like Home* in their all-too-classy neighborhood. One highly respected (by his immediate academic kin) Yale Professor who, until his mind began to fade, made it known audibly that he was the most liberal of men. He was audible among those who objected to someone building such a place in *their* neighborhood. Rosa deLauro was *not* among those objecting to Marge's domestic project. Others, however, tried to sue Marjorie for the very fact that she was caring for kids. Imagine that! Some even offered to pay her to back out of the home's purchase. In due course HUD, the FBI, and the Department of Justice entered the fracas on behalf of the family and prevailed in a landmark early case under the newly passed Americans with Disabilities Act in 1990.

Marjorie withstood the abuse and carried on her work. She supports *There's No Place Like Home* on some small regular donations, Medicaid and Medicare for some of her children, her own hard work—for a long while she worked at one of the local high schools and today for an agency that provides oversight for adults with developmental disabilities. Marjorie has kept the house clean and orderly, all the while struggling to find money to repair the roof or replace industrial size refrigerators and more.

The irony of the location of *There's No Place Like Home* is that it is up a hill that looks down on New Haven's most wealthy while also being just down the hill from Prospect Street which is the virtual dividing line between Yale and its proud folk to the East and, to the West, Newhallville—one of the City's neighborhoods that holds itself together while being beset by urban poverty, crime, struggling schools, and without nearby shopping and service amenities.

Hence another important feature of Marjorie's *There's No Place Like Home*. Because it is so close to the top of Prospect Street, down from which is Newhallville, the heart of New Haven's Black community, her family of mostly Blacks, while housed alongside uppity whites, is close enough to a neighborhood of mostly poor Black folk. When there is sad news in their lives it rises up and over Prospect Street to the wealthy and others on the other side. From this down side of the Prospect Hill there arose, decades before, a deeply serious, life-long Black Revolutionary. When George Edwards died on September 16, 2022 at 85, sad news of his passing and good memories of his work spread even among those who wanted to turn a deaf ear. Until the very end George Edwards remained an unembarrassed radical, whose fame began when he was among the Black Panthers who, in the 1960s, were subjected to federal surveillance, arrest, accusations, even suffering in the hands of others while in jail awaiting court hearing. New Haven's famous on-line news site[7] said this of George Edwards:

> The state tried to frame George Edwards and lock him up for life. His fellow revolutionaries tortured him and tried to kill him. They didn't know whom they were messing with. He survived — and kept at his Black Panther mission for another half century, long after generations of fellow fighters left the theater. ... It was kidney cancer that finally claimed the life of George Edwards. ...Until his final months, he remained one of New Haven's most visible and engaging voices, challenging the power and supporting grassroots social justice crusades. Perhaps the most spied-on and messed-with political activist in New Haven history, he combined theatrical training with an unshatterable suspicion of government power to speak out wherever people gathered: on city buses, at library gatherings, at outdoor protests. ... It was impossible not to listen. Or to appreciate the man speaking. [8]

---

7 When once I was in Honolulu for a talk at the East-West Center, to my amazement a Pacific-Island news site carried a link to the *New Haven Independent*.
8 Paul Bass, "A Panther Passes On," *New Haven Independent* (September 21, 2022).

Marjorie is not an out-in-the-open radical, as George was. She can't afford to be because she relies on public and state agencies for funding and medical care for those she cares for. When George was a Panther, she was just getting started on her radical-in-fact, if not in-public, mission. They are two of a kind, fighting against the crushing power of a dominant society—of the over-others who think of themselves as above it all.

Wealth, Power, Domination

Wealth breeds power and power breeds domination of others. No matter, how liberally minded the powerful are, they gain their way by dominating, often unconsciously, the subaltern poor and others excluded. Those put off by *There's No Place Like Home*'s mission are deep down offended by Marge's hard work trying to keep her kids from slipping into the subaltern excluded by giving visible access to a better world.

Power and domination, however quietly it is whispered, is still tragic in this small city where a single noble woman is looked down upon, ignored, and mistreated by her all-too well-off neighbors is a story that has been told for centuries upon centuries. Wherever people live together they sort themselves as if ordained by the order of things—whether by myths and legends however they are assigned to one or another sector of their tribal culture. Always whether open or hidden, local cultures worship virtual totems or other signs and symbols that assign higher or lower, sacred or profane, statuses to all who gather around the local camp fire.

In the Christian era it became the Church that outgrew its early sects.[9] That grand Church was historically a hierarchy in which the heavenly powers sent down angels then saints then papal fathers, then priests who locally lorded over their faithful while ascertaining the doom of outcasts and sinners. The sects remained after the Council of Nicaea in AD 325 outside the allegedly *only true* Church, then in the sixteenth-century Protestant Reformation after Martin Luther's *Ninety-five Theses* in 1517 a protesting (as the name *protest-ant* implies) sectarian tradition. Early sixteenth-century protestants opposed the bloated Catholic Church's hierarchical scheme. In due course these protesting sects established their own sometimes tyrannical hierarchies that expelled, often viciously, those untrue to their pure rules of order. Hence, among much else, New Haven was settled as a rebelling colony in 1638. Irony of ironies.

The point in this is that there have always been and ever will be regimes of power and domination. The modern ones differed only by more subtly insidious means, working eventually through mass culture to control the minds and means of common people.

C. Wright Mills and Herbert Marcuse, among others, diagnosed this deceptively powerful treachery. They wrote at a decisive conjuncture in late modern history. The 1960s, in America and throughout the world, was a moment when well-established regimes were forced to take account of a drastic change in the world as they had long known it. Colonized people particularly in sub-Saharan Africa and northern Africa, the Caribbean, certain parts of the lesser Americas, indigenous communities the world over, and here and there in South and East Asia were throwing off or challenging the controlling powers of their colonizers. It all began with Gandhi's overthrow of Britain in India in 1947 and Mao's defeat of the nationalists in China in 1949 and continued down into the 1960s and, one could say, continues even today as new nations in Africa and elsewhere are still trying to sort their freedom out, often as they try to rid themselves of despotic postcolonial leaders from Mobutu Sese Seko in Congo to Muammar Gaddafi in Libya.

---

9 Ernst Troeltsch, *The Social Teaching of the Christian Churches* (Westminster John Knox Press, 1992 [1912]).

In America, and in due course elsewhere in the North Atlantic World, early in the 1960s the global revolutions were coming home to roost. It hardly need be said that Martin Luther King, Jr. and Malcolm X were significant figures. Both of their movements were inspired by figures from the peripheral world that had undergone decolonization. King's non-violent Civil Rights Movement owed a deep cultural debt to Mohandas Gandhi in India and South Africa where he led his movements. Malcolm X's Black nationalist movement in the United States was clearly drawn from Islamic Culture even as it was distorted by the Nation of Islam's Elijah Muhammad. But by the mid-1960s, King's Civil Rights Movement had arrived at a position close to that of the Black Power movement that changed the revolutionary agenda of domestic rebels. Similarly, after Malcolm's assassination on February 21, 1964, the Nation of Islam also faded away as new social movements arose.

Immanuel Wallerstein who coined the expression the World Revolution of 1968 out of his analytic view that, since the years on either side of 1500, the modern world came to be as a *world-system*—a system in which the world was organized around a series of Core States (for example the United States after World War II) that dominated a series of colonized Peripheral States in Africa and elsewhere was influenced by the French-Algerian revolutionary thinker, Frantz Fanon.[10] They had met in Accra, Ghana in 1960 and enjoyed a close relation until Fanon's death the following year.[11] Wallerstein, very much an American, was, until his death in 2019, as much a citizen of France as of the world he wrote about. This is worth saying because he viewed the events in 1968 from a global perspective, which they were. In Spring 1968 most major American universities from Berkeley to Columbia were in what one can only call revolutionary turmoil. Paris *Mai '68* was the most unruly among international capitals, but bouleversements were happening from Mexico City to Prague and Berlin. What all these different internal rebellions had in common, directly or indirectly, is that they were provoked by the global decolonizing movements since 1947 that had changed how the new global generation thought about the world they were inheriting. In America, as elsewhere, by the 1960s the young were criticizing their parents' generation for the world they meant to leave for them—a weirdly out of tune world of comfort and consumption, of televisual silliness and pandering politicians who were fighting a war in Vietnam.

The pervasive effect on the young was to at themselves—not psychologically but personally to understand better who they wanted and needed to be. This was the generation of personal politics. Many of the young read and reread C. Wright Mills and Herbert Marcuse. Some knew that unless things changed, they were destined to be one-dimensionally empty. Kwame Ture, Angela Davis, Adrienne Rich, and Audre Lord were among those they read and followed. New politics of race, femininity, sexuality, and more gushed from the pens, speeches, actions of men and women who saw the world afresh and themselves anew. Marjorie, a very local figure in New Haven, was one of the many who breathed the new air and thought a new world.

C. Wright Mills: Imagining the Power Elite

C. Wright Mills was the first *American* social theorist to write explicitly and extensively about the relationship of knowledge to power. In this and many other ways Mills was

---

10 See, for example Fanon, *The Wretched of the Earth* (Grove Weidenfeld, 1961). It should be said that Fanon was French only in the sense that he went to medical school in Lyon. He was born and grew up in Martinique.
11 Immanuel told me that he thought he had been the only white person to visit Fanon in hospital in Washington D.C.

an American original. He has been called a radical nomad by no less a figure than Tom Hayden who coauthored the Port Huron Statement, the political program of the 1960s student movement.[12] Hayden's characterization of Mills is fair enough especially when set against Mills's upbringing in Texas and his intellectual journey from graduate school at the University of Wisconsin Madison to his important books in the late 1950s and his teaching at Columbia University where the faculty denied him promotion to full professor. Mills's books were certainly among the best known to the general public. He was a public figure, known by many for a photograph of him riding around Manhattan on his motorcycle.

Mills was certainly a maverick.[13] Politically, he was a radical, a central figure to the 1960s radical students like Tom Hayden, but even more he was one who earned what was then a badge of honor of New Left-radicals—the over-wrought concerns of the FBI over his visit to Cuba in 1960 just after Fidel Castro rose to revolutionary power.[14]

As for Mills's sociology, some might argue with the claim that he was the first American sociologist to write a social theory of knowledge and power. Robert K. Merton, polymath that he was, certainly touched on the issue in his massive text, *Social Theory and Social Structure*—a collection of articles continuously revised over the years.[15] The book's classical article "Social Structure and Anomie," originally published in 1938, is implicitly a theory of how, in effect, power determines and orders the ways cultures determine and distribute the access of people to institutionally normal means of conforming to a society's guidelines for normal status. The book also contains an important but oft-ignored section on the Sociology of Knowledge which includes an essay that dates to 1941, "Karl Mannheim and the Sociology of Knowledge," that includes serious references to such important works as Marx's "German Ideology."[16] Yet, Merton's few writings on and about power fell short of the direct and explicit writings on power by Mills. Then too, it should be said that Merton's student, Alvin W. Gouldner published in 1954 *Patterns of Industrial Bureaucracy* and *Wildcat Strike: A Study of Worker Management Relationships*—both works indebted to Merton but also drifting toward Marx's thinking on power. It would be another 16 years before Gouldner's *Coming Crisis in Western Sociology* in 1970 which many on the sociological Left considered a companion book to Mills's wildly popular *The Sociological Imagination* in 1959.[17] Still, this being said, C. Wright Mills who died in 1962 at but 45 years, had set down a new path for the study of what Michel Foucault famously called *power/knowledge*. Then too, while doing comparisons, *White Collar and the American Middle Class* in 1951 at about the same time as David Riesman, Erik Erikson, and Edwin Lemert wrote, differently, on the pull of conformity on inner-directed individuals. There was little mention of power in their books—except for Riesman's Chapter 10 in *Lonely Crowd*, "Images of Power," where interestingly he says, that "the other-directed person, if he is political at all,

---

12 Tom Hayden, *Radical Nomad: C. Wright Mills and His Times* (Routledge, 2006). Mills will appear a second time below because he was such a pivot figure, not because he was more important than others.

13 Dan Geary, "Maverick on a Motorcycle? The Thought and Times of C. Wright Mills" from the Introduction to *Radical Ambition: C. Wright Mills, the Left, and American Social Thought* (University of California Press, 2009).

14 Kathryn Mills with Pamela Mills, "The Last Two Years: New York and Cuba," in *C. Wright Mills: Letters and Autobiographical Writings* (University of California Press, 2000), 311–341. Mills's daughters provided other records of his travels to Europe and Mexico where, in both, he had become well-known for his radical politics.

15 Robert K. Merton, *Social Theory and Social Structure* (The Free Press, 1949 [revisions: 1957, 1968]).

16 *Ibid*, 629–630—for the sources of these early articles.

17 For side-by-side discussions of Mills and Gouldner in the context of other contemporaries on the subject of power and knowledge, see Charles Lemert's "Variations on the Theory of Power and Knowledge," in Anthony Elliott and Charles Lemert, *Introduction to Contemporary Social Theory* (Routledge, 2022 [2013]), 243–280. The Mills entry there is the source of much of this entry.

is a member of a veto group."[18] The chapter ends with the tragic observation that "he ends up being what he plays, and his mask becomes the perhaps inescapable reality of his style of life."[19] By contrast, the year following in *White Collar*, Mills begins the book by citing George Orwell's *Coming Up for Air* in 1939 to an acutely political effect when he concludes that the basic trouble with Orwell's Mr. Bowling, a salesman, is like us all in that "we imagine we have something to lose." Eerily, Orwell's salesman anticipates the affliction of Arthur Miller's in *Death of a Salesman*.[20] As we do, or, in the day, we did. The difference for Mills is that the new middle class, white-collar worker is the victim of social forces, while Riesman portrays the other-directed as willing conformist to the world's changes, whose politics are not much more than an occasional veto.

More to the point, hardly anything Mills wrote after *The Power Elite* in 1956 was *not* concerned with power both as a subject in his social theory and as a primary preoccupation of his own political life. In particular, after *The Power Elite* he published *The Cause of World War Three* in 1958 and *Listen Yankee: The Revolution in Cuba* in 1960, after his trip to Castro's Cuba the same year. Then too, an important collection of his papers edited by Irving Louis Horowitz contains essays from his early days in 1939 to the end in 1962. The collection ends with a 1955 essay, "Knowledge and Power," which tells the basic truth of Mills's long and determined interest in the subject.[21]

Among social theorists, the best known of Mills's ideas is that bearing the title of his 1959 book, *The Sociological Imagination*:

> The sociological imagination enables its possessor to understand the larger historical scene in terms of its meaning for the inner life and the external career of a variety of individuals. It enables him to take into account how individuals, in the welter of their daily experience, often become falsely conscious of their social positions. Within that welter, the framework of modern society is sought, and within that framework the psychologies of a variety of men and women are formulated. By such means the personal uneasiness of individuals is focused upon explicit troubles and the indifference of publics is transformed into involvement with public issues.[22]

It is plain to see in the last line of this passage that Mills's sociological knowledge was linked indistinguishably to his politics. The ideal of the sociological imagination was, for Mills, a call for people (and not just sociologists) to see their personal troubles as embedded in society's structural issues—thus to turn away from self-blame which is discouraging to a bold knowledge of the history of societal issues formed in the well-structured public sphere. In practical effect, Mills was broadcasting a manifesto to use the sociological imagination as a work ethic (for all, the common and high-minded) to deploy knowledge of the wider social forces—thus to move beyond indifference or despair to engaged political action.

Too often academics treat the sociological imagination as a methodological maneuver able to generate more imaginative data leading to a wider and better knowledge of social things. Certainly, this is one of the idea's entailments but to focus on this alone is to miss the extent to which Mills, late in his short life, was turning sociology on its head by reframing

---

18 David Riesman, *The Lonely Crowd* (Yale University Press, 1950), 223.
19 *Ibid*, 224.
20 On George Orwell, see C. Wright Mills, *White Collar* (Oxford University Press, 1951), xi. Just below on the same page, Mills says the same of Arthur Miller's *Death of a Salesman*, which opened on Broadway in 1949.
21 C. Wright Wills, "Knowledge and Power," in Irving Louis Horowitz, *C. Wright Mills: Power, Politics and People: The Collected Papers* (Ballantine Books, 1967), 599–613.
22 C. Wright Mills, *The Sociological Imagination* (Oxford University Press, 1959), 5.

hard-won empirical knowledge with much more than hard scientific findings. Sociology is among the arts, intellectual and practical, whereby knowledge is key to a necessary politics of life in an all-too-well-structured social world. In his "Letter to the New Left" he inspired the student radicalism that would take shape in the 1960s.

> This refusal to relate isolate facts and fragmentary comment with the changing institutions of society makes it impossible to understand the structural realities which these facts might reveal; the longer-run trends of which they might be tokens. In brief, fact and idea are isolated, so the real questions are not even raised, analysis of the meanings of fact not even begun.[23]

Mills wrote these words in *The New Left Review*, the year after he published *The Sociological Imagination*. Here again, a manifesto read, not so much by sociologists, as by young New Left radicals the world over. Important to add that the New Left, along with the American Civil Rights Movement, were among the forces that called into question the 1950s culture of conformity that David Riesman and others worried about.

So, for Mills, knowledge and power were part and parcel of each other. Knowledge that reverts to isolated facts and local perceptions is powerless. The powerful who use knowledge to weaken opponents too often cause the powerless to suffer by taking on society's failures as their own. Mills, thus, called out liberal self-sufficient knowledge—the sacred cow of Enlightenment modernity. For him the truth of power is ubiquitously perverse. Again, in 1960, Mills's theory of power's relation to knowledge was not as sophisticated as Michel Foucault's *power/knowledge* later in the 1960s. Yet, there was in that decade something in the air that breathed life into a new theory of knowledge. Mills and Foucault were kin, born of a kind of global weariness, not just of war, but of mindless warmongering, colonizing by dominant political powers, and the deadly state powers of exclusion.

Mills, it could be said, did not discover this radically new and important theory until his last few years of life. Yet, it was always on his sometimes-hidden agenda—an agenda informed by his reading of Marx alongside academic sociology, of pragmatism alongside Parsons and Merton, of Weber alongside liberal political theory. Of Mills's sources, Weber could be said to have been the most important to his thinking as it would come to be.

Early in his scholarly career, Mills with Hans Gerth edited *From Max Weber*. At the time in 1946, few of Weber's texts were available in English. Weber's massive *Economy and Society* would not be translated and widely available until 1978 when the University of California Press edition appeared. Until then, American and other English language readers depended on *From Max Weber*—still today a brilliant selection of Weber's key texts. It begins unsurprisingly with Weber's *Politics as a Vocation* and generally represents Weber's writings on science, religion, politics, and social structures. Of these, none was more important to Mills, and those of like mind, than *Class, Status, and Party*—in which Weber laid down a theory of relations among economic, cultural, and political spheres. The very use of the term *spheres* served as a correction to Marx's severe doctrine of class structures—which in turn made possible Weber's most widely read book, *The Protestant Ethic and the Spirit of Capitalism* in 1905 with its stunningly original idea that the sixteenth-century religious sphere gave rise to the twentieth-century economic sphere of capitalist economic ethics.

---

23 C. Wright Mills, "Letter to the New Left," *New Left Review*, No. 5, September-October 1960: 18. @ https://www.marxists.org/subject/humanism/mills-c-wright/letter-new-left.htm. Also in Horowitz, *C. Wright Mills: Power, Politics and People*, 248.

Weber's essay on class, status, and party was crucial to Mills's theoretical innovations. The three were for Mills as they had been for Weber interconnected phenomena. The one that lent Mills's thinking a distinctive edge was status. Of course, the importance of status rankings had long been a primary consideration in modern societies where, as opposed to traditional societies, status was achieved not ascribed. When an individual advances up the social ranks there is the likelihood that what status may be attained will become a badge of honor—hence, Weber's expression *status honor*. This then is the means whereby status transformed into an element of cultural prestige. Hence, the concerns of 1950s social critics like Riesman who saw the preoccupation with conforming other-directedness as a dangerous cultural turn. In the words of Vance Packard's popular 1959 book they were *Status Seekers*. Status seeking came to be a widely familiar expression that was a symptom of a culture in which achieving status requires the acquisition of the symbols and fads whereby a given status is made evident to others. Kings inherit their crowns and domains. The new American middle class in the day earned their second cars, kitchen gadgets, scrubbed children, and tract homes with picture windows exposing the family's up-to-date televisions. Those days are now gone for the most part. But in Mills's day they were thriving. That he agreed so much with Riesman, in spite of differences, signifies the extent to which he read closely and well *and* kept good relations with those with whom he enjoyed mutual respect.

Yet, the status of those who rise above rural or working-class origins can be real but fragile, and far from a sure thing. This is the subject of Mills's 1951 book, *White Collar: The American Middle Class*. In general terms, this book can be viewed as a systematic historical discussion of Marx's idea of the working proletariat—in Mills's day, the wage earner—was a victim similar to the bosses of industry in Marx's day. In the American 1950s, however, the new middle class of white-collar workers had achieved a status superior to the wage-earners. Not only that but Marx could not have conceived of them as effectively bourgeois in their ways. Their work was increasingly in offices. The new middle class earned enough that they could afford their own homes that served as bases from which they pursued the middling values of people who aspired to something more while achieving something less than their dreams. In a different, though oddly similar, fashion, their circumstances were not unlike Marx's exploited workers. The white-collar worker was, and is, to the less overtly cruel but still arbitrary whim of the dominant managers. Their salaries were meager. Their positions could be taken away in a sudden economic downturn. They could be ordered about, even if in a more superficially reasonable way than the bosses of industry had deployed. Thus, Mills explained, the white-collar workers suffered a constant state of status panic. Their status was real but in an instant it could disappear. The arbitrariness of their status was the tool by which management controlled them. They could never be sure of what they had. As Mills so poignantly put it in 1951 in *White Collar*:

> There is a curious contradiction about the ethos of success in America today. On the one hand, there are still compulsions to struggle, to "amount to something"; on the other, there is a poverty of desire, a souring of the image of success.[24]

Here again, it is plain to see how Mills's *White Collar* drew significantly from Weber's theory of the interrelations among class, status, and power. Class, if economic, is never purely economic. Statuses are sought-after because cultural prestige is important to the modern social system. The new rich seek more wealth. The new middle class seeks to hold on to what they have.

---

24 Mills, *White Collar*, 285.

In 1956, in his most important and popular book, *The Power Elite,* Mills completed his account of the instabilities of post-war America. Here his subject is typified by the book's first chapter, "The Higher Circles." Here Mills put particular emphasis on the then (and still) powerful and worrisome elite sectors—the economic, the political, and the military. More to his main point, in an uncommonly succinct summary of his theory, he writes:

> The idea of the power elite rests upon and enables us to make sense of (1) the decisive institutional trends that characterize the structure of our epoch, in particular, the military ascendancy in a privately incorporated economy, and more broadly, the several coincidences of objective interests between economic, military, and political institutions; (2) the social similarities and the psychological affinities of the men who occupy the command posts of these structures, in particular the increased interchangeability of the top positions in each of them and the increased traffic between these orders in the careers of men of power; (3) the ramifications, to the point of virtual totality, of the kind of decisions that are made at the top, and the rise to power of a set of men who, by training and bent, are professional organizers of considerable force and who are unrestrained by democratic party training. ... Negatively, the formation of the power elite rests upon (1) the relegation of the professional party politician to the middle levels of power, (2) the semi-organized stalemate of the interests of sovereign localities into which the legislative function has fallen, (3) the virtually complete absence of a civil service that constitutes a politically neutral, but politically relevant, depository of brainpower and executive skill, and (4) the increased official secrecy behind which great decisions are made without benefit of public or even Congressional debate.[25]

Mills's exposition of the history, tastes, powers, and cultures of the power elite made the lasting contribution of being the first description of the interlocking directorate of the post-war American dominant strata. In this he solved, or began to solve, a problem Marx had left unsolved. If power, as Marx held, is from the societal top down, how does the dominant class do its *dirty* work? Mills's answer: By sharing common interests and a common elite culture, and by acting behind the scenes in the higher circles. Ever after social theorists in America took his notion of an interlocking directorate as the starting point for the study of power.

For Mills, their power was not so much in what they did as in what they knew. The elite know what their shared interests are, who their status allies are, and how they can work their will against the much larger number of lesser folk. What then are the lesser powers to do if they are not to blame themselves for their fate? To begin with, they must use their informed imagination to study the ways of the power elite and all of forms by which structural powers limit them.

Herbert Marcuse: Eros and the One-Dimensional Man

Herbert Marcuse was born July 19, 1898 in Berlin to an upper-middle class Jewish family, which at the time was safely assimilated into the local society. In 1916, after Gymnasium, he entered military service where he first developed his critical attitude toward Germany that, in turn, sparked his interest in Marxism. In 1919, after the War, Marcuse studied first at Humboldt University in Berlin before beginning doctoral studies in literature, philosophy, and economics at Freiburg. Marcuse's thesis on literature and art was accepted in

---

25 C Wright Mills, *The Power Elite* (Oxford University Press, 1956), 296.

1922—and there began his lifelong theoretical interest in aesthetics, always shaped by a strong but original Marxist theory. After graduate studies, he returned to Berlin and worked for a while in the book business while being supported by his father. This allowed him the relative freedom to read Martin Heidegger's *Being and Time*, which led to his mature knowledge of philosophy, after which he returned to Freiburg to study with Edmund Husserl and Heidegger. His relationship with Heidegger ended in 1932 due to political differences.

When the Nazis rose to power, an academic position in Germany was out of the question. So, Marcuse joined the Frankfurt Institute for Social Research which was itself at risk in the face of the ominous and ubiquitous Nazi threat to free critical thinking. The Institute, since its founding in 1923, had rapidly become Europe's most prominent center for critical social research. Marcuse joined Max Horkheimer, Theodor Adorno, Walter Benjamin, Erich Fromm, and other of the great Critical Theorists, as they came to be called. In 1933 the Institute closed down and moved to New York City, where it remained until 1951 when most—excluding Marcuse and Fromm—returned to Frankfurt eventually to be joined by a new generation of theorists, chief among them Juergen Habermas.

This being said one might ask why is Marcuse a subject in the history of *American* social thought? The answer is that, as important as he was to global social thought, he was one of the most important figures at a crucial moment in post-war America. Marcuse's renowned book, *One-Dimensional Man*, was published in 1964 in the United States just when student and other revolutionary movements were heating up. Two years earlier, in 1962, Students for a Democratic Society (SDS) circulated its *Port Huron Statement*. In many ways, Marcuse's book could be considered the textbook to SDS's declaration of political independence from the old, soft ways of an affluent America and still troubled world.

Consider how each began. *The Port Huron Statement*: "We are people of this generation, bred in at least modest comfort, housed now in universities, looking uncomfortably to the world we inherit." *One-Dimensional Man*: "The society is irrational as a whole."[26] To be sure, the students knew and appreciated other books, including Mills's *The Sociological Imagination*. But Marcuse's book took aim at much the same issues that the students were living with uncomfortably. The SDS students in *The Port Huron Statement* followed their declaration—much as Thomas Jefferson did in his in 1776—with the desiderata of their complaints against the regime that so troubled them. They put racism, poverty, climate change at the head of their list of doléances—after which they turned to their trouble with what was, in fact, at the heart of Marcuse's concern with the ideology of modern societies; namely:

> The worldwide outbreak of revolution against colonialization and imperialism, the menace of war, overpopulation, international disorder, *supertechnology*—these trends were testing the tenacity of our commitment to democracy and freedom and our abilities to visualize their application to a world in upheaval.[27]

In much the same way, Marcuse wrote:

> If we attempt to relate the causes of the danger to the way in which society is organized *and organizes its members*, we are immediately confronted with the fact that advanced

---

26 Herbert Marcuse, *One-Dimensional Man: Studies in the Ideology of Advanced Industrial Society* (Beacon Press, 1964), ix.
27 Students for a Democratic Society, *Port Huron Statement* (Port Huron Michigan, 1962) of which there are many online copies, including at the University of Michigan's 50th anniversary conference site with photos and other documentary material at *The New Insurgency: The Port Huron Statement In Its Time and Ours* (Ann Arbor, Michigan, November 2, 2012). Emphasis added.

industrial society becomes richer, bigger, and better as it perpetuates danger. The defense structure makes life easier for a greater number of people and extends man's mastery of nature. Under these circumstances, our mass media have little difficulty in selling particular interests as those of all sensible men. The political needs of society become those individual needs and aspirations, their satisfaction promotes business and the commonwealth and the whole *appears to be the embodiment of Reason*.[28]

Then immediately following, Marcuse's coda: "The society is irrational as a whole."

How did Marcuse develop these more-than-radical sensibilities of the irrationality of modern societies, for which even in the early 1960s America was the exemplar? Upon leaving Germany, Marcuse had thoroughly immersed himself in the study of American institutions and culture. He had, during World War II, served in the US Office of War Information that, after the War, became the CIA. He taught thereafter at Columbia, Harvard, and Brandeis where he was embraced by its Left-Jewish Culture. It was at Brandeis that Marcuse wrote *One-Dimensional Man* (1964, which became a companion piece of sorts to his nearly as famous *Eros and Civilization*, 1955). Marcuse then taught at the University of California at San Diego from 1965 to 1970, where his fame as a radical left thinker caused Governor Ronald Reagan to terminate his employment. He lived another nine years as a citizen of the United States often visiting Germany. He died of a stroke on July 29, 1979 in Germany while on the way to fulfill an invitation by Juergen Habermas to lecture at the Max Planck Institute. His ashes found their way to the United States but were returned for burial in Berlin.

In Marcuse's earlier years a good portion of his intellectual energy was spent on developing a critical theory of aesthetics that called attention to capitalism's investment in mass culture and its debilitating effects on populations. For Marcuse, what may have been true of theatre and the arts in Greece and other premodern democracies was no longer the case when technology turned popular, even high culture, into a repressive mechanism. Marcuse, however, was by no means a critic of culture in general or even of high culture. In one sense, he agreed with Theodor Adorno in this respect and shared one foundational point with his Frankfurt colleagues—as Martin Jay describes it in *The Dialectical Imagination: A History of the Frankfurt School and the Institute for Social Research, 1923–1950*: "What distinguished the Frankfurt School's sociology of art from its more orthodox Marxist progenitors, however, was its refusal to limit cultural phenomena to an ideological reflex of class interests."[29] Adorno and Horkheimer were hardly orthodox, even if their critique of mass culture was a seemingly orthodox attack on the Culture Industry as a capitalist enterprise.[30] Marcuse's general theory of art, however, enjoys a degree of accord with Adorno's, but he went beyond him in writing a systematic aesthetic theory. In *The Aesthetic Dimension: Toward a Critique of Marxist Aesthetics* (1978 [1977]), Marcuse writes of the revolutionary nature of art: "Art's separation from the process of material production has enabled it to demystify the reality reproduced in this process."[31] More generally, Marcuse provides a nuanced account of art critical of the bourgeois status quo:

---

28 Marcuse, *One-Dimensional Man*, ix. Emphases added.
29 Martin Jay, *The Dialectical Imagination: A History of the Frankfurt School and the Institute of Social Research, 1923–1950* (Boston: Little, Brown, 1973), 178.
30 Max Horkheimer and Theodor Adorno, "The Culture Industry as Mass Deception," in Horkheimer and Adorno, *The Dialectic of Enlightenment* (Stanford University Press, 2002 [1944]).
31 Herbert Marcuse, *The Aesthetic Dimension: Toward a Critique of Marxist Aesthetics* (Beacon Press, 2014 [1977]), 22.

I shall submit the following thesis: the radical qualities of art, that is to say, its indictment of the established reality and its invocation of the beautiful image (*schoener Schein*) of liberation are grounded precisely in the dimensions where art transcends its social determination and emancipates itself from the given universe of discourse and behavior while preserving its overwhelming presence. Thereby art creates the realm in which the subversion of experience proper to art becomes possible: the world formed by art is recognized as a reality which is suppressed and distorted in the given reality.[32]

Art can be, in certain forms, a means to portray the distortions of civil society's false claim to freedom and liberty.

It is evident thereby that Marcuse's Marxist aesthetics is a theory able to identify the refinement with which art *can* expose the duplicitous nature of bourgeois art: "Deception and illusion have been qualities of established reality throughout recorded history. And mystification is a feature not only of capitalist society. The work of art on the other hand does not conceal that which is. It reveals."[33] Later, he adds a boldly revolutionary idea: "Art breaks open a dimension inaccessible to other experience, a dimension in which human beings, nature, and things no longer stand under the law of the established reality principle."[34]

The argument in *The Aesthetic Dimension* would seem to be a carryover from the optimistic elements in his earlier book *Eros and Civilization* in 1955 and a break from the shatteringly negative theory of mass art in *One-Dimensional Man* in 1964. Yet Marcuse corrects the false impression of the earlier book in a 1966 Political Preface to the 1955 version—this by granting that there are grounds for a more positive sense of culture and art: "*Eros and Civilization*: the title expressed an optimistic, euphemistic, even positive thought, namely, that the achievements of advanced industrial society would enable man to reverse the direction of progress, to break the fatal union of productivity and destruction, of liberty and repression ..."[35] Then immediately after, Marcuse forthrightly corrects himself:

> This optimism was based on the assumption that the rationale for the continued acceptance of domination no longer prevailed, that scarcity and the need for toil were only "artificially" perpetuated — in the interest of preserving the system of domination I neglected or minimized the fact that this "obsolescent rationale" had been vastly strengthened (if not replaced), by even more efficient forms of social control.

Eros and Civilization is Marcuse's most systematic contribution to one of the projects of the Frankfurt School—to fuse Freud and Marx into a critical social theory. To this end, he necessarily (as the words in the Preface imply) turned to Freud's idea of the dual drive theory of the Unconscious psyche. This is to juxtapose the struggle between life and death in the psyche of an individual and by extension (as Freud argued in 1929 in *Civilization and Its Discontents*) in the modern world itself. At the least, Freud allowed Marcuse to introduce a dynamic notion of the struggle between social life and social death, that is, between those aspects of culture and art that encourage critical, even revolutionary, thinking and those aspects that undermine critical thinking:

> Mass democracy provides the political paraphernalia for effectuating this introjection of the Reality Principle; it not only permits the people (up to a point) to choose their own

---

32 *Ibid*, 7.
33 *Ibid*, 56.
34 *Ibid*, 72.
35 Herbert Marcuse, *Eros and Civilization: A Philosophical Inquiry into Freud* (Beacon Press, 1966), xi. Quote below, same place.

> masters and to participate (up to a point) in the government which governs them — it also allows the masters to disappear behind the technological veil of the productive and destructive apparatus which they control, and it conceals the human (and material) costs of the benefits and comforts which it bestows upon those who collaborate. The people, efficiently manipulated and organized, are free; ignorance and impotence, introjected heteronomy is the price of their freedom.[36]

Here, Marcuse is supremely clear about the dual drives of mass democracies. They can, on the one hand, give life to human freedom when the people choose freely their leaders, but on the other, they can be death dealing by introjecting them with attitudes of "ignorance and impotence." This, again, is from the Political Preface in 1966—two years after the publication of *One-Dimensional Man* where Marcuse's aesthetic theory turns precisely to the debilitating effects of mass and even high cultures. But, in addition, here too is Marcuse's nod to the two sides of the modern world in respect to its technologies: on one side, "A comfortable, smooth, reasonable, democratic unfreedom prevails in advanced industrial civilization, a token of technical progress,"[37] while on the other side: "Freedom of enterprise was from the beginning not altogether a blessing."[38] The latter alternative he then immediately pounds home with a thoroughgoing critique of the modern:

> The distinguishing feature of advanced industrial society is its effective suffocation of those needs which demand liberation... Here, the social controls exact the over-whelming need for the production and consumption of waste; the need for stupefying work where it is no longer a real necessity; the need for modes of relaxation which soothe and prolong this stupefaction; the need for maintaining such deceptive liberties as free competition at administered prices, a free press which censors itself, free choice between brands and gadgets.[39]

The very mention of "brands and gadgets" serves as a lead to the most important political concept associated with Marcuse: *repressive desublimation.*

Repressive desublimation is the malignancy Marcuse diagnoses as the cause of one-dimensional thought and behavior—which, to put it all-too-simply, is the condition whereby individuals no longer have the ability to think critically and act politically against the prevailing social order. Sublimation, by contrast, is the psychic (and social) process by which thoughts and feelings are repressed in the Unconscious mind (and in culture) by the semiconscious Superego (or the dominant cultural values). Here, the mind/culture distinction is partially collapsed. In Freudian theory, the Superego is the aspect of the psyche that imposes external cultural norms on the mind where the Ego does the work of repressing them into the Unconscious where they encounter the Unconscious libidinal drives—there to create a largely Unconscious struggle between the life and death drives and more generally between the repressed desires and the expectations of society. Sublimation is when repressed desires express themselves in a subliminal form different from their repressed form. A classic example of the process is the archetypical Puritan for whom sexual desire is impure; yet being unable completely to resist it, they act it out in not so obviously external action. In the case of the ideal typical Puritan, they work to create a pure community by expelling those

---

36 *Ibid*, xii.
37 Herbert Marcuse, *One-Dimensional Man* (Beacon Press, 1964), 1.
38 *Ibid*, 2.
39 *Ibid*, 7.

who will not conform to their norms (or by hanging witches). Hanging Salem's witches was, in effect, an expression of forbidden sexual desire. It is, of course, hard to imagine the Puritan as a kind of critical theorist before the fact when in his reality he was acting to affirm and protect a community's values.

Unsurprisingly, Marcuse describes this in very different terms; for example, in respect to his aesthetic theory:

> Artistic alienation is sublimation. It creates the images of conditions which are irreconcilable with the established Reality Principle but which, as cultural images, become tolerable, even edifying and useful. Now this imagery is invalidated. Its incorporation into the kitchen, the office, the shop; its commercial release for business and fun is, in a sense, desublimation—replacing mediated by immediate gratification. But it is desublimation practiced from a "position of strength" on the part of society, which can afford to grant more than before because its interests have become the innermost drives of its citizens, and because the joys which it grants promote social cohesion and contentment.[40]

In this apparently bland statement, Marcuse packs all the explosiveness of his mind-jarring concept of repressive desublimation. It may not seem so, but the passage reflects the basic principle of his aesthetic theory in general. If art is alienated from reality—in Freudian language, the Reality Principle—art is thereby alienated from both political and social realities themselves. In earlier modern times, art enjoyed a degree of distance that allowed for the sublimation of an impulse toward criticism of the governing order. Then comes the distinguishing "Now"—artistic imagery which had a degree of critical efficacy is "invalidated." Art, such as it is under the reign of techno-society, becomes shopping, business, and entertainment that are considered "fun." This is the happiness society to which Marcuse refers throughout the book. Happiness seals the dominant culture's authority to repress the established order's democratic impulse for political criticism. "...[T]here are many ways in which the unhappiness beneath the happy consciousness may be turned into a source of strength and cohesion for the social order," but chief among these ways is the power of mind-numbing but comfortable familiarity with the goods and services sold by the dominating capitalist social order. Hence, the single most telling paragraph in *One-Dimensional Man*:

> The productive apparatus and the goods and services which it produces "sell" or impose the social system as a whole. The means of mass transportation and communication, the commodities of lodging, food, and clothing, the irresistible output of the entertainment and information industry carry with them prescribed attitudes and habits, certain intellectual and emotional reactions which bind the consumers more or less pleasantly to the producers and, through the latter, to the whole. The products indoctrinate and manipulate; they promote a false consciousness which is immune against its falsehood. And as these beneficial products become available to more individuals in more social classes, the indoctrination they carry ceases to be publicity; it becomes a way of life. It is a good way of life—much better than before—and as a good way of life, it militates against qualitative change. Thus, emerges a pattern of *one-dimensional thought and behavior* in which ideas, aspirations, and objectives that, by their content, transcend the established universe of discourse and action are either repelled or reduced to terms of this universe.[41]

---

40 *Ibid*, 72.
41 *Ibid*, 11–12.

To which, Marcuse adds the basic assumption of his aesthetic theory of art in late modern times: "The absorbent power of society depletes the artistic dimension by assimilating its antagonistic contents."[42]

In such times as these, art is reduced to flashy cars, empty promises, nifty fashions, titillating television, sex in the backseat of cars, desire for the newest and best dishwashers, the purported joy of a tract home in a suburb named Country Way, or such like. For Americans old enough to remember, this was the collective dream of the 1950s. *One-Dimensional Man*, published in 1964, was a book about this America projected onto the whole of the then still enveloping inert new social order where literary art, television melodramas, highway cigarette ads, and more stimulate desire for a vague, apolitical happiness:

> In contrast, desublimated sexuality is rampant in O'Neill's alcoholics and Faulkner's savages, in the *Streetcar Named Desire* and under the *Hot Tin Roof*, in *Lolita*, in all the stories of Hollywood and New York orgies, and the adventures of suburban housewives. This is infinitely more realistic, daring, uninhibited. It is part and parcel of the society in which it happens, but nowhere its negation. What happens is surely wild and obscene, virile and tasty, quite immoral—and, precisely because of that, perfectly harmless.[43]

Marcuse's aesthetic theory goes far beyond the mass culture industry that Horkheimer railed against. For Marcuse, everything is mass culture produced by a capitalist industry aiming to please the masses in order to castrate their political organs.

In the end, Marcuse did not give up hope. The global resistance movements of and around 1968 led him to publish *An Essay on Liberation* in 1969, which began: "Now, … this threatening homogeneity has been loosening up, and an alternative is beginning to break into the repressive continuum."[44]

Kwame Ture: Black Power in America and the World

Kwame Ture [aka Stokely Carmichael] was born in 1941 in Port of Spain, Trinidad and Tobago to the name by which he came to be known in America, Stokely Carmichael. His primary schooling was at Tranquility School in Port of Spain until he migrated to Harlem at 11 years to join his parents who had settled in New York when he was but two years old. His secondary schooling was at the highly selective Bronx Science High School. After graduation in 1960 he went to Howard University in Washington, D.C. to study philosophy. There Carmichael continued his vocation as an activist begun already in high school where he organized a protest against a hamburger joint in the Bronx that refused to hire Blacks. At Howard he was a prominent participant in the 1961 Freedom Rides organized by the Congress of Racial Equality (CORE), during when he was arrested multiple times and served hard time in Mississippi's Parchman State Prison Farm. Also at Howard, Carmichael joined the campus affiliate of the Student Nonviolence Coordinating Committee (SNCC).

Upon completing university studies in 1964 he became a fieldworker with SNCC during Freedom Summer in Mississippi where he worked with Bob Moses and Fanny Lou Hammer. After the summer Carmichael engaged in SNCC racial politics and practice throughout the American South, notably with the Selma, Alabama movement and the March to Montgomery in 1965. There he came to know Martin Luther King, Jr., a giant in the field

---

42 *Ibid*, 61.
43 *Ibid*, 76.
44 Herbert Marcuse, *An Essay on Liberation* (Beacon Press, 1969), vii.

but from whom he would soon part ways. Just a year later, in 1966, he became chairman of SNCC, succeeding John Lewis a hero of the 1961 Freedom Riders who would become a revered leader in the United States Congress representing Atlanta and Georgia's 5th congressional district.

During Carmichael's tenure, SNCC expanded its program to include opposition to the War in Vietnam and began to emphasize Black Power as the purpose of Black political action. Carmichael soon became a national and global celebrity for his defiant ideas and charismatic manner which also led to the FBI investigating him. In 1967 he stepped down from SNCC's chairmanship, in part because his celebrity detracted from its political work. Soon after, he began his association with the Black Panther Party, while also publishing, in 1967, the book *Black Power: The Politics of Liberation in America,* coauthored with Charles V. Hamilton. He was by then a figure of global importance.

In 1968 he married Miriam Makeba, the South African singer, who was known as Mama Africa. The following year they moved to Guinea where he changed his name to Kwame Ture out of respect for his African mentors Sékou Touré and Kwame Nkrumah. Ture thereafter devoted his efforts to revolutionary movements in Africa, notably Nkrumah's All-African People's Revolutionary party. In 1996 he learned he had prostate cancer from which he died in Conarky, Guinea in 1998. Significantly, at first Ture was treated for the cancer in Cuba with the support of the Nation of Islam.[45] Like Marcuse, Ture was born abroad and died abroad, but he made an enduring contribution at a turning point in American racial politics.

Kwame Ture's life was devoted to political action that served directly, in the expression of the day, to raise the consciousness of Black people the world over to their political power. The first of Ture's statements of Black Power was a 1966 speech at the University of California Berkeley, which began with poignant humor: "Thank you very much. It's a privilege and an honor to be in the white intellectual ghetto of the West." In America in 1966, Black Power was both practically and ideologically aimed at white power, but with the emphatic focus on black consciousness beginning with the virtual exclusion of whites from the more radical post-integrationist civil rights activities. The idea in the speech reflected his background as a philosopher: "The philosophers Camus and Sartre raise the question whether or not a man can condemn himself. The black existentialist philosopher who is pragmatic, Frantz Fanon, answered the question. He said that man could not."[46] In effect, whites must deal with their own racism. "Now then, before we move on, we ought to develop the white supremacy attitudes that were either conscious or subconscious thought and how they run rampant through the society today." The speech then declaims a bill of particulars of the issues affecting the American people generally—from poverty and the War in Vietnam to riots and other instances of social and racial violence. Most notably, Ture was perfectly clear about the role of capitalism's resistance to movements seeking to change the order of racial things.

> Now we articulate that we therefore have to hook up with black people around the world, and that that hookup is not only psychological, but becomes very real. If South America today were to rebel, and black people were to shoot the hell out of all the

---

45 Richard T. Schaefer, *Encyclopedia of Race, Ethnicity, and Society* (Sage Publications, 2008), 523. After the treatment in Cuba he sought care from Columbia-Presbyterian Medical Center in New York City before returning to Africa to die.

46 Stokely Carmichael, "Black Power," a speech at the University of California Berkeley, October 29, 1966 at Voices of Democracy Site, Academic Web Pages. There are no page numbers but the quotations here are from paragraphs numbered 3, 12, 42, 63—from first to last of a long but engaging speech. Note that many of the paragraphs begin with the inviting locution "Now we ..."

white people there—as they should, as they should—then Standard Oil would crumble tomorrow. If South Africa were to go today, Chase Manhattan Bank would crumble tomorrow. If Zimbabwe, which is called Rhodesia by white people, were to go tomorrow, General Electric would cave in on the East Coast. The question is, how do we stop those institutions that are so willing to fight against "Communist aggression" but close their eyes to racist oppression? That is the question that you raise. Can this country do that?

In the end, Ture's charisma is evident in his call for white people to change their ways:

The question is, will white people overcome their racism and allow for that to happen in this country? If that does not happen, brothers and sisters, we have no choice but to say very clearly, "Move over, or we goin' to move on over you."

In the 1967 book, *Black Power*, with Charles Hamilton, the full range of issues announced in the 1966 speech are spelled out chapter by chapter. But here the authors make it clear in the preface to the 1992 edition that Black Power is a global issue: "We are both far more sensitive to the international implications of our struggle. ... We both believe that until Africa is free, no African anywhere in the world will be free. To us, this is self-evident. It is also self-evident that the revolutionary struggle for that goal will not be deterred."

In the book, Ture was unsparingly critical of bourgeois American values and institutions:

We reject the goal of assimilation into middle-class America because the values of that class are in themselves anti-humanist and because that as a social force perpetuates racism. We must face the fact that what, in the past, we have called the movement has not really questioned the middle-class values and institutions of this country. If anything, it has accepted these values and institutions without fully realizing their racist nature. Reorientation means an emphasis on the dignity of man, not the sanctity of property. It means the creation of a society where human misery and poverty are repugnant to that society, not an indication of laziness or lack of initiative. The creation of new values means a society based on, as Killens expresses it in *Black Man's Burden*, free people not free enterprise. To do this means to modernize—*indeed, to civilize*—this country.[47]

These are words from 1967 on the eve of the 1968 world revolution. The world has surely changed since then. But early in the 2020s—a good half century later—the American middle-class has not. In some parts, it has grown worse, if anything. Kwame Ture was not a sociologist, but he was a practical social theorist who knew enough truth to speak it to the dominating powers of his day and ours.

Bob Moses, Fannie Lou Hammer, Ella Baker: Freedom Summer 1964/The Algebra Project

Freedom Summer in 1964 Mississippi was a turning point in the broader Civil Rights Movement. Martin Luther King's *Southern Christian Leadership Conference* (SCLC) and other organizations including the NAACP Legal Defense Fund and CORE participated, but SNCC lent the project its mover and shaker. Bob Moses, SNCC's field secretary and a prominent civil rights leader organized and directed the activities of Freedom Summer.

---

47 Stokely Carmichael and Charles V. Hamilton, *Black Power: The Politics of Liberation* (Random House, 1967). The reference is to John Oliver Killen, *Black Man's Burden* (Trident Press, 1965).

Robert Parris Moses (1935–2021) had quite a different background from Stokely Carmichael. He was born and grew up in Harlem to hard working but poor parents.[48] They lived in public housing at Harlem River Houses. From the first Moses showed himself interested in his education. He was an avid reader in New York City's Public Library. He studied at Stuyvesant High School, one of the city's two most selective secondary schools. After, he went to Hamilton College, then Harvard for graduate studies in philosophy. The illness of his father and death of his mother prevented him from finishing the PhD. After this ordeal, he taught at Horace Man School, then in time he became engaged in anti-war and civil rights activism.

In 1961, on the advice of Bayard Rustin and Ella Baker, Bob Moses started work in Mississippi and as field secretary for SNCC. Baker and, eventually, Fannie Lou Hammer were his advisors throughout. Hammer, in particular, was the Mississippi activist behind Freedom Summer. Planning for the Freedom Summer began as early as February 1964. By one estimate more than 1,000 volunteer white people and a comparable number of Black volunteers joined the SNCC led movement. The goal was to increase Black voter registration. The Freedom Summer Project in 1964 with its army of whites from the North built and expanded Freedom Schools where Blacks from Mississippi were trained to deal with challenges from white registrars who regularly presented Black voters with multiple question registration forms that asked questions from the state constitution. Freedom Schools also tried to help people know how exactly they were to cast their votes. With Fanny Lou Hammer's guidance and that of many others in local communities, most of them women, some three years of preparation came together in June 1964. Mississippi was chosen because in 1962 only 6.7% of Black voters were registered even though Blacks constituted one-third of the population.

White resentment led to harassment and violence—churches, businesses, and homes were burned, volunteers and workers were beaten, four were killed. Most notoriously, James Chaney, a Mississippi Black, Andrew Goodman, a white volunteer, and Michael Schwerner, a CORE activist also white, were viciously beaten and murdered in Philadelphia, Mississippi, then buried in a mound of dirt where the killers thought they would never be found. But they were. Robert F. Kennedy sent down FBI agents who found the Klan members who were convicted of the murder and sentenced.[49]

The penultimate success of the Summer Project was the creation of the Mississippi Freedom Democratic Party (MFDP) for which Fannie Lou Hammer was Vice-Chair. MFDP elected its own delegates to the national Democratic Party's Convention, when the Mississippi Democratic Party refused to accept their delegates. The Freedom Democratic Party presented themselves to the national Party expecting to be seated instead of the Mississippi Democratic Party's all-white delegates. Lyndon B. Johnson, who became President in 1963 after John F. Kennedy's assassination, was seeking his own full term as President. He had thought perhaps that his success in passing the 1964 Civil Rights Act had earned enough credit so that he could, as he did, refuse to seat the MFDP delegates. He

---

48 Some of the following relies on the Wikipedia entry "Bob Moses (activist)," also: "Robert Parris Moses *The Martin Luther King, Jr. Research and Education Institute* (Stanford.edu), as well as: NPR Obituaries, "Civil Rights Activist, Bob Moses, dies at 86" (July 25, 2021 [Associated Press]). See also, Clayborne Carson, *In Struggle* (Harvard University Press, 1981). But the most important source of the work, experience, and thinking of Bob Moses is Robert Parris Moses and Charles Cobb, *Radical Equations: Civil Rights to the Algebra Project* (Beacon Press, 2001).

49 A 1988 film *Mississippi Burning* staring Gene Hackman and Willem Dafoe kept the story alive for years after even though it presented white agents from the North as central characters in the tragedy and its resolution, while allowing Blacks to function as background to them.

feared he would lose the South in the November election. He won that election but in the long run failed in his only term because his political conniving led him astray into the War in Vietnam. Then too the Freedom Summer Project failed to capitalize on its successes in a long summer's dangerous work. Even though it may well have been at the time the best organized direct-action event of the Civil Rights Movement other than the 1963 March on Washington and Martin Luther King, Jr.'s early direct action protests.

In another sense SNCC was, if not a loser, at least thrown into confusion. In November 1964 it held its first Waveland, Mississippi conference to reflect on the summer's work and its own future. For starters, the presence of so many whites in the group led Blacks to question SNCC's racial agenda. Then too, there arose the question of how they should work together. Early on, SNCC had a plain, if simple, democratic method of talking things through. But in the Freedom Summer Project this was impossible. So many worked here and there in a relatively large state that regular consultation and communication was clearly out of the question. Decentralizing a mass movement is at best awkward, if not downright naïve. The Waveland conference did not go well.

Then, perhaps in an attempt to relieve the common stress, someone asked Stokely Carmichael, "What is the position of women in SNCC?" He, being a comedian of sorts, answered, "Prone." There had been, of course, more than a little random sexual activities among the Freedom Summer and SNCC people. This was, after all, the 1960s. Some took Stokely's allusion to sex in SNCC as a joke. But others seized the occasion to talk about the true place of women in SNCC. Many remarked that women had always been asked to take minutes and do other menial tasks.

Of course everyone at Waveland knew of the central roles played by the great women in the movement especially Ella Baker and Fannie Lou Hammer and countless others across the South without whom SNCC would never have been what it became. The SCLC ministers were, in relation to women, superior, even condescending in spite of the fact that these women were the ones who kept the organization going. SNCC was different, whatever its limitations. Members were young, open, initially mixed race, and intent on open dialogue of the kind necessary when recruiting Blacks to register and vote. In this particular, if flawed, democratic movement not even Stokely could or would command members to do what he wanted. Martin Luther King's Southern Christian Leadership Conference was, by contrast, a minister's organization in which male clergy were leaders not strictly beholden to the masses. As a result, even though Ella Baker had worked for SCLC, as she had for virtually every other civil rights organization in the South, she was always committed to getting to know and be known by those she worked with. Bob Moses had one early meeting with Martin King in which, he felt, the great man was more interested in what Moses could do for him than in who this brilliant young man was.[50]

It is therefore fair to say that Ella Baker was often thought of as the "godmother" of SNCC, as Fannie Lou Hammer was the soul of Freedom Summer. As the story of Stokely Carmichael's joke about the position of women in SNCC got out, many were outraged. Among those present were Casey Hayden and Mary King who had taken careful notes that were circulated, eventually published online as *Sex and Caste: A Kind of Memo*.[51] They took the "Prone" remarked seriously but more in a political sense than as sheer sexism. They (especially Hayden) were against a move at the Waveland retreat to reorganize in a more hierarchical manner with strong central leadership. Hence, *Sex and Caste* was not

---

50 Moses and Cobb, *Radical Equations*, chapter 2, "Learning from Ella: Lessons from Mississippi, ca 1961."
51 Casey Hayden and Mary King, *Sex and Caste: A Kind of Memo* (1965) (at the website History is a Weapon).

aimed at Carmichael but at the wing of the Waveland group that wanted to abandon the decentralized, radically democratic organizational policy.

After Waveland in 1964, SNCC carried (or limped) on. Stokely Carmichael resigned his leadership role in 1967 because of the national uproar over his radical (allegedly Communist) ideology. The year before Bob Moses left SNCC, eventually to become, with the support of a MacArthur "Genius" Grant, the organizer and leader of the Algebra Project. In this his commitment to local community organizing was at work. By 1982, when he had won the MacArthur grant, he had carefully thought through the role of technology and science in late modern America. This of course was well-after Marcuse's *One-Dimensional Man*. But Moses's idea was that young Black children were permanently limited economically and socially when they lacked basic knowledge of the abstract representations of algebra. Knowledge of the abstract formulations of algebra was, and is, a pathway into the technical language of computer arts but, more important, for the techno-culture of the world as it was then emerging—as now, more than a half-century later, it has become the undergirding aspect of economic culture in what some might call postmodern America and the world. Marcuse was dead when the Algebra Project got under way. It is not clear whether he influenced it directly. At the least it is evident that Bob Moses influenced the 1960s generation in several ways at once.

But with due credit to SNCC and to its efforts during and after 1964, it could well be said, at some risk of saying too much, that the long-term contribution of SNCC was the argument over the position of women in SNCC and everywhere else. 1964 was but a year after Betty Friedan's *Feminine Mystique* and two years before she and others founded the *National Organization for Women* (NOW) in 1966. There can be no question that Friedan's works were important to feminism as it developed in the two decades after NOW. At the same time, the work of women like Ella Baker and Fannie Lou Hammer could be said to be *more* important in the long run of feminist culture because what they did was on-the-ground face-to-face work in homes, on streets, in churches, and juke joints. Ella Baker, in particular, can well be ranked (as so far, she has not been) as a mother of modern feminism. Baker with those she mentored—notably Bob Moses, Casey Hayden, and Mary King—were the true leaders of the kind of feminist action that changes communities and more.

It would not be until the early 1970s when Feminist Standpoint Theory took shape that social theory turned to the practical everyday lives of women for its theoretical inspiration. In 1970 and after, radical feminists like Angela Davis became the feminist equivalent to Stokely Carmichael's threats to right wing opponents of women's power in the world. But, unlike and more than Stokely, Angela Davis wrote with scholarly sophistication of women's worlds. Then too in due course so have others. Adrienne Rich and Audre Lorde were important in the formation of a radical line of Third-Wave feminists. Their poetry, nonfiction essays, and public speaking generated powerful and memorable theories of damages done in the name of social order by power and domination. Here, for one example is Adrienne Rich's *Diving Into the Wreck* which many consider her most notable poem, written in the early 1970s when feminism was becoming more openly political:

> We are, I am, you are
> by cowardice or courage
> the one who find our way
> back to this scene
> carrying a knife, a camera
> a book of myths
> in which
> our names do not appear.

But it is Angela Davis, who remains the exemplar of a radical and unsparingly honest theory of *Women, Race, and Class*—as she put it in the title of her still important book on the history of radical Black feminism from the Civil War until late modern American times.

Angela Davis: The Raw Truth

Few social theorists knew or know their minds better than Angela Davis who from the first, when she was just beginning to become what she is now, took a strong and well developed statement of her intent to be a radical activist *and* theorist of Black, feminist, and class liberation from the evils of capitalism.[52] And, Angela Davis knew those from whom she had come, spiritually, as she made clear in 2013:

> Fannie Lou Hammer ... was a sharecropper and a domestic worker. She was a timekeeper on a plantation in the 1960s. And she emerged as a leader of SNCC and as a leader of the Mississippi Freedom Party. She said, "All my life, I have been sick and tired. Now I am sick and tired of being sick and tired."[53]

Angela Davis always spoke the raw truth as here to a largely white audience at Birkbeck College in the University of London where she was more than willing to challenge assumptions. Yes, she meant to say to this crowd, there were virtual plantations in the 1960s in the American South with *timekeepers* taking close account of the rate at which cotton was being picked.[54] Really? In the 1960s so long after Emancipation and long enough after the decline of Jim Crow? Yes, she meant to say. Get used to it!

Not since Frederick Douglass' *Narrative of the Life of Frederick Douglass, A Slave* has anyone of similar importance written and revised their memoir over close to half a century of life. *Angela Davis: An Autobiography* first appeared in 1974, then again in 1988, and 2021.[55] Writing in *The New York Review of Books* in 2022, Keeanga-Yamahtta Taylor reviews the 2021 edition of *Angela Davis: An Autobiography* by putting its latest edition in context: "The fiftieth anniversary of Davis's acquittal of murder, kidnapping, and conspiracy, charges that once threatened her execution, was little acknowledged this past June, but *as a thinker she may be as influential as she has ever been.*"[56] How could this be so long after her radical politics in the 1960s and 1970s? Davis answers the question in the first pages of the 2021 edition of *Angela Davis: An Autobiography*:

> As I write this preface, many narratives are emerging that center the uprisings and organizing efforts related to the police murders of George Floyd, Breanna Taylor, and so many others, which helped to define a period that will be remembered for the collective awareness of structural racism during the Covid-19 pandemic. My contributions, like the work of others who attempted to narrate aspects of others of the anti-racist struggles of the late twentieth century, will hopefully help us to understand where we are

---

52 Angela Y. Davis, *Women, Race, & Class* (Vintage Books/Random House, 1983).
53 Angela Y. Davis, *Freedom Is a Constant Struggle: Ferguson, Palestine, and the Foundations of a Movement* (Haymarket Books, 2011), 68.
54 For example, Sharon Ledwith, *The Last Timekeepers and the Noble Savage* (Mirror World Publishing, 2021).
55 Angela Davis, *Angela Davis: An Autobiography* (Haymarket Press, 2021 [1988, 1974]). Douglass' *Narrative of the Life of Frederick Douglass, A Slave* appeared in 1845, 1855, and 1892—the same span as Davis's *Autobiography*: 47 years! Douglass was 37 when he wrote his first volume. Davis was but 30.
56 Keeanga-Yamahtta Taylor, "'Hell, Yes, We Are Subversive'," *The New York Review of Books* (September 22, 2022), 58. Emphasis added.

today. ... Just as the names of Travon Martin, Freddie Gray, George Floyd, and Breanna Taylor will always be etched into the memories of politically conscious contemporaries today, my Southern comrades of the late 1960s will never forget the names of Leonard Deadwyler, Gregory Clark, and of course, Jonathan and George Jackson.[57]

Even among those sympathetic to today's anti-racist movements, it may seem a bit much to compare today's movements to those of Angela Davis's youth. Yet, those old enough to have lived through both who may have forgotten some of the names, we remember many as we remember the times. Then the social movements faced dug-in late Jim Crow racism in the South and lukewarm liberal "concern" in the North. Today the structural situation is much different. Today anti-racist movements face a most virulent racial nationalism rooted in the South but present across the land—a racialized ideological movement like none other since the KKK which was local by comparison; and the ghosts of the long racial past borne today by our Black children who hear the stories of other Black children killed by police.[58] Davis is quite clear on the difference. She writes that "our collective aspirations were emboldened by revolutionary struggle all over the world—from the People's Movement for the Liberation of Angola, the Mozambique Liberation Front, and the African Party for the Independence of Guinea and Cape Verde in Guinea-Bissau to the National Liberation Front in Vietnam and the successful revolutionary overthrow of Fulgencio Batista in Cuba."[59] It is plain to see that Davis was, as she is now, familiar with revolutionary movements the world over.

Angela Davis is one of a very few social theorists who is both multilingual and multiply and seriously engaged in both academia and in-the-streets political activism. She has been, and is, both feminist and Marxist as, formerly, she was an unflinching member of the Communist Party. In college days she studied French at Brandeis University and German at the University of Frankfurt. It was at Brandeis that she met Herbert Marcuse who led her not just into the study of philosophy and political activism but, later, to the University of California San Diego. At UCSD she studied with Marcuse before moving on to the Humboldt University in Berlin to complete doctoral studies. Back in the United States, her feminism grew more prominent, she joined protests against the War in Vietnam, joined the Communist Party, and took her first academic position in philosophy at UCLA.

Then in 1969 her life took a momentous turn when the University of California Regents fired her for her political views and Party membership. The decision was eventually overturned, but she declined an offer to return to her faculty position in order to devote herself to political activism. Then came the events that, more than anything, determined the course of her life after—a fact supported by her 1974 autobiography. Even the 2021 edition of *Angela Davis: An Autobiography* is all-but entirely about her experiences with the so-called criminal "justice" system in the early 1970s. Davis's early formation was in a sea of legal troubles from which she emerged, in the long run, safely and all-the-more focused politically. As she put it in 1988: "The political threads of life have remained essentially continuous since the early 1970s."[60]

---

57 *Angela Davis: An Autobiography*, x.
58 For one example, Elizabeth Alexander: "I call the young people who grew up in the past twenty-five years the Trayvon Generation. They always knew these stories. These stories formed their world view. These stories helped instruct young African Americans about their embodiment and their vulnerability. The stories were primers in fear and futility. The stories were the ground soil of their rage. These stories instructed them that anti-black hatred and violence were never far." Alexander, "The Trayvon Generation," *The New Yorker* (June 15, 2020), 20. Also: Alexander's *The Trayvon Generation* (Grand Central Publishing, 2022).
59 *Angela Davis: An Autobiography*, xi.
60 *Ibid*, xxvii.

On August 9, 1970, she learned that a friend, Jonathan Jackson, had been killed with three other San Quentin prisoners during an assault on a courtroom in Marin County, California. He had a gun she had lent him. She owned it for self-protection. Perhaps because of her friendship with Jackson and her well-known radical politics, she went into hiding. On October 13, 1970 she was arrested, charged with conspiracy to murder, and jailed for more than a year.[61] One unsurprising fact is that the prosecutor claimed that her association with Jonathan Jackson was a crime of passion and that she could not possibly have been motivated by true political commitments. It was the early 1970s when few in such a position could imagine otherwise about a young woman.[62] In her defense on March 2, 1972, Davis defiantly challenged the prosecutor's case, speaking to the jury:

> Now he would have you believe that I am a person who could commit the crimes of murder, kidnapping, and conspiracy, having been motivated by pure passion. ... Members of the jury, this is utterly fantastic. It is utterly absurd. Yet, Mr. Harris would like to take advantage of the fact that I am a woman, for in this society women are supposed to act only in accordance with the dictates of their emotions and passions. I might say that this is clearly a symptom of the male chauvinism which prevails in this society.[63]

Again, a 29-year-old Black woman addressing white authorities in 1972—Davis here revealed her incipient feminist and social theoretical determination. She was acquitted.

Her trial was widely covered in the US and around the world. She immediately set off on speaking engagements, eventually in Cuba, USSR, and East Germany. She began teaching again in Black Studies at Claremont Colleges, Women's Studies at the San Francisco Art Institute, in Ethnic Studies at San Francisco State College before entering a permanent position in the History of Consciousness and Feminist Studies programs at the University of California at Santa Cruz from 1991 until retirement in 2008. All this long while she remained active in politics and public speaking. In 2019 she was elected to the National Women's Hall of Fame, which took particular note of her years of work toward dismantling the prison industrial system.[64] In 2020 she was named by *Time* magazine as one of the world's most influential persons. Then in 2021 she was elected to the American Academy of Arts and Sciences.

Angela Davis's social theory was always, one way or another, applied to the concerns of her political life. None more so, though differently, than the book she wrote just after her initial, post-trial period of public fame. *Women, Race, & Class* first appeared in 1981. The book bears up well after these many decades because it is systematically historical in the sense that she presents the general theme of its title in carefully historical terms. It begins, for example, with "The Legacy of Slavery: Standards for a New Womanhood." This first chapter sets the tone for the book. It is replete with historical facts and a review of the essential literature—W.E.B. Du Bois's "The Damnation of Women" in *Darkwater* (1920), Eugene Genovese's *Roll Jordan, Roll* (1974), Herbert Gutman's *The Black Family in Slavery and Freedom, 1750–1925* (1976), and ever so much more, including of course the abolitionist Harriet Beecher Stowe's *Uncle Tom's Cabin* (1852) with obligatory critical remarks on Daniel Moynihan's *The Negro Family* (1976) misguided treatise on Black matriarchy. Davis's review of the literature is unlike the tiresome, always tendentious academic reviews

---

61 *Ibid*, Part One, "Nets."
62 *Ibid*, Part Six, "Bridges," 312–319.
63 *Ibid*, 317.
64 https://www.womenofthehall.org/inductee/angela-davis/

of the literature. *Women, Race, & Class*, rather, means to pull together a considerable lineage of works on the degradation of enslaved women to call attention to standards for a new womanhood for which Black women are set forth as the standard. Under slavery women were "breeders" and housemaids when not working the fields. In the new dispensation after the revolutionary 1970s, the abolition of housework became "a strategy goal of women's liberation" in which "the socialization of housework—including meal preparation and childcare—presupposes an end of the profit-motive's reign over the economy."[65] The working concludes on an insistent political point: "Working women have a special and vital role in the struggle for socialism."[66]

Davis traces the general theme of this book and of her political work to the triangulated relations of women, race, and class so well expressed in the Combahee River Collective which held to the following principles:

> During our time together we have identified and worked on many issues of particular relevance to Black women. The inclusiveness of our politics makes us concerned with any situation that impinges upon the lives of women, Third World and working people. We are of course particularly committed to working on those struggles in which race, sex, and class are simultaneous factors in oppression. We might, for example, become involved in workplace organizing at a factory that employs Third World women or picket a hospital that is cutting back on already inadequate health care to a Third World community, or set up a rape crisis center in a Black neighborhood. Organizing around welfare and daycare concerns might also be a focus. The work to be done and the countless issues that this work represents merely reflect the pervasiveness of our oppression.[67]

For herself, Davis took particular interest in critical action and writing in opposition to the prison-industrial complex which she viewed in global perspective. "The notion of a prison industrial complex insists on understandings of the punishment process that take into account economic and political structures and ideologies, rather than focusing myopically on individual criminal conduct and efforts to 'curb crime'."[68] Just after, she goes on to say with ever more theoretical refinement:

> Thus, the prison-industrial complex is much more than the sum of all the jails and prisons in this country. It is a set of symbiotic relationships among correctional communities, transnational corporations, media conglomerates, guards' unions, and legislative and court agendas. If it is true that the contemporary meaning of punishment is fashioned through these relationships, then the most effective abolitionist strategies will contest these relationships and propose alternatives that pull them apart. What, then, would it mean to imagine a system in which punishment is not allowed to become the source of corporate profit? How can we imagine a society in which race and class are not primary

---

65 Davis, *Women, Race, & Class* (Vintage Books/Random House, 1983 [1981]), 143.
66 *Ibid*, 144.
67 *Combahee River Collective Statement* @ http://circuitous.org/scraps/combahee.html (Part 4, 1980). Angela Davis made many references to the Collective which goes back to Harriet Tubman's role on June 6, 1863 in leading Black Union forces by sea to a plantation on the Combahee River in South Carolina. Seven hundred slaves are thought to have been liberated. See Davis, "Reflections on Race, Class, and Gender in the USA" in *The Angela Davis Reader*, edited by Joy James (Blackwell, 1998), chapter 22.
68 Angela Davis, *Are Prisons Obsolete?* (Seven Stories Press, 2003), 36. At the same time, *Combahee River Collective Statement*, refers prominently to Davis's "Reflections on the Black Woman's Role in the Community of Slaves," *The Massachusetts Review* 13:2 (1972), 81–100.

determinants of punishment? Or one in which punishment itself is no longer the central concern in the making of justice?[69]

Davis's theoretical sophistication and her experience with Marcuse when she describes the prison-industrial complex as a set of symbiotic relations by which she means the complex and intrusive socio-technologies by which all, or virtually all, members of any given society are effectively imprisoned in the late modern period. She did not go as far as Michel Foucault did in *Discipline and Punish* in 1974, nor was her view as directed to a one-dimensional society as was Marcuse's. At the same time, neither Foucault nor Marcuse was imprisoned as she was—an incarceration from which she emerged fully Marxist, feminist, and determinedly Black. Plus which by 1974 the symbiotic social technology of the late modern era had already become, as she observes, the instruments of capitalism enterprise—multinational corporation, guard and police unionization, multimedia corporations, and much more. For Davis, global society was itself a conglomerate of socio-technological incorporation. At the core of Angela Davis's thinking is that crime and punishment are not an absolute dichotomy. Many are punished without committing a crime—especially Black men who are, as Alice Goffman and others have shown, subjected to all-but constant surveillance from which there is little chance of escape.

---

69 *Ibid*, 46.

Part V
Reprise

Social Theories in America and the Six Elements

Culture, this acted document, thus is public,
like a burlesque wink or a mock sheep raid.
—Clifford Geertz, *The Interpretation of Cultures*, 1973

Burlesque Winks and Mock Sheep Raids

If there was one thinker in the modern period who was more inventive in reformulating social thinking in his field, and beyond, it was Clifford Geertz of whom I wrote at length in Chapter 13 and in another book.[1] I am not saying that others were not just as, or more, important in what they did. Before the modern period James Madison and Abraham Lincoln were, one could say, *more* inventive in creating something out of nothing—a stable Bill of Rights that made the Constitution work over the years in Madison's cases; a unified, if not healed, nation after many years of Civil War the odds were against the Union defeating Robert E. Lee's army. But this kind of thing is tricky business.

I dare to invoke Geertz instead of others because it was he whose most surprising ideas still puzzle readers today.

> Culture, this acted document, thus is public, like a burlesque wink or a mock sheep raid.
> Though ideational, it does not exist in someone's head; though unphysical it is not an occult entity. ...Once human behavior is seen as (most of the time there <u>are</u> true twitches) symbolic action—action which, like phonation in speech, pigment in painting, line in writing, or sonance in music, signifies—the question as to whether culture is patterned conduct or a frame of mind, or even the two somehow mixed together, loses sense. The thing to ask about a burlesqued wink or a mock sheep raid is not what their ontological status is. It is the same as that of rocks on the one hand and dreams on the other—they are things of this world. The thing to ask is what their import is: what it is, ridicule or challenge, irony or anger, snobbery or pride, that, in their occurrence or through their agency, is getting said.[2]

Geertz settled for many the question of infinite regress—and what elsewhere is called the below the bottom turtle issue. In effect he insisted that in the social sciences we should not try to dig deep into what evidence might be found to explain a phenomenon. Instead, as he says: "The thing to ask about a burlesqued wink or a mock sheep raid is not what their ontological status is." Rather we should look closely at the many sides of a phenomenon

---

1 Charles Lemert, *Silence and Society* (Routledge, 2025), chapter 1.
2 Clifford Geetz, *The Interpretation of Cultures* (Basic Books, 1973), 10.

but at the nuances of actions that have been observed. Hence: "Culture, this acted document, thus is public, like a burlesque wink or a mock sheep raid." The wink and the sheep raid are taken from studies he comments on in which, he argued, the wink, for example, is the sign at issue. If there was a wink, was it a dismissal of what was being said, or a signal to a companion to act a certain way, or the fact of the matter at hand? Better he said to study even the most modest event or sign that is likely to give the answer, than to probe endlessly to all the possibilities—which, after all, are not empirical, even if they are explored numerically.

This short discussion is not, however, an attempt to say that Geertz is the be-all-and-end-all of American social theorists. I mean instead to express a strong instance as to where and how theories change and grow. This after-all is what the book is about—especially in this *Reprise* which is a pulling together of the historical elements by which *Americans Think America*.

Doers and Thinkers in a Small Town

In my church in New Haven there is a smaller group that meets most Monday evenings—a House Church, so to speak. The group has been together for more than 40 years, carrying on as some left town, died, or quit. The group eats a pot luck meal with the main course prepared by that night's host. We spend a good half-hour chatting about whatever, sipping drinks of various mild kinds, nibbling on plates of cheese, crackers, olives, cut veggies—things of that sort. We eat the meal often held in our laps because few of our homes or apartments have a big-enough dining room. After, we read some or another text, usually a biblical passage often the gospel lesson for the coming Sunday. Three members have advanced theological education, several are published scholars, all are smart enough to often have interesting things to say about the text the group reads every week. We usually drift beyond the subject, sometimes into current events in the world that week—this until someone pulls us back to the text before us. Over the years, we've gotten to know each other and gotten to know the story each has to tell.

Kate Walton, for example, grew up mostly in New Haven. After school and Goddard College in Vermont where she studied anthropology, she took a year off to travel overland across equatorial Africa developing primary source curriculum for teaching about Africa. As part of that adventure, she volunteered at Imeloko Hospital in the Democratic Republic of the Congo about 200 kilometers north of the Congo River at its north central curve, after which she returned to Kinshasa by river boat to complete a 2,328-kilometer boat trip on the Congo River from Kinshasa to Kisangani and back.

Upon her return to the United States, she obtained a Master's degree in Education at George Washington University. Over the years she returned to Africa including a year teaching biology and English at Kericho Tea Secondary School where she established a branch of the Wildlife Clubs in Kenya. Then also, Kate served in Belize as a USAID Surplus Food Distribution volunteer. Back home in New Haven, she joined the Fellowship Place serving people with severe mental illness recently discharged from Connecticut Valley Hospital. She spent fifteen years as Chief Executive Officer of Fellowship Place. After 20 years working in the Behavioral Health realm, she decided to move on to addressing the pressing problem of food insecurity in the local population. She was Program Director for the Connecticut Food Bank for eight years. After which, she became President and CEO of Interfaith Caregivers of Greater New Haven which provides free services to the elderly who need help to remain in their homes. These three long-term commitments lasted from 1985 to 2018—before and during which she worked at the Peabody Museum of Archaeology and

Ethnology at Harvard and served as manager of collections at the Social Science Library at Yale. And on it goes. Just recently Kate became President of North End Club, an intellectual endeavor started by and for women, that over more than a century has presented monthly lectures by the likes of Robert Frost, Norman Thomas, May Sarton, and Margaret Mead.

One (me included) wonders how all this is possible given the range and seriousness of Kate's activities. If I were to venture an armchair psychoanalytic diagnosis, it might be because when she was young her Yale professor father disappeared leaving her mother with kids and home to manage. In time, the mother recovered and life became more orderly. Once secure, her mother found and bought a small cabin on Paradox Lake in the Adirondacks. Then, as the years went by, she and her siblings together bought part of the camp across the Lake which closed in 1969 and left abandoned until 1980 when Kate and her siblings purchased six of the buildings and 24 acres.

Today Kate spends late Spring to early Autumn there. She invites individuals and groups from New Haven to visit her in the Adirondacks to visit Fort Ticonderoga Museum and to spend time at her camp Nawita. Then too, she has written and published in 2022 *Paradox Lake of Memories* which is more than a memoir. The book, like her life, is a story that uses her family and their experience on Paradox Lake to tell the story of earth science at Yale in the 1950s and 1960s, and the geology of the Lake which was important for its puzzling origins and the quest to decipher what became the Theory of Plate Tectonics. She also delves into the unique mineral resources that spurred the quest for iron in the early days of New York State after the Revolution. *Paradox Lake* also uncovers the stories of early forgotten feminists. Notably, she writes of the early women geologists who coincidentally were first to study Paradox Lake's enigmatic geologic character—while also describing the experiences of the Mohawk Tribe and other Native Americans whose ancestral lands are in the region. All this is woven together by the surprising ways that Yale and New Haven played important scientific and historical roles in the wider region of New York and Connecticut as early as the 1750s. I spend this much time on Kate Walton so that she can stand as an exemplar of others in our local group about whom just as much, though different, could be said.

In the House Church group there were others who came to town and did good things, thoughtfully. Dr. Bob, as he is called by the group, is from Ohio where he went to college at Case Western Reserve, then trained as a physician at Tufts University School of Medicine in Boston. In New Haven, Robert Windom, M.D. had a long career as a pediatrician at Cornell-Scott Hill hospital and clinic in the Hill neighborhood where he treated children from poor and otherwise struggling families. In addition, he is so well read that there is hardly a topic about which he fails to have something stimulating to say, including race about which he knows much from personal experience.

Then too there is Bob Sandine who was born in a rural Midwest town of a family of modest means and was an excellent student who got himself admitted with a fellowship to the prestigious and costly DePauw University in Greencastle, Indiana. DePauw sparked his interest in theatre. After college he studied theology at Yale Divinity School and soon became the Reverend Robert Sandine, an ordained Methodist minister. Bob's life has been devoted to many activities including ministries in various church venues. But none more than the production of dramatic plays from Sophocles to Thornton Wilder. Bob enjoyed a long career as teacher of English and Director of the Program in Theater Arts at the prestigious private K-12 Foote School in New Haven. He was so good at Foote that when he retired the school's theater was named after him. He was so beloved that even today, years later, many say that he should have been appointed Head of School. Since my daughter went to Foote under an unimaginative Head who was appointed instead, I know he should have been Foote's leader. Among the plays Bob Sandine has directed at the church are those of Neil Olsen, who is also a member of the group.

By profession, Neil Olsen is an electronics engineer with a graduate degree from Rensselaer Polytechnic Institute. He worked for thirty years all over the world for, among other companies, ITT's Advanced Technology Center. Neil then turned to a second life as an historian, author, and book publisher. Among his books are *God's Spy: William Tyndale and the Book that Conquered England* (2013) and *The End of Theocracy in America: The Distinguishing Line of Harry Croswell's Election Sermon* (2013), among others published since 2013. Another of the group is Lois Read, who founded the Art Department at Hopkins Grammar School in New Haven. Lois is a fabled local artist whose paintings can be found on the walls of many homes the town over. In time she switched to writing poetry and has published nine books, including her latest, written in her 98th year, titled *Torches* (2023). Among others in the group is Chris Janis who holds degrees in theology and has served for many years as an unordained pastor and social worker in Newhallville, then as now among the poorest and least white neighborhoods in the town.

There are others in the group but I introduce these individuals in order to make the point that even in very local groups in not so big towns there are gatherings of people who have come from and gone on to far and wide places, while gathering experiences and training that lent them the gift of vocations in service to others where they live. One of them wrote the following without any knowledge of Saskia Sassen or Manuel DeLanda: "Each organization of human beings that share some communal experience in relation to a particular social geography are an organism. If organs organize cells which either systematic ally or randomly bind its parts, the overall health of the organism relates to how well each cell's part relate to input from the outside world. ... The process is eternal, we hope for all human beings."[3]

This we hope in the face of the fact that chaos often tugs at who we are through the wide culture from which chaos descends on us.

Chaos, Self, and Culture

Those who live in a chaotic environment must deal with people moving in and out and other tensions between the ordering and disordering forces of a late- or post-modern society. As a result what any particular individual considers his or her personal identity is itself a constantly changing thing. Those closest to us may have what they consider a full and honest sense of one's identity. But as Erving Goffman taught, we all necessarily keep personal secrets from, even, intimate others. It can be dangerous for the on-going performance of an identity to reveal all of our personal secrets. In this sense, long-married partners all cheat on each other—not necessarily sexually but in some other ways that may in fact be so deeply repressed that the cheater himself doesn't remember them. The emotional force of repression is in the fact that, more times than not, the cheater "forgets" to tell-all. As Goffman put it: "And in truth he will have accepted a self for himself; but his self is, as it necessarily must be, a resident alien, a voice from the group that speaks for and through him."[4] This, some will realize, is an application of Goffman's most famous idea that an individual's self depends on her ability to perform a self-with-others who accept her for what she presents herself to be.[5] Whatever one thinks of Goffman's theory of the presented self, it is hard to

---

3 Kate Walton, "Comment on Mental Health," *Fellowship Place* (May 5, 1994).
4 Erving Goffman, *Stigma: Notes on the Management of Spoiled Identity* (Simon & Schuster, 1963), 123.
5 Erving Goffman, *Presentation of Self in Everyday Life* (Doubleday, 1959). (And see also Chapter 15, "The Fungible Interaction Order.")

deny that any identity we have—or think we have—depends entirely on the extent to which others accept it on the basis of the impression we make on them.

In short, if cultures make a range of identities possible, then social theories are the means by which we can have a personal notion of who we think we are. Personal identity theories are, in a sense, our own social theories of who we are. Such like, however defined, cannot help but be deeply influenced by the culture that, in turn, teaches us to think. It is easy to see that here we are talking about a complex but on-going reciprocity of many trajectories between the individual and her world. More simply put, social theories are means by which we come to think our worlds including their cultures.

The basic elements of American social theory could therefore be said to be the practical means whereby people, like Kate Walton and most others, figure out their own theories of who and what they imagine themselves to be in the world such as it is, on the ground of daily life. So it is for us all, even when we (often) disappoint ourselves. I, for one, think of myself as a first-rate public speaker, but just last night in a darkened Taizé service at church I fumbled and flubbed the reading of a Gospel passage I know by heart. No one there thought I was as brilliant as I hoped to be. This happens to me all the time, as I suppose it does to all of us. We are not always, not even often, who we think we are. If we were and we thought perfectly well of ourselves then one day we'd be Lord of something or another and there might even be a gospel according to Charles. This joke is no joke. In fact, we would be lost (and some are), if we are not able to imagine ourselves better than we are or could be. Such is the moral psychology of modern human nature—a psychology that seems to live on even after modernity itself has slipped into a kind of historical crevice out from which modern people cannot make progress as once they believed they could.

Here then is the conundrum of modern cultures and their almost pathological *sequelae*. Cultures make individuals. Individuals learn from them who they ought to be. The oughts we derive from our cultures are the most basic and practical theories by which we navigate life with others and ourselves. In time the cultures change, even deteriorate, leaving generations of individuals in an unthinkable quandary. It is possible to reframe all this in respect to the American nation's cultural values in an all-too-general but plausible historical comment, as follows.

Once the first settlers of our land *may have* enjoyed an exceptional nature. But somewhere along the way—from 1565 when the Spanish settled St. Augustine, Florida, and from 1619 when the English, then the French, settlers came to North America through revolutions and wars to the 1950s when many Americans moved into all-too-settled suburbs and began to give in to the affluence that fell to the winners of a second Great War—Americans began to lose the world of their fathers and mothers. Yet, culturally speaking, worlds don't die off all at once. America's traditional culture began to die more morbidly in 1989, when the world revolution of 1968 swamped the globe at large with millions and millions of formerly preyed-upon peripherals who refused any longer to stand by as their people and resources were abused and stolen.[6] Even when the peripherals did not win what they wanted, they complicated the liberal ideal of history as progress. Of course there has been progress, much of it good but good mostly for the global well-off who had a free hand over what goods the lesser regions would get. The economic foundation of liberal democracies like America's and others in the Global North were based on free markets that would benefit all who

---

6 Immanuel Wallerstein, *The End of the World As We Knew It* (University of Minnesota Press, 1999) and *Utopistics: Or, Historical Choices of the Twenty-First Century* (The New Press, 1989). And: "The Modern World-System in Crisis: Bifurcation, Chaos, and Choices," in *World-Systems Analysis* (Duke University Press, 2004).

would partake of them. This idea was a deceitful neo-liberal sham pretending that Stuart Mill's invisible hand was what it never was. The old geo-economic regime is no longer.

Still, this being said, what is culture?

Cultures Live and Do Things

Still today, there are those who shy away from anything written by Talcott Parsons. Yet, even if his writings, like those of us all, deserve criticism to ferret out the good from the not-so-good, there remains much in Parsons's theories that is still good enough. Parsons's theory of culture's systemically distinctive qualities is important when one sets out to explain, perhaps define, culture—and especially when the subject is the culture of a complex society like the American one. "Systems of culture," he wrote, "have their own forms and problems of integration which are not reducible to those of personality and social systems or both together. ... and are on a different plane."[7] Parsons got this right, in two ways. Culture stands on its own; and (as he put it) culture is an action system. Or, more simply: *Cultures live. Cultures do things*.

All cultures live and do. American culture is no exception. So, in a sense this book is a kind of macro-ethnography of the ever-changing, multiplex, often-disorderly American people over the relatively few centuries since they first settled here and there on its East coasts. This book is about culture—what a people think about themselves. *Americans Thinking America!*

In the modern world since the Peace of Westphalia in 1648, when the idea of independent nations with borders was first planted, nations have grown up well enough to allow different people to thrive under one or another banner of their cultures that serve their purpose in dynamic relation to their economies, their political systems, their societies. America was, and is, no exception—except perhaps in the sense that its culture taught Americans that their nation was better than all others. Of course, this cannot be true of any nation in a global environment when everything everywhere is constantly changing.

America has been good in its way, but not *the* very best. No nation is. Truth be told, it would be hard to say how so whopping a distorted dream of American life made its way into the cultural heart of collective America. To this point, *Americans Thinking America* has argued that there have been distinctive aspects of American social thought. Otherwise, there would be no reason to write and publish a book like this.

Since their earliest settled days centuries ago, the new Americans brought with them the experience of their journeys across the mysterious and troubled seas. This first dangerous leg of their search for a new world was one that required each among them to find practical ways to deal with their fear of seas greater and more tumultuous than any could have imagined. Then, arriving, they had to settle on strange shores against mile-upon-unknown-mile of woods and forests. This is why it is fair to say that the foundational values of the new American people were, plainly put, *individualism, pragmatism*, and *the promise and threat of Nature*'s *seas, lands, and forests*. Practical reasoning—and in time pragmatism itself—have been considered decidedly American ethical principles. But, even here, practical ethics and pragmatism are not exclusively American values. There are pragmatic people (in the generic sense of the word) everywhere—people who in their wayback, began against the odds dealing with forbidding natural environments like the Mediterranean or the Bering Straits. Plus which, it is righteously stupid even to suggest that other people lack a deep

---

[7] Talcott Parsons and Edward Shils, eds., *Toward a General Theory of Action* (Harvard University Press, 1951), 7.

appreciation of their individual needs and wants. Truth be told the American culture and its society has been like—if not the same as—those of many other nations. The huffing and puffing of its culture may have arrogated America's self-understanding ever since its first settlers fled Europe for something else, and better.

That North America's settlers survived to flourish against terrible natural and geopolitical odds certainly justified their descendants' satisfying, if extreme, conviction that they were special—that their destiny was manifestly exceptional. In one sense they were not far wrong. Late in the 1700s no other North Atlantic nation had so decisively cut ties with its traditional types of political authority. Such a venture properly encouraged them to launch a cultural claim to being better than those they left behind. *Errand into the Wilderness,* at first; then *Manifest Destiny,* early on; and *American Century* later; to *Make America Great Again,* closer to our time. Slogans they were and are. Slogans like these, when held widely among a people, inspire attitudes. *American exceptionalism,* however, embraces them all. Still, it is basically a mantra that moves many souls because there is *some* truth in it. Quite apart from the fact that, strictly speaking, all nations are different from all others, thus exceptional in their own ways, certain aspects of early American history are, at least, above the norm. The early American nation was clearly the first to fashion a working democratic system that has endured even when, from time to time, it has wobbled.

Then again, *Make America Great Again* and other slogans of the kind tell a truth that never seems to have occurred to those who boast in such words. The *great* of any social thing is at best a figure of speech. Bob Dylan may be a great song writer and performer deserving of his Nobel Prize. But, even he is necessarily ranked among others who once were held in similarly high esteem. When the Voyager One space probe in 1977 was launched in order to meet and greet others who may be somewhere in outer space, it contained a pure gold record meant to tell unknown others who we are. Bob Dylan's was not the popular music inscribed. Chuck Berry's *Johnny B Good* was. All attributions of greatness to individuals are necessarily relative and fungible. But to a nation? A social thing so grand and complicated as a nation cannot be, in and of itself, greater than all others—not even for an historical moment. National things are necessarily wobbly and susceptible to failure. For that matter, so are the greatest of empires. They rise and fall. What is Rome today but a religious center for some and a tourist destination with great art and fabulous food for others?

Then too what is America today but a military and economic power nervous before its cultural troubles? Power in and of itself does not and cannot calm the cultural nerves of a nation. Especially not when that nation is constantly changing as always it has. People immigrate without legal right. Some who belong want them out. A once white majority is losing ground to people of various colors. Some hate that reality, a few hate it enough to kill phenotypically alien others. The USA once, just after WWII, was the sole great world power. Soon after, rival powers arose in the USSR and China, which gave birth, first, in the 1950s, to a Red Scare at home and, second, a war in Korea. Then later, in the 1960s, a war in Vietnam led to countercultural divisions that were the political obverse of the divisions over the Red Scare attacks on innocent people. Then, in the 2020s, America was ever more the world's (and history's) strongest military muscle, with scant ability to exercise that muscle against smaller technologically armed rebels and larger troubled national war machines in Russia and China.

In effect, ever since the American Civil War in the 1860s, the United States have suffered deep structural conflicts. None perhaps so deep as the threat of an entire section to secede from the Union. What remained after that Civil War was, it hardly needs saying, still a cavernous difference between Blacks and dominating Whites—a conflict sealed by the Planter

Class reinventing a virtual slavery by holding Black Workers on the plantations with the support of White Workers who were paid the racial wage—by which being accepted as White was the only pay they got working for scant wages and supporting the Planter Class.[8] A century later, with the 1964 Civil Rights Act the last vestiges of this kind of racial double-dealing-began to be called for what it was. Progress of a sort followed but not so much that some sixty years later in the 2020s shadows of this dark past cover the national society and disgrace its better culture.

These are but a few of the vectors in America's all-too-normal matrix of latent social conflicts. As much as most people, and especially believing Americans, want to believe that their nation is at least very good, perhaps the very best, the underlying and undeniable fact is that no nation perfectly achieves its own high values. On the contrary, to live in a nation is to be drenched by storms arising from the vortex of the many wants and needs of others who often want exactly what you have.

Gloomy as this argument is, the fact is that even the most troubled cultures seldom forget their better moments—their great leaders, their good wars, their fine art and music, and the like. One of the best books on this subject is Bernard Bailyn, *To Begin the World Anew: The Genius and Ambiguities of the American Founders*. Generally put, the book's concluding maxim is that challenges will continue and intensify as the years go by, and the people need to know why. "One needs '*some reason*'" for the uncertainty.[9] He comes to this provocative insistence, at the end of a book that begins with the dilemma that haunted American culture from the first then came to a head at its best moment, when the founding fathers won independence and made a workable Constitution that is meant to tolerate stubborn differences and to permit tolerable solutions to differences. The founders "...were truly creative people, [but] their creative efforts, the generations-long enterprise that elevated this obscure people from their marginal world to the center of Western civilization, were full of inconsistencies, logical dilemmas, and unresolved problems."[10] There you have it in a nutshell. Even the best succumb to faults of their own doing. Cultures all are imperfect because they are meant to guide and govern unruly populations. That they do as well as they do is credit against the bad hand they are dealt.

The Culture Problem

If there are differences among the similarities of modern nations this is because *modern* nations since the late eighteenth century have experienced a common thirst for some or another version of democratic values. This is what makes them modern. Premodern and traditional social orders were governed by imperial powers that won their power not by the will of their people but by the ability of leadership to claim a natural right to power by which they could put down or destroy those who would resist them.

Since democracies permit citizens to act more or less freely, nations so organized tend to drift toward socially complicated orders. The risk of social freedom is societal chaos. More freedom necessarily means more chaos from angry disputes to rebellions to civil war. As Reinhold Niebuhr so well explained, "All social co-operation on a larger scale than the most intimate social group requires a measure of coercion. While no state can maintain its

---

8 W.E.B. Du Bois, *Black Reconstruction in America, 1860–1880* (Macmillan Publishing, 1992 [1935]),700–708. Also, David Roediger, *The Wages of Whiteness: Race and the Making of the American Working Class* (Verso Books, 1999).
9 Bernard Bailyn, *To Begin the World Anew: The Genius and Ambiguities of the American Founders* (Vintage Books, 2003), 149.
10 *Ibid*, 1.

unity purely by coercion neither can it preserve itself without coercion."[11] The best modern states can do is provide enough justice so that people can pursue, if not realize, their own values.

This fact of political life is where culture gets into normal trouble. Theorists of culture from Talcott Parsons to Stuart Hall, from Clifford Geertz to Alvin Gouldner have all, one way or another, identified culture's role in relation to the chaotic strains of society as that of maintaining a degree of control or, in the more leftish version, of provoking the changes that might encourage more freedom for its members. Either way, try as many might, it is difficult to say what culture is. Some definitions may be strange. Clifford Geertz for example:

> Culture, this acted document, thus is public, like a burlesqued wink or a mock sheep raid. Though ideational, it does not exist in someone's head; though unphysical it is not an occult entity. ... Once human behavior is seen as (most of the time; there *are* true twitches) symbolic action—action which, like phonation in speech, pigment in painting, line in writing, or sonance in music, signifies—the question as to whether culture is patterned conduct or a frame of mind, or even the two somehow mixed together, loses sense. The thing to ask about a burlesqued wink or a mock sheep raid is not what their ontological status is. It is the same as that of rocks on the one hand and dreams on the other—they are things of this world. The thing to ask is what their import is: what it is, ridicule or challenge, irony or anger, snobbery or pride, that, in their occurrence or through their agency, is getting said.[12]

Complicated, certainly. Hard to understand, perhaps. Just the same this is a definition by the one scholar of culture who may be more universally respected than any other. The point here is not what it means. The point, here, is that cultures are messy things. They don't conform to forthright formula. That is the way they are. *Cultures live. Cultures do things.* What they do is make meaning for other living things who would perish without it. This high-minded purpose, if it is to do what it is meant to do, requires that cultures must dip into the dirt of ordinary life where nothing is clean, little is certain, and trouble is normal. As hard as it is for cultures to do what they are meant to do, it is harder still to define their nature which, as Geertz said, is not ontological but a thing, like a rock or a dream.

So, what are serious thinkers to make of this riddle of a thing that is often drowned in the flux of other things? One thing to say about "culture," the term, is that it has a long but surprising history going back to Greco-Roman times when Cicero thought of the nurturing of the soul as cultivation, an agricultural figure. In the centuries since, culture as cultivation has appeared in several nuances from agriculture to the biomedical research practices of culturing bacteria to culture as a word in the vocabulary of early anthropologists of far away and strange early people. Among early anthropologists, Edward Burnett Tylor's *Primitive Culture* in 1871 was among the first to use "culture" as it is used today in the social sciences. This was two years after Matthew Arnold's *Culture and Anarchy* (1869) in which he made the strong argument that high culture is important to protect society from anarchy. Curiously, an anthropologist has claimed that Arnold's "culture" was closer to the social scientific meaning than was Tylor's.[13] Since early anthropology looked at culture from the bottom-up, one wonders how Arnold's top-down use of the term could be the

---

11 Reinhold Niebuhr, *Moral Man and Immoral Society* (Charles Scribner's Sons, 1935), 3.
12 Clifford Geertz, *The Interpretation of Cultures* (Basic Books, 1973), 10. For more on this definition, see the section on Geertz in Chapter 13.
13 George W. Stocking, Jr., "Matthew Arnold, E.B. Tylor, and the Uses of Invention," *American Anthropologist* 65:4 (1963), 783–799.

same—except for the common sense that both, differently, looked upon culture as a kind of umbrella covering the full range of social actions and structures. In either case, culture eventually found its way into sociology and other of the human sciences to occupy an umbrella-like purpose of holding off social trouble, when not serving as a drum beating the tune of social change.

Still, the trouble remains. How does one presume to write a book about any national culture when we are all nervous on the sea of chaotic troubles? The presumption is even more treacherous when *American* culture is the topic. First, as many have said, American culture is many and various with more moving parts and people demanding to be heard than most other cultures would deal with. Chaos is ever always in the offing. At the same time, secondly, Americans have long thought of their national society as exceptional—by which they do not mean exceptionally troubled. The best that can be done is to not even consider putting forth a pure perfect theory of American culture. As a result, I came upon the concept of *elements*, a term I knew since my college days in the late 1950s. I was then preparing for medical school and studying organic chemistry which in the day taught us the basic elements arrayed in a periodic table. I soon quit preparation for medicine to study theology which, in a strange way, introduced me to what Paul Tillich called the ground of Being in respect to which he wrote of the "ontological elements" in the whole of Being *including human being*.[14] Whether chemistry or theology, the notion of elements came back to me as a good enough way of characterizing whatever elements there might be in a culture of so variegated and duplicitous vectors as the American one.

A Social Theory of America's Cultural Elements

In still another way elements are at play in *Americans Thinking America* derive from the fact that social theory itself is a bit of a bastard—neither fully legitimate social theory as such, nor a well born history in the best sense of that endeavor. As the reader must have noticed so far, social theory appears here and there amid an apparent historical narrative. Yet, in the end even a book of this one's considerable length cannot be both at once if its goal is to chart the periodic table of America's cultural chemistry. A nation's organic chemistry cannot be formulaic as laboratory organic chemistry is. Culture's chemistry is metaphoric, yet its literary link to the real thing is fair enough. Cultural action systems do their work with, amid, and against political, economic, and legal systems (Parsons again). It would be brazen of me, if not downright impudent, to suggest that anyone could possibly write the narrative formula for such a muddle of dynamics. Real organic chemistry tries to do just this with compounds that are in fact named and numbered so that biochemists can mix and match them in the laboratory. Social theorists cannot do this because their compounds are too big, too dynamic, too fungible—and ever changing. By contrast, here is the diagram of the atomic structure of acetic acid, a relatively simple compound.

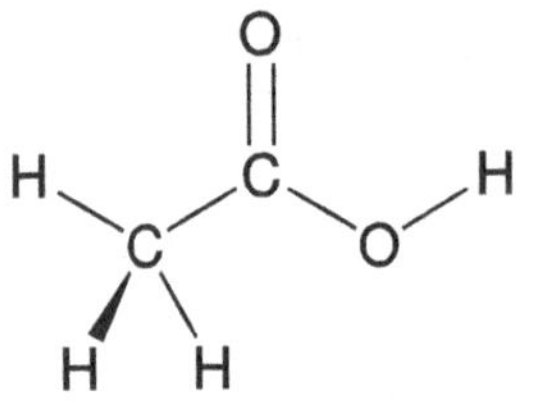

Figure R.1 Diagram of the atomic structure of acetic acid

---

14 Paul Tillich, "The Basis Ontological Structure" and "The Ontological Elements," *Systematic Theology, Volume 1* (University of Chicago Press, 1951), 163–185.

What the chemist can do is draw a diagram representing the elements of a compound. Such a possibility is all but impossible in social theory and the social sciences of culture. Some have tried but their structural diagrams are naïve relative to those in organic chemistry and other of the high sciences. We know why.

Social things cannot be understood as structures comprising the equivalent of subatomic particles. But metaphorically they *can* be said to have created, and been created by, cultural *elements*—by, that is, structural parts that have a beginning in time and a reason for being, parts so basic that many nit-pick over what they are to be called or whether they are sufficient. The names we give to changing social things are necessarily arbitrary—birds, for example. Ornithologists equivocate occasionally but in general they have the advantage of hearing and describing bird songs, watching their flight patterns, timing their migrations, and the like. For them a duck is a duck. Human beings sing and migrate and fly with the help of machines or balloons. Yet, no one thinks of qualities like these when defining the species nature of human beings.

Therefore, when it comes to classifying the structural features of a human culture, the best we can do is describe the apparently essential elements that have made them work. Otherwise put: Cultures are unstable and manifold because the human societies on, and in which, they act are unstable and manifold. As a result, cultures cannot be represented by reductive formulae, diagrams, and numeric terms. When social theorists attempt to deploy formulaic or diagrammatic schemes to describe the finer details of cultures and societies, they come up short of making good sense. I once tried this myself. The result was a silly, utterly abstract, diagram.[15] (I was young and ambitious enough to try anything.) Now, decades later, I have chosen to represent the *elements* of American culture as the more modest means to discuss the umbrella of societal parts so dynamic and manifold that they cannot be definitively captured in formal schemes. Even numeric terms, thus applied, cannot do more than convey rates, percentages, velocities, and such like. But how does anyone measure cultural elements that do not speed at any measurable rate and cannot be measured by rates and percentages? How would they measure what?—perhaps by counting how many people lived by those elements over time. In this case one would need to count how many people at a given time *claimed* they were pragmatists, when their claims could not be measured by their actions. Where does one find data of the sort? The best one can do is measure how many scholars who know what pragmatism is agree with the elements described by the one describing them? Here the problem turns on itself. Such a measure is little more than an opinion survey of what specialized people think about culture. Not very interesting.

The Six Elements

It is fair enough to begin here with what was said at the beginning and the end of Chapter 1. The distinctive qualities of American social theory as they came to be are:

1) an inclination toward the *individual*,
2) who is seen as understanding *nature* as both a challenge and a resource, and,
3) in respect to which, the individual must possess a strong sense of *pragmatism*. Yet, in their social relations, Americans thinking must come to terms with
4) the disordering obstacles to the ability of its culture to maintain a vital *interaction order*,

---

15 Charles Lemert, "Language, Structure, and Measurement: Structuralist Semiotics and Sociology," *American Journal of Sociology* 84:4 (1979), 951.

5) in which what common cultural knowledge that could be had must be had against the powerful effects of historically formed *identity differences*,
6) which, in turn, came to be as waves of immigrants and their social movements struggled among themselves to unsettle the nation state which itself struggles with *exclusions* inevitable to the fact that no one nation, especially not a Global one, can be everything to everyone.

Here, the key words are italicized only to introduce the focal feature of each element. But the key words cannot stand on their own.

The presumption of identifying the elements of so grand and obscure a social thing as a nation's culture must be brought down to earth by accompanying text, as here, that sets each in an historical context. Of course, the "historical" here is itself a presumption. History enters only in the still larger discourse of the book that sets elements gingerly in relation to concepts and historical conditions that arose over time. Even when stated in so many words, as here, the elements are qualified not just by their reliance on the others but by a necessary, if implicit, step back from pure certitude; as in "1) An *inclination* toward the individual." To be sure, this phrase is itself left hanging in discursive air. On its own, it makes no sense, until 2) the *individual* "is seen as understanding *nature* as both a challenge and a resource ... ." The word "individual" has as many meanings as there are particulate beings or things that can be thought of as somehow distinct from others of their species. A duck is a duck is a duck—except along the Mill River where one of them keeps her ducklings in the marshes while another minds hers on the banks of a quiet stream below the waterfalls. Bird watchers may not name a given duck but they do photograph them, record their plumage or practices.

So, the not-so-periodic table of cultural elements must go on from *individuals* and *nature* "3) ...in respect to which the individual *must* possess a strong sense of *pragmatism*." So, in completing the trilogy of primal cultural elements finally an insistent verb, *must*, is required to make sense of the three linked elements. Individuals who orient to nature *must* do something in this relationship. History is full of stories of cultures in which people hunker down or hide from whatever nature they are given to live in and against. Other, more utopian, people see themselves as overcoming their natural environments, often religiously, when they suppose there is a better nature beyond the one at hand.

Individuals, nature, pragmatism—the three first social theoretical elements of the new American culture—from their settlement to their slow-in-coming but inevitable revolution against their colonizing nation,—then to the early half-century before the Civil War when Americans began to explore and settle their far West that Lewis and Clark mapped out for them in 1806,—but then the Civil War changed everything. The deep cultural division between white European settlers and the young nation's people of color—Black slaves and Native American first peoples—gathered force over the years after the Revolutionary Generation. The Missouri Compromise after 1820 and Andrew Jackson's trail of tears after 1831 came to a boiling point in the early Indian Wars and the terrible Civil War that killed so many. After that War's end in 1865, as the North was industrializing and the South was looking for ways to keep a version of slave labor intact in spite of the Emancipation Proclamation, a then still-newer America was forced, ever after, to come to terms with deep structural differences that would not fade away. Far from it.

Hence the hanging thread of the third element that leads to the fourth:
Yet, in their social relations, Americans who believed that America had to come to terms with "*[4] the disordering obstacles to the ability of its culture to maintain a vital <u>interaction order</u>, ...*" With the Union at relative peace, the differences that led to War and more, became an enduring fact of national life. The modern nation was then coming into being

and modern nations were increasingly brimful of differences and latent disruptions. In the United States, industry and farming required workers from abroad—first the Irish, then the Germans, then the Chinese, then more who came under ethnic banners more and more different from descendants of the way back first settlers.

This may be the one way in which America was, and still is, exceptional among modern nations. It invited others in. It needed them. It found a way to accept most of them and their differences. White and European immigrants worked alongside and lived nearby those who descended from the just as White, earlier Northern European settlers. It wasn't an easy mix until in time in the new industrial cities like Chicago where people lived in Nature's Metropolis on the industrial border with Nature's improbable truly Great Plains.[16] Still, some fled the East to settle in the far West. But, on the whole, Americans, whether in towns or cities, somehow had to get along. This required a degree of interaction order however fungible it may have been. People had to get along, which means know the rules of the streets and markets and all that is needed to be with others, some of whom may not speak your language. Historically, it seems fair to say that only modern, therefore complex, societies can have an interaction order because the concept is predicated on a social condition in which interactions tend not to be always orderly, and occasionally are downright disorderly. All modern societies, to varying degrees, are constantly at risk of coming apart. This because they grant members enough freedom to think, and sometimes to say, what comes to mind. A democracy thereby is like a bar or pub late at night, when talk flows freely, sometimes too freely.

So, to posit as America's fourth cultural value the need and necessity of a viable *interaction order* is to attend to the fact of modern life that "[5] *a common cultural knowledge ... must be had against the powerful effects of historically formed identity differences*. ..." that, in turn, spawn "[6] *social struggles that unsettle the nation state, which itself struggles with exclusions inevitable against the fact that no one nation, especially not a Global one, can be everything to everyone.*"

Perhaps even more than with the first three, the second three, the elements of a modern America necessitate each other. *Interaction order, identity differences,* and *exclusions* fit together as hand and finger in a glove. No single one of these elements of American culture can be thought without the others. This is reality, not theory.

So Far So Good. Now to The End

Close readers will look back on what has come before this *Reprise*, and note that at least one element, *individualism*, has been hidden under the covers of *social and political spaces*. This in turn raises the question of where is *nature*? A skeptic will wonder if these first two elements being partly concealed by politics and pragmatism suggest that neither individualism nor nature are primary elements in this social compound.

The short answer is that, strictly speaking, the elements at work in chemical compounds are never distinct from the other elements with which they make the compound. This is just as true of elements at work and play in a compound like American culture. Though stated metaphorically, this fact of collective life is caught, always and necessarily, on the horns of the analytic dilemma. To attempt, as I am, to isolate the elements of a culture is, in its own way, an analytic procedure. The word "analysis" originally meant in the ancient Greek "to loosen up." By 1600 in French it came to mean "to dissect, to take to pieces." In effect

---

16 William Cronon, *Nature's Metropolis: Chicago and the Great West* (W.W. Norton, 1991).

today "analysis" may be properly defined as "to cut into pieces." Social scientific analysis is the cutting into the elements of a social compound in order to determine just how its parts actually work together. Therefore, to state the obvious, *American culture* is not, and cannot comprise, any one unbreachable thing. This digression into the meaning of "analysis" is meant to say that *Americans Thinking America: Elements of American Social Theory* is, and must be, a sketch and not a formula. As a sketch it is meant to present the essential elements of the culture's social theory of itself without cutting them utterly apart.

Again a riddle: Social theories are part of their cultures, even as these cultures make them what they are. Americans, like all other peoples, think themselves because the only honest way to live as an American is to think as an American—even if not necessarily consciously. Paul Crowe is a practical social theorist who may or may not know what he knows about being his kind of American. Here then is the riddle. *If any given instance of thinking is thinking, then what are we to think of the fact that almost no one thinks about why we do what we do when we're doing it.* Even a professional social theorist who attempts to analyze how cultures affect what people think, turns off the computer for dinner with loved ones who could not care less about what he *was* thinking. Still, they ask, "So, how did your day go?"—or the similar. When they do, they do not want to hear a disquisition on Erving Goffman's theory of the presented self, or such like. What they mean to do is to bring you back into their more practical reality. Dinner with loved ones is not a seminar. It is a very practical—and not thought through—attempt to bring you back into life with others.

Crudely rephrased the riddle might be: *If cultures do and think, how do those who do on the ground think their cultures while doing?* To be sure, I realize that this has become so riddled with riddles that it is hard to know how to think about social theories of culture. The simple answer is just do it and don't worry. Instead, worry about the issues with which you must live. Or, if you aim to be more than a practical social theorist try to resolve the issues that comprise the second three elements of culture, namely: How do thinking Americans think:

[4] *the disordering obstacles to the ability of its culture to maintain a vital <u>interaction order</u>,*
[5] *in which what common cultural knowledge that could be had must be had against the powerful effects of historically formed <u>identity differences</u>,*
[6] *which, in turn, came to be as waves of immigrants and their social movements struggle among themselves to unsettle the nation state which itself struggles with <u>exclusions</u> inevitable to the fact that no one nation, especially not a Global one, can be everything to everyone.*

Hence, the three elements that come together in the last major section of this book: *Identities, Differences, and Global Exclusions.* It goes without saying that all of these were present in the early history of American social and cultural thought—again, often hidden in the mix of primary elements and their historical contexts.

Still, the date when these three elements came fully to the fore among America's social theorists could be said to have been 1968, the year of a world revolution in which, among much else, voices from the Global South rose up and shouted to the rest of the world. Then and there, the once unchallenged dominant core states and their semi-peripheral allies were forced to listen to the shouts and songs of those who had been silenced or ignored— Blacks of course, new immigrants from Central and South America and the Caribbean, also women, white and of color, and gays and lesbians who then in time came to stand with all those of the several post-heteronormative sexual orientations. Then, and increasingly, identities entered the fray of an already, and necessarily, social world in which the tensions between order and disorder had become ever more acute. National exclusions, then framed by Global exclusions, soon enough made it impossible to deny that global differences and struggles went far beyond wars, which in fact became commonplace in the lesser, often remote global places. Not *WORLD WARS* but local wars became the normal, if terrible, language of Global reality. As I write, the people trying to live in Bhakmut and other cities in the Ukraine are the target of a possible world war involving Russia. Meanwhile, in Somalia, El Paso, and Uvalde, then too perhaps in Istanbul had Erdogan been defeated in the 2023 run-off—or when and where else in some unpronounceable place on the face of our Globe trouble is already brewing. This is the story of an uncertain world since 9/11/2001.

We live in a world where "Who knows?" is always and everywhere the question to ask—even, and surprisingly, in the all but unthinkable America!

Part VI

Identities and Differences in an Unsettled America, 1968 and Beyond

19 The Feminist Standpoint as Critical Theory
Charlotte Perkins Gilman, Dorothy Smith, Nancy Hartsock, Sandra Harding, bell hooks

It is not motherhood that keeps the housewife on her feet from dawn till dark;
it is house service, not child service.
Women work longer and harder than most men,
and not solely in maternal duties.
The savage mother carries the burdens and does all menial service for the tribe.
The peasant mother toils in the fields, and the working-man's wife in the home.
Many mothers, even now, are wage-earners for the family,
as well as bearers and rearers of it.
        —Charlotte Perkins Gilman, Women and Economics, 1898

Women's standpoint ...discredits sociology's claim
to constitute objective knowledge independent of the sociologist's situation. ...
The only way of knowing a socially constructed world is knowing it from within.
We can never stand outside it.
The standpoint of women situates the inquirer in the site of her bodily experience
and the local actualities of her working world.
        —Dorothy Smith, Women's Experience as A Radical Critique of Sociology, 1974

The feminist standpoint epistemologies ground a distinctive feminist science
in a theory of gendered activity and social experience.
They simultaneously privilege women or feminists ... epistemologically and
yet also claim to overcome the dichotomizing that is characteristic of the
Enlightenment/bourgeois world view and its science.
        —Sandra Harding, The Science Question in Feminism, 1986

My analysis which begins from the sexual division of labor—understood not as taboo,
But as the real, material activity of concrete human beings—could form the basis of an analysis of the real structures of women's oppression ...
Feminist theories must be grounded in women's materiality, as well as men's and must as well be part of a political struggle...
Clearly a systematic critique of Marx on the basis of a more fully developed understanding of the sexual division of labor is in order.
        —Nancy Hartsock, The Feminist Standpoint:
        Developing the Ground for a Specifically Feminist Historical Materialism, 1998

To be in the margin is to be part of the whole but outside the main body.... Much feminist theory emerges from privileged women who live at the center, whose perspectives on reality rarely include knowledge and awareness of the lives of women and men who live in the margin. As a consequence, feminist theory lacks wholeness, lacks the broad analysis that could encompass

a variety of human experiences. Although feminist theorists are aware of the need to develop ideas and analysis that encompass a larger number of experiences, that serve to unify rather than to polarize, such theory is complex and slow in formation. At its most visionary, it will emerge from individuals who have knowledge of both margin and center.
—bell hooks, *Feminist Theory from Margin to Center,* 1984

Women Stand as Women Must: Critically

Feminist Standpoint got its name in the 1970s from Dorothy Smith, a Canadian who influenced feminist theory everywhere.

> The feminist standpoint epistemologies ground a distinctive feminist science in a theory of gendered activity and social experience. They simultaneously privilege women or feminists ... epistemologically and yet also claim to overcome the dichotomizing that is characteristic of the Enlightenment/bourgeois world view and its science.[1]

Smith made the foundational standpoint idea well-defined which made it so influential, but she was not the first to write systematically against cultures that confined women to the home.

Charlotte Perkins Gilman writing in 1898 in *Women and Economics* made much the same point as Smith:

> It is not motherhood that keeps the housewife on her feet from dawn till dark; it is house service, not child service. Women work longer and harder than most men, and not solely in maternal duties. The savage mother carries the burdens and does all menial service for the tribe. The peasant mother toils in the fields, and the working-man's wife in the home. Many mothers, even now, are wage-earners for the family, as well as bearers and rearers of it.[2]

Gilman wrote some seven decades before Dorothy Smith who inspired others to take the feminist standpoint into their research and writing.

Sandra Harding, for example, has focused on women and science from which she drew her own standpoint theory:

> The feminist standpoint epistemologies ground a distinctive feminist science in a theory of gendered activity and social experience. They simultaneously privilege women or feminists epistemologically and yet also claim to overcome the dichotomizing that is characteristic of the Enlightenment/bourgeois world view and its science.[3]

This from her 1986 book, *The Science Question in Feminism*, which won the Jessie Bernard Award of the American Sociological Association.

---

1 Dorothy Smith, "Women's Experience as a Radical Critique of Sociology," *The Conceptual Practices of Power: A Feminist Sociology of Knowledge* (Northwestern University Press, 1990 [1974]), 22.
2 Charlotte Perkins Gilman, *Women and Economics: A Study of the Economic Relation Between Men and Women as a Social Factor in Evolution* (Boston, Small, Maynard & Company, 1989), chapter one (@ https://digital.libr ary.upenn.edu/women/gilman/economics/economics.html).
3 Sandra Harding, *The Science Question in Feminism* (Cornell University Press, 1986), 141–142.

Then too there is Nancy Hartsock's strikingly original essay "The Feminist Standpoint: Developing the Ground for a Specifically Feminist Historical Materialism," in which she wrote:

> My analysis which begins from the sexual division of labor—understood not as taboo, but as the real, material activity of concrete human beings—could form the basis of an analysis of the real structures of women's oppression ...Feminist theories must be grounded in women's materiality, as well as men's and must as well be part of a political struggle ... Clearly a systematic critique of Marx on the basis of a more fully developed understanding of the sexual division.

Few are the feminists, or for that matter academic political theorists, who take Marx with such care and seriousness.

Gloria Jean Watkins, who for good personal reasons asked to be known as bell hooks, died in 2021. Yet, one of her books has appeared on *The New York Times* non-fiction bestseller list years later. Though the following passage is theoretical, it is easy to see why her clear-minded prophetic vision inspired so many to want to read her books.

> To be in the margin is to be part of the whole but outside the main body.... Much feminist theory emerges from privileged women who live at the center, whose perspectives on reality rarely include knowledge and awareness of the lives of women and men who live in the margin. As a consequence, feminist theory lacks wholeness, lacks the broad analysis that could encompass a variety of human experiences. Although feminist theorists are aware of the need to develop ideas and analysis that encompass a larger number of experiences, that serve to unify rather than to polarize, such theory is complex and slow in formation. At its most visionary, it will emerge from individuals who have knowledge of both margin and center.[4]

The titular turn of phrase—from margin to center—says all that needs to be said about the feminist standpoint as critical theory.

Critical theory has long played an important role in modern American and European social thought. This sample of feminists demonstrates what may be the most uncommon way that critical theory can be understood as arising from a particular social standpoint.

Homeless on Main Street: The Shakespeare Lady Stands Out Among the Men

Chapel Street is New Haven's downtown main street replete with shops, restaurants, and other mostly high-end commercial enterprises. At the center of this venue is the Union League Café, the town's most famous and elegant restaurant. On the block from just west of the Town Green past the Union League on to the two Yale University art museums, is where apparently un-housed people ask passers-by for money.

Most of them are men who literally beg for money from wheelchairs or crutches or standing-up. The most notorious of them was Morgan who generally asked me for $40. Once or twice I gave him something, until his begging was almost daily. Morgan is gone now. I hope he lives on in a better place, but most think he died. We usually hear about the deaths, so his story is open. Several others don't beg. They just shout to some remote, often absent, person. The noise they make disturbs everyone, including the homeless who are just

---

4 bell hooks, *Feminist Theory from Margin to Center* (South End Press, 1984), ix–x.

trying to get bread money. Morgan, it seemed to me, had a female partner. Presumably he was the breadwinner for both of them. I assumed they were a couple.

Then for the longest while, there was a lovely, older woman who was known about town as the Shakespeare Lady. To make this more personal, I'll call her Elizabeth. She didn't really beg. She entertained those passing along by reciting elegant, stage-crafted passages from Shakespeare. This is why I call her Elizabeth. She was always charming but not obsequious. As much as the men, she needed bread money, but she gained it by giving before she gained. In a certain sense, it is fair to say that she stood her ground in a determined way that could not be taken as begging. Someone told me that she had been a graduate of Yale's drama program. It never occurred to me to doubt this factoid that could not be confirmed. She is gone now. Perhaps she's somewhere charming angels with her Elizabethan poetry.

For now, the most telling part of her story is how dramatically Elizabeth stood out in contrast to the men. There are good men of marginal means in town. One of whom spent time in prison, belongs to a spiritual group where he both preaches and sings. He is well-enough housed and has no need of public begging. Just to be clear, begging for money is embarrassing, even humiliating. People now without shelter were once housed, some well-housed. How they lost their better life is usually due to mental or physical illness, criminal conviction, or, in some cases, just plain bad luck managing personal finances. New Haven is not an easy place for the not-well-off to live. Rents are high. Most of the shopping in and around town is for the better-off. There is only one supermarket on Chapel Street, on the first floor of a massive apartment complex filled with well settled people. Those living on the margins are caught in the lurch created by America's lingering idea that men ought to be breadwinners for others, at least for themselves. This idea goes back to days later in the nineteenth century and well into the twentieth when, in middle-class and higher families, the men worked, the women kept house. This of course was little more than a norm for a small sliver of the population. In poor families, Black and white, the men worked when they could but all-too-often fled from the humiliation. Well-off women, for whom Eleanor Roosevelt is the model of the day, did what they wanted to do while their husbands did whatever they did.

Returning to Elizabeth, I have no idea what she did when younger. She had the Yale degree which suggests she did well enough. Yet, and here is the point, she was not embarrassed to be on the street and recite Shakespeare for her bread. If she was, she didn't show it. The men begging on the same street did. Some shouted, some asked for outrageous donations, others just begged usually by modestly holding out a hand or a cup. I have yet to see a man begging on the street who was not hiding his embarrassment. In one case I know rather well, the husband (or partner) had his wife ask for money. When she did, he said it was for medicine at a drug store. Men in such a situation hide behind their women or tell lies to get their bread and drug money.

For those who may doubt what I say about Elizabeth and the men about her, consider the women in Carol Stack's *All Our Kin* and their difference from the men in Elliot Liebow's *Tally's Corner*—or, better yet, Benita in Waverly Duck's *No Way Out*.[5] These are among the documented cases of women in hard conditions finding a way to get along, while their men succumb to their failure to earn bread money to keep their lives with others together. Elizabeth the Shakespeare Lady is a conspicuous local case of what theorists call the feminist standpoint.

While none of the urban ethnographers discussed in *Americans Thinking America* take up, in so many words, the feminist standpoint position hinted at here, the long history

---

5 See chapters 15 and 16, chapters on order and disorder, above.

of American culture has again and again opened the blinds on the sun light of feminine autonomy—from Abigail Adams, to Margaret Fuller and Harriet Tubman, to Jane Addams and Charlotte Perkins Gilman, to Zora Neale Hurston and Paula Gunna Allen, and more. And by contrast when prominent men as men usually do their prominence was challenged—Alexander Hamilton when Aaron Burr called him out to the duel that killed him. When John Adams's garrulous temper ruined his presidency, he left town for his home in Quincy to live in comfort with Abigail. These are historical scraps, but they can be tested by looking up and down your neighborhoods or behind what doors you have visited where the differences are often still, this late in the game, there to be seen.

Thus it is that, in due course, slowly at first but faster in the 1970s and after, there came to be a strong identity movement among feminists who, one way or another, wrote social theories of the difference between their subject position and that of men. Stated this way the feminist standpoint emerges as a critical theory of the traditional cultural attitudes on the autonomous nature and power of women in society.

In a certain sense standpoint feminism has a long but indefinite history. In the United States the first book in the lineage was Margaret Fuller's 1845 *Woman in the Nineteenth Century*—a theory that turns on her most striking lines:

Male and female represent the two sides of the great radical divide.
But in fact they are perpetually passing into one another.
Fluid hardens to solid, solid rushes to fluid.
There is no wholly masculine man, no purely feminine woman.

As I said previously,[6] these 40 words in her book of some 200,000 were prescient in the day. They, and *Woman in the Nineteenth Century* as a whole, cut to the heart of what, more than a century later, would become feminist standpoint theory. At the same time they cut apart the pure feminine in the line "There is no wholly masculine man, no purely feminine woman"—a line that, late in the twentieth century, would fit comfortably with fractured identities theory that deconstructed pure standpoint feminism by opening it to its deeper social meaning.

Some might argue that, strictly speaking, Charlotte Perkins Gilman was not a precursor of feminist standpoint theory as it came to be in the 1970s. She was, however, the first American social theorist to begin systematically to study the many ways that, in the late nineteenth and early twentieth centuries, women were viewed as different and lesser. Her *The Man-Made World; or Our Androcentric Culture* in 1911 is a prime instance of this idea. Yet, in spite of Gilman's important contributions it would be much later in the 1970s when the social upheavals of the 1960s continued to have a lasting effect as the full theory came clear. Of course, feminism in America began in earnest in the 1950s when women in SNCC challenged male dominance of the movement. Leaders of the 1954 Mississippi Freedom Summer were led and inspired by Black women leaders, notably Fannie Louis Hammer and Ella Baker.[7] In 1963, what one can fairly call white feminism began with Betty Friedan's *The Feminine Mystique* and her participation in the founding in 1966 of NOW, the National Organization of Women. It would be another few years in the early 1970s when standpoint feminism began to surface in full bloom.

---

6 See Chapter 6 above, "America Faces Its Fate."
7 See "Power, Domination, and the World Revolution of 1968," chapter 18 above.

Dorothy Smith's 1974 essays "Women's Experience as a Radical Critique of Sociology" and "The Ideological Practice of Sociology"[8] began what others advanced. About the same time as Smith, Sandra Harding, beginning from a more philosophical approach, began the journey that led to her full-blown standpoint theory in *The Science Question in Feminism* in 1986.[9] Smith was a sociological theorist, Harding a philosopher, and Nancy Hartsock a political theorist who began with a 1974 essay, "Political Change: Two Perspectives on Power."[10] These three theorists suggest two important features of feminist standpoint theory. First, it began across the human science disciplines. Second, from the first it was straining toward new and, in effect, destabilizing directions. It was never simply a question of sociology's failures, nor of traditional philosophical epistemologies, nor of political science's limited theories of power—but ever something other.

Also with Nancy Hartsock's much later book, *The Feminist Standpoint Revisited* in 1998, the reach of standpoint theory is well into a massive range of classical social theories—from Marx's estranged labor to Louis Althusser's structural Marxism, to Gayle Rubin's rereading of Claude Lévi Strauss's work on the exchange of women in traditional societies, to Richard Rorty and Michel Foucault's crypto-postmodern studies. Just a decade after it began, standpoint theory was already deeply planted in global social thought. Then also there is Gloria Watkins, which is to say bell hooks, who wrote countless books beginning with *Ain't I A Woman: Black Women and Feminism* (1981) which began a standpoint theory that was written by and for Black women as well. Not only this, bell hooks wrote books with notable Black men like Cornel West, *Breaking Bread: Insurgent Black Intellectual Life* in 1991, and Stuart Hall, *Uncut Funk: A Contemplative Dialogue* in 2018. Some would say that bell hooks was not actually a standpoint feminist. If she was not, she was at least a leader who firmly located race as part of women's standpoint—this, amid an early wave of changes in the understanding of the standpoint, was vastly more complex than most in the early 1970s supposed.

Charlotte Perkins Gilman: Escaping the Yellow Wallpaper

> Charlotte Anna Perkins Stetson Gilman was a woman of several names; many hats, and controversial fame. Initially acclaimed for her gifts as a poet and lecturer, she sealed her reputation by writing a series of books on women's economic dependence, domestic confinement, and desire for public service. The theories that inform these efforts were wrung from her own difficult experiences as a woman, wife, daughter, mother, and worker.[11]

This is how Cynthia Davis began her excellent biography of Gilman. It could hardly be better or more honestly said.

Charlotte Perkins Gilman was born in 1860 in Hartford to a father who abandoned her family. Her mother was poor, but they were supported, it seems, by their extended family which included Harriet Beecher Stowe but also Isabella Beecher Hooker and Catherine Beecher. These relations were, more than likely, a source of Charlotte's social values and

---

8 Both are reprinted in Smith's *Conceptual Practices of Power* (University of Toronto Press, 1990), in the first two chapters.
9 Harding, *The Science Question in Feminism* (Cornell University Press, 1986). The earliest background essay to this book is "Feminism: Reform or Revolution?" *Philosophical Forum* 5 (1973), 271–284.
10 Hartsock, "Political Change: Two Perspectives on Power," *Quest/A Feminist Quarterly* 1:1 (1974), 10–25.
11 Cynthia J. Davis, *Charlotte Perkins Gilman: A Biography* (Stanford University Press, 2010), xi.

literary interests, which by 1898 and the publication of *Women and Economics*, made her a pioneer in feminist thought in America. In *Women and Economics* she systematically sketched a sociological study of women, and thereby feminism, in which sex *and* gender play a part in sociology's attitude toward women. Though this book's sociological framework was explicitly social Darwinist, Gilman's foundational social study of gender differences was, as the title suggests, economic—a perspective that, in due course, put her on the map of general sociology. Gilman brought the economic factor to the fore in an original and non-Marxist way.

Gilman's subsequent writings, like *Human World* (1904), moved significantly beyond the first book's all-too-simple evolutionary themes to become what today we would recognize as a serious structural sociology. Later, Gilman's *Our Androcentric Culture; or The Man-Made World* (1911) became the single most important theoretical statement of her sociological feminism. *Man-Made World* opens with an acknowledgment that the sociologist, Lester Frank Ward, influenced Gilman's thinking by identifying the difference between the Androcentric and the Gynaecocentric theories of society. Among her contributions to sociology was a research note in *The American Journal of Sociology*, "A Suggestion on the Negro Problem" (1908). Gilman's early structural sociology was less a formal theory of structures than a tacit theory that addressed the wider and systematic social aspects of women's lives. Hence, books like *The Home* (1903), *The Dress of Women* (1915), *His Religion and Hers* (1923), the brilliant *Concerning Children* (1903), even her *Social Ethics* (1914), extended Gilman's foundational assumptions to cover related issues that, still today, are central to feminist sociology.

Gilman's 1892 short fiction "The Yellow Wallpaper" was the first of her writings to call attention to a then prevailing androcentric prejudice. This idea and its counterpart, gynaecocentric experience, were in effect the *locus classicus* of the structural sociology that Dorothy Smith would later call the problematic of the everyday world of women. Though Gilman's "The Yellow Wallpaper" was a sociological fiction, it remains important today because, as feminist standpoint sociologists like Smith put it, she identified a feminist issue by drawing on her personal experience as typical of the woman's standpoint. Gilman herself had been laid low by post-partum depression after her daughter, Katherine with Charles Walter Stetson, was born in 1895.

"The Yellow Wallpaper" should not be underestimated. It is the short story of a woman being driven crazy by medical treatment for a vague diagnosis of working too hard. "The Yellow Wallpaper" was based on her own experience of confinement for depression. Gilman's then husband, Walter Stetson, called on S. Mitchell Weir, the leading medical expert in the day on health issues among women. Weir prescribed complete bed rest and no work of any kind. Hence, the room with appalling yellow wallpaper that, in the fiction, all but drove the patient out of her right mind. In her own life, Gilman quit the room and in time, in 1894, divorced her husband.

Yet, "The Yellow Wallpaper" remains true to Gilman's biography and to the standpoint of white middle-class women in the day. It helps to understand the dreadful wallpaper images to know that she had been a student at the Rhode Island School of Design. Her artistic sensibilities were as natural as her literary impulses. Here's how she describes the room:

> It is a big, airy room, the whole floor nearly, with windows that look all ways, and air and sunshine galore. It was nursery first and then playground and gymnasium, I should judge; for the windows are barred for little children, and there are rings and things in the walls. [T]he paint and paper look as if a boys' school had used it. It is stripped off—the paper—in great patches all around the head of my bed, about as far as I can reach, and

> in a great place on the other side of the room low down. I never saw a worse paper in my life. One of those sprawling flamboyant patterns committing every artistic sin. It is dull enough to confuse the eye in following, pronounced enough to constantly irritate, and provoke study, and when you follow the lame, uncertain curves for a little distance they suddenly commit suicide—plunge off at outrageous angles, destroy themselves in unheard-of contradictions. The color is repellant, almost revolting; a smouldering, unclean yellow, strangely faded by the slow-turning sunlight. It is a dull yet lurid orange in some places, a sickly sulphur tint in others.[12]

Then, after straight narrative of the husband coming and going, urging her to think that the cure is good for her and her own realization that he loves her very much, there is another passage about the wallpaper:

> I didn't realize for a long time what the thing was that showed behind,—that dim subpattern,—but now I am quite sure it is a woman. By daylight she is subdued, quiet. I fancy it is the pattern that keeps her so still. It is so puzzling. It keeps me quiet by the hour.

Clearly Charlotte, the author, sees herself and her madness in the wallpaper. One of her biographers concludes that "Charlotte presented insanity as a form of rebellion, a crucial turning point toward independence."[13]

If we stop to think of it, in the day, and to an extent now, this is a normal experience of many mostly white, usually bourgeois women who are imprisoned in a home cut off from the world. Even today women who work still do double time at home.[14] And more than a few of them go mad if not outright insane—mad at the injustice of it all.[15]

Soon after Charlotte recovered from her depression, she moved to California where she became a progressive writer and public figure. Katherine was sent back to live with her father. Gilman eventually moved to Chicago where she joined Jane Addams of Hull House in progressive politics. Gilman's radical feminist writings, beginning with *Women and Economics* in 1898, were, thus, rooted in her personal experience that led to the public writings and politics that, in turn, influenced her sociological writings—all of which called particular attention to the indignities women suffered by their exclusion. Gilman's standpoint argument appeared first in 1911, in *Our Androcentric Culture; or The Man-Made World*. Though *Women and Economics* (1898) is Gilman's most robust standpoint argument, *Our Androcentric Culture; or The Man-Made World* is the more mature feminist argument. It is free of the evolutionary baggage of her early thinking and is straightforwardly feminist.

> The scope and purpose of human life is entirely above and beyond the field of sex relationship. Women are human beings, as much as men, by nature; and as women, are even more sympathetic with human processes. To develop human life in its true powers we need full equal citizenship for women.[16]

---

12 Charlotte Perkins Gilman, "The Yellow Wallpaper," 1892 at, among other online sources: https://www.gutenberg.org/cache/epub/1952/pg1952-images.html . Passage just below, same place.

13 Mary A. Hill *Charlotte Perkins Gilman: The Making of a Radical Feminist: 1860–1896* (Temple University Press, 1980), 151.

14 Arlie Russell Hochschild, *The Second Shift and the Revolution at Home* (Penguin/Random House, 1989).

15 Elaine Tyler May, *Homeward Bound: American Families in the Cold War Era* (Basic Books, 1989).

16 This passage and the quoted lines just below the following appear at the very end of *Our Androcentric Culture; or the Man-Made World*. See the Gutenburg eBook @ https://www.gutenberg.org/cache/epub/3015/pg3015-images.html#link2H_4_0016.

Compared to standpoint feminism as it emerged in the early 1970s Gilman's argument comes short, but for its day when women like her were rarely, if at all, thought of as equal to men it was a good enough sketch of the woman's standpoint in society. Where she comes closer to what would come is in the final words of *Our Androcentric Culture; or The Man-Made World*:

> The great woman's movement and labor movement of today are parts of the same pressure, the same world-progress. An economic democracy must rest on a free womanhood; and a free womanhood inevitably leads to an economic democracy.

Our Androcentric Culture in 1911, appeared after Charlotte Perkins had been happily married to Houghton Gilman since 1900. They lived in New York City until 1922 when they moved to Norwich, Connecticut. From 1909 to 1916, Charlotte edited the *Forerunner*, a journal of her invention to which she contributed the content, mostly but not exclusively fiction and poetry. Some have said that the *Forerunner* is her "greatest single achievement."[17]

In the end, Charlotte found her way out of the indignities she had suffered in early life, by her flourishing work in *Forerunner*, her marriage to Houghton, and by enjoying life with him until his death in 1934. The following year, she took her own life, saying, in a final defiance of prevailing customs: "I have preferred chloroform to cancer."

Dorothy Smith: Knowing Society from Within

Dorothy Smith (1926–2022) did not mince words. She wrote and said what she thought and what she thought grew out of a difficult early life in her native England. In a short memoir written in 2004, she said this about her beginnings in sociology:

> I was born in the north of England in 1926 – a long time ago, another world. It's hard to connect who I am now with the girl and young woman who lived back there then. I had worked as a young woman in a variety of jobs, ending up doing secretarial work in the book publishing industry. When I was twenty-five, I was fed up. I'd tried to get on in publishing, but it was a no go for women at that time. I thought I could get a better secretarial job if I had an undergraduate degree, so I applied to the London School of Economics and was accepted. I took a degree in sociology, with a major in social anthropology. I was fascinated.[18]

After the London School of Economics, Smith went to graduate school in sociology at The University of California, Berkeley. She married. She bore children. Her husband left. She divorced. She goes on to admit that she was shocked "to be the one responsible not only for the children and household, but also for earning a living." She carried on as did Gilman and so many other women then and now. After gaining the PhD in 1963, she taught here and there—in Berkeley, in New York, at the University of British Columbia, where in 1968 she played a role in establishing an early women's studies program. But her most important position was after 1977 at the Ontario Institute for Studies in Education where

---

17 For example, Davis, *Charlotte Perkins Gilman*, 287.
18 Dorothy Smith, Collection "Les sciences sociales contemporaines" (Université de Quebec, 2004). Or: http://faculty.maxwell.syr.edu/mdevault/dorothy_smith.htm. All of the following biographical statements are from the same source.

she remained until retirement in 1994 when she returned to British Columbia for a position at the University of Victoria.

Smith's career was long and productive. She wrote in the same 2014 biographical source:

> In my intellectual life there have been three big moments: One was going to the London School of Economics when I was twenty-six and becoming fascinated with sociology; the second was a course given by Tamotsu Shibutani at Berkeley on George Herbert Mead which laid the groundwork for a later deep involvement with the phenomenology of Maurice Merleau-Ponty (I encountered his work accidentally by picking up one of his books in a bookstore and knowing instantly that that's where I belonged); and finally and perhaps biggest of all, the women's movement which was for me a total transformation of consciousness at multiple levels. It led me into the strange paths I'm still pursuing of undoing, among other things, the sociology I'd learned so thoroughly to practice.

These short biographical accounts by, and of, Smith can't begin to do justice to a woman who spent a long life of 95 years exploring and analyzing the differences of women's experiences from those of men. In 2022, when Dorothy Smith died, her several North Atlantic worlds remain, for the most part, dominated by men—some of them good men, but men, nonetheless. To be sure, some of these men looked out on a world they would lead in search of objective means to end wars, govern belligerent citizens, control crime, feed the sick and hungry, more. These are all issues that must be addressed. Dorothy Smith leaves us with the searching question, *What would women's experience tell us?*

Sandra Harding: The Science Question in Feminism

Sandra Harding was born in 1935. After finishing the BA in 1956 at Douglass College at Rutgers and for some years working here and there as schoolteacher, legal researcher and editor, she entered graduate school to study philosophy at New York University. After the PhD in 1973 she taught first at SUNY Albany (as the University of Albany was then called), then at the University of Delaware where she was instrumental in developing its women's studies program, then in 1994 when she accepted a position at UCLA where she soon enough became Distinguished Professor of Education and Gender Studies. Along the way she also served as editor of *Signs: Journal of Women in Culture and Society*. Through all this, she became the leading theorist of feminism and science by being a prodigiously published social theorist on the subject.

One test of the reliability of any social theoretical publication is whether it wins the approval of those outside the theoretical position from which it is written. The bar is even higher when a feminist standpoint paper is accepted by a leading journal in the sciences, plain and simple. That Sandra Harding's "Women, Science, and Society" 1998 article appeared in *Science*—a leading journal by and for scientists on their endeavors—says quite a lot about her and her intellectual sophistication. Here is a longish part of what she wrote:

> Consider two changes in the traditional philosophy of science to which women's movements have contributed. The first has to do with the assumption of neutrality in the research process. Is maximizing the objectivity of research always advanced by maximizing the social neutrality of research processes? The neutrality ideal is maximally effective when it is invoked in contexts where social beliefs differ among members of the scientific community. But how is it useful in detecting social assumptions shared by an entire scientific community—women and men alike—such as assumptions about women's biological inferiority? In such cases it

takes political involvement to move scientific institutions to question prevailing assumptions. Moreover, the neutrality ideal cannot recognize or provide resources for distinguishing between social or political assumptions that tend to obstruct the growth of knowledge and those that could advance it. We need "strong objectivity," as I have referred to it, to detect the most foundational assumptions that shape our own belief systems.[19]

At the heart of Harding's standpoint theory is this idea of "strong objectivity."[20] As she puts it, strong objectivity is meant to overcome methodological neutrality which, in turn, requires "... political involvement to move scientific institutions to question prevailing assumptions." The politics of the feminist standpoint, Harding says, starting with research on any aspect with women's knowledge of their social situation strengthens the objectivity of the outcome.

This very astute theoretical turn is one of the reasons Sandra Harding may rightly be considered one the most inventive and opulently informed among feminists and, for that matter, social theorists generally. The very idea of a strong objectivity founded on women's experience is at least compelling, at most brilliant. For one, it turns the wrong-headed proposition of the subject-object dichotomy on its head—and especially when it is deployed, as for long it has been, as a methodological principle. Harding uses "strong objectivity" as an oxymoron. The supposed neutrality of objective sciences is one thing, but when it comes to the human and political sciences objectivity is something else. Either way it is controversial. Harding is, in effect, arguing that, in the human sciences in particular, there can only be objectivity when the position of those traditionally relegated to the lesser statuses are taken as, at least, a starting point if not as *the* first order of investigative business.

This is the argument first outlined in what may be Harding's most famous article, "The Instability of the Analytic Categories of Feminist Theory,"[21]—in which, among much else, she points to the instabilities of the feminist standpoint in relation to "Other 'Others' "—the standpoints of women in African, Native American, and Asian cultures.[22] Then too, she associates analytic instabilities to the famous (notoriously difficult to some) idea of fractured identities by Donna Haraway[23]—about which, more to come in the chapter following. But for now, two further points about Harding's work over the years. First, she always reaches beyond whatever at the time may have been her active circle of ideas, notably in *Feminism & Methodology* (1987), a collection of essays by leading feminists of the day. The book is a sign of Harding's unfailing commitment, here and elsewhere, to study and embrace different feminist theories—from those of Carol Gilligan and Joyce Ladner, from Dorothy Smith to Bonnie Thornton Dill, from Catherine MacKinnon to Nancy Hartsock.

---

19 Sandra Harding, "Women, Science, and Society," *Science* 281 (11 Sept. 1998), 1599–1600.
20 Sandra Harding, " 'Strong Objectivity': A response to the new objectivity question," *Synthese* 104 (September 1995): 331–349. Or: Harding, chapter 3, in *Feminist Epistemologies*, edited by Linda Alcoff, Elizabeth Potter (Routledge, 1992). And in: *Feminist Theory: A Philosophical Anthology*, edited by Ann E. and Robin O. Andreasen (Blackwell Publishing, 2005). And reprinted many other places, for example: http://www.jstor.org/stable/23739232 .
21 Sandra Harding, "The Instability of the Analytic Categories of Feminist Theory," *Sex and Scientific Inquiry*, edited by Sandra Harding and Jean F. O'Barr (The University of Chicago Press, 1987), 283–302. This article also appeared in *Signs: Journal of Women in Culture and Society* 11: 4 (1986).
22 Sandra Harding, "Other 'Others' and Fractured Identities: Issues for Epistemologists," in Harding, *The Science Question in Feminism* (Cornell University Press, 1986), chapter 7.
23 Donna Haraway, "A Cyborg Manifesto: Science, Technology, and Socialist Feminism in the Late Twentieth Century," in Haraway, *Simians, Cyborgs, and Women: The Reinvention of Nature* (Routledge, 1991), chapter 8.

For now, and relatedly, the important consideration is just how widely read Sandra Harding is in social theories that once one might never have imagined could be important to feminism as such. Though there are many instances of this achievement the best, I think, is her *Sciences from Below* in 2008. The very title focuses attention on her axiom that politics are epistemologically necessary for standpoint feminism. The idea of revolutions from below has been all-but canonical since Marx. But sciences from below? We already know about this turn in Harding's thinking, but to what exactly is she referring?

She means not just to incorporate non-northern standpoints but to begin with them. Harding therefore began *Sciences from Below* with a section that some surely will find controversial—"PROBLEMS WITH MODERNITY'S SCIENCE AND POLITICS: Perspectives from Northern Science Studies." Here, Harding examines Bruno Latour's theories on the natural as opposed to social environment, Ulrich Beck's risk society, and the European sociologists—Michael Gibbons, Helga Nowotny, and Peter Scott and others—, who, as she puts it, "focus on how concepts and practices of "the social" and "the political" must themselves be transformed in order to transform the sciences into more competent knowledge-producers as well as into resources for democratic social relations."[24] Harding does not shrink from criticism of those she introduces, while keeping a clear eye on what they offer. Here the theorists serve to lay down the foundation stone upon which she builds her argument: Northern Sciences, however original they may be, are nonetheless, in a word, Northern, therefore not-Southern.

Sciences from Below goes on in chapters 4, 5, and 6 to cover such topics as "Women as Subjects of History and Knowledge," "Postcolonial Science and Technology Studies: Are There Multiple Sciences?" "Women on Modernity's Horizons: Feminist Postcolonial Science and Technology Studies." There's not a gap in Harding's blanketing of any and all aspects of social theories that ignore or present the theme of sciences from below.

The book's second section, therefore, is "VIEWS FROM MODERNITY'S PERIPHERIES" which begins another important chapter: "Woman As Subjects of History," which comes to an important note on the beginnings of standpoint feminism:

> Standpoint theory's development in feminism originated in attempts to explain two things. One was how what was widely recognized as "good science" or "good social science" could produce such sexist and androcentric research results as feminist social scientists and biologists were documenting. The other was to explain the successes of feminist work which violated the norms of good research, such as engaging in research that was guided by feminist politics.[25]

After which, in chapter 5, the *Sciences from Below* poses the challenging question: "POSTCOLONIAL SCIENCE AND TECHNOLOGY STUDIES: Are There Multiple Sciences?" Her answer is yes (if not "of course")—an answer that begins with reference to subjects who have enjoyed none of the benefits of Northern sciences, among them— peasants, women, subalterns. No one who knows what she's driving at will be surprised to read next of Gayatri Spivak's "Can the Subaltern Speak?" (1988) and others like Eric Wolf's *Europe and People Without a History* (1982).[26] In the same place, Harding continues with other references to those who have put the underdeveloped peripheral world in perspective—Gunder Frank's *Capitalism and Underdevelopment in Latin America* (1967)

---

24 *Ibid*, 17.
25 Sandra Harding, *Sciences from Below* (Duke University Press, 2008), 114.
26 *Ibid*, 134–135.

and Immanuel Wallerstein's multi-volume *Modern World-System* (1974 and after). The social science references to Postcolonial Science and Technology Studies (PSTS) are a subject, and a project, on which she would later publish the definitive book.[27] PSTS is a project meant to support and represent postcolonial scientific work against the odds of global exclusion. Again: *Science from Below*. In the book as a whole one encounters a richly textured cloth that envelops nearly-all the major social theorists who have touched on science.

The third and concluding section of *Science from Below* turns, in effect, toward a summary and what comes next—especially in the final chapter "Moving On" where she says:

> As long as the modern conceptual framework of philosophy, sciences, science studies, and other research disciplines in the West leads us to believe that what happens in households around the globe constitutes obstacles to the advance of objective and reliable knowledge projects and to the achievement of social justice, even progressive research and activism guided by such a framework is doomed to defeat. Women and modernity's Others cannot achieve social justice and make social progress on their own terms as long as this modernity vs. tradition contrast continues to shape the exceptionalist and triumphalist ways in which privileged groups (and the research disciplines that serve them) think and interact with others and the world around them.[28]

Then too there is Harding's most widely read and honored book, *The Science Question in Feminism* in 1986, which presents, with the same systematic care, all the subjects at issue in a feminism of and about science.[29] Again she spares none from criticism—for examples in chapter 4, "Androcentrism in Biology and Science" and 9, "Problems with Post-Kuhnian Stories"—while also including the most revolutionary of new ideas in chapter 7, "Other 'Others' and Fractured Identities: Issues for Epistemologies." Altogether the book does not shy away from identifying the inherent tensions in any science that seeks to be feminist. This is what the chapters in *The Science Question in Feminism* do without a lot of arm waving. They simply and plainly name and explain those tensions, as Harding also does in the chapter on Androcentrism in Biology and Social Science. She does not mention Charlotte Gilman's classic work on Androcentrism early in the century, but (again without using Gilman's more classical term, gynaecocentric) Harding means to establish a thoroughgoing plan for a Gynocentric feminism that delivers a truth serum for the falsely objectivistic man-made sciences.

To this end Harding deploys the five points set down in the introduction of a much earlier book by Marcia Millman and Rosabeth Kanter, *Another Voice: Feminist Perspectives on Social Life and Social Science* (1975). Though in the 2020s many have gone far beyond Millman and Kanter, Harding's listing of the five sources of Androcentrism that still corrupt the social sciences was in her day and still plain and to the point:

1. Social sciences tend to neglect emotions.
2. Sociology tends to focus on public policy definitions of the situation, ignoring the private and less visible.
3. Sociologies, for the most part, assume a "single society" picture of social life.
4. Sex is too often ignored.
5. Quantoid methodologies cannot and do not study the hidden aspects of what they measure.[30]

---

27 Sandra Harding, *Postcolonial Science and Technology Reader* (Duke University Press, 2011).
28 Harding, *Sciences from Below*, 233.
29 Harding, *The Science Question in Feminism* (Cornell University Press, 1986).
30 *Ibid*, 85–92. This is a section poignantly titled: "The Five Sources of Androcentrism in Social Inquiry."

To be sure—and in large part because of—the challenges of feminist social theories, progress in dismantling Androcentrism has been made since 1975. Still, even now, take a field like demography that is willing numerically to announce differences in fertility rates from region to region without mention of differences in sexual practices. Against this kind of thing Harding in *The Science Question in Feminism* describes, in her conclusion, the "Valuable Tensions and a New 'Unity of Sciences' ". To be sure that unity is not the smooth, easy unity of numeric tables and definitive formulae, but the ongoing tensions between, if I may use the terms again, androcentric and gynocentric sciences and theories: "I have argued that it is only coercive values—racism, classism, sexism—that deteriorate objectivity; it is participatory values—antiracism, anticlassism, antisexism—that decrease the distortions and mystifications in our culture's explanations and understandings".[31]

It is hard for me to name another social theorist, whatever their preoccupation, who has more deeply thought through the problems and promises of any subject, much less one so gnarly as feminism.

Nancy Hartsock: Engaged Feminism/Women Staying Alive

Sandra Harding and Nancy Hartsock, in different ways, represent a maturing of feminist standpoint theory that had the effect of turning feminist theory toward the wider field of social theories domestic and internationally.

Nancy Hartsock (1943–2015) wrote most eloquently of her commitment to feminist theory as a collective enterprise in *The Feminist Standpoint Revisited and Other Essays* (1998), the second of her two major books:

> I have for many years believed that feminist theory must be understood as a fundamentally collective enterprise. Despite the fact that these essays appear under my name, I view them as not simply indebted to others but as the representation of the work of many who are involved in dense webs of communities—both inside and outside the university.[32]

This is how she began *The Feminist Standpoint Revisited*, a collection of essays she brought to life so that they could be read as if they were born together in the same theoretical moment. For those who knew her, even if only through her writings, Hartsock's ability to pull diverse sources and writings together would not be surprising.

Nancy Hartsock was born in 1943 in Utah to a family of modest means. After school, she found her way to Wellesley College, perhaps the most elite of elite women's colleges. There she immediately committed herself to the school's Civil Rights group. This led to her tutoring in Roxbury, then a poor Black neighborhood, while also working with the Boston NAACP. When Hartsock began graduate studies at the University of Chicago, she began to work with Saul Alinsky's community organizing projects and with Martin Luther King's effort to bring the Movement to the North.[33] Somehow amid all this, she finished her PhD in political science in 1972, after which she taught at Michigan and Johns Hopkins before moving to a permanent position at the University of Washington—from where she lectured the world over, and of course wrote and taught.

---

31 *Ibid*, 249.
32 Nancy Hartsock, *The Feminist Standpoint Revisited and Other Essays* (Westview Press, 1998), ix.
33 Much of the biographical information here is confirmed in the remarkable collective essay in *Signs: Bringing Together Feminist Theory and Practice: A Collective Interview* Author(s): Heidi Hartmann, Ellen Bravo, Charlotte Bunch, Nancy Hartsock, Roberta Spalter Roth, Linda Williams, Maria Blanco. Source: *Signs*, 21:4 (Summer, 1996), 917–951.

Nancy Hartsock's interest in politics, while active in her younger years, was also central to her writing in later years. Her first major book, *Money, Sex, and Power: Toward a Feminist Historical Materialism* (1985 [1983]) turns on a concise statement that at once deploys ideas of Marx and Engels while also criticizing their ignorance of women as front line laborers:

> In capitalism, women contribute both production for wages and production of goods in the home, that is, they, like men, sell their labor power and produce both commodities and surplus value, and produce use values in the home. Unlike men, however, women's lives are institutionally defined by their production of use values in the home. Here we begin to encounter the narrowness of Marx's concept of production. Women's production of use values in the home has not been well understood by socialists. It is no surprise to feminists that Engels, for example, simply asks how women can do the work in the home and also work in production outside of the home. Marx too, takes for granted women's responsibility for household labor.[34]

Money, Sex, and Power is a disciplined exposition of Marx's basic ideas presented in respect to themes she names for her purpose—to develop a feminist historical materialism. Hartsock's exposition of Marx in Chapter 6, "Power and Class Struggle: Toward a Theory of Class Domination." If the title suggests, at first look, pure Marx, soon it becomes clear where she's heading.

The extraordinarily succinct five-point summary early in this chapter is in fact a deep analytical interpretation of Marx's epistemology. When a feminist theorist writes of epistemology then standpoint theory cannot be far behind. Hartsock's five points are:

1. Material life structures and limits the understanding of social relations.
2. Material life is structured accordingly to opposing groups such that the vision of one is the inverse of the other, making the vision of the ruling class "partial and perverse."
3. The idea that "the ruling class structures the material relations" of all others "cannot be dismissed as false."
4. As a result, "the vision of oppressed group must be struggled for and represents an achievement that requires both science ... and education to grow from political struggle."
5. *"Because the understanding of the oppressed is an engaged vision, the adoption of a standpoint exposes the real relations among human beings as inhuman, points beyond the present and carries a historical and liberatory role."*[35]

These words were first published in 1983 a good 15 years before Hartsock's definitive book on the subject, *The Feminist Standpoint Revisited* (1998) which may be rightly considered the most complete statement of feminist standpoint theory. Even so, it is hard to find even then—or for that matter in any other work of the day on the standpoint—a more succinct and powerful statement on the subject.

---

34 Nancy Hartsock, *Money, Sex, and Power: Toward a Feminist Historical Materialism* (Northeastern University Press, 1985 [1983]), 234–235.
35 *Ibid*, 118, also 232. Emphasis added. Parts are paraphrased. Also it is in her *The Feminist Standpoint Revisited*, 229. This version of her oft-reprinted essay on the Feminist Standpoint is worth reading because Hartsock here summarized her view of the standpoint in the context of her career-long interest in Marx and feminism. *The Feminist Standpoint Revisited* ends with a moving quotation from Gloria Anzaldúa's *Borderlands*.

Money, Sex, and Power: Toward a Feminist Historical Materialism, however, had another purpose, as the book's subtitle makes evident—to move social thought *toward a feminist historical materialism*. This book does just that. It is composed in two major parts. The first, roughly speaking, is on the radical ground necessary for a feminist theory. Each chapter here is nuanced, and each serves a different purpose; for examples: "Rational Economic Man and the Problem of Community" (2), "Toward an Understanding of Domination: Critiques of Mainstream Theories of Power" (4), and the chapter just discussed: "Power and Class Struggle: Toward a Marxist Theory of Class Domination" (6). These are a sampling of the six chapters in Part I where Hartsock's independent theory-making is applied to critical issues in Marxist theory in the broadest sense.

The second part of *Money, Sex, and Power: Toward a Feminist Historical Materialism* turns straight on to the elements of her idea of a feminist historical materialism. Unsurprisingly, Chapter 7 is "Gender and Power: Masculinity, Violence, and Domination" which is, among much else, proof that Hartsock pulls no punches. Then, in Chapter 8, she reaches beyond what all but a few American feminists in the 1980s would have paid prominent attention to: "The Erotic Dimension and the Homeric Ideal." The next two chapters attend to "Women on Power" (9) and, of course, "The Feminist Standpoint" (10) before coming to the concluding Chapter 11, "Power, Class, and Gender: Questions for the Future." It is daring, I know, to list only chapter titles but, here, even in the titles one can begin to see how her critical theory is tinged with unexpected details that at once draw careful thought down into the depths and out to external contexts that lend force to the arguments.

Not inconsequentially, the book ends with three appendices on subjects often mentioned but seldom worked-through as Hartsock has. The first is "The Kinship Abstraction in Feminist Theory" in which she deals with Claude Lévi-Strauss's *The Elementary Structures of Kinship* (1955) which is, she thinks, too often taken as a latently Marxist scheme useful to feminist theory. Hartsock, however, pulls no punches, in saying that "Lévi-Strauss's thought, then, represents a contradictory amalgam that is at once deeply phallocratic, abstract, antimaterialist, and even mystical."[36] Even though this is a wildly over-the-top statement, the essay is a thoughtful review of the rights and wrongs of Lévi-Strauss's theory of kinship.

The remaining two appendices are in the same vein. The second, "Simone de Beauvoir: Liberation or Escalating Domination," where she argues that de Beauvoir's *The Second Sex* (1949) is for her too Hegelian and, by consequence, too little Marxian. "Political theorizing must be understood as an historical act structured by and dependent on material social relations."[37] Instead, Hartsock accuses de Beauvoir of adopting an abstract masculinity though not one as abstract as Lévi-Strauss's. Faint praise that holds out for a "Sisterhood ... yet to be discovered." Then, third, Hartsock writes an appendix on "Gayle Rubin: Abstract Determinism of the Kinship System" where, once again, Lévi-Strauss's structural theory of kinship system serves as the fall-guy. Then when the book comes to its end Hartsock concludes:

> I have attempted to demonstrate the ways feminist theorists can be led into abstraction by adopting theories built either on the categories central to the exchange abstraction or those which constitute abstract masculinity. ... Women's lives, like men's, are structured

---

36 *Ibid*, 279.
37 *Ibid*, 291.

by social relations that manifest the experience of the dominant gender and class. And feminists are not immune to the consequences of this fact.[38]

Though these lines are the conclusion to the third appendix, they could just as well serve as a conclusion not just to the book but also to Hartsock's life work which in 1983 with *Money, Sex and Power* was just beginning to take on a more settled form. Few are they who have written such a good first book—one so good that it is fair to overlook the nit-picking in the appendices.[39]

Money, Sex and Power was, in effect, her first serious publication after graduate studies except for a now all-but forgotten essay Nancy Hartsock wrote, in 1974, that revealed her determination to make feminist theory seriously political. This in a short-lived feminist journal, *Quest: A Feminist Quarterly*, for which she was an active associate:

A feminist redefinition of the concept of political change requires an understanding of the women's movement's concern for the relationships of the personal and the political; a perspective on the struggles within the movement over the nature and uses of power, leadership and organization; sensitivity to the importance of process and interaction in social change; and finally, recognition of the fundamental links between economics and social relationships.[40]

Yet, reading this earliest of her publications closely, it is evident that even a person just out of school can possess a definite sense of method and theory. In an early section of the *Quest* essay she touches decisively on all that would occupy her thinking for years to come. From an early section, "Patriarchy, Capitalism, and White Supremacy," Hartsock lays down the trilogy of structures that put so many at social and personal risk—women, workers, Blacks, and others. Here, in a paper of 15 pages, Hartsock touches on a breathtaking range of thinkers—Bertrand Russell, Hobbes, Marx (of course), Marge Piercy, Eli Zaretsky, Anais Nin, W.E.B. Du Bois, and on and on. In 1974, almost no one wrote seriously of Du Bois, least of all in relation to Marge Piercy and Anais Nin. Together they all serve to sketch the mature standpoint feminism that was soon to be.

It is hard not to think of Angela Davis's *Women, Race, & Class* that would not appear for another decade after Hartsock's 1974 essay.[41] But Davis went about things in ways different from Hartsock. Davis's life has been less devoted to systematic scholarship of the kind Hartsock did. Hartsock regularly focused her attention in the 1980s on issues that then were just beginning to come to attention among social theorists. This while always making insistent mention of the importance of political engagement.

One of her notable later essays in 1987 would be published as "Foucault on Power: A Theory for Women?" Hartsock was respectful, to a degree, of Foucault (and others she considered "postmodernists"), but, ultimately, she was critical because, she thought, Foucault "recapitulated the effects of Enlightenment theories which deny the right to

---

38 *Ibid*, 301. Gayle Rubin's essay, "The Traffic in Women," appeared in Rayna R. Reiter, ed., *Toward an Anthropology of Women* (Monthly Review Press, 1975), 169.
39 As for the enduring value of Rubin's "Traffic in Women" see the importance some twenty years later of the essay Hartsock dismissed: Gayle Rubin with Judith Butler, "Sexual Traffic: An Interview," *Difference: A Journal of Feminist Culture Studies* 6:2–3 (1994), 63–99.
40 Nancy Hartsock, "Political Change: Two Perspectives on Power," *Quest: A Feminist Quarterly* 1:1 (Summer, 1974), 13. Also at https://archive.org/details/questfeministqua11wash/page/13/mode/1up?view=theater
41 For Angela Davis, see Chapter 17 above.

participate in defining the terms of interaction."[42] In this Hartsock makes what in the day was a common error of seeing Foucault as retaining too much allegiance to a tradition that cannot include the oppressed, including women. She's wrong in this. Foucault's theory explicitly transgressed the traditions and, as time went by, he wrote more and often from his own gay experience.[43] Just the same, immediately after her first remarks about Foucault, Hartsock makes a quite remarkable recovery in a section, "The Construction of the Colonized Other," where she introduces Albert Memmi's *The Colonizer and the Colonized* (1967) and Edward Said's *Orientalism* (1978). Ever critical, Hartsock points out that "the Orient is often feminized." Still, here she finds much that serves her feminist standpoint well enough. This essay concludes with an astute statement of the standpoint as she understands it. All-too-simply put, five points (each critical of Foucault): 1. Don't get rid of the subject. 2. Begin from an epistemology that makes knowledge possible. 3. Think of power as a practical daily activity. 4. Theories of power "must recognize that creating alternatives is difficult." 5. All such theories must be engaged and include a theory, preferably also the practice, of political action.[44]

Interestingly, Hartsock makes the same points much more persuasively (and shorn of reference to Foucault), in her 1998 book *The Feminist Standpoint Revisited and Other Essays* where they are reformulated in a more positive Marxist framework: 1. "Material life (class position in Marxist theory) not only structures but also sets limits on understandings of social relations." 2. "If material life is structured in fundamentally opposing ways for two different groups, one can expect that the understanding of each will be an inversion of the other." 3. "The vision of the ruling group can be expected to structure the material relations in which all people are forced to participate and therefore cannot be dismissed as simply false consciousness." 4. "In consequence, the vision available to an oppressed group must be struggled for and represents an achievement that requires both systematic analysis and the education that can only grow from political struggle." 5. "As an engaged vision, the potential understanding of the oppressed, the adoption of a standpoint, makes visible the inhumanity of relations among human beings and carries a historically liberative role."[45] The five points are not a tidy fit with the five on Foucault, but the elements are present here and there, with the important fifth standpoint: *an engaged vision*. Important to add that Hartsock says: "These five points are my restatement with only a few changes of the formulation that appeared in *Money, Sex, and Power: Toward a Feminist Historical Materialism* (1983), 232."[46] This may be true, but, as good as this book was, *The Science Question in Feminism* (1998) could fairly be considered a masterpiece.

A true cynic might think to say that between 1983 and 1998, Hartsock was unable to change her mind. But the fact is that she rewrote the five points as a template for the intervening 1987 "Foucault and Power" essay. What she does do from the beginning in 1974

---

42 Nancy Hartsock, "Foucault on Power: A Theory for Women?" in Linda Nicolson, *Feminism/Postmodernism* (Routledge, 1990), 159–160. Compare Hartsock, *The Feminist Standpoint Revisited and Other Essays* (Westview. 1998), Chapter 10, "Postmodernism and Political Change."
43 See, for one example, Charles Lemert and Garth Gillan, *Michel Foucault: Social Theory and Transgression* (Columbia University Press, 1982), 63–83). Also, among many other places, Michel Foucault, "Sex, Power, and the Politics of Identity," *Ethics: Subjectivity and Truth / The Essential Works of Foucault 1954–1984*, edited by Paul Rabinow (The New Press, 1994), 165–174.
44 Harding, "Foucault on Power," in Nicholson, *Feminism/Postmodernism* (previously cited, 1990), 170–172. Again, Harding misreads Foucault, especially in her point 3, where his power/knowledge is nothing if not practical.
45 Harding, *The Feminist Standpoint Revisited and Other Essays* (Westview, 1998), 229.
46 *Ibid*, note 6, 245–246.

to her second book in 1998 is to think and rethink historical materialism in order arrive at a coherent feminist standpoint theory while, along the way, exploring ideas from a variety of thinkers—Foucault, yes, and Rorty; but also Althusser and Lévi-Strauss; not to mention the large circle of feminists who were her constant intellectual (and one might say spiritual) companions. All this led to her (to use a better word than the masculinist *masterpiece*) *magnum opus*, a truly *most grand work*—grand, that is, in the sense of a book that pulls together some three decades of work. If there is a simple, but strong critical statement, it is:

> Whether we work for wages or not, most of us have come to accept that we work because we must. We know that the time we spend on things important to us must be found outside the time we work to stay alive. Work is an especially important question for feminists since in our capitalist and patriarchal society the work that women do goes unrecognized, whether it is done for wages or not.[47]

These lines appear in a chapter entitled, "Staying Alive." One is tempted to believe that the title is a quote from the Bee Gees,[48] when in truth it is a serious existential line. Hartsock's intellectual purpose in life was to deploy academic resources and languages to compose a feminist theory that allows women to know their realities in order to engage in political work that will, indeed, help them and others to stay alive, and to thrive.

bell hooks (Gloria Jean Watkins): The Standpoint Is Caught in the Matrix

Gloria Jean Watkins (1952–2021) is universally known as bell hooks—the name she took to honor her great grandmother. She always spelled bell hooks in lower case because she wanted attention paid to her books, not who she was.[49] She was, just the same, a personage hard to dismiss, especially in her many public talks, like the 2014 New School conversation she had with Cornel West, who himself is anything but a shrinking violet.[50] Plus which, her thirty-four books are challenging in several ways at once—*Appalachian Elegy: Poetry and Place* (1921), *Teaching To Transgress* (1994), *Feminist Theory from Margin to Center* (1984), *Uncut Funk: A Contemplative Dialogue with Stuart Hall* (2018), many others.

Gloria Watkins was born in a small, segregated Kentucky town. Her father was a janitor; her mother a domestic worker. Yet she grew up with self-confidence and pride in her origins—a story told in *Bone Black: Memories of Girlhood* (1996) where she writes of her mother's love and thoughtfulness that encouraged what would come to be for the adult bell hooks. She was an avid reader which allowed her to overcome the severe limitations of the segregated schools of her youth, eventually to attend college at Stanford University, take an MA at the University of Wisconsin, Madison, and a PhD at the University of California, Santa Cruz (UCSC) in 1976. After which she taught at a number of places, UCSC, Yale, Oberlin, City College New York, before returning to Berea College in her native rural Kentucky, where she founded the Bell Hooks Center to teach and support young Black women to become teachers themselves. There she died of kidney disease at the all-too-young age of 69.

---

47 *Ibid*, 45.
48 See, for example, John Badham, director, *Saturday Night Fever* (with John Travolta), Paramount Pictures, 1977.
49 Heather Williams, "bell hooks Speaks Up," *The Rollins College Sandspur* 112: 17 [no year given].
50 *A Public Dialogue between bell hooks and Cornel West at Eugene Lang College*, The New School, 2014. Easily found on YouTube under the title given. See also their book: bell hooks and Cornel West, *Breaking Bread: Insurgent Black Intellectual Life* (South End Press, 1991).

bell hooks' first prose book, *Ain't I a Woman: Black Women and Feminism* in 1982, set the terms of a Black women's standpoint as growing, originally, from silence.

> At a time in American history when black women might have joined together to demand equality for women and a recognition of sexism on our social status, we were by and large silent. Our silence ... the silence of the oppressed—that profound silence engendered by resignation and acceptance of one's lot."[51]

Then, later, after developing the early history from slavery on when Black women were devalued, she makes no bones about patriarchy as a system but also white feminists who look down on Black women as niggers.[52]

Then too she calls out Michele Wallace author of *Black Macho and the Myth of the Superwoman* in 1979, in which Angela Davis is praised not for her political achievements and her brilliant writing but "for her beauty and devotion to Black men."[53] In the end, after clearing the table of dried up leftovers she serves the key point of early Black standpoint feminists: "We, black women who advocate feminist ideology, are pioneers. We are clearing a path for ourselves and our sisters."[54]

Three years later in 1984 hooks advanced this argument in *Feminist Theory from Margin to Center*. Beginning most directly with an entirely proper attack on Betty Friedan's alleged founding document of late modern American feminism. She makes the claim that Friedan was the founder of modern feminism seem absurd:

> Betty Friedan's *The Feminine Mystique* (1963) is still heralded as having paved the way for contemporary feminist movement—it was written as if [Black] women did not exist. Friedan's famous phrase, "the problem that has no name," often quoted to describe the condition of women in this society, actually referred to the plight of a select group of college-educated, middle and upper class, married white women-housewives bored with leisure, with the home, with children, with buying products, who wanted more out of life. [55]

Then hooks continues in the first chapter, the title of which makes it clear who were the true founders of feminist theory—"Black Women: Shaping Feminist Theory." Even today, so many decades later, there are white feminists outraged by this claim. But bell hooks supports her insistence with an assertion that hints at what came to be called intersectionality.

> A central tenet of modern feminist thought has been the assertion that "all women are oppressed." This assertion implies that women share a common lot, that factors like class, race, religion, sexual preference, etc. do not create a diversity of experience that determines the extent to which sexism will be an oppressive force in the lives of individual women.[56]

---

51 bell hooks, *Ain't I a Woman: Black Women and Feminism* (South End Press, 1982), 1.
52 *Ibid*, 141–142.
53 *Ibid*, 183.
54 *Ibid*, 196.
55 bell hooks, *Feminist Theory from Margin to Center*. Routledge, 2015 [South End Press, 1984], 1.
56 *Ibid*, 5.

In the 2015 revised edition, she adds, more decisively: "We needed theory mapping thought and strategy for a mass-based movement, theory that would examine our culture from a feminist standpoint rooted in an understanding of gender, race, and class."[57] Again, it is hard not to hear the whispers of Angela Davis's *Women, Race and Class* which was published just a few years before in 1981.

The twelve chapters of *Feminist Theory from Margin to Center* present what at the time was the first comprehensive feminist theory—comprehensive because it covers nearly every basic aspect of feminism and did so then well before those who developed the themes fully— sexist oppression, sisterhood: solidarity among women, men: comrades in struggle, work and educating women, ending violence, revolutionary parenting. Some of these topics were in the day just coming to the fore. The book ends with the two most political goals: "Ending Female Sexual Oppression" and "Revolution: Development Through Struggle." At the very end she quotes Paolo Freire, *Pedagogy of the Oppressed* (1967–1968): "Dialogue cannot exist, however, in the absence of profound love for the world and for women and men. The naming of the world, which is an act of creation and re-creation, is not possible if it is not infused with love." These words may seem a little too gentle for a revolutionary unless one remembers that here[58] and elsewhere Freire is often mentioned in the same breath as Albert Memmi, Frantz Fanon, Aimé Césaire—decolonizing revolutionaries all.

The next step worthy of discussion in respect to bell hooks' social theory of the Black women's standpoint—and of her radical thinking in general—is her 1991 book with Cornel West, *Breaking Bread: Insurgent Black Intellectual Life*. There must be other books of the kind, but none I can think of that are as engaging a discussion of so important a subject as insurgent Black intellectual life. Its value is, to be sure, enhanced by the coming together of these two exceptional thinkers who knew each other since they both taught at Yale in the mid-1980s. Their friendship and intellectual companionship endured well after the book to the 2014 conversation at the New School, and beyond. Anyone who watches the conversation on YouTube can see both how warm their friendship was and how synergistic was their thinking. West, for example, says:

> bell hooks' bold project locates her on the margins of the academy and the Black community—in search of a beloved community whose members will come from these very same margins. Her kind of Black feminism—or womanism—puts a premium on reconstructing new communities of Black people (of whatever gender, sexual orientation, and class) and progressives (of whatever race) regulated by thoroughly decolonized visions, analyses, and practices.[59]

Then later on, West adds in words compatible with hooks' earlier writings: "The future of the Black intellectual lies neither in a deferential disposition toward the Western parent nor a nostalgic search for the African one. Rather it resides in a critical negation, wise preservation, and insurgent transformation of this hybrid lineage which protects the earth and projects a better world."[60]

bell hooks begins her concluding chapter, "Black Women Intellectuals," with epigrams from Zora Neale Hurston's *Dust Tracks on the Road*, Kay Lindsey's *The Black Woman*

---

57 *Ibid*, xiii.
58 *Ibid*, 39.
59 bell hooks and Cornel West, *Breaking Bread: Insurgent Black Intellectual Life* (South End Press, 1991), 61.
60 *Ibid*, 146.

as a Woman, and (again) Angela Davis's *Women, Race, and Class*.[61] She goes on to agree with Cornel that being a Black intellectual is an act "of self-imposed marginality."[62] But adds that when the Black intellectual is mentioned, all-too-often it is men like W.E.B. Du Bois and Martin R. Delaney who are mentioned—while Anna Julia Cooper, Mary Church Terrell, and Ida B. Wells are not.[63] She then concludes: "Within a White supremacist, capitalist, patriarchal social context like this culture, no Black woman can become an intellectual without decolonizing her mind."[64]

After *Breaking Bread* hooks went on to write a good many books on an astonishing range of topics. In 1994, in *Teaching to Transgress*, she wrote:

> When education is the practice of freedom, students are not the only ones who are asked to share, to confess. Engaged pedagogy does not seek simply to empower students. Any classroom that employs a holistic model of learning will also be a place where teachers grow and are empowered by the process.[65]

Then in 1995, she began *Killing Rage: Ending Racism* with a very personal line. "I am writing this essay sitting beside an anonymous white male that I long to murder."[66] She was at the time on an airplane and a racist airline worker had denied her friend the first-class seat she'd paid for. Her friend was Black. The worker assumed she did not belong in first-class. The man she was sitting beside supported the exclusion, sharing the racism of the flight attendant. Such a snippet might seem too small to begin a big book. But bell hooks meant to be outraged at the beginning of a very good book on racism and rage.

But then in 2001 she wrote at the beginning of her book on love and political progress. "As the title *All About Love: New Visions* indicates, we want to live in a culture where love can flourish. We yearn to end the lovelessness that is so pervasive in our society. This book tells us how to return to love."[67] Even well into the 2020s it appeared atop *The New York Times* mass market bestsellers list. Then, final example, in 2018, she published a dialogue with Stuart Hall, the founder of the Birmingham Centre for Cultural Studies and *New Left* contributor, *Uncut Funk: A Contemplative Dialogue*.[68] And on and on. She never seemed to slow down or fail to write and speak on each and every conceivable aspect of the politics of the Black feminist standpoint.

This section was composed under the header *bell hooks (Gloria Jean Watkins): The Standpoint Is Caught in the Matrix*. Too often it is ignored that she was an important contributor to Patricia Hill Collins's thinking on the matrix of domination in *Black Feminist Thought*. Collins's idea of the matrix paved the way, without acknowledgment, for what later came to be called intersectionality. Collins writes at the beginning of her discussion of the matrix of domination: "Certain basic ideas crosscut the three systems [race, gender, and class oppression]. Claimed by Black feminist bell hooks to be 'the central ideological

---

61 *Ibid*, 147. [Kay Lindsey's essay is in Toni Cade Bambara, ed., *The Black Woman: An Anthology* (Washington Square Press, 1970).]
62 *Ibid*, 148
63 *Ibid*, 151.
64 *Ibid*, 160.
65 bell hooks, *Teaching to Transgress: Education as the Practice of Freedom* (Routledge, 1994), 21.
66 bell hooks, *Killing Rage: Ending Racism* (Henry Holt, 1995), 8.
67 bell hooks, *All About Love: New Visions* (HarperCollins, 2001), xxix.
68 bell hooks and Stuart Hall, *Uncut Funk: A Contemplative Dialogue* (Routledge, 2018).

components of all three system of domination in Western society. ...'"[69] Of course, hooks was not the sole contributor to this idea. She was, one might say, first among equals in a short tradition going back, first, to Angela Davis, then to Anna Julia Cooper, ultimately to Sojourner Truth.

---

69 Patricia Hill Collins, *Black Feminist Thought* (Unwin Hyman, 1990), 68. Collins's quote is from bell hooks, *Feminist Thought: From Margin to Center* (South End Press, 1984), 29. For Collins on intersectionality, see her *Intersectionality As Critical Theory* (Duke University Press, 2019).

20 Fractured Identities and Queer Analytics
Anna Julia Cooper, Patricia Hill Collins,
Donna Haraway, Kimberlé Crenshaw Williams,
Gloria Anzaldúa, Judith Butler

What a responsibility it is to have the sole management of the primal lights and shadows!
Such is the colored woman's office.
She must stamp weal or woe on the coming history of this people.
May she see her opportunity and vindicate her high prerogative.
—Anna Julia Cooper, A Voice From the South, 1892

In addition to being structured along axes such as race, gender, and social class,
the matrix of domination is structured on several layers. People experience and resist oppression
on three levels: the level of personal biography;
the group or community level of the cultural context created by race, class, and gender;
and the systemic level of social institutions.
—Patricia Hill Collins, The Matrix of Domination in
Black Feminist Thought, 1990

I do not know of any other time in history when there was greater need for political unity
to confront effectively the dominations of "race," "gender," "sexuality," and "class."
I also do not know of any other time when the kind of unity we might help
build could have been possible.
None of "us" has any longer the symbolic or material capability of
dictating the shape of reality to any of "them."
Or at least "we" cannot claim innocence from practicing such dominations.
—Donna Haraway, The Cyborg Manifesto and
Fractured Identities, 1985

Looking at historical and contemporary issues in both the feminist and the civil rights communities,
one can find ample evidence of how both communities' acceptance of the dominant framework
of discrimination has hindered the development of an adequate theory and praxis to address
problems of intersectionality. ...
This adoption of a single-issue framework for discrimination not only marginalizes Black women
within the very movements that claim them as part of their constituency but it also makes
the elusive goal of ending racism and patriarchy even more difficult to attain.
—Kimberlé Williams Crenshaw, Demarginalizing the
Intersection of Race and Sex, 1989

The U.S.-Mexican border <u>es una herida abierta</u> where the Third World grates against the first
and bleeds. And before a scab forms it hemorrhages again, the lifeblood of two worlds merging
to form a third country—a border culture. Borders are set up to define the places that are safe
and unsafe, to distinguish us from them. ...A borderland is a vague and undetermined place
created by the emotional residue of an unnatural boundary.

It is in a constant state of transition. The prohibited and forbidden are its inhabitants.
<u>Los atravesados</u> live here: the squint-eyed, the perverse, the queer, the troublesome, the mongrel, the mulato, the half-breed, the half dead...Gringos in the U.S. Southwest consider the inhabitants of the borderlands transgressors, aliens—whether they possess documents or not, whether they're Chicanos, Indians or Blacks.
—Gloria Anzaldúa, The Homeland, Aztlán in
Borderlands/La Frontera: The New Mestiza, 1987

The female sex is thus also the subject that is not one. ...
I have tried to suggest that the identity categories often presumed to be foundational to feminist politics, that is, deemed necessary in order to mobilize feminism as an identity politics, simultaneously work to limit and constrain in advance the very cultural possibilities that feminism is supposed to open up.
—Judith Butler, Gender Trouble: Feminism and the Subversion of Identity, 1990

Fracturing What Was Once Thought To Be Rock Solid

Since, at least, Plato's *Republic* in 375BE and Aristotle's *On the Soul* in 350BC, if not earlier, many assumed that internal to the human psyche is a *soul*, which, late in the 1900sCE, became a *self*. From ancient times there had been a long history from which came what was thought to be a rock solid feature of human being.

But, as the modern world unraveled in the century from 1890 to 1990, the very idea that we are internally centered on a definite soul, or self, that makes us what we are or who we think we are. The first to launch this departure from psychic singularity was Anna Julia Cooper, in *A Voice From the South* in 1892:

> What a responsibility it is to have the sole management of the primal lights and shadows! Such is the colored woman's office. She must stamp weal or woe on the coming history of this people. May she see her opportunity and vindicate her high prerogative.[1]

This was but a good generation after slavery. Cooper's bio-father was master of her mother. Yet, Cooper found her way north to Oberlin College and literary career. Her belief in the colored woman's office came from a conviction that women of color, as we say today, were at once *both* racial and gendered people—not one or the other but both.

A century later Patricia Hill Collins wrote of the *matrix of domination* in her 1990 book *Black Feminist Thought*:

> In addition to being structured along axes such as race, gender, and social class, the matrix of domination is structured on several layers. People experience and resist oppression on three levels: the level of personal biography; the group or community level of the cultural context created by race, class, and gender; and the systemic level of social institutions.[2]

Patricia Collins was not by any means alone in developing a theory of the many elements at work in one's identity.

---

1 Anna Julia Cooper, *A Voice From the South* (Schomburg Library of Nineteenth Century Black Women Writers/ Oxford University Press, 1988 [1892]), 145.
2 Patricia Hill Collins, *Black Feminist Thought: Knowledge, Consciousness, and the Politics of Empowerment* (Unwin Hamlin, 1990), 227.

It was, however, Donna Haraway who conceived what came to be the defining concept of this line of thought: *fractured identities*. She wrote as part of her development of the idea:

> I do not know of any other time in history when there was greater need for political unity to confront effectively the dominations of "race," "gender," "sexuality," and "class." I also do not know of any other time when the kind of unity we might help build could have been possible. None of "us" has any longer the symbolic or material capability of dictating the shape of reality to any of "them." Or at least "we" cannot claim innocence from practicing such dominations.[3]

It is apparent that with Haraway and the others presented here, each, in different ways, was political.

It is possible that Kimberlé Crenshaw is best known, if poorly understood, by the general public among whom those on the right of the right have expressed indignation at the Critical Race Theory that Crenshaw joined with others to develop.

> Looking at historical and contemporary issues in both the feminist and the civil rights communities, one can find ample evidence of how both communities' acceptance of the dominant framework of discrimination has hindered the development of an adequate theory and praxis to address problems of intersectionality. ...This adoption of a single-issue framework for discrimination not only marginalizes Black women within the very movements that claim them as part of their constituency but it also makes the elusive goal of ending racism and patriarchy even more difficult to attain.[4]

But it must also be said that some of those who partook of creating what is also called Queer Analytics were not merely queer but serious analytic thinkers.

Most striking of these was Gloria Anzaldúa who was born and bred on the borderlands between American Southwest and Mexico but also was a borderlands personality as we shall see.

> The U.S.-Mexican border *es una herida abierta* where the Third World grates against the first and bleeds. And before a scab forms it hemorrhages again, the lifeblood of two worlds merging to form a third country—a border culture. Borders are set up to define the places that are safe and unsafe, to distinguish us from them. ...A borderland is a vague and undetermined place created by the emotional residue of an unnatural boundary. It is in a constant state of transition. The prohibited and forbidden are its inhabitants. *Los atravesados* live here: the squint-eyed, the perverse, the queer, the troublesome, the mongrel, the mulato, the half-breed, the half dead...Gringos in the U.S. Southwest consider the inhabitants of the borderlands transgressors, aliens—whether they possess documents or not, whether they're Chicanos, Indians or Blacks.[5]

While Anzaldúa wrote serious analytic literature, she almost never failed to refer to all the fracturing identities she and others from the Borderlands experienced.

---

[3] Donna J. Haraway, "The Cyborg Manifesto," *Simians, Cyborgs, and Women: The Reinvention of Nature* (Routledge 1991 [1985]), 157.

[4] Kimberlé Crenshaw Williams, "Demarginalizing the Intersection of Race and Sex," *The University of Chicago Legal Forum Vol 1989:* 152.

[5] Gloria Anzaldúa, "The Homeland, Aztlán" in *Borderlands/La Frontera: The New Mestiza* (Spinsters/Aunt Lute, 1987), 3.

But the principal analytic theorist of them all was Judith Butler who, in her 1990 book, *Gender Trouble*, decisively insisted that identity itself was out of tune with the growing number of those feminists who all-but-dismissed not just the idea of gender, but also, race, class, heteronormativity.

> The female sex is thus also the subject that is not one. ...I have tried to suggest that the identity categories often presumed to be foundational to feminist politics, that is, deemed necessary in order to mobilize feminism as an identity politics, simultaneously work to limit and constrain in advance the very cultural possibilities that feminism is supposed to open up.[6]

These theorists may represent the larger and growing number of those prepared to give up much of the traditions that too often served to diminish and exclude others.

Many Identities in One Self/Struggling to Deal with the Uncertainty

KC Eichler-Mosier is a dear friend of many. She is an accomplished actress and one who cares for those she loves. She says of herself on Facebook: "I'm a self-made, trans-goddess, who takes care of the ones she loves, and always lives her truth." We who have known her over the years, even when she was Mel, know this to be true. KC is Black and beautiful. KC recently married Jaimie, who from all appearances is phenotypically white. They have recently posted a picture of the newly married couple lounging on a sofa with one of her very young nieces. The love among them moves one's soul.

Those who do not know KC well or have only seen her at a distance or perhaps heard about her, might not know what to make of her. This in spite of the fact she never is less than perfectly clear who she is. Their confusion is, in the world as it is, quite common. Sometimes we don't even know what to make of ourselves—or, better put, who we want to be in the presence of others. Because of Erving Goffman's idea that we become who we are by the dramatic cooperation of those to whom we present ourselves, it is well known that we are never one precise person with an impermeable identity.[7] Again, remember Goffman's serious joke on the pure identity: "In an important sense there is only one complete unblushing male in America: a young married, white, urban heterosexual Protestant father of college education, fully employed, of good complexion, weight and height, and a recent record in sports."[8] Turn this line around and it means that, in principle, any given identity always runs the course of self-identifying qualities to the extreme of qualifying characteristics. To be sure no one can live at such a pure-perfect extreme. We all live with and within a coherent range that allows us, first, to keep ourselves sane and, second, to allow those—whether intimates, acquaintances, or passers-by—to assign to us some several natures that fit somewhere in our society's scheme of real people.

Of course, Goffman was not a feminist (though he did explore one important aspect of gender differences[9]). But his idea of the individual's ability to manage even spoiled (or spoilable) aspects of who we are is not far off from the issue that owes to early third wave feminists—that all identities are fractured. Think then of Donna Haraway's sharply honest

---

6 Judith Butler, *Gender Trouble: Feminism and the Subversion of Identity* (Routledge, 1990), 11.
7 Goffman's *Presentation of Self in Everyday Life* (Bantam Doubleday, Dell, 1956) is discussed in chapter 15 above.
8 Erving Goffman, *Stigma: Notes on the Management of Spoiled Identity* (Simon & Schuster, 1963) 128. Also in Chapter 14 above.
9 Erving Goffman, *Gender Advertisements*, introduced by Vivian Gornick (Harper & Row, 1976).

1985 statement in *The Cyborg Manifesto and Fractured Identities:* "It has become difficult to name one's feminism by a single adjective—or even to insist in every circumstance upon the noun."[10] At first, Haraway's manifesto with its compounding of biology (cyborg) to social and feminist theory (fractured identities) shocks—but, in time, with patience, it makes original sense.

For those confused by talk of cyborgs and fracturing, Judith Butler offers little relief. Butler, in her 1990 classic, *Gender Trouble* began, philosophically, with statements like this one:

> And what is "sex" anyway? Is it natural, anatomical, chromosomal, or hormonal, and how is a feminist critic to assess the scientific discourses which purport to establish such "facts" for us? Does sex have a history? Does each sex have a different history, or histories?[11]

If Haraway's manifesto was a turning point for an emerging tradition of feminist thought, Butler caused gender trouble by directing that tradition in an entirely different direction beyond sex and gender to what some still call queer analytics.

> The female sex is thus also the subject that is not one. ... I have tried to suggest that the identity categories often presumed to be foundational to feminist politics, that is, deemed necessary in order to mobilize feminism as an identity politics, simultaneously work to limit and constrain in advance the very cultural possibilities that feminism is supposed to open up.[12]

As identities are many, so are feminisms—from which came the radical change in sex and gender thinking caused by queer analytics.

This brief commentary on the theoretical subject of the chapter is a long way from the story of KC, the queer trans-goddess[13] who loves with honesty those in her life. Yet, as the chapter proceeds through one feminist theory after another, it is important to keep well in mind that the subject so to speak (not withstanding Butler's line) is all who must and do contend with the perplexing intrusion of social differences on their personal lives.

KC like all the rest of us has suffered hard times. So too have social theorists of all kinds, including (perhaps especially) feminist theorists. Yet, the personal trouble with trying to develop a personal theory of who or what we are is that it is hard to include the personal sufferings that make us what we've become for better or worse. Once again, Angela Davis, in her powerful autobiography, and bell hooks, in her memoirs and literary writings, are among the exceptions. As it happens poets like Audre Lorde and Adrienne Rich, as we've seen, and other more exclusively literary authors, are often able to make stirring allusion to the deeper personal moments that made them what they became. A recently translated written exchange between two such women brought that suffering down to the heart of any

---

10 Haraway's manifesto was first available to the public in 1985 as samizdat passed around among an ever-growing elite of theorists. It has been republished in Donna Haraway, "A Cyborg Manifesto: Science, Technology, and Socialist Feminism in the Late Twentieth Century," in *Simians, Cyborgs and Women: The Reinvention of Nature* (Routledge, 1991), 149–181 (where the line quoted is at page 158).
11 Judith Butler, *Gender Trouble: Feminism and the Subversion of Identity* (Routledge, 1990), 6–7.
12 *Ibid*, 11 and 147.
13 The moniker she applies to herself.

message by anyone who, whether consciously or not, represents a tradition of persons who have endured the deepest inner pain.

Natalia Ginzburg and Alba de Céspedes, in the recently translated "On Women: An Exchange,"[14] write, in Ginzburg's words:

> I've never met a woman without soon discovering in her something painful and pitiful that doesn't exist in men—a constant danger of falling into a deep dark well, a danger that comes precisely from the female temperament or maybe from an age-old condition of subjugation and servitude that won't be easy to overcome.

To which de Céspedes responds, in part:

> And not only do men not know of the existence of these wells and everything we learn when we fall into them, they're also unaware that they're the ones who push women into them with such ruthless innocence. ... And it's not fair that at least half the beings who inhabit the earth live in a state of subjugation owing to the incomprehension of the other half, the half that acts, decides, and governs.

It is not by chance that these all-too-cutting words were published in September 1944, when the Nazis were thrown out of Italy. Italian women in that day had suffered doubly—yes, by the "age-old condition of subjugation" but also by the years of oppression by evil Fascist men.

Many decades later, well into the 2020s, many are aware that others, even certain men, suffered similar subjugations. A most moving case of a woman understanding the suffering of another woman is Rhiannon Giddens' indescribable dance and musical ode to the slain Breaonna Taylor, *Cry No More*.[15] The lyrical thread words are "we cry no more" sung mostly by Black Women, but also white women and some men. The latent word is, therefore, that many are subjugated for many reasons and in many ways, but it is Black women in America who are the prototype of subjugated suffering.

Though Anna Julia Cooper did not dwell on her subjugation, after Harriet Tubman and Sojourner Truth, she is a prototype of the subjugated Black woman who speaks from the political heart of women's global suffering. But she is not alone. It is no accident that the fractured identity feminists are often Black, yes, but also queer and women of many colors and many tongues.

Anna Julia Cooper: The Colored Woman's Office

Anna Julia Cooper was born in Raleigh, North Carolina probably in 1858. Her mother was a slave; her father her mother's master. She never spoke of him. She often spoke of her. "My mother was a slave and the finest woman I have ever known."[16] Sometime in the late 1860s she was a star pupil at St. Augustine's College in Raleigh, and soon after was tutoring younger ones.[17] In 1877, she married George A.C. Cooper, an Episcopal priest. He was a

---

14 Natalia Ginzburg and Alba de Céspedes, "On Women: An Exchange," translated from the Italian by Allasandra Bastagli and introduced by Ann Goldstein, *The New York Review of Books* LXIX: 20 (2022), 56–57.
15 At YouTube: Rhiannon Giddens, *Cry No More*.
16 Anna Julia Cooper, "Autobiographical Fragment," in Charles Lemert and Esme Bhan, eds., *The Voice of Anna Julia Cooper* (Rowman & Littlefield, 1998), 331.
17 The principal printed source for biographical data on Cooper is Louise Danielson Hutchinson, *Anna J. Cooper: A Voice from the South* (Smithsonian Institute Press, 1981). Some of the biographical and

good man, who died two years later of unrecorded causes. Never after did she marry nor, so far as it is known, enjoy an intimate personal relation with a man.

Cooper's own Episcopalian faith, encouraged by her mother and her husband, was consistently in the background of her writings and actions, no more so than in her 1892 book, *A Voice from the South*, where she announced the colored woman's office in all matters racial and moral:

> What a responsibility it is to have the sole management of the primal lights and shadows! Such is the colored woman's office. She must stamp weal or woe on the coming history of this people. May she see her opportunity and vindicate her high prerogative.[18]

These lines come at the end of the first part of *A Voice from the South* for which the header is *Soprano Obligato*—an obligatory high-pitched musical line. Cooper's literary effect could, indeed, be musical, even as she insisted, in this passage—a gently phrased defiant feminist line—that the colored woman has the sole management of the primal lights and shadows!

Soprano Obligato begins with "Womanhood: A Vital Element in the Regeneration and Progress of the Race," a lecture Cooper delivered in 1886 to, in her words, "the convocation of the colored clergy of the Protestant Episcopal Church at Washington D.C.". In this she delivers but slightly pulls her punch. Those colored clergy in 1886 were, obviously, all men. She is, thus, beginning the quarrel she announced in her short prefatory note, "Our *raison d' être*" in which she puts the Black man on trial for the racial silence he has condoned and caused. She wrote: "One important witness has not been heard from. The summing up of the jury has been made—but no word from the Black Woman."[19] *A Voice from the South* begins with legal defiance of those who have put the Black Woman in the shadows. But *Soprano Obligato* turns to a more religious theme appropriate for the clergy she addressed in 1886. Yet, even here, the supremely refined and learned woman is anything but piously demure.

In "Womanhood: A Vital Element in the Regeneration of and Progress of a Race" Cooper presents at the start a curious but compelling history of religion and civilization from Ancient China and Old Norse through more than nineteen centuries—this interspersed with secular authors from Tacitus, Madame de Stael, Waldo Emerson, to Thomas Babington Macaulay and François Pierre Guillaume Guizot. Then she turns to the chapter's theme directed to an audience of religious Race Men: "It seems not too much to say then of the vitalizing, regenerating, and progressive influence of womanhood on the civilization of to-day. ..."[20] After which she turns to the religious argument itself:

> Christ gave ideals not formulæ. The Gospel is a germ requiring millennia for its growth and ripening. It needs and at the same time helps to form around itself a soil enriched in civilization, and perfected in culture and insight without which the embryo can neither be unfolded or comprehended. ... By laying down for woman the same code of morality,

---

interpretive information here is from Charles Lemert, "Anna Julia Cooper: The Colored Woman's Office," in Charles Lemert and Esme Bhan, *The Voice of Anna Julia Cooper* (Rowman and Littlefield, 1998), 1–43. The bulk of the material in the Cooper archives at Howard University are included in this book. The dates of her birth and early schooling are uncertain as they often were for most of those born into slavery.

18 Anna Julia Cooper, *A Voice from the South* in The Schomburg Library of Nineteenth Century Black Women Writers (Oxford University Press, 1988), 145.
19 *Ibid*, ii.
20 *Ibid*, 18.

the same standard of purity, as for man,...—throughout his life and in his death he has given to men a rule and guide for the estimation of woman as an equal...[21]

It may be too much to observe that, unlike elsewhere, she is a bit too wordy. She again was addressing a body of distinguished gentlemen. She was not yet thirty.

Soon enough the chapter comes to its main point, made by singling out Martin R. Delany, a Harvard graduate, a physician, journalist, abolitionist, more. He was, in a word, *the* Race Man of the days before Booker T. Washington. Cooper said of him that he was "an unadulterated black man who used to say when honors of state fell upon him, that when he entered the council of kings the black race entered with him."[22] It is all-but-impossible that the men to whom she spoke did not shudder or shrink at this. If not then, surely they would have sat up straight when she followed with

> "Only the BLACK WOMAN can say, 'when and where I enter, in the quiet undisputed dignity of my womanhood, without violence and without suing or special patronage, then and there the whole *Negro race enters with me.*'"[23]

In this powerful but calm assault on the dominating man of Black America Cooper stakes out a polite but discernibly political position for Black women.

As Elizabeth Alexander has observed, Anna Julia Cooper was writing at a time when the historically Black colleges of the South—Howard, Tuskegee, Fisk, Hampton, others—were doing their work for variously educated freed Blacks just a few years after the end of Reconstruction in 1877. The 1890s, when *A Voice from the South* was published, were a decade of political and cultural ferment for American Blacks, by then no longer merely "from the South." Booker T. Washington was ascendent. W.E.B. Du Bois was emerging. Washington's opposition to the latter's talented tenth policy for racial regeneration was in the offing. Cooper was unflinchingly on Du Bois's side in this debate and would eventually be subject to attacks by Washington's political machine. Her book was published just the year before the *Plessy v. Ferguson* 1893 brazenly racist decision. Alexander astutely characterizes Cooper's exceptional role amid this turmoil:

> Looking at *A Voice* as a whole, rather than at its parts, reveals a textual strategy to find a new form in which to house the contemplations of an African American women's intellectual movement. The essays are at once allegory, autobiography, history, oratory, poetry, and literary criticism, with traces of other forms of address. Only such a diverse structure could encompass the tensions of forging an African American, female, demonstrably thinking self from whatever intellectual material was at hand. Additionally, Cooper's strategic use of the first person "I" reveals the ways in which she allows her own experience—her own existence, even—to inform the rhetoric of her text as evidence for the feminist strategy she advocates.[24]

No one has been more apt than Alexander in summarizing Cooper's theoretical means and method.[25]

---

21 *Ibid*, 17–19.
22 *Ibid*, 30.
23 *Ibid*, 31.
24 Elizabeth Alexander, *The Black Interior* (Graywolf Press, 2004), 101.
25 Alexander, however, is well aware of the leading others who in the day wrote on the African American woman; see *ibid*, 211 n41. For a somewhat more complete account of those who have written on Cooper's feminism, see Charles Lemert, "Anna Julia Cooper: The Colored Woman's Office," previously cited, 14–28.

But Cooper's raid on the political territory of Black religious Race Men was not all. The second, and truly formative, aspect of *Soprano Obligato* was her no less determined exception to then prominent white feminists. The second chapter in *Soprano Obligato* is "The Higher Education of Women," Cooper's statement of the talented tenth for Black Women. Du Bois wrote of the Talented Tenth of the Negro race in a short but richly empirical article published in 1903, when he was already engaged in his emerging argument with Booker T. Washington's Tuskegee working men's movement. Du Bois put his view this way: "The Talented Tenth of the Negro race must be made leaders of thought and missionaries of culture among their people. (No others can do this work and Negro colleges must train men for it.) The Negro race, like all other races, is going to be saved by its exceptional men."[26] Yet, today, one can hardly miss the, to us, strange fact that the concept refers exclusively to Black men. Thus the very title of Anna Julia Cooper's 1890 speech before the American Conference of Educators must have caused even Black women to look up. The higher education of women was not a general policy among Negroes. Yet she and others had enjoyed higher education by dint of special effort to gain admission to schools like Oberlin where Cooper and others, including Mary Church Terrell and Ida Gibbs Hunt, studied.[27]

> A visitor in Oberlin once said to the lady principal, "Have you no rabble in Oberlin? How is it I see no police here, and yet the streets are as quiet and orderly as if there were an officer of the law standing on every corner."
>
> Mrs. Johnston replied, "Oh, yes; there are vicious persons in Oberlin just as in other towns—*but our girls are our police.*"[28]

If anything, this chapter is more biting in its attitude toward Talented Tenth men who know not what woman can do. It also is progressive, looking beyond the 1890s: "We must thank the general enlightenment and independence of woman (which we may now regard as a *fait accompli*) that both these forces are now at work in the world, and it is fair to demand from them for the twentieth century a higher type of civilization than any attained in the nineteenth."[29]

But after this, *Soprano Obligato* turns full force from men to women as its sardonic title makes all-too-evident: "Woman Vs the Indian." The words are the title of a talk presented by the white feminist, the Reverend Anna Shaw presented in 1891—a naïvely racist opposition that was shared by the more famous white feminist, Susan B. Anthony. But it is not just the stupid notion that the Indian is somehow other-than the Woman, but, even more, the disgrace is how Shaw and Anthony are joined "in the sacred halls of Wimodaughsis"—a term then emerging of associations of women. Cooper, however, puts her own piercing spin on the term: Referring to Wimodaughsis club of which Shaw was president, Cooper wrote of the club's secretary: "She has not calculated that there were

---

26 These lines appear as the conclusion to the article which can found at http://moses.law.umn.edu/darrow/documents/Talented_Tenth.pdf . Important to note that this article was published that same year as his *Souls of Black Folk* (Bantam Books, 1989 [1903]), which includes the important essays on his idea: "Of Booker T. Washington and Others" (3) and "Of The Training of Black Men"(6). Also, the idea of a "talented tenth" first arose in 1896 in reference to the men educated at Negro colleges established in Reconstruction.
27 By 1890 when Cooper presented her talk to the American Conference of Educators, there were a number of colleges that accepted women: Fisk (12), Oberlin (5), Wilberforce (2), Wellesley and Ann Arbor (3), Livingston (2), Atlanta University (1) and Howard (0!). See Louise Daniel Hutchinson, *Anna J. Cooper: A Voice from the South*, previously cited, 92. Also, Cooper, *A Voice, ibid,* 74.
28 Ibid, 55–56.
29 Ibid, 57.

any wives, mothers, daughters, and sisters, except white ones; and she is really convinced that *Wimodaughsis* would sound just as well, and then it need mean just *white mothers, daughters and sisters.*"[30]

Could even a white feminist mean such a thing? Well, yes, Cooper would answer. "Susan B. Anthony and Anna Shaw are evidently too noble to be held in thrall by the provincialisms of women who seem never to have breathed the atmosphere beyond the confines of their grandfather's plantation."[31] Then too there is the question of Shaw's title disparaging the Indian. "Miss Shaw is one of the most powerful of our leaders, and we feel her voice should give no uncertain note."[32] Cooper continues in this frankly disparaging, if superficially polite, vein. "All prejudices, whether of race, sect, or sex, class pride and caste distinctions are the belittling inheritance and badge of snobs and prigs."[33] Until she comes to what may be read as an early standpoint feminist position, here directed at the extreme insensitivity of a white feminist who ought to know better:

> Why should woman become plaintiff in a suit versus the Indian, or the Negro or any other race or class who have been crushed under the iron heel of Anglo-Saxon power and selfishness? If the Indian has been wronged and cheated by the puissance of this American government, it is woman's mission to plead with her country to cease to do evil and to pay its honest debts.[34]

I quote too much because, in spite of the attention she has recently won, there is the temptation to treat Cooper as less than she was—as less than a precursor of what would not become current among feminists until a good century later. She was at the least a precursor of feminist standpoint position:

> Woman should not, even by inference, or for the sake of argument, seem to disparage what is weak. For woman's cause is the cause of the weak; and when all the weak shall have received their due consideration, then woman will have her "rights," and the Indian will have his rights, and the Negro will have his rights, and all the strong will have learned at last to deal justly, to love mercy, and to walk humbly...[35]

But, even more, she was also one who, without using the words, would have understood Patricia Hill Collins's matrix of domination and, thereby also, tacitly an early version of Donna Haraway's fractured identity theory, if not Judith Butler's gender trouble. Bold, even aggressive, though it may be to say so, this implicit theory peeks out in "Woman VS the Indian" in one of her anecdotes about riding a segregated train that had stopped for rest and relief.

> ...Our train stops at a dilapidated station, rendered yet more unsightly by dozens of loafers with their hands in their pockets while a productive soil and inviting climate beckon in vain to industry; and when, looking a little more closely, I see two dingy little rooms with "FOR LADIES" swinging over one and "FOR COLORED PEOPLE" over the other; while wondering under which head I come ...[36]

30 *Ibid*, 81.
31 *Ibid*, 83.
32 *Ibid*, 117.
33 *Ibid*, 118.
34 *Ibid*, 123–124.
35 *Ibid*, 117.
36 *Ibid*, 96.

One might suppose that this is little more than a normal story—except for the fact that in "Woman VS the Indian" just after, for the first time, Cooper has unequivocally identified herself as a <u>Black</u> Woman. Here one might see these first early intimations of what would come to be known as the concept of fractured identity theory.

To this point *Soprano Obligato* has spoken primarily of women in general, with the exception of the line already quoted in which she counters Martin R. Delaney's presumption of being the pure perfect Race Man: "Only the BLACK WOMAN can say 'when and where I enter, in the quiet, undisputed dignity of my womanhood, without violence and without suing or special patronage, then and there the whole *Negro race enters with me.*' "[37] And in this chapter she had been castigating the white women feminists of the South.

Then a few paragraphs before the anecdote about the bathroom signs, she writes: "So the Black Woman holds that her femineity [sic] linked with the impossibility of popular affinity or unexpected attraction through position and influence in her case makes her a touchstone of American courtesy exceptionally pure and singularly free from extraneous modifiers."[38] This, the third chapter in *A Voice from the South*, is slowly but decidedly edging toward not only the book's title theme but to something like a full-bodied theory of the Black Woman's office. She announces this theory in the last section of *Soprano Obligato* under a title that, out of context, would seem innocuous.

"The Status of Woman in America" is the coda of the *Soprano Obligato* section of Cooper's book. Here one might ask, if this section includes previously written and delivered speeches alongside new material, how can one assume that *Soprano Obligato* is a well-knit statement of a theory? For which the obvious, but ill-considered, literary fact that this section of *A Voice from the South* Cooper is painting for all to see a picture of Woman as such, a picture framed by the long-ignored Black Woman—in which she allows herself to stand-in for the Black Voices from the South in a day, just two generations after slavery, when at long-last the Black Woman has migrated North to the center of Womanhood as such.

> The colored woman of today occupies, one may say, a unique position in this country. In a period of itself transitional and unsettled, her status seems *one of the least ascertainable and definitive of all the forces which makes for our civilization*. She is confronted by both a woman question and a race problem and is as yet an unknown or unacknowledged factor in both.[39]

It is important to note the emphasized line. Cooper's Black woman is the least of all the forces in an unsettled world. Cooper means to say that the unique and powerful force of the Black woman owes to her being at the bottom, so to speak, of the hierarchy of the forces then prevailing in America.

Then as she nears the end of *Soprano Obligato*, Cooper repeats her almost sociological vision of the 1890s, but with a more hopeful note:

> In this last decade of our century, changes of such moment are in progress, such new and alluring vistas are opening before us, such original and radical suggestions for the adjustment of labor and capital, of government and the governed, of the family, the church and the state, that to be a possible factor though an infinitesimal in such a moment is pregnant with hope and weighty with responsibility.[40]

---

37 *Ibid*, 31.
38 *Ibid*, 93.
39 *Ibid*, 134, emphasis added.
40 *Ibid*, 143–144.

With these words she introduces the coda to her narrative which is also her most important single statement of Black feminism:

> What a responsibility it is to have the sole management of the primal lights and shadows! Such is the colored woman's office. She must stamp weal or woe on the coming history of this people. May she see her opportunity and vindicate her high prerogative.[41]

Read out of context one is tempted to think that the people whose history is at stake are African Americans alone. But, as we have seen, she also means America and perhaps even modern civilization itself. In the day—and in another sense, in ours—there has not been a more powerfully poetic feminist statement by anyone who understands the very idea of a colored woman's office.[42] All the more so because it is the Black Woman, still from the South who "is to have the sole management of the primal lights and shadows!"

Here was Cooper at her best. She went on to write much more, including the second half of *A Voice from the South* which is a collection of essays mostly on race in America. In 1892 she was in her early years teaching at M Street School where in 1901 she would become its principal. She lived until 1964, 106 years. Along the way she traveled far and wide, supervised the Colored Settlement House in D.C., began doctoral studies at Columbia, became, at age 57, guardian of 5 orphaned children, translated a manuscript from the French *Le Pèlerinage de Charlemagne*, worked in 1919 at the War Camp in Indianapolis that welcomed those who had fought in the Great War, began in 1924 and completed doctoral studies in 1925 at the Sorbonne, after retiring from M Street she served as president of Frelinghuysen University for Black adults without education, and much more.[43]

Yet, as many as her accomplishments were over a long life, she was not without the woman's pain of which Natalia Ginzburg and Alba de Céspedes and others through the years have written. She suffered the loss of her husband after but two years marriage, the grief of that loss and the loneliness of the many years after, and she, worst of all, suffered professional abuse at the hands of Booker T. Washington who was opposed to her Talented Tenth teaching that sent many M Street students to the best universities. In 1906 Washington had her fired after which she taught in Missouri for five years before returning to M Street (when, by the way, Washington's power had faded due to an indiscretion on his part). Cooper may have seemed in her writings upbeat and above it all. She was this, in her way, but in spite of the pain she endured for more than a century's life.

Patricia Hill Collins: The Matrix of Domination

Patricia Hill Collins (1948-) was born and grew up in Philadelphia where she attended the Philadelphia High School for Girls (the first public high school for girls and women) before college at Brandeis University, then graduate studies for the MA in Teaching at Harvard. After which she taught public school in Boston for a few years, before returning to Brandeis for the PhD. Anyone who reads these basic biographic facts or has seen one of many very dignified photos of Collins online, or who superficially read her very serious books, may assume that she arose from the elite, if Black, classes of the East. Truth be told, Collins was born into a Black working class family—her father was a factory worker, her mother a secretary. Neither well-off, nor elite, but well-enough off, and more than decently equipped

---

41 *Ibid*, 145.
42 She was a life-long Episcopalian, hence "office" as in calling or vocation.
43 See chronology in Lemert and Bhan, previously cited, 345–346.

to send her on her way. As a consequence, she transferred to the Philadelphia High School for Girls, when the inadequacy of her city's primary schools that focused on white-middle class pupils became unbearable—after which she indeed went on to elite schools of higher education.

This being the facts of the matter, even though in her neighborhood she enjoyed friendship and fun on the streets, Collins felt the abject dismissal and structural racism of her childhood schools and the wider community—so much so that she began her first important book in 1990, *Black Feminist Thought*, with these words:

> Beginning in adolescence, I was increasingly the "first," "one of the few," or the "only" African American and/or woman and/or working class person in my schools, communities, and work settings. I saw nothing wrong with being who I was, but apparently many others did. My world grew larger, but I felt I was growing smaller. I tried to disappear into myself in order to deflect the painful, daily assaults designed to teach me that being an African American, working-class woman made me lesser than those who were not. And as I felt smaller, I became quieter and eventually was virtually silenced.[44]

Middle-class white folk brought up, as I was, may have struggled in adolescence but they never experienced anything like this. Ours was not the same experience as abiding unbridgeable poverty or drug wars on the streets, to be sure. Still, it is all-too-easy to dismiss Collins's experience and that of so many in her situation as, if not normal, at least a mere condition of being Black in urban America. There is nothing "mere" about it, as my Black daughter will testify.

What followed in the first edition of *Black Feminist Thought* in 1990 was the first systematic pulling together of the strands of earlier standpoint theories into something other and new—not quite fractured identity theory, but a well-thought-through early development of the theory that Donna Haraway had sketched in 1985.[45] What was unique to Collins's statement in 1990 was her forthright linking of feminist knowledge to power—a step made long before many American social theorists were attuned to Michel Foucault's concept of *power/knowledge*. Collins's revolutionary idea picked up Angela Davis's earlier thinking in *Women, Race, and Class* in 1981—that the power of Black women must be understood in relation to this triangle of interposing themes. This entailed a paradigmatic shift that locates resistance in its necessary relation to domination, namely: *Reconceptualizing Race, Class, and Gender as Interlocking Systems of Oppression*. This is the header for the pungent conclusion to the book—a conclusion that is packed not just with the leaves of her own argument but with those of other Black feminists who had nurtured the seeds Angela Davis sowed at the beginning of the decade.[46] This, then, is where Collins cultivates one of the too-often-overlooked but most important concepts not just in feminist theory but in social theory in general—the matrix of domination.

But, before tackling this somewhat mysterious idea, a note on Collins's first published sociological article: "Learning from the Outsider Within: The Sociological Significance of Black Feminist Thought"[47] which appeared in 1986 soon after she finished her doctoral

---

44 Patricia Hill Collins, *Black Feminist Thought* (Unwin Hyman, 1990, first edition), xi.
45 Donna Haraway, "A Manifesto for Cyborgs: Science, Technology, and Socialist Feminism in the 1980s," *Socialist Review* 80 (1985); also in Linda Nicholson, ed., *Feminism/Postmodernism* (Routledge, 1990), 190–233. And republished in Haraway, *Simians, Cyborgs, and Women: The Reinvention of Nature* (Routledge, 1991).
46 See Collins, *Black Feminist Thought* (1990), 222–238.
47 Collins, "Learning from the Outsider Within: The Sociological Significance of Black Feminist Thought," *Social Problems/Special Theory Issue* 33:6 (1986), 14–32.

studies at Brandeis. Here Collins clears the ground for *Black Feminist Thought* in 1990 by identifying herself, first, as a sociologist, and, second, as a theorist able to offer a rigorous review of both sociological and feminist literature on the outsider/within concept. The article is notable in several ways. For one, Collins's early paper may well be among the most important first papers of any sociologist with whom I am familiar. It even could be said to rank with Robert K. Merton's "Social Structure and Anomie" which appeared in the *American Sociological Review* in 1938, the year he finished his doctoral studies at Harvard. Some might see this as an overblown comparison. Merton's famous article has been widely read ever since; Collins's not as much. Merton's article laid the corner-stone for his career as a middle-range sociologist of enduring importance. Collins's, though, is less well recognized, did similar in that it should be seen as a classic piece in Black feminist thought—one that could still play a central role in redefining sociological theory and sociology itself. That it has not (yet), is the fault of sociologists (the author of this book included) who have been late to discover this classic essay of late modern times.

"Learning from the Outsider Within: The Sociological Significance of Black Feminist Thought" starts off with references seldom to be found in a major sociological article: Zora Neale Hurston, Audre Lorde, and bell hooks alongside Georg Simmel, Karl Mannheim, Robert E. Park, and Robert K. Merton.[48] The idea is to lay down the lineage of sociological ideas of the stranger, of marginals, outsiders—against which she strikes the keynote of her fugal composition in which Black feminist theory sings the hard tune of the prototypically excluded marginal who by her social position is the all-but-pure-perfect outsider/within—the Black woman herself, who brings clarity to traditional sociological thinking. "Sociologists might benefit greatly," she writes (just after introducing the sociologists), "from serious consideration of the emerging, cross-disciplinary literature that I label Black feminist thought, precisely because, for many Afro-American female intellectuals, 'marginality' has been an excitement to creativity."[49] This was early in mainstream sociology's awareness of the then rising authority of Black feminist thought among generic social theorists. Collins continues the idea:

> Black feminist scholars may be one of many distinct groups of marginal intellectuals whose standpoints promise to enrich contemporary sociological discourse. Bringing this group—as well as others who share an outsider within status vis-à-vis sociology—into the center of analysis may reveal aspects of reality obscured by more orthodox approaches.

Collins's intention is to deploy the experience of women like her to transform orthodox disciplinary thinking.

The three core themes of "Learning from the Outsider Within" are, precisely, the ways Black feminists are able (if not always willing) to discern the creative value of their experience as outsiders within. The work of the intellectuals among them is to think through and express them, which is what Collins does in the central sections of her paper. First, Black women, having been denied by white male dominated culture the right to define themselves, understand *themselves* better than the definers understand themselves. The very act is political: "Defining and valuing one's consciousness of one's own self-defined standpoint in the face of images that foster a self-definition as the objectified 'other' is an important way of resisting the dehumanization essential to systems of domination."[50] Hence, the second

---

48 Collins, "Learning from the Outsider Within," 15–16 [footnotes included].
49 *Ibid*, 16. The quotation just following, same place.
50 *Ibid*, 18.

theme follows from the first, "The Interlocking Nature of Oppression." Here is a precursor to "The Matrix of Domination" that would appear four years later in her 1990 book, *Black Feminist Thought*. Here, in the article, Collins cites the lineage of those who gave rise to her idea: Sojourner Truth, Anna Julia Cooper, and bell hooks. From hooks's *From Margin to Center* she takes the most telling of ideas—that the complex idea of *systems* of oppression are multiple in their effect. Collins quotes hooks to the effect that "either/or dualistic thinking ... is the central ideological component of all systems of domination in Western society."[51] Both hooks and Collins in the mid-1980s, were way ahead in the sociological game that had not begun to hit the ball that Pierre Bourdieu and Anthony Giddens had been swinging at since the late 1970s—that somehow sociology must overcome the strangling effect of the classic subject/object dualisms.[52] Black women, in particular, cannot afford to think in dichotomies, which are to them destructive. To Collins's credit she is able to soften the harshness of this insistence by quoting a seldom read passage from Anna Julia Cooper's 1893 talk, "Intellectual Progress of Colored Women in the United States since the Emancipation Proclamation":

We take our stand with the solidarity of humanity, the oneness of life, and the unnaturalness of and injustice of all special favoritisms, whether of sex, race, country, or condition. ... The colored woman feels that woman's cause is one and universal; and that ... not till race, color, sex, and conditions are seen as accidents, and not the substance of life; not till the universal title of humanity to life, liberty, and the pursuit of happiness is conceded to be inalienable to all; not till then is woman's lesson taught and woman's cause won—not the white woman's nor the black woman's nor the red woman's, but the cause of every man and of every woman who has writhed silently under a mighty wrong.[53]

Collins follows with the generous statement that she cites Cooper "because it represents one of the clearest statements of the humanist vision extant in Black feminist thought."[54]

The third theme, "The Importance of Afro-American Woman's Culture," might seem to be an afterthought. In fact, it is where Collins returns to politics by commenting on the problems associated with the apparently simple idea of "activism," of which she says: "While Black women's reality cannot be understood without attention to the interlocking structures of oppression that limit Black women's lives, Afro-American women's experiences suggest the possibilities for activism even within such multiple structures of domination."[55]

This one article offers, as I've suggested, a systematic introduction to the subject that would preoccupy her and others for years to come. To be sure, analytic sociologists obsessed by dualistic cause-and-effect thinking would reject it, which is why, one assumes, it appeared not in the *American Sociological Review* that, then and now, publishes with rare exception strictly analytic articles, while *Social Problems* has long been known for its openness to the real world.

But that is not all. Though brief, too brief I think, Collins comes to her conclusion as a sociologist critical of sociology. Writing in a day when mainstream sociology indeed had no serious clue as to the sociological situation of Black women in America, Collins's

---

51 *Ibid*, 20. The quoted line is at bell hooks, *From Margin to Center* (South End Press, 1984), 29.
52 For a discussion of Bourdieu and Giddens, see Charles Lemert, "Three Ways to Think Structures and Ignore Differences," in Lemert, *Sociology After the Crisis* (Routledge/Paradigm, 2004), 131–166.
53 Anna Julia Cooper, "The Intellectual Progress of Colored Women," in Lemert and Bahn *The Voice of Anna Julia Cooper* (Rowman & Littlefield, 1998), 204–205.
54 Collins, "Learning from the Outsider Within," 21.
55 *Ibid*, 23.

sociological vision stands apart, in large part because her doctoral studies were at Brandeis, then the most radical department in the field. Her most biting criticism of sociology is that, in the day, it was governed by two altogether negative, even ignorant, assumptions about Black women: "... (1) white males are more worthy of study because they are more fully human than everyone else; and (2) dichotomous oppositional thinking is natural and normal."[56]

In the 1980s, when Collins began publishing, many of the white males then still new to sociology came to the field because of their experiences of the radical 1960s. We were well prepared to be critical of this field we found ourselves in. But more than a few of us were ignorant of the situation of Black women. We were more inclined to take our lead from sources like C. Wright Mills *The Sociological Imagination* (1959) and Alvin Gouldner's *The Coming Crisis of Western Sociology* (1970). Though both Mills and Gouldner were radical, neither had anything to say of women in general, much less Black women. To make matters worse, both deployed a version of sociology's dichotomous paradigm. For Mills, sociological imagination was the act of looking beyond one's personal struggles to their structural causes. For Gouldner, the key to sociology's salvation was, in his words, "reflexive sociology looks at itself."[57] We of what then was to us a radical temperament thought this kind of thing was the cat's meow—never mind that both formulations applied exclusively to men of our kind, while also urging us to find ways to reflect on ourselves and our situations. Few of us, save for those who had had experience in civil rights work in the Black south, even knew a Black woman unless she had cleaned our childhood house. If only we had read Angela Davis, bell hooks, or Patricia Hill Collins or heard of Fannie Lou Hammer things might have been different. But few among us knew of them—except for those who had been involved in Mississippi Freedom Summer of 1964. Otherwise we were the young and left-liberal With-ins for whom all others were Out-siders.

Surely this *explication de texte* of Collins's first article is a strange way to begin. Yet, I dare to do so because the work that came after was all foreshadowed in Collins's "Learning from the Outsider Within." This is not to say that she has a one-track mind—far from it. The books that followed all expanded, filled-in, and moved-forward the basic ideas in her first article. This is worth saying, in its own right, because academic scholars who try the same very often, in time, find themselves (if they are willing to look) in a rut. This because formal academia, they think, requires one to build reputations for a particular brand they believe they have invented. I could name names but won't because some who have done this are friends and they have done good work of a different, if less critical, kind.

Once again, it is possible to see the special importance of Black feminist intellectuals. They, first of all, do what they do as part of a collective enterprise—one that, from the beginning, necessarily reached deep into their shared experiences of Black culture. And nowhere is this more true than in America where, since 1619, slaves and their descendants had no choice but to think of themselves as outsiders to an essentially white nationalist culture. One might suppose things are better today in the 2020s. But look again, imagine yourself Black living in deepest Mississippi and or in a poor neighborhood in any major city, where the projects having been taken down, you must work harder than any others just to survive.

Black Feminist Thought: Knowledge and the Politics of Empowerment in 1990, by its subtitle, shows just how in the four years since the Outsider/Within article Collins focused her theoretical (and political) concerns. She begins with a mention of Maria W. Stewart's 1831

---

56 *Ibid*, 27.
57 Alvin Gouldner's *The Coming Crisis of Western Sociology* (Basic Books, 1970), 510–512.

early, perhaps first, Black feminist question: "How long shall the fair daughters of Africa be compelled to bury their minds and talents beneath a load of iron pots and kettles?"[58] After which Collins again recites the litany of early Black feminists from Sojourner Truth and Anna Julia Cooper to Ida B. Wells and Toni Morrison—to which she adds others including bell hooks, Gloria Anzaldúa, Ella Baker, and Pauli Murray (her advisor at Brandeis). Listings of this sort are, in a sense, obligatory for Black thinkers who are unwaveringly committed to the tradition. But this litany is particularly interesting because it includes activists like Baker, radicals like hooks and, if in a different sense, Murray, and those like Anzaldúa who, while not Black, are otherwise in the same outsider position.[59] As she was in the 1986 article, Collins here again is writing as a sociologist who is also a Black feminist. Even more to the point, she means to define an epistemological position based on the latter but pertinent to the former. She is aware of the risk:

> [B]y identifying my position as a participant in and observer of my own community, I run the risk of being discredited as being too subjective and hence less scholarly. But by being an advocate for my material, I validate the epistemological stance that I claim is fundamental for Black feminist thought.[60]

The book itself is a voyage through the history of Black women's exclusion and the theories that described their fate. Chapter 3, for example, "Work, Family, and Black Women's Oppression," while it doesn't go into detail on slavery and its history as Angela Davis did in *Women, Race, and Class* in 1981, Collins's chapter is a compact history of the subjugation of Black women. Collins here traces the history of their oppression—in slavery, then after Emancipation in the share cropping system, to urbanization and domestic work, to even the marginalization of Black women in the war-time industry in the 1940s. Rosie the Riveter was white. Black women were paid substantially less and kept on employment tenterhooks. Collins also goes into the economic disadvantages of the Black middle-class which, as still now, was unable to accumulate wealth in some good part because they were excluded from home ownership.

Then, Chapter 4, "Mommies, Matriarchs, and Other Control Images," is thought by many to be the most original feature of the book especially in the day. 1990 was early in the culture studies rage in the academy, but here Collins offers a powerful cultural study of the instances when the dominating culture turned the Black woman into a media caricature that re-enforced white racial prejudices. Collins describes four of these controlling images. First, the "Mammy" came to be after slavery—"a faithful, obedient, domestic servant."[61] This was the woman who worked in white homes. The second image, however, is its corollary in the Black home and community, "The Matriarch," a negative image. This because the "Mammy" had to work in white homes, from which she gained an income that put her in economic charge of family and community matters in the Black community where men were often unable to find paid work. Collins notes that these two images "of the mammy and matriarch place African-American women in an untenable position"[62] in large part because

---

58 Patricia Hill Collins, *Black Feminist Thought: Knowledge and the Politics of Empowerment* (Harper Collins / Unwin Hyman, 1990), 3.
59 Still, Collins says: "The vast majority of thinkers discussed in the text are *to the best of my knowledge* Black women." *Ibid*, 16.
60 *Ibid*, 17.
61 *Ibid*, 71.
62 *Ibid*, 75.

the domestic work left them drained of energy when they came home late in the day. Then, after Franklin D. Roosevelt's New Deal, there was federal welfare support for them, which led quickly enough to the "Welfare Mother" image that demeaned mostly Black women who had babies allegedly for the sole purpose of gaining the welfare checks. Thus, relatedly, the fourth image of Black Women as "The Jezebel"—the "whore, or sexually aggressive woman—is central to this nexus of white male images of Black womanhood because efforts to control Black women's sexuality lie at the heart of Black women's oppression.[63]

More generally, Collins makes the telling point that "race, gender, and sexuality converge on this issue of evaluating beauty" which is perhaps the most important, if tacit, way that Black women are objectified.[64] Chapter 4 ends with "Constructing an Afrocentric Feminist Aesthetic for Beauty." Then, instead of objectifying white women as ugly, Collins writes: "[N]o individual is inherently beautiful because beauty is not a state of being. Instead beauty is always defined as a state of becoming. All African-American women as well as all humans become capable of beauty."[65] It is hard to imagine a more exquisite social theoretical line.

Thereafter the book covers a range of related subjects associated with Collins's view of Black womanhood: the power of self-definition, Black women and motherhood, rethinking Black women's activism, the sexual politics of Black womanhood, sexual politics and Black women's relationships. Each concerns traditions that require continuous rethinking and each is its own orthogonal issue in the tradition of Black Women's history. Collins respects and represents that tradition well but at nearly every turn she cuts open a new line across it. Black women's activism, for example, must transcend its lineage. "It remains to be seen whether African-American women facing challenges of contemporary race, class, and gender oppression will continue this tradition and create new ways to 'lift as we climb'."[66] Throughout, Collins is always looking ahead, realizing that history is not fair to Black women who will, again and again, face new challenges. This was 1990. Who among us in the 2020s can say she was wrong?

Black Feminist Thought concludes with the normal pulling together of its argument but with, again, Patricia Hill Collins' own theoretical restructuring of the issues Black feminists must contend with when thinking and living in a matrix of domination:

> In addition to being structured along axes such as race, gender, and social class, the matrix of domination is structured on several levels. People experience and resist oppression on three levels: the level of personal biography; the group or community level of the cultural context created by race, class, and gender; and the systemic level of social institutions. Black feminist thought emphasizes all three levels as sites of domination and as potential sites of resistance.[67]

Yes, this matrix of domination must be resisted. Yes, race, class, and gender are the axes that create the environment Black women must come to terms with. At the same time, Black women and all others, high or low, in the matrix must deal with it on three levels—their individual consciousnesses, the cultures that have shaped their worlds, and the level of social structures that always and ever have been, and are, controlled by a dominant group.[68]

---

63 *Ibid*, 77.
64 *Ibid*, 79.
65 *Ibid*, 89.
66 *Ibid*, 160.
67 *Ibid*, 227.
68 *Ibid*, 227–228.

Hence here, the conclusion promised in the book's subtitle: *Knowledge, Consciousness, and the Politics of Empowerment.*

Patricia Hill Collins had more to say on many different subjects, even on the first edition of this book. The second edition of *Black Feminist Thought* in 2000 reveals the extent to which she will not stand pat. I know of few books revised into second (or more editions) that are as seriously well revised. Though the basic argument of the first edition of *Black Feminist Thought* remains much the same, often with further appropriate references. One important to notice difference is that intersectionality—a subject she would eventually consider—peeks its head. Kimberlé Crenshaw's first major article that began her foundational work on intersectionality, "Mapping the Margins: Intersectionality, Identity Theory, and Violence against Women of Color," was published in 1991.[69] Collins clearly took Crenshaw's idea to heart, especially in *Fighting Words: Black Women & the Search for Justice*[70] but even more so in the second edition of *Black Feminist Thought* where she embraces Crenshaw (who in the day had not embraced Collins's thinking), for example: "Having determined, then, that everyone was equal in the sense that everyone had a skin color, symmetrical treatment was satisfied by a general rule that nobody's skin color should be taken into account in governmental decision making."[71] (Crenshaw, important to say, is a lawyer first and foremost which may be why she was not, at the time, familiar with Collins's *matrix of domination*—that anticipated *intersectionality* as it came to be.) Pat Collins's second edition of *Black Feminist Thought* in 2000 was clearly more than a mere revision of the 1990 edition in many ways—of which the attention paid to Crenshaw is an instance of primary importance because in due course, in the 2020s, Collins would, as she once said, make her work on intersectionality a major concern of hers.[72] It is worth mentioning this because it says a lot about her readiness to take on new projects that may have been hinted at in her early writings—then to advance them robustly years later when she had retired and was well into her 70s.

Collins's first book-length venture into intersectionality is a 2016 book in the Polity Press Key Concepts series entitled simply *Intersectionality*. It was written with the *Université de Montréal* sociologist, Sirma Bilge. They first met in 2006 at an international conference in Durban, South Africa. Then six years later they met again in Lausanne, Switzerland, at a conference that brought together French-speaking researchers from Europe, Africa, and North America. From this came their *Intersectionality* which is distinguished by being the first important book that examines intersectionality as a global phenomenon. They have said of their work together "Neither of us could have done this book alone. We felt the need for a book that would introduce the complexities beyond the audiences that were comfortable to each of us."[73]

---

69 Kimberlé Crenshaw, "Mapping the Margins: Intersectionality, Identity Theory, and Violence against Women of Color," *Stanford Law Review* 43:6 (1991), 1241–99. Also Kimberle Crenshaw, Demarginalizing the Intersection of Race and Sex, 1989 U. CHI. LEGAL F. 139.

70 Patricia Hill Collins, *Fighting Words: Black Women & the Search for Justice* (University of Minnesota Press, 1998).

71 Kimberlé *Crenshaw,* "Color Blindness, History and the Law," in Wahneema Lubiano, ed., *The House That Race Built* (Pantheon, 1997), 284. Collins discusses Crenshaw in Collins, *Black Feminist Thought* (2000), 278–279.

72 In a personal communication on October 31, 2022, Collins remarked that intersectionality had indeed become a major interest. I had written her to say that I was so glad she had dipped her oar into the intersectionality waters. She replied that it was more an ocean liner steaming away in those waters. As often before, I was again swimming in the wake of changes I had to catch up with.

73 Patricia Hill Collins & Sirma Bilge, *Intersectionality* (Polity Press, 2016), vii.

Though the authors respect what Kimberlé Crenshaw had done, their purpose was to go beyond. "Intersectionality has expanded beyond the civil rights framework suggested featured in Crenshaw's early articles (1989, 1991) to a framework within a transnational context explored in her position paper for the Durban conference (Crenshaw 2000)."[74] They later conclude: "When we broaden our lens to include intersectionality as critical praxis, both its initial expression within social movements as well as its global dispersion beyond the academy, the practices and ideas of diverse people past and present, in the Global North and in the Global South, come into view."[75] And this is the line they follow in *Intersectionality* starting with Chapter 2, "Intersectionality as Critical Inquiry and Praxis," then continuing on to chapters on intersectionality's global dispersion, its effect on identity, its capacity for protest (especially against Neoliberalism), and its promise of critical education.[76] Each chapter is replete with global references that document the book's accounts of the discussions of the global dispersion of intersectionality accompanied by illustrations of its presence in scholarship, journalism, and most importantly on the ground of social movements. Among the book's many ingenious observations is the question "Is gay the new black?" It also stretches the reader's mind by giving an example of the ties between protestors in Turkey and others in Brazil. In 2013 in Turkey there were wild demonstrations in Istanbul's Taksim Geri Park against the government's plan to invade the Park with urban development projects. Brazilian protestors took Turkish protests as their own, chanting "the love is over, Turkey is right here ... Everywhere is Taksim, resistance is everywhere."[77] The example does two things at once—it illustrates the global spread in intersectional politics, while turning "Gay is the new black" into a general slogan for the global political concerns.

Collins's 2013 book *On Intellectual Activism* is in many ways more of the working-through of her thinking over the years on the relation between intellectual work and on the ground activism. But here also Collins defined a next step in the evolution of her thinking and that of those who comprise the collective of Black women theorists who all were as interested in changing the world as in thinking it. In the end she asks the crucial question: "*How can we transcend the barriers created by our experiences within intersecting systems of oppression to build coalitions that foster social justice?*"[78] What she didn't achieve in this book, she did in her second major book on intersectionality.

Intersectionality As Critical Social Theory in 2019 is, very possibly, Collins's second classic—one in which she not only pulls together elements of her early thinking from *Black Feminist Thought* in which feminist theory and sociology are said to be complementary to one another. But in this book she takes as a given the global historical aspects of intersectionality and advances a more systematic social theoretical program that, first, reviews and revises prior schools of critical social theory and, second, inserts intersectionality as a new and dynamic approach to these several intellectual traditions that advance a certain route to social praxis. "Intersectionality offers a window into thinking about the significance of ideas and social action in fostering social change."[79] This is an unsettlingly simple statement which, one assumes has been done before. There are whispers of Marx, Du Bois,

---

74 Ibid, 97. Kimberlé Crenshaw's paper is "Background Paper for the Expert Meeting on the Gender-Related Aspects of Race Discrimination" (Zagreb/ *World Conference Against Racism*), Documents: November 21–24, 2000.
75 Collins & Bilge, *Intersectionality* (Polity Press, 2016), 203.
76 The references to critical praxis were present (if not in so many words) in Collins's *Black Feminist Thought* in 1990.
77 *Ibid*, 109–110.
78 Patricia Hill Collins, *On Intellectual Activism* (Temple University Press, 2013), 241.
79 Patricia Hill Collins, *Intersectionality As Critical Social Theory* (Duke University Press, 2019), 286.

Horkheimer, Reinhold Niebuhr, Mao, Sartre (if not de Beauvoir), Gouldner (C. Wright Mills, after a fashion), Cornel West, Wallerstein, Angela Davis and other early feminists (Black and white), still others. But none, so far as I can remember, quite braided together praxis, critical thinking, and social change as has Collins.

Intersectionality As Critical Social Theory is a book rich in nuance that covers its many subjects systematically, as few books of such ambition do. This is plain to see in its four structural parts, which one after the other follow a path from first things to final ones. Part I Framing the Issues, Part II How Power Matters, Part III Theorizing Intersectionality, Part IV Sharpening Intersectionality's Critical Edge. Each excites the reader's attention. None is entirely predictable.

Part I frames the issues associated with intersectionality that are obvious but basic enough to bear scrutiny: 1. What is meant by critical inquiry? 2. And how does it relate to critical *social* theory? Here again Patricia Hill Collins, the social theorist, explores an issue that social theorists have not fully come to terms with. Or, one might ask, what does insectionality contribute to the ideal of critical inquiry and its deployment in various social theories?

At first, Collins accepts Crenshaw's reference to intersectionality as a metaphor, but immediately goes on to say why metaphors matter. Intersectionality doesn't go very far if it remains as it was in Crenshaw's public explanation—a simple traffic intersection where race and gender run over the Black woman in the intersection where she is neither one or the other.[80] This said, Collins turns immediately to Gloria Anzaldúa, whose borderlands figure brings together such a number of identities that a simple intersection cannot handle them, even if a matrix might. But the important issue here is that, whichever the metaphor, intersectionality cannot be reduced to identities, least of all dualistic identities—like white/black, male/female, straight/gay, able-bodied/disabled, and so on. What Collins sees is, in effect, that the actual cross-currents of social life can*not* be reduced to anything so close to personal identities.[81] They are social, even spatial—a point made by Anzaldúa's geographical vision for which Collins cites Patrick R. Grzanka's *Intersectionality: A Foundations and Frontiers Reader* (2004):

> Anzaldúa's "borderland" metaphor as signifying a geographic, affective, cultural, and political landscape cannot be explained by binary logic (black/white, gay/straight, Mexican/American, etc.) or even by the notion of liminality, that is *the space between*. For Anzaldúa, the borderlands are a very *real* space of actual social relations that cannot be captured within existing social theory.[82]

After this, it might surprise some that Collins, in the book's second chapter "What's Critical about Critical Social Theory?", goes on to attack, in a well-mannered way, one of the sacred cows of cultural left theories. In short (and in my words, not hers): Critical social theories as many are do not *begin* from a theoretical position located in the actual social position of the oppressed from whom one would expect *resistance* to arise. Or, differently put, critical

---

80 Crenshaw, "The urgency of intersectionality," TED talk, November 14, 2016, on YouTube / @ https://www.ted.com/talks/kimberle_crenshaw_the_urgency_of_intersectionality?language=en She of course gives a more technical explanation in her legal briefs, for example, Crenshaw, "Mapping the Margins: Intersectionality, Identity Theory, and Violence against Women of Color," *Stanford Law Review*, ibid.
81 *Ibid*, 37.
82 Collins, *ibid*, 33. For Grzanka's own words, see Patrick R. Grzanka's *Intersectionality: A Foundations and Frontiers Reader* (Westview Press, 2004), 106–107.

social theory is insufficiently critical when it is not an empirical (by extension, experiential) theory of resistance.

Collins's second chapter, though critical, is an extraordinarily useful review of critical social theories, as she defines them: the Frankfurt School, especially Horkheimer; the British School of Cultural Studies, especially Stuart Hall; and Francophone Social Theory, Bourdieu, Foucault, Frantz Fanon. She says of Fanon: "Significantly, Fanon also looked beyond liberation struggles that surrounded him, analyzing how the same national culture that was essential to liberation struggles could become a problem for new nation-states." The liberation movement of the Democratic Republic of Congo, for an example (of my choosing), was led by Patrice Lumumba. In 1960 they won independence from Belgium and, they thought, from the terrible and deadly tradition of Belgian rule of the Congolese people that was first established early in the twentieth century by King Leopold II.[83] A new nation came to be in 1960. But within a year, the army mutinied, Lumumba was assassinated, and an ever more ruthless regime under Mobuto Sese-Seko was installed. Belgian rule continued for all intents and purposes with the no less deadly rule of Sese-Seko enforced under a patina of free world advertisements like Muhammad Ali's *Rumble in the Jungle* defeat of George Foreman in 1974.[84]

Returning to Fanon, it is fair to note that Pat Collins's allusion to him, in particular, supports the conviction about what happens when critical social theories fail to originate with the resistance of the oppressed. Academic theorists, like charismatic rebel leaders, are unlikely to get to the heart of the matter, if they resist those who are the first order resisters.

Then, in Part 2, "Intersectionality and Resistance Knowledge Projects," Collins does the similar in fairly describing the projects before she criticizes them. She begins with antiracism and critical race theory and the book that collects the movement's key writings, Kimberlé Crenshaw's *Critical Race Theory*. Cornel West (who is pretty much everywhere) gives a sharp definition of the intersectionality movement:

The genesis of Critical Race Theory as a scholarly and politically committed movement in law is historic. Critical Race Theorists have, for the first time, examined the entire edifice of contemporary legal thought and doctrine from the viewpoint of law's role in the construction and maintenance of social domination and subordination.[85]

Collins appreciates Critical Race Theory but that does not keep her from criticizing its all-too-tight relationship with legal theory. She sponsors a broader sort of racial formation theory. "Conceptualizing race, racism, racial inequality, and racial injustices, and cultural representations, racial formation theory explains both racial order and racial change."[86] She also insists that the criticism of racism must focus first on Black institutions. "The Combahee River Collective broke a long-standing taboo within African American social and political thought: they criticized practices within Black women's needs and changes that need to

---

83 Adam Hochschild, *King Leopold's Ghost* (Houghton Mifflin, 1999).
84 See, among other sources, Thomas Hauser's *Muhammad Ali: His Life and Times* (Simon and Schuster, 2006 [1991]). Also for those interested in the range of writings by and about Ali in which the 1974 fight in Kinshasa is always the story from which explanation begins, see Charles Lemert, *Muhammad Ali* in the *Oxford University Press Bibliography Dictionary*, 2023. [Hence the reason I chose the example, now hoping that I haven't offended Pat.]
85 Cornel West, "Foreword" to *Critical Race Theory: The Key Writings*, edited by Kimberlé Crenshaw, Neil Gotanda, Gary Peller, Kendall Thomas (The New Press, 1995), xi.
86 Collins, *Intersectionality*, ibid, 307 [note 9].

occur in wider society."⁸⁷ It is no surprise that at this crucial juncture in her book she would cite the one Black women's collective that would declare their political purposes in a 1977 statement that includes the following personal and on the ground truth: "Black feminists often talk about their feelings of craziness before becoming conscious of the concepts of sexual politics, patriarchal rule, and most importantly, feminism, the political analysis and practice that we women use to struggle against our oppression."⁸⁸

Collins's criticism of Critical Race Theory is now easily understood as part of a lineage of race-concerned feminisms, postcolonial theories, and intersectionality itself that seek to establish a paradigm shift in thinking about social inequalities and social injustice. Then she concludes: "Intersectionality itself could easily become a discourse in which resistance is hollowed out, primarily because it fails to attend to the particulars of resistant knowledge projects within its own genealogy and whose futures inform its own."⁸⁹

Intersectionality goes on to bring experience, and community, as well the question of freedom into Part III, "Theorizing Intersectionality / *Social Action as a Way of Knowing*." Then in Part IV, "Sharpening Intersectionality's Critical Edge," Collins tries to untangle what she calls "relationality" before turning to the question: Can intersectionality be what it wants to be without social justice? If not every step in the book's argument is as enticing as the main points, the fact that the argument ends with a question—of social justice—is very much in keeping with Collins's gracious but circumspect way of doing theory.

This said, it is clear enough what Collins's main point is. Intersectionality, with all its merits, cannot become a full-blown critical social theory until it leaves the rarefied air of high theory to dig into the dirt of daily oppressions from which resistance movements arise. This goal is as basic for racial oppressions as for all others. The book concludes simply enough: "Intersectionality is not just ideas, but has an important role to play in the social world."⁹⁰

As *Black Feminist Thought* broke open new possibilities in Black feminist theory, then is it possible that *Intersectionality as Critical Social Theory* will do the similar for not just a startlingly important new movement in race theory but, just as much, in critical social theory? Both are important, but neither is fully what it could be and should be. We will see.

Donna Haraway: Cyborgs and Fractured Identities

The writings of Donna Haraway (1944-) have puzzled many a reader, some of whom admit to having given up trying to understand them. Others, more nastily, reject her work as incoherent, not worth the while. She is a theorist, to be sure, but one who could well be called a post-theoretical theorist. Her background suggests a reason for this. She studied in several quite different fields. At Colorado College, she majored in biology with minors in philosophy and English, after which she went to Paris to study theology under the auspices of an organization devoted to advancing the thinking of Pierre Teilhard de Chardin, a Jesuit paleontologist and philosopher whose writings were, in the day, nearly as hard to understand as Haraway's. In 1972 she finished doctoral studies in biology at Yale with a thesis titled *The Search for Organizing Relations: An Organismic Paradigm in Twentieth-Century Developmental Biology*, that in 1976 appeared in a book of no less challenging

---

87 *Ibid*, 97.
88 See *Combahee River Collective Statement 1977*, in *BLACK PAST* @ https://www.blackpast.org/african-ameri can-history/combahee-river-collective-statement-1977/
89 Collins, *Intersectionality, ibid*, 120.
90 *Ibid*, 290.

title: *Crystals, Fabrics, Field*. Soon enough Haraway began teaching at the only department that then, and still, might hire someone with a background like hers—the History of Consciousness program at the University of California at Santa Cruz. In due course Haraway became Distinguished Professor (now, in 2023, *Emerita*) for having over the years published astonishingly many papers and books, most with no less astonishing and (to some) inscrutable titles. Many, perhaps most, of the titles, mean to represent her brand of science fiction [*sic*]; for example: "In the Beginning Was the Word: The Genesis of Biological Theory" in *Signs* 6:3 (1981); "Teddy Bear Patriarchy: Taxidermy in the Garden of Eden, New York City, 1908–1936," in *Social Text* 11 (1984–85); and, most famously, "Manifesto for Cyborgs: Science, Technology, and Socialist Feminism in the 1980s" in *Socialist Review* 80 (1985). This small sample further illustrates the range of her readership such as it is—from feminists (*Signs*), those of the cultural left (*Social Text*), to Socialist/Marxists (*Socialist Review*). These instances and many more, owe to Haraway's prodigious scholarship across many quite different sectors of science studies and her many intellectual affairs. Bruno Latour, the late French polymath, was, she reports, one of her friends in the trade—a friendship that was not always peaceful. But the list goes on to include feminists from Sandra Harding to Patricia Hill Collins, information specialists like Leigh Star, and all-around engineers and physicists as well as a feminist prominent in medical studies, Evelynn Hammonds, and more.[91]

Then too, Haraway is seldom plainspoken as in an interview for *The Guardian* where she said, apparently to no one's surprise:

> Play captures a lot of what goes on in the world. There is a kind of raw opportunism in biology and chemistry, where things work stochastically to form emergent systematicities. It's not a matter of direct functionality. We need to develop practices for thinking about those forms of activity that are not caught by functionality, those which propose the possible-but-not-yet, or that which is not-yet but still open.[92]

Few among those familiar with all (or most of) Haraway's writings would flinch at the language which itself can only be understood with stochastically playful attention. This because play is a common figure in her thinking and writing—especially in her 1989 book *Primate Visions: Gender, Race, and Nature in the World of Modern Science* where she first systematically writes at book-length of science and science fiction.

Primate Visions begins: "I am writing about primates because they are popular, important, marvelously varied, and controversial."[93] One might add "and playful." But then Haraway goes on to bemoan the fact that global, nuclear culture threatens their survival. And all members of the Primate Order—monkeys, apes, and people—are threatened. Late twentieth-century primatology may be seen as part of a complex survival literature in global, nuclear culture. She continues: "Many people, including myself, have emotional, political, and professional stakes in the production and stabilization of knowledge about the order of primates." What begins as a seemingly playful fact of natural life turns quickly to a crisis of survival and, by implication, death. This is the first clue that science fiction is in the offing. If the end is at hand, then we can only imagine stories of what might come after.

---

91 Yesmar Oyarzun and Aadita Chaudhury, "Interview with Donna Haraway," (August 27, 2019) @ http://doingsts.com/cms/wp-content/uploads/2020/10/haraway-talks-march.pdf
92 Moira Weigel, An Interview "Feminist Cyborg Scholar Donna Haraway: 'The Disorder of Our Era Isn't Necessary'," *The Guardian* (June 20, 2019).
93 Donna Haraway, *Primate Visions: Gender, Race, and Nature in the World of Modern Science* (Routledge, 1989), 3. All quotes in this paragraph are from the same place.

But, before that, Haraway makes a telling point that "monkeys and apes occupy a privileged relation to nature and culture: they occupy the border zones between those mythic poles."[94] Shades of Bruno Latour! The nature/culture divide is mythic because primates, in particular, live in and *between* them. Latour called this the democracy of all things. Haraway, more austerely, says: "The sciences that tie monkeys, apes, and people together in a Primate Order are built through disciplined practices enmeshed in narrative, politics, myth, economics, and technical possibilities."[95]

Yet, these sciences are not the result of cool "objective" work. They are, she goes on to say, "cultures of contention." Admittedly, a student studying these subjects in schools will be confused, largely because the illusion of "objectivity" itself has been taught them from the early days of schooling. Yet, anyone who has spent time in any of the professional academic circles experiences the malice of this breed when it comes to competition for promotions or fellowship, or—worst of all—reviews of the work of others which can be all the more nasty even when the future of a young person is at stake. "Professional" is another myth of these "disciplined" areas of work. They are no different from labor in other areas—business, politics, investments, police work, and so on. Monkeys and apes, by comparison, are the more professional of the primates.

Primate Visions goes on to present a number of essays, including "Teddy Bear Patriarchy," on the general subject of primatology, presented of course with a righteous sense of scientific irony. After some fifteen chapters on aspects of the history of primatology, as she sees it, Haraway comes to her conclusion, *Reprise: Science Fiction, Fictions of Science, and Primatology* which begins with a quotation from *Primate Societies* which in the day had surely been a standard reference work in the field: "[B]ecause the genetic interests of individuals are not identical (unless they are clones), conflicts of interest perpetually endanger the survival of cooperative relationships."[96] After which, Haraway refers again to *Primate Societies* to make a revealing point—this to ground her argument in the knowledge of unqualifiedly professional primatologists:

> I read *Primate Societies* as an exemplar of a widespread groping in 1980s western biopolitical and other cultural discourse for ways to narrate differences that are as deeply enmeshed in feminism, anti-colonialism, and searches for non-antagonistic and non-organicist forms of individual and collective life, as by the hyper-real worlds of late capitalism, neo-imperialism, and the technocratic actualization of masculinist nuclear fantasies. The persistent binarism between antagonistic versus complementary or organicist ("cooperative") difference, coded in primate evolutionary biology in terms of the opposition between group selectionism or genic/individual selection, is what is cracking apart in these hydra-headed, medusoid gropings in the Primate Order.[97]

All this may be strange to some, but here Haraway deeply rereads the nature of the primate order as being, in a word, *medusoid*—which is to say, jellyfish like. Others, especially feminists, have, for good reason, attacked the prevalence of dualisms in social theories. Haraway takes the attack one giant step further to argue that identities themselves, wherever they are postulated, are, at best, hydra-headed gropings for something that cannot be—at least not among primates, and perhaps by implication among the subjects of all

---

94 *Ibid*, 1.
95 *Ibid*, 2.
96 Barbara Smuts, Dorothy Cheney, Robert M. Seyfarth, Richard W. Wrangham, eds., *Primate Societies* (University of Chicago Press, 1987), 287.
97 Haraway, *Primate Visions*, 373.

sciences. Ultimately, for example, the macro-physics of unimaginably distant stellar bodies comes down to earth as nicely-colored but computer-generated pictures that appear daily on Google-*News*, itself a literary figure because when it comes to stellar bodies all "news" is old, especially these days. Some are quite vivid and seemingly true to life, as in the story of Opportunity, the long serving Mars rover.[98] Even so the vivid images of Opportunity took a good ten minutes to come to the NASA Space Center, while those from Pluto take four hours—not to mention the hard-to-imagine billions of light years that it took the image of the planets to come into telescopic view. "In the end, non-identity is antagonistic; it always threatens 'the survival of cooperative relationships'."[99] After which, Haraway narrows the primate scheme of humans.

> Gender is kind, syntax, relation, genre; gender is not the transubstantiation of biological sexual difference. The argument in *Primate Visions* works by telling and retelling stories in the attempt to shift the webs of intertextuality and to facilitate perhaps new possibilities for the meanings of difference, reproduction, and survival for specifically located members of the primate order—on both sides of the bio-political and cultural divide between human and animal.[100]

Primate Visions ends with the science fiction of Octavia Butler's *Dawn*—one of Butler's many much lauded works that earned her a MacArthur genius grant and many other awards. "Butler's is a fiction predicated on the natural status of adoption and the unnatural violence of kin."[101] *Dawn* is the story of Lilith, an African-American woman meant to represent the postcolonial people who suffer first and most acutely from all global crises. In *Dawn* the catastrophe of nuclear war has made earth unlivable. Lilith has lost everything—her son and husband, everything. Butler has Lilith flee earth. She is taken in and suspended in time by the Oankali, who are a non-human kind "webbed into a universe of living machines."[102] The Oankali are, however, interested in human beings whom they perceive as beautiful but also sources of the kind of genetic code that might, so to speak, bring them down to earth. "Lilith is chosen to train and lead the first party of awakened humans. She will be a kind of midwife/mother for these radically atomized peoples' emergence from their cocoons." Again, Lilith is trapped in this post- or proto human situation. The Oankali are, however, unable to become human. Hence, Butler leaves the characters (if that is what in science fiction they are) in this unresolved dilemma.

Haraway's book ends, with a quote from Octavia Butler about Lilith that may seem to be a joke but one that is perfectly serious in respect to primates and their sciences:

> In the narrative of *Primate Visions*, the terms for gestating the germ of future worlds constitute a defining dilemma of reproductive politics. The contending shapes of sameness and difference in any possible future are at stake in the primate order's unfinished narrative of traffic across the specific cultural and political boundaries that separate and link animal, human, and machine in a contemporary global world where survival is at stake. *Finally, this contested world is the primate field, where, with or without our consent, we are*

---

98 For a completely charming narrative of the life and of the Opportunity Mars rover, see "Good Night, Oppy," directed by Ryan White, *Prime Video*, 2022.
99 *Ibid*, 368. But note that "kind" is not a typo. She means "Gender is kind, syntax, relation, genre…"
100 *Ibid*, 377.
101 *Ibid*, 378.
102 *Ibid*, 378. The full Lilith story is from 378 to the book's end at 382.

located. "She laughed bitterly. 'I suppose I could think of this as fieldwork—but how the hell do I get out of the field?' "[103]

Primate Visions in 1989 appeared two years before Haraway's "magnum opus"—a term she would likely reject.

Simians, Cyborgs, and Women: The Reinvention of Nature in 1991 is the place to go for any who are flabbergasted, or the like, by other of her books. To this point it may appear that I am trying, at once, to concede that Haraway's ideas are not for the impatient reader *and* easy enough that, with hard work, one can appreciate what she is up to. This book is a collection of writings since "Animal Psychology and the Nature Economy of the Body Politic: A Political Physiology of Dominance" in 1978 to "The Biopolitics of Postmodern Bodies: Determinations of Self in Human Society" in 1989—in other words, her work throughout the decade of the 1980s. This fact is not incidental. The 1980s were the decade when those concerned with the news of the world were faced with a rising tide of conservativism and global unrest. Critical social theorists the world over had to rethink what they might have begun but not yet achieved. In Europe, for example, Michel Foucault's writings in the 1970s spawned attention to a very different theoretical vocabulary, while *Thousand Plateaus* in 1987 [1980] by Gilles Deleuze and Félix Guattari puzzled readers evermore than anything Haraway wrote. Then too, Slavoj Žižek's *Cynicism as a Form of Ideology* in 1989 seemed impossible to ignore. The 1980s were also when Juergen Habermas's major two volume work, *Theory of Communicative Behavior* (1984, 1987 [1981]), appeared—but also when there were new departures in feminist social theory from Nancy Hartsock's *Theory of Power for Women* (1987), Gayatri Spivak's *Can the Subaltern Speak?* (1988), Trinh T. Minh-ha's *Woman, Native, Other: Postcoloniality and Feminism* (1989), Patricia Hill Collins, *Black Feminism* (1990), others. Why all this in an era of rampant political conservativism—Ronald Reagan in the US and Margaret Thatcher in the UK who were partners in giving birth to neoliberalism and its ludicrous theory of global capitalism. While also in the 1980s, there was rebellion and political turmoil in Iraq, Sudan, Uganda, Laos, and elsewhere not to mention the rise of Al Qaeda and other jihadist movements. But also at the end of the decade the Velvet Revolution in East Europe, the defeat of the Soviets in Afghanistan, and the fall of the USSR and the end of the Cold War in 1991. To be brief, the 1980s were a decade of bouleversements in the global order made all the more chaotic by the countervailing conservativisms of the day. The world was turning topsy-turvy, which may be said to be a kind of global order that requires and encourages new thinking—new theories.

In the midst of all this, in 1985, Haraway published an early version of *A Cyborg Manifesto: Science, Technology, and Socialist-Feminism in the Late Twentieth Century*—her best-known paper that stands as the center-piece of *Simians, Cyborgs, and Women* in 1991. (It might be helpful to remind that "Simians," monkeys and apes, completes the link of this book to *Primate Visions*.) "The Cyborg Manifesto" was circulated as, in effect, *samizdat*, before publication in 1985 in *The Socialist Review*. In *Simians, Cyborgs, and Women* in 1991 it appears as Chapter 8 in the important Part Three, *Different Politics for Inappropriate/d Others*, alongside the just as often read Chapter 9, "Situated Knowledges: The Science Question in Feminism and the Privilege of Partial Perspective." The latter, unsurprisingly appeared in *Feminist Studies* (in 1988) and, indeed, takes up what some (if not Haraway) might refer to as woman's standpoint in relation to science, and begins (again unsurprisingly) with the toxic nature of the key word in overwrought dualistic social sciences—the word that academic and activist feminist inquiry has repeatedly tried to come to terms with

---

103 *Ibid*, 381–382. Emphasis added.

what *we* might mean by the curious and inescapable term "objectivity." "We have used a lot of toxic ink and trees processed into paper decrying what *they* have meant and how it hurts *us*."[104] *We/they/us*! *They* are those who take scientific objectivity for granted.

> The only people who end up actually *believing* and, goddess forbid, *acting* on the ideological doctrines of disembodied scientific objectivity enshrined in elementary textbooks and technoscience booster literature are non-scientists, including a few very trusting philosophers.[105]

Haraway always means what she writes and says—even when, as here, more than a few elements in a single sentence might well confound the speed reader, if she slows down enough to ponder.

Then, in the same paragraph, Haraway compounds the riddle that from time to time riddles her statements with a relatively plain theorem: "Gender, race, the world itself—all seem just effects of warp speeds in the play of signifier in a cosmic force field. All truths become warp speed effects in a hyper-real space of simulations." This may not be everyone's cup of literary tea but, words aside, your average teenager probably gets it because she is on her phone where hyper- or sur-real truths (alleged truths) travel around the globe at warp speeds. Haraway first wrote these words well-before the cyber-age of cell-phones, social media, and the like, but she was able to anticipate such a state of affairs because of her principled and well-argued notion that "objectivity" is, if not nonsense, an illusion. If so, then everything moves about at warp-speed—at impossibly great velocities—that can only be imagined. Hence, sooner-or-later, all scientific "truths" are a special case of science fiction.

Another way to put this is that all signifiers—whether uttered, or written, or otherwise conveyed—once sent out into the world are free-floating meanings searching a recipient somewhere in a force-field all around that is so vast and indefinite as to be cosmic. We live, and move, and have our being in a cosmos of possibilities where no *object* is definitely grounded—which means that our *subjecthood* is necessarily and constantly subjected to force fields that are cosmic because in principle their force is cosmic, global, or transcendental.

Or we are who and what we are because in some locale, or another, some others attend to the self we offer, as Erving Goffman put it to our performances of who we think we are in that instance. Apart from his *Presentation of Self in Everyday Life* (1959), Goffman dealt with this not-always-recognized fact of life in many other writings like *Interaction Ritual*, where he makes an observation particularly apt to Haraway's view of meanings and the question how to propose, or search, for them:

> Serious action is a serious ride, and rides of this kind are all but arranged out of everyday life. As suggested, every individual engages in consequential acts, but most of these are not problematic, and when they are (as when career decisions are made that affect one's life) the determination and settlement of these bets will often come after decades, and by then will be obscured by payoffs from many of his other gambles. Action, on the other hand, brings chance-taking and resolution into the same heated moment of experience; the events of action inundate the momentary now with their implications for the life that follows.[106]

---

104 Donna Haraway, "Situated Knowledges," in Haraway, *Simians, Cyborgs, and Women: The Reinvention of Nature* (Routledge, 1991), 183.
105 *Ibid*, 184.
106 Erving Goffman, *Interaction Ritual: Essays on Face-to-Face Behavior* (Anchor Books, 1967), 261–262. For a discussion, see Charles Lemert, "Goffman," in Lemert and Ann Branaman *The Goffman Reader* (Blackwell Publishers, 1997), especially x–xxi.

In a few words, whether by Haraway or Goffman, all attempts to speak the truth of things—especially things like gender, race, the world itself—speed away into an open cosmos in the hopes that some others will take them in. Such a world cannot *ever* be reduced to objects and subjects or dualisms of any kind.

Haraway's *Cyborg Manifesto* actually emphasizes this very point at its conclusion where, important to note, she treats the cyborg as an image:

> Cyborg imagery can help express two crucial arguments in this essay: *first*, the production of universal, totalizing theory is a major mistake that misses most of reality, probably always, but certainly now; and *second*, taking responsibility for the social relations of science and technology means refusing an anti-science metaphysics, a demonology of technology, and so means embracing the skillful task of reconstructing the boundaries of daily life, in partial connection with others, in communication with all of our parts. ... Cyborg imagery can suggest a way out of the maze of dualisms in which we have explained our bodies and our tools to ourselves. This is a dream not of a common language, but of a powerful infidel heteroglossia. It is an imagination of a feminist speaking in tongues to strike fear into the circuits of the super savers of the new right. It means both building and destroying machines, identities, categories, relationships, space stories. Though both are bound in the spiral dance, I would rather be a cyborg than a goddess.[107]

For those who find Haraway difficult to understand, they should ponder this passage—metaphoric yes, but apt to her points of rejecting dualism, and embracing the warp speed of the multiplicities in and with which we must live.

With this passage in mind, the best way to understand "A Cyborg Manifesto: Science, Technology, and Socialist-Feminism in the Late Twentieth Century" is to take notice of the headers for its sections:

1. An Iconic Dream of Common Language for Women in The Integrated Circuit
2. Fractured Identities
3. The Informatics of Domination
4. The 'Homework' Economy Outside 'Home'
5. Women in the Integrated Circuit
6. Cyborgs: A Myth of Political Identity

The first conglomerate of issues—*1. An Iconic Dream of Common Language for Women in The Integrated Circuit*—, when translated into a somewhat more common theory-speak, have to do with the fact that the cyborg pays no heed to Western culture's origin story of "the myth of original unity, fullness, bliss, a terror represented by the phallic mother from whom all humans must separate."[108] The irony, she argues, is that the cyborg overcomes the liberal ideology of the radically individual self. Instead, "the cyborg is resolutely committed to partiality, irony, intimacy, and perversity."

Lines like these help us to understand why Haraway's theory is puzzling. We who would dare read such an essay have been born into and brought up in this culture of the radical individual who inhabits our dreams of what we are meant to be. These were the days of The Marlboro Man and Ayn Rand and their well-advertised descendants. It is very difficult

---

107 Haraway, "A Cyborg Manifesto: Science, Technology, and Socialist-Feminism in the Late Twentieth Century," in Haraway, *Simians, Cyborgs, and Women: The Reinvention of Nature* (Routledge, 1991), 181.
108 *Ibid*, 151. Quote just below same place.

to think of ourselves as partial, perverse, and ironic, because we have been taught to be individuals pure and simple—as a result, when all is said and done, we are not very good at intimacy. That is the way we are—allegedly less so with women but they, like generic men, have trouble sharing their innermost secrets. Goffman again—"some secrets must always remain secret, kept from others even from those we think of as close".[109] If a young woman once turned tricks to pay for college, she is unlikely to tell an adult partner or an employer.

Haraway then extends her argument by identifying the three crucial taken-for-granted boundaries that must be and, in the world as it is, are being broken down.[110] They are, first, that between nature and culture. There is no boundary here. We humanoids are animals. Nothing could be more obvious, even as it is denied. Here she inscribes a remark that is, in its way, hilarious: "Teaching modern Christian creationism should be fought as a form of child-abuse."[111] In a word, we have not risen "above" our animal nature. The second "leaky" distinction is implied in the first—that between animal and human; which in turn leads to the third—that between physical and non-physical. If we are bound to nature in our animate being then, as Fernand Braudel showed years ago,[112] we are close to rocks and water. If this makes sense, the next section makes better sense.

2. *Fractured Identities* fits more easily into feminist theories—especially those associated with Anna Julia Cooper and Patricia Hill Collins. Still, one must remember that Haraway's is an essay in feminist theory. For her, in this instance, it is women whose identities are fractured. "Painful fragmentation among feminists (not to mention among women) along every possible fault line has made the concept of *woman* elusive, an excuse for the matrix of women's dominations of each other."[113] Later she adds that this was the time when women must confront all the dominations they face, especially those of race, gender, sexuality, and class. Again Haraway speaks as a member:

> None of 'us' have any longer the symbolic or material capability of dictating the shape of reality to any of 'them'. Or at least 'we' cannot claim innocence from practicing such dominations. ... Cyborg feminists have to argue that 'we' do not want any more natural matrix of unity and that no construction is whole.[114]

Such a remark might well offend upbeat liberal/progressive social theorists or theorists of all kinds, even feminists seeking relief from oppression. For Haraway, there can be no *manifesto* without an honest *diagnosis* of the crisis at hand.

Then, at the end of her discussion of fractured identities, she takes apart socialist feminism as, in effect, a caricature of the very social justice Marxism claims to describe—this by excluding race or treating it as an add-on, an after-thought. In the same place, she takes on white radical feminism.

> Embarrassed silence about race among radical and socialist feminists was one major, devastating political consequence. History and polyvocality disappear into political

---

109 Erving Goffman, "Information Control and Personal Identity," in Goffman, *Stigma: Notes on the Management of Personal Identity* (Simon & Schuster, 1963), chapter 2.
110 *Ibid*, 152–153.
111 *Ibid*, 152.
112 Fernand Braudel, *Civilization and Capitalism, Vol 1: The Structures of Everyday Life* (Harper & Row, 1981). Also, Braudel, *The Mediterranean and the Mediterranean World in the Age of Philip II* (Harper & Row, 1973).
113 Haraway, "Cyborg Manifesto," *ibid*, 155.
114 *Ibid*, 157.

taxonomies that try to establish genealogies. There is no structural room for race (or for much else) in theory claiming to reveal the construction of the category of woman and social group women as a unified or totalizable whole.[115]

The fractured identities section ends with a marvelously stunning thought: "Some differences are playful; some are poles of world historical domination. 'Epistemology' is about knowing the difference."[116]

The following section, *3. The Informatics of Domination*, is it seems an elaboration of what Haraway began at the end of 2. A Cyborg Manifesto. "I argue," she writes, "for a politics rooted in claims about fundamental changes in the nature of class, race, and gender in an emerging system of world order analogous in its novelty and scope to that created by industrial capitalism; we are living through a movement from an organic, industrial capitalism to a polymorphous information system—from all work to play, a deadly game."[117] *Play*, again! Here it is plain that play is not frivolous. It is deadly serious. Everything, one may say, is loose, without a singular trajectory, without a particular or strong foundation. Everything grows every which way. One is reminded of Gilles Deleuze and Felix Guattari who saw the rhizome as a deep underground growth of plant and animal life without roots—limbs, leaves, branches that grow in every possible direction. In respect to human communications, a "rhizome ceaselessly establishes connections between semiotic chains, organizations of power, and circumstances relative to the arts, sciences, and social struggles."[118] Among social things, the hierarchical dominations give way to networks—hence, what Haraway calls the informatics of domination, in respect to which she boldly charts the differences in two columns that compare the older white, male, capitalistic hierarchy with the newer informatics of domination.[119] The white, male, and capitalist hierarchically driven cultures begin in representation and proceed through the bourgeois novel thereby creating deep *roots* for organic divisions of labor—the nature/culture *dualisms*, racial chains of being to sex, labor, mind, to white capitalist *patriarchy* (and more in the betweens). By contrast, Haraway's informatics of domination begins in simulation and *science fiction* and the cybernetics of efficient labor, then neo-imperialism, to fields of difference, to genetic engineering (instead of sex), then to *robotics* (instead of labor), *artificial intelligence* (instead of mind), and informatics of domination (instead of white capitalist patriarchy).[120] When Haraway charts the two lists, some thirty-two comparative elements presented side-by-side, she leaves the reader breathless with a mixture of excitement and confusion. The important thing is to accept that this is not a bad/good comparison of cultural elements nurtured by white capitalist patriarchy compared to those leading to the informatics of domination. They are *both* about domination. Informatics may be in some sense *better* but, again, the informatics of domination is rhizomatic. Strictly speaking, "informatics" is the study of how information and technology affect human behavior, for better or worse. This precisely is what Haraway writes about in respect to domination, in general, and to women, in particular.

After this, she discusses how informatics is at play [*sic*] on two associated topics: *4. The 'Homework Economy' Outside the 'Home'* and *5. Women in the Integrated Circuit*.

---

115 *Ibid*, 160.
116 *Ibid*, 161.
117 *Ibid*.
118 Gilles Deleuze and Felix Guattari, *A Thousand Plateaus: Capitalism and Schizophrenia* (University of Minnesota Press, 1987 [1980]), 7.
119 Haraway, "A Cyborg Manifesto," ibid, 161–162.
120 In my presentation of Haraway's two columns (161–162), the emphases are mine—meant to highlight the more striking features of the different cultures of domination.

The former, quite simply, concerns how the new informatic, and post-industrial, economy changes the most basic issues for women who were once confined to *homework* that has become *housework*. Haraway starts: "The extreme mobility of capital and the emerging international division of labor are intertwined with the emergence of new collectives and the weakening of familiar groups."[121] She cites a 1983 conference paper on "the homework economy" on the feminization of work that was previously done mostly by men, work that under informatics made possible "at home" by new communications technologies that, yes, allowed skilled work in the home but, also, aggravated the difference between male and female wages. Among the particular cases of this change, and its consequences is, for example, that "teenage women in industrialized areas of the Third world find themselves the sole or major source of cash wages for their families, while access to land is ever more problematic."[122] Examples of change like this one radically affect family structures, but also sex and reproduction practices—a change so ubiquitous that, Haraway observes, the speculum allows women private diagnostic access to their vaginas and freedom from male dominated medical and family practices.

With Haraway, nothing is ever standard. In section 5. *Women in the Integrated Circuit*, the main part of the discussion is presented as, again, a series of lists of issues in the new economy. One supposes she is composing here a written version of the circuits in which women find themselves (or would if they had read her essay). For example:

Home: Women-headed households, serial monogamy, flight of men, old women alone, technology of domestic work, paid housework, re-emergence of home sweat-shops, home-based businesses and telecommuting, electronic cottage, urban homelessness, migration, module architecture, reinforced (simulated) nuclear family, intense domestic violence.[123]

There are no verbs or acute modifiers—just a list of the way things are becoming. Remember, Haraway was writing in the mid- to late-1980s, very early in the everyday life effects of cultural informatics, yet she gets the historical drift of changes that today, some four decades later in the 2020s, are evident to almost everyone alert to the world one must live in and with. Haraway goes to do the similar with the *Market*, the *Paid Work-Place*, the *State*, *Schools*, *Clinic-hospitals*, *Churches*. To illustrate, again, take her informatics diagram for one structural network that would seem to be immune to informatics:

Churches: Electronic fundamentalist 'super-saver' preachers solemnizing the union of electronic capital and automatic fetish gods; intensified importance of churches in resisting the militarized state; central struggle over women's meanings and authority in religion; continued relevance of spirituality, intertwined with sex and health, in political struggle.

You'd have to be dead-set against anything Donna Haraway says (as some are), not to be struck, even moved, by her stochastic descriptions of the world as it has become for women, to be sure. Even a man, like me, who happens also to be an ordained minister, has seen it all. Hereabouts there is an enterprise that calls itself the *Vox Church*. It started not long ago when its minister rented New Haven's largest public theatre for Sunday services. Within a

---

121 *Ibid*, 166.
122 *Ibid*, 167.
123 *Ibid*, 170. Just below, the informatic network of *Churches*, is on 172.

few years it has grown to nine campuses in Connecticut and Massachusetts plus online programming that offers preaching of the kind Haraway describes, excellent Christianized rock music, and other entertainments including revivals in all campuses throughout the weeks. After all these lists and theoretical declamations, Haraway ends this section with a confession: "I am conscious of the odd perspective provided by my historical position—a PhD in biology for an Irish Catholic girl was made possible by Sputnik's impact on US national science-education policy."[124]

For those who may have followed Haraway through the thickets of her own complicated cultural informatics, the final section 6. *Cyborgs: A Myth of Political Identity* can be no more than a summary of the threads she has thrown down throughout the essay. One can only repeat part of her already quoted conclusion:

> This is a dream not of a common language, but of a powerful infidel heteroglossia. It is an imagination of a feminist speaking in tongues to strike fear into the circuits of the super savers of the new right. It means both building and destroying machines, identities, categories, relationships, space stories. Though both are bound in the spiral dance, I would rather be a cyborg than a goddess.[125]

Anyone not intrigued, even moved, by this may well be in the wrong business.

Kimberlé Williams Crenshaw: Race and Gender at an Intersection

To begin, important to say, that the earlier presentation on Patricia Hill Collins required covering the central points of both Kimberlé Crenshaw and Gloria Anzaldúa, two very different but equally important feminist theorists. Though each has been reasonably well-introduced in the Collins section, each deserves the independent consideration that follows.

Kimberlé Crenshaw (1959–) was born in Canton, Ohio. After studying at Canton McKinley High School, she went on to Cornell University where she majored in government and Africana Studies. In 1984 she received the J.D. at Harvard Law School, then the year following she earned the LL.M from the University of Wisconsin Law School. After Wisconsin she began her teaching career in 1986 at UCLA School of Law where she remains today, even as she simultaneously holds a professorship at Columbia School of Law (since 1995). At UCLA Crenshaw joined the Critical Race Theory (CRT) movement that had roots in the post-Civil Rights Movement in the 1970s. The classic work in this early period is Derrick Bell's *Race, Racism, and American Law* first published in 1972 with many subsequent editions through the years. Bell was, therefore, the leading figure in one of two major introductions to CRT—*Critical Race Theory: The Key Writings That Formed the Movement* in 1995, for which Crenshaw was one of the editors.[126] Richard Delgado was another early leader in the CRT movement along with Jean Stefancic with whom he would publish several books on Critical Race Theory including their own version of *Critical Race Theory: An Introduction* in 2012.[127]

---

124 *Ibid*, 173.
125 Again: *ibid*, 181.
126 Kimberlé Crenshaw, Neil Gotanda, Gary Peller, Kendal Thomas, *Critical Race Theory: The Key Writings That Formed the Movement* (The New Press, 1995).
127 Richard Delgado and Jean Stefancic, *Critical Race Theory: An Introduction* (New York University Press, 2012), 2nd Edition. [The first edition appeared in 2001 and the third in 2017.]

Though Crenshaw was but 27 when she began at UCLA she fit naturally into Critical Race Theory—a relationship made all the more certain when she published her first two, still widely read, articles just another few years after finishing graduate school and beginning at UCLA. They were: first, in 1989, "Demarginalizing the Intersection of Race and Sex," published at the *University of Chicago Legal Forum*; and, second, in 1991, "Mapping the Margins: Intersectionality, Identity Theory, and Violence against Women of Color," at *Stanford Law Review*. These two articles could be said to have consolidated her precocious reputation in the Critical Race Theory movement, even as they were the beginning of her writing on intersectionality, which, of course, went beyond this movement to mark her as a prominent scholar in her own right—hence, the Columbia Law School appointment a few more years on.

Crenshaw's "Demarginalizing the Intersection of Race and Sex" in 1989 was her first and, some might say, clearest statement of intersectionality.[128] Elsewhere, she examines the traffic intersection metaphor,[129] previously introduced in the Collins section above. The article itself retains, of course, the race/gender problem, but examines it in respect to three important legal cases, each illustrating a difficult aspect of the dilemma that, unless Black women can bring and win cases for their rights, the courts will continue to treat race and gender as quite distinct legal matters. "Demarginalizing the Intersection of Race and Sex" proceeds to examine three cases bearing on this dilemma.

She introduces her argument by announcing the title to a 1982 Black Feminist book: *All the Women Are White; All the Blacks Are Men, But Some of Us are Brave*.[130] After which, she writes: "I have chosen this title as a point of departure in my efforts to develop a Black feminist criticism because it sets forth a problematic consequence of the tendency to treat race and gender as mutually exclusive categories of experience and analysis."[131] Then right off, Crenshaw begins with the first, and most important of the three cases: *DeGraffenreid v. GENERAL MOTORS ASSEMBLY DIV., ETC., 413 F. Supp. 142 (E.D. Mo. 1976)*.[132] In 1976, Emma DeGraffenreid led the complaint of five Black women against General Motors for their having been discriminated against as Black women during a 1970 layoff in which they lost their jobs. The defendants argued dismissal on the basis of the Company's seniority policy under which General Motors claimed, remarkably, that because they hired Black men and White women they never categorically hired Black women. The Court summarily reject Emma Graffenreid's argument. Among other judgements the Court said:

> While it does not have the force of *res adjudicata* it must be noted that defendant General Motors and the Equal Employment Opportunity Commission entered into a consent decree on January 9, 1973, with respect to the hiring of female employees. ... To the

---

128 Crenshaw, "Demarginalizing the Intersection of Race and Sex: A Black Feminist Critique of Antidiscrimination Doctrine, Feminist Theory and Antiracist Politics," *University of Chicago Legal Forum* 1:8 (1989).
129 Crenshaw, "The urgency of intersectionality," TED talk, November 14, 2016, on YouTube / @ https://www.ted.com/talks/kimberle_crenshaw_the_urgency_of_intersectionality?language=en
130 Akasha Gloria Hull; Patricia Bell-Scott, Barbara Smith, eds., *All the Women Are White, All the Blacks Are Men, But Some of Us Are Brave: Black Women's Studies* (Feminist Press, 1982).
131 Kimberlé Crenshaw, "Demarginalizing the Intersection of Race and Sex: A Black Feminist Critique of Antidiscrimination Doctrine, Feminist Theory and Antiracist Politics," *University of Chicago Legal Forum* 1:8 (1989), 139.
132 Perhaps it is worth saying that this is how court cases are identified; here with "E.D.MO" meaning Eastern District of Missouri.

Court, this is a further indication that the seniority practices of defendants do not discriminate on the basis of sex.[133]

Needless to say the Court made the same judgment with respect to the Company's racial hiring on the basis that it had hired Black men. Crenshaw concludes: "The district court granted summary judgment for the defendant, rejecting the plaintiffs' attempt to bring a suit not on behalf of Blacks or women, but specifically on behalf of Black women."[134] Again, Black women are left alone in the intersection between race and gender.

The second case is *Moore v Hughes Helicopters, Inc.* United States Court of Appeals, 9th Circuit (16 June 1983).[135] Crenshaw, writing as the lawyer entering her own critical brief on the Court, says:

> The Ninth Circuit noted approvingly: "... Moore had never claimed before the EEOC that she was discriminated against as a female, but only as a Black female .... [T]his raised serious doubts as to Moore's ability to adequately represent white female employees." The curious logic in Moore reveals not only the narrow scope of antidiscrimination doctrine and its failure to embrace intersectionality, but also the centrality of white female experiences in the conceptualization of gender discrimination.[136]

Here, the disqualifying argument is that Moore, a Black woman, never claimed to be representing white females at Hughes. Crenshaw's brilliance is in turning legal screws to tighten the legal discriminatory judgments against Black women.

The third case is *Payne v. Travenol Laboratories, Inc.,* 416 F. Supp. 248 (N.D. Miss. 1976)[137] which completes Crenshaw's triad of different intersectional cases, notably in a succinct summary of the three.

> In sum, several courts have proved unable to deal with intersectionality, although for contrasting reasons. In DeGraffenreid, the court refused to recognize the possibility of compound discrimination against Black women and analyzed their claim using the employment of white women as the historical base. As a consequence, the employment experiences of white women obscured the distinct discrimination that Black women experienced. Conversely, in Moore, the court held that a Black woman could not use statistics reflecting the overall sex disparity in supervisory and upper-level labor jobs because she had not claimed discrimination as a woman, but "only" as a Black woman. The court would not entertain the notion that discrimination experienced by Black women is indeed sex discrimination-provable through disparate impact statistics on women. Finally, courts, such as the one in Travenol, have held that Black women cannot represent an entire class of Blacks due to presumed class conflicts in cases where sex additionally disadvantaged Black women. As a result, in the few cases where Black women

---

133 Emma DEGRAFFENREID et al., Plaintiffs, v. GENERAL MOTORS ASSEMBLY DIVISION, ST. LOUIS, a corporation, et al., Defendants United States District Court, E.D. Missouri May 4, 1976, 1441; @ https://casetext.com/case/degraffenreid-v-general-motors-assembly-div
134 Crenshaw, "Demarginalizing the Intersection of Race and Sex," 141.
135 See https://casetext.com/case/moore-v-hughes-helicopters-inc-a-div-of-summa-corp
136 Crenshaw, "Demarginalizing," 144.
137 See *Payne v. Travenol Laboratories, Inc., 416 F. Supp. 248 (N.D. Miss. 1976).* US District Court for the Northern District of Mississippi - 416 F. Supp. 248 (February 19, 1976) @ https://law.justia.com/cases/federal/district-courts/FSupp/416/248/1500534/

are allowed to use overall statistics indicating racially disparate treatment Black men may not be able to share in the remedy.[138]

I quote Crenshaw's words at length to demonstrate the degree to which she writes her own legal brief that is also critical social theory.

This fact of her method is apparent in the remainder of "Demarginalizing the Intersection of Race and Sex" where, first, under the startling header, "The Significance of Doctrinal Treatment of Intersectionality." In the three cases presented, the Courts all took a doctrinal attitude toward Black women that deprived them of both their distinctive race and gender identities. A Black woman, it seems obvious to say, is neither one nor the other, but both at once and inseparably. "Black women's Blackness or femaleness sometimes has placed their needs and perspectives at the margin of the feminist and Black liberationist agendas."[139] This upon reflection ignorant attitude is a profoundly uncritical dogma about how discrimination works—and, as she says, how feminist theory operates (even in 1989).

"Demarginalizing the Intersection of Race and Sex" ends in a long section under a header that paraphrases Sojourner Truth's famous line *Feminism and Black Women: Ain't We Women?* She quotes the seldom quoted passage in which Truth's line was first uttered in 1851: "Look at my arm! I have ploughed and planted and gathered into barns, and no man could head me—and ain't I a woman? I could work as much and eat as much as a man—when I could get it—and bear the lash as well! And ain't I a woman?"[140] One here sees that Sojourner Truth's 1851 speech was an early version of the categorical intersection which is as much about men as women and both of course about Blacks. Then a third section turns to Anna Julia Cooper whom in 1989 almost no one had read and studied: *When and Where I Enter: Integrating an Analysis of Sexism into Black Liberation Politics.* Sojourner Truth forced those who would read to attend to her gender and race by rebuking the feminist to whom she spoke in 1851, so Anna Julia Cooper did the same in her section in *A Voice from the South*, where she rebuked that Black clergy before whom she spoke in 1892. Crenshaw digs deep into the history of Black women in America to develop this first published statement of intersectionality. In both sections she makes many references to both legal case law and also recent political statements including Moynihan's regrettable 1965 report. To which she adds careful discussion of William Julius Wilson's *Truly Disadvantaged: The Inner-City, the Underclass, and Public Policy* in 1987 in which he corrected Moynihan's early thinking. (Years later, Moynihan repented.) Crenshaw's first article was remarkably textured both in covering the legal precedents and the feminist theories that enriched the notion of intersectionality. She does so with a definitive idea that seldom is found in a scholar's first paper. "Neither Black liberationist politics nor feminist theory can ignore the intersectional experiences of those whom the movements claim as their respective constituents."[141]

Though feminists like Patricia Hill Collins, also a precocious scholar when she started out, made important contributions to Crenshaw's thinking on intersectionality, criticisms were, to a degree, misplaced. Kimberlé Crenshaw is a lawyer who crossed over into feminist theory, as Patricia Hill Collins is a sociologist with an abiding commitment to feminist theory. Both are committed to a political activism that is a given in their scholarly work. And both from their earliest days pushed for a more structural approach to theories of Black

---

138 Crenshaw, "Demarginalizing," 148.
139 *Ibid*, 150.
140 *Ibid*, 153.
141 *Ibid*, 166.

women. For Collins this was natural, given her sociological training. For Crenshaw this was, in a different way, natural given her training in the law where all legal statements are "briefs," in the sense of the points entailed in the case at hand. Crenshaw's structural thinking became more evident in her second article in 1991 where she clearly insists that while identity politics are part of the game, in the end the score is settled structurally: "The problem with identity politics is not that it fails to transcend difference, as some critics charge, but rather the opposite—that it frequently conflates or ignores intragroup differences."[142] Not full throated sociology but moving that way. Black feminists like Crenshaw and Collins teach others who profess to be social theorists of one or another kind. Perhaps Crenshaw didn't know about Collins's matrix of domination, but she wrote in such a way that moved Collins beyond her original concept to her own more completely sociological interpretation of intersectionality. Too often scholars in the social sciences fail to work as, for example, astrophysicists must—always without exception reading, challenging, rethinking, rewriting their own work.[143] Perhaps they together, along with all their colleagues, might in a weird way be making Black Feminist Theory a core aspect of a new astrophysics of the social world as it truly is.

Gloria Evangelina Anzaldúa: Borderlands and the New Mestiza

Gloria Evangelina Anzaldúa (1942–2004) was born in Harlingen, Texas in the Rio Grande Valley of South Texas—in precisely the kind of place she writes of as Borderlands/*La Frontera*. Anzaldúa was obviously a Chicana in a white dominated land. Though her family owned land, they lost what wealth they had to the ugly mischief of white people in the Valley. As a result, she was more than acutely aware of her differences from others—a sensibility made all the more acute by the awful effect of the sudden onset of puberty at age six and the embarrassment of trying to "hide the persistent pain, the bloody rags, the menstrual odors" from school mates and teachers—as AnaLouise Keating notes.[144] For Keating, Anzaldúa's childhood bodily affliction was just the first among many differences—her borderland birth, her skin color, her languages, and, as she came of age, her sexuality, and more.

School abuses notwithstanding, Anzaldúa graduated as valedictorian of her high school class in Edinburgh, Texas before studying at the University of Texas Rio Grande Valley (also in Edinburgh, Texas). She graduated college with majors in English, Art, and Secondary Education, after which she took an MA in English and Education at the University of Texas Austin. Anzaldúa taught school for a while before moving to California to pursue her writing career and teaching at San Francisco State, UC Santa Cruz, and other universities. She had begun political engagement in Austin, a lifelong commitment that is even evident between the lines of her writings.

Anzaldúa's first important book appeared in 1981—*This Bridge Called My Back: Writings By Radical Women of Color*, edited with Cherríe Moraga. As AnaLouise Keating has shown in *The Anzaldúan Theory Handbook*, Gloria Anzaldúa was a prolific author who generously left her papers to an archive at the Nettie Lee Benson Latin American Collection in the University of Texas Austin Library—some 128 feet of materials, a truly astonishing

---

142 Kimberlé Crenshaw, "Mapping the Margins: Intersectionality, Identity Theory, and Violence against Women of Color," *Stanford Law Review* 43:6 (1991), 1241–99: 1242.
143 For a challenging and instructional presentation of how astrophysicists work, see the film *Einstein's Quantum Riddle* (NOVA and PBS, 2019).
144 AnaLouise Keating, *The Anzaldúan Theory Handbook* (Duke University Press, 2022), 15–16. Please note that Keating here and elsewhere quotes from Anzaldúa's unavailable writings. In this case, her "Autohistoria de la artista as a Young Girl."

collection.[145] This being said, the first book by Anzaldúa that one should read is *Borderlands/La Frontera: The New Mestiza* in 1987.

Borderlands/La Frontera is part prose/part poetry and part in English/part Spanish. But it is also the most unusual while also compelling social theory of, precisely, those like her, the New Mestizas. One selection from the beginning of the book says what one needs to know about her theory—a theory that is not always easy for monolingual readers seeking a straightforward standpoint theory to follow.

Beneath the iron sky
Mexican children kick their soccer ball across,
run after it, entering the U.S.

       I press my hand to the steel curtain—
   chainlink fence crowned with rolled barbed wire—
rippling from the sea where Tijuana touches San Diego
    unrolling over mountains
        and plains
          and deserts,
this "Tortilla Curtain" turning into *el río Grande*.
    flowing down to the flatlands
        of the Magic Valley of South Texas
    its mouth emptying into the Gulf.

1950, mile-long open wound
        dividing a *pueblo*, a culture, running down the length of my body,
staking fence rods in my flesh, splits me splits me
             me raja me raja

    This is my home
    this thin edge of
    barbwire.

    But the skin of the earth is seamless.
    The sea cannot be fenced,
el mar does not stop at borders.
To show the white man what she thought of his
        arrogance.
   Yemaya blew that wire fence down.

This land was Mexican once,
    was Indian always
    and is.
    And will be again.

Yo soy un puente tendido
    del mundo gabacho al del molado,
lo pasado me estirá pa' tras
y lo presente pa' 'delante.

---

[145] Keating, *ibid*, Chapter 5, "The Gloria Evangelina Anzaldúa Papers: Creation Story, Treasure Map, and More," and Chapter 6, "Anzaldúa's Archival Manuscripts: Overview, Insights, Annotations."

Que la Virgen de Guadalupe me cuide.
AY ay ay soy, mexicana de este lado.[146]

Right off, it is evident that Anzaldúa can make Donna Haraway's writing look plain and simple. The book as a whole is not just bilingual but also poetry that calls the reader into the very borderland culture of which she writes—an actual geographic place in the American Southwest where the new mestiza live.[147] Anzaldúa's *mestiza* is a quite intentional reworking of the word's original reference to European Spanish and American indigenous peoples. Also, it is important to remember, if you have not read the book, that throughout *Borderlands/La Frontera*, Anzaldúa intersperses Anglo English and Mexican Spanish to make the book itself *mestizan*. Anzaldúa obviously expands the meaning of the word in a way that locates the indigenous people in the Southwest with, and outside of, their ties to Mexican people. But that is not all! Many other qualities and persons are part of *mestiza* mix. She writes under the header *Una lucha de fronteras/A Struggle of Borders*:

> Because I, a *mestiza*,
> continually walk out of one culture
>   and into another
> because I am in all cultures at the same time.[148]

This is the lead verse in Chapter 7, *La conciencia de la mestiza/Toward a New Consciousness*. Anzaldúa follows immediately with a comment that should take the breath away from those who see intersectionality, even matrix of domination, as a celebration of differences some must deal with. Better, the verse suggests, is to see this new consciousness as, simply, the beginning of liberatory power. Concepts of this kind may well be just that, but they also must take into account the suffering those afflicted by so many differences must endure. Anzaldúa: "These numerous possibilities leave *la mestiza* floundering in unchartered seas."[149] Then immediately following on the same page:

> The *new mestiza* copes by developing a tolerance for contradictions, a tolerance for ambiguity. She learns to be an Indian in Mexican culture, to be Mexican from an Anglo point of view. She learns to juggle cultures. She has a plural personality, she operates in a pluralistic mode—nothing is thrust out, the bad and the ugly, nothing abandoned.

Later, she adds: "The struggle is inner: Chicano, *indio*, American Indian, *mojado*, *mexicano*, immigrant Latino, Anglo in power, working class Anglo, Black, Asian—our psyches resemble the bordertowns and are populated by the same people."[150]

Then Anzaldúa lists and discusses the range of contradictions *a mestiza* can, and often must, work-through—living in the dark with no country and no homeland; being indigenous; like corn, being a product of cross breeding; enduring the loss of dignity and respect under machismo rule; as Chicanos needing white society to accept that we are different but human, and that we are visible; being the *mestizo* and queer at the same time while pointing to an evolutionary continuum; having divided loyalties such that many men and women of color do not

---

146 Anzaldúa, "The Homeland, Aztlán / *El otro México*," *Borderlands/La Frontera* (San Francisco: spinsters/aunt lute), 2–3.
147 Grammar notwithstanding here *the new mestiza* is a category of women; hence the plural verb "live".
148 Anzaldúa, *Borderlands/La Frontera*, 77.
149 *Ibid*, 79. [Quote just following same place]
150 *Ibid*, 87.

want to have dealings with white people; and more.[151] Not only does the book invite in those who are willing to experience the *mestizo* way, but, for the empathetic, it also stirs and juggles the heart. Another's experience of Anzaldúa's world may not be the same. Even so, the experience of others might be emotionally and intellectually similar enough to teach social theorists just how unfathomably the sometimes hidden states of mind and life are for others—including those others who may be caught in a matrix of many vectors. Anzaldúa turns academic social-psychology and its affines into a scientific joke. Again, experience on the ground is the soil from which honest theory arises. And no one has planted their ideas more deeply in a geographic locale as has Anzaldúa.

Not withstanding her enormous archives of which AnaLouise Keating writes, much of Anzaldúa's published work is collectively done with others. Of these *This Bridge Called My Back: Writings By Radical Women of Color*, edited with Cherríe Moraga, is exceptionally important—in part because it appeared in 1981 before anything like what is all-too-simply called women of color feminism had come fully into its own. It is also important because, date of origin aside, it is still today in the 2020s perhaps the best anthology of texts by authors who do not always come to mind when one is searching for writings by feminists who may or may not be *mestizan* but are in a borderland situation—queer, Asian American, Puerto Rican, Native American in urban ghettos, and otherwise radical feminists.[152] Included among the less familiar are Toni Cade Bambara, as well as the Black Feminist Statement of the Combahee River Collective, Nellie Wong, Audre Lorde. Still another special quality of this book is its expression of understanding of others who live with or have lived through dangerous times. Anzaldúa writes with emphasis in her foreword to the 1983 second edition of *This Bridge Call My Back*: "Women, let's not let the danger of the journey and the vastness of the territory scare us—let us look forward and open paths in these woods."[153]

Also, strange though it may be to say so, it is as if Anzaldúa's ghost co-wrote AnaLouise Keating's *The Anzaldúan Theory Handbooks* in 2022. Anzaldúa had long before succumbed to diabetes. Yet Keating so faithfully (one might even say, lovingly) represented her that she reasonably can be thought of as, if not a primary source, more than a secondary source. Then too it is important to mention the book they edited together in Anzaldúa's last years, *this bridge we call home: radical visions for transformation* in 2002. Anzaldúa's contribution is short but pungent. In "(Un)natural bridges, (Un) safe places" in *this bridge we call home*, she writes: "While *This Bridge Called My Back* displaced whiteness, *this bridge we call home* carries this displacement further. It questions the terms *white* and *women of color* by showing that whiteness may not be applied to all whites, as some possess women-of-color consciousness, just as some women-of-color bear white consciousness."[154] This we now know is a very important bridge to cross.

Excursus: Feminist Theories as the New Astrophysics of Social Things

Astrophysics? Why this, one might ask? Too much a play on words? Too cute perhaps? Perhaps, but think again about what is going on with these feminists from Anna Julia

---

151 This list of experiences and thoughts of the mestizo people is part direct quotation and part paraphrase of Anzaldúa's main points at *ibid*, 80–88.
152 Cherríe Moraga and Gloria Anzaldúa, eds., *This Bridge Called My Back: Writings by Radical Women of Color* (New York: Kitchen Table/Women of Color Press, 1983 [1981]). See the book's short self-composed autographical paragraphs, 246–250.
153 *Ibid*, v.
154 Gloria Anzaldúa and AnaLouise Keating, eds., *this bridge we call home: radical visions for transformation* (Routledge, 2002), 2.

Cooper to Gloria Anzaldúa and now, next, Judith Butler. As I said earlier, they all work with a consciously patient regard for all others who work on similar matters while, also, looking at those quite beyond feminisms—primatologists, ethnographers, poststructuralists, historians, psychoanalysts, more.

One should never forget that, again for an oft mentioned, example, E=mc², does more than require an unfathomably long and, to the amateur, inscrutable mathematic discourse. It also entails a penetrating, almost poetic, imagination about worlds so far beyond seeing that it was only until most recently that they became visible with the eye of NASA's Webb Telescope which allowed astrophysicists and cosmologists actually to see the ice-laden rings around Saturn. Some of them were surprised to learn that those rings contain the atomic elements of life. Astrophysics as such requires much more than mere quantoid imagination. The late twentieth and early twenty-first century feminists who may be said to be in the tradition of Anna Julia Cooper's and Patricia Hill Collin's matrix of domination theory of the social world and its oppressions were, and are, at least as wildly imaginative, even deeply poetic, as were Albert Einstein or Werner Heisenberg and the many remarkable others who followed or contested their ideas.

Then too, in the long run, feminists came to a crucial point exemplified by Sandra Harding, Gloria Anzaldúa and Judith Butler and others of similar theoretical ingenuity. Their point, so to speak, was that feminism as such *and* feminist theory had to rethink both the term and the practice in ways that saw the feminist stars as cast in a surrounding space that hitherto had been unimaginable—again a link to astrophysics itself which has always held that micro-particles obey the same laws as stellar ones. The more than small, invisible atoms of which all life—human, simian, bacterial, vegetable—is constituted to obey the same beyond-logical rules of motion, order, and being as stellar things. Otherwise, the NASA astrophysicists would not have been able to imagine the possibility of extra-terrestrial life in Saturn's rings. Nor, years earlier, the 1989 Voyager 2 fly-bys of Neptune, the outermost planet in our solar system some 2.8 billion miles from our Sun, would not have become visible to earth-bound eyes. Near or far, we now know which of the planetary gases contain the elements necessary to the *possibility* of biologically vital beings. Life itself, even certain elements of the universe, may be strewn hither and yon. The small and the grand are part and parcel of all stuff, even living stuff.

This is why feminist theorists have, in many ways, led the way among those who think about social things in attacking and dismissing, but also deconstructing and rethinking the micro-macro/subject-object and all other dichotomies of the kind. None more so than Judith Butler:

> If there is a fear that, by no longer being able to take for granted the subject, its gender, its sex, or its materiality, feminism will founder, it might be wise to consider the political consequences of keeping in their place the very premises that have tried to secure our subordination from the start.[155]

In other words, this kind of social physics must not take-for-granted any particular social thing or thought that ignores the macro force of subordination which must be rethought as a political reality free of constraining dichotomies. Social things, small or large, near or far, are ever and always more frozen than Neptune, which interestingly is warmer than Saturn more than 2 billion miles closer to the Sun, our home fire—mysteries abound.

---

155 Judith Butler, "Contingent Foundations: Feminism and the Question of 'Postmodernism'," in *Feminists Theorize the Political*, edited by Judith Butler and Joan Scott (Routledge 1992) [1991]), 19. Butler's insistence

Judith Butler: Gender Trouble and the Politics of Queer Analytics

Judith Butler (1956-) was born in Cleveland, to Jewish parents. They made sure that she enjoyed the benefit of Hebrew School and that she was otherwise steeped at a young age in Jewish philosophy and ethics. Butler attended the more radical-than-thou Bennington College in Vermont for a year or so. After which she moved on to Yale where she completed her BA then the PhD in 1984. She taught at Wesleyan, George Washington, and Johns Hopkins universities before accepting a position at the University of California Berkeley where she remains today. In 2002, Butler accepted the Spinoza Chair of Philosophy at the University of Amsterdam, just one of many prestigious positions and lectureships she has held worldwide.

Like others of her generation (and younger), Butler began her writing life with a book and article prelude to what was to come. First, in 1987 she published her 1984 Yale dissertation as *Subjects of Desire: Hegelian Reflections on Twentieth-Century France* with Columbia University Press. Then, the year following, she published an article which sowed the seeds of what would later blossom—"Performative Acts and Gender Constitution: An Essay in Phenomenology and Feminist Theory" in 1988.[156] Striking though *Subjects in Desire* was in its study of France's Hegelian moment, "Performative Acts and Gender Constitution" was itself a kind of phenomenology. In the article Butler broadened the range of her sources by turning to Anglo-American philosophers like John Searle's "speech act" theory and, even, to George Herbert Mead's symbolic interactionist crypto-phenomenology, among others. This to supplement Hegel, Merleau-Ponty, and especially Simone de Beauvoir–whose famous line begins the article: "One is not born, but rather becomes a woman"—a statement that Butler commented on in order to plant the early roots of her fecund theory of gender:

> When Beauvoir claims that "woman" is a historical idea and not a natural fact, she clearly underscores the distinction between sex, as biological facticity, and gender, as the cultural interpretation or signification of that facticity. To be female is, according to that distinction, a facticity which has no meaning, but to be a woman is to have become a woman, to compel the body to conform to an historical idea of "woman," to induce the body to become a cultural sign, to materialize oneself in obedience to an historically delimited possibility, and to do this as a sustained and repeated corporeal project.[157]

Here, early on, Butler deploys her distinctive theory of performativity as it applies to women—then also to feminist theory and, importantly, to the necessarily political aspect of feminist theory that opposes subjugation:

> Gender is not passively scripted on the body, and neither is it determined by nature, language, the symbolic, or the overwhelming history of patriarchy. Gender is what is put on, invariably, under constraint, daily and incessantly, with anxiety and pleasure,

---

is sufficiently enthralling as to be featured in a newspaper column just after the 30th anniversary of *Gender Trouble*. See Jules Gleeson, "We Need To Rethink the Category of Women," *The Guardian* (September 7, 2021).

156 Judith Butler, "Performative Acts and Gender Constitution: An Essay in Phenomenology and Feminist Theory," *Theatre Journal*, 40:4 (December 1988), 519–531.

157 *Ibid*, 522.

but if this continuous act is mistaken for a natural or linguistic given, power is relinquished to expand the cultural field bodily through subversive performances of various kinds.[158]

Already it is evident how richly informed Butler was from the earliest days, and how she would use a mélange of sources from many theoretical cultures to formulate enduring ideas.

One of the more memorable of those ideas is *necessary drag* which appeared in a 1989 conference paper later published in 1991 as "Imitation and Gender Insubordination."[159] Perhaps this idea does not appear prominently after this paper because drag is a tacit but necessary element in her theory of gender:

> Drag constitutes the mundane way in which genders are appropriated, theatricalized, worn, and done; it implies that all gendering is a kind of impersonation and approximation. If this is true, it seems, there is no original or primary gender that drag imitates, but *gender is a kind of imitation for which there is no original*; in fact, it is a kind of imitation that produces the very notion of the original as an *effect* and consequence of the imitation itself.[160]

If so, then queens and butches and femmes are not imitations of heterosexuality which is falsely assumed to be the one and only real sexuality against which imitation is assumed to be derivative, a copy. Any claim to a gender, whether hetero-, homo-, trans-, queer-, bi-, or more, is a theatrical performance not of what one is told she is born into but of an unequivocally political sexual being.

In *Bodies That Matter: On The Discursive Limits of "Sex,"* first published in 1993, Butler took up the question of drag in quite a different context. She interprets Nella Larsen's 1929 novel *Passing* in which, for Butler, racial passing is an archetypal case of, if not drag, all other forms of passing, including of course sexual ones. Clare and Irene, two childhood friends, meet again in adult life. Both have Black ancestry and both are passing as white. When Clare's white racist husband Jack enters the scene their shared fear of discovery of their secret becomes acute. At a party in Harlem, Clare and Irene and Jack (Clare's suspicious but unknowing husband) are thrown together. Irene fears that Jack is having an affair with Clare. The sexual tension is then interrupted by a racial conflict when Jack accuses Clare of being a "dirty damn nigger." Irene approaches Clare who is standing by an open window. Clare then falls to her death on the street below. The story ends leaving no clue as to whether Clare jumped or was pushed by Irene or Jack.[161]

Butler is interested here in sexual desire as a complicating aspect of racial passing. "The question of what can and cannot be spoken, what can and cannot be publicly exposed, is raised throughout the text, and it is linked with the larger question of the dangers of public exposure of both color and desire."[162] Butler quotes Henry Louis Gates as to racial passing that "carries the double meaning of crossing the color line and crossing over into

---

158 *Ibid*, 531.
159 Judith Butler, "Imitation and Gender Insubordination," in *Inside/Out: Lesbian Theories, Gay Theories*, edited by Diana Fuss (Routledge, 1991 [1989]).
160 *Ibid*, 21.
161 This is my telling of the story which may not be completely in accord with Butler's. See, if you care, Charles Lemert, "The Queer Passing of Analytic Things: Nella Larsen, 1929," in Lemert, *Dark Thoughts: Race and the Eclipse of Society* (Routledge, 2002), 197–220.
162 Judith Butler, *Bodies That Matter: On the Discursive Limits of "Sex"* (Routledge, 1993 [2011]), 169.

death: passing as a kind of passing on."¹⁶³ *Bodies That Matter* ranges vividly and broadly across other literary sources, like "Willa Cather's Masculine Names," and other psychoanalytic theories from Freud to Lacan, and more. But the common principle is one she takes from Norma Alcarón:

> If women of color are "multiply interpellated," called by many names, constituted in and by that multiple calling, then this implies that the symbolic domain, the domain of socially instituted norms, is composed of racializing norms, and that they exist not merely alongside gender norms, but are articulated through one another. Hence, it is no longer possible to make sexual difference prior to racial difference or, for that matter, to make them into fully separable axes of social regulation and power. ¹⁶⁴

If this, then sexual and racial differences, and in principle all other "identities," derive not from nature but from responses to political and cultural regulation.

At the very end, *Bodies That Matter* returns to "Gender Performativity and Drag." Here drag reappears in respect to the theatricality behind the performativity of genders. "To the extent that gender is an assignment, it is an assignment which is never carried out according to expectation, whose addressee never quite inhabits the ideal s/he is compelled to approximate."¹⁶⁵ Gender is a performance against both prevailing expectations that are never completely able to determine a given state of being, which may mean that whatever self we perform is drag. Hence, the somewhat disguised answer to the question that began *Bodies That Matter*: "Is there a way to link the question of materiality of the body to the performativity of gender "sex" figure within such a relationship?" Yes, in a word; but not perfectly obvious until more is said. The more is found in the one book that, more than any other, has puzzled and enlightened Butler's readers for years.

Gender Trouble and the Subversion of Identity was first published in 1990. Ever since, it has been a topic of conversation for both fans and weak-kneed readers who cannot follow Butler's prose style. In the Preface to the 1999 second edition, she makes her purposes clear: "*Gender Trouble* sought to uncover the ways in which the very thinking of what is possible in gendered life is foreclosed by certain habitual and violent presumptions."¹⁶⁶ Then in the same place, she goes on to say how important that book was to her and others: "Much of my work in recent years has been devoted to clarifying and revising the theory of performativity that is outlined in *Gender Trouble*."¹⁶⁷ Then also, Butler makes two revealing confessions. The first is the difficulty of its style, a complaint that Butler has had to face throughout her career.¹⁶⁸ But then, again in the 1999 Preface, she makes an important point about any seriously complicated theory:

---

163 *Ibid*, 183. [Henry Louis Gates, *Figures in Black: Words, Signs, and the "Racial" Self* (Oxford University Press, 1987), 202.
164 *Ibid*, 182. [Norma Alcarón, "The Theoretical Subject(s) *This Bridge Called My Back* and Anglo-American Feminism," in Gloria Anzaldúa, ed., *Making Face, Making Soul: Haciendo Caras* (Aunt Lute, 1990), 356–369.]
165 *Ibid*, 231.
166 Butler, *Gender Trouble and the Subversion of Identity* (Routledge/Taylor and Francis, 1999 [2e]), viii.
167 *Ibid*, xv.
168 For what it is worth, I think her style is just fine—much like Walt Whitman's. One must read it like poetry (even though it is not poetic) before the deeper meanings come clear. Then too since she relied on French theory, sometimes confusing as well, some may assume her writing is too French. But she did not imitate the French who were in the day *sui generis*. See, if it matters: Charles Lemert, "Reading French Sociology," in Lemert, ed. *French Sociology: Rupture and Renewal Since 1968* (Columbia University Press, 1981), 3–32.

It is no doubt strange, and maddening to some, to find a book that is not easily consumed to be "popular" according to academic standards. The surprise over this is perhaps attributable to the way we underestimate the reading public, its capacity and desire for reading complicated and challenging texts, when the complication is not gratuitous, when the challenge is in the service of calling taken-for-granted truths into question, when the taken for grantedness of those truths is, indeed, oppressive.[169]

As a short-hand way of introducing the book and its resources, here are Butler's first lines of the book's first chapter:

1. Subjects of Sex/Gender/Desire
One is not born a woman, but rather becomes one. —Simone de Beauvoir
Strictly speaking, "women" cannot be said to exist. —Julia Kristeva
Woman does not have a sex. —Luce Irigaray
The deployment of sexuality ... established this notion of sex. —Michel Foucault
The category of sex is the political category that founds society as heterosexual.
—Monique Wittig

When the first edition of *Gender Trouble* was published in 1990, French theory was still a riddle to many in the United States who knew something was going on but to them confusedly. Still when Butler turns to her discussion of "gender trouble" she writes in her own high-analytic style:

For the most part, feminist theory has assumed that there is some existing identity, understood through the category of women, who not only initiates feminist interests and goals within discourse, but constitutes the subject for whom political representation is pursued. But politics and representation are controversial terms. On the one hand, representation serves as the operative term within a political process that seeks to extend visibility and legitimacy to women as political subjects; on the other hand, representation is the normative function of a language which is said either to reveal or to distort what is assumed to be true about the category of women. For feminist theory, the development of a language that fully or adequately represents women has seemed necessary to foster the political visibility of women.[170]

From this theorem (if I may call it that) she continues by insisting that representational politics cannot be gotten around. Butler allows that such a move is in effect "postfeminist" but then comes down hard on the notion that sexed bodies are somehow distinct from "culturally constructed genders." Then:

The presumption of a binary gender system implicitly retains the belief in a mimetic relation of gender to sex whereby gender mirrors sex or is otherwise restricted by it. When the constructed status of gender is theorized as radically independent of sex, gender itself becomes a free-floating artifice, with the consequence that man and masculine might just as easily signify a female body as a male one, and woman and feminine a male body as easily as a female one.[171]

---

169 Butler, *Gender Trouble*, 1999, xvii.
170 Butler, *Gender Trouble*, 1999 (2e), 2.
171 *Ibid*, 10.

In one sense it is fair to say that Butler is making trouble for the traditional or received notion that gender is somehow determined by the form and particulars of the sexual body. Against which she argues that:

> If sexuality is culturally constructed within existing power relations, then the postulation of a normative sexuality that is "before," "outside," or "beyond" power is a cultural impossibility and a politically impracticable dream, one that postpones the concrete and contemporary task of rethinking subversive possibilities for sexuality and identity within the terms of power itself.[172]

Hence the book's subtitle: *Feminism and the Subversion of Identity*.

To get to Butler's idea of identity here it is necessary to plow through the several French theorists she lists at the beginning of the book, and more. But shorn of her always nuanced, if not subtle, documentation of her ideas, it is possible to summarize her main idea as to rethinking—if not utterly subverting—identity in relation to gender. Here there are several working principles: 1. Gender is not a natural or biological endowment. 2. If anything, gender serves a theory of identity only to the extent that is political, which is to say representational. 3. For an identity to serve this end it cannot be fixed in stone (which is to say, in a prior determining nature). "Paradoxically, the reconceptualization of identity as an effect, that is, as produced or generated, opens up possibilities of 'agency' that are insidiously foreclosed by positions that take identity categories as foundational and fixed. For an identity to be an effect means that it is neither fatally determined nor fully artificial and arbitrary."[173] Which in turn leads to the strong conclusion of the book: "If identities were no longer fixed as the premises of a political syllogism, and politics can no longer be understood as a set of practices derived from the alleged interests that belong to a set of ready-made subjects, a new configuration of politics would surely emerge from the ruins of the old."[174]

This leads to the very proper readerly question: Can all (or some) of this be stated in plain and simple language? Here's my attempt:

> *Gender is trouble whenever, as some think, a woman owes her identity to a gift of the gods of nature. All-too-simply put, such an idea fixes all things feminine about women such that they are themselves wooden—unable to bend away from dominant males, unable to invent and engage the schemes by which they present themselves to the world about. This deprives them of the representational quality that is at the heart of meaningful politics—which is to say: politics that present their sense of who they are and mean to be. As a result, it is necessary deeply to rethink identity in a way that sets aside the dogmatic notion that women are natural first and foremost, and active human beings secondarily.*

Butler is entirely serious about politics as necessary to feminism, beginning with feminist theories of who women are and what they need and want.

Well after both editions of *Gender Trouble* (1990 and 1999), Butler published *Notes Toward A Performative Theory of Assembly* in which she makes a strong political claim for the importance of assembly to politics itself. Her thesis here is that "acting in concert

---

172 *Ibid*, 40.
173 *Ibid*, 187.
174 *Ibid*, 189.

can be an embodied form of calling into question the inchoate and powerful dimensions of reigning notions of the political".[175] The very presence of public demonstrations, strikes, sit-ins are in and of themselves politically potent and especially so for those, like many women, who use the "precarity" of their bodily lives to mobilize political action for change. To which she adds: "If there is a fear that, by no longer being able to take for granted the subject, its gender, its sex, or its materiality, feminism will founder, it might be wise to consider the political consequences of keeping in their place the very premises that have tried to secure our subordination from the start."[176]

One could go on and on considering Butler's many works. For now, however, it is enough to say that beyond her important works on topics on and around gender, she has explored a good many other subjects of popular as well as intellectual interest. Among these are: *The Psychic Life of Power* in 1997; *Frames of War: When Is Life Grievable?* in 2009; *The Force of Non-Violence* in 2020; *What World Is This: A Pandemic Phenomenology* in 2022. To mention these several of many is, for now, to do no more than allude to what Butler has done over the last most recent of three decades or so. Some will belligerently dismiss much of it because it is too, too complicated. Yet, few when they step back and look would find it hard to deny that behind it all is a protean imagination that spares nothing to dig deep and look beyond the norm.

It is also fair to say that, of all the feminists discussed in this very long chapter, Butler is one who respects others alongside of whom she thinks and works. And she is also one who, like all those in this chapter, has set feminist theory on a new trajectory—one that is never narrowly feminist but ambitiously social in the best sense of the word.

---

175 Butler, *Notes Toward A Performative Theory of Assembly* (Harvard University Press, 2015), 9.
176 *Ibid*, 19.

21 States, Social Movements, and Revolutions
The Roosevelts, Reinhold Niebuhr, Charles Tilly, Theda Skocpol, James Scott

We are determined to make every American citizen the subject of his country's interest and concern; and we will never regard any faithful law-abiding group within our borders as superfluous. The test of our progress is not whether we add more
to the abundance of those who have much;
it is whether we provide enough for those who have too little.
—*Franklin Delano Roosevelt, Second Inaugural Address, 20 January 1937*

A realistic analysis of the problems of human society reveals a constant and seemingly irreconcilable conflict between the needs of society and the imperatives of a sensitive conscience. This conflict, which could be most briefly defined as the conflict between ethics and politics, is made inevitable by the double focus of the moral life. One focus is the inner life of the individual, and the other in the necessities of man's social life. From the perspective of society the highest moral ideal is justice. From the perspective of the individual the highest ideal is unselfishness. Society must strive for justice even if it is forced to use means, such as self-assertion, resistance, coercion and perhaps resentment, which cannot gain the moral sanction of the most sensitive moral spirit. The individual must strive to realize his life by losing and finding himself in something greater than himself.
—*Reinhold Niebuhr, Moral Man and Immoral Society, 1932*

It is especially at the level of culture that a defeated or intimidated peasantry
may nurture its stubborn moral dissent from an elite-created social order.
—*James Scott, The Moral Economy of the Peasant, 1976*

For true democratization to become possible within any given advanced industrial society,
it would surely be necessary for democratizing movements to proceed simultaneously in all advanced countries,
with each movement making it a key objective to achieve steady progress toward disarmament and peace.
—*Theda Skocpol, States and Social Revolutions, 1979*

A social movement is a kind of campaign, parallel in many respects to an electoral campaign. This kind of campaign, however, demands right of a wrong, most-of-all a wrong suffered by a well-specified population. The population in question can range from a single individual to all humans, or even all living creatures.
—*Charles Tilly, Stories, Identities, and Political Change, 2002*

Good Social Love as Radical Resistance

In the all-but-completely walled-off Hill section of New Haven those in the know can find a small but remarkable institution—one that belies the idea the area is isolated from the wider world of trouble and need for change. That institution is the local Amistad Catholic Worker home and shelter. It is led by Mark and Luce Colville who have converted their home and yard into a shelter for the needy. They open their home as a kitchen for meals to feed the hungry. Together they are so serious about their Catholic politics in the tradition of Dorothy Day that they set themselves against the Church itself. For a while they took over direction of Trinity Church Sunday afternoon program outdoors on the Town Green that provides food and spiritual nurture to the poor and the unsheltered homeless. When their Roman Church relented, they recommitted themselves to their Amistad Catholic Worker project—which is meant to honor the movement that Dorothy Day founded in 1933 in the depths of the Great Depression. The Amistad Catholic Worker project in New Haven is based in and around their small house and yard. It welcomes all those in need who can be served in such a small space. At one point, they built in their yard a warming hut that keeps those in need off the ground and out of the merciless rains and falling temperatures. In February of 2023, the home and hut were invaded, as Mark writes on their website:

> Today the Human Rights Zone at the Amistad Catholic Worker suffered an armed intrusion, as two police officers trespassed on our common home unannounced, neither seeking permission nor identifying themselves, and threatening violence if anyone made any sudden movements. Their victim was my friend Philip, a neighbor and economic refugee who has been tending a home here since being evicted from an apartment on the other end of our street about three months ago.[1]

One of the two cops who entered without notice came for Philip on the grounds that they had a warrant for his arrest. When Mark confronted them, one of the officers belligerently gave him his name and address and said "Give this to your attorney. Good luck with your lawyer." As it happens this same officer had previously been indicted for criminal impersonation in another town where he was working as a bouncer. This is just a little on what those who get down on the ground with the poorest of people must deal with.

This is far from all that the Amistad Catholic Worker Project does in the city. Mark speaks around town. He attends any event that concerns those with whom he is concerned such as the annual Memorial Service for those who died unsheltered. He represents a tent city alongside New Haven's West River that, because of his efforts, seems to have gained grudging acceptance of City officials who, in the day, would sweep down and trash the tent homes.

True to the vision of Dorothy Day, Mark and Luce believe, as Day famously said: "The only solution is love, and love comes with community." Plus which, their love is tough love—the love of resistance to official neglect and downright oppression. This is the kind of love that can open eyes of otherwise deaf politicians—a love in action that can lead to revolution even in local social orders, perhaps even in the wider world.

But love must be tough enough to resist when necessary. Late in 2023 Mark and Luce raised money to install six very tiny houses in their small back yard. Trouble loomed. But

---

1 https://amistadcw.wordpress.com/2023/02/18/armed-intrusion/

their tiny house project came on the heels of the City destroying the tent city on the far West border of New Haven. One day bulldozers arrived to tear the place up after those who had lived there for some time had a chance to remove their belongings. There was a minor storm in the City by citizens who saw no reason for this very degraded urban development. Then Mark and Luce did what they could to find housing for those displaced, but Amistad House couldn't care for the many. So they set about to raise money to buy and install the tiny houses. Of course, the righteous complained that the tiny houses were illegal and the Colvilles were violating laws that none of the complainers could name. Then the voices of those who cared for the needs of the poor became a shout. One person entered his support for the project in the online *New Haven Independent*. Within weeks the debate sparked the concern of many others.

Just the same the city handed down a cease and desist order to the Amistad Workers—to which Mark responded emphatically that he would do neither! As I write, it is not clear what will become of the tiny houses. It is likely that they will survive, if only because the Mayor, Justin Elicker, is a good person. He led the way in acquiring state and local funds ($1.5 million) to buy a motel near the Walmart store. The plan is that motel would be redone so that once unsheltered people could live independently with their families and loved ones while having food, medical care, social services on site. One supposes that Justin will also relent on the tiny houses.

Sometimes resistance to the powers that be works for the good, which is a decent enough way of defining love for those in need.

The Unstable Link Among States/Social Movements/Revolutions

This chapter links three aspects of social life that can lead to important changes in a given society. The changes among the relations of *States/Social Movements/Revolutions*, when they occur seriatim—as rarely they do, are meant to turn worlds upside down. Yet when they come together, the result usually turns sour—as it did in Russia in 1917 and China in 1949, both of which soon failed to be truly people's republics. Even in France in 1789 which turned bloody under Robespierre, before it turned imperial under Napoleon and the spirit of the revolution was buried. Some would argue, not unfairly, that only George Washington's American Revolution of 1776 was a successful social revolution. But even here it required Abraham Lincoln and Civil War to begin to lend more than rhetorical weight to Jefferson's "all men are created equal." At the extreme, one could say that Cuba in 1959 was successful in a half-baked sort of way. Fidel Castro was able to free Cuba from corrupt American business corporations to build a society where health care and indigenous culture are world class, but this at the cost of exclusion from the global world and relative economic misery of Cuba's citizens. Then too, as for social revolutions, even those that fail in the long run, like China's, may come to be in an even longer time eventually. Mao's inspiration for the long march began in 1911. The revolution did not succeed in ousting the Nationalists until 1949. Perhaps China much later will become what the younger Mao had hoped. At the same time, even when revolutions succeed, then fail, they can also revert to something worse than what they replaced—as in Russia's Stalin and then Putin.

But a social revolution is only the rare outcome of an historical process that begins with a state against which social movements arise, from time to time, to challenge a given state's failure to do what its people think it ought to do. It is not by accident that when one tries to illustrate possible social revolutions, it is not hard to name names—Robespierre, Washington, Castro, Stalin, Mao, and so on. The named leaders stand in for their state's revolutionary movement aspired to change. One could just as well name the leaders of the old regimes under assault—Louis XVI, George III, Fulgencio Batista, Nicolas II, Yuan ShiKai, then Sun Yat-sen, then Chiang Kai-Shek. Leaders define, for better or worse, a given state, as leaders of social revolutions broadcast their complaints against their states, typified and identified by a purportedly evil state leader. It goes without saying that states may be led by those who create policies and practices to which the people object.

At this point another theoretical bugaboo rears its frightful head—that of the subject/object dichotomy and its numerous derivatives. When one speaks of states and social movements, even social revolutions that occasionally transpire, it is sheer nonsense to speak of individual subjects arguing with or overthrowing more powerful subjects. Leaders are individuals to be sure, but they never rule or dominate their people by themselves alone. They have royal police, palace knights, secret service or the like who defend them. Or, when they are more skillful politicians, they have cabinets, courtesans, parties, and such like who carry out the leader's wishes or demands as best they can. Leaders are what leaders do and not even Hitler or Genghis Khan did what they did alone, even when, in Hitler's case especially, they issued from the deranged mind behind the Nazi Regime.

Likewise some social movements have leaders like Mark and Luce Colville. But they, like others trying to make changes, must begin locally working with those who will join in to get a movement rolling. Sometimes movements remain local. Other times, they reach a wider following like Fannie Lou Hammer and Bob Moses during Mississippi Freedom Summer in 1964 who put Voter Registration on the map of the American Civil Rights Movement. And occasionally they become national and international like Greta Thunberg who, at 18 years, began an enduring climate change movement. All leaders of social movements must begin locally by meeting in backyards or pubs or conferences where their visions take shape and they find the followers. Saul Alinsky, the truly great community organizer, famously had rules for radicals, including[2]:

- Power is not only what you have but what the enemy thinks you have.
- Make the enemy live up to its own book of rules.
- Ridicule is man's most potent weapon. There is no defense. It is almost impossible to counterattack ridicule. Also it infuriates the opposition, who then react to your advantage.
- A tactic that drags on too long becomes a drag.
- The threat is usually more terrifying than the thing itself.
- Whenever possible go outside the expertise of the enemy.

Alinsky had thirteen rules in all, but in the end the one tacit one was: Work in such a way that when the goals are achieved, the people will in time forget you were there. "Once a people are organized they will keep moving from issue to issue."[3] Still, to change things such that the people in a movement no longer need a leader means dealing with the trouble movement action creates. "Change means movement. Movement means friction. Only in the frictionless vacuum of a nonexistent abstract world can movement or change occur without that abrasive friction of conflict."[4]

States/Social Movements/Revolutions takes into account that radical ideals for change must ever always be practical. States are never easily changed. Movements can be "good trouble," as John Lewis famously said, but they are also *hard trouble*. This because when they succeed locally they may succeed for a time but then may weaken because, for some,

---

2 Saul Alinsky, *Rules for Radicals: A Pragmatic Primer for Realistic Radicals* (Random House, 1971).
3 *Ibid*, 180.
4 *Ibid*, 34.

the frustration of failing to create a social revolution that turns a state and its social structures inside/out for the good is deeply frustrating. Some just go on to graduate school or some other preoccupation. Those who join a movement must live by their vision of a better world—and visions can fade into the ether as proponents can no longer see where it all leads.

Yet, when it comes to social theories, it is all but impossible to think real truths if one begins, so to speak, either with subjects or objects—or, better put, with either individuals on the ground and structures in the air of social imaginations. Societies carry on, for better or worse, in the interstitial space between states and movements. Even when dramatic change does not take place, lives lived with others are lived in the between of individuals and structures where real people thrive or fail, then die, satisfied or disappointed with what has been done in their days. Mark and Luce Colville do what they do on a side street in an oft-forgotten neighborhood because they see a better world for which they are willing to endure the troubles at hand—when cops intrude, friends fall ill, others suffer hunger in the cold by a remote river.

The Roosevelts: Traitors to Their Class

The header here comes, many will recognize, from H. W. Brand's *Traitor to His Class: The Privileged Life and Radical Presidency of Franklin Delano Roosevelt* in 2000. The phrase applies equally well to Eleanor, Franklin's wife, and Theodore, her uncle. After Theodore's death and Franklin's rise to power, the two branches of the Roosevelt clan grew competitive and hostile toward each other. This came to be known as the tensions between the Oyster's Bay Roosevelts (Theodore's mansion retreat on Long Island) and the Hyde Park branch (Franklin's palatial home on the Hudson River).

The tensions between their families were only partly because Teddy was a Republican and FDR, a Democrat. They seem to have been driven by Teddy's sons during Franklin's presidency. Whatever the cause, over time the two branches of the Roosevelt clan maintained tolerably good relations—as members of the elite class often do. In the day, still now, the moneyed elite assume a certain cultural responsibility to respect their shared and presumed rights as the nation's highest class.

This was especially true on Theodore's side, given that, as President, he presided over the last decades of the Gilded Age comprising America's new ultra-rich upper class from, roughly, the end of Reconstruction in 1876 to the mid-1890s, then into the early years of the twentieth century. They were Captains of Industry who grew wealthy by controlling and building the industries most essential to the new industrial age—steel, railroads, oil, banking and finance, automobile manufacture —all necessary to the rapid rise of the modern American economy. It was then that they also became known as the Robber Barons of the Gilded Age—Andrew Carnegie, Cornelius Vanderbilt, John D. Rockefeller, J.P. Morgan, Henry Ford. They literally, if then legally, stole from the poor and working classes who were subjected to their greed. Henry Ford was the final pillar of their structure because he completely overhauled manufacturing by introducing the assembly line method of mass manufacturing. Their wealth was so great that J.P. Morgan is known to have, more than once, personally bailed out the U.S. government when it was in financial crisis.

Theodore Roosevelt became President September 14, 1901, upon the death by assassination of President William McKinley. Almost immediately he established his politics in a way that came to be called Progressive—different perhaps from what the term denotes in the 2020s, but still intent upon change. Like all three of the Roosevelts, Teddy (as he was called endearingly by his first wife), suffered debilitating afflictions as a child. Physically, he endured asthma attacks in a day when medicines available today were unavailable. Emotionally, his father (and namesake) died when Theodore Jr. was just out of his teen years. He admired his father to an extreme and missed him dearly. The asthma was so severe that a physician told him that he need to withdraw from all out-of-doors activities and keep himself close to home. Teddy did just the opposite. Ever, and always, when the occasion arose he escaped to the outdoor life—sports in school, hunting in the West in later life, travel to the wildest corners of the world including an unexplored branch of the Amazon where he almost died. It also seems that his determination in politics to stand up to the Bosses of Industry and other of his opponents was part of his life's routine—but so too was the example of his father, a wealthy man who committed significant portions of his days to charitable work to, for example, founding The Children's Aid Society as well as the Metropolitan Museum of Art in NYC and other projects with the poor that entailed on-hand presence.

Teddy overcame all, always with uncommon achievements—among these: while at Harvard he began *The Naval War of 1812* which was published in 1882 and remains today in print as a respected source for the history of the US Navy. After graduating Harvard in 1878, he returned to New York City and began dabbling in politics. Then in 1880 he married Alice Hathaway Lee who may have been the love of his life. She died, however, just four years later while giving birth to a daughter, Alice. His mother died the same day. Theodore was devasted. He sent his daughter to live with a sister. Soon thereafter he left for the far West, to build a ranch and settle in North Dakota where he encountered the hard and earthy men of the plains and cattle herding. When teased by one tough guy for being an Eastern "boy" he stood up and threatened to kick him in the balls and beat him senseless. He was soon accepted into a world he'd never known in his early life among the wealthy at Groton and Harvard. He lost his ranch in 1887 when a winter storm killed his cattle—thereafter to return home to New York and a prodigious career beginning as a New York Assemblyman at the age of 24 years while also

So why in a book on social theory, the Roosevelts? Neither Teddy nor Franklin nor Eleanor was a social theorist! They weren't to be sure. But all three, in different ways, contributed to changes in America that made it what it is today. They were, in this sense, practical social theorists. At some risk, it could be said that if Lincoln completed Washington's revolution, then the Roosevelts, beginning with Theodore, completed Lincoln's. They spoke and wrote, each in a different manner, but always with the thought of changing what was socially wrong in the new urban world with its roots in the dirt of the Gilded Age. It took the Great Depression of 1929, well after TR was gone, to change all that. TR was, of course, the one whose intimate knowledge of hard life on the plains formed him in a way that his upper class background could not. He was tough-minded and hard bitten such that when the Gilded-elite about him were doing wrong, he was more than ready to set them right.

Theodore Roosevelt's first, most famous, encounter of this kind was with J.P. Morgan, than whom none richer and more cocksure. Several times previously, and notably during the economic crisis of 1893, Morgan covered America's debt when President Grover Cleveland had neither means nor clue how to do it. It may have been reasonable in Morgan's way of thinking that he could and should do the same with President Roosevelt in 1902. In September 1901, when Roosevelt was in office but a few months after President McKinley's death, he had to deal with J.P. Morgan's attempt to merge his National Securities Company with Northern Pacific Railroad to create a rail monopoly across the American West. On February 22, 1902, Roosevelt brought suit against Morgan for violation of the 1890 Sherman Anti-trust Act. Edmund Morris describes the bracing matter-of-factness of the new President's character:

Whatever qualms the President may have had in granting an interview, he had little difficulty handling Morgan. Or at least Roosevelt chose not to remember any, when recounting the conversation afterward that included his Attorney General Philander Chase Knox. Morgan had seemed less furious than puzzled. Why had the Administration not asked *him* to correct irregularities in the new trust's charter.

Roosevelt: This is just what we did not want to do.
Morgan: If we have done anything wrong, send your man to my man and they can fix it up.
Roosevelt: That can't be done.
Knox: We don't want to fix it up, we want to stop it.
Morgan: Are you going to attack my other interests, the Steel trust and others?
Roosevelt Certainly not—unless we find out that in any case they have done something we regard as wrong.[5]

In the end, the Supreme Court sided with TR. After Lincoln all presidents had been weak or passive (even Grant) until this Roosevelt. He was every bit as decisive when possible in the Coal Strike later the same year, in May 1902. This time, Morgan relented and settled with the striking miners. Roosevelt brought 41 actions against leaders of industry. No prior president brought half as many.

TRs support of labor against the capitalists was not, however, ideological. He was not a crypto-Socialist or anything of the like. His support for labor was, in his famous phrase, nothing more than giving a *square deal* to all Americans—a phrase that his cousin Franklin had in mind thirty years later when he promised a *new deal* to all during the Depression. The three Roosevelts—including Eleanor—were, one could say, radical for their times, but none was an ideologue. They were political to be sure but with rare exception they were, in their own way, concerned with being practical social activists for common people. This precisely is the way they were traitors to their class.

Just the same, TR was, if anything, more outspoken than his fifth cousin, FDR, and his niece, ER, on the economic injustices in America at the beginning of the twentieth century. Late in his presidency, for example, on January 31, 1908, he sent the following message to Congress:

> Predatory wealth—of the wealth accumulated on a giant scale by all forms of iniquity, ranging from the oppression of wageworkers to unfair and unwholesome methods of crushing out competition, and to defrauding the public by stock jobbing and the manipulation of securities. Certain wealthy men of this stamp, whose conduct should be abhorrent to every man of ordinarily decent conscience, and who commit the hideous wrong of teaching our young men that phenomenal business success must ordinarily be based on dishonesty, have during the last few months made it apparent that they have banded together to work for a reaction. Their endeavor is to overthrow and discredit all who honestly administer the law, to prevent any additional legislation which would check and restrain them, and to secure if possible a freedom from all restraint which will permit every unscrupulous wrongdoer to do what he wishes unchecked provided he has enough money.[6]

---

5 Edmund Morris, *Theodore Rex* (Random House, 2001), 91–92. For a full discussion of the new attitude Roosevelt brought to the presidency, see Morris' second chapter, "Turn of the Tide—1902."
6 Theodore Roosevelt, "Special message to Congress, January 31, 1908," in Elting E. Morison, ed., *The Letters of Theodore Roosevelt* (Harvard University Press, 1952), Vol 5: 1580.

Yet, TRs moral judgments remained firm even well after he left the White House. In his 1913 autobiography: "There can be no nobler cause for which to work than the peace of righteousness; and high honor is due those serene and lofty souls who with wisdom and courage, with high idealism tempered by sane facing of the actual facts of life, have striven to bring nearer the day when armed strife between nation and nation, between class and class, between man and man shall end through the world."[7]

Still it must be said that Theodore Roosevelt's high moral ideals did not keep him from vulgar political deeds. His notorious Rough Riders and the Battle of Kettle and San Juan hills in Cuba during the Spanish-American War in July 1898 was all-but pure theater in which men died. TR considered it the best day of his life. It was a self-serving performance meant to bolster his sense of his manhood. So too, but to good effect, was how he tricked and deceived the Republic of Colombia to cede the Panama territory, thus, in time, to create Panama as an independent republic. More to TR's purposes, his meddling in the affairs of a foreign nation opened the way for the United States to be the builder and governor of the canal in what became an American foreign territory, the Panama Canal Zone. The Canal itself became, and remains, a global waterway that serves shipping the world over. Some good came from geo-political nasty business. TR did many things of the ilk—most more good than not. One was unqualifiedly excellent. This was his contribution to land conservancy in the United States created for the world the very idea of set-aside national lands as parks for the public. At home, he established 150 national forests, close to 60 national game and bird reserves, and millions of acres of public land as well as a good many national monuments. No other president comes close to this record. None even imagined it.

Theodore Roosevelt essentially created the activist presidency that Woodrow Wilson tried but failed to achieve and which Franklin Roosevelt perfected in order to save the nation from economic disaster and the world from a deadly War. This unarguable fact of their lives is strangely related to the further fact that so much of their biographical and political trajectories were so similar as to suggest that FDR meant to follow in the way of TR, his fifth cousin.[8] FDR began his political life elected to a seat in the New York State Assembly, then he was appointed Assistant Secretary of the Navy, then became Governor of the State of New York, then a vice-presidential candidate, before becoming President of the United States—all steps TR took a full generation before FDR.

But, in respect to events neither could have chosen, they both went through character forming experiences that made them who they became. FDR grew up and lived much of his life emotionally beholden to an over-weening mother who spoiled her son from being able to form intimate relations with Eleanor, which fact drove him to his several notable affairs—a kind of triangulated oedipal compulsion. TR, on the other hand, was caught in what might be called an enduring attachment to a dead father that inspired his overdetermined will to stand tall against bullies of all kinds. TR's asthma was obviously a lesser trouble than FDR's polio. Asthma, TR proved, can be overcome. Polio, in the day, could not—even though FDR committed himself to years of physical therapy to no avail. After 1921, when first his polio took away his legs, nothing worked, not even the pools at the Warm Springs resort after 1925.

---

7 Theodore Roosevelt, *Theodore Roosevelt: An Autobiography by Theodore Roosevelt* (Charles Scribner's Son, 1913); here quoted from the Gutenberg Press edition, Chapter XV: 1 @ https://www.gutenberg.org/files/3335/3335-h/3335-h.htm#link2HCH0015 .

8 The following comparisons between TR and FDR are partly drawn from *The Roosevelts: An Intimate History* (Walpole NH: *Florentine Films*, 2014) which was written with Geoffrey Ward as well as Ken Burns; also books cited elsewhere on the two men and Eleanor.

Still, in a sense, Warm Springs was to FDR what the Dakota ranch was to TR—a place where he was forced to come down to the reality of common people. TR did this by being tougher than the cowboy tough guys. FDR did so by buying the resort and turning it into a retreat not just from the pain in his legs but from the deeper confinement of a long limiting confinement in his mother's all-too high class Hyde Park culture. FDR came to be called "Rosy" by the patients and local people in and around Warm Springs. He died there in 1945. According to William Leuchtenberg, Eleanor said of her husband's dealing with polio: "I know that he had real fear when he was first taken ill, but he learned to surmount it. After that I never heard him say he was afraid of anything."[9] Doris Kearns-Goodwin added: "The paralysis that crippled his body expanded his mind and his sensibilities."[10] Though TR was a different character, he too worked-through childhood illness and the limitations of his life in Manhattan at his retreat at Oyster Bay on Long Island. Though FDR was the more charming, TR came to understand people who could not even dream of having a family resort. Still, both were admired, sometimes grudgingly, even by their political enemies. Both left Groton and Harvard behind in order to dip deep into the nation's troubles.

Then too, and important to their times and their successes, each of the Roosevelt presidents had a unique way of communicating with the public. TR was known for his determined and stern public pronouncements. FDR will forever be remembered for his Fireside Chats that were plain-spoken yet eloquent talks with ordinary folk who listened thoughtfully by their radios. And he was wise not to overdo them. According to Doris Kearns Goodwin, he had only 30 of them in his 12+ years in office.[11] Of them all, the first on March 12, 1933, a week after his inauguration, illustrates FDR's gift for making others feel an improbable sense of intimacy with their President:

> I want to talk for a few minutes with the people of the United States about banking—with the comparatively few who understand the mechanics of banking but more particularly with the overwhelming majority who use banks for the making of deposits and the drawing of checks. I want to tell you what has been done in the last few days, why it was done, and what the next steps are going to be. I recognize that the many proclamations from state capitols and from Washington, the legislation, the treasury regulations, etc., couched for the most part in banking and legal terms should be explained for the benefit of the average citizen. I owe this in particular because of the fortitude and good temper with which everybody has accepted the inconvenience and hardships of the banking holiday. I know that when you understand what we in Washington have been about I shall continue to have your cooperation as fully as I have had your sympathy and help during the past week.[12]

These words were spoken directly to ordinary people who had good reason to fear that the bank crisis would ruin them, as the Depression had already ruined many. FDR spoke as though they were partners. He expressed sympathy for those who knew quite well that he

---

9 William E. Leuchtenburg, *Franklin D. Roosevelt: A Life in Brief* (University of Virginia: The Miller Center @ https://millercenter.org/president/fdroosevelt/life-in-brief)
10 Doris Kearns-Goodwin, *No Ordinary Life: Franklin and Eleanor Roosevelt: The Home Front in World War II* (Simon & Schuster, 1995), 198.
11 Doris Kearns-Goodwin, in Ken Burns and Geoffrey Ward, from *The Roosevelts: An Intimate History* (Walpole NH, *Florentine Films*, 2014), episode 6.
12 All of FDR's Fireside Chats are kept at the *Franklin Delano Roosevelt Library and Museum* (Hyde Park, New York: Springwood on the Roosevelt family property). They can be downloaded according to the dates they were given, at: http://docs.fdrlibrary.marist.edu/firesi90.html

would never suffer the economic hardships they faced. Yet, FDR assured them that, with their cooperation, all would be well. In fact, when the banks opened, those who days before had withdrawn their cash redeposited it. Imagine if you can, in our time, a president able to move people so surely for the good of all.

Just more than a year later, on April 28, 1935, in another of his Fireside Chats, he would introduce his Social Security Program then before Congress by fully describing the six principles the program's projects would follow:

(1) The projects should be useful. (2) Projects shall be of a nature that a considerable proportion of the money spent will go into wages for labor. (3) Projects will be sought which promise ultimate return to the federal treasury of a considerable proportion of the costs. (4) Funds allotted for each project should be actually and promptly spent and not held over until later years. (5) In all cases projects must be of a character to give employment to those on the relief rolls. (6) Projects will be allocated to localities or relief areas in relation to the number of workers on relief rolls in those areas.

In a later chat, on July 24, 1935, he added less abstract assurances rooted in common American experiences:

On the basis of this simple principle of everybody doing things together, we are starting out on this nationwide attack on unemployment. It will succeed if our people understand it – in the big industries, in the little shops, in the great cities and in the small villages. There is nothing complicated about it and there is nothing particularly new in the principle. It goes back to the basic idea of society and of the nation itself that people acting in a group can accomplish things which no individual acting alone could even hope to bring about.

Once again we might ask: How long has it been since, in our day, we have heard an American president go into such detail as to the reasoning behind a major social policy, expressed in clear cut rational principles.

By April 14, 1938, FDR felt he was forced to explain the unexpected consequences of the progressive economic programs he had begun. In plain language he said, roughly speaking, that the robust production of goods and services "outran the ability to buy." This much was at least partially clear to those who could not buy the commercial goods available. To which he explained: "There were many reasons for this overproduction. One of them was fear—fear of war abroad, fear of inflation, fear of nation-wide strikes. None of these fears have been borne out." While his listeners could only grasp the theory behind the programs intuitively, they could readily understand the several fears around the corner. Inflation and strikes were common in the day. But also this was 1938. The Nazis were already doing their dirty work. *Kristallnacht* was months away. FDR was deft in alluding to a war few wanted but all knew was brewing. His nod to a possible future war was a stroke of genius. Already in 1938 FDR was in constant communication with Winston Churchill. The War was inevitable. The US had to enter it. But he knew he had to wait for an attack on America before he could engage. Pearl Harbor, on December 7, 1941, was three full years in the future.

FDR's Fireside Chats were original to him in the early days of public media, well before anything like television, when radio was itself still a crude medium. He was brilliant, even when he was called upon to speak in person to large audiences, he performed just as brilliantly. It took a while until he mastered the painful art of struggling to his feet and "walking" awkwardly to a podium. When he did, his rhetorical gifts were not chatty but, in their necessarily different way, they were effective in much the same way. When speaking to large groups, his most memorable line was in his first Inaugural Address on March 4, 1933. "The only thing we have to fear is fear itself." The line has been called poetic nonsense, but it touched the heart. By contrast, his speech on July 2, 1932, accepting the nomination at the Democratic National Convention was jam-packed with details—from the economy to farm prices, with social and political ideas in between, and a history of the Democratic Party's social responsibilities (this at a time when the Party was dominated by those soon to be labeled Dixiecrats and who were anything but socially responsible). But Roosevelt, on this score, pursued robust economic programs for the people, many more generous than those of the early years of the Depression. Of them the G.I. Bill of Rights gave millions of returning war veterans education, housing, and enough income to essentially invent the Post-War middle class.

Still, his communication skills were basic to all he did. FDR's second most famous line was pronounced before Congress the day after Pearl Harbor—"A day that will live in infamy." War was a different matter, and not one in which rhetoric was primary as it was when selling economic policy. In respect to WWII, FDR was tough-minded, yet politically savvy. He was, however, always cautious before committing himself, as when he resisted Churchill's early pleas for armaments and naval support and when waiting before declaring war. He knew he had to wait for something like Pearl Harbor to enter the fray. He knew that Americans knew they had to fight. Only an attack would mobilize them.

The War was also the occasion of his most offensive moral decision to incarcerate Japanese nationals in California, followed closely by his ineptitude in regard to civil rights and failure to desegregate the military. Though he died after the Normandy Invasion, FDR did not live to the War's end. His last major international event before his death was the conference with Churchill and Stalin at Yalta in February 1945. He was visibly ill. Still FDR played a strong role in the controversial agreement at Yalta—to divide Europe among the three major allies. But he was not too ill to deliver words of insight and hope in a press conference aboard the USS *Quincy* returning home from Crimea. Among them were his prescient remarks on Vietnam: "For two whole years I have been terribly worried about Indo-China. I talked to Chiang Kai-shek in Cairo, Stalin in Teheran. They both agreed with me. The French have been in there some hundred years. The Indo-Chinese are not like the Chinese."[13] FDR saw trouble coming, as it would after Dien Bien Phu in 1954. And he was of the clear conviction that the world needed the United Nations—which Eleanor would later serve with distinction. His health declined thereafter. He died of a stroke as an age weary man of but 63 years at Warm Springs on April 12, 1945. FDR went to his grave knowing in his worn soul that he had given all he had to his nation and the world.

Eleanor Roosevelt, like her husband and uncle, was born to wealth and status in Manhattan—she in 1884. Her parents were a problem for her and each other. The father Elliott died at 34 years of a seizure following upon an alcoholism-induced suicide attempt. The mother Anna had died of diphtheria two years before the father. Eleanor had but eight years with her—long enough for the mother to have pronounced her ugly. So much for the feeble human nature of the very rich. Eleanor suffered from this abuse for years to come. The one reprieve in her early teen years was when an aunt encouraged her guardian to send her to Allenswood School in Wimbledon, London. Allenswood was led by Marie Souvestre who was humane as well as progressive in her educational philosophy—so much so that, in

---

13 Franklin D. Roosevelt, Excerpts from the Press Conference Aboard the U.S.S. Quincy En Route From Yalta. Online by Gerhard Peters and John T. Woolley, The American Presidency Project https://www.presidency.ucsb.edu/node/210046

Eleanor's case, she took a personal interest in her, a commitment that continued even after Eleanor's aunt forced her to come home after three years so she might come-out to New York City society. Needless to say the very idea was repulsive to Eleanor. At Allenswood she had been loved by staff and students without need of a social credential. She knew none of the girls at the debutante ball. Her childhood misery returned but soon relented.

This was 1902. She met Franklin that summer. Soon they were engaged. His mother Sara did her best to keep them apart. But they married March 17, 1905, left for a long honeymoon in Europe, then moved into a house in NYC that Franklin's mother bought for them—one attached to hers (no surprise). Thus began Eleanor's living in places that would never become hers until, many years later, when Franklin helped her build her own home in Hyde Park, Val-Kill. FDR and ER had six children, most of whom had trouble finding their way in life. This, at least partly, because, as Eleanor frankly confessed, she had neither taste nor talent for parenting—again, not a surprise given her unkind, long dead mother. Then misery again descended. In 1918 Eleanor discovered Franklin's love-letters to and from Lucy Mercer, ER's secretary. FDR thought of leaving ER but was told by Louis Howe, his political confidant, that it would end his political career. Sara, FDR's mother, added that, if he did, he would lose his inheritance. They carried on. Then in 1921, when they gathered at Campobello Island, Franklin fell to polio. Eleanor nursed him lovingly at least until he came to terms, emotionally as well as physically, with his permanent limitations. ER's care of Franklin, it seems, won her praise at long last.

Eleanor's parental and marital abuse amounted to a weird extended family bond with TR and his asthma, and with FDR's polio. In time, she got over the pain of Franklin's extra-curricular intimacies. When she learned that Margaret Suckley, one of Franklin's longtime, off-and-on, intimate companions had been with him when he died at Warm Springs, it clearly hurt. Still, she must have suspected they were seeing each other over the years, if only because he had built Top Cottage on the estate essentially for them. Still, even at the end, Eleanor carried on making the state funeral and the burial in Sara's rose garden at Hyde Park special. She said in due course, referring to the marriage, that life must be lived as it is. This is how she lived hers. Starting at least with moving into Val-Kill with Marion Dickerman and Nancy Cook. Eleanor had her own friends and, it seems, lovers. Later in life, she enjoyed a most ardent love affair with Lorena Hickcok. Blanche Wiesen Cook, ER's most important biographer, writes: "ER lived a life dedicated to passion and experience. She honored relationships, and their privacy. After 1920 many of her closest friends were lesbians. ... She protected their secrets and kept her own."[14] The most exceptional of her personal relationships was her late-in-life friendship with David Gurewitsch who, first, became her physician in New York City, and in time a close personal friend. Eleanor said to him of their relationship: "You know without my telling you that I love you as I have never loved anyone else."[15] Even more remarkable is that this line featured in the book about David and Eleanor by Edna Gurewitsch who had married David well into his friendship with ER. Edna joined in their friendship. She wrote at length of it in *Kindred Souls* after both had died. She wrote with nothing but affection for them both.

Eleanor's capacity for love in her personal life could well be thought of as the emotional source of her life in service to those in need. Her political activism began in earnest when FDR was governor of New York. Then, during his Presidency from the first, she engaged in New Deal related programs including working to establish the National Youth Administration.

---

14 Blanche Wiesen Cook, *Eleanor Roosevelt: Vol. I: 1884–1933* (Penguin Books, 1992), 13.
15 Edna P. Gurewitsch, *Kindred Souls: The Friendship of Eleanor Roosevelt and David Gurewitsch* (St. Martin's Press, 2002), 12.

One of the more remarkable products of her social activism was the building of Arthurdale, a planned community for impoverished coal-mining families in West Virginia.[16] At every turn, she was criticized as little more than a do-gooder. But this complaint was often turned-back by the way her visits to those in need, like injured military during the War, who could not say enough about how attentive and caring she had been with them. She took time at each wounded man's bedside, learned their names, wrote their families. These quiet acts of human grace were among many other truly good works for civil rights, worker's rights, and, during WWII, the rights of Jewish refugees—to mention but a few.

Like the other two Roosevelts, Eleanor had a distinctive way of communicating with the public. She spoke of course, and often—but most amazingly for many years she wrote *My Day*—a 6-day-a-week newspaper column for various newspapers. In 1936, for example, she wrote just shy of 310 published short commentaries on her experiences and the world's events—of these none was more moving than a column on August 17, 1945—12 days after Franklin died: "When you have lived for a long time in close contact with the loss and grief which today pervades the world, any personal sorrow seems to be lost in the general sadness of humanity. For a long time, all hearts have been heavy for every serviceman sacrificed in the war."[17] FDR was her dead serviceman.

No wonder that when Harry S. Truman appointed her as a delegate to the United Nations, she immediately became the Chair of the UN Commission on Human Rights. As usual, her fellow delegates, Midwest conservatives both, thought the appointment was ludicrous. But they too soon learned how wrong they were. She led the Commission with a kind but iron hand, demanding long work days and on one occasion calling the Soviet representatives out-of-order. They walked out. The work went on to produce the Universal Declaration of Human Rights on December 10, 1948. The General Assembly vote was unanimous. After, she was given a standing ovation, which is said to have been the only time an individual was so honored in that way. Later she chaired John F. Kennedy's first Presidential Commission on the Status of Women. She kept at a life of service until she was too ill to carry on. She refused treatment because life without service meant little to her. She died in her bed at home in New York City, November 7, 1962.

Why the Roosevelts? They were not social theorists by any stretch of the imagination. Yet, they did shape American values at a time when the nation faced troubles as deep as any since the Civil War. The extreme economic unfairness set in motion by the Gilded Age from the end of Reconstruction in 1877 to at least the Great War of 1914; —then the Great Depression of the 1930s; —then another great World War from 1939–1945;—then the need of the United States after 1945 to come to terms with the Cold War globally as well as the continuing racial strife that aggravated social differences in America. The several contributions of the three Roosevelts to healing, or trying to heal, the consequences of these national and global events may to many, including professional social theorists, be ill-remembered. One way to look at this is that the new urban world was a world of differences but also exclusions. The more social orders grow in size, the more they become hierarchical—and hierarchies, by their structural nature, exclude. Societies thereby do not come close to anything like a seriously just society. The best they can achieve is fairness, which is not, as some think, the operative aspect of justice. Fairness, in the world as it has

---

16 Blanche Wiesen Cook—in *Eleanor Roosevelt: Vol II: 1933–1938* (Penguin Viking, 1999),134—makes the important point about Arthurdale that "housing and community development were only vaguely on the national agenda when ER began her crusade."

17 *My Day, August 17, 1945*, at the Eleanor Roosevelt Papers Project, George Washington University https://erpapers.columbian.gwu.edu/defense-curiosity.

come to be since, say 1991, is measured, if not always monetarily, in some other quantifiable yard stick—the number of years a category of people may expect to live, the degree to which the poor and middling of a group have access to ordinary needs like health care and medications, the number of years a criminal may be incarcerated, the degree to which people of a despised class are stopped for no good reason, and so on. The more the world is globalized, the less the poor figure in the needs and goods of ordinary life. As for desires—whether for sex or good neighborhoods or some, however modest, surplus income—are all but out of the question for the excluded.

Theoretically, it may not be the case that global structures are *necessarily* unfair. But practically they are. This is why the central practical theoretical dilemma of our still new century is how to think global structures in relation to the exclusions they seem to breed.

Reinhold Niebuhr: Moral Man and Immoral Society

Reinhold Niebuhr (1892–1971)[18] was a Protestant minister, the author of many books on social ethics and religion, and a leader of left politics in what might be called the second Rooseveltian era when Franklin, then Eleanor were at the height of their powers and prominence. Niebuhr had a degree of respect for both Roosevelt presidents but always bound in critical wraps. Elizabeth Sifton who was one of America's greatest literary editors, and Reinhold's daughter, said this of his view of TR and FDR: "My father was skeptical: the progressivism of Teddy Roosevelt wasn't going to be enough; his cousin's New Deal wasn't going to be either. The problems seemed to be insurmountable. Still it was a great deal better than elsewhere."[19]

Niebuhr was a man of several minds—all of them stemming from a deeply rooted religious attitude that looked at the world suspiciously. His doubts about this-worldly things had at least partly to do with his birth to immigrant parents. His father, Gustav, was an ordained minister in the German Evangelical Church. Reinhold was born when the family was living in Wright City, Missouri just west of St Louis where his father served a small German speaking church. Reinhold grew up in several such rural churches his father pastored. His mother, Lydia, looked after the family and served in the always-treacherous role of minister's wife. Churches and family were, again, German speaking. Important to add that children brought up in parsonages are almost always generous of heart and serious of commitment.[20] All members of this family went on to become prominent figures in America. Reinhold's sister, Hulda, was a leader in religious education; his brother, Helmut Richard a much admired professor at Yale Divinity School; his eventual wife, Ursula, founded the religion department at Barnard College; Helmut's son, Richard Reinhold, taught theology at Harvard Divinity School; then there was Elizabeth, Reinhold and Lydia's daughter. Their son, R. Gustav Niebuhr was the religious editor at *The New York Times* before becoming a journalism professor at Syracuse University.

As for schooling, after graduation from small rural schools, Reinhold studied at Elmhurst College and Eden Theological Seminary, after which he went to Yale Divinity School where in but two years he earned enough credits to be ordained to the ministry in what later became the United Church of Christ. His schooling represents how Reinhold grew in other ways. In 1947 the United Church of Christ brought together the Evangelical and

---

18 Much of what follows is based on, or taken from: Charles Lemert, *Why Niebuhr Matters* (Yale University Press, 2011).
19 Elizabeth Sifton, *The Serenity Prayer: Faith and Politics in Times of Peace and War* (W. W. Norton, 2003), 154.
20 One example among prominent sociologists is Craig Calhoun.

Reformed denomination to which his father's German Evangelical Reformed denomination had belonged. This listing of denominational transitions may seem beside the point, but Reinhold Niebuhr had passed from an isolated, backward looking immigrant church to, in a relatively few number of years, the United Church of Christ, the most ethically progressive of Christian denominations in America. So too his political and intellectual views evolved from small and rural to grand and global.

In 1915 Reinhold Niebuhr became pastor of the Bethel Evangelical Church in Detroit, a German speaking congregation. In the day, Detroit was the hub of the new industrial America dominated by Henry Ford's motor car factories. At the time, Henry Ford (another Gilded Ave grifter) was widely praised for paying workers $5/day—a generous wage in the day. Niebuhr wasn't fooled. He soon came to understand that Ford put workers on unpaid leave during manufacturing down-seasons, thereby reducing their annual income to an amount that paid them only marginally above the poverty line, if that. Niebuhr fought Ford openly and aggressively. One result of his resistance is that over his years in Detroit from 1915 to 1928, when he left for Union Theological Seminary in New York City, his congregation increased in membership from 70 to 700. This, no doubt, because of his genuine first-hand experience of what the workers suffered:

> We went through one of the big automobile factories to-day. ... The foundry interested me particularly. The heat was terrific. The men seemed weary. Here manual labour is a drudgery and toil is slavery. The men cannot possibly find any satisfaction in their work. They simply work to make a living. Their sweat and their dull pain are part of the price paid for the fine cars we all run. And most of us run the cars without knowing what price is being paid for them. ... We are all responsible. We all want the things which the factory produces and none of us is sensitive enough to care how much in human values the efficiency of the modern factory costs.[21]

He was not yet forty when he wrote these lines that exhibit the bottomless sympathy from which grew his criticism of the social and economic order as it had become.

At the same time Niebuhr's sympathies did not quell his unequivocally severe idea of public morality. His higher education before Yale, especially at Eden Theological Seminary, had been politically influential. The biblical scholar at Eden was Samuel D. Press who taught Niebuhr the prophetic values of Amos, the eighth century BCE Hebrew prophet who was an unrelenting critic of the kings and people of Israel. For example (Amos 5:21): "I hate, I despise your religious festivals; your assemblies are a stench to me." Then, stronger still (Amos 9:9–10): "For, lo [says the Lord], I will command and I will sift the house of Israel among all nations, like as corn is sifted in a sieve, yet shall not the least grain fall upon the earth. All sinners of my people shall die by the sword." Amos's God was not interested in pious ceremonies but in righteousness and justice—themes that would be central to Niebuhr's moral theory of politics. His *Moral Man and Immoral Society* (1932), written in his early days at Union Seminary, is the most explicit statements of his rejection of the possibility that the state and its society could be moral.

Moral Man and Immoral Society was the first of Niebuhr's great books. It is not perfect. In time he admitted that "immoral society" was too clumsy a term. What makes it great, nonetheless, is that it is a tacit social theory of politics—one that grew out of his objection, formulated in the Detroit years, to the Social Gospel still then persuasive among liberal Protestants. Simply put, the Social Gospel believed that Christian individuals could

---

21 Reinhold Niebuhr, *Leaves from the Notebook of a Tamed Cynic* (Westminster John Knox Press, 1929), 79–80.

lead the way toward a good society. Niebuhr found this naïve, both religiously and politically. Theologically it was all-too-simply based on a failure to appreciate the depth of sin in human nature. Politically, it saw the social world in America as inclined toward progress that would better the lives of ordinary people. One might add that historically the Social Gospel movement pretended the Gilded Age bosses had not selfishly ignored their role in debasing the poor who were cogs in the wheels of industry. The Social Gospel movement began to unravel during Niebuhr's Detroit years. Just the same, he had its naivety well in mind when he wrote *Moral Man and Immoral Society*. The main, and most famous, idea of this book is that structural society is immoral, thus resistant to moral man's idealized ethic of love.

By the early 1930s when *Moral Man and Immoral Society* was written the Great Depression had put the final nail in the coffin of all innocent economic or religious beliefs of a better world. Niebuhr looked at the situation clearly enough to put structured societies in a proper theoretical place. The state, and the society it means to govern, cannot escape its roots in power—domination, in particular. He continued:

> All social cooperation on a larger scale than the most intimate social groups requires a measure of coercion. While no state can maintain its unity purely by coercion, neither can it preserve itself without coercion. Where the factor of mutual consent is strongly developed, and where standardized and approximately fair methods of adjudicating and resolving conflicting interests within an organized group have been established, the coercive factor in social life is frequently covert—and becomes apparent only in moments of crisis and in the group's policy toward recalcitrant individuals. Yet it is never absent.[22]

Niebuhr is here setting himself hard against both religious and secular liberalism, thus against the dominant core of American popular politics. It is worth adding at this point that Niebuhr declined to consider himself a theologian. He was, he said, a social ethicist. Fair enough. It would not be far wrong, however, to say that he was at least a tacit social theorist. In 1932 no one in America thought about power this way—as the distinguishing line between individuals and social justice. Oh that sociologists (especially) had read Niebuhr's book!

Then too, Niebuhr's thinking, after moving to Union Seminary in 1928, was clearly informed by his thirteen years in Detroit. Here is a partial list of the social justice activities that grew out of Niebuhr's political engagements in those early years:

> Industrial Committee of the Detroit Council of Churches, the Federal Council of Churches, the American Association for Democratic Germany, the Bi-Racial Commission of the City of Detroit, the Highlander School in Tennessee, the Delta Cooperative Farm in Mississippi, the Council on Foreign Relations, Freedom House, Christianity and Crisis.

More than a few of these were life-long commitments. The Highlander School in Tennessee was founded in 1932 by Myles Horton, one of his Union students. At first, it aimed to provide voter education and literacy education for young Blacks. In time it became a civil rights organization serving those often ignored by other social change groups—notably the poor in Appalachia. It continues the work today. The Delta Cooperative Farm in Mississippi

---

22 Reinhold Niebuhr, *Moral Man and Immoral Society* (Charles Scribner's Sons, 1932), 3–4. Also on the general issues around this book, see Charles Lemert, "Powers, Pulpits, and Politics" in *Why Niebuhr Matters* (Yale University Press, 2011), Chapter 3.

began in 1936 to serve the needs of sharecroppers who had been forced off their Jim Crow plantations. It too expanded to other related programs serving the Black and white rural poor.

One of the truly important of Niebuhr's political associations was Americans for Democratic Action (ADA) founded in 1947 by Niebuhr, Arthur Schlesinger, Jr., Eleanor Roosevelt, the labor leader Walter Reuther, the civil rights lawyer Joseph Rauh, Hubert Humphrey, and others of like mind. ADA was to the left of the Democratic Party's left, working politically on behalf of labor for civil rights interests and issues that were particularly urgent for Eleanor Roosevelt, who shared Niebuhr's concern with the then not-so-liberal Democrats. Southerners dominated the Democratic Party through FDR's presidency until Lyndon Johnson's Great Society changed all that. ADA came undone late in the 1960s when the War in Vietnam divided its ranks. Just the same, Niebuhr had become so influential beyond religious circles that its founders appear to have thought first of him. Then too, he never hid his religion. Truth be told, his most famous lines known to millions the world over are the Serenity Prayer, he wrote in 1943:

> God, give us the *grace* to accept with serenity the things that *cannot* be changed,
> *Courage* to change the things that *should* be changed,
> and the *Wisdom* to distinguish the one from the other.[23]

The middle verse rises clearly from his commitment to social change, as the first and the third are foundational to serious social activism.

At the same time, returning to Niebuhr's intellectual work, he kept working ever more after 1928, benefitting from the academic luxury of reading and writing time. Over those years until a stroke in 1952 forced him to cut back on work and social action he was a leader in many social causes serving the poor and excluded. Even after the stroke, he continued these righteous labors once he adjusted to his physical limitations until his death in 1971. In a sense he was born a global person who, when fully mature, could not ignore the reality that across his life from youth to old age this was a time when global affairs were increasingly on everyone's mind. His tenure in Detroit began in 1915 when the Great War was already killing men and other victims in Europe, the Near East, Asia, the Pacific, and Africa. The US would not enter the fighting until Spring 1918. When the War ended in November 1918 many American boys were added to the dead. Woodrow Wilson's League of Nations came to be but failed to establish a peace that would end all wars. During Wilson's presidency, American isolationism prevented the US from becoming the world leader he had hoped it would be. But most damaging was the Versailles Peace Treaty in November 1919 that was so extreme in the terms imposed on Germany as to be the rhizomatic tangle of European underground relations that caused Hitler to sprout above ground in Germany in 1933. Then began the Nazi regime of hatred so severe that another World War was inevitable. When Germany required France to sign an armistice in June 1940, Hitler demanded that it be signed in Compiègne in the same railroad car in which the French had forced Germany to sign their armistice to the Great War in November 1918. At a deeper lever still, what came to be after the ill-conceived end of the First World War was, as some put it, the modern Thirty Years' War from 1914 to 1945. This war led to Stalin's rise to power in the

---

23 Over the years the Serenity Prayer has been variously modified by members of Alcoholics Anonymous and other 12 Step recovery groups for whom it is recited at most weekly meetings. This is Niebuhr's original version. On this point see Elizabeth Sifton, *The Serenity Prayer* (W.W. Norton, 2003), 291–305 [emphasis added]. Also for Sifton's view of the Prayer's relationship to *The Nature and Destiny of Man*, see *ibid*, 225–230.

Soviet Union that, but a few months after the Second World War, led also to a Cold War until 1991 between the West and the Soviets their awkward alliance with Chairman Mao's People's Republic. The hot and cold wars of the twentieth century served as cooker and freezer for these near century-long globalized wars.

Niebuhr lived through many of these changes in global structures. His personal Germanic culture was essentially reformed by his emergent American culture which, as things turned out, could not, and did not, allow him to ignore the global realities through which he lived. This fact of his life affected his thinking usually in quite obvious ways as in *Moral Man and Immoral Society* in 1932. But, less obviously, it was a tacit feature of many of the writings that followed, none more so than the book based on his 1939 Gifford Lectures in Scotland, *The Nature and Destiny of Man* (1943 [1941]). Not only was this book Niebuhr's *magnum opus* twice over in two big volumes in one—it remains today one of the most important works of nonfiction in the twentieth century.[24]

The Nature and Destiny of Man begins and ends, some 600-plus pages later, with statements that, even today, would rock the boat of what remained, then and still, of a common liberal culture of human nature:

> Man is a problem to himself. Man has always been his most vexing problem. How shall he think of himself? Every affirmation which he may make about his stature, virtue, or place in the cosmos becomes involved in contradictions when fully analysed. The analysis reveals some presupposition or implication which seems to deny what the proposition intended to affirm. ... Furthermore, the very effort to estimate the significance of his rational faculties implies a degree of transcendence over himself which is not fully defined or explained in what is connoted by "reason."[25]

Here and throughout the book, Niebuhr is attacking the modern view of man by showing that its all-too-optimistic view of human nature is due to the way it adopted and adapted classical thinking about man. Though understated, amid a wealth of allusions to classical and biblical literatures, Niebuhr presents the evolution of Western history's idea of man—in which the classical Greco-Roman and biblical theories were merged after the Roman era, then in the high Middle Ages when St Thomas Aquinas fused Aristotelian and Augustinian ideas of human nature. All this, he argues, was turned inside out when Liberal Protestantism tried to combine the two, only to destroy what united them.

It is not far wrong to use Max Weber's famous *Protestant Ethic and the Spirit of Capitalism* as the social theoretical exemplar of the origins of Liberal Protestantism. Weber's argument was that puritanical Calvinism's sixteenth-century Protestant doctrine of God as the divine rational author of the ultimate fate of all human souls gradually escaped the religious sphere to become in the nineteenth century the secular ethic of the modern rational Capitalist ethic. In his words:

> The Puritan *wanted* to work in a calling: we are *forced* to do so. For when asceticism was carried out of monastic cells in everyday life, and began to dominate worldly morality, it did its part in building the tremendous cosmos of the modern economic order. ... For of the

---

24 The Modern Library ranked *The Nature and Destiny of Man* 18th of the top 100 nonfiction books of the twentieth century, though with the laughable remark: "Highly recommended for fans of ontology"—as if there were any after that century. It is probably right to say that the book was written in the 1930s well before feminism called into question uninflected use of "Man." See: https://sites.prh.com/modern-library-top-100#top-100-nonfiction

25 Niebuhr, *The Nature and Destiny of Man, Volume I* (Charles Scribner's Sons, 1941), 1.

last stage of this cultural development, it might well be truly said: "Specialists without spirit, sensualists without heart; this nullity imagines that it has attained a level of civilization never before achieved."[26]

Niebuhr was more philosophical than Weber—but he sang from the same hymnbook. He began: "Modern culture has been a battleground of the two opposing views of human nature."[27] Battleground yes, but modernism won the battles on three fronts: [1] First off, in the battle between idealism and naturalism "modern culture slips from the essential Platonism of the early Renaissance to the Stoicism of Descartes and Spinoza and the seventeenth century generally and then to the more radical materialistic and Democritan naturalism of the eighteenth century."[28] In effect, modern man puts Nature in the primal philosophical place—for which Ralph Waldo Emerson and the Concord Transcendentalists were the near perfect modern instance. Niebuhr goes on to stipulate two remaining primordial contradictions. "[2] The concept of individuality in modern culture belongs to a class of certainties of modern man about himself which his own history has gradually dissipated. ... [3] The final certainty of modern anthropology is its optimistic treatment of the problem of evil."[29] The outcome of these desiderata of the modern idea of him- [her-] self is the naïve idea that history is progress—ever onward and upward.

The Nature and Destiny of Man proceeds from these principles to elaborate them and their implications in the book's first volume in chapters with predictable, but sometimes surprising titles, for examples: "The Problem of Vitality and Form in Human Nature," "Individuality in Modern Culture," "The Easy Conscience of Modern Man," "Man as Image of God and as Creature," "Man as Sinner," and "Original Sin and Man's Responsibility." The drift toward what many would call theology is apparent, which would seem to contradict his assertion that he was more an ethicist than a theologian. Yet, the underlying and continuous narrative line is of man who lives, works, and trusts in a contradictory world where neither the true or the good is clearly seen or righteously done. The individual lives in a welter of *thises* and *thats*, as he says in his own way (in italics!):

> *The "I," which from the perspective of self-transcendence, regards the sinful self not as self but as "sin," is the same "I" which from the perspective of sinful action regards the transcendent possibilities of the self as not the self but as "law." It is the same self; but these changing perspectives are obviously significant.*[30]

Then, interestingly, Niebuhr goes on to criticize theologians from Augustine to the Protestant Reformers in order to deny this complex idea of sin and man by reverting to "a simpler emphasis upon the corruption of man [that] must be attributed not just to the illusions of the Fall, but also to the fear that any concessions to man's self-esteem would immediately aggravate the sin of pride."

Admittedly those without training in theology will find this kind of thing obscure. Yet, in the first of the two books of *The Nature and Destiny of Man*, Niebuhr leaps back to the

---

26 Max Weber, *The Protestant Ethic and the Spirit of Capitalism* (Charles Scribner's Sons, 1958 [1904-05]), 181 and 184. Emphasis added.
27 Niebuhr, *The Nature and Destiny of Man*, 5.
28 *Ibid*, 19. [Democritan refers to the philosophy of Democritus, the fifth century BCE Greek atomist philosopher who popularized a view of all things as either atoms or void.]
29 *Ibid*, 21 and 23. [Anthropology here refers not to the social science but to the science or theory of man.]
30 *Ibid*, 279. Quoted line immediately following same place.

simple and clear theme of *Moral Man and Immoral Society*. The concluding chapter of the first book is *Justitia Originalis*—literally, original justice, which he translates as original righteousness—which, important to say, is not the idea that all human beings are righteous from the beginning. Rather, it is a question of faith. "The love of neighbor, the perfect accord of life with life and will with will, is ... a derivative of perfect faith and trust with God."[31]

The second book of *The Nature and Destiny of Man* concerns, as the title says, human destiny. It begins:

> Man is, and yet is not, involved in the flux of nature and time. He is a creature, subject to nature's necessities and limitations; but he is also a free spirit who knows of the brevity of his years and by this knowledge transcends the temporal by some capacity within himself. ... [And:] Man's ability to transcend the flux of nature gives him the capacity to make history.[32]

The words introduce a book that is more openly theological—though always with just as explicit references to the inscrutability of religious logic, as in "the foolishness of God is wiser than men; and the weakness of God is stronger than men." The line is from 1 Corinthians where Paul of Damascus, the onetime persecutor of Christians, had become their missionary to the early churches where very human believers had, as all humans do, lapsed into arrogance as to their wisdom and strength. Biblical history aside, the Bible throughout rebukes believers of various kinds for their having reached too far. From here it is a short step to the secular idea that whatever humans do in their own right they are limited by, at least, the "brevity of their years" even if they also possess "a free spirit...[that allows them]... to transcend time and nature...to make history." Shorn of any doctrinal religious content, Niebuhr is saying—and as we know—that the ability to see beyond the limitations of their time and natures is a universal human quality. Otherwise they would not act in a way as to make histories that carry on after their time is over and they would be buried back into nature's dirt.

The second book of *The Nature and Destiny of Man* is a long discourse on the Protestant idea of human destiny. At every point it contains the basic human quality of, if I may say it this way, *doing in order to have done something that lasts*. Even if the doing is a rain dance or the worship of ancestors without the least idea of making history, it is, just the same, a doing that transcends the fate of a human being who one day will be gone. This ironic fact of human nature and fate raises its head again and again in *The Nature and Destiny of Man*, which otherwise could be seen as nothing but a special brand of religious thought. It is that, but in a way goes beyond what most religious thinking, even that of Protestant Christianity, seldom acknowledges. Nowhere is Niebuhr's supple thinking more apparent than in Book II, Chapter 9 "The Kingdom of God and the Struggle for Justice."

Again justice is the keynote: "The struggle for justice is as profound a revelation of the possibilities and limits of historical existence as the question for truth. In some respects it is even more revealing because it engages all human vitalities and powers more obviously than the intellectual quest."[33] He then follows with an idea that is not only the foundation to his theory of justice but also was the theme of *Moral Man and Immoral Society* ten years before.

---

31 *Ibid*, 193.
32 Niebuhr. *Nature and Destiny of Man, Vol II* (Charles Scribner's Sons, 1943), 1.
33 *Ibid*, 244. Quote just below, same place. [Reminder: This and references to follow are from *The Nature and Destiny of Man* from Book II.]

> Community is an individual as well as social necessity; for the individual can realize himself only in intimate and organic relation to his fellowmen. Love is therefore the primary law of his nature; and brotherhood the fundamental requirement of his social existence.

Here he adds an element not so prominent in the earlier book, love. As much as the reader would rightly suppose, his use of love is basically *agape* then *philos* and *eros* only by accident of right relationships.[34] Niebuhr then adds that love is simultaneously the "fulfillment and the negation of all achievements in human history." In *Moral Man and Immoral Society*, love appears sixty-nine times but never so prominently as here in *The Nature and Destiny of Man*. The earlier book was more or less all-but-pure social ethics. The later book puts those ethics in cosmic even global context—as the primary law of nature/as the fundamental requirement of social existence.

The fact that *The Nature and Destiny of Man* is more theological requires some religious notion that conveys the entirety of social and cosmic life. Hence, *The Kingdom of God and the Struggle for Justice*—title of the ninth chapter in the second volume—turns on the entangled relationship of justice with power (again much like *Moral Man and Immoral Society*).

> No human community is, in short, a simple construction of conscience or reason. All communities are more or less stable or precarious harmonies of human vital capacities. They are governed by power. The power which determines the quality of the order and harmony is not merely the coercive and organizational power of government. That is only one of two aspects of social power. The other is the balance of vitalities and forces in any given social situation. The two elements of communal life—the central organizing principle and power, and the equilibrium of power—are essential aspects of community organization; and no moral or social advance can redeem society from its dependence upon these two principles.[35]

So subtle a theoretical logic as this is seldom, if ever, found in social theories. For a prime example, just imagine how Talcott Parsons's theory of society as a functional interaction of actors[36] would have endured longer to better effect had he read and applied Niebuhr's theory of "the balance of vitalities and forces in any given social situation." Niebuhr, in other words, took power and coercion as the necessary opposing poles of an ever dynamic social movement.

The corollary here is that all social structures are global because, as it is clear to anyone who is able and willing to look at the social worlds on this earth, where it is hard not to realize that these social worlds are always and necessarily in motion, driven in their different searches for power and equipoise—never at rest. Though Niebuhr does not get to the idea of social movements as such, he does provide an implicit theoretical principle that requires them. The dynamo of Global powers requires social movements able to reset the equipoise.

In the between of global power and social movements is the ever-present risk that an over-emphasis on one of the dynamics of this relationship will disturb their equipoise. In

---

34 Perhaps it is worth saying that here *agape* is religious love, while *philos* is brotherly love (as in Philadelphia), and *eros* is sexual love which in the tradition is limited to right relationships (to which I would add that, had Niebuhr lived in our day, his idea of *eros* would have included faithful non-heterosexual relations). But this is a guess on my part based on the fact that Niebuhr was a preternaturally fair-minded person.
35 Niebuhr, *The Nature and Destiny of Man Vol II*, 257–258.
36 See Chapter 12, above.

The Irony of American History (1952) Niebuhr makes it evident that to him in America an exaggerated belief in the individual is that always ironic element:

> Sometimes the irony in our historic situation is derived from the extravagant emphasis in our culture upon the value and dignity of the individual and upon individual liberty as the final value of life. Our cherished values of individualism are real enough; and we are right in preferring death to their annulment. But our exaltation of the individual involves us in some very ironic contradictions. On the one hand, our culture does not really value the individual as much as it pretends; on the other hand, if justice is to be maintained and our survival assured, we cannot make individual liberty as unqualifiedly the end of life as our ideology asserts.[37]

For Niebuhr everything always comes down to a critical sensibility even and especially to his native nation.

Charles Tilly: Social Movements and the Invisible Elbow

Charles Tilly (1929–2008) was the scholar's scholar, author of over 50 books and countless articles and essays, invited talks, and interventions of various kinds. Yet, those who knew him, even those who knew him in passing, were always welcome to call him Chuck. We who have been given the name Charles endure all manner of nicknames—Chas, Charlie, as well as Chuck. Many of us insist on the more dignified Charles—not Chuck Tilly.

Tilly's humanity appeared in many ways, none more so than in his way of writing on extremely complicated topics—into which he often inserted startlingly down-to-earth metaphors that make the telling point with surprising clarity. Two among many examples are short essays: "Invisible Elbow" and "Micro, Macro, Megrim?". Both take on grand and often ill-considered topics in social and political theory. "Invisible Elbow," put simply, renames the metaphor that Adam Smith in *Wealth of Nations* in 1776 alleged to be the dynamic governing economic markets, "The Invisible Hand." It is always dangerous to rely on metaphors when trying to illuminate so big an economic thing as the circulation of wealth. Still, Tilly writes:

> For the Invisible Hand, let's substitute the Invisible Elbow. Coming home from the grocery store, arms overflowing with food-filled bags, you wedge yourself against the doorjamb, somehow free a hand to open the kitchen door, enter the house, then nudge the door closed with your elbow. Because elbows are not prehensile and, in this situation, not visible either, you sometimes slam the door smartly, sometimes swing the door halfway closed, sometimes miss completely on the first pass, sometimes bruise your arm on the wood, sometimes shatter the glass, and sometimes—responding to one of these earlier calamities—spill groceries all over the floor.[38]

Tilly is quick to say that he is not arguing for a world of irrationality, but for the normal experience of unintended consequences. Then he quotes Robert Frost's *Road Not Taken* and a poem from Paul Auster's *Disappearances* along with social scientists Herbert Simon,

---

37 Niebuhr, *The Irony of American History* (Charles Scribner's Sons, 1952), 7; or http://media.sabda.org/alkitab-2/Religion-Online.org%20Books/Niebuhr,%20Reinhold%20-%20The%20Irony%20of%20American%20History.pdf Chapter 1, page 4.
38 Charles Tilly, "Invisible Elbow," in his *Roads from Past to Future* (Rowman & Littlefield, 1998), 39.

Max Weber, and Robert K. Merton who earlier and in different ways gave the Invisible Hand a rest. This was Tilly's way of rethinking handed-down Grand Assumptions with alluring mentions of the irregularities of daily life. Another example, among the many, is his reframing of the taken-for-granted idea that social things must be studied as if they were either macro or micro, "Micro, Macro, Megrim?" The third of this trilogy is the onset of the migraine headache one suffers by trying too fastidiously to deploy all-too-lofty analytic categories that neglect the archaeological fact "that social processes are path-dependent—that sequences and outcomes of causal mechanisms vary by space-time setting, that the order in which events happen affects how that small-scale or large-scale collective experience congeals as culture..."[39] To ignore this fact of life is be afflicted by a severe analytic headache of being wrong-headed.

One can now see that Tilly always dug deep into classic but ill-gotten ideas that, over time, had won too permanent a hold on the thinking of philosophers and social theorists. A third example is worth the mention because it introduces his primary intellectual activity as a political theorist and researcher. He was more than any one thing—an historian, sociologist, as well as a political scientist. He was always looking first and foremost at the largest possible scale of social orders without neglecting the small-scale realities in which social lives are lived. *The New York Times* obituary baptized Tilly "the founding father of 21st century sociology," an honor he would not have thought as his.[40]

Charles Tilly uses these metaphoric stories always to shed light on a more complicated issue of importance to his work. His 1995 essay, "Democracy Is a Lake" is an exceptionally good example of this aspect of his literary method—in this case one central to his social and political theory of democracies. Plus which the essay appears, along with "Invisible Elbow," in *Roads from Past to Present*, arguably the most important collection of his shorter writings late in life. The book is introduced by a generous review essay by Arthur Stinchcombe one of the few major thinkers in sociological social theory who rivaled Tilly's stature.

"Democracy Is a Lake" serves to explain democracy in seriously analytic terms in just more than ten pages. It is, as always, jam-packed with references to pertinent sources—some familiar, others not so much—including several in the original Swedish (just one among the languages Tilly knew)—this to pull democracy along by a "chain" of constituting elements: State, Polity, Rights, Citizenship. Chain? One begins to get how the figure of a chain ties these four concepts together in Tilly's way of defining them:

> *State*: an organization controlling the principal conceptual means of coercion within a delimited territory and exercising priority in some respects over all other organizations with the same territory. *Polity*: the set of relations among agents of the state and all major political actors within the delimited territory. *Rights*: enforceable claims, the reciprocal of *obligations*. *Citizenship*: rights and mutual obligations binding state agents and a category of persons defined exclusively by their legal attachment to the same state.[41]

---

39 Charles Tilly, "Micro, Macro or Megrim?" in his *Stories, Identities, and Political Change* (Rowman & Littlefield, 2002), 76.
40 Douglas Martin, "Charles Tilly, 78, Writer and a Social Scientist, Is Dead," *The New York Times* (May 2, 2008). [I once asked Chuck if he might one day win a Nobel Prize. He said, of course not—there isn't one for what I do. He then turned the question from himself by quickly proposing that Art Stinchcombe should. CL]
41 Charles Tilly, "Democracy Is a Lake," in his *Roads from Past to Future* (Rowman & Littlefield, 1998), 197–198.

With this chain of concepts in mind, it helps to say that Tilly took both his BA and PhD at Harvard in the heyday of Talcott Parsons's Department of Social Relations. He knew very well Parsons's AGIL paradigm which always was drawn into a fourfold scheme of action systems. One might be tempted to interpret Tilly's four elements of democracy as borrowed from Parsons. Yet, Tilly does two things quite at odds with Parsons's scheme. One is to stipulate the constitutive elements as a chain of path-dependent social processes (as he put it in "Micro, Macro, Megrim?") and not at all a network of action systems as Parsons had it. Tilly's chain passes from the State through the political relations associated with states, to the turnkey of any democracy—the rights of citizens and their obligations to the State and others engaged therein. The second contrast to Parsons's relatively peaceful modern social order was for Tilly the key political feature of (even) a democratic State is that it is "an organization controlling the principal conceptual means of coercion." Or as Tilly puts it more succinctly elsewhere: "States themselves operate chiefly as containers and deployers of coercive means, especially armed force."[42] One must give Reinhold Niebuhr credit for seeing, in *Moral Man and Immoral Society* in 1932, the necessary place of coercion in state politics well before Tilly and others pointed to its crucial role in modern—supposedly democratically free—political life.

One might well wonder how this tough-minded concept of coercion works in a seemingly natural figure of a lake. Again, Tilly's metaphors articulate the nature of the concept at hand in relation to the alternatives:

> Democracy does not resemble an oil field or a garden, but a lake. A lake—a large inland body of water—can come into being because a mountain stream feeds into a naturally existing basin, because something dams up the outlet of a large river, because a glacier melts, because an earthquake isolates a segment of the ocean from the main body of water, because people deliberately dig an enormous hole and channel nearby watersheds into it, or for any number of other reasons.[43]

First off, it is easy to see the path-dependent flow in this extended figure that serves as Tilly's chain. A lake's water comes down from the mountains, over or through dams, absorbing glacier melts, and flowing through other barriers and basins to the oceans. Tilly elsewhere frequently cited Fernand Braudel's idea of long enduring time that arises from geographic and climatic sources. It may be a stretch to interpret these waterways as the coercive forces from and through which lake water rises and drains, but it works well enough. Lakes, he goes on to explain, are different from oil fields and gardens that *might* be thought good enough sources of a democratic chain. Yet, he writes: "experts cannot produce a new oil field" and gardens "will not flourish everywhere"... [In both cases,] "experts know what aspects they cannot influence."[44] Or, he means to say, other possible figures for the origins of democracies that they are walled off in contrast to the flow of lake waters—channel, if not path, dependent.

Otherwise put, these three metaphorically composed essays touch on the major features of Tilly's theoretical work—1) classical thought early in the modern age, 2) contemporary theory gone astray, and 3) democracy, then and now, as the hope and trouble of modern life. Tilly wrote very many books, all of them replete with historical data focused on

---

42 Charles Tilly, "The Long Run of European State Formation," *Actes du colloque de Rome* (18–31 mars 1990), 140.
43 *Ibid*, 209–210.
44 *Ibid*, 194.

historical issues, many with serious numeric statistics, almost all with a flood of charts and diagrams mean to illuminate his concepts. Even a listing of several of his major single-authored books (selected from almost as many co-authored ones) is very long: *The Vendée* (1964), *Migration to an American City* (1965), *An Urban World* (1974), *From Mobilization to Revolution* (1978), *As Sociology Meets History* (1981), *Big Structures, Large Processes, Huge Corporations* (1985), *The Contentious French* (1986), *Coercion, Capital, and European States, A.D. 990–1990* (1990), *European Revolutions, 1492–1992* (1993), *Popular Contention in Great Britain, 1758–1834* (1995), *Roads From Past to Future* (1998),[45] *Durable Inequality* (1998), *Politics of Collective Violence* (2003), *Stories, Identities, and Political Change* (2004), *Trust and Rule* (2005), *Identities, Boundaries, Social Ties* (2005), *Why?* (2006), *Democracy* (2007), *Explaining Social Processes* (2008), and *Contentious Performances* (2008). This list alone tells a lot about Tilly, the person and the author. He was, very likely, the most disciplined prolific author of historical nonfiction of his time. And, he worked even harder in the years and months before his death by lymphoma in 2008.

Then too, as much as he reached for maximum clarity for his readers, Tilly was not shy about criticizing common fallacies among his colleagues in social science. In *Big Structures, Large Processes, Huge Comparisons* (1984) he began with an oft-quoted list of erroneous views that led thinking astray on the many subjects he cared about.

- The view that societies are not connected with each other;
- The view that collective behavior can be explained in terms of the mental state of individuals;
- The view that societies can be understood as blocs, lacking parts or components;
- The view that societies evolve through fixed stages (an assumption common in modernization theory);
- The view that differentiation is a master process, common to all societies as they modernize;
- The view that quick differentiation generates disorder;
- The view that rapid social change causes behaviors that are not considered normal, such as crime;
- The view that "illegitimate" and "legitimate" kinds of conflict originate in different processes.[46]

What is missing from this list of false propositions? What did Tilly identify as the important concept that changes everything? So far as I know he was never so reductive to have posed and answered such a question. Yet, it is not far wrong to say (as you might well have already guessed): *coercion*! But why? How might this one concept change everything when it comes to social theories of state and other political structures? The answer is that, as his analytic scheme for State process and its path dependent consequences makes clear,— states, especially democratic ones, are never static, much less always in a state of equipoise. Crudely put: *Democracy means people rule; people are unruly; democratic states must prevent chaos; democratic states are themselves ruled by unruly people; state embedded people, like all people, often go too far when coercing; for over-coerced people to rein-in their states, they must engage in social movement; individuals never change states; only social movements can—however imperfectly.*

---

45 *Roads from Past to Future* contains, at the end, a list of Tilly's publications from 1959–1996.
46 Charles Tilly, *Big Structures, Large Processes, Huge Comparisons* (Russell Sage Foundation, 1984), 11–12.

Tilly may never have put it this way. Still, if one just scans the titles of his books, it is hard not to see that, structurally speaking, *States* and *Social Movements* are the operative structures in democratic politics. The difference between democratic states and autocratic ones is that the autocrats have managed to suppress, if not eliminate, anti-state social movements. In the book where he defines and discusses social movements historically, *Social Movements: 1768–2004* (2004), Tilly begins by making the sharp point that the concept "social movement" took on a political and, eventually, social theoretical meaning in the late eighteenth and early nineteenth centuries when the public politics and revolutionary tone of the day, as he put it, lent the term the meaning it enjoys today among social and political scientists of all brands. "That political complex" he continues, "combined three elements: 1) campaigns of collective claims on target authorities; 2) an array of claim-making performances including special purpose associations, public meetings, media statements, and demonstrations; 3) public representations of the cause's worthiness, unity, numbers, and commitment."[47]

The first giant step to a full-blown study of social movements occurred in the early 1970s after the American Civil Rights Movement made it evident that social movements were more than instances of collective violence in an otherwise stable if dynamic societal order. Jack Goldstone, in the introduction to his *Revolution and Rebellion in the Early Modern Era* (1991), states persuasively that the historical study of revolution and rebellion "changed markedly in the 1970s, ... [when] the historically grounded work of Tilly and his collaborators challenged the validity of general theories of violence, arguing that more attention needed to be paid to how conflicts developed and how resources for opposition were mobilized in specific historical contexts."[48] It is then that resource mobilization theory began as one of the significant new fields in American social thought. Craig Jenkins introduces his 1983 *Annual Review of Sociology* on "Resource Mobilization Theory and the Study of Social Movements," with the defining statement that: "Resource mobilization theory has recently presented an alternative interpretation of social movements. The review traces the emergence and recent controversies generated by this new perspective. A multifactored model of social movement formation is advanced, emphasizing resources, organization, and political opportunities in addition to traditional discontent hypotheses.[49]

Though Tilly is counted among the founders of resource mobilization theory, he went well beyond. Resources, he argued, were important, but not by any means their necessary cause. For a social movement to begin, it requires the kind of collective action that *might* become open rebellion and, in turn, *might* lead to a social revolution—which are very rare. Tilly's *From Mobilization To Revolution* in 1978 is the paradigmatic text (in Thomas Kuhn's sense) that changed everything for social movement theory. It begins with another homespun expression, "The Stuff of Collective Action," followed by a nuanced description of the turmoil in England in 1765–1767 that was inspired, he observes, by the rebellion of its American colonies against the Crown's imposition of the 1765 Stamp-Act Duty. Shortly after, *From Mobilization To Revolution* turns to the basics of a theory of collective action: "The analysis of collective action has five big components: interest, organization,

---

47 Charles Tilly, Ernesto Castañeda, and Lesley J. Wood, *Social Movements: 1768–2004* (Routledge/Paradigm 2020 [2004]), 7.
48 Jack A. Goldstone, *Revolution and Rebellion in the Early Modern Era* (University of California Press, 1991), 18. Needless to say, though Goldstone's book is a major contribution to the history on revolutions in the modern age, he does not agree with Tilly in all things.
49 J. Craig Jenkins, "Resource Mobilization Theory and the Study of Social Movements," *Annual Review of Sociology*, 9, (1983) 527.

mobilization, opportunity, and collective action itself."[50] Then in Chapters 2, 3, and 4, Tilly carefully sets forth the elements and their troubles in these five components. For example, on the vexing question of opportunity, the study of collective action must work with the following assumptions: 1) Collective action costs something. 2) All contenders count costs. 3) Collective action brings benefits, in the form of collective goods. 4) Contenders continuously weigh expected costs against expected benefits. 5) Both costs and benefits are uncertain because (a) contenders have imperfect information about the current state of the polity; (b) all parties engage in strategic interaction.[51] Chapter 5 studies "Changing Forms of Collective Action" where strikes serve as the case study; and Chapter 6 examines "Collective Violence" where he offers several cases of political violence in America and Europe in the early years of the Great Depression and before Hitler's rise to power.

Then, in Chapter 7, "Revolution and Rebellion," the reader comes to the heart of the book's argument. "Revolutionary reality is complex. And, whether it includes coups, assassinations, terrorism, or slow, massive changes such as industrialization, it is controversial—not only because the world is complex but also because to call something revolutionary is, within most forms of western political discourse, to identify it as good or bad."[52] Again, Tilly's language is pithy. Amid a series of violent political actions he includes industrialization which many would not think of as revolutionary—with the unexpected qualifier that the outcomes can be "good or bad." Then, he cites Leon Trotsky's *History of the Russian Revolution*, on the 1917 October Revolution to the effect that revolutions, successful or not, pass through a pre-revolutionary situation:

> The historical preparation of a revolution brings about, in the pre-revolutionary period, a situation in which the class which is called to realize the new social system, although not yet master of the country, has actually concentrated in its hands a significant share of the state power, while the official apparatus of the government is still in the hands of the old lords. That is the initial dual power in every revolution.[53]

As a matter of fact, Trotsky's historical theory of the Russian revolution is a major source for Tilly's pivotal section "Revolutionary Situations and Revolutionary Outcomes." Tilly accepts the idea that a revolutionary situation exists when there is a "dual power" dynamic that in effect threatens the old order still in power. At the same time he rejects Trotsky's suggestion that this is a two-class situation implying that the rebelling fraction is already a structural element in the fluid political situation. Rather, Tilly proposes a still more fluid solution.

"Multiple sovereignty is then the identifying feature of revolutionary situations. A revolutionary situation begins when a government previously under the control of a single, sovereign polity becomes the object of effective, competing, mutually exclusive claims on the part of two or more distinct polities. It ends when a single sovereign polity regains control over the government."[54]

From Mobilization to Revolution then turns to the still more dynamic circumstance in which situations and outcomes are part and parcel each of the other, not structurally discrete fixtures. Here again, his notion of path-dependent historical chains comes into play. Tilly proposes to soften that hard edge of political concepts in order to rethink them as "*continua*

---

50 Charles Tilly, *From Mobilization to Revolution* (Addison-Wesley, 1978), 7.
51 *Ibid*, 99.
52 *Ibid*, 189.
53 Leon Trotsky, *The History of the Russian Revolution* (London: Gollancz, 1965 [1930]), 224.
54 Tilly, *From Mobilization to Revolution*, 191.

[in that]...a situation can be more or less revolutionary."⁵⁵ The chapter proceeds through a thicket of alternative theories (most of them familiar names), more than a few charts meant to illustrate the un-illustratable dynamics, and historical accounts of failed and successful revolutions that support or contradict the theories present. But, when all is said and done, he comes to a rather simple summary of a long discussion: "Three sets of conditions appear to be powerful proximate causes of significant transfers of power: (1) the presence of a revolutionary situation: multiple sovereignty; (2) revolutionary coalitions between challengers and members of the polity; (3) control of substantial force by the revolutionary coalition."⁵⁶ In other words, he untangles hard-nosed conceptual schemes beginning with Trotsky's into a visibly evident and continuous line of historical actions that apply in those rare instances when a revolution succeeds.

And that is not all, when it comes to clarifying surprises. In 1985, Tilly contributed an essay to what then was a major and controversial collection, *Bringing the State Back In*. His contribution, even now when the truth of its title is apparent, will likely raise hackles on the necks of many rightists who read and of more than a few center-left liberals: "War Making and State Making as Organized Crime." From its first lines, one sees that here Tilly is casting new light on a dark corner of social and political theory: "If protection rackets represent organized crime at its smoothest, then war making and state making – quintessential protection rackets with the advantage of legitimacy – qualify as our largest examples of organized crime."⁵⁷ He quickly adds that he is not accusing those who make wars and lead states of being themselves murderers and thieves. Then to finish this remarkable opening paragraph he adds:

At least for the European experience of the past few centuries, a portrait of war makers and state makers as coercive and self-seeking entrepreneurs bears a far greater resemblance to the facts than do its chief alternatives: the idea of a social contract, the idea of an open market in which operators of armies and states offer services to willing consumers, the idea of a society whose shared norms and expectations call forth a certain kind of government.

Later on, after a thoughtful presentation of Fernand Braudel on the subject, he comes to the question readers of *Bringing the State Back In* had been asking, What do states do? Tilly's answer, as usual, is elegantly straightforward:

As should now be clear, [Frederic C.] Lane's analysis of protection fails to distinguish among several different uses of state-controlled violence. Under the general heading of organized violence, the agents of states characteristically carry on four different activities: 1) *War making*: Eliminating or neutralizing their own rivals outside the territories in which they have clear and continuous priority as wielders of force. 2) *State making*: Eliminating or neutralizing their rivals inside those territories. 3) *Protection*: Eliminating or neutralizing the enemies of their clients. 4) *Extraction*: Acquiring the means of carrying out the first three activities—war making, state making, and protection.⁵⁸

---

55 *Ibid*, 194.
56 *Ibid*, 211–212.
57 Charles Tilly, "War Making and State Making as Organized Crime," in *Bringing the State Back In*, edited by Peter B. Evans, Dietrich Rueschemeyer, and Theda Skocopol (Cambridge University Press, 1985), 169. Long quote just following, same place.
58 *Ibid*, 181. [Reference to Fredric C. Lane is to "The Economic Meaning of War and Protection," in *Venice and History: Collected Papers of Frederic C. Lane* (Johns Hopkins University Press, 1966 [1942].]

Each of these entails violence. He explains each as being interdependent. Simply put: States are made by war making that eliminates or controls external enemies which, in turn, requires the exploitation of a state's operating apparatus—all of which require extracting resources from members *and* the wider world. Perhaps the key word here is "extracting" as opposed to borrowing, buying, trading, and other terms of a more generous concept of civil societies might suggest. State making is a tough business requiring hard-headedness as to the role of violence as, one might say, the penultimate resource.

Chuck Tilly was kind and warm to the people in, or on the margins of, his life, but stern, if not harsh, toward the legacy of concepts history served up to him.

Theda Skocpol: States and Social Revolutions

Theda Skocpol was born in 1947 in Detroit, Michigan and later, against the wishes of her parents, went to college at a public university, Michigan State. Michigan was a place she came to consider one of the reasons her sociology has been consistently based on the ground of people and their issues. In a 2019 interview she said: "I think it's very important that I came from the Midwest, and I never feel as comfortable as when I am in the Midwest, and I know what the vast heartland of the country looks like and feels like."[59] After Michigan State, she went to Harvard to study sociology with leading figures like Barrington Moore, a major figure in political sociology, whose *Social Origins of Dictatorship and Democracy* (1966) was then, and still is, a modern classic in comparative historical research on politics. Skocpol's own classic in the field, *States and Social Revolutions: A Comparative Analysis of France, Russia, & China* (1979), starts off by identifying Moore's book, along with two others, as the exemplars for her research on social revolutions.[60]

Upon publication, *States and Social Revolutions* immediately became one of the influential books of the late 1970s and for a good while after. Any number of positive reviews soon appeared. One, in the prestigious *American Journal of Sociology*, began: "Theda Skocpol is perhaps the most ambitious and exciting of a new generation of historical-comparative sociologists who have focused their attention squarely on the big issues of social change that once preoccupied the classic sociologists."[61] Then after correctly praising the details of *States and Social Revolutions*, the reviewers close with a criticism that amounts to the denunciation of precisely what Skocpol did—that she set aside voluntaristic theories of revolution for structural ones. The complaint, in fact, turns on a flimsy remark that Skocpol gave away "the delicate synthesis that Marx struggled to achieve—the coincidence of changing circumstances and of human activity."[62] This observation is worth the while for the way it illustrates an important difference between social scientific theories and social theories, in particular, feminist ones. As we've seen, feminists can differ sharply but never bitterly. They embrace each other with rare exception. Scientifically minded sociologists seem to feel obliged always to denounce some or another aspect of what they review—in this case the very basis of Skocpol's structural project. There's a lesson here.

---

59 Theda Skocpol and Eric Schickler, "A Conversation with Theda Skocpol," *Annual Review of Political Science* 22 (2019): 1–16. A good many of the comments here on Skocpol's biography come from this excellent and thorough interview. They are taken from on-line versions of the discussion for which there are no page numbers. See https://www.annualreviews.org/doi/pdf/10.1146/annurev-polisci-030816-105449

60 Theda Skocpol, *States and Social Revolutions: A Comparative Analysis of France, Russia, & China* (Cambridge University Press, 1979), 6.

61 Jerome L. Himmelstein and Michael S. Kimmel, "States and Revolutions: The Implications And Limits Of Skocpol's Structural Model," *American Journal of Sociology* 86:5 (Mar 1981), 1145–1154.

62 *Ibid*, 1154.

Just the same, *States and Social Revolutions* has held up well over the years so much so that it was celebrated in another review on its 40th anniversary in 2019 that concludes, after a review of the book's strengths and contributions, with: "What is needed is a new Skocpol for a new age of revolutions."[63] Of course, it is true that now, in the 2020s, not only have revolutions changed but so too have states. Theda Skocpol, when she is read as a theorist, is in the long run a productive scholar on many fronts. She said of herself in 2019: "I'm not theoretically driven, I'm a theory user. I use different theories to try to understand real-world patterns and outcomes"[64] Her *States and Social Revolutions* fits this remark to a T. The book's long introductory chapter is perfectly well entitled: "Explaining Social Revolutions: Alternatives to Existing Theories." It begins with a theoretical statement that is more a working theorem: "Social revolutions are rapid, basic transformations of a society's state and class structures; and they are accompanied and in part carried through by class-based revolts from below."[65] After which she offers a precise but careful summary of Marx's idea of the state entrenched as it was in his deeper thinking on the forces and relations of production. Then Skocpol turns to the short list of theorists from whom she borrowed, in particular Ted Gurr's *Why Men Rebel* (1970), Charles Tilly's *From Mobilization to Revolution* (1978), and Chalmer Johnson's *Revolutionary Change* (1966)—who, in the day, were the classic sociological texts of revolution—as, for her, Barrington Moore's *Social Origins of Dictatorship and Democracy* (1966) was basic to her thinking on state politics. Soon after, she comes to the principles in her working theorem shared also by currently prevalent theories of state-revolutions: 1) non-voluntarist, 2) "cannot be explained without systematic reference to *inter*national structures and world-historical developments," 3) in which states are "conceived as administrative and coercive organization—organizations that are potentially autonomous from (though of course conditioned by) socioeconomic interests and structures."[66]

Having set down her principles, Skocpol then proceeds to show that there is light between her and major figures on the general subject of the history of social change—Immanuel Wallerstein is an economic reductionist, she claims; Tilly, Gurr, and Johnson, she argues, reduce the state to "an arena in which social conflicts are resolved"; while, in her view, Tilly, like the Marxists, "regards the state as a system of organized coercion that invariably functions to support the superordinate position of dominant classes and groups."[67] It is possible to forgive the exaggerations here on the grounds that this was her first book. She was untenured. She had to stake out her turf. She would be judged by hard-bitten academic sociologists at Harvard, who as it turned out judged her harshly (about which more to come). Skocpol returns with grace to her main idea:

> We can make sense of socio-revolutionary transformations only if we take the state seriously as a macro-structure. The state properly conceived is no mere arena in which socioeconomic struggles are fought out. It is, rather, a set of administrative, policing, and military organizations headed, and more or less well coordinated by, an executive authority.[68]

---

63 George Lawson, "Happy Anniversary? *States and Social Revolutions* Revisited," *International Affairs* (July 2019) @ https://eprints.lse.ac.uk/101503/1/International_Affairs_Skocpol_review.pdf.
64 "Skocpol," ibid, 2019.
65 Skocpol, *States and Social Revolutions*, 4.
66 *Ibid*, 14.
67 *Ibid*, 26.
68 *Ibid*, 29.

Before turning to her main empirical question—Why France, Russia, and China?—she offers what turns out to be a simple but convincing methodological statement: "Comparative historical analysis is, in fact, the mode of multivariate analysis to which one resorts when there are too many variables and not enough cases."[69]

Why then these three cases?—1) because they all were states beset by debilitating failures in their Old Regimes; 2) all were afflicted by a rebellious lower class; 3) the Old Regimes had to deal with mass-mobilizing political leaders and parties intent upon winning state power.[70] She might have said, but, if memory serves, she didn't explicitly add: These were the only *major* social revolutions of the day.

In any case, here endeth the first 43 pages of a more than 400 page book—in which the remainder is, precisely, comparative historical analysis that covers the three cases with a fine tooth comb. Too fine for this discussion but it is possible to summarize the comb she deployed. There are two major parts. Part I is Causes of Social Revolutions in France, Russia, and China, while Part II covers the outcomes of those revolutions. One gets an idea of the specifics of Skocpol's analysis by attending to the introduction to Part II by turning to its Chapter 4, "What Changed and How: A Focus of State Building." The chapter begins with the expected statement that all three revolutionary states went through similar political and class struggles that produced basic structural "transformations." Yet, there were differences among them. In Russia and China, the revolutions resulted in states led by parties that "asserted control over the entire national economies of the two countries." But in France the post-revolutionary state was organized by a professional and bureaucratic dominating order. In Skocpol's words:

> In contrast to France, Soviet Russia and Communist China resembled each other as development-oriented party-states. But otherwise they differed in key respects, with the Russian regime exhibiting some important similarities to France. For like the French Revolution, the Russian Revolution gave rise to a professionalized and hierarchical state oriented to the firm administrative supervision of social groups. This applied in particular to the domination of the peasant majority in society in the name of urban interests.[71]

A close reading of just this one paragraph gives a taste of Skocpol's fine dish of historical details presented on a delicate structural plate. The whole of Part II continues in the same vein with three chapters each comparing and linking the three cases: Chapter 5, "The Birth of a 'Modern State Edifice' in France"; Chapter 6, "The Emergence of a Dictatorial Party-State in Russia"; Chapter 7, "The Rise of a Mass-Mobilizing Party-State in China."

Even today, more than four decades later reading through the entire book, it is a delight for the way in juicy paragraphs or overflowing chapters, *States and Social Revolutions* treats the reader with the way it bakes its factual *and* theoretical into a loaf that rewards the patience required and stimulates the desire for more. In the end, Skocpol offers a stunning observation:

> Yet for true democratization to become possible within any given advanced industrialized country, it would surely be necessary for democratizing movements to proceed roughly

---

69 *Ibid*, 36.
70 *Ibid*, 40–42.
71 *Ibid*, 162. [Quoted lines just above are from 161.]

simultaneously in all advanced countries, with each movement making it a key objective steady progress toward disarmament and international peace."[72]

These lines stun because, while honest and likely correct, they point to a future in which democratic social revolutions are all but impossible.

When it was published in 1979 *States and Social Revolutions* won widespread recognition in Skocpol's field at the time, sociology. The Society for the Study of Social Problems awarded it the prestigious C. Wright Mills Award and the American Sociological Association gave it, and her, its award for a significant contribution to scholarship. The Association's then-president, Lewis Coser, writing in the Book Review section of *The New York Times* called it a landmark in the study of revolutions.[73] To be sure, given the benighted attitudes of academics, a good number complained about such things as its failure to take into account the individual—the very point she covered as political leadership, not as a primal analytic category. Just the same most who cared about her subject enough to read and discuss *States and Social Revolutions* thought it brilliantly important, especially in the context of political sociology in the day when sociologists, whether seriously centrist or leftish, were trying to come to terms with Marxism and the world revolution of 1968. Yet, Harvard's Department of Sociology denied her tenure in 1980 on a split vote the school's president declined to overturn. Interestingly the split vote was not on the question of personal politics so much as a then-raging dispute on qualitative versus quantoid research.[74] These were the days in Harvard Sociology after Talcott Parsons (who died in 1979) had kept the house in order.

Skocpol did not take the denial as the final word, anything but. She immediately met with Derek Bok, Harvard's then-president, who offered no immediate reversal but did say that he might reconsider the case at a later date. But Skocpol wasted no time in filing a grievance that she was denied tenure because she was a woman—a time when there were no academic women in Sociology and very few in the university. As she did in her first book, Skocpol wrote lengthy and well-documented analytic histories on the facts of her case and the fact of the gender matter at Harvard. This before she accepted a position at the University of Chicago in political science which she liked quite a lot and rose quickly through the academic ranks. But she was not done with Harvard (plus which, her husband was a physicist then working in the East). She won her case at Harvard in 1984 and returned to joint positions in Government and Sociology. She knew the sociologists would not welcome her. The 1981 *The New York Times* sexual harassment article wrote, quoted her:

> Theda Skocpol is not a person who makes small talk. Even her closest friends describe her as capable of being cold and somewhat brusque initially. "Abrasive" is a word often used to describe her, but she has never found this quality much of a career impediment at Harvard. "On a nastiness scale of 1 to 10 in my department, I'd say I'm about 5," she once told a friend.[75]

Those who know Theda are unlikely to object. She can be all-business and, rightly I think, above and beyond the obsequiousness of academics. Part of her business is teaching, which

---

72 *Ibid*, 293.
73 Lewis Coser, "The Sources of Revolt," *The New York Times Book Review* (October 31, 1979), 44–45.
74 "A Question of Sex Bias at Harvard," *The New York Times Book Review* (October 18, 1981), 96. [This article, published in a day when staff-writers were not often given by-line recognition, is a superb account of the story of Skocpol's tenure denial.]
75 *Ibid*, "A Question of Sex Bias at Harvard," 96.

she takes very seriously. The same *NYT* article went on to quote one of her students: "Most professors pay attention to you after you become one of the greats. Theda spent time with us from the beginning. She treated graduate students as serious scholars, said one student. Her courses were tough and her students respected her for it."

After the five years at Chicago, she kept her principal Harvard office in Government and in time won as much recognition in Political Science as she had in Sociology.

In 1985 Skocpol took the State as a subject in a book she co-edited, *Bringing the State Back In: Strategies of Analysis in Current Research*. It began as one might expect with the basic issues, documented with lengthy footnotes identifying the sources:

> A sudden upsurge of interest in "the state" has occurred in comparative social science in the past decade. Whether as an object of investigation or as something invoked to explain outcomes of interest, the state as an actor or an institution has been highlighted in an extraordinary outpouring of studies by scholars of diverse theoretical proclivities from all of the major disciplines. The range of topics explored has been very wide. [1] Students of Latin America, Africa, and Asia have examined the roles of states in instituting comprehensive political reforms, helping to shape national economic development, and bargaining with multinational corporations. [2] Scholars interested in the advanced industrial democracies of Europe, North America, and Japan have probed the involvements of states in developing social programs and in managing domestic and international economic problems. [3] Comparative-historical investigators have examined the formation of national states, the disintegration and rebuilding of states in social revolutions, and the impact of states on class formation, ethnic relations, women's rights, and modes of social protest. [4] Economic historians and political economists have theorized about states as institutors of property rights and as regulators and distorters of markets. [5] And cultural anthropologists have explored the special meanings and activities of "states" in non-Western settings.[76]

Yes, a long quotation from a long essay, but it is a pithy summary of the book's contents and purposes. Yes, she means to put before scholars the work that has been done in their area—work that her 1979 book went a long way toward drawing attention to crucial issues that needed rethinking. It is important to note that, in a sense, Skocpol is, as she put it in *States and Social Revolution*, a theory-user, while also being a proponent of her methodological attitude toward the validity of comparative historical research.

As for her own original research, she began work on a book that became *Protecting Soldiers and Mothers/The Political Origins of Social Policy in the United States* (1992). From the title one might conclude that here she is moving beyond the state, if not social revolutions. Not quite. Here the state is not the primary mover and shaker of early welfare policies from, roughly, 1868 to 1929, but it plays a central role. She makes a counterintuitive argument. To many it would seem obvious that America's social welfare system, such as it is, began in 1933 under FDR with the Social Security Act. She says no. It began in the aftermath of the Civil War in which so many soldiers survived with terrible disabilities leaving their mothers and loved ones suffering without support. This is another chapter in what Drew Gilpin Faust called, *The Republic of Suffering*. Though the development of

---

[76] Theda Skocpol, "Bringing the State Back In: Strategies of Analysis in Current Research," Peter B. Evans, Dietrich Rueschemeyer, and Theda Skocpol, eds., *Bringing the State Back In* (Cambridge University Press, 1985), 3.

a modern social welfare system took many "twists and turns" as she put it—but over the years, even in the nineteenth century, it came to be in its earliest version. She writes:

> Between the 1870s and the 1920s, the paths explored in U.S. social policy were especially distinctive. In an era when many industrializing Western nations were launching fledgling paternalistic welfare states for workers—that is sets of regulations and benefits by male bureaucrats and politicians for male workers and their dependents—the United States sought to help not workers but soldiers and mothers.[77]

The state was, to be sure, a factor but less as the primary mover. These policies came to be because of the efforts of social groups to meet evident needs that even reluctant politicians could not ignore.

Beyond this, Skocpol has published, according to her 2022 *curriculum vitae*, at least 13 single or jointly authored books and another 12 edited books along with countless other shorter writings and monographs. To list just a few of the books is to show how wide ranging her interests are, as well as how deep she has plunged into public policy issues. For examples: *Social Revolutions in the Modern World* (1994), *Social Policy in the United States: Future Possibilities in Historical Perspective* (1995), *Boomerang: Clinton's Health Security Effort and the Turn Against Government in U.S. Politics* (1996), *The Missing Middle: Working Families and the Future of American Social Policy* (2000), *Diminished Democracy: From Membership to Management in American Civic Life* (2003), *The Tea Party and the Remaking of Republican Conservatism* (with Vanessa Williamson, 2012), *Upending American Politics: Polarizing Parties, Ideological Elites, and Citizen Activists from the Tea Party to the Anti-Trump Resistance* (co-edited with Caroline Tervo, 2020), more. This while accumulating honor upon honor.

But all this is not the most remarkable of her recent achievements. When she was a young student, Skocpol had been, like many of her generation, active in civil rights and anti-war activism. Yet, few when they grow older and well-honored, do what she did in 2009 when Skocpol founded the Scholars Strategy Network (SSN). The defining purpose of SSN could be described as bringing academic knowledge out into the world in plain language. In 2014 *Harvard Magazine* reported an example of how SSN makes a difference:

> [Skocpol] cites immigration debates in which legislators clamor for taller fences, ignorant of research showing that fortified borders don't reduce illegal immigration, but do increase costs, keep undocumented workers from going home—and ultimately prompt them to bring in their families. "It's a perfect example," Skocpol remarks, "of how policy produced the exact opposite of what was intended, because people didn't understand how immigration works." Such examples prompted SSN, she continues, to try linking scholars to policy: "How can their work, their voices, their persons get more connected to the broader process of democratic politics?"[78]

Soon after its founding, SSN grew to 400 academics committed to its policy with chapters in 40 states—all avoiding the cost of publishing in outlets unlikely to be read by ordinary readers. To become a member-academic requires, at least, a two-page essay that, Skocpol rightly says, poses a serious challenge for those writing and reading at much greater length.

---

77 Theda Skocpol, *Protecting Soldiers and Mothers/The Political Origins of Social Policy in the United States* (Harvard University Press, 1992), 525.
78 Michael Zuckerman, "Citizen Scholars," *Harvard Magazine* (Sept–Oct 2014).

SSN holds retreats and meetings across the nation usually with the participation of local congresspersons like Rosa DeLauro (D-Conn) who praised its "beyond the Beltway" purposes.

However today Skocpol would calibrate her "nastiness" coefficient, it would be hard for anyone who cares about this world to consider her anything less than an heroic exemplar of what an academic can and *should* be.

James Scott: The Arts of Resistance

James Scott (1936–2024) was born in Mount Holy, New Jersey a relatively well-off town, today a suburb of Philadelphia. He studied at elite schools—Moorestown Friends School, Williams College, and Yale from where he earned a PhD in political science in 1967. With such a trajectory one might assume he remained in an elite groove thereafter. Not so. Anything but. By the time he went to Moorestown, a Quaker School, his father had died (when he was 9) and his mother was coping with depression and alcoholism. Scott started there in the second grade and credits Moorestown for taking over where his parents could not—both in terms of his growing up well and by introducing him to social activism, another quality of Quaker culture.[79] A teacher there encouraged him to go to Williams where, again, he was a scholarship student in economics, who felt quite out of place in what he calls "a rich kid's school." In time Williams realized that its students knew little about common or poor life in America and began a program in which students spent a semester living in (Scott's example) a greengrocer's home. By chance he met William Hollinger, who took him on to write an honor's essay on economic development in Burma, which upon graduation led to a Rotary International Fellowship to study in Burma. While there he was also involved in a good many political activities. Here and there, his life's work was determined, beginning with doctoral studies at Yale, which led to a year in Paris studying at *Sciences Po*, after which he switched from economics to political science. At the time the Yale Department was at its empiricist zenith led by Robert Dahl. Scott did what they required before turning, almost by accident, to study with Robert E. Lane who taught him the scholarly virtue of long, in-depth interviews—a method he employed in his thesis interviewing high civil servants in Malaysia (published by Yale University Press in 1968 as *Political Ideology in Malaysia: Reality and the Beliefs of an Elite*—a book he later thought ill of). It hardly need be said, in this time in Malaysia and after, Scott was an active opponent of the war in Vietnam, including oddly and by accident work with the backhanded efforts of the CIA.

After Yale he accepted a position at the University of Wisconsin Madison. He was eventually tenured, promoted, and popular among faculty and students. After eight years there, Scott returned to Yale where he remained until his death in 2024. When they moved to Connecticut, Scott and his wife Louise bought a farm in Durham, Connecticut—a rural town not that far from New Haven. For years he raised and shepherded sheep and goats and later two cows. He worked in a shed alongside his sheep, until, after many years, it burned down, destroying much of his then current work. Yet, no longer young at the time, he carried on, lecturing the world over, winning any number of prizes and other honors. In 2020, he won the Social Science Research Council's Albert O. Hirschman Prize—the equivalent of the Fields Medal in Mathematics. Over the years, his Yale affiliations increased with joint appointments in

---

79 Most of the biographic details of Jim Scott's life are drawn from one of the best interviews of the kind (over 3 hours) in which he reveals more than a few intimate stories of his childhood—no better way to learn who Jim Scott became and is: Allan MacFarlane, "Interview with James Scott," *Cambridge University Interview Series* (2009) @ https://www.sms.cam.ac.uk/media/1130301 .

the Agrarian Studies Program (which he founded), the School of Forestry & Environmental Studies, Anthropology and Institute for Social and Policy Studies, as well as Political Science. All this, a long journey from a lost childhood reclaimed by Quakers and many accidents in early life that led him to rural villages in Southeast Asia and Yale and the world over.

Scott's intellectual journey began, by his own account, after the initial field work experiences in Southeast Asia with, ironically, an archivally researched book, *The Moral Economy of the Peasant: Rebellion and Subsistence in Southeast Asia* in 1976. Later, when he would be asked where he had done the field work for this book, he had to reply, with no more than a tinge of embarrassment, "in the archives." This of course was a sign of how his reputation in more than a few fields is based on field work in places few others have studied, and many knew not of, as well as ones in a relatively long ago (in this case, the Global Depression of the 1930s). Archival though it may be the central argument of *The Moral Economy of the Peasant* "arises from the central dilemma of most peasant households. Living close to the subsistence margin and subject to the vagaries of weather and the claims of outsiders, the peasant household has little scope for the profit maximization calculus of traditional neoclassical economics."[80] Later, he adds as the book's central idea—that the peasants of whom he writes created a *moral economy*. "An understanding of informal social guarantees of village life is crucial to our argument because, as they are sustained by local opinion, they represent something of a living normative model of equity and justice."[81] Just after, Scott sets forth the findings of his research with a note naming the major works on Southeast Asia that report of this moral economy, followed by graphic and analytic representations on the "Distribution of Risk in Tenancy Systems," an analytic scheme, and, curiously, a "hypothetical case" comparing "Crop Division under Sharecropping and Fixed Rent."[82] These occur in a second chapter on the choices and values available to, and accepted by, the peasants when it comes to "subsistence security"—in many ways the contrapuntal theme of the book's subtitle: *Rebellion and Subsistence in Southeast Asia* is its main point. Here the book offers some actual archival data in Table 3. Comparative Effect of Proportional and Fixed Assessments on Peasant Income—that (if I understand the footnote associated with this table) comes from the *Report on Land Revenue Systems* (Rangoon, Burma.)[83] Even if I am wrong in interpreting Jim Scott's source, I am right to point out that here the book's theoretical claim as to the moral economy of peasants faced with precarities imposed on their actual income by historical changes in the state's role in changing its taxation policies which can have real consequences for the subsistence of the ever-vulnerable peasantry. The data actually show that, between proportionate and fixed taxes on yields, the differences are slight (even though the actual income remains at the subsistence level). Peasants are not necessarily taxed to death, which also means they have some room to maneuver within the limits of their own, local moral economy. Scott concludes:

> I have tried to demonstrate in this chapter (2) that there is a correspondence between the logic of the subsistence ethic and the concrete choice and values of much of the peasantry in Southeast Asia. At the level of village reciprocity, occupational preferences, and the evaluation of tenancy and taxation there appears to be a clear inclination to favor those institutions and relationships which minimized the risks to subsistence, though they may

---

80 James C. Scott, *The Moral Economy of the Peasant: Rebellion and Subsistence in Southeast Asia* (Yale University Press, 1976), 4.
81 *Ibid*, 41.
82 *Ibid*, 45 and 47.
83 *Ibid*, 53.

claim much of the surplus. These preferences grow out of the precarious human condition of subsistence farmers but they also take on a moral dimension as a claim on the society in which they live.[84]

Only those (I include myself) who know next to nothing about the global peasantry could romanticize this last statement. Local life among these peasants, Scott reports, is like local life among poor or otherwise common people everywhere. They bicker, gossip, long for something more, and pose a soft but real threat of sorts to the higher classes who have a say in keeping them down. At the same time, Scott's peasants "are not radically equalitarian. Rather they imply only that all are entitled to a *living* out of the resources in the village."[85] They put up with a relatively bad deal in exchange for "subsistence insurance."

But, as things go, what these peasants had, before *their* modern era, was defenseless when historic global changes came down on them from 1900 to 1940. Among the major changes were the intrusions of a more greedy global market that, first, made their products—rice for example—vulnerable to this market preferences. This while colonialism altered regional populations, among other deep structural changes that weakened the village accords by altering the delicate balance between local and regional forces and by limiting their ability to control the lands and prices that, in turn, weakened their ability to protect themselves economically and culturally. Then too, these dynamics had the effect of all-but destroying the market value of their secondary resources such as selling local craft products. Then Scott adds the deterioration of agrarian class relations that came with a greater more ruthless colonizing capitalism that controlled not only land and taxes but its full arsenal of intrusive measures from the growing inequality in landholding to protecting property rights of land-holders.[86]

The threats to the well-being peasant in Southeast Asia became all-but lethal when the Global Depression of the 1930s set in. "The depression delivered the coup de grâce to an agrarian order already weakened by structural changes begun well before 1930."[87] Then, in parts of the region, rebellions in the summer of 1930 were followed in September by violence directed at the fading colonial regimes. "[A] good many assassinations were traceable directly to the failure of the local official/notable to respect the redistributive norms of village life."[88] After describing the causes and effects of the violence, Scott offers a pungent analysis of the rebellion of the peasants and the role played by their moral economy:

> Regardless of the particular form it takes, collective peasant violence is structured in part by a moral vision, derived from experience and tradition, of the mutual obligations of classes in society. The struggle for rights that have a basis in custom and tradition and that involve, in a literal sense, the most vital interests of its participants is likely to take on a moral tenacity which movements that envision the creation of new rights and liberties are unlikely to inspire. It is for this reason, perhaps, that:
> ... the chief basis for radicalism has been the peasants and the smaller artisans in the towns. From these facts one may conclude that the wellsprings of human freedom lie not only where Marx saw them, in the aspirations of classes about to take power, but

---

84 *Ibid*, 55.
85 *Ibid*, 5.
86 See Scott's tabular listing of these changes and their effects at *ibid*, 66 (Table 4).
87 *Ibid*, 114.
88 *Ibid*, 145.

perhaps even more in the dying wail of a class over whom the wave of progress is about to roll.

Only the moral vision of these classes and the moral indignation that it fosters can begin to explain why peasants may embark on revolt despite seemingly hopeless odds.[89]

The book ends with what may or may not be a shocking fact—that the rebellions did not lead to revolutions. Still what one takes from *The Moral Economy of the Peasant* is a serious fact of peasant life:

> It is especially at the level of culture that a defeated or intimidated peasantry may nurture its stubborn moral dissent from an elite-created social order. This symbolic refuge is not simply a source of solace in a precarious life, not simply an escape. It represents an alternative moral universe in embryo—dissident subculture, an existentially true and just one, which helps unite its members as a human community and as a community of values. In this sense, it is as much a beginning as an end.[90]

Some will be moved by this conclusion, others chilled by the way it turns the mental table on many a reader—that the most marginal of local cultures encourages, perhaps, the wider world of excluded people *and* those who care for them to look under their rebellious moments for the values that could begin, for them and others, a movement toward a better—at least good enough—life.

I have gone on at length covering Jim Scott's first important book for a reason. In the years after its publication he wrote many just as great and interesting books. But in *The Moral Economy of the Peasant* he gave social theory a reason to look in another direction to understand revolutionary social movements and why so few succeed. To put it too simply, when reading Theda Skocpol's *States and Social Revolutions* anyone who cares about the subject should read both of their arguments side by side. For one, they each put Marx in the deep but telling background of their thinking as both keep Barrington Moore in the foreground of their theories. Yet, Skocpol took seriously the social revolutions in prominent early modern states while Scott focused on rebellions in remote and peasant villages that in the day were remote from that modern world as it was still emerging.

The final statement of Skocpol's *States and Social Revolutions* is that "for true democratization to become possible within any given advanced industrialized country, it would surely be necessary for democratizing movements to proceed roughly simultaneously in all advanced countries..."[91]—a condition that in the world as it has become makes a democratic social revolution all-but impossible. While Scott's *The Moral Economy of the Peasant* ends with the reality that peasant rebellions do not rise into revolutions—even while their rebellions are energized by "an alternative moral universe in embryo [that] is as much a beginning as an end." Oddly (perhaps) Scott's conclusion is more in keeping with Marx's determined optimism in a way that Skocpol's is not. Of course, one cannot read too much into this comparison. But one can also say that Scott teaches social theorists that, when it comes to social movements and revolutionary social transformations, it is necessary to look as closely at the weakest, as at the strongest, socially structured societies.

---

89 *Ibid*, 192. [The internal quote is from Barrington Moore's *The Social Origins of Dictatorship and Democracy: Lord and Peasant in the Making of the Modern World* (1966).]
90 *Ibid*, 240.
91 Skocpol, *States and Social Revolutions*, 293.

Scott's second significant book on peasants and their politics appeared a good decade later, *Weapons of the Weak: Everyday Forms of Peasant Resistance* (1985). It began where *The Moral Economy of the Peasant* in 1976 left off by calling biting attention to field studies on peasant social movements that were written after the Vietnam War. They were of course written from a Western perspective and looked for "large-scale structural change at the level of the state." He continues:

> What is missing from this perspective, I believe, is the simple fact that most subordinate classes throughout most of history have rarely been afforded the luxury of open, organized, political activity. Or, better stated, such activity was dangerous, if not suicidal. Even when the option did exist, it is not clear that the same objectives might not also be pursued by other stratagems. Most subordinate classes are, after all, far less interested in changing the larger structures of the state and the law than in what Hobsbawm has appropriately called "working the system . . . to their minimum disadvantage."[92]

He goes on to say that commonplace forms of resistance by peasants were less the beginning of rebellion than an ongoing "struggle between the peasantry and those who seek to extract labor, food, taxes, rents and interests from them [but instead] the ordinary weapons of relatively powerless groups: foot dragging, dissimulation, desertion, false compliance, pilfering, feigned ignorance, slander, arson, sabotage, and so on."[93] Then, to complete Scott's line that carries over from *The Moral Economy of the Peasants*:

> The struggle between rich and poor in Sedaka is not merely a struggle over work, property rights, grain, and cash. It is also a struggle over the appropriation of symbols, a struggle over how the past and present shall be understood and labeled, a struggle to identify causes and assess blame, a contentious effort to give partisan meaning to local history.[94]

In these introductory lines, Scott points to the empirical evidence from which he unearths an important theory—one seldom, if at all, considered by other theorists of social movements.

Weapons of the Weak was a field study. Scott spent fourteen months in 1978–1980 in a Malaysian village of 74 households, he called it Sedaka. In contrast to the earlier book, this one is filled with meticulously gathered accounts of life on the ground in Sedaka. It begins, for example, with a chapter on a marginal individual foremost among the "down and out" of the village. Razak became the center of attention when his daughter, Maznah, died of a seasonal fever. At the viewing, Razak was ignored, unpardonably by the men. Just the same, when passing by the body, villagers would leave small donations to cover the costs of burial. However, Razak stopped Jim from leaving a donation. Jim perhaps, but Razak especially, would have been rebuked—for, presumably, receiving too generous a donation. Later Jim made the donation of M$20 privately and several days later Razak came to his home to thank him for the large donation.

---

92 James Scott, *Weapons of the Weak: Everyday Forms of Peasant Resistance* (Yale University Press, 1985), xv. Also available at https://voidnetwork.gr/wp-content/uploads/2020/04/Weapons-of-the-Weak_-Everyday-Forms-of-Peasant-Resistance-James-C.-Scott.pdf
93 *Ibid*, xvi.
94 *Ibid*, xvii.

Before long we passed on to the topic I had been raising recently in conversations with villagers: the enormous changes that have come to Sedaka since the beginning of double-cropping eight years ago. It was clear to Razak that things were generally worse now than before irrigation. "Before it was easy to get work, now there's no work in the village and the estates (rubber and oil palm) don't want anyone." The trouble, he added, is mostly because of the combine-harvesters that now cut and thresh paddy in a single operation. Before, his wife could earn over M$200 a season cutting paddy and he could earn M$150 threshing, but this last season they only managed M$150 between them. "People weren't happy when the machines came. You can't even glean anymore." What distressed him about the machine as well was how it removed money from the village and gave it to outsiders. Money that might have gone to paddy reapers and threshers from the village and in turn been used partly for local feasts within Sedaka was now paid directly to the owners of these expensive machines. As Razak put it, "They carry it away for their own feasts."[95]

After introducing Razak to begin the first chapter "Small Arms Fire in the Class War," then another local personage of strangely similar but different status is introduced—a personage by which villagers cleverly shot cultural snippets at the higher classes.

Scott introduces Haji Broom as Razak's "mirror image twin his fellow outcast from the opposite end of the social pyramid."[96] The peasants in the village prefer the English language word "broom" here because of onomatopoeic value best represents "to sweep away"—which also covers the sense of one has "cleaned up" at poker (that is, swept up all the chips on the table) or "cleaned out" one's opponents.[97] In Sedaka, Haji Broom was the one who had earned considerable wealth by a Ponzi scheme whereby he (and others of like purpose) took land from people by offering credit that was never paid back—a local instance of usury, which in the Koran is forbidden. Haji Broom was, it seems, as much loathed as Razak and lived in comparably dilapidated quarters in spite of his wealth. Hence, the deep-woven irony in the local culture of these and other South Asian peasants. Attacks on the higher classes, who stole from them (and worse), become a taxonomic species in the local lives by creating a cultural opposite to the poor Razak in Haji Broom, who was despised and rejected to the same degree, social differences notwithstanding. Yet, as Scott carefully explains:

> The tales about Razak and Haji Broom suitably embroidered, elaborated, and retold have far more than mere entertainment value. They amount to an exchange of small arms fire, a small skirmish, in a cold war of symbols between the rich and poor of Sedaka. Hostilities, in this war, as in most, are conducted over a shifting terrain in which there are many neutrals, bystanders, and reluctant combatants with divided loyalties. For the time being, at least, it remains a cold war both because many of the potential participants have important shared interests that would be jeopardized in an all-out confrontation and because one side, the poor, is under no illusions about the outcome of a direct assault.

95 *Ibid*, 8–9. [Important note that after "The poor are poorer and the rich are richer" in the passage, Scott offers one of many instances of explanations of the Malaysian terms used, here: *Orang susah, lagi susah; orang kaya, lagi kaya*. The fact that he should use the term *susah*, which might be translated as "hard up," for his class rather than the term *miskin* (poor) and the term *kaya* (rich) for those who are well-to-do rather than the term *senang* (comfortable), which would make a logical pair with susah, is significant. Other quoted lines in the passage are footnoted to provide the Malaysia language original.]
96 *Ibid*, 13.
97 *Ibid*, 15.

Thus, the "war news" consists almost entirely of words, feints, and counterfeints, threats, a skirmish or two, and, above all, propaganda.[98]

How can this be? The answer: "The rich, while they may be relatively immune to material sanctions, cannot escape symbolic sanctions: slander, gossip, character assassination."[99] It is all too easy for readers today to imagine such a thing. We of the urban North are accustomed to a more complicated and elevated higher status structure where the very, very rich live in another sphere purchased by a wealth so extreme as to make the very poor totally other. In Sedaka, all classes live close by each other in a common ground and culture where, material differences aside, what is said and heard can penetrate and cut. Those with power are unable to silence those without power, much less control what they say and do. The verbal cuts may not break the flesh of the social order, but they obviously hurt.

The introduction to *Weapons of the Weak*, is powerful as few introductions to big books are. Scott does not here outline what is to come chapter by chapter, but his telling of the ethnographic story of Sedaka paints a picture of what is to come—and there is very much to come. There are seven chapters following the first, each covering his topic in ever more generous detail and broad theoretical scope. For example, "History According to Winners and Losers," the fifth chapter, concludes with a powerful point too often missed by others:

> As in any history, assessing the present forcibly involves a reevaluation of what has gone before. Thus, the ideological struggle to define the present is a struggle to define the past as well. Nowhere is this more apparent than in the accounts given by poor villagers, who have had the least to be thankful for over the past decade and whose current prospects are bleak. They have collectively created a *remembered village* and a *remembered economy* that serve as an effective ideological backdrop against which to deplore the present.[100]

By remembering better days, the poor come to terms with what they lost when the rich took over crops and profits, leaving the poor worse off than even in the not-so-good old days. Nor is it just a matter of economic loss. It is personal. Hence they say: "The well-to-do are throwing those who are hard up aside." "The more we want to lift ourselves, the more we are pushed down, the more cruel [they are] to us." "They want to bury us." "As he says this last phrase, Pak Yah thrusts the heel of his hand toward the ground at his feet as if pushing something into the earth and adds, We want to be higher." These strung together lines are translations of Malaysian everyday life sayings in which the pain bleached anger of the villagers is apparent. To illustrate what he means, Pak Yah notes that in the past it was possible to get loans of rice from well-off villagers. But now, he claims, they sell their rice for cash and then claim they have no money.[101] I might add my personal opinion that this is the genius of Jim Scott's books, especially the ethnographically based ones: He seldom fails to present the most basic aspects of everyday life framed by a powerful general theory, almost always interlaced with references to notable authors like, here, Clifford Geertz on thick description whereby the smallest clues can and often do express general cultural meanings.[102] Then too Marx is ever present, if not exclusively so, in the theoretical background.

---

98 *Ibid*, 22.
99 *Ibid*, 25.
100 *Ibid*, 177.
101 *Ibid*, 142. [My summaries and all quotes, same place.]
102 *Ibid*, 139.

The book's concluding chapter, "Hegemony and Consciousness: Everyday Forms of Ideological Struggle," begins with a first section: "The Material Base and Normative Superstructure in Sedaka." At the first *Weapons of the Weak: Everyday Forms of Peasant Rebellion* begins with the most basic of Marxian doctrines—that the ideological struggles in Sedaka arise from changes in the relations of production issuing from a wealthier dominant class, "double-cropping and mechanization backed by the state". Then:

> It is these exogenous changes in the material base that have allowed large landowners and farmers to change the tenure system, raise rents, dismiss tenants, replace wage workers with machinery, and either to lease out large plots for long periods or to resume cultivation themselves. This shift in the balance of economic power has also allowed rich farmers to eliminate or curtail a host of social practices that were part and parcel of the earlier scheme of production relations: feast giving, Islamic charity, loans and advance wages, and even much of the social recognition and respect previously accorded to poorer villagers. What has occurred, in short, is that those facets of earlier relations of production that are no longer underwritten by the material interests of wealthy farmers are being abandoned piecemeal or wholesale.[103]

Scott makes the oft-overlooked point that the true feelings of the poor are not obvious to the innocent observer. On the surface all may seem normal, even imperturbable. No class conflict here. Yet, there is trouble. "The poor ... display an impressive capacity to penetrate behind the pieties and rationales of the rich farmers and to understand the larger realities of capital accumulation, proletarianization, and marginalization."[104] The poor are not stupid. They know what is going on and they act as best they can against the oppressive regime in their everyday lives. When one looks and listens closely and deeply to what they say and what they do, it becomes clear, as it did to Scott, that there are many acts of defiance. These acts of resistance within and against the prevailing ideology are directed at the ruling class but based on, to be sure, the injuries suffered by their material deprivations in crop management and lower profits. Then, as often, Scott comes to a pungent conclusion: "The main point for my purposes is that the peasants of Sedaka do not simply react to objective conditions per se but rather to the interpretation they place on those conditions as mediated by values embedded in concrete practices."[105] Later, after describing the methods of the landowners and the plight of the poor, Scott moves on to an enlightening discussion of ideology that, it seems, only one close to the ground could come up with—his references to Bourdieu, Gramsci, Orwell, Lukács, others on ideology fit the stories he tells.

> On my reading of the evidence it is in fact more plausible to contend that so far as the realm of ideology is concerned, no social order seems inevitable, even in this larger sense, to all of its subjects. The fact that serfs, slaves, or untouchables have no direct knowledge or experience of other social orders is, I believe, no obstacle to their creating what would have to qualify as "revolutionary" thought.[106]

As in *The Moral Economy*, Scott, however, remained skeptical that a true revolution could take place in Sedaka where "resistance by subordinate classes begins close to the ground,

---

103 *Ibid*, 305.
104 *Ibid*, 304.
105 *Ibid*, 305.
106 *Ibid*, 331.

rooted in firmly in the homely but meaningful realities of daily experience. The enemies are not impersonal historical forces but real people. That is, they are seen as actors responsible for their own actions and not as bearers of abstractions."[107] And, again, their complaints about their sense of being wronged come from what they knew or had been told were the belief and actions of the past of those in like position.

Those already familiar with Scott's many books may wonder why here I would focus so much on two of his earliest. The answer is that in *The Moral Economy of the Peasant* and *Weapons of the Weak* he makes important, and original, contributions to social theories of social movements and revolutions. And he does this on the basis of empirical and archival research on peasant life in remote Southeast Asia where few are equipped, even willing, to work, live, learn the languages in order to appreciate what those he came to know have to tell the wider academic world they know not of.

All too-often states are assumed to be the object of social movements that might turn them over into a new social order. None of this is true in places like Sedaka where, first, there are no states that serve as a first order topic of ordinary life complaints. States figure, of course, but only, it seems, in the deep background of the concerns of the poor whose circumstances are due to those better off on the other side, so to speak, of Sedaka. As a result, we learn that, for these peasants, revolution may be a figure of speech in a political vocabulary derived from the far past and oppressive present. Their political ideologies, such as they are, do not, and cannot, contain the high minded notions of a Marx, and certainly not of a Bourdieu—even if their ideas may serve those, like Jim Scott, who seek to understand their lives, traditions, and cultural attitudes.

At the very least, any early twenty-first-century social theory *must* think in global terms. But, when they do, they seldom ask two practical questions that, in theory, must be asked at *one and the same time*. First, how, precisely, are global things imposed on those who today are peasant-equivalents? And, second, even harder to figure, how do those so severely on the margins contribute to global structures in ways that go beyond providing cheap labor and watching as global corporations steal their local resources? If these two questions can be asked, say, of Nairobi and its desperately poor precinct, Kibera or, even Detroit and its vast deteriorated neighborhoods reaching out to Eight Mile Road and beyond, why have they not been asked of the Sedakas and their all too distant global cities wherever they are? This in effect is what Scott did a good many years ago when, for most, the question was all but unaskable.

What is at issue here is the still strange proposition that the poorest of the global poor are more than victims of long distance global structures but that they *share* in the *authorship* of global realities. "Authorship" here is a metaphor, but it serves to raise the question of how the very poor might be active co-creators of the global order. Even the most expansive of micro-theorists could not imagine a macro-world built from and by the lowest micro-settlements. But they may be telling a bad story. To be sure, Scott, in his first books, does not see a revolution coming from villages like Sedaka. But in other books he does hint at this possibility, most impressive is *The Art of **Not** Being Governed* (2009) where he considers the question in an interesting way.

*The Art of **Not** Being Governed*, very late in a long social science fieldwork game, introduces Zomia, the name he and others have coined for a vast elevated, but oddly state-free area in a hill super-region in Southeast Asia. He calls the region "a world of peripheries."

---

107 *Ibid*, 374. [Quote just following, same place.]

Scott offers enigmatic descriptions of a region of "hill-people" who, though on the margins of the global order, have, nonetheless, a social and cultural order of some specific gravity:

> Most, if not all, the characteristics that appear to stigmatize hill peoples—their location at the margins, their physical mobility, their swidden agriculture, their flexible social structure, their religious heterodoxy, their egalitarianism, and even the nonliterate, oral, cultures—far from being left behind by civilization, are better seen on a long view as adaptations designed to evade state capture and state formation. They are, in other words, political adaptations of nonstate peoples to a world of states that are, at once, attractive and threatening.[108]

Then, just after this eye-opening quote, Scott cites Charles Tilly to the effect that places like Zomia are much the same as the world once was: "A thousand years ago, people throughout the earth lived either under loose-knit empires or in situations of fragmented sovereignty."[109]

Thus begins a section with, I assume, an intentionally sardonic, header, "Creating Subjects." Those unfamiliar with Scott's always unpredictable way of thinking and writing might assume that here he's about to discuss *subjects* as in the personal aspect of subjecthood. Yes, and no! This is actually the beginning of an unusual theory of States (capital S intended) as social instruments of the subjugation of individuals seeking relief from the crushing power of States on others. Hence, Zomia is an instance of places that serve as "havens for peoples resisting or fleeing the state."[110] Hence, the book's title *The Art of Not Being Governed*. It's empirical basis is then introduced with another hard-to-ignore header: "The Great March Kingdom; or, "Zomia"; or, The Marches of Southeast Asia." Again, by the way, here is a term that many (me included) could not have gotten without Google: "Marches" refers to the borderlands separating states or regions, as in England and Scotland where the border, even today, is the ancient boundary marked by Hadrian's Wall.

Zomia is home (if the word applies here) to more than a million minority populations within a bordering Marches this distinguishes the region of the hill peoples region from that of state controlled low lands of the valley peoples—lands the hill people left for relief in a stateless upland territory. The Zomia hill peoples live in a region that extends from Cambodia, Thailand, Laos, Vietnam, as well as Burma and parts of Bangladesh and India and four provinces of China—a region "marginal in almost every respect ...[and] a great distance from the main centers of economic activity [that] bestrides a contact zone between eight nation-states and several religious traditions and cosmologies."[111] Yet, the region possesses a unique political order that might variously be built to serve a range of groups and towns "from nuclear families to segmentary lineages, bilateral kindreds, hamlets, larger villages, towns and their immediate hinterlands, and confederations of such towns."[112] In other words, he adds, "the term *political order* ... can avoid conveying the mistaken expression that outside the realm of the state lay mere disorder."

In other words *The Art of Not Being Governed* is a social and political theory of these non-state places on the global map. It serves alongside the works of Chuck Tilly and others who describe the histories of coercive states. This book may not seem to be theoretical unless one looks closely at its chapter titles—"State Space: Zones of Governance and Appropriation,"

---

108 Scott, *The Art of Not Being Governed* (Yale University Press, 2009), 9.
109 Tilly, *Coercion, Capital, European States AD 990–1992* (Blackwell, 1990), 162. [Scott, *ibid*, 9.]
110 *Ibid*, 13.
111 *Ibid*, 14. [See pages 14 and 16 for maps.]
112 *Ibid*, 36.

"Concentrating Manpower and Grain: Slavery and Irrigated Rice," "Civilization and the Unruly," "Keeping the State at a Distance: The Peopling of the Hills," and "State Evasion, State Prevention: The Culture and Agriculture of Escape." Each of these can be (to those willing to think this way) described as the elements of a core theory of non-states. Then too, in its last four chapters, *The Art of Not Being Governed* could serve as a coda or, even, a benedictory word of affirmation. Then too "Orality, Writing, and Texts" (chapter $6^{1/2}$!) includes pithy passages like "oral traditions are to written traditions more or less what swidden agriculture is to wet-rice agriculture or what small, dispersed kin groups are to settled, concentrated societies."[113] Few who get this point, will not be stupefied by the chapter's section headers: "On the Disadvantages of Writing and the Advantages of Orality" or "The Advantage of Not Having a History"—the second of which concludes that when a people make the "choice" to not have a history, it "is always an active choice, one that positions them vis-à-vis their powerful text-based neighbors."[114] Puzzled? Perhaps, but read Scott before making up your mind. "Ethnogenesis: A Radical Constructionist Case" which includes "Identities: Porosity, Plurality, Flux" and" "Radical Constructionism: The Tribe is Dead, Long Live the Tribe"—the second of which ends with a highlands identity theory that would make proponents of Erving Goffman or Harold Garfinkel swoon: "The only defensible point of departure for deciding who is an X and who is a Y is to accept the self-designations of the actors themselves."[115]

It is, however, the third chapter (8) in this Coda that rings an intellectual bell for those who have read Scott's earlier two entries in his trilogy on peasant culture in Southeast Asia. *The Moral Economy of the Peasant* in 1976 and *Weapons of the Weak* in 1985 are, perhaps, less overtly theoretical than *The Art of Not Being Governed* in 2009—each written a good many years apart, so apart that it may make little sense to call them a trilogy as Scott himself does not. And yet they are (or might be) because, empirically, he follows the facts over more than thirty years to an important conclusion that all who think of themselves as social theorists should be a bit embarrassed if they have not followed Scott's sometimes arduous intellectual trail.

So many social theories, even those based on historical and other empirical evidence, mostly begin with a conclusion pretty much already in mind. As much as I admire the works of Charles Tilly and Theda Skocpol this would be said of theirs—and said without diminishing their importance. But few are they who, midstream, change their minds. I would nominate Immanuel Wallerstein as the only one who, after the world revolution of 1968/89, saw that the world-system he had spent so many years defining and explaining had come to an end. He saw that the two final volumes of his sextet of books on *The Modern World-System* would begin to cover the collapse and the whatever after. But he didn't (and couldn't) live long enough to finish more than the first four volumes. It will have to wait for someone other to pull up those final covers on the uncertain worlds in which we now live.

Scott, however, achieved what he has because he chose as his subject peoples in a region where worlds do not change rapidly. When he began in the 1970s villages in Southeast Asia were not particularly under the sway of global things. Still, Scott teaches social theorists a lesson. Think of real people and continue to think on them as long as possible.[116] The last

---

113 *Ibid*, 230.
114 *Ibid*, 237.
115 *Ibid*, 259.
116 The most famous instance of one sociologist who did this is W. Lloyd Warner whose Yankee City series was researched and published between 1930 and 1959. But the difference from others is that Warner's fieldwork was mostly done between 1930 and 1935. As a result there was no possibility of studying changes

substantive chapter of Scott's *The Art of Not Being Governed*, "Prophets of Renewal," is a concluding word on the three volumes of his empirical service. *The Moral Economy of the Peasant* said that rebellion was local and underground. *Weapons of the Weak* admitted that they possessed a hint of possible rebellion. But *The Art of Not Being Governed* starts off differently. It begins with "A Vocation for Prophecy and Rebellion: Hmong, Karen, and LaHue." Here the theme is that potent, if not powerful, prophets in Zomia are no mere "safety valves serving harmlessly to release tension, the better to impose hierarchy ..., these ritual sites have always been zones of struggle, threatening to spill over into actual revolt."[117] Here Scott refers overtly to the first lesson of an earlier and widely read book, *Domination and the Arts of Resistance: Hidden Transcripts* (1990), where he defines *hidden transcripts*—or the kind of hot rebellion that *could* burn over in Zomia:

> The first declaration of the hidden transcripts, then, has a prehistory that explains its capacity to produce breakthroughs. If, of course, the first act of defiance meets with decisive defeat it is unlikely to be emulated by others. The courage of those who fail, however, is likely to be noted, admired, and even mythologized in stories of bravery, social banditry, and noble sacrifice. They themselves become part of the hidden transcript. .. When the declaration of the hidden transcript succeeds its mobilizing capacity as a symbolic act is potentially awesome.[118]

In *The Art of Not Being Governed*, and its implicit use of hidden transcripts of revolution, Scott opens a new door—one that leads to the most poor as more than passive victims but as potential agents of change. Among much else, this is an easy-to-miss departure from Marx for whom revolution was the instrument of those already engaged in the capitalist system. Marx's *lumpenproletariat* was disorganized and in, but not of, the industrial order. Peasants were out of any political order altogether, as Marx wrote in *The Eighteenth* Brumaire: "Their mode of production isolates them from one another instead of bringing them into mutual intercourse."[119] Marx was writing about the French peasantry, who were in a revolutionary moment after 1848, as were others later, like Skocpol whose long discussion of the French peasantry is informed by Marx.[120] Scott, by contrast, is writing about a later and different Southeast Asia peasantry who were quite excluded, by choice, in a state-less environment—thus, they were able to imagine prophetically a better world. Hence Scott's conclusion: "In the valley imagination," the hill peoples are, what he calls, "pre-people"—"pre-padi cultivation, pre-towns, prereligion, preliterate, pre-valley subject."[121] But the valley people had the hill peoples all wrong. They are not pre-anything. Scott continues with open reference to Fernand Braudel's theory of time: "They represent, in the longue durée, a reactive and purposeful statelessness of peoples who have adapted to a world of states while remaining outside their firm grasp." This, to be sure, does not make them revolutionaries. But it does

---

even though it is well known that the region where he found his Yankee City had undergone many changes as Boston grew well beyond its once province borders. See W. Lloyd Warner, *Yankee City* [abridged five volumes] (Yale University Press, 1963), xiii.

117 *The Art of Not Being Governed*, ibid, 298.
118 Scott, *Domination and the Arts of Resistance: Hidden Transcripts* (Yale University Press, 1990), 227. [Definition of *hidden transcript* is at *ibid*, 4.
119 Karl Marx, *The Eighteenth Brumaire of Louis Bonaparte* (Progress Press, 1974 [1852]), 105–106.
120 Skocpol, "Agrarian Structures and Peasant Insurrections," *States and Social Revolutions*, 112–157 [notably 116, note 13].
121 Scott, *The Art of Not Being Dominated*, 337. [Quoted line just below, same place.]

allow for the possibility that, as stateless people outside the grasp of state power, their prophetic urges *could* cause them to rebel more, even revolt.

Among much else over the years, Scott has written other important books on and around those on revolt and revolution against the state. *Domination and the Arts of Resistance: Hidden Transcripts* (1990), is one, in which, it could be said, his idea of hidden transcripts points to what the distant or otherwise blind observer cannot see. Then too Scott makes it clear why states understand little about those they govern—and, as a result, they get so much wrong: *Seeing Like a State: How Certain Schemes to Improve the Human Condition Have Failed* (Yale, again, 1998). Another, *Against the Grain: A Deep History of the Earliest States* (also Yale, 2017) takes the grain that the people of Sedaka and the region grew and lived by a topic for discussing the history of early hunting-and-gathering peoples the world over. How many are they who study empirically a given group, or a more general subject, over many years, while in and among the publications from that work reach out to collateral subjects for which the people of Sedakas and the Zomias are the intellectual backdrop?

Among other things, Jim Scott teaches those who might be in the early innings of the social theory game: stick to the ground, stay with a theme, branch out if you wish from that theme, but never forget it. He, of course, is not alone in this regard. But he does stand out for the patient way he has done it—learning strange languages, living among village people who struggle, finding a way there or back home to read widely among those who have done the similar. I might add one other lesson Scott taught well: Examine your life to see whether it has or has not given you sufficiently challenging experiences that would allow you to be what you might want to be if only you knew what it was. I spent some time, earlier, describing Scott's growing up without present or able parents but, perhaps by chance, he found a Quaker school that cared for him enough to let him see the wider world. Those with growing up troubles without such good luck, if they somehow want to live revolutionary lives, need to be courageous enough to avoid falling into the rut of life in a settled state of things. They should find their Zomia and become hill people who at least can be different and do the different, without a lot of arm waving. What Jim Scott has done in his own way is that, among much else, he has given social theory the idea that neither the state nor society nor culture, nor any other of the standard social categories are given by the gods or by nature or by any transcendent order. One can escape them and think statelessly so to speak. *States, social movements, revolutions* like any other chapter titles in books aiming to account for so strange a land as America must be thought outside professional boxes, looking for the prophets among us who might stir the mind afresh.

22 Rethinking the World in the Unsettled 1960s
W.W. Rostow, Daniel Bell, C. Wright Mills,
Students for a Democratic Society

There may not be much civilization left to save unless we of the democratic north face and deal with the challenges implicit in the stages-of-growth, as we now stand in the world, at the full stretch of our moral commitment, our energy, our resources.
—W.W. Rostow, The Stages of Economic Growth:
A Non-Communist Manifesto, 1960

For the radical intellectual who had articulated the revolutionary impulses of the past century and a half, all this has meant an end to chiliastic hopes, to millenarianism, to apocalyptic thinking—and to ideology. For ideology, which was once a road to action, has come to a dead end.
—Daniel Bell, The End of Ideology, 1960

The sociological imagination enables the possessor to understand the larger historical scene in terms of its meaning for the inner life and the external career of a variety of individuals. ... By such means the personal uneasiness of individuals is focused upon explicit troubles and the indifference of publics is transformed into involvement in public issues.
—C. Wright Mills, The Sociological Imagination, 1959

Today the world alternatively drifts and plunges towards a terrible war when vision and change are required, our government pursues a policy of macabre dead-end dimensions — conditioned, but not justified, by actions of the Soviet bloc. Ironically, the war which seems to close will not be fought between the United States and Russia, not externally between two national entities, but as an international civil war throughout the disrespected and unprotected human civitas which spans the world.
—Students for a Democratic Society, The Port Huron Statement, 1962

Turmoil Arouses Both Sides of the Political Coin

Around 1960, events were unfolding that caused serious thinkers to evaluate the then present to look to the future. There were two sides at the moment. On the one hand, former and older liberals, W.W. Rostow and Daniel Bell, were concerned about what was happening to economic and political thought; on the other were new and young radicals, C. Wright Mills and the SDS students, who proposed what should be done.

W.W. Rostow published *The Stages of Economic Growth: A Non-Communist Manifesto* in 1960. The book canonized a long held theory of Capitalist economic development.

> There may not be much civilization left to save unless we of the democratic north face and deal with the challenges implicit in the stages-of-growth, as we now stand in the world, at the full stretch of our moral commitment, our energy, our resources.[1]

The theory became a policy for democratic nations just when a new and younger generation were about to call for social and economic change.

Also in 1960, Daniel Bell published *The End of Ideology* that asserted that ideology, in particular Marxist ones, had come to "a dead end."

> For the radical intellectual who had articulated the revolutionary impulses of the past century and a half, all this has meant an end to chiliastic hopes, to millenarianism, to apocalyptic thinking—and to ideology. For ideology, which was once a road to action, has come to a dead end.[2]

Bell cloaked his declaration in vitriol meant to allow for his new-found neoconservatism.

Rostow and Bell in 1960 carried on without recognizing the seeds of a new radical political philosophy inspired by C. Wright Mills' idea of the *sociological imagination*.

> The sociological imagination enables the possessor to understand the larger historical scene in terms of its meaning for the inner life and the external career of a variety of individuals. ... By such means the personal uneasiness of individuals is focused upon explicit troubles and the indifference of publics is transformed into involvement in public issues.[3]

Mills would publish in 1960 an explicitly radical "Letter to the New Left." He died but two years later and would not live to see the movement it inspired.

Students For a Democratic Society (SDS) began to bring students from major universities together before it held its now June 1962 meeting at a UAW retreat center in Michigan. That meeting discussed and approved the Port Huron Statement in which SDS presented a comprehensive political agenda on many subjects, including war:

> Today the world alternatively drifts and plunges towards a terrible war when vision and change are required, our government pursues a policy of macabre dead-end dimensions — conditioned, but not justified, by actions of the Soviet bloc. Ironically, the war which seems to close will not be fought between the United States and Russia, not externally between two national entities, but as an international civil war throughout the disrespected and unprotected human civitas which spans the world.[4]

---

1 W.W. Rostow, *The Stages of Economic Growth: A Non-Communist Manifesto* (Cambridge University Press, 1960), 167.
2 Daniel Bell, *The End of Ideology* (Free Press, 1960), 369.
3 C. Wright Mills, *The Sociological Imagination* (Oxford University Press, 1959), 5.
4 *The Port Huron Statement* by Students for a Democratic Society (1962) Published and distributed by Students for a Democratic Society 112 East 19 Street New York 3, New York Gramercy 3-2181) @ https://www.sds-1960s.org/PortHuronStatement-OCR.pdf.

Never before, and not since, had America seen such a movement of university students who stood behind so unflinching a political manifesto, some for many years. Students usually graduate and leave youthful things in their past. Not SDS students.

Of course manifestos are not meant to guide politics forever but this one was a blueprint for leftist thought and action that dug itself into the soul of the nation.

Global Presence Locally:
From Icelandic Eyes on the Trail to Health Care Initiatives in Kenya

One morning not long ago I was on my morning walk along the Mill River with our dog Alice when I came upon a young woman with her dog. We'd passed each other many times before, always pausing as her dog and mine sniffed each other. This day, not sure why, I told her that her blue eyes were wonderful, especially set against her very black hair. She immediately responded: "I'm from Iceland so the eyes are Scandinavian, but the hair was left for us by French and Spanish sailors." (Apparently in the past, and perhaps still, ships docked in Reykjavik for more than a few days.) I offered the woman with the blue eyes a few aimless remarks about how I've always wanted to visit Reykjavik. Then I stopped, realizing perhaps that an old man should not be telling a lovely young woman how much he liked her beautiful eyes—but on these trails people often say such things to each other. That same morning another young woman said she liked my cap, I replied "My wife got it somewhere." Then she leaned over to pet Alice, asking if it was okay. She said she's so sweet. I said, "So are you." Still people, on the trails, don't hit on one another. We stop for moments to exchange brief words of good day or the like. Much of the same happens most days.

But the woman from Reykjavik haunted me. Why was she here? Because of Yale there are many from far parts of the globe in and around town. Still I wondered. I kept our brief chat in mind, perhaps because I was then just beginning this chapter on Global structures. She may have settled New Haven after finishing studies at Yale or marrying or taking a job in America. Still I was struck, and still am, by this and other such momentary meetings by the Mill River. Struck I was, I now think, because she brought home to me how much global people and their stories come into our lives. She made me ponder why haven't I gone to Iceland? Then too, I thought of my many years off and on in Paris and one trip when we visited the South of France where hair is often colored by relations with North Africans. Then also I began to think of a television police show set in the rural north of Iceland that enchants me. Another why not! But this is the way of the world today. We live with others around the world through telemedia or by walking on local paths. This is normal today, and has been normal for years. When I was a boy in the early 1940s, my father went to war somewhere in the Pacific. He came back with mementos I still have—but also he came back somehow broken by what that foreign venture did to him. While he was gone to war Adele, my maternal grandmother lived with us. She had given birth to a brood that included my mother Helen somewhere in the Austro-Hungarian Empire, probably today's Croatia. They fled to America and Cincinnati—already a German city of sorts—when the Great War was on the horizon. This was a good 80 years before my chance passing with a woman from Reykjavik. Then, no television; but the global wars and migrations were then very much with us even in a provincial Midwestern city. The world was then, as today, a world of Global affairs that cannot be avoided—and one from which many are excluded.

Today in the 2020s there are people nearby who live in that world. Among them are two who have changed their lives in order to develop personal and helping relationships with people in deep Africa. Ralph and Mary Ann Stroup, for example, go to our church. But more importantly they have made a life in one of the poorest rural regions of Kenya.

There, in 2008, they founded the non-profit Kenyan Health Care Initiatives. This was a big step that came after Ralph cut back on his medical practice—and by chance renewed contact with a Rutgers classmate, Bruce Williams. Bruce was by then an educational workshop facilitator in Chicago. They met and renewed their friendship after a 40-year absence. Then, soon enough, Ralph joined Bruce on a trip to Kenya where he was facilitating an HIV/AIDS training workshop for Kenyan health care workers. While in Kenya, Ralph, a urological surgeon, was taken to several remote sites in the Il Ngwesi Conservancy where the health infrastructure was in need of support. After he had made several trips back to Kenya on his own, Ralph and his wife, Mary Ann, a nurse with an MBA and experience in nursing administration, began raising funds through their non-profit in Connecticut to help with some of the needs the people in Kenya identified.

An early beneficiary of KHCI's fund raising was a partially built clinic in the Il Ngwesi Conservancy in Laikipia County North district of Kenya. The Conservancy comprises seven villages of some 12,000 Maasai living hard scrabble lives in a region where drought, the torrential rainy season, and the volcanic soil make farming a hit-or-miss operation.

After several joint visits to Kenya, and when the Kenyan Health Care Initiatives had raised enough financial support to begin their own work in the region, Ralph and Mary Ann realized that they needed to organize their work in Kenya among four areas of critical need: 1. Health, 2. Education, 3. Water, and 4. Gender Equity. The first three were acute needs because clinics were rare, children seldom went beyond primary school, the villages had no clean water—and what they had was often carried from a source 60 minutes out and back.

Gender Equity is a different kind of problem—one rooted in the still traditional Masai patriarchal hierarchy. In the Il Ngwesi Conservancy the hierarchy starts with, at the very top, Senior Elders and just lower are Junior Elders. This is followed by Morans, ages 18–30. Young boys are at the bottom of the hierarchy. Morans were the traditional providers of security from marauders, both animal and human, but their role has been diminished with the passage of time. In actual daily life the Morans are herders at best, impoverished at worst, and, not infrequently, they prey on young women.

The alert reader will now wonder: All men or boys? Yes, women and girls are, in fact, at the very bottom of the hierarchy, and quite literally excluded from many forms of decision making in a society that itself is excluded from the benefits of the Global economy. In Il Ngwesi, women who marry are in effect bought for a negotiated price for which a given number of cows is the coin of the realm. They move to the husband's house. When they are having their menstrual periods, they are kept out of the house. When they deliver a baby, they spend some twelve hours in a post-op delivery hut called a manayetta, straw shelter very much in the open. Post-partum mothers are sheltered there and cared for by women in the community. Of course, most will realize, the adverse cultural practice that most afflicts girls in very rural Kenyan and sub-Saharan Africa is FGM—feminine genital mutilation. Still today girls are dipped in cold stream water, then immediately cut by any sharp instrument available. They bleed. They are commonly infected. Some die. But all who survive are marked for life by these deep vaginal cuts that tear away their femininity.

Of late, the Mukugodo Girls Empowerment Program—to which the Ralph and Mary Ann contribute time and money from their donors—works to educate girls and, importantly, men, who in fact often have no sense of the damage they are doing to their daughters. They, it seems, were just following tradition and obeying the expectations of those higher in the patriarchal hierarchy. Closer to the daily needs of the girls, Mary Ann especially has played a role in the Chumvi Days for Girls program. Women from the Conservancy sew and fold washable menstrual napkins that allow the girls to stay in school when they have their period. For a long while women at their church in New Haven made thousands of these kits—until the international Days for Girls Program and the Kenyan Government declared that the kits should be made in Kenya. Hence, still another of the ridiculous bureaucratized mandates by otherwise good national and international programs that ill-serve girls on the ground in Kenya.

These are just a few of the programs in the Il Ngwesi Conservancy that the Stroups have had a part in supporting and building. One of extraordinary importance in the Conservancy is the Ntalabany Clinic and Greenhouse. Before this clinic was built and furnished with medical supplies that made treatment of local Masai people available, the nearest clinic was a *six hour walk* distant. It is today staffed with, as Mary Ann puts it, "very, very kind people." The adjacent Ntalabany Greenhouse provides vegetables not readily grown in the dry ground. Relatedly, Ralph and Mary Ann played the key role in getting water filters manufactured by the Kenyan division of Aqua Clara, International in Holland, Michigan. As a result people in the Conservancy's 19 schools, and 14 preschools, many dispensaries, and over 1200 homesteads can drink clean, clear water.

Their current major project requested by Conservancy members is the building and furnishing of the Il Ngwesi Community Resource Center and Library, which was very much needed, especially for girls who do not have the same educational opportunities as boys. Statistically, 85% of girls attend primary school but only 30% go on to secondary schools. Plus, which, many classrooms are sparsely furnished and have few books or a functioning library.

Unsurprisingly, many young people within the Conservancy are poor readers and many read below grade level. Literacy is one of the keys to keeping girls safe and uncut. The Il Ngwesi Library was built by Kenyan Health Care Initiatives with significant participation from members of the Conservancy to address a wide range of problems not easily addressed by local Kenyan government resources. Yet, the Il Ngwesi Library has continuing need for more books, as do all libraries. But in rural Kenya libraries are rare and ill-stocked with the books and other literature necessary for teaching reading to the illiterate and supporting children able to move on beyond primary school. So, in 2017 Mary Ann joined the North Branford, CT Rotary and teamed up with members interested in international projects, to help with these needs. Meanwhile, back in Kenya community networks have been established, and a school in each community will have a designated room for a library which will be accessible during school vacations and some holidays.

Ralph and Mary Ann have done much good against mighty odds. They have helped develop health care, education, safe water, and gender equity projects that are now stable programs promising ever more progress. They've given a lot of their lives to this work, with no regret. Mary Ann even talks frankly of what will have happened in their Kenyan community after she dies. While others of means, spend time and money on second homes on sea shores or in distant woods, Ralph and Mary Ann have invested much of what wealth and time they have in life with people in Kenya where, one might say (if they wouldn't), they have a second home in Africa. Whatever they would call it, they are truly global people who care about the world's excluded.

Then too, many who live their good lives in prosperous parts of New England, and elsewhere in well-off communities may think of Africa, not to mention the Middle East, East and South Asia, the South and far North Americas as consigned to—to use the now tired and worn out term—the *underdeveloped* world. For those who think and talk this way, globalization is no more than the latest stage of socio-economic progress. Not so long ago this was the way many experts thought. Around 1960 such thinking was taken-for-granted, even as younger people found it wrong. It was then, when high-minded policy makers and intellectuals assumed without serious evidence that, in effect, the world was organized along a path of progress that, while some nations fell behind, most were moving upward and onward to the higher prospects of economic and social well-being. One in particular codified this doctrine of economic growth.

Walt Rostow, the prominent economic advisor to American presidents Kennedy and Johnson in the early 1960s, may well even now inspire those who think as he did. Rostow's *The Stages of Economic Growth: A Non-Communist Manifesto* (1960) set down the influential theory that all global economies from the poorest to the richest are arrayed along a strict linear scale from the traditional societies that are out the capitalist world—or, in some cases are beginning to enjoy the early pre-conditions of take-off toward capitalist growth—Kenya perhaps. All others on the scale may be driving toward economic "maturity" then perhaps on the mass consumption. The pinnacle of progressive movement, Rostow thought, would be those that are beyond mass consumption—Norway today surely. At the same time a prominent sociologist at Harvard saw the world around 1960 as having outlived the need for ideology. In *The End of Ideology* (1960) he argued, among much else, that the coming generations had lost all awareness of the old political debates and "had no secure tradition to build on [and that] in their search for a 'cause,' there is a deep pathetic anger." Tough talk that turned out not to be true.

Just two years after Rostow and Bell published their dogmatic ideas on current history, a group of young college students meet at a United Auto Workers retreat near Port Huron, Michigan to consider the future as they saw it. The result was the now still famous Port Huron Statement and the organization of Students for a Democratic Society (SDS). The Statement made it clear that they were not at all satisfied with the world that had been left to them by parents and teachers, much less pundits like Rostow and Bell. The Port Huron Statement went on to give quite specific criticisms and proposals for their new world. The SDS, itself, was an early institutional embodiment of a New Left. This was 1962. Just two years before an older but still young Immanuel Wallerstein was in West Africa studying the political conflict and the urge for change toward independence from colonial rule. Those studies appeared in 1960. They grew in the first of four volumes on *The Modern World-System* in 1974. Wallerstein's world-system began around 1500 and lasted at least until the end of the 1900s. He took a view of the capitalist world-system that was the diametric opposite of Rostow's—the global capitalist system, he argued, had been more or less fixed for nearly a half-millennium and, instead of progress, the rich economic states weakened the poor regions of the world. Wallerstein argued that the world-system of the day was dominated by wealthy Core-States (usually one at a time from Spain around 1500, then Holland, France, and the UK in the Victorian Era, then America after WWII). At the bottom of this world-system were the impoverished Peripheral Regions (today much of sub-Saharan Africa, parts of Caribbean and South America, indigenous North America and outback Australia, among others).

Here then are the book ends that hold up academic and policy thinking about globalization. There are those who, more or less, still insist on Rostow's review of the world—in particular neo-liberals spawned by Ronald Reagan and Margaret Thatcher in the 1980s as well as avid members of the annual Davos conference in Switzerland. Those who believe and think as did Rostow see every world economy as either moving ever forward and upward—or, either already arrived at a this-worldly economic heaven or stuck in the deep mud out from which it is hard to get.

Ralph and Mary Ann Stroup have lived and worked in the mud and dirt of rural northern Kenya. They are not the least bit naïve as to what it takes to get out and move on up to a better life. They are not theorists to be sure. Ralph and Mary Ann live in the relatively wealthy part of a declining Core State, so they know what better can mean. Yet, they are not satisfied to retire to the lovely country house they bought in 1986. They could, but they haven't and won't. It remains for those of us who are willing to make and read theories of the world to take time-out in order to learn from people like Mary Ann and Ralph—of whom there are many more than one might suspect. The reason we might not know of these others is we are too busy thinking, while they are busy doing.

W.W. Rostow's Overwrought Stages of Economic Growth

Walt Whitman Rostow was born in 1916 to Russian Jewish immigrant parents who changed their son's name from Rostowsky to Rostow, and gave him the name of the great American poet, because they so loved their new country. Plus which, the family spoke English not Yiddish. Walt was prepared by his upbringing for what he became—a major public intellectual and policy advisor in the Cold War Era. He attended Yale at a preternaturally young age, graduated as a Rhodes Scholar, studied at the University of Oxford, Balliol College, before returning to Yale for a PhD in economics in 1940.

Rostow began his policy making career in World War II as Target Selector for pilots in the Office of Strategic Studies. It is reported that Nicolas Katzenbach (later Lyndon Johnson's Attorney General) said: "I finally understand the difference between Walt and me [...] I was the navigator who was shot down and spent two years in a German prison camp, and Walt was the guy picking my targets."[5] This turned out to be the story of Rostow's career as a policy advisor—always influential, seldom in the line of fire—except, that is, for his later advice to Lyndon Johnson on the War in Vietnam that led to America's disastrous involvement in a war it could never, and did not, win. After WWII Rostow became a national policy advisor par excellence, eventually serving presidents John F. Kennedy and Lyndon B. Johnson for whom he was National Security Advisor. But, again, the War in Vietnam was his reputational undoing. It was Rostow, as much as Secretary of State Robert McNamara, who made the arithmetically wrong and militarily catastrophic miscalculation that massive bombing of the North would bring Hanoi to its knees. It did not because the Viet Cong, allied with troops from the North, could fight on their knees in the woods against the American-backed regime in the South. Among other things, it has been estimated by David Milne that the Northern troops and their Southern allies built some 30,000 miles of tunnels and hideouts in its all-out war against the US.[6] Rostow never apologized for his role in the Vietnam war policy, which all but destroyed his legacy as a prominent public figure. Rostow left public service in 1969 when Nixon became president, but MIT told him that because of his role in the Vietnam War he was no longer welcome to return. In spite of his academic accomplishments none of the most prestigious, if arrogant, universities invited him. Rostow had to settle for the University of Texas that then was not the prestigious institution it is today.

A sure sign of the kind of liberal Rostow was in the day is evident in the full title of his still famous (to some notorious) 1960 book *The Stages of Economic Growth: A Non-Communist Manifesto*. At the least, the book is a landmark of modern social and economic

---

5 David Milne, *America's Rasputin: Walt Rostow and the Vietnam War* (Hill and Wang, 2008), 94. I should add that this Milne is the English political scientist (not the artist of the same name) who enjoys a strong reputation for his writing and scholarship. I say this because much of the biographical information used here is from an extraordinarily long and detailed Wikipedia entry on Rostow that seems reliable in all important ways.

6 *Ibid*, 176. McNamara's role in all this was particularly striking because he had earlier executed a statistical study of mass bombing against the Nazis including the destruction of the beautiful city of Dresden. These bombings served no military purpose.

theory. This in spite of the fact that it opens with what today is an almost laughable reason for its writing. On the book's very first page, Rostow states that ever since his days at Yale he had been preoccupied with one question. What is the relationship between economic and social and political forces? In the day just before the 1960s began to change popular ideologies, this was a fair enough question. "I found Marx's solution to the problem linking economic and non-economic behavior—and the solutions of others who had grappled with it—unsatisfactory..."[7] At the risk of performing a literary post-mortem, these words seem to reveal that, even as he made such a bold gesture, Rostow had his doubts. Fine, if you wish, to reject Marx but why the addition of "the solutions of all others"? Really?—no one else in human history had any good ideas on the subject? Clearly he knew he was on shaky grounds in writing a manifesto meant to dismiss Marx when the book itself is a serious, closely argued, theory of economic growth in which Marx serves as a foil for his own ideas—this with the exception of the book's last chapter where Rostow offers his own anti-communist manifesto,[8] followed by a strange appendix, "The Diffusion of the Private Automobile." Neither may be pointless, but his concluding complaint about Marxism and Communism was that philosophically they are deterministic. "What is it in our view of men and of life that reacts equally against Marx's economic determinism and Communism's Hegelian power determinism, its insistence that the correct judgment of history by the Communist élite justifies any use of power that élite judges necessary to fulfill history's laws or its own interests."[9] Wooden dogma like this notwithstanding, otherwise Rostow had a fair attitude toward Marx as one who "created his remarkable system full of flaws but full also of legitimate partial insights, a great formal contribution to social science, a monstrous guide to public policy." The book was a series of lectures at the University of Cambridge, an audience that no doubt brought his own deeper seriousness of intellectual reasoning. The last words of *The Stages of Economic Growth* were true to the times around 1960 when, at nearly every social level of most global societies, the world was changing in ways that put liberals of whatever stripe in a quandary: "There may not be much civilization left to save unless we of the democratic north face and deal with the challenge implicit in the stages-of-growth, as they now stand in the world, at the full stretch of our moral commitment, our energy, and our resources."[10] In its best moments, as in these lines, *The Stages of Economic Growth: A Non-Communist Manifesto* means to rewrite classical economics for a new era.

For readers in the 2020s and after, we need to realize that in 1960, more than half-a-century before, the world was different. For one, globalization was not yet a term in the vocabulary of those who then wrote and spoke of the world as it was becoming. America was very much embroiled in the Cold War that began to heat-up with the Cuban Missile Crisis in October 1962. Crisis it was, to be sure, but it was not understood, even a little bit, as a consequence of the ways Rostow's democratic north was still fixed in a colonizing attitude toward what came to be called the Global South—which it was. Though after 1959 when Fidel Castro's revolution defeated the regime of Fulgencio Batista that was colonized by American corporations, Cuba had joined other colonized nations of the Global South in breaking away from its northern colonizers. This and more were beginning to crest over the political mountains that had so long occluded what Rostow called the "moral commitment" of the then still-dominating Global North.

---

7 W.W. Rostow, *The Stages of Economic Growth: A Non-Communist Manifesto* (Cambridge University Press, 1960), ix.
8 *Ibid*, "Marxism, Communism, and the Stages-of-Growth," 145–167.
9 *Ibid*, 164.
10 *Ibid*, 167.

To his credit Rostow saw something peeking its head over the hedges of public consumption—hence the weird appendix on the diffusion of private cars. Only a few years earlier in Dwight Eisenhower's presidency that ended in 1961 America's Interstate Highway System was begun. Automobiles were no longer a luxury. Everyone who could afford a car *had* to have one. They were but one of the many commodities for home and play that made Americans the consumption oriented, other-directed people that David Riesman and Erik Erikson had diagnosed a decade earlier in 1950.[11] Rostow deserves credit for defining the trouble here as an economic problem. As a result his first chapter defining the stages-of-growth ends with two telling sections—"Beyond Consumption" and "A Dynamic Theory of Production."

Rostow's dynamic theory of production is, perhaps, the surest indication of his genius as a writer and thoughtful literary economist. It is packed with dense but to the amateur more-or-less clear language; for example: "The stages-of-growth also require ... that elasticities of demand be taken into account, and that this familiar concept be widened; for these rapid growth phases in the sectors derive not from the discontinuity of production functions but also from high price- or income-elasticities of demand."[12] While this is not plain English, it can be read to mean that growth, when it occurs, requires a production system able to meet the demands of the consumer able to afford high-prices without disrupting production which itself must adapt to ever increasing technologies.

> When technological maturity is reached, and the nation has at its command a modernized and differentiated industrial machine, to what ends should it be put, and in what proportions: to increase social security, through the welfare state; to expand mass consumption into the range of durable consumers' goods and services; to increase the nation's stature and power on the world-scene; or to increase leisure? [13]

Plain enough English. These remain today questions any society with a robust economy must ask and answer. Rostow puts the point in unmistakable terms: "Babies, boredom, three-day weekends, the moon, or the creation of new inner, human frontiers in substitution for the imperatives of scarcity?" A fair enough practical question in his day.

Returning to the book's economic theory, there are five stages of growth which he briefly introduces with traditional society as the base where growth is absent, yet from which, in principle, the five-stages grow, then 1) the preconditions for growth, 2) take-off, 3) the drive to maturity, 4) the age of mass consumption, 5) beyond consumption. With these stages in mind it is important to say that the general theory can be, and has been, used in two different ways. The *first* is to describe analytically any given society—or category of societies. This is what Rostow does at the beginning of chapter 3 in identifying those societies in Europe, the Middle East, Africa, and Asia in which "the preconditions for take-off required fundamental changes in well-established traditional society: changes which touched and substantially altered the social structure and political system as well as the techniques of production."[14] The *second* way Rostow's scheme has been used is to serve as taxonomy by which the economies and nations of the world can be mapped. The policy idea of developed and undeveloped nations is the most familiar version of this use, even when it is not taken directly from Rostow's book.

11 See chapter 15 above.
12 *Ibid*, 14–15.
13 *Ibid*, 16.
14 *Ibid*, 17.

The stages can be relatively straightforwardly introduced without the economic data and historical cases offered in the book. *Stage 1. Preconditions For Growth* is when agriculture and extractive industries develop sufficiently efficient methods including the application of what technologies are available to produce a surplus beyond what is needed to feed their populations. The surplus allows the nation's economy to plow back investments into improved transport systems which require social overhead capital at least to manage the new systems.[15] Obviously Stage 1 requires early but necessary non-economic costs acutely needed when a poor and marginal nation is beginning to move ahead. "[T]he government must be capable of organizing the nation so that unified commercial markets develop; it must create and maintain a tax and fiscal system which diverts resources into modern uses, …[and more]."[16] The central government must then deal with "essential, major tasks to perform in the period of preconditions."[17] Then too almost always take-off occurs in a nexus of "demonstration effect" by other national economies moving the same direction, of which Europe's drive to economic change in the late-eighteenth and early-nineteenth centuries.

To renege on my promise to keep this simple, the story is incomplete without reference to "the first take-off" which poses, Rostow says, an interesting historical problem. Namely: "If the break-up of traditional societies is judged to have been induced by the transmission of demonstration effects from other societies, how shall we account for the first take-off, that of Great Britain?"[18] Why not France, for example? Or, Holland, and its Dutch East India Company, an early global power after 1602? Rostow's answer is clean and clear:

> Britain, with more basic industrial resources than the Netherlands; more non conformists, and more ships than France; with its political, social, and religious revolution fought out by 1688—Britain alone was in a position to weave together cotton manufacture, coal and iron technology, the steam-engine, and ample foreign-trade to pull it off.[19]

In addition to demonstrating that Rostow—whatever he became during the Vietnam War—was intellectually brilliant and fair minded, passages like this show that as a scholar he was no fool. In addition the whole of chapter 3 makes it clear why the whole of his five stages turn on the fact and theory of these preconditions to take-off.

Stage 2, The Take-Off, is more heavily laden with economic details that cover topics like the supply of loanable funds, the sources of entrepreneurship, leading sectors in the take-off—each offer with analytic details like, in the third: primary growth sectors, secondary growth sectors, derived growth sectors. As for the growth sectors listed they may not mean much to the untrained in economic history (as they don't to me), but theoretically they indicate the extent to which economic growth, once take-off has begun, is unexceptionally oriented to future and greater growth.

By *Stage 3, The Drive to Maturity*, the game is on. Here Rostow begins with a list of the economies and when they reached technological maturity: Great Britain, 1850; United States, 1900; Germany and France, 1910; Japan, 1940; Russia and Canada, 1950.[20] After this, he identifies the crucial role an expanded railroad system able to transport grains and

---

15 One might suppose that more than "transport systems" would benefit from the plowed back investments. But remember that this was 1960 when he was writing about the poorest peripheral nations and regions many of which had dirt roads and scant train or bus systems.
16 *Ibid*, 30.
17 *Ibid*.
18 *Ibid*, 31.
19 *Ibid*, 33.
20 *Ibid*, 59.

raw materials as well as products like cotton textiles and steel. The discussion of Stage 3 (in chapter 5) ends with a warning. "[M]aturity is a dangerous time as well as one which offers new, promising choices."[21] Dangerous because choices must be made, as he said earlier, whether maturity ought to bring increased security, welfare, perhaps leisure, or simply enlarged incomes able to purchase new "gadgets of consumption," or increased security for the nation on the world stage.

When he gets to Stage 4 (in chapter 6), the worm begins to turn with the Age of High Mass-consumption. Chapter 6 begins in a strange way—with the history of the American case from the Progressive Period, 1901–1912, to the Booming 1920s, to the Great Depression in the 1930s, then the Post-War Boom after WWII, followed by a Phase Five: Where next? Since he wrote late in the 1950s, it was a question he couldn't answer but perhaps he should have been vigilant enough to wonder "Where next?" in the 1960s during the War in Vietnam. He did say, interestingly, "American society as of 1959 is not quite as affluent as it looks."[22]

More curious still, when it comes to "Where next?"—after the five-stages, he turns to two chapters on war and peace. Chapter 8, "Relative Stages-of-Growth and Aggression," works its way into the tangle between nuclear weapons and more advanced—then an unknowable future. In Chapter 9, Rostow offers "Relative Stages-of-Growth and the Problem of Peace" in which the problem is that: "Technically, the problem of peace consists in the installation of a system of arms control and inspective within the level of armaments agreement, which could offer all powers greater security than that now afforded by an arms race."[23] It hardly need be said that the drift in these two chapters toward the global situation where the Soviet Union (which he refers to as Russia) and the United States are the opponents who could make war or peace. When one reads this far it is possible to see how Marx and Communism figures in the subtitle and the final chapter.

Like it or not, Rostow's five elements in *The Stages of Growth* made for a good book for the day. Looking back, however, true globalization has set in to good and bad effect such that national economies, if advanced, are no longer national. Rostow meant to write about the world of capitalism but he never arrived at the idea of a world-system. Had Vietnam might not have ruined his reputation. Just the same, his scheme allows us to imagine what some might still call post-modern economies—the utopias in Norway and Scandinavia or, at the other extreme; or the villages on Zomia in Southeast Asia where his fast advancing world would, even today, be a dystopia.

Daniel Bell: The End of Ideology and Capitalism's Contradictions

Daniel Bell (1919–2011), like W.W. Rostow, was born in Manhattan to immigrant Jewish parents who also changed names from Bolotsky to Bell. Otherwise their trajectories were notably different. Where Rostow went to Yale, Bell went to City College of New York, in spite of the fact that he had graduated from Stuyvesant High School, then as now one of the City's most selective and prestigious high schools; after, we went on to Columbia for the PhD in 1961 somewhat late even for one not on Rostow's Rhodes Scholarship path. Bell's PhD he already had 40 years is explained by the fact that he had a good many years in journalism—as managing editor of *The New Leader* (1941–1945), as labor editor of *Fortune* (1948–1958), then with Irving Kristol at *The Public Interest* (1959–1973). For all

---

21 *Ibid*, 72.
22 *Ibid*, 81.
23 *Ibid*, 128.

he wrote and published numerous articles of general interest first to the cultural left then to the emergent neo-conservative culture. His literary impact was so important that he presented articles from this early writing that came to comprise his 1960 book, *The End of Ideology* as his doctoral thesis. By then he was teaching sociology at Columbia, before moving to Harvard in 1969, where he remained until retirement and as emeritus until his death in 2011. Like Rostow, Daniel Bell traveled through and over several political positions, ending unlike Rostow as a respected academic figure only a bit tainted by the neo-conservative moment he helped found. Bell began as a socialist, like so many in the day from the Lower East Side or Brooklyn. He was, for years, proud of this association that he eventually abandoned (as did others of the same political ilk). So proud he was of his past that, as the years went by, he repeated this story: "When I had my Bar Mitzvah, I said to the Rabbi, 'I've found the truth. I don't believe in God ... I'm joining the Young People's Socialist League.' So he look at me and said ... 'Kid, you don't believe in God. Tell me, do you think God cares'?"[24] Harvard, whatever else it does, is elevated enough in its own collective mind to allow, even encourage, a bit of humor, even humanity.[25]

But from his career in journalism Bell published three enduring books, beginning with *The End of Ideology: On the Exhaustion of Political Ideas in the Fifties* (1960), the subtitle of which is significant. He lived believing that 1960 was an ending of political ideas that had had their time in the 1950s. Again, one sees in this a similar attitude (with a different political orientation) to his Harvard colleague David Riesman, whose *Lonely Crowd* (1950) bemoaned the decline of future-oriented individualism for a deleterious social conformity. They and others wrote at either end of the transformative 1950s during when the blush of America's post War affluence when for a short while she was the one and only global power. The solitary global power ended abruptly on March 5, 1946, when Winston Churchill brought down the Iron Curtain in a speech in Westminster College in Missouri where it was heard by few, then broadcast the world over that changed everything. The Cold War broke the allure of America's economic and military triumph. In the 1950s serious social thinkers, some of theme crypto-social theorists, enjoyed an open field on which new ideas could play out. Some of the young generation ran one way—eventually to a new kind of left in which culture began to play the leading role. Older others were attuned to a different, more conservative, wave length.

The End of Ideology: On the Exhaustion of Political Ideas in the Fifties in 1960 was a major text for a New Right. Bell wrote:

> This age, too, can add appropriate citations—made all the more wry and bitter by the long period of bright hope that preceded it—for the two decades between 1930 and 1950 have an intensity peculiar in written history: world-wide economic depression and sharp class struggles; the rise of fascism and racial imperialism in a country that had stood at an advanced stage of human culture; the tragic self-immolation of a revolutionary generation that had proclaimed the finer ideals of man; destructive war of breadth and scale hitherto unknown; the bureaucratized murder of millions in concentration camps and

---

[24] Quoted from the entry on Bell in *New York Intellectuals/Arguing the World* (PBS https://www.pbs.org/arguing/nyintellectuals_bell.html)

[25] A personal example: One of my Harvard advisors was Harvey Cox in the Divinity School. Cox in the day was everywhere on campus and around town where for a long while he organized grand parties for the young and those who wished they still were. One of these events, in the 1960s, featured—if I remember correctly—The Fifth Dimension, or some other similarly down musical group of the day. But, to the point of what Harvard allowed, when Harvey retired in October 2009, he took over Harvard Yard with cows and sheep and more from the school's earliest rural days late in the 1630s.

death chambers. ... For the radical intellectual who had articulated the revolutionary impulses of the past century and a half, all this has meant an end to chiliastic hopes, to millenarianism, to apocalyptic thinking—and to ideology. *For ideology, which was once a road to action, has come to a dead end.*[26]

These words and the very long book itself were influential through many years. Today it is still in print and functions in the deep intellectual consciousness of those of a certain age who, in our day, can hardly believe what people of the right the world over are saying and thinking about our world. Somehow a failed reality show personality was elected in 2016 in the US and since he has spawned many believers to adopt his ideology without content. This one is not alone, neither here nor abroad.

Bell's critical attitude toward ideology in general and American ideologies in particular led him to conclude that by the 1950s nothing was left. All was a void. The young knew nothing of the ideas of their older generation, and had "no secure tradition to build upon, finding itself seeking new purposes within a framework of political society that has rejected, intellectually speaking, the old apocalyptic and chiliastic visions."[27] So, for Bell, it is not thinking alone but social programs that suffered from the vacuity of the 1950s.

> Unfortunately, social reform does not have any unifying appeal, not does it give the younger generation the outlet for "self-expression" and "self-definition" that it wants. The trajectory of enthusiasm has curved East, where, in the new ecstasies for economic utopia, the "future" is all that counts.[28]

In these lines, the quoted words seem to hint at the fact that Bell knew he was overdoing it. By "future"—much less "self-expression" and "self-definition"? Who is he quoting if not his own all-too-clever sarcasm that ripples through the 1960 edition of *The End of Ideology*.

But as time went by, his nasty digs, fall away in a rather remarkable two part commentary in 1988, *The End of Ideology Revisited*. Here, he admits that the 1960 book was, as he put it: "...a 'political' book, in the sense that I have been a participant in these intellectual wars, intertwined with the politics is also a sociological concern, the effort to break free of the 'conventional' sociological categories; and in that context Marxism is also 'conventional' in its 'holistic' or 'totalistic' view of society".[29]

By 1988, Bell was well into the Harvard academic culture and had become more balanced when he responded to the many criticisms directed at his book in the 18 years since its publication. He wrote:

> There were five different criticisms levelled at the book. 1) The end of ideology was a defence of the 'status quo'. 2) The end of ideology sought to substitute technocratic guidance by experts for political debate in the society. 3) The end of ideology sought to substitute consensus discourse. 4) The end of ideology was an instrument of the Cold War. 5) The end of ideology was disproved by the events of the 1960s and 1970s, which

---

26 Daniel Bell, *The End of Ideology* (Free Press, 1960), 369.
27 *Ibid*, 374.
28 *Ibid*, 375.
29 Daniel Bell, "The End of Ideology Revisited," *Government and Opposition* (Cambridge University Press 23:2, 1988), 134.

saw a new upsurge of radicalism and ideology in Western societies, as well as in the Third World.³⁰

Here is a more mature scholar who understands what others think and is willing to respond, which he does wordily:

> Why these many 'misreadings' of the book? The intellectual reason, I believe, is due to my unwillingness to put forth a formulation of the single problem, or of a single answer to questions, because a modern society contains many different currents (in part because of the disjunctions of culture and social structure; in part because of the 'co-existence' of many overlapping social forms, such as property and technical skill as the basis of power), so that my central aim has been to avoid a single conceptual term (such as 'capitalism') and to make analytical distinctions relevant to the complexities. These analytical distinctions run through almost every discussion of structural changes in this volume. Thus it has been easy for polemical critics to pick up one or another side of these distinctions in order to enter a critical objection.³¹

He is vastly more interesting in his replies if one can get over the persistent barbs which can be enticing in their way, for example: Bell considers the complaint that his main idea is a defense of the status quo "a resounding vacuity"—by which he means, in a name: C. Wright Mills whom he criticizes for engaging in personal attacks on himself (which would be the pot calling the kettle black).

Looking back, Bell in 1988 took the position that the famous "upsurge of radicalism" in the 1960s and 1970s was not new. The Beat Generation, he argued, was little different from generations of Bohemians. The race movement was nothing more than liberal political policy beginning with John F. Kennedy. The Black Panthers, he wrote, are nothing more than an iteration of Marx's lumpenproletariat. "If there was a striking new word—a word derived from the Third World—it was 'liberation' ".³² Here he attacks Franz Fanon's *Wretched of the Earth* as being merely a political insistence drawn from Fanon's practice of psychiatry. The Vietnam War was, again, a liberal mishmash for efforts to, in effect, win the Cold War at its last moments. The student movement of 1968 was, he thought, a utopian dream by children of the post-War baby boom in which the new and numerous young found the world handed down to them "harsh." In this regard he pays particular attention to SDS, about which more soon. Bell concludes:

> But all this was a reaction, as I indicated, against the 'organizational harnesses' that societies were imposing on individuals entering into the new bureaucracies of the world. With some hyperbole, yet with some truth, I described these as the first 'class struggles' of post-industrial society, just as the Luddite machine breakers had reacted a hundred and fifty years earlier to the factory discipline of the first industrial revolution. Yet without any hard-headed sociological analysis and understanding, it could, again, only erupt as a romantic protest.³³

---

30 *Ibid*, 139–140.
31 *Ibid*, 140.
32 *Ibid*, 146. [My paraphrase of Bell's theories are based on *ibid*, 144–147.]
33 *Ibid*, 149.

What is to be learned from all this? Bell represents an all-but pure perfect instance of, depending how you see it, either a defense of the past he knew or an attack on the new he hated. It was anything but "hard-headed sociological analysis."

Yet, Bell's 1960 book endures down into our time for lessons it teaches if not for its theoretical wisdom. His other two major books bore a certain but not precise relation to *The End of Ideology*. In 1973 he published *The Coming of Post-Industrial Society* which, in the words of its subtitle, was "a venture in social forecasting." Bell's vision including five points (put here mostly in my words): 1) In the economic sector (as he puts it), services gradually over-take the production of goods; which necessarily entails, 2) the emergence of a professional and technical class among whom, 3) theoretical as opposed to market knowledge is primary; then also: 4) a "future oriented" ethos arises with and from the primary importance of industrial technology, resulting in 5) a "new intellectual technology".[34] *The Coming of Post-Industrial Society* was indeed a venture not just in new ideas but in a certain markedly more disciplined "hard-headed sociological analysis" (as he would say in 1988 in the retread of *The End of Ideology*). Bell goes on to say: "An *intellectual* technology is the substitution of algorithms (problem-solving rules) for intuitive judgements."[35] Remarkable, really—in that after presenting his own hard-nosed sociological analysis, he resorts to *intuition* as humankind's most basic intellectual virtue that is destroyed in the efficiency of Post-Industrial society.

Interestingly, not long after Bell in 1973, Alvin Gouldner in 1976 would publish *The Dialectic of Ideology and Technology*. Gouldner, the reader may recall from chapter 12 in this book, was at once a leader of left intellectuals in his day—one who was also a Marxist of sorts, and a serious critic of Marxism. Yet, in his last years he too turned to the study of the new technology and its culture but in a very different way. For one, Gouldner saw the new ideology associated with technological reasoning he proposed was a form of critical theory for a new age. Far from accepting the end of ideology position of the by then more than a few like Bell, Gouldner sought to renew ideology while also insisting that it was central to what he called the Culture of Critical Discourse. No less, Gouldner denounced the Post-Industrial Age theme as a fantasy. "A technocratic model, then, which sees technicians dominating officials and management as governed by an exclusive reliance on a standard of efficiency is a fantasy, a utopia, an ideal type."

Bell's third major book, *The Cultural Contradictions of Capitalism* in 1976, is in many ways his best. As literature it is far more elegant than the two previous—this in large part because its social theory is relatively free of rants and full of astute ideas on culture as, in the day, it had become. One supposes that even Gouldner would have appreciated *The Cultural Contradictions of Capitalism*. Bell himself said of it

> This book stands in a dialectical relation to my previous book, *The Coming of Post-Industrial Society*. In that volume, I sought to show how technology (including intellectual technology) and the codification of theoretical knowledge as a new principle for innovation and policy were reshaping the techno-economic order, and with it, the stratification system of the society as well. In these essays, I deal with culture, especially the idea of modernity, and with the problems of managing a complex polity when the values of the society stress unrestrained appetite. The contradictions I see in contemporary capitalism derive from the unraveling of the threads which had once held the culture and

---

34 Bell, *The Coming of Post-Industrial Society: A Venture in Social Forecasting* (Basic Books, 1973), 14.
35 *Ibid*, 29.

the economy together, and from the influence of the hedonism which has become the prevailing value in our society.[36]

The last sentence here is, to be sure, touched by his earlier penchant in the use of *hedonism* to characterize the dominating value of the day in the 1970s. Looking back on, much less living through that decade, this is ridiculous. Yet Bell does a good job of defending the idea itself.

While granting that modern society is in a state of flux, Bell makes an important distinction. The economy and its technology, even politics, have built-in brakes to control the rate and extent of changes. Each is slowed down by a demand for resources—natural, financial, and the ability of groups in the polity to veto and otherwise slow the apple cart. But when it comes to culture, by contrast, "changes in expressive symbols and forms, difficult as it may be for the mass of people to absorb them readily, meet no resistance in the realm of culture itself."[37] He then goes on to offer a general characterization that some would resist in spite of its being very interesting:

> Culture, for a society, a group, or a person, is a continual process of sustaining an identity through the coherence gained by a consistent aesthetic point of view, a moral conception of self, and a style of life which exhibits those conceptions in the objects that adorn one's home and oneself and in the taste which expresses those points of view. Culture is thus the realm of sensibility, of emotion and moral temper, and of the intelligence, which seeks to order these feelings.[38]

Almost no one in the day, or since for that matter, would reduce culture to those emotions and thoughts that function to control feelings in concert with intelligence. Yet, here Bell, absent the wise guy language of the earlier books, makes an important contribution that deserves more attention than it has received—this, one supposes, because *The End of Ideology* so thoroughly sucked up the reading energy of teachers and readers.

In any case, the book is about the effects of culture on capitalism, for which he wrote of the "new capitalism" which since at least the 1920s was culturally split between requiring the older Protestant Ethic of a disciplined work ethic when the individual is at work but, simultaneously, when not at work, it incites individuals to play and pleasure seeking. "The disjunction was bound to widen. The spread of urban life, with its variety of distractions and multiple stimuli; the new roles of women, created by the expansion of office jobs and the freer social and sexual contacts; the rise of a national culture through motion pictures and radio—all contributed to a loss of social authority on the part of the older value system."[39] In effect, Bell's argument comes to the strong conclusion that in America capitalism has lost its traditional moral commitment to the work ethic, for which it has instead drifted toward a pleasure principle, with the consequence that "the culture has been dominated (in the serious realm) by a principle of modernism that has been subversive of bourgeois life, and the middle-class life-styles by a hedonism that has undercut the Protestant ethic which provided the moral foundation for the society."[40] Unsurprisingly, Bell endorses David Riesman's *Lonely Crowd* that verges in a similar direction without extremes about destroying the middle-class and such like.[41]

---

36 Bell, *The Cultural Contradictions of Capitalism* (Basic Books, 1976), xxx.
37 *Ibid*, 34.
38 *Ibid*, 36.
39 *Ibid*, 75.
40 *Ibid*, 84.
41 For Bell on Riesman, see *ibid*, 43.

All-in-all, Daniel Bell came around to a serious, balanced, theory of culture before the days when culture theory would become the academic rage. Plus which, he could be almost poetic as in the words that end the book: "Within limits, men can remake themselves and society, but the knowledge of power must coexist with the knowledge of its limits. This is, after all, the oldest and most enduring truth about the human condition—if it is to remain all too human."[42]

Yet, for better or worse, *The End of Ideology* remained and remains the book for which Daniel Bell is known, for good, if insufficient, reasons. It joins a growing company of books of similar thinking that together changed popular thinking. One telling comment on this fact is by John T. Yost, a psychologist who like all academic psychologists writes with mountains of data. Here is Yost's summary statement of the political consequences of the end of ideology theorists:

> The end-of-ideology thesis originated with neoconservatives such as Daniel Bell, Edward Shils, and Francis Fukuyama; their work helped to marginalize the radical left and to give neoconservatives a fresh start. Dinesh D'Souza wielded the end-of-ideology excuse to distance conservative policies from unpopular legacies such as racism. Soon thereafter, it was liberals who, following the collapse of socialism in Eastern Europe, abandoned their commitment to robust social welfare programs, and professed the need for a "third way" (Anthony Giddens) to defeat the heirs of Thatcher and Reagan. The strategy worked for Bill Clinton and Tony Blair—but arguably at the cost of taking historically leftist concerns such as exploitation, egalitarianism, and social and economic justice off the political bargaining table.[43]

C. Wright Mills: A New Left for a New Day

C. Wright Mills (1916–1962) was born in Waco, Texas. In later life when he rode about on his motorcycle, it was tempting for some to conclude that this was somehow a hint of his cowboy days. He didn't quite deny it:

> I grew up in Texas, curiously enough on no ranch but in Waco, Wichita Falls, Fort Worth, Sherman, Dallas, Austin, and San Antonio—in that order. My family moved around a bit. The reason I was not stabilized on a ranch is that my grandfather had lost my ranch. He was shot in the back with a .30-30 rifle, always it's in the back, but he really was.[44]

Cowboy or not—this is the way Mills was: brash, bare bones honest, one who cut to the truth as he saw it; and more.[45] Mills was also uncommonly ambitious and brilliant. By the time he finished undergraduate studies in sociology and philosophy at the University of Texas Austin, he had published articles in sociology's two leading academic journals, the *American Sociological Review* and the *American Journal of Sociology*. Even so, he came close to letting self-doubts keep him from going on to graduate studies.[46]

---

42 Ibid, 282.
43 John T. Jost, "The End of the End of Ideology," *American Psychologist* (Oct. 2006), 667.
44 C. Wright Mills, "Growing Up: Facts and Fantasies, 1957," in Kathryn Mills, ed., with Pamela Mills, *C. Wright Mills: Letters and Autobiographical Writings* (University of California Press, 2000), 25.
45 As for Mills' brashness see his 1939 letter to Read Bain, editor of the *American Sociological Review* about his article "Logic, Language, and Culture." He would not graduate college studies until later in 1939, yet he declined to make many of the recommended revisions and wrote to Bain as if they were pals [in Kathryn Mills, ibid, 35.] It may surprise that Mills is covered here a second time. It is not because he was more important than others. But because at a crucial time he was a pivotal figure.
46 Irving Louis Horowitz, *C. Wright Mills, An American Utopian* (Free Press, 1983), 40.

In September 1939, he and his wife, Freya, moved to Madison, Wisconsin where he began doctoral studies. The following summer they divorced, then in the spring of 1941 they remarried just before Mills finished his course work for the PhD. At Wisconsin, he met and began to work with Hans Gerth. Together they translated, edited, and published in 1946 *From Max Weber: Essays in Sociology* which for a long while was a primary source book for students of Weber without German. After the PhD from Wisconsin in 1943, he began teaching at the University of Maryland with the support of Robert K. Merton— than whom no major figure in the field was more generous to younger sociologists getting started. While at Maryland Mills was hired by Columbia University's Bureau of Applied Research which led in short order to an appointment at Columbia in 1947. Through these years his marriage was on and off again. They divorced for good this time in July 1947. Such was the story of his life. From UT Austin in 1939 to Columbia in 1947 with major publications along the way, his days sped on and away. Everything went by fast. In 1942 his high blood pressure exempted him from military service. This was the first sure sign that his heart would fail him. He died of a heart attack twenty years later at 45 years of age on March 20, 1962.

But before that final moment he published 19 books and pamphlets; and 185 articles, essays, and reviews; as well as countless other lectures and interventions—and was the inspiration and subject of 171 books and shorter commentaries.[47] His major and still influential books, among the many, are *White Collar: The American Middle Class* in 1951, *The Power Elite* in 1956, and *The Sociological Imagination* in 1959. Tom Hayden classified Mills' writings as falling into four time periods each with its own characterization:

- *Apprehension and Maturation*, 1939–1949
- *Pessimism Formulated*, 1950–1956
- *Radical Polemics, Analyzing the Default*, 1956–1960
- *Tentative Hopes*, 1960–1962[48]

Hayden, famous for many things in politics and his relationships with Casey Hayden, Jane Fonda, and Barbara Williams is important here because he was among the founders of the *Students for a Democratic Society* (SDS) and the principal author of its Port Huron Statement. Hayden's MA thesis at Michigan was on C. Wright Mills. He was thus ahead of the others in SDS and other radical student movements in that he saw the importance of Mills to a New Left—an importance left unfulfilled because of Mills' early death in March 1962 just more than a year after his famous "Letter to the New Left" in *The New Left Review*, published September 1960. For this reason, among others, Hayden's classification of Wright Mills' literary career is particularly helpful.

As for the 1939–1949, *Apprehension and Maturation*, we have seen already the strange fact about this man who otherwise was always out there doing whatever, yet nonetheless suffered a period of severe self-doubt before starting graduate studies. But the apprehension faded quickly once he moved to Madison such that Hans Gerth said this of him in the day:

---

47 See for a sample: C. Wright Mills, *Power, Politics and People: The Collected Essays of C. Wright Mills*, edited with an introduction by Irving Louis Horowitz (Oxford University Press, 1963). For a listing of his own writings and of those who commented on his writings, see in this collection "Bibliography of the Writings of C. Wright Mills," 613–641.

48 Tom Hayden, *Radical Nomad: C. Wright Mills and His Times* with commentaries by Stanley Aronowitz, Richard Flacks, and Charles Lemert (Routledge/Paradigm, 2006), 67–69.

> Mills came from Texas University with Thorstein Veblen in one hand and John Dewey in the other. He was a tall, burly young man of Herculean build. He was no man with a pale cast of the intellect given to self-mortification. He was a good sportsman with bat and man, a dashing swimmer and boatsman, sailing his shaky dory on Lack Mendota. We would walk with machetes to make our way to the boat. Mills dashed with his motor-boat past the more imposing houses of midwestern corporation executives to the pier of the village store.[49]

Whether this was part of the maturation in Hayden's scheme is not clear. What was clear is that the books of this period were serious in every way—his 1946 book with Gerth, *From Max Weber* and in 1948 *The New Men of Power: America's Labor Leaders* which was, among other things, an implicit if not quite fully mature theory of social and political structures in the United States. Here he wrote: "The American labor leader, like the politician and the big businessman is now a public figure, different groups hold various images of him. He is reviled and acclaimed by small and politically alert publics, he is tolerated and abused by the mass public. As always, like other men of power, he is carefully watched by men inside his own organization."[50]

This of course is but a hint of Mills' view on the new Post-War American society which was thriving economically and socially—when, by contrast to the 1930s, labor leaders were rebels who represented down and out workers in a collapsed economy. If Mills was ebullient like many others, it is easy to understand why he would soon become a more and more left liberal critic of that society. If that, then it would seem that labor leaders and the business elite could work cooperatively for the good of all. *The New Men of Power* is not one of Mills' great books but it is an important marker on the road he would soon travel.

The second phase, *Pessimism Formulated: The Analysis of the Power Elite and the Mass Society*, 1950–1956, came to be during the events of the 1950s that, Daniel Bell thought, were times when Post-War youth and the culture they imbibed had lost their grip of the traditions that, to Bell, mattered politically and socially. Even though Bell spoke at the memorial service at Columbia for Mills, his early characterization of Mills was nothing if not the bitter personification of a younger generation unable to think and do what needed to be done to make America real. Here's how Bell ends his essay on Mills:

> Much of Mills' work is motivated by his enormous anger at the growing bureaucratization—this is his theory of history—and its abettors and this gives [*The Power Elite*] its appeal and pathos. Many people do feel helpless and ignorant and react in anger. But the sources of helplessness ought to be made clear, lest one engage, as I think Mills does, in a form of "romantic protest" against modern life.[51]

Compare, if you want to deconstruct Bell's unqualifiedly psychological reading of *The Power Elite*, Mills' own words:

---

49 Hans Gerth, "On C. Wright Mills" (remarks at the memorial meeting for Mills at Columbia University) quoted in Horowitz, *C. Wright Mills: American Utopian*, ibid, 46–47.
50 Mills, *The New Men of Power: America's Labor Leaders* (University of Illinois Press, 1948), 13.
51 Daniel Bell, "*The Power Elite* Reconsidered," in G. William Domhoff and Hoyt B. Ballard, eds., *C. Wright Mills and the Power Elite* (Beacon Press, 1968), 224. The chapter was originally a 1958 *American Journal of Sociology* essay when Bell was himself in the early stages of transition from a red-blooded journalist to an academic.

The idea of the power elite rests upon and enables us to make sense of (1) the decisive institutional trends that characterize the structure of our epoch, in particular the military ascendancy in a privately incorporated economy, and, more broadly, the several coincidences of objective interests between economic, military, and political institutions; (2) the social similarities and the psychological affinities of the men who occupy the command posts of these structures, in particular the increased interchangeability of the top positions in each of them and the increased traffic between these orders in the careers of men of power; (3) ramifications, to the point of virtual totality, of the kind of decisions that are made at the top, and the rise of men who, by training and bent, are professional organizers of considerable force and who are unrestrained by democratic party training.[52]

Oddly, it is almost as if one of President Dwight Eisenhower's speech writers had written these lines into the President's 1961 Farewell Address in which he warned the nation that "In the councils of government, we must guard against the acquisition of unwarranted influence, whether sought or unsought, by the *military-industrial complex*. The potential for the disastrous rise of misplaced power exists and will persist."[53] In the last words of *The Power Elite* Mills offers a soft form of righteous anger which may have been too much for Bell. "Commanders of power unequaled in human history, they have succeeded within the American system of organized irresponsibility."[54]

The years 1950–1956 were indeed a period, as Tom Hayden put it, when Mills began to formulate a serious pessimism about American Society which was apt to those few years. America had in 1948 instituted the Marshall Plan—which is to say, the European Recovery Program—to rebuild Europe, including Germany, that it and its allies had so thoroughly destroyed in the War. Of course Stalin wanted nothing to do with such a thing. The Cold War heated up, while at home Senator Joseph McCarthy and his House Un-American Activities Committee injected a virulent Red Scare in what had been months before America's warm optimism blood. Then too the Korean War began June 25, 1950. For three years, and still today, that War divided the Korean Peninsula and world opinion. The nation was torn every which way. Then also these were the years when televisual media took over domestic entertainment attention and, as Herbert Marcuse would argue a decade later in Herbert Marcuse's *One-Dimensional Man* in 1964, all-but destroy the critical component of human consciousness. Less than a decade before Marcuse, Mills was prominent among those who began to recognize just how sterile Mass Culture could be. Hayden had it just right when he named this stage of Mills' thinking *Pessimism Formulated*. Just as Dick Flacks was right in criticizing Mills for preferring "…to say that he was diagnosing the 'main drift' in society rather than claiming to be making predictions."[55] It is true that, as Irving Louis Horowitz said, from the days of *From Max Weber* in 1946 with Hans Gerth "Mills began to see himself carved in a Weberian mold."[56] Yet, even in Weber's *Protestant Ethic and the Spirit of Capitalism* that, amid the absurdly numerous footnotes and wandering themes of his portrayal of Martin Luther's traditionalism and John Calvin's latent rationalism as progenitors of the Capitalist ethic, there was a loose kind of causal argument—loose in

---

52 Mills, *The Power Elite* (Oxford University Press, 1956), 296.
53 "Military-Industrial Complex Speech, Dwight D. Eisenhower, 1961," Part IV @ https://avalon.law.yale.edu/20th_century/eisenhower001.asp
54 Mills, *The Power Elite*, 361.
55 Dick Flacks, "C. Wright Mills, Tom Hayden, and the New Left," in Tom Hayden, *Radical Nomad: C. Wright Mills and His Times* with commentaries by Stanley Aronowitz, Dick Flacks, Charles Lemert (Routledge/Paradigm, 2006), 7.
56 Irving Louis Horowitz, *C. Wright Mills: An American Utopian* (Free Press, 1983), 47.

the same way that Mills from *The White Collar* in 1950 and *The Power Elite* in 1958 describes the beginnings of a Mass Society and its Higher Circles that end up as an irresponsible Power Elite. Mills wrote, in effect, of Weber's spirit of capitalism run amok—a conviction that Weber himself announced at the end of *The Protestant Ethic and the Spirit of Capitalism*: "Specialists without spirit; sensualists without heart; this nullity imagines he has attained a level of civilization never before achieved."[57]

As Mills furiously worked to outrun his bad heart, the changes in his literary work fell into shorter and shorter periods—from 1939 to 1949, from 1950 to 1956, then from 1956–1960 a period of *Radical Polemics: Analyzing the Default*—in which Mills grew more and more isolated from American radicals. As Tom Hayden put it, Mills' isolation "was so complete that his writing turned into bitter inquiries into the default of the liberal and radical movements, and especially into the default of the intellectuals in their role as guardians of reason and freedom."[58] The three books of this period are either outside the realm of what radicals then could or would think—*The Causes of World War Three* (1958) and *Listen Yankee* (1960)—or against the norms of liberal academics who were failing to protect reason and freedom—*The Sociological Imagination* (1959).

H. Stuart Hughes was a brilliant teacher but a bit of a sourpuss in regard to Mills: "*The Causes of World War Three* is just as disheveled as it predecessors. If anything, it is even more disorganized and repetitious."[59] Here is proof positive of Hayden's observation that Mills' isolation from left liberal intellectuals was all but complete. For many he could do no right. Still, to Hughes' credit he adds: "Yet once again, as in the past, in *The Causes of World War Three* Mr. Mills has something arresting and important to say. And once again it is something that no one else seems to be saying—or at least in so forthright and explicit a fashion." This is the basic intellectual truth about Mills especially in the books of the *Pessimism Formulated* where he had neither time nor intention to persuade those he considered irresponsible—whether economists, politicians, preachers, or intellectuals. In *The Causes of World War Three* Mills renders a stern judgment on any and all, mostly in regard to the then two major opponents in the Cold War.

> Both the Russian and American elites, and intellectuals in both societies, are fighting the Cold War in the name of peace, but the assumptions of their policies and the effects of their interactions have been, and are, increasing the chances of war. War, it is assumed in their military meta-physic is the most likely outcome of the parallel existences of the two types of political economy. Such is the official lay of the land, the official definition of world reality, the contribution to peace of the national spokesmen among the power elite.[60]

In 1958, I was intellectually still politically wet behind the ears, yet for me and many of my generation words like these dried the ears and opened the mind.

Even more, Mills here has in mind the defaulted company of those who should have, but did not, criticize the power elites in a society that was on the way to being fully massified. *Listen, Yankee: The Revolution in Cuba* (1960) properly drew widespread attention in part because it was based on an unauthorized visit to Cuba where he met with Castro, Che, and

---

57 Max Weber, *The Protestant Ethic and the Spirit of Capitalism* (Charles Scribner's Sons, 1983 [1904–1905]), 182.
58 Hayden, *Radical Nomad*, ibid, 68.
59 H. Stuart Hughes, "The Politics of Peace; A Reflection on C. Wright Mills, *The Causes of World War Three*," *Commentary* (February 1959).
60 C. Wright Mills, *The Causes of World War Three* (Simon & Schuster, 1958), 49–50.

other leaders of the new Cuba after Castro's 26th of July Movement removed Batista from office and took-over the island nation in early 1959. One might assume that book was a kind of intellectual and political travelogue. It was that in a sense, but much more.[61] *Listen Yankee* was a prophetic book. It reads today as slightly weird—framed too much in the Cold War rhetoric he so despised; too optimistic as to the likelihood that Castro's political revolution would lead to a social revolution; still too bound to the logic that any who opposed the American power elites were *ipso facto* on the side of progress. Yet, *Listen, Yankee* provides much more than a hint of where Mills would have gone had he survived the heart attack in 1962. First, and most disgusting to his opponents—and especially the sociological method makers—he wrote in the first person as if he were a Cuban revolutionary. The conceit was that he could visit Cuba, meet with Fidel and Che, tour the country, and presume to write, but a few months after, in and for the voice of the Cuban people.

> So, this is who we Cubans are:
> We're part of Latin America.
> We're fed up with Yankee corporations and governments.
> We've done something about it.
> You're corporations and governments don't like.
> We are not alone.[62]

Audacious, yes; but also telling, simple, and the truth of things to come. Just the year before in 1959 in *The Sociological Imagination* he advised the sociological imaginer: "Keep your eyes open to the varieties of individuality, and to the modes of epochal change."[63] The sociological imagination, he thought, is never cautious, always willing to err, and always open to social changes the cautious will miss. Mills understood that the Cuba of 1959 was part of a global movement. *Listen, Yankee*, he said from the first, "...is about more than Cuba. For Cuba's voice is the voice of a hungry-nation bloc, and the Cuba revolutionary is now speaking. ... In Africa, in Asia, as well as in Latin America the people behind his voice are becoming strong in a kind of fury they had never known before. As nations, they are young, the world is new to them."[64]

That Mills had published *The Sociological Imagination* the year before his visit to Cuba means certainly that the 1959 book was deep in his head and heart. In *Listen, Yankee* in 1960 he was already imagining a new world beyond his personal troubles with other left intellectuals. Hence the all-but-scriptural lines in *The Sociological Imagination*:

> The sociological imagination enables the possessor to understand the larger historical scene in terms of its meaning for the inner life and the external career of a variety of individuals. It enables him to take into account how individuals, in the welter of their daily experience often become falsely conscious of their social experiences. Within that welter, the framework of modern society is sought, and within that framework the psychologies of a variety of men and women are formulated. *But such means the personal uneasiness of individuals is focused upon explicit <u>troubles</u> and the indifference of publics is transformed into involvement in <u>public issues</u>.*[65]

---

61 Some of the following is drawn from or based upon Charles Lemert, "After Mills: 1962 and Bad Dreams of Good Times," in Hayden, *Radical Nomad*, 48–50.
62 Mills, *Listen, Yankee* (Ballantine Books, 1960), 28–29.
63 Mills, *The Sociological Imagination* (Oxford University Press, 1959), 225.
64 Mills, *Listen, Yankee*, 7.
65 Mills, *The Sociological Imagination*, 5. Emphasis added.

Just imagine what American sociology might have accomplished after it began to break away from Talcott Parsons late in the 1970s—when, that is, it theoretically settled upon the ideal types provided by the differences between Columbia University and the then still prominent Chicago School. Columbia sociology, led by Robert K. Merton and Paul Lazarsfeld, was, if not thoroughly quantitative, robustly structural. By supposed contrast, the University of Chicago School which long had been focused on the ethnographical study of smaller, more personal social groups. Hence, a foundation of the macro/micro differences conveyed by exaggerated institutional differences. This caricature is, like all others, not fully accurate even if, through the years, sociologists have sorted themselves between the study of subjects on the ground and structures in the theoretical air.

Mills—perhaps because from the early days at Wisconsin he thought of himself as in a Weberian mode—was not drawn in this either/or. Yet he had well informed, if extreme, views of academic sociology. The bulk of *The Sociological Imagination* is devoted to varieties of sociological method, beginning with his famous condemnation of Talcott Parsons' Grand Theory, mostly castigating the writing as unintelligible. "I suppose one could translate the 555 pages of *The Social System* into about 150 pages of straightforward English."[66] Think what you want, but this is not a helpful criticism. Mills does better in the next chapter on "Abstracted Empiricism," which is always easier to criticize when it is too abstracted. "What has happened in the fetishism of the Concept is that men have become stuck way up on a very high level of generalization, usually of a syntactical nature and they cannot get down to fact."[67] Fair enough. This would have been a better way to criticize Parsons.

Then in a chapter on "Types of Practicality," Mills, having dismissed an all-too-lofty empiricism, turns to the local. "The social scientist who spends his time on the details of small-scale milieux is not putting himself outside the political conflicts and forces of his time."[68] Then he goes on to examine what for him in 1959 was a contemporary issue. Sociology had lost, he said, "its reforming push ... [while reframing] ... the practical [as] that which is thought to serve the purposes, of ... great institutions"[69]—of, that is, corporations, the army, and the state and especially industry where he has in mind Elton Mayo's school of human relations in industry, of which the Hawthorne Bank Wiring Room Study was the most famous. It is an important micro study but one that showed that the workers responded to different issues than sheer profit—the physical environment, for example. Social reform was nowhere to be found in this kind of research, which was not practical in any way that appealed to Mills. After his exposé of that basic types of social research, *The Sociological Imagination* strays into a number of interesting essays on bureaucracy, philosophies of science, history and the like culminating in the marvelous appendix that everyone beginning in most fields should read, "On Intellectual Craftsmanship."

All in all, the enduring importance of *The Sociological Imagination* is its scriptural lesson on the relation between *personal troubles* and *public issues*. If only more than a few had taken this relationship seriously back in Mills' day we might have avoided the dichotomies problem—subject/object, micro/macro, on and on. What Mills saw and thought was that in the real world these distinctions hurt any serious attempt to come to terms with the social world all about. First, he proposed, we must identity the personal troubles we are experiencing when rethinking them as public issues—as what affects all those to a similar degree

---

66 *Ibid*, 31. [This is Mills the wise-guy. Cute but not quite right. I found Parsons a brilliantly clear teacher and his books difficult but clear enough. But then again I'd spent years before that reading theologians like Paul Tillich and Karl Barth, who in dealing with other-worldly matters made sense only if one trusted them. CL]
67 *Ibid*, 74.
68 *Ibid*, 78.
69 *Ibid*, 92.

in the larger worlds we live in. *Think troubles/think public issues—this is how to live and how to think.*

Students for a Democratic Society: Tom Hayden, Dick and Mickey Flacks, So Many Others

Students for a Democratic Society (SDS) came into being at the United Auto Workers retreat in Port Huron, Michigan June 11–15, 1962. There and then came radical students intent on rethinking politics with an eye on their generation of university students. The important document that was agreed upon at the meeting was *The Port Huron Statement*—an astonishingly thorough political manifesto of just shy of 9,000 words. Imagine nearly a hundred still young people agreeing on a document of that length and detail. Tom Hayden, who wrote an early draft before the meetings, was largely responsible for the Statement. Others played a role, Al Haber, SDS's first President, contributed, as did Dick Flacks, who among much else, organized the documentation for the 1962 meetings.[70] Todd Gitlin, then a student at Harvard College, was present and would become an early President of SDS. Gitlin went on to teach at UC Berkeley, ultimately at Columbia—more importantly he became a prodigious author and a public notable until his death in 2022. Al Haber, after a while became disillusioned with SDS and lowered his political eye to local issues when he became a cabinet maker living in Michigan. From Todd Gitlin to Al Haber one gets a sense of the range of voices in the early days and how the cohort after their student days drifted into other lives.

For now, I choose to focus on those who remained committed over their lifetimes to the kind of politics SDS meant to inspire. Chief among them were Tom Hayden and Dick Flacks and his wife Mickey Flacks. They remained friends over the years until Tom's death in 2016 and Mickey's in 2020. Who knows what keeps people in touch over the years? It's never one thing. But in these cases it could be said that C[harles] Wright Mills was chief among their reasons. For one, as we've seen already, Hayden quite extraordinarily wrote his MA thesis at Michigan on Mills, while being totally involved in SDS. And, Dick and Mickey Flacks, in recognition of Mills' importance to them, named their first son Charles Wright. More importantly they all lived lives that one would expect proponents of the Port Huron Statement to live. Though the expression "politics are personal" was invented by late second wave feminists in the 1970s, one could say Dick and Mickey exemplified it. They held meetings in their apartment in Ann Arbor, always kept and held strong friendships with political allies, but most of all their family exemplified the kind personal relations people of their political purposes ought to have. More broadly, Dick Flacks has written:

> I would like to highlight several particular intellectual sources for the ideological orientation expressed at Port Huron. An immediate model and resource was C. Wright Mills, who died at age forty-two, two months before the meeting at Port Huron. In the year after Port Huron, Hayden wrote his master's these on Mills. The language of the Statement is quite consciously resonant with Mills' style—a style that is both muscular and academic, with strong moral challenges couched in direct address to the reader. More important

---

70 Al Haber and Dick Flacks. *Peace, Power and the University: Prepared for Students for a Democratic Society and the Peace Research and Education Project*. Ann Arbor: Peace Research and Education Project, 1963), Mimeographed, 12p. [The documentation has grown into *Students For A Democratic Society Papers, 1958–1970* (State Historical Society of Wisconsin, Microfilm.]

than stylistic borrowing was that the Statement as a whole tried to fulfill Mills' call for the cultivation of "sociological imagination."[71]

Hayden and the Flackses all lived lives that one would expect of proponents of the *Port Huron Statement*. They *lived the life* of the *Statement*. Though he lived and died before the fact, Mills was the source of this manifesto, but he did not live it. His marriages and relationships and his intellectual ambitions overwhelmed whatever good intentions he had.

In this respect, Dick and Mickey went far beyond what Mills was capable of. More than any in the movement, they *lived the life* Port Huron imagined for their generation. Mills did not. His marriages and relationships were overwhelmed by his intellectual ambitions and his personality. Mills was not an easy ticket. Here is what, Irving Louis Horowitz, one of Mills' biographers (and his literary executor), said of the trouble Mills made for himself:

> Mills was a strong character. He disguised his faults by admitting to even worse faults. He responded to others' claims that his behavior was boorish by behaving even more outlandishly. ... Mills quite personal style led to a near-unanimous negative consensus about him. However much those who knew him firsthand differed about the quality of his work, they were unanimous about his personality. ... Mills only infrequently mentioned any of his three wives, Freya, Ruth, or Yaroslava. They seemed to have entered into his consciousness only at the work level.[72]

Among those familiar with him and this thinking in the early days of SDS, Tom Hayden and Dick Flacks, in their writings, neither mentioned nor dwelt on his personality.

What they did care about was Mills' thoughts on the British New Left, of which he wrote in his *Letter to the New Left* in 1960—that, in turn, became the principal text in Tom Hayden's fourth category in his classification of Mills' literary trajectory, *Tentative Hopes: The New Left, 1960–1962*. Mills' *Letter to the New Left* was brief with two main concerns. The first is a long and rambling disquisition on the end of ideology that reminds those that Mills had a previous relationship with Daniel Bell going back to the early 1940s when Bell was editor of *The New Leader* to which Mills contributed several pieces.[73] Whatever their relationship was in those early days, by 1960 Mills, in *The Letter*, characterized Bells' intellectual style as "gossipy," then goes on to the general topic:

> Practitioners of the no-more-ideology school do of course smuggle in general ideas under the guise of reportage, by intellectual gossip, and by their selection of the notions they handle. *Ultimately, the-end-of-ideology is based upon a disillusionment with any real commitment to socialism in any recognizable form. That* is the only "ideology" that has really ended for these writers. But with its ending, *all* ideology, they think, has ended. *That* ideology they talk about; their own ideological assumptions, they do not.[74]

---

71 Richard Flacks, "Philosophical and Political Roots of the American New Left," in Richard Flacks and Nelson Lichtenstein, eds., *Sources and Legacies of the New Left's Manifesto* (University of Pennsylvania Press, 2015), 332.
72 Horowitz, *C. Wright Mills: An American Utopian*, 4–5.
73 *Ibid*, 76–78.
74 Mills, "Letter to the New Left," *New Left Review* (No. 5, September–October 1960). Emphasis added. @ https://www.marxists.org/subject/humanism/mills-c-wright/letter-new-left.htm . Quotations immediately following are from this source, for which there are no page numbers.

The end-of-ideology is very largely a mechanical reaction—not a creative response — to the ideology of Stalinism. Here then is the clue to why the second general topic of *The Letter* is Russia and global Communism. "The end-of-ideology is very largely a mechanical reaction—not a creative response—to the ideology of Stalinism." Though surely he knew Daniel Bell's thinking on the subject, here Mills was not concerned with the ideas published in Bell's *The End of Ideology*. Here he is taking a position about the wider end-of-ideology discussion in the UK, in particular E.P. Thompson's edited 1960 book, *Out of Apathy*, that included chapters by Norman Birnbaum, Stuart Hall, Alasdair Macintyre. Thompson himself, wrote the introductory chapter, "At The Point of Decay," that says all one needs to know about the British new left version of the end of socialism debate.[75] Mills had been thinking about the problem of the Left for some time. In "The Decline of the Left" he began: "There is no Left establishment, anywhere that is truly international and insurgent. ..." But he ended with a call to arms that many in SDS read into his *Letter to The New Left*: "[What] we must do is define the reality of the human condition and to make our definitions public ..."[76]

Taken together, the two aspects of Mills' *Letter to the New Left* suggest how he turned for a moment to the situation in Great Britain while thinking of fashioning a New Left for his day in America. As Dick Flacks points out, in the 1950s in America there had already been discussions of this possibility, among them Paul Goodman's *Growing Up Absurd* in 1960. Others too including many at Port Huron were intent upon forcing the academic world to "connect to the critical analysis and collective action that was emerging."[77] Mills, in *Letter to the New Left*, put this idea as his final word: "Let the old men ask sourly, "Out of Apathy—into what?" The Age of Complacency is ending. Let the old women complain wisely about "the end of ideology." We are beginning to move again. Mills himself had little to say specifically about the New Left in America except that it should stress "agencies of change" and the expectation that its young adherents would be moral, humanistic, intellectual. At the very end of *Radical Nomad*, Tom Hayden did something both clever and important. Hayden imagined what Mills might have said about the New Left had he lived. For example:

> We know the importance of talking about and organizing around issues that are at one and the same time meaningful to people and radical. ... We think economic problems are the fundamental ones that connect most others, but we don't neglect cultural and personal problems that can't be postponed ... We figure it will take a long time, and much experimental work, before we come to reach all the people the movement needs to take power—which is one of the things we are seeking.[78]

Mills' *Letter To The New Left* assuredly figured in Tom Hayden's thinking when he wrote the *Port Huron Statement*. The statement was not a translation of Mills' thinking. In fact they went far beyond him. For one, an important section of the Port Huron Statement on racial discrimination began with "Our America is still white." Mills, however, in all he wrote, had nothing important to say about race in America, while the SDS statement

---

75 E. P. Thompson, ed., *Out of Apathy* (Stevens and Sons, London, 1960). For Thompson's "At The Point of Decay," see https://www.marxists.org/archive/thompson-ep/1960/decay.htm [To my surprise along with this webpage an article that I had written and forgotten about was mentioned: "End of Ideology, Really," *Sociological Theory* 9 (Fall 1991): 164–172.]
76 Mills, "The Decline of the Left," in Mills, *Power, Politics, and People* (edited by Irving Horowitz), *ibid*, 235.
77 Mickey and Dick Flacks, *Making History Make Blintzes* (Rutgers University Press, 2018), 120–125.
78 Hayden, *Radical Nomad*, 191–192.

provided a long list of issues that demanded political attention, chiefly: literacy, income, work, unemployment, housing, education, voting—and each was presented with key facts of the matter.

This was 1962. The Civil Rights Movement was less than a decade old and was on the verge of fading away into SNCC and Black Power. Casey Hayden was not yet 25. Todd Gitlin was not yet 20. Al Haber, often call the father of SDS, was the oldest at 26. The principal life experience of most was school. Mississippi Freedom Summer was two years off. SNCC was yet to become the force in student civil rights actions it would be after 1964.

The Port Huron Statement is, in retrospect, a remarkable contribution to political and social theory in its day—one that, in many ways, is at least as important well into the twenty-first century when the world is different but the basic issues of life with others the same. One of its still enduring aspects is the plain but potent ideal of politics as *participatory democracy*.

> As a *social system* we seek the establishment of a democracy of individual participation, governed by two central aims: that the individual share in those social decisions determining the quality and direction of his life; that society be organized to encourage independence in men and provide the media for their common participation.[79]

By *participatory* the Statement means that political decisions were to be collective and made in public; and made in such a way as to create better social relations "by bringing people out of isolation" into meaningfully different and better social lives. Democracy, thereby, is meant to be fully social and life-giving. As one small sign of how the students at Port Huron operated in keeping with these professed values, Dick Flacks notes that the theory of "participatory democracy" was introduced by Arnold Kaufman, a University of Michigan philosopher professor who had taught a number of SDS members, including Tom Hayden.[80]

The SDS statement then covers a wide range of issues that mattered in the day (as still they do[81]) to students and all others seeking a better world, including student life in universities, the wider society, the needs of the helpless in society, labor and politics—this and more before coming to the famous concluding section on the university's role in social change stated as the desiderata of an American New Left:

1. Any new left in America must be, in large measure, a left with real intellectual skills, committed to deliberativeness, honesty, reflection as working tools. ...
2. A new left must be distributed in significant social roles throughout the country.
3. A new left must consist of younger people who matured in the postwar world, and partially be directed to the recruitment of younger people.

---

79 The Port Huron Statement published by Students for a Democratic Society. (Published and distributed by Students for a Democratic Society 112 East 19 Street New York 3, New York Gramercy 3-2181) @ https://www.sds-1960s.org/PortHuronStatement-OCR.pdf.
80 Flacks, *Making History Making Blintzes*, 118. [Perhaps it should be said that the authors of this book, Mickey and Dick Flacks, labeled sections according to who was addressing the topic at hand. Dick was the author of this section on SDS.]
81 Ironically, just yesterday (in early November 2023) I gave a zoom talk to a class of a hundred or so sociology students at Dick Flack's department at the University of California at Santa Barbara. I asked them: how many of you are active in politics? One person only raised her hand. But she raised the key question of the 2020s: Will capitalism's interest in gas and oil make it impossible for us to save the world from climate change? I answered, yes, but I'm 86! No one objected.

4. A new left must include liberals and socialists, the former for their relevance, the latter for their sense of thoroughgoing reforms in the system. ...
5. A new left must start controversy across the land, if national policies and national apathy are to be reversed.
6. A new left must transform modern complexity into issues that can be understood and felt close up by every human being. It must give form to the feelings of helplessness and indifference, so that people may see the political, social, and economic sources of their private troubles, and organize to change society.

Each of these working principles ends with a strong statement that shows how the university early in the 1960s offered the environment in which each of these aspects of political life in the day could grow.

In our day, in the 2020s, when universities have a very different place in American culture—when higher education is much more oriented to qualifying students for the job market, these words from the 1960s may seem utterly romantic if not, to some, absurd. But it must be remembered that the 1960s were the days when the postwar baby boom was still sprouting university students. Student populations were soaring. From 1965 to 1975, the number of higher education students doubled—from 592million to 1,118million—a rate that continued even into the early 2020s by when the number of students doubled again from 1,118million to 2,015million, though with signs of a decline corresponding to the demographic decline in birthrate.[82] Then also in the 1960s in the universities many SDS members had attended schools places like Michigan and Harvard, and their like. Still, even schools like these were seen less as havens for prep school pupils preparing to become masters of the corporate world than as hotbeds of new ideas and new visions of the American future. Even all-too-precious Harvard had its days of student rebellion.

Then too, though it seemed quite at odds with SDS politics, the counterculture that blossomed late in the 1960s, grew from its early roots in the 1950s with the Beat Generation. Books like Alan Ginsberg's *Howl* (1956) and Jack Kerouac's *On the Road* (1957) were all but required reading for young rebels. At first they were part of what was then known as the *San Francisco Renaissance* that soon enough migrated across the nation landing with a particular thud in New York City where Kerouac, attending Columbia on a football scholarship [!], studied literature with English professors who influenced some of his later writings. Similarly, Ginsberg was among those who engaged in critical discussions of the formal literary methods of Lionel Trilling and others of the older guard.[83] By the end of the 1950s there was considerable Beat community in Greenwich Village. The Beats were not a particular influence on the SDS crowd but their countercultural ideas and life style were in the air combining in due course with later trickster icons from Muhamad Ali to Jerry Rubin whose 1970 book *Do It!* was introduced by Eldridge Cleaver.[84] Also Jack Whalen and Dick Flacks, in *Beyond the Barricades*, their study of later student radicals active in 1970, conclude that student radicals were significantly influenced by political events in the 1960s.[85]

---

82 https://www.google.com/search?q=https%3A%2F%2Fwww.statista.com%2Fstatistics%2F183995%2Fus-college-enrollment-and-projections-in-public-and-private-institutions
83 Robert Genter, "I'm Not His Father: Lionel Trilling, Allen Ginsberg, and the Contours of Literary Modernism," *College Literature* 32:2 (2004), 22–52.
84 Charles Lemert, *Muhamad Ali: Trickster in the Culture of Irony* (Polity Press, 2003). Jerry Rubin, *Do It!* (Simon and Schuster, 1970). Also, for an excellent sample of primary sources from the 1960s with a section on the counterculture in the 1970s see Judith Clavir Albert and Stewart Edward Albert, *The Sixties Papers: Documents of a Rebellious Decade* (Praeger Publishers, 1984).
85 Jack Whalen and Richard Flacks, *Beyond the Barricades: The Sixties Generation Grows Up* (Temple University Press, 1989).

All this happened, while the Civil Rights Movement was stirring the political consciousness of young and old since the Montgomery Bus Boycott of 1955–1956. Times were truly changing and SDS was part of those changes.

It would be too much to say that SDS and its Port Huron Statement were somehow *the* pivotal moment in the bouleversements of the 1960s. But they were, at least, an exemplar of what the best young people were thinking then and what they aspired for themselves *and* their country. SDS was strong in conviction and action in the years just after 1962. By the time of its 1963 convention in Pine Hill, New York, there were 9 chapters and perhaps 1000 members nationwide, of which 200 attended the annual convention, for which Dick Flacks wrote a kind of manifesto, "America and the New Era."[86] It began with four new trends that were then coming into view: 1. The emergence of a New Europe, 2. The emergence of the Third World, 3. The disruption of the international communist movement, 4. The obsolescence of nuclear weapons. Had there been any doubt earlier, "America in the New Era" clearly sent SDS on a global trajectory. Plus which, as Flacks wrote in "The New Left and American Politics After Ten Years," in 1971, in 1963 there still "appeared to be a heady political climate for radical reform."[87] In this one year, it was moved, he goes on to say: "The very token adjustments of the New Frontier confirmed the criticisms of the New Left and reinforced aspirations for more far-reaching change. Moreover, the civil rights movement had catalyzed black protest in urban areas by the spring of 1963; the peace movement had begun to develop grass-roots political organization during the 1962 congressional elections and in the heat of the test-ban debate; and campus ferment was rapidly growing." Yet, whatever lease on political life these events gave SDS, it soon ran into trouble of its own making. How to protest the Vietnam War divided factions that would never heal. Flacks again:

> By the SDS convention of 1969, the organization had split into bitterly hostile and contending factions. Essentially, this fragmentation was rooted again in the problem of agency. There were some who found comfort in a peculiarly dogmatic revival of traditional Marxist faith in the industrial working class. There were others who argued that the only white group that was authentically revolutionary was the youth, that the primary radical goal was the destruction of the American empire, that therefore the primary agency had to be the revolutionary black movement within the country, together with the Third World revolutionary movements outside, and with the white youth playing only a supportive, destructive role. For most of the thousands of rank-and-file SDS membership, this debate seemed bizarre. The year 1969 saw the total demise of SDS as a national organization and the thorough fragmentation of the New Left as a political force.[88]

Still, the open question about SDS is: How can we know which of the aspirations embodied in the Port Huron Statement outlived SDS? This is a tough question to answer. Even so, there is an answer in the offing. The world of the 1962 generation of New Left students dreamt of has not come to be. Still students marched on in the decade following 1962, as Jack Whalen and Richard Flacks demonstrated in their 1989 book, *Beyond the*

---

86 Richard Flacks, "America in a New Era," personal photocopy sent to me by Dick.
87 Richard Flacks, "The New Left and American Politics After Ten Years," *Journal of Social Issues* 27:1 (1971) 27.
88 *Ibid*, 32.

Barricades: The Sixties Generation Grows Up. In an earlier 1984 essay, they write of the 1960s generation:

> The New Left and the counterculture of the sixties were crucibles of identity, agencies of adult socialization whose effects have been durable. The 'liberated generation' when young tended to be extremely naïve about its liberation from the constraints and orientations of mainstream society.... Even so, this does not justify the rejection of the New Left; these young, just the same, the study showed that they developed at least a keen sense of what adult development and the future might expect from them a commitment to social change.[89]

In *Beyond the Barricades*, Whalen and Flacks tell the stories of a 1970s group of New Left student radicals.[90] They meant to tell the truth through them—that those then young and engaged were far from perfect. Their longitudinal interviews with the former students continued well into their adult lives provide the most intriguing all-but experiment view of what became of their generation. Some had drifted away from politics, others maintained a degree of left-liberal consciousness, others dropped out of it altogether.

Whalen and Flacks interviewed some 40 activists who had been engaged in a protest in Isla Vista, California that began February 25, 1970, in the evening. The protestors were young and mostly white students at the adjacent University of California at Santa Barbara. Police arrived in considerable number but not enough to prevent students from pushing back on the barricades. More police were called in. The Bank of America, a local instance of corporate wealth, was burned to the ground. Students eventually retreated. Students were arrested and jailed. Most avoided federal prison. A June 7th gathering was called to protest police brutality. Some 1,500 students filled a local park before the nightly curfew went into effect. Helicopters and sound trucks intervened to disperse the crowd. Faculty tried to get the curfew lifted. The students sat down and began singing patriotic songs. At 7:30 the police began making arrests. By 9:30, 667 students were arrested.[91]

Whalen and Flacks had access to essays written of activists in the Isla Vista protests. One of the protestors wrote in the summer of 1971:

> It's the end of another year, and the war is still going on. It's the end of another year, and the revolution hasn't come. ... How can we be militant and not isolate ourselves from the masses of people in this country, who want the war ended, who want clean air, good jobs, and the pursuit of happiness? Can the war and racism be ended with a revolution? How do we make a revolution? What is revolution?[92]

This is a common reaction among young activists once a radical moment had come to an end. Many of us had reflections like this—especially so in a time when so many beyond those engaged in on the ground actions shared the concerns others acted on when we did not.

In *Beyond the Barricades*, Whalen and Flacks tell a California version of how the wider generation grew up. They ask, in the end was there a Sixties Generation? To which their answer is yes. Some among the many who marched in those days remained true to the

---

89 Jack Whalen and Richard Flacks, "Echoes of Rebellion: The Liberated Generation Grows Up," *Journal of Political and Military Sociology* 12:2 (1984): 76–77.
90 See Jack Whalen and Richard Flacks, *Beyond the Barricades: The Sixties Generation Grows Up* for their presentations of events in Santa Barbara that began in 1970.
91 A good bit of this all-but-literal account is from *Beyond the Barricades*, 29–35.
92 *Ibid*, 116.

values of one or another Left—no longer New, but not quite Old, as had been the Left of their parents' generation who lived through the 1930s and its terrible economic crisis. "Alongside the myths of lost and betrayed youthful idealism, there is a contrary belief—namely, that the people of the sixties are still 'different' and continue to feel a bond with their agemates."[93] If their slogan *participatory democracy* was not sung aloud, for many, as they grew older, believed that the whole point of democracy was simply to make a society in which all have a say that is heard about how that society has its being.[94] *Beyond the Barricades* ends with a prophecy: "The spirit of the sixties did not die as its bearers got older, nor did they betray that spirit. Perhaps the spirit waits for a new opportunity that will permit the tide of collective action once more to rise."[95]

If so, then that spirit was carried forward by people like Tom Hayden, Mickey Flacks, and Dick Flacks and many younger others. This June morning's New Haven News site, *The Independent*, carried a story of students at Wilbur Cross High School who have joined together as the Socialist Scholar's Party—a *political* party! One of the Party's founders, Dave Cruz-Bustamante, a rising senior, was recently elected to the New Haven Board of Education. In the school just ending in June 2023, members of the Party worked "with the teachers union, community leaders, and grassroots organizations like the Citywide Youth Coalition to increase student advocacy within high schools." *The Independent* also reports that among their concerns are "that New Haven High School students are granted input in school district decision making, a more socially relevant curriculum, and increased investment in student well-being and restorative justice."[96] It is unlikely that these students in our time knew anything about SDS. Perhaps, but what is evident is that their political movement bears many of the traces of the early history of student political movements. Things happen that way. Examples from the past somehow escape into the cultural air to return to the political ground to stir souls at some much later time.

As it happens in May 2006, *The Santa Barbara Independent* published a cover-story "UCSB's Most Dangerous Professor Dick Flacks Looks Back." Though the *New Haven Independent* story on student radicals was published a good twenty years later than the one in the *Santa Barbara Independent*, they tell much the same story. Student radicalism long after SDS in 1962 may be diluted but it is still alive. Flacks began teaching at University of California Santa Barbara in 1969 when the 1968 rebellions were still hot. He had left a tenured position at the more prestigious University of Chicago for California, another world from New York City where he and Mickey came of age, even from Michigan in the early 1960s. Santa Barbara was then, as it still is, an all-but suburban community. Its university was still finding its way out of the teacher's college days early in the twentieth century. It became a University of California campus in 1958. People at UCSB were worried that Dick Flacks would be a "most dangerous professor." When the *SBI* article appeared in 2006 those worries were damp if not dry. Yet: "Instead, Flacks spent the next thirty-seven years on campus advocating a pragmatic brand of radical politics coupled with nonviolent civil disobedience. As a result, Flacks was allowed to operate with a relatively free hand, helping to radicalize generations of students. Both through his classes on social movements and his work with student groups, Flacks inspired young people to go into the world and 'make history'."[97] He and Mickey set about to encourage students in the 1970s and through

---

93 *Ibid*, 272.
94 *Ibid*, 253–254.
95 *Ibid*, 283.
96 Maya McFadden, "Socialist Scholars Speak Truth to School Power," *New Haven Independent* (June 20, 2023).
97 Nick Welsh, "UCSB's Most Dangerous Professor Dick Flacks Looks Back," *The Santa Barbara Independent* (May 11, 2006), 1. Quotes following in this paragraph are from the same source.

the years in Santa Barbara, as they had at Michigan in 1962. Many of the radical activities were local and to some not that radical. "Dick and Mickey Flacks helped start the slow-growth Citizens Coalition, which succeeded in electing a more environmentally minded council majority." When these groups faded away, they turned into what *for Santa Barbara* was a radical project.[98]

> In 2000 they got together with other concerned citizens — some of them ex-students — to form SBCAN. Its charge is to fuse the goals of the environmental and the social-justice movements — not an easy task when two visions of a perfect Santa Barbara are colliding: affordable housing versus small-town neighborhoods. How is it possible to have either in a market of million-dollar cottages?[99]

Now 23 years later, and three years after Mickey's death, Dick is 85, and still active as only those our age can be. His oldest son, Charles Wright, has moved to Santa Barbara. His second son, Marc, with a PhD in Sociology, left a California State College position for Yuba College where he is committed to organizing students for work in their worlds. The Yuba College *Spotlight* says of him: "Coming from a long line of activists, including a famous sociologist, Marc Flacks has no intention of staying in line."[100] All this over many years and still Dick continues to serve UCSB students and faculty as friend and mentor—not to mention a network of former students and colleagues far and near.

I have barely mentioned the very many books and articles Dick has published. He has been, through all this, a productive scholar, fulfilling in his way what Tom Hayden did in his. "Any new left in America must be, in large measure, a left with real intellectual skills, committed to deliberativeness, honesty, reflection as working tools." This is the complete version of the first of the principles of New Left that concludes the Port Huron Statement. But perhaps the best conclusion for their joint words at the end *Making History/Making Blintzes*:

> As Mickey says one point of this book is to show that the full-time and single-minded organizer/activist identity isn't necessarily the best standard for defining serious political engagement. Social change seems to require such work. But movements defined by the perspective of the most committed activists can risk losing connection with the everyday needs and the perspectives of the people to and for whom they claim to be speaking.[101]

---

98 Dick told me in July 2023 that he does not think it was radical.
99 Nick Welsh, "UCSB's Most Dangerous Professor Dick Flacks Looks Back," *ibid*.
100 Somer Hansom, "Marc Flacks," *Yuba College Spotlight* (June 8, 2022) @ https://yc.yccd.edu/spotlight/staff/2022/06/marc-flacks-community-focused
101 Mickey and Dick Flacks, *Making History/Making Blintzes: How Two Red Diaper Babies Found Each Other and Discovered America* (Rutgers University Press, 2018), 475.

23 Global Structures and Exclusions
Immanuel Wallerstein, Saskia Sassen, David Harvey, Nancy Fraser

Almost all of West African countries have seen the emergence of a single party which has led the nationalist struggle, is now in power, and dominates the local political scene. In the struggle against colonial rule, these parties forged a unity of Africans as Africans.
—**Immanuel Wallerstein, Ethnicity and National Integration in West Africa, 1960**

Perhaps the opposite kind of imbrication of law and territory from that of global finance is evident in a domain that has been equally transformed by digitalization but under radically different conditions. The key digital medium is the public access Internet and the key actors are largely resource-poor organizations and individuals.
—**Saskia Sassen, Territory Authority Rights, 2006**

The theoretical argument I have here set out is, I hold, as fundamental to the elucidation of our present plight as it is to the interpretation of the historical geography of capital. If I am correct, and I hasten to add that I hope I am grossly in error and that history or others will quickly prove me so to be, then the perpetuation of capitalism in the twentieth century has been purchased at the cost of death, havoc and destruction wreaked in two world wars.
—**David Harvey, Spaces of Capital, 2001**

Theories of justice must become three-dimensional, incorporating the political dimension of <u>representation</u> alongside the economic dimension of <u>distribution</u> and the cultural dimension of <u>recognition.</u>
—**Nancy Fraser, Scales of Justice, 2010**

New Global Realities:
A World System, Assemblages, Spaces of Capital, Rethinking Justice

Just when W.W. Rostow was publishing his tract on *The Stages of Economic Growth* in 1960, Immanuel Wallerstein published his report on a research visit to West Africa which turned out to be an early text that grew into his massive four volumes on *The Modern World System*.

> Almost all of West African countries have seen the emergence of a single party which has led the nationalist struggle, is now in power, and dominates the local political scene. In the struggle against colonial rule, these parties forged a unity of Africans as Africans.[1]

---

1 Immanuel Wallerstein, "Ethnicity and National Integration in West Africa," *Cahiers d'Etudes africaines* 3 (1960), 138.

There could hardly be a more different view of world order from Rostow's development model than Wallerstein's world-system in which the poor regions of the world are dominated by the more developed.

Saskia Sassen in 2006 published *Territory Authority Rights* [sic] which is a theory of the digital Global Era covered by her deviant use of the concept of global assemblages.

> Perhaps the opposite kind of imbrication of law and territory from that of global finance is evident in a domain that has been equally transformed by digitalization but under radically different conditions. The key digital medium is the public access Internet and the key actors are largely resource-poor organizations and individuals.[2]

Sassen does not view herself as necessarily a political radical, but she is a *theoretical* radical. Not even Immanuel Wallerstein has set out to invent so unreservedly a new set of concepts.

David Harvey *is* a political radical in the sense that he has devoted years to writing about Marx and Marxism, which is interesting because one doesn't usually think of geographers as Marxists. His *Spaces of Capital: Toward a Critical Geography* in 2001 is nothing if not balanced in method and presentation:

> The theoretical argument I have here set out is, I hold, as fundamental to the elucidation of our present plight as it is to the interpretation of the historical geography of capital. If I am correct, and I hasten to add that I hope I am grossly in error and that history or others will quickly prove me so to be, then the perpetuation of capitalism in the twentieth century has been purchased at the cost of death, havoc and destruction wreaked in two world wars.[3]

Harvey is as much an historian who looks wisely at the way Capitalism has been, and still is, deadly.

Nancy Fraser, like others discussed in this chapter, is also a re-inventor of preexisting theories. When one reads the following statement, it might seem just plain everyday social theory. It is more.

> Theories of justice must become three-dimensional, incorporating the political dimension of *representation* alongside the economic dimension of *distribution* and the cultural dimension of *recognition*.[4]

When she wrote in the early 2000s, social theory was torn in respect to how, and if, her three categories might be used in a three-dimensional scheme. As you will see later, she quite brilliantly resolved the issue for those willing to rethink their theoretical habits.

Social theorists are meant to be inventive as to traditional theories. The four discussed here are exceptional in the degree to which they have taken this expectation seriously.

Immanuel Wallerstein:
From Ghana in 1960 to the End of the Capitalist World System in 1989–1991

---

2 Saskia Sassen, *Territory Authority Rights* (Princeton University Press, 2006), 338.
3 David Harvey, *Spaces of Capital: Toward a Critical Geography* (Routledge, 2001), 343.
4 Nancy Fraser, *Scales of Justice: Reimagining Political Space in a Globalizing World* (New York: Columbia University Press, 2010), 15.

In 1960, when students at the University of Michigan were moving toward forming *Students For a Democratic Society*, Immanuel Wallerstein was, as I've said, in West Africa studying how Ghanaians and others in the region were moving toward freedom. "In the struggle against colonial rule, these parties forged a unity of Africans for Africans."[5]

Wallerstein, like Dick and Mickey Flacks, was born in New York City where he, like them, knew the Old Left very well. But he was born in 1930, making him a generation older than the SDS students. Just the same, in 1960, his first research trips to West Africa taught him how Africans, young and old, were struggling with a colonialist world that was worse—much worse—than issues that concerned university students in America. Still, in May 1968, during the student take-over of administration offices in the now famous Columbia Crisis,[6] he was chief among a small band of faculty who interpreted the students' demands to tone-deaf Columbia University administrators.[7] All of Wallerstein's higher education was at Columbia University, where he took an MA in 1954, and a PhD in sociology in 1959, after which he taught at Columbia until 1971 when he moved to McGill. In 1976 he moved again to Binghamton University in New York where he founded the Fernand Braudel Center for the Study of Economies, Historical Systems, and Civilization. Upon retirement in 1999, he became a Senior Research Scholar in Sociology at Yale while continuing his service as *Directeur d'études associé* at the *Ecole des Hautes Etudes en Sciences Sociales* in Paris.

Over the years, he has been engaged in, among many other commitments, the World Social Forum since its founding in Porto Alegre in 2002 and has visited Subcomandante Marcos, leader of the Zapatista Army of National Liberation, at his mountain headquarters in Chiapas. Then too, until his last weeks in 2019, Wallerstein wrote a bi-monthly series of Commentaries on geo-political events—each informed by a life-time of scholarly and intellectual work, but also each an implicit call for critical understanding and political action.[8] Through all this, he was primarily devoted to research, writing, and lecturing the world over. After his love of family and friends, Immanuel was an intellectual above all else. As things turned out, he was an intellectual native to the Global Sixties—while, as he put it, at best a "fellow traveler of the New Left."[9]

After an initial scholarly interest in India, early in his doctoral studies at Columbia Wallerstein received a Ford Foundation grant to support research trips to Africa. He eventually visited nearly all of the nations of that continent. This was surely a key turning point in his thinking on the way to developing his program of World-Systems Analysis—a scrupulously documented four volume argument that, since it first appeared in 1974, has become the most influential systematic but critical analysis of the history of the capitalist world-system. This thoroughly academic work of scholarship grew up over four decades preoccupied with the global spread of Western capitalism from the Iberian colonizing penetrations of the then virginal new world around 1500 to the time when the capitalist world-economy fell into uncertainty after 1989–1991.

Wallerstein's view of modern Euro-American capitalism grew from roots laid in his own early experiences in Africa. "If my intellectual quest led me early on away from the familiar

---

5 Immanuel Wallerstein, "Ethnicity and National Integration in West Africa," *ibid*, 138.
6 See The Cox Commission Report, *Crisis at Columbia: Report of the Fact-Finding Commission Appointed to Investigate the Disturbances at Columbia University in April and May 1968* (Random House, 1968).
7 "Faculty Committee Submits Proposals," *Columbia Daily Spectator* (Sunday, April 28, 1968), 1.
8 The Commentaries appear on his website: https://www.iwallerstein.com. The 500th and last one: "This Is The End; This Is The Beginning" appeared on July 1, 2019.
9 Immanuel Wallerstein, Charles Lemert, Carlos Aguirre Rojas, *World-Systems Analysis in Changing Times* (Routledge/Paradigm, 2012), 17.

grounds of my own country to that of contemporary Africa, which was still a colonized continent when I first visited it and began to study it, it was because I had the gut feeling in the 1950s that the most important thing that was happening in the twentieth-century world was the struggle to overcome the control by the Western world of the rest of the world."[10]

Wallerstein met Frantz Fanon in Accra, Ghana in the summer of 1960. He was just beginning his long productive life. Fanon, who died at 36 years in 1961 was productive in his way because of his two classic books, *Black Skin/White Masks* and *Wretched of the Earth*. Fanon was one of the three most indelible influences on Wallerstein's modern world-systems research program. The other two were Fernand Braudel, the French social historian, and Ilya Prigogine, the Nobel Prize recognized chemist. The three influenced Wallerstein at different, but crucial, times as he developed his extensive study of the capitalist world-system. Fanon, of course, came first. Apart from his books, Fanon introduced Wallerstein on his 1960 visit to West Africa to what became the global periphery exploited by the capitalist core and its allies in the world-economy. But also Fanon was an exemplar of the power of political commitment that underlay the world-systems project.[11]

> Rereading Fanon in the light of revolutionary movements in the twentieth century should lead us *away from* polemics into a closer analysis of the realities of class structures. ... He pushed us to look for who would take what risks and then asked us to build a movement out of such a revolutionary class. Have the history of the years since he wrote disproved this instinct? I fail to see how and where.[12]

This is Wallerstein writing in 1979 well after what he called the world revolution of 1968 and nearly two decades after he met the revolutionary Fanon in Ghana.

The influence of Braudel was revealed to his readers as early as 1974 in *The Modern World-System, Vol I: Capitalist Agriculture and the Origins of the European World-Economy in the Sixteenth Century*. "Braudel more than anyone else made me conscious of the central importance of the social construction of time and space, and its impact on our analyses."[13] He initially took from Braudel the concepts of a world-economy and, especially, that of *la longue durée* which was the first-hint of the importance of TimeSpace in his thinking. After 1974, Braudel, was so impressed by *The Modern World-System Vol I*, that they jointly taught a seminar in Paris. Then began a continuous relationship until Braudel's death in 1985. Since then, with rare exception, Wallerstein visited Paris in the winter months and, notably, named his research center at the University of Binghamton after Braudel.

It was Ilya Prigogine who influenced Wallerstein on the theoretical interstices of Braudel's scheme. Prigogine, in *The End of Certainty: Time, Chaos, and the New Laws of Nature* (1996), among other writings, provided the idea that led Wallerstein, somewhat later in his theory of the capitalist world-system, to sharpen his use of Braudel's concepts of time. Prigogine's general attitude toward the physical sciences entailed the clarifying concept of chaos as the necessary correlate to scientific determination. Wallerstein makes it clear that Prigogine's notion of uncertainty is already present in Braudel's tripartite theory of time in which events and even structures which may appear to the naive observer as fixed in time

---

10 Wallerstein, "Introduction," *The Essential Wallerstein* (The New Press, 2000), xvi–xvii.
11 On Fanon, see Charles Lemert, *The Modern World-System, 1500–1991* in Kristin Plys and Charles Lemert, *Capitalism and Its Uncertain Future* (Routledge, 2022), 41–51. A good bit of the discussion of Wallerstein here is from this earlier source.
12 Wallerstein, "Fanon and the Revolutionary Class," in *The Essential Wallerstein*, ibid, 31.
13 *The Essential Wallerstein*, xxii. Also in "The Development of an Intellectual Position," https://iwallerstein.com

become chaotic when they are seen as vulnerable to the intervention of conjunctures arising in the systemic space between the long enduring and the particular event.[14]

Then too, it is important to realize that no analytic system so many years in the making and of such a (literally) global range could derive from as few as three influences. Wallerstein's *World-Systems Analysis: An Introduction* (2004) is the best resource for an appreciation of the many connections in Wallerstein's critical method—including the role of Karl Polanyi in relation to Braudel's idea of the world economy, Andre Gunder Frank as the source of world systems (plural), and of course of his response to the many Marxist critiques of world-systems analysis.[15] The enormity of the project being granted, its nuances must be taken into account, even in respect to the three pivotal influences that are not easily reconciled by those who wish to follow the thread of Wallerstein's critical attitude toward the capitalist world-economy.

The thread is there to be followed. All too simply put: *Fanon* was basic to what came to be the global periphery from which capitalism extracts its supplies of cheap labor-power and natural resources necessary to its production process by which surplus value is accumulated. Braudel was crucial to Wallerstein's central analytic reference that capitalism works within particular nation-states—including the historical series of core states, beginning with Iberia in the sixteenth century—, but is always and necessarily a world-economy. Then, it was Prigogine who provided the principles of uncertainty and chaos as just as important to historical as to natural systems. Hence there is a story behind Wallerstein's four volumes of critical social history of the capitalist world-system—the story of the long history of Capitalism's role in the world order: 1) *Capitalist Agriculture and the Origins of the European World-Economy in the Sixteenth Century*; 2) *Mercantilism and the Consolidation of the European World-Economy, 1600–1750*; 3) *The Second Great Expansion of the Capitalist World-Economy, 1730s–1840s*; 4) *Centrist Liberalism Triumphant, 1789–1914*. Two additional volumes were projected ("if I can last it out," as he put it[16]): 5) 1873–1968/89 on blossoming and bust of the capitalist system; 6) 1945/1968–2050 on the structural crisis of the capitalist world-economy. That anyone already in his eighties (as he was when the fourth volume appeared in 2011) would project these last two of six volumes is a tribute both to the genius of the work and to its logic.

Genius is what genius does, but it is the logic that is important. Whether anyone could in a lifetime do all this is one thing. That it could be imagined is another and this is what counts. Marx, in a fashion, attempted something similar. But, only *Capital I* in 1867 was a more-or-less polished book. What Marx aimed to do was to generate a theory of Capitalism. Wallerstein, always dismissive of theory as such, has produced a critical historical description of actual capitalisms from the transition out of agricultural beginnings in the sixteenth century to the crisis and uncertainty of the capitalist world-economy after 1968–1989. In this last mentioned aspect, is where Prigogine's influence again comes into play. In 2004, Wallerstein wrote:

> The modern world-system in which we are living, which is that of a capitalist world-economy, is currently in precisely such a crisis, and has been for quite a while. ... One plausible moment at which to start the story of this contemporary systemic crisis is the

---

14 Immanuel Wallerstein, "Time and Duration," in *Uncertainties of Knowledge* (Temple University Press, 2004), 71–82.
15 See especially, Immanuel Wallerstein, *World-Systems Analysis: An Introduction* (Duke University Press, 2004), chapter 1 ("Historical Origins") and chapter 2 ("Capitalist World-Economy").
16 Immanuel Wallerstein, *The Modern World-System IV: Centrist Liberalism Triumphant 1789–1914* (University of California Press, 2011), xvii. [Sadly, Immanuel "didn't last it out." He died early morning August 31, 2019.]

world revolution of 1968, which unsettled the structures of the world-system considerably. This world revolution marked the end of a long period of liberal supremacy, thereby dislocating the geo-culture that had kept the political institutions of the world-system intact.[17]

He is quick to add that 1968 was at best the beginning of the crisis—a prelude of sorts to the end of the Cold War in 1989 and collapse of the *liberal* world-culture. But which liberalism?

When it comes to liberalism Wallerstein is not playing with double-entendres. By liberal, he means, rather, the geo-culture that emerged after the revolution of 1848 when both radicalism and conservatism (symbolized all-to-neatly by the extremes in France after 1789) were replaced by a global culture in the Euro-American core states. In effect, this was the beginning of formally democratic, open societies, and qualified assurances of citizenship rights; in other words, the rationally organized modern nation-states that served the purposes of the capitalist world-economy. The world revolution of 1968 began the erosion of naive confidence in such a system—an erosion encouraged by the decolonizing movements of the late 1950s (Cuba and Tunisia for example) and early 1960s (Algeria, most of Africa, the Caribbean). In other words these were movements inspired by Fanon among others in the Négritude movement.

Wallerstein has written extensively on the period from 1945 to 1990—from the rise of the American hegemony after World War II to the stagnation in economic growth associated with the end of the Cold War and the ironic decline of American power.[18] These writings, in effect, cover—however episodically—the periods meant to be discussed systematically in the proposed volumes 5 and 6 of *The Modern World-System* series. Historically, the argument on the period between 1945 and 1990, is four-fold.[19] The US was the core state in the world-system with Japan and Europe as its alliance of semi-peripheral states. The Cold War was a "formal conflict, in which the U.S.S.R. acted as a semi-imperialist agent of the United States." The third-world seized on the conflict to assert its right to self-determination and national development. But the 1970s and 1980s was, he continues, "a period of global economic stagnation" during which the US fell into decline in part because of the third-world's disillusionment with global capitalism's fatuous promises of progress. The crisis after 1990 was the revolts in the Global South that unhinged the Global North's optimism.

Wallerstein relies, in particular, on Prigogine to describe (and predict) a bifurcation in the world-system, the surfacing of the chaos that lay below the surface all along, and a long crisis in the capitalist system perhaps extending even to mid-21st century. Whether capitalism as we know it can or will prevail is far from certain. But Wallerstein does believe that some version of a world-system will reassert itself. Here we are dealing with social-science fiction but, precisely, the kind of fiction good social-historical thinking ought to provide. Its genius, if that is what it turns out to be, is that it is fiction based on an empirical history of the capitalist world-system since the sixteenth century.

Thus, the conclusive purpose of Wallerstein's project is to assert the Braudelian idea that capitalism was *a* world-system among others actual and possible. If capitalism is (or even can be conceived as being) historically bound—*a* world economy not *the* world economy—then we have a macro-scope with which to view the early decades of the new millennium

---

17 Immanuel Wallerstein, *World-Systems Analysis: An Introduction*, 77.
18 Immanuel Wallerstein, *Geopolitics and Geoculture: Essays on the Changing World-system* (Cambridge University Press, 1991); *The End of the World As We Know It: Social Science in the Twenty-first Century* (University of Minnesota Press, 1999); *The Decline of American Power* (The New Press, 2003).
19 Immanuel Wallerstein, "Cold War and the Third World: The Good Old Days?" in *After Liberalism* (The New Press, 1995), 10–11. Quotes following the same source.

and, especially, those most acute after 2016 or so. The crisis of our times is more than simply the rise of authoritarian politics based on the racist hatred of immigrant populations. It is or, perhaps we must say looking back, it may have been due to the utter collapse of the liberal democratic culture that was (and may be no more). World-systems are cultures, politics, and economies—all at once. Hence the abiding uncertain future of Capitalism itself. An uncertainty that is assured by the series of global events that were hidden in the necessary chaos of a world-system dominated by core states.

Wallerstein's world-system makes Rostow's linear scheme look shabby. The very notion that all the weakest economies of the world contain the sperm that *will* give birth to an ever growing economy is more than shabby, it is at least silly in spite of the fact that Rostow himself, a product of his times and culture, was anything but silly. The very notion that all the weakest economies of the world contain sperm that will give birth to an ever growing economy may seem silly. But important to remember, even forgive, that Rostow's 1960 was the very brand that SDS, in one way, and Immanuel, in another, criticized. It was hard then in the JFK and LBJ White Houses to see what they saw. What Wallerstein saw and said is that the long-enduring capitalism world-system was without a linear myth of necessary progress. In his world-system the weakest economies were a periphery managed by and for the interests of the world's core states.

This world-system had a beginning, he argued, around 1500 when Europe's wealthiest powers sent merchants around the world to trade in whichever commodities could be bought and sold—of which the most valuable commodity was slaves.[20] But, while in principle Rostow's scheme could have no end, Wallerstein's did. For him, the capitalist world-economy began to experience such a degree of global chaos that no Core State could manage it because so many states in the Periphery were rebelling. Thence a once well-ordered system slipped into a multi-polar system of which the BRIC nations—Brazil, Russia, India, China—were considered rivals to the US and EU nations in a multipolar world. But chaos played its nasty game again. Brazil declined after a series of political revolts of which that of Jair Bolsonaro in 2018 was the most outrageous. Then too Russia fell into economic decline about the same time culminating in other words beginning of formally democratic, vaguely open civil societies, and qualified assurances of citizenship rights seemingly in the political decline of Vladimir Putin, after his ill-conceived attempt to take back Ukraine in February 2022. Then also, China's economy fell away in part because of the global COVID crisis that came when its economic growth rate fell to a low of 2.24% in 2020 from a high of 14.23% in 2007. And as India's population is close to exceeding China's, it has been slow to develop the export economy that would make it a global economic power. This is but one example of the chaos that reigns among the world's economies, all of which are beholden to US/EU capitalisms.

While these dynamics are associated with the rise of economic and political revolutions in the 1950s, 1968 was a year when they turned on the Global North. Wallerstein's year of a world revolution was 1968 that came out fully dressed in 1989 when the Cold War collapsed and with it the all-too over determined, if a half-millennium long, world-system. Chaos broke it apart. Today, chaos reigns alongside local sometimes stable time/spaces. Wallerstein may have been a fellow traveler with SDS and domestic political radicals of the day, but soon enough he simultaneously justified the global concerns of the students in 1962 but pressed their mostly domestic vision of radical politics into a global framework. Wallerstein was an activist, yes; but his political actions mostly arose from his intellectual

---

20 Andre Gunder Frank, in *ReOrient: The Global Economy in the Asia Age* (University of California Press, 1998), argued that it was Asia not Europe that founded a world-economy.

work. Still because of him it is now very difficult, if not impossible, to think of the world as tidily ordered by any particular global power. For one thing we can no longer think of this world as one in which a Global South is the passive victim of those in the North. To be sure, these new truths were not all directly taken from Wallerstein's writings. But they do diagnose the chaos better than any other social theoretical scheme. As much as he refused to call what he did a theory, it was so much the fodder for healthy theory that even those closest to him did what he would not do.[21]

Saskia Sassen: Global Cities and TAR, Territory Authority Rights

Saskia Sassen was born in 1947 in The Hague, in the Netherlands. In her youth she and her parents lived there until it became evident that her father had been a Nazi collaborator, whereupon Saskia and her mother left to live in Italy. Her higher education was every bit as international—in France, Italy, Argentina, then in 1974 a PhD at the University of Notre Dame in Indiana. She held a number of academic positions nationally and internationally, including Harvard and the University of Chicago before becoming the Robert S. Lynd Professor of Sociology at Columbia University and, for a time, a Centennial Visiting Professor of Sociology at the London School of Economics where her husband, Richard Sennett, a distinguished sociologist, has long held an appointment.

Few have written so much over so many years of globalization. One can hardly imagine any aspect of collective life that Sassen has not examined. For examples, among the many: *Expulsions: Brutality and Complexity in the Global Economy* (2014), *Territory Authority Rights: From Medieval to Global Assemblages* (2006), *The Global City: New York, London, Tokyo* (2001), *The Mobility of Labor and Capital: A Study in International Investment and Labor Flow* (1988), *Losing Control? Sovereignty in an Age of Globalization* (1996)—the first on this list is the one of particular importance when it comes to Global Structures and Exclusions.

Digging in to any of Sassen's writings requires a sharp shovel able to dig and lift the dense material she has laid before the reader. It is worth the effort, however, but motivation and patience must be generated by the reader's interest in the author's large, complex, and many subjects—cities, labor, sovereignty, or the explosive power of the global economy. Not least among the challenges Sassen put to serious readers is her titles. They seldom reveal the underlying truths of the book at hand which is often a bramble of concepts that turn again and again over each other, often to become branches no less tangled. This may seem to be a reckless criticism. It is not. I am just telling the reader that Sassen's books are worth the while *and* the intellectual effort. She wouldn't be discussed in this book were it not that the tangles come with an uncanny originality on issues that could not be more important.

Yet, Sassen understands the problem of which a prime example is *The Global City: New York, London, Tokyo*, which was first published in 1991 then revised in 2001 with what she calls a "slash and burn attitude."[22] Right off, a reader is likely to assume that the concept she has in mind refers to *any* city of international importance, of which the three cities named are examples of a larger phenomenon. But not so—not in the 1991 edition, not in the revision. It helps to consider that in 1991 social theorists had just begun to think of Global Cities, which meant that it was perfectly normal to think of these three as somehow the sum and substance of such cities. By 2001 and since that had begun to change

---

21 See Charles Lemert, "Wallerstein and Uncertain Worlds," in Wallerstein, Lemert, and Rojas, *Uncertain Worlds: World-System Analysis in Changing Times* (Routledge/Paradigm, 2013), 156–157.
22 Sassen, *The Global City: New York, London, Tokyo* (Princeton University Press, 2001), xv.

in a big way. Still, even then, it was fair to think of New York, London, Tokyo as more than case studies—as the waves, of a rising urban tide. Then too, Sassen has lived, off and on, in two of these three. Anyone who knows even one of them knows any one of them is global without being *merely* global:

> These cities contain a *multiplicity* of international markets, major *concentrations* of foreign firms, and of producer services selling to the world market, and they are key locations for the international property market. The sharp concentrations of such activities constitute *internationalized spaces* at the heart of the large, basically domestic urban areas.[23]

It is clear enough, if not obvious, that Sassen's idea here turns on the free play between *multiplicities* and *concentrations* in which the game is defined by *international spaces* that are urban, to be sure, but also and simultaneously large *and* domestic spaces. The uninitated reader endowed with common sense might stumble on the large/domestic juxtaposition because large when bound so tightly to domestic confounds the belief that domestic spaces are small when compared to larger spaces. Along the way, Sassen reflects on what she had discussed in the previous chapter on postindustrial sites and their connections to the three cities with national urban systems. Here, I am trying to summarize the main idea of a 450 page book by offering my own exegesis of a single, if long, paragraph on page 172. Sassen's theoretical and literary methods make such a thing possible, if not easy. She has a gift for packing many, seemingly different ideas into a relatively few words (sometimes too few).

Saskia Sassen is not, however, playing word games. She thinks and writes with an uncommon grasp of all of the apparent empirical and analytic issues for which the topic at hand is something like a solar magnet holding them all together. This is an unusual literary method for a social theorist. Others working in the field tend all-too-often to present their ideas in a linear fashion from an alpha to an omega—from, that is, a premise to a conclusion. Sassen lays it all out at the start. *The Global City* begins with the questions she intends to answer. Normal enough, but then she gives a strong sketch of her answer under the header, "New Conceptual Architecture," that summarizes her main theoretical idea of a global city: "Economic globalization and telecommunications have contributed to produce a spatiality for the urban which pivots both on cross-border networks and on territorial locations with massive concentrations of resources."[24] She is not of course the only author to present her main, conclusive idea at the start. What she does, more or less uniquely, is to keep rolling over the idea so that by the end her readers have turned over and over with her as she adds yeast that rises dough into nutritious bread. "The concept of a global city-region adds a whole new dimension to questions of territory and globalization."[25]

The Global City is many things at once—not all of them things of the same kind. Then at the end of the paragraph on *internationalized spaces* she goes on to ask: "Does a ranking emerge? Is there a global hierarchy?"[26] Before she answers the question, she returns, still on the same page, to a general empirical comment on her three cities:

> The first question here is, How do these three cities relate to one another and to the global market? The typical view in the 1980s was that New York, London, and Tokyo vis-à-vis other major cities competed among themselves and would sharpen that competition by

---

23 *Ibid*, 172. Emphases added.
24 Sassen, *The Global City* (2001), xxii.
25 *Ibid*, 351.
26 *Ibid*, 172.

providing joint 24-hour coverage of the markets. What is emerging out of the analysis of the multiplicity of financial and services markets concentrated in these cities is possibility of a systematic connection other than competition—an urban system with global underpinnings.

Here, with social scientific restraint, she paints a picture of how the *internationalized spaces* that embrace both domestic and global qualities may have arisen in the 1980s. She asserts that New York, London, and Tokyo left competition behind in favor of, again, an "urban system with global underpinnings."

The importance of what Sassen is doing in *The Global City* in 2001 is that she is staking out her own theory of globalization—one different from two of the leading theorists of globalization in the day. Her idea of an urban *system* is more than a "driving force" transforming political, economic, and cultural sections, as David Held put it in *Global Transformations: Politics, Economics, and Culture* (1999). Sassen knows specifically what she means by the term she deploys, while Held et al. tend to emphasize a more general if not abstract concept "transformationalist thesis" in which globalization is understood as "a reordering of the framework of human action" that inclines toward "the end of the nation-state."[27] By contrast, Sassen writes and thinks in quite a different way (as I've tried to show). She tends to dive into the subject and turn a variety of key possibilities over and over on each other, as a "driving force" that *may* generate "the possibility" of "global underpinnings" for the world as she saw it then. She and Held were looking at the same globalizing world and seeing similarities comprising quite different desiderata. If anything, her concept of a *global system* is closer to Manuel Castells in *The Rise of the Network Society* (1996) where he wrote in bold: **"Our societies are increasingly structured around a bipolar opposition between the Net and the Self."**[28] You'd think Castells was bogged down by the micro/Self and the macro/Net dichotomy, but the distinction itself disappears in the rest of the book and in the series for which this is the first of three volumes.[29] Just the same, Sassen's *global system* is an independent internalized space that is systematic in its own right. Plus which, she asks a second question: What about other financial centers like Paris, Frankfurt, Hong Kong? All, she reckons, also have "a strong global orientation"[30] to be sure. But by the 2020s China had absorbed Hong Kong such that Shanghai is now what that once-sheltered island to the South had been. Then too, a quarter century into the twenty-first, Tokyo is no longer Asia's solitary financial center as Seoul and Taipei have joined the club with Shanghai. In 2001, Sassen could not have foreseen these changes, but her over-all scheme allowed for them.

In the end, Sassen offers a well-decided position that is, many years later now, more compelling than those of Held and Castells—and certainly better than those who have dipped an oar in the globalization waters—and especially Francis Fukuyama whose *End of History and the Last Man* (1992) was a bad joke on more serious efforts to get somewhere with a

---

27 David Held & Anthony McGrew, David Goldblatt, Jonathan Perraton, *Global Transformations: Politics, Economics, and Culture* (Stanford University Press, 1999), 10, which displays a quite interesting table of analytic issues arrayed in three columns comparing hyperglobalists, skeptics, transformationalists.
28 Manuel Castells, *The Rise of the Network Society* (Blackwell, 1996), 3. Bold is in original.
29 The series is *The Information Age: Economy, Society, Culture*. [I venture to guess that one of the reasons that Castells and Sassen arrived at a similar view of the emerging world is that both travelled far and wide in their formative years—Castells from Spain, to Paris, to Berkeley; Sassen from the Netherlands, to Argentina, to Italy, to New York and London. Held, on the other hand, while not a homebody, spent most of his all too short life in the UK. He died of cancer at 67 in 2019.]
30 Sassen, *Global City*, 172, again.

rapidly changing world. Samuel Huntington's *Clash of Civilizations and the Remaking of World Order* (1996) and Stanley Hoffman's "Clash of Globalizations," in *Foreign Affairs* in 2002 made important contributions to the debate as to what globalization was at the same time as Sassen was sharpening her theory. There were many other contributions to this debate in a 2010 book meant to introduce both the idea of globalization and its then major interpretations of its process.[31] Yet few of the then emergent theories do not offer systematic theories comparable to those of Held, Castells, and Sassen, who in *The Global City* comes to a serious and still compelling conclusion on the matter:

> The global city represents a strategic space where global processes materialize in national territories and global dynamics run through national institutional arrangements. In this sense, the [global city] model overrides the zero-sum notion about the global economy and the national economy as mutually exclusive.[32]

Yet, if there is a criticism to be made, it would be that the book, apart from the limitation of its triad of global cities, does not begin to take into account cities in the Global South that are in a different way beginning to have an effect on the globalizing North. Cities like Kinshasa and Nairobi in Africa, and Jakarta in Indonesia, not to mention Jim Scott's anti-urban extended zone, Zomia, in upland Southeast Asia. To be sure, then, even now, places like these were not important primary players in the global urban system, but they conspire to inspire a vision that already unsettles the urban centers in the Global North. However one thinks of these and similar peripheral urban zones, to consider them as one must resort to a global theory that never claimed to be a theory of globalization—Immanuel Wallerstein's world-system. He considered globalization to be more prescriptive than descriptive.[33] He may have had a point, except that he stubbornly refused to refer to world-systems analysis as a theory,[34] which strictly speaking it wasn't—at least not in the way that Saskia Sassen and others were doing their theories. No matter how hard one tries to change them, social theories are necessarily prescriptive in that they operate outside, even above, whichever empirical facts that may seem to have sent them aloft. To each his or her own.

A good while after Sassen's *The Global City* appeared and she had published books on labor and capital, global economics, and sovereignty, among others, she published in 2006 what some (not her) might call her field theory, *Territory Authority Rights: From Medieval to Global Assemblages*. This book won six best book awards from professional associations, perhaps because it covers so many central and associated issues in late modern society. Oddly she gives *Territory Authority Rights* the acronym *TAR*. I have no idea what is suggested by *TAR* in Dutch or any of the many languages she has, but in American English it calls to mind the sticky substance that trapped trickster Brer Rabbit and served as the title of Toni Morrison's *Tar Baby*, a novel about a woman stuck in an inescapable relationship she, like many Black women, held together. It may seem that I am playing a game here, except for the fact that *TAR* does convey a sense of the way in modern times authority

---

31 Charles Lemert, Anthony Elliott, Daniel Chaffee, and Eri Hsu, editors and authors, *Globalization: A Reader* (Routledge, 2010), parts 4, 5. 6; pages 201–421.
32 Sassen, *The Global City*, 347.
33 Immanuel Wallerstein, *World-Systems Analysis: An Introduction* (Duke University Press, 2004), 93.
34 Wallerstein, "The Itinerary of World-Systems Analysis; or How to Resist Becoming a Theory," in Wallerstein, Charles Lemert, Carlos Aguirre Rojas, *Uncertain Worlds: World-Systems Analysis in Changing Times* (Routledge/Paradigm, 2013) chapter 4; also in Wallerstein's *The Uncertainties of Knowledge* (Temple University Press, 2004) and other places.

and rights are always buried—thus stuck in territories. Cross any given territorial border and your rights might well be challenged, inviting local authorities to pull you over.

Sassen's *TAR* is an acronym that is almost a singular word-phrase as if, in a globalized world, one cannot make sense without a conceptual, even practical, relation to all three elements. Hence the book itself examines how these three came to be assemblage makers. "I have taken three transhistorical components present in almost all societies and examined how they became assembled into different historical formations. These three components are territory, authority and rights (*TAR*). They assume specific contents, shapes, and interdependencies in each formation."[35]

Thereafter, the book offers an historical overview of *TAR* through the centuries in which Sassen generates her version of assemblage theory as it appears, she thought, in three important period markers. Part One is *Assembling the National*. It begins with the medieval period when a legal order came to be an admixture "of Church and 'Roman vulgar law' as well as custom, including elements of folk law, developments such as the formalizing of the status of nobility and, over time, a variety of particular legal orders."[36] Then, just after, she declares that the "vested interests of burghers aligned them with Roman law which had well-developed theories of private property and the means of ensuring compliance."[37] These conditions stabilized the Medieval towns in which leaders valued "written, evidentiary law" that provided a fixed political order from which emerged the Capetian Dynasty after the death of Charlemagne in 804 C.E. and the end of the Carolingian Dynasty. This complicated historical process began of course as the Holy Roman Empire, during when, in an oft-used formula, *Lex est Rex*—law is king. Thus, from 800 C.E. and Charlemagne to 987 C.E. when the last Carolingian King, Louis V, died to be succeeded by Hugh Capet, the Capetian King, these two political orders laid the foundation for subsequent centuries when the late Medieval French State came to be. Oddly, but necessarily, the succession of kings, most of them weak and uninteresting, invented royal systems limited by local lords who operated in relation to laws that were born in the earlier Medieval towns. Here Sassen makes a strong statement as to how "a new political order characterized by the aim of a centralized territorial administration came to be...":

> Precisely because these kings were weak and confronted by lords with far more power, the rational administration could intermediate between king and the nobility. These two medieval institutions—territorial kingship and medieval towns—both suffused in church authority could become agents in the project to develop and institute rational written law. [38]

This is one of the more pungent analytic statements in a long book that turns to and fro along the way to Sassen's *TAR* assemblage theory.[39]

---

35 Sassen, *Territory Authority Rights*, 4.
36 *Ibid*, 62.
37 *Ibid*, 62–63.
38 *Ibid*, 63.
39 Another guess: It is hard not to assume that Sassen's knowledge of and interest in this period when the Church slid into proto democratic politics is due to her doctoral studies at the premier Catholic university in America, Notre Dame. Whether the guess is right she deserves credit for this historical point that few others among social theorists might think to identify. I studied at two different theological graduate schools and back in those days read a fair amount of medieval history and literature and Sassen's pithy statement shook what I had believed to have been the case.

Part One. Assembling the National, however, cannot end with a brilliant statement that merely points to the promise of the national—and it does not. Its concluding chapter is "Assembling National Political Economies Centered on Imperial Geographies." This is where Sassen, as she does from time to time, unpacks *TAR* with concepts loaded for the historical period at hand. Readers who expect a general historical frame for the TAR assemblage theory are likely to be puzzled by these large chunks of history over which the narrative leaps. From the early medieval period after 800 C.E. the story skips to the modern era in the 1500s and beyond. Sassen begins by rather carelessly identifying the differentiating link between the early medieval rational law-making period and the middle modern banking and industrial period in the late 1800s. This is meant to open the way to an understanding of her argument that the modern moment is different from the global period in the 2000s. This point is made rather clumsily: "My argument is that the organizing logic of the world scale of the 1800s was foundationally different from today's global phase, and thus so was the relational system within which those capabilities functioned, no matter their shared modernity."[40] In this she seems to be nodding toward her own brand of assemblage theory.

After these rather obscure introductory lines, she redeems it all by an excellent section on the range of theories that moves from classical medieval thinking to the modern era—from Max Weber to Theda Skocpol and Charles Tilly, and more. She concludes this splendid discourse with:

> From its first formation then capitalism was both national and global, shaped by the key actors from both the private and state sector. As has been amply documented in the scholarship, the actual move toward capitalism took place over a long period of time and through many different, complex, and interlocking processes that produced rising levels of capital and merchandise, better ships, and more powerful weapons.[41]

This is one of Sassen's best summary passages that goes straight to the heart of *Dissembling the National*, which is central to the book's most basic argument. Historically, the crucial moment for Sassen's theory, as it was for most places and institutions the world over, was the end of World War II in 1945.

The post WWII era was conjunctural, in part because of the War itself, but also because, Sassen argues, it was a tipping point that disassembled the preeminence of the nation as the source of national power and wealth. One view is that change began with the Bretton Woods international money conference in 1940 where the IMF (International Money Fund) was established to become today a Fund that touches all the nations of the world. Sassen prefers a later tipping point because, even now, the IMF and the World Bank, as well as the post-War Marshall Plan "weakened the other players (Western European States) by raising the interdependence/dependence vis-à-vis the United States, forcing or pressuring them to adopt policies they did not necessarily want."[42] Sassen continues with a long and elaborate discussion of world history after WWII with a focus on the 1970s and 1980s when there transpired a redistribution of power inside the state, where again the American state is the prime example. Here the important fact of this matter was the rise of executive power in the national government, which in turn produced a radically different relation between public and private—which in another turn, limited the private sphere to being a source of

---

40 *Ibid*, 74.
41 *Ibid*, 89. [Footnote 24 on this page is a short but data-rich note on this process. Why it is not in the text itself is a mystery.]
42 *Ibid*, 167.

informed critical authority. But more important is the way "the deregulation of the economy and the privatization and marketization of private functions not only expand the private sphere but also remove economic activities from any public scrutiny and accountability."[43] Remarkably, as well as mind numbingly, she concludes this section with a 21 page analytic appendix: *Executive Secrecy and Discretionary Abuses—Bush Administration, 2001–2007*. For the patient reader, it is well worth careful reading. It is hard to imagine a better illustration of the problem at the highest level of government.

Part Two. Disassembling the National then offers a long and theoretically subtle chapter 5, "Denationalized State Agendas and Privatized Norm-Making." At issue here is the global market for capital. In the 1970s "banks provided three-fourths of all the short- and medium-term credit; ... by 1999 the share of commercial banks in total financial assets was less that 20 percent."[44] States, to be sure, are still players in the global economy, but they are in a global economy in which state authority is more diffuse as nonstate actors, privatization, and deregulation changed the dynamics of state authority.

> The national as container of social process and power is cracked, opening up possibilities for geography of politics that links subnational spaces. Cities are foremost in this new geography. One question this engenders is how and whether we are seeing the formation of new types of politics that localize in these cities. ... The large city of today is a strategic site for these new types of operations.[45]

Sassen ends the chapter with another illuminating appendix *Vulture Funds and Sovereign Debt/Examples from Latin America (November 2004)*. A vulture fund exists when investment funds buy out distressed funds that have over-sold and can be re-sold at a high-profit when their market position improves. Brazil, Panama, Peru, and Ecuador were among the examples given. In each case either the government itself or a private corporation was distressed such that their debt was bought and resold on the global market.

As may now be plain, *Disassembling the National*, is a step-by-step historical presentation of how a state's authority declines as the global economy gains more and more control of capital markets. So, no surprise, the last chapter in *Part Two* concerns how citizenship rights in the Global City aggravate the ways certain populations lose rights. In a nutshell:

> If we consider that large cities concentrate both the leading sectors of global capital and a growing share of disadvantaged populations—immigrants, poor women, people of color generally, and in the megacities of developing countries, masses of shanty dwellers—then cities have become strategic terrain for a series of conflicts and contradictions.[46]

Those affected have less and less connection to the national state as they struggle in their isolated neighborhoods to deal with the rising tide of conflict.

Part Three. Assemblages in a Global Digital Age will not surprise any reader who has followed the *TAR* argument so far, except for the one important change in her theoretical tune. While *Part One* and *Part Two* were about the *assembling* of the national and its disassembling, *Part Three* seems at first to strike down hard on the concept *assemblage*—as if she were playing a major chord like other assemblage theorists. Yet, at best, Sassen's *Territory*

---

43 *Ibid*, still 167.
44 *Ibid*, 261.
45 *Ibid*, 314.
46 *Ibid*, 315.

Authority Rights is a minor chord when she refers to what some would call the post-modern state. For Sassen the global digital age may be an assemblage in the classical sense, it is true, but it is also hard to imagine just how the time/space we live in is, even for a moment, settled into something so calm as the *TAR*-like state of affairs announced in the title of chapter 7 (the first chapter in *Part Three*), "Digital Networks, State Authority, and Politics." If she means something loud and bright then her pitch is way too low when *TAR*'s first note presumes to cover *territory* with *digital rights*. Granting that, as she does, whatever the global digital order is, it requires a new logic. "Among these new logics are those that constitute a variety of global digital assemblages and novel spatio-temporal framings for social activity."[47] This is how she introduces her third grand historical age that, she appears to assume, is—if not traditionally territorial—still capable of *framing social activities*. Don't get me wrong. She has every right to theorize this or some other thing. My problem is with her using a concept, *assemblage*, that has a long, serious, and still vital tradition to describe something other than the irreconcilable movements *assemblage* is meant to define.[48] This being said, and granting that many concepts have different meanings to different theorists, I turn now to what she means by *Assemblages of a Global Digital Age*.

As I said, Chapter 7, "Digital Networks, State Authority, and Politics" appears at first to cover the transformation of Sassen's *TAR* so as to have digital networks function as a kind of territory. She starts right in with a section, "A Politics of Places in Cross-Border Circuits," that begins with an inscrutable concept that nonetheless is central to the book's basic ideas: "One key assumption is that understanding the [here's that word:] *imbrications* between digitalization and politico-economic processes requires *digital space* and resisting purely technological readings of the technical capabilities entailed by digitalization."[49] This is the first use of *imbrications*—which means the necessary structural folding in and under of layers, as in the asphalt tiles on some roofs or of spoken words that cut back and forth among the meanings in a sentence or paragraph; or, at the extreme, novels like James Joyce's *Ulysses* where Leopold Bloom's day is spent traveling hither and yon through Dublin—just as Joyce's novel folds Homer's *Odyssey* over into another time that (as anyone who has spent Bloomsday in Dublin knows) is everywhere and nowhere at once. The present folds into the past, as the real slides under fiction.

Sassen's *imbrications* between digitalization and politico-economic processes is a way of keeping, while simultaneously dismissing *territory*, as somehow folded into, if not under, *digital space* which some may suppose is a mere metaphor. While I cannot read Sassen's mind, my interpretation is that it is not. To speak of a "Global Digital Age" is to play with what Wallerstein called Time/Space, and what astrophysicists call Space/Time—and what the late Stephen Hawking called Wormholes, as in "… when space-time is warped enough to make travel into the past possible, virtual particles moving on closed loops in space-time become real particles traveling forward in time at, or below, the speed of light."[50] I once taught Hawking's *A Brief History of Time* in a college class of very bright students, one of whom came up after the discussion to say: "I love this class. I've always loved science *fiction*." For a long while I believed he got Hawking wrong. But now,

---

47 *Ibid*, 325.
48 Other than what has been said here, Sassen's last chapter in *Part Three*, *Assemblages of a Global Digital Age*, summarizes and gives references to the vital tradition of assemblage theory. Also, I want to say, that *my* last section to this presentation of Saskia Sassen's theory is my portrayal of recent shifts in assemblage theory that are different in certain ways from Sassen's.
49 *Ibid*, 329.
50 Stephen Hawking, *A Brief History of Time* (Bantam Books, 2017), 169.

years later, I can say that wormholes and such like in physics, not to mention Leopold Bloom in *Ulysses*, are imbrications of fact and fiction—perhaps even the same as *territory and digital networks*.

It seems to me that Sassen is doing something like this in *Part Three* of the book which is decidedly less historical and more analytically theoretical—one might even say, programmatic. Sassen, writing early in the twenty-first century, realized that something like what she calls the Global Digital Age has dawned, even if the, as now, several decades into that new century, enough empirical sunlight has shown us what this Age is really about. *Assemblage* may not be the best term, but *imbrication* can be very helpful as in: "The argument I develop is that while the digital is specific and in many ways irreducible in the sense of nonfungible, it does nonetheless evince often complex imbrications with the nondigital. I use the concept imbrication to accommodate both independence and this irreducibility of each the digital and the nondigital."[51] Then, just after, Sassen begins the following paragraph with: "In this examination, the questions of territory, authority, and rights are revisited through the lens of the formation of digital domains we easily think of as not territorial, not subject to conventional state authority, and not involving any formal rights to speak of." Then, at the end of the next paragraph, she says that "territory plays a specific role and, further, that a particular kind of territoriality gets shaped via imbrication with these global digital assemblages." One can be excused for supposing that Sassen is trying to have it both ways at once. But if one grants, as I do, her special interpretation of assemblages, which may not be as dynamic and willing to cut ties with a past, she does here bring together aspects of the *TAR* model in ways that allow for a decisive change from the Medieval to the Modern Age (a change that took a good millennium to complete).

Sassen then turns, in an important section, to the question of—in her words: "A Politics of Places on Cross-Border Circuits." She begins here, referring to the issues dealt with in the book's earlier sections on the modern era:

> Perhaps the opposite kind of imbrication of law and territory from that of global finance is evident in a domain that has been equally transformed by digitalization but under radically different conditions. The key digital medium is the public access Internet and the key actors are largely resource-poor organizations and individuals.[52]

Then just after, she remakes an earlier point that the Internet "has enabled a new type of cross-border politics [that allow] ... small resource-poor organizations and individuals" to participate in the Internet—thus creating "a sharp growth in cross-border politics by actors other than states."[53] Having just strung together partial quotes is my way of trying to make sense of Sassen's arguments that are all-too-often so abstract that the reader longs for an example—simply mentioning Osama bin Laden and 9/11 would have gone a long way toward illustrating how the very poor using the Internet can provoke cross-border effects.

Sassen is trying to get to how digital networks comprise and function in a new sort of electronic territory that, however different, still works on hard-grounded territories—Lower Manhattan after 9/11 for example. She is talking/writing about the power of poor and excluded activists with cell phones who want to attack or remake some or another part of their worlds. Put this way (and all too simply) the section following makes manifest

---

51 Sassen, *Territory Authority Rights*, 326.
52 Ibid, 338.
53 These rather chunky lines are from the same paragraph on 338 as the previously quoted lines.

sense—*EMBEDDING THE DIGITAL*.[54] Embedding gets to the, until now, missing *territory* in *TAR*, "to embed" is to plant something down deep in some substance, such as the soil of a territorial place. Sassen writes:

> Digital networks are embedded in both technical features and standards of hardware and software, as well as the actual societal structures and power dynamics. ... This means that power, contestation, inequality, and hierarchy inscribe electronic space and shape the criteria for what types of software get developed."[55]

One gets the idea that here Sassen wants to nail down her idea. For one thing, she offers a rich list of references, which is always a signal that the author is herself embedded in a group of experts accomplished in respect to the subject at hand. In particular, in this case among many others, Sassen has the particularly brilliant, but now late, Bruno Latour for his justly famous 1991 article "Technology is Society Made Durable":

> If we abandon the division between material infrastructure on the one hand and social superstructure on the other, a larger dose of relativism is possible. Unlike scholars who treat power and domination with special tools, we do not have to start from stable actors, from stable statements, from a stable repertoire of beliefs and interests, nor even from a stable observer. And still, we regain the durability of social assemblage, but it is shared with non-humans thus mobilized. ... It is as if we might call technologies the moment when social assemblages gain stability by aligning actors and observers. Society and technology are not two ontologically distinct entities but more like phases of the same essential action.[56]

Even if one takes Latour as context for Sassen's argument, *EMBEDDING THE DIGITAL* brings her to the crux of *Part Three: Assemblages in a Global Digital Age* and just how global digital media are simultaneously embedded in their own digital world and in the social territory of structures and powers. Even though the remainder of chapter 7 tends to drudge through a swamp of complicated notions, this one section brings us to the conclusive chapter 8 of the main argument *Assembling Mixed Spatial and Temporal Orders: Elements for a Theorization*—which starts with another of the book's decisively important sections, *ANALYTIC BORDLERLANDS: SPECIFICITY AND COMPLEXITY*. Importantly, Fernand Braudel enters the story for his theory of Time-Space that influenced Immanuel Wallerstein. Sassen agrees that times and spaces are not mutually exclusive even though, in her scheme they are related by extension: "[T]he specificity of the global does not necessarily reside in being mutually exclusive with the nation."[57] Here then is territory in the *Global Digital Age*. In brief, the digital creates a space of its own that necessarily is imbricated with time such that: if time/space are one then the digitalized world may exhaust the rough distinction between the medieval and modern eras in which *TAR* came to be. Hence the third dispensation in which *Territory Authority Rights* change only to become at once different from what they once were and the same—Analytic Assemblages.

---

54 It is worth saying, for those who are still following my reading of Sassen's book, that she uses various typographical methods for introducing new and important topics—here *ITALICIZED CAPS*, even as elsewhere in a book of many layers I use my own typographical method.
55 Sassen, *Territory Authority Rights*, 341.
56 Bruno Latour, "Technology Is Society Made Durable," in John Laws, ed., *A Sociology of Monsters* (Routledge, 1991), 129.
57 Sassen, *Territory Authority Rights*, 381.

Again, for the most part, Sassen uses *assemblage* in her own way—one that tends to protect the basic truth of *TAR* while allowing for the obvious, yet hard to figure, realities of the Digital Age. Take her ideas for what they are—at the least important. Just the same I conclude this long section on Saskia Sassen with a brief presentation of the other perplexing, yet vital, assemblage theories that entail what Sassen does not seem to see. Zones of Exclusion are the ultimate but impossible to avoid outcome of a hard won global era infused with never settled dynamic relations that are, at once, both connected and disconnected—while also being necessary, if not life-giving, to the world as it becomes again and again something other than what it once was.

Assemblages, Exclusions and Zones of Exclusion

Joshua Scannell in *Cities: Unauthorized Resistances & Uncertain Sovereignty in the Urban World* (2012) strikes quite a different global key from Sassen's. This relatively short but jam-packed book begins:

> Cities, especially in countries with large peasant populations, are young, largely male, and volatile. Many strangers to a city do not expect to settle and, once there, will certainly not remain. ... Global squatters, perhaps measuring in the billions, are especially vulnerable to forcible relocation by urban governments. The governments may decimate their communities to appear "modern" to a patronizing West (that would rather not see shantytowns while celebrating Olympic festivals or the latest round of trade talks).[58]

He goes on to describe elements of "constantly morphing units of assemblage," including gangs, criminal activities, shadow economies, self-organizing tactics that often lapse into violence, attempts to use conventional methods of mobilization, resistance to language appropriation, and what Scannell cleverly calls "general metaphysical resistance."[59]

The key word here is a term Sassen uses in her own way—*assemblages*—that has a rich history in European social thought, that has been present in plain language by Manuel DeLanda in *A New Philosophy of Society: Assemblage Theory and Social Complexity* (a book that was published the same year as Sassen's *Territory Authority Rights*, 2006). DeLanda:

> "...[A]ssemblages, being wholes whose properties emerge from the interactions between parts can be used to model any of these intermediate entities: interpersonal networks and institutional organizations are assemblages of people; social justice movements are *assemblages of several network communities; central governments are assemblages of several organizations; cities are assemblages of people, networks, organizations, as well as a variety of infrastructural components, from buildings and streets to conduits for matter and energy flows, nation states are assemblages of cities, the geographical regions and cities, and the provinces that several such regions form.*[60]

---

58 Joshua Scannell in *Cities: Unauthorized Resistances & Uncertain Sovereignty in the Urban World* (Routledge/Paradigm, 2012), xvii.
59 Ibid, 82–83.
60 Manuel DeLanda, *A New Philosophy of Society: Assemblage Theory and Social Complexity* (Continuum Books, 2006), 4–5. [Emphases added.] It may be important to add that DeLanda attributes his theory of assemblages to Gilles Deleuze and Felix Guattari, *A Thousand Plateaus* (University of Minnesota Press, 1987 [1980]), 337 and elsewhere.

He is at least thorough in this conceptual liturgy that has the aura of the Christian Nicene Creed—in which everything that can be said is said. Still, in DeLanda's creed one can find the important, integrating idea that the "interactions between parts" are *not* resolved into totalizingly integrated wholes. The parts are always and unrelentingly at odds with one another—always thereby in dynamic conflict.

The concept *assemblage* comes from a famously inscrutable but paradigmatic book—*A Thousand Plateaus: Schizophrenia and Capitalism*, by Gilles Deleuze, a major French philosopher, and Felix Guattari, a French philosopher who was also a psychoanalyst—hence the subtitle and the ability of both to invent and think through a concept that refers to deep and serious differences. They write:

> The assemblage has two poles or vectors; one vector is oriented toward strata, upon which it distributes territorialities, relative deterritorializations, and reterritorializations; the other is oriented toward the plane of consistency or destratification, upon which it conjugates processes of deterritorialization, carrying them toward the absolutes of earth.[61]

Or, one of the lines that particularly influenced DeLanda, occurs where Deleuze and Guattari summarize their argument: "We have gone from stratified milieus to territorialized assemblages and simultaneously, from forces of chaos, as broken down, coded, transcoded by the milieux to the forces of the earth."[62] Either way, confusion notwithstanding, it is easy to see that Saskia Sassen's idea of assemblage is similar to but not entirely the same as that of Deleuze and Guattari. In the one place where she mentions them in a long and careful footnote that summarizes their idea of "*assemblage* as a contingent ensemble of practices and things that can be differentiated (that is, they are not collections of similar practices and things) and that can be aligned along the axes of territorialization and deterritorialization." This is a fair one sentence summary but Sassen, while respecting what they have accomplished, goes on to say that she prefers a dictionary definition that "is profoundly untheoretical… I locate my theorization elsewhere."[63] Personally I'm not sure that any concept can be untheoretical, especially when dealing with *TAR* assemblages but as much as she sees this key concept differently it is to her credit that she has read *A Thousand Plateaus* and staked a different position from those who were the rage in the generation before hers.

If there is an empirical and theoretical near opposite to Sassen it is AbdouMaliq Simone who has studied cities with large often poor integrated assemblages of migrants from arid lands or villages and homes torn by civil wars in Africa, Indonesia, and beyond. Always he looks for what the poor and excluded in these cities have traveled far and hard for. They want what others want, even when it is hard to get and keep:

---

61 Deleuze and Guattari, *ibid*, 145.
62 *Ibid*, 337. [This may be the place to say to those new to these theorists: I understand how hard they are to understand because it took me years to get the picture. I even tried reading them in French but that didn't help. But in time it came clear. I don't regret at all the time and energy I invested in reading all of these thinkers from Lacan and Foucault to Deleuze and Guattari and to Derrida then DeLanda and Sassen. I believe they have told their hard-working readers the basic truth of the new world that is still, as it may be forever, becoming whatever it is—something like: *imbricated assemblages in never ending time/space*. In this sense it is a social theoretical version of the astrophysics of our uncountable trillions of stars and planets. And why not?]
63 Sassen, *Territory Authority Rights*, page 5, footnote 1.

The desire for citizenship is the desire for a space of maneuverability and becoming for the kinds of collaborations, the kinds of being-with others — in work, residence, movement, worship, and so forth — that one wants. The issue becomes, quite simply, what kinds of political assemblages most effectively embody the urban worlds that Africans seek to conjure on the basis of their memories, skills, and aspirations? What kinds of political mechanisms best facilitate the capacity of urban residents to act, and act with the autonomy necessary to make best use of the particular resources present within a given city?[64]

Of his 20 books *City Life From Jakarta to Dakar: Movements at the Crossroads* (2010) covers, as we have seen,[65] key urban centers along a wide territorial range of the Global South from Jakarta and Phnom Penh in far Southeast Asia to Dakar on the far western edge of West Africa—a distance of about 9,000 miles. *City Life From Jakarta to Dakar* is not about cities so much as *cityness*—which is to say a much more global phenomenon *and* one intractably local and irregular. For Simone, *cityness* captures those elements of city life that cannot be fully captured, least of all by the organizing categories of modern social science. *Cityness* is about surprises and contradictions that are the source of human enterprise that includes absurdly illegal activities about which ordinary people possess the finest detailed knowledge—they see what is below the surface appearances of terrible human misery but also of people working together in order to live. What Simone sees is the startling possibility that in the most peripheral regions of city life, where there is neither clean water nor sewage systems, it is possible for people themselves to be the infrastructure. City life is about local living, not life in abstract planned cities. *Cityness* is about assemblages of people coming and going. In Simone's words:

> Buildings, layouts, provisioning systems, and organizations try to hold together and stabilize relationships between materials, environments, bodies, and institutions. Urban infrastructure attempts to bring these elements into circuits of association that constitute both bodies and territories in ways that must be continuously calibrated and readjusted. … As a result things and people come and go, intensify and withdraw their engagements and, in the end, every engagement is temporary. Connections break down, collectivities generate unanticipated outcomes, penetrate across territories and associations for which they are unprepared.[66]

One does not have to live and work in Kibera outside Nairobi which is considered by many the worst urban slum in Africa, to know that things break down. Then too Greenwich, Connecticut, considered by another many the wealthiest suburb in America. Things breakdown everywhere, leaving people unprepared. The question is: How do we think about global cities in a way that tells of this deeper truth as fundamental and ubiquitous.

Ultimately the issue here is Zones of Exclusion and even, to borrow Achille Mbembe's term, Necropolitics. AbdouMaliq Simone and Achille Mbembe are among a group of social theorists who have taken seriously assemblages as zones of exclusion—Michel Foucault's

---

64 AbdouMaliq Simone, "The Visible and Invisible: Remaking Cities in Africa," Part One: *A Practicing Urban Politics The Ghost in the (Political) Machine* at www.documenta-platform6.de/wp-content/uploads/simone_the-visible-and-invisible.pdf
65 In Chapter 17 above on The New Ethnographers of Urban Disorder.
66 AbdouMaliq Simone, *City Life From Jakarta to Dakar: Movements at the Crossroads* (Routledge, 2010), 7–8.

carceral archipelago, Gilles Deleuze and Flexis Guattari's rhizomatic assemblages, Giorgio Agamben's bare life.[67]

However we may use a term like *assemblages* or otherwise consider the world today as it is, it would be hard to make much sense of it without admitting that this world as it has become is structured in such a way that some are excluded while they and still others must deal with a world-wide politics of death.

David Harvey: The Marx Whisperer[68]

David Harvey has been called The Marx Whisperer because for so many years, the world over, he has gently but also loudly called readers to ride Marx again and again.[69] Today as I write in 2023, Harvey is in his late eighties (an age some of us consider not yet old), his internet course on Marx's *Capital* has over a million followers.

So much does he come to mind that I *believe*, without being sure, that he was an officemate in the *Centre International* just off Boulevard Raspail, a few blocks from the *Maison des Sciences de l'Homme*. If indeed he was the one I remember, why we weren't in that day at *MSH*, I can't say. Was that really David Harvey? What I can say is that he whispered Marx in my ear soon after, and through the years, even back then in Paris, when Pierre Bourdieu whispered in the other ear until we amicably parted ways. Anyhow:

David Harvey (1935–) was born in Gillingham in Kent, UK. There, he attended a grammar school for boys before becoming a student at St. John's College, Cambridge, where, also, he took his PhD with an empirical historical study of hops production in the region. Hence, the irony that he did not stray all that far from home until he began a writing life of books that influenced thinking the world over. Harvey's first major book was a popular and well-regarded text, *Explanation in Geography*, after which he moved on intellectually. While at the University of Bristol in the 1960s, he began, as did others in the day, a turn toward Marxism, a step that played a role in his move to Johns Hopkins University, where Geography and other programs were similarly inclined toward radical left ideas.

In 1973, Harvey published *Social Justice and the City* in which his Marxist philosophy inspired a theory of urban spaces that was critical of capitalism's avaricious domination of social spaces. Ever since, his radical ideas have grown more expansive and focused on a variety of subjects (even as Marxism grew less exotic among academics). He remained at Johns Hopkins with an interlude at Oxford (1987–1993), until leaving Baltimore for New York City and a distinguished professorship at the CUNY Graduate Center, where he remains today.

One of Harvey's most discussed books in the early New York period was *The Condition of Postmodernity* (1987), which began with the often ignored distinction between modernity and modernism—hence also: that between, as he puts it: POSTmodernISM and postMODERNism, a distinction that is a little too cute and not well explained. What he means becomes easier to understand in the book's two chapters in the last section where he distinguishes between "Postmodernity as an historical condition" and "Postmodernism as a hall of mirrors." In a stand-alone, half page preface to the book, Harvey's distinction and

---

67 Charles Lemert, "Capitalism's Zones of Exclusion and Necropolitics," in Plys and Lemert, *Capitalism and Its Uncertain Future* (Routledge, 2022), 343–353.

68 My discussion here of David Harvey is nearly the same as my discussion of his ideas and person in Kristin Plys and Charles Lemert, *Capitalism and Its Uncertain Future* (Routledge, 2022), 254–260.

69 "The Marx Whisperer" owes to Owen Hatherley who wrote under this title about David Harvey in *The New Statesman* (June 28, 2023).

the main argument of the book are concisely summarized, so much so that one wonders why the similar has not been offered to readers by other authors:

> There has been a sea-change in cultural as well as in political-economic, practices since 1972. This sea-change is bound with the emergence of new dominant ways in which we experience space and time. ... While simultaneity in the shifting dimensions of time and space is no proof of necessary or causal connection, strong a priori grounds can be adduced for the proposition that there is some kind of necessary relation between the rise of postmodernist cultural forms, the emergence of more flexible modes of capital accumulation, and a new round of "time-space compression" in the organization of capitalism. ... But these changes, when set against the basic rules of capitalistic accumulation, appear more as shifts in surface appearance rather that as signs of the emergence of some entirely new postcapitalist or postindustrial society.[70]

The book itself thus follows the steps in this argument.

Part One of his *The Condition of Postmodernity* examines the modernity-to-postmodernity issue in culture. Part Two outlines the stages of twentieth-century capitalism from Fordism to what he calls flexible accumulation (roughly finance capitalism). Part Three concerns the compression of space and time, by which is meant the degree to which new technologies have changed how the spatial and temporal worlds are experienced as closer and faster-moving to the degree that time overwhelms space. Part Four, "Cracks in the mirrors, fusions at the edges," is the conclusion of the argument as to the condition of postmodernity, which ends with the entirely ambivalent statement:

> There are some who would have us return to classicism and others who seek to tread the paths of the moderns. From the standpoint of the latter, every age is judged to attain 'the fullness of its time, not by being but by becoming.' I would not agree more.[71]

To call this "ambivalent" is not to disparage. Harvey, the urban geographer, aims to take cultural postmodernism seriously, while attending to the way the world is experienced as compressed down from its classically remote and fixed modern state of affairs. Harvey, the Marxist geographer, cannot leave modernism because capitalism is inherently so modern that even its post-Fordist flexibilities do not make something other and radically different.

That Harvey is not by any means a vulgar Marxist is apparent in his *Justice, Nature & the Geography of Difference* (1996), which is, in its way, a *tour de force*. Some might suppose that *The Condition of Postmodernity* suffers from being a bit too schematic as to structure and programmatic as to content. But *Justice, Nature & the Geography of Difference* serves the function of defining the troubling vectors that form an asymptote at some distant point toward which space, time, and nature rise without ever meeting—a point that is no place in particular. Harvey puts it this way: "I try to define a set of workable concepts for understanding space-time, place, and environment (nature)."[72]

For this book, the prefatory text is Adrienne Rich's poem, *An Atlas of the Difficult World*, in which the final lines are:

---

70 David Harvey, *The Condition of Postmodernity* (Basil Blackwell, 1987), vii.
71 *Ibid*, 359.
72 David Harvey, *Justice, Nature & the Geography of Difference* (Basil Blackwell, 1996), 2.

> I promised to show you a map you say but this is a mural
> then yes let it be these are small distinctions
> where do we see it from is the difference.

This book is more down to earth, in some good part because Harvey's Marxism is wrapped around political issues of which those discussed in Part Four are pivotal: Justice, Difference, and Politics; or, as he defines the concepts in Chapter 12: "Class Relations, Social Justice, and the Political Geography of Difference." These convergent political problems are a result of the straightforward historical fact of capitalism's global expansion. Global capitalism has the effect of creating new places that become "permanences with the flux and flow of capital circulation," a fact central to the geography of capitalism that Harvey develops later on the same page:

> New territorial divisions of labor and concentrations of people and labor power, new resource extraction activities and markets form. The geographical landscape which results is not evenly developed but strongly differentiated. "Difference" and "otherness" are *produced* in space through the simple logic of uneven capital investment, a proliferating geographical division of labor, an increasing segmentation of reproductive activities and the rise of spatially ordered (often segregated) social distinctions ...[73]

These lines, coming as they do after, again, a careful explanation of facts and concepts necessary to a "political geography of difference," are brilliant, even poetic in an abstract sort of meter. They achieve the necessary ambivalence with which *The Condition of Postmodernity* ended. Harvey repairs the cracks in cultural postmodernism's mirror to reflect just how its high theory of "otherness" and "difference" can be brought down to earth. Marx's vocabulary can be reworked to speak the truth of justice, nature, and a geography of difference. Harvey doesn't go as far as Bruno Latour in collapsing the neoclassical dichotomy nature/culture. Instead, he leaves them as they were received after the nineteenth century in order to bring environment justice under a new sun (1966, 431): "The work of synthesis has to be on-going since the fields and terrains of struggle are perpetually changing as the capitalist socio-ecological dynamic changes."[74]

No wonder then that the title of his next book *Spaces of Hope* (2000), a collection of published essays and lectures of the 1990s, fills in gaps in his line of thought with topics such as "Uneven geographical developments and universal rights" and "Responsibilities toward nature and human nature." But also, Harvey opens up new topics that once, few, if any, would have expected a serious Marxist to entertain: "The body as an accumulation strategy," and "Body politics and the struggle for a living wage." What the entries in this compendium have in common is precisely, as he says at the first, "The difference a generation makes." This organizing theme owes to the biographical fact that 1998, when the book came together, was the 30th anniversary of 1968 from which he dates his own revolutionary generation, when, for him, "the streets of Baltimore burned" from rioting, as did the streets of Paris, Berlin, Mexico City, and other cities the world over. The hope of a new generation, and those of his who are still engaged, is that they and he will seize "the courage of our own minds and are prepared to take an equally speculative plunge into the unknown." After which, he concludes: "What Marx called 'the real movement' that will

---

[73] Ibid, 295.
[74] Ibid, 431.

abolish 'the existing state of things' is always there for the taking. That is what gaining the courage of our minds is all about."

The year after *Spaces of Hope*, Harvey published another collection of essays *Spaces of Capital: Towards a Critical Geography* (2001) that covers writings more or less in and of the saga of the generation of 1968, from 1974 to 1989, beginning with "Reinventing Geography"—an interview with the editors of the *New Left Review* (previously published by the same group of editors in 2000). The interview itself is instructive because there is no better place to follow Harvey's account of his thinking from *Explanation of Geography* in 1969 to his then present 2000, when, at 65 years, his Marxist geography had achieved a considerable maturity. For example:

> ...While the adaptability of capitalism is one of its prime weapons in class struggle, we should not underestimate the vast swathe of opposition it continues to generate. The opposition is fragmented, often highly localized, and endlessly diverse in terms of aims and methods. We have to think of ways to help mobilize and organize this opposition, both actual and latent, so that it becomes a global force and a global presence.[75]

It would be hard to imagine a more mature political assessment based on years of intellectual and empirical study of capitalism and the world it dominates. As all collections do, the book wanders quite a bit, even as it is packed with *aperçus* such as "Geography is too important to be left to geographers."[76] And, "Geographical knowledges occupy a central position in all forms of political action."[77] The latter crystallizes the former. Disciplines displace those who earn their daily bread from academic writing about the worlds they aim to study. But political actions are always and necessarily on the ground in given spaces.

Most poignant of all his memorable observations occurs in his discussion of the production of spatial organization in the 1985 essay "The Geopolitics of Capitalism," where he appropriates a line from Marx's *Grundrisse*: "Capitalism, Marx concludes, is necessarily characterized by a perpetual striving to overcome all spatial barriers and 'annihilate space with time.'"[78] Though *Spaces of Capital: Towards a Critical Geography*, as a whole, is a disappointment for its disjointed putting together of divergent essays, this one line and its chapter are worth the price of a heavy book. Here, Harvey points us to *Notebook V* in the *Grundrisse* where, more than any other place in Marx's many writings, the point of time–space compression comes sparklingly clear. Unfortunately, in my edition of the *Grundrisse*—which seems to be the same as the one Harvey's cites—I do not find the exact line he quotes, but I could find the longer passage from which the quote is drawn:

> *Circulation time thus appears as a barrier to the production of labour* = an increase in necessary labor time = a decrease in surplus labour time = a decrease in surplus value = an obstruction, a barrier to the self-realization process of capital. Thus, while capital must on the one side strive to tear down every spatial barrier to intercourse, i.e. to exchange, and conquer the whole earth for its market, it strives on the other side to annihilate this space with time, i.e. to reduce to a minimum the time spent in motion from one place to another. The more developed the capital, therefore, the more extensive the market over which it circulates, which forms the spatial orbit of its circulation, the more does it strive

---

75 David Harvey, *Spaces of Capital: Toward a Critical Geography* (Routledge, 2001), 24.
76 *Ibid*, 116.
77 *Ibid*, 233.
78 *Ibid*, 327.

simultaneously for an even greater extension of the market and for greater annihilation of space by time.⁷⁹

The passage is so wonderfully literary (even in translation) and, to the point of labor time's space, one wonders why Marx did not include it in Part Five of *Capital I*, where he discusses the working day and surplus value with its page after page of clumsy formulaic notions meant, one supposes, to make the facts of the matter plain to the common reader when, in fact, it bores the reader to tears. It is to Harvey's enduring credit that in getting to the key passage in Marx he used it to formulate capitalism's compression of time/space as central to its vulgar methods for accumulating capital.

The balance of this chapter in Harvey's *Spaces of Capital* is in effect an *explication de texte* in which he demonstrates, step by step, how the time-space problem works to destructive ends:

> *The theoretical argument I have here set out is, I hold, as fundamental to the elucidation of our present plight as it is to the interpretation of the historical geography of capital. If I am correct, and I hasten to add that I hope I am grossly in error and that history or others will quickly prove me so to be, then the perpetuation of capitalism in the twentieth century has been purchased at the cost of death, havoc and destruction wreaked in two world wars.*⁸⁰

In the two decades since he wrote these lines, Harvey, who turned 88 in 2023, has published a good many books, none of which—so far as I can tell (it is all too much for me to read in the finite time available to an 86-year-old)—gives evidence that he has *not* been proven wrong about capitalism's deadly havoc. Still, in 2005, for example, *A Brief History of Neoliberalism* provides the best history of neoliberalism from its beginnings early in the 1970s to early in the 2000s. It begins with a devastating portrayal of what it has wrought:

> The process of neoliberalization has, however, entailed much "creative destruction" not only of prior institutional frameworks and powers (even challenging traditional forms of state sovereignty) but also of division of labour, social relations, welfare provisions, technological mixes, ways of life and thought, reproductive activities, attachments to the land and habits of the heart. Insofar as neoliberalism values market exchange as "an ethic in itself, capable of acting as a guide to all human action, and substitution for all previous ethical beliefs," it emphasizes the significance of contractual relations in the marketplace. It holds that the social good will be maximized by maximizing the reach and frequency of market transactions, and it seeks to bring all human action into the domain of the market.⁸¹

It would be hard to say worse about any form of capitalism.

---

79 Marx, *Grundrisse* (Penguin Books [with *New Left Review*] (1973 [1857–1858]), 539.
80 Harvey, *Spaces of Capital*, ibid, 343. Emphases added.
81 David Harvey, *A Brief History of Neoliberalism* (Oxford University Press, 2005), 3. [The internal quotations are from Paul Treanor, "Neoliberalism: Origins, Theory, Definition," at web.inter.nl.users/Paul Treanor/neoliberalism.html. In any case, Treanor works in Amsterdam and all I could find was blurbs about how great this article is. I wish I could find it.]

In *Seventeen Contradictions and the End of Capitalism* (2014), Harvey is empirically explicit, as always he is, in describing the then current crises of capitalism. Then, too, as usually he does, Harvey states his purpose, which turns out to be intriguing:

> So what I am seeking here is a better understanding of the contradictions of *capital*, not of *capitalism*. I want to know how the economic engine of *capitalism* works the way it does, and why it might suffer and stall and sometimes appear to be on the verge of collapse. I also want to show why this economic engine should be replaced and with what.[82]

Overlooking the first line which requires the thinking reader to wonder how the contradictions of capital would not entail the same in capitalism, the final sentence is, if not new to him, extraordinarily inviting. Readers may therefore be motivated to immediately skip the book's main chapters on the 17 contradictions and turn to its conclusion "Prospects for a Happy but Contested Future: The Promise of Revolutionary Humanism." Here the reader is, as often before, treated to a wide-ranging discussion of religion and world religions, of the Renaissance, and much more, before coming to Frantz Fanon to whom he returns often in previous writings—but never quite so warmly as:

> …[W]hat is so stunning about *The Wretched of the Earth*, and what indeed brings tears to the eyes on a close reading and makes it so searingly human, is the second half of the book, which is taken up by devastating descriptions of the psychic traumas of those on both sides who found themselves forced by circumstances to participate in the violence of the liberation struggle.[83]

The liberation struggle in Africa and wherever it takes place is a struggle (if I may say it this way) not so much about capital as about Capitalism's avaricious greed, yes, to extract surplus value, hence capital, wherever it can be had. But where historically it was first had and remains to be had is on the backs of colonized people beginning with the first waves of conquest and colonization in the sixteenth century, which were unarguably the first seeds of a global Capitalism. Of course, Harvey is not naïve on this point even if he surprises by his primary distinction as to where the contradiction in capital resides.

His last line in this book is telling: "There are, as we have seen, enough compelling contradictions within capital's domain to foster many grounds for hope," that is, the hope of those able to cry openly at the suffering caused by capitalism's greed for endless capital accumulation. Those tears may be where a revolutionary humanism begins and ends. Harvey makes the point less succinctly and more fully in *Marx, Capital, and the Madness of Economic Reason*:

> To be sure, capital is not the only possible subject for any thorough and complete reckoning of current ills. But to pretend that it has nothing to do with our current ailments and that we do not need a cogent, as opposed to fetishistic and apologetic representation of how it works, how it circulates and accumulates among us, is an offence that human history, if it manages to survive that long, will judge severely.[84]

---

82 David Harvey, *Seventeen Contradictions and the End of Capitalism* (Oxford University Press, 2014), 11.
83 *Ibid*, 290.
84 *Ibid*, 290.

Nancy Fraser: Global Justice as Representation, Distribution, and Recognition[85]

Nancy Fraser (1947–) was born in Baltimore, Maryland. She was educated at Bryn Mawr College outside Philadelphia, after which she earned the PhD at the CUNY Graduate Center in New York City. She then taught at Northwestern University for a good while, before joining the faculty of the New School for Social Research as Henry A. and Louise Loeb Professor of Political and Social Science and Professor of Philosophy. She remains there still.

Since its founding in 1919, the New School has been home to Left thinkers, including John Dewey, Thorstein Veblen, and Charles Beard in the early years. After 1933, the New School became known as the University in Exile because it served as a home for Europeans fleeing Italian and German Fascism. Even now, the New School offers a course devoted to the careful appreciation of Theodor Adorno and Max Horkheimer's 1947 book *The Dialectic of Enlightenment*, written during their exile in the United States. All this is to say that Nancy Fraser remains at the New School because it is for her the all-but-perfect intellectual home. She has devoted her writing life to her own version of critical theory and is recognized in Europe as one of the world's leading social theorists—this so much so that she was introduced for a talk in Germany as one of North America's leading intellectuals. Such recognition is rare for any American, because even now (with some exceptions) the nation's philosophers resist taking deep consideration of the major German and French philosophies. The New School has long been an exception to this cultural silliness.

Nancy Fraser's first, and still important book, *Unruly Practices: Power, Discourse and Gender in Contemporary Social Theory* in 1989, is all the proof one needs of her early close reading of European social theories. She began the book with a statement of method that has guided her academic and political thinking over the years to come:

> I argue repeatedly that politics requires a genre of critical theorizing that blends normative argument and empirical sociocultural analysis in a "diagnosis of the times." In this, I am affirming a fairly classical left view found in Marx and in the Frankfurt school of Critical Theory. At the same time, I am opposing a tendency in some sections of the academic Left to engage in what can only appear as esoteric forms of discourse unless and until connections to practice are elaborated, indeed mediated, through sociopolitical analysis.[86]

Though the second sentence in this passage inclines toward an esoteric discourse of its own, her position is clear enough.

Fraser's book itself is a fair elaboration of these principles. In the book's three sections—roughly: Foucault and power, Derrida and deconstruction, Habermas and gender—she respectfully interprets each tradition with an eye to important political issues, including the sexual body, technocracy, women and welfare, and more generally Late Capitalism. Given that, from the first, she made her theoretical and political preferences clear, Fraser is fair but predictably critical of the Foucauldian and Derridean lines (with Richard Rorty thrown in). A tribute to her broader sense of fairness is that she also criticizes Habermas in respect to what, for her, is a crucial political issue, the needs of women in the late capitalist lifeworld.

---

85 Much of this section is taken from my contribution to Kristin Plys and Charles Lemert, *Capitalism and Its Uncertain Future* (Routledge, 2022), 254–260.

86 Nancy Fraser, *Unruly Practices: Power, Discourse and Gender in Contemporary Social Theory* (Minneapolis: University of Minnesota Press, 1989), 6.

Habermas, she writes, "…fails to address the issue of how to restructure the relation of child rearing to paid work and citizenship."[87] In the same place, she continues:

> Habermas's categories tend to misrepresent the causes and underestimate the scope of the feminist challenge to welfare state capitalism. In short, the struggles and wishes of contemporary women are not adequately clarified by a theory that draws the battle line between system and lifeworld institutions.

Fraser obviously parts with Habermas and German critical theory in general over more than a principle of theoretical feminism. Her feminism has always been, to varying degrees, concretely focused on practical problems of women living in a patriarchal world in which the feminine, in all its manifestations, is diminished, often eradicated from the dominant culture. Looking back from the 2020s to Fraser's 1989 book, some might suppose that this is an extreme statement. It may be, but only in the sense that she did not write in such a stern manner of the realities for women then still so stark. Even today, when many women are prominent in public positions of power and authority, the starkness of patriarchy casts a cloud over women who still must struggle on meager, irregular government payments, while their children must go to inferior public schools, and their partners, if men, are all too often away in prison, to their graves, or in wandering lives; then too, women's political successes are met with scorn and in several notorious cases they are deprived of the victories they fairly won. In 1989, all was not bleak for women, but neither was it bright. Though a third-wave feminism moved out into its own in the 1970s, in 1974 when Dorothy Smith's now classic article on feminist standpoint theory "Women's Experience as a Radical Critique of Sociology" challenged the masculinist aloofness of mainstream social theory. Also in the same year, Carol Stack's *All Our Kin* told the story of women getting by in public housing on slim pickings by cooperating with each other as if they were kin. These and other feminist ventures began a slow but definite shift on how those bold enough to care ought to think about women's experience. Yet it would be a good while until feminism's *annus mirabilis* in 1990, when books like Judith Butler's *Gender Trouble* and Patricia Hill Collins' *Black Feminist Thought* as well as Fraser's *Unruly Practices* in 1989 brought forth a major advance beyond these earlier pioneering works. A plainspoken token of what was then advanced is Patricia Hill Collins' phrase (borrowed from bell hooks), the *matrix of domination*, which conveys the fact of life that all who live in Capitalist societies are caught on one or another or several dominating vectors.

Yet even these advances required time for readers to digest in order to nourish the will to work on the streets. Still now, more than three decades later, on the verge of a return of a version of sanity in 2021, the success of women's public efforts is good if not dazzling. Yet, when Nancy Fraser, in the subtitle to her 1989 book used the words "power, discourse, and gender," she was in a sense teasing the reader to look down and deep at the practical problems of women who seek to live self-consciously as feminists. Many still are caring for children alone, paying ever higher rents, while participating, when they can, in political actions that might support both their sense of womanhood and the needs and wants of daily life. In other words (again, so far as I know, Fraser doesn't say it this way), she is writing about capitalisms, in all their several natures, as at least the most important, if not the sole, pillar of the patriarchal State since Marx began writing about the capitalism of his day.

---

87 *Ibid*, 137.

Fraser made a series of theoretically political steps after *Unruly Practices* in 1989. *Justice Interruptus: Critical Reflections on the "Postsocialist Condition"* (1997) is a collection of her articles published in the 1990s. By *postsocialist* she means to retain socialism as a critical ideal after the events of 1989 when the collapse of the Soviet Union and its East Bloc spelt an historical end to more than the Cold War. Second, but interestingly, she suggests that this event might be causally related to the rise on the cultural Left of identity politics, in respect to which she says that the events of 1989 led to a shift in the political imaginary with, to her, an important difference:

> More deeply, ... we are witnessing an apparent shift in the political imaginary, especially in terms in which justice is imagined. Many actors appear to be moving away from a socialist imaginary, in which the central problem of justice is redistribution to a "postsocialist" imaginary, in which the central problem of justice is recognition. With this shift, the most salient social movements are no longer defined in terms of "classes" who are struggling to defend their "interests," end "exploitation," and win "redistribution." Instead, they are culturally defined "groups" and "communities of value" who are struggling to defend their "identities," end "cultural domination," and win "recognition." The result is a decoupling of cultural politics from social politics, and the relative eclipse of the latter by the former.[88]

With this poignant statement as preface, Fraser begins the collection with an article previously published in 1995 in *New Left Review*, "From Redistribution to Recognition? Dilemmas in Justice in a Postsocialist Age," which is the first of a good many subsequent discussions of the dilemma framed in relation to economic issues such as "After the Family Wage: A Postindustrial Thought Experiment" interspersed with astute, but argumentative, comments on the views of other major feminist theorists such as "False Antitheses: A Response to Seyla Benhabib and Judith Butler." *Justice Interruptus*, thereby, is the first readily available book-length discussion of Fraser's contestation with those she considered "recognition" or identity theorists of social justice.

Fraser takes a mediating position between the two Left political extremes—redistribution and recognition—a position she argues is made possible from within the experience of a social movement, in particular, feminist politics: "Within social movements such as feminism, for example, activist tendencies that look to redistribution as the remedy for male domination are increasingly disassociated from tendencies that look instead to recognition of gender differences."[89] That social movements engaged in real on-the-ground politics might clarify relations that otherwise would remain philosophical is a telling point as to Fraser's underlying beliefs about the world as lived, and important to remind, this is the significant difference with Habermas. A lifeworld is an analytic category. Fraser, though not known for being a social activist, is clear enough about the importance of sociopolitical movements to an understanding of her philosophical principles. Important to add that when her topic changes, she knows to change her theoretical structure, as in her 2010 book *Scales of Justice: Reimagining Political Space in a Globalizing World*, where she writes of how Globalization requires a reframing:

> I shall argue, first, that theories of justice must become three-dimensional, incorporating the political dimension of *representation* alongside the economic dimension of *distribution* and the cultural dimension of *recognition*. I shall also argue that the political

---

88 Nancy Fraser, *Justice Interruptus: Critical Reflections on the "Postsocialist Condition"* (Routledge, 1997), 2.
89 Nancy Fraser, "Recognition without Ethics?" *Theory, Culture & Society* 18 (2001): 21.

dimension of representation should itself be understood as encompassing three levels. The combined effect of these two arguments will be to make visible a third question, beyond those of the "what" and the "who," which I shall call the "how." This question, in turn, inaugurates a paradigm shift: what the Keynesian-Westphalian frame cast as the theory of social justice must now become a theory of *postWestphalian democratic theory*.[90]

The literary genius of Nancy Fraser is her ability to express enormously complicated ideas in a kind of plain language that allows the reader to assume that she gets the drift of what is being said. There are occasionally notions that require unpacking. One of them is *post-Westphalian democratic theory*. The Treaty of Westphalia in 1648 demarcated the territorial limits of what thereafter came to be known as the modern nation-states. Hence the idea that a nation is defined first and foremost by its territorial borders. Once, centuries later, globalization took hold as the reality of late-modern States able to deploy late and all-but-post-modern technologies and their military and financial methods, the Westphalian norm fell when, as Fraser puts it (following Hardt and Negri's *Empire*), states were able "to govern at a distance through flexible fluctuating networks that transcend structured institutional sites."[91]

What Fraser is doing here is an important example to other social philosophers. Justice emerges, after *Unruly Practices* where it was the latent theme, to become the prevailing theme that guides her from "Gender and the Politics of Need Interpretation" in the 1989 book to a more focused theoretical gaze on the redistribution versus recognition controversy among feminists in and about 1995. Then, a decade later, in the essay "Mapping the Feminist Imagination: From Redistribution to Recognition to Representation" (2005),[92] she refined the 1995 two-dimensional model (if that is the word) into three dimensions where political *representation* takes a coequal theoretical place alongside *redistribution* and *recognition*. Then, in 2007, a *NLR* essay "Reframing Justice in a Globalizing World"[93] resets the tripartite scheme in the salient, more general terms of justice and globalization—which then becomes, one must say, the literary frame for this reframing in *Fortunes of Feminism: From State-Managed Capitalism to Neoliberal Crisis* (2013). This is a book of essays organized in what she calls a "Drama in Three Acts."

Fraser thus returns to feminism after State-Managed Capital after the 2010s in the economic crisis of Neoliberalism. The three acts of the drama of feminism's relations to Capitalism are instructively identified:

1. Feminism Insurgent: Radicalizing Critique in the Era of Social Democracy
2. Feminism Tamed: From Redistribution to Recognition in the Age of Identity
3. Feminism Resurgent? Confronting Capitalist Crisis in the Neoliberal Era

One might say that this is a little too much already with the titles. I think not for two reasons. Fraser's titles and headers are remarkably lucid as to which ideas are pursued

---

90 Nancy Fraser, *Scales of Justice: Reimagining Political Space in a Globalizing World* (Columbia University Press, 2010), 15–16.
91 *Ibid*, 126.
92 Nancy Fraser, "Mapping the Feminist Imagination: From Redistribution to Recognition to Representation," *Constellations: An International Journal of Critical and Democratic Theory* 12 (2005): 295–307.
93 Nancy Fraser, "Reframing Justice in a Globalizing World," in *Global Inequality: Patterns and Explanations*, eds. David Held and Ayse Kaya (Polity Press, 2007). Also in the *NLR*, 2005.

at each turn. But also, when Fraser's literary *oeuvre* is followed from the beginning to the present, the reader learns a good lesson in just how central feminism is to a better understanding of Capitalism as it has come to be.

In a tiny 2019 book (or pamphlet) with huge implications, *The Old is Dying and the New Cannot Be Born*, Fraser traces what she considers the dying of, yes, the old capitalist order but also of the moribund Neoliberal order down to the waning years of the Trump regime which, she argues, put an end to the "hegemony of progressive Neoliberalism." As oxymoronic as this may sound, her original interpretation of the times makes sense: "The progressive-neoliberal bloc combined an expropriative, plutocratic economic program with a liberal-meritocratic politics of recognition. The distribution component of this amalgam was neoliberal."[94] Here she refers to the Reagan-Thatcher-Clinton era in which government support for the poor was cut in favor of direct and indirect benefits to the wealthy. Against which, so-called progressive "New Democrats" pursued policies of recognition that did little more than name and identify those excluded while subjecting them to policies of redistribution that kept them in place—hence the progressive-neoliberal hegemony that encouraged a reactionary Neoliberalism comprising "Christian evangelicals, southern whites, small town Americans, and [the] disaffected working class"—in other words, the base that elected Donald Trump which he eventually lost control of as the years passed him by. Against all this, Fraser proposes a "Strategy of Separation," arising from two basic splits:

> First, less privileged women, immigrants, and people of color have to be wooed away from the lean-in feminists, the meritocratic anti-racists and mainstream LGBTQ+ movement, the corporate diversity and green-capitalists who hijacked their concerns, inflecting them in terms consistent with neoliberalism … . Second, Rust Belt, southern, and rural working-class communities who have to be persuaded to desert their current crypto-neoliberal allies. The trick is to convince them that the forces promoting militarism, xenophobia, and ethnonationalism cannot and will not provide them with the essential material prerequisites for good lives, whereas a progressive populist bloc just might.[95]

Shades of the Occupy Wall Street Movement in 2011!

Fraser wants, however, to make something clear: "I am not suggesting that a progressive-populist bloc should mute pressing concerns about racism, sexism, homophobia, Islamophobia, and transphobia."[96] What she is against is "moralizing condescension, in the mode of progressive neoliberalism." What she helps us to be clear about is not, primarily, adopting the smug, commonplace, *neoliberal* attitudes that run through the media. Rather, she insists that the paralyzing pseudo-progressive ideas are so much a presence in our times *because* of the global force of neoliberal Capitalism. If, on this point, there is reason to pause before Fraser's theoretical acuity, it is because of her political locutions. When she writes of *hegemonic progressive neoliberalism*, the phrase suggests that progressive attitudes are somehow on an equal hegemonic footing with Neoliberalism (with a capital N). Neoliberal Capitalism is the scam that plays with the stages of Capitalist development to suggest that it was still somehow "liberal" in the classic sense of "free market" economies in which all would thrive by a simple devotion to their self-conceived best interests, protected, of course,

---

94 Nancy Fraser, *The Old is Dying and the New Cannot Be Born* (Verso, 2019), 11–12.
95 *Ibid*, 31–40.
96 *Ibid*, 33.

by a mysterious Invisible Hand. That—as now we who would think know—Adam Smith was a philosophical mythmaker who did little more than give permission to the mythmakers of our time. Whatever the Capitalisms that came to be after the eighteenth century were in point of economic reality: "Capitalism" was, as still it is, a metaphor to suggest the way the world is. In actual historical fact, there have been any number of political, social, and economic experiments—none of them permanent; all of them ever changing.

What makes Nancy Fraser's writings so instructive is that since the 1980s, she has sought to calibrate these changes while using, as she and we must, a variant of the preexisting nomenclature. That one must do as has been done, does not demand that the names we give to the various stages of whatever we are commenting upon prevent us from making the fine, nonobvious discrimination of the deeper changes that exhaust the utility of preexisting vocabulary to name. Nancy Fraser does this about as well as it can be done. Yet, her resort to locutions like *hegemonic progressive neoliberalism* should be called into question, as one can assume she will in a forthcoming book. That *neoliberalism* pretends to be a new and better, if necessary, kind of Capitalism is all but absurd. Fraser gets this. But still, she has not yet gotten the full force of the historical reality that, by whatever name, economic reason—practical and scientific—dooms the possibility that any political movement can fundamentally change the sordid nature of Capitalism's now global economic reasoning. Her call for a "separation" of progressive from Neoliberal is a good beginning, one made good by her method of making the contentions among feminist thinkers a hard drive for reprogramming social and political theory.

No one, so far, has gotten this quite right. Fraser in many ways is a leading light, so to speak, of thinkers who have begun the process of not just "rethinking" economic reason but reworking it on the grounds of daily life. As a measure of what she has done against what needs to be done, it helps to turn now to a thinker, different in many ways from Fraser, yet just as clear about, in David Harvey's phrase, "…capital and the madness of economic reason".

Why Marx Now?

In a book on the way Americans think of themselves, some might wonder: Why now all this on Marx? For which, it needs to be said that Marx and Marxism itself are the intellectual sources to which America have *not* paid close enough attention. If, as I do, you understand 1619 as the actual first year of the nation as it has become, then it must be granted that Americans would have done better had they thought about how Capitalism has done the dirty deeds that made slavery and, still now, race so central to our culture. Capitalism in 1619? Yes, to be sure. The settlers in the Virginia Colony and their English backers brought and bought slaves who in due course made for them a profit in cotton production. One of Marx's basic rules is that profit is surplus value gained when labor is cheap or free (except in the case of slavery where there are costs in housing and feeding a slave population).

Think of what Thomas Jefferson—than whom none in this day knew more about European philosophies—would have thought about his slaves had he studied Marx as he did so many others. Jefferson likely sent a copy to James Madison who might well have written a Federalist Paper on the anti-democratic effect of surplus value in the cotton trade. The global cotton empire[97] was led by American cotton growers who pressed their slaves to produce the economic raw material that passed through Lowell and Lawrence in

---

97 Again, Sven Beckert, *The Empire of Cotton: A Global History* (Vintage, 2015).

Massachusetts and Manchester in the UK to be fashioned into fabrics that, in turn, became clothing marketed across the known world. Hence, from cotton we have America's role in the North Atlantic Trade Triangle—African men and women (and their children) shipped west to the Americas where they were pressed to hard work in fields to grow the balls that could be spun into fabric that could be sold and sewn into clothing then sold across the world, from which the profits were plowed back into Capitalism's triangle.

Yet in the day Americans had no Marx and little like him. Thomas Paine may have come closest to a radical thinker but he had other revolutionary fish to fry. In 1848 when Marx wrote for the *New York Daily Tribune* Americans paid scant attention to the scraps of Marx's thinking that could only be found if only more had looked. Think of Waldo Emerson, Henry Thoreau, and Margaret Fuller in mid-nineteenth century Concord who were major intellectuals and for the times radicals in America and beyond. What if Fuller in her days in Italy had absorbed the Marxism that was known well by many across Europe? She might have realized she was into something important and stayed in Europe and not boarded that ship for home that sank and killed her just yards before it arrived. All could have been different here on our side of the Atlantic if any of these twists and turns in America's literary history had turned left.

Americans, however, had nothing until recently that might have helped them come up with a serious sense of how their nation has been, and is, complicit with sad, even tragic, dialectic between Global Structures and the Exclusions they have bred. As Immanuel Wallerstein said in his way, and David Harvey said in his, the time-space of capital is global in a way that cannot be understood without a critical geography the space of capital.

Part VII

American Futures, 1542 and 1619 to When?

Part VII

American Indians, 1542 and
1610 to Winter?

24 The TimeSpace of Traveling Theory
Edward Said, Sam Han, Trịnh Thị Minh Hà, Cabeza de Vaca, Black Elk, Phillis Wheatley, Gyatri Chakravorty Spivak, Howard Zinn, E.O. Wilson

Like people and schools of criticism, ideas and theories travel
—from person to person, from situation to situation, from one period to another.
Cultural and intellectual life are usually nourished and often sustained
by this circulation of ideas… .

—Edward Said, *Traveling Theory*, 1982

So far as I know it was Edward Said who invented the idea of traveling theory:

> Like people and schools of criticism, ideas and theories travel—from person to person, from situation to situation, from one period to another. Cultural and intellectual life are usually nourished and often sustained by this circulation of ideas… .[1]

Said himself lived this idea. From birth in Palestine to school in Egypt, and eventually to Columbia University from where he continued to travel the world of places and ideas.

What follows in this concluding chapter of *Americans Thinking America* are introductions to a number of writers listed above who have, in their different ways, also been traveling theorists. I discuss them briefly here as a suggestion for any who would one day write a book that completes this one. No single book is ever complete. Those mentioned here are but a sample of those who could well be in a book on this subject that reaches deeper in time and space.

Traveling Theory Always Moving

Among Edward Said's many justly famous and important books, some would say that "Traveling Theory" is the text everyone must read. Its simplest line is the epigraph for this chapter, repeated now: "Like people and schools of criticism, ideas and theories travel—from person to person, from situation to situation, from one period to another." On closer reading, the line is more theoretically subtle than a quick reading would allow. In a strong paragraph at its beginning Said outlines the three ingredients of theoretical travel that are the same as any kind of traveling: persons, places, times. So far as I know he has never used the expression *TimeSpace*, but he might as well have since his major and most often read books could be seen as books on *time—Beginnings: Intention & Method* (1975)—and,

---

[1] Edward Said, "Traveling Theory," in *The Edward Said Reader*, edited by Moustafa Bayoumi and Andrew Rubin (Vintage Books, 2000), 195–196.

second, on the politics and global space to and from which culture travels—*Culture and Imperialism* (1993).[2]

Said is on topic now because of his more general theme that too often is overlooked—theories travel every which way and, he writes of the four major ways. 1) there is always a point of *origin* from which 2) they travel a distance passing through various contexts where upon 3) they deal with *conditions* of acceptance or resistance that may alter them such that 4) "the now fully (or partly) accommodated (or incorporated) idea is to some extent transformed by its new uses, *its new position in time and place.*"[3] This is enough to justify (as if Said needs justification for anything he has done) using this one idea among his many, to frame the concluding chapter of *Americans Thinking America*. Which in itself requires an explanation.

In what sense is Edward Said American? This is a question that could just as well be asked of others in this book: Herbert Marcuse from Germany, David Harvey from Britain, Saskia Sassen from the Netherlands, Trjnh Thj Minh Hà from Vietnam, Gayatri Spivak from India, not to mention Thomas Paine who came to America from the UK and Alexander Hamilton who was born in Charlestown and St Kitts. The question would be reversed if we think of Kwame Ture who was born in Trinidad and Tobago and died in Conakry, Guinea. Though he is famous for what he did here, was he really American? Then there are those like Thomas Jefferson, Immanuel Wallerstein, and James Baldwin who all lived in France long enough and fluently-enough to pass as French.

Said was very much aware of the effects of growing up in the Middle East on his education and writing life in America. He was born in the British mandate of Palestine, grew up in Cairo and Jerusalem, attended British private schools in both cities, visited Lebanon with his Lebanese mother, before the family moved to the United States where he studied at Northfield Mount Hermon, Princeton, then Harvard for a PhD in English Literature. He then taught at Columbia University until his end. All this while identifying as a Palestinian-American and being politically active on behalf of the Palestinians. Near the end of his life, after a cancer diagnosis, he wrote *Out of Place* about how, through his years, he was, like so many others, dispossessed.

> *Out of Place* is a record of an essentially lost or forgotten world. Several years ago I received what seemed to be a fatal medical diagnosis, and it therefore struck me as important to leave behind a subjective account of the life I lived in the Arab world, where I was born and spent my formative years, and in the United States where I went to school, college, and university. Many of the places and people I recall here no longer exist, though I found myself frequently amazed at how much I carried of them inside me in often minute, even startling, concrete detail.[4]

Edward Said spent his life traveling, staying, and traveling again—just as his own literary and social theories were born of his travels hither and yon.

---

2 *Beginnings: Intention & Method* (Johns Hopkins University Press, 1975; and *Culture and Imperialism* (Knopf, 1993).
3 "Traveling Theory," in *The Edward Said Reader*, ibid, 196.
4 Edward Said, *Out of Place* (Random House, 1999), ix. For more context and my attempt to put in perspective of how his dispossession and nostalgia worked their effect on his thinking and politics, see Lemert, "Said and 'Edward' / Dispossession and Overcoming Nostalgia," in Lemert, *The Structural Lie: Small Clues to Global Things* (Routledge/Paradigm, 2011), Chapter 8.

A Local Beginning for a Global Thinker and Traveler

Sam Han is a social theorist with an exceptional range of interests. His eight books and many featured journal contributions are important, though not as important as Said's fewer books—but then few are they whose books are as enduringly important as those of Said. There is no shame in being less than him, but there is justifiable pride to be had of Sam Han's work—a pride I hold dear because he was a student of mine at Wesleyan University. When at Wesleyan he spent time in New Haven with us and was a regular in my advanced theory seminar that occasionally met in our home. In the acknowledgments to his first book, he graciously thanked me for being his teacher but, more importantly, he thanks Geri and Annie for making him feel part of our family. Even though Wesleyan in Middletown and New Haven were little more than a stop along the way of his travels around the world, he knew our town and how it was such a comfort to the family. Still, after college he moved on and lived many places. This beyond his regular visits to his extended family in Korea.

Apart from Sam's scholarship (about which more to come), if anything, he has traveled more globally than Edward Said. Sam Han was born in South Korea to parents who spoke little English. When they moved to the U.S. Sam attended the prestigious Fieldston School in the Bronx before going to Wesleyan where he majored in English and Sociology and earned high honors. Then he moved back to New York City where he began teaching at the College of Staten Island/CUNY and doctoral studies at the Graduate Center of the City University of New York. Upon completing the doctorate in sociology in 2012, Sam began a six-year tenure at Nanyang Technological University in Singapore where, in addition to being tenured, he had also become a research fellow at the Hawke Center at the University of South Australia in Adelaide. In 2018 Sam moved to the University of Western Australia in Perth where he became Director of the Korean Research Institute of Western Australia. Then, he moved to London in 2002, as lecturer in Sociology, Media Studies and Communication in the School of Social and Political Sciences at Brunel University.

But Sam Han is not just a traveler plain and simple. His mind, and therefore his books, travel far and wide over a range of topics very few others would ever consider exploring and especially not when they are as young as Sam was when he started out. He began with *Navigating Technomedia* (2008) and *Web 2.0* (in 2011)—both published before he finished graduate studies, in addition to (pardon me) *The Charles Lemert Reader* with Daniel Chaffee in 2010. Then *Digital Culture and Religion in Asia* (2015) and *Technologies of Religion: Spheres of the Sacred in Post-Secular Modernity* (2016) followed by *(Inter) Facing Death in Global Uncertainty* (2020) and *The Concept of Tragedy: Its Importance for the Social Sciences in Unsettled Times* (2023), and more. You can see the trajectory along which he traveled from technomedia to digital culture to unsettled global times each set in respect to Asia, and religious cultures.

As things have turned out these days, no one lives in any one place. With rare exception, we all live in a world that has weirdly come down upon us—through the improbable mechanics of twenty-first century technomedia that have created the global digital territory in and with which we must live. Sam Han has put it simply: "Technomedia is unlike prior media and technologies precisely because of its ability to break down and reconstitute the classic categories of knowledge, space, time, and politics. ... *It challenges thought and pushes it toward the future.*"[5] This may not, at first, sound simple. But it is nicely explained when Sam Han tells of a visit he made to Seoul, his home town. Sam had long

---

5 Sam Han, *Navigating Technomedia: Caught in the Web* (Rowman and Littlefield, 2008), 18. The example just below is drawn from one Han uses late in his book.

lived in America but on this trip, as before, he was in Seoul to visit family and to meet a few South Korean sociologists. He had made an appointment with one, an author of a book in one of my book series, Kyung-Man Kim. The appointment was made for a given time and place months before Sam had left for Korea. Yet, he arrived at the appointed hour in Professor Kim's office at Sojang University, an institution where I would give a lecture years later arranged by another professor, Sang Jin-Han, whom I had taught at Southern Illinois University at Carbondale years before. You can see that part of the story is that by the turn to the twenty-first century people the world-over enjoyed quite a few international relations made possible by what Sam calls navigating technomedia that small and more sophisticated technological tools that make the computer of my middle age look museum bound. The point of Sam's story, however, is that he appeared for the appointment right on time and Professor Kim greeted him by saying, "Sam you're here. I wasn't sure you'd come."[6]

This was early in the technomedia regime in global culture. Just the same, it shows that there were those comfortable with technomedia as today many are. Decades later some might not yet be totally at ease with technomedia, even as we use cell-phones, iPads, lap tops, *KardiaMobile EKG* monitors, and more. The lesson Sam Han teaches is well-put in the subtitle of his first book: *Caught in the Web*. Everyone on the planet, from the remote grassland steppes in Mongolia, to the isolated village of Tanana on the Yukon in Alaska, to the Arctic Archipelago in Canada's Arctic Seas, to Russia's Vostok Station in Antarctica—everyone in places like these and places everywhere are caught in the web by settlers from Ulaanbaatar, poachers in the woods off the Yukon, expensive cruise shippers in the Arctic Ocean, to bio-scientists in Vostok. All can be, and some are, caught even as they walk in the wild woods searching their cellphones for news.

Sam Han begins *Web 2.0* with the forgotten to others fact that in 2006 *Time Magazine* named its Person of the Year "You"—by which he means that by naming "You" as its Person of the Year, *Time* was branding 2006 as the year in which there was a "marked shift toward 'user-generated' technoculture" that many call "Web 2.0."[7] As part of his explanation of this new technoculture, Han gives the example of "the de-expertization of journalism" by which anyone anywhere can say what they think about anything on any of the platforms like Meta, X, and others that come and go, or change their names, day by day. Americans know this very well by their experience with a former President of the United States who shouts whatever comes to his mind as if it were well-reported news.

Sam Han first gave us this news of the effects of technomedia in his book of 2008, two years after 2006 when Saskia Sassen published the similar in *Territory Authority Rights* [again: without commas] that would mark these three fluid aspects of her *TAR* as somehow distinct instead of being all-at-once, always-changing, never-ending. Hence the strange global effect that Charles Lemert met Sang-Jin Han in Carbondale, Illinois in the 1970s and Sam Han in Middletown, Connecticut in the 2000s, during when Sang-Jin brought Charles to Korea to give talks, one of which was at Sojang University where Sang-Jin's wife Young-Hee was teaching and where he met Kyung-Man Kim whose book Charles published—and whom he disappointed when he could not attend dinner at his home outside Seoul because Ming Yan was in Seoul from Beijing and Charles felt that he should not leave Ming alone. They had become friends when he spent a long week in Beijing where, among much else, Ming had him speak at the Chinese Academy of Social Sciences before showing him her research neighborhood just off Tiananmen Square.

---

6 *Ibid*, xvi–xvii.
7 Sam Han, *Web 2.0* (Routledge, 2011), 1. The reference following to 'de-expertization" is at *ibid*, 40.

There was a time when such a spiraling circle of relationships all over the world would not have come together as it did among such an open network of people who met because that circle turned again and again, embracing more and their others. Then too, there is that fact that Ming lives in Beijing much of the year while her husband and sons live in the Bronx which home allowed the oldest boy, Alfred, to attend Stuyvesant High School from where he has gone to university then began a career as a teacher in English, his second language, and more to come. This because of technomedia and *TAR* by which territory becomes digital as the politics of authority and rights change for the better or the worse—one never quite knows which.

An Explanation/On to a New Beginning, Parsimoniously

Admittedly I have done a great deal of outside-the-normal writing in this book. For one, academics seldom write about themselves as I have. I have tried, however, always to return to the narrative at hand after beginning each chapter with a local story of my town and its people and places. I have had in mind, as I said in the Preface, and the first two chapters, two things.

First, by this unconventional practice I hoped to make the major point that America (like most, if not all, well-named societies) is what it is because of the habits and practices of people who live down-deep in its many local communities. *Americans can think America* because all thoughts about who we are must, and do, begin in the dirty soil and sometimes clean air of local life.

Second, and relatedly, I tell these local stories because in towns and neighborhoods—as opposed to faculty meetings and classrooms—people tend to tell each other the truth more often than not. If this were not true there could be no livable community as there was not in Nazi Germany, or Folsom Prison except when Johnny Cash sang the truth for all to hear. Truth, such as it is, is nothing more than a story told well among people at a coffee hour in a *schul,* or in a bar somewhere the wife won't find you, or when one tries to explain why she was speeding when a cop pulled her over, or just about everywhere when you have to tell a truth that may or may not convince the other addressed. Theory, therefore, is, as I said at length in the first two chapters, a well-baked story often rung through the shredder of one's high-minded colleagues and students who, one hopes, will buy and read your books. I am not here claiming that academics and book writers try too hard to tell their truth stories. Where and whenever we tell our stories we tell a full range of truths—from gossiping at the urinals in a men's room or publishing in a thought-to-be prestigious scientific journal—we are passing on truths of varying degrees of truthfulness. Whether the story told is that a mutual friend is having an affair with another friend's wife or the broadcasting of $E=mc^2$ for some select few to ponder, theory telling is *always* partially true, never the whole story. $E=mc^2$ is wonderous gossip, so to speak, of an intimate affair between energy and mass married by the speed of light squared but *without* taking into account the well-known story of the other affair that mass must have with gravity. As for local stories introducing sometimes grand social theories there is always some venal, if not mortal, sin in any attempt to marry the small and the large, the local and the ubiquitous. This is why so many righteous social thinkers insist on the micro/macro dichotomy. For social theorists, and philosophers of all kinds, dichotomies are, in effect, a rule of chastity preventing the two members from joining together so as to produce a progeny of stories about how little things grow up to become big ones. Truths must never be chaste. They live by thinking and doing in a world where gossips threaten to turn them in, which requires truth tellers to distance their gossip as much as possible. In a sense we are all unfaithful in our marriage to truth. This is why, earlier in this book, I have said, that ethnography, however it is conducted, should be considered the only method able to show the way into the larger facts of life. Ethno-graphy is writing about *and with* people.

I return now to my point about including myself and those I live among as the source of stories that can introduce coupled or divorced theories that themselves, variances aside, can be joined to tell the story of what Americans came to think of themselves over five centuries going on six.

From here on I will dash, perhaps too quickly, through the stories of authors and their writings about whom I would like to write in some other book. I am probably way too old to do that since I'm already committed to books with, if I may say it this way, beloved friends. So if I fail in this project, perhaps someone younger might do what I wish I could but probably cannot. The field is so rich. Just today, for example, a book I bought from Amazon arrived on the porch outside my work room. It begins the story of Americans thinking America where it should begin: Ned Blackhawk's *The Rediscovery of America: Native Peoples and the Unmaking of American History*. The title alone says what needs to be said and done. My failure in this book is that, by comparison, I have bought into America's story as having begun in 1619 when settlers came with slaves. Obviously now the story should begin in a far longer ago when the first real Americans settled across the continent, lived according to the stories of their civilizations, built homes and empires, and so much more in the plains and deserts, hills and mountains, along rivers and lakes that white settlers thought of as *their* prime real estate.

Short Stories of Some Who Came to America and Made Its Story Different

The short stories that follow are not short because they are less important than what came before. They are important for another book that better accounts for how theory should travel next in order to get into the meat of this new world, which we can only begin to understand by rethinking the American world as so far we have thought it—*as members, as theorists, as travelers*.

These stories are not of any one categorical type. Some are by those who have come here from abroad—Trịnh Thị Minh Hà and Gayatri Spivak—who teach us lessons of our complicity in the global fear of their differences from us, *and* of the way those who clean and scrub homes are battered and beaten, *and* of the silence of those in the deep basements of global living. Another, Álvar Núñez Cabeza de Vaca, came here to march across America's far west Southern lands to encounter people and places strange to Europeans who in the early 1500s were just settling their modern world-systems. Still another, Phillis Wheatley, rose up and out of the darkness in which Black people were considered incapable of writing fine poetry. Then too, there are those like Howard Zinn who taught us to look down the social ladder to understand the truth of America's ignorance of her most poor. And also, all must listen to E.O. Wilson, who taught us what we do not want to learn—that life of the human and natural kind is dying and needs to find a future.

Walking With the Disappeared: Trịnh Thị Minh Hà

Trịnh Thị Minh Hà was born in Hanoi in 1952 but moved to the South during war with the Americans. Trịnh studied music at the National Conservatory of Music in Saigon. She migrated from Vietnam to the United States in 1970—a fact that shouts out in her creative work as film maker, artist, author, and composer (if you read her books with an open ear you will hear the music). She begins *Elsewhere, Within Here: Immigration, Refugeeism, and the Boundary Event*: "The epoch of global fear has provoked extreme reactions and sentenced the world to indefinite confinement behind the bars of homeland security. With the political backlash against marked foreigners, foreign-born or foreign-looking members, asylum and refugeeism remain a key political issue."[8] This opening line is prelude to the story of how she found herself suspended in a nether land of time and space:

> When I first came to the United States from Vietnam in 1970, for several months I could not get a good sleep during the night. No matter how hard I tried to surrender to it, I repeatedly found myself lying still, eyes wide open in the dark, waiting. Waiting for what? Waiting, I thought, for dawn, so that I could finally fall asleep a few hours before starting my morning activities. So I waited, unable to figure out my uneasiness, until one night a distant shooting in the streets outside unexpectedly shed a light on the situation. I realized I was briefly home again.[9]

Home again by imagination in Hanoi, where she grew up with the reality of war always near. Though she is not, in this passage, writing about dreams, it is important to realize that dreams are the emotional moments when the line between time and space is erased. Daydreams especially yank us out of conscious life to speed us into a faraway place.

Speaking of dreams, there is also an element of cinema in Trinh's writing and thinking—of, that is, the infinite layers by which film imbricates time layered over space in a darkened room where one is meant to lose herself in the no-place and ever-shifting times on a screen. Watching a film can be said to be an instance of dreaming out loud. *Woman Native Other*, Trinh's first book and still the most important for many, turns on the critical section "Infinite layers: I am not I can be you and me." She writes:

> A critical difference from myself means that **I** am not **I**, am within and without **i**. **I/i** can be **I** or **I**, **you** and **me** both involved. **We** (with a capital **W**) sometimes include(s), other times exclude(s) **me**. **You** and **I** are close, **we** intertwine; **you** may stand on the other side of the hill once in a while, but **you** may also be **me**, while remaining what **you** are and what **I** am not. The differences *between* entities comprehended as absolute presences—hence the notion of *pure origin* and *true* self—are an outgrowth of a dualistic system of thought peculiar to the Occident.[10]

As strange as this may be to those new to Trịnh, do not overlook the last sentence which puts all that precedes it in perspective. Make no mistake about it, Trịnh here is pushing the micro/macro dichotomy, and all dualistic logics in their place. And that place is masculinist. Men dividing the worlds in two to prevent those undesirable to their male fantasies from getting into their world. Also, it is no accident that the above passage is framed by

---

8 Trịnh Thị Minh Hà, *Elsewhere, Within Here: Immigration, Refugeeism, and the Boundary Event* (Routledge, 2011), 1.
9 *Ibid*, 11.
10 *Woman Native Other* (Indiana University Press, 1989), 90. **Bold** emphases added. Also for a similarly sophisticated and spot on analysis, see Patricia Clough, *AUTOaffection: Unconscious Thought in the Age of Teletechnology* (University of Minnesota Press, 2000), especially Patricia's poem: "There Is a Story; or a Home Movie Rerun," 62–68; and her discussion of Trịnh, 166–170. Then too, in a letter to me about writing *AUTOaffection* Patricia said: "I see it as a secret writing where I left my thoughts, without knowing. For that, it was a mysterious time. Still I am glad to be in less mysterious times." It seems she wrote the letter in August 2001 just after *AUTOaffection* had been published. I've lost touch with Patricia who, in another time, was a best buddy. I believe she has now become a psychoanalyst—an all but perfect next move for one who can see many things, many of them hidden—and see them all at once.

two pages of still shots of women from the world over. She is thinking as the film-maker she became after studying and performing music in Saigon and earning the PhD in music at the University of Illinois. Both arts could be said to be powerful tools for dismantling false dichotomies.

Trịnh's films may be better known the world-over than her books, especially *Surname Viet Given Name Nam* (1989) which, as the title clearly suggests, is a filmic account of her uncertain but still serious relation to her beginning in war-torn South Vietnam.[11] Few are as accomplished in so many of the arts—a fact suggested by her double-appointment as Professor of Gender and Rhetoric at the University of California Berkeley.

One last mention of all of Trịnh's many public interventions that must not go unsaid: *Lovecidal: Walking with the Disappeared* in 2016 is, for me, the most powerfully poetic of Trịnh's books. The subtitle says it all about those who come here from war-torn places where loved ones are killed as much by their own refusal to flee as their inability to get out of war's way. We die from the wounds remembered:

> The call of the Disappeared continues to haunt and move women around the world. It gains in new resonances as it spreads and intensifies across the continent. ... Each time a new victim emerges to visibility, the wounds open anew and trauma deepens among terrified mothers and relatives of the disappeared.[12]

Gayatri Chakravorty Spivak: America's Subaltern?

Gayatri Chakravorty Spivak was born in 1942 in Kolkata, which the author of her Wikipedia page insists on calling Calcutta, its name until 2001, when the Imperial British name was replaced by the Bengali, Kolkata. Personally I would remark that there are two moves here that bear a relationship to Gyatri Spivak's ideas. Since India's independence was won in 1947, when also the partition from Pakistan was agreed to, the Wikipedia scribe may have been honoring the fact that Gayatri Spivak's native city was not renamed Kolkata until 2001—a Bengali name deferred by 54 years. I am sure there was a reason, but I have no competence in this aspect of India's history (though I should have). I introduce this fact because of the importance of the word *deferral* in my display of ignorance of India's history.

In 1947 Gayatri Spivak was but 5 years old. By 2001 she was 59 on the way to becoming, in 2007, University Professor in Humanities at Columbia University—this after passing through college in Kolkata, then graduate studies at Cornell University in way-remote Ithaca. In those 50 or so years she published at least ten books, a comparable number of translations, and countless essays and talks the world over. Of all these works, two stand out to many.

One is Spivak's translation of, and 89 page preface to, Jacques Derrida's 1967 book *De la Grammatology* which was published when *tout Paris*[13] was on fire with new ideas—among them those of Derrida, as well as Michel Foucault, Pierre Bourdieu, Jacques Lacan, many others. Derrida's book was very much at the center of all that. The *second* is Gyatri Spivak's matchlessly famous "Can the Subaltern Speak?"—published in a 1988 collection that was itself the book to read by those who wanted to understand the resurgence of cultural studies in America in the 1980s (itself a kind of tamed-down borrowing of the so-called French

---

11 See: https://www.youtube.com/results?search_query=Surname+Viet+Given+Name+Nam+(1989).
12 Trinh, *Lovecidal: Walking with the Disappeared* (Fordham University Press, 2016), 105.
13 For my version of *tout Paris* and 1968, see Charles Lemert, "Reading French Sociology," in Lemert, ed., *French Sociology: Rupture and Renewal Since 1968* (Columbia University Press, 1981), 3–32.

post-structuralism twenty years before). "Can the Subaltern Speak?" is a short but key paper that functions for many as the definitive text of subaltern studies.

These two texts—a long preface to her translation of a nearly 400 page book and an essay of but 45 pages—are the reason Gayatri Spivak must be at least mentioned in *Americans Thinking America*. We, then and now, need Derrida to disrupt our nation's long history of imagining America as being somehow at the leading edge of human progress—is being a *presence* obviously to itself and *its* world. One would hope that—after all these years and so many recent failures at wars in Korea, Vietnam, Iran, Iraq, Afghanistan, and those now boiling in Ukraine, the Sudan, and Gaza—Americans will soon get off the Make-America-Great bandwagon and its cognates. So far we have not. I believe we haven't because deep in our collective theoretical mind we still seem to see world problems as ones we are *obliged* to solve. With power comes responsibility—but not insistence on being the mover and shaker of all that happens everywhere. National interests, which are real, can get in the way of national clear-headedness.

What Gayatri Spivak has done in these two works on Derrida and the Subaltern is to present an alternative for Americans willing to rethink how they think America. Gayatri Spivak's presentation of Jacques Derrida's philosophical and social thinking could change how Americans think about themselves. Admittedly this proposition, not to mention the writings of Derrida, can make one's hair hurt. Believe me when I say that I wouldn't bother if I didn't think it important. So here goes:

At a crucial moment in Gayatri Spivak's Translator's Preface to *Of Grammatology*, she quotes a key passage from Derrida's book, namely:

> As for the concept of *experience*, it is most unwieldy here. Like all the notions I am using, it belongs to the history of metaphysics and we can only use it under *erasure*. "Experience" has always designated the relationship with a presence, whether that relationship had the form of consciousness or not. Yet we must, by means of the sort of contortion and contention that discourse is obliged to undergo, exhaust the resources of the concept of experience before attaining and in order to attain, by *deconstruction*, its ultimate foundation. It is the only way to escape "empiricism" and the "naive" critiques of experience at the same time.[14]

Now, keeping close to the ground of the words, Gayatri Spivak has here selected a key passage on Derrida's philosophical attitude on *experience*. Since we are here dealing with the imbrication of two thoughts on the same notion, I repeat now for emphasis-sake Derrida's important line: "As for the concept of *experience*, it is most unwieldy here. Like all the notions I am using, it belongs to the history of metaphysics and we can only use it under *erasure*." In effect, he is saying that, while *experience* has been central in the history of metaphysics, it is not actually present to thought itself. Here is Gayatri Spivak quoting Derrida on this point:

> The history of metaphysics, like the history of the West, is the history of these metaphors and metonymies. Its matrix—if you will pardon me for demonstrating so little and for being so elliptical in order to bring me more quickly to my principal theme—is *the determination of being as presence* in all the senses of this word. It would be possible to show that all the names related to fundamentals, to principles, or to the center have always

---

14 Spivak, "Translator's Preface," in Jacques Derrida, *Of Grammatology* (Johns Hopkins University Press, 1976 [1967]), xvii. Quotation from Derrida is *ibid*, 60. Emphases added.

designated the constant of a presence—*eidos*, *arché*, *telos*, *energeia*, *ousia* (essence, existence, substance, subject) *aletheia*, transcendentality, consciousness, or conscience, God, man, and so forth.[15]

In short, *being*—as in human *being*—has always been *thought of* as *being present to itself* (which is to say to the self that thinks itself) and to the world. For an example used at the beginning of this book, consider Descartes' *Cogito ergo sum*. *I think therefore I am* is a familiar example of Derrida's idea: We *are* because we are present to ourselves in thinking; or, conversely: we exist because we can think ourselves as present. This is a very crude illustration of Descartes, but it is not far off from Derrida's philosophical complaint against the long line of philosophical ideas that make *presence* first and foremost among the principles by which we think.

This is at the heart of his poorly understood method of *deconstruction* which is definitely more than *destruction*. To deconstruct is, to put it simply, is "to better, more deeply understand." In an interview, Gayatri Spivak put it this way:

> It's not just destruction. It's also construction. It's critical intimacy, not critical distance. So you actually speak from inside. That's deconstruction. My teacher Paul de Man once said to another very great critic, Fredric Jameson, "Fred, you can only deconstruct what you love." Because you are doing it from the inside, with real intimacy. You're kind of turning it around. It's that kind of critique.[16]

Returning to Spivak's Derrida—"Like all the notions I am using, it belongs to the history of metaphysics and we can only use it under *erasure*." This of course, given what we've seen her say, does not mean *erase* as in *get rid of*. In the French, the concept is *sous rature*, or "under erasure" like the traces on our kitchen chalk board where it is impossible to clean off earlier notes completely. Spivak's translation of Derrida puts it with unusual clarity:

> The trace is not only the disappearance of origin—within the discourse that we sustain and according to the path that we follow it means that the origin did not even disappear, that it was never constituted except reciprocally by a non-origin, the trace, which thus becomes the origin of the origin. From then on, to wrench the concept of the trace from the classical scheme, which would derive it from a presence or from an originary non-trace and which would make of it an empirical mark, one must indeed speak of an originary trace or arche-trace. Yet we know that that concept destroys its name and that, if all begins with the trace, there is above all no originary trace.[17]

This is the best passage I could find for the moment. I could go on, were it to suit present purposes, to discuss how Derrida borrowed the key concept from Heidegger and thereby notoriously invented the word *différance* as opposed to *difference* that functions to suggest that meanings, however different, are always *deferred* much as the name of her native city Kalcutta was.

---

15 Spivak, "Preface," *ibid*, xxi. Emphasis added.
16 The interview was in 2016 with Steve Paulson of *Los Angeles Review of Books*: https://web.archive.org/web/20180310010714/https://conversations.e-flux.com/t/gayatri-spivak-on-derrida-the-subaltern-and-her-life-and-work/4198
17 Derrida, *Of Grammatology*, 61 [Quoted by Spivak at xviii].

But enough already. This disquisition of Spivak/Derrida, while obtuse at times, is meant to make a point I now consider essential to a book like *Americans Thinking America*. With no exception I can remember, all the major thinkers on America's history have in fact thought of *America* as ever already *present*. Not even Thomas Paine's celebrated lines read to George Washington's troops on Christmas eve 1776—important as they were to the crossing of the Delaware and the victory that eventually won America her independence— declared a cultural presence that promised the sought-after new national state. They were:

These are the times that try men's souls; the summer soldier and the sunshine patriot will, in this crisis, shrink from the service of his country; but he that stands it now, deserves the love and thanks of man and woman. Tyranny, like hell, is not easily conquered; yet we have this consolation with us, that the harder the conflict, the more glorious the triumph.

Paine's *Common Sense* begins with an idea of an America that could have been, but was not yet. Through the years many have dreamed of that America and written of it as though it were already present. But it was not—*and never will be*. Cultural theories are thought to be theories that embrace a reality but that reality is never more than a trace.

Hence, the first lesson that Spivak's Derrida has for those who want to think America is: look for the trace of a culture that has disappeared— trace that has never been, nor could have been, purely present. We Americans live in, and by, a culture that, like all cultures, has long been to those who inhabit that nation no more than a trace of what they thought it was. *Make America Great Again* may be the only wise thing the phrase's inventor blathered on about when he was in fact trying to make America what Americans thought it was or could be. In a strange sense, in that man's defiance, he accidentally stumbled on a saying that should be buried but won't because historians don't erase. They inscribe. All we can do is cover over the slogan, and deconstruct its object—the America that exists as a trace into which we must dig for its deeper meaning. This is a task hard to do. Even so Spivak's Derrida is a beacon.[18]

---

18 There is an interesting note about Spivak's relationship with Derrida. After she finished graduate education she began teaching English at the University of Iowa in 1965 and quickly rose to full professor in 1970. She was by then a proven talent, but not even remotely a specialist in French theories. Then in 1967 she came upon Derrida's *De la Grammatology*. She thought it interesting and decided to translate it, knowing nothing about its author. But soon after publication her now famous "Translator's Preface" and the English edition became a startling success. She did not meet Derrida until 1971 when he introduced himself to her. "*Je m'appelle Jacques Derrida.*" She reported that "I almost died"! They soon became fast friends to the point that when they were together in public people asked him if he too was Indian—to which he replied, tongue in cheek, *Oui!* Later in the 2016 interview with Steve Paulson, she spoke to this point when asked: "Today you are best known as one of the founders of postcolonial studies. Is there a connection between this work and your earlier work on deconstruction and translating Derrida?" [Her reply:] "You know, I was not at all part of the French theory coterie. So as an outsider I had been the tiniest bit of a trendsetter with deconstruction. It had become so internalized that I certainly wasn't making connections. But the postcolonial business had come as a sort of autobiographical moment that comes to most middle-class metropolitan migrants—like Edward Said, thinking "I was Orientalized." [She later said:] "In 1981 when I was asked by the Yale French Studies to write on French feminism and by Critical Inquiry to write on deconstruction, I asked myself, how is it that I have become an authority on French material? So I turned around to think differently. Therefore, it was an engagement with that part of deconstruction, which looked at what is excluded when we construct systems. That part of deconstruction which is said to be the best way to proceed is a very robust self-critique. And that part of deconstruction which said that you do not accuse what you are deconstructing. You enter it. Remember that critical intimacy? And you locate a moment where the text teaches you how to turn it around and use it. So this had become part of my way of moving. So clearly, there was a connection. But one thing I've never done is apply theory. Theorizing is a practice. It becomes internalized. You are changed in your thinking and that shows in your work. So that's what happened." [The footnote below here: Leon De Kock, "Interview with

Then, there is the second lesson that Gayatri Spivak teaches those who want to think America, namely, those so buried in a false history that we wonder if they can speak. "Can the Subaltern Speak?" was a question that, for her, could only be asked out of her understanding of Indian culture. She writes as part of the subaltern study group well formed by 1988 when her essay first appeared. She quotes the then major figure in the movement, Ranajit Guha:

> The historiography of Indian nationalism has for a long time been dominated by elitism—colonialist elitism and bourgeois-nationalist elitism . . . shar[ing] the prejudice that the making of the Indian nation and the development of the consciousness-nationalism which confirmed this process were exclusively or predominantly elite achievements. In the colonialist and neo-colonialist historiographies these achievements are credited to British colonial rulers, administrators, policies, institutions, and culture; in the nationalist and neo-nationalist writings—to Indian elite personalities, institutions, activities and ideas.[19]

But then, mentioning Guha's interpretation of "the politics of the people"—a concept subject to the criticism of essentialism (with which she agrees), Gayatri Spivak acknowledges Guha's attempt to complicate the idea of a politics of the people. Then she sketches the outline of class distinctions in India:

1. Dominant foreign groups.
2. Dominant indigenous groups on the all-India level.
3. Dominant indigenous groups at the regional and local levels.
4. The social groups and elements included in this category [*the subaltern*] represent *the demographic difference between the total Indian population and all those whom we have described as the 'elite.'*[20]

In one interview Gayatri Spivak points out that the term *subaltern* owes to Antonio Gramsci when he had been silenced during his long imprisonment.[21] The best instance of a subaltern unable to speak is the traditional Hindu practice of Sati where a widow sacrificed her life silently upon the funeral pyre of her dead husband. More generally, these are the people in India who are so below even the next highest rung on a morbid ladder—the dominant local and regional indigenous groups that themselves are below even the national indigenous classes which are silenced in effect by foreign colonial rulers and interests.

There are no truly silenced subaltern classes in America. Spivak is not here commenting on the racially or economy oppressed groups, but she does refer to others who might be considered subaltern were it not that they served the interests of the proletariat. As a result the long list of excludeds are not really silent. She quotes Michel Foucault on this point:

Gayatri Chakravorty Spivak *I* in *New Nation Writers Conference in South Africa* (The Wayback Machine, 1991) at https://web.archive.org/201107006205400/http://.synergiesprairies.ca/ariel/article/viewFile2505/2458]

19 Ranajit Guha, in his edited collection *Subaltern Studies I: Writings on South Asian History and Society* (Oxford University Press, 1982), 1.
20 Gayatri Chakravorty Spivak, "Can the Subaltern Speak?," in Cary Nelson and Larry Grossberg, eds., *Marxism and the Interpretation of Culture* (Macmillan, 1988), 79. Italics in text.
21 Leon De Kock, *Interview With Gayatri Chakravorty Spivak: New Nation Writers Conference in South Africa* (The Wayback Machine, 1991) @ https://web.archive.org/web/20110706205400/http://ariel.synergiesprairies.ca/ariel/index.php/ariel/article/viewFile/2505/2458 . Also Kylie Smith, "Gramsci at the margins: subjectivity and subalternity in a theory of hegemony," *International Gramsci Journal*, No. 2 (April 2010), 39–50.

As allies of the proletariat, to be sure, because power is exercised the way it is in order to maintain capitalist exploitation. They genuinely serve the cause of the proletariat by fighting in those places where they find themselves oppressed. Women, prisoners, conscripted soldiers, hospital patients, and homosexuals have now begun a specific struggle against the particular form of power, the constraints and controls, that are exercised over them. [22]

Thus, if there is a *de facto* subaltern group in America it would be "our" indigenous people who were, and still are, silenced by confinement to distant impoverished reservations. This book refers to them, but its inadequacy as a book on *Americans Thinking* America is that, while I discuss important indigenous women like Gloria Anzaldúa and Paula Gunn Allen, they are but the beginning of a history of America that takes seriously not just the normal erasures of our history but the erasure of the systematically silenced.

Some Other Travelers Before America Became a Trace of Itself

What follows is a strange, very partial, even debatable list. Just the same I mean for this section to be a prelude to *later*, larger discussions—ones that emphasizes those who represent American subalterns, the traces of which have been ignored. They are also figures in the long American story of traveling theory.

Ned Blackhawk

Ned Blackhawk was born in 1971 to the Te-Moak tribe of the Western Shoshone in Nevada.

He grew up in Detroit, went to college at McGill University, then took his PhD in history at the University of Washington—after which he taught at the University of Wisconsin-Madison before moving to Yale in 2009, then becoming the Howard R. Lamar Professor of History and American Studies while working with Yale's Group for the Study of Native America. In 2023 Blackhawk won the non-fiction National Book Award for *The Rediscovery of America: Native Peoples and the Unmaking of U.S. History*, which began with the question that must be asked of America: "How can a nation founded on the homelands of dispossessed Indigenous peoples be the world's most exemplary democracy? This question haunts America."[23]

Haunts it should, but the poignancy of Blackhawk's question is that so few, over many years, down to present times are truly spooked by a fact so abidingly obvious. *The Rediscovery of America* is a book of 600 pages including a hundred pages of notes replete with maps of locations of Native Nations. It begins with "American Genesis: Indians and the Spanish Borderlands" in which the early Spanish settlers even before their settlement of St Augustine in 1565, had begun to explore the Southwest lands where New Mexico would be founded in 1598. The Spanish were not kindly settlers, needless to say. Their relations with indigenous peoples were, to say the least, troubled. Still, in the 1550s "nearly one hundred Pueblo communities confronted the Spanish."[24]

---

22 Michel Foucault, *Language, Counter-Memory, Practice: Selected essays and interviews*, trans. Donald F. Bouchard and Sherry Simon (Cornell University Press, 1977), 216.
23 Ned Blackhawk, *The Rediscovery of America: Native Peoples and the Unmaking of U.S. History* (Yale University Press, 2023), 1.
24 *Ibid*, 19.

The history continues through centuries of confrontation and decimation which marked the times of Native resistance to the dominating whites. Hence, Blackhawk writes of "The Indigenous Origins of the American Revolution" to and through the Civil War era, down to the nineteenth century where the discussion continues under the title "Indigenous Twilight at the Dawn of the Century: Native Activists and the Myth of Indian Disappearance," and concludes with "From Termination to Self-Determination" on events through the end of the twentieth century. The book concludes on a deeply qualifiedly optimistic note:

> By the end of the century the dark days of termination had faded. A series of "new partnerships" had begun. [Still] nearly a third of all tribal members lived below the poverty line, as the challenges of health, education obtainment, and economic development continued to impair tribal nations. Language loss, continued ecological destruction, and innumerable legacies of colonialism endure, making the challenges of Native America among the most enduring."[25]

The story told is that, given what America's Indigenous people have endured, any history of America must, as it has not, look deep into the sufferings of its subaltern people. Hence, Ned Blackhawk's thesis that America needs to go through all this ignored history in order to rediscover itself:

> Encounter—rather than discovery—must structure America's origin story. For over five hundred years peoples have come from outside North America to the homelands of Native peoples, whose subsequent transformations and survival provide one potential guide through the story of America.[26]

Álvar Núñez Cabeza de Vaca

Álvar Núñez Cabeza de Vaca (ca. 1490–1559) was not even remotely subaltern, but he was a traveling theorist in the sense that from 1528 to 1537 he traveled, mostly on foot, from the Gulf of Mexico in Florida across the length of the Southern borderlands from Texas across today's New Mexico and Arizona and back-and-forth south of the border in Mexico. He was not a theorist in our sense of the word but he wrote, upon returning to Spain, *La relación de Álvar Núñez Cabeza de Vaca* which remains to this day one of only two written records on Indigenous people encountered along the way.[27]

Cabeza de Vaca's long walking journey across the Southwestern Borderlands began in 1527 as part of the Pánfilo de Narváez explorations of the American South. When they arrived in Hispaniola the expedition lost a good many of its men before moving on to Cuba where Cabeza de Vaca had been sent to gather provisions for the company. Soon enough, Cabeza de Vaca fell out of agreement with Narváez and set out on his own mission. He met native peoples along his way, capturing some as slaves, killing others.

By 1528 Cabeza de Vaca made his way to the Gulf of Mexico where he encountered other Indigenous people who turned the tables on his by then smallish group by capturing and holding them as prisoners. Cabeza de Vaca was among the few who escaped, whereupon he embarked on a truly remarkable walk across of the Southern borderlands from Texas

---

25 *Ibid*, 445.
26 *Ibid*, 3.
27 *La relación de Álvar Núñez Cabeza de Vaca*, translated in 1905 as *The Journey of Alvar Nuñez Cabeza De Vaca* (1542) @ https://web2.qatar.cmu.edu/~breilly2/odyssey/Cabeza_de_Vaca.pdf . The only other such record of the day was Hernando de Soto's record of his travels in Mexico's Yucatan Peninsula.

to New Mexico to Arizona. Though at first the encounters were fraught with trouble, the more striking stories in *La relación de Álvar Núñez Cabeza de Vaca* are of his thoughtful, admiring, field notes of the Indigenous people he met:

> Of all the people in the world, they are those who most love their children and treat them best, and should the child of one of them happen to die, parents and relatives bewail it, and the whole settlement, the lament lasting a full year, day after day. Before sunrise the parents begin to weep, after them the tribe, and the same they do at noon and at dawn. At the end of the year of mourning they celebrate the anniversary and wash and cleanse themselves of all their paint.[28]

Throughout, the bands and nations he encountered are seldom identified in part because he knew little of their languages. Then too, remembering that his mission was sponsored by Spain, then the leading imperial power in the world—which is to say, he was telling stories for his sponsors and their people, not necessarily for us centuries later. Just the same, it would not be wrong to consider Cabeza de Vaca an ethnographer before the fact. His report on the native people of America's southern borderlands is an indispensable resource for thinking about Americans before America. If the descendants of the traveling theorist, Cabeza de Vaca, wrote about became subalterns when white settlers took over their lands, they were not during their centuries of living on the borderlands before Cabeza de Vaca came upon them.

Phillis Wheatley

Somewhere on the lands that became Gambia and Senegal, she was enslaved and sold to a trader who took her to Boston where she was sold again to the Wheatley family that gave her the name Phillis. She was then thrust into a subaltern position, but one that offered freedoms uncommon for slaves like her and Frederick Douglass. In Wheatley's case it was her virtual siblings, the daughter and son of her owner, who taught her reading and writing, including Greek and Latin. The Wheatley family also took her to London with them, widening still more her cultural vision.

Phillis Wheatley's first collection of poems was ready for publication in 1772 when she was probably 18 years old. Try as she might she could not find a publisher for so young and indentured a Negro woman. To publishers in that day such a one was literally unthinkable, in spite of the fact that her poetry, while not great, was brilliantly classical. As in *To M Æ C E N A S*, an ode to Gaius Maecenas an advisor to the Roman Emperor Octavian:

> M Æ C E N A S, *you, beneath the myrtle shade,*
>   *Read o'er what poets sung, and shepherds play'd.*
> *What felt those poets but you feel the same?*
> *Does not your soul possess the sacred flame?*
> *Their noble strains your equal genius shares*
> *In softer language, and diviner airs.*[29]

---

28 *Ibid*, 17.
29 This was the lead poem in *Poems of Various Subject by Phillis Wheatley Negro Servant to Mr. John Wheatley of Boston in New England* (printed for Cox and Berry, King Street, Boston, 1773), 9 @ https://www.gilderlehrman.org/sites/default/files/GLC06154.pdf

It is not difficult to imagine why in 1792 no white publisher would believe that a young Negro slave could write such lines. Just the same, they were eventually published as *Poems on Various Subjects, Religious and Moral by Phillis Wheatley, Negro Servant to Mr. John Wheatley, of Boston, in New England* in September 1773 on the testimony of 18 of Boston's most distinguished gentlemen who interviewed Phillis Wheatley in October 1772 and assured her eventual publisher that she and the poetry were authentic in every way.

Phillis Wheatley thereafter became a notable on both sides of the Atlantic and most importantly among several of America's founding fathers. Thomas Jefferson, however, ever true to his racist judgment about Negroes writing in *Notes on the State of Virginia*, had nothing good to say for Wheatley's poems.[30] But George Washington, upon reading a poem for, and sent to, him praised her literary gift which was evident in "'Twas mercy brought me from my *Pagan* land":

> 'Twas mercy brought me from my *Pagan* land,
> Taught my benighted soul to understand
> That there's a God, that there's a *Saviour* too:
> Once I redemption neither sought nor knew.
> Some view our sable race with scornful eye,
> "Their colour is a diabolic die."
> Remember, *Christians, Negros*, black as *Cain*,
> May be refin'd, and join th' angelic train.[31]

Phillis Wheatley had but 33 years when she died in 1784. In so few years, she mastered the art that gave her freedom to rise out of and above America's subaltern for the enslaved—who in her day were confined in the nation's dark basement where they were meant to be silent. Yet, she was a subaltern woman who learned how to speak, and to find her place in America's Revolutionary era:

> So, she becomes, in effect, the most famous person of African descent in North America and Europe at a time when the question of slavery, its rightness, its wrongness, who's to blame for it, how it might be changing or not changing, is newly controversial, and becomes inseparable from the controversy over the empire, and the place of the North American and Caribbean colonies in the British Empire. So she really is a poet of the Age of Revolution, and helps make the issues of slavery and the issues of liberty inseparable and mutually reinforcing in many different ways that I explore in tracking her life from the 1760s to her untimely death in 1784.[32]

Black Elk

Black Elk, which is to say *Heȟáka Sápa* (1863–1950[33]), was a Holy Man of the Oglala Lakota people, for whom Pine Ridge, South Dakota is their home. It was there in 1890 that

---

30 Henry Louis Gates, "Phillis Wheatley On Trial," *The New Yorker* (January 20, 2003) @ https://www.sas.upenn.edu/~cavitch/pdf-library/Gates_Phillis.pdf
31 *Ibid*, 13. The poem is found under the header "On Being Brought from Africa to America."
32 David Waldstreicher (interview with Jeffrey Rose, on Waldstreicher's *The Odyssey of Phillis Wheatley: A Poet's Journeys Through American Slavery and Independence* (Farrar, Strauss & Giroux, 2023). For the interview see: https://constitutioncenter.org/media/files/The_Odyssey_of_Phillis_Wheatley_Transcript.pdf (Thursday, July 27, 2023)
33 There is disagreement as to Black Elk's death day and year.

the Ghost Dance movement so threatened the U.S. government that its army massacred as many as 300 Lakota people just outside town, many of them women and children. Black Elk was there at Wounded Knee that day December 29, 1890 but escaped the slaughter. He had already been tamed, so to speak, by traveling to Europe with the Buffalo Bill Wild West Show and was present at a celebration of Queen Victoria's golden jubilee. The Lakota called her "Grandmother England." Earlier he had been present at the Battle of Little Big Horn in 1876. Where he told John Neilhardt, who would become his amanuensis:

> There was a soldier on the ground and he was still kicking. A Lakota [Sioux] rode up and said to me, 'Boy, get off and scalp him.' I got off and started to do it. He had short hair and my knife was not very sharp. He ground his teeth. Then I shot him in the forehead and got his scalp. ... After a while [on the battlefield] I got tired looking around. I could smell nothing but blood, and I got sick of it. So I went back home with some others. I was not sorry at all. I was a happy boy.[34]

This snippet tells the story of a Sioux hero during the dying days of what Ned Blackhawk calls "The Indigenous Twilight" for which the Wounded Knee Massacre in 1890 was the turning point in a troubled time for Native People.[35] Black Elk was a hero among his people. He was with Crazy Horse at Little Big Horn where, legend has it, he had been told to kill one of Custer's men and returned home "a happy boy." Black Elk was still a teenager of not quite 14 years. But years later as the Lakota were pressed hard by the *Wasichus* [the white people] he was pressed to theatrical service in Buffalo Bill's traveling show of Native people whose lives *as a people* were fast fading away. Yet, even though he was at Wounded Knee 1890, and survived, Black Elk soon after converted to Catholicism—which must have been a sad historical moment for a Lakota Holy Man.

The principal town for the Lakota Sioux, Pine Ridge, lingers on. To the North a Bureau of Indian Affairs looks down on the town which comprises a few streets, simple housing, schools, tribal buildings, offices of the Bureau of Indian Affairs all arrayed around an all-too-very white American gas station and fast order café. From there to the South a crudely paved road leads to a smaller town just over the Nebraska border where those afflicted with alcoholism walk to drink. Many die on the road back to Pine Ridge. Alcohol is forbidden on the reservation. One of the more vibrant institutions in Pine Ridge is the Catholic Church which supports a good school, commonly staffed by college educated volunteers who serve for a year or so before going on with their lives. One of my Wesleyan students, Thandi Emdon, served there shortly after she graduated college when I visited her in Pine Ridge. The days with her house mates were a highlight of my visit—less so were my memories of a settlement that seemed perpetually grey even in bright light. There is a darkening that covers emotional perception when what is perceived is a sad history of loss—of living on the plains when the buffalo are gone, where all that remains is a distant, ever unfinished mountain top memorial to Crazy Horse.

Black Elk lived through the times where Wounded Knee stood for what was so heartlessly destroyed. When he died, he left behind two, among other, records, both passed down by a faithful scribe. One is *The Scared Pipe: Black Elk's Account of the Seven Rites of the Oglala Sioux* recorded and edited by Joseph Epes Brown and prominently republished by the Penguin Metaphysical Library in 1971 [1953]). This is a book that describes the Sacred Pipe ritual of the Lakota in stirring language that is unmistakably the language of a Holy

---

34 Ian Frazier, "Another Version of Black Elk," *The New Yorker* (26 December 2017).
35 Ned Blackhawk, *The Rediscovery of America*, ibid, 363–370.

Man still committed to his Lakota Great Spirit, even while professing faith in the Roman Catholic God:

> O Grandfather, *Wakan-Tanka*, I shall now make this your sacred place. In making this altar, all the birds of the air and all the creatures of the earth will rejoice, and they will come from all directions to behold it! All the generations of my people will rejoice! This place will be the center of the four great Powers. The dawn of the day will see this holy place! When your pure light approaches, O *Wakan-Tanka*, all the moves in the universe will rejoice![36]

Against the pure light of Black Elk's remembrance of the Lakota's O *Wakan-Tanka* is the shadow story of their surrender to Army troops in Pine Ridge on January 15, 1891. At the end of *Black Elk Speaks*, John Neilhardt writes for us the words of Black Elk:

> It was nearly dark when we passed north of Pine Ridge where the hospital is now, and some soldiers shot at us, but did not hit us. We rode into the camp, and it was all empty. We were very hungry because we had not eaten anything since early morning, so we peeped into the tepees until we saw where there was a pot with papa (dried meat) cooked in it. We sat down in there and began to eat. While we were doing this, the soldiers shot at the tepee, and a bullet struck right between Red Crow and me. It threw dust in the soup, but we kept right on eating until we had our fill. Then we took the babies and got on our horses and rode away. If that bullet had only killed me, then I could have died with papa in my mouth.[37]

Then, at the very end, this ever more morbid benediction:

> I did not know then how much was ended. When I look back now from this high hill of my old age, I can still see the butchered women and children lying heaped and scattered all along the crooked gulch as plain as when I saw them with eyes still young. And I can see that something else died there in the bloody mud, and was buried in the blizzard. A people's dream died there. It was a beautiful dream. And I, to whom so great a vision was given in my youth,—you see me now a pitiful old man who has done nothing, for the nation's hoop is broken and scattered. There is no center any longer, and the sacred tree is dead.

The Lakota had journeyed across the American Great Plains, thriving for many centuries back in time from the ninth to the twelfth centuries CE. Members of the seven bands of the Sioux people spoke and danced freely until the European whites came and took it all away in the course of less than a century, from 1820 to 1891. Before, they had never been subaltern, after they were thrust into something like that dark dungeon of silence from which, in the century after that, when some among the *Wasi'chu* began to see what their white ancestors had done.

---

36 *The Scared Pipe: Black Elk's Account of the Seven Rites of the Oglala Sioux* recorded and edited by Joseph Epes Brown (Penguin Books, 1971 [1943]), 89.
37 Black Elk, "End of the Dream," *Black Elk Speaks: The Story of the Holy Man of the Lakota*, with John Neilhardt (University of Nebraska Press, 2014 [1932]), chapter 25. [My online edition has no page numbers, see: http://public.gettysburg.edu/~franpe02/files/%5BJohn_G._Neihardt%5D_Black_Elk_Speaks__The_Complete_(z-lib.org).pdf]

When Theory Travels It Moves Through Silences

It would be fair to conclude that this ending of *Americans Thinking America* mingles and mixes theories about theory—the more familiar one is that theory travels across time and space; the more inscrutable one is the silencing of others to a subaltern world or its functional equivalent where those confined cannot speak. The latter of these plays loosely with Gayatri Spivak's *subaltern* dug so deeply into a now more open Indian caste system where the excluded are not only forbidden to speak but they themselves believe they must live with a system of *Sati* ritual wherein widows once threw themselves on the funeral pyres that burned their dead husbands.

Yet, having cut and pasted different ideas from Edward Said's travelling theory to Gayatri's subaltern silence, I come to a conclusion that another book or books need to be written, even if I am unlikely to live long enough to write them.

For my last word on all this I conclude with the possible and the beyond possible:

Thinking Down and Beyond the Dead: Howard Zinn and E.O. Wilson

Howard Zinn (1922–2010) and Edward O. Wilson (1929–2021) lived in the same town and taught across the river from each other at Boston University and Harvard. Zinn was born Jewish in Brooklyn; Wilson was born in Birmingham, Alabama to a family constantly on the move. Zinn's father was a ditch digger who had immigrated from Austro-Hungary at the start of WWI. Wilson's father was an alcoholic who died by his own hand. Yet, he had encouraged his son's childhood interests in nature. Zinn's experience with a hard working labor family led to his career as a historian and political theorist of the downtrodden. Wilson began collecting insects at age nine—the first steps toward his career as an entomologist. Today Zinn stands alone among social theorists who have studied America's most poor and excluded; while Wilson stands as the inventor of sociobiology based on his years studying the social behavior of ants. Zinn needed company in an all-too-small corps of those who could have, but did not, write a book like *The People's History of the United States*. Wilson needed the company of sociobiologists who made it possible to write a book on *The Future of Life*. Both were perfectly clear as to what those who came after them must do about America and the world.

Howard Zinn ended *A People's History of the United States* with a dire but true assessment of his country—as overrun by the owners of corporate wealth, as a nation with two antiquated political parties abiding in a "permanent adversarial culture" that offers little to say about America's real, long-term future. Then he concludes:

> I think of the words of the poet Shelley,
> recited by women garment workers in New York to one another
> at the start of the twentieth century:
> *Rise like lions after slumber,*
> *In unvanquishable number!*
> *Shake your chains to earth, like dew*
> *Which in sleep had fallen on you—*
> *Ye are many, they are few!*[38]

---

38 Howard Zinn, *A People's History of the United States* (Harper Perennial Modern Classics, 2003 [1980]), 688.

E. O. Wilson's *The Future of Life* begins with a letter to Henry David Thoreau asking: "Henry! May I call you by your Christian name? Your words invited familiarity and make little sense otherwise."[39] The letter continues in a familiar tone meant to show Thoreuvians that Henry's world in the mid-nineteenth century Concord is not far in space and time from Edward's in early twenty-first century Lexington—neighborhood towns still. Again, Edward writing to Henry:

> You brought me here. Our meeting could have just as well been a woodlot in Delaware, but here I am at the site of your cabin on the edge of Walden Pond. ... You once said that old deeds are for old people, and new deeds are for new. You were the new and we are the old. Can we now be wiser? For you here at Walden Pond, the lamentation of the mourning dove and the green frogs *t-r-r-onk!* across the predawn water were the true reason for saving this place. For us it is an exact knowledge of what that truth is. So, two truths. We will have them both you and I and all those now and forever to come who accept the stewardship of nature.[40]

This well-imagined letter serves to link Thoreau himself and his contemporary Charles Darwin to the natural and human history of the world between the two times when modern mechanics had begun to shred a natural world that today is on life-support, if that. In Henry's day, it was the railroad across the pond that blared the noise of the then rising modern world over the pond where he had sought peace. The modern world's disturbance at Walden was an early first of the global crises that, in Wilson's day, became, as he put it, "Nature's Last Stand." In a focused yet reader-friendly book of 200 pages, Wilson covers a near end game of that destructive reality.

Unlike what you might expect of a Harvard sociobiologist, Wilson's *The Fate of Life* is about a new fact of biological life—that Nature's destiny is intimately wed to Humankind's. Hence the problem that still looms well-into Wilson's new century:

> The central problem of this new century ... is how to raise the poor to a decent standard of living worldwide while preserving as much of the rest of life as possible. Both the needy poor and the vanishing biological diversity are concentrated in the developing countries. ... The natural environments where most biodiversity hangs on, cannot survive the press of land-hungry people with nowhere else to go.[41]

Truths like this one, which is, after all, unqualifiedly universal roll down like thunder. Unless this problem is solved somehow, sooner rather than later, such a thing as America won't be thinkable.

In a sense it is hard to think America because of the ways human nature twists and turns between the human and the natural. For social theory and for all other kinds of serious thinking, the future must at least take seriously what Zinn and Wilson each demand: dig deep below the surface of those who are heard each night on cable news—dig down to those most at risk as we all will be one day if we fail to think straight about a world in which its space and time could well fall from its final precipice into a sea the depths of which are unknowable.

---

39 Edward Wilson, "A Letter to Thoreau," *The Future of Life* (Vintage Books, 2002), xi.
40 *Ibid*, xi and xxiv.
41 *Ibid*, 189.

Index

Adams, Henry: life of 223; theory of culture 223–6
Alexander, Jeffrey: career 253; on culture 254–7
Alinsky, Saul 479
Allen, Paula Gunn: family background 273; and Native American culture 274–6; and women 276–7
American Civil War 35; causes of 142–3; death in 123–4; effects of 192–3; key battles 125–6, 181; legacy of 123, 144, 194; memorials to 122; Reconstruction program 126–7, 266–7; *see also* Lincoln, Abraham
American culture 20; and capitalism 234, 539; elements of 33, 37–8, 399–401; evolution of 129–31; and geography 28–31, 93; idea of exceptionalism 130, 394–5; individualism 31–2; influence of settler history 28–30, 198, 394–5; migration and 17, 31, 34, 401; and print technology 97; race and 395–6; and violence 78; *see also* culture
American Revolution: Battles of Lexington and Concord 80; post-war difficulties 77, 79–80; as main successful decolonising revolution 57
Anderson, Benedict 97
Anderson, Elijah 337–9
Anthropocene 99
Anzaldúa, Gloria Evangelina: collaborations 496; early life 466; and the New Mestizo 467–9
Articles of Confederation and Perpetual Union 78–9
assemblage: AbdouMaliq Simone on 575; history of theory 573–4; Saskia Sassen on 569–70

Baker, Ella 380
Baldwin, James: career 278–9; feelings towards Civil Rights leaders 280–1; personal life 282–3; *see also* I'M NOT YOUR NEGRO
The Beat Generation 551
Bell, Daniel: career 534–5; on changing ideologies post-WWII 535–6; on culture 538–40; revisiting of earlier writings 536–7; on social movements 537

Bellah, Robert: on culture 243–5; life 240–1; on religion 241–2
Bill of Rights 79
Black Elk 606–8
Blackhawk, Ned 603–4
Bronte, Charlotte *see* Jane Eyre
Brown, John: Harper's Ferry 138; influence of Oliver Cromwell on 135; legacy 137; other influences 136
Burke, Edmund 52
Butler, Judith: approach to feminism 474; on drag 472–3; early career 471; on gender 471–5; political approach 475–6
Butler, Octavia 455–6

Cabeza de Vaca, Àlvar Núñes 604–5
Calvinism: and the *Protestant Ethic* 494; and the world system 242
Carmicheal, Stokely *see* Ture, Kwame
civil rights movement 365: Black Power 377; Freedom Summer 378–9; *see also* Du Bois, W.E.B; King Jr., Martin Luther; Ture, Kwame; Student Nonviolent Coordinating Committee
Church, Edwin: *West Rock New Haven* 42, 109
Cold War: Cuban Missile Crisis 531; impact on global system 291, 561
Collins, Patricia Hill: approach to theory 465–6; black feminist theory 443–7; criticism of sociology 444–5; on intersectionality 448–52; life 441–2
colonialism: and capitalism 26, 142, 581; early expeditions 29–30; resistance to 364–5
Constitution of the United States 9, 79; primary concerns 81
Constitutional Convention 8, 81
contemporary anti-racist movements 383
Cooper, Anna Julia: life 435–6, 441; on religion 436–7; on the role of black women 436–7, 440–1; and white feminism 438–9
Counts, Dorothy 279–80
Covey, Edward 155–7
Crenshaw, Kimberlé Williams: approach to theory 465–6; analysis of court cases 463–5;

early career 462–3; *see also* Critical Race Theory; intersectionality
Critical Race Theory: Kimberlé Crenshaw on 462–3; Patricia Hill Collins on 451–2
culture: and belonging 43, and borders 43, and capitalism 539; definitions of 243, 246, 396; development of theory 238–9, 397–8; elements of 8, 21; function of 223, 397; and the individual 393; and memory 129; and power 34–5

Davis, Angela: politics 83; on U.S. prison system 385–6; trial 384; *Women, Race and Class* 384–5
democracy 501–2
Derrida, Jacques: on experience 599–600; *see also* Spivak, Gayatri Chakravorty
Descartes, René: and the self 317, 600
Desmond, Matthew: approach 350; work 348–9
Dewey, John 210; social thought 211–12
Douglass, Frederick 126, 140–1; life as a slave 156–7; life's work 148–9; philosophy of 158–9; *What to the Slave Is the Fourth of July?* speech 149–55
Du Bois, W.E.B 24, 66; on black labor 266–7; early career 264–5; on the Talented Tenth 438; work with the NAACP 266
Duck, Waverly: on interaction order 342–5; interpretation of prior ethnographic research 340–1

Edwards, Jonathan: departure from Calvinism 47–8; impact 50; life 44–5; *Sinners in the Hands of an Angry God* sermon 47–8; social theory of 47–9
Emerson, Waldo: conception of nature 101; and Kant 100; on materialism 18; *Nature* 101–3; on power and wealth 104–5; as social theorist 104; as storyteller 17–18
Erikson, Erik: career 294–5; *Childhood and Society* 295–6
ethnography: beginnings/history of research 308–9, 316, 321–2; Chicago and 308, 320–1; criticisms of 325–8; developments in 337; importance of 312–14, 329; and race 323–5
Evers, Medgar 281

The Federalist Papers 82–5
feminist critical theory: characteristics of 470; key thinkers 408–9, 432–3; origins of 410–12
Franklin, Benjamin: character 15–16, 45–6; early writing career 44; impact 50; and voluntary associations 45–6
Fraser, Nancy: on declining neoliberalism 586–7; and feminist thought 583–5
Fuller, Margaret: feminist social theory 113, 116–17; life and work 112–13, 115; *Summer on the Lakes* 114–16

functionalism: origin of 222
fungibility 284–5, 289–90, 305–6

Gaia Hypothesis 98–100
Garfinkel, Harold: career 302; theory of sociology 302–5
Geertz, Clifford: on culture 246–7, 389–90; life 245; on semiotics 246
General Motors 463–4
The Gilded Age: and the Progressive-Era 24; ultra-rich industrialists 481
Gilman, Charlotte Perkins: life 412, 414–15; sociological fiction 413–14
Gilpin Faust, Drew 121–22, 123
Goffman, Alice: criticisms of 354–5; work 356–8
Goffman, Erving: on selfhood 392–3, 433; on social character 298–9; on social interaction 300–1
Goldstone, Jack 57
Gouldner, Alvin W: on culture 248–9
Grant, Ulysses S. 192
The Great Awakening 49
The Great Depression: economic advancements post-WWII 290
Greenwood School 172–3

Hamilton, Alexander: affair 86–7; on factions 82–3; life 86; *Report on Manufacturers* 89–91; *Report on a National Bank* 87–8
Hammer, Fanny Lou 381
Haraway, Donna: academic background 452–3; on capitalist hierarchies 460–1; and feminist theory 458–9, 461; on objectivity in social sciences 456–7; primates and social identity 453–6
Harding, Sarah: career 416; feminist social theory 416–17, 419–20; political social theory 418–19
Harlem Renaissance *see* Du Bois, W.E.B; Hurston, Zora Neale
Hartsock, Nancy: career 420; feminist social theory 421–5; on Marx 421
Harvey, David: on capitalism and its decline 581; Marxist geography 578–9; on neoliberalism 580; on postmodernity 576–7
Hegel, Friedrich; 5
Holmes, Oliver Wendell: legal writings 196–7; social pragmatism 195–6
hooks, bell: feminist social theory 426–8; life 425; on race 427–8
Hurston, Zora Neale: career 269; and folktales 269–70; narrative theory 272–3

I'M NOT YOUR NEGRO 277–8
Indian Removal Act 134
intersectionality: key texts 448–52, 463–5; precursors to 426, 448, 465; *see also* Collins, Patricia Hill

James, William: idea of the Self 206–7; life and academic career 204–5; *Pragmatism: A New Name for an Old Way of Thinking* 207–8; *Principles of Psychology* 205–7
Jane Eyre 14–15
Jay, John 60–1
Jefferson, Thomas 15; personal life 63; relationship with John Adams 63–4; on slaves 70–2; time in France 67; *see also* Notes on the State of Virginia
Jim Crow laws 24; New Jim Crow 127–8, 194
Jones, Nikki 351–3

Kaplan, Justin 164
Kansas Nebraska Act 134–5, 176
Kant, Immanuel 5; and idealism 100
Kenyan Health Care Initiatives 527–8
King Jr., Martin Luther 365; on Black Power 261; the Southern Christian Leadership Conference 382

Latour, Bruno 99
Lemert, Edwin 296–8
Lincoln, Abraham 16, 184; Civil War policy 124–5, 192; Copper Union Address 176–8; death of 187; early life 173–4; *Emancipation Proclamation* 125, 180–1; foray into politics 174–5; Gettysburg Address 181–3; legacy 190–1; and slavery 175–6, 179; pragmatic social ethic 173, 175, 192; and Stephen A. Douglas 177
The Louisiana Purchase: expeditions after 30; history of 68
Lovelock, James 99

Madison, James: on factions 80, 83–5; *Notes on Ancient and Modern Confederacies* 81–2; relationship with Hamilton 85
Marcuse, Herbert: life and career 370–1, 372; political theory 373–6; theory of aesthetics 372–3, 374–6
Marx, Karl: absence of Marx in American theory 587–8; on ideals 18; *lumpenproletariat* 522; on profit 587; scale of work 10; and social theory 5; time and space 579–80; and women 421
Massachusetts 64
Mead, George Herbert 212; idea of the Self 213–14
Merton, Robert K: on culture 223–5; social theory 232–3
migration: in the 1820s 123; changes to cities 334–6; The Great Migration 193; Polish settlement in the USA 321–2
Mills, C. Wright: career 540–1; on class 369–70; classification of writing periods 541; criticisms of sociology 546; and Cuba 544–5; on knowledge and power 366–8; and Max Weber 368–9; on the New Left 548–9; pessimism around post-War America 542–4; politics 368
Missouri Compromise 77, 134
Morgan, John Pierpont 482–3
Moses, Bob 379, 381

nation-state: development of 7–8; disassembling of 568–9; and national consciousness 97; precursors to 567; role of the leader in 478–9; social order in 396–7; The Treaty of Westphalia 7, 585
National Association for the Advancement of Colored People 281
National Mall 77–8
Neighborhood Housing Services 287–8
New Haven: black churches 262; Civil War monument 122; demography 262–3; Fair Haven 333–4; the Hill 309–11; history of first Colony 74–6; homelessness in 12–13, 203–4, 239–40, 409–10, 478–9; House Church group 390–2; indigenous population 261–2; inner city 361–2; local natural geography 92–3; Newhallville 286–8; Sam Han 593–4; *There's No Place Like Home* adoption program 362–4
The New School 582
Niebuhr, Reinholt: early life 490–1; opinion on the Roosevelts 490; social justice actions 492–3; social theory 491–2, 494–5, 497; support for workers 492; theology 491, 495–6
Notes on the State of Virginia: background 66–8; content 68–72

Paine, Thomas: *Common Sense* 50–1; early life 50; inspiring revolution 50–1; political theory of 52–4; *Rights of Man* 51–3
Parsons, Talcott: on culture 229–31, 394; early career 227; social theory 227–9
Peirce, Charles Sanders 201; theory of language 208–9
Pennsylvania 64
The Port Huron Statement: background 529, 547; and Herbert Marcuse 371; on the New Left 550–1; and *participatory democracy* 550
pragmatism: essence of 173, 201–2, 207–8; fix-it culture 185–7; as an indigenous American philosophy 198, 201; important contributors 201–3; proto-pragmatists 195–6; *see also* Holmes, Oliver Wendell; Lincoln, Abraham; James, William; Roosevelt, Theodore

queer analytics: development of 434

revolution: definition of 56–7; leaders in 478–9; study of 502; successes and failures 479
Riesman, David: career 292; *The Lonely Crowd* 292–4
Rios, Victor: life 345–6; on racial criminalization 346–7

rituals: social 59–60
Roosevelt, Eleanor: personal life 487–8; political work 488-9 relationship with Franklin 488
Roosevelt family: parallels between Franklin and Theodore 484–5; tensions 481
Roosevelt, Franklin Delano: affairs 488; during World War Two 487; Fireside Chats 485–6; social policy 486; struggle with polio 485
Roosevelt, Theodore: action against industrialists 482–3; personal life 481–2; political failings 484; social pragmatism 198–9
Rorty, Richard 215–16
Rostow, Walt Whitman: economic theory 532–4; on Marx 531; public service career 530

Said, Edward 591–2
Sassen, Saskia: career 563; and the digital age 569–72; on globalization 563–6; on the nation-state 567–9
Scott, James: approach 521, 523; career 511–12; ethnographic storytelling 515–17; research on peasant life 512–14, 518; on social movements 518–19, 522–3
Second Great Awakening 49
sex work 341–2
Simone, AbdouMaliq 336; on cities 334–5
Skocpol, Theda: on the nation-state 509; place amongst other sociologists 505–6, 508; on revolutions 56–7, 65–6, 507–8; Scholars Strategy Network 509–10
slavery: as economic capital 134; and religion 153; *see also* The American Civil War; Douglass, Frederick; Lincoln, Abraham; The Missouri Compromise; Tubman, Harriet
Slotkin, Richard 78
Smith, Dorothy: life and career 415–16
Social Gospel movement 491–2
sociology: androcentrism in 419–20; changes of theory in 1980s 456; knowledge and power 366–8; origins in philosophy 4–6, 317–18; structures and subjects 318–20
Spivak, Gayatri Chakravorty: *Can The Subaltern Speak* 602–3; and Jacques Derrida 598–601
story: and culture 21–2; elements of 8–10; and the listener 312; and theory 8, 306, 314–15, 595; trickster tales 132–3, 270–1; (un) reliability of 12–15
Student Nonviolent Coordinating Committee: demise of 380–2; Freedom Summer 379; legacy of 381; *see also* Moses, Bob; Ture, Kwame; Women
Students for a Democratic Society: and C. Wright Mills 547–8; convention of 552; divisions within 552; formation of 547; legacy of 554–5; political atmosphere surrounding 529, 551–2; *see also* The Port Huron Statement

technology: and changes to world system 291, 538, 571–2, 594; and truth 457
Thanksgiving 22
theory: of America 5–6, 8, 393; definition of 6–7; kinds of 4–6, 393
Thomas, W.I. 321–2
Thoreau, Henry David: and life by pond 20; and Goethe 105–6; relationship with Emerson 19; 37; and self-culture 107; *see also* Walden
Tilly, Charles: on collective social movements 502–4; criticisms of social sciences 501; on democracy 499–500; on the nation-state 504–5; use of metaphors 498–9
TimeSpace: and American culture 30–1, 38, 143; original hypothesis 25–6
Tocqueville, Alexis de 5–6
transcendentalism: Concord 17, 32, 95–6; influence of European thought 94, 100; impact of 123, 146; and nature 96, 98–100; Transcendentalist Club 97, 104; *see also* Emerson, Waldo; Thoreau, Henry David
Treaty of Paris 60
Trịnh, Minh Hà Thị 596–8
Tubman, Harriet 141; comparison with John Brown 137–8; The Underground Railroad 138–9; post-Underground Railroad 142
Ture, Kwame: life and career 376–7; politics 377–8

United States of America: and British colonial rule 46; formation of nation-state 77; historical evils of 127–8; indigenous peoples 602–3; and international conflict 130, 599; and geography 93, 96; and race 24, 146–7, 193–4; voluntary associations 36–7; *see also* American Civil War; American Culture

Virginia 64–5

Wacquant, Loïc 325–8
Walden 19–20; *The Bean* Field chapter 110–12; social theory of 105, 110–12; temporality in 108–10
Wallerstein, Immanuel: on capitalism 560–2; career 558; influences on 559–60; work in Africa 558–9; World Revolution 365; on world systems 25–6, 561–2; *see also* TimeSpace
Washington, George: character 58; legacy 58, 61–2; presidency 61; self-presentation 59
Washington, D.C. 76–7
West, Cornel 215; and race politics 216–17
Wilson, William Julius 324–5
women: black women 353, 385–6, 426, 446–7; in capitalism 421, 425, 461; in Kenya 528; and kin groups 344–5; Native American 276–7; in sociology 412–13, 444–5; in the SNCC 380–1; *see also* feminist critical theory

World War Two: effect on world system 291, 493–4
Wheatley, Phillis 605–6
Whitefield, George 46
Whiteman, Walt 159, 169; and the American Civil War 165–7; and the death of Abraham Lincoln 167–9; poetic method 164–5; and race 160; sexuality 165–6; social theory of 161–3; *Song of Myself* 161–4

Zomia 519–20
Znaniecki, Florian 321–2